KU-775-759

The Victoria History of the Counties of England

EDITED BY WILLIAM PAGE, F.S.A.

A HISTORY OF WORCESTER

VOLUME II

A HISTORY OF WORCESTER

EDITED BY J. W. WILLIS-BUND, M.A., LL.B., F.S.A. AND

WILLIAM PAGE, F.S.A.

THE VICTORIA HISTORY OF THE COUNTIES OF ENGLAND

WORCESTER

WITHDRAWN

PUBLISHED FOR
THE UNIVERSITY OF LONDON
INSTITUTE OF HISTORICAL RESEARCH
REPRINTED FROM THE ORIGINAL EDITION OF 1906
BY
DAWSONS OF PALL MALL
FOLKESTONE & LONDON
1971

THE LIBRARY
NEWMAN COLLEGE
BARTLEY GREEN
BIRMINGHAM B32 3NT
Class No. LH 942 44
Barcode. 00828238
Author. WOR

802571

X062010X ✓

Issued by
Archibald Constable and Company Limited
in 1906

Reprinted for the University of London
Institute of Historical Research
by
Dawsons of Pall Mall
Cannon House
Folkestone, Kent, England
1971

ISBN: 0 7129 0480 8

Printed in Great Britain
by photolithography
Unwin Brothers Limited
Woking and London

INSCRIBED
TO THE MEMORY OF
HER LATE MAJESTY
QUEEN VICTORIA
WHO GRACIOUSLY GAVE
THE TITLE TO AND
ACCEPTED THE
DEDICATION OF
THIS HISTORY

EVESHAM.

THE
VICTORIA HISTORY
OF THE COUNTY OF
WORCESTER

EDITED BY

J. W. WILLIS-BUND, M.A., LL.B., F.S.A. AND WILLIAM PAGE, F.S.A.

VOLUME TWO

PUBLISHED FOR

THE UNIVERSITY OF LONDON

INSTITUTE OF HISTORICAL RESEARCH

REPRINTED BY

DAWSONS OF PALL MALL

FOLKESTONE & LONDON

CONTENTS OF VOLUME TWO

CONTENTS TO VOLUME TWO

LIST OF ILLUSTRATIONS

LIST OF ILLUSTRATIONS

LIST OF MAPS

EDITORIAL NOTE

The Editors wish to express their thanks to all those who have assisted in the compilation of this volume. They desire, however, specially to state their indebtedness to Mr. Oswald G. Knapp, M.A., of Evesham, who has given much valuable help and advice, particularly with regard to the accounts of the parishes in the Hundred of Blackenhurst ; to Mr. William Pearce, J.P., F.S.A., of Pershore, for suggestions and help ; to the Reverend W. H. Shawcross, of Bretforton Vicarage, Evesham ; Mr. John Brinton, of Moor Hall, Stourport ; Mr. Edmund H. New, of Evesham ; Mr. Percy J. Pond, of Droitwich ; Mr. F. Grazebrook, of Dudley ; and the Reverend Eustace Havergal, M.A., of Feckenham, for information on various points ; to Mr. Arthur W. Ward, Honorary Survey Secretary of the Vale of Evesham Camera Club, for many photographs generously given for use in this volume, and to the Society of Antiquaries for the use of blocks for illustrations.

TABLE OF ABBREVIATIONS

Abbrev. Plac. (Rec. Com.)	Abbreviatio Placitorum (Record Commission)
Acts of P.C.	Acts of Privy Council
Add.	Additional
Add. Chart.	Additional Charters
Admir.	Admiralty
Agarde	Agarde's Indices
Anct. Corresp.	Ancient Correspondence
Anct. D. (P.R.O.) A 2420	Ancient Deeds (Public Record Office) A 2420
Ann. Mon.	Annales Monastici
Antiq.	Antiquarian or Antiquaries
App.	Appendix
Arch.	Archæologia or Archæological
Arch. Cant.	Archæologia Cantiana
Archd. Rec.	Archdeacons' Records
Archit.	Architectural
Assize R.	Assize Rolls
Aud. Off.	Audit Office
Aug. Off.	Augmentation Office
Ayloffe	Ayloffe's Calendars
Bed.	Bedford
Beds	Bedfordshire
Berks	Berkshire
Bdle.	Bundle
B.M.	British Museum
Bodl. Lib.	Bodley's Library
Boro.	Borough
Brev. Reg.	Brevia Regia
Brit.	Britain, British, Britannia, etc.
Buck.	Buckingham
Bucks	Buckinghamshire
Cal.	Calendar
Camb.	Cambridgeshire or Cambridge
Cambr.	Cambria, Cambrian, Cambrensis, etc.
Campb. Ch.	Campbell Charities
Cant.	Canterbury
Cap.	Chapter
Carl.	Carlisle
Cart. Antiq. R.	Cartæ Antiquæ Rolls
C.C.C. Camb.	Corpus Christi College, Cambridge
Certiorari Bdles. (Rolls Chap.)	Certiorari Bundles (Rolls Chapel)
Chan. Enr. Decree R.	Chancery Enrolled Decree Rolls
Chan. Proc.	Chancery Proceedings
Chant. Cert.	Chantry Certificates (or Certificates of Colleges and Chantries)
Chap. Ho.	Chapter House
Charity Inq.	Charity Inquisitions
Chart. R. 20 Hen. III. pt. i. No. 10	Charter Roll, 20 Henry III. part i. Number 10
Chartul.	Chartulary
Chas.	Charles
Ches.	Cheshire
Chest.	Chester
Ch. Gds. (Exch. K.R.)	Church Goods (Exchequer King's Remembrancer)
Chich.	Chichester
Chron.	Chronicle, Chronica, etc.
Close	Close Roll
Co.	County
Colch.	Colchester
Coll.	Collections
Com.	Commission
Com. Pleas	Common Pleas
Conf. R.	Confirmation Rolls
Co. Plac.	County Placita
Cornw.	Cornwall
Corp.	Corporation
Cott.	Cotton or Cottonian
Ct. R.	Court Rolls
Ct. of Wards	Court of Wards
Cumb.	Cumberland
Cur. Reg.	Curia Regis
D.	Deed or Deeds
D. and C.	Dean and Chapter
De Banc. R.	De Banco Rolls
Dec. and Ord	Decrees and Orders
Dep. Keeper's Rep.	Deputy Keeper's Reports
Derb.	Derbyshire or Derby
Devon	Devonshire
Dioc.	Diocese
Doc.	Documents
Dods. MSS.	Dodsworth MSS.
Dom. Bk.	Domesday Book
Dors.	Dorsetshire
Duchy of Lanc.	Duchy of Lancaster
Dur.	Durham
East.	Easter Term
Eccl.	Ecclesiastical
Eccl. Com.	Ecclesiastical Commission
Edw.	Edward
Eliz.	Elizabeth
Engl.	England or English
Engl. Hist. Rev.	English Historical Review
Enr.	Enrolled or Enrolment
Epis. Reg.	Episcopal Registers
Esch. Enr. Accts.	Escheators Enrolled Accounts
Excerpta e Rot. Fin. (Rec. Com.)	Excerpta e Rotulis Finium (Record Commission)
Exch. Dep.	Exchequer Depositions
Exch. K.B.	Exchequer King's Bench
Exch. K.R.	Exchequer King's Remembrancer
Exch. L.T.R.	Exchequer Lord Treasurer's Remembrancer

TABLE OF ABBREVIATIONS

Exch. of Pleas, Plea R.	Exchequer of Pleas, Plea Roll
Exch. of Receipt	Exchequer of Receipt
Exch. Spec. Com.	Exchequer Special Commissions
Feet of F.	Feet of Fines
Feod. Accts. (Ct. of Wards)	Feodaries Accounts (Court of Wards)
Feod. Surv. (Ct. of Wards)	Feodaries Surveys (Court of Wards)
Feud. Aids	Feudal Aids
fol.	Folio
Foreign R.	Foreign Rolls
Forest Proc.	Forest Proceedings
Gaz.	Gazette or Gazetteer
Gen.	Genealogical, Genealogica, etc.
Geo.	George
Glouc.	Gloucestershire or Gloucester
Guild Certif. (Chan.) Ric. II.	Guild Certificates (Chancery) Richard II.
Hants	Hampshire
Harl.	Harley or Harleian
Hen.	Henry
Heref.	Herefordshire or Hereford
Hertf.	Hertford
Herts	Hertfordshire
Hil.	Hilary Term
Hist.	History, Historical, Historian, Historia, etc.
Hist. MSS. Com.	Historical MSS. Commission
Hosp.	Hospital
Hund. R.	Hundred Rolls
Hunt.	Huntingdon
Hunts	Huntingdonshire
Inq. a.q.d.	Inquisitions ad quod damnum
Inq. p.m.	Inquisitions post mortem
Inst.	Institute or Institution
Invent.	Inventory or Inventories
Ips.	Ipswich
Itin.	Itinerary
Jas.	James
Journ.	Journal
Lamb. Lib.	Lambeth Library
Lanc.	Lancashire or Lancaster
L. and P. Hen. VIII.	Letters and Papers, Hen. VIII.
Lansd.	Lansdowne
Ld. Rev. Rec.	Land Revenue Records
Leic.	Leicestershire or Leicester
Le Neve's Ind.	Le Neve's Indices
Lib.	Library
Lich.	Lichfield
Linc.	Lincolnshire or Lincoln
Lond.	London
m.	Membrane
Mem.	Memorials
Memo. R.	Memoranda Rolls
Mich.	Michaelmas Term
Midd.	Middlesex
Mins. Accts.	Ministers' Accounts
Misc. Bks. (Exch. K.R., Exch. T.R. or Aug. Off.)	Miscellaneous Books (Exchequer King's Remembrancer, Exchequer Treasury of Receipt or Augmentation Office)
Mon.	Monastery, Monasticon
Monm.	Monmouth
Mun.	Muniments or Munimenta
Mus.	Museum
N. and Q.	Notes and Queries
Norf.	Norfolk
Northampt.	Northampton
Northants	Northamptonshire
Northumb.	Northumberland
Norw.	Norwich
Nott.	Nottinghamshire or Nottingham
N.S.	New Style
Off.	Office
Orig. R.	Originalia Rolls
O.S.	Ordnance Survey
Oxf.	Oxfordshire or Oxford
p.	Page
Palmer's Ind.	Palmer's Indices
Pal. of Chest.	Palatinate of Chester
Pal. of Dur.	Palatinate of Durham
Pal. of Lanc.	Palatinate of Lancaster
Par.	Parish, parochial, etc.
Parl.	Parliament or Parliamentary
Parl. R.	Parliament Rolls
Parl. Surv.	Parliamentary Surveys
Partic. for Gts.	Particulars for Grants
Pat.	Patent Roll or Letters Patent
P.C.C.	Prerogative Court of Canterbury
Pet.	Petition
Peterb.	Peterborough
Phil.	Philip
Pipe R.	Pipe Roll
Plea R.	Plea Rolls
Pop. Ret.	Population Returns
Pope Nich. Tax. (Rec. Com.)	Pope Nicholas' Taxation (Record Commission)
P.R.O.	Public Record Office
Proc.	Proceedings
Proc. Soc. Antiq.	Proceedings of the Society of Antiquaries
pt.	Part
Pub.	Publications
R.	Roll
Rec.	Records
Recov. R.	Recovery Rolls
Rentals and Surv.	Rentals and Surveys
Rep.	Report
Rev.	Review
Ric.	Richard

TABLE OF ABBREVIATIONS

Roff.	Rochester diocese
Rot. Cur. Reg.	Rotuli Curiæ Regis
Rut.	Rutland
Sarum	Salisbury diocese
Ser.	Series
Sess. R.	Sessions Rolls
Shrews.	Shrewsbury
Shrops	Shropshire
Soc.	Society
Soc. Antiq.	Society of Antiquaries
Somers.	Somerset
Somers. Ho.	Somerset House
S.P. Dom.	State Papers Domestic
Staff.	Staffordshire
Star Chamb. Proc.	Star Chamber Proceedings
Stat.	Statute
Steph.	Stephen
Subs. R.	Subsidy Rolls
Suff.	Suffolk
Surr.	Surrey
Suss.	Sussex
Surv. of Ch. Livings (Lamb.) or (Chan.)	Surveys of Church Livings (Lambeth) or (Chancery)
Topog.	Topography or Topographical
Trans.	Transactions
Transl.	Translation
Treas.	Treasury or Treasurer
Trin.	Trinity Term
Univ.	University
Valor Eccl. (Rec. Com.)	Valor Ecclesiasticus (Record Commission)
Vet. Mon.	Vetusta Monumenta
V.C.H.	Victoria County History
Vic.	Victoria
vol.	Volume
Warw.	Warwickshire or Warwick
Westm.	Westminster
Westmld.	Westmorland
Will.	William
Wilts	Wiltshire
Winton.	Winchester diocese
Worc.	Worcestershire or Worcester
Yorks	Yorkshire

A HISTORY OF
WORCESTER

ECCLESIASTICAL HISTORY

WITH only the vague facts that must necessarily serve as a foundation for the history of Christianity in England up to the sixth and seventh centuries, it is unprofitable to speculate as to the possible existence of Christianity in the district now known as the county of Worcester[1] during those early years. British Christianity has left no visible record,[2] although part of the county west of the Severn was held by the Britons until after Gildas wrote, about 550.[3] British Christianity would with difficulty survive the battle of Deorham and the conquest of the Severn valley by the West Saxons about 577.[4] Before the Christianity of Wessex[5] could penetrate to the Severn valley it had to pass into the rule of the heathen Penda, the all-conquering king of Mercia.[6] Thus, probably, the province remained heathen with the rest of the Middle Angles. According to Bede, and Florence of Worcester, the Middle Angles were converted on the death of Penda at Winwaed in 655,[7] when his son Peada, who had become a Christian in 653 and married the daughter of the Christian Oswy, king of Northumbria,[8] succeeded him. St. Finan, who had baptized the young king, sent a Scot, Diuma, to convert Mercia at the request of Peada,[9] and ordained him bishop of the Middle Angles and Mercians.[10] While it is uncertain how far west this conversion reached, it is probable that St. Augustine reached the Severn about this time on his way to his celebrated interview with the British bishops, though the attempt to locate the meeting in Worcestershire, probably, is mistaken.[11] Moreover, it seems that by the year 661 Worcester was under the rule of a Christian family, which governed it as tributary to the king of Mercia. Bishop Stubbs proved this point by showing that the ruling family was in all probability

1 See App. i.

2 William of Malmesbury states that there was a church, probably of British origin, on the spot where St. Egwin founded Evesham, but this is doubtful (Will. Malmes. *Gesta Pontif.* (Rolls Ser.), 296).

3 Gildas' *De excidio Britanniæ* (Eng. Hist. Soc.), 33–5.

4 Yet Bishop Stubbs suggests that Worcester contained 'a fair sprinkling of native British Christians in the seventh century' (*Arch. Journ.* xix. 238).

5 Converted by St. Birinus in 635.

6 Penda succeeded Cearl as king of Mercia in 626. At the battle of Cirencester in 628 he defeated the West Saxons, and probably received the Severn valley under the agreement. *A. S. Chron.* (Rolls Ser.) i. 44, 45.

7 Bede, *Hist. Eccl.* iii. cap. 24.

8 Ibid. iii. cap. 21. *Flor. Wigorn.* (Engl. Hist. Soc.) i. 21.

9 Bede, *Hist. Eccl.* iii. cap. 21.

10 Ibid.

11 Ibid. ii. cap. 2. The meeting was at St. Augustine's Oak. 'Id est robur Augustini in confinis Huicciorum et occidentalium Saxonum appellatur.' Two Worcestershire spots are mentioned; one in the parish of Rock, for which there is nothing to be said more than that some writers have conjectured it possibly might have been there, as the parish is not far from the borders of Wales, where Bede says the interview took place. Any other spot on the Welsh border has exactly the same claim as Rock to being the site of the supposed interview. The other place is the Mitre Oak, near Hartlebury. Except the name Mitre Oak, there is nothing to identify this place more than there is in the case of Rock. The name is nothing, for the Mitre Oak was a tree in the forest of Ombersley, on the boundary of the parish of Hartlebury, and, doubtless, marked the boundary of the bishop's lands or of his rights within the forest.

connected with the royal house of Northumbria, from whom Mercia had received Christianity.[1] Eanfrith, Eabba, Oswald, Osric, Oslaf, and Osred are names common to both families,[2] and Eabba, the wife of Ethelwealh of Sussex, baptized in 661, was herself baptized before that date in the court of her brothers Eanfrith and Eanhere of the Hwiccas.[3] Hence it may be, Eanfrith and Eanhere, governors of Worcester, were Christians before 661.

It was during the rule of Osric, the next governor or king of the Hwiccas,[4] that the diocese of Mercia was divided[5] into the five dioceses, of which the province of the Hwiccas formed one.[6] This division was completed in 680 at the council of Hatfield,[7] when Ethelred,[8] the third son of Penda, was king of Mercia, and Osric and Ethelred together may be regarded as the founders of the see of Worcester. The connexion with Northumbria was strengthened by the early bishops of Worcester coming from the monastery of St. Hilda at Whitby. Tatfrith, the first appointed, died before consecration.[9] He was succeeded by another monk of Whitby named Bosel, who was consecrated by Archbishop Theodore in 680,[10] but was 'so pulled down with such extreme infirmitie of hys bodie as he could not of himself execute the office.'[11] Thereupon Oftfor was chosen to officiate under Bosel, 'a man of singular merit and rare sanctity,' who, 'preaching the word of faith and giving in his life an example to those who heard and saw him, dwelt there for a long time.'[12] A trace of this is seen in the dedication of a disused church adjoining Worcester to St. Cuthbert. On Bosel's resignation, in 691, Oftfor was appointed his successor,[13] but he held the see only one year. He was succeeded in 692 by St. Egwin,[14] the founder of Evesham Abbey, who resigned the bishopric in 710[15] to become abbot of that house.

In the meantime, the organisation of the church in the diocese had begun. The bishop made Worcester his central station, and founded here the first church, dedicated to the honour of St. Peter. Round him gathered his secular priests,[16] and from thence he sent them out to teach and baptize. Up to the beginning of the eighth century Worcester was, probably, the one religious centre of the district. All the religious life gathered round this church, and the chief endowments were granted to it. The other settlements were her colonies, and in a greater or less degree under her influence. But as the 'monastic phase of the church' gained a stronger hold in Worcester, then the monastic element of the cathedral church separated from the secular,

[1] *Arch. Journ.* xix. 237.
[2] Bede, *Hist. Eccl.* iii. cap. 1; iv. cap. 13 and 23.
[3] Ibid. iv. cap. 13.
[4] Ibid. Osric also was connected with the Northumbrian royal family. See *Arch. Journ.* xix. 237–238.
[5] See decision of Synod of Hertford in 673.
[6] *Flor. Wigorn.* (Engl. Hist. Soc.), i. 36.
[7] Birch, *Cart. Sax.* i. 84–6.
[8] Habington says of Ethelred that he 'enlarged here the empire of Christ . . . such rare fruite did God produce out of the soure stock of Penda.' *Surv. of Worc.* (Worc. Hist. Soc.), ii. 325.
[9] Bede, *Hist. Eccl.* iv. cap. 21: 'Vir strenuissimus ac doctissimus atque excellentis ingenii vocabulo Tatfrid de ejusdem abbatissæ monasterio electus est antistes; sed, priusquam ordinari posset, morte immatura præreptus ist.'
[10] Ibid. iv. cap. 12.
[11] Habington (Worc. Hist. Soc.), ii. 327. Bede, *Hist. Eccl.* iv. cap. 21: 'tanta erat corporis infirmitate depressus ut officium episcopatus per se inplere non posset.'
[12] Bede, *Hist. Eccl.* iv. cap. 21.
[13] *Flor. Wigorn.* (Engl. Hist. Soc.), i. 42.
[14] *Chron. de Evesham* (Rolls Ser.), 4.
[15] Ibid. 12.
[16] These may have been the missionary monks who became the clergy of the church. But in the eighth century the distinction between monks and clerks was of little importance. Later on, when the distinction was marked, the bishop of Worcester as monastic bishop of a secular cathedral 'lived as an abbot in his own house and presided as a bishop in the church.' As monasticism developed, the monastic bishop drove the secular clergy from the cathedral. See *Mem. of Ric. II.* (Rolls Ser.), ii. Introd. xxi–iii.

and became the monastic society of St. Mary, distinct from the secular college of St. Peter until the time of St. Oswald.[1] At this date also the episcopal monastery was confronted by two powerful monastic bodies, Evesham and Pershore. As early as 691 there is said to have existed a monastery at Fladbury,[2] but here, as at Bredon, the 'monastery' was, probably, a 'family monastery,' a colony of priests and monks living together and dependent on the cathedral church.[3] Evesham and Pershore were distinct from these, and rivals of, rather than dependent on, the church of Worcester.

From the resignation of the see by St. Egwin in 710 to the accession of St. Dunstan in 957, the ecclesiastical history of the county is mainly a record of endowment after endowment to the three houses of Worcester (the two churches of St. Peter and St. Mary benefitting equally), Pershore, and Evesham. Whatever form of discipline was observed in these houses during this period, it seems possible that the members of the communities were sometimes secular canons and not regular monks of the true Benedictine Order, although in the Council of Clovesho of 747 the members of all religious communities were ordered to live 'secundum morem monasticæ vitæ.'[4] It was not until the tenth century that the movement was inaugurated which was to bring the strict Benedictine rule into the district, and to substitute regular monks for secular canons. In Worcester the work was done by St. Oswald, who succeeded to the see in 959. St. Dunstan had held the see for two years (957–9) after the death of Cynewald, but during this time there is no evidence that he attempted to introduce the rule of St. Benedict into the diocese. Whether he advocated or only acquiesced in St. Oswald's work is uncertain, but it would appear that the impulse towards a stricter life came to St. Oswald from within rather than by any outside influence.[5] After a stern training at Fleury he came to England and became a staunch friend of St. Dunstan, who persuaded Edgar to make him his successor at Worcester.[6] The necessary consent of the clergy and laity of the diocese was obtained, and Oswald became bishop.[7]

Without delay St. Oswald began his work of introducing the stricter Benedictine rule. According to his biographer he was watchful over his clergy and laity, and gave them an example of good living in his own life ; and, since many were wandering from the right way, he sent for a certain Germanus and many others from France to help him to introduce the rule of Fleury into the diocese.[8] Seven monasteries in the diocese were reformed,[9] and seculars gave way to monks. With the church of Worcester his task was difficult. The clerks refused to accept the rule of St. Benedict, so, according to Eadmer, he had recourse to the curious device of building, or more probably rebuilding and enlarging, the church of St. Mary at Worcester, adjoining that of St. Peter,[10]

1 *Arch. Journ.* xix. 244.
2 Birch, *Cart. Sax.* i. 110.
3 See *Arch. Journ.* xix. 245–249.
4 Wilkins, *Concilia*, i. 95.
5 *Vita S. Oswaldi, Historians of York* (Rolls Ser.), ii. 6–10.
6 Ibid. ii. 15.
7 Ibid. 16 : 'Primo tamen requiritur voluntas cleri et populi super re ipsa, et cum ingenti exultatione et vociferatione fit vox omnium una.'
8 Ibid. ii. 16. Germanus had been taken to Fleury by Oswald, and remained there when the latter returned to England. See ii. 14.
9 Ibid. ii. 20.
10 Ibid. ii. 23. Eadmer distinctly says, 'monasterium . . . construere cœpit ; in quo quibuscum conversaretur monachos adunaret' ; but it seems almost certain that the church of St. Mary was in existence before 770. See *Arch. Journ.* xix. 244–5. One possibility is that the earlier church of St. Mary was really part of the church of St. Peter (it certainly shared the same cemetery), and Oswald may have built the separate church.

and filling it with monks; he transferred thither the bishop's chair which had always belonged to St. Peter's.[1] Thus says William of Malmesbury, the 'claviger paridisi' gave way to the 'janitrix cœli.'[2] The laity attended now the one and now the other church, but little by little the Benedictines gained favour among the people, and they deserted the church of St. Peter for that of St. Mary.[3] By this means the seculars were gradually drawn into the new system. Winsinus, the vicar of St. Helen's church, provost of the cathedral, was persuaded to become a monk, and was sent by St. Oswald to be trained at the monastery of Ramsey.[4] In 969 he surrendered the keys of St. Peter's cathedral with all emoluments and territories to the monks of St. Mary's monastery,[5] and was placed at its head as the first prior.[6]

Besides strengthening and extending the order of St. Benedict in the county, St. Oswald attempted to strengthen the power of the bishop by contesting the claims of Evesham to be exempt with all her possessions from all episcopal control. The famous charter *Altitonantis*, supposed to have been obtained by Oswald from King Edward in assertion of his episcopal rights, is unquestionably spurious as it stands, though it has many genuine elements, and 'the story that it tells is in the main true.'[7] It purported to give the bishop full rights, civil as well as ecclesiastical, within the hundred of Oswaldslow, excluding the sheriff, and securing the bishop's right of jurisdiction over all the churches in the hundred to whomsoever they might belong.[8] Some belonged to Evesham, but Evesham itself and most of its property was in another hundred.

In another way the bishop established episcopal supremacy. He strengthened the temporal power of the bishop as a landowner by introducing a system of leasing the lands of the see for life or three lives, with reversion to the bishop at the end of the time. Leases meant services to the bishop, and in this way he ensured the cultivation of the lands he retained in his own hands, as well as of those which he let out, and had a large force ready at hand in case of war or tumult. Oswald is said to have leased 190 hides out of the 300 included in the bishop's hundred.[9] Thus a large number of tenants were secured for the see. The spread of population over the county was encouraged; the cultivators resided on the land they cultivated; villages sprang up in many places previously uninhabited. Round the houses lay the cultivated land, and beyond these so much waste or common, thus each grant or group of grants was the nucleus of a new settlement, which became a township, and either alone or with its neighbour required a church to supply its spiritual needs. Thus Oswald's policy led to the building of new churches, many of which were chapelries, but by the time of Edward the Confessor had resident priests.

[1] *Vita S. Oswaldi, Historians of York* (Rolls Ser.), ii. 25-78.
[2] Will. Malmes. *Gesta Pontif.* 248.
[3] *Vita S. Oswaldi, Historians of York* (Rolls Ser.), ii. 24, 25.
[4] Ibid. ii. 25, 78.
[5] Wharton, *Anglia Sacra*, i. 542.
[6] *Vita S. Oswaldi, Historians of York* (Rolls Ser.), ii. 25, 78. *Flor. Wigorn* (Engl. Hist. Soc.), i. 141. *Ann. Mon.* (Rolls Ser.), iv. 268.
[7] Maitland's *Dom. Bk. and Beyond*, 269.
[8] By virtue of the charter the episcopal control over any churches belonging to Pershore or Evesham could only be doubted if they could be proved outside this hundred. In the time of Edward the Confessor the charter proved useful, for when the king granted the 200 hides that had belonged to Pershore to his abbey of Westminster he granted special privileges and exemptions which might have been held to exclude such of the Westminster churches as were in the hundred of Oswaldslow from the bishop's power had it not been for the charter of Edgar.
[9] *V. C. H. Worc.* i. 287–298.

Oswald held the see of Worcester for twenty-nine years (962–991); for nineteen of those years (972–991) he was archbishop of York as well as bishop of Worcester.[1] His biographers say that St. Dunstan, fearing lest the monks of Worcester should once more become seculars without the guiding hand of St. Oswald, gave him permission to hold the two sees.[2] In spite of his care for the diocese of York,[3] St. Oswald seems to have spent much of his time in Worcester, and was brought there to die in February 992.[4] From his death to the Conquest his work was tried by tests of various kinds, but it stood the trial. The violent anti-monastic reaction that set in after Edgar's death failed to permanently affect it, while the encouragement Oswald had given to the growth of new centres of spiritual life resulted in the rapid development of churches in the bishop's hundred. Of his two successors, Aldulf of Peterborough (992–1002)[5] and Wulstan (1002–17),[6] little is known, except that they both, like Oswald, held the sees of York and Worcester.[7] During both episcopates, as during that of Leofsin (1017–1033),[8] Wulstan's successor, the county was several times raided by the Danes.[9] Probably at such a time as this the services on sea and land which the bishops could demand from their tenants proved useful to the church and justified Oswald's policy.[10] In 1033 Leofsin died[11] and Brihtegus, the abbot of Pershore, was appointed bishop.[12] The Worcester monks complained of him that he provided for his relations out of the revenues of the see;[13] this was probably an exaggeration due to jealousy at the appointment of a rival abbot. Brihtegus died in 1038[14]; and Harold gave the see to Living or Lyfing, bishop of Crediton.[15] He is spoken of by William of Malmesbury as an 'ambitious and arrogant despiser of ecclesiastical law,' unscrupulous and greedy.[16] Whether he deserved this character is uncertain, but in 1040 he was deposed by Hardicanute on the grounds that he had been accessory to the death of Alfred, King Ethelred's eldest son.[17] On payment of a large sum he was restored,[18] and on his restoration he denounced Sweyn, the son of the great Earl Godwin, for carrying off the abbess of Leominster and keeping her as his mistress for a year. Backed by the archbishop he compelled Sweyn to send the abbess back to her convent.[19] His successor Aldred (1046–1062)[20] was chiefly employed in fighting pirates. In 1049 a band of Irish pirates landed in Monmouthshire, and being joined by the Welsh, started on a plundering expedition up the Wye. Aldred was bishop both of Worcester and Hereford, and with the united forces of the two sees he followed up the pirates. The Irish, with the help of Gruffyd the Prince of South Wales, surprised the bishop in the early morning and completely defeated him.[21] On a vacancy occurring in the see of York

1 Wharton, *Anglia Sacra*, i. 472.
2 *Vita S. Oswaldi*, *Historians of York*, ii. 28.
3 Ibid. 27.
4 *Flor. Wigorn.* (Engl. Hist. Soc.), i. 149.
5 Ibid. i. 149, 156.
6 Ibid. 156, 180.
7 Wharton *Anglia Sacra*, i. 473.
8 *Flor. Wigorn.* (Eng. Hist. Soc.), i. 180, 189.
9 Ibid. i. 166, 176, 177.
10 The charter of Edgar made the provision of sea service one of the liabilities of the church of Worcester. That such a force was actually provided is clear from an entry in Domesday, where one Turchill, who held lands at Pershore, is spoken of as the steersman ('stermannus regis Edwardi'). *V. C.H. Worc.* i. 300a. Also 10 hides at Bishampton, which was also in the hundred, were held by four free men from the bishop for service by land and water. Ibid. 290b.
11 *Flor. Wigorn.* i. 189.
12 Ibid.
13 Heming, *Chartul.* ed. Hearne, 255. Without the consent of the monks he handed over lands of the monastery at Eardistone and Sapey Pitchard to his brother-in-law Adlehem.
14 *Flor. Wigorn.* i. 193.
15 Ibid.
16 Will. of Malmes. *Gesta Pontif* (Rolls Ser.), 200, 201.
17 Ibid. i. 321.
18 Ibid.
19 Heming, *Chartul.* ed. Hearne, 275, 276.
20 *Flor. Wigorn.* i. 199, 219.
21 Ibid. i. 203.

Aldred considered that his constant fights with the Irish and Welsh entitled him to have that see as well as those of Worcester and Hereford ; he went to Rome to persuade the Pope to give it him.[1] Pope Nicholas II. considered an archbishopric and two bishoprics were too much for any one man, but agreed to give him York if he would resign Worcester.[2] This Aldred promised to do, but on his return to England persuaded Edward the Confessor to transfer the see of Worcester to the province of York.[3] The genuineness of the charter of transfer is not above suspicion, but undoubtedly a very intimate relation existed between the sees of Worcester and York. Aldred was called the protector of the diocese of Worcester, and it was to him that the Worcester house appealed against the encroachments of Urse d'Abitot.[4] The Pope sent legates to England to see that the agreement to give up Worcester was carried out and a new bishop elected, and they on their arrival were lodged in the Worcester monastery under special charge of the prior Wulstan, whose piety they so much admired that they resolved[5] he should be the new bishop.[6] The Worcester house elected him, and the king and the Witan confirmed the election in 1062.[7] Probably under the influence of the papal legates, in whose eyes Stigand was a usurper, Wulstan refused to be consecrated by that archbishop, and made a protest on the Canterbury Profession Rolls.[8] He was therefore consecrated by Aldred[9] on 8 September, 1062, and held the see of Worcester until his death in January 1095—the last Saxon bishop who survived so long.

St. Wulstan's episcopate connected the two periods of the pre and post Conquest churches. With Aldred of York he made an early submission to the Norman. Partly because of this and partly because his well-known personal holiness gave William confidence in him he retained his diocese after the Conquest, for a certainly submissive Saxon could better be trusted in the vicinity of the rebellious Welsh and Marcher Lords than a possibly rebellious Norman.[10] His position was a very difficult one, and it speaks well for the man that he was able to maintain it. He had to submit to the spoliation of the church, but on the whole he was able to maintain his rights with a fair amount of success. He maintained the bishop's authority in the hundred of Oswaldslow, and the rights of the see not only against Evesham but also against the Norman archbishop of York.

Almost any measures were justifiable to withstand the spoliation of the church by the Normans, either by men like Urse d'Abitot or Osborn

1 *Flor. Wigorn.* (Eng. Hist. Soc.), i. 204.

2 *Historians of York* (Rolls Ser.), iii. 5, 6, 7.

3 Ibid. 7, 8, 9.

4 This was the occasion of the famous words of reproof told by William of Malmesbury, as spoken to Urse by the bishop telling him that his posterity should not inherit the patrimony of St. Mary. Will. Malmes. *Gesta Pontif.* (Rolls Ser.), 253.

5 This proceeding had not been used since the time of Offa, and evidently the papal legates had to proceed cautiously in their selection of a papal nominee, and thus it was that their choice fell on Wulstan, who was likely to be popular with the clergy and people as well as with the monks.

6 *Flor. Wigorn.* (Engl. Hist. Soc.), i. 220 : 'Hi videntes dum ibi morabantur ejus laudabitem conversationem in ejus electione non tantum consentiebant immo tam clerum quam plebem maxime ad hoc instigabant suaque auctoritate ejus electionem firmabant.'

7 Ibid.

8 *Simeon of Durham* (Rolls Ser.), ii. 176, 177.

9 In this way the link between York and Worcester was strengthened, and Wulstan's refusal on the plea that Stigand was uncanonical may have really been manufactured to help to make good the claim that York was bringing forward to include Worcester in the northern province.

10 This was proved by the rebellion of 1073, for if Worcester had then favoured the rebels they would have been able to gain the line of the Severn.

Fitz Richard, who plundered under the form of law,[1] or like Odo of Bayeux, the 'lupus rapax' of the monks, without any semblance of law.[2]

It might have been expected that the religious houses would have united against the spoiler, but Evesham then as ever was ready to enforce its claims against Worcester or Pershore. An attempt to despoil Pershore is noted in Domesday. Concerning a hide of land at Bransford, 'the county says that in time of King Edward it belonged to the church of Pershore, and yet the abbot of Evesham held it on the day of King Edward's death, but how they know not.'[3] In 1077 Athling the abbot of Evesham died, and his Norman successor Walter put forward a claim to lands which the church of Worcester held partly as her own, partly as belonging to the hundred of Oswaldslow. The case was heard before the bishop of Coutances, and Wulstan was successful in making good his rights over the lands at Hampton and Bengeworth by producing a charter supposed to have been given to Worcester by Offa in 780, which included a grant of Hampton and Bengeworth to the bishop.[4] Against Thomas of Bayeux, the Norman archbishop of York, Wulstan fought to win back the manors belonging to Worcester which Aldred had retained when he became archbishop. He met Thomas of Bayeux's claim that Worcester was part of the province of York by demanding back these manors, and supported by Lanfranc he was successful.[5]

Besides bearing valuable witness to the plunder of the church by the Norman, the Domesday survey gives very important details as to the ecclesiastical state of the county. It shows, in the first place, the great preponderance of the ecclesiastical over the lay landowners. Taking the county at 1,200 hides, the church held 786 to the lay 414.[6] Moreover, the lands held by the church were held with special privileges[7] or exemptions, so that the shire court had practically no rights within them.[8] The survey furnishes valuable evidence as regards the distribution of the parish churches in the county before the Conquest. It gives the number of priests in the county, and since where there was a priest there was in all probability a parish church or a chapel, a rough estimate of the number of the churches can be obtained.[9] In all, some sixty priests are mentioned stationed at fifty-seven places. The distribution of these places proves that the population in the north or centre was very

1 Two methods were chiefly employed:—(1) Many of the leases made by Oswald were falling in; and, instead of allowing the church to retake possession, the sheriff Urse seized them on behalf of the crown as being lands without an owner. Thus land at Pershore, held by service to Pershore by a certain Azor to revert to the church on his and his wife's death, is given in Domesday as held by the sheriff. Azor was holding on King Edward's death, but was afterwards outlawed, and the sheriff thereupon seized the land. *V. C. H. Worc.* i. 304. (2) Fitz Richard seized on the lands of those whose title was in any way weak. Thus, since the title of Adlehem, the brother-in-law of Brihtegus, who had granted him lands at Eardistone and Sapey Pitchard, was very uncertain, Fitz Richard seized the lands, well knowing that Adlehem could not resist. *V. C. H. Worc.* i. 313b.

2 According to the Domesday return Odo held Acton Beauchamp, which he had got in some way from the Evesham monks, and also Sheriff's Lench, which according to Domesday he took away from the church of Evesham which had owned it for many years, and let it to Urse d'Abitot. *V. C. H. Worc.* i. 308.

3 *V. C. H. Worc.* i. 305b.

4 Heming, *Chartul.* ed. Hearne, i. 77.

5 Wilkins, *Concilia*, i. 324.

6 *V. C. H. Worc.* i. 285–323.

7 Among these are especially noteworthy the payment of corn duty, 'circ-set,' 'sepultra,' and other similar payments due to the church.

8 Domesday says that the county was divided into twelve hundreds. For the profits of the hundreds, the sheriff had to pay a fixed sum—17 pounds by weight and 16 by tale—and if he did not receive so much, he had to make it up himself. He complained that seven of the hundreds were so exempt that he lost much on the ferm. Five of these seven hundreds belonged to the church.

9 Only four churches are mentioned by name, at Astley, Doverdale, Belbroughton, and Halesowen.

small as compared with that of the south, where most of the church lands lay.[1] Thus, there are twenty-eight priests mentioned in the return of the Worcester lands, nine in that of Westminster, two in that of Pershore, four in that of Evesham; while only eighteen are given in the return of the lands of all the lay landowners. In some cases the worldly wealth of the priests is given, ranging from that of the priest of Nafford, who had no plough and no cattle, to the priest of Cleeve and Lench, who had one hide and two ploughs.[2] Evidently these priests were the Saxon rectors, probably educated in the monastic schools and submissive to the discipline of St. Oswald as given in the Canons of Edgar.[3] By these the priests were bidden to have care in the service and worship of God,[4] preaching every Sunday to their people and always offering a good example themselves;[5] distributing the people's alms so as to please God;[6] eschewing all unbecoming occupations;[7] abstaining from oaths and forbidding them;[8] not consorting with women, but loving their own spouse, that is, their church;[9] not being hunters or hawkers or dicers, but occupying themselves with their books 'as became their order.'[10] This was the rule by which the Saxon clergy were ordered to direct their lives, but there is little doubt that the Norman Conquest brought a considerable change in the lives and status of the priests. Patronage in Saxon times had been in the hands of Saxon lords or Saxon abbots, whose nominees were likely to be Saxon in sympathy with their parishioners. After the Conquest Norman lords and Norman abbots filled the vacant rectories with men not only out of sympathy with the Saxon parishes, but usually untrained in the discipline of the Saxon clergy, and who, in many cases, were either monks or hired priests.

Since the possession of the church usually went with that of the manor, it seems that the majority of churches in Worcestershire must have been held from early times by the religious houses. Hence, the county was spared much of the litigation of the twelfth century between monasteries and lay patrons on the subject of advowsons. Norman founders, after the Conquest, increased this tendency by endowing their monasteries, not only with land and moneys, but also with the churches on those lands. Moreover, English benefices went as thank offerings of the Norman lords to monasteries in Normandy and elsewhere. To the abbey of Cormeilles, that of Tenbury, with a share in the churches of Martley and Suckley;[11] to the abbey of Lyra, that of Hanley Castle with the tithes of Malvern Chase, Queenhill, Bushley,

[1] In the north (8):—
Old Swinford, Hagley, Ombersley (2), Halesowen ('a church with two priests'), Northfield, Alvechurch.
In the centre (13):—
Bromsgrove, Droitwich (2), Elmley Lovett, Hanbury, Stoke Prior, Hartlebury, Wolverley, Doverdale, Hampton Lovett, Upton Warren, Chaddesley Corbett (2).
In the south (26):—
Kempsey, Fladbury, Inkberrow, Rous Lench, Bishampton, Cutsdean, Ripple (2), Blockley, Daylesford, Tidmington, Hindlip, Churchill, Overbury, Sedgeberrow, Lippard, Comberton, Nafford, Severn Stoke, Cropthorne, Cleeve Prior, Broadway, Church Honeybourne, Church Lench, Broughton Hackett, Besford.
West of the Severn (12):—
Holdfast, Mathon, Eardiston, Tenbury, Longdon, Powick, Abberley, Astley, Eastham, Clifton-upon-Teme, Sapey Pitchard, Rock.

[2] *V. C. H. Worc.* i. 303b, 297a.
[3] Wilkins' *Concilia*, i. 225–239.
[4] Ibid. 225–7.
[5] Ibid. 228, art. lii.
[6] Ibid. art. lv.
[7] Ibid. art. lviii.
[8] Ibid. art. lix.
[9] Ibid. art. lx.
[10] Ibid. art. lxiv.
[11] *V. C. H. Worc.* i. 299b, 320b, 323a.

Forthampton, Eldersfield, and Feckenham, of which latter the abbott of Lyra himself became rector.[1] The religious houses were in these cases 'rectors'; they had the spiritual direction of the parish, and at the same time the possession of all the temporal rights of the rector.[2] In many cases the spiritual duties were handed over to one of the monks in holy orders or to a hired priest, and the bulk of the temporal profits went to the monastery. Hired priests, removable at the pleasure of the monastery, could only have a transient influence, if any, on the parishioners, while a monk could have few of the wide human sympathies required of a parish priest. An attempt was made to remedy this evil in the national synod of 1102.[3] In the next century a further remedy was found in the foundation of perpetual vicarages.[4]

In 1095 St. Wulstan died.[5] It was to his active support in 1073[6] and again in 1076 that William owed his victory over his rebellious barons. It was Wulstan who was one of the most active adherents of William Rufus against Roger Montgomery when helped by the rebel Welsh in 1088,[7] and who hurled the curse on the foe and gave the blessing to the royal troops which was supposed to have brought the defeat of the rebels.[8] Thus he tided the church of Worcester over a difficult period, and made it appear a supporter of the Norman, not by compulsion but by its own free will.

One mark of St. Wulstan's episcopate still exists. In 1084 he ordered new buildings of the monastery of Worcester to be begun.[9] A portion of these works was his new cathedral, the crypt of which, one of the finest Norman crypts in the country, still remains. In the same year the priory of Great Malvern was founded at St. Wulstan's advice by the hermit Aldwin, as a cell to Westminster, and the power of the Benedictines strengthened in the county.[10]

From the death of St. Wulstan to the end of the twelfth century the long line of bishops of Worcester added little to the history of the county. Bishop Samson, his immediate successor, was a canon of Bayeux, brother of Thomas, archbishop of York. He was elected and consecrated in 1096,[11] and held the see until his death in 1112.[12] He was only in minor orders at the time of his election, and married, as his son Thomas became archbishop of York.[13] There is little that is noteworthy in Samson's episcopate except that in 1109 he successfully upheld the claim of Canterbury to include the diocese of Worcester against the claim of parity with Canterbury once more made by his son, Thomas, archbishop of York.[14] Being high in court favour he was able to make rich grants to the prior and monks of Worcester, and brought ornaments for the church from London; but he won the hatred of the whole monastic order by ousting the regulars from the church of Westbury

1 *V. C. H. Worc.* i. 321b, 322a, 322b.

2 See Cutts' *Parish Priests*, 96–97.

3 The Synod of Westminster in that year decreed that monks should not possess themselves of parish churches without the sanction of the bishop, and should leave the stipendiary priest a sufficient endowment. (Wilkins' *Concilia*, i. 383, art. xxii.)

4 By a decree of the Lateran Council in 1179.

5 *Flor. Wigorn.* (Eng. Hist. Soc.), ii. 35.

6 Ibid. 10, 11.

7 Will. Malmes. *Gesta Pontif.* (Rolls Ser.), 285.

8 Ibid.

9 *Ann. Mon.* (Rolls Ser.), iv. 373. Will. of Malmes. *Gesta Pontif* (Rolls Ser.), 283.

10 *Ann. Mon.* (Rolls Ser.), iv. 373. Will. Malmes. *Gesta Pontif* (Rolls Ser.), 285.

11 Ibid. 290.

12 Ibid. *Flor. Wigorn.* (Eng. Hist. Soc.), i. 66.

13 Will. Malmes. *Gesta Pontif* (Rolls Ser.), 289: 'Samson, frater archiepiscopi Eboracensis Thomae senioris junoris pater.'

14 Ibid. 261.

in Gloucestershire and putting secular canons in their place.[1] It is perhaps for this cause that his faults were so fully analysed by the monkish chroniclers. Thus William of Malmesbury enlarged on his gluttony, although he confesses that the bishop was very charitable.[2] His successor, Theolf, was also a Norman courtier and canon of Bayeux. He was elected in 1113, but not consecrated until 1115.[3] The consequent two years' vacancy of the see gave the abbots of the different religious houses, notably Worcester and Evesham, an opportunity for putting forward claims to exercise acts of jurisdiction which were regarded as precedents in after years.[4] William of Malmesbury characterised Theolf as similar to his predecessor Samson, a courtier with few of the qualities of a bishop.[5] The same might be said of his successors—Simon, chaplain of Queen Adela, mother of King Stephen,[6] John de Pagham, and Alvred, who had been chaplain of Henry I. Two years after the death of Theolf Simon was elected, and held the see twenty-five years (1125-50).[7] When elected he was only in deacon's orders, but was ordained priest one day and consecrated bishop the next.[8] He seems to have spent his time disputing with the Worcester house as to the respective rights of the bishop and monks to the estates of the church. It was the time when the church, taking advantage of the political anarchy of Stephen's reign, consolidated its strength and became the most important ally that Stephen or the empress could gain. Simon, however, seems to have taken little personal part in the struggle, but the Worcester house was evidently in favour of Stephen, for during the bishop's absence at Rome in 1139,[9] in spite of the influence of the earl of Gloucester in the district, they, in accord with the citizens, opened the gates of Worcester to the king.[10] John de Pagham (1151-58)[11] and Alvred (1158–63)[12] have left little but their names to mark their tenure of the see.

Their successor, Roger, the son of Robert, earl of Gloucester, lived during stirring times for the church, and took part in the Becket controversy as a staunch supporter of ecclesiastical rights against the return to 'ancient custom' urged by the king. He is the reputed author of a letter to Henry in 1165 interceding for the archbishop and his fellow exiles.[13] He was denounced by the king as an enemy to the commonwealth[14] and forbidden to join Becket abroad.[15] He evidently disobeyed the order, went without royal licence,[16] and was forbidden to return;[17] thereupon he wrote to the Pope for directions as to the terms by which he might return to his diocese. The Pope bade him go back provided he exercised his episcopal office without obeying the royal 'customs.'[18] He then joined the court in Normandy, where he was reported to have spoken against Becket and his cause.[19] However, he defended his constancy to Becket's principles and continued friendly with the archbishop until his murder.[20] As the well-known friend of Becket, Bishop

1 Will. Malmes. *Gesta Pontif* (Rolls Ser.), 290.
2 Ibid. 289. n. 3.
3 *Flor. Wigorn.* (Eng. Hist. Soc.), ii. 66, 68.
4 *Chron. de Evesham* (Rolls Ser.), 99.
5 Will. Malmes. *Gesta Pontif* (Rolls Ser.), 290: 'Antecessori suo non absimilis moribus.'
6 Ibid. 290.
7 *Flor. Wigorn.* (Eng. Hist. Soc.), ii. 79. *Ann. Mon.* (Rolls Ser.), i. 47, iv. 26.
8 Thomas, *Surv. of Worc. Cath. Acc. of Bishops*, 106.
9 *Flor. Wigorn.* (Eng. Hist. Soc.), ii. 114.
10 Ibid. ii. 115. The result was, that soon after the Empress's party retook the city and burnt it. Ibid. ii. 118-21.
11 *Ann. Mon.* (Rolls Ser.), iv. 26, i. 48.
12 Ibid. iv. 30, i. 49, ii. 56.
13 *Mat. for Hist. of Thos. Becket* (Rolls Ser.), v. 169.
14 Ibid. iv. 63.
15 Ibid. vi. 74.
16 *Ann. Mon.* (Rolls Ser.), i. 50.
17 *Mat. for Hist. of Thos. Becket* (Rolls Ser.), vii. 301.
18 Ibid. vi. 390, 393.
19 Ibid. 270, 276, 321.
20 Ibid. 394.

Simon, 1125–1150.

Walter de Cantilupe, 1237–1266.

Godfrey Giffard, 1268–1302.

William de Gainsborough, 1302–1307.

Worcester Episcopal Seals.—Plate I.

To face page 10.

Roger was then sent as envoy to the Pope to deny the king's complicity in the murder.[1]

Engaged as he was in matters which affected the history of the English Church generally rather than the Church of Worcester especially, Roger had little influence in his diocese. The period of his episcopate was one series of quarrels between the monasteries and the secular clergy, and between the different monasteries as to their respective rights. For monasticism was becoming a still more important force in the county with the foundation of the Cluniac priory at Dudley in 1160, the Cistercian abbey at Bordesley in 1138, the priory of Little Malvern in 1171, and the three nunneries at Cookhill, Westwood, and Whistones about the same time. The church of St. Augustine, Dodderhill, had been granted to the Westwood nuns; the Worcester monks claimed it as theirs, and a long contest as to this church began which in one form or another lasted over a century.[2] Worcester also fought Westminster as to the right to elect a prior to Great Malvern[3] and denied Osbert Fitz Hugh's claim to present to the churches of All Saints and St. Clement, Worcester.[4] The Cistercians were now gaining a foothold in the county, and the next bishop came from their order. Baldwin, abbot of Ford, in Devon, was consecrated on Roger's death in 1180,[5] but only held the see four years, being translated to Canterbury in 1184.[6] His successor, William de Norhale, prebendary of St. Paul's and archdeacon of Gloucester died in 1190.[7] In the next nine years three bishops held the see, but nothing noteworthy is recorded of any one of them. Robert Fitz Ralph, archdeacon of Nottingham, was consecrated in 1190 and died in 1193.[8] Henry de Soilli, abbot of Glastonbury, held the see from 1193 to 1195, his successor, John de Constantiis, from 1195 to 1198.[9] Of the latter, the Worcester Annals tell how he 'irreverently and of night' removed the relics of St. Wulstan from the cathedral, where they were afterwards replaced by his successor.[10] Bishop Mauger had a more remarkable episcopate. He was elected on the death of John de Constantiis in 1199,[11] but his election was annulled by Pope Innocent III. on account of his illegitimate birth.[12] Against this, Mauger appealed to the Pope, who was so pleased with his mind and person that he issued a decretal to Archbishop Hubert Walter in his favour,[13] and consecrated him at Rome.[14] Mauger had been physician to Richard I.;[15] had probably accompanied him to the Holy Land and learnt many of the Eastern arts of healing. When he became bishop miracles began to be numerous at St. Wulstan's tomb;[16] in 1203 the saintly bishop was canonised,[17] and the offerings to his shrine supplied a fund apparently devoted to the repair of the cathedral and the other buildings burnt down in the spring of 1202.[18] The monks of Worcester disputed the bishop's right to these offerings, but the

1 *Mat. for Hist. of Thos. Becket* (Rolls Ser.), vi. 474, 476, 485.
2 Nash, *Hist. of Worc.* i. 337.
3 See *V. C. H. Worc.* ii. *Relig. Houses* under Great Malvern.
4 Reg. i. D. and C. Worc. fol. 24. Cited by Nash, *Hist. of Worc.* ii. App.
5 *Ann. Mon.* (Rolls Ser.), i. 52, iv. 39, 384.
6 Ibid. i. 53, ii. 62, iii. 23, iv. 39, 40, 385.
7 Ibid. i. 54, iv. 43, 387.
8 Ibid. i. 54, iv. 44, 387, i. 55, ii. 249, iv. 47, 388.
9 Ibid. i. 55, iv. 388, 389.
10 Ibid. iv. 392: 'Ossa beati Wulstani ab episcopo Johanne de Constantiis noctu et irreventer levata noctu etiam reponuntur ab episcopo Malgerio.'
11 Ibid. i. 56.
12 *R. de Diceto* (Rolls Ser.), ii. 168.
13 Migne, *Patrologia*, ccxv. 1193-5.
14 *R. de Diceto* (Rolls Ser.), ii. 168.
15 Ibid.
16 *Ann. Mon.* (Rolls Ser.), iv. 391.
17 Ibid. 392.
18 Ibid. 391.

question was settled by a compromise, the offerings being divided between them.[1] Evidently Bishop Mauger had high ideas of episcopal authority, for he determined to control the exempt abbey of Evesham. Bishop Simon had attemped to visit the abbey in 1139, but Abbot Reginald appealed to Rome and the bishop's claims were declared illegal.[2] Mauger's letter announcing his proposed visitation seems to have fallen unexpectedly on the abbey in 1202; a discussion of the question among the monks resulted in a protest to the bishop and a threatened appeal to Rome.[3] The bishop applied to the archbishop, who gave no decision, but left the matter to be discussed before the papal legates appointed to examine the cause in England.[4] The latter gave sentence in 1204 that the jurisdiction over the abbey belonged to the bishop, and that of the vale to the abbey.[5] On further appeal to Rome the monks gained the judicial decree of Innocent III. proclaiming the exemption of the abbey from the bishop's visitation.[6] But the interdict of 1208 came before the dispute as to the churches of the vale could be finally settled, and Bishop Mauger having pronounced the interdict and incurred the king's enmity was among those who, according to Roger of Wendover, fled into parts across the sea and lived there among comforts, not setting themselves up as a wall for the house of the Lord, but, 'seeing the wolf coming, left their sheep and fled.'[7] His possessions were confiscated by the king,[8] and, although he came back to England in 1209, and attempted to come to terms with the king, he did not return to his diocese, since John would not make full restitution, but retired to the abbey at Pontigny, where he died in July 1212.[9]

The next bishop, Walter de Gray, resigned the Chancellorship of England to become bishop, but only remained at Worcester for two years, when he was translated to York.[10] It was during this period that the two orders of Friars, the Preachers or Dominicans and the Minorites or Franciscans, first came to England.[11]

The episcopate of Bishop Sylvester, the next bishop,[12] was chiefly remarkable for the two great functions which were celebrated during it; the first the burial of King John, who was brought from Newark to be interred, according to the directions in his will, in the church of St. Mary and St. Wulstan, at Worcester. He was buried before the high altar, Oswald on one side of him and Wulstan on the other, thus fulfilling Merlin's prophecy that he should be placed among the saints.[13] The second event was the dedication of the new cathedral in 1218 to the honour of St. Mary, the Apostle St. Peter, and the confessors Oswald and Wulstan. The young King Henry III., five English bishops, the four Welsh bishops, seventeen abbots, the earls of Essex and Hereford, seven barons, and an infinite number of noblemen and gentlemen were present.[14] For the bishop it was an unfortunate day. A new and very gorgeous shrine had been prepared for St. Wulstan since the precious metals on the old one had been melted down to pay the fine placed on the monastery for submitting to Prince Louis and

[1] *Reg. Beatæ Mariæ Wigorn* (Camden Soc.), 24a.
[2] *Chron. de Evesham* (Rolls Ser.), 99.
[3] Ibid. 109-115.
[4] Ibid. 123.
[5] Ibid. 131.
[6] Ibid. 179, 183.
[7] *Roger of Wendover* (Eng. Hist. Soc.), ii. 224.
[8] *Gervase of Cant.* (Rolls Series), ii. 107.
[9] *Ann. Mon.* (Rolls Series), ii. 267. 'Obiit Maugerius Wigorniensis episcopus apud Pontinacum suscepto habitu monachali.'
[10] Ibid. iv. 403.
[11] Ibid. 405.
[12] Ibid.
[13] *Ann. Mon.* (Rolls Ser.), 407.
[14] Ibid. 409.

the French.[1] There was some difficulty in getting St. Wulstan to fit into his new shrine, which was not long enough for him. The bishop thought that if all the bones were placed within it the mode in which they were placed did not very much matter; so, 'with his own hand,' says the chronicler, 'he cut them up, placed them in the shrine, and praised himself for the deed.'[2] This impious act took place on the 6 June; on the 16 July the bishop was dead; St. Wulstan had avenged himself!

The Worcester monks had their candidate for the see; so had the legate Gualo, and he put such pressure on the monks that they elected his nominee, William de Blois,[3] who for eighteen years was a strenuous upholder of episcopal rights against the attempted encroachments of the religious houses—notably, Worcester, Malvern and Evesham.[4] He established the bishop's right not only to visit the Worcester house, but also to depose a prior for inefficiency and to have the final word in the election of future priors.[5] In a further struggle with the monastery concerning the profits from certain parish churches, especially St. Helen's and Claines, he effected a compromise—the bishop was to have the profits of and maintain the vicar of the churches east of the river, the monastery of those west of the river.[6] In spite of the opposition of the abbot of Westminster, the bishop maintained his right to visit and receive procuration from Malvern.[7] He does not seem to have questioned the right of Evesham to remain exempt, but he would not allow the abbot to exhibit outward signs of his independence. At the first diocesan synod of his episcopate the abbot wore his mitre. This the bishop would not allow, nor would he permit the abbot to sit next to him at the synod.[8]

Another feature of William de Blois' episcopate was his successful attempt to increase and maintain the revenues of the see; sometimes by exchange of lands, sometimes by purchase. Thus during his episcopate he did much to increase both the spiritual and temporal power of the bishop. His great work in Worcester was the building of the Carnarie chapel between the cathedral and the bishop's palace; under this he placed a very large crypt, to be used for the more reverent disposal of the bones of the dead. When finished it was dedicated to the honour of St. Thomas the Martyr, the murdered Becket, and was probably one of the earliest, if not the earliest, dedication to him in the county.[9] One of his last acts was to hand over the church of Bromsgrove to the priory.[10] He died in 1236 at Alvechurch,[11] having done more for the see than most of his predecessors since the Conquest.

His contests with the monasteries, and his efforts to reform the mode of living, point to the fact that the early religious zeal of the Benedictines had to a great extent departed; that their cares were now more for matters temporal than for matters spiritual; that if the religious life of the time had to be quickened, some new movement was required. The same idea had been conceived, the same want experienced abroad. To meet it two new

[1] *Ann. Mon.* (Rolls Ser.), 407.

[2] Ibid. ii. 289. 'Ipse propria manu cum securi secuit et per loca multa divisit ac de hoc facto semetipsum laudavit.'

[3] Ibid. 290, iv. 410.

[4] *V. C. H. Worc.* ii. *Relig. Houses.*

[5] *Ann. Mon.* (Rolls Ser.), iv. 411–417.

[6] Ibid. iv. 426.

[7] Ibid. 424.

[8] Ibid. iv. 411.

[9] Thomas, *Surv. of Worc. Cath. Acc. of Bishops*, 129.

[10] Ibid. 427.

[11] Ibid. i. 101.

religious orders, the preaching friars and the minorite friars, had arisen who were to work a change in the life of the times. Abroad their main work was to extirpate heresy, here it was to revive the religious life.

Before describing their work, a word should be said as to the state of the diocese on the death of William de Blois in 1236. The middle of the thirteenth century may be taken as the time when the development of the church in the diocese had reached its highest point. It will, therefore, be well to see how the church stood at the beginning of the contests she was about to undertake. Roughly, the county in the Worcester diocese was divided into 115 parishes, the most valuable of which belonged to the church. It is not easy to give a detailed list of the church patronage in the thirteenth century, but, speaking generally, out of the 115 parishes the patronage of 84 was in ecclesiastical hands, and that of 31 belonged to laymen, including the Crown.[1]

With so large an amount of the patronage of the county in the hands of the religious houses it is hardly surprising that the evils arising from appropriate benefices were becoming more and more apparent in Worcestershire. A large part of the revenues of the church was kept in the hands of the monasteries or bishop, and generally inefficient and ill-paid priests were hired to have the spiritual care of the parishes. Some idea is given in the bishop's registers of the position of the persons ordained.[2] Possibly a large percentage of the candidates are named from the places whence they came, as 'John of Cleeve Prior,' 'Richard of Powick,' and that implies that they were of the yeoman class and possessed no surname. The worldly position of some of the ordained is clearly shown by the rules concerning 'persons ordained who had not sufficient means of support.' The bishop, if he ordained such, was obliged, if not to keep them, at least to see they were provided with a sufficiency to live upon. In some cases the title by which each candidate was ordained is given in the ordination lists.[3] The 'living wage' of an ordained person, possessing which he was supposed to need no help from his patron, varied in different dioceses; but in Worcester 30*s.* a year seems to have been the lowest limit, 40*s.* the more usual sum.[4] This shows to some extent the class from which the candidates for orders were taken. They would often be the children of the tenants of the religious houses in the different parishes, and would serve as another link to bind the parishes and the religious houses together. If the house received the monies from the parish it also provided for the children, and was in other ways in close relations with them. It cannot be wondered that the hold upon the county of the ecclesiastical bodies was too firm to be easily shaken.

Another point which would tend in the same direction was the fact that in many of the parishes where the patronage was in lay hands the living was

[1] The chief ecclesiastical patrons were :—

Bishop of Worcester	19	benefices
Worcester monastery	27	"
Evesham	13	"
Pershore	11	"

[2] In 1282 as many as 386 were ordained (*Worc. Epis. Reg. Giffard* [Worc. Hist. Soc.], 158-164), and two years later 333, of whom 122 were sub-deacons, and, therefore, recruits to the ranks of the clergy since the previous ordination. (Ibid. 237).

[3] e.g. *Worc. Epis. Reg. Giffard* (Worc. Hist. Soc.), 161. Geoffrey de Sokelege, at the presentation of Thomas de Bentleye ; Nicholas de Croppethorn, at the presentation of the rector of the place.

[4] In the Year Book 10 Edw. III. the living wage of an ecclesiastic was put at 5 marks a year.

given either, as in rare cases, to a person not in orders at all, or to a person who was only in minor orders.[1] To remedy this the Council of Lyons, in 1273, ordered that unless the holders of benefices obtained priests' orders within one year of the date of the Council they should forfeit their benefices. The Register of Bishop Giffard has a number of entries of attempts to enforce this provision.[2]

In the meantime the Council of Westminster, following the directions of the Lateran Council of 1179, had in the year 1200 inaugurated the great ecclesiastical experiment of the thirteenth century, the foundation of perpetual vicarages as a remedy against the many disadvantages of appropriation. The stipendiary priest, removable at the pleasure of the monastic or lay patron, was now to give way to a competent parish priest, instituted perpetual vicar by the bishop. The vicar was answerable to the bishop only, and was to be sufficiently endowed out of the revenues of the parish, usually receiving the small tithes, while the religious house received the great tithes.

In many early cases the actual date of foundation is difficult to discover. Probably many of the Worcestershire vicarages were founded in the early part of the century, but there is no direct evidence to that effect. The earliest mention of a vicarage is in the Annals of Worcester, under the year 1234. The chapels of Wick and Wichenford were then evidently regarded as vicarages, since the settlement of the jurisdiction and appurtenances belonging to them on the Worcester house was 'in proprios usus salvis honestis vicariis.'[3] Also a later entry stated the claim of the Worcester house to present vicars to the chapels of Wick and Wichenford.[4] St. Helen's, Worcester, was a vicarage by 1235,[5] and Bromsgrove by 1236.[6] The vicarage of St. Andrew's, Pershore, was in existence by 1256,[7] and of Grimley[8] and Tardebigge before 1269.[9] In 1270 the perpetual vicarage of Wolverley was founded, 'and William de Mepham, rector of the same,' granted the bishop and his successors the right to collate to the vicarage.[10] The vicarage of Severn Stoke was constituted before 1273,[11] that of Hartlebury by 1280,[12] that of Dodderhill before 1281,[13] that of Inkberrow by 1282,[14] and that of Beoley by 1285.[15]

In the taxation return of 1291, Kempsey, Hanley Castle, Lench Rokulf (Church Lench), Feckenham, and Dodderley (Dudley) are also mentioned as vicarages.[16] Thus by the end of the thirteenth century there had been, at the lowest estimate, some twenty vicarages created in the county. In the early

[1] This shows the contrast between lay and ecclesiastical patronage. The lay patrons gave the living as a provision to a man, whether he was or was not fitted for the post, or was or was not in orders; the ecclesiastical patrons, whatever they did with the money, did not appoint a man who could not perform the duties.

[2] e.g. *Worc. Epis. Reg. Giffard* (Worc. Hist. Soc.), 103. Mandate of bishop of Winchester citing clerks 'who have received any benefice since the Council of Lyons who have not been ordained priests within a year from their receiving the same.'

[3] *Ann. Mon.* (Rolls Ser.), iv. 426. [4] Ibid. iv. 427. [5] Ibid. [6] Ibid. [7] Ibid. 444. [8] Ibid. 26. [9] Ibid. 31.

[10] *Worc. Epis. Reg. Giffard* (Worc. Hist. Soc.), 42. In 1322 the vicarage was appropriated to the scholars of Merton College, Oxford, and the arrangements as to tithes of wool and milk, etc., for the vicar recapitulated. (Worc. Epis. Reg. Cobham. f. 81).

[11] *Worc. Epis. Reg. Giffard* (Worc. Hist. Soc.), 54.

[12] Ibid. 123. In this year Walter, the parochial chaplain of the rectory of Hartlebury, was ordained vicar of the rector of the same.

[13] Ibid. 132. The profits of the vicarage of the church of Dodderhill were in the May of that year sequestered, and later in the same year the portion of the vicarage united to the portion of the rectory (Ibid. 136).

[14] Ibid. 152. [15] Ibid. 252. [16] *Pope Nich. Tax.* (Rec. Com.), 216–224.

part of the fourteenth century there were further foundations at Powick,[1] Tibberton,[2] Ombersley,[3] Bishampton,[4] Astley,[5] Pershore,[6] Longdon,[7] Kidderminster,[8] Blockley,[9] and Broadway.[10]

In spite of these strenuous attempts made to raise the status of the clergy and improve the parochial conditions of the county, there were many glaring abuses and much disorder in the church of the thirteenth century. Non-residence and pluralities were, as usual, among the most general, and although the bishops seem in some cases to have attempted to check both these forms of abuse,[11] they more often encouraged them by licences to the clergy to absent themselves for different purposes such as to study, to travel, or to go to the court of Rome.[12] Absence for study seems to have been used as a fiction to allow foreigners who belonged to some of the religious houses to hold their benefices while the work was done by a substitute. In one case, that of Feckenham, the Norman abbot of Lyra was the vicar, and some of the monks from Newent appear to have taken the duty.

The southern portion of the county was practically under the control of the Benedictine monks ; the north was so thinly populated and so uncultivated that it did not furnish any great opportunity for church work. Any new religious body that came must be ready to fight the Benedictines, and as far as could be seen the Benedictines were all powerful.

The new religious orders who went forth to revive the work of the church were not to be deterred by so unpromising an outlook. The Franciscans came to Worcester about 1225.[13] They established themselves in the lower or eastern side of the town, on the city wall, and Frater de Leycestria was appointed the first head of the house.[14] 'Friar Street' still serves to mark the spot. It was a marshy place, hardly inhabited, but the settlement throve, and Worcester became one of the nine centres of the Franciscan Order in England, the only Minorite house in the county, probably because nowhere else could the friars obtain a footing, since the ground was too fully occupied by the other religious houses.

The Dominicans or Black Friars came to Worcester after 1221 ;[15] their house was off Broad Street, close to the city wall. The place is still known as Blackfriars. The Dominicans, however, never obtained such hold in the county as the Franciscans, and had comparatively little effect on the history of the county.

At first the friars, especially the Franciscans, were true to their mission. They worked and laboured among the poor and sick, classes the Benedictines had never tried to reach. Perhaps their greatest and best work

1 Worc. Epis. Reg. Maidstone, 1314, fol. 21d.
2 Ibid. fol. 35d.
3 Ibid. Cobham, 124d.
4 Ibid. Orleton, 1331, fol. 23.
5 Ibid. bk. ii. fol. 8d.
6 Ibid. fol. 44d.
7 Ibid. Simon de Montacute, 1333, fol. 18.
8 Ibid. 1336, fol. 24.
9 Ibid. Thoresby, 1352, fol. 41.
10 Ibid. Wakefield, fol. 75.
11 *Worc. Epis. Reg. Giffard* (Worc. Hist. Soc.), 103. Mandate of bishop ordering 'clerks who were rectors of churches to return and make personal residence at their cures.' Ibid. 299. Citation of rectors of churches of Evenlode to answer concerning plurality of benefices.
12 Ibid. 91, 380, etc.
13 *Ann. Mon.* (Rolls Ser.), iv. 416 (1224) : 'Fratres Minores isto anno primo venerunt in Angliam.' *Monum. Franc.* (Rolls Ser.), i. 16: 'Intravit autem Ada de Mariseo apud Wygorniam zelo scilicet majoris paupertatis,' 1225.
14 Ibid. i. 28.
15 *Ann. Mon.* (Rolls Ser.), iv. 413 (1221) : 'Transitus Sancti Dominici ordinis Prædicatorum. Item hoc anno venerunt fratres Prædicatores primo in Angliam.'

was among the lepers and the outcasts ; and whatever may be thought of the later conduct of the friars, the Franciscans are always entitled to be spoken of with respect, as they made the first really systematic attempt to deal with the sick and suffering. No body of men that the Church of Rome has ever produced has so shown its heroism and self-denial in working among the sick and suffering as the early Franciscans, the true followers of St. Francis. No higher ideal has ever been put before mortal man than the ideal of absolute poverty for Christ's sake, which lay at the root of his teaching. Even in those days men saw and realized the beauty of the conception ; so the Franciscans prospered. But they soon departed from their first teaching. They considered it was necessary to get a firm foothold in Worcester, and circumstances favoured them. One of the great feudal families, the Beauchamps, held the castle of Worcester which adjoined, if it did not encroach upon, the Benedictine priory. Consequently the monks were always on bad terms with the Beauchamps, and they and the bishop were not always friendly. A quarrel over their rights had been nominally settled in 1258.[1] In 1260 the general chapter of the Franciscans was held at Worcester,[2] and it is probable that then the policy of conciliating the Beauchamps as the opponents of the Benedictines was resolved upon. Whether it was or not, the Franciscans followed this course. In January, 1268, William Beauchamp, fifth baron of Elmley, died, and in his will directed his body should be buried in the church of the Friars Minor of Worcester, 'et coram corpore meo equum ferro coopertum ut decet cum stramentis militaribus.'[3] Some years later his son became possessed with the idea, the Worcester monks said at the suggestion of the friars, that the monks had dug up the earl's body and carried it away, why does not appear. So convinced was he of this that in 1276 he came to Worcester with his brother and had his father's grave opened to see whether the body was there. It was found and recognized, and, the annals say, he departed excommunicated ;[4] but the excitement caused by this raised a prejudice against burials in the cathedral or in the churchyard of the cathedral. The Franciscans established a burial ground which became popular, and caused considerable loss to the monks in the falling off of the fees for burials and the offerings for masses for the repose of the dead. The monks, however, determined not to lose their rights, as they regarded them, without a struggle. In 1289 a citizen of Worcester named Poche died ; the Franciscans alleged that in his will he ordered his body should be buried in the Franciscan cemetery. The monks, however, stated that he wanted to be buried in the cathedral, and in spite of the resistance of the friars they carried off the body by force and buried it in the churchyard of the cathedral.[5] The Franciscans complained to Archbishop Peckham, himself a Minorite Friar, that they had been assaulted and wounded by the monks ; this the monks alleged was untrue. The king interfered in the dispute and ordered that after mass had been said for the deceased in the cathedral, provided the monks lost nothing, if the friars could prove that the body was left to them for burial they were to have it and bury it.[6] Peckham was not

[1] *Reg. Beatæ Mariæ Wigorn* (Camden Soc.), 160b.
[2] *Ann. Mon.* (Rolls Ser.), iv. 446.
[3] *Worc. Epis. Reg. Giffard* (Worc. Hist. Soc.), 7, 8, 9.
[4] Ibid. 471.
[5] *Ann. Mon.* (Rolls Ser.), iv. 499, 500.
[6] Ibid. 500 : 'In cathedrali ecclesia post missam dictam pro mortuo, proviso quod ecclesia nihil perdat si Fratres Minores possunt legitime probare quod corpora sibi sint legata, ea libere ad suam efferant sepulturam.'

satisfied, he boldly stood up for his order, writing to the monks, complaining of their conduct to the friars, adding that he did not intend to allow their wickedness to pass by uncorrected, as he could not and ought not to endure the complaints of his brethren.[1] For a time the friars obtained the upper hand. Sir Nicholas de Mitton of Bredon by his will dated 1 January, 1290, directed his body to be buried in the church of the Blessed Mary of Bredon, but his heart in the place of the Friars Minor of Worcester, and with his heart he gave '£40 for the fabric of six altars in the same place.'[2] He left legacies to the Minorite Friars of Worcester, the preaching Friars of Gloucester, the Minorite Friars of Gloucester, the Friars of Mount Carmel at Gloucester, and the preaching Friars of Warwick. This shows clearly the popularity of the friars and helps to explain the deep-rooted hostility between them and the Benedictines.

Another element at work in the diocese probably produced a good deal of discontent, but it is difficult precisely to measure its extent, the influence of the alien priories. Altogether a good deal of property was held by foreign religious houses, including some church preferments; it is not clear to what degree the foreign houses filled up the benefices with the foreigners, but they did it to a considerable extent, and the fact of having a constantly changing number of foreigners must have had some influence especially on the language and literature of Worcestershire. In an account in Giffard's Register of a dispute between the monks in the alien house at Wotton Warren, a cell to Conches, some of the witnesses said they could not depose to what the disputants had said because they were ignorant of their language (idoma).[3]

Walter Cantilupe succeeded William de Blois in 1237.[4] His episcopate lasted until 12 February, 1266, and included the stormy time of the Barons' War. He was a son of Lord Cantilupe, and both by connexion and by inclination took the side of the barons against the king. His first fight of importance was in a synod in London in 1237. The papal legate Otho was about to deprive a number of the holders of ecclesiastical benefices in order to have the patronage, but Cantilupe protested against the deprivation of these men, many of whom were noble, saying some would sooner take up arms than give up their benefices.[5] Here he struck the note of the policy he followed during his episcopate, that in defence of their rights the holders of property, even of ecclesiastical property, were justified in making armed resistance. There was never a more strenuous defender of the rights of the see against all comers, whether lay, regal, or papal, than this bishop of Worcester. His next fight was for an outlying part of the county, Dudley, to decide whether it was to be in the diocese of Worcester or of Coventry and Lichfield. Here the pope compelled a compromise. The town and churches were given to the Worcester diocese, the castle and priory to Lichfield, and in spite of all the changes in six hundred and fifty years this settlement is still in force.[6]

[1] *Ann. Mon.* (Rolls Ser.), iv. 501: 'Nos non intendimus istam nequitiam dimittere incorrectam qui plagas fratrum nec debemus nec possumus sine lacrymis tolerare.'

[2] *Worc. Epis Reg. Giffard* (Worc. Hist. Soc.), 388.

[3] Ibid. pt. ii. 131.

[4] *Ann. Mon.* (Rolls Ser.), iv. 83, 428.

[5] Thomas, *Surv. of Worc. Cath. Acc. of Bishops*, 130.

[6] *Ann. Mon.* (Rolls Ser.), iv. 429. 'Tota villa de Duddeleia cum ecclesiis et earum pertinentiis lege diœcesana pertinebit ad episcopum Wygorniæ: situs vero castri ejusdam villæ et cella monachorum cum pertinentis scilicet in comitatu Staffordiæ pertinebit ad episcopum conventrensem.'

Having fixed the external limits of the diocese, Cantilupe began to enforce his rights within. Peter de Saltmarsh claimed rights in the manor of Upton upon Severn, which Cantilupe said belonged to the see: the bishop sued him with many others who made like claims in the King's Court and was successful.[1] In a quarrel with William Beauchamp, fifth baron of Elmley, Cantilupe had a more difficult struggle. William Beauchamp had levied assize of bread and ale in the hundred of Oswaldslow at Elmley Castle, and had held view of frankpledge in all his manors in the hundred to the prejudice of the same liberty; he also withdrew his manor of Bengeworth from the hundred of Oswaldslow to his court of the barony, and impeded the bishop from having free warren granted to him by the king in the demesne lands of Bredon.[2] Cantilupe excommunicated him,[3] and himself proceeded to Lyons in 1250 to procure the papal condemnation.[4] The pope ordered Beauchamp to seek the bishop's absolution;[5] and on his refusal confirmed the sentence of excommunication.[6] However, on 1 May, 1251, he was absolved by the bishop under the pope's direction, evidently at the king's request.[7]

The bishop's attitude towards the religious houses shows the same determination to uphold episcopal rights. When the priory of Malvern fell vacant he took possession of it, and in spite of the opposition of the abbot of Westminster installed John of Worcester as prior.[8] It was during his episcopate that the long-standing quarrel between the bishop and the abbey of Evesham concerning disputed rights in the churches of the vale of Evesham was decided by a compromise. The controversy at Evesham had begun under Bishop Mauger in 1202,[9] and had practically meant a success for the abbot, since the bishop, driven from England by the interdict of 1208, had been forced to leave the point in dispute undecided.[10] No bishop of Worcester from the time of Mauger to that of Cantilupe had raised the question, but some definite settlement was absolutely necessary. In 1248 on appeal to Rome the final agreement was made. The bishop renounced all jurisdiction in the vale except in the church of Abbots Morton, where the vicars were to hold the vicarage taxed to the bishop;[11] in return for this he received the patronage of the churches of Hillingdon (Middlesex), Weston (Gloucestershire), and Kinwarton (Warwickshire), with pensions of one mark from Hillingdon and half a mark from Weston.[12] At the same time the convent was allowed to withhold some of the tithes[13] and the advowson of the church of Abbots Morton, and to have a chapel in their court at Morton.[14] Thus, although the abbey had been really successful, the bishop made the sacrifice look like a concession.

Another interesting side to Cantilupe's work in the diocese is his strict attention to the local organization of the churches. At a diocesan synod held at Worcester in 1240, he issued fifty-nine constitutions to be observed by his clergy.[15] In these he made systematic regulations as to the various sacraments and ceremonies, entering into extraordinary detail,

1 *Ann. Mon.* (Rolls Ser.), iv. 429.
2 *Worc. Epis. Reg. Giffard* (Worc. Hist. Soc.), 75.
3 *Ann. Mon.* (Rolls Ser.), i. 142.
4 Ibid. iv. 440.
5 Ibid. i. 142.
6 Ibid. i. 143, iv. 440.
7 Ibid. i. 145, iv. 440.
8 Ibid. iv. 434.
9 *Chron. de Evesham* (Rolls Ser.), 109.
10 Ibid. 225.
11 Liber Albus (Worc.), f. 101, 2. *Ann. Mon.* (Rolls Ser.), iv. 439. *Cal. of Papal Letters*, li. 252. *Worc. Epis. Reg. Giffard* (Worc. Hist. Soc.), pt. i. 9–10.
12 Liber Albus (Worc.), f. 49.
13 *Pope Nich. Tax.* (Rec. Com.), 217b.
14 *Worc. Epis. Reg. Giffard* (Worc. Hist. Soc.), pt. i. 10. Liber Albus (Worc.), ff. 101, 102.
15 Wilkins, *Concilia*, i. 665–678.

ordering that children who were to be confirmed should wear new garments,[1] and that the poor who communicated might not be compelled to give alms.[2] His exhortations went further and followed the parishioners to their homes, bidding them rear up their children carefully.[3] The clergy themselves he exhorted to put on humility and guard against envy and jealousy, and to be zealous in visiting the sick.[4] He forbade them to let out their churches to farm without episcopal licence,[5] ordered vicars to make residence and rectors not to absent themselves without licence.[6]

But it is not as a diocesan bishop that Cantilupe is best known to history; it is rather as the sturdy supporter of Simon de Montfort and the friend of Grossetête. In 1252, and again in 1255, he supported Grossetête in the policy of opposition to the papal mandate demanding a tenth of the church revenues for the king.[7] In 1255 the bishops of London and Worcester made two famous speeches, in which the one said he would rather be beheaded, and the other that he would rather be hanged, than see the church so spoiled.[8] In 1258 Cantilupe joined the barons, was elected on their side in the Provisions of Oxford,[9] and became a faithful ally of Simon de Montfort, entertaining him at Kempsey before the battle of Evesham in 1265, and urging him and his followers to fight valiantly for their liberties, absolving them from their sins so as to make them fight more valiantly.[10] For this the legate Ottoboni deprived him of the right to the sacraments, and when the bishop persisted in aiding the rebels, excommunicated him.[11] How much further his resistance would have gone is uncertain. He was ill with a mortal disease, and desiring to die in communion with the church, submitted and was absolved. His death is recorded in the chronicle of Thomas Wykes as that of so good a bishop that 'but for his close adherence to Simon de Montfort he would have been worthy of canonization.'[12]

His episcopate was epoch-making both within and without his diocese. Within his diocese his work was one of definition; defining episcopal rights, defining modes and methods of local church organization. Without, his work was also one of definition, defining the rights of the English church, in defence of which he was ready to join with the alien Simon, and remain faithful to him when the majority of the barons had deserted or become only half-hearted supporters.

On Cantilupe's death Nicholas, archdeacon of Ely, who had been Lord Chancellor, Lord Keeper, and Lord Treasurer, was appointed to Worcester. He only held the see for a few months, and was then translated to Winchester.

During the vacancy on Bishop Nicholas' translation came one of the most important changes in the administration of the diocese. An agreement was at last made with the archbishop as to the custody of the spiritualities of the see whilst it was vacant. This had always been a source of dispute whenever a vacancy occurred. The bishop was the king's feudal tenant, and on his death the temporalities of the see went to the Crown and remained in the king's hands until he granted them to the new bishop—usually when the latter did homage on his appointment. But

1 Wilkins, *Concilia*, i. 667.
2 Ibid. 671.
3 Ibid. 668.
4 Ibid. 670.
5 Ibid. 672.
6 Ibid. 673.
7 Matt. Paris, *Chron. Maj.* (Rolls Ser.), v. 326, 525.
8 Ibid. 525.
9 *Ann. Mon.* (Rolls Ser.), i. 447.
10 Ibid. iv. 168.
11 Ibid. 455–456.
12 *Ann. Mon.* (Rolls Ser.), iv. 180.

in addition to the revenues the bishop derived from his temporal possessions, he received an income for performing various spiritual functions, such as consecrating churches, granting licences, dispensations, and receiving fees on visitations. These spiritualities went when the see was vacant to the archbishop of Canterbury. In what capacity opinions differed ; the Roman view was that the archbishop, being papal legate, received them for the pope ; the Anglican, that he received them as the English metropolitan. In whatever capacity, they had to be collected, and the collection gave rise to a difficulty. A local man would know better than a stranger of what the fees consisted, so would be able to get more money, but the honesty of the local guardian of spiritualities was not invariably above suspicion, and although he might collect more than a stranger, it by no means followed that the archbishop received more. A stranger did not know the different sources from which to collect, and would probably lose a good deal from ignorance, so that even assuming he was strictly honest, there would be a considerable leakage. It was therefore necessary to choose between two evils, the honesty of the stranger and the dishonesty of the resident. Archbishop Boniface devised a happy means which combined the advantages of each ; he allowed the local man to collect, and paid him a percentage on the sum received. The same difficulty had arisen in the large diocese of Lincoln, and in 1262 it had been settled there by a formal agreement that on a vacancy the prior of Lincoln should act as the archbishop's collector and be allowed a commission. In 1268 an agreement similar in principle but varying in detail was made as to Worcester, and confirmed by Archbishop Peckham in 1283.[1] The prior got in all he possibly could, paid over two-thirds to the archbishop, and retained one-third for his trouble. To us thirty-three per cent. seems a very handsome commission. The record of the acts of the priors while acting as 'official and administrator of the spiritualities in the city and diocese of Worcester, the see being vacant,' from 1301 to 1435, is contained in a register of the Dean and Chapter of Worcester, known as the Sede Vacante Register,[2] which is a most important document for the ecclesiastical history of the county, showing what the bishop's rights were supposed to be, since the prior did all he could to enforce them to the uttermost farthing.

The Worcester agreement differed from the Lincoln in one very important particular, as to the right of the prior, while acting as guardian of the spiritualities, to visit the monasteries. In the Lincoln agreement the prior could only visit two religious houses in each archdeaconry. In the Worcester agreement there was no limit to his power wherever the bishop's right of visitation extended. Naturally the prior seldom failed to exercise his right, for it was both profitable and pleasing to him to hold an episcopal visitation into the other religious houses. In this way Worcester, though by no means the most powerful or most privileged of the monasteries of the diocese, was placed in an exceptionally important position in comparison with the other houses. Moreover its attitude to the bishop and his claims to jurisdiction was then changed. It was now to the priory's interest to uphold and extend the bishop's rights as far as possible, so, except when the bishop attempted to make good his claims over Worcester itself, the bishop could always count upon its support. Thus no alliance of all the religious houses against the

[1] *Reg. Epistolarum Peckham* (Rolls Ser.), ii. 632.

[2] Printed by the Worc. Hist. Soc.

bishop could arise. If they fought him they did it separately, not collectively. The way the monks of Worcester came to regard the bishop is perhaps best shown by the case of Giffard. He had many contests with them, and fought them on several occasions, but he was also a great benefactor, and the prior recognized the importance of upholding the bishop's authority. So in 1292, considering the things both spiritual and temporal bestowed upon them by the bishop, they granted with unanimous consent that every year after the decease of the same bishop they would feed thirteen poor persons on the day of his anniversary, and that this might be observed inviolate they inserted it in the martyrology of the monastery.[1]

Another change in the administration of the diocese which had been begun in Cantilupe's episcopate, but which probably was not fully carried out for some years, was the attempt to arrive at a uniformity of the services in the churches. What was the original use which prevailed in Worcestershire is by no means clear, though it is alleged to have had its own use based on a service book Oswald had obtained from Corbie; but if this was so it belonged to the Worcester house and no other, for probably there was no one use. Worcester had the Sarum Use, but from a memorandum in a thirteenth-century antiphon in the cathedral library, one of the Worcester service books that has survived, it would seem that the Benedictine monasteries in the county were greatly lacking in uniformity. It appears from this that the observances, even if the use was the same, differed in the four great Benedictine houses in the county.[2] The Benedictines, unlike the Cistercians, had no common monastic missal, but to a great extent adopted the local use of the diocese in which their houses were situated.[3] It would have been expected that certainly as part of the county was in the Hereford diocese in that part and in so much of the Worcester diocese as is west of the Severn the Hereford Use or something like it would have prevailed, but this does not appear to have been the case. The use of Sarum seems to have become the one usually employed. Cantilupe prescribed it for the services that should be held in the Carnarie Chapel in Worcester, and directed that all Divine offices that should then be sung and all canonical hours then observed should be according to the use of Sarum.[4]

Godfrey Giffard succeeded Nicholas in 1268. He was bishop for thirty-four years (1268-1301). Like Cantilupe he belonged to a noble family, but his family had no local connexion with Worcestershire. Although a strong upholder of episcopal rights, probably quite as strong as Cantilupe, Giffard was also a royalist, and in spite of occasional quarrels with the king, he was a most loyal servant of the Crown. Giffard resigned the Lord Chancellorship to become bishop of Worcester. He retained much of the lawyer, and in his administration of the see his legal training often appears. His first act was to complete the fortifications of Hartlebury, thus giving the bishop a stronghold on the line of the Severn.[5] He then tried to clear the diocese of rebels. Here he had no easy task, especially as he had to deal with one who had

[1] *Worc. Epis. Reg. Giffard* (Worc. Hist. Soc.), 432.

[2] Worc. Cath. MSS. f. 120. 'Isti domus habebunt martilogium cum dirige cum monachi in eis obierint scilicet Glostoma Ramasey Abyndoma Westmonasterium Burgo St. Petri Malmesbury Wenlok Monasterium Sti Remisii Remensis. Mutteley habebit Martilogium sive dirige. Et isti domus habebunt dirige sive martilogium viz Radyngia Gloucesteria Teukesberia Evesham Wynchelcombe Persora Malvernia major et Malvernia minor.'

[3] *Introduction to Westminster Missal* (Henry Bradshaw Soc.), xii.

[4] Thomas, *Surv. of Worc. Cath.* App. No. 43.

[5] Ibid. *Acc. of Bishops*, 136.

been a source of much of the trouble, Gilbert, eighth earl of Gloucester, seventh earl of Hertford, and ninth earl of Clare. Fortunately for Giffard he assumed the Cross.[1] The bishop gave leave to two of the Cantilupes, Thomas who had been chancellor to Simon de Montfort and afterwards became bishop of Hereford and a saint, and Hugh, archdeacon of Gloucester, to absent themselves for three years to study theology.[2] In May, 1269, William Beauchamp, tenth earl of Warwick, did homage to the bishop in the chapel of Bredon.[3] They, however, quarrelled the same year over the patronage of Hampton which the earl claimed,[4] and subsequently the bishop revived the litigation which Cantilupe had begun against the earl exercising any jurisdiction in Oswaldslow.[5] The litigation extended over several years, but terminated in the bishop's favour, and was of importance as showing his power over one of the great lay barons of the county.

The bishop's next fight was with Archbishop Peckham, who, as it was stated, did all in his power to take away the rights of his suffragan bishops and transfer them to his own court.[6] Richard de Swinefeld, bishop of Hereford, who was the prime mover, was excommunicated,[7] and Giffard charged with simony, disobedience, and perjury.[8] This dispute, however, ended in a mutual reconciliation, Giffard having other fights on hand.

In 1282 his fight with Great Malvern began. Malvern was a cell to Westminister, and the Malvern house first and the Westminster house afterwards claimed that the bishop of Worcester had no right to visit Malvern since it was a cell to a royal house, and as such was exempt from visitation. Against this there was the fact that the bishop of Worcester had on various previous occasions visited Malvern without protest.[9] In the abstract it would seem that Westminster was right, but the case on legal grounds was quite arguable. On the merits Giffard was clearly right, and the knowledge that this was so probably gained him many supporters. In his visitation in 1282 Giffard went to Malvern and preached there. Whether his text, 'I will come and descend on you,' had any hidden meaning, does not appear ; but he ascertained, and the fact was not denied, that the prior, William de Ledbury, kept twenty-two women at various houses and farms connected with the priory ; the bishop thereupon deposed him and absolved him from the rule of the house.[10] The contest was not therefore a mere question of visitation. To depose the prior of the cell of another house without any notice to that house was an assertion of power which required a great deal to support it. Giffard appears to have excommunicated for contumacy all the monks of the priory who did not recognize and obey his sentence of deposition.[11] In spite of the censure of Archbishop Peckham[12] the abbot of Westminster, Richard de Ware, held his own against Giffard. When the monks of Great Malvern, in spite of excommunication, elected as prior William de Wykewane, and sent him to the abbot, the latter imprisoned him

[1] *Ann. Mon.* (Rolls Ser.), iv. 218, 458.
[2] *Worc. Epis. Reg. Giffard* (Worc. Hist. Soc.), 2–3.
[3] Ibid. 9.
[4] Ibid. 36.
[5] Ibid. 75, 77, and *Ann. Mon.* (Rolls Ser.), i. 139, 440, iv. 439.
[6] *Reg. Epistolarum Peckham* (Rolls Ser.), i. 328–334. The complaints of the bishop concerning the exercise of the archiepiscopal jurisdiction with the archbishop's answer to the same are here given.
[7] Ibid. iii. 1068.
[8] Ibid. 757.
[9] *Ann. Mon.* (Rolls Ser.), iv. 424, 429, 430.
[10] *Worc. Epis. Reg. Giffard* (Worc. Hist. Soc.), 178.
[11] Ibid. 165.
[12] *Reg. Epistolarum Peckham* (Rolls Ser.), ii. 516.

and his attendants. The bishop appealed to the king and to the pope and pronounced excommunication after excommunication, but to no avail. The king took the part of the abbot and forced a settlement. Giffard had to admit that as he had seen Apostolic letters saying that Westminster and all its cells and priories were free from diocesan law and ordinary jurisdiction, he would so regard them.[1] He, however, retained the right to visit the churches. Prior Ledbury was reinstated and made to convey to the bishop the manor of Knightwick as an indemnity against the costs he had incurred.[2] The abbot of Westminster released his prisoners and there was a general absolution from excommunication on both sides.[3] It would seem that the abbot of Westminster cared nothing for the fitness of the man, as it was not till 1287 that he deposed Prior Ledbury and appointed Richard de Estone.[4] But doubtless he was fighting simply for his rights; not so much to reinstate an immoral prior, as to deny the bishop's right to depose him. Still, disputes such as these, which must have been publicly known, as all the bishop's sentences were ordered to be read in the parish churches, doubtless led to that feeling of discontent which gradually grew up against things as they were. Nothing could speak more forcibly for reform than the reinstatement of William of Ledbury without any censure on his conduct, even though it was only meant to prove the legal right of the abbot.

Another of Giffard's great fights, and it is by considering them that the real state of the county is best seen, was his resistance to the demands continually made on the clergy for money. No complaint was more frequent, and on the whole none better founded, than the protests against the constant payments made to the pope or his agents, or rather nominally raised for such purposes. A good instance of this is shown in the case of Peter's Pence. In 1301 the sum raised from the diocese under this head was £34 2*s.* 7½*d.*, of which £14 came from the Worcester archdeaconry. The bishop paid annually for Peter's Pence a fixed sum of £10 5*s.* 0*d.*, and the balance appears to have been retained for the trouble of collecting. A letter from Pope Gregory X. stated that the sum received from the Worcester diocese for Peter's Pence was £10 5*s.* 0*d.* and requested the collection.[5] The letter gives the contribution of thirteen other dioceses, and Worcester stands seventh on the list as regards the sum paid. Whatever sum the Worcester officials collected they did not pay it over unless they were obliged. In 1282 Pope Martin IV. wrote to the archbishop of Dublin directing him to compel those who had not paid the tenth for the Holy Land to pay it at once. On this the archbishop wrote to the bishop of Worcester giving particulars of the sums due and requesting payment.[6] The particulars are interesting as showing the difficulty there was in getting these ecclesiastical extortions paid. Evesham was sworn, according to the oath of the proctor, as to value at 1,000 marks, and owed £48 6*s.* 3½*d.* for each of the last six years. Worcester was sworn at £214 5*s.* 0*d.* and owed 39*s.* 4*d.* for each of the first five years, and for the sixth year £6 6*s.* 9½*d.* Great Malvern was sworn to be of the value of £75 2*s.* 4*d.* and owed £4 2*s.* 3*d.* for each of the six years. This shows that however keen the religious houses might be to get in their resources there was not an equal

1 *Worc. Epis. Reg. Giffard* (Worc. Hist. Soc.), 219.
2 Ibid. 218.
3 Ibid. 219.
4 *Ann. Mon.* (Rolls Ser.), iv. 494.
5 *Worc. Epis. Reg. Giffard* (Worc. Hist. Soc.), 57.
6 Ibid. 143.

alacrity to pay the pope. Another tax that was greatly resented was the payment of the papal nuncios. These officials, when on papal business, were paid by a tax on ecclesiastics, called procurations, usually fixed at so much a day. In 1282 the Nuncio Geoffrey de Vezano, canon of Cambray, not receiving his procurations regularly, wrote to Giffard to request payment, and as this had not the desired effect applied to Archbishop Peckham, who enclosed a list of arrears and ordered immediate payment. Among those who had not paid were the priories of Worcester, Pershore, Evesham, Great Malvern, Little Malvern, Bordesley, Astley, Besford, Westwood, and Cookhill. None of them, it is said, 'have paid the last year, many of them are in arrears for the preceding years.'[1] It is plain that Rome was always in one way or the other asking for money, and the English authorities were doing all they could to refuse. In Worcester Giffard himself seems to have headed the opposition. As a patriot, he hated to see English money go to Rome, as a bishop, he needed the money for his diocese, and for the heavy taxation made necessary by the king's wars.

The period of Giffard's episcopate marks in Worcestershire, as elsewhere, the beginning of the foundation of chantries. The Statute of Mortmain had discouraged endowments on so large a scale as was necessary for the foundation of monasteries, and a new form of spiritual investment was wanted. Thus chapels attached to churches were founded by some benefactor for masses and prayers for the soul of the founder, his family, and all faithful dead. The endowment of the chantry was usually supplied by the founder, and he appointed the priest who performed the necessary services. Hence at many of the churches there were two priests, the regular parish priest and the chantry priest. The first mention of a chantry is in 1269, when Osbert de Alne, chaplain, was admitted to the chantry, with a rent of 12 marks left by William Roculf in his will.[2] In 1280 a priest was admitted to say divine service for the soul of a former citizen of Worcester and receive in return the rents left by will for this purpose.[3] In 1287 the bishop's great chantry of the Carnarie, Worcester, was endowed;[4] in 1298 a priest was presented to the chapel of Abbots Morton,[5] and in 1300 a memorandum is given as to 'a chantry in the court of the manor of Walter Beauchamp at Powick.'[6] Later registers show how general the practice became, until by the fifteenth century most of the larger parish churches had chantries annexed to them, which in some cases were endowed to support three or more chaplains.[7] The same practice went on in some of the conventual churches. In Little Malvern the monks agreed to let a priest pray at the altar of the Holy Cross for 'the souls of Henry, Geoffrey, Matilda, and Nicholas de Mitton, Edith and Robert de Clipston, Richard de Clipston, Alice and Richard de Boudon, and Ellen,' in return for the food portion of a monk and 20*s.* a year.[8] Another feature of the time is also to be found in the bishop's confirmation of the rules as to anchorages or cells. Thus he confirmed those of the anchorage of St. John, Worcester, founded by Juliana, the anchoress there in 1269.[9]

1 *Worc. Epis. Reg. Giffard* (Worc. Hist. Soc.), 146.

2 Ibid. 34. The entry does not say where the chantry was, but it may have been at Rous Lench, as the Roculfs had property there, and Rous Lench used to be called Lench Roculf.

3 Ibid. 124.
4 Ibid. 308.
5 Ibid. 507.
6 Ibid. 544.

7 Worc. Epis. Reg. Carpenter, fol. 26.

8 *Worc. Epis. Reg. Giffard* (Worc. Hist. Soc.), 114.

9 Ibid. 35.

Giffard thought it well to encourage both orders of friars. He was 'conservator of the Order of Friars Preachers,' the Dominicans,[1] and was admitted by Brother Bonagratia, the Minister General of the Minorites, into all the benefits of that order in 1282.[2] On the Sunday following the feast of St. Francis in that year he celebrated mass in the Franciscan church at Worcester, and served (procuravit) all the brethren of the house.[3] It shows the hold the friars had acquired, that the bishop should be the conservator of the one order and a member of the other.

One mark of the united action of Giffard and the bishop of Hereford, Richard Swinefeld, has survived to this day. Gilbert de Clare claimed various rights in Malvern chase and tried to exclude the two bishops from it.[4] The bishops appealed to the courts to settle the question, and the bishop of Hereford was ready with a champion to decide the matter if it had come to wager of battle. This was not necessary, as the case was decided before the king's judges, with a jury composed of men from Herefordshire and Worcestershire. They decided in favour of the bishops, and the great trench still called 'the Earl's ditch' was dug along the top of the Malvern Hills to show where the rights of the earl of Gloucester ended, a trench which to this day forms the boundary between the counties of Worcester and Hereford.[5] The earl had made the ditch on Giffard's land, so Giffard, by way of settlement, made him agree that he and his heirs should furnish annually to the bishop and his successors at his manor at Kempsey from the chase at Malvern two couple of bucks and does on the Vigil of the Assumption and Christmas Eve.[6]

A glimpse of the state of Worcestershire parishes in the diocese of Hereford is given from the roll of Bishop Swinefeld's household expenses in the years 1289, 1290, when the bishop visited them.[7] At Tenbury the agent of the abbot of Lyra, who managed the abbey's property there, attended the bishop and paid his procurations. Lindridge had been both a rectory and a vicarage, but on the death of the last rector the rectory and vicarage were united under the then rector, John de Betterley, to comply with the canon against the division of benefices. The union did not last long, for in 1305 the great tithe was appropriated to the priory of Worcester. Rock was the next parish visited, and the vicar paid procuration.

Like Cantilupe, Giffard had spared no effort to maintain episcopal rights. Like him too he had been involved in struggles which seemed rather secular than religious, yet he did not neglect the spiritual side of his office. The visitations recorded in his register prove his work in his diocese was thorough, if not systematic. He did not attempt to visit Evesham, but paid no regard to claims of the Cistercian abbey of Bordesley to be exempt.[8] In 1284 he visited Pershore and corrected the monks, bidding them 'apply themselves more to the divine offices and attending the sick in the infirmary,' and shut the cloister door against the entrance of seculars, 'whereby a stumbling block is prepared for those contemplating Christ.'[9] In 1285, after his official had

1 *Worc. Epis. Reg. Giffard* (Worc. Hist. Soc.), 126.
2 Ibid. 156.
3 Ibid. 165.
4 *Ann. Mon.* (Rolls Ser.), iv. 476.
5 Ibid. 494. Here it is said that the earl made the foss against the wild beasts: 'Quia bestiæ sylvæ transeuntes terminos Herefordenses frequenter ibant et non revertebantur, G. comes Gloucestriæ super Malverniæ montes fossatum fecit.'
6 *Worc. Epis. Reg. Giffard* (Worc. Hist. Soc.), 526.
7 *Roll of Household Expenses of Bishop Swinfeld* (Camden Soc.).
8 *Worc. Epis. Reg. Giffard* (Worc. Hist. Soc.), 6, 243, 379.
9 Ibid. 242.

visited Cookhill, the bishop sent a letter to the nuns forbidding them to go out of the cloister unless compelled by necessity.[1] The Worcester monks he condemned because they went out 'wandering and leading harriers.'[2] Such instances as these show his determination to preserve strict discipline in his diocese.

Giffard died in February, 1301. On his death the agreement under which the prior acted as guardian of the spiritualities came in force, and Prior John de la Wyke tried to enforce his rights. When the prior acted as guardian of the spiritualities[3] his first step was always visitation. The other monasteries not unnaturally resented this, and a fight began between the monasteries of St. Peter's, Gloucester, and Tewkesbury, and the prior as to his right to visit them. They refused him admittance, so he excommunicated them, but the archbishop ordered him to withdraw the excommunication.[4]

Before the election of the new bishop had been settled the bishop of Llandaff, John of Monmouth, was engaged by the prior to come to Worcester to hold an ordination, and the correspondence between him and the prior is given in the registers. The bishop wanted to come, but was afraid to do so without the consent of the archbishop, who had already disputed the prior's authority.[5] The prior assured him that he might come without any fear of consequences, quoting the composition of Archbishop Boniface to prove his own authority.[6] The bishop, however, 'unwilling to offend the archbishop, without prejudice to the prior,' felt it but right to gain the archbishop's consent.[7] Having gained it, he held the ordination on the Saturday of Ember week next after the feast of St. Matthew the Apostle in 1302.[8]

In the meantime the question of the election of the new bishop had to be settled. The prior had called the chapter together in March, 1301, immediately on the death of Giffard, and as soon as they had received a *congé délire* they proceeded in April, 1302, to elect John St. Germain, 'a priest of lawful age . . . and wise in temporal and spiritual matters.'[9] The election was referred to the archbishop for confirmation, but in August the archbishop submitted the matter to the pope, stating many alleged irregularities in the procedure.[10] John St. Germain himself proceeded to Rome to defend his election.[11] The prior wrote in his behalf, promising a pension to Francis, cardinal of the Apostolic see, archdeacon of Worcester, if he supported him.[12] The pope, however, quashed the election[13] and appointed William Gainsborough, a Franciscan, who was so poor that he had to borrow money

[1] *Worc. Epis. Reg. Giffard* (Worc. Hist. Soc.), 267. [2] Ibid. 392.

[3] From the prior's accounts some idea of the value of the spiritualities of the see is obtained. An account of the receipts for the year 2 Feb. 1301—2 Feb. 1302 is given, the total amounting to £109 11*s.* 11*d.* The sums received from the different deaneries are given separately and divided into summer and winter accounts. For Worcester they run:—Powick, summer £2 11*s.* 4*d.*; winter £2 9*s.* 0*d.*: Pershore, summer £3 12*s.* 10*d.*; winter £2 3*s.* 4*d.*: Kidderminster, summer £3 7*s.* 4*d.*: winter £1 19*s.* 0*d.*: Worcester, summer £1 18*d.* 8*s.*: winter 15*s.* 10*d.*: Wych, summer £3 14*s.* 8*d.*: winter £1 17*s.* 4*d.* Total amount £24 9*s.* 4*d.*

[4] *Sede Vac. Reg.* (Worc. Hist. Soc.), 11, 12. Some letters that passed between the prior and his agents in Rome show the state of things very clearly. The prior told his agent that the archdeacon of Worcester, who was a cardinal residing at Rome, might help his cause against the monasteries. The agent replied that the cardinal would not move unless 'urged, not by words, but by presents as is usual.' (Ibid. 41.) *Hist. MSS. Com. Rep.* xiv. App. viii. 196.

[5] *Sede Vac. Reg.* (Worc. Hist. Soc.), 11. [6] Ibid. 15, 16. [7] Ibid. 17, 18. [8] Ibid. 21.

[9] Ibid. 1. [10] Ibid. 12. [11] Ibid. 14, 15. [12] Ibid. 18.

[13] This step was often repeated. Between 1301 and 1435 fifteen out of nineteen elections were quashed and the pope's nominee appointed. On four occasions the monks elected their own prior, Wulstan of Bransford; three times he was set aside by the pope in spite of the support of the archbishop and the king and it was only on the fourth time that the pope confirmed the election.

on all sides to pay the expenses of his enthroning. The register contains an angry letter from the bishop to the prior complaining that they would not advance him money.[1] It appears he had to borrow £100 from the archdeacon of Dorset, who wrote rather sharply to the prior, telling him to pay that sum to the bishop at once so the bishop might repay him, or else he will take other means.[2] The account of Gainsborough's enthronement shows how the poor man was plundered of everything he had by the different officials by way of perquisites—his horse, his saddle, his boots, his cape—and he was at last left standing bare-footed and half-clothed at the cathedral door.[3] One claim was made against him by the king. While the temporalities were in the royal hands the arable lands of the see were sown with corn, and on their restoration the king made the bishop pay the cost of cultivation and sowing, amounting to 512 marks.

The most noteworthy feature of Gainsborough's episcopate was the growing importance of the friars and the consequent struggle between them, the rectors of parish churches, and the secular clergy in general concerning their right of preaching and hearing confession.[4] The bishop, himself a Franciscan, was naturally in sympathy with the friars and in their cause appealed to Rome. Popes Benedict XI. and Clement V. both supported them and confirmed their privileges of preaching and hearing confession and of immunity from excommunication without special Apostolic letters, while the bishop, as 'conservator of the said privileges of the said brothers,' saw that the papal mandates were enforced.[5]

Otherwise Gainsborough's episcopate is not marked by anything of importance. He was sent to negotiate the marriage between Edward II. and the 'She-Wolf of France,' and died at Beauvais before he could return.

The period between his death and the appointment of his successor is marked by a curious incident. Edward II. was most desirous to place his old tutor, Walter Reynolds, in the see, but was afraid that the pope would appoint before this could be done. He therefore wrote a most remarkable letter to the prior and convent of Worcester to hasten the election, pointing out the dangers that followed from a see being left vacant, dangers not only to the see but also to England,[6] and making an uncompromising statement of the rights of the Crown against the pope as to the appointment of bishops. This document is such as would hardly have been expected from Edward II., for it places very simply and very clearly the rights of the English kings as to bishops, and is therefore of more than local importance. Moreover, it

[1] *Sede Vac. Reg.* (Worc. Hist. Soc.), 46.

[2] Ibid. 52.

[3] Ibid. 53. Even then the proctor of the archdeacon of Canterbury still wanted more and claimed a cup and 10 marks for his expenses. This last was too much for the bishop, who replied he would see about it.

[4] Worc. Epis. Reg. Gainsborough, fol. 6*d.*

[5] Ibid. ff. 6*d*, 7, 7*d.* 8, 9.

[6] *Sede Vac. Reg.* (Worc. Hist. Soc.), 104. He states that before the time of King John all his ancestors, kings of England since Christianity had been established in England and bishoprics ordained, freely gave bishoprics without any contradiction as they give prebends now in their free chapels. King John gave to cathedral churches the right of free election; Pope Innocent confirmed this. The king always reserved the patronage of the bishoprics and the gift of all things during the vacancies. When a bishop dies the chapter should ask for a *congé d'élire;* when they have elected anyone they should present him to the king, who can accept or refuse him, for the king, dealing with his own prelate, has the right to confirm or quash the election, as the elect may be a traitor or an enemy of the king or the realm, or of another nation and not understand the language. The king has never relinquished the right of his Crown. The pope cannot confer bishoprics in England or reserve them, as the matter concerns lay patronage.

had its effect; the pope, although he annulled the election, gave up the idea of filling the see with a nominee of his own and appointed Reynolds himself.[1] Whether his appointment was judicious may be doubted, for, 'being absent from his diocese on the affairs of the king,' one of his first acts was to appoint John de Monmouth, the bishop of Llandaff, to execute the episcopal office,[2] and shortly afterwards, without ever having visited his diocese, he went to Rome, having appointed Benedict de Paston vicar-general of the diocese during his absence.[3] In 1311 he became Lord Chancellor of England, and on Winchelsey's death in 1313 he was translated to Canterbury.

Reynolds was the first bishop who tried to work the diocese by deputy; the system which he inaugurated formed a precedent, for the course was afterwards taken of appointing foreigners to the see of Worcester who never came near the diocese, and did all episcopal work that had to be done by deputy. At the same time, although Bishop Reynolds gave over his work to his deputy he did not leave everything to him, but constantly interfered in the affairs of the diocese. His register gives various commissions issued to the vicar-general ordering him to threaten an unruly brother with excommunication[4] or to enforce personal residence on vicars and priests;[5] or to 'examine the lives and conversations of clerks,' and present them for ordination to any bishop whom the bishop of Worcester himself should appoint to hold ordination in his stead.[6]

One incident of the vacancy on Reynolds' translation marks how the crusading spirit had subsided. Clement V. wrote that the Council at Vienne in 1312 had imposed 'a tithe for six years on the faithful to redeem the inheritance of our Redeemer which had become the property of aliens, . . . most filthy Saracens.' Hence he directed the archbishop of Canterbury to enforce the payment of the subsidy; the archbishop sent to the prior ordering him to get in the money. The prior ordered that one moiety of the tithe be paid before the exaltation of the Holy Cross on penalty of the greater excommunication; but even this did not produce the money, for in December there was a further order to pay by the feast of St. Hilary. It would thus appear that it was then quite as difficult to get money for a crusade as for any other object.

On the translation of Reynolds to Canterbury in October, 1313, the monks of Canterbury had elected Thomas Cobham, canon of York, but the pope, urged by Edward II., set aside this election, since 'the appointment was reserved to the Apostolic see,'[7] appointed Walter Reynolds to Canterbury and Cobham to Worcester.[8] But Cobham refused Worcester, so the pope 'absolved him from the chain by which he was bound to Worcester'[9] and appointed Walter Maydeston in his stead.[10] The new bishop was very poor, and had to borrow considerable sums of money in order to carry on the business of the see; as he could not pay his creditors he gave them yearly pensions payable out of the revenues of the diocese, some of them to last until the bishop could give the recipients a suitable living. There is little of importance in the four years of his episcopate. Like his predecessor

[1] *Sede Vac. Reg.* (Worc. Hist. Soc.), 111.
[2] Worc. Epis. Reg. Reynolds, f. 13.
[3] Ibid. f. 9.
[4] Ibid. f. 64d.
[5] Ibid. ff. 68d, 84d.
[6] Ibid. ff. 78, 81d, 84.
[7] *Cal. of Papal Letters*, ii. 115.
[8] *Sede Vac. Reg.* (Worc. Hist. Soc.), 144.
[9] Ibid. 145.
[10] *Cal. of Papal Letters*, 115.

he was a friend of the king, and interfered in the king's behalf to see that the tenths due to the Exchequer for the war in Scotland were paid. Those who refused were to be excommunicated, and absolution of the same was reserved for the bishop.[1] He was twice absent 'on the business of the realm of England.' As early as January, 1314, he had given licence to Simon Walpole and John Bloyrn to admit and institute to the churches of the diocese during his absence;[2] in March, 1317, he died abroad,[3] probably at Orleans.[4] In the early part of the year 1315 the bishop paid a series of visitations, receiving full procuration in most cases. After the visitation he wrote a general letter to 'his beloved sons' denouncing the practice of keeping churches vacant, and bidding them appoint fit persons in place of those rectors who had been removed.[5] He also sent a special mandate to John, the prior of Worcester, to correct the excesses of the monks of the said monastery.[6]

During the vacancy of the see on his death two cases came before the prior which it is to be hoped were exceptional. William de D., parish priest, was charged with sacrilegious theft, common usury, perjury, and glaring immorality. He was, however, allowed to purge himself and to re-enter his benefice.[7] Master R. de A. B., chaplain, was accused of immorality, usury, drunkenness, homicide, brawling, and negligence of his duties. He also was allowed after purgation to re-enter his benefice.[8]

Thomas Cobham, whom the monks of Canterbury had intended to be archbishop on Winchelsey's death, but whose election the pope, at the king's request, set aside in favour of Reynolds, was the next bishop. The pope appointed him to Worcester in April, 1317,[9] and he held the see until August, 1327. One of the chief points in his episcopate was his refusal to muster his tenants to go to the Scotch war. His refusal was based on the ground that he had already sent all that were fit for service and had none left who were able to go; he, however, sent the king £50, excusing the smallness of the present on account of his many losses and the spoiled and naked condition of the bishopric.[10]

The struggle over the election of the new bishop in 1327 and the final appointment of Adam Orleton showed the necessity for Edward's protest about the king's right to appoint bishops. The monks elected and the king approved the election of Wulstan de Bransford, prior of Worcester, a royal partisan. The archbishop was afraid to consecrate Wulstan, and the monks of Canterbury, in spite of the king's orders, were afraid to call upon the suffragans of Canterbury to do so, as it was stated the bishopric had been reserved by the pope.[11] This proved true, and the see was handed over to the king's greatest enemy, the bishop of Hereford, Adam Orleton.[12]

At Worcester Orleton could do even more to harm the royal cause than at Hereford. The Mortimers already had a strong hold on the county, such an ally as bishop of Worcester gave them a stronger. The bishop's attitude was shown in a sermon he preached at Oxford before the

[1] Worc. Epis. Reg. Maidstone, f. 28d.
[2] Ibid. f. 20d.
[3] *Sede Vac. Reg.* (Worc. Hist. Soc.), 180.
[4] *Cal. of Papal Letters*, ii. 140.
[5] Worc. Epis. Reg. Maidstone, f. 26.
[6] Ibid.
[7] *Sede Vac. Reg.* (Worc. Hist. Soc.), 180.
[8] Ibid.
[9] *Cal. of Papal Letters*, ii. 140.
[10] Worc. Epis. Reg. Cobham, f. 73.
[11] Thomas, *Surv. of Worc. Cath. Acc. of Bishops*, 169 and App. N. 92.
[12] *Cal. of Papal Letters*, ii. 263.

queen and the Prince of Wales, the text being, 'And I will put enmity between thee and the woman, and between thy seed and her seed ; it shall bruise thy head.'[1] The obvious reference was to the king and queen, although the bishop, when taxed with it in 1333, alleged that it applied to Hugh Despenser and the queen.[2] With such a strong supporter in Worcester the queen and Roger Mortimer were able to send the king as a prisoner to Berkeley Castle in the diocese of Worcester. It was the bishop who privately conveyed orders to the royal keepers in the famous line which served as a death warrant, 'Edwardum occidere nolite timere bonum est.' As bishop, Orleton is chiefly noted for the number of persons he ordained. He held the see six years (1327–1333), and ordained over one thousand persons. At one ordination at Tewkesbury he ordained 406, at one at Campden 419. Probably he is the only bishop of Worcester who ever held an ordination for the diocese of Worcester in Paris.

In the early years of Edward III. Orleton was translated to Winchester by the pope,[3] who sent Simon de Montacute to Worcester,[4] and described him as 'of elegant morals, fair honesty, and bright chastity.' His chief acts were to enrich the Worcester house, for which they ordered the day of his death to be placed in their Martyrology.[5] He was translated to Ely in 1337, and was followed by Thomas Hemenhale, who was also appointed by the pope.[6] He only held the see one year, dying at Hartlebury in 1338.[7]

Wulstan de Bransford, the prior of Worcester, on his fourth election by the monks of Worcester was at last confirmed in the episcopate by the pope.[8] Had he been made bishop when first elected he would probably have been one of the celebrated bishops of Worcester, but when at last the pope allowed his election he was too old. When summoned to Parliament he asked to be excused on the ground of his infirmities ; he, however, promised if the king would release him for life from attending Parliament he would go as long as he lived and was able to celebrate mass on the anniversary of Edward II. at St. Peter's, Gloucester.[9] Wulstan ordered masses, prayers, and processions to be made, and granted a forty days' indulgence to all who would attend the service for Edward III.'s great naval victory at Sluys.[10] A large part of his time was occupied in confirming endowments of chantries and anniversaries. The two acts by which he was most remembered were building a bridge over the Teme at his native place, Bransford, thus improving the route into Wales and Herefordshire ; and building, while prior, a large hall to the priory, known as the Guesten Hall, for the entertainment of strangers and for holding courts.[11]

The closing years of Wulstan de Bransford were marked by that scourge of the fourteenth century, the 'Great Pestilence' or 'Black Death.' Rumours of the coming plague reached England in the early summer of 1348, and towards the end of the year 'the cruel pestilence, terrible to all future ages, came from parts over the sea to the south coast into a port called Melcombe (Weymouth),

1 Gen. iii. 15.
2 Thomas, *Surv. of Worc. Cath. Acc. of Bishops*, 173.
3 Ibid. 512.
4 Ibid.
5 Ibid. 174.
6 *Cal. of Papal Letters*, ii. 541.
7 *Sede Vac. Reg.* (Worc. Hist. Soc.), 256.
8 Worc. Epis. Reg. Wulstan de Bransford, f. 3.
9 Rymer, *Fœd.* v. 191, 310.
10 Worc. Epis. Reg. Wulstan de Bransford, f. 154.
11 This fine hall with a splendid roof lasted till within living memory, when it was pulled down by the dean and chapter as it was supposed to interfere with the view from the windows of one of the canon's houses. The chapter said they had no money to restore it and no one would find any.

in Dorsetshire.'[1] The wave of contagion swept over Dorset, Devon, and Somerset, and passed on into the Midlands and the rest of England. Prayers and processions, fasting and humiliation, were ordered by king and prelate, but still the Black Death spread havoc in all parts of the realm. In the county of Worcester it was at its height in the summer months of the year 1349. Burials in the churchyard of the cathedral were forbidden as early as the April of that year,[2] and 'in these sad times' all funerals were ordered to take place outside the walls in the cemetery of the hospital of St. Oswald.[3] It is difficult to form any exact idea of the proportion of the population swept off by the plague. It may be that the long list of institutions to benefices in Wulstan de Bransford's register from March, 1348, to July, 1349, is due to the heavy death roll among the clergy in these years.[4] The register for the six months' vacancy on the death of Wulstan, from July to December, 1349, is one long series of institutions. To no less than 67 out of 138 parishes a presentation was made, in some cases more than one.[5] On 10 July and again on 21 August a priest was presented to Great Malvern; institutions to Powick are registered on 15 May and 10 July.[6] In nearly every case it is stated that the institution took place on account of the death of the late rector.

So great was the alarm and distress the pestilence created that every Catholic usage and canonical right was set aside. The 'Quatuor Tempora' of the Ember seasons were disregarded, and ordinations were held where and how they could. When the plague was at its height, during the vacancy, no ordinations are recorded, but all candidates were granted letters dimissory to be ordained in any diocese they could.[7] Probably this was the only possible expedient, since the other bishops were too busy with their own ordinations to come to Worcester, while the need was too pressing to wait until the new bishop was appointed.[8] John Thoresby was made bishop in January, and between January and September he held eight large ordinations.[9]

On Thoresby's election, one of his first acts was to appoint the prior of Llanthony his vicar-general.[10] In his own words he wished 'to appoint a remedy for the want of rectors and parish chaplains, owing to the loss of so many priests in so many churches.'[11] He also realized the scope for extortion and neglect given to those who held benefices by the state of the county. Thus he admonished such to have the cure of souls without extorting excessive payments for burials or masses for the dead, but to be satisfied with a reasonable salary.[12]

The Black Death in Worcestershire was chiefly felt by the loss of labourers, which affected considerably the income of the religious houses, as they could not get the land cultivated, their services performed, nor the rents from the tenants. The monks so often complained of poverty that too much

[1] Gasquet, *Great Pestilence*, 1. [2] Worc. Epis. Reg. Wulstan de Bransford, f. 146d.

[3] Leland mentions this cemetery in his *Itinerary* as the place 'where corses were wont to be buried in the time of pestilence as in a public cemetery for Worcester.' (Quoted from Leland in Gasquet's *Great Pestilence*, 122.)

[4] Worc. Epis. Reg. Wulstan de Bransford, bk. ii. ff. 10-19. The list is too long to quote, but it is significant enough that it fills nine folios of his register.

[5] *Sede Vac. Reg.* (Worc. Hist. Soc.), 225-239. [6] Ibid. [7] Ibid. 247-9.

[8] The number of candidates thus ordained was as follows:—Sub-deacons, 89; deacons, 14; priests, 37; acolytes, 42; total, 182.

[9] Worc. Epis. Reg. Thoresby, fol. xiii-xviii. [10] Ibid. fol. 6. [11] Ibid. [12] Ibid.

importance should not be attached to their complaints, but now they really felt the strain, for, as far as can be made out, the number of the monks in the different houses was less than it had been, probably because of the diminution of rents preventing so large a number being maintained, and of the difficulty in filling vacancies.

A result of the Black Death on the parochial clergy is stated by Langland: 'Parsons and parish priests complain to the bishop that their parishes have been poor since the time of the pestilence, that they may get license and leave to dwell in London and sing there for simony, for silver is sweet.'[1] It is very difficult to compare the number of licences for non-residence given before and after the Black Death so as to test the truth of the statement, but it does appear from the registers that in the last half of the century there was a good deal of non-residence among the parochial clergy, but whether more than before cannot be stated.[2] In February, 1350, the bishop issued a mandate to the sequestrator-general to remove from their benefices all who did not make personal residence.[3] In 1362 Bishop Barnet issued a general mandate to the archdeacon to enforce residence under pain of excommunication, recounting how 'many make it a practice to depart without obtaining a licence, and others let their churches to farm and do not return to them again.'[4] It is tempting to censure the parish priests for this non-residence, but there is much to be said on their side. Their stipends were limited by appropriation of tithes and dues 'by worldly bishops and rich abbots that have many thousand marks more than enow,'[5] until 'many priests were forced to steal,'[6] while at the same time the archbishop and the Parliament tried to keep down these stipends by ordinances or statutes parallel with the Statutes of Labourers.[7] Papal demands were also increasing. Revenues might fail, estates be uncultivated, but the papal court must have money, and it is perhaps as much to its exactions as to any other cause that the deep discontent is due which arose against the clergy. One instance will suffice. In 1374, at the time when the pressure was heavy in the county, three papal nuncii were sent to Flanders by Pope Gregory, and a letter was addressed to the Worcester authorities by the prior of Canterbury, the see being vacant, by which all ecclesiastical persons in the diocese of Worcester were ordered to pay a halfpenny on every mark of their goods and benefices within twenty-four days.[8] It may be imagined what discontent such a demand created to a poor impoverished country. This was in September. In December came another order to levy a further farthing, as the nuncii had stayed in Flanders longer than was expected,[9] and yet

[1] Langland, *Piers the Plowman*, ed. Skeat, p. 9.

[2] The probability is that during the plague men had been ordained with little regard to their fitness, and that these men, when they had gained a benefice, were 'wanderers, and made no personal residence, not celebrating zealously nor ministering to their parishioners.' Worc. Epis. Regis. Thoresby, fol. 15d: Mandate of the bishop condemning such rectors.

[3] Worc. Epis. Reg. Thoresby, fol. 19d.

[4] Ibid. Barnet, fol. 2d.

[5] *Engl. Works of Wicliff*, ed. Thos. Arnold, iii. 215.

[6] Thos. Walsingham, *Hist. Ang.* (Rolls Ser.), i. 297.

[7] (*a*) Wilkins, *Concilia*, iii. 30, 1354, Archbishop Islip limited priests' stipends to seven marks a year.
(*b*) *Stat. of Realm*, 36 Edw. III. cap. 8. Limit set at six marks.
(*c*) Worc. Epis. Reg. Wakefield, fol. 130, 1379. Archbishop Courtney ordered them not to exceed six marks.
(*d*) Ibid. Philip Morgan, 1421. Archbishop Chicheley set the limit at seven marks or three marks with 'cibariis.'

[8] *Sede. Vac. Reg.* (Worc. Hist. Soc.), 322.

[9] Ibid. 323.

another order to pay a further farthing towards an allowance of 12 florins a day to Pileus, archbishop of Ravenna, papal nuncio to France and England.[1] In January came a further demand for a farthing for the three nuncii in Flanders, since they had continued to stay.[2] Naturally there was considerable difficulty in getting in the money. A small part was collected by some means, and sent to the abbot of Winchcombe, who had been appointed collector, but when he came to pay it over to the papal agents they refused to receive the amount by instalments, but insisted on having the whole levied at once, and in one sum ![3] To make matters worse, in February came a writ from the king ordering that the arrears of a tenth granted to the Crown by the clergy should be at once levied and paid.[4] The clergy had to get this money, which they could only do by enforcing their rights to the full extent. All writers of that date join in speaking of the rapacity of the clergy and the religious houses. This is, doubtless, true, but they leave out of sight how the unfortunate ecclesiastics were pressed for payment of taxes and charges.

Probably the enforcement of their rights by ecclesiastics, made necessary by the constant drain of Papal demands, increased the cry for reform, and this cry gathering force extended also to the religious side of things. Hatred of the pope led to his claims being questioned and denounced, and with his claims those of his ministers, whether bishops, priests, or deacons. With so large a part of the county in ecclesiastical hands, with ecclesiastical exactions so strictly enforced, it is not wonderful that Worcestershire soon became a hotbed of the movement against ecclesiastics. Wiclif began by repudiating the claims of Rome and speaking plainly as to church endowments. He embodied in himself the spirit of the continental reformers of the preceding century, of Arnold of Brescia, of St. Bernard of Clairvaux, of St. Francis of Assisi, who attacked the secularization and corruption of the church as it gathered together worldly property, honour, and power. Like them he aimed at renewing the church by leading it back to a condition of Apostolic poverty. This part of his opinions found a ready sympathy in Worcestershire,[5] doubtless because the county had especially felt the heavy hand of ecclesiastical rule and was glad of any excuse to weaken its power. But Wiclif's teaching involved the idea of the importance of each individual as a unit, and this idea, which logically demands equality of opportunity for every man, could be and was twisted into meaning that 'all men are equal.' From this followed the socialistic teaching, spread and exaggerated by Wiclif's followers, that 'all should belong to all in common.' It was this side of his teaching that had such considerable effect in Worcestershire as in all England at the end of the fourteenth century. There was yet another result from the theory of equality, an attack first on the government and then on the doctrine of the Church. If there was no right of supremacy, except that given by righteousness, then the priest was not necessarily above the people. Thus the priest who sinned could not fulfil any of the priestly offices. The prayers of a priest 'in mortal sin,' preached the Lollards, are of no more avail than 'the lowing of cattle or the grunting of pigs.'[6] The Registers of Bishop Wakefield

[1] *Sede Vac. Reg.* (Worc. Hist. Soc.), 323.
[2] Ibid. 324.
[3] Ibid. 325.
[4] Ibid. 329.
[5] Worc. Epis. Reg. Wakefield, fol. 112. One of the charges against the heretics is that they say it is contrary to Holy Scripture for ecclesiastics to have temporal possessions.
[6] Ibid. Morgan, fol. 17d.

and Bishop Philip Morgan prove conclusively that this form of 'heresy' was very strong in Worcestershire. William Taylor, Thomas Drayton, and John Walcote were three of the more notorious heretics who again and again came under the denunciation of the bishop's vicar general.[1] How far Wiclif's attack on the doctrines of the church, as to transubstantiation, affected Worcester it is difficult to tell. Like Abelard and Berenger of Tours Wiclif believed, as a result of his theory of the direct relation of each individual, according to his merit, with God, that the actual recognition of the Real Presence would only come with the revelation in the individual himself. This doctrine spread into Worcester, as proved by the mandate of Archbishop Courtney in 1394[2] issued 'against divers conclusions, heresies, and errors which are dogmatically asserted and publicly preached by persons eternally damned,' and setting forth these conclusions and errors at length. Before that, in 1387, Bishop Wakefield issued orders that no one suspected of Lollardy was to be allowed to preach, especially naming Nicholas Hereford, John Ashton, John Perney, John Parker, and Robert Swynderby, 'who have honied words in their mouths, but venom under their lips.'[3] Also he forbade any layman under pain of excommunication either to hear such persons preach or give them any encouragement.[4] Further proof of the influence of Wiclif's doctrinal views on Worcestershire is given by the grounds, distorted as they were,[5] on which the Worcester victim Badby was executed during Thomas Peverell's episcopate. Archbishop Arundel had caused the laws as to heresy to be revived, and the facilities to execute heretics increased. A tailor of Evesham named Badby declined to believe in transubstantiation, and the bishop held a court in the Carnarie Chapel to try him for heresy and blasphemy. Badby, if the account is to be believed, from the irreverent language he used at the trial, proved himself guilty of both charges. Excommunication had no effect on him; he insisted he was right in his belief and refused to abjure. He was then brought before Convocation, Archbishop Arundel and the clergy. He still persisted in his views as to transubstantiation and was therefore handed over to the secular arm. Finally, in spite of Arundel's petition to the Lords, he was ordered to be burnt in Smithfield. The Prince of Wales, afterwards Henry V., was present at the execution, and urged him to recant : he declined, and was burnt to death.[6] His was, it is believed, the first execution under the Statute of Henry IV. of 1401, under the provisions of which two of Peverell's successors in the see were later to suffer. Apart from this trial and the general accusation brought against Worcestershire by Archbishop Courtney, there seems little to prove that the doctrinal controversy had a specially marked effect on the county. In fact disbelief in the doctrine of transubstantiation does not seem to have been generally included in the accusations brought against the Worcester Lollards, and the probability is that in Worcester, as elsewhere, the revolt was against the temporal rather than against the spiritual side of ecclesiasticism.

1 Worc. Epis. Reg. Morgan, vol. i. ff. 13, 16 and 17d, vol. ii. ff. 6, 46d. Ibid. Polton, ff. 53, 54, 55.

2 Ibid. Wakefield, fol. 112.

3 Ibid. f. 128. Hereford and Ashton were the Oxford leaders of the movement and next in importance to Wiclif himself.

4 Ibid.

5 Thos. Walsingham, *Hist. Ang.* (Rolls Ser.), ii. 282 'Pertinaciter defendit hanc hæresim quod videlicet non est corpus Christi quod sacramentaliter tractatur in ecclesia sed res quædam inanimata, pejor bufone vel aranea, quæ sunt animalia animata.'

6 Ibid.

The history of the Worcester bishops after Wulstan de Bransford shows a decline in their position and that they were sinking into a different and inferior class from what they had been. On Wulstan's death the Worcester monks, not dismayed by past rebuffs, had elected their prior John de Evesham. The pope promptly set him aside, and translated the bishop of St. David's, John Thoresby.[1] He was made Lord Chancellor while bishop and shortly afterwards transferred to York.[2] The pope filled up Worcester by another translation from St. David's, Reginald Brian,[3] who fell a victim to the plague, dying at Alvechurch in 1361.[4] The pope again filled up the vacancy by appointing John Barnet.[5] He was enthroned by the abbot of Winchcomb, since the archdeacon of Canterbury, who ought to have performed this ceremony, was a Roman Cardinal, and the archdeacon's proctor appointed the three abbots of Gloucester, Tewkesbury, and Winchcomb in the archdeacon's place.[6] His chief act at Worcester was to grant an indulgence of forty days to all who prayed for the benefactors of the cathedral or became benefactors thereof. In April, 1364, he was made Lord High Treasurer and translated to Bath and Wells.[7] In the register during the vacancy on Barnet's translation one of the earliest lists is given of the sums received for synodals in the archdeaconry of Worcester:—Worcester Deanery, 20*s.*; Powick Deanery, 13*s.*; Pershore Deanery, 39*s.*; Wick Deanery, 27*s.*; Kidderminster Deanery, 24*s.*; Warwick Deanery, 26*s.*; Kineton Deanery, 25*s.* Total £8 14*s.*[8]

The pope filled up the vacancy by another translation, this time by the appointment from Rochester of William Wittelsey,[9] who held the see for four years, and was then translated to Canterbury.[10] Another translation by the pope, that of William de Lynn from Chichester, followed.[11] He was bishop for seven years, 1368–1375, but his episcopate made no history. Henry Wakefield, who succeeded, was also appointed by the pope;[12] he was archdeacon of Canterbury, and is described as being in spiritual matters prudent, in temporal matters circumspect. He held the see for nineteen years, 1375–1394. During his episcopate the last of the fights between the prior of Worcester and the bishop as to their position took place. The prior, taking advantage of his extended powers during the vacancy of the see, had gradually assumed the use of certain vestments and ornaments which were of an episcopal character, but he had done this under papal sanction. Clement VI. granted the right to use mitre, ring, and pastoral staff; Innocent VI. provided that these should not be used in the presence of the bishop or his ordinary, and that the mitre should have no precious stones or other ornaments.[13] Urban V. gave the right to wear the mitre and ring in the presence of the bishop, but without pearls or gems. In the absence of the bishop the prior might wear the mitre jewelled and ornamented, the ring, the tunic or dalmatic, the sandals and the gloves of a bishop, and carry a bourdon of silver with silver knobs or bosses, but without other ornament. This bourdon or short staff was not, however, to

[1] *Hist. of Ch. of York* (Rolls Ser.), ii. 419. *Cal. of Papal Letters*, iii. 311.
[2] Ibid. iii. 469.
[3] Ibid.
[4] *Sede Vac. Reg.* (Worc. Hist. Soc.), 203.
[5] Ibid.
[6] Worc. Epis. Reg. Barnet, fol. 11d.
[7] *Sede Vac. Reg.* (Worc. Hist. Soc.), 217.
[8] Ibid. 222.
[9] Thomas, *Surv. of Worc. Cath. Acc. of Bishops*, 183.
[10] Ibid.
[11] Thos. Walsingham, *Hist. Ang.* (Rolls Ser.), i. 307.
[12] Worc. Epis. Reg. Wakefield, fol. 1.
[13] *Cal. of Papal Letters*, iii. 571.

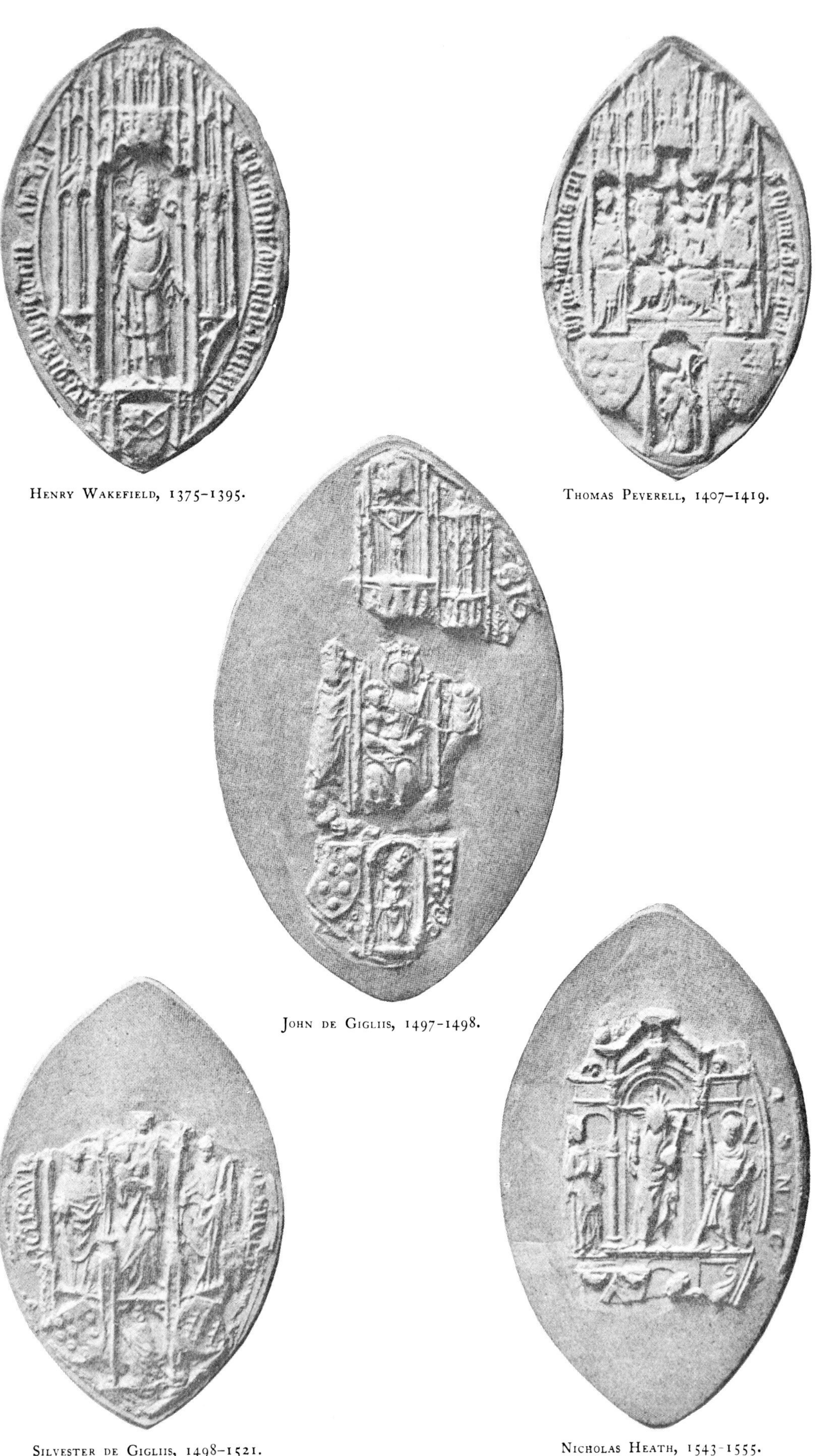

Henry Wakefield, 1375–1395.

Thomas Peverell, 1407–1419.

John de Gigliis, 1497–1498.

Silvester de Gigliis, 1498–1521.

Nicholas Heath, 1543–1555.

Worcester Episcopal Seals.—Plate II.

To face page 36.

be used as a pastoral staff.[1] Pope Boniface IX. confirmed these rights. The bishop of Worcester would not hear of the prior arraying himself in episcopal robes or having a pastoral staff. The matter, however, was compromised by the intervention of the archbishop, and it was agreed that when the bishop was present the prior was not to wear a mitre with gold fringe or precious stones ; when he was absent he might. When the bishop was present the prior was to have no pastoral staff ; when the bishop was absent he might have one, but it was to be shorter than the episcopal, painted in only two colours, white and blue ; no gold and no precious stones.[2]

On Wakefield's death the usual practice was followed ; the pope translated Tideman de Winchcomb, bishop of Llandaff, to Worcester and set aside the elect of the monks.[3] It is said that this was done at the express request of Richard II. He was at all events a staunch friend of the king, and remained so until the end. Tideman died in June, 1401.[4] The monks elected Richard Clifford to succeed him, and for once the pope did not set aside, but confirmed the election.[5] Clifford was sent as ambassador to Germany, and in 1407 translated to London. Thomas Peverell, a Carmelite friar, bishop of Llandaff, was translated by the pope to Worcester.[6] The most noteworthy event in his episcopate was the trial and execution of the Lollard victim Badby.[7]

Peverell died in March, 1418,[8] and as a Carmelite he was buried in the Carmelite church at Oxford.[9] The monks elected Philip Morgan, the chancellor of Normandy, as bishop,[10] who was accepted by the pope, and was consecrated in the cathedral at Rouen. His chief work was outside the diocese, as he was one of the bishops who acted on the Privy Council during the minority of Henry VI. In 1425 the pope translated him to Ely, and in 1426 translated Thomas Polton from Chichester to Worcester.[11] Polton held a synod of his clergy in 1427, and drew from them a subsidy of 1*s.* in the pound on the value of their livings ; on being sent by the king to the Council of Basle he got another subsidy of 2*d.* in the pound towards his expenses.[12] From this council he never returned, dying at Basle in August, 1433.[13] The prior and convent at once met to select a successor, and the man of their choice was Thomas Bourchier, who according to Canon Law was not able to be elected bishop as he was under the requisite age, thirty.[14] The monks asked the pope, Eugenius IV., to dispense with this and to confirm him, because he was 'very useful to the cathedral church of Worcester and to all the English church, and very necessary in expelling . . . heresies which are daily exercised in divers parts of the diocese of Worcester, and to correct the . . . invasion and usurpation of the jurisdiction, liberties, and rights of ecclesiastical matters and persons which by the secular powers are exercised in these days more than usual, . . . bearing in mind the birth, discretion, and power of the same, being born of the noble blood of the kings of England.'[15] The pope had

1 Worc. Epis. Reg. Wittesleye, fol. 2. Mr. St. John Hope calls attention to the bourdon which is held by a figure of the last abbot of Evesham, Philip Hawford or Ballard, at the back of the high-altar screen in the Lady Chapel at Worcester.

2 Ibid. Wakefield, fol. 93d. *Cal. of Papal Letters*, iv. 48.

3 *Sede Vac. Reg.* (Worc. Hist. Soc.), 369.

4 Ibid. 371.

5 Worc. Epis. Reg. Clifford. Note at beginning of register.

6 *Sede Vac. Reg.* (Worc. Hist. Soc.), 390.

7 See supra.

8 *Sede Vac. Reg.* (Worc. Hist. Soc.), 391.

9 Ibid. 407.

10 Ibid. 405.

11 Worc. Epis. Reg. Polton, fol. 1.

12 Thomas, *Surv. of Worc. Cath. Acc. of Bishops*, 192.

13 *Sede Vac. Reg.* (Worc. Hist. Soc.), 431.

14 Ibid. 431–434.

15 Ibid. 433. Bourchier was the son of Ann Countess of Eure, daughter of Thomas Woodstock, and grand-daughter of Edward III., and was at the time twenty-eight years old, having been born in 1405.

promised the see to the dean of Salisbury, Thomas Brown, but the king at the request of the Commons in Parliament denied the right of appointment, and solicited the pope to consent to Bourchier's election, while he himself promised the see of Rochester to Brown. To this compromise the pope agreed, dispensed with Bourchier's lack of age, and confirmed him in the see of Worcester, which had now been vacant for nearly two years.[1] After all the reasons of the monks Bourchier did but little for Worcester. As bishop, he visited the hospital of St. Wulstan and directed certain reforms to be carried out,[2] but beyond that his episcopate has left no mark. In 1443 he was translated to Ely by papal provision.

On his translation the pope appointed John Carpenter, the provost of Oriel, Oxford, bishop of Worcester.[3] He held the see for thirty-three years (1443–1476), during the greater part of the Wars of the Roses. Throughout his register there is a noticeable increase in the number of indulgences given ;[4] one of the most remarkable being that offered to all contributing towards the subsidy for Elizabeth, widow of John Holt, who was taken captive in the war in Normandy by the adversary of the king, and was redeemed for 1,140 marks, by the payment of which all her possessions were gone.[5]

Carpenter was a strong man who set himself to work to reform the corruptions and remove the lethargy into which the church seemed sinking. There can be no plainer proof of this than his systematic visitation of the diocese in 1461 and 1466. On Tuesday, 22 September, 1461, he proceeded firstly to the cathedral church, and 'was received there with great state.' He remained there, receiving procuration in food and drink for himself and his servants, until Thursday, 24 September. On that day he visited the hospital of St. Wulstan, and received four marks procuration. Thence he proceeded through his diocese, visiting not only monasteries, but deaneries and parish churches, either in person or by his commissioners.[6] In 1466 he made another personal visitation quite as thorough and systematic.[7] Several years before, in 1460, he had sent special injunctions to the archdeacon of Worcester to cause all rectors and vicars throughout the archdeaconry 'to exhort their people in the vulgar tongue, between solemn masses, on the nearest feast day,' to observe the articles that the bishop himself had drawn up concerning the parochial clergy.[8] Moreover the archdeacon was to take the name of all rectors and vicars and possessors of all churches, and inquire by what title they held, in what orders they were, and whether any were pluralists.[9] These injunctions and the articles which follow clearly show the strong reforming attitude of this bishop.[10]

[1] *Sede. Vac. Reg.* (Worc. Hist. Soc.), 435. *Proc. & Ord. Priv. Coun.* iv. 183, 285, 286.

[2] Worc. Epis. Reg. Bourchier, fol. 71, 72, and 72d.

[3] Ibid. Carpenter, fol. 1.

[4] Worc. Epis. Reg. Carpenter, ff. 24d, 52, 58, 60d, 61d(3), 65(2), 81, 83, 83d, 84, 90, 124d, 185, 192, 212.

[5] Ibid. 24d.

[6] Ibid. ff. 168–9.

[7] Ibid. fol. 218.

[8] Ibid. fol. 95–96.

[9] Ibid. ff. 95–96.

[10] The articles are as follows :—

'1. That no curate coming from another diocese to ours shall celebrate or minister sacraments beyond a month without showing letters of commendation to us or our commissary-general, from the diocese where he last dwelt.

'2. That no ecclesiastical benefice in the diocese shall be let to farm, either to laymen or laymen and clerks jointly, but only to clerks. If this rule is broken, a third part of the revenues of the benefice shall be applied to the fabric of the cathedral church. And if before this order any benefices have been farmed out to laymen or laymen and clerks jointly, the lease shall be revoked within

His was the first systematic attempt to check the inefficiency of the parochial clergy, and to ensure their proper care of the parishes, and he also deserves respect for his efforts to increase learning among the clergy. He endowed a library in the Carnarie Chapel, Worcester, possibly the original of the present Chapter Library.[1] Also he encouraged preaching[2] in a way very different from any of his predecessors. Among the bishops of Worcester in the fourteenth and fifteenth centuries, Carpenter, in spite of his faults, stands out as one who realized that the most vital part of church affairs must be the relation of the individual parish priest to his people.

On Carpenter's death, in 1476, the bishop of Rochester, John Alcock, was translated to Worcester. He was a statesman rather than an ecclesiastic, Lord President of Edward IV.'s Court of the Welsh Marches, and afterwards Lord Chancellor. Thus, in 1481, when a visitation of the diocese was planned, the bishop, being hindered by the business of the king and the kingdom of Italy, left the work of his diocese to his commissary. In 1486 he was translated to Ely.[3]

The new bishop, appointed by papal provision, was Robert Morton, archdeacon of Gloucester,[4] nephew of that more celebrated Morton, the archbishop of Canterbury under Henry VII. Morton was a good instance of the new type of bishop that for the future was to fill the see of Worcester. He was so much employed by the king on public business that he had to resign the mastership of the Rolls, yet he was considered to have leisure for the bishopric of Worcester. His episcopate is chiefly marked by two thorough visitations which he made in person in 1488 and 1491 through the whole diocese, preaching in many of the churches, issuing special mandates to those which most required visitation.[5]

Robert Morton was the last English bishop of Worcester before the Reformation. His four next successors were all Italians. Henry VII. and

six months after this edict, or a third part of the revenues of the benefice shall be applied as above stated.

'3. That whereas the naughtiness of unbridled ambition so occupies the minds of certain religious persons that, unmindful of their profession, they attempt those things which are forbidden them, by wandering outside their monasteries, and by celebrating divine offices and ministering sacraments in parish churches and chapels without the consent of their superiors, all curates of the diocese are ordered that they shall not permit any religious person of any order to celebrate in their churches or chapels beyond one month (the article of necessity only excepted), unless it shall appear to them that such religious person is qualified, and has the licence of his superior, approved by the bishop or his commissary-general, and all religious persons are in like manner forbidden to celebrate.

'4. That in every year there shall be collections for the poor on the feasts of All Saints, Palm Sunday, and Whitsunday, by the churchwardens of every parish, and in augmentation of such alms the bishop grants the sums coming to them for penances throughout the diocese, according to the discretions of the commissary-general.

'5. That whereas perilous error exists as to the sacraments of baptism (which our Saviour instituted as the door of all sacraments), matrimony, and extreme unction, it is ordered that all rectors and vicars cause their churchwardens to provide a fit book of the said sacraments, called a Manual, within six months of the time that this mandate is published in the general chapter.

'6. That no curate or other priest shall celebrate on portable altars not having crosses and characters (caretteres), according to the dictates of the holy canons, not firmly enclosed in wood or boxes (capsulis), or removed from the same, or that are broken within the crosses and characters, under pain of suspension for a month.'

[1] Worc. Epis. Reg. Carpenter, i. f. 175 and 175d, vol. ii. f. 59d. The chaplain who celebrated in the Carnarie Chapel was to be the Librarian, and was to have '£10 a year and 4 yards of linen cloth for a dress.' See also Ibid. Silvester de Gigliis, ff. 132–6.

[2] Ibid. The same chaplain was to make a solemn preaching in the parish church of Worcester, or at the city cross. Various licences and stated qualifications for preachers are given throughout the register, ff. 84, 114, 128, 168, etc.

[3] Ibid. Morton, fol. 1. [4] Ibid. [5] Ibid. ff. 32, 33.

Henry VIII. recognized the necessity of having well paid diplomatic agents at Rome and elsewhere. The persons best fitted to act as such agents were ecclesiastics, and in addition to their training there were more posts with high salaries that could be held by ecclesiastics than by any other class. An ecclesiastic could hold a rich bishopric which would pay him well for his work at no cost to the Crown, and Henry VII. and Henry VIII. regarded bishoprics as a means of paying their agents.[1] The king had to consider what sees would do without resident bishops. The Court of the Welsh Marches had taken away all the temporal administrative work of the bishop of Worcester, the spiritual work could be done either by the archdeacons or by someone specially appointed, and bishops in particular cases could be hired as the priors of Worcester had hired the bishop of Llandaff and others to do such ecclesiastical work as could only be done by a bishop at a fixed rate. The three sees—Lichfield, Hereford, and Worcester—did not each require a resident bishop,[2] and their revenues could be used as the king desired. For some reason, probably because it was not required when the vacancy arose, Lichfield escaped having an alien, but Worcester was regarded as a place that could be handed over to the king entirely, and Hereford in a less degree. In 1497 there was in London an Italian, John de Gigliis, who had been resident in England some years as papal agent, and had become archdeacon of London and prebendary of Hoxton in St. Paul's Cathedral.[3] Among his pursuits was that of writing Latin verses. He wrote a marriage ode on the wedding of Henry VII. and Elizabeth of York,[4] and did what he could to ingratiate himself with the new king, and successfully, for he was sent to Calais on a mission in 1487,[5] and so satisfied the king that he was made archdeacon of Gloucester.[6] In 1489 he published an indulgence granted by Innocent VIII., and soon afterwards went to Rome as Henry's agent.[7] When, in 1497, the see of Worcester became vacant, a bargain seems to have been arrived at between the pope, Alexander VI., and the king that John de Gigliis should be bishop of Worcester. The plan had two advantages; the English agent had a recognized position, and also received a handsome salary at no cost to the king. The pope, by bull dated 30 August, 1497, appointed Gigliis bishop of Worcester. He was consecrated at Rome on 10 September. On 5 December he received the temporalities.[8] He was enthroned by proxy, his vicar-general representing him, on 12 April, 1498. He died at Rome on 25 August in that year, and was buried in the English college there.[9]

John de Gigliis's term of office had been too short to see if the experiment was a success. It was, however, determined to persevere with it. A nephew of the late bishop, Silvester de Gigliis, who had been in his household and had assisted in his work, was, though only thirty-three, selected by the king and the pope as the successor.[10] Henry designated him in the confirmation of the temporalities of the see as 'causarum nostrarum in curia Romanum solicitator.'[11] Like his uncle, he was enthroned by proxy,[12] and

[1] See Creighton, *Hist. Essays*, 203. 'Bishoprics were frankly regarded as affording salaries for such officials as the rapid development of the State required for its increasing needs.'

[2] See Ibid. 203-204.

[3] Newcourt, *Repert. Eccles.* i. 61.

[4] The poem is in the British Museum, Harl. MSS. 366.

[5] Bernard Andre in Gairdner's *Memorials*, 56.

[6] Browne Willis, *Cathedrals*, i. 666.

[7] Wharton, *Anglia Sacra*. i. 538.

[8] Rymer, *Fœd.* xii. 657-670.

[9] Thomas, *Surv. of Worc. Cath. Acc. of Bishops*, 202.

[10] Worc. Epis. Reg. Silvester de Gigliis, fol. 1.

[11] Thomas, *Surv. of Worc. Cath.* App. 130.

[12] Worc. Epis. Reg. Silvester de Gigliis, fol. 3.

left the work of his diocese to be done by his vicars-general—Thomas Alcock, Thomas Wodyngton, and Thomas Hannibal. In 1504 Silvester came to England the bearer of a present of a papal cap and sword from the pope to Henry. He does not appear to have visited his diocese, but remained at court, and seems to have continued in England during the life of Henry VII., but there is nothing to show he condescended to visit Worcester or to do anything for the diocese beyond drawing the salary. On his accession, Henry VIII. showed a preference for another agent, an Englishman, one of the cardinals, Christopher Bainbridge, archbishop of York, and to him the greater part of the English political work was entrusted. In 1512 Silvester was sent to Rome as one of the English representatives on the Lateran Council; Worcester thus had the honour to have her bishops selected as representatives at both the last two great Councils before the religious changes in England, Basle and the Lateran. Silvester soon found that the bishop of Worcester, although the king of England's agent, was overshadowed by the cardinal of York. Jealous of Bainbridge, and more versed in the subtle diplomacy of the court, Silvester took up a policy utterly opposed to his. In May, 1514, Bainbridge wrote to Henry VIII. accusing the bishop of Worcester of plotting with the French ambassador in betraying England's secrets.[1] In the July of that year Bainbridge was dead, poisoned by a priest, Raynald de Modena, who had formerly been a servant of Silvester's household. Raynald was imprisoned, and confessed his crime, stating that he administered the poison at the instigation of the bishop of Worcester, who gave him 15 gold coins, saying: 'If we do not get rid of this cardinal we shall never live quietly in Rome.'[2] Before his death Raynald withdrew the charge 'through the means of Worcester,'[3] and the bishop, exculpated, 'hath marvellous great favour "ad occultandam veritatem, sed immortalis Deus tam horrendum scelus videtur odisse."'[4] The probability seems to be that Silvester was working as agent for Wolsey, who was 'urgent for the cardinal's hat,' and wrote to the bishop complimenting him on his acquittal, and begging him 'by his politic handling to induce the pope to make me a cardinal,' then 'ye shall singularly content and please the king.'[5]

Through the long tangled skein of Wolsey's dealings with the papacy the bishop of Worcester was his agent, and so judiciously did he carry out his policy that he was in favour both with Wolsey and the pope. In July, 1515, Leo X. wrote to Henry VIII. in praise of the bishop, begging him advance him to some richer diocese, 'considering that the whole anxiety of the bishop hath ever been to serve you and your father.'[6] He also sent a letter to Wolsey begging him to second his request.[7] But promotion for Silvester hung on the result of his attempt to get the 'red hat' for Wolsey. In the same month Wolsey wrote to the bishop: 'The king is well pleased with your services, and intends to reward them,' but 'the king's grace marvelleth that the pope delayeth so long sending the red hat to me, seeing how tenderly and instantly and often his grace hath written.'[8] By the end of 1518, as no preferment had come, although Wolsey was now a

[1] *L. and P. Henry VIII.* i. 809.
[2] Ibid. i. 844.
[3] Ibid. i. 867. Letter from Secretary Burbank to Henry VIII.
[4] Ibid. i. 877. Letter from Secretary Pace to Wolsey.
[5] Ibid. i. 892. Letter from Wolsey to Silvester.
[6] Ibid. ii. 200.
[7] Ibid.
[8] Ibid.

cardinal, and the negotiations for 'the universal peace' had been safely carried through by the help of Silvester, the bishop was 'very anxious to be advanced to the cardinalate,' and was 'willing to sacrifice for that honour every other promotion.'[1] But Wolsey did not support his suggestion for two years after this appeal. In March he was so satisfied with Worcester's long service that the king wrote to Leo X. urging him to make Silvester a cardinal.[2] Silvester himself was very hopeful, and wrote to Wolsey that he expected to be promoted at the next creation of cardinals.[3] But the pope, 'considering that the bishop of Worcester does not possess such qualities as are suitable to so high a promotion,' would not risk the infamy he might draw upon himself by such a creation.[4] In November, 1520, the Cardinal de Medici wrote to the auditor of the chamber: 'The pope would rather not receive any further letters respecting the promotion of Worcester . . . he is constantly pestered by Worcester . . . if Worcester cannot take the hint, his holiness will have to tell him openly since he does not wish to incur this infamy.'[5] On 18 April, 1521, Silvester died in Rome, and was buried on the next day.[6] Early in the month, when he lay dying, Cardinal Campeggio wrote to tell the king and Wolsey and to beg 'for the bishopric in his place, to be translated to Salisbury when it is vacant.'[7] But Henry wanted a more powerful man as his agent, and offered the see to Julius de Medici,[8] although it was 'a gift all unequal to his merits.' The cardinal accepted 'the favour which he had neither expected nor asked for,'[9] but at the beginning of the next year, on the death of Pope Leo, he aspired to the papacy,[10] and wrote to the king resigning the see of Worcester in favour of the papal nuncio in London, Jerome Ghinucci, subject to certain stipulations as to the revenues of the see, probably meaning that Cardinal Medici was to receive a considerable annuity as the price of his self-denial. Meanwhile Medici continued to act as administrator of the see, and his connexion with it went on until after the election of the pope, Hadrian VI., who appointed Ghinucci, who was already bishop of Ascoli.[11]

The new bishop was not to be envied. As Wolsey's agent in Rome he had much questionable work to do. He had still more questionable work after Wolsey's fall in urging the pope to proclaim the marriage between Henry and Catherine null and void. His failure led to his fall. The 'memorable Parliament' of 1534 deprived the two Italians who held English sees, Campeggio of Salisbury and Ghinucci of Worcester, of their bishoprics, and authorized the king to appoint to them as if the bishops had died.[12] So ended the Italian bishops of Worcester. The chapter is a unique one in the history of English episcopacy, and one that deserves careful study. From the time of Carpenter to 1534 the see of Worcester was practically a means of paying state officials. But the business of the see of Worcester was not administered less satisfactorily under bishops who lived at Rome than were other English bishoprics under bishops who lived in London. In both cases the bishops only exercised a general supervision from a distance, and left the

[1] *L. and P. Hen. VIII.* ii. 1366. Letter of Silvester Darius to Wolsey. [2] Ibid. iii. 203, 217, 269.
[3] Ibid. 218. [4] Ibid. iii. 296. Letter from Cardinal de Medici to ——.
[5] Ibid. iii. 394. [6] Ibid. 471. [7] Ibid. 466-467.
[8] Ibid. 516. [9] Ibid. iii. 540. [10] Ibid. 840.
[11] Ibid. 1093. Bull of Pope Adrian VI. nominating Jerome bishop of Worcester.
[12] *Stat. of Realm*, 25-26 Hen. VIII. c. 27. 'The act is an excellent example of Henry's legislation and of his magnificent audacity in finding good reasons for doing right in an unjust and tyrannical fashion,' Creighton, *Hist. Essays*, 226.

rest of the work to be done by deputies. The system of delegation was very complete, and the spiritual functions were carried on by suffragan bishops.[1] The legal part of the episcopal business was undertaken by the vicars-general, who were able men, perfectly capable of administering the see.[2] Sometimes they applied to a friendly bishop for help. In 1515 Thomas Hannibal had trouble with 'three young fools,' unruly canons of St. Augustine's, Bristol, and applied to Fox, bishop of Winchester, who handed over the matter to Wolsey.[3] The management of the temporalities of the see was entrusted to supervisors, who were chosen generally from the important families of the

[1] Of these bishops little is known but their names and titles.

1322.—Robert le Petit, bishop of Clonfert, Ireland. (Eubel, *Hierarchia Catholica medii aevi*, i. 200, ii. 303.)

1350.—Richard, bishop of Nazareth. (Ibid. i. 375, ii. 303.)

1373–5.—Robert, bishop of Prischtina or Prizzen in Albania. (Ibid. i. 430, ii. 303.)

1395.—William Northbridge, bishop of Pharen (Faröer-Insulae) in Norway. (Ibid. i. 253, ii. 303.)

1416.—John Stockes, bishop of Triburnien (Brefny in Ireland). (Ibid. i. 523, ii. 303.)

1420.—Thomas Botyler, bishop of Christopolis. (Ibid. i. 193, ii. 303.)

1420.—Stephen Brown, bishop of Ross (Ireland). (Ibid. i. 447, ii. 303.)

1426–33.—Richard Belmer, bishop of Achonry (Ireland). (Ibid. i. 68, ii. 303.)

1433.—Robert Windel, bishop of Emly (Ireland). (Ibid. i. 295, ii. 303.)

1443.—James Blakedon, bishop of Achonry. (Ibid. ii. 303.)

1443.—John Heyne, bishop of Clonfert. (Ibid.)

1465–79.—Richard Wolsey, bishop of Down Connor (Ireland). (Ibid. 304.)

1480.—William Westkarre, bishop of Sidon. (Ibid.)

1497.—George Brann, bishop of Dromore (Ireland). (Ibid.)

1498.—Thomas Cornish, bishop of Tenos. (Creighton, *Hist. Essays*, 230.)

1498–1500.—Donatus, bishop of Emly. (Eubel, ii. 304.)

1501.—Ricard, bishop of Olonne, i.e. Richard Wycherley, a Dominican of Warwick employed by Bishop Morton in 1487 and 1493 (Worc. Epis. Reg. Morton). Died at Worcester in 1501, and buried there in the church of the Black Friars. (Walcott, *Notes and Queries*, 2nd ser. ii. 1.)

1503.—Edward, bishop of Callipolis in Thracia. (Eubel, ii. 304.)

1503–23.—Ralph Heylesden, a Franciscan, consecrated 3 March, 1503, bishop of Ascalon (Wadding. *Ann. Minorum*. xv. 271). He received a pension of 150 gold ducats out of the see (Stubbs, *Reg. Sac. Anglicanum*, 146), and was instituted vicar of Cropthorne on 15 October, 1508. (Worc. Epis. Reg. Silvester de Gigliis, fol. 54d.)

1524–26.—John Stanywell, bishop of Poletensis, abbot of Pershore, 1527. (Stubbs, *Reg. Sac. Angl.* 202.)

1526–41.—Andrew Whitmay, bishop of Chrysopolis (*L. and P. Hen. VIII.* vi. 683), appointed master of Hospital of St. Bartholomew, Gloucester, on resignation of Thomas Aparell in 1510. (Worc. Epis. Reg. Silvester de Gigliis, fol. 66d.)

[2] The following is a list of the vicars-general under the Italian bishops :—

1487–1503.—Thomas Wodyngton, LL.D. In office under Bishop Morton (Worc. Epis. Reg. Morton) and Bishop Silvester. (Ibid. Silvester de Gigliis, fol. 15, etc.)

1503–4.—Thomas Alcock, archdeacon of Worcester, 1503, and preceptor of St. Wulstan. (Ibid. fol. 33.)

1504–11.—Robert Holdsworth or Hallesworth. (Ibid. fol. 60.)

1511–18.—Thomas Hannibal, D.C.L. (Ibid. fol. 94 and 123), prebendary of Gevendall in the church of York, 1504 (Wood, *Athenæ*. i. 654) ; employed by Wolsey in Rome (*L. and P. Hen. VIII.* ii. 262, iv. 7, 50, 71, 99, 132, 159, etc.) and helped to promote Clement VII. (Julius de Medici) to the papacy. Clement wrote to Wolsey in 1524 commending Hannibal and saying 'he would retain him till the spring, as a journey during the winter was unfit for his age,' then 'he would send him with a golden rose to the king' (Ibid. iv. 11). In 1524 Hannibal was made Master of the Rolls. (*L. and P. Hen. VIII.* iv. 125, 169.)

1518–26.—John Bell, LL.D. 'vicar-general of Julius de Medici, commendator of the see of Worcester' (Ibid. ii. 927). He seems to have been 'official of Worcester' as late as 1526 (Ibid. iv. 932). He was employed by Henry VIII. to influence Oxford University in favour of the king's divorce (Ibid. iv. 2,834, 2,570, 2,520, 2,441, 2,309, 1,429, 1,872–4). He was afterwards archdeacon of Gloucester and warden of the collegiate church of Stratford-on-Avon and prebendary of Lincoln and Lichfield, master of St. Wulstan's Hospital (Thomas, *Surv. of Worc. Cath.* 205), and in 1539 he became bishop of Worcester. (Ibid.)

1526–32.—Thomas Parker. (Thomas, *Surv. of Worc. Cath. Acc. of Bishops*, 205 ; *L. and P. Hen. VIII.* iv. 2,700.)

1532.—Thomas Bagarde, LL.D. (Ibid. vi. 112 and viii. 51). He became Latimer's chancellor. (Ibid. xi. 548.)

[3] Ibid. ii. 194.

county.[1] The local agents, as formerly, collected the rents, accounted for them to the Receiver-general, who in turn submitted them to the bishop's agent in London. In June, 1533, John Hornyold, receiver-general, wrote to Cromwell, 'I have levied of the diocese of Worcester £200, which shall be paid to your hands to the king's use if you desire.'[2] In the December of that year he wrote again that he was not able to come to London himself, but the account and the moneys should be ready there. 'You know,' he told Cromwell, 'that it is the king's pleasure I should retain in my hands the temporalities of the bishopric until his pleasure (probably touching the already planned suspension of Ghinucci) shall be known.'[3] The rental all told was about £975 a year, or something like £10,000 of our money.

It is hardly possible to imagine a greater change from the crafty Italian, who never came near his diocese, to his successor, Hugh Latimer, the son of a sturdy English yeoman, the first Protestant bishop of the see, who, having been chaplain to Anne Boleyn, was promoted by her favour.[4] He was consecrated by Cranmer, Gardiner, and Shaxton at Winchester on 26 February, 1535, and confirmed in the bishopric by the king in August of that year,[5] but did not receive the temporalities of the see until September.[6] Six days before he was consecrated a report was spread that he had 'turned over the leaf.' A certain Richard Clotton wrote to a Mr. Fowler that Latimer had preached before the king 'acknowledging the pope's authority as the highest on the earth, and that if he should misuse himself he ought to be reformed by a general council and not otherwise.' At the same time he was said to have confessed a belief in pilgrimages and prayers to saints.[7] Other reports were also circulated, and in 1536 the bishop preached at St. Paul's Cross and 'openly purged himself of the false lies surmised by the enemies of the truth.'[8] The complaints of the rebels in the various insurrections when 'every man cried out against Cromwell, Cranmer, Latimer, the two chancellors, and the king's visitors'[9] would show clearly enough Latimer's reforming attitude if any proof were needed beside his resignation in 1539 and his death in 1555. It is to Latimer's credit that, opposed as he was to all papal claims, he was also opposed to the way in which the dissolution of the monasteries was carried out. He wrote to Cromwell asking that the monastery of Great Malvern might be retained, 'not for monkrye, but for hospitality,' adding that the country is poor and full of penury, and expressing a hope that two or three of the religious houses in each shire might be 'charged to such remedy.'[10] If any evidence was wanting of the purely secular character of the spoliation, it is shown in the letter of Latimer. He gravely states that if the house is allowed to remain the prior would pay 500 marks to the king and 200 to Cranmer.[11] During Latimer's episcopate the dissolution of the monasteries produced very wide reaching effects on the county, but not so great as often supposed, for although the priory of Worcester was dissolved, yet the bulk of the lands went to form the endowment of the dean and chapter, which took the place, the property, and the duties of the religious house. Therefore, practically the great estates of the church of Worcester still remained in

[1] In 1523 Bishop Jerome appointed John Gostewick, John Russell of Strensham, and Thomas Russell his son, supervisors for a salary of £100 a year. (*L. and P. Hen. VIII.* iii. 1193.)
[2] Ibid. vi. 308.
[3] Ibid. vi. 609.
[4] Wharton, *Anglia Sacra*, i. 539.
[5] *L. and P. Hen. VIII.* viii. 80. Stubbs, *Reg. Sac. Angl.*
[6] *L. and P. Hen. VIII.* viii. 90, 154, 246 and Pat. 27 Hen. VIII. pt. i. m. 39.
[7] *L. and P. Hen. VIII.* viii. 98, 114.
[8] Ibid. x. 503.
[9] Ibid. xii. 90.
[10] Ibid. xiii. pt. ii. 443.
[11] Ibid.

ecclesiastical hands, although the lands belonging to the cell of Little Malvern were confiscated and passed into lay hands. One of the most noteworthy effects of the dissolution in Worcestershire was the revival of the old struggle concerning jurisdiction in the vale of Evesham, no longer between the bishop and the abbot, but between the bishop and the dean and chapter of Christ Church, Oxford, to whom the king had granted the right of visitation of these churches.[1] In Bishop Freake's register (1583–8) there is 'a memorandum concerning the privileges particular in the vale of Evesham, granted to Christ Church, Oxon.' Here the bishop by an ingenious argument proved that the king had no right to grant away the right of jurisdiction as part of the possessions of the abbey. The right of jurisdiction in the special churches of the vale was granted not by any king, but by the 'part consent of the bishop of Worcester, as appeareth in the white booke of the bishopric'[2] and by the 'collateral grant from the pope or prescription.' Thus the grant was to the persons of the abbot and his convent, and when they no longer existed the right reverted to the bishop, for 'before Egwin, the third bishop of Worcester, founded Evesham, and three or four hundred years after, all these were of the jurisdiction of the bishop.' If the king had had any right to make such a grant then the grant itself fell 'short of that which they wolde have,' for the grant is 'præfatis Decano et Capitulo' only, and therefore reacheth only to them and not to their successors.[3] In spite of the bishop's arguments Christ Church maintained the right of visitation, and did so up to our own day.

Latimer was a strong reformer, but his administration of Worcester has no very noteworthy event beyond his attempts to confirm Protestantism. When the Act of the Six Articles[4] was passed he was too advanced in his views to subscribe to it, and set an example of preferring his opinions to his income, by resigning the bishopric on 1 July, 1539.

In August John Bell was appointed bishop. He had been preceptor of St. Wulstan's Hospital, archdeacon of Gloucester, and vicar-general to Bishop Silvester, so was not unfamiliar with the diocese. He remained only four years, resigning the see in 1543.[5] He was followed by Nicholas Heath, 'a most wise and learned man of great policy and of as great integrity,'[6] who held the see from 1544[7] till 1552, when, as he declined to subscribe to the Edwardian Prayer Book, he was committed to the Fleet and deprived of his see by the King's Authority as Supreme Head of the Church.[8] In his place Hooper, the bishop of Gloucester, was appointed, and the two sees were once more temporarily reunited.[9] Hooper seems to have been four times enthroned for the two sees, once on his appointment at Gloucester, once on his appointment at Worcester, and a third time when the two sees were united, at Worcester and again at Gloucester. Unfortunately his register consists only of a few fragments, and what is known of him as bishop has chiefly to be collected from Fox's *Martyrs*, not always a most reliable authority. On Mary's accession he was deprived. In the Sede Vacante register of the dean and chapter of Canterbury (1553–5) an account of the

1 Pat. 38 Hen. VIII. pt. viii.
2 See supra.
3 Worc. Epis. Reg. Freake, ff. 31d, 32.
4 *Stat. of Realm*, 31 Hen. VIII. c. 14.
5 *L. and P. Hen. VIII.* xviii. 214.
6 Prattinton Coll. (Soc. Antiq.).
7 *L. and P. Hen. VIII.* xix. 39 and 175.
8 Thomas, *Surv. of Worc. Cath. Acc. of Bishops*, 207.
9 *Cal. of S. P. Dom.* 1547–80, 39.

reason why various of the sees then became vacant is given and Worcester is there mentioned.[1]

From this the official reason for Hooper's deprivation seems to be that Heath's deprivation was illegal, since the king had no power to deprive and so Heath remained bishop. Acting on this he was restored in July 1553, for in his register it is stated : 'Here Nicholas, bishop of Worcester, was restored to his bishoprick.'[2] In August he was summoned to Convocation as bishop of Worcester and Queen Mary made him President of the Council of the Welsh Marches.[3] He had not much time to show what he could do in that capacity, for in 1555 he was translated to York.

It will have been noticed that a different ground is put forward for depriving Hooper of Gloucester, namely that he was married. The question of clerical marriages was one of the burning questions of the time, and led to a number of clerical deprivations, not only among the bishops but also among the inferior clergy. What was the precise number of deprivations for marriage has always been a disputed point ; some writers allege that the deprivations were carried out on a very large scale.[4] So far as Worcestershire is concerned it is unfortunate that the registers are defective when the deprivations took place, but they only record five deprivations during the whole of Mary's reign ; on the other hand, no institutions are mentioned during 1554 and 1555.[5] In the absence of evidence it cannot be affirmed that the county felt to any great extent the deprivations which the changes under Mary brought about. It may be that Heath on his restoration did not enforce the law against married clergy very rigidly, or that since there was a large Roman Catholic population in the county the clergy had not taken advantage of the Act of 1548[6] allowing priests to marry. It is possible that a good deal of the apparent tranquillity in the diocese was due to the bishop who succeeded Heath at Worcester, Richard Pates. He had been provided by the pope in 1541, but did not come to Worcester until 1555.[7] He seems to have been more of a scholar than a politician, and is said to have been averse to any persecution. On the death of Queen Mary, Pates was imprisoned and deprived.[8] On his release he went abroad, attended the Council of Trent, and died at Louvain.[9]

With the deprivation of Pates a new order of things began. The diocese appears to have been in a deplorable state : the churches ruined and neglected, the church furniture dilapidated. The plunder of the churches had gone on to such an extent that everything connected with it seemed to be lawful prey.[10] The confiscation of the monasteries had been followed by the confiscation of the chantries, and throughout the district the church revenues had been devoted to other purposes than ecclesiastical objects. A number of the more

[1] Sede Vac. Reg. Dr. C. Cant. 'Johannes Hooper Wigorn et Glocestrer destituebatur ab eis ex hic causis viz. A sede Wigorn per restitutionis et restitutionis processus fuit penes Willelmum Gay registrarium. A sede Glocestrer propter coniugium et alia male merita et titulum vitiosum ut supra. In sede Glocestrem surrogabatur Jacobus Broks.'

[2] Thomas, *Surv. of Worc. Cath. Acc. of Bishops*, 209.

[3] *Cal. of S. P. Dom. Add.* 1547-1565, 219.

[4] Gairdner in his *Hist. of the Engl. Church, Hen. VIII. to Mary*, 337, states that the number so deprived is supposed to have been one in five or probably one in six.

[5] Thomas, *Surv. of Worc. Cath. Acc. of Bishops* 209.

[6] Stat. 2 and 3 Edw. VI. c. 21.

[7] Thomas, *Surv. of Worc. Cath. Acc. of Bishops* 209.

[8] Strype, *Hist. of Reform.* 146.

[9] Ibid.

[10] In 1559 Sandys wrote to Lord Burghley begging him to forgive the smallness of his New Year's gift, for 'such ys the barrenness of this contie that it bringeth nothing forth fit to remember you with all.' (Prattinton Coll. (Soc. Antiq.).

prominent of the reformed clergy were in exile, and those that remained were probably not best fitted to discharge the task of building up again the religious life in the county. It was most important for Worcestershire that the new bishop should be a man of tact and discretion, not extreme in one way or the other, and one who would not enforce too strictly the *via media anglicana.* It is hardly too much to say that the man selected, Edwin Sandys, was wanting in every qualification that the bishop of Worcester then required. He had gone abroad during Mary's reign and married 'a daughter of Mr. Sandes of Essex, a gentlewoman beautiful both in body and mind, which died at Strasburg.'[1] On his return he became one of the queen's chaplains, and had a good deal to do with the preparation of the Elizabethan Prayer Book.[2] In addition he was a great believer in the queen's supremacy. In fact, he was almost an ideal Elizabethan bishop, cringing to the Crown and tyrannical to his subordinates. In one way his attitude was singularly like that of the queen. Zealous a reformer as he was, he shared with her a distrust of Puritanism when it led men to extremes which threatened the basis of civil government. He looked askance at such Puritans as 'pretended favourers and false brethren who, under colour of reformation, seek the ruin and subversion of learning and religion and at the same time give a push to the civil polity. Their colour is sincerity under the appearance of simplicity, but in very truth they are ambitious spirits and can abide no superiority.'[3] But he had nothing of the queen's toleration for Roman Catholicism. While she realized how much greater political dangers might become if she aroused sympathy for the Romanists by persecution, Sandys, as he himself said at a later date when he had become archbishop, grew weary at her cautious policy, and felt that no measures against these 'lying papists' could be too severe. Directly he was made bishop he gave vent to his zeal. The interval between Bishop Pates's imprisonment and Sandy's appointment had given the opportunity, but the bishop found a strong opposition organizing against him. Instead of trying to propitiate this party, 'before he was scarce warm in his seat'[4] he held a visitation of his diocese, sweeping away all outward tokens of Roman Catholicism and rigorously enforcing a formal adhesion to the Act of Uniformity on clergy and laity alike. His determined attitude led to the various accusations that were brought against him, notably by Sir John Bourne, who represented the feeling of the Romanist layman of the diocese. Sir John had been Secretary of State to Queen Mary, and during her reign had shown his enmity to Sandys, petitioning the Queen to keep him in prison, for he was 'the greatest heretic in Cambridge.'[5] The old feud broke forth again when the bishop, in one of his visitations ordered the altar stone left standing in the church of St. Peter, Worcester, belonging to the parish where Sir John lived, to be pulled down and defaced. Sir John, in contempt of the bishop, carried it intact to his own house. Accused of this crime before the queen's council, he asserted that the stone had been taken away a year before the bishop came and was laid aside for the pavement of one of the aisles, and had never been brought to his house.[6] In his turn he made counter charges against the bishop, accusing him of wasting and alienating the patrimony of the diocese of Worcester. The

1 Prattinton Coll. (Soc. Antiq.). Foxe, *Eccl. Hist.* (ed. 1610), p. 1893, col. 1.
2 Ibid. Strype, *Annals*, i. 81, and *Life of Archbishop Grindal*, 33.
3 Prattinton Coll. (Soc. Antiq.).
4 Strype, *Parker*, i. 156.
5 Prattinton Coll. (Soc. Antiq.).
6 Strype, *Annals*, i. 388, etc.

episcopal manors of Grimley and Northwicke had been allowed to go to ruin, bricks had even been taken away from Grimley to the palace of Worcester to make a 'washing-house necessary for the women's laundry.'[1] Besides this he had granted leases of the best of his parsonages to his children and reversions of farms and leases to others for a term of forty years or more.[2] It seems reasonable to assume that these charges were fashioned by Sir John and his confederates to quicken the opposition of the county against the bishop. The charge of waste and alienation of the revenues of their dioceses has been often levelled against the Elizabethan bishops, but this charge must be modified in the light of the Act of Parliament passed in 1558–9 empowering the queen to take into her hands certain of the temporal possessions of any archbishopric or bishopric which fell vacant, recompensing the value with parsonages impropriate.[3] In the case of Worcester, it was under this Act, before Sandys became bishop, that the queen took into her hands the manors of Hanbury, Wick Episcopi, Bredon, Welland, and Knightwick.[4] Further, the bishop's own words may be quoted in his defence. He who drew up the orders for bishops and clergy in which the bishops were warned that as temporary possessors of the bishopric they had no right to 'let or alienate by lease or grant except for their own term of office any of the manors or whatsoever heretofore hath not been in lease,'[5] unless he added hypocrisy to his other vices could scarcely have been a notable offender against his own injunctions, especially as in one of his letters he showed his hatred of the practice: 'These be marvellous times. The patrimony of the church is laid open as a prey unto all the world.'[6] Further charges brought against Sandys by Sir John Bourne were those of neglect of duty and looseness of morals.[7] Against both these charges the bishop can be defended. His orders for bishops and clergy, issued about 1562, may be cited in his defence against neglect of duty, entering as they do into detail concerning those who are to be ordained for the ministry, that each one be 'fit and learned to teach the people' and only admitted with the 'consent of six learned ministers, who shall all lay their hands upon his head at his admission'; concerning the catechism of the children and youths in the parish churches; concerning presentations to benefices that 'none shall be presented except such as are learned and fit for the office'; and, lastly, concerning the exclusion from communion of 'whoever is a common swearer in the diocese.'[8] The charge of immorality was the natural view of those whose ideal was celibacy among the clergy. The bishop himself had married twice, and doubtless did all in his power to raise the status of the wives of the clergy. But the impression that the married clergy made on those of the old way of thinking is clear from the opposition that met the bishop on all sides. Sir John Bourne and his son Antony used the fact that the canons were married to insult their wives. Not content with attacking the bishop, Sir John drew up a pamphlet setting forth the abuses among the dean and chapter of Worcester. That the canon's wives persuaded them to have the organ pipes 'molten into dishes,' and of 'the cases had they made them bedsteads.' That their wives sold the grain allotted to their portion, not in Worcester, but at the dearest market.

1 Prattinton Coll. (Soc. of Antiq.). A paper written by Sir John quoted.
2 Ibid.
3 *Stat. Revised*, i. 487.
4 Mins. Accts. 2 and 3 Eliz. no. 38.
5 Wilkins, *Concilia*, iv. 240.
6 Strype, *Whitgift*, i. 546.
7 Strype, *Ann. of Reform*, i. c. 25.
8 Wilkins, *Concilia*, iv. 240.

That the dean and chapter put all fines, perquisites, profits of corn, etc., into their own pockets, 'wherewith they decked their wives so finely . . . as none were so fine and trim in the city. And as by their habit and apparel you might know the priests' wives, and by their gait in the market and the streets from a hundred other women, so in the congregation and cathedral church they were easy to be known by placing themselves above all other of the most ancient and honest calling of the said city.'[1]

In strong contrast to the power of the bishop, and the luxury of the dean and chapter, was the state of the county clergy. They had to struggle for existence, and were gradually sinking lower and lower. It would be difficult to find a time when the religious life of the country was deteriorating to a greater extent. Exaggerated as the evils among the clergy of the time doubtless have been, there is much to prove that marriage tended to lower the standard of living among the clergy in the county. Meagre provision had been made for their support in pre-reformation times, since most of the benefices had belonged to the monasteries,[2] and the rectorial tithes had been appropriated to some monastic purpose. At the dissolution these great tithes had passed into the hands of the Crown, leaving the priest only his 'living wage.' Thus the income that had been almost too small for an unmarried clergy had now to support a married clergy and their families. It could hardly be expected that a very high class of men could be looked for as incumbents. In position they were little better than labourers, and if this was the state of the vicars, that of the curates, where there were curates, must have been worse. Sandys admitted the state of his clergy to have been very bad, and alluded to it in one of his sermons.[3] He felt that some remedy must be found, and the remedy that he hit upon brought him into trouble with Archbishop Parker. It is a rule of ecclesiastical law that a bishop cannot without the leave of the archbishop hold two visitations in one year. Without even applying for leave for a second visitation, Sandys determined to make a second in 1561 to inquire into the habits of his clergy. They resented this and complained to Parker, who at once forbade the bishop to hold two visitations in one year without his express permission.[4] Thus the bishop was thwarted on all sides in his attempts at reform; the degradation of the clergy became a disgrace, which continued for at least two centuries and a half, and which was a source of danger to the Church. When deprivation meant starvation not only for themselves but for their families, and when the bishop was practically president of the Court of the Welsh Marches, which had general jurisdiction even over the clergy, it was natural that the clergy should become a cringing, down-trodden class, as subservient to the bishop as the bishop was to the Crown. For the Court of the Welsh Marches, as part of the Queen's Council, exercised an ecclesiastical as well as a temporal jurisdiction, and although in some respects it protected ecclesiastics against the laity, yet since the bishop of Worcester was a powerful member, he seldom failed to use his power to enforce obedience on his clergy.

1 Prattinton Coll. (Soc. Antiq.).

2 See supra.

3 *Sermons of Archbishop Sandys* (Parker Soc.), 120.

4 Strype, *Parker*, 78. The bishop deprived two of his clergy 'which, as savouring of too much rigour, the archbishop disliked and surmised that he had covetous ends thereby, as in a letter which he sent to the said bishop he hinted, and therein spake of "Germanical natures," as though that bishop, who had been an exile in Germany, ... had sucked in some principles of Germany more than were good.'

Sandys' episcopate had certainly been a failure, but the times were difficult and there were very few men living who had caught the spirit of toleration and could have filled his post more successfully. In 1570 he was translated to London, 'which he would willingly have avoided as being easy here at Worcester.'[1] He excused himself to Cecil 'being conscious of his own inability for so great a charge, not caring so much to be placed in the view of the court and the whole realm,' and pleading his 'want of health and bodily infirmity,' but hearing that Cecil was offended, and 'Her Majesty misliked to alter her determination,' and that the people of London 'descried' him with 'universal joyfulness,' he determined to take the office 'whatsoever may become of me.'[2]

His successor at Worcester was Nicholas Bullingham, for Dr. Calfhill, archdeacon of Colchester, whom the queen had nominated, died before he could be consecrated. Like Sandys, Bullingham had been abroad during the reign of Mary, and on his return at Elizabeth's accession was made bishop of Lincoln. He was also, like his predecessor, a married man, and like him a strong upholder of the Anglican church. But he came to Worcester an old man wanting to be quiet, and the only great event that stirred his episcopate was the visit the queen paid to Worcester.

Of John Whitgift, Bullingham's successor, there have been many varying opinions. He was a stern and arbitrary disciplinarian with a strong determination to maintain the Anglican church, as established by Acts of Parliament, against both Romanists and Puritans, and his position enabled him to enforce his will. Thus Macaulay and Hallam, judging him from the modern standpoint of toleration, could only condemn him. To those of his contemporaries who felt with him the need of enforcing ecclesiastical uniformity against 'contentious Protestant and stubborn Papist,'[3] he appeared as a 'devoute man, verie mercyfull, free from malice or practise of revenge . . . borne for the benefite of his country and the good of the Church, wherin he ruled with admirable moderation, suppressing such new sects as in his tyme began to ryse.'[4]

Worcester offered no easy task for the new bishop. During Bullingham's episcopate the effect of Sandy's unwise policy, which had alienated both Romanist and Puritan, began to be felt. Recusancy was rife, especially among the Papists, for the county was 'much warped towards Popery.'[5] The strength of the Papists in the county may be gathered from the general statement made by Whitgift to the Lords of the Council in 1577. Mass was said at various houses by persons 'so apparelled that they could not be known.'[6] Priests who had come 'from beyond the seas' taught the children, christened them anew, and 'swore their parents should not come to church.'[7] They also buried men secretly at night 'because they would not admit nor receive the service now used.'[8] People went to mass in the night season 'carrying in mails and bags all things pertaining to the saying of mass.'[9] Whitgift was by no means loth to use his power against the recusants, and, anxious that they should not be sheltered by the magistrates of the county, he 'sought

1 Prattinton Coll. (Soc. Antiq.).
2 Ibid.
3 Strype, *Whitgift*, 85.
4 Prattinton Coll. (Soc. Antiq.).
5 Strype, *Whitgift*, 82, concerning recusancy in the counties under the jurisdiction of the Court of the Welsh Marches.
6 Strype, *Whitgift*, 82.
7 Ibid.
8 Ibid.
9 Ibid.

from the Privy Council for a special commission to him and some of the Welsh bishops, exclusive of others, to be his assistants.'[1] The lords of the Council sent 'their hearty thanks' to the bishop for 'his pains in these examinations and discoveries,' and promised speedily to send him a special commission of oyer and terminer for proceeding against the heretics in those counties over which the jurisdiction of the Court of the Welsh Marches extended.[2] Thus the work of maintaining ecclesiastical uniformity in Worcester was put into the hands of the bishop, who was ordered to send up to the Council from time to time the names of persons who would not go to church and also of popish recusants.[3] The first class included the names of both Puritans and Romanists, the last of Romanists only. Whitgift sent up his first list in November, 1577, begging that no lenity might be shown towards the 'many men and women of great countenance and revenues who by common report are noted to be great mislikers of the religion now professed . . . lest others by their example fall to the like contempt.'[4] Among those named in the special list of Papists were Lady Windsor, Sir Robert Throckmorton, Thomas Throckmorton, John Talbot of Grafton, Thomas Blount of Kidderminster, and Dorothea Heath of Alvechurch.[5] The list of recusants shows the following numbers :—

In the Deanery of Worcester	13
,, ,, Powick	7
,, ,, Kidderminster	5
,, ,, Droitwich	4
,, ,, Pershore	6
,, ,, Evesham	4
	39[6]

In December, 1582, Whitgift reported to Walsingham the capture of two massing priests in Worcestershire 'of some account among our recusants.' He also gave information against other Papists in the county, notably Thomas Moore and Rees Moore, 'poor men but very dangerous,' the former of whom was Bonner's porter in the reign of Queen Mary.[7] In the same year the Council ordered the bishop and his officers to hold conferences with the recusants 'now in hold,' and 'publickly confute their errors' according to the rules set down by the Council. According to these rules those named by the Council to hold conferences, 'while abstaining from angry and opprobrious words,' were to base their arguments on the authority

[1] Strype, *Whitgift*, 83. S. P. Dom. Eliz. vol. cxviii. no. 11. [2] Strype, *Whitgift*, 83. [3] Ibid. 97.
[4] S. P. Dom. Eliz. vol. cxviii. no. 11. [5] Ibid. [6] Ibid. vol. cxviii. no. 11.
[7] Ibid. vol. clvi. no. 29. John, bishop of Worcester, to Thos. Walsingham. 'Right Honorable,—There are taken here in Worcestershire by Monday and his fellowe, two old and very ignorant massing priestes whose examinations I have sent unto you here enclosed. It seemeth that they are of some accompt among our recusantes. There are also dwelling at Rippell in this county two brethren, one called Thomas Moore, the other Rees Moore, pore men but very dangerous. Thomas Moore was Bonner's porter in Queen Marie's tyme. Many Papistes resort to their house (as it seemeth) to heare masses and to have other conference. I have sondry tymes layed wayte for them, but could not by any meanes have them taken before this tyme. They are watermen and dwelling hard upon Severn syde and in the edge of Gloucestershire. Rees Moore is nowe here in prison in Worcestre, but will confess nothing to any purpose. The other, who is the "lewder," cannot yet be come by.

'I think there are not two worsse asserted anywhere of their calling that doo more harme, etc.

'Youre honoure to remane,

'Jo Wigorn.'

The Moore family was strongly recusant, and remained so into the eighteenth century. In 1715 there were five Papists reported in Ripple, and all five belonged to the Moore family. (Forfeited Estate P. (P.R.O.), 110.)

of the Scriptures and the Fathers. When Papists and Jesuits could give no passage of Scripture as the special ground of their faith, then they should testify to those listening that such men based their faith 'not on the rock of Holy Scripture . . . but on the uncertain sands of tradition.' When they gave any ground of Scripture and 'wrested it to their sense' then the defenders of Protestantism should confute them by the interpretation of the old doctors.[1] Such orders were sent to every diocese, but were probably nowhere better obeyed than in Worcester, where the bishop himself was so learned and keen a disputant. The work of enforcing ecclesiastical uniformity, through the agency of the Court of the Welsh Marches, involved the bishop in the tasks of a civil magistrate as well as those of a spiritual judge. This gave him considerable power over his clergy. To the bishop was also given the right of nominating the justices of the peace for the county.[2] Under his province came quarrels between Papists and Puritans, and in times when so few words could be taken to mean so much these quarrels were only too frequent. 'Notwithstanding his diligence in this place' and the strict discipline he maintained, misreports were carried to the court against the bishop, asserting that there were 'certain murders and other great misdemeanours' happening in Worcestershire between the friends of a Mr. Abingdon, a Papist, and those of a certain Mr. Talbot.[3] Whitgift cleared himself in a letter to the Lord Treasurer, saying that there was no shire more quiet nor in better order than Worcestershire. The facts of the quarrel between Abingdon's men and Talbot's men had been exaggerated; there were as few misdemeanours as at any other time, and 'those which he heard of and fell out in proof were as severely punished as ever they were for any thing he could perceive by any record.'[4] Apart from Whitgift's work on the Court of the Welsh Marches there are two points of interest in his episcopate. His opposition to the alienation of the revenues of the diocese led to the reversion of the manors of Hallow and Grimley to the see.[5] In 1578 commissioners for inquiring into concealed lands came into Worcester, and among other lands they 'had in their eye Hartlebury, the chief seat and manor of the bishop.' Whitgift wrote to the Lord Treasurer for redress, and evidently succeeded, for the next month he wrote again saying that Hartlebury had not been taken from him. In defence of church lands in general against these 'concealers' he wrote a bold letter to the queen, begging her to dispose of them as the donors intended, not to friends and flatterers.[6] In one other way Whitgift asserted the rights of the church against the Crown. In 1578 he wrote to the Lord Treasurer making suit to the queen to bestow on him the right of disposing of the prebends of his church. His aim was to present such persons as were learned preachers to forward the established religion and 'bring the people off from Popery.'[7] His suit was successful, although the right was only given him as a personal favour during his continuance in the see. Elizabeth had granted the same to Bishop Sandys

1 Strype, *Whitgift.*

2 Ibid. 93, quoting a paper of state (MSS. G. Petyt. Armig.), 'Justices of Peace for Worc. John Talbot of Salwarpe and such other as the bishop shall think fit.'

3 Ibid. 84.

4 Ibid. quoting a letter of Whitgift's in the author's possession.

5 Sir George Paul, *Life of Whitgift*, pp. 27, 28.

6 Strype, *Whitgift*, 87. Strype's comment is 'Words becoming the mouth of a truly Apostolic bishop!'

7 Ibid.

in 1562 for his lifetime,[1] but the right was too precious for the Crown to relinquish altogether.

It is difficult to form a clear idea of the state of religion in the county under Whitgift's successor, Edmund Freke (1584–1591). Under a less severe rule than that of Whitgift recusancy probably increased. The trial and death of Campion in 1581 had inspired rather than trampled down the hopes of the Papists. Among the Worcester Papists who were suspected of helping Campion and Parsons was a William Bell, deputy clerk of the peace in Worcester and a friend of the Throckmortons. He was examined in December, 1583, as to his knowledge of Parsons, but the result of the examination is not given.[2] In 1586, the year of the Babington conspiracy, George Throckmorton, son of Sir John Throckmorton, was examined as to his knowledge of Anthony Babington. He confessed that he was acquainted with Babington, but knew nothing of his plot, asserting that he himself had been brought up in France and to the Roman Catholic religion, but that he had had no communication with 'seminary priests or others of that mind for two years.'[3] The recusancy laws of 1581, imposing a fine of £20 a month on recusants, meant in many cases ruin or conformity. In Worcester it was the Papists who suffered most under these laws, for militant Puritanism does not seem to have been strong in the county. In June, 1586, the justices of Worcester certified to the Privy Council the offers made by certain recusants in the county to be discharged of the penalties of the statute.[4] The pathetic tone of some of these letters shows that there were many Papists in Worcestershire who could ill afford to pay so dearly for their conscience sake. Elizabeth Pakington, a widow, notwithstanding her 'great charge and smal habilitye as havynge three daughters all unmarried and nearly all unprovided for and one sonne also in the licke case,' offered a contribution of 20 nobles a year to the queen as a compensation for the removal of the penalties of the statute.[5] 'I have strayned me unto the uttermost,' she says, 'in respecte of such gratious favour and clemency to be extended towards me.' Another recusant was John Middlemore, of Hawkesley in King's Norton, who pleaded that his family were such a tax on him that already he was forced into debt. 'I have one daughter unmarried, but marriageable if my purse were as ready; I have lately bestowed one daughter in marriage, the greatest portion of whose marriage portion I remain yet a debtor for.' Yet rather than forego his religion he would pay a yearly sum to Her Majesty. These are typical of the seventeen letters forwarded to the Council, but some have other excuses, as John Woolmer of Kington, who pleaded that he was a 'pore younger brother with neither landes, leases, annuity, nor any other lyvinge.' To others like William Breadstorke of Staunton, husbandman, and Rees Moore and Thomas Moore of Ripple, watermen, the fine must have meant more than their living.

Bishop Freke died in March, 1591, and was succeeded in 1593 by Richard Fletcher, dean of Peterborough, who held the see for one year and was then translated to London.[6] While dean of Peterborough he was present with Mary Queen of Scots when she suffered death at Fotheringhay in 1586. 'At which time being the person appointed to pray with her and for her,

[1] Pat. 4 Eliz. pt. vi. m. 53.
[2] S. P. Dom. Eliz. vol. clxiv. no. 19.
[3] Ibid. vol. cxciv. no. 42.
[4] Ibid. vol. cxc. no. 11.
[5] Ibid.
[6] Prattinton Coll. (Soc. Antiq.).

did persuade her to renounce her religion, contrary to all Christianity and humanity (as it was by many there present so taken), to her great disturbance.'[1] A bishop with such a record would be likely to show little lenity to the Papist recusants of Worcestershire. Moreover, the danger from both Spain and France was over; the defeat of the Armada had crippled Spain; Henry of Navarre had defeated the Leaguers at Ivry and was king of France. Thus Elizabeth could attack the Papists with impunity. The year 1592 marks the beginning of the Recusant Rolls, and in 1593 all recusants not having goods and lands to a certain amount were ordered to leave the country or be deemed felons, while suspected Jesuits and seminary priests refusing to answer on examination were to be imprisoned without bail until they should confess.[2]

This year 1593 was a hard one for Puritans as well as for Papists. 'Obstinate recusants,' whether Papist or Puritan, those who denied the queen's power in ecclesiastical causes and those who were frequenters of conventicles, were included among those who should abjure the realm within three months and lose all their lands and goods.[3] It is difficult to gauge the difference in the number of Papists and Puritans in the recusant rolls for Worcester, but most of the names are those of well-known Romanist families, and seem to prove the strength of the Papists as compared with the Puritans. The rolls also show very clearly the state of the majority of the recusants. Bishop Bilson, who was appointed successor to Fletcher in April, 1596, after the see had been vacant from January, 1594,[4] wrote to Cecil in the July of 1596 concerning the recusants in the county. He reported that Worcester was as dangerous as any place he knew: 'Nine score recusants of note besides retainers, wanderers, and secret lurkers' were dispersed in 'forty several parishes and six score and ten households.' Of these about forty were 'families of gentlemen who either themselves or their wives absent themselves from church. . . . Many of them are not only of good wealth but great alliance, as the Windsors, Talbots, Throgmortons, Abingdons, etc.' He named thirty-two of the 'wealthier sort,' and eighteen gentlewomen who 'refused the church though their husbands did not,' besides 'fourscore and ten several householders of the meaner sort where man or wife or both are recusants, besides children and servants.' On the whole the bishop's estimate seems to agree with the lists on the Recusant Rolls. The Windsors, Throckmortons, Abingdons, Talbots, Middlemores, Blounts, Packingtons, Foliots, Lygons, and Woolmers appear as the 'wealthier sort.'[5] But the majority of the recusants are of the working class. Labourers from Chaddesley Corbett, and Yardley, and Stoke Prior; fishermen and watermen from Ripple; husbandmen from Elmley Lovett and Chaddesley Corbett; a baker and a 'wheeler' from Stoke Prior,

[1] Prattinton Coll. (Soc. Antiq.).

[2] *Stat. of Realm*, 35 Eliz. c. 2.

[3] Arber, *The Pilgrim Fathers*, 34.

[4] The Cecil MSS. show how difficult it was to find anyone who was willing to become bishop of Worcester now the see was so impoverished. The queen offered the office to Wm. Daye, dean of Windsor, who at first accepted (Hist. MSS. Com. *Rep. on Cecil MSS.* pt. v. 48), but afterwards refused, finding that 'he had been much deceived in his choice' and that 'the change was little greater and yet the charge far greater' (Ibid. 79). Again he wrote to Cecil, 'it would utterly beggar me to take it. . . . I pray you therefore to move her highness to be gracious unto me and in my old age not to put me to seek another county, a strange air, new acquaintance, and another living without sufficient maintenance.' 14 Jan. 1594. (Ibid.).

[5] *Recusant R.* (Pipe Off. Ser.), 34–45 Eliz. nos. 1–12. There is no distinct evidence to prove whether Papists or Puritans were in the majority on the rolls themselves. But the greater number of the names occur elsewhere as those of Papists, and the inference naturally is that the Papists were in the majority.

and a tailor from King's Norton;[1] three yeomen from Stoke Prior, Halesowen, and Yardley,[2] but in all the rolls the majority of recusants are women.[3] To cope with the number of recusants in the county Bishop Bilson pleaded that the queen would trust him with 'the commission ecclesiastical,' since ordinary authority was 'weak to do any good on either sort, excommunication being the only bridle the law allows to a bishop, and either side despise that course of correction as men that gladly and of their own accord refuse the communion of the church.' If the queen would grant him this power he would endeavour 'to serve God and Her Majesty' 'by viewing the qualities, retinues, abilities, and dispositions of the recusants, by drawing them to private conference,' 'lest ignorance make them perversely devout,' by restraining them from maintaining 'any wanderers and servitors that feed their humours.' Also he promised to certify what were the causes of 'so much revolting.'[4] There is no evidence that the queen granted this 'commission ecclesiastical,' but anyhow the bishop had not time to carry out his plans, for in 1597 he was translated to Winchester.

His successor Gervas Babington[5] was the last of the Elizabethan bishops of Worcester, who, translated from Exeter in 1597,[6] held the see until his death in 1610. The period of his episcopate was one of general unrest. The accession of James I. roused the Papists to their final effort, since his religious training made it seem likely that his sympathies would be all for Puritanism. Nowhere in the country were the Papists more active than in Worcestershire, and their activity culminated in the Gunpowder Plot of 1605. The details of the plot, the capture and subsequent execution of the various ringleaders, hardly belong to the ecclesiastical history of Worcester, but at the same time nothing proves the strength of Roman Catholicism in the county more conclusively than the examinations of the various Papists, rich and poor, connected with the plot.[7] The foremost ringleaders were of the Worcester Papist families, the Winters, the Talbots, the Abingdons. At Hindlip, the home of the Abingdons, most of the negotiations were carried on. When the plot had failed and search for the plotters was being made in January 1606 Sir Henry Bromley, sheriff of Worcester, was ordered to search thoroughly Hindlip House.[8] The sheriff reported the difficulty of his search and that Mr. Abingdon and all the household 'denied any knowledge of the priests.' But when they had given up hopes two men crept from a secret place and surrendered through hunger and cold. These were Owen and Chambers.[9] It was at Huddington, the home of the Winters, that Garnet the Jesuit was

1 *Recusant R.* (Pipe Off. Ser.), 35 Eliz. no. 2.

2 Ibid.

3 Ibid. In 1594–5 there were 3 in Elmley Lovett to 1 man, 5 in Northfield to 3 men, 3 in Kington to 1 man, 5 in Hanley Castle to 3 men, 7 in Yardley to 3 men, 3 in Stoke Prior to 3 men, 2 women were the only recusants in Longdon, only one in Oldberrow, Bredon, Bretforton, and 3 the only recusants in Alvechurch.

4 Hist. MSS. Com. *Rep. on Cecil MSS.* pt. vi. 266–7.

5 There are two interesting stories concerning Babington quoted by Dr. Prattinton. The first tells that Bishop Babington had a little book containing three leaves only, which he turned over night and morning. The first leaf was *black* to remind himself of Hell and God's judgment due for sin. The second *red* to remind him of Christ's passion. The third *white* to set forth God's mercy to him through the merits of His Son in his justification and sanctification.

The other pictures him while chaplain to the earl of Pembroke helping 'his noble countess,' Mary Sidney, in translating the Psalms, 'for it was more than a woman's skill to express the tense so right, as she hath done in her verse!' Prattinton Coll. (Soc. Antiq.).

6 Prattinton Coll. (Soc. Antiq.).

7 *Cal of S. P. Dom.* Jas. I. (1603–10), 240–314.

8 Ibid. 281.

9 Ibid. 283.

arrested,[1] and it was in Worcestershire that most of the conspirators sought refuge and 'lay hid in barns and poor men's houses.'[2] The financial burdens of recusancy were now heavier than ever before. Not only were the ordinary fines paid to the crown, but the fines were farmed out for a fixed sum, leaving the 'farmer' to make what profit he could. Moreover the 'benefit of the recusancy' of particular Roman Catholics was now conferred on court favourites and officials, particularly in the reign of James I. In 1604 Sir William Anstruther was granted the benefit of the recusancy of John Talbot of Grafton,[3] and Archibald Napier that of Gertrude Winter of Huddington.[4] In 1608 Thomas Williams was granted the benefit of the recusancy of William Sparry of King's Norton,[5] and Thomas Dixon that of William Middlemore of Hawkeslew and of Leonard Smallpeece.[6] In 1610 the valuable recusancy of no less than eleven Romanists, six of whom belonged to Hanley Castle, was granted to Thomas Dixon.[7] Various other like grants were made in the following years, and are one more proof of the vast sums extorted from the Romanists. It is scarcely to be wondered that occasionally, but only very occasionally, men were forced into becoming 'Church Papists,' and going to church simply to escape the penalties of recusancy. In 1613 a certificate was given by John Hall, vicar of Kington, the constable and the two churchwardens 'that Rees Woolmer of Kington came to his parish church the Sunday following the Quarter Sessions and upon the Sunday next after received the Holy Communion in the parish church of Kington at a general Communion then had and ever since that time hath frequented his parish church every Sabbath and other days in the time of divine service and sermons with dutiful behaviour and reverence as a good subject ought to do.'[8] This seems as if Woolmer had been proceeded against for not going to church and had been required to attend church, receive the sacrament, and produce a certificate of his having done so to the court. This is borne out by the fact that about the same time Woolmer took the oath of allegiance before the justices.[9] He, however, still continued to be a Catholic, and in subsequent presentments of popish recusants for the parish of Kington his name appears. The act of being a 'Church Papist' was alleged as a ground for disqualifying a person from keeping an alehouse. In a letter to the clerk of the peace a charge is made against the licensed victuallers of Droitwich that they neither frequent the church themselves nor warn their guests to do so in the time of divine service. The letter then goes on to ask that the licence of one Adam Partridge be taken away, 'as his mother is a "Church Papist" who hath neither received the Communion according to her promise to the Lord Bishop nor taken the oath of allegiance.'

While there is no definite evidence of an active display of Puritanism, there is evidence that Puritan ideas were influencing the county. As early as the reign of Edward VI. there is an entry for the purchase of 'two forms for the Communion to be received at,' in St. Michael's, Worcester.[10] There are doubtless other proofs of the influence of Puritanism on the ceremonial of the Worcestershire churches, but there is no clearer proof of the prevalence of Puritan ideas than the various presentments for divers kinds of Sabbath-breaking

1 *Cal. of S. P. Dom.* Jas. I. (1603–10), 283.
2 Ibid. 281.
3 Ibid. 146.
4 Ibid. 356.
5 Ibid. 423.
6 Ibid. 430.
7 Ibid. 593.
8 *Sess R.* (Worc. Hist. Soc.), 188.
9 Ibid. 189.
10 Dr. Gee, *Elizabethan Prayer Book*, 179.

given on the quarter sessions rolls. In 1602 William Thomas of Wickhamford was charged with 'railing with his neighbours on the Sabbath dayes in the church and churchyard.'[1] In 1606 the grand jury presented that Francis Doune of Doddenham kept an alehouse without licence, receiving lewd persons, 'whereby it is suspected that the church is robbed by some of them and two very good surplices stolen forth of the same church.' Also he hired 'one Brinton, a lewd and bad person to play there holiedays and the Sabbath dayes in prayer times. It causeth men's sons and servants from their business.'[2] In 1607 two victuallers of Pershore were punished for 'using unlawful vices and manners every Saboth day in the morning as drinkinge swearinge and bowlinge out of order and measure.'[3] In 1608 Henry Dingley of Hanley Castle petitioned the justices of the peace to call on the churchwardens and constables of Hanley Castle to prevent the great abuses done there on Sabbath days, 'and especially the great riot and unlawful assembly on Sunday last being Whit Sunday by forty persons at least many of them being recusants who daily increase in the said Parish.'[4]

Another instance of the growth of Puritan feeling was the beginning of the treatment of immorality as a temporal crime, punishable at the sessions. The ancient discipline of the church was still exercised, for persons of immoral lives were first sent to the spiritual courts and put to penance. But if they still persisted in their crime, temporal punishment, which was far more effectual, was awarded.[5] This tendency to transfer 'spiritual' cases to temporal courts, which follows in the wake of Puritanism, is further seen in the strict watch kept in the civil courts over cases of non-observance of the church fasts, etc. The royal reason for this was not ecclesiastical, but what the king thought statecraft. By not allowing flesh to be eaten it was thought the people would be compelled to eat salt fish, and this would encourage the fishing trade and so the navy: he would therefore do good both in temporal and in spiritual matters by making the people either fast or eat only fish. In 1619, Richard Wylson, of Stourbridge, was summoned to appear at the sessions for dressing flesh during the time of Lent.[6] In the same year John Tillet, of Kidderminster, innkeeper, was summoned for not observing Lent,[7] while in 1620 a butcher named Harris was charged for 'killing flesh in Lent.'[8] This strange survival of ancient discipline is again seen in the various sentences of excommunication passed by the spiritual courts. At the same time these sentences were often repeated and were evidently difficult to enforce. If other charges were brought against those excommunicated then a statement to that effect seems to have been added in aggravation of the other offences, otherwise excommunication does not seem to have had much effect. In 1604 Joan Bassell was said to be 'a common bawde, a friend of thieves, and a common scold,' and a receiver of stolen goods; it is then added: 'also she is an excommunicated person

[1] *Sess. R.* (Worc. Hist. Soc.), 52. [2] Ibid. 81. [3] Ibid. 102.

[4] Hanley Castle was and had been a great Romanist stronghold. (*Recusant R.* (Pipe Off. Ser.), 34 Eliz. onwards, and *Cal. of S. P. Dom.* Jas. I. (1603–10, 593.) Probably this was partly owing to the proximity of the district to the county boundaries and the opportunities it gave for escape into either Herefordshire or Gloucestershire. Moreover it was within Malvern Chase and offered every facility for concealment.

[5] *Sess. R.* (Worc. Hist. Soc.), 119. In 1609 John Phillips of Flyford Flavell and Elizabeth Sherman were bound over to appear for continuing to lead immoral lives even though they had been once sentenced in the spiritual court and had done penance according to their sentence. Cases such as this are very frequent.

[6] Ibid. 275. [7] Ibid. 274. [8] Ibid. 324.

and shall and doth stand excommunicated for these four years last past.'[1] Margaret Bache, wife of John Bache, nailer, of Chaddesley Corbett, was alleged to be a common scold and a source of strife among her neighbours, and had been presented as a scold at the court leet for Chaddesley. She was also presented at a visitation at Bromsgrove in 1603 for misbehaving her tongue towards her mother-in-law and excommunicated.[2] Hence it appears she had been excommunicated for twelve years and had not yet experienced any evil results.

While Romanism and Puritanism were so effectively influencing the county there was little attempt on the part of the clergy of the church of England to cope with either. Indeed, the state of the clergy had not improved since the accession of Elizabeth. The right which Sandys and Whitgift had wrung from the queen of appointing the prebends of Worcester had reverted to the crown. Bishop Parry, the great court preacher of the day,[3] who succeeded Babington in May, 1610, was more of a courtier and a scholar than a bishop, and was not likely to interfere with the king's right of appointment. Indeed, there is little trace of his tenure of the see in its history. On the death of this 'good, godly, and learned prelate' in December, 1616,[4] the king appointed[5] a very different man, John Thornborough, who had been bishop of Limerick (1593-1603) and of Bristol (1603-16).[6] By his time, however, the royal right of presenting to the prebendaries was a settled fact.[7] The king promised the offices during the lives of the holders, and when a vacancy occurred all that the bishop or chapter had to do was to obey by installing the royal nominee. In some cases the king seems to have granted the prebendaries to men who were not likely even to visit the cathedral.[8]

This right in the king's hands necessarily meant that not only the dean and the canons were nominees of the crown, but that they were likely to appoint those whom the king selected to the livings in their patronage. Considering how large a number of the church livings had passed into the patronage of the dean and chapter at the dissolution,[9] it is clear that the court could then control the distribution of the majority of the benefices in the county. Thus, in 1608, although Wickhamford was under the patronage of the dean and chapter, Salisbury remonstrated with the bishop because he had not admitted Mr. Wyncott to the rectory of Wickhamford on the king's presentation.[10] In another instance, in September, 1611, the king

[1] *Sess. R.* (Worc. Hist. Soc.), 67.

[2] Ibid. 211.

[3] Dr. Prattinton describes him as 'an able divine, well read in the fathers, a thorough disputant, and so eloquent a preacher that King James always professed he seldom heard a better. The king of Denmark also gave him a very rich ring for a sermon preached before him and King James at Rochester.' Prattinton Coll. (Soc. Antiq.).

[4] *Cal. of S. P. Dom.* Jas. I. (1611–18), 427.

[5] 'Buckingham's kinsman, Henry Beaumont, was to have been bishop, but failed from the dislike felt of Snowden and Bailey, very unworthy men who are bishops of Carlisle and Bangor.' Ibid. 422.

[6] Prattinton Coll. (Soc. Antiq.).

[7] In January, 1637, he wrote to Laud saying that 'the dean and chapter denied his right of jurisdiction over them, for 'heretofore they are now immediate donatives from the King' and so claimed exemption from the jurisdiction of the bishop. *Cal. of S. P. Dom.* (1636–7), 359.

[8] Ibid. (1623–5), 158. John Hanmer, bishop elect of St. Asaph, petitioned the king for permission to retain the prebend in Worcester which he held, and to have the archdeaconry of St. Asaph and various other benefices as well as his bishopric.

[9] See supra. *E.g.*, almost all the possessions and advowsons that had belonged to the Worcester house went to the dean and chapter.

[10] *Cal. of S. P. Dom.* Jas. I. (1603–10), 448.

presented John Archibald to the vicarage of Bromsgrove with the chapel of King's Norton, which was also under the patronage of the dean and chapter.[1] In this way royal nominees were preferred to many of the livings.[2] The king tried in the same way to secure the livings under the patronage of the bishop for his nominees. With a subservient bishop, such as Babington or Parry, the task was easy. So sure was the king of his influence over the bishop that in 1604 he granted to Robert Maxwell, one of the gentlemen of the privy chamber, the advowson of the rectory of Ripple 'immediately and as soone as the same shal be void,'[3] notwithstanding the fact that the bishop had been the patron at least from the time of Giffard.[4] But Bishop Thornborough, although he finally gave way to the king, opposed the royal claim to nominate for the livings of Hartlebury and Upton upon Severn. On the death of the rector of Hartlebury, in 1623, Secretary Conway wrote to the bishop 'recommending' Dr. Lesly for the parsonage.[5] The bishop wrote back to say that he had given the benefice of Hartlebury to 'an ancient grave preacher,' his son-in-law, before he received Dr. Lesly's application. He was 'sorry to hear that the king is displeased,' but had promised Hartlebury to his son-in-law three years ago, and at the same time had promised Upton upon Severn, which the king also wanted for a Mr. Woodford, to his chaplain.[6] The king wrote back to the bishop that his excuses for not admitting Lesly and Woodford were not sufficient, and required him to admit them at once and provide otherwise for his son-in-law and chaplain.[7] The bishop answered that, 'trusting in the royal justice and clemency,' he would comply with his request and put Dr. Lesly in possession of Hartlebury, his son-in-law having resigned. Mr. Woodford would resign his benefice in London to his chaplain, 'whom Woodford makes a conscience of ruining,' and then be appointed to Upton upon Severn.[8] At the same time the bishop wrote to Secretary Conway that he would have maintained his right to his benefices, 'but would rather lose twenty such than hazard the loss of His Majesty's favour.'[9] The king wrote later thanking him for his 'dutiful conformity,' and telling him that he had procured the living of St. Faith's for Mr. Smith, the chaplain.[10] In June, 1628, Thornborough wrote to Charles I. saying he had given the archdeaconry of Worcester to his son, 'a learned divine of a good and frequent preacher.' Though he 'had very few preferments in his gift,' yet when two of his best benefices worth £400 per annum became void and were disposed of 'to a son-in-law and another,' it pleased the late king to require them for Dr. Lesly and Dr. Woodford. Then 'with much ado,'

[1] S. P. Dom. Docquet, vol. x. Sept. 9, 1611.

[2] In one instance there is evidence of a strong opposition and virtual success of the dean and chapter against a royal nominee. In March, 1627, Secretary Conway wanted the rectory of Broadwas for his chaplain, Thomas Archbold, and wrote to the dean and chapter recommending the same. *Cal. of S. P. Dom.* (1627–8), 112. The dean, Joseph Hall, pleaded his own engagement 'to one of their body' (ibid. 113), and the chapter excused themselves for not presenting Archbold as they had already nominated Richard Potter thereto (ibid. 157). This evidently involved a struggle, for in November, 1677, Secretary Conway wrote to the newly appointed Dean William Juxon begging him put an end to the litigation between the dean and chapter and Archbold concerning his presentation to Broadwas, made, according to Conway's statement, by Dean Lake, Hall's predecessor (ibid. 454). In the end the case was referred to the bishop (ibid. 1628–9, 166), and the result seems to have been a compromise and an eventual victory for the dean and chapter. Inst. Bks. (P.R.O.) Ser. A. Worc.

[3] S. P. Dom. Docquet, vol. vi. Sept. 17, 1604.

[4] Nash, ii. 299.

[5] *Cal. of S. P. Dom.* (1623–5), 362.

[6] Ibid. 370.

[7] Ibid. 373.

[8] Ibid. 385.

[9] Ibid. (1623–5), 386. The bishop further says 'it is thought a retribution on him for procuring from his prebendaries two of their best benefices to please the king.'

[10] Ibid. 423.

he procured on the resignation of his son-in-law and chaplain, and would do so again if the king should require the archdeaconry from his son. Still he expressed a wish that the king would not do so as his son was 'a worthy man without preferment' from his father.[1]

With so much of the patronage of the county under royal influence there was little hope of promotion for any of the poorer clergy who had no court favour. Such a state of things was likely to encourage carelessness on the part of the clerks and curates in the county since it accentuated the bareness of the 'living wage' allotted to them now that there was no prospect of increasing it. It is unsafe to generalize from a few examples, but several cases brought before the grand jury at the sessions seem to show no very high standard of conduct among some members of that section of the clergy.[2]

If these instances are typical of the state of the clergy, the lack of any evidence that the bishops from Sandys until the time of the Laudian revival made any strict inquiry into the lives and discipline of the clergy becomes still more strange. Bishop Thornborough was in many ways an ideal bishop of the Arminian type in his hatred of both Puritans and Romanists. He was translated to Worcester in the spring of 1617, and by July had already begun his attacks on the recusants of the county. Three yeomen of Belbroughton were bound over before the bishop to appear at the next Quarter Sessions, 'touching Mr. Apleton, a recusant.'[3] In the same month William Fownes, a constable of Belbroughton was summoned for letting Mr. Apleton escape his hands.[4] At the next session Matthew Walford, churchwarden of Belbroughton, was indicted for not presenting recusants according to the statute.[5] This first year is typical of Thornborough's proceedings against recusants.[6] The position that he was called upon to fill was no easy one. While Romanism was so little on the decrease that in October 1625 there were rumours of a 'plot to be sped in Worcester,'[7] the spread of Puritanism was already evidenced by the continued presentations for Sabbath breaking, which had reached a stage of open opposition. In 1617, William Jeffries, of Longdon, petitioned the justices of the peace against various 'sports and morrices and dancings held by the youth or inhabitants of Longdon on the Sabbath days, by reason whereof many rude ruffians and drunken companions have come there from other towns adjoining to the said sports, and have made much quarrelling,

[1] *Cal. of S. P. Dom.* (1628–29), 574.

[2] *Sess. R.* (Worc. Hist. Soc.), 50, 52, 101, 328, 703.

[3] Ibid. 236.

[4] Ibid. 237.

[5] *Sess R.* (Worc. Hist. Soc.), 244. Evidently the constables were very lax in presenting recusants. In the Session Rolls the constables from Abberley, Badsey, Belbroughton, Doddenham, Eastham, Grimley, Hartlebury, Mamble, Old Swinford, Paxford, St. John-in-Bedwardine, St. Michael's-in-Bedwardine, and Stock and Bradley presented there were no catholics in their parishes. That these statements were not true is proved by the Recusant Rolls for the same date or by a special case in St. John's-in-Bedwardine, where after a return of 'no catholics' had been made, a Roland Davis of the parish was indicted at the Middlesex Sessions.

[6] His harshness towards recusants is further shown by his suggestion, in 1627, that 'recusants should be charged to maintain their own arms, though taken from them.' *Cal. of S. P. Dom.* (1627-8), 315.

[7] Ibid. (1625-6), 122. Besides this, the story of Anderson, the 'high priest' of the Jesuits in Worcester, and his supposed conversion of the bishop's daughter, show the length to which the Romanists dared to go in the county. The pretended conversion of Benjamin Thornborough, the bishop's son, in order to reveal the residence of Anderson and secure his imprisonment, shows that, where Romanists were concerned, any means in Thornborough's eyes were justified by the end. (*Hist. MSS. Com. Rep.* viii. p. 40.) The practice of being a 'professed Romist,' in order to betray the priests, seems to have been in favour. In 1612 Sir James Perrot had written to Salisbury telling him how Jesuits and priests kept up 'intelligence among the recusants dwelling in Worcester,' and wishing 'that some trusty professed Romanist would come among them and reveal much of their haunts and practices.' Ibid. (1611–18), 123.

ready to murder one another.'[1] The same hatred of Sunday sports gave rise to the long continued quarrel between Gerard Prior, vicar of Eldersfield, and his parishioners. Prior, if not a Puritan, had Puritanical ideas, and was supposed to have preached a sermon against profaning the Sabbath by dancing; and, knowing it was done under royal sanction, to have added a prayer that 'the king's heart might be turned from profaneness, vanity, and popery.'[2] Jeffreys, a justice of the peace for Worcester, being informed of his 'improper words,' bound him over to appear at the sessions. He also informed the bishop, who on proof of the words spoken suspended Prior.[3] Further, many of his parishioners, 'William Rumney and his confederates,' brought a charge against their vicar of irreverence and immorality.[4] But others of them, with many of the clergy of the diocese, petitioned the bishop to restore the vicar, saying that he had been falsely accused, and had 'often prayed for the king.'[5] The bishop sent these petitions to the archbishop, saying that the words had not been spoken by Prior himself, but unknown to him by a James Roades, of Herefordshire, who had once preached in Prior's pulpit.[6] The bishop added that Prior was very penitent for any improper words he had spoken, and offered to recall them in the pulpit.[7] Nevertheless the bishop would not restore him until he had had the archbishop's advice. The archbishop gave his opinion for Prior;[8] Archdeacon Swaddon also wrote to Sir Julius Cæsar, one of the Privy Council, in his favour.[9] The case was then referred

[1] *Sess. R.* (Worc. Hist. Soc.), 254–5. The petitioner gives fully detailed examples. 'On a Sabbath day in 1614 some of Forthampton's men coming to the said sports made an affray upon the smith's man of Longdon, whereby the townsmen then had been much troubled to part the said affrays, to keep the peace, and to bring them before some of His Majesty's justices for the county, the principal actor in which last-mentioned affray was one Sandys, of Eldersfield, who since has cut off his neighbour's arm for doing the office of constable upon him a little before, and when, as on a Sabbath day, 1615, there was much sport made in Longdon by morrices and dancings, and because at evening service the same day they were forced to cease their sports, some of the youth of Longdon procured a poor woman, then being excommunicated, to go into the church in service time and make another poor boy follow her into the church, and then tell the minister (being then saying the service of Almighty God) that the excommunicate person was in church, hoping thereby to put an end of God's service that so they might again return to their sports. All which being done by the excommunicate person and poor boy as they were directed, the minister was thereby interrupted in God's service and the whole congregation much disturbed. And whereas upon Trinity Sunday, 1616, the dancing again taking place in Longdon aforesaid, your poor petitioner being the constable there for the preventing and suppressing these abuses, endeavoured peaceably to take the minstrel then playing, and to punish him upon the statute against rogues, thereupon one of the dancing company strake up your petitioner's heels and said he would break your petitioner's neck down the stairs if he departed not from them and let them alone, whereby your petitioner being much terrified by them departed, and afterwards many other abuses were committed that year by the said company too long here to relate unto you, and whereas now again, the present year 1617, they were again there dancing sports upon every Sabbath day, whereby it is to be feared the like quarrels may ensue as before, to the great dishonour of the Almighty and contempt of His Majesty's laws and proclamations against the same, may it therefore please your worships, these premises considered, to make some order in this your open session for the suppressing the profanation of the Lord's Day, and so shall give commands to the high constable to see the same executed.' This thoroughly Puritanical petition well represents the views that party held as to Sunday. All sports were to be put down. The petitioner must have been greatly disappointed with the order the court made. Sandys was ordered to be of good behaviour, and the constables of the parish were ordered not to stop all morrices, dancing, and games on Sunday as the Puritans wanted, but to bring all morrice dancers who danced in the time of Divine Service and all who practised unlawful games before the local magistrate. It is an interesting touch of the manners of the time, the device to stop the evening service, by sending an excommunicated person to church, and it is unfortunate the result of the experiment is not given.

[2] *Cal. of S. P. Dom.* (1619–23), 73.
[3] Ibid.
[4] Ibid. (1611–18), 164.
[5] Ibid. (1619–23), 72.
[6] Ibid.
[7] Ibid.
[8] Ibid. 78.

[9] Ibid. He speaks of Prior as a 'learned, painful, and zealous preacher of good character' . . . falsely attacked by his parishioners, who 'being punished for disorderly conduct,' had revenged themselves by repeating slanderous words he had uttered thirteen months before against the king, but 'they ought to be prosecuted for concealing such a thing so long!'

'to the Lord President[1] and the bishop,' who evidently released Prior from his suspension.[2] This case illustrates the bishop's attitude both towards Puritanism and discipline among his clergy. He suspended Prior not because of the complaints of the parishioners of his immorality, whether true or no, but because of his Puritanical attack on Sabbath breaking. At the same time the state of the clergy was such that it could not be overlooked even by so staunch a friend as Archbishop Laud. He made a visitation of the diocese as metropolitian in 1634, and at that he gave the dean and chapter of Worcester certain articles of inquiry to answer. On those answers he issued certain orders,[3] so that it may be safely taken that the abuses that these orders were designed to redress were admitted to exist by the dean and chapter themselves. A perusal of the orders shows that the dean and chapter were still unreformed, that the complaints Sir John Bourne had made against them seventy years before were still to a great extent true. The choristers were not appointed because they could sing, the timber was sold for the profit, and the chapel at the cathedral door[4] turned into a hay barn. Concerning this latter charge, the bishop seems to have been more to blame than the dean and chapter.[5] In 1637 he wrote to Laud that 'the decayed chapel standing over the charnel without the church was used by the bishops for a house to put hay in ever

[1] It is not clear if 'the Lord President' meant the Lord President of the Council or the Lord President of the Marches; but it may be the latter, since Prior petitioned the council that his parishioners who had causelessly accused him might be punished and compelled to pay his expenses, and that the usage he had sustained might be redressed by the Council of the Welsh Marches. *Cal. of S. P. Dom.* (1619–23), 78.

[2] Prior was vicar of Eldersfield until 1627.

[3] 'Orders enjoined by the most reverend Father in God, William, lord archbishop of Canterbury, His Grace Primate of all England and metropolitan, to be observed by the dean and chapter of Worcester made upon their joint and several answers to the articles of inquiry given them in charge in his grace's metropolitan visitation depending in the diocese of Worcester, Anno Dom. 1635 :—

1. 'Imprimis, all your prebendaries and other ministers of your church be constantly resident in their several places as the statute of your church requires.

2. 'Item, that none be admitted to any place of your quire before he be first approved of for his voice and skill in singing by such of your church as are able to judge thereof, and that the places there as they fall void be supplied by men of such voices, as your statutes require.

3. 'Item, that hoods, square caps and surplices be constantly used, according to the canon in that behalf provided by the dean, residentiaries, petty canons and other ministers belonging to your church whensoever they come to administer or hear divine service.

4. 'Item, that no timber trees growing upon your ground be hereafter sold, wasted, or made away but that they be carefully preserved for the only use and repair of your church.

5. 'Item, that your choristers be duly and diligently catechised, which hath been formerly too much neglected.

6. 'Item, that your churchyard be decently and without profanation kept, and that you take care that the bones of the dead may not lie scattered up and down, but that they be gathered together and buried, and that the chapel called Capella Carnaria, situate at the entry of your cathedral, now profaned and made a hay barn, be restored and employed to the wonted use, and that the encroachments made upon your churchyard and other hallowed ground about your church be likewise restored and laid open for those ancient uses to which they were dedicated.

7. 'Item, that as much as in you lies you prevent the common thoroughfare made through your close.

8. 'Item, that the muniments which concern the public state of your church be publicly taken from every particular and private person that hath any of them in his custody, and that for ever hereafter they be carefully preserved and kept together in some convenient place which shall be thought fit for that purpose by the dean and chapter.

9. 'Item, that your porters, sextons, and other your church officers (if they be able), serve their own places in their own persons.

10. 'Item, we require that these our injunctions be carefully registered and observed.'—Wilkins, *Concilia*, iv. 519.

[4] This was the Carnarie chapel.

[5] In 1637 the dean, Christopher Potter, claimed to have reserved 'their charnal house from the bishop's profanation, who passionately desired to keep it for his hay house.'—*Cal. of S. P. Dom.* (1636–7), 391.

since the dissolution.'[1] Nevertheless in obedience to Laud he had delivered the same over to Mr. Tomkins, the prebendary, 'who promised the same should be converted to prayers at six in the morning.' But Mr. Tomkins removed 'all things of the spacious old school into this little chapel,' and as it was joining on to the bishop's court, the bishop pleaded that he should be much disquieted by the noise of the two hundred boys, besides which 'there will be more profanation by swearing and lying among the boys than when the hay was in it.'[2] The bishop himself was at issue with the dean and chapter for suffering two houses to be built over graves in the churchyard, not because of the desecration, but because one was 'over-looking the bishop's palace.'[3] Also he pleaded that they should not be allowed to take away his 'bake-house and slaughter-house, with a garden, coach-house, and chamber over it,' on the ground that he only held them by sufferance and lease, 'all which, notwithstanding,' the bishop hoped 'lawfully to keep for his successors.' Thus Bishop Thornborough only raised his voice against the dean and chapter when they made personal attacks on him, otherwise he cared little about their irreverence and irreligious spirit. But Roger Mainwaring, appointed dean in November, 1634, was a more thorough reformer. In September, 1635, he wrote to Laud telling him of the work he had done in the cathedral. Among the seventeen items he enumerated he showed that he had begun to enforce high Anglican vestments and ornaments. An altar-stone of marble was erected and set on four columns. The wall behind the altar was covered with 'azure coloured stuff with a white silk lace down each seam.' The altar itself he had adorned with a pall, an upper and a lower part, and had fenced 'the holy table' with a rail. Vestments which had been polluted and turned into 'players' caps and coats' he had caused to be burned, the silver extracted and put into the treasury of the church. He showed his archæological spirit by preserving 'thousands of rolls lying in the tower,' removing them from 'a damp stone wall and from under a window where the rain beat in upon them,' and by repairing and beautifying 'His Majesty's Audit Hall there.' He showed also his love of order and reverence by ordering the forty king's scholars, instead of 'coming tumultuously into the choir,' to 'come in binatim and to do reverence toward the altars.'[4]

The evils that existed among the dean and chapter necessarily pointed to evils among the lower clergy. At last the idea that some reform was absolutely necessary seemed to have come to Worcester as to the whole of England. In Worcester, as elsewhere, an attempt had been made to supplement the work of the parochial clergy by utilising the system of 'lecturers' appointed to preach to the people on Sunday afternoons.[5] Encouragement was given to religious men and women to found lectureships in different parishes, so that people might hear a profitable sermon at least once a Sunday. But in Worcester, as elsewhere, the system involved a struggle between the Arminian dean and chapter and the Puritanical 'lecturers.' For the most popular preachers of that day were the Puritans, and they succeeded in completely monopolising the lectureships. In 1614 the Corporation of Worcester

[1] *Cal. of S. P. Dom.* (1636–7), 360. [2] Ibid. [3] Ibid. [4] Ibid. (1635), 394–5.

[5] This system was at first directed to the supply of good preachers in cathedral churches. It had gradually extended to parish churches in towns, and afterwards to churches in the larger villages.

founded a lectureship on condition that they were to appoint the lecturer, who was to be entitled to preach at the cathedral every Sunday 'at the charge of the city of £40 per annum.'[1] With the spread of Puritanism this meant the appointment of Puritan lecturers, and the dean and chapter with their strong Arminian bias could not stop them from preaching. But in 1633 the king and the archbishop determined to check these lectures, and issued orders to the bishops to 'take great care concerning the lecturers in their several dioceses' that they should conform to Arminian ceremony and doctrine.[2]

But the lecturers had become too firmly fixed for any such proposals to be effective. The archbishop was required to make returns to the king as to the different dioceses and how the orders were observed. In 1634, Laud, in his return to the king, reported that he had received no account from four of his dioceses, of which Worcester was one;[3] but in 1636 he gave details as to Worcester:—'My Lord Bishop of the see (Thornborough) certifies that your Majesty's instructions are carefully observed, and that there are only two lecturers in the city of Worcester, but very conformable, and that they are so, and that one of them preaches on Sunday in the afternoons after catechizing and service in the parish churches, and ending before evening prayers in the cathedral. I may not here forbear to acquaint your Majesty that the Sunday lecture was ever wont to be in the cathedral, and that it was removed because the city would suffer no prebend to have it, and evening prayer in the parish church must needs begin betimes and their catechizing short and the prayers at the cathedral begin very late if this lecture can begin and end in the space between, but if it can be so fitted I think the dean and chapter will not complain of the remove of the lecture to a parish church.'[4] In 1637 there is a further certificate from the archbishop: 'My Lord the Bishop certifies that he is less troubled with nonconformists since Mr. Wheatley of Banbury gave over his lectures at Stratford within that diocese, and that during this heavy visitation at Worcester[5] he hath caused the lecture there to cease.'[6] It is difficult to understand Bishop Thornborough's attitude towards the lecturers and the citizens. It seems as if his personal antagonism towards the dean and chapter made even him encourage the Puritanical leanings of the citizens. In January, 1637, the dean wrote to Laud telling him how the bishop took 'every course likely to plant faction and contempt of the church in the citizens,' telling them not to come to the choir service and allowing them to sit covered during prayers. Also he highly favoured 'their beloved lecturers . . . one of whom lately at the mayor's house called the choirmen "altar-mongers."' Also he hated Mr. Tomkins, their prebend, 'a worthy, true, honest, and true-hearted churchman,' and his hatred 'so inflamed the

[1] *Cal. of S. P. Dom.* (1636–7), 359–497. Among some of the famous divines who held the pulpit were Dr. Abbot, archbishop of Canterbury, and Dr. Wright.

[2] The special directions were as follows:—

1. That in all parishes the afternoon sermon be turned into catechising.

2. That every bishop take care in his diocese that all lecturers do read divine service according to the Litany printed by authority in their surplices and hoods before the lecture.

3. That when a lecture is set up in a market town it may be read by a company of grave and orthodox divines near adjoining and of the same diocese, and that they ever preach in such seemly habit as belong to their degrees, and not in cloaks.

4. That if a corporation maintain a single lecturer, he be not suffered to preach until he professes his willingness to take upon him a living with cure of souls within that corporation, and that he do actually take such benefice or cure so soon as the same shall be fairly procured for him. (Rymer, *Fœd.* viii. pt. iv. 23.)

[3] Ibid. 103.

[4] Ibid. ix. pt. ii. 76.

[5] In 1637 there was a bad outbreak of plague in Worcester.

[6] Rymer, *Fœd.* ix. pt. ii. 135.

citizens' that this good man had all possible insults and affronts put on him by the schoolboys, even by those to whom the dean and chapter presented exhibitions.[1] The citizens were determined to maintain the right of the lecturers against the dean and chapter, and with the support of the bishop they sent a petition to the archbishop in March, 1637. They stated that within the city of Worcester there were nine parishes, whereof many incumbents were not 'preaching ministers,' whereby a great many of His Majesty's subjects are not so well instructed in the Word of God as they ought to have been.' The lecturer at the cathedral had been the remedy, but now the dean would not have the sermons, although the congregation had attended divine service in the cathedral as well. They prayed Laud that they might 'continue their former liberty, and present to the bishop a sufficient preacher to preach in the cathedral.'[2] In November, 1639, they sent up a further petition. A new method of attack on the lecturers had been tried. Time out of mind there had been in the west end of the cathedral church 'an ancient pulpit for daily prayers and preaching of the Word of God, with convenient seats and kneeling for the citizens and others, to which place very great numbers were wont to resort . . . . and which for decency and comeliness has been commended by most who have seen it for a graceful ornament.' In 1637 Laud's vicar-general ordered these seats to be removed and the pulpit moved to the west end of the choir, hoping that the congregation would be crowded out of the choir and unable to listen to the preachers. Thereupon the citizens petitioned that the pulpit might be restored to its former place, since the west end of the choir was 'very unwholesome for the auditory,' as there were 'so many doors near the same.' Moreover when the pulpit was moved into the choir 'the sixth part of the auditory' was crowded out, and many 'ancient men and women were constrained to forbear coming thither' because of the 'want of convenient seats.'[3] Bishop Thornborough with several of the prebends joined in the petition. In reference to it the dean, Dr. Christopher Potter, wrote later in the same month to Laud stating the case from his point of view. The vicar-general had seen that these seats dishonoured the goodly fabric of the church since during choral service many 'gathered auditors about them in the seats and read to them some English divinity so loudly as that the singers in the choir were much disturbed by them.' But his order to take the seats down enraged the citizens, who hereupon fled 'to their oracle and asylum, the old bishop (of late feeble, now lusty), who has indeed debauched the people, otherwise tractable to reason, by his popular fawning and flattering them in all their fancies.' He begged Laud to 'yield a little to their folly . . . and gratify them with their own beloved place till that mistress of fools, their own experience, show them the vanity of their desires and the wisdom of your direction and choice for them.'[4] On the

[1] *Cal. of S. P. Dom.* (1636–7), 391. 'Very lately when Mr. Tomkins was coming out of choir service,' relates the dean, 'as he was doing his adoration to God, purposely to hinder him the boys came thrusting upon him in such an insolent manner that he hit one a box on the ear. The town triumphs at this, and the boy's father means to sue him for striking in the church.' [2] Ibid. 496–7. [3] Ibid. (1639–40), 79–80.

[4] Ibid. 107. The dean also gave various reasons why the west end of the choir was a fitter place than the west end of the church for the pulpit:

1. It was more spacious, and capable of opening into a large cross aisle.
2. More commodious for the eminent sitting of their magistrates upon the ascending steps.
3. It was warmer; no door opening out of the cathedral there save one small one into our cloister behind a great pillar, and a large cold north door opening a little above their old desired place.

This is almost a direct contradiction of the statements made by the citizens.

29 November, 1639, the answer came. His Majesty was 'well content' that the 'preaching place' should be returned to the west end; but, instead of the old seats, movable seats, 'decent, handsome, and easy,' should be placed there for the mayor and his brethren, the bishop and the dean and prebends, with forms for the other citizens. No seat was to be raised higher than the ordinary except that of the bishop, mayor, and dean and chapter, and these only 'for decency sake.'[1] This meant that the Crown had yielded, for the sermons of the lecturers had become too popular for Charles or Laud to silence them. Not only was this the case in Worcester city itself but in various parishes of the county. Perhaps one of the most striking instances is the deliberate stand made by the inhabitants of Kidderminster against their vicar, and their election of a lecturer who was destined not only to do more than anyone else in furthering Puritanism in the county, but also to make for himself a great and enduring name in English history. The vicar at Kidderminster, George Dance, instituted 1627,[2] was certainly not of 'such parts as fitted him for the care of so great a congregation,' even if it was exaggeration to say that he was 'a weak and ignorant man who preached only once a quarter.' The parishioners determined to supplement a weak vicar with a strong lecturer, and tried to find the man they wanted. Their first attempt was a failure; their next was more successful. They engaged as lecturer a man from Bridgenorth, who was to make Kidderminster famous; that man was Richard Baxter. The story of his life need not be given here, only so much as refers to the Kidderminster lectureship, for it will illustrate both the good and the bad side of those institutions. In 1640 the inhabitants of Kidderminster petitioned against their vicar; they alleged that he was an ignorant, weak man, a frequenter of alehouses and at times drunk, and kept a curate who was a common tippler, drunkard, railer and trader in unlawful marriages. On this, Dance offered a compromise that, if they allowed him to retain the living, a sum of £60 a year should be paid out of the profits to support a lecturer; the curate should be got rid of, and a committee of fourteen appointed to select the lecturer, who was to be at liberty to preach whenever he pleased, but Dance was to be allowed to read the prayers and do any other part of the formal work of the church.[3] On these terms the petition was withdrawn. The committee first selected a man named Lapthorn, but he did not approve himself to the committee; he was therefore discharged, and on 9 March, 1641, Baxter was invited from Bridgenorth to become the lecturer.[4] After some hesitation he went, 'feeling inwardly called upon to do so,' and was appointed on 6 April, 1641, after preaching his first sermon. Baxter remained at Kidderminster until the Civil War broke out in 1642. It is probable that his preaching was the most effective means of establishing a Puritan party in the county. On recommending his hearers to sign the Protestation he was censured by the Royalists, and had temporarily to leave Kidderminster, but soon returned, and was there when the Civil War began.

It was to a great extent owing to the lecturers that the Parliament had any following in the county. The Roman Catholics almost without exception took the side of the Crown in the Civil War, and their numbers in the

[1] *Cal. of S. P. Dom.* (1639–40), 130.
[2] Nash, *Hist. of Worc.* ii. 57.
[3] Prattinton Coll. (Soc. Antiq.).
[4] Ibid.

county was one of the reasons that made Worcester take the king's side so strongly. Moreover, with but few exceptions, bishop, dean and chapter and gentry were High Church Royalists. The patronage of the majority of the benefices was in their hands, and under the influence of the king they almost invariably appointed Royalist nominees; therefore it may be said with truth that the county was a stronghold of the High Church party. Their strength in the county was witnessed by the various petitions sent up to the king and Parliament by 'the justices and gentry and commended by the whole county.' In December, 1641, they petitioned as men 'bred up in the true Protestant religion' that all attacks on government by bishops and the ancient and uniform liturgy should be quelled, and the 'uniform service of God continued amongst us.'[1] In 1644 they addressed another petition asserting that with the expense of their lives and fortunes they would continue still 'in the maintenance of the Protestant religion . . . against all seditions and factious innovations.'[2] Against this strength of High Church influence and feeling the Puritans could only contend by the lectureships, and these had only been established in towns and in the larger villages. There were lecturers at Worcester, Dudley, Kidderminster, King's Norton, and Evesham, and this band of men who considered they had been especially sent by Providence to do its work and to overthrow spiritual wickedness in high places, formed the strength of the Worcestershire Puritans.

Among the clergy themselves there were several whose inclinations led them to forsake their cures and join the Parliamentary forces. In January, 1642, Charles wrote to Prideaux, who had succeeded Thornborough in 1641,[3] that Henry Hacket and John Halcister, parsons respectively of St. Helens and St. Nicholas, Worcester, had long been seditious and schismatic preachers, and that having abandoned their said cures, were then 'actually joined to the rebels.' Therefore the king recommended the bishop to admit a certain Nathaniel Marston, who had 'exceedingly suffered in his poore estate by the coming of the rebels into the city,' to officiate one of the said abandoned cures and receive the full profits and benefits thereof, and finally, if the incumbent did not return to his cure, to institute Nathaniel to the same.[4] In February the king wrote again concerning Humphrey Hardwicke, rector of St. Mary Witton, 'a person who, for his seditious carriage in those parts, was formerly silenced preaching in the parish.' He had not only stirred up his parishioners to rebellion, but had also himself joined the army under Essex, for which the king ordered the bishop to proceed against him, 'that a man of better merit may be appointed in his place.'[5] In July, 1643, he wrote further concerning Humphrey Hardwicke that the bishop should eject him and put in his place Richard Jennings, 'one of the gentlemen of the chapel royal.' Meantime the proceeds of the benefice from the time of its desertion by Hardwicke were to go to Richard Jennings.[6] Another case of sequestration for desertion was that of Nathaniel Salway, rector of Severn

[1] Prattinton Coll. (Soc. Antiq.), Townshend's Annals (1640–60). [2] Ibid.

[3] Prideaux's absence from London on his enthronement at Worcester prevented him from joining with the other bishops in the Protestation, and so enabled him to escape from being impeached with them. He, however, in 1642 signed the protest as a peer against the Bill for excluding the bishops from Parliament. He appears to have been at Worcester during the Civil War and the siege in 1646, and on the surrender of the city he retired to Bredon, where he died.

[4] Prattinton Coll. (Soc. Antiq.). Both returned and were in Worcester when it was occupied by Essex at the end of September, 1642. [5] Ibid. [6] Ibid.

Stoke. The bishop suspended him for desertion, and in April, 1643, the king wrote that the said Nathaniel was then in London, where he had 'invaded the profits of the rectory of St. Martin's Vintry, of right belonging to our trusty and well-beloved chaplain Dr. Bruin Ryves.' Therefore the king willed the bishop to commit the cure of the said rectory to Dr. Ryves.[1] Mr. Burroughs, rector of Oldberrow, was another 'great promoter and stirrer up of this horrid and unnatural rebellion,' who had deserted his cure 'contrary to the duty of a good pastor and subject.' The king wrote in October, 1643, requiring the bishop to admit Anthony Harwood, one of the chaplains of the royal army, to execute that charge and receive the fruits of the said rectory.[2]

The sects of Anabaptists, Antinomians, Brownists, and Quakers, were well represented in Worcestershire. In December, 1642, the king wrote to Prideaux that 'a principal cause of the said rebellion hath been the great increase of Brownists, Anabaptists, and other sectaries and persons mistaken and mispersuaded in their religion'; and in order that the bishop might remedy anything of that nature in his see the king bade him attend with vigilance to his pastoral charge, do his utmost endeavour to reform all abuses, 'correcting the ill lives of the clergy and all scandalous persons, advancing pious and learned preachers, and providing that all that have the care of souls do diligently preach God's Word, and, residing at their cures, perform what to their duty and places doth appertain.'[3]

While the county was thus a stronghold of the High Church party and yet a place where the sectaries flourished, as far as definite evidence goes there is nothing to prove that the number of ejections under the rule of the Commonwealth was greater in Worcestershire than in other less biassed counties. The nomination of the Committee for Scandalous Ministers in 1640,[4] followed by that of the Committee for Plundered Ministers, marked the beginning of the work of Parliamentary sequestration.[5] The ordinance doing away with the use of the prayer book and setting up the directory came into force in 1645,[6] and from that time ejections and sequestrations began in earnest. Bishop Prideaux, as a staunch Royalist and Episcopalian, was naturally one of the first to suffer.[7] With him the dean and chapter, as the central forces of the High Church feeling, were sequestered.[8] But the sequestrations among the parochial clergy hardly seem, so far as general evidence goes, to have been a large proportion of the whole number of the clergy in the county. Dr. Walker, in his attempt 'to record the sufferings of the loyal clergy,' could only name twenty-four sequestrations, and some of these are uncertain. Various other sequestrations may have been made, since there are noticeably few livings held by the same incumbents in 1660 as in 1640. But from this it is unsafe to generalize, since in many cases the incumbents may have resigned or died within a period of twenty years. Evidence from the journals of Parliament shows no Worcester minister in the list of sequestrations of 'superstitious, innovating or malignant clergy,'[9] and only three Puritan nominations are given, two on the resignation of the

[1] Prattinton Coll. (Soc. Antiq.). [2] Ibid. [3] Ibid.

[4] Shaw, *Hist. of the Eng. Church*, 1640–60, ii. 177. [5] Ibid. 185. [6] Ibid. 354, 355.

[7] Walker, *Sufferings of the Clergy*, pt. ii. 78. [8] Ibid. pt. ii. 79–82.

[9] Shaw, *Hist. of the Eng. Church*, 1640–60, ii. App. ii. 295.

late incumbents,[1] and one on sequestration. The latter was the appointment of Richard Warde to Upton-upon-Severn, on the sequestration of William Woodford, 'of whose fitness the Assembly disapproved.'[2] In 1645 a cause was pleaded after a petition to the Committee for Plundered Ministers, between Mr. Williams, to whom the rectory of Beoley was sequestered, and Mr. Sugard, the late incumbent, who 'loudly claimed that he was presented thereto by Sir Edward Spenser.' The Assembly of Divines decided that Sir Edward should make good his claim, and, failing that, the rectory should be handed over to Mr. Williams.[3] Evidently Mr. Williams did not enter into the cure, as in September, 1646, 'Alexander Clogie, minister to the Assembly,' was admitted to officiate the cure of the church of Beoley.[4] He was probably ejected in July, 1660, when David Bordall was instituted.[5] There was evidently a sequestration of the rectory of Tredington also, since in March, 1646, 'copies of the articles in the cause of Dr. Smith, rector of Tredington,' were ordered 'to be delivered forth to parties on all sides according to the petition of Thomas Betts.'[6] Moreover, Walker mentions Dr. Smith among the sequestered clergy, and gives the name of Richard Durham, who succeeded him in the living in 1658.[7] The other ejections given by Walker are those of Thomas Archbold from Harvington,[8] George Benson from Lindridge,[9] Herbert Bowton or Boughton from Wolverley,[10] Edwin Brace from Doverdale,[11] Francis Charlet from Salwarpe,[12] Edwin Cooper from Hampton Lovett,[13] George Dance from Kidderminster,[14] George Durant

1 Ralph Nevil was nominated to Evenlode in May, 1647, on the resignation of Jervis Clarke (*Lords' Journal*, ix. 185), who had been instituted in 1636 by Charles I. (Nash, i. 395). In 1661 Ralph Nevil's institution was confirmed, probably on his conforming, by Charles II. (Ibid.). Jonathan Grant was nominated to Astley (*Lords' Journal*, ix. 511), void by the resignation of John Wood (*Commons' Journal*, v. 367; *Lords' Journal*, ix. 543, x. 20).

2 Plundered Min. Com. Add. MSS. 15,672, 27 May, 1647. Walker, *Sufferings of Clergy*, pt. ii. 408.

3 Ibid. Add. MSS. 15,670. 4 Ibid. 5 Nash, i. 73.

6 Minutes of Plundered Min. Com. Add. MSS. 15,670.

7 Walker, *Sufferings of the Clergy*, pt. ii. 373, and Comp. Bks. (P. R. O.), Ser. i. Worc.

8 Walker, *Sufferings of the Clergy*, pt. ii. 188. According to Walker, Archbold was sequestered not so much for his zeal for Episcopacy and the Royalist cause as for his opposition to a design on the part of some of his parishioners to enclose part of the common field. The articles of sequestration were brought against him about August, 'so that he lost all the crops for that year.' His wife and family were 'plundered and thrown out of doors, and not so much as a bed was allowed him for himself, a wife, and his ten children.' His wife in a few years died of grief, and he himself 'removed to London and died there in a short time.' His successor was one William Bridges, who had some time before been curate at the living during the vacancy of the church, and 'could get no preferment until he thrust out Mr. Archbold.' William Bridges died in 1654 and was succeeded by William Hopkins (Nash, i. 578), who was evidently ejected in 1656 when Stephen Baxter was appointed (Comp. Bks. (P. R. O.), Ser. i. Worc.), but who was restored in 1662 (Nash, i. 578).

9 Walker, *Sufferings of the Clergy*, pt. ii. 211. Sequestered and succeeded by John Giles (Aug. of Livings (Lamb. Lib.), cmlxxix. 451).

10 Walker, pt. ii. 212. He was evidently succeeded by Thomas Baldwin, a Puritan nominee (Aug. of Livings (Lamb. Lib.), mxvi.). Ejected in 1661 (Nash, ii. 474). 11 Walker, pt. ii. 212.

12 Ibid. 227. He was succeeded by Richard Woolley (Calamy, *Nonconformist's Memorial*, iii. 413, and Comp. Bks. (P.R.O.), Ser. i. Worc.), ejected at the Restoration.

3 Walker, 227. He was succeeded by John Fraston, ejected in 1660 (Calamy, *Nonconformist's Memorial*, iii. 3 2).

14 Ibid. 233. Concerning his sequestration Richard Baxter wrote that 'the people at Kidderminster had again renewed articles against their old vicar and his curates, and upon trial of cause the committee had sequestered the place but put no one in it, but put the profits into the hands of divers inhabitants to pay a preacher till it was disposed of.' Baxter himself refused to take anything but the lectureship, and the cure was handed over to a Mr. Richard Serjeant, 'a harmless man of no learning' (*Reliq. Baxterianæ*, ed. Sylvester, p. 79). Yet Baxter seems to have been looked upon as the vicar, and when Serjeant was transferred to Stone in 1657, Baxter himself tells how all the time he abode at Kidderminster he did not remove the old sequestered vicar so much as out of his vicarage house. But at the Restoration, when Dance was restored and 'times had changed, the instigation of others made him as malapert again as if he had been awakened out of a sleepy innocence' (*Reliq. Baxterianæ*, p. 97).

from Blockley,[1] Richard Farley from Upton Warren,[2] Emanuel Smyth from Hartlebury,[3] Nathaniel Holihead from Church Lench,[4] William Hollington from Alvechurch,[5] Francis Kerry from Eastham,[6] Samuel Lee from Chaddesley Corbett,[7] Benjamin Masters from place unknown,[8] John Moseley from White Lady Aston,[9] Edward Pilkington from Ombersley,[10] William Spicer from Stone,[11] Henry Sutton from Bredon,[12] William Harewell from Old Swinford and Stourbridge,[13] Thomas Taylor from Knightwick and Doddenham,[14] Thomas Warmestry from place unknown.[15] This may not be a full list of the sequestrations in Worcester, but there seems to be no definite evidence to prove that other institutions made under the Commonwealth followed on sequestrations and not on the resignation or death of the incumbent. At Earl's Croome Richard Fletcher was presented on the cession of the late incumbent Edmund Fleetwood,[16] who had been instituted in 1646,[17] on the ejection, or possibly resignation, of Richard Bury, instituted in 1641.[18] John Hall, the vicar of Bromsgrove, instituted in 1624,[19] may have conformed in 1645, for in 1650 he was still holding the living.[20] Whether he was ejected after this it is difficult to tell; but in October, 1655, Joseph Ayne was mentioned as 'late minister of Bromsgrove';[21] while in September, 1654, John Spilsbury was 'exhibited to the Committee for Approbation and Presentation of Ministers for presentation to Bromsgrove.'[22] In November, 1656, he was called 'vicar

[1] Walker, 233. George Durant was dispossessed by a party of horse, 'who dragged his children (whereof he had then ten living, and most of them very young) out of doors; and the neighbours out of charity put them into a poor cottage in the same town and relieved them.' Mr. Giles Collier was 'thrust upon the parish' on Durant's ejectment, and conforming at the Restoration, was confirmed in the living by Charles II. (Nash, i. 105).

[2] Walker, 247. His successor evidently conformed at the Restoration, since there is no new institution to Upton Warren until 1699 (Nash, ii. 451).

[3] Walker, 277; Nash, i. 574. One of Emanuel Smyth's successors was Thomas Wright, who also evidently conformed after the Restoration, 1670.

[4] Walker, 277; Nash, ii. 82. He was turned out and cruelly treated with his wife and children, and died a few years after. His successor was evidently ejected at the Restoration, since Thomas Twitly was appointed in 1662.

[5] Walker, 277. His successor was Richard Moore, who held the living until 1661, when he was forced to surrender it to Mr. Hollington, who survived the usurpation. This may have been the same vicar, Mr. Hollington, who in 1642 was brought before the quarter sessions. See supra.

[6] Ibid. 290. Kerry was succeeded in 1649 by Edward Benson (Comp. Bks. (P.R.O.), Ser. i. Worc.), who probably conformed at the Restoration, since no new institution was made until 1667 (Nash, i. 367).

[7] Walker, 300. According to Walker one of Lee's successors was Thomas Baldwin or Badland (Calamy, *Nonconformists' Memorial*, iii. 389), who was ejected in 1661 when Mr. Lee was restored.

[8] Ibid. 313. The name of the living is given as Flyford, but this does not tally with Nash.

[9] Ibid. 313. One of his successors was Robert Brown, ejected in 1660 (Calamy, *Nonconformists' Memorial*, iii. 415).

[10] Ibid. 336. His successor, George Boraston (Aug. of Livings (Lamb. Lib.), cmlxxi. 282), may have conformed at the Restoration, as no new institution seems to have been made until 1688 (Nash, ii. 220).

[11] Ibid. pt. ii. 373. William Spicer was turned out of the living, but he was succeeded in 1657 by Richard Serjeant, who had married his daughter (Comp. Bks. (P.R.O.), Ser. i. Worc.). At the Restoration Spicer was restored and Serjeant ejected (Calamy, *Nonconformists' Memorial*, iii. 414).

[12] Walker, 373. Richard Beeston who succeeded him was ejected in 1660 and Sutton was restored (Calamy, iii. 387).

[13] Walker, 373; Nash, ii. 214. Jervis Bryan who succeeded him was ejected in 1662. He was succeeded by Richard Pierson, 'who was very kind to him, but sorely distressed at his own conformity, often saying, "Were it to do again, I would not do it for all the livings in England"' (Calamy, iii. 415).

[14] He was succeeded by Matthew Bolton in 1654 (Walker, 385), who seemingly conformed at the Restoration and held the living until 1674 (Nash, ii. 69).

[15] Walker, 385.

[16] Pres. to Benefices under the Commonwealth (Lamb. Lib.), cmxlvi. No. 27.

[17] Comp. Bks. (P.R.O.), Ser. i. Worc.

[18] Nash, i. 269.

[19] Ibid. 167.

[20] Aug. of Livings (Lamb. Lib.), cmlxxix. p. 449.

[21] Ibid. mviii. p. 326.

[22] Ibid. cmlxviii. p. 56.

approved of Bromsgrove,'[1] and was instituted either in that year or in 1657.[2] The probability is that Joseph Ayne was ejected and sequestered, as in 1665 he brought up a petition before the Committee for Maintenance of Ministers, evidently directed against John Spilsbury, the newly-approved vicar.[3] John Hancox, instituted to Elmley Castle in 1636,[4] evidently conformed in 1645, for in 1650 he was still holding the living.[5] Thomas Batchelor, vicar of St. Andrew's, Pershore, also evidently conformed. He was instituted in 1636,[6] and in 1650 was holding the living, and was specially mentioned in a grant by the Committee of Plundered Ministers as a 'godly and orthodox divine.'[7] It can be quite well understood that some may have been forced by an outlook of poverty to conform rather than starve. Others, like Gerard Prior, who had Puritanical leanings, would gladly welcome any system opposed to 'Laudian idolatry.'

It is difficult to gather a clear idea of the state of the church under the Commonwealth, but one point stands out very clearly with regard to Worcestershire, and that is the determined attempt the Presbyterians made to increase the revenues of some of the poorer parochial clergy. In some cases this was done out of the better-endowed livings,[8] but the majority of augmentations was made out of the confiscated property of the dean and chapter of Worcester in accordance with the general scheme for the appropriation of a portion of the revenues of dean and chapters to this purpose. Thus £40 yearly was granted to Roger Turner, minister of Castle Morton, out of that part of the revenue of the dean and chapter coming from rents and tithes of the rectory of Longdon;[9] £50 to John Taylor, minister of Dudley, of the revenues of the dean and chapter;[10] £50 out of the same to James Warwick, rector of Hanley Castle;[11] £40 13*s.* 4*d.* to Thomas Bromwich, minister of the church of Kempsey;[12] £50 to George Drake, minister of the church of the Holy Cross in Pershore;[13] £50 to Thomas Batchelor, of St. Andrew's, Pershore;[14] £25 6*s.* 8*d.* to William Fincher, of Moseley, the then value of which living was only £4 13*s.* 4*d.*[15] In one instance, that of Elmley Castle, the augmentation was made out of the rent of the impropriate rectory of Elmley, reserved for the bishop of Worcester.[16] In spite of this attempt to better the lot, and so probably the status, of the poorer clergy,[17] there is little in the history of Worcestershire, as in that of all England, to justify the rule of the Directory.

There is, however, one bright spot in the history of the county during this time—Kidderminster. There it was shown to what results the Puritan rule could attain when it was entrusted to competent hands. In 1646 Baxter had returned to Kidderminster. The living was pressed upon him, but he

1 Aug. of Livings (Lamb. Lib.), cmlxxii. p. 628.

2 In the proceedings of the Committee for the Maintenance of Ministers he is called 'minister of Bromsgrove' in 1656 (Ibid. cmlxxi. 282), but in the Comp. Bks. at the Record Office his institution is given in June, 1657.

3 Aug. of Livings (Lamb. Lib.), cmlxviii. p. 56.

4 Nash, i. 389.

5 Aug. of Livings, cmlxxix. 453.

6 Nash, ii. 252.

7 Aug. of Livings (Lamb. Lib.), cmlxxix. 453.

8 Ibid. 450. £16 13*s.* 4*d.* granted out of the impropriate rectory of Inkberrow to and for the maintenance of the minister of the chapel of Moseley.

9 Ibid. cmlxxxvii. 170.

10 Ibid. cmlxxix. 456.

11 Ibid. 454.

12 Ibid. 453.

13 Ibid. 449.

14 Ibid. 453.

15 Ibid. mxvi.

16 Ibid. cmlxxix. 450.

17 Evidently there had been little improvement in the status of the lower clergy, since in 1660 Baxter wrote that in one of the next parishes to Kidderminster, called Rock, there were two chapels where the poor ignorant curate of one got his living by cutting faggots, the other with making ropes, their abilities answerable to their studies and employments. Prattinton Coll. (Soc. Antiq.) Extracts from *Reliq. Baxterianæ* MSS. fol. 1696.

declined to take it, refusing to turn the old vicar Dance, incompetent though he was alleged to be, either out of the living or out of the vicarage, declining to receive more of the profits than £100 a year, residing at the top of another man's house, devoting himself body and soul to the work of evangelizing Kidderminster.[1] Although he complained of his want of success, he to a very great degree succeeded, the best proof being that he had to enlarge his church. In spite of the very rigid discipline he exercised, he was able, after applying every test of conduct and morals which he considered necessary, to receive as constant communicants one-third of the number that could possibly communicate. Bigoted, impetuous, quarrelsome as Baxter was, there were few in the seventeenth century who presented a nobler pattern of Christian holiness: there was no place where Christian work was more thoroughly carried out than at Kidderminster. He found the inhabitants, to use his own words, 'a people who had never had any awakening ministry before, but a few formal cold services from the curate'; when he left them he could say that they were 'as godly a people as any in the kingdom,' and he could boast, 'we were all of one mind, one mouth, one way, not a separatist, Anabaptist, Antinomian, or any other sectary in the town.'[2] There is no more significant proof of the failure of the system of the Directory in the county than Baxter's own attack on it in his attempt to establish a system of church government on a new basis. He strove to unite the ministers of all the Worcestershire churches into a voluntary association for mutual and spiritual help, and the maintenance of church discipline.[3] No act of Baxter's life proves more clearly than this how utterly impossible it was to work with him. His ideas had to be accepted or else Baxter would not join, but would demur in no measured terms. This association can only be described as the Baxterian idea of church government. It declared the equality of all the ministers who belonged to it as ministers of God; they were all equal, and none superior to the other. It denied any ministerial authority above that of their congregations, for it asserted that the people not only had, but ought to exercise, the right of correcting the acts of their minister. It recognized that the State was supreme over the Church, as it sanctioned the use of the civil power over ministers and congregations when required. It recognized the necessity of each minister having a fixed local district to work in, and not merely to address himself to the people generally. It was therefore opposed to all the rival parties of the day—Episcopalians, Presbyterians, and Independents. Strange to say, it obtained a considerable amount of support in the county.[4] That it would ever have become a real working scheme is not likely, but it served to show where the Presbyterian system of government had been found wanting.

In other ways it had failed also. Men who looked for a spiritual awakening turned not to the Presbyterians, but to the divers sects of Quakers, Anabaptists, and Antinomians, whom the Presbyterians delighted to persecute. The question of toleration was difficult. Cromwell's ideal was 'that liberty to know, to reason, and to argue freely according to conscience.' Baxter said of him, that he 'kept fair with all saving his open enemies. He carried it with such dissimulation that Anabaptists, Independents, and Antinomians did all think that he was one of them. But he never endeavoured to persuade

[1] *Reliq. Baxterianæ*, ed. Sylvester, p. 97.
[2] Ibid. p. 90.
[3] Shaw, *Hist. of the Eng. Church*, 1640–60, ii. 152–5.
[4] Ibid. 1640–60, App. iii. c. 454.

the Presbyterians that he was one of them, but only that he would do them justice and preserve them, and honour their worth and piety . . . for he knew they were not so easily deceived.'[1] Incomprehensible to men like Baxter, Cromwell's ideal went down before the strength of Presbyterianism and the fact that the only means he had to combat Presbyterian intolerance was the army, itself an instrument of intolerance. It was persecution more than anything else which brought so great an increase among the sectaries in Worcestershire during the Commonwealth. This increase was seen chiefly among the Quakers. Divers of them 'went naked through divers chief towns and cities . . . some famished and drowned themselves in melancholy, and others undertook by the power of the spirit to raise them.'[2] One instance relates to Claines parish, where 'they took a man out of his grave that had so made away with himself and commanded him to live but to their shame.'[3] According to Baxter many Franciscan and other Papists were found as disguised speakers in the Quaker assemblies, 'and its like are the very soul of their horrible delusion.'[4] At the same time Baxter acknowledged that the Quakers, when persecuted under the Conventicle Act of 1663, 'were so resolute and so gloried in their constancy and sufferings that they assembled openly, although they were dragged away to the common gaols.'[5] George Fox, 'the founder of the Friends,' in his journeyings through Great Britain visited Worcester five times. His first visit was in 1655, when he found that at Evesham 'the magistrates had cast several Friends into divers prisons, and hearing my coming they had made a pair of high stocks.'[6] However, Fox went on to Evesham, and in the evening had 'a large precious meeting wherein Friends and people were refreshed.' The next morning he rode to the various prisons and visited the Friends there, among them one Humphrey Smith, 'who had been a priest, but was now a free minister of Christ.'[7] As Fox was leaving Evesham he 'espied the magistrates coming up the town' to seize him, but he managed to escape, although 'the priests and professors were exceeding rude and envious about this time in these parts.'[8] From Evesham he went on to Worcester, where he had 'a precious meeting,' and a heated discussion after it, so that 'there was like to have been a tumult in the city' had not Fox himself intervened and 'got them quiet.'[9] Among the 'priests and professors' Richard Baxter was pre-eminent. Fox came into conflict with him over the question of tithes. In 1652 the army under sectarian influence presented a petition to the Council urging the abolition of tithes. In Baxter's view it was impossible to have a regular ministry without a regular system of support, and the best means of providing that support was by tithes. With all the energy of his nature Baxter strove to defeat the proposal to abolish tithes, and for this end he organized the celebrated Worcestershire petition.[10] Concerning it, he himself says, 'when the Quakers did openly reproach the ministry and the soldiers favour them, I drew up a petition for the ministry and got many thousand hands to it in Worcester . . . and when a certain Quaker (Fox) wrote a reviling censure of this petition I wrote a defence of it, and caused one of them to be given to each Parliament man.'[11]

1 *Reliq. Baxterianæ*, p. 100.
2 Ibid. 77.
3 Ibid.
4 Ibid. 77.
5 Ibid. 436.
6 *Fox's Autobiography*, ed. H. S. Newman, 105.
7 Ibid. 106.
8 Ibid.
9 Ibid.
10 Prattinton Coll. (Soc. Antiq.) Extracts from *Reliq. Baxterianæ* MS.
11 Ibid.

Fox's account of his second visit in 1659 shows that the Quakers were active in the city of Worcester. 'At Worcester,' he says, 'the Lord's truth was set over all, people were finely settled therein, and Friends praised the Lord, nay, the very earth rejoiced.'[1] But in that year there was 'a great fear and trouble in many, looking for the king's coming in and that all things should be altered.'[2] Although there had been little toleration for Quakers under Parliamentary rule, there was to be less under Charles II. Yet the severity with which persecution was carried on depended to a great extent on the men who were justices of the peace. In March, 1661, Mr. Townshend and Mr. George Symmonds, as justices of Worcestershire, bailed out of the castle gaol in the city twenty-two Quakers and fourteen Anabaptists upon their promise to acknowledge Charles as king, to live peaceably, and to appear at the next assizes.[3] But the spirit of persecution showed itself in Fox's third visit in 1667. At Pershore 'the Friends' feared that officers would be sent from the sessions court to break up the meeting.[4] At Worcester, since it was fair time, Fox held a 'very precious meeting.'[5] But there was in Worcester one Major Wild, 'a persecuting man,' and he sent soldiers to the meeting inquiring after Fox, who again managed to escape, 'leaving the Friends settled in good order.'[6] His next visit in 1673 was less fortunate. A meeting was held in a barn at Tredington, and after the meeting Henry Parker, a justice of Worcester, and Rowland Haynes, a priest of Hunnington, came to the house of John Halford, where Fox was staying, and took him and Thomas Lower, a Friend, prisoners, and sent them to Worcester gaol.[7] When there they presented a petition to Lord Windsor, lord lieutenant of Worcester, who spoke them fair but could not set them at liberty.[8] The account of the trial at the sessions, then at the King's Bench, and again at the sessions, gives some idea of the state of feeling among the justices of the county.[9] Some were 'very loving' towards Fox and the Quakers,[10] others like Justice Parker were determined to carry out the letter of the law and compel men to take the oaths of supremacy and allegiance. It is interesting to see that the Quakers found followers among the better classes of the county and not only among the poor. Fox himself tells how when he was in prison many visited him, and amongst others the earl of Salisbury's son, 'who was very loving and troubled that they had dealt so wickedly by me . . . and stayed about two hours with me and took a copy of the errors of the indictment in writing.'[11]

The Anabaptists, on the other hand, seem to have found favour solely among the poorer classes. They were most numerous in the centre of the county. In 1670 Thomas Wilmot, vicar of Bromsgrove, reported at the Epiphany Sessions, that being ready to attend the funeral of Jane, the wife of John Echols of Bromsgrove, he was 'by a tumult of Anabaptists affronted and disturbed' while reading the burial service. They no sooner came to the place but they 'irreverently threw the corpse thereinto, and, having their hats on their heads, immediately, contrary to the orders of the church, without the least respect to the service of the same, and without either clerk or minister with them who should first cast in the mould, covered

[1] Prattinton Coll. (Soc. Antiq.), 181. [2] Ibid. [3] Ibid. Townshend's Annals, 1640–60, 422.
[4] Fox, *Autobiography*, 256. [5] Ibid. [6] Ibid. [7] Ibid. 318.
[8] Ibid. In the calendar of prisoners awaiting trial in the gaol at Worcester, in 1673, the name of George Fox occurs. The indictment against him is also among the county records.
[9] Ibid. 320–25. [10] Ibid. 323. [11] Ibid. 325.

the corpse amongst a tumult. There was one, Henry Waldron, who, entering into the bellman's house without his leave, took away his spade, wherewith John Price, contrary to all civility and decency, notwithstanding he was checked by the minister, with his head covered, persisted to throw the mould into the aforesaid grave.' In a record of the conventicles in the diocese in 1669 there was a conventicle of Anabaptists at the house of John Fryers at Feckenham,[1] another of 'twenty or thirty mean persons' at the house of John Poole at Dormston,[2] two at Kington, both of about thirty 'mean persons,' at the houses of William Haynes and Samuel Roper, and under the leadership of Mr. Eagleston, a clothier, and Thomas Feckenham, a cobbler.[3] At Bewdley there was another conventicle under the same leadership[4]—evidently that mentioned by Baxter in 1660 when he reported that there was 'a church of Anabaptists' at Bewdley.[5] The same record of 1669 shows that there was a large conventicle of Quakers at Inkberrow, some three hundred meeting at the house of widow Stanley,[6] another at Kington, and one of twelve families at Pershore.[7]

There were a few, but it would seem only a few, of a still more violent sect, the Fifth Monarchy men. Beyond the fact that they had a chapel at Oldbury in the extreme north-east of the county, little is known about them. In September, 1667, Major Wild, Fox's 'persecuting man,' the commander of the troop of horse stationed at Stourbridge to keep the Nonconformists in order, sent a detachment of his troop to Oldbury. There they found a crowd of about 2,000 gathered outside the chapel listening to a Fifth Monarchy man.[8] The preacher from his pulpit saw the troop coming, suddenly stopped in the midst of his sermon, and saying, 'Friends, here is a party of horse,' threw off his black gown and periwig and rushed from the pulpit, put on a grey coat, told the people he must shift for himself, and disappeared. Meanwhile the soldiers surrounded the chapel, and after some fighting, made a number of the men in it prisoners. These were brought before a magistrate and bound to appear at sessions. One of their sureties was Thomas Wilmot of Wolverley.[9]

The Restoration meant fiercer persecution for the sectaries; it also meant persecution for both Presbyterians and popish recusants. The Clarendon Code made civil and political rights dependent on conformity to the State Church and the principles set down in the Act of Uniformity of 1662, and it erased for the time being all traces of the attempt at toleration, which, failure as it was, was nevertheless the ideal of some at least of the men who fought under Cromwell.[10] The restoration of the old order of things meant that

[1] MSS. Tenisonii (Lamb. Lib.), dcxxxix. fol. 272. [2] Ibid.
[3] Ibid. fol. 272. [4] Ibid. [5] *Reliq. Baxterianæ*, p. 90.
[6] MSS. Tenisonii (Lamb. Lib.), dcxxxix. fol. 272. [7] Ibid.

[8] One who was present has described the service. 'As soon as the Psalm was over the preacher went into the pulpit and offered up a strange prayer, but one that was suitable to the sermon. His text was, "Thy kingdom come" (St. Luke xi. 2). He proved, or tried to prove, from various texts that here on earth Christ had established an actual kingdom of temporal rewards for his suffering saints and working servants, which in His own good time He would hand over to them. That it was their duty to strive for the coming and bringing in of that kingdom; that there was such a kingdom, and that it was upon earth, not in heaven; it was not the kingdom of glory, but one quite distinct in nature and in administration. To prove this he cited texts from Daniel, Revelation, and other mystical places.'

[9] Sess. R. In the next year this Thomas Wilmot of Wolverley married a lady named Johusua Smith, daughter of the minister of Elmley Lovett, and the year after was made vicar of Bromsgrove, and drew up a petition against the Anabaptists.

[10] See The Humble Petition and Advice of 1657.

bishop, dean, and chapter came back into their old places in Worcester with their old powers rather enhanced than curtailed. On 31 August, 1660, the first morning prayers were said in Worcester Cathedral since July, 1646,[1] and on Sunday, 2 September, there was a great assembly at 'morning prayer' at six o'clock in the morning, and 'at nine there appeared again all the gentry and many citizens,' and Dr. Dodeswell, a prebend, preached the first sermon.[2] On 12 September George Morley, the new bishop, was 'brought into Worcester by Lord Windsor and most of the gentry and all the clergy,' accompanied by the 'blare of the trumpets, the volunteer militia, and the trained bands of the city and of the clergy.'[3] On the next Sunday he preached 'an admired sermon' in the cathedral.[4] On 13 September Dr. Oliver was made dean of Worcester,[5] but was a year later succeeded by Dr. Thomas Warmstry, installed on 27 October, 1661.[6] The Act of Uniformity of 1662,[7] enforcing the use of the Prayer Book as at present composed seemed contrary to the 'liberty to tender consciences' promised under the Declaration of Breda.[8] It meant that ministers must either conform or be ejected, and when they were ejected the patronage of the majority of the livings went back nominally to the bishop or dean and chapter, really to the king, and thus once more a loyalist clergy could be secured for the county.

On the whole, few of the Worcester clergy seem to have conformed to the revised system. According to Calamy,[9] thirty-five ejections were made at the Restoration. Evidently this is not a full list of those who gave up their livings between 1660 and 1663, for besides these thirty-five there were more than sixty inductions to livings in the county in those years.[10] In some cases the incumbent seems to have conformed and been reinducted. At Blockley Giles Collier, who had succeeded George Durant on his sequestration in 1646, conformed and was reinstituted in 1660.[11] At Evenlode also in the same year Ralph Nevil, who had succeeded Jervis Clerke in 1647, conformed and was reinstituted.[12] At Church Lench Joseph Treble conformed 'thro' the importunity of his wife,' but removed into Warwickshire.[13] In some cases the old incumbents were living, and where this was so there was a greater likelihood that the Nonconformist minister would be ejected or would himself make a

1 Prattinton Coll. (Soc. Antiq.), Townshend's Annals, 412.
2 Ibid.
3 Ibid. 430.
4 Ibid.
5 Ibid. 414.
6 Ibid. 414.
7 See Gee and Hardy, *Doc. Illus. of Eng. Ch. Hist.*, 600–2.
8 Ibid. 587.
9 Calamy, *Nonconformists' Memorial*, iii. 383–419. Richard Moore from Alvechurch, Henry Oasland from Bewdley, Richard Beeston from Bredon, Mr. Wall from Broadway, John Spilsbury from Bromsgrove, Thomas Baldwin from Chaddesley Corbett, Edward Boucher from Churchill, William Westmacott from Cropthorne, Thomas Francis from Dodderhill, Timothy Jordan from Eckington, George Hopkins from All Saints' Evesham (according to Anthony Wood Hopkins 'constantly frequented the parish church after his ejection, received the Holy Communion, and did all things required of a lay member of the Church of England'), Thomas Matthews from St. Lawrence's Evesham, John Freeston from Hampton Lovett, Stephen Baxter from Harvington, Thomas Bromwich from Kempsey, Richard Baxter from Kidderminster, John Giles from Lindridge, Ambrose Sparry from Martley, Joseph Cooper (Calamy quotes concerning him that 'his deportment was so graceful and majestic that "Here comes Mr. Cooper" hath often charmed a rude society into civil order and composed lewd persons into a proper decorum') from Moseley, Thomas Franks from Naunton Beauchamp, Thomas Hall from King's Norton, Cornelius Wood from Peopleton, William Kimberley from Redmarley d'Abitôt, Richard Woolley from Salwarpe, Giles Woolley his brother from place unknown, Richard Serjeant from Stone, Jarvis Bryan from Old Swinford, Benjamin Baxter from Upton upon Severn, Robert Brown (a Fifth Monarchy man who died at Plymouth 'from excessive preaching') from White Ladies Aston, Joseph Read from Great Witley, Joseph Baker from St. Andrew's Worcester, Simon Moor from the Cathedral church, Richard Fincher from St. Nicholas Worcester, Thomas Juice from place unknown, Richard Durham from Tredington.
10 Nash, *op. cit.* vols. i. and ii.
11 Ibid. i. 105.
12 Ibid. i. 395.
13 Calamy, *Nonconformists' Memorial*, iii. 418.

surrender.[1] On the whole, there seems to have been comparatively little conformity in the county, and many ejections or surrenders. Men like Thomas Batchelor of St. Andrew's, Pershore, who had gladly conformed in 1646, would not be likely to conform to the Act of Uniformity. Some like Bromwich of Kempsey partially conformed and gained freedom to preach.[2]

The Presbyterians were not the only sufferers under the Clarendon Code, and after 1673 under the Test Act.[3] In 1643 all sects had united in denouncing the Romanists. Sequestrators were appointed for the several counties to seize two-thirds of the estates of the Papists for the use of Parliament. No Papists were to receive the benefit of public protection, all soldiers were first to be billeted on Papists' houses, and no horses were to be taken until theirs had first gone.[4] Even Cromwell had seen no possibility of toleration for the Romanists, and under the Commonwealth they had either fled or been persecuted. He ordered all priests to quit the kingdom and no Romanist to go within twenty miles of London.[5] The officers who were placed over militia districts had orders to 'take care that Papists and other disaffected persons should be deprived of their arms.'[6] With the Restoration the services which the Romanists had rendered the Crown during the Civil War were rewarded by penalties and punishments, since loyalty was now measured by adherence to the state church. Worcester was still a Romanist centre, but the actual numbers in the county are difficult to discover. A return made in 1676 gave 727 Romanists and 1,533 Nonconformists out of the whole diocese population of 43,378.[7] Of these thirty-three Romanists were in the rural deanery of Worcester, and twenty-four in Worcester city, sixteen of whom were in St. Nicholas', Worcester. In 1693 the number of Papists in Worcester above the age of sixteen was given as 719, as against 37,489 Conformists and 1,325 Nonconformists.[8] The probability is that these returns, while giving the full strength of the orthodox, do not give that of either the Romanists or Nonconformists;[9] at least, it seems evident that in Worcester, as elsewhere, in spite of persecution, the number of Papists steadily increased during the reign of Charles II. The uneasiness of Parliament at the increase of Popery was shown by the petition of the House of Commons in 1670, by the stringent Conventicle Act of the same year, and by the Test Act of 1673.[10] It was well known that by this time many private houses in Worcester were

[1] E.g. Stephen Baxter was ejected from Harvington and William Hopkins reinstated (*Nash.* i. 578). George Dance was reinstated at Kidderminster (ibid. ii. 57). Sutton at Bredon (Walker, *Sufferings of the Clergy*, pt. ii. 373).

[2] Calamy, *Nonconformists' Memorial*, iii. 393.

[3] See Gee and Hardy, *Doc. Illus. of Engl. Ch. Hist.* 632–40.

[4] Prattinton Coll. (Soc. Antiq.).

[5] Ibid.

[6] Ibid. Townshend's Annals, 1640–60.

[7] Bishop Compton's return (Salt Soc. Lib.).

[8] *Cal. of S. P. Dom.* 1693, p. 448.

[9] In Kidderminster only 14 Nonconformists and 8 Catholics against 1,578 Conformists is not likely to be right.

[10] Gee and Hardy, *op. cit.* A great number of the certificates under the Test Act still exist among the Sessions Records. The Act required anyone who held any office under the Crown to produce a certificate signed by the minister and churchwardens and others that the person named had attended divine service and received the Sacrament in accordance with the rites of the Church of England. The way in which the certificates were made out probably shows their value. Three or more persons, A, B, and C, would go to a church. All would receive the Sacrament. The minister and churchwardens signed all the certificates. Then B and C certified A had done so, and A and C certified for B, and A and B for C. The certificate was then filed with the clerk of the peace, and A, B, and C were considered legally qualified to hold any office under the Crown. Probably the chief value of the certificates is that they are a record, and a fairly complete one, of the clergy and churchwardens for the different parishes in the county from 1673 to 1828, when the Roman Catholic Emancipation Act was passed, and the necessity for the certificates done away with.

regularly used for Mass, and were frequently visited by priests.[1] Father Benwick, alias Sanders, was the resident priest in Worcester in 1678,[2] but he escaped the persecution which followed on Titus Oates' discovery of the supposed plot to establish the Papal supremacy. Designed as this discovery was to work up the nation against the Papists, it succeeded only too well. Men were executed if they were only suspected of being priests, and priests were executed for the mere fact that they were priests. In 1679 Father Wall, alias Francis Johnson, a Franciscan, was put to death in Worcester because he refused to accept the oaths of supremacy and allegiance, and was charged, but the charge was not proved, with being a priest in England.[3] In his speech at his execution he claimed to be of a Lancashire family and to have studied at Douay, where he took the habit of St. Francis in 1652.[4] In 1656 he was sent to Worcester as 'priest,' and 'being in London on All Saints' day when the proclamation came forth to command all Catholics to depart from thence by the Friday following,' he came to a friend's house in Worcestershire, but only to hear the second proclamation 'that no Catholic should walk above five miles without being stopped and carried before a justice to have the oaths tendered.' He therefore decided to remain where he was; but a magistrate who came to the house to take another man for debt, took Father Wall by mistake, and suspecting him, tendered the oaths. He refused 'for his conscience sake,' but bravely defended himself through a long and painful trial, making a strong stand on his loyalty to the king and to his father.[5] One other instance shows how irksome life was made for the Romanists even when they were not persecuted. Dame Mary Yate, a Catholic, when about seventy years old, sought leave to go beyond the seas for the benefit of her health. She received permission under condition that she should 'give security not to enter into any plot or conspiracy, and should not repair to the city of Rome or return unto this kingdom without first acquainting one of His Majesty's principal secretaries of state.' If she did this she might 'embark with trunks of apparel and other necessaries, not prohibited at any port in the kingdom, and pass beyond seas, provided she departed the kingdom within fourteen days.'[6] With the reign of James II. there was a brief respite from persecution. About 1685 the Roman Catholic chapel was erected in Worcester, and in the same year marks the beginning of the register of baptisms among the Worcester Catholics.[7] In 1687, when James II. visited Worcester he went to hear Mass at the chapel, to the indignation of the mayor and corporation, who refused to accompany him further than the door.[8] With the Revolution and the accession of William of Orange the breathing space which the Romanists had gained was over. Their chapels were ruthlessly destroyed and they were specially exempted from the Toleration Act of 1689.[9] It was not until 1778 that any attempt was made to exempt them from the penalties of their religion, but the Roman Catholics of Worcester seem to have clung to their old religion[10] until the Emancipation Bill of 1829 finally gave them full civil and political rights.

[1] Noake, *Worc. Sects.* 50, 51.
[2] Ibid. 52.
[3] Prattinton Coll. (Soc. Antiq.), Tracts, *Trial of Mr. Francis Johnson.*
[4] Ibid.
[5] Ibid.
[6] Ibid. Her passport is among the sessions papers.
[7] Noake, *Worc. Sects.* 62, 63. These registers have been published by Mr. Crispe.
[8] Ibid.
[9] Geé and Hardy, *op. cit.* 663.
[10] Noake, *Worc. Sects.* 66 onwards.

In 1662 Bishop Morley was translated to Winchester. His task at Worcester to establish the Act of Uniformity was no easy one, especially to a man who had so little sympathy with his opponents. His treatment of Richard Baxter was not only ungenerous, but unjust. Clarendon and the king, thinking that they might win over Baxter by preferment, offered him the bishopric of Hereford. He declined, not in the most courteous terms, saying that his sole aim was to go on with his work at Kidderminster.[1] He had refused to turn out Dance during the Commonwealth, and now all he asked was that Dance should not be allowed to silence him. He proposed therefore that Dance should have some prebend or place of profit given him, but should not be allowed to preach. Morley promised to license Baxter to preach and make terms with Dance. But after a quarrel with Baxter at the Savoy Conference, the bishop ignored his promise. Thereupon Baxter wrote *The Mischiefs of Self-Ignorance and the Benefits of Self-Acquaintance*, showing up the bishop's false dealing.[2] The bishop answered that it was 'the bishop of Worcester and not Mr. Baxter' who was 'pastor of Kidderminster, as well as all the other parochial churches in the diocese.'[3] On these grounds he claimed justification for his act, stating that Baxter had proved himself unworthy of the right of preaching, and therefore as he (the bishop) had the care of the souls of the men of Kidderminster he had the right to prohibit Baxter.[4]

A well-known Royalist, John Gauden,[5] succeeded Morley at Worcester, but only survived his translation a few months, dying in September, 1662.[6] John Earl, his successor,[7] held the see for less than a year, and was translated to Salisbury in 1663.[8] Robert Skinner, the next bishop, was translated from Oxford.[9] He held the see until his death in 1670, leaving but little trace of his tenure. Nor has his successor, Walter Blandford, who was also translated from Oxford, and who held the see four years. Blandford was followed in 1675 by a still more firm Royalist, Fleetwood, who when young was tutor to the children of Charles I., was present at the battle of Edgehill, and when Essex destroyed the Royalist centre had earned the king's gratitude by carrying off the young princes to a place of safety, a service which was held sufficient to excuse the fact that his brother was the regicide Fleetwood. Under staunch Royalist bishops such as these, conformity was a necessary qualification for office among the parochial clergy. The necessity led men like Thomas Wilmot, of Wolverley, who had been surety for a disloyal sectary in 1667,[10] to appear at the sessions in 1670 as an active proscriber of Nonconformists, after he had obtained the vicarage of Bromsgrove.[11] So long as the clergy were loyal there seems to have been little care for their spiritual fitness. Moreover, many of the clergy suffered, as their fathers had done at the beginning of the century,

[1] *Reliq. Baxterianæ.*

[2] Prattinton Coll. (Soc. Antiq.), Tracts.

[3] Ibid. He adds, 'The truth is that Mr. Baxter was never either parson, vicar, or curate there or anywhere else in my diocese . . . for he never came in by the door into that sheepfold, but climbed up some other way by violence and intrusion, and therefore by Christ's own inference he is a thief and a robber.'

[4] Ibid. Tracts, *Bishop Morley's Defence of Himself against Baxter.*

[5] The probable author of the 'EIKON BASILIKE,' the title of which Nash suggests was given 'to humour the false taste of the times.' (Nash, ii. App. clviii.)

[6] Prattinton Coll. (Soc. Antiq.).

[7] Ibid. Townshend's *Annals*, 1640–60.

[8] Ibid. Isaac Walton says of him in his *Life of Mr. Richard Hooker*, 'since Mr. Hooker died none have lived whom God hath blest with more innocent wisdom, more sanctified learning, or a more pious, peaceable, primitive temper than John Earle.'

[9] Ibid.

[10] See supra. Thomas Wilmot was surety for a Fifth Monarchy man at Oldbury.

[11] See supra, his petition at the Epiphany Sessions of 1670.

from a cruel poverty. All the attempts that had been made under the Commonwealth to better the livings of the poorer clergy had been nullified at the Restoration when the lands and revenues of bishop and dean and chapter, from which these augmentations had mostly come, were restored. Doubtless too the growth of Nonconformity had deprived the clergy of many of the offerings they had before received. The statements of a satirist like Echard [1] may be overdrawn, but there is a residuum of truth in them, and evidently the poverty of the clergy was such that a country clergyman had not the means to study or keep himself informed.[2] The great difficulty was to provide for their families, and want of means compelled their children in many cases to sink back into the position of labourers and servants, and tended to lower the social status of the clergy as a class. Had measures been taken at the Restoration to improve the condition of the county clergy much subsequent trouble might have been saved, but no attempt seems to have been made until the eighteenth century. The Tory ministry of 1702--8 won over the clergy by restoring to the church the tenths and first-fruits which had belonged to the Crown since 1534, and under the influence of Harley, the Tory Secretary of State, an effort was made to utilize these tenths to relieve the distresses of the poorer clergy. In order to find out the real state of the various parishes advertisements were sent to the minister of each parochial church or chapel in England begging him to answer various questions concerning his parish.[3] The advertisements and the answers for fourteen Worcestershire parishes are preserved in the Lambeth library.[4] Of these the most poverty stricken clergyman was the rector of St. Andrew's, Droitwich. The two parishes of St. Mary Witton and St. Nicholas had been united to the parish of St. Andrew's under the Commonwealth, since both the churches had been destroyed during the war [5] and St. Andrew's was 'a fair large church

[1] *The Grounds for Despising the Clergy considered.*

[2] Aug. of Liv. (Lamb. Lib.). Even allowing for the depreciation of money since the seventeenth-century and recognizing that the Worcestershire clergy were not alone in their poverty in the country, it still remains a fact that the value of some of the benefices can hardly have been a sufficient living wage ; *e.g.*

Benefice.	Annual Value in the Seventeenth Century.		
Moseley	£4	13	4
Pershore, St. Andrew's	6	10	0
St. Andrews', Worc.	12	0	0
St. Martin's, Worc.	13	0	0
Naunton Beauchamp	13	10	0
Harvington	13	16	0
Ombersley	13	16	0
Halesowen	13	17	0

[3] Notitia Parochalis (Lamb. Lib.) The questions were as follows :—

'1. Whether the tithes are impropriate and to whom ?
2. What part of the tithes is your church or chapel endowed with ?
3. What augmentation has your benefice received ?
4. Has your church or chapel been founded since the Reformation ?
5. What union or dismemberment has been made of your church and by whom ?
6. What Library is settled in your parish and by whom ?
7. If the yearly value of your rectory, vicarage or chapel be under £30—if so, how much ?
8. To whom the advowson belongs ?
9. If co-nominal with any other place and what the distinction ?
10. If not taken notice of in the Valor Beneficorum, pray say what Deanery it is in ?'

[4] The fourteen parishes are :—

Birtsmorton (Notitia Parochalis, f. 8), Bransford (f. 32b.), Broadway (f. 896), Coston Hackett (f. 982), St. Peter's, Droitwich (f. 981), St. Andrew's, Droitwich (f. 984), Hadzor (f. 983), Halesowen (f. 1559), Lindridge (f. 1030), Great Malvern (f. 45), Pendock (f. 34), Salwarpe (f. 715), Stanford-on-Teme (f. 1032), Welland (f. 35.)

[5] Aug. of Livings (Lamb. Lib.).

sufficient for all the parishioners.' The rector had therefore 'the care and burden of these three parishes.' He received nothing from the impropriators of the tithes of St. Nicholas, and ''tis a pity' he says, 'that these matters were not rectified and the impropriators called to account.' From St. Andrew's the tithes were 'not worth mentioning, coming to so little more than what goes to pay Her Majesty's tenths and procurations.' Further, there was no glebe land belonging to the church, and such was the 'tenuity of the rectory that his sole dependence is upon the charity of some gentlemen in the town and the small ecclesiastical duties accustomably paid at Easter, all which seldom exceeds six or seven pounds a year.' Of the tithes of St. Mary Witton the rector received only £10 yearly, the rest being 'settled upon — Beck, minister in or near Ipswich during his life.' Thus the whole value of the rectory was 'much short of £20 a year.'[1] The vicar of Broadway was only endowed with 'half the tithes lamb,' and the yearly value of the vicarage was uncertain 'according to the year for lambs and fruits, but it never exceeded £17 a year.'[2] The benefits of 'Queen Anne's bounty' and the joining together of some of the smaller parishes have brought the lowest benefice up to not less than £40 a year. But of the 155 modern parishes some 41 are still under £200 a year.

The poverty of the seventeenth-century clergy had doubtless been accentuated by the fact that there were now other channels for the charity of those who before had made their offerings to the church alone. The Declaration of 1672, declaring that the 'church of England shall remain as at present, all paying tithes, and no person holding office who is not conformable, but all penal laws against the Nonconformists and recusants (except popish recusants) shall be suspended, and a certain number of places licensed for their worship,'[3] meant the beginning of the formation of the Nonconformists into a body separated off from the church, with its own places of worship, and its own methods of worship and entirely dependent on private subscription. In the same year twenty-four buildings were licensed in Worcestershire. For Presbyterians at Bewdley, Bromsgrove, Eastham, Hagley, Honeybourne, Kidderminster, King's Norton, Old Swinford, Oldbury, Halesowen, Stourbridge, Suckley, Weathercock Hill, Withall, and Worcester. For Congregationalists (the original Independents) at Birlingham, Broadway, Bromsgrove, Evesham, Ombersley, and Worcester. For Baptists at Kyrewood, and for Nonconformists undefined at Cropthorne and Dudley.[4] Under James II. the Nonconformists were tolerated under the Declaration of Indulgence, primarily intended to relieve the Romanists. It was merely an accident, his absence from London in May, 1688, that prevented William Thomas, the new bishop of Worcester, who had succeeded Fleetwood in 1683, from being one of the celebrated band who were prosecuted for publishing a 'false, slanderous, and malicious libel' in their petition to the king against the Declaration of Indulgence. Thomas refused to read the declaration or to sanction its reading in the churches of his diocese. Soon afterwards he received a reprimand from the court for his disobedience, to which his answer was 'sincere without any tincture of collusion, but declaratory of his firm

1 Notitia Parochalis (Lamb. Lib.), fol. 984.
2 Ibid, fol. 896.
3 *Cal. of S. P. Dom.* 1671–2, p. 203.
4 Ibid. 1672–3, p. lviii.

resolution not to comply.'[1] The turn events took saved him from any punishment from thus following his conscience.

With all his hatred of James's attempted toleration for Romanists and Nonconformists the bishop would not act contrary to his former oaths and homage to James and take the oath of allegiance to William and Mary. 'If my heart do not deceive me,' he wrote to John Kettlewell, 'and God's grace do not fail me, I think I could suffer at a stake rather than take this oath.'[2] He prepared to vacate his see rather than submit, but he died on the 25 June before the oath could be tendered to him.[3] The dean, Dr. George Hickes,[4] followed the example of the bishop and headed the ranks of the Worcester non-jurors. Among these were Dr. Ralph Taylor, rector of Severn Stoke, Dr. Joseph Crowther, prebend of Worcester and rector of Tredington, Henry Panting, rector of St. Martin's, Worcester, and Upton upon Severn, John Griffin, non-juror bishop, rector of Churchill, John Griffith, rector of St. Nicholas, Worcester, John March, vicar of Long Compton, Thomas Maurice, curate of Claines, minor canon of Worcester, Thomas Roberts, rector of St. Nicholas or St. Swithin's, Worcester, Ralph Norrice, vicar of South Littleton, Thomas Beynon, curate of Upton upon Severn, John Worthington, curate of Offenham,[5] Thomas Keyt, rector of Binton, Samuel Sandys, vicar of Willoughby, and Thomas Wilson, rector of Arrow. But with these exceptions, Worcester seems soon to have settled down under the new system. Yet there was a certain amount of Jacobite feeling dormant in the county, especially among the county gentry, and it is probable that this and the desire of the Church party to counteract it led to those constant charitable gifts which became so common in nearly all the parishes between the Revolution and the middle of the eighteenth century, when they were checked by Parliament.[6] Gifts of land and of money to be dealt with in promoting the interests of the Church and to be distributed by the vicar and the churchwardens were made in most of the parishes both in the town and the country, and these gifts were made not so much by the great landowners, the Tory squires, as those of the middle class who had become rich by trade and who were desirous of supporting the new order of things. The fact that the gifts were often confined to members of the Church of England, in some cases to communicants, that they often consisted of money for services to promote the controverted doctrine of the church, for books for children to be brought up in the principle of that church—all point to the fact that one result of the non-jurors was an attempt by the middle class of the county to keep the clergy loyal to the Hanoverian dynasty, and possibly to the Walpole Ministry.

[1] Nash, ii. App. clxi.

[2] Ibid. Concerning the bishops who refused the oaths at the Revolution, Mark Noble says:—'If moderation had swayed their tender consciences would never have been an inconvenience to the State . . . candour will not blame them. Delicacy might have united with prudence to have let them remain unmolested. No interest would have been injured and a disagreeable division would have been prevented.' Prattinton Coll. (Soc. Antiq.).

[3] Nash, ii. App. clxii.

[4] It is a strange instance of the irony of history that in the latter part of the seventeenth century Fleetwood, one of the Worcester bishops, should have been the brother of a regicide, while Hickes, the non-juror dean, was the brother of a nonconformist minister executed as a traitor for his part in the Monmouth rebellion.

[5] *Life of Rev. John Kettlewell*, prefixed to his works. App. vi. Overton. *The Non-jurors*, 471–496.

[6] Stat. of Realm, 17 Geo. II. cap. 15.

The new bishop, Edward Stillingfleet, instituted in 1689, was one of the best representatives of the scholarly latitudinarian school of the time. He had learnt the lesson that the greatest virtue of a bishop is toleration, and, strong Hanoverian and Anglican though he was, he met the opposition of Jacobites, Romanists, and Nonconformists in his diocese by controversies on paper rather than by any active measures. But he was more than a controversialist, and his book *Origines Britannicæ* still holds its own. During the ten years he held the see he was a trusted servant of the Crown, and was one of those employed by William III. in the work of settling the church in Ireland.[1] His successor William Lloyd was a very different man, a violent Whig, whose political views were the guiding star of his actions as bishop. Determined to support the Hanoverian system he looked on the Jacobites as accursed. Before his translation to Worcester he had made himself very unpopular in his Lichfield diocese, 'his conduct rather becoming a cruel inquisitor than a Christian bishop.' So zealous was he for William III. that 'next to himself he thought him truly inspired . . . advanced his interest, and did all he could to blacken gentlemen of good fame and English reputation.'[2] In Worcester his strong anti-Jacobitism aroused the indignation of the Tory gentry. The Act of Settlement, strengthening the Bill of Rights, struck a blow at the Jacobite cause and insured the succession of Anne. Bishop Lloyd was determined to help her cause, and if he did not inspire, he signed and supported an address to the king promising a change in the county members at the next election. One of those members was the then Sir John Pakington. At the next election, in 1702, the bishop used every effort, legal and illegal, to turn out Sir John. But all his efforts were in vain. Sir John was elected, and brought the bishop's conduct before the House of Commons. His charge was that the bishop 'soon after the late Parliament rose' sent to him and bade him desist from offering himself at the next election, threatening him that if he did 'he would speak against him to his clergy.' Also that the bishop and his secretary sent letters to several of his clergy 'to make interest' against Sir John in their parishes, 'aspersed him and his ancestors with several vices to his clergy and at confirmations and visitations,' soliciting them to vote against him on pain of the bishop's displeasure. The bishop's son also gave Sir John 'a scandalous character,' and said that he had 'voted to bring in a French government,' and that they 'might as well vote for the Prince of Wales as for him.'[3] The House decided that the charges were fully made out against the bishop, and he was voted 'guilty of malicious, unchristian, and arbitrary conduct, in high violation of the liberties and privileges of the Commons of England.'[4] He was removed, on petition to the queen, from being Lord Almoner, but still held in favour at court.

Yet in spite of all this Lloyd was by no means one of the indifferent bishops who have filled the see of Worcester. Much of his Whiggery must be forgiven when it is remembered that he was one of the few English bishops who had seen the inside of the Tower of London as a state prisoner, having been, when bishop of St. Asaph, one of the celebrated seven who were sent there by James II.[5] The Nonconformists were usually Whigs; the

1 *Cal. of S. P. Dom.* 1690–1, 158.
2 Prattinton Coll. (Soc. Antiq.), Anonymous letter in the Coles MSS.
3 *Journ. of the House of Commons*, iv. 37. Nov. 18, 1702.
4 Ibid. iv. 39.
5 York Powell and Tout, *Hist. of Eng.* 676.

memory of his imprisonment for conscience sake, and his dislike to do anything against his party made Lloyd one of the most tolerant bishops to protestant Nonconformists that ever filled the see of Worcester. Except that he refused to allow the celebrated high-church Tory Sacheverell[1] to preach in the diocese or to permit the bells to be rung in his honour, Lloyd seems to have subsided from the partisan into the scholar, most of his time being taken up with considering questions of unfulfilled prophecy and the application of the books of Daniel and Revelation to the affairs of Queen Anne.[2] The memory of Lloyd the election agent and partizan prelate has long ago passed away, but the memory of Lloyd the bishop is still preserved in Worcester. A Mrs. Palmer, of Upton Snodsbury, was supposed to be possessed of considerable property; her house was broken into and she was murdered by a number of masked and armed robbers, among whom was her son. They were tried, convicted, and executed, and, in consequence, a considerable estate came to the bishop by escheat.[3] One result of the bishop's studies was that he regarded this as the price of blood, and so refused to receive it. As he was legally bound to do something with the land he handed it over to maintain a school in the city of Worcester, which still exists, and is known as Bishop Lloyd's school. Lloyd lived to see the great Whig wish carried out, the heirs of the Electress Sophia of Hanover settled on the throne. He died in 1717, and curiously, another of the victims of James II. followed him to Worcester,—John Hough, who had been deprived of the presidentship of Magdalen College, Oxford, to make room for a Catholic. So far as the history of the county is concerned Hough made none; for twenty-six years he filled the see (1717–1743), and except for numerous instances of his kindness and liberality the story of those years is a blank.

Maddox, his successor (1743–59), had been a controversialist before coming to Worcester;[4] he endeavoured to reply to Neale's *History of the Puritans*.[5] He was chaplain to Caroline of Anspach, and probably learnt from her and her favourite minister, Sir Robert Walpole, the virtue of the policy 'Quieta non movere.' His great act as bishop was to found the Worcester Infirmary in 1745.[6] His successor, Johnson, repaired the palaces of Worcester and Hartlebury, while Brownlow North, the next bishop, founded the charity for the poor clergy that has now become known as the Musical Festival of the Three Choirs, Worcester, Hereford, and Gloucester. On his translation to Winchester, Richard Hurd, the tutor of the Prince of Wales, afterwards

[1] In January, 1710, he wrote to the archbishop of Dublin, concerning the 'turbulent preaching and practices of an impudent man, one Dr. Sacheverell, . . . now riding in triumph over the middle of England, stirring up people to address Her Majesty for a new Parliament. . . . I need hardly tell your grace who are they by whom this work is carried on. . . . The heads of them are such as have been formerly in the ministry. . . . This is likely to be the overturning of all . . . and surely so understood by all the Papists and Nonjurors of the Kingdom . . . they push for it with all their might.' *Hist. MSS. Com.* Rep. ii. App. xv.

[2] Prattinton Coll. (Soc. Antiq.). 'A letter from Swift among the Coles MSS. in 1712, tells how the bishop pretends to be a prophet, and went yesterday to the Queen by appointment, to prove that four years hence there would be a war of religion, and that popedom would be destroyed, and if it were not true, he would be content to give up his bishopric. . . . Lord Treasurer Harley confounded him sadly in his own hearing, which made the old fool very quarrelsome. He is near 90 years old.'

[3] Sess. R.

[4] Horace Walpole wrote to Sir Horace Mann in 1743, 'Madox of St. Asaph has wriggled himself into the see of Worcester. He makes haste! I remember him only domestic chaplain to the late bishop of Chichester, Dr. Waddington.' Prattinton Coll. (Soc. Antiq.).

[5] Nash, ii. App. clxiv.

[6] Ibid.

George IV., became bishop. His reputation for piety, scholarship, and liberality was great. He added to it by refusing the archbishopric of Canterbury, preferring to stay in the quiet of Hartlebury.[1] He did his duty thoroughly as bishop as is witnessed by the numerous ordinations and visitations recorded between 1781 and 1808.[2] One remarkable note in his episcopate is the number of licences for non-residence granted to rectors or vicars either on account of the unfitness of the vicarage or rectory, or on account of bodily infirmity or actual illness on the parts of the incumbents.[3] This is all the more remarkable in the face of the growing strength of Nonconformity and especially of Wesleyanism in the county. But the church of the eighteenth century had all along been characterized by the greatest apathy, especially among the parochial clergy, and as yet all the force and zeal of John Wesley had not succeeded in breaking through this. Bishop Hurd himself was perfectly contented with the state of things as they were. In 1792 he wrote to the king an address of thanks for his proclamation against seditious writings and publications. 'Nothing but experience,' in his opinion, 'could make it conceivable that any subjects . . . could be so weak and wicked as to raise groundless jealousies in the minds of the people, and to disseminate such principles and writings as tend to destroy under pretence of reforming excellent customs in church and state.'[4] Neither of his successors, the courtly prelate Cornewall (1808–1831), very dignified, very respectable, and 'who never mentioned Hell to ears polite,' nor the politically minded Carr (1831–41), whose corpse was taken in execution for debt, were likely to have felt or cared to feel the need for some upheaval in the Church to meet the vigour and activity of the Nonconformists.

The Toleration Act of 1689, and the episcopate of Bishop Lloyd had given the Worcester Nonconformists comparative freedom in the early part of the eighteenth century. The number of places licensed for the performance of religious worship rapidly increased under the new régime, and very many earnest minded men were driven by the deadness of spiritual life in the Church to join the Dissenters in their worship. Attempts were made to stay this tendency by prosecutions of Dissenters at the sessions and in the Consistory Court,[5] but the attempts were, in most cases, crushed by the wiser policy of the central authorities and had no effect. A letter written by the dissenting minister of Stourbridge, about 1784, to the Rev. R. Foley, rector of Old Swinford, as an answer to the charges brought against the Dissenters of Stourbridge, gives an interesting picture of the relations between the Churchmen and Dissenters.[6] About this time the Birmingham riots had 'produced a frenzy' in that part of the county. Before the riots the rector had been 'candid, liberal, and christian' towards the Dissenters, but now his conduct had entirely changed. Dr. Priestly, whose house was destroyed by the rioters in 1791, had unwisely written an attack on some of the feoffees of

1 'This learned and ingenious prelate published at one time *Moral and Physical Dialogues*, with a wonderful Whiggish cast. Afterwards, having thought better, he republished the work with a more constitutional spirit.' When he declined the archbishopric, Johnson, who disbelieved in his political conversion, said 'I am glad he did not go to Lambeth, for after all I fear he is a Whig at heart.' Boswell, *Life of Johnson* (ed. Croker), v. 67, 68.

2 Prattinton Coll. (Soc. Antiq.), Acts of Bishop Hurd.

3 Ibid.

4 Ibid. fol. 368.

5 Sess. R.

6 Prattinton Coll. (Soc. Antiq.), Tracts. 'Answer of B. Carpenter, Dissenting minister of Stourbridge to the Rev. R. Foley.'

a hospital which had admitted Dissenters, but from which Dissenters were now excluded. This gave the rector of Old Swinford a pretext for making a counter-attack on the Dissenters in general, charging them with a determination to set themselves up as better men than the members of the Established Church, to withdraw all their custom from Churchmen, and above all to increase the numbers of their ranks by proselytizing, by founding Sunday schools and meeting houses wherever possible, and drawing in the 'honest and industrious orders in those parts.'[1] This latter charge was true, but true only because the Dissenters were zealous to supply a need which the church seemed to ignore. The projected meeting house at Lye Waste near Stourbridge was to supply means of worship for the population of the district, which was so rapidly increasing with the influx of trade, commerce, and manufacture into those parts. Even the rector of Old Swinford confessed that 'the pastor can no longer know the faces of half his parishioners, the church will not contain one-tenth of their numbers, and the result, a growing inattention to religion and depravity of manners, since the poor have not the gospel effectually preached to them.'[2] Thus, when the Church was deaf to every appeal, the Dissenters seized and used the opportunity.[3]

There was another force beside the growth of the Dissenters as an independent and proselytizing community which was to arouse the Church to an awakening in the middle of the eighteenth century. Perhaps this force was the greater because John Wesley was essentially an English Churchman to whom the services and ceremonies of the church appealed, and who declared himself no Dissenter, but 'one anxious to labour in the ground left untilled by the Church.' At first Wesley, unlike Whitfield, 'thought the saving of souls almost a sin if it had not been done in a church,' but when the Church rejected him he followed Whitfield's example of field preaching, and gradually established an organized society apart from the Church. His first recorded visit to Worcestershire was in 1761, when he preached at Evesham, in the 'Abbey church.'[4] Evidently the county had before this come under the influence of the new movement, for he says, 'I found at Evesham a poor shattered society, almost sunk to nothing, and no wonder since they have been almost without help till Mr. Mathen came.'[5] At Dudley he found 'a large and quiet congregation . . . the scene here is changed since the dirt and stones of this town were flying about me on every side.'[6] In 1765, and again in 1768, he visited the county,[7] preached at Upton and then rode on to Worcester. In the city the difficulty was where to preach, 'since no room was large enough to contain the people and it was too cold for them to stand abroad.' At length they found a barn where a large congregation assembled, and 'nothing was wanting but a commodious building.'[8] Evidently the Wesleyan spirit was very strong in Worcester itself.[9] In 1770 Wesley speaks of the society there as 'all of one heart and mind, so lovingly and closely united together that I have scarcely seen the like in the kingdom.'[10] In 1772 a new chapel

[1] Prattinton Coll. (Soc. Antiq.), Tracts.
[2] Ibid. Letter of the Rev. R. Foley.
[3] Ibid. Answer to the Rev. R. Foley.
[4] Wesley, *Extracts from Journal*, 1755–62.
[5] Ibid.
[6] Ibid.
[7] Ibid. 1762–70.
[8] Ibid.
[9] The rector of St. Andrew's seems to have been highly favourable to the Wesleyan movement, and allowed Wesley to preach in his church, and in 1784 Wesley was 'agreeably surprised to find the congregation deeply attentive while he applied the story of Dives and Lazarus.' Ibid. 1738–86.
[10] Ibid.

was built in the city,[1] and in March of the same year Wesley preached in it, but 'for a time the work of God was hindered by a riotous mob; but the mayor cut them short, and ever since we have been in perfect peace.'[2] In 1774 Wesley found the society in Worcester 'walking in love, and not moved by all the efforts of those who would fain teach them another gospel.'[3] Every year Wesley visited the city and found 'the flame still increasing,' and the chapel much too small for the increasing congregation; and in 1788 he says, 'the Methodists here have by well-doing utterly put to silence the ignorance of foolish men, so they are now abundantly more in danger by honour than by dishonour.'[4] A record of the names and numbers of the Methodists of Worcester city in that year gives the numbers as 209; of these 60 were men and 139 women, besides a large number of casual attendants.[5] Besides Worcester city there were many other Wesleyan centres in the county, and by 1770 a circuit was organised including Worcester, Bengeworth, Church Honeybourne, and Bewdley, and other places in Gloucestershire and Warwickshire. In 1787 the Worcester portion was separated from the Gloucester, and a circuit direction of 1797 shows the standing of Wesleyanism in the county. At Ombersley a new society of eighteen members was formed that year; at Droitwich a new society also, of which 'we have very good prospect'; at Bromsgrove a society of nineteen members, 'steady, but not very lively'; at Bengeworth were the four remaining members of what was once 'the oldest and largest society in this part of the kingdom'; at Pershore preaching had been renewed at the 'earnest request of some poor people.'[6] In 1795, four years after Wesley's death, the Wesleyans of Worcester city bought an old chapel which had belonged to a branch of the Independents.[7] In 1813 with the increase of the congregation the present chapel was built.[8]

As early as 1763 something of the warning that Wesleyanism was offering to the church had been realised in Worcester. In that year, and in 1766, Warren, the archdeacon of Worcester, delivered two charges to the clergy of the diocese of Worcester against 'the sophistical arts of the Papists and the delusions of the Methodists.'[9] It is to his credit that he advocated a toleration for the Papists by law, but his toleration was only based on the fact that toleration for Papists by law would be better for the Church than the toleration they enjoyed *against* law. Evidently the Romanist feeling was still strong in the county, for he bade his clergy be vigilant against 'the Romish priests maintained under the protection of families of rank and opulence,' and 'not to

[1] In 1861, one of Wesley's congregation, who had heard him preach in the Riding House before the chapel was built, was living in a cottage close by the spot. Her name was Jane Crump, she was ninety-three years old, but she delighted to tell her visitors how well she remembered Wesley's sermons, and how 'the people used to rise as early as five in the morning to hear him preach,' and so far from insulting him would go some distance from the city to meet him, when they knew of his coming to Worcester, and escort him into the city. Noake, *Worc. Sects.* 313.

[2] Wesley, *Extracts from Journal*, 1738–86.

[3] Ibid.

[4] Ibid. 1786–9.

[5] Noake, *Worc. Sects.* 315. 'The majority of these members were engaged in the glove trade (then flourishing in Worcester), others were servants, cordwainers, milk-sellers, water-carriers, bricklayers, hatters, coopers, dyers, patten-makers, smiths, watermen, one or two china workers, a milliner or two, and several gentlewomen.'

[6] Noake, *Worc. Sects.* 316 et seq. From the circuit directories of 1797.

[7] Ibid.

[8] Ibid.

[9] Prattinton Coll. (Soc. Antiq.), Tracts.

suffer tares to be sown while they sleep.' Also, he gave a list of the popish books he had met with in the diocese, and especially condemned the subtle influence of Bossuet.[1] As for the Methodists they differ from the church in 'doctrines relating to faith and grace . . . they draw multitudes of men and women after them into the fields, and barns, and tabernacles, and churches . . . the spirit, they say, bears witness to their preaching . . . they are received with sighs and groans, many forsake all and follow them, and their converts are so very sure of it that they can name the very instant when they received the Holy Ghost.' The archdeacon saw that they were an especial danger to the church, since 'the common people are more apt to give ear to passionate effusions, be they ever so wild and incoherent, than to sensible and sober discourses, and are more attracted by addresses to their imagination than to their reason.' To fight against this the clergy were warned to 'avoid lukewarmedness and unconcernedness *that too generally appear in religious matters* . . . anxious concern for the world and the world's manners and pleasures and vanities of any sort that give the Methodists great advantage in the censure of our conduct.'

But in spite of the archdeacon's warning the 'lukewarmedness and unconcernedness' was too deeply rooted to be easily shaken off. It was only when Oxford was once more full of real intellectual life, and when the Oxford movement had spread itself beyond the bounds of the University, that a revival of religious activity in the church itself began in Worcestershire as in all England. Schools and churches were rebuilt, and at length an effort was made to extend church life into the different parts of the diocese, especially into the manufacturing districts, where the need had been so long felt and so long supplied by the efforts of those outside the church. Hugh Pepys,[2] who succeeded Carr, and was bishop during the beginnings of the revival, retired in 1861, after an episcopate of twenty years. Under his successor, Henry Philpott[3] (1861–91), the work was pressed forward, and to him, perhaps, more than to any other man is due the present position of the church in the county.[4] On his retirement in 1891, Bishop John Perowne was appointed (1891–1902); under him the religious activity continued. A new archdeaconry, Birmingham, taken partly out of that of Worcester and partly out of that of Coventry, was made, and a suffragan bishop of Coventry appointed. Under Bishop Gore (1902–5) the work was steadily carried forward. The almost unique position in the manufacturing world that Birmingham has assumed, and the consequent ever increasing population of the northern districts, shaped the project of forming a new diocese of Birmingham carved out of the Worcester diocese. The idea was started by Bishop Perowne, but Dr. Gore has carried it out, devoting a large part of his own fortune to the object. To the new see he has been translated (1905), Yeatman-Biggs, bishop suffragan of Southwark, being his successor in what is left after this third dismemberment of the mother diocese of Worcester.

[1] In the nineteenth century several new Roman Catholic churches were built in the county. One of the most notable of their buildings is the Benedictine convent of nuns at Stanbrook near Powick, with a beautiful church adjoining, served by two priests of the Benedictine order.

[2] The brother of the Chancellor Lord Cottenham.

[3] He was chairman of the Prince Consort's Committee, when he, as Prince Albert, contested the chancellorship of Cambridge with Lord Powis.

[4] But see Creighton's Letter, as to candidates for ordination.

ECCLESIASTICAL HISTORY

APPENDIX No. I

ECCLESIASTICAL DIVISIONS OF THE COUNTY

In accordance with the early organisation of the Church in England, when the diocese coincided with the kingdom, the district that became the county of Worcester was, as part of Mercia, included in the Lichfield diocese.[1] About 679, as a result of Archbishop Theodore's work, Lichfield, like the other bishoprics, was divided into six dioceses, taking as their boundaries those of the still existing tribes or under kingdoms. Thus the kingdom of Hwiccas became the new diocese of Worcester,[2] but this was by no means identical with the later county. None of the five regions into which the Mercian kingdom was divided bore the name of shire, since these districts were not divided into shires and named after their chief towns until after the reconquest of Mercia from the Danes by Edward the Elder in 922.[3]

From this date until the time of the taxation of Pope Nicholas of 1291, there is no definite date to mark the progress of the ecclesiastical organisation of the county. However, the formation of the archdeaconries of Worcester and Gloucester, comprising the diocese of Worcester, evidently came with the institution of territorial archdeaconries after the Conquest,[4] and these archdeaconries were probably identical with those given in 1291. That of Gloucester included such part of Gloucester as was within the diocese of Worcester, with one Worcester parish—Broadway in Campden deanery. That of Worcester included the deanery of Warwick, comprised of such part of the county of Warwick as was within the diocese of Worcester, together with the parishes of Blockley and Evenlode, in the county of Worcester, excepting the parish of Broadway, and the north-western corner of the county stretching from Ribbesford to Tenbury, which formed the deanery of Burford (Hereford diocese), and the northern parish of Oldbury, part of the Hereford deanery of Stottsdon.[5] Hence the county of Worcester, while not identical with the diocese of Worcester, was wholly within the diocese, with the exception of the parish of Oldbury and the fifteen parishes of Abberley, Bayton, Bockleton, Clifton upon Teme, Hanley Child, Hanley William, Kyre-Wyard, Lindridge, Mamble, Rock, Ribbesford, Stanford on Teme, Stockton on Teme, Sapey, and Tenbury, included in the Herefordshire deanery of Burford.

The names and limits of the deaneries in the county were fixed certainly before 1291, though it is difficult to say at what date. Evidently the deanery of Worcester existed as early as the late twelfth century, since in 1206 the death of Roger Dod, dean of Worcester, is noted in the Worcester annals.[6] In 1291 there were six deaneries in the county and diocese of Worcester, containing altogether 115 parishes, viz. :—

Worcester, containing the twenty-six parishes of Astley, Broadwas, Grimley, Hindlip, Holt, Kempsey, Kenswick, Martley, Ombersley, Pirton, Severn Stoke, Shelsley, Shrawley, Spetchley, Tibberton, Warndon, Wichenford, Wick Episcopi, Witley, St. Andrew Worcester, All Saints Worcester, St. Clement Worcester, St. Helen Worcester, St. Martin Worcester, St. Peter Worcester, St. Swithun Worcester.

Powick, containing the sixteen parishes of Acton Beauchamp, Birtsmorton, Eldersfield, Hanley, Leigh, Longdon, Madresfield, Great Malvern, Little Malvern, Mathon, Pendock, Powick, Redmarley D'Abitôt, Suckley, Staunton, Upton upon Severn.

Pershore, containing the thirty-three parishes of Abberton, Abbots-Morton, Bredon, Bishampton, Churchill, Cleeve-Prior, Great Comberton, Croome D'Abitôt, Hill Croome, Dormston, Eckington, Elmley Castle, Feckenham, Fladbury, Flyford Flavell, Grafton Flyford, Harvington, Himbleton, Inkberrow, Kington, Church Lench, Rous Lench, Naunton Beauchamp, Overbury, Holy Cross Pershore, St. Andrew Pershore, Peopleton, North Piddle, Ripple, Sedgeberrow, Strensham, Twining, Upton Snodsbury.

Kidderminster, containing the thirteen parishes of Belbroughton, Clent, Chaddesley Corbett, Doverdale, Dudley, Elmley Lovett, Hagley, Halesowen, Hartlebury, Kidderminster, Old Swinford, Yardley, Wolverley.

Droitwich, containing the fifteen parishes of Alvechurch, Beaulieu or Beoley, Bromsgrove, Dodderhill, St. Andrew Droitwich, St. Peter Droitwich, Hampton Lovett, Hanbury, Martin

[1] Bede, *Hist. Eccl.* iv. cap. 3.
[2] Stubbs, *Const. Hist.* i. 246.
[3] Ibid. i. 123 and *A. S. Chron.* (Rolls Ser.), i. 195.
[4] Stubbs, *Const. Hist.* i. 255 n.
[5] *Pope Nich. Tax.* (Rec. Com.), 216–225.
[6] *Ann. Mon.* (Rolls Ser.), iv. 395.

Hussingtree, Northfield, Salwarpe, Stoke Prior, Tardebigge, Upton Warren, St. Mary-next-Witton.

Vale of Evesham, containing the ten parishes of Badsey, Bengeworth, Bretforton, Church Honeybourne, St. Lawrence Evesham, Hampton, Littleton, Norton, Offenham, Wickhamford.

The five deaneries of Worcester, Powick, Pershore, Kidderminster and Droitwich, were entirely under the bishop's jurisdiction; the Vale of Evesham was exempt after the year 1268.[1] The area of the two northern was nearly equal to that of the four southern, but the value of the four southern seems to have been greater than that of the two others.[2]

Between the years 1291 and 1524 the deaneries remained almost unchanged. Hence in the latter year the numbers of parishes in the six deaneries of the county were given as follows: Worcester, 26; Powick, 17; Kidderminster, 14; Droitwich, 16; Pershore, 30; Evesham, 9.[3] These numbers show that there could have been little material alteration.

In 1535, the date of the Valor Ecclesiasticus, the deaneries were the same, but the divisions in the deaneries themselves had slightly altered. The deanery of Worcester then comprised thirty-five parishes, consisting of twenty-five rectories and ten vicarages. The chapels of Claines, Areley and Knightwick had become rectories, and that of Hallow a vicarage; the church of Kenswick had become a free chapel. The five new parishes were those of Oddingley, White Ladies Aston, Cotheridge, St. Michael Bedwardine Worcester, St. Nicholas Worcester, and St. Alban Worcester.

In the deanery of Powick there were three new parishes. The chapel of Berrow and the chapel of Welland, which had been in Pershore deanery in 1291, had become vicarages and been annexed to Powick, and the vicarage of 'Chocknell' had been created.

In the deanery of Pershore, also, three new parishes had been created, Broughton Hackett, Earl's Croome, and Crowle, while the chapelry of Birlingham had become a rectory. The parish of Twining had been transferred to the archdeaconry and county of Gloucester.[4]

In the deanery of Kidderminster there were two new parishes; the rectories of Rushock and Stone had been created, while the parish of Clent had been transferred to the diocese of Hereford.[5]

In the deanery of Droitwich there were two new parishes, the rectories of St. Nicholas Droitwich, and Hadsor.

In the Vale of Evesham the only alteration was that the parish of Littleton had been divided into the two parishes of South, and Middle and North.

In the clergy lists from 1841 to 1861 the same names of deaneries are given, with practically the same schedule of parishes. Fourteen new parishes had been created; two in Worcester deanery: Bredicot and Stoulton; three in Powick: Bushley, Chaceley and Newland; two in Pershore: Huddington and Wick-juxta-Pershore; four in Kidderminster: Broom, Cradley in Halesowen, Dudley Eve Hill, and Pedmore; three in Droitwich: Catshill, Moseley and Wythall. The parish of Oldbury had been transferred from Hereford diocese to Kidderminster deanery, and that of Broadway from the archdeaconry of Gloucester to the Worcester deanery of Evesham.

In 1861–2 the deaneries were completely reconstituted. The deanery of Worcester was split up into East and West Worcester, and four new deaneries were created. The schedule of parishes under the different deaneries was as follows:—

Worcester East, containing the sixteen parishes of Bredicot, Hindlip, Kempsey, Oddingley, Ombersley, Pirton, St. Martin Worcester, St. Michael Worcester, St. Nicholas Worcester, St. Swithun Worcester, Severn Stoke, Spetchley, Stoulton, Tibberton, Warndon, and White Ladies Aston, or Aston Episcopi.

Worcester West, containing the twenty-one parishes of Areley Kings, Astley, Broadwas, Claines, Cotheridge, Grimley, Holt, Knightwick, Martley, All Saints Worcester, St. Andrew

[1] The final settlement between the bishop and the abbot was made in that year and the exemption of the churches of the Vale confirmed. *Worc. Epis. Reg. Giffard* (Worc. Hist. Soc.), 9.

[2] *Pope Nich. Tax.* (Rec. Com.), pp. 216-217.

Southern	£	s.	d.	*Northern*	£	s.	d.
Worcester	285	4	0	Droitwich	208	1	4
Powick	189	10	4	Kidderminster	226	6	10
Pershore	339	17	2				
Vale of Evesham	104	7	10				
	£918	19	4		£434	8	2

[3] *L. and P. Hen. VIII.* iv. (i.) 424.

[4] *Valor Eccl.* (Rec. Com.), 226.

[5] This alteration must have been made later than the fourteenth century, since Clent appears in the bishop's registers as portion of Kidderminster deanery until the late fourteenth century. *Worc. Epis. Reg. Giffard* (Worc. Hist. Soc.).

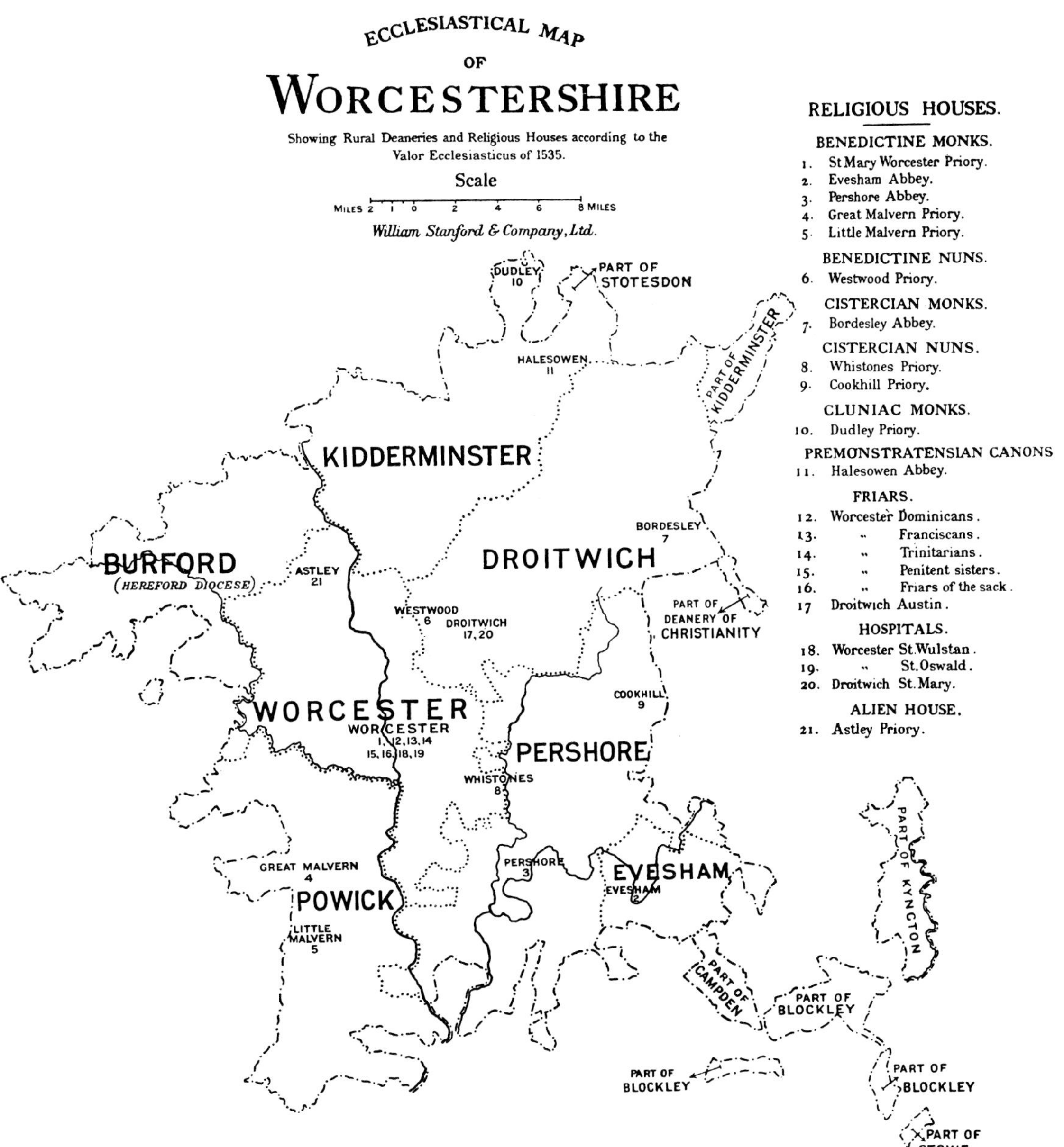

To face page 90.

Worcester, St. Alban Worcester, St. Clement Worcester, St. Helen Worcester, St. John Bedwardine Worcester, St. Martin Worcester, St. Peter Worcester, Shelsley, Shrawley, Wichenford, Witley.

Powick, containing the fourteen parishes of Acton Beauchamp, Guarlford, Leigh, Madresfield, Great Malvern, Little Malvern, Malvern Link, North Malvern, Malvern Wells, Malvern West, Mathon, Newland, Powick, Suckley.

Pershore, containing the twenty parishes of Besford, Bricklehampton, Birlingham, Churchill, Crowle, Great Comberton, Little Comberton, Defford, Elmley Castle, Flyford Flavell, Grafton Flyford, Himbleton, Huddington, Naunton Beauchamp, Peopleton, St. Andrew Pershore, Holy Cross Pershore, North Piddle, Upton Snodsbury, and Wick-juxta-Pershore.

Kidderminster, containing the thirty-seven parishes of Acock's Green, Belbroughton, Blackheath, Broom, Chaddesley Corbett, Churchill, Clent, Cradley, Doverdale, Dudley, St. Edmund Dudley, St. James Dudley, St. John Dudley, St. Thomas Dudley, Elmley Lovett, Hagley, Halesowen, Hartlebury, Kidderminster, St. George Kidderminster, St. John Kidderminster, St. Mary Kidderminster, Langley, Lye in the Waste, Old Swinford, Butler's Marston, Lower Mitton, Oldbury, Pedmore, Quinton, Romsley, Rushock, Stone, Stourbridge, Old Swinford, Wolverley, Wribbenhall, Yardley.

Droitwich, containing the twenty-four parishes of Alvechurch, Balsall Heath, Beoley or Beaulieu, Bromsgrove, Christchurch Catshill, Dodderhill, St. Andrew Droitwich, St. Mary Droitwich, St. Nicholas Droitwich, St. Peter Droitwich, Hadsor, Hampton Lovett, Hanbury, Lickey, Martin Hussingtree, Moseley, Northfield, King's Norton, Redditch, Salwarpe, Stoke Prior, Tardebigge, Upton Warren, Wythall or Wythewood.

Evesham containing the thirteen parishes of Badsey, Bengeworth, Bretforton, Broadway, Cleeve Prior, All Saints Evesham, St. Lawrence Evesham, Great and Little Hampton, Church Honeybourne, Norton, Offenham, Sedgeberrow, Wickhamford.

Bredon containing the eight parishes of Bredon, Croome d'Abitôt, Earl's Croome, Eckington, Hill Croome, Overbury, Ripple, Strensham.

Upton, containing the thirteen parishes of Berrow, Birtsmorton, Bushley, Castle Morton, Chaceley, Eldersfield, Hanley Castle, Longdon, Pendock, Redmarley D'Abitôt, Staunton, Upton upon Severn, Welland.

Feckenham, containing the twelve parishes of Abberton, Abbots Morton, Bishampton, Church Lench, Cropthorne, Dormston, Feckenham, Fladbury, Harvington, Inkberrow, Kington, Rous Lench.

The parishes in the county belonging to Hereford diocese were in the deanery of Burford. They were as follows :—Abberley, Bockleton, Burford, Clifton-on-Teme, Dowles, Eastham with Hanley Child, Hanley William and Orleton, Edvin Loach,[1] Kyre Wyard, Lindridge with Pensax, Mamble with Bayton, Ribbesford with Bewdley, Rochford, Rock, Lower Sapey, Shelsey Walsh, Stanford-on-Teme, Stockton-on-Teme, and Tenbury.

At the present time (1905) the list of parishes under the deaneries is as follows :—

Worcester East, containing the twenty-three parishes of Aston Episcopi, Broughton Hackett, Churchill, Crowle, St. John Claines, St. George Claines, Rainbow Hill Claines, Tything Worcester Claines, Hindlip, Kempsey, Norton by Kempsey, Ombersley, Spetchley, Tibberton with Bredicot, Warndon, St. Martin Worcester, St. Michael Bedwardine Worcester, St. Nicholas Worcester, St. Paul Worcester, St. Peter with Whittington Worcester, St. Stephen Worcester, St. Swithun Worcester, Holy Trinity Worcester.

Worcester West, containing the eighteen parishes of Areley Kings, Astley, Broadwas, Cotheridge, Grimley, Hallow with Broadheath, Holt, Knightwick with Doddenham, Martley, Shelsley Beauchamp, Shrawley, Wichenford, Great Witley with Little Witley, All Saints Worcester, St. Andrew Worcester, St. Clement Worcester, St. Helen with St. Alban, St. John Bedwardine.

Powick, containing the seventeen parishes of Acton Beauchamp, Guarlford, Leigh with Bransford, Madresfield, Great Malvern, Holy Trinity Great Malvern, Christ Church Great Malvern, Malvern Link, Little Malvern, Malvern Wells, Malvern West, Cowleigh, Mathon, Newland, Powick, Suckley with Alfrick and Lulsey.

Pershore, containing the nineteen parishes of Great Comberton, Little Comberton, Cropthorne Defford with Besford, Eckington, Elmley Castle, Flyford Flavel, Grafton Flyford, Nafford with Birlingham, Naunton Beauchamp, Peopleton, St. Andrew Pershore, Holy Cross Pershore, Broughton Pershore, Pinvin and Bricklehampton, North Piddle, Stoulton, Upton Snodsbury, Wick-juxta-Pershore.

Kidderminster, containing the twenty-six parishes of Amblecote, Belbroughton with Fairfield, Broom, Chaddesley Corbett, Churchill in Oswaldslow, Clent, Elmley Lovett, Hagley with Blakedown, Hartlebury, St. Mary with Trimpley and Franche, Kidderminster, St. George Kidderminster, St. John Kidderminster, Lye, Mitton, Wribbenhall, Old Swinford, Pedmore, Rushock, Stamber

[1] Transferred to the county of Hereford in 1893.

Mill, Stone, St. John Stourbridge, St. Thomas Stourbridge, All Saints Wilden, Wolverley, Wollaston, Cookley.

Droitwich, containing the sixteen parishes of Dodderhill, Elmbridge, Wychbold, Doverdale, Witton Droitwich, St. Nicholas Droitwich, St. Peter Droitwich, Hadsor with Oddingley, Hampton Lovett, Hanbury, Himbleton, Huddington, Martin Hussingtree, Salwarpe, Stoke Prior, Upton Warren.

Evesham, containing the thirteen parishes of Badsey with Aldington, Bengeworth, Bretforton, Broadway, Cleeve Prior, All Saints with St. Lawrence Evesham, Hampton, Honeybourne, South Littleton with Middle and North Littleton, Norton with Lenchwick, Offenham, Sedgeberrow, Wickhamford.

Bredon, containing the eight parishes of Bredon, Croome D'Abitôt, Earl's Croome, Hill Croome, Overbury with Alston, Teddington and Washbourne, Ripple, Severn-Stoke, Strensham.

Upton, containing the fourteen parishes of Berrow, Birtsmorton, Bushley, Castlemorton, Chaceley, Eldersfield, Hanley Castle with St. Gabriel, Longdon, Pendock, Queenhill, Redmarley D'Abitôt, Staunton, Upton upon Severn with Good Shepherd, Welland.

Feckenham, containing the eleven parishes of Abberton, Abbots Morton, Bishampton, Bradley, Church Lench with Abbots Lench, Feckenham, Fladbury with Wyre Piddle and Throckmorton, Harvington, Inkberrow with Cookhill, Kington with Dormston, Rous Lench.

Bromsgrove, containing the eight parishes of Alvechurch with Beoley, Bromsgrove with All Saints' vicarage, Catshill with The Lickey vicarage, Cofton Hackett, Finstall, Tardebigge with Webheath, Redditch with St. George Redditch.

Of the parishes in the Hereford diocese Bockleton Burford, Eastham with Hanley Child, Hanley William and Orelton, Kyre Wyard, Rochford, Lower Sapey, and Tenbury still belong to the deanery of Burford. Abberley, Bewdley—now become a separate parish—Dowles, Lindridge, Mamble with Bayton, Ribbesford, Rock, Shelsey Walsh, Stanford-on-Teme have been transferred (1905) to the newly-formed deanery of Bewdley, and Clifton upon Teme to that of Bromyard.

THE RELIGIOUS HOUSES OF WORCESTERSHIRE

INTRODUCTION

Benedictinism both at its best and worst was the dominant feature of the monastic life of Worcestershire. In Worcester itself the Benedictine rule was possibly introduced by the time of the Council of Clovesho, 747, while St. Egwin, who founded the monastery of Evesham in 703, was himself a Benedictine. The house of Pershore was also in existence by the beginning of the eighth century, and came under the injunctions to follow the Benedictine rule imposed in the Council of Clovesho. But the beginning of strict monastic life and the ousting of secular canons from the monasteries did not come until the tenth century when St. Oswald came to Worcester imbued with the true Benedictine ideal, which he felt to be irreconcilable with communities of secular canons. With such an early footing in the county the Benedictines could not but prosper. Early endowments were showered upon them by devout kings and princes until prosperity brought rivalry and jealousy and a constant and irritating struggle over their possessions. An impetus to the rivalry was given by the foundation in 1085 of the Benedictine priory of Great Malvern which was subject to Westminster Abbey, and of Little Malvern in 1171, especially as the latter, though locally connected with Great Malvern, was really dependent on the Worcester house. Finally, in the twelfth century, the strength of Benedictinism was completed in the county by an appeal to women as well as men in the foundation of the nunnery of Westwood.

With the Benedictine power so well developed it might well be almost impossible for any other order to become of importance in the county. Yet by the middle of the twelfth century the Cistercians, themselves part of a revival within the Benedictine order, gained a footing in the county, and a Cistercian house was founded at Bordesley. Following this in the thirteenth century came the establishment of the two Cistercian nunneries of Whistones and Cookhill in 1255 and 1260. In the meantime Gervase Paynel, in the middle of the twelfth century, had founded and endowed the Cluniac house of St. James of Dudley, and Peter des Roches in 1218 the Premonstratensian house of Halesowen on the borders of Shropshire.

By this time also a new influence had come into the county with the settlement of the Franciscans at Worcester between 1225 and 1230. The monastic orders had been drawn into difficulties produced by worldliness and had deserted their former ideals in their thirst for temporal power. The Friars Minor came with the gospel of simplicity and poverty to meet the needs, hitherto unheeded, of the poor and suffering. In their fight to gain a firm foothold they too departed from their ideal perhaps because it drew too much on the heroism of mankind. Besides the Franciscans the Friars of the

Sack were settled in Worcester by 1271, and there was a small body of Penitent Sisters mentioned in 1240. In the fourteenth century William de Beauchamp founded the house of the Black Friars or Dominicans in Worcester, but they, unlike the Franciscans, seem to have had little practical effect on the county. The Austin Friars settled at Droitwich in 1331.

Of the three hospitals of the county, that of St. Mary, Droitwich, was founded in 1285, that of St. Wulstan, Worcester, better known as the Commandery, in about 1085, and that of St. Oswald, Worcester, before 1268, probably much earlier. The last alone has survived as a charitable organization.

The one alien house of the county was that of Astley, founded somewhere in the twelfth century.

Rich in religious houses, the county of Worcester is also rich in materials for their history, especially for that of the greater Benedictine houses. For Worcester itself it is natural there should be much in ordinary sources as well as in the Priory register and the chartulary compiled by Heming. There is much also for the other Benedictine houses of Pershore and Great Malvern, while for the Premonstratensian house of Halesowen the visitations of the conservator-general of the order are most valuable. But the most interesting and by far the most valuable of all the sources is the chronicle of the abbey of Evesham, being as it is for the greater part a rare picture of the internal life of a monastery, and a contemporary history of the house written by one who had no mean share in making that history.

It would be interesting, but almost impossible, to estimate the effects of monasticism in any one county, but especially so in Worcestershire, where monasticism was the pivot round which all else seemed to turn. Episcopal power, great though it might be, had to eventually give way before the claims put forward by Evesham. The religious houses were the greatest landowners, and what was more, since the patronage of the county was almost exclusively in their hands, the influence they possessed was incalculable. They were, too, the centres of learning in the county and of all organized almsgiving; and although they so often neglected what Wiclif would call the 'universal' for the personal, and forgot the good they might do in struggling for more power and more possessions, it is not well to underestimate, in spite of all their failures, their effect on the county as a refining and educating force.

HOUSES OF BENEDICTINE MONKS

1. PRIORY OF ST. MARY OF WORCESTER

The origin of the cathedral at Worcester may be traced far back to the establishment of the episcopal see of the Hwiccas, in 680, on the division of the unwieldy diocese of Mercia carried out by Archbishop Theodore, with the co-operation of the Mercian King Ethelred and other Hwiccan princes.[1] Numerous grants and privileges were bestowed by Ethelred and subsequent kings and viceroys on the bishop and his *familia*, the first occupants of the cathedral monastery, dedicated, like most Hwiccan foundations of an early date, to St. Peter. It is difficult to define the precise character of these early societies and 'families.' Bede states that they were originally composed of a mixed company of clerks and monks, but which of the two elements preponderated is still open to conjecture. The first mention of another society composed entirely of monks, destined eventually to swallow up and supersede the earlier establishment, occurs in a charter of Ethelbald, king of the Mercians, dated 743, granting to the monastery of St. Mary

[1] *Ann. Mon.* (Rolls Ser.), iv. 365.

Worcester Priory.

Worcester Priory.

Worcester Priory.

Hospital of St. Wulstan.

Hospital of St. Oswald.

Little Malvern Priory.

Worcester Monastic Seals.—Plate I.

To face page 94.

of Worcester the reversion of lands at Cold Ashton and Notgrove in Gloucestershire which he had bestowed on Osred, a member of the royal family of the Hwiccas.[1] Nothing is known of the earliest origin of St. Mary. Green suggests, but gives no authority, that it may be identified with the monastery at Worcester founded by Alfred and presided over by his daughter, the abbess Ethelburga.[2] The more probable theory is that this second society was the outcome of the separation of the dual elements of which the first establishment was composed, and that the mixed society which had early formed the bishop's 'familia' resolved itself into the secular college of St. Peter and the monastic society of St. Mary.[3] In support of this theory Dr. Stubbs[4] notes that the earliest references to St. Mary occur about the time of the Council of Clovesho, which laid a definite obligation on all monks and nuns to follow the rule of St. Benedict.[5] The distinction between the two establishments continued up to the time of St. Oswald, by whom the bishop's chair, which had hitherto belonged to St. Peter's church, was transferred to St. Mary's, which henceforth became known as the cathedral church of St. Mary of Worcester. In the centuries intervening the two churches existing side by side benefited equally from the liberality of Mercian princes. About the year 757 Eanberht, viceroy of the Hwiccas, with his brothers Uhtred and Aldred, granted land at Tredington-on-Stour to Bishop Milred and the church of St. Peter, 'where our parents lie buried,' that prayers and masses might be offered to God daily.[6] His brother, the viceroy Uhtred, gave land at Stoke Prior on the east of the river Salwarpe to the brethren serving God in the monastery at Worcester dedicated to the Virgin Mary, and in 775 bestowed on the church of St. Mary,[7] 'where the bodies of my parents lie buried,' Shipston-on-Stour, for the better keeping of a good table and for the use of Christ's poor inhabiting there.[8] Probably the two churches shared the same cemetery, though St. Peter's churchyard is generally given as the burial ground of Hwiccan princes. Wigferth, duke of the Mercians, with his wife Alta, considerable benefactors to the see, and of whose gift the monks of Worcester claimed the manor and church of Lindridge,[9] was buried here about the year 781 under a stone cross in the cathedral cemetery.[10] St. Oswald is said to have preached to the people too numerous for St. Peter's church from the stone cross in the churchyard before St. Mary's was built; we read that it was taken down in the time of Edward the Confessor in order to repair the church of St. Peter.[11] Aldred the viceroy added Sedgeberrow, which he had obtained from King Offa, to the possessions of St. Mary.[12] Offa made numerous grants to both churches, but the authenticity of his charters as well as those of Uhtred the viceroy is regarded as more than doubtful.

The see, and consequently the cathedral chapter, profited largely by a practice in vogue during the eighth and ninth centuries for rich laymen to make temporary provision for their families, and at the same time testify to their devotion to religion by making over large grants of money or land for the foundation of monasteries where relations of the donor could be established for life, but with the intention of their final reversion to the episcopal see. Fladbury was one of the earliest of these foundations thus absorbed into the college at Worcester. Bishop Oftfor obtained it by grant of King Ethelred about the year 961,[13] and it was regranted by Bishop Ecgwin to Ethelheard, son of Oshere the Mercian sub-regulus and early benefactor of the see, in exchange for Stratford, on condition that its monastic state should be maintained.[14] It descended to the viceroy Aldred by inheritance, and was by him granted to the Abbess Ethelburga his kinswoman on condition of its reversion to the see.[15] On her death it was confirmed to Bishop Deneberht and his *familia* by King Kenulf. The Danish raids fell heavily on the diocese during the ninth century, and the bishops were obliged to make considerable grants of church lands in order to purchase protection.[16]

Bishop Oswald, destined to end the long rivalry between the sister churches of St. Peter and St. Mary,[17] was appointed to the see in 961 by the influence of Dunstan.[18] He proceeded at

[1] Birch, *Cart. Sax.* i. 239.

[2] *Hist. and Antiq. of Worc.* p. 25. The monastery of Withington, the site for which had been granted by the viceroy Oshere to the Abbess Dunna and Bucga her daughter, was by a synodal decree confirmed to the see of Worcester after the death of the Abbess Hrotwar, grand-daughter of Bucga (Birch, *Cart. Sax.* i. 225). It fell in during the pontificate of Bishop Milred, who granted it to the Abbess Ethelburga for life on condition that both it and her monastery at Worcester should after her death devolve to the see. Heming, *Chartul.* (Hearne ed.), ii. 464, 465, 466.

[3] Stubbs, *Arch. Journ.* xix. 244.

[4] Ibid.

[5] Wilkins, *Concilia*, i. 97.

[6] Birch, *Cart. Sax.* i. 261.

[7] Ibid. p. 289.

[8] Ibid. p. 291.

[9] *Reg. of the Blessed Mary of Worc.* (Camd. Soc.), p. 10b.

[10] Heming, *Chartul.* (Hearne ed.), ii. 341, 342, 343.

[11] Ibid.

[12] Birch, *Cart. Sax.* i. 310, 311, 312.

[13] *Codex Diplo.* i. xxxiii. and Heming, *Chartul.* (Hearne ed.), i. 21.

[14] Ibid. 23.

[15] *Codex Diplo.* i. 146.

[16] Heming, *Chartul.* (Hearne ed.), i. 6.

[17] Grants appear to have been made to both by King Athelstan, who in a charter dated 929 refers to St. Mary's as a *basilica*. Birch, *Cart. Sax.* ii. 343.

[18] William of Malmesbury, *Gest. Pont. Angl.* (Rolls Ser.), 248.

once to bring about the reforms for which he had been selected, but chose a gentler method than that adopted by his fellow-reformers Dunstan and Ethelwald: instead of forcibly expelling the secular canons who refused to comply he undermined and supplanted them.[1] He began by showing a marked preference for St. Mary's church, and by frequent attendance there at divine offices so drew off the people who flocked to hear him preach and receive his blessing that St. Peter's became practically deserted.[2] He then proceeded to build a new and stately church in St. Peter's churchyard, which he dedicated to the Blessed Mary. By these and other means[3] the seculars found themselves so reduced that, with Wynsin, a creature of Oswald's, kirkward of St. Peter's and vicar of St. Helen's church, at their head, they peaceably handed over the keys, deeds, etc. of the college to the bishop, and with but two exceptions consented to receive the habit.[4] Wynsin was sent to Ramsey, and after undergoing three years' probation was installed dean of St. Mary's, whither the inmates of St. Peter's had been transferred. In this manner the possession of the bishop's seat passed over to St. Mary's church, or, in the language of William of Malmesbury, 'the saint who bears the keys of paradise made way for her who keeps the door of heaven.'[5] The date of the completion of this transfer is generally given as 969,[6] though the famous charter of King Edgar, now generally regarded as a forgery, referring to the reforms effected by St. Oswald, and commenting severely on the previous occupants of the cathedral, is dated 964.[7] By it the lands and possessions of the bishop and chapter were consolidated into the hundred of Oswaldslawe, containing 300 hides in Worcestershire, to be held under the legal jurisdiction of the bishop with privileges and exemptions, excluding that of the hundred or county courts.

The new cathedral church, with its twenty-eight altars,[8] was completed in 983.[9] The bishop was not allowed to resign Worcester on his promotion to York in 972, lest in his absence the reforms established by him in the cathedral chapter should be undone.[10] On his death in 992 he was buried in the church which he had built from the foundations. Ten years later his remains were translated by Aldulf, then archbishop of York, and placed in a shrine.[11]

The church of Worcester suffered severely under the Danish invasion of the early part of the eleventh century. A schedule of its possessions lost about this time states that during the reign of King Ethelred the country was wasted and depopulated under Sweyn, the pagan king of the Danes, and that in order to meet the heavy tax laid on the whole of England nearly all the ornaments of the cathedral were taken, the altars despoiled of their gold and silver tables (*tabulæ*), crosses and chalices melted down, and large sums of money carried off.[12] The citizens of Worcester rose in rebellion under the extortion of Hardicanute, and pursued the two house-carls sent to enforce payment, and slew them in the monastery whither they had fled. The army sent by the king to take vengeance laid waste the city for four days, and left on the fifth day carrying plunder with them.[13] The cathedral thus ravaged with fire and sword remained until replaced by the foundation of Wulfstan II., the last Saxon prelate, who succeeded on the eve of the conquest. His predecessor, Archbishop Ealdred, will be remembered for his curse of the usurping sheriff of Worcester, Urse D'Abitôt, against whose encroachments on their burial ground the monks of St. Mary's had applied for protection.[14]

Wulfstan began his career under Bishop Brihteah, by whom he was ordained deacon and priest. Urged by his parents, and especially his mother, he proceeded to take monastic vows and entered the monastery of St. Mary, of which his father was already an inmate. He filled the offices of *scholasticus*, or master of the school, and treasurer in succession, and on the death of Ethelwin, or Agelwin, was made prior.[15] He was chosen, it is said, against his will to fill the see vacated by the promotion of Bishop Ealdred to York in 1061.[16] He was the friend of Harold, but after the battle of Hastings when all was lost he met the Conqueror at Berkhampstead and with others made submission to him.[17] An entry in Heming's chartulary records a grant of two hides of land at Cullacliffe made as early as 1067 to the bishop and his monks on condition that

[1] William of Malmesbury, *Gest. Pont. Angl.* (Rolls Ser.), 248.

[2] Ibid.

[3] Much stress is laid by earlier writers on the alleged impoverishment of the canons by Oswald in making extensive grants of the estates of the college to laymen (Thomas, *Surv. of the Cath. Church of Worc.* 39). It has been pointed out that the conditions of tenure amounted to a sort of leasehold, 'with ample provision reserved for the lords and owners.' Stubbs, *Arch. Journ.* xix. 252.

[4] Wharton, *Angl. Sacr.* i. 542.

[5] William de Malmesbury, op. cit. (Rolls Ser.), 548.

[6] Wharton, *Angl. Sacr.* i. 546.

[7] *Reg. of the Blessed Mary of Worc.* (Camd. Soc.), p. 21b.

[8] Browne Willis, *Hist. of Mitred Abbies*, i. 302.

[9] Heming, *Chartul.* (Hearne ed.), i. 188.

[10] *William de Malmesbury* (Rolls Ser.), 249.

[11] *Roger de Hoveden* (Rolls Ser.), i. 67, 70.

[12] Heming, *Chartul.* (Hearne ed.), i. 248.

[13] *Flor. Wigorn.* (Engl. Hist. Soc.), i. 195.

[14] *Hightest thou Urse!*
Have thou God's curse!
William de Malmesbury, op. cit. (Rolls Ser.), 253.

[15] *Roger de Hoveden* (Rolls Ser.), i. 104, 105.

[16] Ibid.

[17] *Ralph de Diceto* (Rolls Ser.), i. 197.

they should 'intercede faithfully for the Conqueror's soul and for those who assisted him when he obtained the lordship of this land.'[1] Worcester is said to have shared the fate of other monasteries plundered in 1069,[2] but the feeling of mutual confidence and respect between bishop and king was maintained during the Conqueror's reign nevertheless, and by another charter William testified to Wulfstan the bishop and Urse the sheriff that he had confirmed to Alstan the dean and the monks of Worcester all customs and privileges pertaining to their priory.[3]

According to the Domesday Survey the church of Worcester[4] at that time held in Worcestershire, besides the triple hundred of the Oswaldslawe, land at Cleeve Prior, Phepson, and Hanbury within the hundred of Esch, at Stoke Prior and Alvechurch within the hundred of Came, at Hartlebury and Wolverley in that of Cresslau, and the two manors of Eardiston in Lindridge and Knighton on Teme assigned to the support of the monks within the hundred of Dodingtree.[5] In addition the church held various manors and estates in the counties of Gloucester and Warwick.[6] By a suit instituted on the death of Archbishop Ealdred in 1069 and on the promotion of his successor Thomas, Wulfstan was able to prove the claim of the subjection of Worcester to York to be groundless, the council confirming the ancient liberties of the church as granted by the kings of Mercia and of the English.[7]

In 1084 Wulfstan began his life's work, the erection of a new cathedral in place of St. Oswald's, which had been so grievously damaged in the Danish raids, and which was now ordered to be unroofed and demolished.[8] In 1089 the work was completed, and the monks entered their new and enlarged monastery on the Day of Pentecost in that same year, the bishop offering upon the altar on the dedication day of the church, built to the pious memory of Blessed Oswald, the manor of Alveston in Warwickshire, recovered from the Conqueror at great labour and cost, and now applied to the maintenance of the brethren whose number Wulfstan had augmented from twelve to fifty.[9] Among other good works for the benefit of the community *Sanctæ Mariæ in Cryptis*,[10] Wulfstan restored the house of Westbury, which had fallen into decay through time, 'the ravages of pirates, and the neglect of provosts' (*prepositorum*), and gave it back to the use of the monks of Worcester, with whom it had been early associated as one of those 'family' monasteries of which mention has already been made.[11] At his wise instigation 'Heming the monk' codified the wonderful collection of charters and documents relating to the see and church of Worcester, known to us as *Heming's Chartulary*, as a means of ensurance against further loss in future.[12] One of the last acts of his life was to convene a synod in the monastery of 'Saint Mary in the crypts' in 1092 to decide a dispute between the parish priests of the churches of St. Helen and St. Alban as to which was the mother church of Worcester. The prior and chapter put in a claim to St. Helen's church, alleging that it had belonged to them since the foundation of the see. The synod found that there was no mother church but the cathedral.[13]

The successors of Wulfstan the last Saxon bishop[14] owed their appointment during the twelfth century to court influence. Indirectly their connexion with the king and official life benefited the cathedral chapter by enhancing the importance of the city and see of Worcester before the sanctity attaching in the following century to the tombs of SS. Oswald and Wulfstan had established its fame. Bishop Sampson, consecrated in 1096, bestowed many gifts on the monks, but was disapproved by them for revoking the constitution of Westbury and re-establishing secular canons there.[15] In the interval between his death and the appointment of his successor the cathedral was considerably damaged by fire, in which it is said the roof was wholly consumed, 'the lead melted, the planks converted into charcoal, and beams as large as trees fell to the pavement'; the escape of Wulfstan's tomb was regarded as miraculous.[16] Bishops Sampson and Theulf were both buried in the nave of St. Mary's before the crucifix.[17] Stephen was received at Worcester in 1139 by the clergy and citizens with open arms; the ring from his finger which the king offered on the altar was scrupulously returned to him the following day.[18]

1 Heming, *Chartul.* (Hearne ed.), ii. 413, 414.

2 Ibid. p. 343.

3 *Reg. of the Blessed Mary of Worc.* (Camd. Soc.), p. 25b.

4 By the church is understood to mean the bishop and monks between them. Of the fifteen manors which composed the Oswaldslawe, eight were held by the bishop and seven by the monastery, viz.: Overbury, Sedgeberrow, Shipston-on-Stour, Harvington, Grimley, Hallow, and Cropthorne, with parts of other episcopal manors consisting of seven hides. Hale, *Intro. to Reg. of Blessed Mary of Worc.* (Camd. Soc.), iv. v.

5 *Dom. Bk.* (Rec. Com.), i 172, 173, 174.

6 Ibid. pp. 184, 185, 239.

7 *Roger de Hoveden* (Rolls Ser.), i. 123, 124, 125.

8 William de Malmesbury, op. cit. (Rolls Ser.), 283.

9 Heming, *Chartul.* (Hearne ed.), ii. 418.

10 Ibid. ii. 528.

11 Ibid. p. 421.

12 Ibid. i. 282.

13 Ibid. ii. 528, 930.

14 After an episcopacy of 32 years that had seen the rise and fall of many, death came to him not unexpectedly on 18 January, 1094–5. For three days his body lay before the altar in sight of the populace that flocked to worship and make offerings, and then received burial at the hands of Robert of Hereford, that intimate friend whom at the moment of departure his spirit had summoned. *Ralph de Diceto* (Rolls Ser.), i. 219.

15 William de Malmesbury, op. cit. (Rolls Ser.), 290.

16 Ibid. pp. 288, 289.

17 Ibid. p. 290.

18 *Flor. Wigorn.* (Engl. Hist. Soc.), 115.

In the later part of the year the city was thrown into commotion by the report of the advance of the Empress's troops. The citizens prepared for assault by depositing their goods and valuables in the cathedral.[1] The monks endeavoured to avert the doom by carrying the relics of St. Oswald in procession. The cathedral appears to have escaped in the firing of the city which ensued.[2] Bishop Simon showed himself a liberal benefactor of the convent, to whom he subjected the priory of Little Malvern with the church of St. Giles,[3] restored the church of Lawern,[4] and gave back to the monks their right in the church of Westbury.[5]

From the reign of Henry I. Worcester frequently became the headquarters of the king and court during the great festivals of the year.[6] Roger de Hoveden states that Henry II. caused himself to be crowned for the third time with Eleanor his wife at Worcester in the solemn feast of Easter 1159. When they came to the offertory the king and queen removed their crowns and laid them on the altar with a vow that they would henceforth cease to wear them.[7] Roger, who occupied the see for the first part of the reign of Henry II., during his rule settled various disputes that had arisen between the convent and Osbert de Say respecting the churches of All Saints and St. Clement, Worcester,[8] delivering judgment in the crypt of the cathedral before the altar of St. Peter. In 1178 he terminated a controversy between the monks of Worcester and the nuns of Westwood respecting the patronage of the church of Dodderhill.[9] In 1175 the new tower of the cathedral is reported to have given way, and a disastrous fire in 1189 did great damage.[10]

Richard I. in the first year of his reign granted to St. Mary's church and the bishop and his successors, for the soul of his father King Henry and the good estate of his mother Eleanor and himself, 614 acres of assarted land, parcel of various manors belonging to the bishop.[11] John de Coutances in the short term of his office is said to have removed irreverently and by night the bones of St. Wulfstan; they were restored to their resting-place by Bishop Mauger in 1204.[12]

The wonderful miracles attributed to the relics of the saint did not begin till 14 January, 1201, 'which for a whole year or more increased to such an extent that sometimes fifteen or sixteen sick were cured in one day.'[13] A deputation of the monks was despatched to Rome to procure the canonization of their patron, and on 1 September, 1202, the archbishop of Canterbury, with other commissioners, visited Worcester at the command of the pope for the purpose of holding an enquiry.[14] As a consequence of this report St. Wulfstan was canonized at Rome on 23 April, 1203.[15] These events had an important bearing, for in 1202 the cathedral with its adjoining offices was again visited by fire,[16] and the revenue accruing to the brethren by the offerings of pilgrims who flocked to the shrine largely enabled them to rebuild their church and monastery. By the year 1224 these offerings had become so valuable that the bishop and convent had to come to some agreement as to their respective shares.[17] In 1216 the men of the earl of Hereford plundered the cathedral and exacted 300 marks from the monks, for which they were compelled to melt down the shrine of St. Wulfstan.[18]

King John visited the city[19] in the Christmastide of 1217, and having been received in solemn procession made his prayer at the tomb of the saint; subsequently at the request of the prior he granted to the brethren full liberties and customs within the manors of Lindridge, Wolverley, Stoke and Cleeve Prior,[20] and commuted the fine to which they were liable for the grant that it might be applied to the repair of their church.[21] On the confiscation of church lands which followed the Interdict in 1208, the king ordered the sheriff to restore to the prior of Worcester all his lands and rents.[22] Following the death of Bishop Mauger the chapter elected their prior to be his successor, but the election was set aside in favour of Walter de Gray, the king's chancellor, and Prior Ralph, having renounced the right of his election, was blessed by the papal legate as abbot of Evesham,[23] of which

1 'Behold,' says the chronicler, 'the mother church of the diocese converted into an inn and council chamber of the citizens! By reason of the number of chests and sacks but little space remained to the servants of God in such a hostelry.' *Flor. Wigorn.* (Engl. Hist. Soc.), p. 119.

2 Ibid. 3 Reg. i. D. and C. Wigorn. f. 9.

4 Ibid. 5 Ibid. f. 13.

6 It appears to have been a practice of the early Norman kings to hold their court at Gloucester during the Christmas festival, at Winchester during Easter, and Westminster at Whitsuntide. Great state was observed on these occasions, and the king always wore his crown.

7 *Roger de Hoveden* (Rolls Ser.), i. 216.

8 *Reg. of the Blessed Mary of Worc.* (Camd. Soc.), p. 133; Thomas, *Surv. of the Cath. Ch. of Worc.* p. 114.

9 Reg. i. D. and C. Wigorn. cited by Nash, *Hist. of Worc.* i. 337.

10 *Ann. Mon.* (Rolls Ser.), iv. 383, 386.

11 Thomas, *Surv. of the Cath. Ch. of Worc.* App. No. 27.

12 *Ann. Mon.* (Rolls Ser.), iv. 392. 13 Ibid.

14 Ibid. 15 Ibid. p. 392.

16 Ibid. p. 391. For a time the inmates were probably distributed in neighbouring houses; two monks, we read, were sent to Evesham. *Chron. of Evesham* (Rolls Ser.), 227.

17 *Reg. of the Blessed Mary of Worc.* (Camd. Soc.), f. 29.

18 *Ann. Mon.* (Rolls Ser), iv. 406, 7.

19 He had kept Easter here in 1200.

20 *Reg. of the Blessed Mary of Worc.* (Camd. Soc.), p. 11.

21 *Ann. Mon.* (Rolls Ser.), iv. 395; Close, 9 John, m. 12.

22 Ibid. 9 John, m. 3.

23 *Ann. Mon.* (Rolls Ser.), iv. 402, 403.

body he was already a member.[1] John wrote to the prior and chapter on the elevation of Gray to York in 1216 pointing out the expediency of making fit choice of those pastors who should be useful to the king and his realm and desiring them on those grounds not to elect their sub-prior or the prior of Little Malvern.[2] Thus admonished the convent elected their prior Silvester de Evesham who had just returned from the Roman council,[3] having received letters of protection from the king earlier in the year.[4] The death of John followed some months later. In obedience to his last wishes [5] the abbot of Croxton, after performing the customary anatomical operation, conveyed the body of the king from Newark to Worcester, where it was buried before the high altar of the cathedral between SS. Oswald and Wulfstan ; the chronicler adds 'that the saying of Merlin might be verified, let him be buried between the saints.'[6] The monks seized the occasion to obtain from the guardians of the infant king Henry III. that part of the castle of Worcester within the king's fee which they had long claimed,[7] the king himself confirmed the grant in 1232,[8] and in the same year bestowed on the brethren the church of Bromsgrove to provide for the yearly celebration of his father's anniversary.[9] In an entry under the year 1224 we read of the king's order to the Exchequer to pay for an embroidered cloth 'to cover the tomb of our father.'[10]

In June 1218 the cathedral church all this time in building was solemnly consecrated and dedicated anew to St. Mary, St. Peter, St. Oswald, and St. Wulfstan, in presence of the young king, his nobles and bishops, and on the same day the remains of St. Wulfstan were translated to a permanent shrine.[11] William de Blois built the charnel-chapel or *Carnarie*, situated between the cathedral and the bishop's palace, with a crypt under it for the bones of the faithful, and dedicated it to St. Thomas the Martyr. He ordained that mass should be said daily in the chapel for the repose of his soul and of his predecessor's. It was endowed by Walter de Cantilupe in 1265 for the maintenance of four priests.[12] The prior, we are told, began to build his house in August 1225, and finished it in December next.[13]

The episcopacy of William de Blois, 1218–1236, was an important one in the building up and consolidation of the power and independence enjoyed by the convent at a later stage when the interests of bishop and chapter had become to a certain extent divorced. The frequent disputes which estranged the community taught them at least the necessity of a clear definition of the extent of the bishop's power in chapter, and the limit of their submission to him as head. Forced on the monks against their will by the papal legate Guala, the convent reluctantly consented to elect William, then archdeacon of Bucks, to the vacant see on the death of Silvester de Evesham. It must be admitted that he showed himself both able and energetic in carrying on the work of building, and enlarging the revenues of the monastery. In 1220 his struggle with the community began. He visited and made a searching examination into the internal and external affairs of the houses, with the object, it appeared, of deposing the prior.[14] The attempt was foiled by the obstinate resistance offered by the brethren, and in the following year they claimed to have received letters of indulgence from Rome forbidding his deposition unless instigated by the pope himself. In the discussions which ensued the sacristan was deposed and three of the monks excommunicated in one day, the enraged community retaliating by violently opposing the bishop when he attempted to enter the chapter-house with his clerks. The pope suspended the prior the following year, and the bishop returning from Rome deposed him and instituted William Norman, prior of Great Malvern, in his place, the monks meanwhile violently protesting.[15] The quarrel lasted till the year 1224, in the course of which the bishop seems to have seized certain pensions and rents of the monks which he was afterwards ordered to restore.[16] The meeting held in the chapter-house on 3 October, 1224, presided over by the archbishop of Canterbury, decided with an object of putting an end to strife that William Norman should resign his office and receive the manor of Cleeve Prior for his lifetime by way of compensation, that the convent should pay his expenses, amounting to 100 marks, in the suit, and that the bishop should appoint another prior from outside the cathedral body. For the future it was provided that on the vacancy of the house the convent should present seven of their number to the bishop, who should appoint a prior out of the seven, and he should not be removed save for just cause, and during such vacancy the bishop should have the presentation to churches belonging

[1] 'In those days,' adds the chronicler, 'it was quite possible for a monk to have a place in the chapter and a stall in the choir of many monasteries.' *Chron. of Evesham* (Rolls Ser.), 255.

[2] Pat. 17 John, m. 5.

[3] *Ann. Mon.* (Rolls Ser.), iv. 405.

[4] Pat. 17 John, m. 7.

[5] On being asked during his fatal illness where he desired to be buried John replied, 'To God and St. Wulfstan I commend my soul and body.' Matt. Paris, *Hist. Minor.* (Rolls Ser.), ii. 193.

[6] *Ann. Mon.* (Rolls Ser.), iv. 407.

[7] Ibid. pp. 407, 408.

[8] Chart. R. 16 Hen. III. m. 10.

[9] Ibid. [10] Close, 8 Hen. III. m. 3.

[11] *Ann. Mon.* (Rolls Ser.), iv. 409–10.

[12] Thomas, *Surv. of the Cath. Ch. of Worc.* App. No. 43.

[13] *Ann. Mon.* (Rolls Ser.), iv. 418.

[14] Ibid. p. 411.

[15] Ibid. pp. 412, 413.

[16] *Reg. of the Blessed Mary of Worc.* (Camd. Soc.), p. 29.

to the priory together with wardships, marriages, and escheats of all free tenants, all other profits remaining to the convent.[1] The appointment of a prior should not be delayed so as to cause injury to the convent.[2] The bishop and chapter should each retain half of the offerings made at the bier and shrine of Blessed St. Wulfstun, and both parties should appoint 'honest clerks' for the custody of the same. It was further enacted that the bishop before entering the chapter-house should warn the convent, and should be attended only by his clerks if he intended to treat of spiritual matters. He might be accompanied by seculars if temporal matters were to be discussed. Finally all were admonished to lay aside rancour and ill-feeling and to forgive mutually all debts and expenses incurred by the other.[3] In 1234 a suit between the bishop and chapter respecting the church of St. Helen, Worcester, was settled by arbitration which ordained that the bishop should have jurisdiction over the church with the chapel of Claines on the east of the Severn and that the convent should hold *in proprios usus* the church with the chapels of Wyke and Wickhamford on the west of the Severn for the hospitality of their house.[4] A composition in 1283 between Boniface, archbishop of Canterbury, and the monks of Worcester ordained that in the vacancy of the see the custody of the spiritualities should be vested in the prior, or in the event of his death or absence in the sub-prior, as the archbishop's official, with the right of exercising such spiritual jurisdiction within the diocese as pertained to the office of custodian. Two-thirds of the profits of administration should go to the archbishop, the prior retaining the other third with all procurations made in kind.[5] It may also be recalled here that St. Wulfstan confirmed the right of the priors of Worcester since the days of Wynsin to be deans over all the churches belonging to the monks so that no dean or archdeacon could have any right therein, all ecclesiastical dues being paid by the prior as dean direct to the bishop.[6]

Bishop Cantilupe obtained from Henry III. grants of various privileges for lands belonging to the church. He took, however, a prominent part on the side of the Barons in the troubles of the later part of the reign, and while under the pope's ban for his complicity with the king's enemies the prior was summoned to the great parliament held at Winchester in 1265 after the fall of De Montfort from which the bishop was excluded.[7] We read that on the eve of these troubles the archbishop of Canterbury visited Worcester in 1260 and was received by the bishop and convent who paid a procuration of four marks.[8]

The thirteenth-century register of the Blessed Mary of Worcester contains a minute account of the internal economy of the convent about this time. This interesting document, besides the larger part, consisting of a specimen rent roll of the monastery for the year 1240, contains entries of public interest such as the re-issue of the Charter in 1224, the charter of the forests, with numerous charters and bulls relating to the possessions and liberties of the cathedral chapter. From it we learn the manner in which its large revenue was applied to the various offices, the provision for lights at the various chapels and altars as well as in the dormitory, the disposition of bequests,[9] the celebration of the anniversary of King John named among other benefactors and departed priors, the wages paid to the servants and to the prior's *familia*, the servants' Christmas gifts, the daily distribution of bread outside the convent body, the portion of St. Wulfstan, their patron and benefactor whom the brethren deemed ever present among them, the forms to be observed on the death of a prior, the notices served on the death of a member of the house to other houses within the bishop's fraternity.[10] It is possible to

[1] The independence of the priory was further secured by the sentence of Henry III. that the custody of the priory during a vacancy did not pertain to the crown, and in the years 1252 and 1260 we are told that it remained wholly and absolutely in the hands of the sub-prior and cellarer. *Ann. Mon.* (Rolls Ser.), iv. 441, 446.

[2] In the 'Liber Pensionum' of the church of Worcester appears the note of a customary payment to the prior on his 'first creation' of a special subsidy from all his manors and demesnes known as '*saddell selver*,' f. 64 and 'Ledger,' i. f. 13d.

[3] *Reg. of the Blessed Mary of Worc.* (Camd. Soc.), pp. 27, 28, 29.

[4] Ibid. f. 36; *Ann. Mon.* (Rolls Ser.), iv. 426.

[5] Add MS. 36,583, ff. 162, 3, 4.

[6] Heming, *Chartul.* (Hearne ed.), ii. 530, 531.

[7] *Ann. Mon.* (Rolls Ser.), ii. 366. The prior was summoned again by writ in 1295, 1299, 1307, and 1314. *Parl. Writs* (Rec. Com.), i. p. 912.

[8] *Ann. Mon.* (Rolls Ser.), iv. 446.

[9] Notwithstanding the wishes of the donor expressed in his will it was ordained that to the prior should go his charger or palfrey (*dextrarius vel palefridus*), to the chamberlain furs and armour, all other clothes to the sacristan, save linen or long clothes which should go to the refectorian, utensils to the cellarer. Bequests of other chattels to places in particular should be allowed to stand, of those granted in general terms to the church by freemen the chapter should take two parts, the sacristan one, those of the order of rustics should all go to the sacristan. The legacies of people who took the monastic habit on their death-bed should belong to the prior. *Reg. of the Blessed Mary of Worc.* (Camd. Soc.), p. 26b.

[10] Ibid. ff. 110b. 131a. According to a document contained in the chartulary of Bath Abbey, Bishop Wulfstan in 1022 entered into an agreement with the abbots of Evesham, Chertsey, Bath, Pershore, Winchcomb, and Gloucester, that they and the priory of Worcester would adopt the Benedictine rule and be in unity as if all the seven monasteries were one monastery, 'with one heart and soul.' They agreed to sing two masses weekly on Monday and Friday for all the

reconstruct much of the routine of this Benedictine house from such abundant material.

Immediately on his consecration in 1268 Bishop Giffard[1] bestowed on the prior and chapter the church of Grimley with the chapel of Hallow;[2] during his rule he confirmed the composition made with William de Blois for the custody of the priory during a vacancy, and in 1275 placed the cathedral under the protection of the pope who confirmed to the church of St. Mary all its possessions and prohibited the custom of the king and bailiffs seizing the movable goods of the priory on the death of its bishop.[3] He augmented the number of priests to officiate in the charnel-chappel from four to six, and added to their endowment the churches of St. Helen in Worcester and Naunton in Cotswold,[4] and shortly before his death bestowed on the priory the church of Dodderhill.[5]

Edward I. was a frequent visitor at Worcester and is said to have had a special love for St. Wulfstan.[6] He held Parliament here on an outbreak of the Welsh in 1282,[7] and made a practice of stopping to hear St. Wulfstan's mass and to implore the aid of the saint's prayers when summoned to quell disturbances in Wales. On the eve of the Gascon expedition in 1293 he sent his clerk with offerings for St. Wulfstan and two golden cloths for the high altar. On the same day the chapter ordained that three masses of St. Wulfstan should be said weekly until the king's return in safety.[8] He came to Worcester by boat in July, 1295, before embarking for France, and heard mass and made offerings to the shrines of St. Wulfstan and St. Oswald, and on the morrow, kneeling before the tomb of St. Wulfstan, the prior and precentor standing by, he vowed to God and the saints that in return for the intercession of St. Wulfstan he would provide for the maintenance of three monks in the convent and two candles to burn before the shrine.[9] In fulfilment of this promise he bestowed on the convent the church of Worfield on the occasion of his visit here with the queen 16 April, 1301.[10] The king in 1302 made a grant to the convent of the offerings of St. Wulfstan's shrine during all future vacancies.[11] The monks had to sustain a suit for their possession of the church of Bromsgrove in 1279 which they won,[12] but were subsequently fined for holding assize of bread within the manor.[13] The convent obtained from the king in 1282 a confirmation of previous charters granted to them by his predecessors.[14]

Despite the evidences of wealth and distinction that attended the rule of Giffard it was not a time wholly of gain to the convent. The bishop and chapter joined in concert in opposing outside interference with their joint rights, but the controversies that rent them internally were long and bitter and did much to foster that growing spirit of rebellion and independence which marked the attitude of the monks. The articles of complaint formulated against the bishop by the convent on the occasion of the archbishop's visitation in 1301[15] contain the gravamen of these disputes.[16] Among other things the monks complained that the bishop had stirred up the sacristan against the prior,[17] had made the best churches in his patronage prebendal to Westbury,[18] and wasted the first fruits of vacant churches within his diocese which should have been applied to the repair of the church of Worcester described as ruinous. He was further accused of impoverishing the convent by making certain grants prejudicial to them without their consent, that he had on one occasion when visiting them made grievous statutes and received fifty marks from the chapter for revoking them, and on another occasion had brought with him so many of his kinsmen that the number of horsemen quartered on the monastery amounted to a hundred. Every grievance, extortion, or encroachment was set down, including the destruction of pots and pans by the bishop's retinue. Many of the charges were denied or explained away by Giffard, but allowing for exaggeration much

brothers of the fraternity both living and departed, and to perform various works of charity in washing, shoeing, and clothing poor men (*Chart. of St. Peter of Glouc.* (Rolls Ser.), iii. xviii.). During the rule of Prior Thomas he and Bishop Wulfstan and the convent of Worcester made an agreement with Abbot Alwyn and the monastery of Ramsey that in memory of St. Oswald, who re-constituted both, they would be as one monastery, and on the death of any brother of either congregation prayers should be offered and alms given to the poor for thirty days, and on the death of the bishop or prior of Worcester or abbot of Ramsey for a whole year. Thomas, *Surv. of the cath. ch. of Worc.* App. No. 3.

1 In 1281 among other bequests to Worcester the sacristan received from the executors of Giffard's predecessor, Nicholas de Ely, 60 marks for the re-building of the tower. *Ann. Mon.* (Rolls Ser.), iv. 480.

2 Ibid. p. 458.

3 Thomas, *Surv. of the cath. ch. of Worc.* App. Nos. 49, 50.

4 *Worc. Epis. Reg. Giffard* (Worc. Hist. Soc.), p. 336.

5 *Ann. Mon.* (Rolls Ser.), iv. 550, 1.

6 Ibid. p. 488.

7 Ibid. p. 484.

8 Ibid. p. 514.

9 Ibid. p. 521.

10 Ibid. p. 544.

11 Pat. 30 Edw. I. m. 26.

12 *Abbrev. Plac.* (Rec. Com.) 196.

13 Ibid. p. 220.

14 Pat. 10 Edw. I. m. 10.

15 *Ann. Mon.* (Rolls Ser.) iv. 550.

16 *Worc. Epis. Reg. Giffard* (Worc. Hist. Soc.), pp. 548–551.

17 It appears however that the prior opened fire by telling the sacristan who was always appointed by the bishop that he should cease attending to the bishop's orders. Ibid. p. 96.

18 The history of this lengthy dispute is given both in Giffard's Register and in the *Annals* of Worcester with the conflicting views of both parties.

truth remains in the complaints. Giffard had picturesque qualities, but he was of an imperious disposition with a stubborn temper that brooked no opposition, fond of state and display, and regardless of scruples that weigh with smaller men.[1] He loved to entertain royally and to do good to those of his kith and kin.

The convent was visited at frequent intervals during the rule of Giffard; his visitations here are recorded in 1282[2] and in the year 1284, when according to his register he found nothing reprehensible.[3] In the intervening year the diocese was visited by Archbishop Peckham; he arrived at Worcester on the morrow of the Feast of the Purification, 1283, and received procuration from the bishop but lay at the priory; the following day he visited the monks.[4] Relations between bishop and convent in the ensuing years became much strained owing to prolonged and bitter dispute, and an incident which occurred in 1288 rendered the contest between them more acute. On the death of Robert de Fangef, archdeacon of Gloucester,[5] John de Ebroicis, a nephew of Giffard, was appointed. In the first year of his appointment he claimed the right of calling the names of the candidates at an ordination held at Westbury; the precentor of the cathedral, to whom the office of custom belonged, attempted to vindicate his claim, but was ignominiously expelled, the bishop apparently assenting; the following year the incident was repeated at Bromsgrove.[6] The convent were up in arms at the slight, and during 1288 protested against the bishop receiving the monks' professions pending their appeal for the rights of their church.[7] The *Annals* record two fruitless attempts on the part of Giffard to enter the chapter-house in 1288. Finally he yielded to the extent of admitting that the rights of the church were whatever they had been before the expulsion of the precentor from Westbury.[8] The monks were not so successful, according to their own showing, in their next controversy, and it served also to stir up the archbishop of Canterbury against them. Their smouldering dislike of the Franciscan friars had in 1289 broken out in open feud; they carried off by force the body of a certain citizen of Worcester, H. de Poche, who the friars asserted desired to be buried by them, and caused it to be buried in their own cemetery.[9] The archbishop interfered,[10] and eventually, after a series of inquiries, the brethren were compelled to dig up and return the body to the brothers minor, who, regardless of their promise to take it away secretly and with all modesty, made the triumph an occasion of great display and public rejoicing to the natural confusion of the monks.[11] Hostilities with the bishop meanwhile continued, and in 1289 the community discerned a fresh grievance in his 'extortion' of the chapel of Grafton which they were at considerable cost and labour to recover at law.[12] The bishop came to visit the convent on 7 November, 1290, and in his official account states that he was impeded on the second day of his visitation as he was examining some of the officials in the chapter-house by the violence of the prior and his adherents.[13] It is not a matter of great surprise after such litigation to find from the bishop's injunctions published the following March[14] that the convent was endeavouring to raise money by the sale of corrodies and by contracting loans. The brethren were also forbidden to wander about or lead out harriers.[15] The monks record that the bishop wrote to them on 6 May, 1291, and visited them the following day. Negotiations followed which resulted in the bishop revoking his former grievous statutes,[16] and possibly it was in gratitude for this concession that the prior and convent agreed the following year that on the anniversary of the bishop's death every year they would feed thirteen poor persons.[17] In 1292 a brawl took place in the cathedral; the monks on hearing that blood had been shed, though it was doubtful if it had touched the pavement, carefully abstained from celebrating, and divine offices were said in the chapter-house until the church had been reconciled by the bishop.[18] A brief entry records that on 11 June, 1300, Giffard visited the monastery,[19] he was breaking up fast

[1] An instance of this may be found in his removal of the tomb of John of Coutances in order to make room for his own.

[2] *Ann. Mon.* (Rolls Ser.), iv. 488; *Worc. Epis. Reg. Giffard* (Worc. Hist. Soc.), p. 165.

[3] Ibid. p. 243.

[4] Ibid. p. 170.

[5] In 1284 the prior and convent granted a licence to Robert to found a chantry of two chaplains at the altar of Holy Cross within the cathedral to pray for the soul of the said Robert and of Walter Giffard, formerly archbishop of York. Ibid. p. 252.

[6] *Ann. Mon.* (Rolls. Ser.), iv. 495, 496, 498.

[7] Ibid. p. 496.

[8] Ibid. pp. 496, 497.

[9] Ibid. p. 499.

[10] Ibid. p. 502.

[11] Ibid. p. 504.

[12] Ibid. p. 498.

[13] *Worc. Epis. Reg. Giffard* (Worc. Hist. Soc.), p. 380. The monks' account says that the bishop descended upon them with a retinue of 140 horsemen and remained three days, and departed on the fourth day in anger at the refusal of the convent to second his schemes for Westbury. *Ann. Mon.* (Rolls Ser.), iv. 504.

[14] *Worc. Epis. Reg. Giffard* (Worc. Hist. Soc.), p. 392.

[15] Ibid.

[16] *Ann. Mon.* (Rolls Ser.), iv. 505.

[17] *Worc. Epis. Reg. Giffard* (Worc. Hist. Soc.), p. 432.

[18] *Ann. Mon.* (Rolls Ser.), iv. 509, 510.

[19] *Worc. Epis. Reg. Giffard* (Worc. Hist. Soc.), p. 525. The account of the Worcester annalist is that the bishop sent two officials to visit the chapter and that they were refused admittance by the prior on the ground that they were not qualified by the terms of the composition to exercise the office of visitation. *Ann. Mon.* (Rolls Ser.), iv. 545

at that time, and in August of the same year being hindered by increasing infirmity he gave instructions for the visitation of the priory by commissioners[1] and wrote to the prior and chapter to notify impending visitation.[2] The archbishop of Canterbury, notwithstanding the bishop's protest,[3] came to visit the diocese in the following spring. He arrived at Worcester on 14 March, 1300–1, and preached to the monks, and afterwards went on to visit the bishop who was lying ill at Wyke.[4] The following day he visited the prior and chapter by his clerks and lodged meanwhile at the prior's house, for the guest-house of the convent was taken up with pilgrims and guests. The annalist speaks of the day on which the archbishop published his corrections as 'a day of tribulation and rebuke,' and with reason, for he deposed the sub-prior, precentor, and chamberlain, and forbad the sacristan, third prior, and pittancer to leave the precincts of the monastery for a year.[5] The fourteenth century opens with the resignation of the prior in 1301[6] and the death of Bishop Giffard in the following January, 1301–2.[7]

The cathedral priory rose during the ensuing century to a position of commanding eminence, notwithstanding papal pretensions which almost invariably on the voidance of the diocese 'provided' to the see regardless of the wishes of the monks, and the fact that from and partly owing to the rule of Giffard it was crippled from the outset by want of sufficient funds to meet the increased outlay required for building and other purposes. The prior's ascendancy in the diocese was also increased by a rapid succession of short episcopates with intervals of voidance occasionally much prolonged, during which as official custodian of the see[8] he exercised powers of spiritual jurisdiction over other monasteries in the diocese, which was much resented in the case of great rival houses like St. Peter of Gloucester, Tewkesbury, Bristol, and Winchcomb, and resulted in much friction and frequent appeals on both sides to the court of Canterbury. How successful the prior was in maintaining his right to visit and exercise the spiritual authority temporarily vested in him may be seen in the register *Sede Vacante*. The frequent absence of the bishop on affairs of the realm also placed him in a position of redoubled trust and honour. In regard to their relations with the diocesan the convent continued to resist strenuously any attempt to impinge on its prerogative or curtail its liberty on the part of the bishop. The chartulary of St. Peter's of Gloucester contains an interesting copy of an agreement dated 1315, whereby the monasteries of Worcester, Gloucester, Cirencester, and Lanthony bound themselves together in opposition to any molestations by their bishop and his officers, and agreed to share law expenses incurred in carrying cases up to Canterbury or Rome.[9] In the middle of the century Pope Clement VI. granted leave to Prior John of Evesham[10] and his successors to wear a mitre, ring, and pastoral staff and give the solemn benediction at mass and table. His successor, Innocent VI., confirmed these privileges, but at the request of Bishop Reginald decreed that the mitre and other ornaments should not be worn in the presence of the bishop, and, lest these should become more magnificent than those of the bishop, ordained that the prior's mitre should be of white with orphreys but without gems or precious stones. The prior petitioned Urban V. for leave to wear his mitre in the bishop's presence, setting forth the privileges obtained by other abbots and priors. He was only able to obtain, however, an indulgence for the use of a mitre ornamented with pearls and precious stones, and other insignia to be worn in the absence of the bishop.[11] It was further decreed by Innocent VI. that the prior or sub-prior should not reconcile churches or cemeteries, save during the vacancy of the see or in the absence of the bishop out of England, as the episcopal income was largely dependent on the dues of such reconciliations.[12]

Building was carried on extensively all through the century. In July, 1302, we are told that a great part of the monks' dormitory fell down, the result of negligence, as for a long time it had been in a threatening condition. The drain of constant litigation and appeals that needed backing by the power of the purse seems to have allowed the brethren but scant means to set their house in order. In a letter to the archbishop in

[1] *Worc. Epis. Reg. Giffard* (Worc. Hist. Soc.), p. 529.

[2] Ibid. p. 529.

[3] Ibid. p. 540.

[4] *Ann. Mon.* (Rolls Ser.), iv. 548.

[5] Ibid. pp. 548, 549.

[6] Ibid. p. 550.

[7] Ibid. p. 551.

[8] The style adopted by the prior of Worcester during a vacancy was as follows: *Prior of the cathedral church of Worcester by authority of the Court of Canterbury Official and Administrator of the Spiritualities in the City and Diocese of Worcester, the see being vacant. Reg. Sede Vac.* (Worc. Hist. Soc.), p. 134.

[9] For this purpose £10 was to be subscribed annually by each house, whether engaged at that moment in litigation or not, in order to furnish a common fund at need. *Chart. of St. Peter, Gloucester* (Rolls Ser.), i. 140.

[10] It is stated in reference to John of Evesham, the proudest and most ambitious of a succession of aspiring priors, that in 1365 a mandate was directed by Cardinal Guillermus to the sub-prior of Worcester, that having heard the charges against the prior of crimes such as the violent laying of hands on his brethren, carrying arms, the playing of unlawful games, entering taverns, not paying the salaries of officers, etc., he, the said sub-prior, was empowered to suspend or absolve the prior as he might find suitable. J. Noake, *The Monastery and Cathedral of Worcester*, pp. 101–2.

[11] Wilkins, *Concilia*, iii. 201.

[12] *Cal. of Papal L.* iii. 571.

March, 1302, the prior reminds him of his promise to help the monastery, which at his visitation he found so oppressed by debt that there was scarcely enough food, and pleads for the confirmation of the church of Dodderhill, appropriated to them by the late bishop.[1] It was urged as a reason for the appointment of John de Sancto Germano that the building of the church would be continued by him, and the state of the monks improved with regard to their food and refection.[2] According to the Taxation Roll of 1291, the prior of Worcester held temporalities in the two archdeaconries of Worcester and Gloucester amounting to £196 16*s.*[3] and £6 2*s.*,[4] and spiritualities of the value of £17 12*s.* 8*d.*;[5] he held also temporalities and spiritualities amounting to £34 18*s.* 2*d.*[6] in the diocese of Hereford, and £4 4*s.* in the diocese of Coventry and Lichfield.[7] The prior and convent added largely to their estates during the present century, but owing to their financial condition on its opening, and its economic changes, were nevertheless constantly made to feel the embarrassment of insufficient means. The usual resort was made to appropriation. In the last year of his reign Edward I. appropriated to the convent the church of Lindridge of their advowson for the maintenance of three more monks in their house, and to provide wax lights to burn before the shrine of St. Wulfstan.[8] In 1313 Bishop Reynolds appropriated to them the church of Dodderhill,[9] the brethren in their petition reciting the loss of eight manors and five churches in the time of the wars and by general extortion, combined with the increased drain on hospitality, so many strangers making their way to the town by the bridge over the Severn, whereby they had become so impoverished that without assistance they would be obliged to reduce the number of their monks.[10] During his episcopacy Reynolds appointed a commission to remove the wooden and stone tombs in the cathedral churchyard for the repair of the fabric.[11] Bishop Maidstone appropriated the church of Tibberton to the office of the precentor at his request, showing that his income was insufficient to defray the cost of writing new books and repairing the old, and of keeping a horse and servant for the affairs of the monastery.[12] In 1330 the convent obtained a grant from Edward III. for the appropriation of the church of Overbury with the chapels of Washbourne, Teddington, and 'Berghes' annexed;[13] the grant was confirmed by the pope in 1346 at the prayer of Queen Philippa, reciting that the priory at that time was burdened with debt, the church ruinous, and its manors in need of repair.[14] Bishop Montacute in 1336 granted a licence to the prior and convent to build a new *domuncula*, and renew the cemetery in view of its age.[15] In the same year he restored to the priory the manor of Crowle Siward, originally granted in the reign of Bertulf, the Mercian king, and since lost,[16] and leased to the brethren certain lands within the manor of Kempsey for a term of thirty years, in order to augment the office of the sacristan.[17] To indemnify the bishop for the loss of the manor, the convent agreed to pay him and his successors an annual pension of one mark from the manor of Tibberton,[18] and in return for his 'paternal kindness' made him a participator in all their prayers and religious exercises, placed his name in their martyrology, and ordained the yearly celebration of his anniversary.[19] Bishop Wakefield, in 1389, appropriated the church of Stoke Prior to the use of the chamberlain's office on account of the poverty of its issues.[20]

Besides numerous pensions granted by the convent,[21] frequent demands came from the king for corrodies and grants to his retainers. In October, 1287, Edward I. wrote to the bishop for the exhibition of Alice, a lay sister, *conversa*, and John her son, within the priory.[22] In February, 1301-2, he wrote to the convent, asking for a corrody to be given to the bearer, John le Traior, which was granted.[23] The prior in 1309 presented, as pertained to his office, a corrody called the corrody of King John, to a certain Nicholas atte Zales of Humelton.[24] During the reign of Edward II. Nicholas de Renty was sent

1 *Reg. Sede Vac.* (Worc. Hist. Soc.), p. 44.

2 Ibid. p. 14.

3 *Pope Nich. Tax.* (Rec. Com.), 227b.

4 Ibid. p. 228. 5 Ibid. pp. 216–7, 222–3.

6 Ibid. pp. 163, 165. 7 Ibid. p. 257.

8 Pat. 33 Edw. I. m. 13.

9 Worc. Epis. Reg., Reynolds, f. 96–7. This church granted to the priory shortly before his death by Giffard was seized by the king in consequence of the monks' action in appropriating the tithes without obtaining the royal licence. (*Abbrev. Plac.* (Rec. Com.) 250); the king eventually restored the patronage of the church on payment of a fine. Pat. 33 Edw. I. pt. ii. m. 23.

10 Reg. i. D. and C. f. 72.

11 Worc. Epis. Reg., Reynolds, f. 22.

12 Ibid. Maidstone, f. 23.

13 Pat. 4 Edw. III. pt. i. m. 12.

14 *Cal. of Papal Pet.* i. 121. A condition of its grant was the sending two monks to study at Oxford.

15 Worc. Epis. Reg., Montacute, ii. f. 22. In 1349, during the visitation of the Black Death, Bishop Wulstan de Bransford ordered the dead to be buried in the cemetery of St. Oswald instead of in the cathedral burial ground, on account of the danger arising from the burial of so many there (Ibid. Bransford, i. f. 146). In 1350 orders were given for the consecration of a piece of ground for the cemetery of the Brothers Preachers of Worcester. Ibid. Thoresby, f. 6.

16 Ibid. Montacute, i. f. 29. 17 Ibid. ii. f. 22.

18 Ibid. f. 20. 19 Ibid. 20 Ibid. Wakefield, f. 64.

21 During the vacancy which followed the death of Giffard a corrody was granted to Robert de Humelton, a citizen of Worcester, and Agnes his wife, such as the buyer of the monastery was wont to receive. *Reg. Sede Vac.* (Worc. Hist. Soc.), p. 34.

22 *Worc. Epis. Reg. Giffard* (Worc. Hist. Soc.), p. 315.

23 *Reg. Sede Vac.* (Worc. Hist. Soc.), p. 39.

24 Ibid. 89.

to receive the necessaries of life, together with maintenance for a horse and groom, within the convent for his life.[1] John le Barber was sent in May, 1316, to receive a similar allowance.[2] On the death of Nicholas, the king requested the prior and convent to admit Geoffrey de Caroune on the same terms,[3] and in November, 1320, to allow Peter Dannyles, or Danviliers, to receive such maintenance in their house as James le Barber had had.[4] In 1322 came a request for admittance and life maintenance for Alice Conan, in return for her good services to the queen.[5] The brethren attempted to evade the last imposition, and were summoned in Michaelmas Term, 1323, by the king for neglecting to comply with his request. The prior protested the inability of the convent, owing to the badness of the times, but the reason being considered insufficient the matter was deferred. On the next hearing the prior acknowledged the admission of previous pensioners at the king's request, but stated that the charter of King Edgar, which he produced in court, granted the convent certain indemnities, and that their lands had been given in such a manner that it was not lawful for any bishop or prince to withdraw or invade any of their privileges so long as the Christian faith endured, consequently the prior was quit of all claim for sustenance. Judgment was finally given in the prior's favour, saving the right of the king to imparl therein.[6] The convent appear to have yielded the point as of courtesy, but secured a promise from Edward III. in the first year of his reign that the grant made by them of £10 a year for the maintenance of her damsel at the queen's request should not prejudice them or their successors as a precedent.[7] The priory received requests for aid in connexion with various incidents in the reign of Edward III.[8] In 1335 John Ussher was sent to the priory to receive such maintenance as John le Traior had had at the request of Edward I.[9] The convent obtained a licence from Edward III. in 1332 to acquire four messuages and 8*s.* rent in Worcester, for the maintenance of a chaplain celebrating daily in the Lady Chapel for the souls of the father and mother of William le Orfevre, of Worcester;[10] by another licence in 1334 they acquired land in aid of the daily celebration in the church.[11] Richard II. in the first year of his reign confirmed previous charters granted to the priory; among these was one of Edward III. in 1369, giving leave to the monks to crenellate their priory.[12]

The chapter of Worcester was visited with other religious houses in the diocese by the prior or his commissaries during the not infrequent vacancies which occurred during the fourteenth century; these occasions provided indeed an opportunity for rigorously enforcing all episcopal rights of spiritual jurisdiction.[13] On 3 September, 1303, Bishop Gainsborough sent a notice to the prior and chaplain of his intention to visit their priory.[14] Bishop Maidstone in October, 1313, appointed officials to visit all religious houses in the diocese on account of his own disability.[15] The prior was ordered in May, 1315, to correct and punish the 'excesses' of his fellow monks in the monastery of Worcester lately visited.[16] Bishop Montacute visited the monastery on Monday before the Feast of All Saints, 1333, and preached and received procuration.[17] In a subsequent letter of corrections the bishop made earnest endeavours to reform existing abuses, and, taking different departments in order, laid down various rules for the guidance of each officer. He desired the brethren also to labour quietly for the spiritual welfare of their house, and advised that the younger members should be kept more usefully occupied, and not suffered to wander from the precincts of the cloister except for some special and approved cause. The eating of meat in times and places prohibited by their rule[18] was forbidden, together with the non-observance of fast, and the sowing of discord; the observance of silence, almsgiving, the care of the sick in the infirmary, enjoined. Various officers came under the bishop's mild censure, the sub-prior was admonished not to absent himself from the priory without reasonable cause, the sacristan ordered to restore two cloths sent for St. Wulfstan's shrine by the king, and the vestments bequeathed by Bishop Godfrey to the altar of

1 Close, 8 Edw. II. m. 28d.
2 Ibid. 9 Edw. II. m. 16d.
3 Ibid. 12 Edw. II. m. 31d.
4 Ibid. 14 Edw. II. m. 13d.
5 Ibid. 16 Edw. II. m. 12d.
6 This record and process was inspected later by Edward III. Pat. 11 Edw. III. pt. ii. m. 30.
7 Ibid. 1 Edw. III. pt. ii. m. 4.
8 The marriage of his sister in 1332 (Close, 6 Edw. III. m. 16d), the war in Scotland (Ibid. 7 Edw. III. pt. i. m. 19; 8 Edw. III. m. 5d), and the Breton expedition in 1342 (Ibid. 16 Edw. III. pt. ii. m. 10d).
9 Ibid. 9 Edw. III. m. 25.
10 Pat. 6 Edw. III. pt. ii. m. 5.
11 Pat. 8 Edw. III. pt. ii. m. 27.
12 Ibid. 1 Ric. II. pt. iv. m. 4.
13 At the same time the prior was obliged during the vacancy of 1302 to submit to decrees respecting the management of his own house by the General Chapter of the Benedictine Order. *Reg. Sede Vac.* (Worc. Hist. Soc.), pp. 34, 35.
14 Worc. Epis. Reg. Gainsborough, f. 20.
15 Ibid. Maidstone, f. 18. 16 Ibid. f. 26.
17 Ibid. Montacute, ii. f. 42.
18 Clement VI. granted the monks an indulgence to eat flesh meat from Septuagesima to Quinquagesima, but not in the refectory, and for the rest of the year in the refectory. Deed cited *Hist. MSS. Com. Rep.* xiv. *App.* pt. viii. p. 169. Another indult dated 1289 empowered the prior and chapter to wear caps (pilleis vel almiciis non curiosis) during divine service in cold weather. *Cal. of Papal L.* i. 501.

the Blessed Mary, and to make up his quarrel with William de Incebergh. The brethren were admonished generally to refrain from the company of women, and to let greater kindness and brotherly love dwell among them.[1] Notice of another visitation was sent to the convent 6 November, 1335.[2] Prior Bransford succeeded to the see on the death of Hemenhale, and in the first year of his rule, 1339, signified to the prior and chapter of Worcester his intention of visiting the convent on Thursday after the Feast of St. Denis (October 9), on which day he desired all absent brethren to be recalled.[3] He remained two days at the priory at the expense of the convent.[4] Notice of another visitation was received in October, 1342.[5] The Black Death ravaged the diocese during the short rule of John Thoresby; the bishop did not visit his diocese till 1351, when he was enthroned.[6] In August of that year he warned the convent to prepare for his visitation by summoning all absent members to be present.[7] Visitations were frequently carried out at this time by the bishop's officials. Innocent VI. issued a bull in 1357 for the visitation of the diocese by the bishop or his vices, the latter were not to receive procuration for more than a day.[8] Towards the close of the century the archbishop of Canterbury signified his intention of visiting the city and diocese, for which he had received a special bull from Urban V.[9] He was received on Wednesday, 12 October, 1384, by the bishop, prior, and chapter in solemn procession, and led to the altar, where he read the collect and prayer and celebrated mass. During his stay he was entertained at the palace, and on Thursday preached to the convent on the text 'Descendam et videbo.'[10] On 29 October, at Kempsey, he confirmed the various churches, pensions, and tithes held by the church of Worcester.[11]

The fourteenth century was a period of lawlessness and strife, and its history abounds in instances of brawl and quarrel, robbery and bloodshed profaning even the cathedral, and breaking out within the hallowed precincts of the ancient sanctuary.[12] In 1302 the prior of Worcester ordered the excommunication of the bailiffs of the city, 'men of blood and craft' who had lured and arrested a clerk taking sanctuary in the crypt of the cathedral. Public penance was enjoined on the officials with their servants at the door of the cathedral.[13] Reynolds in August, 1313, ordered the prior of Worcester to reconcile the cemetery from bloodshed,[14] and in the following year Bishop Maidstone excommunicated certain persons who had dragged a fugitive out of sanctuary and appealed to the king to enforce observance of ancient privilege.[15] The cathedral cloister was the scene of an affray in 1318,[16] and in the course of Cobham's rule the monks complained of interference with the pipes conveying their water supply.[17] In July, 1337, an official of the city appeared before the vicar-general to make submission, having incurred sentence of excommunication by distraining on the house of one John atte Green, situated close to the cathedral cemetery and within the church's fee.[18] In 1349 a serious riot took place between the monks and townsmen in which the bailiffs and commonalty 'comming in warlike manner with armes' attacked the church and priory, broke the priory gates, made assault on the prior's servants and beat them, and 'with bows and arrows and other offensive weapons' pursued the prior and the monks and endeavoured to set fire to the monastery.[19] The case was brought up before the justices, who decided that trespasses had been committed against the prior and assessed the damages at £100 12*s.*[20] Thieves broke into the the 'elemosinaria' within the cathedral cemetery in the year 1350, and carried off whatever they could lay hands on.[21] On 27 January 1390–1, Bishop Wakefield reconciled the cathedral from effusion of blood and afterwards absolved those who had taken part in the affray.[22] Henry IV. in the second year of his reign confirmed the ancient grant of sanctuary within the church by

[1] Worc. Epis. Reg. Montacute, ii. f. 42, 43, 44.

[2] Ibid. f. 42. The bishop wrote to the prior and chapter on 10 April, 1335, respecting a visitation of the house by his vice, and the prior's liberty to manumit; the bishop conceded the right as far as custom permitted, and desired other matters to be left to his vice's and the prior's own discretion. Ibid. f. 48.

[3] Ibid. Bransford, i. f. 9d.

[4] Ibid. f. 12.

[5] Ibid. f. 60.

[6] The bishop was diligent in enforcing personal residence on his clergy. Ibid. Thoresby, f. 19d.

[7] Ibid. f. 26.

[8] Ibid. Brian, i. ff. 77, 80d.

[9] Ibid. Wakefield, f. 112.

[10] Ibid. f. 113.

[11] Deed cited *Hist. MSS. Com. Rep.* xiv. *App.* pt. viii. p. 168.

[12] The church of Worcester possessed the very fullest privileges of sanctuary from its earliest period. Its boundaries were declared on 21 May, 1460, during the prelacy of Carpenter. Starting from the door of the north entrance of the cathedral near to the Carnarie and including the churchyard, they extended to the great gate of the priory, thence to the stone wall bounding the Severn, and from the Severn reached to the Carnarie, again including it as far as the door of the church and dividing the palace from the churchyard. Ledger i. D. and C. f. 35, and see Habington, *Surv. of Worc.* (Worc. Hist. Soc.), ii. 387–9.

[13] *Reg. Sede Vac.* (Worc. Hist. Soc.), p. 36; *Ann. Mon.* (Rolls Ser.), iv. 554.

[14] Worc. Epis. Reg. Reynolds, f. 91.

[15] Ibid. Maidstone, ff. 3, 4.

[16] Ibid. Cobham, f. 11d.

[17] Ibid. f. 115.

[18] Ibid. Hemenhale, f. 10.

[19] Habington, *Surv. of Worc.* (Worc. Hist. Soc.), ii. 390–1.

[20] Ibid.

[21] Worc. Epis. Reg. Thoresby, f. 10.

[22] Ibid. Wakefield, f. 76.

which it was ordained that no 'bailiffs, sergeants, minister, or other person of the city of Worcester shall hereafter carry or bear any mace or maces but only in the presence of the king or his children within the churchyard, priory, and sanctuary of Worcester, nor intermeddle within the aforesaid liberties.' [1] An indenture, dated in the time of Bishop Carpenter, between the prior and convent of the cathedral church of Worcester and the bailiffs and commonalty of Worcester gave licence to the said bailiffs and their successors 'for their worship and honour' to have their maces borne before them by their sergeants in the church or cemetery and in the parish of St. John.' [2] During the rule of Prior John Fordham the convent obtained from the bailiffs of Worcester the privilege of conveying water from the city conduits to their own precincts, on condition that for this grant they and their successors should present annually to the bailiffs and their successors a red rose at the feast of St. John Baptist.[3] A lengthy agreement was arrived at in 1509, during the rule of John Weddersbury, respecting the lead pipes which conveyed water from a spring at Henwick Hill to the monastery [4] by which the convent agreed to mend the pipes whenever broken within seven days. The city authorities and the monastery agreed that if in future either party should have a grievance, four monks and four citizens should have 'loving meetings and communications before anything be attempted at lawe.' [5]

According to the number of the brethren assembled for the election of Bishop Clifford in 1401 the chapter at that time numbered forty-four; there was a third and fourth prior as well as prior and sub-prior.[6] The number appears to have dwindled to forty in 1419, [7] but forty-five brethren and monks assembled in chapter for the election of Thomas Bourchier in 1433.[8] The brethren engaged in a dispute in the early part of the century with the scholars of Queen's College, Oxford, respecting the non-payment of a pension due for the church of Newbold Pacy during a vacancy.[9] In 1432 they came to an amicable agreement with the Hospital of St. Wulfstan, Worcester, as to the provision of a chaplain for the chapel of Claines within the parish of Bromsgrove.[10] An indenture dated 1412, and another in 1460, between the two monasteries of Malmesbury and Worcester transferred to the use of the latter certain chambers at Gloucester College, Oxford, for the convenience of their monks studying there.[11]

In 1437, in consequence of the long continuance of disastrous rains and the threatened failure of crops, the prior and convent were ordered to cause the shrine of St. Oswald to be carried about in solemn procession 'as we byn enformed that hyt hath byn afore this time for cessyng of such continual reyne.'[12]

The prior and chapter received various requests for aid during the wars of the Roses. Henry VI. in 1458 asked for an allowance to be restored to Richard Hertlebure, brother of a former prior, who had been grievously wounded 'in our warres beyond sea,' and reduced to poverty.[13] In 1459 he acknowledged the loan of a hundred marks to aid him against the rebels.[14] Edward IV. wrote to the prior of Worcester in the second year of his reign asking for a benevolence to be raised in order to meet the invasion of 'oure grete Adversary Henre namyng hymselfe Kyng of England by the malicious counseille and excitation of Magarete his wife namyng her selfe Quene of England.' Instructions were given to assemble the brethren with all other persons, householders, and inhabitants within the precincts of the age of sixteen and upwards and to read these letters and inscribe their names in a book.[15] The convent obtained a pardon for divers transgressions from Henry VII. in the first year of his reign, 1485–6.[16]

The visitations of the monastery during the fifteenth century throw little light on its condition. In April, 1429, Bishop Polton commissioned his official to finish the visitation of the priory, being himself hindered,[17] and in June, 1432, Parliament then claiming him, ordered the master of St. Wulfstan's Hospital, Walter London, his

[1] Pat. 2 Hen. IV. pt. i. m. 16. This grant confirmed by Henry VI. had the further privilege added to it 'that no sheriff, escheator, coroner, constable, etc., shall arrest any man for any cause whatsoever (treason against the king's person only excepted) within the churchyard and precincts of the monastery.'

[2] Reg. i. D. and C. f. 86b.

[3] Habington, *Surv. of Worc.* (Worc. Hist. Soc.), ii. 401.

[4] The convent received a licence from Henry VI. to carry a conduit over Severn bridge to convey the water from Henwick. *Hist. MSS. Com. Rep.* xiv. *App.* pt. viii. 193.

[5] Habington, *Surv. of Worc.* (Worc. Hist. Soc.). In 1406 the pope ordered the abbot of Pershore to enforce by ecclesiastical censure the observance of the ancient custom now held in abeyance by bold despisers, whereby after the ringing of the curfew in the cathedral church, and before the ringing of prime in the morning, no other bell in any other church or chapel in the city should be rung to the injury and disturbance of the prior and chapter. *Cal. of Papal L.* vi. 79.

[6] *Reg. Sede Vac.* (Worc. Hist. Soc.), p. 373.

[7] Ibid. p. 405.

[8] Ibid. p. 431–2.

[9] Ibid. p. 386.

[10] Worc. Epis. Reg. Polton, f. 134.

[11] Reg. D. and C. xii. f. 138, cited *Hist. MSS. Com. Rep.* xiv. *App.* pt. viii. p. 182.

[12] J. Noake, *The Monastery and Cathedral of Worc.* p. 116.

[13] *Diocesan Hist. of Worc.*, p. 125.

[14] Ibid.

[15] Reg. i. D. and C. f. 22.

[16] Deed cited *Hist. MSS. Com. Rep.* xiv. *App.* pt. viii. p. 199.

[17] Worc. Epis. Reg. Polton, f. 62.

commissioner-general, to visit the prior and chapter.[1] During the vigorous rule of Carpenter the convent was twice visited. On the first occasion the bishop arrived 22 September, 1461, at the priory, where he was received by the sub-prior, the prior being ill,[2] and the convent with great state and entertained with his household for two days; his visitation sermon was preached by the sacristan.[3] On the next occasion, in October, 1466, he remained three days and 'reformed' the church and brethren, preaching himself from the text 'Fili quare fecisti nobis sic.' In his register is enrolled a copy of ordinances for the cellarer previously confirmed by Bishop Bourchier in 1443.[4] The bishop in his zeal for the spread of learning added to the cathedral library which was in the charnel-house, and in 1458 endowed it with £10 a year for the support of a chaplain who should be a Bachelor in Theology and act as librarian.[5] Bishop Alcock issued a special mandate in December, 1481, for the visitation of the priory, which was carried out on 8 January following by his commissary, all the brethren being present save those studying at Oxford.[6] In 1480 during his rule there was a bold robbery in the Lady Chapel; the bishop issued a mandate that all gold, silver, rings, jewels, drapery on the image of the Virgin Mary which had been removed should be restored within fifteen days.[7] The visit of his successor, Robert Morton, in 1488 is described in the register of his acts; he arrived at Worcester, Friday, 19 September, and was received at the gate of the city 'called the Forgate' by the clergy, aldermen, and bailiffs. The prior and convent according to precedent met him in procession in the middle of the cemetery and escorted him into the cathedral up to the high altar, where he bestowed on the prior Robert Multon and on the brethren the kiss of peace. The following day he preached to the brethren from the text 'Vide et visite vineam istam' and exhorted them to continue in the worship of God and in the observance of their sacred religion.[8]

From the brief notices of the formal visitations made by the vicars-general of the Italian bishops who followed, little information can be gathered. Thomas Wodyngton commenced a tour of the diocese in 1497, and visited the prior and chapter on Monday, 7 May, of that year;[9] as vicar-general for Silvester de Gigliis he visited here again on 19 June, 1500.[10] Thomas Alcock visited on 19 June, 1503,[11] Master Thomas Hannibil came to visit on 25 April, 1512, and again on 14 April, 1516; on both occasions he received procuration for three days.[12] In 1506 during the rule of Mildenham a dispute was referred to the bishop as to the right of his chancellor to any allotted seat or 'place of dewty' in the cathedral. Silvester de Gigliis in a temperate letter signed 'Gilbert' made reply that he was informed by credible persons that the chancellor should sit next the prior and that the prior should not usurp the bishop's place, but sit with his brethren 'after ye old custom,' which advice he deemed best until he could come himself or depute the matter to be examined indifferently.[13]

A vivid description is given by Leland of the burial of the young prince Arthur in the cathedral church in 1502.[14] The body of the prince, who died on 2 April, was removed from the castle of Ludlow on St. George's Day and conveyed to the parish church, whence the procession set out for Worcester, where it was met at the city gate by the 'bayliffs and the honest men of the cittie on foot' and in the churchyard by the abbots of Gloucester, Evesham, Chester, Shrewsbury, Tewkesbury, Hales, and Bordesley, and the prior, of Worcester, the bishop not being present. At *Dirige* there were nine lessons, of which the first was read by the abbot of Tewkesbury and the sixth by the prior of Worcester. The embroidered coat of arms, the sword, shield, and crested helmet of the prince were conveyed up the choir with the earl of Kildare's son wearing the armour of the dead prince and mounted on his charger, the abbot of Tewkesbury as gospeller receiving the offering of the horse. At the conclusion of the great ceremony the corpse was borne to the grave at the south end of the high altar of the cathedral. It is said that no offerings were allowed to be made by those of the city on account of the sickness or pestilence that then raged there.[15]

[1] Worc. Epis. Reg. Polton, f. 131. Notices of impending visitations were served on the cathedral chapter 28 September, 1428, and 30 March, 1433. Ibid. ff. 47d. and 127d.

[2] Thomas Musard seems to have suffered constant ill-health; he was laid up during the bishop's next visit.

[3] Worc. Epis. Reg. Carpenter, i. f. 168d.

[4] Ibid. ii. f. 126.

[5] He should also celebrate mass in the chapel and read a moral lecture from the Old or New Testament once or twice a week, and preach in the cathedral or at the churchyard cross every Friday at the bishop's discretion. Ibid. f. 175.

[6] Ibid. Alcock, f. 98.

[7] Ibid. f. 64.

[8] Ibid. Morton, f. 32.

[9] Ibid. John de Gigliis, f. 9.

[10] Ibid. Silvester de Gigliis, f. 175.

[11] Ibid. f. 185.

[12] Ibid. ff. 94, 123.

[13] J. Noake, *The Monastery and Cathedral of Worc.* 127. This reads like the revival of an old controversy. In an MS. cited by J. Noake (p. 94) we read that 'after ye mitre was procured by Johannes de Evesham and ye prior of Worcester became lord prior, in some triennial visitation of the bishop of Worcester ye bishop's chancellor sate him down in ye prior's seat in ye quire, and ye prior was fain to take ye next stall, which was much stomached by ye lord prior and great complaints made even to Rome.'

[14] Leland, *Collect.* v. 374-381.

[15] Ibid.

We read that a corrody in the priory of Worcester was granted in reversion to William Gowre, groom of the chamber, by Henry VIII. in the year 1513.[1] George Heynes, groom of the buttery, was granted it on its next vacancy in 1532.[2] In 1522 Arthur Purde, student at Oxford, obtained at the suit of his father the pension which the bishop elect was bound to give to a clerk of the king's nomination.[3] The journal left by Prior William Moore who succeeded to the rule of the house in 1518, on the death of John Weddesbury, gives a very fair idea of the mode of life of the head of a great religious house at that time. It exhibits the prior in the pleasant light of a hospitable magnate entertaining the gentry of the county, and as a kindly, easy-going man who did not forget the ties of blood or neglect the claims of dependents. It shows him travelling about, for comparatively little of his time was spent at Worcester. It gives details as to the entertainment provided when he received distinguished visitors, among whom was the Princess Mary, taking a share in humbler festivities and family rejoicings withal, and bestowing gifts on his father, mother, and other relations. There are allusions to the sports and amusements of the day, otter hunting, the visits of players, minstrels, and jugglers, the feasting of the citizens and their wives, entries occasionally interrupted by pious ejaculations and versifications on the part of the writer. The prior was also a man of refined taste, and bought books, furniture, 'peynted cloths'; there is an entry for stained glass windows. He is entered as a justice of the peace in 1531 and the following year.[4] But the luxury, ostentation, and show that may be natural to a man of no spiritual profession consorts ill with the ideal of one who has embraced that state implying poverty and renunciation. In the frequent absence of the head at his many manor residences the government of the house largely devolved into the hands of the sub-prior, and its condition furnishes the reverse side of this picture of easy-going, kindly existence, which is not as attractive. The officers were at variance and the convent split up into two parties, the one headed by the sub-prior, Dr. Neckam, opposed to the prior and resenting his open-handed liberality with consequent financial difficulties, the other favourable to a head whose pleasant qualities made him universally popular. In 1528 we are told that 'the cellarer intends to ask Wolsey for the office of sacrist and expel the present holder, who,' the writer continues, 'had it of the gift of Wolsey and has exercised it with much modesty.'[5] In 1534 the prior, sub-prior, almoner, and cellarer with thirty-seven other brethren subscribed to the oath of the royal supremacy, denying the authority of the pope in England,[6] and at the beginning of the following year received a visit from Archbishop Cranmer. His 'iniuncciones et provisiones' for the order and discipline of the convent dated 22 February, 1534-5, relate to the reading of the Bible and its exposition in English, the use of the common seal, the need of making an inventory of the movable goods of the monastery, the provision of properly cooked food, and the general conduct of the officers of the house.[7] On the occasion of Dr. Leigh's visit here on the king's commission at the end of July, 1535,[8] the smouldering embers of discord burst into a flame. John Musard, a monk, took the opportunity to bring an accusation of treason against one Richard Clyve, and to prefer a charge against the prior of deposing two discreet men, Dr. Neckam from the office of sub-prior without any alleged lawful cause, and William Fordham from the cellarer's office 'for standing unto the right of the house.' He also complained that 'he and several others of the convent' had been oppressed for sixteen years and several times confined in the bishop's prison 'simply for telling the truth,' and that he was imprisoned on 2 March by a party in the convent for appealing to 'my lord of Canterbury's' visitation.[9] Two of the monks were already lying under a charge of using 'seditious words' and 'unfitting' demeanour,[10] and the house was divided on the question of the merits of the former and present cellarer. William Fordham writes to Cromwell immediately after Leigh's visitation stating that the 'saddest' men of the convent desire that he shall be reinstated;[11] on the other hand a petition was addressed to Cromwell on the part of the sub-prior and twenty-five of the brethren praying that he will retain their present cellarer Thomas Sudbury in his office, and stating it as their experience that 'Sudbury has been a good husband to the profit of the monastery,' while Fordham they describe as 'a troublesome person who has put our house to great expense and vexation.'[12] The possibility of the prior's resignation as a result of the allegations brought against him was early expected. On 15 August, 1536, the archbishop writing to Cromwell prays him on the vacancy of the house 'to be good to Mr. Holbech, D.D., of the house of Crowland, or to Dan Richard Gorton, B.D., of the house of Burton-on-Trent.'[13] On 19 October we read that Neckam 'has got the rule of the priory' for the time being, and that 'he and his brethren are still troubled by the cellarer.'[14] The disgraced prior meanwhile

[1] *L. and P. Hen. VIII.* i. 5384.
[2] Ibid. v. 1499 (18).
[3] Ibid. iii. 2862 (6).
[4] Ibid. v. 166 (46) and p. 706.
[5] Ibid. iv. pt. ii. 4589

[6] P.R.O. Acknowl. of Supremacy, No. 122.
[7] Ledger ii. D. and C. f. 187. An inventory of the goods of the priory is given under date 7 September, 1535. *L. and P. Hen. VIII.* ix. 297.
[8] Ibid. 5.
[9] Ibid. 52.
[10] Ibid. 108.
[11] Ibid. 6.
[12] Ibid. 653.
[13] Ibid. 97.
[14] Ibid. 639.

retired or was banished to Gloucester, whither the kindness of his friends followed him.'[1]

The Valor of 1535 gives the priory an income of £1,386 9*s.* 8¾*d.*, a not unconsiderable return; nevertheless, John Musard, writing from his prison 'this cold winter,' to which he had been condemned 'in consequence of the complaints of false conspirators to your under visitors,' says 'your Lordship's farmary (infirmary) is down, your kitchen is down, your cloister had been down before this time if Mr. Doctor, your officer,[2] had not underset him with timber, your ostry and brewery ready to fall with much more that 1,000 marks will not repair.' He proceeds to lay the cause of 'the decays of your honourable Lordship's monastery' against the prior and his reckless hospitality, ostentation and love of display. 'Our untrue master,' he continues, 'kept great hospitality upon our chancellor and bishop's officers . . . with great fees and rewards, for he has been most of his time at law with gentlemen, the convent, and tenants, on account of the affection he has to his kindred and servants. He gives to them the alms the monastery is bound to give in our prince's name to fourteen poor people, viz., 16 bushels of corn each a year, and they hold the greatest farms and profits belonging to the monastery. There are three goodly mitres and staves in the cathedral, but he has sold plate to the value of £80 to buy a new mitre and staff. . . . He has as servants 4 gentlemen, 10 yeomen, and 10 grooms, of whose wages the convent officers pay much. Besides these, 10 yeomen belonging to the convent go in his livery for whom he is not charged. Even this number would not satisfy him, but he has gentlemen waiters[3] as well, and has increased their wages, diminishing the portion of the convent. I wish you knew of the poor service the convent has on fish days.'[4]

The writer describes the failure of his efforts to obtain a hearing at visitations within the last sixteen years and their result—'pore Musard to prison for telling truth,' and begs Cromwell to remove him to Westminster. There is a reference in the prior's journal under the year 1531 to John Musard which rather upsets the idea he evidently desired should be entertained of him: a reward to the beadle and others for 'fetching and conveying Dan John Musard home from Overbury after he robbed his master of certain plate and other things';[5] it explains the reason why his complaints were lightly treated by Dr. Leigh and other visitors, as is evidently the case. William Moore's resignation must be dated between 11 February, 1535–6, when he came over to Worcester from Gloucester, according to the account given by Neckam, and applied for the use of a horse and money to go and see Cromwell,[6] probably with a view of coming to terms as to his retiring pension,[7] and the 7 March following, when the sub-prior and convent received a licence to elect, *vice* William Moore, resigned.[8] On the 13 March they made choice of Henry Holbech, S.T.P., monk of Crowland, and prior of the black monks studying at Cambridge,[9] and his election was confirmed by Henry VIII. on 22 March, 1535–6.

Little is recorded of the rule of the last prior. In November, 1536, he sent Cromwell, 'as a remembrance of his duty,' an annuity of twenty nobles from the manor of Alvestone.[10] Bishop Latimer visited the priory in 1537, and left injunctions reproving the neglect of the king's ordinances for the suppression of idolatry and superstition, desiring that in future they should be observed, and that the prior should have a whole Bible in English to be fast chained in some open place either in the church or cloister, and that each religious person should have at least a New Testament in English by Christmas next. He also laid down rules that all singing and other ceremonies should be laid aside during the preaching time, and that a lecture in English should be read every day except holidays.[11] A report is given under date of 27 August, 1537, of the examination of malcontents against the stripping of the ornaments and jewels of the image of the Virgin Mary in the Lady Chapel.[12] The following year the prior was appointed bishop suffragan of Bristol;[13] after the suppression

1 The personal popularity of prior Moore comes out strongly in his disgrace. The bishop of Coventry and Lichfield, advising caution in dealing with the charges laid against him and his house, says 'the party is a great possessioner, and at assizes the gentry of the county have been familiarly entertained by him.' (Ibid. 510.) Lady Margery Sandys pleading for him to Cromwell says he 'is a true monk to God and the king,' and adds a little spitefully, 'his accuser, Dr. Neckam, is very well known.' (Ibid. 656.) Bishop Latimer while doubting the advisability of restoring him, shows evidence of kindly feeling for the 'simple' man. *L. and P. Hen. VIII.* x. 56.

2 Neckam.

3 In a ledger of the church of Worcester is contained an entry relating to the appointment in 1472 of John Salwey, gentleman, to the office of 'gentylmankervery,' Ledger i. f. 74b.

4 *L. and P. Hen. VIII.* x. 216.

5 J. Noake, *The Monastery and Cathedral of Worc.* 202.

6 *L. and P. Hen. VIII.* x. 311.

7 The terms on which he retired were extremely favourable; he obtained apartments within the monastery for himself and his servants, with fuel, household implements and necessaries, silver, plate, etc., as well as the use of the manor house at Crowle and a sum of money.

8 Ibid. 597 (8).

9 Ibid. 597 (8).

10 Ibid. xi. 1198. In the same year the priory was charged with having suppressed the hospital of Dodderhill and the priory of Bromsgrove, without licence of the king, and of converting the profits to their own use. Ibid. 1429.

11 Ibid. xii. 842.

12 Ibid. 587.

13 Ibid. xiii. pt. i. 646 (2).

of the house, 18 January, 1539-40,[1] he was reappointed as first dean of the cathedral church on its newly-constituted basis, according to the charter of foundation of Henry VIII., dated 24 January, 1541–2.

Priors of Worcester [2]

Wynsin or Wynsius or Winsige, 971, died before 992.[3]
Ethelstan, circa 992.[4]
Ethelsinus.[5]
Ethelsinus II.[6]
Godwin.[7]
Ethelwin or Agelwin.[8]
St. Wulfstan, before 1057,[9] made bishop of Worcester 1062.
Elfstan, 1062.[10]
Egelred,[11] circa 1088.
Thomas,[12] circa 1089; died 1113.
Nicholas,[13] died 1124.
Gwarin or Warin,[14] circa 1130.
Ralph,[15] died 1143.
David,[16] succeeded 1143, deposed 1145.
Osbert or Osbern,[17] succeeded 1145; died the same year.

1 *L. and P. Hen. VIII.* xv. 81. Pensions were assigned to the following 'divers superfluous persons late religious' in the monastery of Worcester, 'now despatched out of the same,' Thomas Sudbury and William Lemster £6 13*s.* 4*d.* each, Richard Calamon and nine others £6 each (ibid.). To Henry Holbech, D.D., bishop suffragan of Bristol, now guardian of the late altered monastery of Worcester, was assigned £266 13*s.* 4*d.* pension with £8 13*s.* 4*d.* for commons, and nine servants £31 4*s.* Total, £306 10*s.* 8*d.* Ibid. 867.

2 Up to the Conquest the heads of the cathedral chapter were known as 'prior,' 'præpositus,' 'primus' and 'decanus.'

3 After serving a probation of three years at Ramsey, he was made dean in 971. Wharton, *Angl. Sacr.* i. 546.

4 He is said to have succeeded before Oswald's death in that year. Ibid.

5 He is said to have died on 7 July, but the year is not given. Ibid.

6 His death is given on 4 December. Ibid. He may be identified with Egelsius, dean in the time of King Ethelred, of whom he purchased for his church the town of Swinford in Staffordshire. Heming, *Chartul.* (Hearne ed.), i. 547.

7 *Angl. Sacr.* i. 547.

8 Ibid.

9 Duke Leofric and his wife Godiva are said to have restored Blackwell to the church when Wulfstan was prior. Leofric died 31 August, 1057. Heming, *Chartul.* (Hearne ed.), ii. 517.

10 He was brother to St. Wulfstan, and succeeded on his promotion to the bishopric. *Angl. Sacr.* i. 547.

11 He had been sub-prior and chanter in the church of Canterbury, and was by St. Wulfstan preferred to the priorship. Ibid. ii. 212.

12 He was prior when St. Wulfstan dedicated the new cathedral. Heming, *Chartul.* (Hearne ed.), ii. 420; *Angl. Sacr.* i. 548.

13 Ibid.

14 Ibid.

15 Ibid.

16 Ibid.; *Ann. Mon.* (Rolls Ser.), i. 46.

17 Ibid.

Ralph de Bedford,[18] succeeded 1146; died 1189.
Senatus,[19] resigned 1196.
Peter,[20] 1196, deposed 1203.
Ralph de Evesham,[21] 1203, made abbot of Evesham 1214.
Silvester de Evesham,[22] 1214, made bishop of Worcester 1216.
Simon,[23] 1216, deposed 1222.
William Norman,[24] 1222, resigned 1224.
William de Bedford,[25] 1224, died 1242.
Richard de Condicote,[26] 1242, died 1252.
Thomas,[27] 1252, died 1260.
Richard de Dumbelton,[28] 1260, died 1272.
William de Cirencester,[29] 1262, died 1274.
Richard de Feckenham,[30] 1274, died 1286.
Philip de Aubyn,[31] 1286, died 1296.
Simon de Wyre,[32] 1296, resigned 1301.
John de Wyke,[33] 1301, died 1317.
Wulstan de Bransford,[34] 1317, made bishop of Worcester 1339.
Simon de Botiler, 1339, died the same year.
Simon Crompe, 1339, died 1340.
John de Evesham, 1340, died 1370.
Walter de Leigh, 1370, died 1388.
John Green, 1388, died 1395.
John de Malvern, 1395, died 1423.
John de Fordham, 1423, died 1438.
Thomas Ledbury, 1438, died 1443–4.
John Hertelbury, 1444, died 1445.
Thomas Musard, 1445, died 1469.
Robert Multon, 1469, died 1492.
William Wenloke, 1492, died 1499.
Thomas Mildenham, 1499, died 1507.
John Weddesbury, 1507, died 1518.
William Moore, 1518, resigned 1536.
Henry Holbech, 1536, surrendered 1539–40.

Deans of Worcester [35]

Henry Holbech (last prior), 1541–2.
John Barlow, 1544.
Philip Hawford, *alias* Ballard, last abbot of Evesham, 1553–4.

18 *Angl. Sacr.* i. 548; *Ann. Mon.* (Rolls Ser.), iv. 386.

19 Ibid. 386, 8.

20 Ibid. 389, 392.

21 Ibid. 392, 402, 3.

22 Ibid. 403, 405.

23 Ibid. 407, 415.

24 He was put in by the bishop against the wishes of the monks. Ibid. 415; *Reg. of Blessed Mary of Worc.* (Hale ed.), p. 28.

25 *Ann. Mon.* (Rolls Ser.), iv. 417, 434.

26 Ibid. 434, 441.

27 Ibid. 441, 446.

28 Ibid. 446, 462.

29 Ibid. 462, 466.

30 Ibid. 467, 492, 493.

31 Ibid. 493, 527.

32 Ibid. 527, 550.

33 Ibid. 550; *Angl. Sacr.* i. 549.

34 Ibid. The rest of the priors will be found in this list, pp. 549–50.

35 The deans of Worcester up to 1845 are taken from Le Neve's *Fasti Ecclesiæ Anglic.* iii. 70, corrected by T. Duffus Hardy.

Seth Holland, 1557.
John Pedder, 1559–60.
Thomas Wilson, 1571.
Francis Willis, 1586–7.
Richard Eedes, 1597.
James Montague, 1604.
Arthur Lane, 1608.
Joseph Hall, 1616.
William Juxon, 1627–8.
Roger Mainwaring, 1633.
Christopher Potter, 1635–6.
Richard Holdsworth, nominated by the king 1646 but never installed. Vacancy 11 years.
John Oliver, 1660.
Thomas Warmestry, 1661.
William Thomas, 1665.
George Hickes, 1683.
William Talbot, 1691.
Francis Hare, 1715.
James Stillingfleet, 1726.
Edmund Marten, 1746.
John Waugh, 1751.
Sir Richard Wrottesley, 1765.
William Digby, 1769.
Hon. St. Andrew St. John, 1783.
Arthur Onslow, 1795.
John Banks Jenkinson, 1818.
James Hook, 1825.
George Murray, 1828.
John Peel, 1845.
Hon. Grantham Munton Yorke, 1874.
Lord Alwyne Compton, 1879.
John Gott, 1886.
Robert William Forrest, 1891.

The description of the pointed oval seal of the eleventh century is taken from a cast at the British Museum.[1] The obverse represents the Virgin crowned, seated on a throne, her feet on an ornamental corbel with the Child in her arms, in her right hand a fleur-de-lis. Legend :—

+ SIGILLVM SČE DEI GENIT[RIC]IS MA[RIE] WIGORNEN[S]IS ECL'E

Reverse : A small oval counterseal representing a woman pouring out a libation to a deity, from a fine antique gem. There is a mark of the handle of the seal. Legend :—

+ HABVNDANS CAVTELA · Ñ · NOCET.

The C is square in 'cautela' and 'nocet.'

A round fifteenth-century seal, red, is attached to the deed acknowledging the king's supremacy.[2] The obverse represents the Virgin crowned, seated on a throne in a carved niche, with elaborate canopy of five cusped arches, holding the Child who is standing on the seat, in the left hand a sceptre. Overhead, in a small niche of similar design, the Trinity. On either side in a small niche an angel, full length, swinging a censer. Outside these niches, on either side, a tree on a mount with a shield of arms slung upon the branches, the left defaced but perhaps the royal arms of England, the right ten torteaux in pile, the arms of the see of Worcester. In base an arcading. Legend :—

SIGILL ' : COM . . . . BEATE : DEI : GENITRICIS : MARIE : WYGORNIE

Reverse : Two carved niches with Gothic canopies, containing on the left St. Oswald with crosier, on the right St. Wulfstan with pastoral staff; each lifting up the right hand in benediction. Over the canopies three small niches containing the coronation of the Virgin between two angels swinging censers. At either side a niche, canopied, containing a kneeling ecclesiastic, with a similar kneeling figure over each canopy. Legend :—

OSWALDVS : PATRES : ꝫ : WLSTANUS : MONACHOR . SERVANT : HOS . . . . . A : REORŪ.

The description of the later seal for the new foundation, 1542, is taken from casts at the British Museum.[3] The impression is chipped, but represents on the obverse the Nativity. In the field are two scrolls inscribed *Gloria in Excelsis* and *Natus est Nobis*. In base a carved shield bearing the arms of the see. Legend :—

+ SIGILLV̄ · DECANI · ET · CAPITVLI [C]ATHEDRALIS · WIGORN . . . AN . 154 . .

The reverse represents Henry VIII. in robes of majesty, seated on a carved canopied throne, on either side a number of ecclesiastics, over them two labels inscribed : *Vivat Rex*. Above the canopy St. Peter, half length, with nimbus, holding a key in the left hand ; in his right hand a label inscribed : *Non* . . . . . Legend :—

QVI + PROVOC . . . + REGEM + PECCAT + IN + ANI . . . . VERBES + 20 +.

2. THE ABBEY OF EVESHAM

No monastery has a more picturesque foundation story than the Benedictine abbey of Evesham. The saintly bishop of Worcester who founded the abbey was the type of man round whom monastic chroniclers loved to weave a halo of miracle and legend. Much of the story of the foundation of Evesham is doubtless the invention of the eleventh and twelfth centuries, yet in the foundation charter of St. Egwin, which Prior Dominic in the chronicle of Evesham claimed to be a transcript 'pœne verbum ex verbo' from the original, the bishop himself is made to introduce the legend concerning the iron fetters with which he had bound his feet, and the key of which he had thrown into the Avon, and found in Rome

[1] Brit. Mus. xxxix. 32.

[2] P. R. O. Acknowl. of Supremacy, No. 122.

[3] Brit. Mus. lviii. 79, 80.

Evesham Abbey. Evesham Abbey.

Pershore Abbey.

Evesham Abbey. Westwood Priory. Evesham Abbey.

Worcester Monastic Seals.—Plate II.

To face page **112.**

in the body of a fish.[1] On his return from Rome he obtained from Ethelred the place called Hethomme (Evesham), where he had cast the key into the Avon, and urged by a vision of the Virgin, who appeared on that spot first to his herdsman Eoves and then to himself, founded a monastery there.[2] According to William of Malmesbury there was already on the spot, among thorns and undergrowth, an ancient church, where Bishop Egwin frequently prayed even before the vision.[3]

The endowment of the new foundation began with Ethelred's grant of Evesham in 701, followed in 703 by a further grant of the fort of Chadbury, lands in Stratford, and the 'old monastery' of Fladbury.[4] The last of these Egwin exchanged with Ethelhard, sub-regulus of the Wicii, for land in Stratford which he had 'unjustly occupied.'[5] In 709 grants came from Kenred, king of Mercia, and Offa, king of Essex, of eighty-four manses round Evesham on the banks of the Avon,[6] and Egwin himself purchased twenty manses in Twiford from Osward the brother of Ethelred.[7] Also Ethelricus, son of King Osher, gave eight manses, and Walter the priest another eight, and altogether by 714 the endowment of the monastery was one hundred and twenty manses.[8] These were at Evesham, Bengeworth, Hampton, Lenchwick, Abbots Morton, Offenham, the two Littletons, Badsey, Worcester, Honeybourne, Bretforton, Ombersley,[9] Oldberrow, and Mathun (Worcester), Salford, Sandburne, Kinwarton, Willey, Mapleborough (Warwick), Willersey, Burton, Maugersbury, Aldestrop, Great Swell, Child's Wickham (Gloucester).[10] Letters from Pope Constantine in 709 and in 713 are supposed to have confirmed the privileges and endowment of the monastery, but these are clearly spurious.[11] In 710 another benefactor, Ceolred of Mercia, is said to have granted land at Ragley, Arrow, Exhall, Wigginshill, Atherstone, Dorsington, Broom, Milcote, Grafton, Hillborough, Bidford, and Binton,[12] but the charter is evidently spurious, as are the supposed grants of Ethelbald of Mercia in 716 and 717.[13]

From the death of St. Egwin, who had resigned his see and become abbot of his new foundation in 710,[14] the history of the monastery is almost a blank until the time of King Edgar. Endowments naturally became less frequent, and the charters purporting to be grants from Offa of Mercia[15] and Beorhtulf king of Mercia[16] are in themselves spurious even if they represent actual grants. But although the possessions of the abbey did not increase, the eighteen abbots who followed Egwin between the years 717 and 940 'kept the possessions entire as they had been at Egwin's death.[17] On the death of Egwin, the last of these, a prince of the Wiccii named Alchelm received a grant of the abbey from Edmund the son of Edward the Elder, and drove away the monks, installing secular canons in their stead.[18] After his death in 946, Wulfric and Oswulf bishop of Ramsbury were among those who encroached on the territories of the

[1] *Chron. de Evesham* (Rolls Ser.), 7, 18. Another version of this story is given by William of Malmesbury, *Gesta Pontif.* (Rolls Ser.), 297. Here the fish is said to have leapt on board the ship on St. Egwin's return journey from Rome.

[2] *Chron. de Evesham* (Rolls. Ser.), 18.

[3] Will. Malmes. *Gesta Pontif.* (Rolls Ser.), 296, 297.

[4] *Chron. de Evesham* (Rolls Ser.), 18, 71.

[5] Ibid. 18. In the anonymous *Life of Egwin* of the tenth or eleventh century Egwin is said to have begged the monastery of Fladbury from the king, and given it to Ethelheard, 'qui mihi alium benigno corde concessit cœnobium quod Stratford noncupatur' (Cotton MS. Nero E. I. fol. 27).

[6] Ibid. Egwin's foundation charter gives the number granted as eighty-four. Another manuscript which claims to give Egwin's statement concerning the lands of Evesham gives the same number (Harl. MS. 358, f. 51b). The extant charter of 709, which is in all probability a forgery of the twelfth century, gives the number as sixty-seven manses, but only enumerates sixty-five (Cotton MS. Vespas. B. xxiv. fol. 68).

[7] Ibid.

[8] Ibid.; Harl. MS. 358, f. 51b.

[9] The charter of Ethelweard granting twelve cassates in Ombersley to Evesham in 706 appears to be the only genuine early charter relating to the endowment of the abbey; Haddan and Stubbs, *Councils*, iii. 278.

[10] Harl. MS. 358, f. 51d.

[11] Cotton MS. Vespas. B. xxiv. ff. 76, 76d. One point that tells against the authenticity of this letter of Pope Constantine lies in the words 'call a council of the whole country of England, being kings, bishops, and religious orders, together with the peers and the nobility.' This would be hardly possible in the early eighth century. William of Malmesbury doubts the whole legend, since Bede would hardly have been silent about the foundation if it had been thus solemnly proclaimed at Rome (Will. Malmes. *Gesta Pontif.* (Rolls Ser.), 297). For these letters and the early charters of Evesham—almost all of which are forgeries—see Haddan and Stubbs, *Councils*, iii. 278–283.

[12] Harl. MS. 3763, fol. 62. Abbot Agelwy evidently acquired these lands in the eleventh century, and this charter was forged to strengthen his claim to the lands.

[13] Harl. MS. 3763, fol. 62b; Cotton MS. Vespas. B. xxiv. fol. 27d; *Chron. de Evesham*, 73.

[14] For his work as abbot, and details of his life and the miracles attendant on his death, and the power attributed to his relics, see the story well told in *St. Egwin and his Abbey of Evesham*, compiled by the Benedictines of Stanbrook, near Worcester.

[15] Harl. MS. 3763, fol. 63; Cotton MS. Vespas. B. xxiv. f. 74b.

[16] Harl. MS. 3763, fol. 63d.

[17] Ibid. 229, fol. 17; *Chron. de Evesham* (Rolls Ser.), 76 and 77.

[18] Ibid.

church,[1] and the pillage went on until the reign of Edgar. Then in 960, by the decree of the Council of that year,[2] and by the influence of St. Oswald, bishop of Worcester, the monks were restored, and Osward was appointed abbot by the king.[3]

In 976, after the death of Edgar, and probably of Osward also, the monks were again expelled by Alfhere, prince of Mercia, who installed a few secular canons, but kept most of the possessions of the monastery for his own use.[4] Falling sick, however, and despairing of his life, with a typical death-bed repentance he sent for a certain monk Freodgar, and restoring all the possessions, made him abbot.[5] But finding it impossible to oust the seculars, Freodgar, with the consent of King Ethelred, exchanged the abbey with Earl Godwin for Towcester.[6] However, shortly afterwards Ethelred granted the monastery to Bishop Ethelsig, who quickly fell under his displeasure and was deposed from his bishopric.[7] Thereupon the king gave the abbey to Bishop Athelstan,[8] and on his death to Adulf, bishop of Worcester.[9] Adulf, it is said, subjected the abbey to episcopal jurisdiction,[10] and appointed Alfric abbot of Evesham. On Alfric's death Alfgar became abbot, and during his rule Earl Godwin seized forty hides of the lands of the abbey in Evesham, Offenham, Ombersley, Burton, and Lenchwick.[11]

Henceforward until the thirteenth century the history of Evesham was one long struggle to preserve its possessions from all encroachments and to maintain its independence of all episcopal control. The encroachments of Earl Godwin heralded the one; Adulf's high assumption of episcopal control the other. Into the history comes the story of a strenuous and successful contest on the part of the monks against a profligate and cruel abbot, foisted upon them by royal command. But the point which most vitally affected the life and welfare of the monastery was the development of that worldly ambition which gradually blotted out every regard for truth if truth meant loss of material privileges and possessions.

Alfgar's successor, Brithmar, about 1012 redeemed the 40 hides of the abbey lands from Earl Godwin,[12] who next year, under his successor Ethelwig, once more took possession of the lands,[13] but was expelled by the next abbot, Alfward, a monk of Ramsey,[14] who about 1034 was made bishop of London, but still remained abbot of Evesham.[15] During his abbacy the first signs of the coming fight against episcopal control appeared. He first asserted the freedom of the abbey, and so far obtained it that he appointed Avitius prior of Evesham Dean of Christianity for the Vale of Evesham.[16] During his rule also King Cnut, his kinsman, endowed the abbey with Badby and Newnham (Northamptonshire) in 1018,[17] and in 1020 with 'five lands' in Gloucestershire, two in Winchcomb, and one in Northampton.[18] Earl Leofric also restored Hampton and Bengeworth[19] and other lands.[20] After thirty years' careful rule over the monastery Alfward, when dying, was refused admittance to the abbey by the monks, who threatened to depart if he came.[21] He was therefore carried to Ramsey, where he died and was buried in 1044.[22]

His successor Manny was chosen by King Edward the Confessor, who in 1055 granted Swell Minor and Grafton Major to the abbey,[23] and seems to have been the last royal benefactor.[24] In 1059 Abbot Manny resigned on account of paralysis, and was succeeded by Ethelwig in the spring of that year.[25] Aldred, archbishop of York,[26] consecrated him, and he became a favourite counsellor of Edward the Confessor,

[1] Harl. MS. 229, f. 17; *Chron. de Evesham* (Rolls Ser.), 77. One of Wulfric's spoils was a manse near Maugersbury, restored by King Ethelred in 986. Ibid. 74, and Harl. MS. 3763, fol. 162d.

[2] Wilkins, *Concilia*, i. 247.

[3] *Chron. de Evesham* (Rolls Ser.), 78; Cotton MS. Vespas. B. xv. fol. 19.

[4] Ibid. 78.

[5] *Chron. de Evesham* (Rolls Ser.), 79.

[6] Ibid. 79, 80. The earl offered the king three hundred 'mancusæ' of gold to have the abbey and its lands confirmed to him and his successors for ever. The king received the gold and gave his consent, but retracted his promise.

[7] Ibid. 80. This may have been Ethelsig or Ethelsius, bishop of Sherbourne from 979–993 (Will. Malmes. *Gesta Pontif.* (Rolls Ser.), 179).

[8] *Chron. de Evesham* (Rolls Ser.), 80. Probably either Alfstan bishop of London, who died in 995 or 996, or Alfstan bishop of Rochester, who died in the same year (Will. Malmes. *Gesta Pontif.* (Rolls Ser.), 145, 136).

[9] *Chron. de Evesham* (Rolls Ser.), 80.

[10] Ibid.

[11] Ibid.

[12] Ibid. 80, 81.

[13] Ibid. 81.

[14] Ibid. 81, 82, 85. Godwin was killed at the battle of Assandun in 1016, so the restoration must have been before this date.

[15] Ibid. 83.

[16] Ibid.

[17] Ibid. 74; Cott. MS. Vespas. B. xxiv. f. 20b; Harl. MS. 3763, f. 65. These lands are not mentioned among the Evesham possessions in the Domesday Survey. Badby is there given as held by the church of Crowland (*V. C. H. Northants*, i. 319b). Moreover these lands are not among those pillaged from the church by Odo of Bayeux (*Chron. de Evesham*, 97).

[18] Ibid. 75. Land in Northampton belonged to Evesham at the time of the Survey, i.e. 4 hides at Litchborough and one house in Northampton (*V. C. H. Northants*, i. 301, 320).

[19] See Topography.

[20] *Chron. de Evesham* (Rolls Ser.), 84, 85.

[21] Ibid. 85.

[22] Ibid.

[23] Ibid. 75.

[24] See list of benefactors, *Chron. de Evesham* (Rolls Ser.), 75.

[25] Ibid. 87.

[26] Ibid. 88, 89.

Harold, and William I.[1] He was one of the most careful and just of abbots, caring for the welfare of his monks, increasing their number from twelve to thirty-six, and leaving money to build a new church.[2] He also increased the possessions of the abbey by redeeming many lands from Edward the Confessor and 'many other good men.'[3] Some he obtained from the church of Worcester 'since the prelates of that church had held them unjustly.'[4] These were Acton and Bengeworth, Milcote, Weston, Evenlode, and Daylesford, and many houses in Worcester. But Stratford and Fladbury he did not recover.[4] Other lands which he gained or regained[5] were in Hampton, Upton, Witton, Sheriff's Lench, Atch Lench, Church Lench (Worcester),[6] Swell, Kineton, Stoke, Weston, Hidcote, Pebworth (Gloucester). A full account of the possessions of the abbey is given in the Domesday Survey, during the abbacy of Walter, monk of Cerisy in Bayeux, who succeeded Ethelwig on his death in 1077.[7] The Survey also bears out the Evesham record of the lands which Ethelwig had won and Odo of Bayeux and Urse d'Abitôt seized from the church. Six hides belonging to Evesham at Acton were held in 1086 by Odo of Bayeux, while Urse d'Abitôt held of the bishop 3 hides in Upton, 'of right belonging to the monastery,' half a hide in Witton,[8] and 4 hides in Hantune.'[9] Odo had

[1] The Conqueror made him governor of the midland counties. *Chron. de Evesham* (Rolls Ser.), 89.

[2] Ibid. 95, 96. By 1086 the number of the monks had increased to sixty-seven (Cotton MS. B. xxiv. fol. 41d).

[3] Ibid. 94.

[4] Ibid. 95. The story is very differently given by the Worcester historian Heming, whose duty was to support the cause of Worcester in the struggle with Evesham concerning the possession of these lands. According to him Acton had belonged to the Worcester house, and was held by a certain Ordwig, by whom it had been restored to St. Wulstan when he was prior. It had afterwards been seized by Ethelwig —'vi magne iniquitatis illata loco rite hereditario villam istam abstulit'—and then by Urse the sheriff, who settled it on his daughter. According to the Evesham monks Acton was part of the patrimony of Ethelwig, and he had given it with Bransford to Urse the sheriff in exchange for Bengeworth, but Urse had kept all three (*Chron. de Evesham* (Rolls Ser.) 95). The account in the Domesday Survey practically agrees with the Evesham chronicle. In it Acton was held in fee by Urse, of Odo of Bayeux, but in the time of King Edward it had belonged to the abbey, and Urse 'received it from the abbot in exchange for other land' (*V. C. H. Worc.* i. 308a). Concerning Evenlode and Daylesford, Domesday also bears out the statement of the Evesham chronicle (*V. C. H. Worc.* i. 293b). The real struggle, however, was over Bengeworth. Evesham seems to have held 5 hides of Bengeworth from the time of Egwin (*Chron. de Evesham* (Rolls Ser.), 18). These were wrenched from the church in the time of Edmund, son of Edward the Elder, but restored to Abbot Alfward by Earl Leofric (Ibid. 84, 85). By the time of Edward the Confessor these hides were held of Evesham by a certain Arngrim, but Urse the sheriff had seized one of the hides by 1086 (*V. C. H. Worc.* i. 307a). Heming's chartulary says that Arngrim held land at Bengeworth of the Worcester house, but that in consequence of Urse d'Abitôt having seized other land belonging to that church in the same place, Arngrim had recourse to Ethelwig as the most powerful patron he could discover, and by Ethelwig's advice renounced Worcester and paid service to Evesham. Thereupon Ethelwig proceeded to oust him from his land and seize it himself (Heming, *Chartul,* ed. Hearne, i. 269–70). In this way he secured the other lands and outskilled Wulstan, who was 'the servant of God only,' and not versed in worldly wisdom (Ibid. 271, 272). The truth is difficult to discover, but the Domesday Survey seems to give valuable evidence in favour of Evesham's claim. Bengeworth was a 10-hide manor, 5 hides had been granted by Bishop Brihtheah to a certain Azor or 'Atsere' or 'Asser,' who had been deprived by Urse (Heming, *Chartul.* 269, and *V. C. H. Worc.* i. 297a), while Arngrim held the other 5 of Evesham. The probability seems to be that the lands in Bengeworth which Ethelwig tried to buy from Urse with his patrimonial lands of Acton and Bransford were the 5 hides which Azor had held, but Urse had kept these with Acton and Bransford and afterwards seized 1 hide of those held by Arngrim (*Chron. de Evesham* (Rolls Ser.), 95). Thereupon, probably, the Worcester house, seeing no hope of gaining back her half from Urse, laid claim to the hides which Evesham held, and to enforce this claim Heming's story was concocted. Domesday states that Abbot Walter made good his claim to 5 hides (*V. C. H. Worc.* i. 307a), and the Evesham chronicle states that he recovered the land which Arngrim had held, but that which the bishop had given to 'Asser' Urse held (*Chron. de Evesham,* 97).

[5] It is difficult in many cases to tell whether Ethelwig acquired these lands or redeemed them. If former charters were true they had for the most part been granted before by Ethelbald, Beorhtulf, or Offa of Mercia. More probably they were acquired by Ethelwig, and the charters forged to strengthen possession. The chronicle itself seems to infer that he acquired many of the lands (*Chron. de Evesham,* 95, 97).

[6] As regards the Worcester lands the Domesday Survey clearly shows how they were acquired (see infra).

[7] *Chron. de Evesham* (Rolls Ser.), 95, 96. *V. C. H. Worc.* i. 306–8. Ibid. *Warwick,* i. 306–307a. Ibid. *Northants,* i. 320a.

[8] Given to the church by a certain Wulfgar 'who placed his gift on the altar when his son Alfgeat became a monk there. Afterwards Ethelwig leased the land to his uncle for life; the latter was killed in Harold's battle, and the church received it back, and held it until the seventh year of Walter's abbacy (*V. C. H. Worc.* i. 319).

[9] Abbot of Evesham held it T. R. E. Ethelwig bought it from a certain thegn who could rightfully sell his land to whom he would, and who gave it, when bought, to the abbey by placing a copy of the gospels on the altar by the witness of the county court (*V. C. H. Worc.* i. 319b).

also seized land in Sheriff's Lench,[1] Daylesford, and Evenlode,[2] and 1 hide at Bransford[3] held by Urse. In Warwick Odo himself held Arrow, King's Broom, and Bidford, and had seized also Temple Grafton, Burton, Exhall, Atherstone, Wigginshill, Milcote, Weston, and Salford, which he gave over to Urse D'Abitôt, Osbern Fitz Richard, William Fitz Corbucion, and others.[4] In Oxon he seized Salford, Cornwell, Chiselton, Shipton, and Deanfield.[5] In Gloucester Hidcote, Pebworth, Dorsington, Weston, Stoke, and Kineton.[6] Thus Odo of Bayeux seized twenty-eight of the thirty-six villages which Ethelwig had won for Worcester.[7]

Of the spiritualities of the abbey it is difficult to form any clear estimate until the time of the taxation of Pope Nicholas, but undoubtedly from their earliest foundation all rights in the churches of the vale[8] belonged to the abbey, and were claimed as included in the gifts of Kenred and Offa confirmed by Pope Constantine. On this ground at a later period the abbey claimed the same rights over nine other churches on lands granted to them by Kenred and Offa, at Ombersley (Worcester), Coughton, Salford, Ilmington (Warwick), Burton, Bradwell, Upper Swell, Stone, and Weston (Gloucester).[9] It is impossible to say how early the abbey asserted its claim over these churches outside the vale, but the appointment of Avitius to be Dean of Christianity for the vale of Evesham[10] about 1040 signified that the abbey considered the churches of the vale under its own rule and in no way subject to the bishop or archdeacon of the diocese. It was not until the thirteenth century that this right was finally won by the abbey, which after 1248 had sole jurisdiction over the churches of the vale only.

Abbot Walter's great task was the carrying out of Ethelwig's design to build a new church. With the money that Ethelwig had left, augmented by that which he himself collected by sending monks round the country with the shrine of St. Egwin,[11] he built the crypts and the upper church as far as the nave, and began the building of the tower.[12] Although a considerable part of Ethelwig's acquisitions had been wrenched from Evesham, Abbot Walter was able to increase the number of the monks and also, the chronicler notes, the rigour of the order.[13] But he seems to have won the disapprobation of the monks by granting abbey lands and offices to his relatives, especially by instituting a secular dean and steward, taking the office of steward away from the prior and making it hereditary in his own family.[14] His successor, Robert de Jumièges, instituted on Walter's death,[15] continued his predecessor's policy of granting out the abbey lands to his relatives. A most interesting record has survived of the internal condition of the monastery under his rule. There were then sixty-seven monks, five nuns (this is the only known reference to nuns in connexion with Evesham), three 'pauperes ad mandatum,' and three clerks who enjoyed equal privileges with the monks. There were sixty-five servants in the monastery, five served in the church, two in the infirmary, two in the cellar, five in the kitchen, seven in the bakehouse, four in the brew-house, four did the mending for the monastery (sertores), two attended the bath, two were shoemakers, two were in the orchard, three in the garden, one attended the stranger's gate, four waited on the monks when they went abroad, four were fishermen, four waited in the abbot's chamber, three in the hall, and two were watchmen.[16] Of the sixty-seven monks, twelve were sent to Denmark by William Rufus,[17] and by permission of King Eric founded a subordinate cell at Odensey, the dependence of which on Evesham was ratified by a charter of Waldemar, king of Denmark, in 1174.[18] Maurice, a monk

[1] Of Sheriff's Lench 2 hides were given to Evesham by Gilbert Fitz Turold for the soul of William Fitz Osbern, and 1 mark was placed in that church from the proceeds. For the other 2 hides Abbot Ethelwig gave 1 mark of gold to King William, and the king granted the said land to the abbey for his soul (*V. C. H. Worc.* i. 308b).

[2] These two lands were 'held by the abbot of Evesham from the bishop of Worcester until the bishop of Bayeux received them from the abbey, and were assigned to the support of the monks' (*V. C. H. Worc.* i. 293b.)

[3] It belonged to the church of Pershore T. R. E. but 'was held by the church of Evesham on King Edward's death; but it is not known how' (Ibid. 305b).

[4] *V. C. H. Warw.* i. 303b, 304a, 319b, 333b, 334a, 337b, 338a.

[5] *Dom. Bk.* (Rec. Com.), i. 155–7.

[6] Glouc. Domesday, ff. 166a, 169a, 167b.

[7] *Chron. de Evesham* (Rolls Ser.), 97. Harl. MSS. 3763, fol. 58b.

[8] The churches of the vale were those of All Saints and St. Lawrence in Evesham, Norton, Lenchwick, Hampton, Badsey, Wickhamford and Aldington, Bretforton, Church Honeybourne, Littleton, Offenham and Bengeworth. *Pope Nich. Tax.* (Rec. Com.), 219 b.

[9] Ibid. 216a, 218b, 219a, 222b.

[10] *Chron. de Evesham* (Rolls Ser.), 83. See supra.

[11] The various stories of the miracles already wrought by the relics of St. Egwin's in punishing those who unjustly claimed the patrimony of Evesham, in mercifully freeing those who were bound and fettered, or in protecting the monastery against fire, are given at length in the *Chronicle*, pp. 39–67.

[12] *Chron. de Evesham* (Rolls Ser.), and Harl. MS. 3763, f. 171b.

[13] Ibid. 97.

[14] Ibid.

[15] Harl. MS. 3763, f. 168b. Cotton MS. Vespas. B. xv. f. 20.

[16] Cotton MS. Vespas. B. xxiv. f. 41 d.

[17] Ibid.

[18] Ibid. ff. 18a and b. This charter was written by William 'a corpore ecclesie de Evesham tunc in priorem electus et ad regimen prioratus transmissus.'

of Evesham, succeeded Abbot Robert, and ruled the monastery until his death.[1]

From this time to the end of the thirteenth century the efforts of the abbots seem to be solely directed to the augmentation of their material welfare and privileges.[2] Already they had settled down into the position of feudal lords, holding their lands by military tenure. As early as the charter of Henry I., granted between 1100 and 1108, the hundred of Blakenhurst was confirmed to the abbey for the service of four knights' fees and a half.[3] The holders of these fees[4] provided knights for the defence of the abbey, and it is recorded that Abbot Reginald 'removed the houses of the knights of Kinwarton and Coughton and others from the place where the garden of the monastery and the croft of St. Kenelm now are, with which the abbey was, as it were, besieged.'[5] Probably the monks felt capable of defending themselves, judging by the action of Abbot William de Andeville (1149–59),[6] who took and destroyed William de Beauchamp's castle of Bengeworth.[7] Besides possessing this military spirit, the abbots of this time made many improvements in the abbey itself. In addition to gifts to the church of Evesham, Abbot Reginald built the wall round the abbey, a refectory, a parlour, a guest chamber, and kitchen. Adam, monk of Cluny, who became abbot in 1160 on the death of Abbot Roger (1159–60),[8] continued the improvement of the abbey,[9] but £20 from land in Burton (Gloucestershire) which had formerly belonged to the monks he appropriated to himself.[10] Though possibly grasping and ambitious, Abbot Adam's failings pale before the open avarice and selfish greed of Abbot Roger Norreys. In him all the desire which other abbots had felt to enrich the abbey was centred in himself.[11] He wasted the abbey lands and revenue,[12] stinting the brethren in clothes and food, while he himself and certain of the brethren enjoyed every luxury.[13] In 1195 the monks headed by Thomas de Marleberge appealed againt him to Hubert, archbishop of Canterbury, then papal legate.[14] For a time he was able to redress their grievances, but after his office had expired the abbot began his oppressions afresh, treating the monks so ill that in 1198 they made a further appeal to the archbishop, who came to Evesham in 1201 to make an inquiry into the case.[15] But Abbot Roger corrupting certain of the monks by bribes and promises, deceived the archbishop and made his peace with him.[16] After that matters grew worse, until the scandal came to the ears of Bishop Mauger, who thereupon asserted his right to visit the abbey and redress the evil.[17] But the monks preferred even personal discomfort to submission to an authority which if once allowed would permanently take away that freedom won by a struggle which dated from 996, when Bishop Adulf first emphasized the question. Until Abbot Alfward[18] no open opposition seems to have been made by the monastery, but as the abbey increased in greatness and wealth, impatience of any outward check became more marked, and led to Abbot Reginald's pilgrimage to Rome in 1139 to plead the liberty of the church against Bishop Simon.[19] He partly succeeded in his claim and obtained also several privileges for his church from the pope.[20] Abbot Adam was the first to gain the right to use all the episcopal ornaments except the ring, and obtained many other privileges from Pope Alexander, all of which worked for the liberty of the church.[21] The monks were not likely to let slip these hardly won privileges even when the bishop interfered to take their part against an unjust and vicious abbot. When the bishop's letter came the abbot himself offered no resistance, thinking that he would come only as a guest. But Thomas de Marleberge seeing the real meaning of the words 'causa visitationis'[22] was foremost in opposition to the bishop and was chosen as

See also a charter by Bishop Riculf (f. 22). The later history of this cell appears to be unknown. The two other cells of Evesham were at Penworth in Lancashire, founded about the end of the eleventh century; and at Alcester, called Our Lady of the Isle, near Evesham, founded about 1140 by Ralph Boteler, but, becoming impoverished, was annexed to Evesham in the fourteenth century.

1 *Chron. de Evesham* (Rolls Ser.), 98.

2 Harl. MS. 3763, fol. 169. *Flor. Wigorn.* (Eng. Hist. Soc.), ii. 91.

3 *Cal. of Chart. R.* 1226–57, 257.

4 In 1166 the holders of two of the knights' fees were Ralph de Coughton and Ralph de Kinwarton (*Liber Niger*, ed. Hearne, i. 175, and *The Red Book of the Exchequer* (Rolls Ser.), 301).

5 *Chron. de Evesham* (Rolls Ser.), 98.

6 Ibid. 100.

7 See Topography under Bengeworth.

8 *Chron. de Evesham* (Rolls Ser.), 100.

9 See Topography.

10 Ibid. 102.

11 Gervase of Canterbury draws his character while monk of Canterbury in no favourable terms, 'erat enim ab adolescentia monachatus sui superbus, elatus, pomposus in verbis, dolosus in factis, cupidus prælationis, aspernator religionis, ad superiores adulator, ad inferiores contemptor, gloriosus in veste, negligens in ordinis observatione, amicus fœminarum, amator equorum, iracundus ad correptiones, paratus ad detractiones in omnibus etiam incorrigibilis. (*Hist. Works of Gervase of Cant.* (Rolls Ser.) i. 382).

12 *Chron. de Evesham* (Rolls Ser.), 105.

13 Ibid.

14 Ibid. 106.

15 Ibid. 107.

16 Ibid.

17 Ibid. 109.

18 See supra.

19 Ibid. 99. There is an interesting letter written by Abbot Reginald to his kinsman Gilbert Foliot concerning this controversy with Worcester, stating the Evesham case very strongly (Ibid. 112 n.). Gilbert Foliot thereupon wrote to the archdeacon of Worcester pleading the cause of Evesham (Ibid. Preface, xii. n.).

20 Ibid. 99.

21 Ibid. 101.

22 Ibid. 109.

spokesmen to explain to him the grounds for their resistance to his visitation.[1] Mauger replied by suspending all except the abbot for contumacy and excommunicating them.[2] Thereupon Marleberge appealed to archbishop Hubert to inquire into the bishop's claim,[3] and the abbot, who had retired to Bradwell when the quarrel began,[4] at last made common cause with the monks against the bishop.[5] The archbishop's inquiry was indecisive, and the suit was referred to the papal delegates, the abbots of Malmesbury, Abingdon, and Eynsham.[6] As abbots they were likely to be partial judges, and Mauger appealed from them to Rome.[7] In the meantime the abbot had taken advantage of his reconciliation with his monks to continue his tyranny and farm out all their lands.[8] This involved the monks in a further quarrel with the king and the archbishop, since they illegally reaped some lands which the abbot had farmed out. Marleberge, who was sent to explain matters, was refused an interview with the king, but was able to satisfy the archbishop. The result was a visitation by the archbishop, as papal legate, but all he did was to refer the questions between the monks and the abbot to arbitrators,[9] who decided that the monks had been at fault in trying to recover lands alienated by their abbot. Marleberge and four others were banished from the house for a fortnight.[10] But Marleberge was needed in the fight against the bishop and was recalled to plead before the papal commissioners in August 1204.[11] In September of that year he hastened to Rome to plead his cause with Innocent III., before the commissioners could pass sentence.[12] But the pope, irritated by his importunity, ignored his appeal and he was forced to retire to Piacenza and then to Pavia.[13] Meanwhile the abbot had also started for Rome, and after a short imprisonment at Chalons arrived there in March, 1205.[14] Marleberge then returned to Rome, but as they were unable to smother their personal enmity [15] he retired to Bologna in April for about six months.[16] It seemed as though his cause was defeated, for in April the commissioners in England awarded the bishop temporary jurisdiction over the abbey although they allowed him none in the churches of the vale.[17] Submission to the bishop was enjoined on the monks, and the bishop himself tried to conciliate them.[18] But he took up an unwise line in enforcing his right too quickly and in excommunicating the abbot on his return from Rome.[19]

Meanwhile Marleberge had been training himself at Bologna in canon and civil law and was ready by October, 1205, when the abbot returned to England, to meet the bishop's advocates in the final suit at Rome. He answered the advocate, Robert Clipstone, by relying on the special priviledges granted to Evesham by Popes Constantine, Innocent II., Alexander III., Clement, and Celestine.[20] By these he maintained the abbot was made supreme under the pope, for as the bull of Pope Constantine had stated 'locus sub monarchia proprii abbatis sit liber . . . salva per omni sedis apostolicæ potestas.'[21] Clipstone's defence was that these bulls were of doubtful authenticity.[22] This the pope denied, examining them himself and passing them round among the cardinals for examination.[23] Then Clipstone took up a different argument. He maintained that the bishop's right was one of prescription, that the abbey had always been subject to the diocesan, who had been admitted into the abbey church and had blessed the abbots, and they had acknowledged his jurisdiction.[24] Marleberge's argument against this was that the abbey was in its turn fortified by prescription. True, the bishops had blessed their abbots and the abbots had owned the bishop's jurisdiction, but this had been in face of the protests of the chapter of Evesham, while the abbots had only submitted 'salvis privilegiis suis.' Moreover the bishops had only been admitted into the abbey church after the monks had stated their privileges and claimed exemption also for the churches under their rule.[25] These limited rights were all the bishop could claim by prescription, and these merely by the sufferance of the monastery. With this sweeping defence Marleberge turned his adversary's weapons against himself, and the abbey was declared exempt in December 1205. Marleberge, worn out by hard work added to long fasting, fainted in court when he heard the verdict.[26]

However, only half of the dispute had been settled, as the jurisdiction over the churches of the vale had not been definitely assigned to the abbey. A commission was ordered to try the case in England [27] before the bishops of Ely and Rochester, and Benedict, canon of London.[28] The bishop claimed a prescriptive right to jurisdiction over the churches of the vale. Marleberge, who had returned to Evesham,[29] asserted that what right the bishop had gained had been the result of carelessness on the part of the chaplains and the

[1] *Chron. de Evesham* (Rolls Ser.), 117.
[2] Ibid. 117, 118.
[3] Ibid. 119, 120.
[4] Ibid. 116.
[5] Ibid. 121.
[6] Ibid. 123.
[7] Ibid.
[8] Ibid. 124.
[9] Ibid. 129.
[10] Ibid. 130.
[11] Ibid. 130.
[12] Ibid. 141, 142.
[13] Ibid. 143.
[14] Ibid. 144.
[15] Ibid. 145, 146.
[16] Ibid. 147.
[17] Ibid. 131–137.
[18] Ibid. 136, 138.
[19] Ibid. 149.

[20] Ibid. 153–160.
[21] Ibid. 156, 157.
[22] Ibid. 160.
[23] Ibid. 161.
[24] Ibid. 161, 162.
[25] Ibid. 162, 163.
[26] Ibid. 168, 169.
[27] Ibid. 92.
[28] Ibid. 193.
[29] Ibid. 198, 200. Marleberge had borrowed money of Roman merchants during the suit to pay for legal advice and was obliged to leave the abbey documents as security, and having no means to make the usual gifts to the pope and cardinals, had to escape secretly from Rome in 1206.

deans of the vale.[1] The deans of the vale, being clerks and not monks, cared rather for the bishop's favour than for the rights of the abbey, and among other things handed over the annual contribution of the abbey towards Peter's Pence to the bishop, who thereby acquired the right to excommunicate the parishioners of the vale if they refused payment to himself.[2] A resolution was made that in future the deans should be members of the abbey removable at pleasure, not secular priests. Roger Fitz Maurice, canon of Hereford, was expelled from the deanship and Marleberge himself appointed, holding the office until he became abbot.[3] The monks were forbidden to admit any bishop or archdeacon of Worcester on any pretext. Neither were they to admit the prior of Worcester or the archdeacon of Gloucester if they came as officials of the bishop or archdeacon of Worcester.[4] It was not until 1207, after the council of Reading of October 1206, in which the exemption of the abbey was finally declared in England,[5] that the question of the jurisdiction of the vale was formally discussed before the English legates.[6] The bishop made various proposals for a settlement. He suggested that the Evesham claim to two thousand marks costs in the late suit should be renounced, for if the bishop were regarded as winner of the suit concerning the churches outside the vale 'neither could demand expenses from the other.' He himself would renounce all jurisdiction over the churches of the vale and would give the churches of Ombersley and Stowe to the abbey providing they surrendered all claim to jurisdiction in the nine churches outside the vale. All attempt at compromise was, however, frustrated by the Interdict of 1208. Bishop Mauger fled from England and the matter was undecided until the time of Bishop Cantilupe. A composition was made between him and the abbot and confirmed by Bishop Godfrey Giffard in 1269, by which the bishop was given jurisdiction in the church of Abbots Morton only, while even there the abbot might hold a chapel in his court. Also the bishop was to have pensions from Hillingdon (Middlesex), from the church of Weston, and from the church of Stanway. Otherwise all rights claimed in the churches within the vale seem to have been confirmed to the abbey.[7] From 1269 the quarrel between the abbot and the bishop was ended. In 1336 Pope Innocent pronounced that the abbey had been wholly exempt from episcopal jurisdiction from its earliest foundation 'only subject to the apostolic see in spirituals and to the crown in temporals.' But while 'in capite' it was thus exempt 'in membris' the abbot 'ought to accede to the diocesan,' and was not exempt from 'showing the bishop reverence, observance, and honour, with which the bishop should remain content.' The pope also expressed a hope that 'the more free the abbey was from secular service the more ardent it might be for the Divine service.'[8] Evidently the bishop remained content with 'honour and reverence,' but in the time of Abbot Zatton, Archbishop Courtney attempted to push the claims of the archbishop of York and to visit Evesham.[9] Abbot Zatton 'gloriose et viriliter et magnis expensis' repulsed him from the monastery[10] and Evesham was thenceforward left to enjoy her dearly won privileges.

To return, however, to the abbacy of Roger Norreys. The monks had once more shown a determination to bear with his tyranny rather than allow the bishop to interfere with their affairs. While the suit for exemption was in progress at Rome, Bishop Mauger, acting in virtue of the decision of the papal commissioners in 1205, drew up an adverse report of Abbot Norreys' conduct, and forwarded it to Rome.[11] Marleberge, who was then at Rome, fearing complications would follow if the abbot were deposed through the bishop, hushed the matter up, and left the abbot to renew his old tyranny.[12] But after the council of Reading, Thomas de Northwich and Marleberge were expelled by him in November, 1206.[13] Upon this thirty of the monks left the abbey with Marleberge 'on foot, with their loins girt, and with staves in their hands.' The abbot seeing them go as he sat in judgment in the chapel of St. Lawrence, called together an armed company and followed them.[14] The monks, however, stood their ground, and though unarmed were able to defeat the armed men of the abbot.[15] Marleberge and his company then pursued their way, hastening to get out of the land belonging to the abbey, so that if there were need they might obtain help 'from strangers who did not fear the abbot.' When they had come into the land of William de Beauchamp, the abbot, fearing they would succeed in gaining help against him, followed them and entreated them to return, promising to do whatever they wished in future.[16] Finally the monks agreed to return when the abbot promised to renounce the special indulgences he had received from the pope by which he had attempted to expel Marleberge and Thomas de Northwich.[17] For a few months there was peace, but on the death of Thomas de Northwich and the expulsion of Adam Sortes,[18] when Marleberge was left alone to head the opposition against

[1] *Chron. de Evesham* (Rolls Ser.), 194.
[2] Ibid. 194, 195.
[3] Ibid. 196.
[4] Ibid. 196.
[5] Ibid. 202.
[6] Ibid. 222.
[7] *Worc. Epis. Reg. Giffard* (Worc. Hist. Soc.), p. 9.
[8] Worc. Epis. Reg. Montacute, f. 25, 25b.
[9] *Chron. de Evesham* (Rolls Ser.), 306.
[10] Ibid.
[11] Ibid. 199.
[12] Ibid.
[13] Ibid. 203.
[14] Ibid.
[15] Ibid. 203.
[16] Ibid. 204.
[17] Ibid.
[18] Ibid. 224.

him, Norreys once more began his persecution.[1] The monks, 'making a virtue of necessity,' bowed their necks to the yoke,' and seeing that there was no one who would see justice done to them, suffered 'as patiently as the weakness of human nature would permit.'[2] It was not until 1213, when Nicholas, bishop of Tusculum, came to England as papal legate to remove the interdict of 1208, that the monks saw any chance of opposition to the abbot. But at that time a further difficulty faced them. The Roman creditors who had been expelled from England by the king in 1208[3] returned to claim their debts in 1213.[4] Marleberge was sent to meet them, and pleaded that the monks were not in fault, since they had not means to pay. The abbot had impoverished all their revenues, and since the interdict had been pronounced the king had held all monastic lands in his hands. An agreement was made with the creditors at Wallingford in October, 1213, by which the monastery was to give them fifty marks as a fine and to pay their expenses.[5] However, on Marleberge's return the abbot refused to pay a penny towards the fifty marks.[6] Marleberge in desperation applied to the archbishop and begged him to visit the abbey.[7] This involved a discussion concerning the extent of the archbishop's power over the abbey, and the point being very indefinite, Marleberge finally applied to the legate,[8] who, reproaching him for not before revealing the state of the abbey, promised to visit and redress grievances.[9] On Marleberge's return to Evesham the abbot met him at Bradwell, and there Marleberge told him he had seen the legate, but said nothing of his proposed visit to Evesham.[10] When his visit was announced the abbot, fearful of the result, questioned Marleberge carefully as to his share in bringing the legate to Evesham, and Marleberge tells how, as the abbot questioned him on the night journey from Bradwell to Evesham, he feared every moment that he would murder him.[11] When the legate arrived Marleberge by his command accused the abbot, and set forth a long list of the ills they had suffered at his hands. He had starved them of food and deprived them of clothing until the brethren were obliged to remain in the infirmary for want of frocks and cowls, and masses were neglected for want of breeches for the celebrants.[12] The necessary result was a general disregard for the statutes of the monastery, and the institution of a begging system among the monks, so that instead of giving alms they received them. Various other charges were brought against him of wasting the abbey revenues and property, of simony and manslaughter, of neglecting to wear monastic dress, and finally of gross immorality.[13] The abbot worked hard to defend himself, and charging his accusers with conspiracy, attempted to bring counter accusations against them.[14] However, he was deposed by the legate in 1213,[15] and early in the following year Randulf, prior of Worcester, on the legate's recommendation,[16] was made abbot of Evesham.[17]

Success in the suit at Rome led to a desire for further privileges, and the second year after his installation Abbot Randulf went in person to Rome and obtained fresh benefits for Evesham, among them a confirmation of his apportionment of the rents of the monastery.[18] The misrule of Abbot Norreys had taught the monks to take precautions, and clearly defined constitutions were drawn up by Abbot Randulf in 1214,[19] and confirmed in a general council at Rome in 1216.[20] Besides showing the determination of the monks to prevent a recurrence of the tyranny of Roger Norreys, these constitutions give an excellent picture of the organization of the monastery. They begin by reciting the right given to the abbot on his visit to Rome to assign and distribute the rents of the monastery.[21] The next section is devoted to a statement of the necessary conduct of the abbot. He must constantly reside within the monastery, leading a regular life among the brethren, managing the temporal concerns of the house to the best of his power, and so as might most conduce to the utility of the church, maintaining the number of the monks, and receiving or rejecting none without the consent of the convent. The election of the prior, sub-prior, and other officers[22] was to take place in the general council, with the consent of the whole convent, or 'of its better and wiser part,' confirmed by the casting vote of the abbot. The prior and sub-priors of the order were charged with the preservation of discipline among the brethren, especially to see that they

[1] *Chron. de Evesham* (Rolls Ser.), 230.

[2] Ibid. [3] Ibid. 225. [4] Ibid. 230.

[5] Ibid. 231. [6] Ibid. 231.

[7] Ibid. 232. [8] Ibid. 233.

[9] Ibid. 234. [10] Ibid.

[11] Ibid. 235. 'Valde timui ne occideret me, erat enim nox.'

[12] Ibid. 238.

[13] Ibid. 236–248. [14] Ibid. 249.

[15] Ibid. 250. *Ann. Mon.* (Rolls Ser.), i. 61; iii. 38; iv. 402. However, in 1218 he was restored to the priory of Penworth, where he remained for almost six years, dying in 1223. *Chron. de Evesham* (Rolls Ser.), 251, 252, 253.

[16] Ibid. 254–6. The monks were unable to agree in their choice of an abbot, and the decision was therefore referred to the legate.

[17] Ibid. 256. *Ann. Mon.* (Rolls Ser.), iii. 38.

[18] Ibid. 266. [19] Ibid. 205, 225.

[20] Ibid. 205, 221. [21] Ibid. 205.

[22] The following officers are enumerated: Prior, sub-prior, third prior, and other obedientiaries of the order, the prior of Penworth, the precentor, dean, sacrist, chamberlain, manciple, cellarer, infirmarer, almoner, keeper of the vineyard and garden, the inspector of the church fabric, the pitanciary, and the attender on strangers.

ate only in the refectory, and did not go out of the convent without the leave of their superiors.[1] To the cellarer was assigned the whole care of the concerns of the abbey, excepting the rents assigned to particular offices, and the duty of administering necessaries for the use of the monks and the entertainment of secular guests and strangers.[2] To the prior were allotted all obventions or fees under the common seal; all tithes of Bengeworth, both great and small, to buy parchment for the writing of books; the manor house of Bengeworth, with its appurtenances,[3] and various other rents. To the office of fraterer belonged certain lands and rents in money and kind 'for the repair and furnishing of spoons, cups, drinking measures (justæ), towels, and other utensils, together with lamps and oil.'[4] There also belonged to him what was left of the ale after the first meal, and every day six measures from the cellar, out of which he owed pittance to the convent after collation on the Sabbath and once in every week at the time the hymns to St. Mary were sung, and at various other times.[5] To the precentor were assigned tithes and rents, with which he was to provide all parchments for briefs, charters, or leases, ink for the scribes, and colours for the illumination of books.[6] To the dean belonged 'a corrody for one servant,' and also the collection of Peter's Pence wherever the bishop did not collect them, from whence he was to pay annually to the pope the sum of 20*s*.' To him also belonged the visitation of the churches of the vale and the fees of all causes appertaining to the deanery, from whence he was to give a pittance to the convent on the Sunday on which the 'Misericordia Domini' was sung.[7] To the sacrist belonged six chapels of the vale, those of Norton, Lenchwick, Morton, and Offenham, with two in Evesham, All Saints and St. Lawrence,[8] and tithes and rents from abbey lands in Worcester, Hereford, and Gloucester.[9] Lands and rents also were portioned to the chamberlain, the infirmarer, and the almoner, whose special possessions included 'all the bakehouses of the Vale in which the tenants are accustomed to bake their bread,[10] and the tithe of all the bread given out within the gates of the abbey, whether baked there or bought. The almoner also had care of the monks' garden, so that he might have materials for broth (pulmentum) for the poor.[11] For the support of the fabric of the church and monastery were apportioned fifteen marks from the church of Ombersley, and if for any cause this should be left unpaid the abbot must himself supply finances for necessary repairs. This, with tithes from the land of William Burn in Offenham, and those of the smith of the same place, was all that was definitely set apart for the church. Further provision was made of sums from 'the preachings of the abbey (prædicationes abbatiæ), the bequests of the faithful, or any other gifts for that purpose.'[12] To the cell provided for the accommodation of strangers belonged the small tithes of the three Littletons for the purchase of towels, cups, and basons for guests.[13] To the kitchen belonged the third fish pond beyond St. Egwin's well, and the old town and market-place of Evesham, from which the kitchener received 5*s*. 1½*d*. every Saturday, and annually at the beginning of Lent four thousand salted fishes. Besides this, further rich provision was made, while from every carucate of land in the Vale of Evesham excepting Aldington, three hundred eggs were due every year, and from every manor 3*d*. to furnish dishes (discos) and twelve jars or pots (ollæ). Also the kitchener ought to have two store pigs (porcos ad plancheram), and as often as he bought fish at the market of Evesham for the whole convent he should have bread and a measure of ale for the refreshment of those who sold the fish. Further, for every kind of food that required sauce in which ale is used ale should be given him from the cellar, and cheese once in the day, for the purchase of which Abbot Randulf assigned the profit of the chapel of Bretforton.[14] The revenue of the kitchen in money would amount to far more than £1,000 at the present day, besides the various rents in kind. Perhaps the most interesting section in the constitution is that devoted to the duties of the cellarer. The curious details of the beans provided from Church Honeybourne to make broth throughout Lent, of the daily portions and the special occasions on which the brethren were allowed extra portions of bread and ale, of the loaf of monk's bread given to the washers as often as the table linen was washed, of the provision of bread and ale for the servants who watch with any dying brother, and so forth, call up a graphic picture of the inner life of the monastery.

A further picture is given of the literature and architecture of the abbey in the account of the works of Thomas de Marleberge. Evidently up to this time the abbey had paid no marked attention to literature, apart from the writing of charters. Doubtless the ordinary amount of manuscript writing had been done by the monks. Abbot Walter of Cerisy 'made many books,'[15] and Prior Dominic wrote the first part of the

[1] *Chron. de Evesham* (Rolls Ser.), 206.
[2] Ibid. 207. [3] Ibid. 208, 209. [4] Ibid.
[5] Ibid. and Cotton MS. Aug. ii. 11.
[6] *Chron. de Evesham* (Rolls Ser.), 210.
[7] Ibid. This seems to mean the 89th Psalm.
[8] Ibid. The chaplains of All Saints and St. Lawrence had a right to bread and beer daily from the buttery of Evesham.
[9] Ibid. 211.
[10] Cotton MS. Aug. ii. 11. *Chron. de Evesham* (Rolls Ser.), 212, 213.
[11] Ibid. 216. [12] Ibid.
[13] Ibid. [14] Ibid. 217. [15] Ibid. 97.

Chronicle of Evesham, but except the gift of books by Abbot Reginald,[1] and of a Bible by Abbot Adam,[2] there is no special mention of library or books until the time of Marleberge. He brought with him the works of Democritus, Cicero, Lucan, Juvenal, and other classical authors, as well as many sermons and notes on theology, with books of grammar and so forth. When prior he made a large breviary, 'the best then extant in the monastery,' and bound up 'Hamo on the Revelation' and the lives of the patrons of the Evesham church, 'with the acts both of good and bad men of that church,' in one volume.[3] He also bought 'the four Evangelists with glosses,' Isaiah and Ezekiel; and completed many books which a certain William de Lith had begun. He also compiled two books which seem to have been the groundwork for the Evesham Book, written later probably for Abbot John de Brokehampton between 1282 and 1316.[4] Of these books the one, 'de grossa litera librum de ordine officii abbatis a Purificatione Sanctæ Mariæusque ad Pentecostem et de professione monachorum et lectiones de Pascha et Pentecosta,' evidently corresponded to the second section of the later book, which deals with the order of the special ceremonial of certain days from Candlemas to Easter. The second book which Marleberge compiled contained 'predictum officium' (possibly, if not probably, equivalent to 'officium abbatis[5] quod officium non prius erat ordinate scripture apud nos), and seemingly corresponded with the first section of the Evesham Book, giving general directions as to the abbot's part in the services and various forms of Benediction.[6] But perhaps the most valuable of Marleberge's works is that part of the chronicle written by him giving details of the abbacy of Roger Norreys, and of the suit at Rome, such as could only have been told by one who took so prominent a part in the events described. During the next abbacy, that of Richard le Gras (1236–42), Walter de Odington, monk of Evesham, 'applying himself to literature, lest he should sink under the labour of the day, the watching at night, and continual observance of regular discipline, used at spare hours to divert himself with decent and commendable diversion of music, to render himself the more cheerful for other duties.' Literature evidently gave way to music, and his only production was a treatise, *De Speculatione Musicæ*,[7] a work which is said to rank second only to that of Franco of Cologne.[8] Apart from this there is no mention of the library or of any gifts to it after the time of Marleberge.

Besides his literary work Marleberge enlarged and beautified the buildings of the abbey, and while he was devoting himself to work within the monastery, Abbot Randulf seems to have been chiefly occupied in improving the abbey lands, building mills and granges, making dovecotes and fishponds and clearings in the forests, and giving licences to his free tenants to make clearings where land seemed possible of cultivation.[9]

John de Brokehampton, who was abbot from 1282 to 1316, followed in the steps of both Marleberge and Abbot Randulf. Besides improving the abbey buildings[10] he built granges and made canals on the abbey lands, and improved many of the churches belonging to Evesham, building altars and chancels.

In many ways this work was typical of the stage now reached in the history of the monastery. After the final settlement of the quarrel with the bishop the abbey privileges were firmly established, and thus the fourteenth and fifteenth centuries were a period of quiet enjoyment of all the privileges and wealth that an earlier age had gained. External events such as the coming of the Black Death might affect for some time the wealth and prosperity of the abbey, but their lands and privileges were ensured against attack, and no outward events could arouse them from this feeling of absolute security in their wealth. Thus, gradually, as in the majority of the monasteries, the way was paved for a dissolution as necessary for the welfare of the church as it was profitable to the king who, seemingly from very different motives, carried out the reform.

The external history of Evesham during this period was mostly the result of political events and difficulties. The baronial wars of Henry III., the Welsh and Scottish wars of Edward I. and II., and, finally, the Hundred Years' war, brought enhanced taxation which fell most heavily on the richest landowners, Evesham among them, and involved them in frequent struggles to maintain their rights. As early as 1229 Henry III. had begun his oppression of the church. Thus on the vacancy at Evesham on

[1] *Chron. de Evesham* (Rolls Ser.), 99.

[2] Ibid. 267.

[3] Ibid. 268.

[4] *Liber Evesham.* (Henry Bradshaw Soc.), vol. vi.

[5] See preface to *Liber Evesham.*

[6] Some book concerning the forms of Benediction would certainly be compiled about this time, since authority to use these forms had been obtained by Abbot Roger Norreys. A series of three papal bulls dating from 1189 to 1191 purpose to give this permission (Cotton MS. Vespas. B. xxiv. ff. 79, 79b). The genuineness of the first two, however, is suspicious, and probably the grant did not come until 1192. See *Liber Evesham.* (Henry Bradshaw Soc.), 187.

[7] Stevens, *Hist. of Abbeys, etc.* i. 205.

[8] Grove, *Dict. of Music*, sub *Notation.*

[9] This policy plunged the church into several quarrels. William de Beauchamp many times raided these cleared lands and carried off the corn. In 1274 the abbot of Evesham presented a charter of Henry VIII. by which he claimed right to clear the woods of Badsey; but in 1280 the men of Fawley impleaded him because they had hitherto had common pasture in these lands. *Abbrev. Plac.* (Rec. Com.), 188, 197

[10] See Topography, under Evesham.

the death of Abbot Randulf the king seized the temporalities and retained them for three parts of a year,[1] while on the death of Thomas of Gloucester in 1255 he kept the temporalities so long that papal interference was necessary, and in 1256 came an exhortation from Rome to the king to assign the temporalities (regalia) to Henry of Worcester, abbot elect of Evesham.[2] Henry of Worcester died in 1263 during the critical period of the struggle between Henry and his barons.[3] Money was welcome to the king, and the temporalities were retained until the election of William de Whitchurch in 1266.[4] During the abbacy of John de Brokehampton in 1309 the king granted the abbey custody of the temporalities during the next voidance, 'saving to the king the knight's fees and the advowsons of the churches,' rendering for the same six hundred marks if the voidance lasted for one year, and a proportionate sum if for less than a year.[5] In 1318, 'in honour of the victory at Evesham when his father freed his grandfather Henry from his enemies,' and by a fine of £200, Edward II. granted the abbey the custody of the temporalities during every voidance, for a payment of 240 marks for every four months or less, and 200 marks and 'pro rata' for every four months or less afterwards.[6] The attitude of the abbots of Evesham towards taxation seems to have been generally constitutional. They were ready to grant loans asked as such, but among the first to oppose exorbitant demands made against their charters. Thus in 1294 the abbot pleaded discharge of a war subsidy of 420 marks levied on his four and a half knights' fees for the war in Gascony.[7] In 1311 Edward II. sent a request that the abbot of Evesham, among others, would give credence to the king's clerk whom the king sent 'to explain certain affairs touching him and his expedition into Scotland,' hoping that they would fulfil his request for money.[8] Various loans in the reigns of Edward II. and Edward III. were granted by the abbots,[9] and in many cases the king besought the abbot and convent to provide sustenance out of their house for certain of his yeomen also who had served the king in Scotland or France, with the saving clause that this should not hereafter 'prejudice the abbey as a precedent.'[10]

It is difficult to gain any clear idea of the internal history of the abbey in the fourteenth and fifteenth centuries, since through its exemption from episcopal jurisdiction no information can be drawn from the episcopal registers. Judging from a papal mandate of 1254 annulling the sentences of excommunication issued against the abbot and convent of Evesham by the archbishop of Canterbury and the bishop of Worcester in virtue of papal letters published by Pope Gregory for the reformation of the Benedictine order, reform was needed in the abbey but hindered by papal indulgence.[11] An indult granted to Thomas Ledbury, a monk of Evesham, in 1400, who as a reward for certain services to the abbot and convent had received a room and cell in the infirmary, gives a curious example of the privileges sought by a monk. Thomas Ledbury desired in addition to his due portion of food the further portion called 'a stagere' wont to be enjoyed by the senior monk of the monastery, and 'to receive honest friends in his said room and to eat and drink with them.' Licence was granted him to receive the extra portion provided it did not exceed 1½*d.* a day, and to eat and drink in his room 'with honest men and one of the monks,' and to repair for two hours with 'an honest companion to honest places for recreation.'[12] In 1403 this indult was revoked by petition of the abbot and convent 'as contrary to the rule of the order against private property among its members, as disturbing obedience in the monastery, and as a pernicious example.'[13] Frequent instances of attacks on the property of the abbot during the fourteenth and fifteenth centuries, and frequent inroads resulting from the old enmity between the monks of Evesham and the earl of Warwick, must have been a great hindrance to order in the monastery and obedience among the monks, and must have tended to make them fighters rather than students. But order and learning had no greater enemy than the Black Death, creating as it did one of those epochs when death and the

[1] *Chron. de Evesham* (Rolls Ser.), 272. Marleberge, after re-election, according to the pope's orders, was consecrated in the July of 1230, but the temporalities were not restored until September of that year.

[2] *Cal. of Papal Letters*, i. 330.

[3] *Chron. de Evesham* (Rolls Ser.), 282.

[4] *Cal. of Papal Letters*, i. 392, 420.

[5] *Cal. of Close*, 1318–23, 153.

[6] Ibid. 1343–6, 424; *Chron. de Evesham* (Rolls Ser.), 288; Harl. MSS. 3763, fol. 134.

[7] *Rolls of Parl.* (Rec Com.) i. 461b. 'Lequele service le dit Abbe n'est mye tenuz a faire, ne luy, ne nul de ses predecesseurs unqs ne le sesoient sinon en la presence nostre seigneur le Roy ou de ses auncestres et ceo solonc le purport des chartres les auncestres nostre Seigneur le Roy avantdit.' Therefore the abbot begged that his church might ever enjoy the privileges granted by the said charters.

[8] *Cal. of Close*, 1307–13, 357.

[9] *Rolls of Parl.* (Rec. Com.) ii. 453b; *Cal. of Pat.* 1330–4, 422, 424, 447.

[10] *Cal. of Pat.* 1330–4, 21; *Cal. of Close*, 1307–13, 554; Ibid. 1313–18, 306, 462, 560, 601; Ibid. 1318–20, 116; Ibid. 1330–3, 281.

[11] *Cal. of Papal Letters*, i. 299.

[12] Ibid. v. 335.

[13] Ibid. 551. It is significant that this indult and its revocation occurred during the good rule of Abbot Zatton, of whom the chronicler says:—'Iste abbas in conventu suo simplex et rectus et mitis semper apparuit non nimis mundanus sed valde religiosus nullinocens sed omnes diligens et omnibus quantum potuit proficiens, semper Deo devotus.' *Chron. de Evesham* (Rolls Ser.), 310.

fear of death sweeps aside all rules and refinements. Impossible as it is to gauge accurately its effects on the monastery when so little evidence is forthcoming,[1] there is little likelihood that Evesham escaped its generally demoralizing and destructive influence. The depopulation of the monastery by the disease is shown by a comparison of the number of monks in 1086 and in 1418. In 1086 there were sixty-seven;[2] in 1418, according to the list of monks taking part in the election of Abbot Richard Bromsgrove, there were only thirty-one,[3] though the chronicle states that there were thirty-eight at that date.[4] But the high death-rate among the monks is most convincingly shown by an entry in the Harleian manuscripts making provision for a priest to celebrate mass 'for the souls of the brethren departed in this fearful pestilence.' It recites how so many of the monks of Evesham had been 'destroyed by the pestilence now raging that on account of their multitude' the customary allowance made to the poor for a year on the death of each monk 'could not conveniently be made,' and to remedy this 'a competent chaplain' was hereby provided to pray for their souls.[5] Moreover the building of the new charnel chapel in the cemetery of Evesham seems to indicate how great was the number of deaths at the time.[6] At the time of the Dissolution the number of the monks granted pensions was thirty-three.[7] It is clear therefore that after the Black Death the monks never reached their original number. As to the results of the Black Death on the material wealth of the abbey the chronicle may or may not be misleading. Other evidence shows that the plague was raging in Worcestershire in 1349, and for the next few years 'on divers manors of the bishopric of Worcester' the king's escheators 'could not obtain more than the small sum they allowed on account of the dearth of tenants and of customary tenants . . . who had all died in the deadly pestilence which raged in the lands of the bishopric.'[8] It is not likely that mortality from the plague was confined to the tenants of the bishop, and Evesham must have suffered ; yet the chronicle says nothing of its losses, but recounts the acquisitions of manors and tenements by the various abbots, and sums up the state of the abbey in 1379 as 'full of all good things.'[9] The first mention of debts is on the death of Abbot Zatton in 1418, and these are attributed to various law suits.[10] Abbot Richard Hawkesbury also contracted a debt of 1,000 marks by entertaining nobles 'who came to the monastery in such numbers that the rents would not suffice.'[11] His successor was able to pay the debt,[12] and at the Dissolution the abbey was out of debt, except the sum of £800 to the king for part of the first fruits.[13]

While the abbey could not pass unscathed through a period of war and arbitrary taxation, which was intensified by the coming of the Black Death, there is another side to its history during this period. It was a time in which the abbey sealed its exemption from the bishop's influence by applying to the pope on such matters as the caps they were to wear in the choir 'in consideration of the cold site of their monastery,'[14] and by obtaining licences and dispensations from him which entirely cut them off from any connexion with the bishop. Before the end of the thirteenth century the abbot had obtained the right to give solemn benediction in the absence of the archbishop, bishop, or legate, in addition to former licence to wear mitre, ring, sandals, and other pontifical insignia.[15] He had also received licence to grant dispensations in regard to the observance of statutes added to their rule by papal or legatine authority.[16] In 1332 the abbey is termed 'a royal foundation directly subject to Rome, having jurisdiction exempt, with power to correct all persons, ecclesiastical and secular alike, dwelling within such jurisdiction, without any bishop being able to interfere.[17] In 1363 a papal indult granted that 'in consideration of the dangers and expenses of the journey to the apostolic see' no confirmation was necessary for an abbot elect of Evesham, but he might be blessed by any bishop of the monastery's choice 'in communion with that see.'[18] Needless to say the choice never fell on the bishop of Worcester.[19] But besides this settlement of ecclesiastical rights and privileges the same period was marked by an increase of

[1] There is no mention of the pestilence in the chronicle of the abbots of that time. In all probability Abbot William Boys died of the plague in 1367, though the chronicle only says, 'multa ægritudine fatigatus apud manerium de Ombersley diem suum clausit extremum.' *Chron. de Evesham* (Rolls Ser.), 299.

[2] Cotton MS. B xxiv. fol. 41d.

[3] Lands, MS. 227, fol. 41.

[4] *Chron. de Evesham* (Rolls Ser.), 310.

[5] Harl. MS. 3763, 159b.

[6] Ibid. f. 160.

[7] *L. and P. Hen. VIII.* xv. 37.

[8] L. T. R. Mem. R. 26 Edw. III. (membrane marked (1) near the end of the roll).

[9] *Chron. de Evesham* (Rolls Ser.), 303.

[10] Ibid. 309–10.

[11] Cotton MS. B. xv. f. 18.

[12] Ibid.

[13] *L. and P. Hen. VIII.* xiii. i. 360.

[14] *Cal. of Papal Letters*, i. 250, 270.

[15] Ibid.

[16] Ibid. 299.

[17] *Cal. of Pat.* 1330–4, 249.

[18] *Cal. of Papal Letters*, iv. 329.

[19] Abbot Richard Bromsgrove received benediction from the bishop of Bangor ; Sir John Wickwan from the bishop of Bath ; Richard Pembroke from the bishop of Hereford ; 'for being made exempt the abbey was careful to prevent all claim of subjection for the future and constantly received benediction from other bishops and not from Worcester.' Letter among MS. Whartoni (Lamb. Lib.) dlxxxv. f. 665.

of material privileges. Many royal grants of markets and fairs, free warren, frankpledge, quittance of suit at the hundred court, rights of assize, and other privileges, were made by Edward III. and Edward IV., and there are many instances of the jealous way in which the house guarded every right, especially in the town of Evesham.[1] Thus during the fifteenth century the state of outward prosperity was reached which is witnessed in 1535 by the Valor Ecclesiasticus giving the yearly revenue of the monastery as £1,183 12*s.* 9*d.* clear,[2] and by the long roll of its possessions, reaching the same value, entered on the Ministers' Accounts for 1540-7.[3]

Clement Litchfield, who was in reality the last abbot of Evesham, summed up in himself all the qualities of his predecessors. From the time of John de Brokehampton, without exception, the abbots had been chosen from officials or monks of Evesham; and although this might be a hindrance to any broadening of interests in the monastery, it ensured that the abbots were men who had the cause of the monastery at heart. Apart from their attendance at parliament none of the abbots from the time of Richard le Gras seem to have held any important political office, but to have devoted all their energies to work within the monastery. Of none was this more true than of Clement Litchfield. Thus in 1535 the royal inquisitors could not but describe the abbot as 'a man chaste in his living' who 'right well overlooked the reparations of his house.' Latimer, however, influenced doubtless by the old enmity between the bishop of Worcester and the abbot of Evesham, termed him a 'bloody abbot,' and in December, 1537, wrote to Cromwell concerning Evesham reminding him that though the abbey was exempt from his own jurisdiction it was subservient to Cromwell. 'I pray God amend them,' he wrote, 'or else I fear they be exempt from the flock of Christ. Very true monks, that is to say 'pseudoprophetæ,' and false Christian men, pervertors of scripture, sly, wily, disobedientaries to all good orders, ever starting up as they dare, to do hurt.'[4]

From 1535,[5] to 1538, the date of his resignation, Abbot Clement was troubled by the attempts of the king's agents to make him surrender. In 1536 he wrote to Cromwell complaining that two years ago a certain Mr. Wever, one of the king's servants, brought letters from the king for certain pastures called Plowdon (in Church Honeybourne), and although when Cromwell had 'received a little fee' from the house 'the king was well contented,' yet ever since Mr. Wever had borne the abbot 'great grudge' and had 'imagined many ways to have him deposed,' saying that he had authority to put him down and make whom he would abbot, and ceased not 'following his malice' towards him.[6] Moreover by 1536 the king had found at least one friend within the monastery, the cellarer of Evesham, Philip Hawford, who was in negotiation with Cromwell in that year and who wrote in May, 1536, telling Cromwell that he would 'gladly accomplish' all the promises he had made and be always ready for 'the call to preferment' promised him by Cromwell.[7] In 1536, Alcester and Penworth, the two cells of Evesham, were dissolved, and Charles Bradway and Richard Hawkesbury once more became monks of Evesham.[8] In October, 1537, Arthur Kelton wrote to Wriothesley, 'after my return from you I certified my kinsman, the cellarer of Evesham (Philip Hawford) . . . that you intended to move the cause with the counsel of Dr. Petre.' Hawford had since written to remind Kelton that the 'audit and receipt came shortly after All Hallows' day and the abbot received all he could get beforehand contrary to custom.' Therefore Kelton begged Wriothesley to abbreviate the time so that he might 'with some receipt be the more abler to content the king's first fruits.'[9] The result of this letter was that in March, 1538, Dr. Petre was sent with letters from Cromwell to the abbot, who was forced 'by the vile arts and low devices of Cromwell' to give in his resignation, since he would not surrender to the king. Petre wrote to Cromwell that the abbot was 'contented to make resignation immediately on sight of your lordship's letters, saving that he desired me very instantly that I would not open the same during the time of my being here, because it would be noted that he was compelled to resign for fear of deprivation. As to his pension he refers to your lordship, submitting himself to be orderly in all things as to your lordship shall be thought to be mete.'[10] 'We have taken the surrender of this

[1] *V. C. H. Worc.* ii. Topography.

[2] *Valor Eccl.* (Rec. Com.), iii. 254.

[3] Mins. Acc. 31, 32 Hen. VIII. L. R. 1330.

[4] *L. and P. Hen. VIII.* xii. ii. 442.

[5] The year 1535 was evidently the year of the first visitation by royal inquisitors. Richard Luton wrote to Cromwell: 'We have so much to do at the abbey of Evesham that we cannot attend you to-night, but will see you to-morrow. We must take Tewkesbury in our way and peruse the inventory, appropriations, and other muniments.' Ibid. ix. 1.

[6] Ibid. x. ii. 236. Mr. Wever's suit did not cease on the resignation of Clement Litchfield, for in June, 1539, Philip Hawford wrote to Cromwell complaining of his continued suit for 'a pasture necessary for the monastery for keeping up hospitality.' Ibid. xiv. i. 520.

[7] Ibid. x. 390.

[8] Ibid. 498, xi. 14, 236, xii. 1. 280.

[9] Ibid. xii. ii. 316.

[10] There seems to be no mention of a grant of a pension, but the 'lodging commonly called the Chamberer's Chamber' together with 'the Tailor's House' and an orchard called the 'Calves Croft' are entered in the Ministers' Accounts as belonging to Clement Litchfield for the term of his life (Ibid. xix. i. 276). On 18 August, 1546, he died and was

priory,' he goes on to say, 'with as much quietness as might be desired and proper for the dispatch of all other things.'[1] Evidently the course to be taken had already been planned out. Philip Hawford was 'called to preferment' on the fourth of April,[2] and in the same month the temporalities were restored to him.[3] Evidently he had bribed Cromwell for his preferment, for in May, 1538, Dr. Petre wrote to Wriothesley that 'touching Mr. Cromwell's matter the abbot says it shall be paid to-morrow morning,'[4] and an entry of 400 marks from the abbot is found in Cromwell's account for that month.[5] In October, 1538, Latimer wrote to Cromwell thanking him on behalf of the abbot of Evesham for his kindnesses which 'few will better remember.' Of the abbot, Latimer spoke in friendly terms as a 'very civil and honest man' and one who 'puts his sole trust in Cromwell.'[6] In January, 1540, Hawford fulfilled his promises and surrendered the monastery to the king, receiving a pension of £240 a year as his reward,[7] and afterwards in lieu of the pension the deanery of Worcester. The abbey church was rased to the ground immediately on the surrender, and the usual reckless destruction and spoliation followed, though the tower of Abbot Litchfield was saved, as it is said, by the intervention of the men of Evesham, who, as Browne Willis suggests,[8] had contributed towards its erection. Even Philip Hawford had attempted to save the buildings of the convent, petitioning that the monastery should be turned into a college when surrendered. The first petition made in November, 1538, set forth the reasons why Evesham should be made into an educational establishment. It was 'situated in wholesome air in the town of Evesham, through which there is a great thoroughfare into Wales.' Also it was near Warwickshire 'where there is no monastery standing,' and was exempt from the bishop. The buildings of the house itself were in good repair and the house free from debt except £800 owing to the king, and noted for its hospitality, for as there were few inns in the town of Evesham 'all such noblemen as did repair and resort to the same town' could not have lodging 'without the said monastery.'[9] The same arguments were repeated in the second petition made in June, 1539, but again were of no avail.

buried in the parish church of All Hallows, in Evesham, giving to the church before his death three kine to have mass and dirge with certain refreshings to the parishioners 'at every yeare's mynde for ever.' (Lands. MS. 1233, fol. 31).

[1] Cotton MS. Cleop. E. iv. fol. 308.
[2] Pat. 29 Hen. VIII. m. 14.
[3] *L. and P. Hen. VIII.* xiii. i. 411.
[4] Ibid. 354. [5] Ibid. xiv. ii. 322.
[6] Ibid. xiii. ii. 272.
[7] Aug. Off. Misc. Bks. vol. 245, f. 105.
[8] Browne Willis, *Mitred Abbeys*, i. 97.
[9] *L. and P. Hen. VIII.* xiii. ii. 360.

With one last glimpse of a monk of the monastery living in the early seventeenth century, the history of Evesham ends. In 1603, Father Augustine Bradshaw reconciled to the Benedictine order 'one Lyttleton, who had formerly been a monk of Evesham, and was now best known by the nickname of 'parson-tinker.' Being reclaimed he went home and 'presently fell blind and so remained almost two years deprived of his benefice and had he not been bedridden had been imprisoned for his conscience and so died with great repentance being near 100 years old.'[10]

ABBOTS OF EVESHAM

St. Egwin, 710-717.[11]

Between the years 717 and 941.[13]
- Ethelwold.
- Aldbore.
- Aldbath.
- Aldfefert.
- Tildbrith.
- Cutulf.
- Aldmund.
- St. Credanus.[12]
- Thincferth.
- Aldbald.
- Ecbrith.
- Elferd.
- Wlfard.
- Kinelm.
- Kinath.
- Ebba.
- Kinath.
- Edwin.

(The abbey possessed by seculars 941–969).[14]

Osward, 969-976.[15]

(The abbey again possessed by seculars 976-c.989).[16]

(The abbey in possession of Bishop Ethelwig, Bishop Ethelstan, and Adulf bishop of Worcester respectively c.989-c.996).[17]

Brithmar, c. 996-1014.[18]
Alfward, 1014-1044.[19]
Manny, 1044-1059.[20]
Ethelwig, 1059-1077.[21]
Walter de Cerisy, 1077-1104.[22]

[10] Bod. Lib. Wood MS. B. 6. f. 16. This was Richard Lyttleton sub-sexton of the monastery at the time of the Dissolution.
[11] *Chron. de Evesham* (Rolls Ser.), 12, 14.
[12] Ibid. 76 n. [13] Ibid. 76.
[14] Ibid. 77. [15] Ibid. 78.
[16] Ibid. 78, 79. [17] Ibid. 80.
[18] Ibid. 81. [19] Ibid. 81, 85.
[20] Ibid. 86, 87. [21] Ibid. 87, 95.
[22] Ibid. 96, 98. The year 1086 is given as the date of Walter's death in Harl. MS. 3763 f. 168d, and in Cotton. Vespas. B. xv. f. 18. However, Walter, abbot of Evesham, was a witness to William Rufus's charter to the monastery of Bath in 1094 (*Adam de Domerham* (ed. Hearne), i. 278) and to Henry I.'s confirmation charter in 1102 (Harl. MS. 358, f. 39). Florence of Worcester gives the date of his death as 1104. *Flor. Wigorn.* (Eng. Hist. Soc.), ii. 53.

Robert de Jumièges, 1104-1122.[1]
Maurice, 1122-1130.[2]
Reginald, 1130-1149.[3]
William de Andeville, 1149-1159.[4]
Roger, monk of St. Augustine's, Canterbury, 1159-1160.[5]
Adam, monk of Cluny, 1160-1191.[6]
Roger Norreys, 1191-1213.[7]
Randulf, prior of Worcester, 1214-1229.[8]
Thomas de Marleberge, prior of Worcester, 1229-1236.[9]
Richard le Gras, 1236-1242.[10]
Thomas of Gloucester, 1243-1255.[11]
Henry, prior of Evesham, 1255-1263.[12]
William de Whitchurch, 1266-1282.[13]
John de Brokehampton, 1282-1316.[14]
William de Cheriton, 1317-1344.[15]
William de Boys, 1345-1367.[16]
John de Ombersley, 1367-1379.[17]
Roger Zatton, 1379-1418.[18]
Richard Bromsgrove, 1418-1435.[19]
John Wykewan, 1435-c.1460.[20]
Richard Pembroke, 1460-1467.[21]
Richard Hawkesbury, 1467-1477.[22]
William Upton, 1477-1483.[23]
John Norton, 1483-1491.[24]
Thomas Newbold, 1491-1514.[25]
Clement Litchfield, 1514-1539.[26]
Philip Hawford or Ballard, 1539-1540.[27]

On the obverse of the common seal of the monastery the swineherd Eoves is represented standing with his feet to the left and his face to the right between two oak trees, leaning on a staff and tending a sow suckling a pig. On a broad scroll with a lancet-shaped cusp in the upper part and curved at the sides, forming a kind of trefoiled outline, the inscription—

EOVES : HER : WONEDE : ANT : W[AS : SWON :]
[FOR] : PI : MEN : CLEPET : þIS :
EOVISHOM

Outside the scroll on either side is a tree. In the upper part a church with a tall spire or central tower, and each gable ornamented with a cross and having a cinquefoil over the roof-line on the right. Between two arches, one plain and one trefoiled on each side, Egwin, bishop of Worcester and founder, kneeling before the Virgin with crown and long cross, attended by a man wearing a cloak and a woman with a book. To him the word ECCE LOC QVĒ ELEGI under the church are addressed. On the right under a tree the Virgin is seated with her feet on a platform, appearing in a vision to Eoves.

SIGILLUM : SANCTE : MARI[E : ET : SANTI :
ECGWINI : ĒPI : E]OVESHAMENSIS :
MONASTER[II]

On the reverse of the seal is a complicated design divided into two portions or storeys by a series of pointed arches, trefoiled and the two larger arches crocketed with oak leaves. In the upper storey between two oak trees Bishop Egwin mitred is kneeling to the left and presenting a small model of a church with a tall central spire and two side towers or turrets, each topped with a cross, and that on the right with a flag, to the Virgin who is seated in a niche crowned with the Child on her left knee. In the lower storey the three royal patrons of the monastery, Kenred, Offa, and Ethelred, seated on a bench with crowns. The one on the left has a falcon on his wrist, the middle one holds a sceptre, the one on the right is turned in profile to the right. The three are presenting a charter inscribed—

DAMUS : REGIE : LIBER : TATI :

On the right is Bishop Egwin mitred kneeling and receiving the charter, behind him a chaplain kneeling.[28] The inscription runs thus :—

DICTI]S :]ECGWI[NI : DANT :]REGE[S :
MUNERA TRINI : OMNIBUS : UNDE : PI]E :
NITET : AULA : SACRATA : MARIE

3. THE ABBEY OF PERSHORE

The abbey of Pershore is stated by William of Malmesbury to have been founded by Egelward, duke of Dorset, in the reign of King Edgar,[29] but this is generally accepted as the date of the re-constitution of a house already in existence and the introduction of Benedictine monks.[30] Leland describes the monastery as originally founded about the year 689 by Oswald,[31] a

1 *Chron. de Evesham* (Rolls Ser.), 98.
2 Ibid.
3 Ibid. 98, 99. Cott. MS. Vesp. B. xxiv. f. 54.
4 Ibid. 99, 100.
5 Ibid. 100.
6 Ibid. 100, 102.
7 Ibid. 102, 250.
8 Ibid. 255, 272.
9 Ibid. 272-278.
10 Ibid. 278, 279.
11 Ibid. 279, 280.
12 Ibid. 281, 282.
13 Ibid. 282, 283.
14 Ibid. 284, 289.
15 Ibid. 289, 293.
16 Ibid. 293, 299.
17 Ibid. 299, 303.
18 Ibid. 303, 310.
19 Ibid. 338.
20 Ibid. 338.
21 Ibid. 339.
22 Ibid.
23 Ibid.
24 Ibid.
25 Ibid.
26 Ibid. 340.
27 Ibid.

28 B.M. Seals. xxxv. 58 (13th century). Dr. Prattinton has recorded the varying interpretations of the inscriptions on the Evesham seal (Prattinton Coll. Soc. Antiq.) A badly executed copy of the seal exists in which the legend on the scroll has been corrupted as follows :—

EOVESHE : VENETIE : AIT : WAS : SWIN :
CORVIMEN : CLEPET : VIS : EOVISHOM.

B.M. Seals, xxxv. 60 (15th cent.) Tindal, Nash, and Dugdale made use of this impression.

29 *Will. of Malmes.* (Rolls Ser.), 298.
30 Ibid. note 4.
31 The brother of Osric, prince of the Hwiccas and founder of St. Peter's, Gloucester, and the abbey of Bath. Leland, *Coll.* (Hearne ed.), i. 240.

nephew of Ethelred, king of the Mercians, who instituted secular canons in the new foundation, monks being subsequently introduced, then the canons reinstated and finally replaced by monks through the instrumentality of King Edgar.[1] The monastic *Annals* say that St. Oswald after introducing monks at Worcester and Westbury constituted the same at Pershore in 983, the name of the first abbot being Foldbriht or Fulbert.[2] According to the chronicle this holy man, famous for the austerities he practised, was raised from death by the prayers of St. Oswald and declared the glorious visions he had seen under the guidance of St. Benedict and that for the merits of St. Oswald he had received forgiveness of sins and assurance of salvation, after which he again expired.[3]

The charter of Edgar, dated 972, recites that he has granted to the convent situated at Pershore and dedicated to the ever blessed Virgin Mary, Mother of Our Lord, and the apostles SS. Peter and Paul, all the privileges bestowed on them by his predecessor Coenulf at the request of Duke Beornoth with the liberty of electing a head according to the rule of St. Benedict after the death of Folbriht, in whose time this liberty had been restored. The document, which runs to great length, enumerates extensive grants of 'manses' in Pershore and elsewhere to be restored to the possession of the monks.[4] The monastery passed through many vicissitudes before the compilation of Domesday, and is said to have sustained great losses amounting to 'more than half her revenues, one part being devoured by the ambition of the rich, another buried in oblivion, and the greatest portion of all bestowed by Edward the Confessor and William the Conqueror on Westminster.'[5] The house was perhaps exceptionally unfortunate; it was several times destroyed by fire and a prey to plunder. According to Leland it became deserted on the first destruction by fire early in the eleventh century, and the abbey of Westminster stepped into the possessions of the monks.[6] The church was rebuilt and opened in 1020.[7] The brethren suffered severely under the depredations of Duke Delfer, or Alphere,[8] who did great injury to the monastic establishments of the diocese. After a life of crime and rapine the oppressor of the church is said to have met with a horrible death, 'being eaten of vermin.' His son Odda restored what his father had plundered and vowed a vow of perpetual virginity lest a son of his should be guilty of similar crime.[9] He adopted the habit of a monk at Deerhurst, and after his death in 1056 his body was carried for burial to Pershore.[10] The *Anglo-Saxon Chronicle* describes him as 'a good man and pure and very noble.'[11] Many years later, after another of these disastrous fires which devasted Pershore, the workmen digging in the Lady-chapel came upon a leaden coffin containing the bones of this 'founder' and inscribed with his epitaph, 'Odda, sometime duke, in times past called Edwin in baptism, a worshipper of God and a monk before his death, lies here. Joy to him in peace with Christ Our Lord. Amen.'[12] Earl Odda or Wadda was the benefactor who purchased the precious relics of St. Edburga and bestowed them on the convent; in honour of this sacred trust, which drew many pilgrims attracted by the report of miracles performed at her shrine, the house was from that time dedicated to the Blessed Virgin and St. Edburga Virgin.[13]

At the time of the Domesday Survey the lands held by the abbey comprised Hawkesbury and Cowley in Gloucestershire, the manor of Pershore with the berewicks or hamlets of Chevington, Abberton [Edbritone], Wadborough, Broughton, Abberton [Edbretintune], Wick and Cumberton containing 26 hides. The monks had a salt pan at Droitwich yielding 36 'mits' of salt. In Beoley with Yardley the convent held 21 hides, 20 in Sture (Alderminster), 30 in Broadway, 3 in Leigh and 5 at Mathon in the hundred of Dodingtree of which one hide lay in Herefordshire. Payment of church scot was due to the abbey for 300 hides, and the abbot had the right of 'forisfactura' or payment for transgression for 100 hides.[14] The value of the land in many cases had fallen considerably since the days of the Confessor, and many of the places mentioned in the charter of Edgar had passed out of the possession of the abbey. It is stated in a ledger of the bishopric of Worcester that half the town of Pershore with its appurtenances had been granted to the abbot of Westminster by King Edward.[15]

The abbot and convent obtained a charter from King John in the first year of his reign confirming to God and St. Mary and Blessed Edburga Virgin and the monastery of Pershore all their lands and possessions within the counties of Gloucester and Worcester to be held free of all secular service, with right of soc, sac, thol, theam, and infangnethef, and a prohibition addressed to the sheriff and king's officers forbad the exaction of toll or custom from the

1 Leland, *Itin.* (Hearne ed.), v. 2.
2 *Ann. Mon.* (Rolls Ser.), iv. 369.
3 Leland *Coll.* (Hearne ed.), i. 244.
4 Birch, *Cart. Sax.* iii. 583.
5 *William of Malmesbury* (Rolls Ser.), 298; cited by Habington, *Surv. of Worc.* (Worc. Hist. Soc.), ii. 237.
6 Leland, *Itin.* (Hearne ed.), v. 2.
7 Ibid. *Coll.* (Hearne ed.), i. 242.
8 Ibid. *Itin.* (Hearne ed.), v. 2; Add. MS. 5847, p. 353.
9 Ibid. *Coll.* (Hearne ed.), i. 244.
10 *A. S. Chron.* (Rolls Ser.), 326.
11 Ibid.
12 Leland, *Coll.* (Hearne ed.), i. 244.
13 Ibid. *Itin.* (Hearne ed.), v. 2.
14 *Dom. Bk.* (Rec. Com.), i. 275–6.
15 Nash, *Hist. of Worc.*, ii. 245.

convent and their servants.[1] Henry III. confirmed the privileges granted by his father, and in 1251 the convent obtained a charter granting them the liberty of free warren over their demesne lands in the manors of Pershore, Leigh, Mathon, Alderminster, Broadway, Cowley, Hawkesbury, and Wadborough.[2]

The Taxation of 1291 gives the abbey an income of £99 12*s.* 6*d.* derived from temporalities in the diocese of Worcester.[3] The spiritualities, amounting to £41 2*s.* 10*d.*,[4] included £6 13*s.* 4*d.* from the altar of Holy Cross in the southern part of the nave of the conventual church which served the parish, and £5 from St. Andrew's church, Pershore, said to have been built by Edward the Confessor for the use of the tenants of the abbot of Westminster to whom he had made large grants in Pershore.[5] Early in the thirteenth century a dispute seems to have arisen between the two abbots as to their respective rights, the abbot of Pershore asserting that the 'atrium' of the church was his and that the free tenants of the abbot of Westminster had no right there; ultimately he agreed that the abbot of St. Peter's should have his seat where he had had it of custom.[6] The abbot and convent of Pershore are said to have obtained the advowson of St. Andrew's in 1241, and to have been thus relieved 'from the oppression of the abbot of Westminster and Guy de Beauchamp.'[7] In addition to St. Andrew's they appear by the end of the thirteenth century to have presented to the churches of Broadway[8] and Cowley[9] in Gloucestershire, Leigh,[10] Mathon,[11] Abberton,[12] Eckington,[13] and St. Peter the Great of Worcester.[14]

Financial difficulties induced the monks at a comparatively early stage to supplement lessened resources by resort to appropriation. At the latter end of the twelfth century the archbishop of Canterbury, Hubert Walter, bestowed on the brethren in consideration of their poverty the church of Hawkesbury 'in proprios usus.'[15] Henry de Soilli is said to have granted them the appropriation of the church of Broadway when it should next become vacant for the maintenance of the infirmary,[16] and the church of Mathon on its next vacancy for the better 'procuration' of the brethren on festivals.[17] The appropriation of the church of Alderminster, granted about this time, was lost until restored by bishop Giffard in 1269.[18] Eudo de Beauchamp bequeathed the advowson of the church of Hill-Croome with his body to the church of SS. Mary and Edburga of Pershore,[19] Osbert Fitz-Pontii gave a fishery in Longney with the church of that town.[20] Geoffrey de Chamville granted to abbot Gervase the chapel of St. Nicholas of 'Kemerford' to provide a pittance for the monks on the feast of St. Mary during his lifetime, and after his death on his anniversary.[21] Among the benefactors of the abbey special mention must be made of Lady Constance de Leigh, who by a charter made during her widowhood and 'after the divorce made between Geoffrey de Avetot my kinsman and me' relinquished for herself and her heirs all rights of stewardship with customs and corrodies pertaining to the same which she and her ancestors formerly enjoyed in the abbey.[22] She also confirmed a bequest of 3*s.* annual rent to the high altar of Pershore made by her father William de Leigh,[23] and by the consent of Mabel her mother, and after a divorce had been 'celebrated' between herself and Stephen de Ebroic', added the gift of a piece of ground in Eckington to enlarge the monks' burial ground which it adjoined.[24] During the rule of abbot Roger, Lady Constance bequeathed her body with the advowson of Holy Trinity church, Eckington, in perpetuity to the monastery and the abbot and his successors.[25] Besides the Lady-chapel there is a mention of the chapel of St. Michael,[26] and on St. David's Day 1514–15 Christopher Westerdall, 'gentyllman,' made a grant for the maintenance of a daily mass called 'Seynt Johny's Masse' in the chapel of St. John the Baptist within the conventual church.[27]

The causes of the dwindling resources which so hampered the abbey are set forth in the petition of the monks for the appropriation of St. Andrew's church, Pershore. This document, dated 1327, states that at the time of its foundation the monastery was sufficiently endowed for the maintenance of a statutory number of brethren, the exercise of hospitality, and the care of the poor; a time, however, subsequently ensued in which owing to wars and disturbances, the power of kings and nobles, and by no fault of the community itself, as many as thirty manors formerly in its possession were lost, while at the same time the charges on the hospitality of the house had so increased on account of its situation near the public way which attracted great

1 Chart. R. 1 John, pt. ii. m. 3.
2 Ibid. 35 Hen. III. m. 3.
3 *Pope Nich. Tax.* (Rec. Com.), 230, 236.
4 Ibid. pp. 217, 218, 220–223.
5 Nash, *Hist. of Worc.* ii. 251.
6 *Abbrev. Plac.* (Rec. Com.), 24.
7 Leland, *Coll.* (Hearne ed.), i. 242.
8 *Worc. Epis. Reg. Giffard* (Worc. Hist. Soc.), p. 39
9 Ibid. p. 106.
10 Ibid. p. 98.
11 Ibid. p. 484
12 Ibid. p. 64.
13 *Reg. Sede Vac.* (Worc. Hist. Soc.), 74.
14 *Worc. Epis. Reg. Giffard* (Worc. Hist. Soc.), p. 544.
15 Aug. Off. Misc. Bks. 61 f. 102.
16 Ibid. ff. 104–5.
17 Ibid. f. 105.
18 *Worc. Epis. Reg. Giffard* (Worc. Hist. Soc.), p. 28.
19 Aug. Off. Misc. Bks. 61, f. 110.
20 Harl. Chart. 50 B. 22.
21 Aug. Off. Misc. Bks. 61, f. 110.
22 Ibid. f. 46.
23 Ibid.
24 Ibid.
25 Ibid. f. 46d.
26 *Reg. Sede Vac.* (Worc. Hist. Soc.), 19.
27 Madox, *Formul. Anglic.* 272.

numbers of people, not only of the rich and powerful, but also of the poor, that the brethren found themselves unable to sustain the burden. The scarcity of the last few years, combined with disease and murrain among the sheep, and the 'extortion of enemies,' had so reduced the capacity of the house that it was impossible without extra assistance to put the church and conventual buildings, the greater part of which had been destroyed by fire, into repair, and the nave of the church, the refectory, dormitory, and guest house still lay in ruins.[1] In addition to St. Andrew's, Pershore, the convent were permitted in 1344 to appropriate the church of Holy Trinity, Eckington, also of their advowson, at the request of John de Beauchamp.[2]

In 1327 the abbot and convent received licence to lease certain lands in Pershore with the advowson of St. Andrew's church to Adam de Herwynton for the term of his life.[3] After his death, about 1345, the convent ordained a chantry of two secular priests at the altar in the southern part of the nave in a chapel within which the late Adam had been buried, to pray for the souls of Guy, late earl of Warwick, and Adam de Herwynton, who had bequeathed a large sum of money with certain lands and rents for this purpose, and for the good estate of Thomas, now earl of Warwick, and Lady Katherine, his wife, while they lived and for their souls 'when withdrawn from this light.'[4] The yearly observance of the anniversary of the said Adam was set down for the last day of March.[5]

No blame seems to have attached itself to the monks for the management of their affairs until the middle of the fourteenth century ; their misfortunes received due commiseration and their kindness to poor travellers was much commended. Their conduct, however, in 1340 attracted the bishop's attention, and he wrote to the late abbot, William de Herwynton, committing the custody of the abbey to him, *pro tem.*, on the ground of reports that certain brethren, 'degenerate sons,' were wasting its goods and creating grievous scandal by applying them to their own licentious pleasures.[6] The charge of alienation of property and general mismanagement was renewed in December, 1352, but uncoupled with a hint of grosser scandal.[7] The economic condition of the last half of the fourteenth century was little calculated to improve the financial position of any religious foundation, and Pope Boniface IX., in 1345, confirming the appropriation of the churches of Broadway and St. Peter the Great of Worcester to the abbot and convent of Pershore, states that their monastery 'is weighed down with debt, and their refectory and dormitory in need of repair.'[8] This is the last reference to the financial condition of the house until the eve of the Dissolution.

The relations of abbot and convent with the king, and their contact with national life, seem of a quite normal and uneventful nature. The abbot received letters of protection from King John in 1200,[9] and on three occasions from Edward I.[10] Henry III., on the occasion of the fire which broke out on S. Urban's day, 1223, and reduced the monastery and the greater part of the town to cinders,[11] issued instructions for the constable of Bristol to allow the convent twelve trees (*fusta*) from the forest of Alveston for the repair of their church and buildings, similar contributions being laid on the forest of Feckenham and forest of Kinver ;[12] the new church was dedicated by Walter de Cantilupe in 1239. A similar fate overtook it in 1288 ; a conflagration broke out on 22 April in the bakehouse and brewery, spread to the bell-tower (*clocherium*), and nearly consumed the whole church.[13] Edward I., who had spent a week at Pershore in January, 1281–2,[14] came to the monks' assistance, and bestowed on them ten oaks fit for timber from the forest of Dean for rebuilding.[15] The entry in the *Annals* records that on 25 June, 1299, the bishop of Llandaff 'reconciled' the church of Pershore, as the church-keeper, deceived by the counsel of a woman, had offered strange fire in the sacred place.[16]

A register containing an account of the estates held of the abbey and the privileges enjoyed by the convent was burnt during one of these fires, and a commission was held to ascertain their extent by the evidence of the monks. Walter the prior stated in evidence that when Bishop Mauger came to Pershore to ordain, he withdrew from the monastery to the chapel of St. Andrew within the precincts of the monks' cemetery on being shown their customs ; subsequently, on the invitation of the brethren, he entered the convent and ordained. On another occasion when the said bishop was invited by the abbot and convent to the feast of St. Edburga, he celebrated mass

1 Worc. Epis. Reg. Cobham, f. 124.

2 Pat. 18. Edw. III. pt. ii. m. 48.

3 Ibid. 1 Edw. III. pt. ii. m. 11.

4 Aug. Off. Misc. Bks. 61, f. 34d.

5 Ibid. This chantry, usually styled 'of Adam Herwynton,' is referred to as the chantry of All Saints in an entry of 1490. Worc. Epis. Reg. Morton, f. 41.

6 Ibid. Bransford, f. 19.

7 Ibid. Thoresby, f. 42.

8 *Cal. of Pap. L.* iv. 524.

9 Chart. R. 2 John, m. 33d.

10 In 1277 (Pat. 5 Edw. I. m. 6) ; 1282 (Ibid. 10 Edw. I. m. 4) ; and 1295 (Ibid. 24 Edw. I. m. 21).

11 *Ann. Mon.* (Rolls Ser.), i. 66, iv. 415.

12 Close, 7 Hen. III. m. 7.

13 *Ann. Mon.* (Rolls Ser.), iv. 314, 495.

14 Close, 10 Edw. I. m. 7. He was here again in September, 1294 (Pat. 22 Edw. I. m. 10). Edward III. came to Pershore in the first year of his reign (Close, 1 Edw. III. m. 3d), and in January, 1329–30 (Pat. 3 Edw. III. pt. ii. m. 3).

15 Close, 16 Edw. I. m. 2.

16 *Ann. Mon.* (Rolls Ser.), iv. 541.

and prepared to carry away the offerings, but restored the same without gainsay on the exhibition of their privileges, by which also Abbot Gervase claimed, and took his place at the right hand of William de Blois when the bishop held a synod. The prior further stated that the bodies of all holding lands in the following places were to be buried in the abbey :—Pershore, Pinvin, Besford, Defford, Woodmancote, Birlingham, Pensham, Wick, Bricklehampton, the village of Eckington, Strensham, Woolashill, Nafford, Pirton, Stoke, Naunton, Great Comberton, Peopleton, North Piddle, Abberton, Broughton Flavel, Martin Hussingtree, Upton Snodsbury, Cowsdoun, Broughton, Walcot, Chevington, Caldwell, Wadborough, Thornton, 'Harlega,' and Little Comberton ; those who held no lands should be buried in the churchyard of Little Comberton. Respecting the wills of the deceased, the principal legacy should be carried before the corpse to the church of Pershore, and having been valued by the sacristan and the chaplain of the place to which the dead belonged, half should belong to the sacristan and half to the chaplains. All offerings made in the monastery for the dead should go to the sacristan. Further, the bodies of the deceased should be carried to the chapel of the place to which they belonged, and mass there said for their souls with the exception of the parishioners of Wick, St. Andrew, Pershore, Bricklehampton next the church, Pinvin, Birlingham, and those of the fee of Walter de Nafford; the oblations offered in the chapels should belong to the chaplains. In conclusion the prior said that he had frequently witnessed the register, and committed its contents to memory, and that the brethren had frequent recourse to each article referred to, being much disturbed in the peaceful possession of their privileges, and had written them down in various places for inspection by judges deputed by the pope or the ordinary. Other indulgences had been granted, but these he admitted he could not recall. His testimony, with some variations, was more or less confirmed by the witness of fifteen of the monks.[1]

The abbot of Pershore was summoned in 1264 to Parliament with other prelates to confer with Simon de Montfort on the affairs of the kingdom,[2] and to the Parliaments held in 1295 and 1299.[3] The service of the house from the year 1155–6 was assessed at two knights' fees.[4] By a deed dated 1166 Reginald, abbot of Pershore, acknowledged that he held all knights' fees of the old feoffment, and that of these William Beauchamp held one, and Geoffrey Blacke and Robert de Lorticote half a knight's fee each of the abbot.[5] In all burdens incident to their position the abbot and convent of Pershore bore their due share, respectable but wholly commonplace.

The king exercised the royal prerogative of imposing pensioners on the house, though it may be questioned whether this imposition was claimed as of right or conceded as by request. The abbot of Pershore in Michaelmas Term, 1813, appeared in suit before Edward II. respecting a corrody, and stated that John Beauchamp, Hugh de Cokesay, and John le Blake held the manors of Beoley, Yardley, Goldicote, and Walcot from the abbot by the service of two knights, and that he held them of the king in chief by the said service quit of all other charge.[6] Stephen le Prest, of Ripley, was sent in May, 1309, to the convent to receive maintenance for himself and one groom,[7] and in 1318 William de Rampton, yeoman of the king's pantry, who had long served the late king, was sent to receive for life the same allowance as Richard Fytel had received in his lifetime.[8] William del Putte, serjeant of the queen's buttery, was similarly sent in December, 1329, to the abbey in place of Robert Squier, deceased.[9] In connexion with this last grant an entry in the patent rolls states that the king made a concession to the abbot and convent that it should not prejudice them in future nor be drawn into a precedent.[10] A few years later, however, Thomas de Mussenden, king's yeoman, after long and faithful service, was sent to receive the maintenance which the late William del Putte had received 'at the late king's request.'[11] In accordance with recent legislation, Edward III. by letters patent in 1340 granted to the abbot and convent that on the occasion of a vacancy by the death, cession, or resignation of the abbot, the custody of the house with the temporalities and goods should devolve into the hands of the prior with full administration of the same, saving to the king and his heirs knights' fees and advowsons of churches, and paying for each vacancy

[1] Add. Chart. 42, 605. Most of the disputes in which the abbey of Pershore engaged relate to these rights of burial and the fees involved. The account of one affray between the tenants of the abbots of Westminster and Pershore is given in the chartulary of the monks ; it is evident that the brethren did not regard the transgression of their men with much horror. The abbot of Westminster complained that the hedges and ditches of his park at Tydesley had been thrown down, his property damaged, and his animals carried off. The matter came before the king's court, and the tenants of the abbey of Pershore were condemned to pay 100 marks and bound over to make good any loss or damage they might in future cause (Aug. Off. Misc. Bks. 61, f. 111).

[2] Rymer, *Fœdera* (Rec. Com.), i. pt. i. 449.

[3] *Parl. Writs* (Rec. Com.), i. 777.

[4] *Red Bk. of the Exch.* (Rolls Ser.), ii. 661, 704 ; i. 28, 41, 51, etc.

[5] Ibid. i. 302.

[6] *Abbrev. Plac.* (Rec. Com.), 331.

[7] Close, 2 Edw. II. m. 6d.

[8] Ibid. 12 Edw. II. m. 31d.

[9] Ibid. 3 Edw. III. m. 4.

[10] Pat. 3 Edw. III. pt. ii. m. 1.

[11] Close, 12 Edw. III. pt. i. m. 25.

that should occur £36 for a period of two months and for a longer time in proportion. It was enacted also that at the commencement of any vacancy the sheriff, escheator, or king's officer should take a simple seisin within the gate of the monastery and then retire, nor should he remain longer than one day for the purpose of taking seisin.[1] By the payment of a fine of £10 the convent obtained a confirmation of the grant from Richard II. in 1379.[2]

The position of the abbot of Pershore from early days was an important one in ecclesiastical circles, and he receives frequent mention during the eleventh and twelfth centuries. The abbey of Pershore was included in a federation which, according to a document dated 1022, contained in the chartulary of Bath Abbey, united the abbots of Evesham, Chertsey, Bath, Pershore, Winchcomb, and Gloucester, and the dean of Worcester, in a bond of agreement pledged to abide by the Benedictine rule, and to live as if all seven monasteries were one monastery, 'quasi cor unum et anima una.' The members of each community should be received as brethren whilst living, and after death benefit by the prayers of all.[3] The abbots of Gloucester, Tewkesbury, Winchcomb, and Pershore when they were blessed were bound to provide entertainment for the cathedral convent of Worcester or pay 40*s.*; the sacristan of Worcester should receive from them vestment and cope.[4] These dues are recorded to have been paid in 1198 and in 1234.[5] On the benediction of William de Leigh, early in 1290, the sacristan received his 'baudekin' and vestment 'de serico cum arbouribus,' but the usual entertainment was excused on account of the late fire.[6]

The efforts of the heads of the community during the twelfth and thirteenth centuries were directed towards lessening the burdens incident to their poverty, and adjusting the affairs of each department in the house. An early entry records that Abbot Wido or Guido assigned the manor of Hawkesbury to the monks for the augmentation of their kitchen and to provide clothing.[7] Abbot Gervase confirmed the grant, but reserved to himself and his successors the right of presentation to the vicarage, homage, reliefs etc., and of visiting the church once a year, with entertainment for himself and twelve horsemen for four days, including the day of arrival.[8] Abbot Eler added a proviso that any increase in the issues should be applied to the office where need should appear greatest; 40*s.* out of Longney was to be expended in procuring herrings for the brethren during Lent.[9] An interesting entry states that Richard, abbot of Whitby, bestowed on the church of Pershore for the sake of Abbot Simon, 'monk of our church,' a toft with houses within the borough for the curing of his fish, with as much wood as should be required.[10] The anniversaries to be observed by the brethren include that of Abbot Simon, whose obit was ordained to be kept on the same day as that of his father, Maurice de Ambersley,[11] and the anniversary of Abbot Gervase, who decreed that on his obit 10*s.* should be expended in wine and a pittance for the monks, and 10*s.* in food for the poor, and the almoner, out of certain rents, of which one mark was bestowed in perpetual alms with Walter de Fonte 'our monk,' should find the abbot and his successors 10*s.* to be distributed annually to thirty poor persons on Maunday Thursday at the 'mandatum,' and 4*d.* to be bestowed by each monk on two poor people, and half a mark to clothe and shoe the brother deputed annually in succession to pray for the soul of the abbot, with a daily allowance from the kitchen.[12] The convent confirming the aforesaid ordination recorded that Abbot Gervase 'ruled this place well and nobly for thirty years, and repaired it after its destruction by fire, and relieved it of debt beyond the ability of the convent, plunged in poverty, to pay, and acquired for it further lands and possessions.'[13] The anniversary of their benefactor Lady Constance de Leigh was ordained by Abbot Roger,[14] and in 1249 the abbot and convent granted an anniversary to Roger de Wigorn', prior of Pershore, and about the same time to the precentor, Richard de Wendelburgh, and Sampson de Bromsgrove, rector of Stoke, who bestowed rents on the convent for the provision of lights for the high altar and the Lady-chapel.[15] Abbot Eler obtained from Walter de Cantilupe the restoration of certain tithes within the parish, and ordained that these should be expended in augmenting the monks' brewery, and for the yearly observance of his own anniversary on the feast of St. Elerius Martyr.[16] The anniversary of Henry de Bideford who augmented the goods of the house, and obtained the restoration of the church of Alderminster, was ordained by William de Leigh to be observed on the vigil of St. Martin 'in hieme' (11 November), and the anniversary of Henry de Caldwell on 2 March.[17]

The abbey of Pershore appears to have been diligently visited by the bishop of Worcester, or, in the case of a vacancy, by the prior of Worcester. Bishop Giffard showed himself a kind, but stern,

1 Close, 14 Edw. III. pt. i. m. 38.

2 Pat. 3 Ric. II. pt. i. m. 28.

3 *Chart. of St. Peter, Glouc.* (Rolls Ser.), iii. xvii.

4 *Reg. of the Blessed Mary of Worc.* (Camd. Soc.), p. 132b.

5 *Ann. Mon.* (Rolls Ser.), iv. 389, 426.

6 Ibid. p. 500.

7 Aug. Off. Misc. Bks. 61 f. 2d.

8 Ibid.

9 Ibid. f. 3.

10 Ibid. f. 97. This grant may probably be assigned to Richard de Waterville, Abbot of Whitby, 1177–1189.

11 Ibid. f. 96.

12 Ibid. f. 97.

13 Ibid. f. 96.

14 Ibid. f. 96d.

15 Ibid.

16 Ibid. f. 96.

17 Ibid. f. 97d.

disciplinarian; during the first year of his rule he restored to the community the church of Alderminster for the maintenance of hospitality and of the infirm monks.[1] In December, 1269, he issued a mandate to compel the abbot and cellarer of Pershore to make satisfaction for the goods of the late rector of Broadway which they had carried off.[2] The bishop paid as many as five recorded visits to the abbey in the course of his rule,[3] but with the exception of a list of corrections published after a visitation in 1284 no comment is recorded which throws light on the internal condition of the house. In that year, after notifying the abbot and convent of his intention to visit them,[4] the bishop arrived at the monastery on the Vigil of the Feast of St. Edburga, and remained two days at the charge of the convent.[5] His amendments denote a somewhat lax discipline. The brethren were admonished to apply themselves more to the divine offices, and to have the door of the cloister more carefully kept to prevent the entrance of seculars 'whereby a stumbling-block is prepared for those contemplating Christ.' The sick and infirm should receive more attention, and a certain ancient custom as to corn for the bread and ale of the convent should be commuted. The abbot was enjoined, other things permitting, to sit in the cloister alone, and Brother Henry de Winchcomb being rather suited for performing divine offices than to attend to matters outside the convent, was ordered to reside within the cloister henceforth. The obedientiaries were reminded of the duty of rendering strict and regular accounts.[6] In a list of complaints formulated towards the close of his rule, Giffard was charged with exacting procuration of more than 30 marks during a visitation of Pershore, and of taking the gift of a palfrey. The bishop in his reply stated that he had not exceeded the customary procuration in food and drink, and had been presented with a foal by the abbot.[7]

Visitations carried out by the successors of Giffard are duly recorded,[8] but between the years 1284 and 1340 afford no light as to the management of the house. The abbot and convent received a licence from Bishop Cobham to have the cemetery of their church reconciled from effusion of blood and homicide.[9] In the last year of his rule the bishop addressed a friendly letter to the abbot requesting that he would make the bearer, Walter de Chalgrove, porter within the abbey, the office of which had fallen vacant.[10] The scandalous behaviour of the monks necessitated the recall of their late abbot in 1340, as has been already mentioned. On his resignation, Thomas de Pyriton was appointed by the bishop in consequence of the double election made by the convent of him and brother Robert de Lutlenton.[11] The number of brethren about that time appears to have been thirty according to a letter, dated 1346, purporting to be signed by all the convent.[12] At the time of the Dissolution it had fallen to about twenty. The abbot and convent were warned by Bishop Thoresby in December, 1352, after a recent visitation made by his official, not to alienate their property, and admonished to observe the ordination of the bishop's deputy of a special allowance of 2*d.* a day per head in lieu of provision from the kitchen 'until the faculties of the house should have increased.'[13] A copy of the bull of Pope Innocent VI. for the visitation of houses within the diocese 'not exempt' was appended to a notice of impending visitation, and the procuration to be required forwarded to the abbey in 1357.[14] The commissioners of the prior of Worcester visited the monastery during a vacancy on 24 April, 1364, and received procuration in food and drink.[15] In 1392 Bishop Wakefield deputed the abbot of Pershore to perform the ceremony of 'blessing' a widow.[16]

The accounts of visitations in the fifteenth and early sixteenth centuries are mostly without colour or interest.[17] In 1412 Bishop Peverell forwarded a list of injunctions to the convent in lieu of visitation. The brethren were admonished therein to study to make their lives conformable to the rule

[1] *Worc. Epis. Reg. Giffard* (Worc. Hist. Soc.) p. 31.

[2] Ibid. p. 23.

[3] He was here at the close of the year 1268 (Ibid. p. 11) and again in 1282 on St. Edith's Day, when he preached in the chapter-house from the text 'Aufer rubiginem de argento,' etc. (Ibid. p. 164). He made a visitation of the abbey on the morrow of the octave of St. Michael, 1289, and preached and received procuration, and again on Saturday before the Feast of All Saints, 1290, when he remained at Bredon at his own expense (Ibid. p. 379).

[4] Ibid. p. 235. [5] Ibid. p. 236.

[6] Ibid. p. 242. [7] Ibid. p. 551.

[8] Bishop Maidstone paid a visit here in 1315 (Ibid. Maidstone, f. 24), and a visit by Cobham is recorded on Monday after Ascension Day, 1319, when he preached from the text 'Be ye prudent and watch unto prayer,' and received procuration (Ibid. Cobham, f. 20).

[9] The date and cause of the brawl are not given; probably it occurred about 1320.

[10] The house was visited in February, 1338–9, by commission of the prior of Worcester after the death of Cobham (*Reg. Sede Vac.* (Worc. Hist. Soc.), 373), and soon after his appointment by Bishop Bransford in 1339 (Worc. Epis. Reg. Bransford, f. 12).

[11] Pat. 14 Edw. III. m. 20.

[12] It was addressed to the bishop for the ordination of Adam de Herwynton's chantry (Aug. Off. Misc. Bks. 61, f. 34d).

[13] Worc. Epis. Reg. Thoresby, f. 42.

[14] Ibid. Brian, f. 80d.

[15] *Reg. Sede Vac.* (Worc. Hist. Soc.), 219.

[16] Worc. Epis. Reg. Wakefield, f. 102.

[17] A visit by the commissioners of the prior of Worcester is recorded on 4 July, 1401 (*Reg. Sede Vac.* (Worc. Hist. Soc.), 383.

of blessed Benedict, to quit vain talk and contentious heresies, and to celebrate masses for the souls of their founders, and keep their names in remembrance. The bishop reminded them of the rule forbidding a good religious to hold personal possessions, and directed that Brother W. B., who contrary to rule held the offices of prior and sacristan, should be absolved from the latter and summoned to make a faithful report of his receipts.[1] Abbot William Newenton appears in some manner to have given rise to scandal in 1426. The bishop ordered him to be admitted to purgation on a specific charge of incontinence.[2] From this ordeal he issued triumphant, and his defamer, John Lockyer, was cited to appear before the bishop, who imposed public penance on him in the cathedral of Worcester and the conventual church of Pershore.[3] Bishop Carpenter paid two visits to the abbey. On the first occasion he arrived at Pershore on Wednesday, 14 October, 1461, and was received in state and with great reverence by the community, and remained at the convent till Friday morning; his visitation sermon was preached by Master William Mogys. A list of special injunctions was issued to the abbot; but, unfortunately, their contents are not stated.[4] The bishop remained at the abbey from Friday, 24 April, until the following Tuesday in the year 1467, and received procuration in food and drink, a special mandate being issued for his visitation.[5] A monk of Pershore received a dispensation from the pope in 1468 enabling him to accept a benefice with cure of souls.[6]

In 1478 the brethren admitted Bishop Alcock into their fraternity in return for his kindness, and ordained that he should participate in all their spiritual exercises and devotions, and after death that a special mass should be said yearly for his soul, with 'dirige' and 'placebo.'[7] Alcock visited the abbey on Friday, 11 January, 1481–2, but left the following day.[8] His successor, Morton, visited the convent Friday, 10 June, 1491, and preached in the chapter house; he remained at the abbey till the following Monday.[9] The abbey, in common with other religious houses, was visited at no infrequent intervals by the vicars-general of the Italian prelates who followed. The duration of these visits, during which they were entertained by the convent, was commonly of three days; no record is preserved of the state and condition of the houses thus visited.[10]

Entries of the grant of corrodies and annuities, the right of which seems to have remained in the hands of the crown, occur towards the close of the fifteenth and beginning of the sixteenth centuries. In 1478 an annuity of 26*s.* 8*d.* was made to a certain John Usher.[11] In the first year of the reign of Henry VIII. John Ashkyrke, yeoman of the Wardrobe of Beds, received the grant of a corrody lately held in the abbey by John Young, deceased.[12] The convent obtained a licence from Henry VIII. in May, 1512, to appropriate the rectory of Mathon with the portion of Chokynhill of their own patronage.[13] In 1514 the convent, probably at this time heavily in debt, consolidated the rents for the endowment of the chantry of Adam de Herwynton of two chaplains, and ordained that in future it should be served by one only.[14] William Compton, who succeeded to the rule of the house in 1504, appears to have been an ecclesiastic of the type represented by William Moore, the last but one of the priors of Worcester; his name occurs in the list of justices of the peace for Worcester and Gloucester in 1512 and 1514[15]; he was evidently popular in the county, and probably took a share in all local doings and events. At the same time his lax government and profuse expenditure added much to the difficulties of his successor. He resigned in 1526, and on 30 September John Stonywell, bishop of Polizzi, received the royal assent to his election.[16]

The history and personality of the last abbot of Pershore is an interesting and notable one. He is said to have been born in the parish of Longdon, Staffordshire, in a small hamlet called Stonywell. In accordance with the early bent of his mind, he was educated in a Benedictine monastery, probably Pershore, and from thence sent to Gloucester College, Oxford, where the monks of Pershore had an apartment for their novices. He became in later years 'prior' of this college, and was noted for his learning and blameless life.[17] He was already bishop of Polizzi when a patent for his election to Pershore was

[1] Worc. Epis. Reg. Peverell, f. 52. Notices of impending visitation were served to the abbey in the vacancy occasioned by the death of Peverell, March, 1418–9 (*Reg. Sede Vac.* (Worc. Hist. Soc.), 400), and during the rule of Thomas Polton, August, 1428 (Worc. Epis. Reg. Polton, f. 48).

[2] Ibid. f. 15.

[3] Ibid. f. 25d.

[4] Ibid. Carpenter, i. f. 169.

[5] Ibid. f. 218d.

[6] Ibid. f. 51d.

[7] Ibid. Alcock, f. 166.

[8] Ibid. f. 98d.

[9] Ibid. Morton, f. 33.

[10] The vicar-general of John de Gigliis was here in June, 1497 (Ibid. John de Gigliis, f. 9d). The vicar-general of his successor came in July, 1500 and 1503, and in May, 1512, and in April, 1516 (Ibid. Silvester de Gigliis, ff. 175, 185, 94, 123).

[11] Pat. 4 Edw. IV. pt. iii. m. 16.

[12] *L. and P. Hen. VIII.* i. 49. A grant in survivorship was made a few months later to Thomas Bell, yeoman of the king's mouth in the cellar (Ibid. 631), and again in 1514 (Ibid. 4686), 1518 (Ibid. ii. pt. ii. 4295), and 1537 a similar grant was made; Ibid. xii. 191 (4).

[13] Ibid. i. 3208.

[14] Worc. Epis. Reg. Silvester de Gigliis, f. 80.

[15] *L. and P. Hen. VIII.* i. 3301, 4764.

[16] Ibid. iv. pt. ii. 2537.

[17] Wood's account cited by Dugdale, *Mon.* ii. 412.

granted by Henry VIII. The task set before him was no light one. He found the abbey, he said, loaded with debt which had been accumulated by his predecessor, offices granted for which no services had either been exacted or returned, and his efforts to lift the house out of this condition, to free it from debts, some of which under the circumstances he considered not binding, and to redeem its offices, earned him the opposition of the tenants and the hatred of the inhabitants of Pershore. He had to meet incessant demands from his predecessor for pension deferred, the insidious attacks of enemies and detractors, and constant pressure from the court party on whom he had relied for support.

The letter written by Richard Beerley, monk of Pershore, to Cromwell in 1536, even allowing for exaggeration, points to a very sad and unsatisfactory condition in the monastery. The writer, addressing it to the 'Most reverent lord in God, second person in this realm of England,' states that 'it is grudging in his conscience that the religion they keep is no rule of St. Benet nor commandment of God nor of any saint, but light and foolish ceremonies . . . and let the precepts of God go.' He has done this for six years, and it grieves his conscience that he has been a dissembler so long, supposes this religion is all vainglory and nothing worthy to be accepted before God or man, has a secret thing on his conscience which moves him to go out of the religion were it ever so perfect, which no man may know but his ghostly father, who shall know of it hereafter, and many other foul vices done amongst religious men. He begs the commissioner to help him out of this vain religion and make him his 'servant, handemayd, and beydman,' promising to tell him how the king's commandment is kept in putting forth from books the bishop of Rome's usurped power. The monks, he continues, drink and bowl 'after collacyon until ten or twelve of the clock and come to matins as dronck as "myss" (mice), and some at cards and some at dice and at tables. Some come to matins at the beginning, some in the midst, and some when it is almost done; and they would not come at all but for the bodily punishment, "nothyng for God's sayck."'[1] This was not the only blow struck at the house or its head. On 22 April, 1538, information was lodged with my Lord Privy Seal by William Harrison, groom of the King's Privy Chamber, 'of such words as the abbot of Pershore did speak at his table . . . sounding to treason.' The substance of the charge being: first, that the abbot in conversation with Mr. Ralph Sheldon (one of his most determined opponents by the way) on 'the usurpation of the Church of Rome,' said, inclining himself over the table: 'I trust as I pray God that I may die one of the chynderne of Rome;' and, further: 'I will prove that he is accursed that withstondyth a power,' giving for his proof this text: 'Omnis potestas a Deo est, quia a Deo ordinatæ sunt.' Secondly, that in reference to the pestilence which was then raging the abbot remarked: 'As for us in this country we be smitten with the plagues of David for David's offences . . . God be merciful to us.'[2]

That the suppression of the house already determined[3] would be unopposed by the much-tried man appears evident in his letter to Cromwell in February, 1538–9, in which he expresses his willingness to resign and 'entreats' of a pension,[4] because he has borne all charges of his monastery from Michaelmas to the Annunciation next, prays he may have this half-year's rent, and then he will leave the house out of debt which he found indebted over £1,000. In the light of past services he begs to have this considered in his pension, and that he may have a house and his monks' pensions according to their virtues; he also petitions for leave to have his books and 'favour for his trusty servant the bearer.'[5] According to the Valor of 1535 the net income of the abbey amounted at that time to £643 4*s.* 5*d.*[6] The pension list, dated January, 1539–40, assigned the following pensions to the dispossessed monks: John Stonywell, bishop of Polizzi, abbot, £160 with the gallery, new lodgings adjoining it, a garden, two orchards 'with the pools in the same';[7] the prior £13 6*s.* 8*d.*, sub-prior £10, almoner £9, fermerer £8, four others, of whom the cellarer was one, £6 13*s.* 4*d.* each, John Glyn £7, and four others the sum of £6 each.[8]

1 *L. and P. Hen. VIII.* xi. 1449. As in a similar case of Thomas Musard of Worcester Priory, there may have been other circumstances which would tempt suspicion of such a letter. Richard Beerley's name does not occur among the inmates of the house at its dissolution, so his wish to be taken into the service of those responsible for its downfall may have been gratified.

2 Ibid. xii. pt. i. 822. If correctly reported, the abbot's simplicity in thus allowing himself to be 'drawn' by his old adversary Sheldon seems very great. It would be more credible that, as reported at another part of the discussion, when challenged 'the abbot made none answer, but scornfully smiled.'

3 Richard Layton, writing to Cromwell in December, 1538, says: 'When you send down your commissioners for the suppression of Winchcomb, Hales, and Pershore.' Ibid. xiii. pt. ii. 1175.

4 In a previous letter to Cromwell he says: 'No doubt the benefice has been sweet to me (as your lordship says), but remember what I left when I came to this . . . I send my servant with this letter desiring you to deliver my age from vexation, of which I have long been weary.' Ibid. 1259.

5 Ibid. xiv. pt. i. 349.

6 *Valor Eccl.* (Rec. Com.), iii. 259.

7 The abbot is said to have died at a great age in 1553. Dugdale, *Mon.* ii. 412.

8 *L. and P. Hen. VIII.* xv. 92.

ABBOTS OF PERSHORE.

Foldbriht or Fulbert[1] 983, died 988.
Bricthegn or Brihteah occurs 1032,[2] made bishop of Worcester 1033.[3]
Edmund, died 1085.[4]
Turstin, died 1087.[5]
Guido or Wido, deposed 1102,[6] died 1137.[7]
William, elected 1138.[8]
Thomas, occurs between 1145–1153.[9]
Reginald, occurs 1157,[10] died 1174.[11]
Simon, elected 1175, died 1198.[12]
Anselm, elected 1198, died 1203.[13]
Gervase, elected 1204, died 1234.[14]
Roger, elected 1234, died 1250–1.[15]
Eler, elected 1251,[16] resigned 1264.[17]
Henry de Bideford, elected 1265.[18]
Henry de Caldwell, elected 1274,[19] died 1289–90.[20]
William de Leigh, elected 1290,[21] died 1307.[22]
William de Herwynton, elected 1307,[23] resigned 1340.[24]
Thomas de Pyriton, appointed 1340,[25] died 1349.
Peter de Pendock, elected 1349.
Peter de Broadway, elected 1363, died 1379.[26]
Thomas de Upton, elected 1379.[27]
William de Newenton, elected 1413.
Edmund Hert, elected 1456, resigned 1479.
Robert Stanwey, elected 1479.
John Pibleton, elected 1497.
William Compton, elected 1504, resigned 1526.
John Stonywell, elected 1526,[28] surrendered 1539–40.

The pointed oval twelfth-century seal of the abbey,[29] chipped at the point, represents the Virgin with crown seated on a carved throne; on her left knee the Child with nimbus, lifting up his right hand in benediction; in her right hand is a sceptre *fleur-de-lizé*. At the left side of her head is a crescent, on the right an estoile of six points. St. Paul stands on the left holding a sword erect by the point, St. Peter on the right holding two keys; over the head of each an estoile, over the keys a quatrefoil. In base under a trefoiled arch St. Edburga, three-quarters length, in her right hand a chalice, in her left an open book. On each side an estoile. Legend :—

[+ SIG]ILL · BEATE · MARIE · ET · SC̄E · EADB[VRGE] · VIRGINIS · ꝑSORENSIS · ECLES[IE]

The pointed oval counterseal of the thirteenth century[30] represents the Virgin with crown, turned to the right, seated on a throne; the Child with beaded nimbus is in her arms, before her St. Edburga kneeling in adoration. Legend :—

+ SIGIL'M · SC̄E · MARIE · ET · SC̄ · EADBVRGE · VIRG · ꝑSOR

The pointed oval seal of Roger de Radeby, abbot, 1234–1251,[31] represents the abbot, full-length, having in his right hand a pastoral staff, in his left hand a book. Legend :—

+ SIGILL' RO . . . . DEI GR̄A . . . . . BATIS PERSORE

4. THE PRIORY OF GREAT MALVERN

The priory of Great Malvern is stated in the *Annales* to have been founded in 1085 by Alwy, a monk.[32] William of Malmesbury narrates how one Aldwin or Alwy, a monk of St. Wulfstan, lived as a recluse with a single companion named Guy 'in that vast wilderness which is called Malvern.'[33] Guy deemed it needful as the

[1] These dates are given in the *Annales* (Rolls Ser.), iv. 369. Foldbriht's name occurs, however, in Edgar's charter dated 972, before the granting of which he must have been dead.

[2] He was a witness to the charter granted by Canute to the abbey of Croyland (Gale, *Rerum Anglic. Script.* i. 59).

[3] *Roger de Hoveden* (Rolls Ser.), i. 89.

[4] Ibid. p. 139. Nash gives the names of two abbots previous to Edmund: Alfric 1044, Roger died 1074 (*Hist. of Worc.* ii. 247); but quotes no authority.

[5] *Roger de Hoveden* (Rolls Ser.), i. 139.

[6] Said to have been deposed in a council held by Anselm, archbishop of Canterbury (Ibid. p. 160), but he is stated to have been present at the enthronement of Simon, bishop of Worcester, in 1125 (Habington, *Surv. of Worc.* (Worc. Hist. Soc.), ii. 363).

[7] *Ann. Mon.* (Rolls Ser.), i. 46.

[8] Ibid.

[9] He addressed a letter to Pope Eugenius III. during the long dispute between the churches of York and Gloucester, *Chart. of S. Peter's Glouc.* (Rolls Ser.), ii. 110.

[10] Ibid. 106.

[11] *Ann. Mon.* (Rolls Ser.), i. 51.

[12] Ibid. and p. 56.

[13] Ibid. and p. 57.

[14] Ibid. and p. 93.

[15] Ibid. and p. 143.

[16] Ibid. iv. 440. He was appointed by Henry III. escheator for the whole of England this side Trent (Pat. 35 Hen. III. m. 4).

[17] Ibid. 48 Hen. III. m. 1.

[18] Ibid. 49 Hen. III. m. 29.

[19] Ibid. 3 Edw. I. m. 36.

[20] *Ann. Mon.* (Rolls Ser.), iv. 500.

[21] Ibid.

[22] Pat. 35 Edw. I. m. 15.

[23] Ibid. m. 11.

[24] Ibid. 14 Edw. III. pt. iii. m. 37.

[25] Worc. Epis. Reg. Bransford, f. 45d.

[26] Pat. 3 Ric. II. pt. i. m. 22.

[27] Ibid. m. 9.

[28] *L. and P. Hen. VIII.* pt. ii. 2537.

[29] Cast at Brit. Mus. lxxiv. 3.

[30] Brit. Mus. D. C., E. 35.

[31] Ibid. 75.

[32] *Ann. Mon.* (Rolls Ser.), iv. 373.

[33] Legend has linked the priory of Great Malvern with a still earlier habitation in the forest. Leland states that it was founded in the eighteenth year of the Conqueror in the vicinity of the chapel of St. John Baptist, the scene of the martyrdom of St. Werstan (Leland, *Coll.* (ed. Hearne), i. 65). St. Werstan is supposed to have been a monk who escaped the destruction of Deerhurst by the Danes and founded a cell in the forest; his life is commemorated in the stained glass in the priory church.

Great Malvern Priory.

Bordesley Abbey.

Bordesley Abbey.

Great Malvern Priory.

Dudley Priory.

Halesowen Abbey.

Cookhill Priory.

Worcester Monastic Seals.—Plate III.

To face page 136.

shortest road to glory to make a pilgrimage to Jerusalem to visit the Lord's sepulchre or meet a blessed death at the hand of the Saracen. Aldwin was also drawn by the same desire, but sought first the counsel of Wulfstan his spiritual father, who dissuaded him, saying, 'Do not, I beseech thee, Aldwin, go anywhere, but remain in this place; believe me you would wonder, if you knew what I know, how much God is about to perform through you in this place.' He relinquished his project and remained to found Malvern. One after another devotee came to Aldwin until the number rose to 300. 'Abundant store of provisions flowed in on them from the neighbouring inhabitants, who counted themselves happy in being permitted to minister to God's servants—nay, if they lacked aught, faith supplied the want, for they deemed it a small thing to be without carnal food when they were nourished on spiritual joys.' [1]

An account of the foundation of Great Malvern in Giffard's register states that the hermit Aldwyn dwelt in the time of Edward the Confessor in a place where the priory was situated, and that at his petition the earl of Gloucester, Hudde by name, granted him the site together with the wood as far as Baldeyate, whereupon the hermit collected monks and adopted the rule of St. Benedict, and made one Andrew sub-prior. Afterwards, but without the consent of his diocesan, he made the priory subject to the abbot of Westminster 'for the time being.'[2] He is said to have died in 1140.[3] The monastery thus founded was dedicated to the Virgin Mary, but occurs occasionally under the patronage of St. Mary and St. Michael,[4] as in a charter of an early benefactor, Richard Fitz Pontii, which recites that the donor for the good of his soul and of his family has granted to God and St. Mary and St. Michael of Malvern and the monks serving God there the church of Eastleach with appurtenances in Gloucestershire.[5]

Henry I. was a great benefactor to the monastery, and by a charter, inspected and confirmed later by Edward III., confirmed to God and the church of St. Mary of Malvern the yardland in Baldenhall which William his father had previously granted for the good of his soul, together with the rent of 4*s*., 2 hides of land, one in Worcestershire and the other at Quatt in Staffordshire, land in Worfield and 'Limberga' bestowed on the monks by Gislebert, abbot of Westminster, the church of the castle of Richard Fitz Pontii in Cantarabohan with 2 carucates of land, the church of Eastleach with land and tithe of the demesne of the said Richard, and the town of Hatfield in Herefordshire obtained by the brethren in exchange from Roger de Chandos, with other grants.[6] By another charter, dated 1127, Henry I. confirmed to the church of Malvern all its possessions granted by his predecessors Edward the Confessor and the Conqueror, to be held by the brethren in free alms with the liberties of soc, sac, thol, theam, and infangnethef, and freedom from the payment of geld or other exaction, and from all suits and quarrels of the shire and hundred courts.[7]

The prior was summoned in the reign of Edward I. respecting his right to hold a court of view of frankpledge within his manor of Longney with exemption from all secular service. He obtained a verdict on the ground that the priory of Great Malvern as a cell of Westminster could claim these privileges by virtue of the charter of Henry III. to the abbot granting that the abbey of Westminster with all its cells should be free from all exactions and fines and should have the right to hold a court of view of frankpledge within all its lands.[8] The prior was impleaded for a corrody in Michaelmas Term, 1318, and stated that before the Conquest there was a congregation of hermits at Malvern, and that the foundation of the priory was laid by Urse d'Abitôt; subsequently by the consent of the founder the abbot of Westminster constituted there a prior and monks, and gave them the manors of Newland, Worfield, and Powick. Henry I. confirmed previous gifts, and added £10 worth of lands in Baldenhall, Malvern, Northwood, and Fulford, to be held free of all charges and secular service.[9]

The Taxation of 1291 gives the priory an income of £87 13*s*. 2*d*. derived from temporalities and spiritualities within the dioceses of Worcester,[10] Hereford,[11] Sarum,[12] Coventry and Lichfield,[13] Lincoln,[14] and Llandaff,[15] by far the largest portion issuing out of Hereford.[16] The prior and convent obtained from William de Whittlesey in the fifth year of his translation a certificate for their title to the appropriation of the parish churches of St. Thomas the Martyr of Malvern, of Powick, and of Longney.[17]

The main feature of interest in connexion with the priory of Great Malvern is to be found in its

[1] William of Malmesbury, *Gesta Pontif.* (Rolls Ser.), 285, 286.

[2] *Worc. Epis. Reg. Giffard* (Worc. Hist. Soc.), p. 178.

[3] Matt. Paris. *Chron. Majora* (Rolls Ser.), ii. 174.

[4] Gervase of Canterbury, *Mappa Mundi* (Rolls Ser.), ii. 435.

[5] Cart. Antiq. L. F. C. xviii. 11.

[6] Pat. 50 Edw. III. pt. i. m. 15, per Inspex.

[7] Dugdale, *Mon.* iii. 448.

[8] *Plac. de quo War.* (Rec. Com.), p. 255.

[9] *Abbrev. Plac.* (Rec. Com.), p. 331.

[10] *Pope Nich. Tax.* (Rec. Com.), 216, 217, 218, 226, 228, 233.

[11] Ibid. 158, 159, 160.

[12] Ibid. 180.

[13] Ibid. 257.

[14] Ibid. 34.

[15] Ibid. 284.

[16] The spiritualities in the Worcester diocese amount to £2 16*s*. 0*d*., the temporalities to £19 19*s*. 8*d*.; the spiritualities in Hereford were worth £38 13*s*. 3½*d*., the temporalities £22 18*s*. 6½*d*.

[17] Worc. Epis. Reg. Silvester de Gigliis, ff. 201–2, cited by Nash, *Hist. of Worc.* ii. 137.

position forming the local stronghold of the abbot of Westminster in the midst of the diocese of Worcester, and the long struggle which resulted between the bishop as diocesan and the abbot as superior to establish more complete supremacy therein.[1] The dispute seems at first to have resulted in a triumph for the bishop, though his authority was evaded whenever possible by the abbot and the community itself. During the reign of Henry II. the monks of Malvern, with the object of throwing off the yoke of the diocesan, elected a certain Walter as their prior who was secretly instituted by the abbot, whereupon the bishop, Roger de Gloucester, suspended the prior until he and his superior had made satisfaction for their 'excess,' and then ordered him to be instituted by his own official.[2] In 1191 another Walter is said to have received the cure of souls and administration of the spiritualities of Great Malvern at the hands of Robert Fitz Ralph, then bishop of Worcester.[3] The register of Giffard also records that Silvester, bishop of Worcester, 1216–1218, made Thomas de Wicke, a monk of Great Malvern, prior and confirmed him.[4] In 1222 William de Blois promoted William Norman, prior of Great Malvern, in the place of Simon prior of Worcester whom he had deposed[5]; the appointment was temporary, but the conference which met to settle the controversy on 3 October, 1224, decided that the sometime prior of Malvern should receive the manor of Cleeve Prior for life on his enforced retirement from Worcester.[6] On Quinquagesima Sunday, 1233, a difference arose between the bishop and his former nominee as to the visitation of the priory; the bishop, however, gained his point, and was solemnly admitted with procession to the monastery and received procuration, and on the morrow entered the chapter-house and preached the cause of his visitation.[7] In 1234 after the death of William Norman the bishop visited his successor, arriving at the abbey as before on Quinquagesima Sunday, and receiving procuration.[8] In the first year of his succession Walter de Cantilupe visited Great Malvern with other religious houses and corrected what required correction,[9] and in the following year he came again to the priory.[10] On the death of Prior Thomas in 1242 the bishop assumed the custody of the house and examined the election of John who succeeded to the rule, and confirmed him in the presence of the abbot and convent of Winchcomb, and caused him to be installed by his official, having first received his profession of obedience.[11] The *Annales* state that the abbot of Westminster protested, but apparently without avail.[12]

The vexed question of jurisdiction received final settlement during the rule of Giffard after one of the most bitter ecclesiastical quarrels recorded in English history. The bishop in accordance with the precedent established by his predecessors came to the priory 22 September, 1282, apparently in the ordinary course of visitation, though probably summoned by the complaint of the monks as to the conduct of their prior, William de Ledbury.[13] In the chapter-house he preached to the assembled community from the text 'I will come and descend upon you,' and afterwards proceeded to examine the charges brought against the superior, who was then and there convicted of the grossest crime and immorality.[14] Giffard left without taking any decided action, and returned to Kempsey, probably to turn the matter over. Some days later as he was at table messengers arrived bearing fresh complaints. The bishop hesitated no longer, but inflamed with righteous anger he returned to Great Malvern and deposed the

[1] A convention between the prior and the abbot and convent of Westminster about 1217 endeavoured to define the extent of the latter's jurisdiction. It was agreed that on the election of a prior he should be presented to the abbot and convent for confirmation and should make profession of canonical obedience according to the rule of St. Benedict, saving that he should not be removed in malice by the abbot. The abbot should visit the priory once a year, bringing with him no more than twenty horsemen, and should remain two days and nights at the charge of the house. He should enter the chapter-house and correct what required correction as abbot. It should not be lawful to remove any monk or substitute one from Westminster without the consent of Great Malvern. The monks should make their profession at Westminster and return to Malvern. The abbot moreover should receive hospitality once a year in the manor of Powick, which had been leased to the priory for an annual rent of £24, and again should not burden his hosts by bringing more than twenty horsemen. Cott. MS. Faust. A. iii. f. 276, 279.

[2] *Worc. Epis. Reg. Giffard* (Worc. Hist. Soc.), p. 199.

[3] Ibid. p. 198.

[4] Ibid. p. 178.

[5] *Ann. Mon.* (Rolls Ser.), iv. 415.

[6] Ibid. 417. A fuller account of this dispute is given in the register of St. Mary of Worcester (Camd. Soc.), pp. 27, 8, 9.

[7] *Ann. Mon.* (Rolls Ser.), 424, and *Worc. Epis. Reg. Giffard* (Worc. Hist. Soc.), p. 178.

[8] Ibid. p. 198, and *Ann. Mon.* (Rolls Ser.), iv. 425.

[9] Ibid. 429, and *Worc. Epis. Reg. Giffard* (Worc. Hist. Soc.), p. 198.

[10] Ibid. and *Ann. Mon.* (Rolls Ser.), iv. 430.

[11] *Worc. Epis. Reg. Giffard* (Worc. Hist. Soc.), p. 198.

[12] *Ann. Mon.* (Rolls Ser.), iv. 434.

[13] In March 1279–80 the sub-prior of Great Malvern wrote to the bishop stating that brother William de Ledbury had been canonically elected prior and presented to the abbot of Westminster. *Worc. Epis. Reg. Giffard* (Worc. Hist. Soc.), p. 188.

[14] Ibid. p. 164. Ledbury's unfitness for the office he held seems never to have been disputed, though in the final adjustment, if not in the ensuing fight, it appears largely overlooked. It was stated that he kept over twenty mistresses, on whom he lavished whatever he could seize, while the community starved. Ibid. p. 178.

offender, who it is said fled and added to the scandal by becoming apostate.[1] The attitude of the community on this decisive action is not stated, but several of the monks incurred sentence of excommunication for their contumacy, from which they were soon afterwards released.[2] Giffard's action in removing Ledbury might have commanded more general sympathy, but his next step was unwise and the reason assigned unjustified. In the vacancy thus created he took the custody of the house in his own hands, stating that he did so 'as patron,' and put in his officer as custodian.[3] This roused the opposition of some of the monks, and they were again excommunicated for contumacy.[4] With the bishop's approval and concurrence the convent elected William de Wykewane in the place of Ledbury, and he was sent to the abbot and convent of Westminster for confirmation. Hitherto the abbot had remained in apparent inactivity; probably he utilized his position[5] to give the king his version of the affair and enlist his support. On the arrival of the prior elect he was seized by the abbot's orders and thrown into prison with his companions. Giffard wrote to the bishop of Bath and Wells, at that time chancellor, acquainting him with what had occurred and asking him to tell the king the truth of the matter.[6] The following day Edward I. addressed a letter to Giffard stating that the abbot had satisfied him as to the justice of the claim of the abbey to be immediately subject with all its members to the holy see and exempt from ordinary jurisdiction, consequently in deposing the prior and removing sundry officers, etc. the bishop had violated the abbot's undoubted rights and should forthwith cease from such molestation and restore the priory to its original state.[7] The letter of Giffard to the abbot threatening him with the consequences of continued detention of the prior elect only evoked a retort from the abbot that the allegations contained in the letter were untrue, nor did the order of Peckham, archbishop of Canterbury, for the release of the prisoners produce the slightest effect.[8] Giffard's high-handed action in seizing the temporalities of the priory moved the king to order the sheriff of Worcester to turn out the bishop's official and take possession of all revenues, manors, etc. for the king.[9] This was a decided rebuff, but Giffard, stating that he 'did not propose to dispute the claim on account of the king being occupied in warfare,' re-appointed his clerk to keep the spiritualities only.[10] On 23 November 1282 the king went further and ordered the sheriff to restore the priory to Ledbury 'now prior of the same,' threatening him with a heavy fine unless he should fully execute the writ.[11] In the meanwhile Giffard ordered the abbot of Westminster to be cited to appear before him and the excommunication of the monks of Malvern to be published in every church throughout the deanery.[12] This again produced no effect; the abbot did not appear, and was declared contumacious, though under the circumstances the penalty was postponed.[13] The bishop wrote again to the archbishop of Canterbury and addressed a petition to the king praying that he might be allowed to have the temporalities and spiritualities of Great Malvern during a vacancy.[14] On 16 November, 1282, he passed sentence of interdict upon the priory, and the dean of Powick was ordered to sequestrate the issues of the parish church appropriated to Great Malvern.[15] This was shortly followed by an interdict laid on all the towns, monasteries, priories, churches, and chapels of the abbot of Westminster within the diocese,[16] and a prohibition under penalty of excommunication against buying, selling, eating, drinking, or holding any communication with Ledbury and the monks of Malvern who were excommunicate.[17] In December, 1282, Peckham signified his intention of visiting the diocese.[18] The tour began on the morrow of the Feast of the Purification, and the archbishop arrived at Malvern on the Saturday following. Having preached in the chapter-house, he asked in due form for admission to visit the brethren, whereupon the proctors of the abbot of Westminster rose up and formally protested on the grounds that the priory was privileged and neither archbishop nor bishop had jurisdiction therein.[19] Peckham gave them a day for the exhibition of the alleged privileges,

1 *Ann. Mon.* (Rolls Ser.), iv. 484.

2 *Worc. Epis. Reg. Giffard* (Worc. Hist. Soc.), pp. 165–6.

3 Ibid. p. 181.

4 Ibid. p. 167. It is difficult to keep count of the excommunications issued by Giffard about this time; the list includes those excommunicated for communicating with the excommunicated members of Great Malvern, those who expelled the bishop's officer, the monks who contemned the bishop's jurisdiction with the laymen who impeded the same, and all who received or communicated with the deposed prior.

5 He was treasurer of the king's household.

6 Ibid. p. 178.

7 Ibid. p. 182. Previous to this there must have been some counter-excommunications, for on the same day the bishop ordered the excommunication of those who aided the excommunicating of persons put by him in the place of Ledbury and others in the rule of the monastery. Ibid. p. 183.

8 *Reg. of Peckham* (Rolls Ser.), ii. 423.

9 *Worc. Epis. Reg. Giffard* (Worc. Hist. Soc.), p. 181.

10 Ibid. p. 186. The bishop wrote again to the bishop of Bath and Wells pointing out that the Treasurer (the abbot of Westminster) had incurred sentence of excommunication by seizing the temporalities of the priory into the king's hand; which, nevertheless, the bishop continued, he had not published, on account of his reverence to the king.

11 Ibid. p. 181.

12 Ibid. p. 179.

13 Ibid. p. 183.

14 Ibid.

15 Ibid. p. 184.

16 Ibid. p. 185.

17 Ibid. p. 186.

18 Ibid. p. 186.

19 Ibid. p. 171.

and, in accordance with the agreement made with the abbot's representatives, wrote that night from Wyke to the official of Canterbury, the dean of Arches, and the examiner of the court of Canterbury, ordering them to proceed at once to Westminster to examine what evidence could be produced in favour of the claim preferred.[1] All this while the prior elect was kept in prison loaded with fetters, and on 9 February, 1282–3, Giffard wrote to Cardinal Hugh of Evesham begging him to use his efforts for the release of his nephew, stating that one of his companions had already succumbed to the cruel treatment meted out to the prisoners.[2] The dowager queen Eleanor, probably at the cardinal's instigation, also appealed to the king for the release of William 'because he is the nephew of the cardinal';[3] the king thus petitioned relented so far as to summon the bishop to appear before him at Montgomery touching the dispute between him and the abbot.[4] Giffard continued to urge his appeal at the Roman Court[5] and went on excommunicating.[6] The inspection of the evidence failed to convince Peckham of the justice of the priory's claim to exemption, and he ordered the bishop to excommunicate the prior, sub-prior, precentor, sacristan, cellarer, and chamberlain of Great Malvern for contumacy.[7] The meeting at Montgomery, if it took place,[8] had no appreciable effect on the condition of the unhappy prior elect and his companions, and on 6 May, 1283, Giffard again petitioned the king on their behalf.[9] Repeated excommunications were followed in June by a notification to the sub-prior and convent of Great Malvern of the bishop's intention to visit them;[10] in the same month he took the further step of sequestrating all pensions, portions, etc. belonging to the monks.[11] The long-delayed bull from Rome arrived at last appointing the priors of Chertsey and St. Frideswyde of Oxford with the precentor of Wells to hear the appeal; the two priors, probably a little shy of the task, delegated others to act in their place.[12] Judgment delivered on 23 July, 1283, confirmed the sentence of excommunication against Ledbury and the sub-prior of Malvern, and communication with them was forbidden until they had obtained absolution.[13] Matters remained much as they were until the autumn, when the king determined on the termination of the quarrel,[14] and ordered the two parties to appear at Acton Burnell, where he himself superintended the compromise at which they finally arrived. The bishop was shown apostolic letters stating the abbey of Westminster with all its cells and priories, and especially that of Great Malvern, to be exempt from diocesan law and ordinary jurisdiction, on the strength of which he acknowledged the exemption of the priory,[15] and agreed to absolve Ledbury and all the monks from the sentence of excommunication and interdict together with their servants.[16] The abbot of Westminster agreed that the prior and convent should make over to the bishop the manor of Knightwick to indemnify him for the loss he had incurred,[17] and on 15 November, 1283, Edward I. wrote to the sheriff of Worcester to announce that a 'firm peace' had been established between the two disputants, and that he should put the bishop into possession of the manor granted him by the prior and convent, and maintain, protect, and defend him therein.[18]

In reviewing this great fight it is impossible to feel greatly edified by its results; the bishop lost a point so strenuously upheld by his predecessors, the right of jurisdiction in the priory, though the loss was sweetened to him by the substantial gain of a manor. It would be ridiculous to assume that the cause of religion was served by the retention of such an ornament to monasticism as Ledbury,[19] the slurring over of his offence seems a blot on all concerned in the affair, and it is to be observed that Peckham, who had so actively upheld the right of his suffragan, with whom he was in other respects so frequently at variance, was left out in the final agreement. On hearing of it he wrote an annoyed letter to Giffard, asking for information respecting a settlement reported to be simoniacal, and warning him if that were the case to revoke it instantly, and refrain from making similar ones in future.[20] The bishop replied to the letter, and the matter was then dropped.

[1] *Reg. of Peckham* (Rolls Ser.), ii. 516.

[2] *Worc. Epis. Reg. Giffard* (Worc. Hist. Soc.), p. 189.

[3] *Reg. of Peckham* (Rolls Ser.), ii. 749.

[4] *Worc. Epis. Reg. Giffard* (Worc. Hist. Soc.), p. 195.

[5] Ibid. p. 189. [6] Ibid. p. 173. [7] Ibid. p. 192.

[8] The bishop excused himself from attendance at convocation on the score of the king's summons and appointed proctors (Ibid. p. 195), to whom in writing he spoke of the 'uncertainty of the king's movements' in connexion with the liberation of William de Wykewane. Ibid. p. 199.

[9] Ibid. p. 199.

[10] He appointed his official to execute the duty, but no entry occurs of its actual fulfilment. Ibid. p. 201.

[11] *Reg. of Peckham* (Rolls Ser.), ii. 569.

[12] *Worc. Epis. Reg. Giffard* (Worc. Hist. Soc.), p. 202.

[13] Ibid. p. 210.

[14] In August he published an order to the effect that the prior and convent of Great Malvern, on account of their claim to be exempt from ordinary jurisdiction, had been excommunicated by the archbishop of Canterbury and bishop of Worcester, whereby they were prevented from buying and selling anything and obtaining food; proclamation should therefore be made that all might communicate with the convent and their servants for buying and selling of victuals. Ibid. p. 211–12.

[15] Ibid. p. 218–19. [16] Ibid. p. 219.

[17] Ibid. p. 219. [18] Ibid. p. 220–21.

[19] He was allowed to remain in office till August, 1287, and then deposed by the abbot. *Ann. Mon.* (Rolls Ser.), iv. 494.

[20] *Reg. of Peckham* (Rolls Ser.), ii. 643.

Subsequent efforts to establish jurisdiction over the priory were made by the bishop or chapter of Worcester without success. In 1290 the monks of Great Malvern obtained a writ for the confirmation of their acquittance from visitation, or, failing that, the restoration of the manor of Knightwick.[1] Archbishop Winchelsey was engaged in visiting the prior and convent of Great Malvern in July, 1301, when articles of complaint against Bishop Giffard were presented to him by the chapter of Worcester. The precise nature of this visit is not stated. Among the procurations due to the church of Worcester, 'sede vacante,' was the sum of 40*s.* which the prior of Great Malvern or his deputy had to place on the high altar within fifteen days of the notice of a vacancy.[3] The monks were cited to appear at Pershore to answer for their resistance to the prior of Worcester's visitation during a vacancy in 1333.[4] In June of the same year the pope sent a mandate to the bishop of Worcester respecting the king's request for the appropriation of the church of Longdon to the abbot and convent of Westminster, to which the bishop had refused consent, unless the abbot would release to him jurisdiction over the priory.[5] The privilege was not yielded by the abbey, as appears in a list of 'houses exempt' appended to a bull of Innocent VI., for the visitation of the diocese during the rule of Reginald Brian.[6]

Bishop Carpenter paid a visit to the priory in July, 1340, for the purpose of consecrating altars within the conventual church. He was received with great ceremony, and remained the night with his household at the charge of the convent. The following day he consecrated the high altar in honour of the Blessed Virgin Mary, St. Michael, St. John the Evangelist, SS. Peter and Paul, and St. Benedict the Abbot; an altar to the right of the choir, in honour of St. Wulfstan and St. Thomas of Hereford; and another on the left, in honour of Edward King and Confessor, and St. Giles the Abbot. A fourth was dedicated in honour of SS. Peter and Paul and All Apostles, St. Katharine and All Virgins; a fifth in honour of St. Lawrence and All Martyrs, St. Nicholas and All Confessors; a sixth in honour of the Blessed Virgin and St. Anne, and a seventh in honour of St. Ursula and the Eleven Thousand Virgins.[7]

With the exception of the long struggle terminating in the furious fight of 1282–1283, which dragged the priory into prominence, its history is uneventful. Much of their property appears to have been lost or alienated by the community between 1217 and 1368,[8] and the brethren found the house unable to bear the charges incumbent on it,[9] and set themselves to the task of adding to their estates. They obtained from Edward I. and his two immediate successors frequent licences for the acquisition of land, and were permitted by Bishop Maidstone, in 1314, to appropriate the church of Powick already of their advowson.[10] The prior and convent shared the incidents of aid and subsidy imposed on religious houses generally, and admitted the pensioners which the kingly prerogative presented to foundations of royal patronage. In February, 1309–1310, Edward II. sent John de Waltham, 'who had long served the late and present kings,' to the priory to receive the necessaries of food and clothing, according to the requirements of his estate, including a chamber to be set apart for his use within the enclosure of the priory.[11] On the death of John de Waltham, Henry de Thornhill, the king's cook, was sent on 2 March, 1317–18, to take his place.[12] In 1346, Edward III. granted a patent for the appropriation of the churches of Upton Snodsbury and Eastleach to the prior and convent.[13] From a letter cited by Nash,[14] we read that the appropriation of Upton Snodsbury church was not confirmed by the bishop of Worcester till 1392, and then at the special request of the archbishop of Canterbury and the bishops of London and Hereford. The letter of the archbishop sets forth that the convent being situated near the public way, and but slenderly endowed from the foundation, the monks have petitioned him on the ground of maintaining their accustomed hospitality.[15]

The custom of the house during a vacancy occasioned by the death or cession of a prior was fully recognized by the king, who desired his escheator in July, 1340, not to intermeddle with the custody of the priory, as it was proved that since the days of Richard I. no entry was ever made for a time of voidance, and divers inquisitions showed that the sub-prior and convent were accustomed from its foundation to elect a prior without licence of the king, and to dispose of its issues without interference from the king or his ministers, so that the custody ought not to

1 *Rolls of Parl.* (Rec. Com.), i. 62.

2 *Ann. Mon.* (Rolls Ser.), iv. 550.

3 *Reg. of Blessed Mary of Worc.* (Camd. Soc.), p. 2.

4 *Hist. MSS. Com. Rep.* xiv. App. pt. viii. 193.

5 *Cal. of Papal L.* iii. 393.

6 Worc. Epis. Reg. Brian, i. f. 74.

7 Ibid. Carpenter, i. f. 155.

8 Judging from a comparison of a confirmation of the estates of the priory by Honorius III. in the earlier part of the thirteenth century with that of Archbishop Whittlesey in 1368.

9 The house is said to have maintained twenty monks and thirty poor men. Habington, *Surv. of Worc.* (Worc. Hist. Soc.), ii. 176.

10 Worc. Epis. Reg. Maidstone, f. 16d.

11 Close, 3 Edw. II. m. 3d.

12 Ibid. 11 Edw. II. m. 9.

13 Pat. 20 Edw. III. pt. iv. m. 18.

14 From the Liber Albus, f. 363, given in full by Nash, *Hist. of Worc.* ii. 138.

15 Ibid.

belong to the king, save of lands which might be acquired or those held of him in chief.[1]

Entries relating to Great Malvern during the fifteenth and early sixteenth century are brief and without great interest until we come to the eve of the Dissolution. The priory was in all probability visited by Dr. Legh in 1535; the prior of Worcester, writing to Cromwell on 1 August, says 'Dr. Lee, who was with us this week on the king's visitation, departed on Saturday to Much Malvern';[2] no report is given of his 'finding' here. According to the Valor of 1535, the income of the prior and convent amounted to £375 0*s.* 6½*d.*;[3] Avecote, in Warwickshire, a cell of Great Malvern, was returned in 1536 as under a less yearly value than £200,[4] and came under the earlier act for suppression.

Efforts were made to save the priory from the fate impending; the prior wrote to the commissioner entreating his favour, stating that he and his brethren deem it 'expedient to ask the king's pleasure how they shall order themselves.[5] Bishop Latimer's letter to Cromwell is a striking testimony to the management of the convent and the character of its then head. The good bishop, writing 'at the request of an honest man, the prior of Great Malvern, of my diocese,' pleads for the 'upstandynge' of his house, and continuance of the same to many good purposes, 'not in monkery . . . but to maintain teaching, preaching, study with praying, and (to the which he is much given) good "howsekepynge," for to the "vertu" of hospitality he hath been greatly inclined from his beginning, and is very much commended in these parts for the same . . . The man is old, a good "howsekepere," feeds many, and that daily, for the country is poor and full of penury. Alas, my good lord, shall not we see two or three in each shire changed to such remedy? . . Sir William Kingston can report of the man further.'[6]

This appeal, backed by an offer to find 500 marks for the king and 200 for Cromwell himself, failed of its object. The actual date of the surrender of the house is not given, but the pension-list for the late prior and monks of 'Much' Malvern is dated 12 January, 1539–40, and assigns to the prior the sum of £66 13*s.* 4*d.*,[7] to the sub-prior £13 6*s.* 8*d.*, to the sexton £8, to four monks £6 13*s* 4*d.* each, £6 each to three monks, to another monk £6 6*s.* 8*d.*; Christopher Aldewyn, *alias* More, scholar at Oxford, received £10.

1 Close, 14 Edw. III. pt. ii. m. 54.

2 *L. and P. Hen. VIII.* ix. 5.

3 *Valor Eccl.* (Rec. Com.), iii. 241.

4 *L. and P. Hen. VIII.* x. 1238.

5 Ibid. xiii. pt. ii. 905.

6 Ibid. xiii. pt. ii. 1036.

7 Ibid. xv. 51. The prior bears the name of Richard Whitborn, *alias* Bedyll. The honest old man, the good 'howsekepere' for whom Latimer pleaded, seems to have died or vanished.

Priors of Great Malvern [8]

Aldwin or Alwy,[9] 1085.
Walcher Lotharingus,[10] occurs 1125, died 1135.
Roger,[11] occurs 1151 and 1159.
Walter,[12] elected 1165.
Roger Malebranche,[13] made abbot of Burton 1178.
Thomas de Wicke,[14] occurs 1217.
William Norman,[15] occurs 1222, died 1233.
Thomas,[16] died 1242.
John de Wigornia,[17] elected 1242.
Thomas de Bredon.[18]
William de Wykewane.[19]
William de Ledbury,[20] 1279, deposed 1287.
William de Wykewane,[21] *durante lite* 1282.
Richard de Eston,[22] elected 1287, died 1300.
Hugh de Wyke,[23] occurs 1305 and 1314.
Thomas de Leigh,[24] 1340, died 1349.
John de Painswick,[25] elected 1349, died 1361.

8 The following list of priors is taken from W. Cole's list copied from Willis; where possible it has been verified and amended.

9 W. Cole, Add. MS. 5811, f. 118d. and *Ann. Mon.* (Rolls Ser.), iv. 373. Other accounts date the foundation of the house before the Conquest, but all give Aldwin as the first head. The date of his death, in 1140, given by Matthew Paris (*Chron. Majora* (Rolls Ser.), ii. 174), does not coincide with the date of his successor.

10 Add. MS. 5811, f. 118d.

11 Ibid.

12 Ibid. and *Worc. Epis. Reg. Giffard* (Worc. Hist. Soc.), p. 198.

13 Add. MS. 5811, f. 118d. and *Ann Mon.* (Rolls Ser.), i. 187.

14 Add. MS. 5811, f. 118d. and Cott. MS. Faust A. iii. f. 276.

15 Add. MS. 5811, f. 118d. and *Ann. Mon.* (Rolls Ser.), iv. 415, 425.

16 Add. MS. 5811, f. 118d. and *Worc. Epis. Reg. Giffard* (Worc. Hist. Soc.), p. 198.

17 Ibid. and Add. MS. 5811, f. 118d.

18 Ibid. and *Worc. Epis. Reg. Giffard* (Worc. Hist. Soc.), p. 178.

19 Ibid. and Add. MS. 5811, f. 118d.

20 Add. MS. 5811, f. 118d. and *Worc. Epis. Reg. Giffard* (Worc. Hist. Soc.), p. 188, and *Ann. Mon.* (Rolls Ser.), iv. 494.

21 Add. MS. 5811, f. 118d. and *Worc. Epis. Reg. Giffard* (Worc. Hist. Soc.), p. 178.

22 Add. MS. 5811, f. 118d. and Pat. 33 Edw. i. pt. i. m. 19, and Worc. Epis. Reg. Maidstone, f. 16d.

23 Add. MS. 5811, f. 118d. and *Ann. Mon.* (Rolls Ser.), iv. 494, 548.

24 Add. MS. 5811, f. 118d.

25 Ibid.

Simon Bysley or Byscheley,[1] elected 1361.
Richard Rolle or Polle, elected 1397.[2]
John Malverne,[3] occurs 1435.
J. Bennet,[4] occurs 1449.
Richard Mathern or Mathon, resigned 1457.[5]
Richard Dene,[6] elected 1457, occurs 1463.
Richard Bone.[7]
Richard Frewen.[8]
Maculinus Ledbury,[9] occurs 1503.
Thomas (Kegworth),[10] occurs 1511.
Thomas Dereham or Dyrham,[11] occurs 1533 and 1538.
Richard Whitborn, *alias* Bedyll, Bedle or Bedill,[12] received a pension 1539–40.

The twelfth-century pointed oval seal of the priory is taken from a cast at the British Museum. The obverse represents the Virgin with crown, seated on a carved throne, in her lap the Holy Child, a sceptre fleur-de-lizé in her right hand. Her feet on a foot-board, ornamented with an arcade of round-head arches. The Child with nimbus lifting up the right hand in benediction, in the left hand a book.[13] Legend :

[+SIGILLVM · S̄C̄]E · MARIE · [M]ALVERNIE

The reverse, a smaller pointed oval counterseal, represents the archangel Michael, half-length, with wings expanded, holding a crown of three points before him, in the act of casting it down on the 'sea of glass,' here shown by three wavy lines.[14] Legend :

[+]SIGILLVM : SCI : MICHAEL[IS]

The later seal is a white, pointed oval seal, attached to a deed of Prior Richard at the close of the thirteenth century.[15] Obverse represents the Virgin, with crown and head-dress of unusual form, seated on an elaborately carved throne, the Child on her left knee. Legend imperfect :

. . . [MALVE]RNI[E]

Reverse, as in the previous seal.[16]

The probable seal of Thomas de Wicke, 1217, is[17] a thirteenth-century, white, pointed oval seal representing the Virgin with crown, seated on a throne under a carved canopy of pyramidal form, the Child on her left knee between Michael the archangel on the left, with nimbus and shield, and a saint, perhaps St. John the Baptist, on the right, with nimbus, lifting up the right hand in benediction, in the left hand the Agnus Dei (?), above his head a wavy estoile. In base, under a trefoiled arch, with a sunken quatrefoil on each side, the prior half-length, praying.

E+SIGILLVM : THOME : PRIORIS : MAIO[RIS : [M]ALVERN'[18]

5. THE PRIORY OF LITTLE MALVERN

The *Annales* record that the priory of St. Giles of Little Malvern was founded in 1171 by two brothers who were born at Beckford, the name of the one who became the first prior being Jocelin, and that of the second Edred. They adopted the habit and rule of St. Benedict, and customs (consuetudines) from the chapter of Worcester.[19] This brief account has been amplified into a story much resembling that of Great Malvern, according to which the first colony was composed of a union of monks who had forsaken the priory of Worcester with the intention of leading in the forest, 'the wilderness of Malvern,' the more austere life of hermits. Of these Jocelin and Edred, 'brethren by nature and religious profession,' either by drawing recluses together or by the bestowal of their temporal goods before they entered into religion, became the founders of this priory dedicated to St. Giles and built within the see of the bishop of Worcester. The subsequent history of Little Malvern differs considerably from that of its greater neighbour, and from the earliest time it was subject to the diocesan and united to the fraternity of the cathedral church in no ordinary degree. In a ledger of the priory of Worcester exists a deed whereby Simon, bishop of Worcester, decreed that Little Malvern and the church of

1 Add. MS. 5811, f. 118d. Cole cites in support of this MS. Widmore, vol. 40, p. 87.

2 Ibid.

3 Ibid. Abingdon, in his description of the priory church, notes the following inscription in one of the six windows of the choir, *Orate pro anima Johannis Malverne qui istam fenestram fieri fecit*, and states that he was prior in 1435. Add. MS. 23,089, f. 88.

4 Add. MS. 5811. f. 118d.

5 Ibid.

6 Ibid. His name is recorded in one of the windows in the nave. Add. MS. 23,089, f. 88.

7 Ibid. and from a window in the nave.

8 Add. MS. 5811, f. 118d.

9 Ibid. His name is also to be found in one of the windows of the priory church. Add. MS. 23,089, f. 89.

10 *L. and P. Henry VIII.* i. 1639. The Cole MS. states that he was elected 5 January, 1505, and that he occurs again in 1516. Add. MS. 5811, f. 118d.

11 Willis' list, quoted by W. Cole, states that Thomas Dereham occurs in 1533, and again in 1538 (Add. MS. 5811, f. 118d). Thomas, prior of Great Malvern, was summoned to convocation in 1529 (*L. and P. Henry VIII.* iv. pt. iii. p. 2700), and Thomas Dyrham is given as prior in the Valor of 1535 (iii. 241). Prior Thomas wrote to the commissioner in November, 1338. *L. and P. Henry VIII.* xiii. pt. ii. 905.

12 The pension list, dated 12 January, 1539-40, assigns the sum of £66 13s. 4*d*. to Richard Whitborn as prior. *L. and P. Henry VIII.* xv. 51.

13 Brit. Mus. xiii. 49, 50.

14 Nott. *Antiq. of Moche Malverne*, 1885, p. 35.

15 Harl. ch. 83 A. 34.

16 Nott. *ut supra*, p. 37.

17 Brit. Mus. xxxix. 35.

18 Nott. *ut supra*, p. 37.

19 *Ann. Mon.* (Rolls Ser.), iv. 382. Wharton, *Angl. Sacra*, i. 476.

St. Giles should be eternally united in frankalmoign with the church of Worcester, that no person should be admitted to the monastic habit without the joint consent of the bishop, prior, and chapter of the cathedral church, that the prior of Worcester might remove the monks of Little Malvern by way of correction and replace them by others from the cathedral chapter, and that the prior of the smaller monastery should be elected in the chapter of Worcester.[1]

The principal benefactors of Little Malvern are said to have been William de Blois, Henry III., and it is conjectured Gilbert de Clare, earl of Gloucester and lord of Malvern Chase, from the fact of 'his honourable coat appearing in the church.'[2] A still earlier benefactor was Mauger, bishop of Worcester, who in 1200 assisted the poverty of the little community by bestowing on them as much fuel from his wood of Malvern as they needed for domestic requirements, with the yearly grant of an oak tree, the only condition attaching to this gift being that the brethren should celebrate their obsequies and anniversaries on the death of the donor and all future bishops of Worcester.[3] The grant was confirmed by the chapter of Worcester, with the addition of 20*s.* pension from the church of Hasfield in Gloucestershire, given by the bishop with the consent of Richard de Pauncefote the patron.[4] Early in the thirteenth century Giles, bishop of Hereford, confirmed assarts 'de la Dirfaud,' the gift of William his predecessor, and land at 'Horton' given by John de Stanford.[5] Gilbert the cook of Longdon gave all his land at Longdon and 5*s.* yearly for the provision of a light before the altar of the Blessed Mary in Longdon church;[6] two further grants placed them in possession of the manor.[7] The advowson and the chapel of Eldersfield in Longdon was granted to the convent by Reginald Folet:[8] a charter of William Folet confirmed to the church of God and St. Giles 'my patron' of Little Malvern the gift of land in the town of 'Bichemers' with further grants, the donor concluding his deed of gift by commending himself and his family to the same church, desiring that the brethren should receive him as a monk.[9] The prior of Little Malvern acquired the manor of Pendock by purchase,[10] and held lands at Naunton in Gloucestershire with the advowson of the church of St. Andrew there, which advowson he made over to Bishop Giffard, reserving a pension of 8*s.*[11] In Worcestershire the monastery possessed the manor of Horwell,[12] a yearly allowance of 40*s.* from Elmley Castle, and the patronage of the church of Coberley in Gloucestershire.[13] The abbot and convent of Lyra in France conveyed to the priory of Little Malvern the churches of Hanley Castle and Eldersfield,[14] and in addition the convent held the rectory of Welland with the chapel said to have been bestowed by Simon, bishop of Worcester,[15] the advowson of the church of Cold Ashton,[16] and later on portions in the chapels of Nafford and Birlingham.[17] According to the Taxation Roll of 1291 the priory had an income of £17 1*s.* 6½*d.* derived from spiritualities and temporalities in the diocese of Worcester,[18] and 10*s.* from temporalities in the diocese of Hereford.[19] Besides their English possessions the prior and convent had property in Ireland, though by what means this was acquired cannot be stated.[20]

The supremacy claimed by Worcester over the small community was rigorously exercised by Bishop Giffard. In May, 1269, he appointed William de Broadway on the death of Richard, late prior of Little Malvern,[21] and similarly in 1280,[22] 1287,[23] and 1299[24] a vacancy was supplied by the bishop's provision. In 1274 he published a grant whereby Prior John and his brethren gave to Henry, son of Geoffrey Bernard, in return for benefits conferred on them the right of presenting two secular clerks to the monastery who should pray for the souls of the said Henry and various members of his family. The right of presentation should descend to Nicholas de Mutton and his heirs and assigns after the death of the said benefactor.[25] Five years later this undertaking was revised, and a chantry ordained at the altar of the Holy Cross within the priory

1 Deed given in full by Nash, *Hist. of Worc.* ii. 155. Heming dates this subjection to Worcester from 1127 (*Chartul. of Worc. Cath.* [Hearne, ed.] ii. 532): if this be correct it would be necessary to date the foundation of the priory some years earlier.

2 Habington, *Surv. of Worc.* (Worc. Hist. Soc.), ii. 190.

3 Worc. Epis. Reg. Orlton, ff. 9, 10.

4 Ibid.

5 Charter given by Dugdale, *Mon.* iv. 449.

6 Harl. Chart. 83 B. 1.

7 Ibid. 83 B. 37, 44.

8 Ibid. 83 B. 25, 6, 7, 8.

9 Ibid. 83 B. 14.

10 *Rot. Hund.* (Rec. Com.), 284. Habington gives an account of the vicissitudes whereby this manor, said to have been originally granted to Worcester by King Edgar, came into the hands of Little Malvern. *Surv. of Worc.* (Worc. Hist. Soc.), ii. 284.

11 It was appropriated by the bishop to the charnel chapel of the Carnarie, Worcester, in 1287. *Worc. Epis. Reg. Giffard* (Worc. Hist. Soc.), p. 336.

12 *Pope Nich. Tax.* (Rec. Com.) 228.

13 Nash, *Hist. of Worc.* ii. 141.

14 Ibid. i. pp. 562, 374; and Habington, *Surv. of Worc.* (Worc. Hist. Soc.), ii. 194.

15 Nash, *Hist. of Worc.* ii. 455.

16 *Worc. Epis. Reg. Giffard* (Worc. Hist. Soc.) p. 331.

17 Habington, *Surv. of Worc.* (Worc. Hist. Soc.) ii. 194.

18 *Pope Nich. Tax.* (Rec. Com.), 217, 222, 224, 228.

19 Ibid. p. 174.

20 In the ecclesiastical taxation of Ireland, 1302–6, appears an entry of the portion of the monks of Malvern in the deanery of Tanehey (Taney) within the see of Dublin rated at £32. *Cal. of Doc. relating to Ireland*, 1302–7, p. 239.

21 *Worc. Epis. Reg. Giffard* (Worc. Hist. Soc.), p. 7.

22 Ibid. p. 122.

23 Ibid. p. 330.

24 Ibid. p. 513.

25 Ibid. p. 65.

church for the benefit of the said Henry and his family.[1] The church was probably rebuilt about this period, as in the course of Giffard's visitation of the diocese in 1282 he stayed two days at the monastery of Little Malvern, and visited the chapter and dedicated their church, the charge of the two days' entertainment being borne by the convent.[2] During the rule of Giffard an inquiry was made concerning one Simon Chamberlayn, who was reported to have entered the monastery of Little Malvern and become professed therein as a monk of the order of St. Benedict, but who, notwithstanding, had returned to the world and married, when he was in no way capable of paternal inheritance, to the prejudice of his brother.[3] The bishop, being appealed to in the face of a serious family problem, made reply 'that of old custom the prior of Malvern is as it were the bishop's minister in that place,' so that the bishop could nominate or put there whom he would without the election of the monks, but that without his consent the prior could not give the habit to anyone or receive anyone for profession 'which makes the monk more than the habit,' and that the said Simon had not made profession to the bishop or to any other in his name.[4] This did not end the matter, but the final conclusion is not recorded.

John de Dombleton, who was appointed prior in 1299,[5] did not retain the office long.[6] After his resignation the annalist who records the appointment of his successor, William de Molendinis or Mills, states that he was not admitted to his former estate by the chapter of Worcester. On being recalled for the election of Giffard's successor in 1302, he sent renouncing all right or voice in the election on the ground that he had been translated to Malvern and there made prior, 'wherefore because of his present condition the same John tarries at the schools of Oxford at the expense of the prior and chapter of Worcester.'[7] The latter received an order from the presidents of their general chapter to re-admit their former member, and quickly complied.[8]

The convent appears to have suffered various losses from time to time. Giffard, in a licence for the appropriation to the brethren of the church of Stoke Giffard, states that it was granted on account of their sufferings during the Barons' War and the war in Wales.[9] Thomas, earl of Warwick, bestowed on them the advowson of the church of Notgrove with the rent of a pound of pepper in 1338,[10] and the prior and convent were permitted to appropriate the church of Whatcote in 1368, in consequence, it is said, of the loss of divers possessions in Ireland.[11]

These distant possessions of the priory proved a charge in many ways, involving the personal residence of the prior or the appointment of attorneys to represent him. One of the monks was as a rule appointed, but the post does not appear to have been much sought after by the brethren. Bishop Cobham, after his visitation in 1323, reproved one of the community for refusing to go, in consequence of which a less suitable person had to be sent, to the loss and injury of the convent;[12] and in 1336 brother Nicholas de Upton, upon whom the duty had devolved, obtained a dispensation from the bishop absolving him from the office on the ground that it was to the danger of his life to cross the Irish Sea.[13] Cobham suggested that it was not fitting for a monk to live alone, and advised that in future two brethren be sent, means permitting.[14] After much loss and expense the brethren were finally relieved of a troublesome charge in 1484, when Bishop Alcock permitted them to lease all their lands, churches, and chapels in Ireland to the abbot and convent of the Blessed Virgin Mary of the Cistercian Order in Dublin in perpetuity for the annual sum of 450 marks.[15]

The spirit of devotion which animated the early founders of the priory does not appear to have largely inspired their successors. It should be remembered that, though the community had their estates apart from the church of Worcester, the terms of the federation which bound them placed the convent in the position of being used as a house of correction by the larger monastery, and no instance is recorded of the head of the smaller house resigning his post to take up a position of greater dignity and responsibility. The bishops of Worcester claimed to hold a veto on all admitted to the monastery, and in 1290 Giffard stopped at Little Malvern to receive the profession of two monks, and remained a day at his own expense. The following day being Sunday he dedicated three altars at Redmarley, but remained on at the priory at the prior's charge.[16] In October, 1303, Bishop Gainsborough warned the convent of his intention to visit their monastery.[17] The prior, William de Molendinis, resigned his office on the occasion of this visitation, and his resignation 'for certain and legitimate causes' was accepted by the diocesan, and appointment made of Roger de Pyrie or Pyribrok

1 *Worc. Epis. Reg. Giffard* (Worc. Hist. Soc.), p. 114.
2 Ibid. p. 165.
3 Ibid. p. 499. 4 Pat. 26 Edw. I. m. 3.
5 *Worc. Epis. Reg. Giffard* (Worc. Hist. Soc.), p. 513.
6 He resigned at Christmas 1300. *Ann. Mon.* (Rolls Ser.), iv. 548.
7 *Reg. Sede Vac.* (Worc. Hist. Reg.), 3. 8 Ibid. 35, 44.
9 *Worc. Epis. Reg. Giffard* (Worc. Hist. Soc.), p. 454.
10 Pat. 12 Edw. III. pt. ii. m. 29.
11 Nash, *Hist. of Worc.* ii. 141.
12 Worc. Epis. Reg. Cobham, f. 88.
13 Ibid. Montacute, i. f. 30.
14 Ibid. Cobham, f. 88.
15 Worc. Epis. Reg. Alcock, f. 137.
16 *Worc. Epis. Reg. Giffard* (Worc. Hist. Soc.), p. 323.
17 Ibid. Gainsborough, f. 21.

to succeed him.[1] The brethren were admonished a year later not to alienate the goods of their house.[2] The priory was visited on the death of the bishop in 1307 by the commissioners of the prior of Worcester, at the special request, it is said, of all the convent.[3] Probably the best description of the state of the monastery may be gathered from Bishop Cobham's injunctions after his visitation in 1323.[4] In regard to the rule of the house the bishop ordained that a sub-prior be appointed to take the place of the prior when absent, that the cellarer and principal officers be appointed by the prior with the consent of the convent or the greater and wiser part of it, 'that it is not usual to choose young leaders whose worth has yet to be proved,' and for that reason the monk who filled the office of bursar, and was but in deacon's orders, should be removed, and a senior monk in priest's orders substituted. The cellarer should be deposed, and the steward (villicus) who was suspected of wasting the goods of the house either removed or compelled to render account of his stewardship. The prior was forbidden to dispose of timber, goods, or valuables without the consent of the chapter, and prohibited from fishing in the fishpond belonging to the sick unless approved by the whole community, and then he should make good what he had taken. The brethren were enjoined to take better care of the sick, and especially of brother Hugo de Crombe, and to restore the ancient portion of the poor on obit days, reported to be reduced by one half. The bishop desired brother Henry de Wigorn, studying at Oxford at the sole discretion of the prior, and spending money which had better be applied to the needs of the sick, to be recalled, 'since whoso does not work in the Lord's vineyard should have no share in the daily wage,' but directed that he and others of studious tastes should have liberty after the completion of the hours to read good works. The novices should have a master to instruct them diligently in manners and habits of discipline. That general discipline was lax appears evident. Several members were warned against meeting to discuss secretly the affairs of the convent and criticize the prior and his friends, etc. The voice of scandal was not unheard, and the prior was enjoined to admit brother Hugh de Pyribrok to purgation respecting a charge of immorality. It is to be hoped that brother Hugh was able to clear himself of the imputation, as he became prior a few years later.[5] The bishop finally forbade the expenditure of any of the goods of the house on relations either of the prior or any member of the convent, or their appointment to offices save by the consent of the greater part of the community.

[1] Worc. Epis. Reg. Gainsborough, f. 23.

[2] Ibid. f. 4d.

[3] *Reg. Sede Vac.* (Worc. Hist. Soc.), p. 121.

[4] Worc. Epis. Reg. Cobham, f. 88. [5] Ibid. f. 112.

Notices of succeeding visitations are very brief in character and throw no light on the condition of the house[6] until we come to the year 1480. The decisive action taken by Bishop Alcock in that year implies that it had been for a considerable time in urgent need of reform. He says 'As it is notary known through all my diocese to the great displeasure of God, disworship of the Church . . . the misliving and dissolute governance of the brethren that hath been inhabit in the place of Little Malvern, being of my foundation and patronage; the rules of that holy religion not observed nor kept, but rather the said brethren in all their demeanance hath been "vagabunde" and lived like laymen to the pernicious example of all Christian men.'[7]

The task of reform was energetically carried out, the prior, John Wyttesham, resigned his office, and was sent to the abbot of Abingdon, as president of the order, with a request that he might be transferred to Batsel (Battle) where he had been professed, the bishop bestowing on him 13*s.* 4*d.* from the common fund of the monastery.[8] Four of the brethren were dismissed for their 'demerits' and sent to St. Peter's, Gloucester, there to be instructed in the rule of St. Benedict and the vow of their profession; to each the bishop gave out of his own purse 10*s.*[9] In September following, Henry Morton, a monk of Tewkesbury, was appointed prior in charge on the grounds that the community by crimes and excesses had shown themselves unfit to elect a superior.[10] The bishop's care did not end here. In the two years which elapsed before the recall of the brethren he rebuilt their church and repaired their lodging, and in October, 1482, wrote that having been for two years 'in worshipful and holy places' he considered they should now be sufficiently instructed in their religion. He laid down regulations that none of the brethren should go into the town or fields without a companion or without obtaining leave of the prior, and asked as sole return for his benefactions that a mass should be said for him daily at 'Our Lady Aulter.'[11] From this time the conventual church appears by his ordinance to have been dedicated to St. Mary, St. Giles, and St. John the Evangelist. On the resignation of Henry Morton in 1484 the convent agreed to elect as his successor whoever the bishop should

[6] The prior and convent were visited in February, 1338-9, by commissioners of the prior of Worcester (*Reg. Sede Vac.* p. 271). In September of the same year they received notice of impending visitation by Bishop Bransford, of which the mere fact of its taking place is recorded (Worc. Epis. Reg. Bransford, i. ff. 10, 11). In 1388 the brethren were again admonished not to alienate the property of the house (Ibid. Brian, ii. f. 19). Bishop Carpenter visited Little Malvern by his commissioner William Vance on 20 October, 1461 (Ibid. Carpenter, i. f. 169).

[7] Ibid. Alcock, f. 111. [8] Ibid. f. 69.

[9] Ibid. [10] Ibid. f. 74d. [11] Ibid. f. 111.

appoint, and confirmed his subsequent nomination of Thomas Colman, a monk of Great Malvern.[1] The convent received the formal visitations paid by the vicars-general of the four Italian prelates who occupied the see of Worcester in succession, but their record contains no hint of the state of the priory. In 1533 a complaint was lodged against John Bristowe, prior of Little Malvern, for a trespass in Malverne Chase for the purpose of killing the king's deer.[2] Among the signatures of those subscribing to the king's supremacy in 1534 appear the names of John Bristowe and seven others dated 31 August,[3] and we are told that the convent assented unanimously. The clear income of the priory amounted at that time to £98 10*s.* 9*d.*, consequently it fell within the scope of the earlier Act for the suppression of religious houses of less yearly value than £200.[4] The precise date of its surrender is not known. John Bristowe, the last prior, appears in a pension list for 1536-7 down for a yearly pension of £11 13*s.* 4*d.*[5] The possessions of the priory were much coveted by John Russell, secretary of the Council of the Marches of Wales.[6] The site of the monastery was granted however with lands in other counties to Richard Andrews and Nicholas Temple;[7] subsequently the manor and demesne of Little Malvern came into the hands of Henry Russell in the reign of Philip and Mary.[8]

Priors of Little Malvern

Jocelin,[9] 1171.
Edred.[10]
Richard,[11] died 1269.
William de Broadway,[12] appointed 1269.
John de Shockeley,[13] occurs 1274 and 1279 died 1280.
John de Colevylle or Colewell,[14] appointed 1280, resigned 1286.
John de Wigornia,[15] appointed 1287, died 1299.
John de Dombelton,[16] appointed 1299, resigned 1300.
William de Molendinis or Mills,[17] appointed 1300–1, resigned 1303.
Roger de Pirie or Pyribrok,[18] appointed 1303, resigned 1326.
Hugh de Pyribrok,[19] appointed 1326, died 1360.
Henry de Staunton,[20] appointed 1360, died 1369.
John de Wigornia,[21] appointed 1369.
Richard de Wenlock,[22] occurs 1378, resigned 1392.
Richard Brewer,[23] appointed 1392.
William Brewer, occurs 1435.[24]
John Estnor,[25] occurs 1445.
John Clement,[26] occurs 1462.
John Wyttesham,[27] resigned 1480.
Henry Morton,[28] appointed 1480, resigned 1484.
Thomas Colman,[29] appointed 1484.
John Bristowe,[30] occurs 1529.

A description of the twelfth-century pointed oval seal of this house, about 2¾ by 1¾ in. when perfect, is taken from a cast in the British Museum.[31] The impression is indistinct, but represents St. Giles the Abbot full-length holding in his right hand a book, in his left hand probably a pastoral staff. Legend:—

. . . LLVM : SCI : E[GIDII : ABB]ATIS : NOVE : MELVE . . . .

A fourteenth-century pointed oval seal 2½ by 1¾ in., represents the Virgin with nimbus standing, in her right hand the Holy Child, in her left hand a sceptre fleur-de-lizé; on her left St. Giles with a fawn, on her right St. John the Evangelist, in a niche with triple canopy and tabernacle work at sides. In base a shield of arms: on a fesse between three cocks' heads, a mitre, Bishop ALCOCK, benefactor.[32] Legend:—

. S' + COE + DOMUS + SIUE + PRIORATUS MALUARNIE : MIOR

The seal for peculiar jurisdiction, a pointed oval, represents St. Giles in a canopied niche with pastoral staff caressing a fawn under a tree, the corbel carved with a triple branch.[33] Legend:—

SIGILL'V JVRISDICCIONIS PARVE MALVERNIE

1 Worc. Epis. Reg. Alcock, f. 164.
2 *L. and P. Hen. VIII.* vi. 1603.
3 Ibid. vii. 891, 1121 (60). It has been conjectured from the ten seats remaining in the choir that the priory consisted of ten monks; the number appears to have varied greatly.
4 Ibid. x. 1238.
5 Ibid. xiii. pt. i. p. 375.
6 Ibid. xii. pt. i. 1295. He presented a petition from the tenants of Little Malvern to be allowed to retain the five bells which had always served the parish church as well as the monastery. Ibid. xii. pt. ii. 279.
7 Deed cited in Dugdale, *Mon.* iv. 447.
8 Ibid.
9 *Ann. Mon.* (Rolls Ser.), iv. 382.
10 Ibid.
11 *Worc. Epis. Reg. Giffard* (Worc. Hist. Soc.), p. 7.
12 Ibid. p. 7.
13 Ibid. p. 65. Nash gives William de Wherham as prior in 1279, but quotes no authority, and his example is followed by Dugdale. 'John, prior of Little Malvern' occurs again in 1279 in the register of Giffard (p. 114.), and his death is recorded in 1280. Ibid. p. 122.
14 Ibid. pp. 122, 300.
15 Ibid. pp. 330, 441, 513.
16 Ibid. 513; and *Ann. Mon.* (Rolls Ser.), iv. 548.
17 Ibid.
18 Worc. Epis. Reg. Gainsborough, f. 23.
19 Ibid. Cobham, f. 112.
20 Ibid. Brian, i. f. 30.
21 Ibid. William Lynne, f. 20.
22 Nash, *Hist. of Worc.* ii. 143; Worc. Epis. Reg. Wakefield, f. 101.
23 Ibid.
24 Nash, *Hist. of Worc.* ii. 143.
25 Worc. Epis. Reg. Carpenter, i. f. 37d.
26 Ibid. f. 172.
27 Ibid. Alcock, ff. 69, 74d.
28 Ibid. ff. 74d. 137d.
29 Ibid. f. 137d.
30 *L. and P. Hen. VIII.* iv. pt. iii. p. 2700.
31 Brit. Mus. lxxiv. i.
32 Ibid. lxxiv. 2. Dugdale, *Mon.* iv. 447.
33 B.M., D.C., F. 57. Classed among 'peculiars' by C. S. Perceval, *Proc. Soc. Antiq.* 2nd Ser. v. 250.

HOUSE OF BENEDICTINE NUNS

6. THE PRIORY OF WESTWOOD

The priory of St. Mary of Westwood of the order of Fontevrault [1] was founded in the early part of the reign of Henry II. by members of the de Say family.[2] The charter of the new foundation, granted by the king at Worcester, confirmed to the nuns of the church of Fontevrault the gifts bestowed on them by Osbert Fitz-Hugh and Eustacia de Say his mother, consisting of the site of their new dwelling, with land at Westwood and Crutch, a salt pit in Droitwich, and the church of Cotheridge, with whatever gifts might be hereafter added to them.[3] Successive royal charters confirmed that of Henry II. and enacted that the nuns should hold their lands free of all exactions, suits, and quarrels, with right of soc, sac, thol, theam, and infangnetheof.[4]

The affection entertained for the order of Fontevrault by the Norman and early Plantagenet kings is very strongly marked. Eleanor, the queen of Henry II., is said to have loved every nun at Fontevrault as if she had been her daughter, and to have desired to take the veil there. She was buried in the abbey with her husband and son.[5] Thus favoured it is not surprising to find other grants following those of the noble founders. Alicia, the lady of Salwarpe, gave the nuns half a yardland in Boicot for the good estate of her own soul and of her children and for the souls of her husband William Beauchamp and her son William, the grant being confirmed by Walter Beauchamp.[6] John English gave them a mill outside Droitwich called Middelmulne and some land for a yearly rent of three marks.[7] William Bray gave with his daughter Amabilia the service or rent of half a hide of land which he held of the Knights Hospitallers in Piddle, and the service of another yardland leased to Henry Luvet at a rent of 3*s.*, with a cottage, four acres of land, and a meadow, for which the nuns agreed to pay annually a pound of cumin at Christmas.[8] From William Fitz-Alewy of Droitwich they obtained a rent of 3*s.* in Estwood from half a yardland at the brook, parcel of the fee of Thomas le Mey, to whom they were to pay annually a clove gilliflower.[9] Cecilia de Turberville, with the consent of Walter her son, and for the soul of William de Turberville her husband, gave to God and the Blessed Mary of Westwood all the land at Kindon which had been granted to her and her husband on their marriage by Hugh de Arderne, for which the sisters were to pay an annual rent of a soar hawk or 12*d.* to Thomas de Arderne and his heirs.[10]

An hereditary right seems to have been possessed by descendants of the founders to have a nun maintained in this house. William de Stuteville, who married Margaret de Say, relinquished this claim and confirmed the charters previously granted by Hugh de Say,[11] Robert Mortimer, and Margaret de Say, according to the tenor of the charter of Osbert Fitz-Hugh, 'founder of the church of Blessed Mary of Westwood.'[12] The church of St. Nicholas of Droitwich was granted to the church of Fontevrault by Matthew count of Boulogne. His daughter Ida, the countess of Boulogne, confirmed the gift of the chapel together with the land forming its endowment at the petition of M. abbess of Fontevrault, whom the countess styles *karissima matertera mia*.[13] The same lady also confirmed the grant made by Robert de Caverugge of the whole of his estate in Cotheridge for the annual payment of 5*s.* to herself and her heirs in remission of all exaction and secular service. The donation was confirmed by Reginald and William de Benhall, descendants of the donor, with the stipulation that the sisters should receive the daughter of Reginald as a nun.[14] Among other benefactors in the neighbourhood were John, the dean of Droitwich, who gave land adjoining the estate which his father held of the church of Deer-

[1] This order, founded in 1101–2 soon after the council of Poictiers by Robert d'Arbrissel, sprang rapidly into fame and favour. The constitution of the order was confirmed by Pope Paschal II. in 1106, and the great abbey church of Fontevrault, built with means largely provided by the kings of France and England as well as by the bishop and inhabitants of the district, consecrated in 1119. Nicquet, *Hist. de l'ordre de Fontevrault*, 1342, p. 57–8. It was the last resting-place of Henry II. and Richard I.

[2] Osbert Fitz-Hugh, generally named as the founder, occurs in Pipe Rolls for 7 and 14 Henry II.

[3] Pat. 17 Edw. IV. pt. 2, m. 14, per Inspex.

[4] Ibid. The inspeximus charter of Edward IV. confirms previous confirmations granted by Henry III., the first and third Edwards, Richard II., Henry IV., and Henry VI.

[5] Nicquet, *Histoire de l'ordre de Fontevrault*, p. 254.

[6] Cott. MS. Vespas, E. ix. f. 2d.

[7] Ibid.

[8] Ibid. f. 3.

[9] Ibid. f. 3d.

[10] Ibid. f. 4.

[11] The two brothers Osbert and Hugh Fitz-Hugh assumed the surname of their mother Eustacia de Say. Hugh succeeded Osbert who died without issue, and was succeeded by his son Richard, who dying also without issue was succeeded by his brother Hugh de Say, whose only daughter, Margaret, became his heiress and took for her second husband Robert de Mortimer, and for her third William de Stuteville in the reign of Henry III. Nash, *Hist. of Worc.* i. 240.

[12] Cott. MS. Vespas. E. ix. f. 5.

[13] Ibid.

[14] Ibid. f. 5d.

hurst,[1] and Osbert Fitz-Osbert Bende, who gave land in Droitwich, parcel of the fee of Deerhurst, with two *helflings* and a half of salt at 'Northeremest Wich' for an annual rent of 4½*d.* and six baskets of salt to the church and a pair of white gloves yearly to his heirs.[2] Richard, priest of St. Augustine of Dodderhill, bequeathed land in Ruinestret, Droitwich, to the nuns of the Blessed Mary of Westwood with his body to be buried in their church,[3] Alured Luverun 2*s.* yearly out of a salt pit in Droitwich to provide tallow for light in the convent,[4] and Adam Fitz-Adam Luvetun of Droitwich 12*d.* for the provision of light in the infirmary.[5] By another concession the nuns obtained a right of transit over the bridge of 'Brerhulle' for their carts carrying hay and corn from haymaking until Michaelmas, and carrying wood from haytime to All Saints.[6] According to the Valor of 1535 the priory appears to have held the manor of Cold Ashton or Little Ashton in Gloucestershire, which was leased at an annual rent of £5 4*s.*[7]

With the exception of detailed grants entries respecting this nunnery are few and information scanty. The order was exempted by Honorius III. in 1224 from episcopal jurisdiction and made immediately subject to the holy see, consequently the registers of the diocese contain but slight reference. During the twelfth century the priory had a lengthy controversy with the chapter of Worcester respecting the church of St. Augustine of Dodderhill[8] which the abbess of Fontevrault claimed for the 'poor nuns' of Westwood by the gift of Osbert Fitz-Hugh and the assent and 'council of A. bishop of Worcester'[9] and of the king. The 'abbess A.'[10] wrote to Roger then bishop of the diocese desiring him 'as strife was unbecoming a servant of God' to determine the dispute with the aid of certain councillors, among whom she named the aforesaid Osbert, promising to abide by their decision.[11] The matter was finally compromised in 1178 by the chapter of Worcester retaining the church and assigning to the nuns all the land in Clerehall with a meadow and its appurtenances, and all tithes of their lands in the parish of Dodderhill, that is to say the tithes of Westwood, Clerehall, and Crutch, with the burial and obventions of all men within these lands.[12] Two bequests to the house are recorded in the register of Bishop Giffard, the one of a mark bequeathed by William Beauchamp in his will dated January, 1268–9,[13] and the other of £10 by Roger de Clifford in 1284.[14] Edward I. is said to have held the order of Fontevrault in great esteem, and the prioress and convent received special royal protection in October, 1277, to last over Easter, with exemption from a general levy on grain made by the king in various counties for the support of the army in Wales.[15]

The house seems, in the absence of direct evidence, to have been distinguished for the piety of its inmates who were largely recruited from noble families, 'for the worthiness of these nuns being of eminent families in this and other shires,' remarks Habington, speaking later;[16] but it does not appear to have been a wealthy establishment. The prior of Worcester as custodian of spiritualities of the see 'sede vacante' directed his commissary in 1312 to exact none of the dues which might pertain to his office from the possessions of the prioress and convent of Westwood, being desirous to spare their poverty.[17]

The connexion of the priory with the diocesan was slight but never unfriendly. Bishop Maidstone soon after his promotion to the see in 1313 granted an indulgence of 40 days to the prioress and nuns of Westwood,[18] and in December, 1337, Bishop Hemenhale admitted the profession of eighteen religious within the conventual church of Westwood.[19]

Foundations of the order of Fontevrault drew to them a community of both sexes living side by side in separate dwellings, the women's division dedicated to the Blessed Virgin and the men's to St. John the Evangelist, the idea of the

1 Cott. MS. Vespas. E. ix. f. 6d.
2 Ibid.
3 Ibid. f. 7.
4 Ibid.
5 Ibid. f. 9.
6 Ibid. f. 9d.
7 *Valor Eccl.* (Rec. Com.), iii. 276.
8 Habington speaking of Westwood says, 'In a vast and solitary wood, for the situation called Westwood in long outworn ages, a limb of St. Augustine's parish, usually called Dodderhill, was founded a house for religious women, who leaving the world, were devoted to God. . . . Westwood, in the territories of the Sayes, barons of Burford, and lords of Wychbold, was by their indulgence made a parish of itself, including Westwood, Crutch, and Clerehall.' *Surv. of Worc.* (Worc. Hist. Soc.), i. 459.
9 Alfred, 1158–1160.
10 Adelburga de Haute-Bruyere as third abbess was head of the order from 1155 to 1180. Nicquet, *Hist. de l'ordre de Fontevrault*, p. 410.
11 Reg. of D. and C. of Worc. f. 22, cited by Nash, *Hist. of Worc.* i. 337.
12 Ibid.
13 *Worc. Epis. Reg. Giffard* (Worc. Hist. Soc.), p. 7.
14 Ibid. p. 283.
15 Pat. 5 Edw. I. m. 4.
16 *Surv. of Worc.* (Worc. Hist. Soc.), i. 459.
17 *Reg. Sede Vac.* (Worc. Hist. Soc.), 62.
18 Worc. Epis. Reg. Maidstone, f. 1.
19 Ibid. Hemenhale, f. 12. The order of Fontevrault, though considered apart, seems to have been placed by the founder before his death under the rule of St. Benedict; but the abbess, Marie de Bretagne, writing in 1459 to Pope Pius II. for the reform of the order, represented that at Fontevrault existed a community composed of religious men and women in separate habitations, of whom the women followed the rule of St. Benedict and the men that of St. Augustine, and yet all were under the supremacy of the abbess, and this seems not uncommon in other houses of the order. It was definitely placed under the Benedictine rule by the statutes of the great reform drawn up by the commissioners of Pope Sixtus IV. in 1494, but continued to qualify as an order apart. Helyot, *Hist. des Ordres Monastiques*, vi. 97–8.

founder being that their relations should be based on the text John xix. 27.[1] Supreme authority over the whole order in matters temporal and spiritual [2] was vested in the abbess of Fontevrault, and in the case of daughter houses in the prioress over the community. Allusions to a prior at Westwood are very slight, and information can hardly be gathered as to the existence of a division for religious men. A note appears on three charters confirming grants to the house, 'acquired by N. de Ambr' then prior,' [3] but this may be a mistake for 'prioress'.[4] An entry under the year 1316 speaks of Richard 'le Prior of Westwood' and Geoffrey 'le Priouresbrother.' [5] In 1344 during the war with France the priors of Westwood and Nuneaton, of the order of Fontevrault, received a licence from the king to attend a general chapter by the order of their superior on condition that they carried nothing beyond their reasonable expenses. An oath was exacted that they would 'behave well' and would not tell the king's adversaries of his secrets, but would rather inform him of any attempts against himself.[6] This is the only recorded instance on the part of Westwood of a representative being sent to attend a chapter of the order. In a deed of the year 1352 it appears that 'the prior, prioress, and canons of Westwood' bestowed on William Was de Shrawley, who held a yardland and a quarter of arable land in the manor of Shrawley, a weekly allowance of half a measure of good, pure, and well-winnowed corn.[7]

It is a question to what extent the priory of Westwood was really dependent on the abbey of Fontevrault. It is not included in any list of alien houses, nor is any mention made of it in the return of the prior of Worcester to the king's writ of 1374 desiring to be certified as to the number of benefices held by aliens.[8] The advowson of the priory in the year 1330–1 appears to have come into the hands of the Talbot family,[9] and in February, 1341–2, the king's escheator was directed to deliver the advowson of the priory of Westwood with other manors and churches to John Talbot 'son and heir of Joan' late the wife of Richard Talbot of Richard's Castle.[10]

There is little material for the history of Westwood during the last half of the fourteenth century until the time of the Great Schism in the papacy, 1378–1447. Edward III. in October, 1356, granted a licence to William de Salwarpe, clerk, and Thomas his brother to assign various lands in Salwarpe and salt works in Droitwich for the provision of two chaplains to celebrate daily in the church of St. Michael, Salwarpe, for the souls of the faithful departed. Subsequently the salt works were bestowed on the prioress and convent of Westwood in accordance with this ordination.[11]

The order of Fontevrault was temporarily discredited for the adherence of the abbess to the anti-pope Clement VII. during the schism. The priory on the death of the prioress Isabella Gros 'extra Romanam curiam' applied to Urban VI. to confirm the election by the convent of Edith de Benacre as her successor, and to appoint a deputy to whom in all future vacancies the nuns might apply during the schism, the abbess by becoming schismatic having forfeited the right of confirmation of elections which undoubtedly belonged to her 'as much by the institution of the order approved by the apostolic see as by ancient and acknowledged custom.' [12] The pope wrote to the prior of Worcester empowering him to examine the mode of election of the elected prioress, and if found canonical to admit and induct her into corporal possession of the priory, committing to him also a similar duty in all vacancies that should occur in the house while the schism lasted.[13] Prioress Edith de Benacre, however, seems to have resigned her office almost immediately, and in her place the sisters elected Mary de Acton, the subprioress, on the feast of Holy Trinity 1384, her appointment being approved by the prior of Worcester who caused her to be installed.[14]

[1] As Fontevrault was founded in a wild rocky region and the first community subsisted entirely on alms sent them and on what they could take from the ground, their duties were divided, the women to sing the praises of God continually, and the men, their religious duties performed, to till and cultivate the ground for the benefit of all, thus approximating to the ideal in the mind of B. P. Robert of the service that should be rendered by the men to the women as St. John rendered it to the Blessed Virgin.

[2] This differentiated the order from that of St. Brigid, where authority was vested in a female head in matters temporal but not spiritual. Robert d'Arbrissel set the example to his followers by submitting himself to the first abbess of Fontevrault, Petronille de Chemille. Helyot, *Hist. des Ordres Monastiques*, vi. 94.

[3] Cott. MS. Vespas. E. ix. ff. 6d. 7, 8d.

[4] Tanner, *Notitia*, Worc. xviii. note 6.

[5] Pat. 9 Edw. II. m. 17d. and 10 Edw. II. m. 3d.

[6] Close, 18 Edw. III. pt. i. m. 7d.

[7] *Reg. Sede Vac.* (Worc. Hist. Soc.), p. 20. Later still, in the years 1433–4, Robert Finch of the diocese of Worcester was ordained deacon and priest to the title successively of the prioress and convent of Westwood and the prior and convent of Westwood. Ibid. 419, 422.

[8] Ibid. 307.

[9] Close, 4 Edw. III. m. 40d.

[10] Ibid. 15 Edw. III. pt. i. m. 34.

[11] Pat. 30 Edw. III. pt. iii. m. 16.

[12] Extracts from Liber Albus, f. 282; Nash, *Hist. of Worc.* i. 353.

[13] Ibid.

[14] Ibid. p. 354–5. The nuncio and collector of the papal camera in England called on the prior of Worcester to show why the first fruits of the priory should not be devoted to the camera by reason of the provision of the house made to the prioress Edith de Benacre by apostolic authority committed to himself. The said prioress having been summoned to appear protested that she could not legally be compelled to pay the demand, and the prior stated that the resignation of Edith had preceded his reception of the papal mandate for her provision and that the nuns had proceeded immediately to elect Mary de Acton.

In 1405 on the resignation of Eleanor Porter the prior confirmed the election by the convent of Isabella Russell and issued a mandate for her induction.[1] According to an entry under date of 8 November Elizabeth Norton was prioress in 1465. Hers is the last name recorded till we come to that of the last prioress, Joice or Joys or Jocosa Acton. According to the Valor of 1535 the estates of that priory at the time yielded a clear income of £75 18*s.* 11*d.*,[2] so that Westwood came within the terms of the earlier act for the suppression of religious houses of less than £200 yearly value.[3] In March, 1536–7, the priory with the rectory was granted to Sir John Packington[4] for the yearly farm of £22, regarded by him as but poor compensation for his 'painful office in North Wales.'[5] This was followed in March, 1539, by a further grant of the reversion and annual rent of a crown lease of the rectory of Cotheridge together with other possessions of the late priory of Westwood to be held in as full a manner as Joyce Acton the late prioress held the same.[9] A yearly pension of £10 was granted to this lady on 11 March, 1536–7,[10] but no mention is made of other inmates at the date of the surrender of the house, nor do they appear as recipients of that measure of compensation.

Prioresses of Westwood

Isabella Gros.[11]
Edith de Benacre,[12] resigned 1384.
Mary de Acton,[13] elected 1384.
Eleanor Porter,[14] resigned 1405.
Isabella Russell,[15] elected 1405.
Elizabeth Norton,[16] occurs 1465.
Joice or Jocosa Acton,[17] surrendered 1536.

The impression of the fifteenth-century seal of this house taken from a cast at the British Museum[18] is very indistinct. It is a pointed oval 1⅝ by 1 in., and represents the Annunciation of the Virgin under a canopy. The legend is defaced.

HOUSE OF CISTERCIAN MONKS

7. THE ABBEY OF BORDESLEY

Although Worcestershire was so great a Benedictine centre the Cistercians obtained a footing within it at Bordesley in the middle of the twelfth century. They came to England in a period of anarchy and unsettlement, which greatly affected the progress of the movement and left a minor trace in the contradictory charters to the various houses of the Cistercian order. Bordesley abbey was undoubtedly founded in 1138[6] by Waleran de Beaumont, count of Meulan and Worcester, and a foundation charter to that effect is to be found among the Hatton manuscripts.[7] Yet it is difficult to reconcile this with the fact that the Empress Maud also gave a charter of foundation and endowment in 1136, stating that by this she and Henry her son founded and endowed the abbey of Bordesley 'for the love of God and of King Henry my father, and Geoffrey count of Anjou my lord, and the queen my mother,' to which Waleran de Meulan was a witness.[8] When this charter was quoted in an inspeximus made by Richard II. no mention was made of any former charter or endowment, but Maud with her son Henry were looked on as sole founders.[19] Moreover, Henry II. in 1157 took the monastery into his custody, considering himself and his mother the founders.[20] The only way to account for these inconsistencies is to suppose that the real foundation was made by Waleran in 1138, in which year he is known to have been in England.[21] But from 1138 onwards to 1141 he was too fully occupied with fighting on Stephen's side to carry out his proposed foundation.[22] After the battle of Lincoln he forsook the cause of Stephen and joined the empress, after having made a pilgrimage to Jerusalem in 1145.[23] It may well be that it was not until then that the planned foundation of Bordesley was remembered, and the count, now subservient to the empress, gave up his right as founder to her.

[1] Liber Albus, f. 424–5 ; Nash, *Hist. of Worc.* i. 356–7.
[2] *Valor Eccl.* (Rec. Com.), iii. 276.
[3] *L. and P. Hen. VIII.* x. 1238.
[4] Ibid. xiii. pt. i. p. 580.
[5] Ibid. xi. pt. 2, 775.
[6] *Ann. Mon.* (Rolls Ser.), iv. 186.
[7] Dugdale, *Mon.* v. 409.
[8] Dugdale (*Mon.* v. 409) quotes the whole charter from an original in the possession of Clement Throgmorton of Haseley. There is a fragment of a like charter preserved in the Harleian Collection (Harl. MS. 537, f. 93), and the whole is given in full in an inspeximus of the lands of the abbey in the reign of Richard II. (Pat. 2 Rich. II. pt. ii. m. 24).
[9] *L. and P. Hen. VIII* i. 651, g. 44.
[10] Ibid. xiii. pt. 1, p. 576.
[11] Extracts from Liber Albus ; Nash, *Hist. of Worc.* i. 354.
[12] Ibid.
[13] Ibid.
[14] Ibid. 356.
[15] Ibid.
[16] Pat. 5 Edw. IV. pt. 2, m. 18.
[17] *L. and P. Hen. VIII.* xiii. pt. i. p. 576.
[18] Brit. Mus. lxxiv. 74.
[19] Pat. 2 Ric. II. pt. ii. m. 24.
[20] Add. Ch. 6039.
[21] *Ord. Vit.* (Eng. Hist. Soc.), xiii. 32, 37.
[22] Ibid. 32–42.
[23] *Chron. Norm.* sub anno.

In both charters the endowment was the same, and included the whole land of Bordesley (Worcester) and 'Cornehall'[1] (Worcester) and Tardebigge (Worcester), the church of Tardebigge, and the whole land of Hollowell (Holloway ?). There were also gifts of lands in Warwick and Worcester made by William and Stephen de Beauchamp, the bishop of Worcester, the earls of Chester and Warwick, and a few others. By 1291 the value of their temporalities was £43 2*s.* 0*d.*,[2] while their spiritualities were valued at £2 15*s.* 4*d.*[3]

The history of the lands of the abbey is to be found in the long list of grants, confirmations, and exchanges which took place in the twelfth and thirteenth centuries. In comparatively few cases does the monastery seem to have been involved in the usual quarrels over its right to its lands,[4] and never in a serious quarrel. Thus, although Bordesley was never richly endowed, its possessions were safe, and by 1535 its temporalities had reached the annual value of £348 9*s.* 10½*d.*[5]

However, the revenues of Bordesley, as of so many of the Cistercian houses, depended to a great extent on its wool-growing, and its position in the forests of Feckenham and Arden was favourable for it. Signs of extensive wool-growing by the monks are to be found in notices of the exportation of their wool to foreign parts and their dealings with the merchants of Florence. In 1224 Henry III. granted to the monks of Bordesley that the thirteen sacks of wool which they had in London should be transported to foreign parts 'sine impedimento.'[6] In 1278 the abbot and convent petitioned in Parliament concerning an obligation made by a former Abbot John with some Florentine merchants who had lent him 300 marks of silver, which the abbot proposed to repay in wool, forty-two sacks of which were worth 300 marks. The present abbot complained that the monastery had paid one hundred of the marks and also the forty-two sacks of wool, so that the merchants had received twelve sacks of wool to the good.[7] There is an interesting note in 1341 of the determination of the abbot and convent to maintain their rights against unjust taxation. They pleaded against 'the assessors and collectors of the wool last granted in that county that they had tried to levy wool of the abbot's moveable goods therein,' whereas his temporalities were taxed as annexed to his spiritualities.[8] A further stand against excessive taxation was made in the reign of Henry VII. when William, then abbot of Bordesley, stood out against 'a double contribution on the part of the monasteries,' but the abbot of Stratford wrote to him advising him 'to be conformable to the same and not to run in danger of censure, and in conclusion be compelled thereto with further cost and little thank.'[9]

As a royal foundation Bordesley received many privileges from the crown. Henry II., as part founder of the abbey, granted that the monks should not be impleaded for any of their lands except before the king;[10] that they should have all the villeins and fugitives belonging to their lands,[11] and should enjoy their lands without encroachment.[12] In 1205 John granted that the monks of Bordesley, 'qui sunt de propria elemosina nostra,' might be quit of toll and all customs both for the things they bought and the things they sold.[13] Rights in the forest of Feckenham, especially right to make assarts or clearings which would serve as pasture land for their sheep, must have been invaluable to the monastery, and were granted in 1230 by Henry III.[14] and in 1464 by

[1] Probably Tutnall in Tardebigge parish.

[2] *Pope Nich. Tax.* (Rec. Com.), 229b, 238, 257b.

[3] Ibid. 217, 217b, 219b, 223.

[4] In Henry II.'s reign a certain Alice claimed lands in Sunger against the abbot, but for half a mark of silver abjured all right which she had against the said abbot (Madox, *Form. Angl.* Preface xv.). About the same time a composition was made, implying a former quarrel, between the monks of Bordesley and the church of St. Mary of Warwick over the tithes of the lordship of Bidford, by which the abbot and convent were to render 15*s.* yearly to a canon of Warwick for the retention of the tithes (Madox, *Form. Angl.* 24). In 1260 came another composition concerning these same tithes, this time between the abbot of Bordesley and the prior of Kenilworth and the perpetual vicar of Bidford, by which it was agreed that if the monastery of Bordesley acquired any lands within the parish of Bidford, which now paid tithes to the church of Bidford, the monastery should pay the tithes to the church (Madox, *Form. Angl.* 26). In 1238 a final settlement was made concerning land in Claverdon claimed by Nicholas de Burley, by which the abbot retained the land but gave up to Julia the wife of Nicholas and Richard her son certain lands for their lives and yearly portions of corn for her life (Madox, *Form. Angl.* 222). In 1244 a settlement was made between the abbot of Bordesley and the bishop concerning common pasture claimed by the bishop in Osmaresley for certain of his tenants of Alvechurch, allowed by the abbot under conditions (Nash, ii. 415, from Liber Albus, Worc. ff. 84, 85).

[5] *Valor Eccl.* (Rec. Com.), iii. 271, 272, 273.

[6] *Cal. of Pat.* 1216–25, 471.

[7] *Rolls of Parl.* (Rec. Com.), i. 1b.

[8] *Cal. of Close*, 1341–3, 310.

[9] Stowe MS. 141, fol. 7.

[10] Add. Chart. 6039.

[11] Madox, *Form. Angl.* 294.

[12] Ibid. 295.

[13] *Rot. Chart.* (Rec. Com.), 145. In 1275 Henry abbot of Bordesley pleaded against Robert Mortimer that he had exacted passage and toll from the abbot and his men passing by his farm of Wycheland against this charter (Ft. of F. 3 Edw. I. No. 59, Coll. 258, file 9).

[14] *Cal. of Chart. R.* 236. The same condition had been made in 1220 and evidently disobeyed. *Rot. Claus.* (Rec. Com.), i. 417b.

Edward IV.[1] and confirmed by Henry VIII. in 1536.[2]

Of the internal history of the house in the twelfth century it is difficult to find any trace. A visitation of the English Cistercian abbeys is recorded in 1188, and as a result William, abbot of Bordesley, resigned, probably on account of some irregularity, and was succeeded by Richard, sub-prior of the house.[3] A brief but fairly detailed description[4] of the state of the abbey in 1332 shows that at that date there were thirty-four brethren, inclusive of the abbot, and one novice, seven lay brothers, and seventeen serving men, with a very considerable quantity of stock. The rent of their farms brought in over £45, and their wool produced nearly £33, the total receipts amounting to £175 10*s*. 2*d*. On the other hand their expenses and debts came to £257 18*s*. 1*d*., showing a deficit of £82 7*s*. 11*d*., which, however, thanks to debts paid off and increase of stock, was £55 better than the previous year. The episcopal registers give some vague indications of the state of the house between the thirteenth and fifteeth centuries, but little that is definite. A letter from the bishop of Worcester on behalf of a novice of Bordesley imprisoned at Newgate in 1286,[5] another letter to the abbot of Bordesley in 1312 acquainting him with the complaint of Alice de Estach of the grievous wrong she had suffered from one of the monks, Thomas de Eryngdon, and of the scandal thereby occasioned,[6] and a pardon granted in 1339 to Henry son of William Mason, a monk of Bordesley, for the death of William de Wandone, monk,[7] hardly speak well for the monks, though it is hard to judge by cases whose very mention goes to prove they were exceptional; and it is significant that although Bishop Giffard, ignoring the exemption of the Cistercians from ordinary visitation, five times visited the monastery,[8] he issued no injunctions or adverse report concerning the state of the house. Again, it is hardly likely that if the house had not been in good repute the pope would have made the abbot of Bordesley his mandatory so often as he did.[9]

However this may be, there is certainly no evidence against the house to be found at the time of the Dissolution. A commission[10] to visit certain monasteries of the Cistercian order issued in 1535 included Bordesley,[11] but the result is not known. No further clue to the steps the commissioners were taking with regard to the abbey appears until 1538. In the May of that year Richard Whittington, cellarer of Bordesley, wrote to Thomas Evaunce[12] that their father and master John Day intended to resign, or had already resigned, the abbey, 'for that he is aged, impotent, sick, and also not of perfect remembrance.' Further, he desired letters to the lord Cromwell, and promised to obey Evaunce's advice, surrendering the monastery into the king's hands, 'trusting in Cromwell for a means of living.'[13] On 8 July, 1538, Evaunce wrote to Cromwell to hurry on the final surrender since harvest was at hand and the rye would be fallen in ten days and wheat anon after, and 'the king had better sell the corn standing to the tenants than in the barn.'[14] Evidently the abbot had already made an informal submission, since Evaunce complained that the abbot 'since his submission' had falsely sold most of the crops to his servants, but he himself had 'cautioned them not to meddle.' As for the state of the revenues of the house, Evaunce stated that the abbot would leave it £200 in debt, with much of its timber felled and its 'household implements' purloined. He therefore advised that a commission should be sent to inquire into the case or a clause inserted in the commission of suppression.[15] On 17 July, 1538, John Day finally surrendered the abbey with all its possessions into the king's hands,[16] and by 31 July the house had been 'defaced and plucked down, and the substance thereof sold to divers persons without profit or lucre paid or answered to the king's majesty's use for the same.'[17] The authorized sale, however, was not made until 23 September of the same year. Evidently much of the fabric of the church and cloisters had been stolen by that time, since the sale of all the glass and iron that

[1] *Cal. of Pat.* 1461–7, 357.

[2] *L. and P. Hen. VIII.* x. 418.

[3] *Ann. Mon.* (Rolls Ser.), ii. 245.

[4] Dodsworth MSS. (Bodl. Lib.), lxxvi. f. 94.

[5] *Worc. Epis. Reg. Giffard* (Worc. Hist. Soc.), 286.

[6] Worc. Epis. Reg. Reynolds, f. 51.

[7] *Cal. of Pat.* 1338–40, 232.

[8] *Worc. Epis. Reg. Giffard* (Worc. Hist. Soc.), 6, 243, 340, 354, 379, 443. These visitations were in 1268, 1284, 1289, 1290, 1294. In 1284 he received procuration and slept at the monastery at the cost of the house. In the other cases he received procuration in food and drink only. Bishop Carpenter also visited the monastery in 1467 and received four marks procuration (Worc. Epis. Reg. Carpenter, f. 218).

[9] *Cal. of Papal Letters*, i. 94; ii. 547; iv. 80.

[10] Issued in accordance with Act of Parliament of 1533–4, appointing that every visitation should henceforward be made by 'such person or persons as shall be appointed by authority of the king's commissioners' (*Stat. of Realm*, Hen. VIII. p. 470).

[11] *L. and P. Hen. VIII.* viii. 24.

[12] Thomas Evaunce received the site of the monastery on the Dissolution, and had already made overtures to Cromwell for it, since in June, 1538, Latimer wrote to Cromwell that he had intended to sue for 'some good piece of the demesne of Bordesley,' but hearing that Mr. Evaunce had begun the same suit he would give up his intention (*L. and P. Hen. VIII.* xiii. i. 437).

[13] Ibid. 350.

[14] Ibid. 500.

[15] Ibid. 501.

[16] Ibid. 518.

[17] Add. MS. 11041, f. 26.

remained, of the pavement and out-buildings and of 'one little bell,' only reached just over seventy shillings.[1] In October, 1539, the pension list for Bordesley was issued. It shows the number of the monks as nineteen besides the abbot, but does not give any particulars as to their respective offices in the monastery.[2]

Abbots of Bordesley

William, occurs about 1160.[3]
Hamo, occurs about 1170.[4]
William, resigned 1188.[5]
Richard, elected 1188,[6] resigned 1199.[7]
William de Stanley, elected 1199,[8] died 1204.[9]
William de Pershore, occurs 1205.[10]
Philip, occurs 1217,[11] died 1223.[12]
Philip, occurs 1244.[13]
John, occurs about 1273.[14]
Henry, occurs 1275.[15]
Thomas Orlecote, elected 1277.[16]
William de Heyford, elected 1293.[17]
John de Edveston, elected 1309.[18]
William de Berkhampstead, occurs 1317[19] and 1319.[20]
John de Acton, elected 1361.[21]
John Braderugge, elected 1383.[22]
Richard, occurs 1384.[23]
John, occurs 1415.[24]
Richard Feckenham, occurs 1433.[25]
John Wykin, occurs 1445.[26]
William Halford, elected 1452.[27]
William Bidford, 1460.[28]
Richard, 1511.[29]
John Day, occurs about 1519,[30] surrendered July, 1538.[31]

The common seal of Bordesley represents the coronation of the Virgin in a carved niche with two trefoiled arches. Below, under another arch, is an ecclesiastic kneeling to the left in adoration.

[SIGI]LL' : ECL'E : BEATE : MARIE : DE : BORD[ESLE] [32]

There are two other seals connected with the monastery extant—one a seal of an abbot of Bordesley and the other a seal of Abbot William Halford. The former represents the abbot standing on a carved corbel with a pastoral staff in his right hand and a book in his left.

SIGILL' : ABBATIS : DE : BORDESLEY [33]

The second represents the Virgin standing in a carved canopy with the Child in her left hand.

. . . . S : DE : BOR . . . .[34]

HOUSES OF CISTERCIAN NUNS

8. THE PRIORY OF WHISTONES

The nunnery of the White Ladies of Aston, otherwise known as the house of St. Mary Magdalene, at Whistones, of the order of St. Bernard of Clairvaux, stood in the parish of Claines, on the north side of the cemetery of the hospital of St. Oswald. It was founded by Walter de Cantilupe before 1255, in which year the site 'et cætera eis collata' were confirmed to the nuns by the prior and convent of Worcester.[35] Further details of this confirmation are given in the Liber Albus, showing the endowment to have included 51 acres of arable land and 2 acres of meadow at Aston Episcopi, or White Ladies' Aston, together with the tithes of the demesne lands at Northwick (Worcester) and Newland (Worcester), and of the land of Richard Blund and

[1] Add. MS. 11041, f. 86.

[2] *L. and P. Hen. VIII.* xiv. i. 597. The list is as follows:—John Day, abbot, £50; also Thos. Wall, Thos. Baxter, Thos. Lyllie, Ric. Weston, Ric. Badger, Thos. Yerdelay, Thos. Tayllor, Thos. Philips, Ric. Soufford, Wm. Steward, John Johnson, Ric. Evance, Wm. Edwardys, Wm. Austen, Roger Shaspere, John Pene, Thos. Tayllor, and John Hantum, monks. Possibly the Richard Weston of this list is the Richard Whittington, cellarer of the abbey, above mentioned.

[3] Willis, *Mitred Abbies*, ii. App. 29.

[4] Tanner, *Notitia*, Preface xlviii.

[5] *Ann. Mon.* (Rolls Ser.), ii. 245.

[6] Ibid. He was sub-prior of Bordesley.

[7] Ibid. 252.

[8] Ibid.

[9] Ibid. 256.

[10] Tanner, *Notitia*, Preface xlviii. W. abbot of Bordesley occurs c. 1210 (*Cal. of Bodl. Charters*, p. 685).

[11] *Ann. Mon.* (Rolls Ser.), iv. 409.

[12] Ibid. ii. 298.

[13] Liber Albus, Worc. ff. 84, 85.

[14] *Rolls of Parl.* (Rec. Com.), i. 1b.

[15] Feet of F. 3 Edw. I. no. 59 (Coll. 258, file 9).

[16] Tanner, *Notitia*, Preface xlviii.

[17] Ibid.

[18] Worc. Epis. Reg. Reynolds, f. 12.

[19] Tanner, *Notitia*, Preface xlviii.

[20] *Cal. of Pat.* 1317–21, 369.

[21] Worc. Epis. Reg. Brian, f. 36b.

[22] Ibid. Wakefield, f. 39b.

[23] MS. E. R. Mores from Nash ii. 407.

[24] Tanner, *Notitia*, Preface xlviii.

[25] Worc. Epis. Reg. Bourchier, f. 10b.

[26] Ibid. Carpenter, i. f. 37b.

[27] Ibid. f. 104b.

[28] Tanner, *Notitia*, Preface xlviii.

[29] Ibid.

[30] Court of Aug. Proceedings (P. R. O.), Bdle. 1, no. 47.

[31] *L. and P. Hen. VIII.* xiii. i. 518.

[32] Cott. Ch. xi. 20 (A.D. 1520).

[33] Ibid. B. M. Seals, lxxiii. 93 (13th cent.).

[34] Ibid. Add. Ch. 4890 (A.D. 1465).

[35] *Ann. Mon.* (Rolls Ser.), iv. 443.

Peter de la Flagge in Claines (Worcester).[1] By 1291 the nuns had also acquired a portion in the chapel of Claines, granted by Bishop Giffard in 1283,[2] and the tithes of the chapel of Aston Episcopi, or White Ladies' Aston.[3] In 1301 the king granted the bishop licence to alienate to the prioress and convent 12 acres of land and 1 acre of wood in Northwick.[4] In 1329 he granted them licence to acquire in mortmain land and rent not held in chief to the value of 100*s*.[5] In 1331 Joan Talbot, widow of Sir Richard Talbot, of 'Richard's Castle,' Hereford, gave them one messuage, 15 acres of land, 1*d*. rent, and half an acre of meadow, with appurtenances, in Flagge, in the manor of Northwick.[6] This grant was confirmed by Bishop Orleton in the November of the same year,[7] and by the prior and convent of Worcester in the December.[8] In 1334 20 acres of land in Northwick were alienated to the prioress and convent by William de Beauchamp, and 2 acres by Hugh de Hanford, chaplain.[9] In 1335 Thomas atte Mulne was given licence to alienate to Whistones 6 acres of land and half an acre of meadow in Northwick, of the yearly value of 14*d*.[10] In 1400 came a royal grant of £10 yearly from the issues of the county of Worcester,[11] and in 1476 Margery Swinfen, prioress, promised in consideration of this grant to cause a mass to be done four times a year 'for the solle of the noble prince of blessed memorie Richard, late Duke of York, father to our sayde soverayne lord'; also three days in the year mass for the 'prosperitie and welfare of our sayde soverayne lord, the quene, my lord prince, and there noble issue'; also every Friday in the week the prioress and convent would 'goo a procession sayinge the lateneye for the tranquylite and peas of this roialme of England . . . . and remembryng our founder the bishop of Worcester in the same.'[12] The £10 annual grant was confirmed to the house by Henry VII. in 1486, and in 1488 the king ordered the sheriff to pay all arrears of the said grant, and to pay the annuity itself from time to time in accordance with the grant.[13] With the help of this gift from the king the temporalities of the house by 1535 had reached the value of £33 9*s*. 8*d*., while their spiritualities were valued at £22 13*s*. 11*d*., and included the rectory of Weston (Warwick),[14] appropriated to Whistones in 1407 by Bishop Clifford,[15] and confirmed by Bishop Carpenter in 1445 or 1446.[16]

The poverty of Whistones, as of Cookhill, was proverbial. In 1240 Henry III. ordered the bailiffs of Tewkesbury to deliver a cask of the king's wine to the White Sisters of Worcester.[17] In 1275 Bishop Giffard, who was a generous benefactor to the house, wrote to the papal legate, on behalf of the nuns of Whistones, pleading their inability to support their own needs, much less to pay heavy taxation.[18] In 1284 the bishop gave a quarter of corn and another of barley, with half a mark to buy herrings, to all the nuns of Worcester, on account of their poverty,[19] and on his death he bequeathed to the nuns of Whistones vestments for their great altar and 100*s*. in money.[20] During the vacancy that followed Bishop Gainsborough's death, the Lady Agnes de Bromwych, prioress of Whistones, died, and the proceedings on the election of the Lady Alice de la Flagge as her successor are given with remarkable detail, and incidentally show the poverty of the house.[21] In 1308 the sub-prioress, Lucy de Solers, wrote to the bishop-elect of Worcester, pleading that in consideration of the smallness of the possessions of the nuns of Whistones, 'which compelled the same nuns formerly to beg to the scandal of womankind and the discredit of religion, for the honour of religion and the frailness of the female sex,' he should grant them by their proctor licence to elect their new prioress, and should confirm the same election.[22] This appeal, addressed strangely enough to the bishop-elect, and not to the prior of Worcester, evidently implied that the nuns had not sufficient means to pay the fees that were due to the bishop on a new election. John, prior of Worcester, wrote to W. Burston, begging him to promote the business of the Whistones nuns,[23] and also to the rector of Hartlebury, praying him that he would 'testify the extreme poverty of the nuns of Whistones to the elect of Worcester,' in order that he might 'incline to the prayer of their proctors' for licence to elect a new prioress, and commit the confirmation of the same to any of the neighbouring prelates that so he might 'relieve the necessity and serve the honour of the order.'[24] On this the bishop-elect wrote giving the prior and the rector of Hartlebury, his commissary general, power to receive and examine the election of a prioress of Whistones, and confirm the same according to the canonical institutions.[25] He also wrote to Lucy de Solers, giving her licence to elect, and as the patronage belonged to

[1] Liber Albus, Worc. f. 62.

[2] The tithes of Claines were granted on condition that the nuns were answerable for the services of the church by a fit priest *Worc. Epis. Reg. Giffard* (Worc. Hist. Soc.) p. 190).

[3] *Pope Nich. Tax.* (Rec. Com.), 239, 216.

[4] *Cal. of Pat.* 1297–1301, 595.

[5] Ibid. 1327–30, 457.

[6] Liber Albus, Worc. f. 139, 140.

[7] Ibid.

[8] Ibid.

[9] *Cal of Pat.* 1334–8, 47.

[10] Ibid. 185.

[11] Ibid. 1399–1401, 374.

[12] Worc. Epis. Reg. Alcock, f. 167.

[13] *Mat. for reign of Hen. VII.* (Rolls. Ser.), ii. 375.

[14] *Valor Eccl.* (Rec. Com.), iii. 230.

[15] Nash, i. 222.

[16] Worc. Epis. Reg. Carpenter, i. f. 31d.

[17] Close, 25 Hen. III. m. 8.

[18] *Worc. Epis. Reg. Giffard* (Worc. Hist. Soc.), p. 78.

[19] Ibid. p. 231.

[20] Liber Albus, Worc. f. 62.

[21] *Sede Vac. Reg.* (Worc. Hist. Soc.) 111–114.

[22] Ibid. 112.

[23] Ibid. 113.

[24] Ibid.

[25] Ibid.

the bishop, he claimed to grant the licence 'without prejudice to the church of Worcester, and without making it a custom.'[1]

Further details of this election and that of Agnes de Monynton in 1349 give almost the only events recorded of the history of the monastery. Lucy de Solers sent a full description to the bishop reciting how on the vigil of the Apostles Peter and Paul she and the whole convent had assembled in their chapter house, and had appointed the Monday following to treat of the election. On that day, mass being over, being instructed in the form of election by two sisters of the priory, Alice de Seculer and Isabel de Aston, all who were present, unanimously, 'as if inspired by the Holy Ghost,' chose Alice de la Flagge, 'a woman of discreet life and morals, of lawful age, professed in the nunnery, born of lawful matrimony, prudent in spiritual and temporal matters.'[2] But, as yet, Alice, with a modesty befitting her virtues, could not be persuaded to agree to the election. But, 'weeping, resisting as much as she could, and expostulating in a loud voice as is the custom,' she was carried to the church and her election proclaimed. At length, on the following Wednesday, 'being unwilling to resist the Divine will,' she consented, and after reference to the bishop's commissary and the prior of Worcester the election was confirmed.[3] In 1349, on the death of Juliana de Power, Agnes de Monynton, sub-prioress, with six other nuns, who probably constituted the rest of the convent,[4] petitioned the bishop that the new prioress might be chosen from among themselves (que le soit une de nous sus nomes). The bishop, as patron, chose Agnes de Monynton.[5]

Little is known of the internal state of the house as regards the maintenance of order and discipline. The injunctions issued by Bishop Wittesleye in 1365 to the prioress and nuns of the diocese showed a marked departure from the rules of the order in the nunneries of the diocese in general, and probably in Whistones among them.[6] However, in no case is there record of special injunctions or corrections following on any of the frequent episcopal visitations to the house.

There is no trace of the actual surrender of Whistones at the time of the Dissolution. It probably took place in 1536 under the statute of that year granting the king the smaller religious houses whose annual value was under £200.[7] It appears in the list of these houses made in 1536,[8] and in 1538 in a list of the houses lately dissolved in the country.[9] Jane Burrell, the last prioress, received a pension of £5 10*s.* on her surrender,[10] and enjoyed the same until 1553.[11]

Prioresses of Whistones

Juliana, occurs 1262.[12]
Agnes de Bromwich, died 1308.[13]
Alice de la Flagge, elected 1308,[14] died 1328.[15]
Juliana de Power, elected 1328,[16] died 1349.[17]
Agnes de Monynton, elected 1349.[18]
Elizabeth Hanbury, resigned 1427,[19] died 1427.[20]
Elizabeth Tewkesbury, elected 1427.[21]
Elizabeth Wotton, elected and died 1472.[22]
Margery Swinfen, elected 1473,[23] died 1485.[24]
Joan Morton, elected and died 1485.[25]
Jane Burrell, surrendered in 1536.[26]

9. THE PRIORY OF COOKHILL

Isabel de Mauduit, countess of Warwick, is said to have founded the Cistercian nunnery of Cookhill in 1260.[27] But it is evident the foundation was made in the twelfth century, though the actual date seems impossible to ascertain. The earliest mention is in an abstract of a deed by William Beauchamp, earl of Warwick, confirming to the nuns of Cookhill the gift which Isabel the countess his mother, William the earl her brother, and Waleran the earl her

1 *Sede Vac. Reg.* (Worc. Hist. Soc.), 112.
2 Ibid. 114.
3 Ibid. 113.
4 Their names are as follows :—Ellen Ryons, Joan Pope, Agnes Groos, Sibyll Shelle, Ellen Spelly. Hence it would seem the house consisted of six nuns and a prioress and sub-prioress.
5 Worc. Epis. Reg. Bransford, ii. f. 156.
6 Ibid. Wittesleye, f. 7.
7 *Stat. of Realm,* 27 Hen. VIII. c. 27.
8 *L. and P. Henry VIII.* x. 516.
9 Ibid. xiii. ii. 502.
10 Ibid. xiii. i. 576.
11 Bks. of. Ct. of Aug. (P.R.O.) 232, f. lxii.
12 Liber Albus, f. 67.
13 *Sede Vac. Reg.* (Worc. Hist. Soc.), 112.
14 Ibid.
15 Worc. Epis. Reg. Orlton, ii. f. 21.
16 Ibid.
17 Ibid. Bransford, ii. f. 156.
18 Ibid.
19 Ibid. Poulton, f. 14d.
20 Ibid. f. 34.
21 Ibid.
22 Ibid. Carpenter, ii. f. 48d.
23 Ibid.
24 Ibid. Alcock, f. 167. According to Tanner (*Notitia,* Preface xlviii.) Elizabeth Wotton died in 1478, and Margery Swinfen succeeded her in that year, but this is impossible in the light of the evidence of the register.
25 Ibid. f. 153d.
26 *L. and. P. Hen. VIII.* xiii. i. 576.
27 Habington unhesitatingly ascribes the foundation to Isabel, quoting a record of John Rous 'quondam capellanus de Gibecliffe juxta Warwick.' 'Venerabilis Isabella uxor nobilis viri Will de Beauchamp . . . filia Aliciae Mauduit domina de Hanslap et soror Will de Mauduit com. War. et de Novo burgi ejusque ob. prolis defectum proxima haeres. Ista Domina apud Cokehull in com. Wigorn est sepulta inter moniales ibi quarum est fundatrix et patrona' (Habington, *Surv. of Worc.* (Worc. Hist. Soc.), 311).

grandfather made to them of the church of Netelton.[1] This carries the foundation back, at any rate, as far as the end of the twelfth century. More decisive than this, as a proof that the foundation could not possibly have been as late as 1260, is a suit, entered on the patent roll of 1227, between Sarah, prioress of Cookhill, and Peter Fitz Herbert and William Boterell, concerning the advowson of the church of Alcester.[2] Tanner says that Isabel 'might be styled the foundress, as having the patronage of this house by descent, or perhaps as restoring it after it might have been forsaken, or she might be a considerable benefactress, but she could not be the original foundress.'[3] Evidently she became a nun of Cookhill, for in the will of her husband, William Beauchamp, a legacy of 10 marks was made 'to the church and nuns of Kokeshull, and Isabel my wife.'[4] It is on record that she was buried among the nuns at Cookhill, and in the seventeenth century a tomb bearing her name and a broken inscription remained in the ruined chapel of the nunnery.[5]

As there seems to be no existing foundation charter it is impossible to say exactly what the original endowment of the nunnery included, but a charter of John, bishop of Worcester, given in 1288, confirming lands and possessions to Cookhill gives a summary of the endowments up to that date. Two hides and a half at Cookhill by the gift of Maud of Crombe D'Abitot;[6] four virgates at Clodeshale (Cladeswell, Worcester) and one virgate at Toidon by the gift of Sibyll, wife of Ralph of Hampton; Tatebecha (? Tachbroke, Warwick) by the gift of Walter de Trecha; lands at Spernovere (Spernall, Warwick) by the gift of William Durvassel; lands at Morton Underhill (in Inkberrow) by the gift of Robert, son of Odo; the mill of Campden (Chipping Campden, Gloucester) by the gift of 'Thomas, nephew of the earl of Gloucester'; churchscot from all the lands of William Beauchamp in Worcestershire which rendered the same; churchscot from Huddington (Worcester) by the gift of Alan Warnesto and his wife Cicely, and from Hatch Lench houses, by the gift of Stephen Beauchamp.[7] In the Taxation of 1291 there were three entries of the spiritualities of Cookhill entered but erased since the nuns were discharged payment on account of their poverty.[8] In 1330 the church of Bishampton was appropriated to the nuns of Cookhill 'for the relief of their poverty,' with reservation of a fit provision for the vicar. In 1535 the house had acquired several other small rents in Church Lench and in Worcester, also in Alcester (Warwick), Campden (Gloucester), and 'Gundycott' (Condicote, Worcester), and in Westhyde and Kempeley (Hereford). These temporalities reached only the value of £16 5*s.* 4*d.* while the spiritualities were worth £19 3*s.* 11*d.*[9]

Only on three recorded occasions was the house involved in any struggle over its possessions and rights. In 1227 Prioress Sarah claimed the advowson of the church of Alcester against William Boterell and Peter Fitz Herbert;[10] in 1331 prioress Cecilia came to terms with the prior and convent of Worcester, probably after some dispute concerning lands or rights, and agreed to pay them an annual pension of one mark;[11] while in 1367 a dispute concerning the right of burial in the churchyard of Spernall between the prior of Studeley and the prioress of Cookhill ended in favour of the former.[12]

The poverty of the house of Cookhill is indeed almost the chief feature of its known history. Almost every reference to the nuns is to speak of their poverty, to exempt them with other slenderly endowed houses from payment of any extraordinary taxation or to grant them respite for the arrears already owing to the king. Thus in 1276 the king granted for the relief of their poverty six oaks from the forest of 'Kanek,' for timber.[13] In 1279 an ordinance was issued by the bishop concerning tithes of sheaves and hay from the parishes of Church Lench and Hatch Lench given 'for the relief of the nuns of Cockhulle.'[14] In 1313,[15] and again in 1402,[16]

1 MS. Macro. 12, ii. 18a (from Tanner, *Notitia*, 624). From this charter Nash deduces that Cookhill was founded by the year 1198.

2 *Cal. of Pat.* 1225–32, 167.

3 Tanner, *Notitia*, 624, n.

4 *Worc. Epis. Reg. Giffard* (Worc. Hist. Soc.), 8.

5 Habington, *Surv. of Worc.* (Worc. Hist. Soc.), 1, 312.

6 Habington quoting from 'The Book of Aydes,' 20 Edw. III. gives the prioress of Cookhill holding two and a half hides in Inkberrow (i.e. at Cookhill) which Osbert D'Abitot of Crombe Dabitot formerly held (*Surv. of Worc.* (Worc. Hist. Soc.), 311).

7 From original charter in hands of William Brome, Esq. of Ewithington, Hereford, quoted in Nash, ii. 17.

8 *Pope Nich. Tax.* (Rec. Com.) 217b, 218b, 239b. These three entries are the church of Lench Roculf, valued at £5 6*s.* 8*d.*; a portion in the church of Alcester valued at £1 13*s.* 4*d.*; and a portion in the church of Spernall valued at £1 0*s.* 0*d.*

9 *Valor Eccl.* (Rec. Com.), iii. 262–3.

10 *Cal. of Pat.* 1225–32, 167.

11 Liber Albus, f. 140b. from MS. Soc. Antiq. cxlix.

12 Worc. Epis. Reg. Wittesleye, fol. 7a. The dispute had arisen on the ground that the right of burial of those of free condition in the churchyard was assumed by the prioress to include those who 'since the epidemic' had become free. The right of burying those of 'free condition' belonged by ordination to the prioress and convent, that of burying the unfree to the prior and convent. The bishop inspected the letter of confirmation to the prior of Stodeley and decided in his favour that he should have the burial of those who beforetime held servile tenements, but were now free.

13 *Cal. of Close*, 1272–9, 312.

14 *Worc. Epis. Reg. Giffard* (Worc. Hist. Soc.), 116.

15 Worc. Epis. Reg. Reynolds, fol. 93b.

16 Ibid. Clifford, 70d.

Cookhill was exempted from payment of tenths because its rents were 'poor and weak.' In 1336 the king ordered the treasurer and barons of the exchequer to cause the nuns of Cookhill to have respite for £15 due from them as arrears to the king, 'as their house is so slenderly endowed that they have not enough to live upon without outside aid (aliena subvencione).'[1] Doubtless their poverty was chiefly due to their slender endowment, but it was perhaps also partly due to the unwise conduct of their 'temporal business,' judging from an entry in the episcopal registers under the year 1285, when the bishop wrote to the prioress and nuns, as a result of the visitation of John de Farley, his official, that for the better conduct of their temporal business Thomas the chaplain should have full charge of their temporal affairs.[2] This letter also gives a valuable light on the history of the house in the thirteenth century. Evidently the rules of the order had not been well observed, for the bishop ordered the prioress and convent not to go out of their cloister unless compelled by necessity, and not to wander about in the town.[3] Similar orders issued in 1365 by Bishop Wittesleye to all the nuns of the diocese of Worcester[4] point to certain irregularities in the nunneries of the diocese and probably in Cookhill among them. At the same time the frequent visitations to Cookhill recorded in the episcopal registers do not generally seem to have been followed by any injunctions or corrections, although offences and irregularities were more likely to come to light in a small and poor nunnery than in a larger and richer.

Of the nuns themselves it is difficult to learn much. In the few mentions of them that exist both the prioresses and the nuns seem to have been of good family, although, judging from the poverty of the house, they could not have been rich enough to be generous benefactors when they took the veil. A Margaret Butler[6] is mentioned in 1272 as desiring to be professed 'in the church of Cookhill,'[7] and in 1365 a Joan Helwene, nun of Cookhill, was made prioress of Pynley.[8] The pension list of 1540 showing the number of nuns at the Dissolution as seven, including the prioress, is the first clue to the numbers of the house.[9] Probably the numbers had never been higher than this.

For some reason hard to discover, since bribing was out of the question, Cookhill was exempted from suppression in 1537, and Elizabeth Hews (Hughes) was appointed prioress.[10] However it may have been granted to her for the purpose of surrender, which evidently took place in 1538 or 1539, and the pension list is dated from 1540.[11] No further details exist concerning the dissolution except the list of scanty possessions entered in the ministers' accounts for 1542.[12]

Prioresses of Cookhill

Sarah, occurs 1227.[13]
Agnes de Alyncester, resigned 1290.[14]
Cecilia de Sarnefend, installed 1290,[15] occurs 1331.[16]
Sarah, died 1349.[17]
Christina Durvassel, elected 1349.[18]
Alice Rous, elected 1361.[19]
Elizabeth Hughes, elected 1537,[20] surrendered 1538 or 1539.

The common seal of the nunnery represents a lady, possibly Isabel de Beauchamp, holding in the left hand a falcon, in the right a destroyed object.[21] Dugdale describing the seal attached to a document in the Augumentation Office describes the figure as holding a book in her left hand.[22] The inscription is very imperfect—

SIGILL' : SANCTE . . . . .

HOUSE OF CLUNIAC MONKS

10. THE PRIORY OF ST. JAMES OF DUDLEY

The Cluniac priory of Dudley was founded about the middle of the twelfth century[5] and furnishes an interesting example of a religious establishment annexed to a baronial castle and subordinate to the lords of the manor. The founder, Gervase Pagnell, states in his charter for the new foundation that, bearing in mind the intention of his father, Ralph Pagnell, to establish a religious community at Dudley, he has fulfilled the design for the good of his father's soul chiefly

1 *Cal. of Close*, 1333–7, 694.

2 *Worc. Epis. Reg. Giffard* (Worc. Hist. Soc.), 267.

3 Ibid. 4 Worc. Epis. Reg. Wittesleye, fol. 7a.

5 The date is approximately fixed by a charter of Walter Durdent, bishop of Coventry and Lichfield 1149–1160, confirming to the monks the church of Wombourn. Harl. MS. 3868, f. 274.

6 A member of the Butler family who were lords of Oversley (Warwick).

7 *Worc. Epis. Reg. Giffard* (Worc. Hist. Soc.), 52.

8 Worc. Epis. Reg. Wittesleye, fol. 12d.

9 *L. and P. Hen. VIII.* xv. 35. The list is as follows:—

Dame Elizabeth Hughes, prioress,	£8
„ Anne Morgan	66*s.* 8*d.*
„ Joan Belamy	53*s.* 4*d.*
„ Alice Wastle	53*s.* 4*d.*
„ Margaret Dyson	53*s.* 4*d.*
„ Alice Reve	53*s.* 4*d.*
„ Elizabeth Oweley . . .	53*s.* 4*d.*

10 Ibid. xii. i. 350. 11 Ibid. xv. 35.

12 Mins'. Accts. (Aug. Off.) 33 Hen. VIII.

13 *Cal. of Pat.* 1225–32, 167.

14 *Worc. Epis. Reg. Giffard* (Worc. Hist. Soc.) 342.

15 Ibid. 16 Liber Albus Worc. fol. 140b.

17 Worc. Epis. Reg. Bransford II. fol. 11b.

18 Ibid. 19 Ibid. Brian, fol. 38a.

20 *L. and P. Hen. VIII.* xiii. i. 350.

21 B. M. Seals, lxxiii. 94. The date is after 1260.

22 Dugdale, *Mon.* v. 736.

and of his ancestors and for the good estate of himself, his wife and son, and has granted and confirmed to God and St. James of Dudley, St. Milburga of Wenlock, and to the monks serving God at Dudley, in free alms the site of their church with the churches of St. Edmund and St. Thomas of Dudley, and the churches of Northfield, Sedgley, and Inkpen. Also the church of Bradfield, half a hide of land in Churchill with the other half which Agnes de Somery bequeathed to the church of St. James with her body, the whole of which was in his fee. He confirmed all gifts made to the monks by any tenant or knight of his, reserving to himself and his heirs all services due to them, and granted that their cattle should feed in whatever pastures his own were pastured except in his parks, that they should have pannage in the forests for their pigs and those of their tenants residing within the limits of his gift, 'in elemosyna mea resedentium,' and a tithe of his bread, venison, and fish while he resided at Dudley or Harden. Under the supervision of his steward they should take whatever wood they required for their buildings and other 'easements' except from his hedges and parks. These liberties were granted with right of soc, sac, thol, thac, and theam.[1] The founder further ordained that the prior of Wenlock should select monks for the new house, and by the consent of the founder and his heirs appoint a prior from his own chapter. When the house could support a convent he was authorized to constitute one, subject to the consent of his convent and the founder and his heirs. This liberty was shortly afterwards exercised and a deed, witnessed by Robert his son, reciting the former grant states that 'we John, prior of Wenlock, and the convent of the same do ordain a convent, so that Osbert, now prior of St. James, and Robert and Hugh his brothers do make wholly and fully a perfect convent.'[2]

Guido or Wido de Hoffeni or Offeni, together with Christiana his wife and William his son, conferred on the monks of Dudley in free alms the church of Wombourn and its appurtenances 'for the redemption of our souls.'[3] Subsequently a question seems to have arisen as to whether this donation included the parishes of Trysull and Seisdon. An inquisition held at Stafford found that these two chapels belonged of right to the church of Wombourn, and they were confirmed by Bishop Richard Peche of Coventry and Lichfield to God and St. James of Dudley and St. Milburga of Wenlock 'as of the pious gift of Wido de Offendi and William his son.'[4]

Pope Lucius III. in the first year of his pontificate[5] issued a bull on behalf of Everad, the prior of Dudley, and his brethren ordaining that in their church the order of St. Benedict should be observed according to the constitutions of Cluny, and confirming to them all previous possessions together with a licence to retain in canonical possession whatever might hereafter be added to them.[6] The possessions enumerated in the bull included the church of St. James of Dudley with the chapels [or churches] of St. Edmund and St. Thomas, the churches of Sedgley and Northfield with the chapel of Coston Hackett,[7] the churches of Ingle . . . . and Bradfield with the chapel of Inglefield the gift of Gervase Pagnell the founder,[8] the church of Wombourn with the chapel of Trysull given by Guy de Offeni, the church of Selly (Seille) by Ralph de Seille, the town of Churchill by Agnes de Somery, the town of Saredon by Osbert de Kenefare, a virgate of land in the town of 'Wolynton' the gift of Robert de Chanden, and lands in Inkpen the gift of John Mansell.[9] The monks also obtained right of sepulture for all who desired to be buried in their church, unless they were excommunicated or under interdict, saving the rights of those churches to whom the said bodies should belong, with the privilege that in the event of a general interdict the monks might in a low voice celebrate divine offices, the doors being closed, bells not sounded, and all excommunicated and interdicted persons excluded. The exaction of tithe of lands cultivated by them or at their expense was prohibited, and the brethren were authorized to present clerks or priests for the parish churches which they held to the diocesan for institution. They might also receive and keep clerks or laymen fleeing from the world, and it was prohibited for anyone having made his profession in the house to depart except for a more rigid rule. The pope also decreed that all ancient and reasonable customs observed up to the present should be retained in future, and that no one should molest or in any way vex them saving the authority of the pope, diocesan law, and reverence due to the church of Cluny.[10]

In obedience to a papal mandate in 1238 the bishops of Worcester and Coventry and Lichfield came to an important agreement as to the bounds of their respective dioceses whereby it was decreed that the town of Dudley with its churches and appurtenances should belong to Worcester, while the castle and priory should remain under the jurisdiction of the bishop of

[1] Harl. MS. 3868, f. 274.

[2] Dodsworth MS. ix. p. 132, cited by Erdeswick in his *Surv. of Staff.* p. 341.

[3] Harl. MS. 3868, f. 274.

[4] Ibid. f. 275. The same bishop confirmed to the monks the church of Sedgeley, the gift of Gervase Pagnell. Ibid. f. 274.

[5] Dugdale dates this bull 1190, but Lucius III. became pope in September, 1181, so the correct date should be 1182.

[6] Harl. MS. 3868, f. 275.

[7] See Habington's *Surv. of Worc.* (Worc. Hist. Soc.), i. 168.

[8] Dugdale, *Mon.* v. 83.

[9] Ibid.

[10] Ibid.

Coventry and Lichfield.[1] The Taxation Roll of 1291 gives the priory an income of £27 11*s.* 4*d.*, including temporalities at Dudley within the diocese of Worcester to the value of £5 14*s.* 6*d.*, and temporalities and spiritualities of the value of £21 16*s.* 10*d.* in the Coventry and Lichfield diocese.[2]

The barony of Dudley in default of male heirs passed from the Pagnell family to the Somerys[3] on the death of Roger de Somery in 1290. Roger, bishop of Coventry and Lichfield, granted an indulgence of forty days to all who having truly repented and confessed their sins should say devoutly the Lord's Prayer with the Angelic Salutation for the soul of Roger de Somery, knight, whose body lay buried in the conventual church of Dudley 'of our diocese.'[4] In 1300, on the death of another Roger de Somery, Pope Boniface VIII. offered another indulgence to the faithful on similar conditions.[5]

The monks seem for the most part to have led a quiet uneventful life under the protection of the great house to which they were so closely united. On various occasions they made known their grievances. The archbishop of Canterbury, in 1281, wrote to the bishop of Salisbury respecting a complaint of his neglect to institute to the church of Inkpen the clerk presented by the prior by the special concession of the archbishop to whom collation had 'hac vice' devolved, attributing this refusal to the false representations of a certain John Russel. The archbishop warned his suffragan to delay the matter no longer.[6] The register of Bishop Giffard of Worcester records that the monks of Dudley in 1274 presented the rector of the church of Wyn', Lincoln diocese, to the church of Northfield to be held by him 'in commendam' on account of the poverty of the rectory.[7] It is also recorded in the same register that the archbishop of Canterbury on 24 September, 1292, confirmed sentence of excommunication passed upon brother Robert de Mallega, 'rector of the parish church of Dudley and prior of the same, for manifest offences.'[8] There appears to have been some trouble in connexion with the church of Northfield. On 3 March, 1292–3, parson Malcolm de Harleye formally renounced a quarrel which he had with Peter de Estcot touching the church in question and undertook to procure a like renunciation from the prior and monks of Dudley. On the 7th of the same month he acknowledged receipt on behalf of himself and the religious men of the sum of twenty marks at the hands of two parties, one of whom was this same Peter de Estcot, in part payment of 100 marks in which the bishop of Worcester was bound by reason of certain business in connexion with the church of Northfield.[9] The conservator of privileges of the Cluniac order[10] in September, 1294, ordered the archdeacon of Worcester to annul the sentence of excommunication passed by the bishop of Worcester and Peter de Estcot, his chaplain, against the late archdeacon of Westminster, procured by the monks of Dudley;[11] the reason for the sentence is not stated. The brethren contended with the abbot of Halesowen in 1297 for a fourth part of the chapel of Frankley as belonging to the church of Northfield. They were compelled however to relinquish this claim and to content themselves with the patronage of Northfield.[12] Robert de Mallega, who gives the impression of an energetic head, occurs again in May, 1298, when his assent was given to the presentation by John Deobul of Suckley of a clerk to the rectory of Churchill near Kidderminster.[13]

The prior of Dudley, like other superiors of Cluniac foundations,[14] was probably suspected or implicated in the rebellion of Thomas, earl of Lancaster, in 1322; he was arrested 'for certain reasons' by the king's order, but released in October, 1323, and his goods restored.[15]

The commissary-general acting for the prior of Worcester during a vacancy in March, 1338–9, reported that he had cited the prior of

1 *Ann. Mon.* (Rolls Ser.) iv. 429.

2 *Pope Nich. Tax.* (Rec. Com.) pp. 228, 243, 251. Many possessions previously mentioned are omitted in this reckoning. Dugdale states that the priory is included in the taxation as being within the diocese of Worcester; probably confusion has arisen between the priory and the churches of Dudley, which, according to the convention of 1238 already mentioned, are placed in Worcester.

3 Robert, the son of Gervase Pagnell, founder of Dudley priory, died before he could succeed, and Hawysia, daughter of Gervase, became his heir. She took for her first husband John de Somery, and Dudley came into the hands of Ralph her son and heir.

4 Dugdale, *Mon.* v. 84.

5 Ibid. This Roger was succeeded by John de Somery his brother, who dying without issue, his estates were divided by his sisters and co-heiresses Margaret and Joan. Margaret, who had for her share the castle of Dudley which included the priory, married John de Sutton, and through her the barony of Dudley lapsed into the Sutton family.

6 *Reg. of Peckham* (Rolls Ser.), i. 218.

7 *Worc. Epis. Reg. Giffard* (Worc. Hist. Soc.), p. 65.

8 Ibid. p. 426.

9 Ibid. p. 441–2. The name of Peter Estcot, rector of the church of Northfield, occurs in a list of those promoted to deacon's orders by the bishop of Worcester at Hartlebury on the Vigil of Holy Trinity 1293. Ibid. p. 431.

10 The archdeacon of Westminster.

11 *Worc. Epis. Reg. Giffard* (Worc. Hist. Soc.), 449.

12 From the Lyttleton charters cited by Nash, *Hist. of Worc.* ii. 192. The monks presented to this church up to the year 1438. In 1479 bishop Alcock of Worcester presented by right of devolution. Ibid.

13 *Worc. Epis. Reg. Giffard* (Worc. Hist. Soc.), p. 496.

14 See *V.C.H. Surrey*, ii. 71.

15 Close, 17 Edw. ii. m. 35.

Dudley to appear to answer for his appropriation of an annual pension of six marks from the rectory of Northfield in the diocese of Worcester without sufficient title, and on his non-appearance had pronounced him in contempt and sequestered the aforesaid six marks.[1] The bishop of Worcester in 1342 summoned the community to exhibit their title for the appropriation of the church of Dudley, which was allowed.[2] In January, 1351–2, a certain Robert de Wymersfeld was attacked at the suit of William, prior of Dudley, for taking 'vi et armis' goods and chattels belonging to the priory at Dudley, during a vacancy in the priory in 1349. Robert appeared in person, and denied the charge. The case was heard for the third time at Bromwich at Whitsuntide and a verdict given for the plaintiff.[3]

Dudley though subordinate to the alien house of Wenlock seems to have escaped seizure into the king's hands during the French war, probably as being reckoned parcel of the estates of the lordship of Dudley.[4] An entry in the patents under date of 7 July, 1346, states in reference to the church of Northfield that it was of the patronage of Dudley notwithstanding any right the king could claim therein.[5] There is no record of its visitation by the delegates appointed for that purpose by the abbot of Cluny, or the prior of La Charité-sur-Loire to which affiliation it belonged, until the middle of the fifteenth century, when in a fragment enumerating the English and Scottish foundations of Cluny, apparently forming part of a report, it is stated that at the priory of Dudley there should be four monks, and two masses celebrated daily, one with music.[6] The house being exempt from episcopal jurisdiction and visitation, entries relating to it in the registers of the diocese are rare, but occur occasionally.[7] In April, 1400, the bishop confirmed an indenture between (1) Richard of Stafford, prior of Dudley, and his brethren; (2) the vicar of the church of Sedgeley, which was appropriated to the priory; and (3) the rector of the church or chapel of Darlaston, whereby it was agreed that the priory and convent should receive 10*s.* from the rector, and that vicar and rector should divide the offerings for the dead, the vicar receiving all the wax and candles.[8] In February, 1402–3, the brethren obtained a certificate from the bishop for their appropriation of the parish churches of Sedgeley and Wombourn and an annual pension of 10*s.* from the chapel of Darlaston.[9]

According to an entry in the patent roll of that year, on 14 July, 1421, the prior of St. Milburga, Wenlock, on the death of brother John Billingburgh, presented William Canke to the priory of St. James, Dudley, to whom the king gave up the temporalities which were in his gift by reason of the minority of John, son of Thomas Sutton, late baron of Dudley.[10] His rule proved a very short one, and in the following October the prior of Wenlock presented three monks of his house to the king praying him to admit one of them to the priory, which was vacant by the resignation of William Canke, and the king admitted John Brugge.[11] A charter and lease by this prior dated in the chapter house of Dudley the Feast of the Nativity of St. John Baptist, 1434, is still in existence.[12] The inhabitants of Dudley in 1483 gave 'three score okes' out of the forest of Kinfare towards the building of their 'chauncell.'[13]

John Webley occurs as prior in the Valor of 1535, giving the annual value of the priory at £36 8*s.* 0*d.*;[14] the pension list of the dissolved priory of Wenlock, 26 January, 1539–40, assigns a pension of £10 to Thomas Shrewsbury, prior of the cell of Dudley.[15] The site of the priory was granted as parcel of the late monastery of Wenlock in Salop to Sir John Dudley in 1545.[16]

Priors of Dudley

Osbert,[17] occurs circa 1160.
Everad,[18] occurs 1182.
William.[19]
Robert de Mallega,[20] occurs 1292 and 1298.

1 *Reg. Sede Vac.* (Worc. Hist. Soc.), 271.

2 Worc. Epis. Reg. Bransford, i. f. 59, cited by Nash, *Hist. of Worc.* i. 361.

3 De Banco R. Hil. 25–26, Edw. iii. m. 135, cited in *Coll. for Hist. of Staffs* (Wm. Salt, Arch. Soc.), xii. (1) iii.

4 The escheator was ordered in February, 1322–3, to restore to Margaret co-heiress of the late Roger de Somery the advowson of the priory of Dudley, co. Stafford, of the yearly value of forty marks. Close, 16 Edw. ii. m. 13.

5 Pat. 20 Edw. iii. pt. ii. m. 16.

6 Duckett, *Chart. and Rec. of Abbey of Cluni*, ii. 213.

7 Isabel de Sutton, countess of Dudley, in her will dated 1396 left directions for her body to be buried beside her husband Richard de Dudley in the church of the Carmelites at Coventry, with bequests to the churches of Sedgeley, and St. Edmund and St. Thomas of Dudley. Lichfield Epis. Reg. Lescrope, f. 49.

8 Ibid. Burghill, f. 170.

9 Ibid. f. 177d.

10 Pat. 9 Hen. V. pt. i. m. 2 and Harl. MS. 6962, p. 160.

11 Pat. 9 Hen. V. pt. ii. m. 18.

12 Cott. ch. xxi. 14.

13 Harl. MS. 433, f. 102.

14 *Valor Eccl.* (Rec. Com.), iii. 104.

15 *L. and P. Henry VIII.* xv. iii.

16 Ibid. xvi. 678 g. 47.

17 He was the first prior when the new foundation, built between 1149–1160, was constituted a convent. Dodsworth MS. ix. p. 132, cited by Erdeswick in his *Survey of Staff.* p. 341.

18 The bull of Pope Lucius III. in the first year of his pontificate is addressed to Everad, prior of Dudley, and his brethren. Harl. MS. 3868, f. 275.

19 *Lyttelton Charters* (Ed. Jeayes), no. 15.

20 He was excommunicated in 1292. *Worc. Epis. Reg. Giffard* (Worc. Hist. Soc.), pp. 426, 496.

Thomas de Londiniis,[1] occurs 1338 and 1346.
William,[2] occurs 1351–2 and 1354
Richard de Stafford,[3] occurs 1400.
John Billingburgh,[4] died 1421.
William Canke,[5] appointed 1421, resigned in the same year.[6]
John Brugge,[7] appointed 1421, occurs 1434.[8]
John Webley,[9] occurs 1535.
Thomas Shrewsbury,[10] received a pension 1539-40.

The pointed oval thirteenth-century seal of Dudley, chipped at the bottom, taken from a cast at the British Museum, represents St. James or a prior, full length, in his right hand a long cross, in his left a book.[16] Legend :—

S'CONVME PRIO . . . DVDELEYE.

A later seal, of which only a fragment remains attached to a charter dated 1434, represents St. James in profile to the right standing under a canopy, with flat cap, staff and book. Legend wanting.[17]

HOUSE OF PREMONSTRATENSIAN CANONS

11. THE ABBEY OF HALESOWEN

The abbey of Halesowen was founded in the early thirteenth century when King John in 1214 gave the manor of Hales (Shropshire) to Peter des Roches, bishop of Winchester, to build there a religious house of 'whatever order he pleased.'[11] In the next year he confirmed the manor with appurtenances to the Premonstratensian canons of Hales.[12] The patronage was given to Bishop Peter who according to the visitation book of the Premonstratensian abbeys founded the monastery in 1218, dedicating it to the honour of the Virgin and St. John the Evangelist.[13] On 6 May of that year, according to the same authority, the abbey was furnished with monks from the abbey of Welbeck (Nottingham), and the abbot of Welbeck became the superior of the newly founded abbey.[14] Hence it seems that the buildings were not inhabitable until the year 1218, and probably to mark the installation of the monks in that year Henry III. granted the bishop of Winchester £17 3*s.* 4*d.* towards the building of the abbey,[15] while in 1223 he granted the bishop sixty 'copula de cablecio' from the forest of Kinver or Kinsare (Staffordshire), for the 'repair of his church of Hales,'[18] and in 1227 confirmed King John's foundation charter and grant of the manor of Hales.[19] Somewhere about this time William Ruff granted the advowson of the church of Walsall (Staffordshire), with the chapels belonging to the same, and the king confirmed the same in 1233[20] and 1245. In 1245 Henry III. confirmed 'the church of Waleshale with its chapels and all appurtenances' to the abbey in a charter worded as though the grant were made by the king himself.[21] This suggests that the king had some claim to the advowson, and in 1293 he put forward the claim. A 'quo warranto' was brought against the abbot at the suit of the crown for the advowson of Walsall and Wednesbury. To this the abbot pleaded that Henry III. by his letters patent gave the convent the church of Walsall, and the chapel of Wednesbury was part of the same. The king conceded the advowson of Walsall, but denied that Wednesbury was part, and the jury found that the chapel of Wednesbury 'fuit matrix ecclesia ante donationem et concessionem quas predictus Henricus Rex fecit.'[22] In 1301, in consideration of a fine made by the abbot, the king granted him the advowson of the chapel of Wednesbury, 'which the king some time ago recovered as his right from Nicholas the predecessor of the present abbot.'[23] At the time of the taxation of Pope Nicholas the church of Walsall and the church of Hales were the only spiritualities belonging to the monastery.[24] But in 1340 the advowsons of

[1] His name occurs among the witnesses to a charter of John de Sutton, lord of Dudley, granted in that year (Dugdale, *Baron.* ii. 215). In 1346 Thomas, prior of Dudley, brought an action against certain persons for breaking his close at Trysull. De Banco R. 20 Edward III. m. 440.

[2] De Banco R. Hill, 25-26 Edward III. m. 135. At Michaelmas, 1354, William, prior of Dudley, was sued with others for trespass. De Banco R. Mich. 28 Edw. III. m. 75d.

[3] Lichfield Epis. Reg. Burghill, f. 170.

[4] Pat. 9 Hen. V. pt. i. m. 2.

[5] Ibid.

[6] Ibid. pt. ii. m. 18.

[7] Ibid.

[8] Cott. Chart. xxi. 14.

[9] *Valor Eccl.* (Rec. Com.), iii. 104.

[10] *L. and P. Hen. VIII.* xv. iii.

[11] *Rot. Claus.* (Rec. Com.), i. 174b. This charter is also quoted in an 'inspeximus' made in 1510 (Chan. Conf. R. 2 Hen. VIII. pt. ii. m. 8.)

[12] *Rot. Chart.* (Rec. Com.), 217.

[13] Sloane MS. 4935, fol. 29.

[14] Ibid.

[15] Pipe R. 2 Hen. III. Rot. i.

[16] Brit. Mus. xxii. 27.

[17] Cott. Chart. xxi. 14.

[18] *Rot. Claus.* (Rec. Com.), i. 530, 547, 550.

[19] *Cal. of Chart. R.* 1227–57, 32.

[20] Dugdale, *Mon.* vii. 927. The charter is undated. It is said to be in the possession of the earl of Dudley.

[21] *Cal. of Chart. R.* 1227–57, 287.

[22] *Plac. de Quo Warr.* (Rec. Com.), 715.

[23] *Cal. of Pat.* 1292–1301, 590.

[24] *Pope Nich. Tax.* (Rec. Com.), 217, 243. A struggle which had taken place between the convent and the dean of Lichfield concerning the advowson of the church of Harborne ended in 1270 by the abbot giving up the advowson. Lich. Epis. Reg. Hales, fol. 154d.

the churches of Clent and Rowley[1] with the chapels attached were granted to the house by John Botetourt, lord of Warley (Worcester), and in 1343 the same churches were appropriated to Halesowen at the petition of the abbot.[2] He pleaded that the situation of the house on the high road obliged them to exercise great hospitality, while they had slender means to support the expenses since they had lately suffered great loss from the fire which had burnt many of their houses within the borough of Hales and from the coldness of devotion among the people to the head of St. Barbara which had formerly been one of the most precious relics belonging to the monastery.[3] By 1535 Halesowen had also acquired the advowsons of the churches of Ludley and Cradley (Stafford), and of Warley (now co. Worcester).[4]

The temporalities of the house kept pace with the spiritualities. The primary grant of the manor of Hales was followed by several minor grants, chiefly of outlying lands, during the reign of Henry III. and Edward I.[5] In 1331 John de Hampton granted the manor of Rowley (Stafford) to Halesowen, reserving to himself the right of nominating a canon who should pray daily for his soul and that of his wife Eleanor.[6] This grant is rather hard to reconcile with a charter of the same year given by Edward III. granting the manor of Rowley to the abbot and convent at an annual rent of £10 6*s.* 8*d.*[7] Probably the king as over-lord superseded John de Hampton's grant by his own and reserved the above rent. In 1337 Joan Botetourt, lady of Warley, granted the manor of Warley (Worcester) to Halesowen providing the abbot found three canons 'of sufficient knowledge of reading and chanting, of the age of twenty and upwards,' to burn six wax candles every year in the church on her annivesary, to give 1 mark to each member of the convent attending this yearly obit for their pittance, and to distribute 20*s.* yearly to the poor coming to the abbey on that day.[8] And in 1473 licence was given to the convent to acquire lands and rents not held in chief to the value of £10 for the sustenance of a chaplain celebrating divine service in the chapel of St. Kenelm, appertaining to the church of Clent, and for the repair of the same chapel.[9] Thanks to these and other grants the temporalities of the house which in 1291 were only worth £22 15*s.* 6*d.*[10] had reached the sum of £294 10*s.* 2½*d.*[11]

The abbots of Halesowen seem to have taken little part in affairs outside their monastery, except as visitors of their daughter house at Titchfield (Hants).[12] Neither do they seem to have been involved in many local land suits, the last recorded land suit in which the abbot was involved being in 1279 when the king claimed the manor of Hales by writ of 'quo warranto.' The abbot quoted King John's charter and secured his right.[13] From several records that have survived it seems probable that at least in the thirteenth and fourteenth centuries the abbots were not on very good terms with their manorial tenants. Nash has recorded, without any further reference, that the abbots exercised a peculiar jurisdiction over their tenants with regard to proving the wills of the deceased.[14] However, the quarrel that arose in the thirteenth century was concerned with the ordinary manorial customs of the manor of Hales. In 1278 the abbot and convent pleaded that their tenants of Hales claimed to be 'de antiquo dominico Domini Regis,' and in spite of the witness of Domesday Book to the contrary refused in virtue of this claim to pay their due services and customs to the abbot, who now begged that his rights in the manor might be thoroughly secured.[15] Evidently the result was the lawsuit brought against the abbot by the king in 1279.[16] In the same year as the petition against the tenants there is an entry in the episcopal register bidding the deans of Warwick, Pershore, and Wick to excommunicate those who laid violent hands on the abbot of Halesowen and his brethren at Beoley.[17] Possibly, although there is nothing except the identical date to prove the suggestion, this may refer to an attack made by the tenants on the abbot. The unquiet years of the period of the Peasants' Revolt gave the tenants of the abbey an opportunity to renew their old protests against services due to the abbot, and in 1387 a commission of oyer and terminer was issued 'on information that divers bondmen and bondtenants of the abbot at Romsley had refused their customs and services for their holdings and confederated by oath to resist the abbot and his ministers.'[18] There is no evidence to prove that the struggle lasted on into the fifteenth century, and in all probability in

1 *Cal. of Pat.* 1338–40, 443.

2 Worc. Epis. Reg. Bransford, fol. 59d.

3 Ibid.

4 *Valor Eccl.* (Rec. Com.), iii. 207.

5 Various charters in the possession of Viscount Cobham at Hagley (Jeayes, *Littleton Charters*).

6 Dugdale, *Mon.* viii. 928.

7 Quoted in an 'inspeximus,' and confirmation given in 1391 (*Cal. of Pat.* 1388–92, 420). This same rent was granted in 1337 to Alice Plowton for good service done to the king's sister (Ibid. 1334–7, 500). It was granted in 1486 to Queen Elizabeth, wife of Edward IV. *Mat. for reign of Hen. VII.* (Rolls Ser.), ii. 349.

8 *Cal. of Pat.* 1334–8, 425, 461, 495.

9 Ibid. 1467–77, 396.

10 *Pope Nich. Tax.* (Rec. Com.), 230–251.

11 *Valor Eccl.* (Rec. Com.), iii. 206.

12 See *V. C. H. Hants.* ii. 185.

13 *Abbrev. Plac.* (Rec. Com.), 197.

14 Nash. ii. App. xxiii.

15 *Rolls of Parl.* (Rec. Com.), i. 10b.

16 See supra.

17 *Worc. Epis. Reg. Giffard* (Worc. Hist. Soc.), p. 103.

18 *Cal. of Pat.* 1385–9, 317.

Halesowen as elsewhere much of the difficulty was smoothed away by the growth of commutation and the new class of labourers.

One of the most noteworthy events in the history of Halesowen was the incorporation with itself of the priory of Augustine canons at Dodford in 1332.[1] By the confirmation charter of Henry III. it appears that Dodford was of royal foundation, being founded by Henry II., probably between the years 1184 and 1191, and endowed with lands lying in Bromsgrove and the adjoining parishes.[2] In 1291 the priory was entered in the taxation roll as holding lands and rents in Dodford worth £4 17*s.*[3] In 1464 Edward IV. 'in consideration of the decrease of the fruits and profits' of the house which had come 'so near dissolution that for a long time only one canon has remained there' appropriated the house and its possessions to Halesowen.[4] From this time one of the canons of Halesowen was to be prior of Dodford and the abbot was to keep in repair the church, refectory, and other buildings of Dodford. Also the abbot and convent were to pay a yearly pension of 6*s.* 8*d.* to the bishop and his successors, 3*s.* 4*d.* to the prior and convent of Worcester, and 2*s.* to the archdeacon.[5] Under the protection of Halesowen the revenues of Dodford increased, and in the Valor of 1535 its demesne lands alone, entered as part of the possessions of Halesowen, were worth £7; while rents and woodland in Dodford which had been part of its possessions were valued at £17 13*s.* 1*d.*[6]

The various rent rolls belonging to Halesowen that still exist bear valuable witness to the material prosperity of the abbey. Among the Littleton manuscripts at Hagley are two rolls of the cellarer of Halesowen for the years 1369 and 1370. In the first the receipts for the sale of corn and oats and other commodities reached the sum of £84 15*s.* 6*d.*; while the expenses for the year, including 19*s.* paid to the vicar of Hales, repairs made on the estates of the abbey, the provisioning of the house and the payment of servants, amounted to £83 19*s.* 4*d.* In the roll for 1360 there is an interesting entry of provisions bought for the abbot of Welbeck and the abbot of Croxton, probably on the occasion of their visit to the house to superintend the election of the new Abbot Richard de Hampton. There was also a gift of 40*s.* to the abbot of Welbeck, and other gifts to his chaplains, his chancellor, his penitentiary, palfreyman, and groom, and further gifts to the abbot of Croxton and his suite. Evidently the year of an election was one of many expenses. Besides entertaining the abbots of Welbeck and Croxton the abbey seemingly had to pay the expenses of the journey to Worcester to gain the confirmation of the new election by the prior and convent.[7] The prior and convent of Worcester also claimed a pittance of 20*s.* and the new abbot's vestments.[8] Apart from the extraordinary expenses that came with an election there is abundant evidence that the ordinary expenses of the house, considering the smallness of its numbers, were very heavy, chiefly owing, as the abbot himself complained in 1343, to the necessary hospitality they extended to strangers and wayfarers. At a visitation of the convent held in 1489, when the canons of the house only numbered seventeen, four of whom were resident on the vicarages belonging to the monastery, 20 bushels of wheat and rye were weekly consumed in bread, and 1110 quarters of barley, 60 oxen and 40 sheep, 30 swine and 24 calves were consumed yearly.[9] Besides indiscriminate hospitality the abbey was called upon to grant several corrodies, the usual grant being 18*s.* 8*d.* 'pro coquina.'[10] Moreover a pension of two marks was due every year to the prior and convent of Worcester,[11] and one of two marks also to the bishop.[12] Besides this 'Walter sometime abbot of Halesowen'[13] had bound the convent 'for divers considerations and causes' to pay the dean and chapter of Lichfield a yearly pension of 40*s.* out of the profits and fruits of the churches of Walsall and Wednesbury for the support of two choristers to serve in the cathedral church of Lichfield. Also Abbot John Derby 'by reason of great sums of money granted to the convent by one Thomas Hayward, dean of Lichfield,' granted the said Thomas £6 a year for the maintenance of one priest perpetually to minister in the said cathedral church.[14] In spite,

[1] *Cal. of Pat.* 1461–7, 321.

[2] Dugdale, *Mon.* vii. 944; *Cal. of Chart. R.* 1226–57, 156.

[3] *Pope Nich. Tax.* (Rec. Com.), 231.

[4] *Cal. of Pat.* 1461–7, 321.

[5] Worc. Epis. Reg. Carpenter, i. f. 186.

[6] *Valor. Eccl.* (Rec. Com.), iii. 206.

[7] MSS. in possession of Viscount Cobham, at Hagley (*Hist. MSS. Com. Rep.* ii. 38).

[8] Two notices show that they carefully maintained their claim. In 1232 on the election of R. canon of the house as the new abbot the Worcester annals note that their house received the vestments and the 20*s.* 'pro pitancia.' *Ann. Mon.* (Rolls Ser.), iv. 424. In 1313 the prior wrote, evidently to Walter de la Flagge who had been elected as long ago as 1305 (Worc. Epis. Reg. Gainsborough, f. 37), begging that the cope in which the same abbot was admitted to the gift of benediction might be transmitted to him, as before asked, in order that discord might not arise between them. *Reg. Sede Vac.* (Worc. Hist. Soc.), 150.

[9] MS. Ashmole. Bodl. Lib. 1519, f. 662d.

[10] Rent roll of 1370 in possession of Viscount Cobham.

[11] MS. Soc. Antiq. cxlix.

[12] Ibid.

[13] Evidently Abbot Walter de la Flagge (elected 1305), since there was no other abbot of that name.

[14] Aug. Proc. (P.R.O.), Bdle. 17, no. 100. The dean of Lichfield, Henry Williams, complained that since the Dissolution of the monastery of Halesowen the dean and chapter had themselves paid the annual sum to the choristers and chantry priest, but had no return from the crown.

however, of all outward drains on the revenues of the monastery an inventory taken in 1505 on the death of Abbot Bruges gives a picture suggestive of internal prosperity. It carefully enumerates the cattle belonging to the monastery and notes how eight oxen from 'Hasmore' were apportioned to the cellarer and four fat beeves from the same place to the kitchen. It describes the abbot's chamber with its two feather beds, and its 'quylte of white wroght with nedyll worke.' In the new chamber was 'a feather bed, a quylte covered with red sylke, a red coverlit with dolphins.' After enumeration of the furniture in the other principal chambers and of the goodly array of plate in the abbot's chamber, the shrine of St. Kenelm bearing the head of the saint 'silver and gilt' with a crown silver and gilt, a sceptre of silver and ornaments, and the shrine of St. Barbara's head also 'of silver and gilt,' are described as being the most precious possessions of the monastery.[1]

As a Premonstratensian house Halesowen until 1512[2] was under the jurisdiction of the abbot of Prémontré, and the abbot of Hales often attended the meetings of the chapter-general at Prémontré,[3] where the decrees were passed which were enjoined on the houses of the order in England at the visitation of the conservator-general. The abbot of Welbeck, from the first foundation of Halesowen, had been styled 'pater abbatie de Hales,'[4] and as such superintended every election[5] and took the abbey wholly under his protection. On one occasion he wrote to the abbot of Halesowen, probably John Derby,[6] begging him to receive back into the abbey a certain brother Thomas Bromsgrove, who had left the convent without leave but now desired to return.[7] The abbot of Hales wrote back that he would obey the wise counsel of the abbot of Welbeck, and admit the penitent once more into the house.[8] The careful visitations of the house that were held by the bishop of St. Asaph, the conservator-general of the order, give much light on the internal state of the monastery in the fifteenth century. At these visitations punishments were inflicted on those who had broken the rules of the order or were guilty of misconduct. Thus in 1478 John Saunders was found guilty of immorality and was banished from Halesowen to the monastery of Dale (Derbyshire) for eighty days. Brother Thomas Cooksey was accused of the same crime, but denying the same was allowed to purge himself.[9] In a second visitation made in that year the bishop reported that all was well, except that one brother had broken the rule of silence and was to be put on bread and water for one day.[10] In 1481 the bishop discovered 'many enormities' in the performance of divine ceremonies and services, and in the observance of the rules of the order. The brethren were ordered not to eat and drink in the houses of laymen within one league from the monastery, and only to eat in the places appointed for refreshment in the monastery itself. The abbot was ordered to remove from the monastery certain evil women, and forbid them access to the monastery in the future. Further the visitor inquired strictly into the temporal affairs of the house, and bade the abbot preserve his woods and groves as far as possible, and not sell or waste them, but guard them carefully as his predecessor John Derby had done.[11] At the next recorded visitation in 1488 the bishop found 'nothing worthy of correction,' but the state of the monastery both spiritual and temporal bore witness to the good rule of the abbot Thomas Bruges[12] and the zeal of the brethren.[13] In 1494 the visitor reported that the tonsures of the brethren were not cut as the rule of the order directed, and that the abbot had felled much timber, though this was forgiven since it was proved to have been necessary.[14] In 1496, however, we read that five of the younger brothers, Roger Walsall the ringleader,[15] Richard Bakyn, Richard Hampton, Roger Wednesbury, and Thomas Dudley, entered into a conspiracy against the abbot, and at least in the case of Richard Bakyn added immorality to the crime of conspiracy. The month of August brought the visitor and the punishment. Roger Walsall was to be banished to the monastery of Croxton (Leicestershire), where he was to be imprisoned for ten years. Richard Bakyn was sentenced to undergo severe punishment for sixty

[1] Sloane MS. 4935, f. 32.

[2] In 1512 all the Premonstratensian abbeys in England were exempted from the jurisdiction of Prémontré and subjected by papal and royal authority to that of the abbot of Welbeck (Rymer, *Fœd.* xiii. 338).

[3] In 1327 the constable of Dover was ordered to allow the abbot of Halesowen to cross from that port with four horses and 20 marks for expenses of himself and his household to attend the chapter-general at Prémontré (*Cal. of Close*, 1327–30, 217).

[4] Sloane MS. 4935, f. 29.

[5] See the account of the election of Thomas de Lech (Sloane MS. 4935, f. 26), of Thomas Bruges (Ibid. ff. 30–31), and of Edmund Grey (Ibid. f. 34).

[6] The letters are not dated, but were written by John abbot of Welbeck, occurs 1468 (Dugdale, *Mon.* vii. 872). Thomas Bromsgrove is last mentioned among the canons of Hales in 1478 (MS. in Ashmolean, 1519, f. 5d), when John Derby was abbot (1446 to 1485) (Worc. Epis. Reg. Carpenter, i. f. 46; Add. MS. 5841, f. 65).

[7] Sloane MS. 4935, f. 27.

[8] Ibid. f. 28.

[9] MS. Ashmole. (Bodl. Lib.), 1519, f. 5d.

[10] Ibid. f. 18.

[11] Ibid. f. 90d.

[12] Elected in 1485 (Worc. Epis. Reg. Alcock, f. 154d).

[13] MS. Ashmole (Bodl. Lib.), 1519, f. 67d.

[14] Ibid. f. 123.

[15] This same Roger Walsall had been the one black sheep in the monastery in the year 1488, but had at that visitation been absolved and restored to his former rank in the house. (Ibid. f. 67d.)

days, and to be sent for a term to the monastery of St. Agatha (Yorkshire). The other three were sentenced to punishment for forty days and then banishment for a term, Richard Hampton to the monastery of Barling (Lincolnshire), Roger Wednesbury to Newhouse (Lincolnshire), Thomas Dudley to West Deorham (Norfolk). However, at the earnest entreaty not only of the culprits themselves (lacrymabiliter misericordiam implorantes) but of the abbot himself and other brethren, and of the abbot of Talley [1] who was helping in the visitation, the bishop referred 'both the crime and the penalty' to the next chapter-general.[2] By the time of the next recorded visitation in 1517, Richard Bakyn had become sub-prior and the other four were 'worthy canons.'[3] While the existence of irregularities is evidenced by these records, it is probable that the Premonstratensian visitations were far more exhaustive and strict than those of the ordinary diocesan, and the bishop of Worcester's visits to Halesowen do not seem to have been followed by any censure on the government of the house. Any idea of excessive laxness is contradicted by the unwillingness of Abbot John Derby to receive back a penitent apostate until recommended to do so by the abbot of Welbeck, and by the punishment in 1478 of the brother who had broken the rule of silence, and by the fact that in 1494 the only correction needful in the house was in the way that the tonsures of the brethren were cut.[4]

There is no report on the visitation of Halesowen previous to suppression, though some such visitation probably took place in 1536, and was evidently followed by the payment of £4 in January, 1536, and in March, 1537, by the abbot of Halesowen to Cromwell.[5] On 9 June, 1538, William Taylor, the last abbot, surrendered the house and all its possessions to the crown.[6] On 12 June Legh wrote to Cromwell that according to the commission and indenture he had dissolved the monastery of Halesowen, and the surrender having been sealed with the convent seal he was sending it to Cromwell to be enrolled.[7] Either in that year or early in 1539 the moveables, plate, lead, bells, and buildings of the monastery were sold, and the receipts were entered in the Augmentation accounts of September, 1539, under the name of the 'late commissioner, John Freman.'[8]

[1] The Premonstratensian house of Talley in Caermarthenshire from the time of its foundation in 1214 was subject to the monastery of St. John at Ambois, but on account of the distance between the houses the patronage was transferred to Halesowen probably in the fourteenth century. Dugdale, *Mon.* iv. 161–165.

[2] MS. Ashmole. (Bodl. Lib.) 1519, f. 133d.

[3] Ibid. f. 147.

[4] See supra.

[5] *L. and P. Henry VIII.* xi. 597, xiv. ii. 318.

[6] Ibid. xiii. i. 431.

[7] Ibid. xiii. i. 436.

[8] Ibid. xiv. ii. 72.

Abbots of Halesowen

Abbot of Hales, translated to Welbeck 1232.[9]
R. elected on this translation, 1232.[10]
Martin, temp. Edward I.[11]
Nicholas, temp. Edward I.[12]
N. died 1298.[13]
John, elected 1298.[14]
Walter de la Flagge, elected 1305.[15]
Bartholomew, elected 1314.[16]
Thomas de Lech, elected 1322.[17]
Thomas de Birmingham, elected 1331.[18]
William de Bromsgrove, elected 1369.[19]
Richard de Hampton, elected 1369.[20]
John de Hampton, elected 1391.[21]
John Poole, elected 1395.[22]
Henry de Kidderminster, elected 1422.[23]
John Derby, elected 1446.[24]
Thomas Bruges, sub-prior, elected 1485.[25]
Edmund Greyne, prior of Hornby, elected 1505.[26]
William Taylor, last abbot, surrendered 1538.[27]

The common seal of Halesowen represents the Virgin seated on a throne with a crown on her head, the Child on her left knee, a sceptre in her right hand, and with her feet on a carved corbel.

. . . . . VĒTUS : ECCL̄IE : SC̄E : MARIE : D . . . . .[28]

[9] *Ann. Mon.* (Rolls Ser.), iv. 424.

[10] Ibid.

[11] *Cal. of Bodl. Chart.* p. 396.

[12] Ibid.

[13] *Ann. Mon.* (Rolls Ser.), iv. 539.

[14] Ibid. 540.

[15] Worc. Epis. Reg. Gainsborough, f. 37.

[16] Ibid. Maidstone, f. 6d.

[17] Sloane MS. 4935, f. 26. Nash and Dugdale, agreeing with a list made by Bishop Littleton (Coles MS. 5841, f. 65), give the date of Thomas de Lech as 1276. The Sloane MS., however, is a transcript of the Premonstratensian register, and plainly gives the date as 1322. Moreover in the entry on the episcopal register of the election of Thomas de Birmingham in 1331 the abbacy is said to be 'vacant by the voluntary resignation of brother Thomas,' who was evidently Thomas de Lech.

[18] Worc. Epis. Reg. Orlton, f. 41d.

[19] Ibid. Lynn, f. 20.

[20] Ibid.

[21] Ibid. Wakefield, f. 80.

[22] *Sede Vac. Reg.* (Worc. Hist. Soc.), 355.

[23] Worc. Epis. Reg. Morgan, i. f. 16.

[24] Ibid. Carpenter, i. f. 47.

[25] Ibid. Alcock, f. 154d ; Sloane MS. 4935, f. 30.

[26] Sloane MS. 4935, f. 34.

[27] Rymer, *Fœd.* xiv. 607.

[28] Add ch. 9207 (A.D. 1531). There is also a seal existing that belonged to Thomas de Birmingham, abbot of Halesowen, representing the abbot standing on a carved corbel with a pastoral staff curved outwards in the right hand and a book in the left. Harl. ch. 44 E 15.

FRIARIES

12. THE BLACK FRIARS, WORCESTER

The house of the Black Friars was founded in 1347 by William Beauchamp lord of Elmley, who on 5 June of that year obtained licence to alienate in mortmain to the Prior Provincial and Friars Preachers in England a plot of land called 'Belassis' within the walls of the city of Worcester, 100 perches long by 30 perches broad, which was said to be held in chief, to build a house for friars of the Order.[1] The foundation was confirmed, or 'conceded to the province,' as the phrase ran, by the general chapter of the Order at Lyons in 1348.[2] It was one of the last, if not the last, house of the Order to be established in England. On 17 February, 1349–50, Bishop John Thoresby commissioned the bishops of Hereford and Llandaff to consecrate or dedicate a place for the cemetery of the church of the Friars Preachers.[3] In 1351 William Beauchamp obtained licence to assign to the prior and brethren 2 acres of land, with their appurtenances, adjoining the house of the Friars Preachers, and said to be held of the king in free burgage. In return for this favour the friars were bound to celebrate divine service every day for the king and his heirs, and a fine of 1 mark was paid in the hanaper.[4] However, more than a century elapsed before the friars acquired full possession of this land, though they had before that built a gateway on it. The reason for the delay was a disputed title: part of the land was claimed by the prior of St. Mary's, Worcester, and part by the prior of Great Malvern. In 1455 Sir John Beauchamp of Powick, on paying 40*s.* in the hanaper, obtained a writ of privy seal authorizing him to carry out his ancestor's wish by granting compensation to the priors of Worcester and Great Malvern from tenements or lands which he did not hold in chief of the crown.[5]

In 1364, at the petition of John Beauchamp, 'kinsman of the earl of Warwick,' son of Giles and nephew of William Beauchamp, Urban V. granted relaxation during ten years, of a year and forty days of enjoined penance to penitents who on the principal feasts of the year visit and give alms for the repair of the church of St. Dominic of the Friars Preachers of Worcester, of which house the said John and his progenitors were founders.[6]

Richard II. in 1391 granted the prior and convent, for the enlargement of their garden, a garden called 'Pynnokeshey,' lying between the city walls on one side and the way called 'Dolday' on the other, at a rent of 6*d.* a year. It was in the king's hands because Audrey, late wife of Adam Barras, had granted it without licence to the church of St. Clement, Worcester, after the Statute of Mortmain.[7]

There was a school of theology here as in all Dominican convents. In 1393 Friar William Shyrburne, and in 1397 Friar Philip son of Raymund, were assigned to this house as lectors by the master-general of the Order.[8]

On 7 May, 1431, a warrant was issued by the Council for the arrest of Thomas Northfield, S.T.P., a Friar Preacher, at Worcester, and for the seizure of his magical books.[9]

The earliest extant bequest to the Friars Preachers of Worcester is contained in the will of Simon Gros of Worcester, dated 1360.[10] Katharine, wife of Thomas Beauchamp, earl of Warwick, and daughter of Roger Mortimer, earl of March, left them £20 in 1369;[11] Henry Wakefield, bishop of Worcester, left them 40*s.* in 1395;[12] John Halle of Worcester left them 60*s.* in 1451.[13]

Sir John Beauchamp, K.G., baron of Powick, in 1475 bequeathed his body to be buried in the friars' church 'in a new chapel there now to be made on the north side of the quire'; the chapel of lime and stone, with the tomb, were to be built according to the 'patroun of the portretour,' or plan specified in an indenture drawn up between the testator and John Hobbes, mason, of Gloucester: on the tomb was to be placed 'a convenient image of alabaster.' For 'the apparelling of the altar' in the chapel, Sir John bequeathed a gilt chalice, two corporax cases, mass book, vestments, and altar cloths of red velvet and cloth of gold, and of white and red silk. He also provided that a priest of the house should say mass daily in the chapel, receiving 8*d.*

[1] Pat. 21 Edw. III. pt. iv. m. 14.

[2] *Acta Capitulorum Generalium Ordinis Prædicatorum*, ii. 324 (in vol. iv. of *Mon. Ord. Præd.* ed. Reichert, Romæ, 1899). 'Item concedimus provincie Anglie unam domum ponendam in civitate Vigorniensi.'

[3] Worc. Epis. Reg. Thoresby, f. 6.

[4] Pat. 24 Edw. III. pt. i. m. 29.

[5] Pat. 33 Hen. VI. pt. ii. m. 9; *Reliquary* xx. 26–7.

[6] *Cal of Papal Reg.: Petitions*, i. 499; *Papal Letters*, iv. 40, 9 May, 1364.

[7] Pat. 15 Ric. II. pt. i. m. 30.

[8] *Reliquary*, xx. 27; B. M. MS. Add. 32,446 (Extracts from the Registers of the Masters-General of the Order of Friars Preachers, by the Rev. C. F. R. Palmer), f. 7. 'Item eodem die (xx. Jun. 1397) frater Philippus Raymundi fuit assignatus pro lectore Wyconiensi.'

[9] Rymer, *Fœd.* x. 504.

[10] Worc. Epis. Reg. Brian, f. 100v.

[11] Nicolas, *Test. Vetusta*, p. 78; Dugdale, *Baronage*, i. 234.

[12] P. C. C. Rous, f. 26.

[13] Ibid. f. 126 v.

a week for ever: all the friars who were in priests' orders were to take this duty in turn. To ensure the due celebration of his yearly obit, he left to the convent 'in augmenting and amending of their fare and diet every day *2d.*' Among his other bequests to the house were 'a pair of organs of mine being within the parish church of Chelsea in the county of Middlesex,' and 40 marks towards building the cloister and repairing the church and houses.[1]

Margaret, wife of Sir John Beauchamp, who died in 1487, left her body to be buried in the same church, by the body of her lord and husband, and 'ordained that a priest should sing for her soul during the term of one whole year after her decease, within the said house of friars, receiving for his pains 100*s.* She also willed that a tablet of alabaster should be made of the birth of our Lord, and the three kings of "Colleyn," to be set on the wall over her body when it should be buried. Likewise an image of alabaster of St. John the Evangelist, containing three-quarters of a yard in length, with the chalice in his hand, to be set over her likewise; also a candlestick of white iron, with three branches, to set on the tapers of wax of 4 lb., to burn before that image every Sunday, as long as they should endure.' Her will also contains elaborate instructions as to her burial, and bequests of vestments to the convent.[2] Richard Wycherley, O.P., titular bishop of Olenus in Greece, in 1502 desired to be buried in the choir of this church, opposite the tomb of Richard Wolsey, O.P.,[3] late bishop of Down and Connor.[4]

It may be noted that Bishops Giffard, Gainsborough, and Reynolds, all of whom lived before the Black Friars were established at Worcester, were conservators of the privileges of the Friars Preachers in England.[5]

The story of the dissolution and grant of this house to the city will be told in part in connexion with the history of the Grey Friars. 'The Black Friars in Worcester,' wrote the bishop of Dover to Thomas Cromwell in August, 1538,[6] 'is a proper house without any lead, and may dispend by year in rotten houses about twenty nobles by year, but all is in decay. There was an "ancres," with whom I had not a little business to have her grant to come out, but out she is.' This friary is mentioned among 'houses of friars lately given up which have any substance of lead:' it is probably a mistake for the Grey Friars.[7]

The vestments of the Black Friars, to judge from the inventory drawn up at the time of the Dissolution,[8] were less elaborate than those of the Grey Friars. Among the ten suits may be mentioned 'a sute of blew branchyd damaske pryst decon and subdecon,' and 'pryst decon and subdecon off blacke worstede lackynge all thynge.' Most of them were incomplete in some respects. There were five single vestments, four old chasubles, twelve copes (among them 'a red cope for marteres,' and 'ii lytyll copys for chyldern'). No mention is made of any books. The church contained a pair of organs, and the steeple a great bell and a small. The inventory gives the contents of the kitchen (down to 'a broken gredyren"), of the brewhouse, and the buttery. The 'chambers' seem to have been the best furnished part of the house, containing 'v fether beddes with ther bolsteres, a tester of greene saye, iiij candelstekes, with ij basons and ij eweres, a payer of aundyeryns and a fyer schwlue, an almery and ij coferes, a tester and a syler grene saye and rede, a cubborde clothe and a towell, a salt of pewter, a carpet and vj cuscheynes, iij couerlettes.' The plate—candelsticks, cross, censer, goblets, spoons, etc.—weighed 178½ oz. In the nether sextry were four great chests, a cross banner, and four staves for the canopy. The ostry, frater, and prior's chamber contained only tables, trestles, and forms.

Some of the friars of this house appear to have accommodated themselves to the religious changes. The sheriff of Gloucester, Thomas Bell, complained to the bishop of London (9 June, 1536) that Bishop Latimer had admitted to preach a Black Friar 'called Two-year old,' who was banished from the diocese of Worcester by Dr. Bell, then chancellor, for his abominable living and drunkenness.[9] And Latimer himself after the surrender wrote to Cromwell on behalf of the prior, Richard Edwards, who, 'when he surrendered up his house, was promised his capacity freely, both for himself and all his brethren. He is honest . . . I tolerate him in my diocese, and trust you will favour him.'[10]

Lawrence Thorold was prior here in 1528.[11]

[1] P.C. C. Logg, f. 99b; Dugdale, *Baronage*, i. 250; Nicolas, *Test. Vetusta*, 338.

[2] P. C. C. Milles, f. 3; Dugdale, *Baronage*, i. 249–250.

[3] Bodl. MS. Wood B. 13 (Wills from the Prerogative Office, St. Paul's, London; Reg. Blamyn); *Reliquary*, xx. 27–28.

[4] A few other bequests may be noted: Maud Longency of Worcester, 1371 (5*s.*), Worc. Epis. Reg. W. Lynne, f. 54; Elias Spelly, 1391, (40*s.* for the fabric of their house), P. C. C. Rous, f. 57; William ap Rees, 1446 (10*s.*), P. C. C. Rous, f. 95.

[5] *Worc. Epis. Reg. Giffard* (Worc. Hist. Soc.), p. 116; Worc. Epis. Reg. Gainsborough, f. 8, 9; Ibid. Reynolds, f. 53, 78v.

[6] Ellis, *Original Letters*, 3rd ser. iii. 189; *L. and P. Hen. VIII.* xiii. pt. 2, no. 49.

[7] Ibid. No 489. 'A porch of a lodging, divers gutters, with part of the steeple, lead.'

[8] R. O. Chapt. Ho. Bks. 153, ff. 76–77; *L. and P. Hen. VIII.* vol. xiii. pt. 1, no. 1513; *Reliquary*, xx. 29.

[9] *L. and P. Hen. VIII.* vol. x. no. 1099.

[10] Ibid. xiii. pt. ii. no. 646 (19 Oct. 1538); Latimer's *Remains*, 405–6.

[11] *Reliquary*, xx. 28.

13. THE GREY FRIARS, WORCESTER

The Franciscans settled at Worcester between 1225 and 1230. It was probably there that Peter of Eport, rector of Stoke Prior, was received into the order in 1226,[1] and it is certain that the famous Adam de Marisco entered the order at Worcester not later than 1230.[2] This house was head of one of the seven custodies into which the English province was divided—the custody comprising in the fourteenth century the convents of Worcester, Coventry, Lichfield, Stafford, Preston, Shrewsbury, Chester, Llanfaes, and Bridgnorth.[3] The special characteristic of the custody under the first custodian, Robert of Leicester, was 'pura simplicitas'; 'for Friar Robert, a man of small body but large heart, was always devoted to the highest simplicity and brought many simple men into the order.'[4]

The site of the original house is unknown; it was probably within the city wall, as Henry III. in 1231 commanded the bailiffs of Worcester to enlarge the postern in the wall before the house of the friars or make them a more convenient way for bringing in firewood and other necessaries.[5] This position did not allow room for expansion, and during the ministry of Albert of Pisa (1236–9) the friars moved to a new site outside the city wall, where they seem to have remained till the Dissolution.[6] In 1246 the friars again received from the king permission to have a postern in the wall of the city, 'if it be not to the damage of the city.'[7] The friary was being enlarged or rebuilt in 1257, when the king granted the brethren six oaks in Kinefare forest for the construction of their buildings at Worcester,[8] and similar grants of 'oaks fit for timber' were made by Edward I. in 1276 and 1282.[9]

The Worcester annalist after relating the death and funeral of William Beauchamp, earl of Warwick, at the Grey Friars in 1298, continues:[10] 'And so they buried him in a place where no one had yet been interred, in which in winter time he will be said to be drowned rather than buried, where I have once seen herbs growing.' As the earl left his body to be buried in the choir of the Grey Friars, it would appear that the church had recently been rebuilt on a new site.

A provincial chapter of the order (of which no records remain) was held at Worcester in 1260.[11] In 1285 Bishop Giffard requested William of Gainsborough, vicar of the English province, to appoint Robert de Crull lector in the convent of Worcester.[12] But in 1337 the principal *studium* of the custody was not at Worcester, but at Coventry.[13]

The Worcester convent does not seem to have produced many learned men; the famous Johannes Wallensis is said by Bale and others to have been a Minorite of Worcester.[14] Ralph of Loxley, regent master at Oxford about 1310, was buried there—probably in his native convent.[15] Roger of Conway, the opponent of Richard Fitz-Ralph, archbishop of Armagh, belonged to the custody of Worcester, but in 1355 obtained papal licence to live in London.[16] The friary seems to have possessed a considerable theological library: two manuscripts in the British Museum can be identified as having formerly belonged to it—one containing the bible,[17] the other the letters of St. Augustine.[18]

It is clear that the Minorites of the diocese, and probably of the city of Worcester, had disputes with the parish priests about their right to hear confessions and to preach,[19] but no details seem to have been preserved.[20]

So far as they can be traced, the relations of the friars to the bishops of Worcester were friendly; their relations to the monks hostile.[21]

[1] *Ann. Mon.* (Rolls Ser.), iv. 419.

[2] Th. de Eccleston, *De Adventu Minorum*, Rolls Ser. (*Mon. Franciscana*, i. 16); Little, *The Grey Friars in Oxford* (Oxf. Hist. Soc.), 135.

[3] Th. de Eccleston, *ut supra*, 27, 28. Eubel, *Provinciale O.F.M. Vetustissimum* (Quaracchi, 1892), p. 12.

[4] Th. de Eccleston, *ut supra*, corrected by MS. Phillipps, 3119, f. 74, where a gloss is added: 'potius promovit sibi subditos simplicis vitæ quam dissolutos magnæ scientiæ vel literaturæ.' On the Franciscan virtue of *pura simplicitas*, cf. Sabatiar, *Speculum Perfectionis*, pp. lxxi. 167, etc.

[5] Close, 15 Hen. III. m. 2 (Dat. Worc. 3 Oct.).

[6] Th. de Eccleston, p. 34. *L. and P. Hen. VIII.* vol. xiv, pt. 1, no. 102, and pt. 2, no. 780. Leland, *Itinerary*, iv. 104.

[7] Close, 30 Hen. III. m. 12.

[8] Close, 41 Hen. III. m. 2 (Worc. 26 Sept.); *cf.* Close, 40 Hen. III. m. 5.

[9] Close, 4 Edw. I. m. 4 and 10 Edw. I. m. 7.

[10] *Ann. Mon.* (Rolls Ser.), iv. p. 537.

[11] Ibid. 446.

[12] *Worc. Epis. Reg. Giffard* (Worc. Hist. Soc.), p 263.

[13] MS. Bodl. Can. Misc. 75, f. 78. *Trans. of the Royal Hist. Soc.* vol. viii. p. 69 (1895).

[14] Bale, *Index Scriptorum*, p. 211. Peterhouse Cambridge, MS. 18, 1. *Dict. Nat. Biog.* lix. 119.

[15] *The Grey Friars in Oxford*, p. 165.

[16] Ibid. 239, and *Bull. Franc.* vi. 289. In *Cal. Papal L.* iii. 563 he is wrongly described as 'warden of Worcester.'

[17] MS. Burney, i. marked 'Biblia 13.'

[18] MS. Royal, 5 B. v. marked 'Augustinus 10.'

[19] *Worc. Epis. Reg. Giffard* (Worc. Hist. Soc.), pp. 371, 372; Worc. Epis. Reg. Gainsborough, f. 6v, *cf. Ann. Mon.* (Rolls Series), iv. 545.

[20] A very curious entry in Bishop Giffard's register, f. 299 (ed. Willis Bund, p. 349), may be noted here. The custody of the church of Shipton, to which Henry de Schypt, whose institution has been deferred, has been presented, is committed to W. de Oldeswell, priest, so that he keep the said presentee according to the orders of the Friars Minors of Shipton, in school and sustenance, until the bishop ordains otherwise (10 Kal. Apr. 1288).

[21] The provincials of the Dominicans and Franciscans were ordered in 1261 by the pope to make inquiries in the diocese of Worcester (among others)

Bishop Giffard in 1275 gave orders that the Friars Minors should be admitted to the churches throughout the diocese to preach the Crusade and grant indulgences.[1] On account of 'the sincerity of his devotion' to the Minorites, he was made partaker of all the suffrages of the order by Jerome of Ascoli, the minister general, in 1278, and the privilege was confirmed by Jerome's successor, Bonagratia, in 1282.[2] On the Sunday following the feast of St. Francis in the latter year the bishop celebrated mass in the Grey Friars' Church, and supplied food to all the brethren.[3] In 1384, 'wishing to help the Friars Minors and the nuns dwelling in Worcester in their poverty,' he ordered the bailiff of Worcester to deliver to the friars 'two quarters of good and pure corn and half a mark of silver to buy herrings,' and supply similar provisions to the nuns.[4] In 1290 the Franciscan archbishop of Canterbury, John Peckham, thought it necessary to remind Giffard of the privileges of the Friars Minors as to hearing confessions and granting absolution without the consent of the parish priest,[5] and about the same time he interfered vigorously in a quarrel between the Minorites and the monks of Worcester.

The quarrel arose over the burial of Henry Poche, a citizen of Worcester. Monks and friars both claimed the body. On 1 March, 1289–90, the sacristan of St. Mary's obtained it by force and buried it in the cathedral cemetery, in spite of the opposition of many friars. There was something of a tumult, and the friars suffered some injury. They appealed to the archbishop, complaining that they had been attacked and wounded by the monks, and demanding redress of grievances. A rumour of the riot reached the king. Peckham took up their cause with energy. He wrote to the bishop of Worcester stating the friars' case and declaring that the wrong could not be endured. Giffard was slow to move, and received in July a peremptory letter from the archbishop, ordering him to have the body exhumed and given back to the friars, or to cite the prior and convent to appear before the archbishop before 1 August. Bishop Godfrey held a formal inquiry into the matter on 24 July, and, according to the monastic annalist, a jury of clerks and laymen found that the last wish of the deceased was to be buried in the cemetery of St. Mary, and that no one had hurt the friars intentionally, but that by the pressure of the crowd they had been forced on to some dung heaps, where they had stumbled and fallen.

Peckham was not satisfied with this result: on 13 December, 1290, the prior received notice that if the body was not restored to the friars within a fortnight, he and the elders of his house would be suspended. The monks yielded, stipulating that the friars should take away the body privately. 'But instead of that,' writes the Worcester annalist, 'on the day after the feast of St. Thomas the Apostle (22 December) with great pomp and uproar, explaining their right to the people in the mother tongue, and inviting all they could to the spectacle, to our confusion, they carried the body away through the great square, singing, amidst an uproarious scene.'[6]

Meantime an attempt had been made to avoid such scandals in future by a compromise: mass for the dead was first to be celebrated in the cathedral church: then, 'provided that no loss accrue to the church, if the Friars Minors can lawfully prove that the bodies have been bequeathed to them, they shall be free to carry them away to their place of burial.' It does not appear whether the friars accepted this settlement.[7]

The next bishop, William of Gainsborough, was himself a Franciscan, and the Worcester friars took a prominent part in the ceremonies of his enthronement.[8] He and several of his successors were appointed by the Apostolic See to the office of 'conservator of the privileges of the Friars Minors in England.'[9]

Among the benefactors of the house the Beauchamps are the most prominent. In 1268 William Beauchamp, lord of Elmley, father of the first earl of Warwick of this family, bequeathed his body to be buried in the church of

into the number of churches held by religious, the stipends of vicars, etc.—the pope having received information as to the 'reported cupidity of religious' in getting churches appropriated to them. Bliss, *Papal Letters*, i. 375.

[1] *Worc. Epis. Reg. Giffard* (Worc. Hist. Soc.), p. 83.

[2] Ibid. pp. 94, 156. Thomas's *Survey of Cath. Ch. of Worc.*, App. no. 51. Giffard was not, as Mr. Willis Bund thinks, a Minorite.

[3] *Worc. Epis. Reg. Giffard* (Worc. Hist. Soc.), p. 165.

[4] Ibid. p. 231.

[5] Ibid. pp. 371, 372.

[6] *Ann. Mon.* (Rolls Ser.), iv. pp. 499–500, 502–3, 504. *Worc. Epis. Reg. Giffard* (Worc. Hist. Soc.), pp. 371, 388. The anonymous chronicle preserved in MS. Cotton Cleop. B. xiii., which is certainly by a Franciscan, and which Hardy (*Descr. Catal.* iii. 276) ascribes without sufficient grounds to a Franciscan of Worcester, merely says (f. 152): 'eodem anno in crastino S. Thome apostoli restitutum est fratribus minoribus Wigorniæ corpus Henrici Poche civis Wigorn., quod eis a monachis injuriose ac violenter ablatum fuerat A.D. MCC. 89.' The dispute is referred to by the Monk of Westminster, *Flores Historiarum* (Rolls Ser.), iii. 75.

[7] *Ann. Mon.* (Rolls Ser.), iv. 500.

[8] Thomas, *Survey*, no. 76.

[9] See Worc. Epis. Reg. Gainsborough f. 8; Wulstan de Bransford, i. f. 13; Thoresby, f. 29; Simon de Monte Acuto, ii. f. 10v.; Adam de Horlton, ii. f. 49v.; Cobham, f. 43. The last entry is a letter of the bishop as conservator of the privileges of the Friars Minors in England to A. de B. concerning iv. marks bequeathed by B. de C. to the said friars, which were sequestrated by A. de B. on behalf of the rector of Tredentone (Worc.) of which parish deceased was a parishioner. The bishop commands that 40*s.* sterling be paid to the warden and brethren (no date).

the Friars Minors of Worcester and directed that at his funeral a horse fully armoured with all military caparisons should go before his corpse. To the convent he gave 40*s*.[1]

William Beauchamp, Earl of Warwick, son of the above, by will made in 1296[2] left his body to be buried in the choir of the Friars Minors, to whom he also bequeathed two great horses, namely those which at his funeral should carry his armour, and further £200 for the solemnizing of his funeral. He died 9 June, 1298. The Worcester annalist[3] attributes his decision to be buried here rather than with his ancestors in the cathedral church, to the influence of Brother John of Olney. 'At length,' he goes on, 'on 22 June, the friars, having got hold of the body of so great a man, like conquerors who had obtained booty, paraded the public streets, and made a spectacle for the citizens.'

Guy, Earl of Warwick, son of William, buried his mother, Maud, daughter of John FitzGeoffrey, here in 1300 next her husband, 'though in her lifetime she arranged to be buried elsewhere.'[4]

Sir Nicholas de Muthon (Mitton), Knt., in 1290 left legacies to the friars of Worcester and other places; he bequeathed his body to be buried at Bredon, and his heart in the place of the Friars Minors of Worcester, and with his heart £40 for the fabric of six altars in the same place.[5]

Sir Walter Cokesey, Knt., in 1295 bequeathed his body to be buried here among the Friars Minors, and gave them 10 marks of silver instead of his armour, which was to go before his corpse, but to be returned to his son Walter;[6] the horse which carried his armour was to become the property of the friars. Bishop Godfrey Giffard left the Friars Minors of Worcester 100*s*.[7] Katharine, widow of Thomas Beauchamp, earl of Warwick, left them £20 in 1369.[8] Henry Wakefield, bishop of Worcester, left them 40*s*. in 1395.[9] William ap Rees was buried here, and left the friars 20*s*. in 1446.[10] John Halle of Worcester left them 40*s*. in 1451.[11] Sir John Beauchamp, K.G., Baron Powick, in 1475 left 'to the house or priory of the Grey Friars of Worcester iiii torches, or some other necessary thing behoveful for their church.'[12] Margaret Leynham, widow of Sir John Leynham, Knt., in 1482 directed she should be buried 'in the quere of the church of the Grey Freres of Worcester,' if she died in that county, and bequeathed to the house 50 marks, and to Dr. Wibbe, 'prior' of the said house, £20. But she subsequently annulled both bequests, 'insomuch as she shall not now be buried there,' and left to Dr. Wibbe 'only 40*s*., over the reward that she gave him afore her departing out of the country.'[13]

Sir Robert Throckmorton, Knt., whose will was proved in 1520, desired that 'ther be said for my soule in as shorte space as it may be doon after my deceas twoo trentalles in the Graye ffrieris of Worceter (and elsewhere), and for every of thes trentalles I will there be gyven x*s*. apece.'[14]

The Grey Friars had also, Nash notes,[15] 'several benefactors amongst the gentry of this county, whose arms are still remaining in the bow window of their great hall, now part of the city gaol; those of Throgmorton, Besford, Russel, Hodyngton, Bridges, and another—sable . . . . between three crescents argent.'[16]

Though Edward II. granted the Friars Minors of Worcester a charter of confirmation in 1322, in which he speaks of the place and areas given to them by 'our ancestors and others,'[17] the house seems to have owed little to royal bounty until the end of the fifteenth century. In September, 1483, Richard III. granted to Friar Thomas Jonys, of the house of the Friars Minors, within the city of Worcester, a meadow called 'Digley' (Diglis), lying under the castle, during pleasure; it was in the king's hands owing to the minority of Edward, earl of Warwick.[18] In December of the same year he granted to Master Peter Webbe, S.T.P. warden, and the Friars Minors of the house of St. Francis, Worcester, the king's moiety of the manor of Pyrye (Perry) by Worcester, and a mill under the castle of Worcester called 'Frogge Mille,' a street adjoining (called Frog Lane till the end of the nineteenth century), with their appurtenances, to hold during the minority of Edward, earl of Warwick, at a rent of £6 a year.[19] In May, 1485, the rent

[1] *Worc. Epis. Reg. Giffard* (Worc. Hist. Soc.), p. 7–9; Nicolas, *Test. Vetusta.* p. 50; Dugdale, *Baronage*, i. 227; Nash, *Worcestershire*, ii. App. p. cli.

[2] Nicolas, *Test. Vetusta.* p. 52; Dugdale, *Baronage*, i. 229 (from Giffard's Register).

[3] *Ann. Mon.* (Rolls Ser.), iv. p. 537.

[4] Ibid. p. 549.

[5] *Worc. Epis. Reg. Giffard* (Worc. Hist. Soc.), p. 388–390.

[6] Nash, *Worcestershire*, vol. ii. App. p. cli. Dugdale, *Antiq. of Warwickshire*, p. 930 (from Giffard's Register).

[7] Worc. Epis. Reg. Gainsborough, f. 17.

[8] Ibid. Lynne, f. 52 v.

[9] P. C. C. Rous, f. 26.

[10] Ibid. f. 95.

[11] Ibid. f. 126b.

[12] P. C. C. Logg, qu. 13.

[13] Ibid. f. 41 seq.

[14] P. C. C. Maynwaring, qu. 2.

[15] *Worcestershire*, ii. App. p. cli.

[16] For further bequests, see the wills of John of Worcester called son of Peter, 1292 (*Worc. Epis. Reg. Giffard* (Worc. Hist. Soc.), p. 422); William de Loriaco, rector of the church of Bredon, 1310 (Worc. Epis. Reg. Reynolds, f. 31); Simon Gros of Worcester, 1360 (Worc. Epis. Reg. Brian, f. 100v); Matilda Longency of Worcester, 1371 (Ibid. Lynne, f. 54); Elias Spelly, c. 1391 (P. C. C. Rous, f. 57).

[17] Pat. 15 Edw. II. pt. i, m. 2.

[18] Cal. Pat. 1 Ric. III. pt. v. m. 7.

[19] Ibid. m. 14.

was remitted, 'because the dormitory of their house, which was ruinous, fell down on the evening of St. Laurence's day' (10 August), and the daily celebration of masses 'for the good estate of the king and the soul of his father' substituted for the money payment.[1]

The religious changes of Henry VIII.'s reign found the friars divided. In 1536 the sheriff of Gloucester sends to the bishop of London information about 'the disorderly and colorable preaching of certain of the bishop of Worcester's preachers.' 'He will not suffer any D.D. or B.D. of the diocese to preach, who are known for discreet men and learned, but has admitted the warden of the Grey Friars, Worcester. . . . and divers other light persons, who follow the parson of Stawton (Staunton near Gloucester) to the disquiet of Christian people,' and preach against Purgatory, prayers for the dead and so on. The writer trusts 'that by you and the duke of Norfolk the premisses will be redressed' (June 9).[2] Next year, Thomas Cromwell is interested in the case of 'a friar, a Scot born,' who is in ward with the bailiffs of Worcester for traitorous words.[3] The nature of these and his fate do not appear.

The visitation of the friaries took place in 1538. On 23 May, Richard Ingworth, bishop of Dover, wrote to Cromwell that he had been to Worcester and other places in the west, visiting the friars' houses, and found everywhere poverty, 'and moche schiffte made with suche as theie had before, as yewellys selling, and other schiffte by leasys.' He put a stop to this by making indentures and sequestering the common seals, 'so that I thinke before the yere be owt ther schall be very fewe housis abill to lyve, but schall be glade to giffe up their howseis.'[4]

The two houses of friars in Worcester surrendered on 4 August into the hands of the bishop of Dover, 'considering that they were not able to live for very poverty, and no charity had come to them as of old, for in the space of six weeks each house had run at least £3 in debt.'[5] The bishop had a good deal of difficulty in getting the Grey Friars to surrender. 'They be so close to each other that no man can come within them to know their hearts.'[6]

The inventory of the Grey Friars at the time of the Dissolution[7] shows that they possessed ten complete suits (priest, deacon, and sub-deacon), many of them elaborately ornamented with fishes of gold, stars of gold, birds, harts, and lions; a number of single vestments decorated with *fleur de lis* of gold, dragons, harts, lions of gold, angels of gold, flowers, stars, Katherine wheels, 'green popinjays and silver heads,' and 'one of silk of divers colours with the ragged staff'—perhaps a gift from the Beauchamps. In the dormitory were two feather beds with their bolsters, two pairs of blankets, five poor coverings, four good mattresses, and two bolsters. In the 'custere's' (custodian's ?) chamber were three bedsteads, two chairs, and three poor forms; and in the minister's chamber two bedsteads, a chair, and a few other articles. Among the contents of the kitchen were 'xiii. platers and dyschys and one sawser and iii. counterfeit dyschys.' The brewhouse and buttery present no features of special interest. The service books consisted of five antiphonars, five graduals and a chanter's book, six psalters, two 'versycull' books, three mass books for the altars, a gospel book, and a 'priest book.' In the quire were a pair of organs and a 'frame for the sepulcher,' and two bells in the steeple. The plate, consisting of two chalices, a pix and cruets, three masers, and two 'paxseys off yuery bonde aboute with sylver,' weighed 86 oz.

The Bailiffs, Aldermen, and Common Council petitioned Cromwell to get the friars' houses granted to the city for the repair of the walls and bridge, which were decayed. 'The stone of the said houses is very meet for the purpose.[8] 'They are set in two barren sides,[9] where is no defence but the said houses joined to the walls.' The churches should be pulled down to make towers and 'fortytudes' in the walls.[10] Latimer also wrote to Cromwell on behalf of the city, mentioning as a third object to which the property should be applied the maintenance of the school, which had hitherto been supported by the guild of the Holy Trinity.[11]

In December, 1539, a grant was made to the bailiffs and citizens for £541 0*s.* 10*d.* of the house and site of 'lez Blacke Frears' in the city of Worcester, and of the house and site of 'lez Grey Frears' near the said city, and within the liberties thereof; the churches, steeple, and churchyards of the said houses, and twenty messuages, lands, etc., in the said city, and in Powick, Warmedon, and Severn Stoke belonging to the said houses. The city was to hold the property of the king by the service of the twentieth part of one knight's fee and an annual rent of 26*s.* 8*d.*[12]

[1] Pat. 2 Ric. III. pt. iii. m. 23.

[2] *L. and P. Hen. VIII.* vol. x. no. 1099.

[3] Ibid. vol. xii. pt. i. no. 969; and pt. ii. no. 1299.

[4] Ibid. xiii. pt. i, no. 1052; and Wright, *Letters relating to the suppression of Monasteries*, p. 193–4.

[5] *L. and P. Hen. VIII.* vol. xiii. pt. ii. no. 32.

[6] Ibid. xiii. pt. ii. no. 49; from Ellis, *Orig. Letters*, 3rd ser. iii. 189–190.

[7] Chap. Ho. Books, 153, ff. 78–79. *L. and P. Hen. VIII.* vol. xiii. pt. i. no. 1513.

[8] *L. and P. Hen. VIII.* pt. ii. no. 540 (5 October, 1538).

[9] Ibid. xiv. pt. i. no. 102 (5 January, 1539).

[10] Ibid. xiv. pt. i. no. 543 (17 March, 1539).

[11] Ibid. xiii. pt. ii. no. 543 (6 October, 1538); Latimer's *Remains*, p. 402.

[12] Ibid. xiv. pt. ii. no. 780, § 9 (9 Dec. 1539); Exch. Ministers' Accounts, 30–31 Hen. VIII. 230 (Worcestershire). In these accounts the receiver

No materials exist from which a list of either the custodians or the wardens could be compiled. Besides those already mentioned, the warden of the Friars Minors, Worcester, acted on a papal commission to investigate charges of disobedience brought by the patriarch of Jerusalem against certain persons in 1287;[1] between 1333 and 1337 the warden was among those commissioned by Bishop Simon de Monte Acuto, in consequence of a papal bull, 'to convoke the clergy and people, and to address the clergy in Latin, the people in the mother tongue, and to preach the word of the cross.'[2]

14. TRINITARIAN FRIARS OF WORCESTER

There is no evidence of the existence of a house of this order in Worcester. Nash says: 'Within this parish of St. Nicholas towards the bottom of the Angel Lane, between that and the Broad Street, was a religious house belonging to the friers of the Holy Trinity, for the redemption of captives.'[3] He also states that the new churchyard in this parish (i.e. All Saints), consecrated in 1644, 'was formerly called the garden-ground in Angel Lane, or Friars' Orchard, and did belong to the Friars of the Holy Trinity over against it.'[4] There can be little doubt that the chantry of the Holy Trinity in the parish of St. Nicholas, founded in 1371, has been mistaken for a house of the Trinitarian Order.[5]

15. PENITENT SISTERS, WORCESTER

Henry III. granted six oaks to the Penitent Sisters of Worcester on 13 February, 1240–1.[6] Nothing more is known about them.

charges 78*s.* 8*d.* for the expenses of himself and his servants during four days at Worcester in June, 1539, 'pro edificiis superfluis infra precinctum earundum domorum (i.e. fratrum Minorum) appreciandis et valuandis.' Cf. Gasquet, *Hen. VIII. and the Engl. Mon.* ii. 74. In the Scudamore Papers (B. M. MS. Add. 11041) Robert Burgoyne refers to 'my painful and long circuit that I am in, in surveying the late friars' houses in Worcester,' 25 June (f. 30). It is not clear to which houses the following passage refers in a letter of Burgoyne, dated 5 July (f. 31): 'Howbeit, Mr. Giffard and I have sold in friars' houses all the building; the cause was for that they were so spoiled and torn by such as sold the goods that in manner were down, and if they should not have been sold the king should have had nothing thereof.'

[1] *Worc. Epis. Reg. Giffard* (Worc. Hist. Soc.), p. 307.

[2] Worc. Epis. Reg. Montacute, bk. ii, f. 15.

[3] Nash, *Worc.* ii. App. p. cxxxix. There is a street still (1905) called the Trinity.

[4] Ibid. p. cxxxiv.

[5] Prattinton MS. collection, Mon. 152d (Soc. of Antiq.). There are several references to the order in the Worc. Epis. Reg. (e.g. Simon de Monte Acuto, i. f. 9; Silvester de Gigliis, f. 199), but none to any house of the order at Worcester.

[6] Close, 25 Hen. III. m. 14.

16. FRIARS OF THE PENANCE OF JESUS CHRIST OR FRIARS OF THE SACK, WORCESTER

There was a house of this order in Worcester at the end of the reign of Henry III. On 5 March, 1271–2, the king granted them in free alms the street (vicus) called 'Dolday,' 120 or 140 ft. in length, and 11 ft. in width, for the augmentation of their place. The jurors who held the 'inquisitio ad quod damnum' in February declared that the grant would not be injurious but 'to the advantage and honour of the king and to the advantage of the citizens.'[7] The Order was suppressed by the Council of Lyons in 1274.[8]

17. AUSTIN FRIARS, DROITWICH

The Augustinian Friary was founded here in 1331, when Thomas Alleyn of Wyche obtained licence to alienate in mortmain to the Provincial Prior and Austin Friars in England a plot of land three hundred feet square in Wyche to build thereon an oratory and habitation.[9]

The prior and brethren of Droitwich in 1343 received from John, son of William Dragoun of 'Wiche,' a plot of land in that town two hundred feet long and sixty feet broad for the enlargement of their dwelling place.[10]

John Bush and William Mercer, chaplains, obtained letters patent, dated 20 November, 1351, authorizing them to grant the friars certain plots of land, five acres in extent, adjoining the friary, for the further enlargement of their house. The friars paid 6*s.* 8*d.* in the hanaper for this privilege.[11]

These three donations were confirmed by letters patent in 1385 for 40*s.* paid in the hanaper.[12]

A deed dated 8 July, 1388, recording the founding of an anchoret's cell in connexion with the convent presents features of special interest. It is in the form of letters patent issued in the name of the convent by Friar Henry Duke, presumbly the prior, and addressed to all the sons of Holy Mother Church. Brother Henry makes known 'that the house, which Thomas Beauchamp, Earl of Warwick, founder of our convent, has recently built at his own expense, next the choir of our church on the south side, for the inclusion and habitation of brother Henry

[7] Inq. a.q.d. file 3 (30), formerly Inquis. p.m. 56 Hen. III. no. 47; Pat. 56 Hen. III. m. 19. According to the Inquisitio the length of the street was 140 ft.; according to the Pat. Roll 120 ft.

[8] Extracts from the constitutions of this little known order are printed in *Eng. Hist. Rev.* ix. 121 seq.

[9] Pat. 4 Edw. III. pt. ii. m. 10. Dated 21 Jan. 1330–1. Inq. a.q.d. 211 (9).

[10] Pat. 17 Edw. III. pt. i. m. 25 (7 May). Inq. a.q.d. 268 (22).

[11] Pat. 25 Edw. III. pt. iii. m. 7.

[12] Ibid. 9 Ric. II. pt. i. m. 4.

de Stokebrugge, where he may lead the life of an anchoret to the honour of God, and pray for the good estate of the founder and his kin, shall henceforth be at the disposition of the said earl and his heirs, who shall have the right of presenting to the same house, after the death of Henry de Stokebrugge and on each vacancy caused by death, religious and devout persons wishing to profess the anchoretic life and to be enclosed there : provided that they be friars of our order, or at least be willing to assume the habit of our religion, and to submit themselves to the obedience and correction of our prior in those things only which pertain to the anchoretic life and to the good name of our order : in such wise however that our convent is bound to perpetual poverty, for our convent may by no means in future be burdened with heavy expenses.'[1]

Henry Wakefield, bishop of Worcester, left the friars of Droitwich ten marks in 1395.[2]

The bishop of Dover visited the house early in 1531 and found great poverty there as elsewhere. He wrote to Cromwell at length on the subject.[3] 'Touching "Wheych," the which is the principal cause of my writing, it is not able to continue a house of religion to keep above one friar, for all is sold. He that was prior, by whom at Easter you sent your letters to the bailiffs to see all their stuff delivered again into the house, he hath in less than one year that he hath been prior there felled and sold seven score good elms, a chalice of gilt of 70 oz., a censer of 36 oz., two great brass pots, each able to seethe a whole ox as men say, spits, pans, and other, so that in the house is not left one bed, one sheet, one platter or dish, nor for all the promise that be made to your lordship he is not able to bring home anything again, nor yet to make a true account where this is spent by 20 marks truly. And in his coffer I found eleven bulls of the bishops of Rome, and above an hundred letters of pardons, and in all the books of the quire the bishop of Rome still standing as he did twenty years past. I have charged the bailiffs that he be forthcoming; and for the house I have set a poor friar to keep mass there, and I have provided for his board and living to be paid 16[*d.*] a week, till your further pleasure be known in it.' 'The house,' he goes on, 'is meet for no man to dwell in, without great costs done on it. It standeth in a good air, and it hath so many "tenauntreys and closeis" about it that be letten for 5 *li.* by year. There be two good bells, a chalice, and a few vestments of little value ; the stuff beside is not worth 40*s.* Lead there is none, except in two gutters, the which the prior hath conveyed into the town, but it is sure. It is meetly wooded in "hege rowys."' Several gentlemen of the county were eager to secure the site—Sir John Russell, the sheriff of Worcester, Mr. Pye, and Mr. Newell, 'servant with my lord of Worcester.' The bishop of Dover favoured the suit of the last, 'for and except he have it I think he shall lose a marriage of forty marks by the year.' Latimer was also soliciting the site on behalf of a lady, with good hopes of success.[4] But on 25 June, 1538, he wrote to Cromwell : 'With an honest gentlewoman my poor honesty I pledged, which is now distained . . . for that in Durtwych and here about the same we be fallen into the dirt and be all to dirted even up to the ears ; we be jeered, mocked, and laughed to scorn. A wily Pye hath wilily gone between us and home, when we thought nothing less, but as good simple souls made all cocksure.' It was now too late to 'call yesterday' again, as Mr. Pye said the king had given the property to him. Mr. Pye did not obtain the property, however, till 1543, at which time it was let out to a number of yearly tenants. The site of the house with all buildings necessary to the farmer together with a close called 'the Conyngre' was let at 13*s.* 4*d.* a year ; the Friars' Orchard, two acres, was let to William Borne at a rent of 8*s.* ; three tenements with gardens were held by Bray, William Bere, and Lawrence Barbour at rents of 8*s.*, 8*s.*, and 5*s.* respectively ; 'the Barley Close,' one acre and a half, was let to John Geffreys for 10*s.*; 'the Vine Close,' one acre, to Gilbert Wheler for 5*s.* ; half of the Friars' Meadow, two acres in extent, was let to William Newport for 12*s.* (the other half belonging to Willian Parkyngton, Esq.), and the close of one acre called 'Friars' Shellengers' was leased to William Wheler for a term of years at an annual rent of 7*s.*

The total annual value was £3 16*s.* 4*d.* In estimating the price the valuer, Richard Rose, deducts a tenth as rent to the crown, leaving £3 8*s.* 8*d.* net ; this is divided into 'Howsing' 41*s.* 8*d.*, 'which being decayed rated at thirteen years purchase doth amount to the sum of £27 20*d.* : and Lands, 27*s.*, which at twenty years' purchase doth amount to the sum of £27.' Total, £54 1*s.* 8*d.*[5]

John Pye of Chippenham in the county of Wilts, Esquire,[6] in purchasing the Austin Friary

[1] Nash, *Worc.* i. 332 : from the Habington MSS. (The deed has been summarized in the translation given in the text.)

[2] P. C. C. Rous, f. 26.

[3] Wright, *Letters relating to the suppression of Mon.* p. 193, seq.

[4] *L. and P. Hen. VIII.* xiii. pt. 1, no. 1258. Latimer's *Remains*, p. 397.

[5] Aug. Off. R.O. Particulars for grants, 34 Hen. VIII. no. 910. Pat. 34 Hen. VIII. pt. 8, m. 14. The summary in *L. and P. Hen. VIII.* vol. xviii. pt. 1, no. 226 (80) is inaccurate in some details.

[6] A John Pye, who had been mayor of Oxford, obtained a lease of the Grey Friars, Oxford, in 1540 : he had been active in bringing about the surrender of the Oxford friaries. Little, *Grey Friars in Oxford*, p. 121.

of Droitwich at this price was acting in partnership with Robert Were alias Brown of Marlborough; the former paid for the Droitwich property, the latter for the property of the White Friars of Marlborough, and the partners became joint owners of the two estates, holding each of the king for the twentieth part of one knight's fee and paying a yearly rent in the one case of 7*s.* 8*d.*, in the other of 9*s.* 5½*d.*[5] It is probable that these gentlemen were speculators in monastic lands and bought to sell again.[6]

HOSPITALS

18. THE HOSPITAL OF ST. WULSTAN, WORCESTER

'There is a fayre suburb without Sudbury gate and it was an hospital called St. Wulstan . . . some called it a commanderye[1] where was a master, priests, and poore men; some say it was originally of the foundation of the queen.'[2] Such is Leland's account of the Hospital of St. Wulstan, recording the traditional foundation. Camden accepted this tradition, but the more generally acknowledged founder was St. Wulstan himself who probably founded the hospital about 1085. It then consisted of a master, two chaplains, and poor brethren whose number was not specified, until 1441.[3] They followed the rule of St. Augustine, professing vows of poverty, chastity, and obedience, but not bound by the rigidity of strict monastic life, since the hospital was intended primarily as a charitable institution. Hence at some period, probably not long after the foundation, an infirmary for indigent sick and infirm was established. By 1294 there were reported to be twenty-two sick persons in the infirmary, and the hospital undertook to provide three beds 'in a decent place' in the infirmary for three indigent chaplains chosen by William de Molendiniis, a benefactor of the house. These chaplains were to have food daily with the brethren, as well as a share of the pittances, ale, and charities, that were given to the sick and infirm.[4] On the death of either of the chaplains another 'indigens et honestus' was to be chosen and instituted by the bishop.

Although the hospital relied greatly on private benefaction for the up-keep of its charitable works, the founder undoubtedly endowed it with the ground on which it stood and the lands adjacent.

The preceptor and brethren of St. Wulstan had the right of nominating a priest to officiate in the chapel on their land at Chadwick near Bunyon, providing the chaplain was approved by the prior and convent of Worcester, and swore that he would in no way injure the mother church of Bromsgrove appropriated to the Worcester house. He was endowed with the small tithes only, the rest went to the church of Bromsgrove, while the preceptor paid 2*s.* yearly to the prior and convent and half a pound of frankincense twice a year to the vicar of Bromsgrove.[7] Moreover none of the parishioners of Bromsgrove were allowed to attend the chapel at Chadwick except the holder of the small tithes and his family, who should also be obliged four times in a year, Christmas, Candlemas, Easter, and Midsummer, to go to the church of Bromsgrove.[8]

Between the thirteenth and fifteenth centuries private benefactors made frequent gifts chiefly of lands in or near the city of Worcester,[9] but the gifts were often very small, and there is evidence to prove that the hospital had a sharp struggle against poverty. By 1535 the temporalities amounted only to £66 8*s.* 11*d.* and the spiritualities to £13 3*s.* 7*d.* The final income of the house, when payment had been made to the chaplains who prayed for the souls of the various benefactors, was £63 18*s.* 10*d.*[10] Hence it was exempted from the payment of certain tithes in 1275,[11] and from the increased taxation of 1291,[12] 1313,[13] and 1402,[14] and in 1368 bishop Wittesleye certified to John de Cabrespinio, the papal nuncio, that the members of the hospital would be forced to beg 'if a half or a third or a fourth part of the fruits of the hospital' should be taken from them.[15] This poverty may to

[1] There seems to be no better explanation of this title than that given by Nash, that the title of Preceptor or Commander was assumed in the time of Edward I. by Walter a master, who had served in the Holy wars (Nash, *Worc.* ii. 329).

[2] Leland, *Itinerarium*, iv. 104.

[3] Worc. Epis. Reg. Bourchier, fol. 74. Of the early brethren nothing is known except that in 1221 a pugilist who had been blinded in a fight, having been miraculously cured by St. Wulstan's relics, was converted, and became a brother of the hospital. *Ann. Mon.* (Rolls Ser.), iv. 413, 414.

[4] Cotton MS. Caligula, A x. fol. 190.

[5] Pat. 34 Hen. VIII. pt. 8, m. 14.

[6] Nash, *Worc.* i. 332, says: 'The land was given to Mr. Thomas Gierse, whose son sold it to Mr. Hugh Dashfield, in whose family it long remained. It is now the property of Hugh Cecil, Esq., in right of his wife.'

[7] Worc. Epis. Reg. Cobham, f. 134d.

[8] Dean and Chap. Reg. 2 Worc. f. 50.

[9] Bod. Lib. Worc. Chart., nos. 1, 3, 6, 7, 9, 12, 13, 14, 15, 18, 27, 38, 42, 44, 46, 57, 64, 69, 71, 99. See 'Topography.'

[10] *Valor Eccl.* (Rec. Com.), 228–9.

[11] *Worc. Epis. Reg. Giffard* (Worc. Hist. Soc.), 78.

[12] *Pope Nich Tax.* (Rec. Com.), 231, 239.

[13] Worc. Epis. Reg. Reynolds, fol. 93d.

[14] Ibid. Clifford, fol. 70d.

[15] Ibid. Wittesleye, fol. 30d.

some extent have been caused by the repressive policy towards the hospital shown by the prior and convent of Worcester. A complaint made to the bishop by the hospital in 1312 illustrates the jealousy existing between the two. The prior and convent had taken away and detained St. Wulstan's pastoral staff by which the brethren of the hospital had been wont to 'seek charities from well-disposed persons.' The bishop wrote desiring the prior to return the staff to the brethren, 'for the better getting of their alms thereby.' The former answered that St. Wulstan's staff had 'not been out of their hands a day nor a night nor an hour,' only the oblations arising therefrom had been granted to the hospital, and 'what was a matter of grace was now asked as a right.'[1]

However, many of the troubles of the house arose not from outward misfortune but from internal irregularity. In 1321 Bishop Cobham bade the master of the hospital make diligent inquiry into the waste of goods and dishonourable lives of the brethren, and correct 'what is wanting persons and things.'[2] But in spite of this warning, waste and irregularity evidently continued in the hospital into the fifteenth century until in 1441 Bishop Bourchier after a visitation wrote to the master and brethren commenting on the mismanagement of the house under past preceptors. One of them, William Moore or Dylew, had made excessive grants of corrodies and liveries, to the injury of the house. Between the years 1401–4 no less than eight such grants are recorded,[3] and this probably was not the full number. Thus the bishop forbade the granting of any corrodies or liveries, but the revenues were to be used for their proper purposes. The organization of the institution was stated afresh since the original charters were lost. There should be one master at the collation of the bishop, to be in priest's orders or promoted thereto within a year of his appointment as master. The said master should have as companions two chaplains secular, perpetual, or temporal, to officiate in the hospital for the souls of the founders and benefactors, receiving yearly from the preceptor 4 marks and 3½ yards of cloth for a robe and a competent room, and food and drink at the master's table. There were to be five brethren and two sisters who should receive 7*d.* weekly from the master.[4]

From 1441 to the time of the dissolution there is little record of the history of the hospital except mentions in the registers of occasional visitation and the collation of a preceptor by the bishop.

The papal bull of 21 August, 1524, granting Wolsey the right to dissolve certain of the smaller religious houses, among which St. Wulstan's was included, seemed to threaten an early dissolution for the house. But Wolsey's fall from power and sudden death brought respite for a few years. On 27 June, 1534, the master and inmates of the hospital were among those who rejected the papal authority,[5] and in August of the same year made their formal subscription to the royal supremacy.[6] From 1534 to 1539 the fate of the religious houses was in the balance, and that of St. Wulstan's among them. In 1539 Master John Bell, a man after the king's own heart, was promoted to the bishopric of Worcester, and the hospital handed over to Richard Morison, a gentleman of the Privy Chamber, obviously for the purpose of surrender.[7] On 20 May, 1540, the final surrender of the preceptory was made,[8] evidently under peculiar conditions. The house and site of the preceptory with the church steeple and churchyard, the manor of Chadwick, the appropriate rectories of Claines and Crowle, and the chapel of St. Godwald,[9] were granted to Richard Morison,[10] who in the same year wrote to Anthony Denny of the Privy Chamber, saying Mr. Chancellor had promised to be very good to him in his petition that the surrender of the house might not be reversed, 'but that I may be bound for ever, as these men shall die, to take new and to be as much charged as I was, the house being in the former estate.'[11] It would almost seem from this that the charitable work of the dissolved hospital was to continue, since 'these men' were presumably sick in the infirmary. In fact there seems to have been some idea of refounding the house, since Morison begged that 'the surrender might not be reversed,' and later in his letter complained that it would be 'a great shame to him to be compelled to buy all the household and chapel stuff again which is now sold.'[12] Evidently the idea fell through, for in 1544 Richard Morison made an exchange with the king of the hospital and its lands, which in 1545 became part of the endowment of Christ Church, Oxford,[13] as had been Wolsey's purpose in 1524.

1 Liber Albus, Worc. ff. 53, 54.

2 Worc. Epis. Reg. Cobham. f. 72.

3 Bod. Lib. Worc. Chart. Nos. 80, 82, 83, 85, 87, 92, 93, 94.

4 Worc. Epis. Reg. Bourchier, ff. 72 and 72d.

5 *L. and P. Hen. VIII.* vii. 329.

6 Ibid. 442. The list of names is as follows:—John Bell, preceptor; Nicholas Bushby, Christopher Morley, chaplains; Thomas Lake, Gilbert Harling, Lawrence Pockenson, John Smith, Richard Brasier, brethren; Alice Newry, Amy Mors, sisters.

7 The same Richard Morison was already made master of the hospital of St. James, Northallerton, Yorks, and surrendered it 19 May, 1540. (*L. and P. Hen. VIII.* xv. 233.)

8 *L. and P. Hen. VIII.* xv. 324.

9 St. Godwald seems to have been a saint of local repute or perhaps of foreign origin, but nothing definite is known about him. There was a chapel dedicated to him in Stoke Prior.

10 *L. and P. Hen. VIII.* xv. 409.

11 Ibid. xv. 338.

12 Ibid.

13 Harl. MS. 4316, f. 56d.

Preceptors of the Hospital of St. Wulstan

Walter de Wredens occurs 1260–70,[1] died 1298.[2]
Peter de Morton occurs 1304[3] and 1312.[4]
Thomas Bromley collated 1313.[5]
Peter Franceys collated 1341,[6] occurs 1349.[7]
David Maynard resigned 1361.[8]
Robert de Dycleston, or Dycheston, occurs 1361,[9] resigned 1364.[10]
Martin Trovel collated 1364.[11]
Lawrence Foyer of Schryvenham occurs 1369.[12]
William Rome resigned 1374.[13]
William Alewy collated 1374.[14]
William Moore, *alias* Dylewe, occurs 1386[15]–1404.[16]
Richard Grafton collated 1421.[17]
Walter London collated 1424,[18] occurs 1433.[19]
John Stokes collated 1441,[20] died 1466.[21]
Edmund Hecker collated 1466.[22]
William Vance, or Valence, collated 1467,[23] died 1479.[24]
Thomas Alcock collated 1479,[25] resigned 1484.[26]
John Burton collated 1484,[27] resigned 1503.[28]
Thomas Alcock collated 1503.[29]
John Bell occurs 1534,[30] resigned 1539.
Richard Morison collated 1539, surrendered 1540.[31]

The common seal of the hospital of St. Wulstan represents a standing figure of St. Wulstan mitred and holding a pastoral staff in the left hand, while the right is raised in benediction.

SIGILLU · HOSPICII · WOLSTANI[32]

1 Bod. Lib. Worc. Chart. No. 8.
2 *Ann. Mon.* (Rolls Ser.), iv. 536.
3 Liber Albus, Worc. f. 22.
4 Ibid. ff. 53, 54.
5 Worc. Epis. Reg. Reynolds, fol. 95.
6 Ibid. Wulstan de Bransford, i. fol. 48d.
7 *Sede Vac. Reg.* (Worc. Hist. Soc.), 225, 232, where he is called *warden* of the hospital.
8 Tanner, *Notitia.* Preface xlix.
9 *Sede Vac. Reg.* (Worc. Hist. Soc.), 204.
10 Ibid. 217.
11 Ibid.
12 Bod. Lib. Worc. Chart. No. 72.
13 *Sede Vac. Reg.* (Worc. Hist. Soc.), 289.
14 Ibid. William Rome, on his resignation, was made rector of La Holte in place of William Alewy (Ibid. 288).
15 Bod. Lib. Worc. Chart. No. 76.
16 Ibid. No. 97.
17 Worc. Epis. Reg. Morgan, ii. fol. 5d.
18 Ibid. fol. 29.
19 Bod. Lib. Worc. Chart. No. 100.
20 Worc. Epis. Reg. Bourchier, fol. 71.
21 Ibid. Carpenter, i. fol. 209.
22 Ibid.
23 Ibid. fol. 215. He was the bishop's chancellor.
24 Ibid. Alcock, fol. 56d.
25 Ibid.
26 Ibid. fol. 123d.
27 Ibid.
28 Ibid. Silvester Gigliis, fol. 33d.
29 Ibid.
30 *L. and P. Hen. VIII.* vii. 329.
31 Ibid. xv. 324.
32 B. M. Seals, DC., G3. A fifteenth-century seal represents the saint as described above, while below him, under a pointed arch, an ecclesiastic three-quarters length is represented in prayer :

SIGILLUM · COMMUNE · HOSPITALIS · SANCTI · WULSTANI · WIGORN. (B. M. Seals, lviii. 92).

19. THE HOSPITAL OF ST. OSWALD, WORCESTER

Although the foundation of the hospital is usually ascribed to St. Oswald himself, there is no charter or evidence existing to prove the truth of the statement.[33] Leland sums up the history of the house by saying that it was 'first erected for monks then infected with leprosy,' then changed into a hospital, and 'there was a master, fellows, and poor folks ; but of later tymes it was turned into a free chapel, and beareth the name of Oswald as a thing dedicated of old tyme unto him.' This outline is probably true, but the detail of the history is difficult to fill in with the scant evidence that survives, especially of the early existence of the hospital. The first mention of the house comes when it had already become a hospital, when in 1268 William de Beauchamp left 10*s.* for the infirm of the hospital of St. Oswald.[34] In 1291 came a gift by the will of Nicholas Mitton, this time to 'the brothers of St. Oswald.'[35] In 1296 William de Molendiniis, who was also a benefactor of St. Wulstan's hospital, died before he could finish the church he was building to St. Oswald, evidently in connexion with the hospital.[36]

Nothing is known of the early endowment of the hospital, but by 1291 it possessed half a virgate of land at Whittington (Worcester), which was not taxed since it was 'hardly sufficient for themselves.'[37] In 1310 a licence was granted to John Blanket to alienate in mortmain 10 acres in Northwyck (Northwich imprint is below) by Worcester to the hospital,[38] and in 1334 came a like grant of 100 acres in Wyke and Northwyck providing the hospital found two chaplains out of the brethren to celebrate divine service for the soul of the king and queen Philippa and various others.[39] By

33 Dugdale (VII. 779), Tanner (*Notitia*, 625), and Nash (i. 224) quote a certain manuscript—Davies MS. Stow—as giving the foundation by St. Oswald, and as founded for a chaplain, master, and four brethren. The manuscript quoted is not in the British Museum, and is not easy to discover.
34 *Worc. Epis. Reg. Giffard* (Worc. Hist. Soc.), p. 8.
35 Ibid. 388.
36 *Ann. Mon.* (Rolls Ser.), iv. 528.
37 *Pope Nich. Tax.* (Rec. Com.), 231.
38 *Cal. of Pat.* 1307–13, 289.
39 Ibid. 1330–4, 283.

1535 the revenues of the hospital amounted to £13 14*s.* 4*d.*,[1] and included rents from the land in Whittington, from Claines, and from Smite, now Smite Hill, in the parish of Claines.[2] With the other small religious houses St. Oswald's was exempted from various taxations because its rents were 'poor and weak.'[3] In 1419, 1420, and 1421 the bishop granted licence to the quæstors of the hospital to collect alms for a year for the support of the same.[4] In 1468 the hospital was evidently in need of repairs, and since it could not pay expenses out of its own funds, indulgence was granted to all who assisted for one year in the repair and construction of the buildings.[5]

The evidence of the episcopal registers shows that at any rate in the fourteenth century there was much irregularity among the brethren of the hospital, and on two occasions after an inquiry into the state of the house the master was deposed. In 1321 Bishop Cobham ordered Thomas Bromley, master of St. Wulstan's, and the dean of Worcester to make inquiry as to the truth of the report that the brethren of St. Oswald led dissolute lives and wasted the goods of the hospital.[6] As a result the master, William de Claines, was deposed.[7] In 1394 Robert de la More, as commissary of the bishop, executed a commission from the same to 'punish and correct the crimes and excesses of the master and brethren of the house of St. Oswald,' and to appoint another master, absolving William Bysseley from the rule of the house. The latter made a public confession, and was found guilty and unfit to have the administration of the hospital.[8] He was thereupon removed, and David Burnard, a brother of the house, who had seemingly not taken part in the late 'crimes and excesses,' was instituted in his place.[9] In the election of Thomas Parker as master in 1454, further provision was made for the good rule of the house. The same 'swore that he would not alienate nor let to farm for more than eight years any meadows, lands, or rents of the hospital without licence of the ordinary,' and 'that he would guard the statutes given out for the hospital by the said ordinary.'[10]

An inquiry made by Bishop Brian in 1356 as to the right of patronage and the true state of the hospital gives valuable evidence as to its organization. The archdeacon of the diocese, at the bishop's request taking the evidence of the rectors and vicars of the deanery of Worcester, stated that the patronage of the house belonged to the sacristan of the Worcester priory; that the master and brethren, except one master, Robert Collesbourne (1311), always wore a habit distinct from the secular; that the said house was neither portionary nor pensionary, except that they owed 15 lb. of wax yearly to the sacristan of Worcester.[11]

In 1539 Nicholas Udal, then master of the hospital, leased the same with the chapel, chapel-yard, etc., to John Hereford. Thus the house was saved from the ordinary dissolution, although its revenue was alienated. The advowson of the chapel, with the 15 lb. of wax owed to the sacristan of the Worcester house, was granted in 1542 to the dean and chapter of Worcester,[12] who henceforth presented the masters, except in the year 1615, when James I. took the patronage into his own hands, when Mr. Coucher, who had bought the lands of the hospital, restored the rents to trustees for the following purposes: £12 a year to his son, £1 to the four poor people in the four almshouses. From this time the hospital, having lost its ecclesiastical aspect, has survived as a charitable institution, which exists at the present day practically on the lines of its reorganization in 1664 and 1753.

In 1665, in the bishop's account of the hospitals of the diocese, St. Oswald's was described as having an annual revenue of £98 9*s.* from lands lying in several parcels dispersedly in the county of Worcester, a certain parcel in the suburbs of the city of Worcester, the tenements on which had been burnt down during the late civil war. Moreover the master, Dr. John Fell, received an allowance in accordance with the Act of 1664, and the steward also. Eight poor men and two poor women were maintained, and received £8 a year according to the statute. The master, Dr. Fell, had at his own expense purchased a house 'for the habitation of the said poor persons, the old hospital being destroyed in late times of war,' and had settled it upon his successors for ever. The house, with its repairs and fencing with brick wall,' cost him £450.[13] The Act of 1664 had attempted to secure the property of the house, empowering the master to let the lands and tenements for a term of years not exceeding three lives, or one and twenty years, and the houses for forty years, reserving on the said grants or leases 'the best improved value that the said lands and houses shall be yearly worth for the respective yearly rents thereof.' In 1681 the revenues were augmented by Thomas Hayes, who erected six additional rooms to the hospital and settled £50 a year, arising from a farm called

[1] In a MS. Sancroft, cited by Tanner, *Notitia*, xxi. 3, it is stated at £14 14*s.* 4*d.*, and upon a new valuation 4 Edw. VI. at £15 18*s.*

[2] *Valor Eccl.* (Rec. Com.), iii. 229.

[3] Worc. Epis. Reg. Reynolds, fol. 93d. Clifford, fol. 70d.

[4] Ibid. Morgan, ff. 3, 4, 19.

[5] Ibid. Carpenter, fol. 22.

[6] Worc. Epis. Reg. Cobham, fol. 72: 'Sinistra plurima referentur, fratribus ipsius bona dilapidantibus et vitam ducentibus inhonestam.'

[7] Ibid.

[8] *Sede Vac. Reg.* (Worc. Hist. Soc.), 360.

[9] Ibid. 361.

[10] Worc. Epis. Reg. Carpenter, fol. 115d.

[11] Ibid. Brian, fol. 18.

[12] *L. and P. Hen. VIII.* xviii. 31.

[13] MS. Tenisoniane (Lamb. Lib.), vol. 639, f. 433.

'Charlstree' and a messuage in 'Stagbatch,' on the hospital.[1] About 1825 an inquiry was made into the management of the property, and information was filed against Dr. Jenkinson, the master, concerning the appropriation of the funds of the charity during his mastership. The vice-chancellor decided that the leases had been made for merely nominal rents to the great detriment of the hospital, and were to be set aside on this ground. An article in the *Worcester Journal* for January, 1832, commented on this decision as being unjust in so far that it deprived the leaseholders without any compensation.[2] At the same time the revenues of the hospital were so far improved by the new leases that they reached almost £20,000 instead of £450. The hospital was rebuilt in 1873, and at the present day it consists of 37 houses for 20 men and 17 women, who receive 8*s.* a week with coals and clothing.

Masters of the Hospital of St. Oswald

Robert de Collesbourne 1311.[3]
William de Claines collated 1321.[4]
William de Shrewsbury,[5] or de Salop,[6] admitted 1349.
Richard Baker resigned 1355.[7]
John Barthelot collated 1355.[8]
William Byssley collated 1361,[9] deposed 1394.[10]
David Burnard collated 1395.[11]
Henry or Hugh Clifton collated 1396.[12]
John Freude died 1429.[13]
John Balle collated 1429.[14]
Thomas Parker collated 1454,[15] resigned 1454.[16]
Thomas Symonds collated 1454.[17]
Thomas Hawkins resigned 1470.[18]
William Fautell collated 1470,[19] resigned 1480.[20]
John Meyre collated 1480,[21] resigned 1506.[22]
John Hale collated 1506.[23]
Thomas Parker died 1538.[24]
Nicholas Udal collated 1538.[25]

1 *Worc. Journal*, 20 January, 1831. Cutting in Prattinton Coll. (Soc. Antiq.).
2 Prattinton Coll. (Soc. Antiq.). Cutting from the *Worc. Journal* for 20 January, 1832.
3 Worc. Epis. Reg. Reynolds, fol. 41.
4 Ibid. Cobham, fol. 28d.
5 Nash, Worc. i. 225.
6 Tanner, *Notitia*. Preface xlix.
7 Worc. Epis. Reg. Brian, fol. 16.
8 Ibid.
9 *Sede Vac. Reg.* (Worc. Hist. Soc.), 203.
10 Ibid. 360.
11 Ibid. 361.
12 Worc. Epis. Reg. Winchcomb, fol. 12d.
13 Ibid. Polton, fol. 82.
14 Ibid.
15 Ibid. Carpenter, i. fol. 115d.
16 Ibid. fol. 123d.
17 Ibid.
18 Ibid. ii. fol. 14.
19 Ibid.
20 Ibid. Alcock, fol. 67.
21 Ibid.
22 Ibid. Silvester de Gigliis, fol. 49.
23 Ibid.
24 Tanner, *Notitia*. Preface xlix.
25 Ibid.

20. THE HOSPITAL OF ST. MARY IN DROITWICH

The hospital dedicated to the Virgin in the parish of Droitwich has little known history. It was founded by William Dover, rector of the church of Dodderhill, in 1285, and endowed with a bullary of salt, half a carucate of land and rents worth 26*s.* 4*d.* in Wich and Witton near Salwarpe (Worcester).[26] These lands had in the same year been granted to William Dover for that purpose by the abbot and convent of St. Peter's, Gloucester, on his payment of 50 marks.[27] In that year also Edward I. confirmed the same grant and the prior and convent of Worcester were assigned patrons.[28] The house consisted of a master and brethren whose number, judging from the endowment, could not have been very great.

Several notices of the appointment of masters occur in the episcopal registers, but no connected list can be obtained. In 1328 Bishop Adam Orlton commissioned the archdeacon of Gloucester to proceed with the appointment of a master to the hospital.[29] This was evidently John de Gloucester whom the prior of Worcester had presented to the bishop for election.[30] In 1349 William Hull was presented to the mastership of the hospital,[31] and on his death in 1361 was succeeded by John Alewy.[32] According to Habington John Froniester succeeded John Alewy in 1392,[33] but there seems to be no entry to that effect in Bishop Wakefield's register. In 1396 Henry Nayne was appointed on the presentation of John, prior of Worcester,[34] and in 1398 Robert Boleyn is said to have been master,[35] although there is no confirmatory evidence on the registers. In 1461 William Norwood was collated to the hospital,[36] and in 1502 another collation, the last recorded in the registers, was made, but the name of the newly elected master not given.[37]

26 MS. Soc. Antiq. cxlix. Reg. D. and C. Worc. fol. 37.
27 Ibid. fol. 38d.
28 Habington, *Surv. of Worc.* (Worc. Hist. Soc.), ii. 305.
29 Worc. Epis. Reg. Orlton, fol. 17d.
30 Habington, *Surv. of Worc.* (Worc. Hist. Soc.), ii. 305.
31 Ibid. Habington also states that Thomas de Saungebury was presented to custody in the same year, but the mention of William Hull's death causing the vacancy in 1361 seems to disprove this.
32 Worc. Epis. Reg. Brian, fol. 40.
33 Habington, *Surv. of Worc.* (Worc. Hist. Soc.), ii. 305.
34 Worc. Epis. Reg. Winchcomb, fol. 9d. Habington states that Nicholas Wilbe and Thomas Nayne by commutation and the prior's presentation were masters of the hospital of Droitwich in 1396.
35 Habington, *Surv. of Worc.* (Worc. Hist. Soc.), ii. 305.
36 Worc. Epis. Reg. Carpenter 1, fol. 159.
37 Ibid. Silvester de Gigliis, fol. 25d.

Instead of falling with the other religious houses at the Dissolution the hospital of Droitwich seems to have been suppressed late in 1535 or early in 1536, not by royal licence but by its patrons the prior and convent of Worcester. In the Valor of 1535 'the hospital or chantry in the parish of Dodderhill' was given at an annual value of £8.[1] In 1536 articles were brought against the prior and convent of Worcester to prove that they had 'suppressed the hospital of Doverhill in Dartewich without licence of the king,' and 'expelled the poor people to their utter destruction,' causing the hospital to be pulled down and the building materials sold for their own use. Also they had 'troubled' Richard Cornewall, clerk and master of the house, putting him 'in jeopardy of his life' and now 'held the lands of the same by intrusion.' They had moreover mowed a meadow which had belonged to the hospital, called Preast meadow in Forde in the parish of Dodderhill.[7] This evidence explains why there is no trace of the hospital in the ordinary records concerning the Dissolution of the monasteries.

ALIEN HOUSE

21. THE PRIORY OF ASTLEY

At the time of the Domesday Survey the manor of Astley was in the possession of Ralph de Todeni, of whom it was held by the abbot of St. Taurinus, Evreux, in France. Four hides were held free of all custom according to the grant of the Conqueror when Ralph bestowed them on the monastery.[2] Probably Ralph de Todeni was the founder of this priory [3] although the date of its foundation cannot be definitely stated ; it was a cell subject to the abbey in France and endowed with the manor and church of Astley. Among the deeds of the abbey of St. Taurinus is a charter granted by Richard I. in January 1195–6 confirming to the abbot and convent all gifts already bestowed on them.[4] Among the benefactors named appears Ralf de Toencio, who gave in England Astley (Heseleia) with its appurtenances by consent of William, king of the English.[5] Of the early history of this cell there seems no record available. During the reign of Richard I. the priors of Malvern and Esseley (probably Astley) were commissioned by the pope to arbitrate in a dispute between the church of Worcester and Sir Thomas Ruppe of Harvington respecting certain tithes.[6] Frequent mention is made of this little community in the register of Bishop Giffard. Perhaps the most interesting feature in its connexion is the pleasant relation it contrived to maintain with the great ecclesiastical magnates of the diocese. No friction seems ever to have existed between the bishops of Worcester and the abbots of St. Taurinus or priors of Astley, and on the only occasion when the bishop was called on to exert superior authority in the management of the affairs of the priory with respect to the provision made by the brethren for the vicarage of the appropriated church of Astley[8] he 'asks them amiably' instead of summoning them peremptorily. Other slight incidents testify to the wish of the diocesan to conciliate and win the confidence of the alien community, while the brethren on their side appear to have submitted willingly to episcopal jurisdiction, admitted the bishop for the visitation of their priory, and on one occasion at least appealed to him for protection in the invasion of their rights.[9] This good understanding between the diocesan and an alien house will not be found so general as to pass without notice. The practice appears to have been, when the priory became vacant, for the abbot of St. Taurinus or his deputy to present a monk selected for the office by the convent to the bishop for admission and institution, profession of obedience having been made to him as diocesan. In April 1268 Bishop Giffard proposed to visit the priory, but was prevented by some cause not stated ;[10] however, at Michaelmas in 1282 he visited it in the chapel of Worcester,[11] and again in 1287 at Michaelmastide he visited it and received procuration there.[12] An incident which occurred in 1280 illustrates the connexion of the priory with the descendants of the attributed founder Ralph de Todeni. Prior Simon appealed to the bishop that although the goods of the house had for certain causes been sequestrated, certain 'sons of iniquity,' representing that the house was void when it was not so, by command of the noble lady Petronilla de Thony had carried off goods and possessions, and these were being consumed and detained to the prejudice of the priory and the contempt of the bishop's jurisdiction. The bishop caused a monition to be published threatening the invaders of ecclesiastical property with excommunication and summoning them to appear before him.[13]

[1] *Valor Eccl.* (Rec. Com.), iii. 270.

[2] Dom. Bk. 1, 176.

[3] Habington, *Surv. of Worc.* (Worc. Hist. Soc.), ii. 1. 13.

[4] *Cal. of Doc. France*, 1, 309.

[5] Ibid.

[6] Nash, *Hist. of Worc.* i. 576.

[7] *L. and P. Hen. VIII.* xi. 571.

[8] Worc. Epis. Reg. Reynolds, f. 86, and Orlton, ii. f. 8d.

[9] *Worc. Epis. Reg. Giffard* (Worc. Hist. Soc.), 122.

[10] Ibid, p. 7.

[11] Ibid. p. 165.

[12] Ibid. p. 334.

[13] Ibid. p. 122.

Probably the lady who was the instigator of this marauding expedition desired to assert her right in the house during a supposed vacancy. The prior received a dispensation from the bishop in 1286 to absent himself in parts beyond the sea until the Feast of the Assumption;[1] probably this was for the purpose of visiting the parent house.

The Taxation Roll of 1291 states that the income derived by the brethren from temporalities in the See of Worcester amounted to £7 15*s*. 4*d*.[2] The church of Astley is rated at £8,[3] but is not included in the possessions of the priory. In a document of a later date it is stated to have been appropriated to the brethren by Walter sometime bishop of Worcester,[4] probably Walter de Cantilupe, as the prior presented to the vicarage of the church of Astley in March, 1295–6,[5] and again in the year 1300.[6]

The estates of the prior were not extensive enough perhaps to bring them much within the region of dispute, and one other difference only is recorded between the community and their neighbours. In 1326 Bishop Cobham wrote to admonish the rector of the church of Witley that the dispute between himself and the prior of Astley respecting certain tithes should be amicably settled.[7]

During the vacancy of the see in 1303 the abbot of St. Taurinus wrote to the prior of Worcester to inquire as to the behaviour of Ralph de Portes, monk of Astley,[8] and received a favourable report.[9]

The supervision exercised by the diocesan over this alien cell seems to have included the duty of receiving the resignation of its head; in October, 1313, Stephen de Meisiaco resigned the office of prior before the bishop in his chapel in London.[10]

It is impossible to gather what the community numbered. During the reign of Edward III. the prior had but one companion; the number had, however, probably fallen considerably owing to the war with France and consequent difficulties. The brethren probably suffered from lessened resources, as Bishop Wulstan remitted half the sum due to him for procuration during a visitation of the priory in 1339.[11] No mention is made of the state of the house either in this or any previous visitation, but absence of comment may be generally interpreted favourably.

Astley was included with other religious houses of the order of St. Benedict which had protection granted to them by Edward I.[12] It was seized into the king's hand as an alien foundation during the French war in the reign of Edward III.[13] Ralph de Walle or Valle, then prior of Astley, was summoned personally in July, 1345, to appear before the council on the morrow of St. Peter ad Vincula next at latest, to speak with them upon matters that would be fully set forth to him there.[14] In December, 1354, Edward III. caused an inquiry to be made into the possessions of this house, certain of whose estates he understood had been fraudulently retained to the prejudice of the Crown.[15] The return made by the prior of Worcester in 1374 to the king's writ requiring to be certified as to the ecclesiastical benefices held by aliens and their true value, stated that 'brother John, prior of Astley, monk of Couches, occupies the said priory and resides there with another monk. The value of the said priory is estimated at £20 a year.'[16] A list of alien houses with a description of their property in 1379–80 gives the priory of Astley with the manor, church, and advowson of vicarage.[17] The king issued an order in September, 1380, for an inquiry to be made touching the removal of goods and chattels from the priory[18]; suspicion was at that time easily aroused in the case of alien cells, lest they should be conveying money and valuables out of the kingdom. Astley was placed in the custody of Richard de Hampton, and by a further grant in February, 1380–1, the appointment was made for life as long as he should continue to pay a yearly rent of £20.[19] Notwithstanding this, the abbot of St. Taurinus seems to have made other arrangements, and in October, 1384, John Beauchamp, esquire of the chamber, obtained a licence from Richard II. to hold the priory of Astley, which had been granted him by the abbot of St. Taurinus in Normandy, for a term of many years on payment of a large sum of money, rent free during the continuance of the war with France and the papal schism, his good services and the expense he had already incurred in connexion with the cell being taken into consideration.[20] Two years later this grant was confirmed and further amplified; pardon was granted to those who had acquired the priory and the advowson of the church of Astley without licence, and they were permitted to grant the premises to Sir John

1 *Worc. Epis. Reg. Giffard* (Worc. Hist. Soc.), 293.
2 *Pope Nich. Tax.* (Rec. Com.), 230.
3 Ibid. 216.
4 Worc. Epis. Reg. Orlton, ii. f. 8d.
5 *Worc. Epis. Reg. Giffard* (Worc. Hist. Soc.), 466.
6 Ibid. p. 526.
7 Ibid. Cobham, f. 115.
8 *Sede Vac. Reg.* (Worc. Hist. Soc.), 57.
9 Ibid. 58.
10 Worc. Epis. Reg. Reynolds, f. 94.
11 Ibid. Bransford, f. 12.
12 Stevens, *Hist. of Abbeys, Monasteries, etc.*, i. 174.
13 Close, 15 Edw. III. pt. iii. m. 5 d. and 6 d.
14 Ibid. 19 Edw. III. pt. ii. m. 22 d.
15 Inq. p. m. 28 Edw. III. (2nd nos.), 64.
16 *Sede Vac. Reg.* (Worc. Hist. Soc.), 307.
17 Add. MSS. 21,344, f. 98.
18 Pat. 4 Rich. II. pt. i. m. 18 d.
19 Ibid. pt. ii. m. 18.
20 Ibid. 8. Rich. II. pt. i. m. 18.

Beauchamp, Knt., and Joan his wife and his heirs, with the provision that neither he, she, nor their heirs should be called on to pay any yearly farm at the Exchequer during the present or any future war, and should be exempt from the payment of all ecclesiastical dues.[1]

From the date of its severance from the parent house the history of Astley as a religious house ceases. By his attainder in 1386–7 the lands of John Beauchamp de Holt became forfeited into the king's hands.[2] In July, 1389, on payment of a sum of 1,200 marks, Thomas, earl of Warwick, obtained a grant of the manor 'called Astley priory, together with other lands of the late John Beauchamp of Holt.[3] This priory was one of the alien monasteries suppressed and confiscated by order of the Parliament held at Leicester in 1414.[4] By a grant of Edward IV. on 11 November, 1468, at the request of Thomas his kinsman, cardinal archbishop of Canterbury, the priory or manor of Astley, sometime cell and parcel of the possessions of the abbey of St. Taurinus, in Normandy, with all its appurtenances, manors, and possessions, was bestowed on Henry Sampson, the dean and college of Holy Trinity, Westbury, in the county of Gloucester, to be held by them in free alms for ever.[5]

List of Priors of Astley

(Founded tempo William the Conqueror)

Simon,[6] occurs 1280.
Robert de Sanarvill,[7] 1290.
Guy de Villaribus,[8] 1294.
Ralph de Porters,[9] occurs 1300, resigned 1304.
Stephen de Meisiaco,[10] 1305, resigned 1313.
Robert de Loueris,[11] 1313, died 1330.
John Heribel,[12] 1330, resigned 1334.
William Busquet,[13] 1334.
Ralph de Valle,[14] 1341.
William Prevot,[15] 1343, resigned 1349.
Hugh de Valle,[16] 1349.
John Egerii,[17] 1360–1, resigned 1361.
John Bomet,[18] 1361.
William de Atrio,[19] 1361–2.
John,[20] occurs 1374.
Richard de Hampton,[21] custodian, 1380.
John Beauchamp,[22] custodian 1384.
Thomas, earl of Warwick,[23] custodian, 1389.
Suppressed, 1414.
Conferred on college of Holy Trinity, Westbury, 1468.[24]

[1] Pat. 9 Rich. II. pt. ii. m. 8.
[2] Inq. p. m. 12 Ric. II. No. 91.
[3] Pat. 13 Ric. II. pt. i. m. 32.
[4] Habington, *Surv. of Worc.* (Worc. Hist. Soc.), ii. 14.
[5] Chart. R. 8 Edw. IV. No. 4.
[6] *Worc. Epis. Reg. Giffard* (Worc. Hist. Soc.), 122.
[7] Ibid. 365.
[8] Ibid. 444 d.
[9] Ibid. 526.
[10] Worc. Epis. Reg. Gainsborough, f. 25d. and Reynolds f. 94d.
[11] *Sede Vac. Reg.* (Worc. Hist. Soc.), 139.
[12] Worc. Epis. Reg. Orlton, f. 19.
[13] Ibid. Montacute, f. 13 d.
[14] Ibid. Bransford, i. f. 47 d. In an entry on the Close Roll 19 Edw. III. pt. ii. m. 22 d., Ralph de Valle or Walle is still mentioned as prior of Astley in 1345 ; a mistake probably arose through his death or cession not being notified to the king.
[15] Ibid. Worc. Epis. Reg. Bransford, i. f. 57 d. and ii. f. 13.
[16] Ibid.
[17] Ibid. Brian, f. 32 d.
[18] Ibid. f. 33 d.
[19] *Sede Vac. Reg.* (Worc. Hist. Soc.), 208.
[20] Ibid. f. 174.
[21] Pat. 4 Ric. II. pt. ii. m. 18.
[22] Ibid. 8 Ric. II. pt. i. m. 18.
[23] Ibid. 13 Ric. II. pt. 1, m. 32.
[24] Chart. R. 8 Edw. IV. No. 4.

EARLY CHRISTIAN ART

SAXON SCULPTURE

FROM the historical data given in the article on the Ecclesiastical History of the county in this volume, it seems most probable that the pre-Norman sculptured monuments of Worcestershire belong to the Anglian school of early Christian art in Mercia rather than to the Celtic school of Wales or the Saxon school of Wessex. Reviewing the evidence as to the date of the monuments, the period when the conditions would have been most favourable for the production of ecclesiastical works of art seems to be the last half of the eighth century and the first half of the ninth century, a time of comparative calm after the incessant fighting for the supremacy between the different Anglo-Saxon kingdoms in the seventh century and before the Viking invasions of the ninth and tenth centuries kept the English fully occupied in fighting for their very existence. It was in the latter half of the eighth century also that Offa made Mercia the leading state in England, and his friendship with his contemporary, Charlemagne, at the time of the revival of learning in France with the assistance of Alcuin of York, must have had an important influence on the development of ecclesiastical art in this country.

The number of examples of pre-Norman sculptured monuments in Worcestershire is so extremely small that it is almost impossible to draw any general conclusions from the style of the art they exhibit. Only two such monuments have been recorded, namely, the cross-head at Cropthorne and the carved stone at Rous Lench.

Cropthorne is an ideally beautiful English village situated on the south bank of the River Avon between Evesham and Pershore. It is at present quite unspoilt by the intrusion of any modern villas, and the distant views of the Bredon and Malvern hills add greatly to the charm of the landscape. Cropthorne is 3 miles west of Evesham and a little over a mile south of Fladbury railway station.

The pre-Norman cross-head now stands on the sill of the east window of the south aisle of the nave of Cropthorne Church. It is 2 feet 9 inches high by 2 feet 10 inches wide by 9 inches thick, and is made of oölite. The cross has rounded hollows and cusps between the arms, and is surrounded by a cable and bead moulding. It is sculptured on four faces thus :—

Front.—On the top arm of the cross, a dragonesque creature with the head, claws, and wings of a bird and a tail terminating in a large leaf. On each of the side arms, a bird with a hooked beak. On the bottom arm, a beast with a long tongue protruding from its mouth and looped round its foreleg. In the centre of the cross, scrolls of foliage springing from two stems and passing behind the legs of the birds on the side arms of the cross.

Back.—On each of the side arms, a beast crouching down and having a protruding tongue tied in a Stafford knot. On the bottom arm, a beast standing erect, with its tail passing at the back of its hind leg and looped round its fore leg. In the centre of the cross, a scroll of foliage springing from a single stem on the back of the beast on the bottom arm, and terminating in an animal's head on the top arm.

Right and Left Sides.—A Greek fret, or square key-pattern, on the ends of the arms and in the cusped hollows between them.

This is a remarkably fine example of an Anglo-Saxon cross-head, and is perhaps one of the best now in existence. The number of complete crosses [1] of the pre-Norman period which still remain *in situ* is extremely small, and we are generally left to conjecture what the perfect monument was like by joining a head found at one place to a shaft and base found at another. Cross-shafts are much more common than cross-heads, partly no doubt because a shaft could be easily chopped up into pieces suitable for use as building material, and would thus be safely preserved inside a wall for centuries until some modern alteration in the fabric revealed its existence. Cross-heads also would be more likely to be mutilated by iconoclasts than cross-shafts.

The shape of the Cropthorne cross-head is Anglo-Saxon rather than Celtic, as is shown by the absence of the circular ring connecting the arms, which is characteristic of the Scottish, Irish, Welsh, Manx, and Cornish crosses.

It will be noticed that the only decorative motives used on the cross-head at Cropthorne are zoömorphs, foliage, and key-patterns; there being none of that interlaced work which is so common on monuments of this period. The most remarkable feature about the zoömorphs is the way in which the texture of the skin is conventionally indicated by a series of parallel lines going in different directions. Only the middle part of the body is treated in this way, there being a narrow plain band forming a margin round the outside. The more elaborately the details of the animals are worked out, the later, probably, the date of the monument upon which they occur. As a general rule, upon the earlier crosses of the pre-Norman period the bodies of the animals are devoid of ornament. The first attempt at decoration was to make a double outline round the body and to introduce little spiral scrolls at the points where the legs join the body.[2] Lastly, the whole of the body was covered with scales or lines intended to convey the idea of the rough hairy hide of the beast.[3]

A very unusual peculiarity in the Cropthorne cross-head is the decoration of the narrow faces with a Greek fret. Occasionally the ends of the arms of crosses of this period exhibit ornament, but it is very seldom continued round the rest of the narrow face, above and underneath the horizontal arms. The elaborate sculpture, the rows of pellets below the bottom arm, and the cable moulding seem to indicate rather a late period. The style of the animals and foliage corresponds almost exactly with that of a fragment of a pre-Norman cross-shaft built into the south wall of Wroxeter [4] church, Shropshire.

[1] Such as those at Gosforth and Irton in Cumberland; Carew and Nevern in Pembrokeshire; Iona and Kildalton in Argyllshire; Dupplin in Perthshire; Monasterboice, co. Louth; Kells, co. Meath; and Clonmacnois, King's co.

[2] As on the cross-slab from Papil, Shetland, now in the Edinburgh Museum (see J. R. Allen's *Early Christian Symbolism*, 359).

[3] As on the fragment of a cross-shaft at Crofton, near Wakefield, Yorkshire (*Proc. Soc. Ant. Lond.* (Ser. 2), vol 4, p. 33).

[4] D. H. S. Cranage's *Churches of Shropshire*, pt. 7, p. 651.

Cross-head in Cropthorne Church.

Front and Right Side of a Pre-Norman Stone at Rous Lench.

To face page 184.

This monument has been described and illustrated in *Gent. Mag.* 1793, 791; and in W. Salt Brassington's *Historic Worcestershire*, 50.

The village of Rous Lench is situated 7 miles north-west of Evesham. A carved stone, the exact purpose of which is not certain, was lately found built into the wall of the church here. It was exhibited by the Rev. W. K. W. Chafy, D.D. at a meeting of the Society of Antiquaries on 15 December, 1898, and is described and illustrated in their *Proceedings* (2nd series, xvii. 259).

It is a block of oölite, nearly rectangular but rounded at one end, 1 foot 11½ inches long by 1 foot 5 inches high by 1 foot 2 inches thick, cracked across the middle and sculptured on two faces thus:—

Front.—At the top a serpent with its body looped in three places, below this a pair of peacocks placed symmetrically facing each other, and at the bottom a man holding a sickle or pruning-hook in his right hand and offering a newly cut bunch of grapes to the peacocks above. The background is formed by a mass of vine branches with foliage and grapes.

Right side.—Three serpents with their bodies looped at intervals and interlaced.

The subject represented upon the front of the stone at Rous Lench is chiefly interesting as affording a unique example of the occurrence of the peacock symbol in Anglo-Saxon art. That this sculpture is a barbarous and debased copy of a Lombardo-Byzantine original will be apparent to anyone who will take the trouble to compare it either with the ivory chair of S. Massimiano at Ravenna[1] (A.D. 456 to 556), or with the fragment of an ambo at S. Salvatore, Brescia.[2] In both the instances mentioned pairs of peacocks are associated with scrolls of foliage, which like those at Rous Lench are no doubt intended for the vine symbolizing 'Christ the true vine.' It is probable that most of the foliage on the Anglo-Saxon crosses of Northumbria and Mercia owes its origin to the classical vine. It is instructive to observe the various modifications which the vine has undergone in the process of successive copying and to note how the bunches of grapes (being the most essential features) have remained, if not altogether unchanged, at least easily to be identified from first to last, while the leaves have been altered quite beyond recognition. The adaptation of the classical vine to Christian purposes may easily be traced. In what is perhaps the earliest instance of the use of the vine in the decoration of a Christian building, namely, in the mosaics of the church of S. Constantia[3] at Rome (A.D. 320 to 350), the design is entirely in the Pagan style. On a sculptured sarcophagus[4] of the third century in the Lateran Museum at Rome a vintage scene similar to that of S. Constantia is associated with distinctively Christian symbols such as 'Christ the Good Shepherd.' On a Merovingian sarcophagus[5] of a somewhat later date at Moissac church in France the vine is found in combination with the Chi-Rho monogram, the Alpha and Omega, and a pair of doves drinking from a vase.

Lastly, the vine is to be seen, with its leaves and bunches of grapes still treated in a thoroughly realistic manner, on a pre-conquest cross-shaft at Nunnykirk,[6] Northumberland. A progressive series of scrolls of foliage from the early sculptured Christian monuments of Northumbria and Mercia might

[1] R. Garrucci, *Storia dell' Arte Cristiana*, vol. vi. pl. 414, and Rohault de Fleury, *La Messe*, vol. ii. pl. 154.

[2] R. Cattaneo, *Architecture in Italy* (transl. by the Contessa Isabel Curtis-Cholmeley), 151.

[3] J. H. Parker, *Hist. Photos of Mosaic Pictures in Rome*, no. 11.

[4] J. H. Parker, *Hist. Photos of Arch. of Rome*, iv.

[5] Cast in the Trocadero Museum, Paris.

[6] *Arch. Æl.* xix. 192.

easily be got together illustrating the various changes due to conventionalizing the classical vine and making successive copies of it. The modifications thus produced are as follows :—(1) alteration in the shape of the bunches of grapes, chiefly due to making them rounder and less pointed so as to fit into the spaces between the scrolls ; (2) reduction in the number of grapes in the bunches; (3) substitution of pointed or other leaves (perhaps suggested by the foliage on Samian ware or by the Tree of Life, which was considered to be a type of the vine symbol of Christ) for the true vine leaf ; and (4) the exaggerated use of spiral curves in the scrolls of the stems, and the introduction of trumpet-shaped expansions at the points where smaller stems branch off from the main stem. As illustrating the successive stages in the degradation of the vine in pre-Norman sculpture, the following examples may be taken :—

Crosses at Eyam and at Bakewell, Derbyshire.—Scrolls with an excessive amount of twist given to the volutes, with trumpet-shaped expansions in the stem, and with pointed leaves.

Cross-shaft at Ilkley,[1] *Yorkshire.*—Scrolls much twisted, bunches of grapes circular, and leaves very degenerate.

Fragment of Cross-shaft at Jarrow, Co. Durham.—Scrolls and bunches of grapes only, the leaves having disappeared.

Lintel of Doorway at Craythorne, Yorkshire.—Scrolls only remaining, and bunches of grapes surviving as single pellets.

Cross at Penally,[2] *Pembrokeshire.*—Leaves of very degenerate form and bunches of grapes reduced to small round knobs, each at the end of a separate stem ; as at Rous Lench.

As a proof of the Italian origin of some at least of the foliage in pre-Norman sculpture in England it may be pointed out that the bunches of grapes on the jambs of the arch in the Saxon church of Britford, Wilts,[3] present a feature which is peculiar to Lombardo-Byzantine art, namely, the enclosing the grapes within a margin representing the outline of the bunch. Exactly the same treatment is to be seen on the ciborium of the church of S. Apollinare-in-Classe[4] near Ravenna (A.D. 806 to 816).

As instances of highly conventionalized, rather than degraded, representations of the vine, the twelfth-century fonts at Montdidier in France,[5] and St. Mary Bourne, Hampshire,[6] may be taken. In both cases the foliage is identical, but on the Montdidier font the figure of our Lord with a vesica is placed in the centre of the foliage, making the meaning of the symbolism, 'I am Christ, the true vine,' perfectly clear. The leaves are entirely conventional, and altogether unlike those of the vine, but the bunches of grapes, although nearly round, can readily be recognized.

The next point to be commented upon in the Rous Lench stone is the little figure of a man amongst the foliage holding a sickle or bill-hook in his right hand, and a bunch of grapes, at which a pair of peacocks are pecking, in his left. This particular incident does not stand alone, for very similar vintage scenes occur in the twelfth-century sculpture at Vezelay, in France,[7] and at Castor, Northants.[8] In the former the man is cutting off a bunch of

[1] *Journ. Brit. Arch. Assoc.* xl. 160.
[2] *Arch. Camb.* (Ser. 5), xvi. 36.
[3] *Wilts Arch. Mag.* xvii. 249.
[4] Cattaneo, *op. cit.* 202.
[5] C. Enlart in the *Mémoires de la Soc. des Ant. de Picardie* for 1898 (Amiens).
[6] *V. C. H. Hants*, ii. 244.
[7] *Builder*, 20 Dec. 1884.
[8] On capital of arch of south transept, east side.

grapes with a knife, and has a basket hung on a forked branch of the vine to hold the fruit. In the latter the man is plucking a bunch of grapes with his left hand and holding a basket in his right. These figures are obviously copies with local colouring of the little naked winged genii which are represented gathering grapes into baskets on the sculptured sarcophagus of the third century in the Lateran Museum at Rome, already mentioned.

Lastly, with regard to the peacocks on the Rous Lench stone there can be little doubt that they are used symbolically, and are not intended to be merely decorative. When peacocks are used as heraldic supporters, so to speak, of the Cross (as on the cathedral at Athens),[1] or of a chalice surmounted by a cross, as on the tomb of Theodota[2] of the eighth century at Pavia, and on one of the carved screens in the church of S. Apollinare Nuovo at Ravenna, or of the Chi-Rho monogram (as on the sarcophagus of Archbishop Theodore at Ravenna),[3] it is obvious that they were not placed in such intimate association with the most sacred emblems of the Christian faith without some very good reason, though what this reason may have been is not quite so easy a question to answer. The writers of the moralized treatises on natural history of the Middle Ages, called bestiaries, derived many of their ideas from Pliny, and where any peculiarity of a bird or animal suggested an obvious analogy with anything relating to Christian doctrines it was readily turned to account. Pliny, however, dwells chiefly on the vanity of the peacock, and mentions that it changes its feathers once a year.

Some writers have endeavoured to trace a connexion of ideas between the renewal of the peacock's feathers and the Resurrection. St. Augustine (*De Civit. Dei*, lxxi. civ.) speaks of the peacock as an emblem of immortality, from the opinion of his time that it was in part or entirely incorruptible.[4] St. Isidore,[5] archbishop of Seville (A.D. 601–636), the great authority on science in the middle ages, shows that this view was still held in the seventh century. He says, '*Pavo*, nomen de sono vocis habet, cujus caro tam dura est, ut putredinem vix sentiat, nec facile coquatur ; de quo quidam sic ait :

Miraris quoties gemmantes explicat alas
Et potes hunc sævo tradere, dure, coco.'

The peacock is described in some, although not all, of the bestiaries, but the account given is so feeble that it would seem that the real meaning of its symbolism had been quite forgotten by the thirteenth century. The bestiary says 'The peacock when it is asleep at night wakes up suddenly because it thinks it has lost its beauty. The peacock is like the soul, which in the night of this world thinks that it has lost the grace of God and cries out in great distress with tears and prayers.'[6] There is a good illustration of the peacock in a thirteenth-century bestiary in the British Museum. (Harl. 4751, f. 54b.)

The earliest example of the occurrence of the peacock in an illuminated MS. is in the Syriac Gospels of Rabula[7] (A.D. 586) in the Medici-Laurentian

1 A. Didron (*Christian Iconography*, transl. by Miss M. Stokes), i. 389.
2 Cattaneo, *op. cit.* 153.
3 Garrucci, *op. cit.* vol. v. pl. 391, fig. 3.
4 Smith's *Dict. of Christian Antiquities*, article 'Peacock.'
5 J. P. Migne's *Patrologia*, lxxxii. 466.
6 Cahier et Martin, *Mélanges d'Archéologie*, ii. 161.
7 Garrucci, *op. cit.* vol. iii. pls. 128–140.

Library at Florence. In later times we find peacocks used in the decoration of some Gospels written for Charlemagne,[1] and now in the National Library at Paris, and in the Book of Kells[2] in the Library of Trinity College, Dublin.

A word in conclusion as to the artistic merit of the Rous Lench stone. Although neither the anatomy of the human figure nor the details of the foliage and birds will bear minute criticism, the general decorative effect is distinctly good. There is an individuality and vigour in the design which is often wanting in works of art of a better period. The marks it bears of having been evolved from something that had gone before, give it an interest it would not otherwise possess, and above all the story told by these quaint uncouth figures of that old serpent the Devil on the one hand, and on the other of Christ who promises immortality to those who partake of the sacrament, is as forcibly and clearly brought out here as it would be in the highest work of art.

Mr. C. R. Peers, F.S.A., has reminded me that there are some architectural fragments of pre-Norman date in Wyre Piddle church. These consist of portions of a pillar piscina, with a capital carved with acanthus foliage; and some mutilated beasts' heads with the tongues protruding between the teeth. This peculiar treatment also occurs on a sculptured horse's head dug up on the site of the Tolsey[3] at Gloucester and now in the Gloucester Museum.

Mr. Peers also mentions the existence of some pre-Norman fragments in Elmley Castle church which I have not seen.

Mention must also be made here of a perforated bronze object found at Pershore about 1779, and thus referred to in the *Gentleman's Magazine* (xlix. 536): 'This piece of antiquity was found a few years ago in a mass of gravel in digging a cellar near the middle of the town of Pershore in Worcestershire.' The accompanying illustration shows it to resemble the cover of a thurible consisting of two parts. The lower part has been lost, but the upper part is now in the possession of Mr. O. G. Knapp, of the Mansion House, Bengeworth, Evesham. It is square in plan with a projecting loop at each of the four corners, the loops having holes $\frac{1}{12}$ of an inch in diameter through each of them. Holes of various shapes are pierced in the top and sides for the smoke of the incense. The design is principally architectural, but it is also partly zoömorphic. The shape is that of a small building with an open arcade of three arches on each side, and surmounted by a roof like that of the tower of the Saxon church of Sompting, Sussex. Above the arcades are triangular gables ornamented with a scale pattern in imitation of roofing-tiles. The pointed top consists of four lozenges filled in with a rude imitation of plants and birds, the background being pierced. The birds are in higher relief than the rest and covered with punched work. At the apex of the roof and at the top and two lower corners of each of the gables are knob-like projections representing the heads of beasts, the eyes of which are punched. The ridges of the roof and the arcades below are ornamented with two kinds of punched work, one like a circle and central dot, and the other like a crescent. On one side there is an inscription on the horizontal band

1 Aug. de Bastard, *Peintures de MSS. 8me au 16me siècle. MSS. Français*, Livraison 1.

2 J. O. Westwood, *Facsimiles of Miniatures*.

3 *Illustrated Archæologist* for 1894, p. 263.

Capital of Pillar Piscina, Wyre Piddle Church.

Thurible Cover, found at Pershore, *c.* 1779.

To face page 188.

between the arcading and the triangular gable in Saxon minuscules mixed with capitals:

+ƷODRICMEƿVORhT

'+ *Godric made me.*'

The final T is on the side of the projecting head.

The formula 'me wvorht' may be compared with 'Drahmal me worhte' on the Anglo-Saxon cross in the church of SS. Michel et Gudule[1] at Brussels, and 'Biorthelm me worte' on the knife from Sittingbourne,[2] Kent, now in the British Museum.

This[3] is the only specimen of a thurible of the Anglo-Saxon period now in existence. Representations of Saxon thuribles will be found in the copy of Cædmon's *Paraphrase*[4] in the Bodleian Library, and in the *Benedictional of Æthelwold*[5] in the Library at Chatsworth.[6]

Norman Sculpture

The specimens of Norman sculpture in Worcestershire are not nearly so numerous as those in the adjoining counties of Hereford and Gloucester, as the following list shows.

Sculptured Norman fonts.—Chaddesley Corbett; Halesowen; Holt; The Nash, Kempsey; Overbury.

Sculptured Norman Tympana.—Alderminster; Castle Morton; Little Comberton; St. Kenelm's; Netherton; Pedmore; Ribbesford; Stockton.

Miscellaneous Norman Sculpture.—Beoley; Bredon; Bretforton; Holt; St. Kenelm's; Leigh; Norton; Rous Lench.

Norman fonts may be divided into three classes as regards their architectural design, namely: (1) those without any supporting column; (2) those supported on a single column; and (3) those supported on a central column with four or more smaller columns surrounding it. The first class is the simplest and therefore probably the earliest, cylindrical or rectangular in shape, and resting sometimes on the floor of the church, but more often on a single step forming a kind of base. The idea of these primitive fonts seems to have been suggested by the early Christian ivory 'situlae'[7] or by the marble well-heads[8] of the tenth century, which are so common in Venice. Some of the best specimens of fonts without any supporting column are to be found in Anglesey.[9]

Fonts belonging to the two remaining classes consist of three separate parts, the bowl, the stem, and the base. The bowl may be cylindrical, hemispherical, or rectangular, and in some cases intermediate forms are produced by rounding the bottoms of cylindrical bowls and the lower corners of rectangular bowls.

1 H. Logeman, *Reliquaire de la Vraie Croix*, etc.

2 *Arch.* xliv. 331.

3 To prevent any confusion, it should be mentioned that another thurible, but of the thirteenth century, has been found at Pershore. This is engraved in *Arch. Journ.* xxxiv. 191.

4 *Arch.* xxiv. pl. 83.

5 *Arch.* xxiv. pl. 20.

6 I am indebted to Mr. O. G. Knapp for kindly sending me the object for examination. It is 3⅝ inches high and 2⅝ inches square. The pierced ornament is not unlike that on some of the bowl-shaped brooches of the Viking period.

7 J. O. Westwood, *Cat. of Fictile Ivories in S. K. M.* 266.

8 R. Cattaneo, *op. cit.* 306.

9 Papers on Mona Mediæva in *Arch. Camb.* (Ser. 1), i. 61, etc.

The sculptured decoration of Norman fonts is usually confined to the bowl, although occasionally the columns and bases are ornamented. When the bowl is hemispherical the sculpture forms one continuous design, when cylindrical the sculpture may be continuous, but is more frequently broken up by arcading, and when rectangular each of the four faces is treated as a separate panel.

The subjects chosen were not so much those referring to the rite of baptism as those which were most suitable for filling the space the sculptor had at his disposal. A rectangular bowl presents four faces available for decoration, two of which can be seen at the same time. The most suitable subjects therefore were those forming either a pair or a set of four, although it is not unusual also to find a separate subject on each face having no connexion whatever with the rest. The subjects were generally taken from the first chapters of Genesis or from the life of Christ.

A cylindrical bowl demands a somewhat different treatment, as there is nothing to show where the design begins or ends, and only a small portion of the curved surface can be seen at one time. A single subject could not be used with advantage, both on account of the difficulty of finding one containing enough figures to go right round the bowl, and because the scene represented could only be taken in bit by bit as the spectator walked round the font. The subjects most often chosen, therefore, were those consisting of several nearly similar figures suitable for being placed under arcading. These often constitute a complete series, such as the twelve apostles, a set of saints, the labours of the twelve months, the virtues and vices, etc. They were sufficiently alike for one or two to suggest the rest, and thus would enable the spectator to comprehend the meaning of the whole series while only seeing one section of it. In other cases the figures were divided into groups, each forming a separate subject which could conveniently be seen from one point of view.

The number of sculptured Norman fonts in Worcestershire is not sufficiently great to afford the material for illustrating the different ways of treating the decorative designs which have been described. The examples, however, at Chaddesley Corbett and Holt show very well how one class of font (that with a hemispherical bowl supported on a stem and base) was beautified by the art of the stone carver of the twelfth century.

The font at Chaddesley Corbett is given in Rickman's *Gothic Architecture* (7th edition, p. 74) as a typical specimen of the style of sculpture prevalent in England during the Norman period. The shape of this font resembles that of an early chalice with a very short stem, and the whole of its surface is covered with elaborate sculpture. The upper edge of the bowl is decorated with a horizontal band of five-cord plaitwork and the remainder with a procession of dragons, each biting the end of the tail of the dragon in front. Each dragon's neck and tail are interlaced with the so-called 'triquetra' knot. The stem has a five-cord plait upon it, and is made convex so as to resemble a cable. The base is ornamented with an interlaced pattern composed of two horizontal rows of Stafford knots.[1]

The general style of the sculpture resembles that of the details of some of the Norman churches in Herefordshire, more especially Kilpeck. In all

[1] Compare the font at Castle Froome, Herefordshire, illustrated in *Arch. Journ.* lx. i.

Bowl of the Font, Overbury Church.

To face page 190.

the work of this school interlaced ornament is a prevalent feature, being probably a survival of the Celtic tradition. Some fanciful persons who believe, with no sufficient reason, that the triquetra knot is symbolical of the Trinity, would no doubt see in its use for hampering the movements of the dragons an allegory of Good restricting the power of Evil. It does not seem likely that the dragons have anything whatever to do with the rite of baptism, because they occur quite as often on tympana and other sculptured details of Norman churches as they do on fonts. Dragons are generally used in Christian art to symbolize the evil principle, as in the contests between St. Michael, or St. George, and the Dragon. Scandinavian mythology also abounds in stories of heroes overcoming similar monstrous foes ; so that it is not surprising that our ancestors with northern blood in their veins should have let their imaginations run riot in portraying the dragonesque creatures with which they were familiar long before they became Christians.

The font at Holt[1] has a round bowl supported on a round stem. The bowl is ornamented with a series of grotesque heads of beasts and has a bold cable moulding round the bottom. The stem is short and is sculptured with mouldings running in a diagonal direction. I am indebted to the Rev. J. B. Eccleston, rector of Holt, for a photograph from which the above description has been written.

The font at Overbury is illustrated in a paper by the Ven. Archdeacon Walters on 'The Fonts of the Archdeaconry of Worcester,'[2] and is described as follows :—

> The bowl seems to belong to the twelfth century and the shaft and base to the fourteenth century. The bottom of the bowl has been cut down to fit an octagonal shaft, with a ball flower in low relief on each face. The bowl is divided into four panels by triple cable-pattern bands. In the panels are : (1) Figure of the founder holding a church[3] in his right hand, and hanging from his left is a pennon.[4] (2) A floral pattern partly restored. (3) A dove in glory over a Latin cross, all modern except the shaft of the cross. (4) A figure with halo under an arch, holding in the left hand a pastoral staff, but the right hand and arm have been restored to match the left.[5]

The font at Halesowen, also illustrated in the same paper, belongs to the class in which the bowl is supported by a large column in the centre surrounded by four smaller columns. Such fonts usually have a square bowl, but in this case it is cylindrical, with four rectangular projections over each of the small columns. The round portions of the bowl are ornamented with interlaced beasts, something like those on the pre-Norman crosses. The bodies of the beasts have a double outline, the part in the middle being covered with a hatching of diagonal lines. On the outer faces of the four rectangular projections are full-length figures. The columns below have cushion capitals.

The original bowl of the Norman font belonging to Pershore Abbey is now in the grounds of The Nash at Kempsey, near Worcester. It is illustrated in F. B. Andrews's *Pershore Abbey*, p. 28. The bowl of the font is round and decorated with an arcade of semicircular intersecting arches. There is a figure under each arch, 'much worn and encrusted with lichen,' according to Mr. Andrews.

1 An engraving is given in Paley's *Baptismal Fonts*.
2 *Ass. Archit. Soc. Rep.* xxvi. ii. 510.
3 Or metal shrine.
4 A maniple or a leather case for the shrine.
5 The right hand should be giving the benediction.

The sculptured Norman tympana in Worcestershire are more numerous than the fonts, and are decorated with the following figure subjects :—

Agnus Dei	at Castle Morton
Christ in Glory	at Pedmore, at Stockton, and at St. Kenelm's
Contest between Man and Monster	at Ribbesford
Dragon	at Netherton
Cross within Circle . . .	at Alderminster
Tree and Animal . . .	at Stockton
Wolf	at Stockton

Of these, the first two, the Agnus Dei and Christ in Glory, are the most common subjects which occur on Norman tympana in England, there being about twenty examples of each. The triumph of Good over Evil (as symbolized by Christ bruising the Serpent's head, St. Michael and the Dragon, St. George and the Dragon, David and the Lion, or the contest between a hero and a monster) was also a favourite subject for the decoration of Norman tympana, of which no less than ten examples are known, and dragons (represented singly or in pairs) occur with nearly the same frequency.

The Agnus Dei at Castle Morton occupies the greater part of a recessed semi-circular space in the middle of the tympanum. The cross carried by the Lamb is of the plain Latin shape ; there is no nimbus round the head, nor is the whole figure enclosed within a circular aureole. This perfectly simple way of representing the Agnus Dei is comparatively rare on Norman tympana.[1]

Speaking generally, each period in the history of Christian art has its own peculiar system of religious symbolism, so that it is possible to say in most cases at what date any particular symbol was first introduced, and also when it went out of use. The length of life enjoyed by each symbol has been different, some having continued to exist from the earliest period to the latest, whilst others have died out in the course of a century or two after they first made their appearance in Christian art. The Agnus Dei is amongst those symbols which have had the longest term of existence, although it has not always been treated in the same way. In the paintings of the Catacombs of Rome (A.D. 200 to 400), on the early Christian sculptured sarcophagi (A.D. 300 to 600), and on the Italo-Byzantine mosaics in the churches of Rome and Ravenna (A.D. 500 to 700), the Divine Lamb is represented as standing on the summit of a mountain, from the foot of which issue the four rivers of Paradise,[2] typifying the four evangelists. The Holy Lamb usually has the Chi-Rho monogram of Christ upon the forehead, sometimes combined with the nimbus. In the art of the twelfth century the Lamb has a cruciform nimbus in place of the monogram, and carries the cross of the Resurrection with its flying banner, the whole being enclosed in a circular medallion.[3] This later treatment is the one adopted in Norman sculpture.

On Norman tympana and lintels of doorways where the Agnus Dei is introduced as the principal subject, it generally occupies a central position within a circular medallion, having in many cases supporters (to use the term in its heraldic sense) on each side, but it is also occasionally placed unsym-

[1] There are other examples of the Agnus Dei without any accessories at Thwing in Yorkshire, and in Cornwall.

[2] Didron, *op. cit.* i. 67.

[3] Probably intended for an aureole or glory ; St. John the Baptist is represented in Christian art as carrying the Agnus Dei on a circular disc.

metrically (not in the centre of the tympanum or lintel) among a group of other figures. Examples of the symmetrical treatment of the Agnus Dei are to be seen on Norman tympana and lintels at Upleadon, Gloucs., and Pen Selwood, Somerset (with two beasts as supporters); at Bondleigh, Devon (with two doves as supporters); at Langport, Somerset (with two angels as supporters); at Pipe Aston, Hereford (with two of the evangelistic symbols as supporters); and formerly at Tetsworth, Oxon (with a bishop on one side and a priest on the other). Of the unsymmetrical treatment of the Agnus Dei on Norman tympana, there are examples at Elkstone, Gloucs. (where the Lamb is introduced in the scene of Christ enthroned in majesty); at Hoveringham, Notts (in the scene of St. Michael and the Dragon); at Stoke-sub-Hamdon, Somersetshire (in association with the Tree of Life and Sagittarius and Leo); and at Parwich and Hognaston, Derby (in association with beasts, birds, and serpents). The form of the cross held by the Agnus Dei varies, and often there is no nimbus round the head, but these minor details need not be referred to here.

Christ in Glory on the Norman tympanum at Pedmore[1] is represented enthroned within an oval aureole supported by the symbols of the four evangelists. The right hand of the Saviour is raised giving the benediction, and the left rests on the knee. The same subject on the tympanum at St. Kenelm's[2] is treated in a somewhat different manner. The aureole is supported by two angels, and our Lord is standing instead of being seated on a throne. He is crowned and has a nimbus round the head. The most remarkable feature is that the right hand of the Saviour, which is held up in the act of benediction, protrudes through a circular ring on one side of the aureole. It has been suggested that the figure within the aureole is not intended for Christ, but for St. Kenelm. The portrayal of a saint in this manner would be quite contrary to the ordinary laws of Christian iconography. Around the outside of the tympanum are four dragonesque creatures with their bodies interlaced, forming a sort of ornamental border round the figure subject.

Representations of Christ in Glory do not make their appearance in Christian art until about the seventh century. Among the earliest examples are those on the leaden flasks of holy oil from Jerusalem,[3] on the sculptured altar of Ratchis[4] at Cividale (A.D. 744–749), in the Syriac Gospels of Rabula[5] in the Medici-Laurentian Library at Florence (A.D. 586), and on the carved ivory diptych of Rambona[6] in the Vatican Museum at Rome. There is hardly any variation in the conventional way in which this subject is treated throughout the whole range of Christian art. The Saviour is almost always seated giving the benediction with the right hand and holding a book in the left. The figure of Christ is enclosed within an oval or a vesica-shaped aureole, either supported by angels or surrounded by the symbols of the four evangelists.

The best examples of Christ in Glory on sculptured Norman tympana, showing the different ways of treating the subject, are to be found at Ely Cathedral (where the aureole is supported by two angels); at St. Peter's,

[1] C. E. Keyser, *Norman Tympana and Lintels*, fig. 113. [2] Ibid. fig. 113.
[3] Garrucci, *op. cit.* vol. iv. pls. 433–435. [4] Ibid. vol. vi. pl. 424. [5] Ibid. iii. pl. 127.
[6] J. O. Westwood, *Cat. of Fictile Ivories in S. K. M.* 56.

Rowlstone, Hereford (where the aureole is supported by four angels); at Betteshanger, Kent (where the aureole has no supporters); and at Elkstone, Gloucs. (where Christ is enthroned but not placed within an aureole).[1]

The sculpture on the Norman tympanum at Ribbesford[2] represents an archer with a helmet on his head shooting with a bow and arrow at a monster. Between the two is an animal apparently intended for a hound. The monster has a muzzle on its snout and a fish-like tail. It bears a certain amount of resemblance to a seal. An endeavour has been made to explain the sculpture by a local legend about killing a fish-monster from the Severn,[3] but it is more probably intended to symbolize the contest between the good and evil principle, as in the St. Michael, or St. George, and the Dragon, which occurs on several Norman tympana in England.[4]

On the tympanum of a blocked doorway of a disused Norman chapel at Netherton[5] there is sculptured a very spirited dragon with huge outspread wings and open mouth. The carving is in a remarkably good state of preservation, but unfortunately a tree has been allowed to grow directly in front of the doorway, partly hiding the sculpture from view.

Among the miscellaneous details of Norman churches in Worcestershire which exhibit figure sculpture, the most interesting are the figures of Christ in niches over doorways at Leigh and at Rous Lench, St. Margaret and the

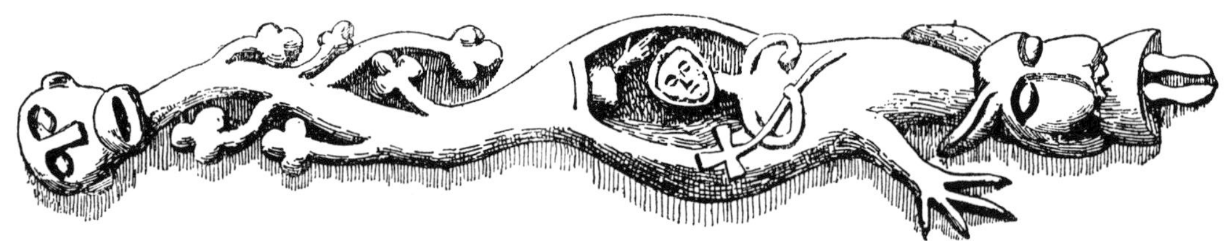

St. Margaret, from a Capital in Bretforton Church.

Dragon on the capital of one of the columns of the north arcade of the nave of Bretforton church, and the eagle and the fish on the left jamb of the doorway of Ribbesford church.

In the round-headed niche over the doorway at Leigh, the Saviour is seen standing with the cross of the Resurrection in the left hand and giving the benediction with the right. The nimbus round the head is cruciferous. Figures of this kind in niches over doorways are somewhat rare in the Norman period, but there are other instances at Lullingstone, Somerset (Christ enthroned); Prestbury, Cheshire (Christ triumphant, standing with the cross of the Resurrection); Patrixbourne, Kent (the Agnus Dei); Haddiscoe, Norf. (a bishop); and on the capital at Bretforton, St. Margaret is shown with a cross in her right hand bursting through the side of the dragon, and at the same time her feet and the lower part of her skirt protrude from the dragon's mouth as she is being swallowed. Above the head of St. Margaret is the Dextera Dei, symbolizing the miraculous

[1] For further information see J. R. Allen, *op. cit.* 262.

[2] Keyser, *op. cit.* fig. 68.

[3] See 'Description of some Curious Sculptures at Ribbesford Church, Worc.,' by Edwin Lees, in *Ass. Archit. Soc. Rep.* xv. 66 (1879).

[4] J. R. Allen, *op. cit.* 271.

[5] Keyser, *op. cit.* fig. 56.

Lectern in Norton Church: probably the Chapter-house Lectern of Evesham Abbey.

To face page 194.

deliverance of the saint by the interposition of the Hand of God. The dragon's tail branches out into trefoils, and terminates in a semihuman, semi-bestial head.

Scenes from the lives of saints not mentioned in the Bible are very rarely represented in Norman sculpture, and the only saints whose miracles or martyrdoms are commemorated are St. Nicholas,[1] St. Laurence,[2] and St. Margaret. Besides the sculpture of St. Margaret and the Dragon at Bretforton, there are other examples on the Norman font at Cotham[3] in Yorkshire, and on the Norman doorway at Tutbury in Staffordshire.

The eagle and fish sculptured on the jamb of the Norman doorway at Ribbesford is a subject which occurs in the decoration of early churches in Italy,[4] in Irish[5] illuminated MSS., on pre-Norman Christian monuments in Scotland,[6] and on Anglo-Saxon metal-work.[7] The symbolism is fully explained in the mediæval bestiaries, as in that of Philippe de Thaun.[8]

Mr. C. R. Peers, F.S.A., has called my attention to the existence of the remarkable marble lectern from the chapterhouse of Evesham Abbey, now at Norton, near Evesham, and to the figure of the so-called abbot of Pershore, in Beoley church. He supplies the following description of the former :—

Front (*i.e. West Face*).—In the middle the seated figure of an abbot or bishop in amice, chasuble, dalmatic, stole, and alb ; right hand raised in blessing ; top of head damaged, so not clear whether mitred or not ; on either side scrolls of foliage.

East Face.—Among foliage, two heads with close-curled hair and short rounded ears.

North Face.—Among foliage a beast's head with long pointed ears.

South Face.—As north.

The top is sunk to take a book, and there are pinholes (perhaps for brackets for lights) at the top corners. It is 2 feet 4 inches square, by 1 foot 6 inches high in front and 6 inches at the back. It has been published in *Arch.* xvii. 278.

The so-called abbot of Pershore at Beoley, and another somewhat similar figure of an ecclesiastic in St. Kenelm's church, are illustrated in W. Salt Brassington's *Historic Worcestershire*, pp. 80 and 109.

1 On fonts at St. Nicholas's Church, Brighton, and at Winchester Cathedral.

2 On font at Cotham, Yorkshire.

3 J. R. Allen, *op. cit.* 317.

4 On the west front of the church of S. Michele at Pavia. Leader Scott, *Cathedral Builders*, 52.

5 In the Book of Armagh in the Library of the Royal Irish Academy at Dublin. Sir William Betham, *Irish Antiquarian Researches*, 221.

6 J. R. Allen, *op. cit.* 384.

7 On an embossed plate of bronze found in the Thames and now in the Brit. Mus. (W. A. Mansell's series of Photographs, No. 918.)

8 Thomas Wright, *Popular Treatises on Science in the Middle Ages*, p. 109.

POLITICAL HISTORY

THE early political history of the county is to a large extent the result of three important factors. The first of these was the geographical position of the shire, intersected by a great navigable river, the Severn. Whoever controlled Worcestershire was able to hold the line of the Severn, and could thus check the piratical raids of Irish, Norse, and Danes, and what was even more important in later times, prevent the junction of insurgents from other parts of England with the lawless marchmen and the ever turbulent Welsh. It was not until the sixteenth century, or later, that the county settled down into a peaceful English shire.

The second great factor was that until the seventeenth century a large part of the county was forest. Originally the whole shire formed part of the great Mercian Forest, in which spots gradually became cleared, settlements formed, and villages built. These settlements occurred usually in its southern half. To the west of the Severn the land remained for long uncleared, and to the east the primæval woodland stretched across from the river banks to the Warwickshire border. One, and not the least important, point in the county history is the story of how villages, little by little, emerged from the forest and caused the curtailment of its boundaries. Not only did the existence of a large woodland area keep much of the county in a wild and uncultivated state, with a sparse and scattered population, but after the Norman Conquest, the special forest laws tended to the increase of the royal power. Thus Hallam spoke of a forest as an 'oasis of despotism in the midst of the old common law.'[1] On the west of the Severn the great forest of Dean extended along the Gloucestershire and Worcestershire borders and on into the latter county as far as the river Teme. The portion of this forest lying in Worcestershire in later times, probably after it was granted to Gilbert of Clare, earl of Gloucester, by Edward I., became known as 'Malvern Chase.' It still, however, remained an area under exceptional forest laws[2] until the crown rights were sold by Charles I. in the seventeenth century.

On the north-west of the county, from a point near the Teme which it is not easy to determine with accuracy, but which is probably at the boundaries of the parishes which afterwards became the hundred of Doddingtree, there stretched the great forest of Wyre, the last vestiges of which the Crown sold towards the end of the nineteenth century. On the east of the Severn a large forest, beginning at Worcester, followed the course of the river till its junction with the Stour, and thence extended to the Clent Hills and the Bromsgrove Lickey, in the direction of the boundary of Warwickshire and Worcestershire. Originally this great forest was called by three distinct names, each referring to a particular part, Ombersley the western, Pyperode the central, and Horwell the eastern, but in time these

[1] *Middle Ages* (1853), ii. 309 note.

[2] Turner, *Select Pleas of the Forest* (Selden Soc.), p. cix. sqq.

names[1] disappeared, and the whole area became known as the forest of Feckenham. Up to the middle of the seventeenth century, when Charles I. sold the forestal rights, this forest formed the great division between the north and south of the county. So near at one time did its boundaries come to the walls of Worcester that the 'Justice Seat' of the Forest Court was held at the hospital of St. Wulstan, the commandery just outside the city walls. This forestal area could not fail to have had the effect in mediæval times of largely enhancing the royal power in the county.

The third great factor was the power of the Church. The largest hundred in the county, Oswaldslow, was the property of the bishop. He ruled it, the courts were his courts, the royal officers had no rights in it, there he was supreme. Whether the charter of Edgar, under which the bishops claimed their rights is or is not a forgery, the fact remains that the bishop's claim to exclusive jurisdiction was recognized fully and absolutely, and as a consequence all the profits of the local courts and other royal rights in the district went to the bishop.[2] But the bishop's jurisdiction over his hundred by no means exhausted the holding of the Church in the shire. The hundred of Blackenhurst was the property of the abbey of Evesham, while the hundred of Pershore had belonged to the abbey of Pershore, whose possessions, although to a large extent lost to that monastery, still remained, and even yet remain ecclesiastical property, first of the abbey of Westminster, then of the dean and chapter of Westminster, and now of the Ecclesiastical Commission. Worcester priory also held a considerable amount of land, which in the same way passed first to the dean and chapter, then to the Ecclesiastical Commissioners, so that even now substantial traces of the old influence of the Church still exist in the county in spite of seizure, spoliation, and sale.

These three conditions naturally determined to a great extent the future history of the county. As a result of the first, the city of Worcester became the strategic base for operations against Mid and South Wales, and to this is due most of the royal visits and royal favours that Worcester received in her history. Long after the need for a military town had passed away, Worcester remained the centre for the trade between London and Wales, as from it branched off the chief roads into all the surrounding districts. Worcester was on the direct line of communication between London and Ludlow, the seat of the court of the Welsh Marches. It was as the centre for men and supplies from Wales that it acquired its great importance in the civil wars, and even yet its old importance lingers, as it now forms one of the most busy railway junctions for Welsh trade. The second and third factors have also left their trace on the county history. To the great possessions both of the crown and the Church we may partly attribute the fact that Worcestershire never has possessed a powerful territorial aristocracy. It is true that some of the great feudal families have from time to time owned lands in the county, but with the single exception of Dudley Castle, one looks in vain for any place in the county which formed the chief residence of a feudal baron. Elmley Castle and Hanley Castle, it is true, belonged to the Beauchamps, but their real home was not in Worcestershire; the Mortimers held lands in the county, but Wigmore was their stronghold.

[1] The name Pyperode still remains in Pepper Wood in the parish of Chaddesley Corbett.
[2] *V. C. H. Worc.* i. 248.

POLITICAL HISTORY

The early history of the county is the history of raids, some by land, some by water; by land the raiders were usually Welsh, by water the raiders are said to have been Danes, but it seems probable that Irish pirates,[1] who are known to have worked up the Severn into Gloucestershire, came further and plundered Worcestershire settlements, carrying away slaves and booty. As the Saxon conquerors had marched along the banks of the Severn past Bewdley to attack Uriconium, so the later Danish raiders must have followed the Severn valley, and their boats sailed up from the Severn sea.[2] Of these raids we know little beyond the fact of their occurrence.[3] In the time of Alfred we may note an important charter[4] by which Aethelred and Aethelflaed are stated to have built a 'burh' at Worcester at the request of Bishop Werefrith, to whom they granted divers privileges. It is possible that just before this both monastery and town had suffered from Welsh or Danish raids.

One of the earliest definite pieces of civil history is the destruction of Worcester in 1041.[5] Two officers of Harthacnute who had come to levy a tax had been killed by the citizens in a riot that arose out of their refusal to pay. To maintain his authority, the king sent a force to lay waste Worcester, whilst the citizens retreated to the island of 'Bevereye,' where the Salwarpe joins the Severn about three miles above the city. There they formed a camp, leaving Worcester to its fate. The town and the castle were burnt, but the citizens four times repulsed the onslaught of the king's army led by Earls Godwin, Leofric, and Siward, with the result that they obtained terms, on which they capitulated and were allowed to return to their homes.[6] This was the first of the many recorded burnings of Worcester, and it gives some clue as to the condition of the town, which was probably a collection of wooden buildings clustering round the church.

From the peculiar distribution of influence in the county, the Norman Conquest produced far less change here than elsewhere. The forests passed to the Crown and became king's land. The English lay tenants-in-chief were dispossessed and their lands given to Normans, but they were relatively few in number.[7] The two leading churchmen in the county, Bishop Wulstan[8] and Abbot Aethelwig, both Englishmen, retained their positions and proved staunchly loyal to the Conqueror. But Normanizing the county took longer here than in other parts. Only one castle, that of Dudley, belonging to William Fitzansculf,[9] is mentioned in Domesday. The castle of Worcester was probably not built on a considerable scale until about the Conquest, as its site encroached on the land of the monastery and thus caused the well-known scene between Archbishop Ealdred, protector of the see at Worcester, and

[1] Note, *Flor. Wig.* (Engl. Hist. Soc.), i. 203; 'Hibernienses piratæ' and *Ang. Sax. Chron.* (Rolls Ser.), i. 310.

[2] See notice of Ribbesford in Heming, *Cartulary*, i. 256.

[3] See *V. C. H. Worc.* i. 310 notes. It is traditionally reported that on one occasion a Dane caught in an act of sacrilege was flayed alive, and his skin, of which portions are still believed to be in existence, nailed to the door of the cathedral. Similar stories for which there would seem to be some foundation are told of several churches in eastern England. See *Arch. Journ.* v. 185.

[4] Heming, *Cartulary*. See *V. C. H. Worc.* i. 242.

[5] *Ang. Sax. Chron.* (Rolls Ser.), i. 296.

[6] *Flor. Wig.* (Engl. Hist. Soc.), i. 195.

[7] *V. C. H. Worc.* i. 262.

[8] In illustration of the important position of Wulstan from the very beginning of the Conqueror's reign, see the English writ reprinted by Round, *Feudal England*, p. 422.

[9] *Engl. Hist. Rev.* xix. 229. There do not seem to have been any stone-buildings here until about the middle of the thirteenth century; a licence to crenellate was granted in 1264.

the sheriff Urse d'Abitot. The Normans who had grants of land in Worcestershire did not live within its limits, so the danger which threatened the county was disruption. This actually began ; Earl Hugh had a grant of land at Halesowen which was transferred to Shropshire, the earl's tenants attending the lord's court there, and the parish of Clent went to Staffordshire.[1] Had William FitzOsborn lived, or rather had his son not committed treason and incurred the consequent forfeiture, it is more than likely that the hundred of Doddingtree would have passed into Herefordshire. As it was in the centre of the county, probably owing to some forestal arrangements Alvechurch went to Warwickshire, while in the south transfers went so far that several Worcestershire parishes were included in the Domesday survey of the adjoining counties, the first step to their becoming incorporated with those counties for all purposes. But the county survived the dangers of disruption, and until 1832 its boundaries remained practically unaltered.

The part the county was destined to play in English history was shown soon after the Conquest. The rebellion of the earls in 1074 would certainly have been serious, and probably successful, if the earls marchers on the Welsh border could have united with the eastern rebels and their Danish supporters. Urse the Worcestershire sheriff, Walter of Lacy, Wulstan the bishop of Worcester, and Aethelwig, abbot of Evesham,[2] called out their tenants and guarded the Severn fords. Earl Roger was thus prevented from crossing, and so the two sections of the rebels, the eastern and the western, were beaten in detail.[3] This result proved the importance of a strong castle at Worcester with a loyal bishop and sheriff. The forfeitures that followed the rebellion brought a new element into the county—the Mortimers. Among the rebels was the son of William FitzOsborn, whose lands were forfeited, and to a good deal of them the Mortimers succeeded. Their influence tended to detach the hundred of Doddingtree and the Teme valley from the county ; a part of it passed into the diocese of Hereford, to which it still belongs. But against this influence was set the fact that the Church of Worcester was an extensive land-owner then in the Teme valley, and it was mainly owing to this that the valley and the hundred remain to the county. The effects of this rebellion do not appear to have extended beyond the Doddingtree hundred, for the hundred of Halfshire, comprising the part of the county lying to the north of the Clent Hills and on to Kidderminster, was under the control of William Fitzansculf, the lord of the castle of Dudley, who remained loyal to the Crown. It was to the west of the Severn that the real danger lay.

In 1088 there was a serious rebellion against William II. headed by his uncle Odo, bishop of Bayeux.[4] The lords marchers had not profited by the lesson of 1074, but again rose in arms. In the west the moving spirit was Roger of Montgomery, earl of Shrewsbury, whose vast territorial influence is summarized in the style given him by Ordericus—[5] 'Rogerius Merciorum comes.' He was probably not present[6] in person during the raid on

[1] *V. C. H. Worc.* i. 238, 239. Both Halesowen and Clent were restored to Worcestershire at a later period.

[2] To whom is addressed the famous writ preserved in the Evesham Chartulary, Cott. MS. Vesp. B. xxiv. fol. 15 (18)—contemporary testimony to the institution of Knight Service by the Conqueror. Mr. Round has attributed this mandate with much probability to the year 1072. *Feudal England*, p. 304.

[3] *Flor. Wig.* (Eng. Hist. Soc.), ii. 11.

[4] *Ang. Sax. Chron.* (Rolls Ser.), i. 357.

[5] *Ord. Vit.* Migne, p. 563.

[6] This may be inferred from the words of Florence, ii. 24 : 'Cum hominibus Rogeri de Scrobbesbyria.'

Worcester, but leaders were found in Roger de Lacy, Osborn of Richard's castle, and his son-in-law Richard de Neufmarché, with the Lord of Wigmore, Ralph de Mortimer, 'all Frenchmen,' says the Peterborough chronicler, thus emphasizing the specially feudal character of the rising, for in their following were the lawless men of the marches and many Welsh.[1] Grievously burdened with the cares of his position, the aged Wulstan prepared, 'like another Moses, to play the man for his people and city.'[2] At the request of his garrison he left his home beyond the church and entered the castle. Already the rebels were burning and slaying all around, when the citizens, encouraged by their bishop's blessing, sallied forth across the Severn bridge and fell upon them while plundering the bishop's lands at Wick. Encumbered with booty, the marauders were swept before the onslaught, and the victors returned to give thanks to God and His servant.

During the reign of Henry I. we have few specific details relating to this county. Perhaps the most important was a terrible fire at the city of Worcester, recorded in 1113, which happened just before midsummer, when the castle, all the churches, and the whole town suffered severely. A monk most useful to his brethren and two servants of the monastery with fifteen citizens perished.[3] It was suspected that the first outbreak was due to the Welsh. Five years after died[4] Florence the Worcester monk, who told as a faithful witness the early history of his city and shire. There is no further notice of importance till the beginning of the next reign.

Stephen marched[5] through Worcester in 1138 on his way to attack Dudley Castle which was held for the empress by Ralph Paganel. Again, in Easter week of the following year, he entered the city in state and offered at the high altar of the cathedral church the kingly ring from his finger. On the morrow by the consent of the monastic community it was returned to him, and he was pleased to accept it, marvelling much at the humility and devotion of the monks.[6] Afterwards the king marched to the siege of Ludlow, and on his return again passed through the city of Worcester. Towards the close of the year Stephen 'to his own hurt'[7] granted to Waleran de Beaumont, count of Meulan, the lordship of Worcester and possibly the earldom of the county.[8]

In the autumn of 1140 the empress arrived at Gloucester and rumours of impending attack were brought to Worcester from the rival city. The earl was absent and Bishop Simon had neither the force of character nor the local prestige of St. Wulstan. The citizens resolved to take sanctuary in the cathedral church, which, as the chronicler bitterly complains, became a repository for furniture, a public inn and a hall of debate, while the chanting of the office blended with the wailing of women and the cries of

[1] *Ang. Sax. Chron.* (Rolls Ser.), i. 357. 'þa men þe yldest waeron of Hereforde and eall þeo scir forþmid, and þa men of Scrobscyre mid mycele folce of Brytlande.'

[2] *Flor. Wig.* (Engl. Hist. Soc.), ii. 26.

[3] Ibid. ii. 66.

[4] Ibid. Cont. ii. 72.

[5] Ibid. ii. 110.

[6] Ibid. ii. 115. In the previous year a like ceremony had taken place at Gloucester, and the ransom paid to the monks for the return of the ring was fifty shillings. Ibid. ii. 105.

[7] *Hen. Hunt.* (Rolls Ser.), 282.

[8] Round, *Dict. Nat. Biog.* iv. 70. The Cont. of Florence speaks of a 'Comes Civitatis' and 'Comes Wigornensis,' which must refer to Waleran. See also *Arch. Journ.* li. 47.

infants at the breast. 'O misery of miseries to behold! The high altar is stript, the cross removed, the image[1] of Mary mother of God, most holy, no longer greets the eye!'[2] Early in November the blow fell. News was brought of the rapid advance of the men of Gloucester, and the clergy vested in their albs, with tolling bells, carried the relics of St. Oswald their patron in suppliant procession through the cemetery, even as the enemy were rushing from gate to gate through the city streets. An attack on a strong outwork near the castle had been repulsed by the townsmen, but on the unguarded northern side an entrance was forced, many houses burnt, cattle and property were carried off, with prisoners 'coupled like hounds' for ransom. But apparently the castle held out and no permanent lodgment was effected. Later in the month Earl Waleran reached Worcester and viewed the blackened ruins of the sacked quarter as a personal insult to himself. Descending on Sudeley, which was held for Maud, he took ample vengeance. As the chronicler remarks, 'What he did is scarce fit to record; he returned evil for evil, seized the people, their property, and beasts for booty, and on the morrow returned to Worcester.'[3] Soon afterwards Stephen arrived and saw with his own eyes what the city had suffered in his cause, and gave the constable's honour, the fief of Miles of Gloucester, to William of Beauchamp, sheriff of Worcester. After a raid into Herefordshire he returned towards Oxford, passing through Worcester on his way, and there confirming the election of one Maurice to the see of Bangor.[4]

Early in 1141 Miles the former constable attacked Winchcomb. Stephen at once made Worcester his base, and Waleran, mindful of the wrongs of his citizens, carried the war into the enemy's territory and sacked the lordly manor-house of Earl Robert at Tewkesbury. At the supplication of the abbot of Tewkesbury and his brethren he spared their possessions and even released his prisoners; but on his return to Worcester the earl gleefully declared that he had scarce ever made such a burning before either in Normandy or England.[5] At Lincoln fight Earl Waleran played the coward, perhaps from policy, and in 1145 he entrusted his lordship of Worcester to the sheriff William de Beauchamp when he set out on pilgrimage to the Holy Land.[6] On his return he adhered to the cause of the empress and held Worcester against Stephen, who in 1150 plundered and burnt 'the very fair city.' but failed to enter the castle.[7] In 1152 the king again renewed the blockade, but by the treacherous counsel of the earl's twin-brother, Robert of Leicester, two counterworks which had been built were levelled and Waleran again escaped, and sought refuge in Normandy.

One of the early acts of Henry II. was to restore the royal authority along the line of the Severn. This was opposed to the views of the lord, marchers, and especially to those of Roger of Hereford, who held Gloucester and Hereford, and Hugh de Mortimer, who fortified Bridgnorth, Cleobury,

[1] Probably the wonder-working image which four centuries afterwards Cromwell stripped of its fair adornment. See Froude, *Hist. of Eng.* iii. 238.

[2] *Flor. Wig.* (Engl. Hist. Soc.), ii. 119.

[3] Ibid. ii. 120.

[4] Ibid. ii. 121.

[5] Ibid. ii. 124.

[6] *Hist. MSS. Com. 5th Rep.* App. p. 301.

[7] *Hen. Hunt.* (Rolls Ser.), 282.

and Wigmore, and determined to keep them against the king. The earl of Hereford at the instance of Bishop Gilbert Foliot soon submitted, but Hugh de Mortimer proved more stubborn, and Cleobury was captured and destroyed before he made his peace.[1] As soon as Henry had reduced the barons throughout the county to their allegiance he turned his attention to Wales, and after the campaign of 1157 he came to Worcester in the following year. At the Easter mass in the cathedral the king and queen taking off their crowns placed them on the altar and vowed that they would never wear them again.[2] The county felt the great judicial reform of Henry II. in 1176, when the kingdom was divided into circuits for the king's judges.[3] One of them consisted of the counties of Worcester, Shropshire, Hereford, and Gloucester, and since that date the judges have with more or less regularity come on circuit in the county. Except that in the year of his accession, 1189, Worcester was again burnt, and that the county in spite of complaints had to bear its share of the heavy demands made by Richard I., the reign of this monarch is almost unmarked in its history. John's reign began with a great fire at Worcester, in 1202, when the cathedral, all the houses near it, and a great part of the city was burnt.[4] In the great struggle between John and the pope the bishop of Worcester, Mauger, took part against the king, being one of the bishops appointed by the pope to put the interdict in force.

King John, with the restless energy of his race, travelled incessantly, and was often in Worcestershire, keeping Easter or Christmas at Worcester itself, or hunting at Feckenham and Kinver.[5] In 1204 he was in the county twice, first in the early spring, and then in August to meet Llewellyn of Wales and Madoc son of Griffin. For the king's need at the Mid Lent of 1205, great provisions of sturgeon and other fish and all manner of spices were sent to Worcester by the purveyors. In 1207, on his way to his hunting seat at Kinver, he worshipped[6] at the shrine of St. Wulstan, for whom he always showed a peculiar devotion. Amongst later visits may be mentioned the Christmas court of 1214. After the king's visit in the August of 1216, he wrote[7] from Berkeley directions as to the defence of Worcester Castle, in the event of a siege by the dauphin. About the same time he informed William de Cantilupe that he had committed to John Marshall the castle of Worcester, the county and its appurtenances, and all the forests of the shire. A few weeks later the castle was in the hands of William Marshall the younger, who declared for Prince Louis. But it was speedily attacked by the earl of Chester and Fawkes of Breauté, when the townsmen fought stubbornly, but the garrison of the castle at length sought refuge in the cathedral. The victors sacked the city and monastery, and the unhappy monks melted the precious adornments of St. Wulstan's shrine to pay their ransom, whilst a climax of evil was suffered in the suspension of divine service till the following Feast of the

[1] *Chron. Rob. de Torigneio* (Rolls Ser.), iv. 184.

[2] *Roger de Hoveden* (Rolls Ser.), i. 216; cf. *Pipe R.* 4 *Hen. II.* (Hunter), p. 175.

[3] *Roger de Hoveden* (Rolls Ser.), ii. 88.

[4] *Ann. Mon.* (Rolls Ser.), i. 56; ii. 78; iv. 391.

[5] For these visits see itinerary of King John in Hardy, *Pat. R.* (1835), and J. Noake, *Worcester Nuggets*, p. 4, sqq. where a collection of record references to these visits will be found. The king as early as 1200 spent Easter Day at Worcester.

[6] *Ann. Mon.* (Rolls Ser.), iv. 395.

[7] Rymer, *Foed.* (Rec. Com.), i. 142.

Assumption.[1] The sufferings of the citizens are reflected in a significant entry on the first patent roll[2] of the following reign, where allusion is made to 'the hundred pounds which the men of Worcester promised King John of good memory, formerly king of England, that the walls of Worcester might not be levelled and the town remain unscathed by fire and destruction.' Meanwhile, John, after his last foray, was brought a dying man to Newark, where he made a will bequeathing his body for burial to the church of Worcester. Thither it was conveyed by Sylvester the bishop and the faithful earl of Pembroke, who laid it before the high altar near the tombs of St. Wulstan and St. Oswald, so verifying, the chronicler tells us, the prophecy of Merlin, 'And he shall be placed among the saints.'[3]

Early in the next reign the long-disputed bailey of the castle at Worcester was handed over to the bishop, the motte being retained in the king's hands,[4] and entrusted to Walter[5] de Beauchamp. The young king, Henry III., was brought to Worcester[6] in 1218 to the consecration of the new cathedral, and visited the city on several occasions afterwards. At varying intervals the itinerant justices and the forest judges held their courts, though in 1261 the men of Worcester declined to admit the justices in eyre, as less than seven years had passed since their last visit.[7] From the year 1237 till 1266 the history of the county practically centres round the bishop, Walter de Cantilupe, son of Lord William de Cantilupe, and an indomitable supporter of the barons against the foreigners. Into the baronial scale he threw the whole weight of his influence, and the ecclesiastical landowners in the main followed the bishop. The lay barons on the other hand had no fixed policy ; the Somerys, who were the owners of Dudley Castle, were in a half-hearted way for the king, as were the Mortimers ; the Clares were at first on the side of the barons, the red earl fighting on their side at Lewes, but afterwards on the side of the king at Evesham. The county being thus divided took no very definite part in the struggle. But the bishop's interest was considerable ; he could, when he mustered his forces, call upon the heads of seven religious houses, six knights, and twelve gentlemen[8] to appear with their vassals to support Earl Simon.

Early in the war in February, 1263, Worcester was attacked by a baronial force led by Robert Ferrers, earl of Derby. After repeated assaults the city was taken and sacked, the cathedral alone being spared. The Jewry suffered especially, and seems to have been utterly destroyed.[9] And later, on Edward's escape from Ludlow, Worcestershire saw the final and decisive settlement of the struggle. The Royalists seized Worcester and Gloucester and broke down the Severn bridges, thus hoping to cut off Montfort from England. Young Simon de Montfort, who had been besieging Pevensey,[10] on the receipt

1 *Ann. Mon.* (Rolls Ser.), iv. 406–7.
2 Pat. 1 Hen. III. m. 16.
3 *Ann. Mon.* (Rolls Ser.), iv. 407.
4 Pat. 1 Hen. III. m. 10.
5 Ibid. m. 9.
6 *Ann. Mon.* (Rolls Ser.), iv. 409.
7 Ibid. 446.
8 *Giffard Reg.* (Worc. Hist. Soc.), p. xix.
9 *Ann. Mon.* (Rolls Ser.), iv. 448. *Matt. West.* (Rolls Ser.), ii. 486. The mention of the Jewry is interesting as an indication of the considerable trade of the city. Reference to the Worcester Jewry will be found in Pat. 2 Hen. III. m. 3, and to their Archa or Chirograph-chest. Ibid. 1 Edw. I. m. 18, and 4 Edw. I. m. 35, which latter references point to a recovery from the sack of 1263.
10 *Ann. Mon.* (Rolls Ser.), iv. 169. 'Frivolam et inutilam relinquens obsidionem castri Pevenesaye.'

of an urgent message from his father set off to join him, and marched as far as the family castle at Kenilworth. Edward waited at Worcester ready to prevent a junction of the two armies. A woman [1] in male disguise employed as a spy brought him word that the younger de Montfort's men slept outside the castle and kept slack guard. Edward seized the opportunity, left Worcester at night on the eve of St. Peter ad Vincula, and entered Kenilworth at dawn on 2 August. The surprise and rout were complete ; many knights were taken in their beds,[2] others escaped half naked,[3] whilst among the most precious captures were the emblazoned banners of young de Montfort's men. Without delay Edward returned to Worcester to meet the elder de Montfort, who was trying to cross the Severn and join his son. Earl Simon had reached Kempsey, four miles below Worcester, and here by a little known and an unguarded ford on the bishop's land crossed with ease, and that night was entertained by the bishop at his manor-house there.[4] The next day, Monday, 3 August, Earl Simon marched towards Evesham on the way to meet the younger de Montfort, and took possession of the town. Evesham is surrounded on three sides by the River Avon, the ground sloping upward from it along the Alcester road. On Edward's return to Worcester he heard that Earl Simon had crossed the Severn and was marching on Evesham. He set off at once, and on reaching Norton, about three miles from Evesham, left a small picket as a guard on the main road at Chardbury, and marched up the valley to the left into the main Alcester road. At dawn on 4 August mass was said, and Bishop Walter preached to the baronial troops, and gave plenary absolution.[5] This was scarcely done when a large force was seen approaching down the Alcester road. Supposing them to be his son's troops Earl Simon set out to meet them, whilst the enemy encouraged the belief by displaying the banners they had taken at Kenilworth. Word was soon brought that the advancing force was Prince Edward's, as the scout on the abbey tower had detected among the banners displayed the ensigns of the royalist leaders. 'By the arm of St. James,' swore the earl, as he watched the improved discipline of the royal forces, 'they come on skilfully, but it is from me they have learnt it, not from themselves.' He at once recognized that all was lost. To charge uphill and cut their way through superior numbers flushed with their Kenilworth victory was a trial too hard for his ill-disciplined band. The Welsh infantry fled at the first onset, and many were drowned in the Avon, which barred their flight.[6] The barons and their immediate adherents fought desperately, and for two hours kept up the unequal contest. Basset and Despenser, his staunchest supporters, and Henry [7] his eldest son died near Earl Simon, who was at last struck down by a blow from behind. His body was vilely outraged,[8] and the severed head and hands were sent to Maud of Mortimer at Wigmore. As an army the baronial force was exterminated, all its leaders were slain or captured. The royalist victory was decisive and complete.

1 *Walter of Hemingburgh* (Engl. Hist. Soc.), i. 322.

2 *Ann. Mon.* (Rolls Ser.), iv. 170.

3 *Chron. of Melrose*, Gale (1684), i. 231.

4 *Chron. Mon. S. Albani* (Rolls Ser.), 35.

5 *Rob. of Glouc.* (Rolls Ser.), ii. 763.

6 Harl. MS. 542. f. 49 ; cf. *Walter of Hemingburgh* (Engl. Hist. Soc.), i. 324.

7 So *Ann. Mon.* (Rolls Ser.), iv. 174. According to other accounts Henry de Montfort was captured after his father's death and ruthlessly butchered. Guillaume de Nangis, *Vie de St. Louis* (Bouquet), xx. 417.

8 *Rob. of Glouc.* (Rolls Ser.), ii. 765, and de Nangis *ut supra.*

It took some time to pacify the county, partly from the vacillating policy[1] of de Clare and partly from the fact that the whole of the clergy, from the influence of the bishop, were either avowed or secret rebels. When Walter de Cantilupe died not the least of the work done by his successor, Bishop Giffard, was the settlement of the county after the Barons' War.[2] Edward had seen enough of the mischief that might ensue in England from a rebellion in Wales, and on succeeding to the throne set himself to work to reduce Wales to submission. This brought Worcester again into importance, and the king's visits there on his various Welsh expeditions were numerous. One of the most important of these visits was in the autumn of 1278, when he sanctioned by his presence[3] the marriage of Llewellyn, prince of Wales, and Eleanor de Montfort. In spite of this alliance the Welsh troubles continued, and a parliament was held at Worcester in the late spring of 1282 to take measures of repression.[4] Many years later, when Scotland had succeeded Wales as the theatre of war, orders were issued to Miles Pychard and Richard de Brightwell to raise 500 men in Worcester for service in the North, and measures were taken to render the levy effective.[5]

In 1278 began the great lawsuit as to the boundary of Malvern Chase between the earl of Gloucester and Swinfield, bishop of Hereford, in which Bishop Godfrey ultimately became involved. The ground of complaint was an alleged encroachment by the earl on the bishop's manors of Colwall and Eastnor, and the case was taken into the king's court. Both the earl and the bishop had their champions ready to fight and maintain the issue, but the justices sent the case to a jury, who decided in favour of the bishop, and a ditch, still known as the Earl's Ditch, was dug along the crest of the Malvern Hills setting out the lawful boundary. Traces of the ditch still remain and are regarded to this day as fixing the line of the county frontier. In cutting the ditch the earl infringed on the rights of the bishop of Worcester and a long litigation followed, which was at last settled by the earl agreeing to pay to the bishop and his successors two deer and two does yearly.[6]

A visit of the king to Feckenham in 1289 was followed by a general inquiry, held on the eve of Lady Day, into the Worcestershire forest administration. As a result some foresters were charged with unlawful hunting in the forest and imprisoned, and in the spring of the following year bound over to appear and answer at Woodstock.[7] These foresters seem to have been employed by the ecclesiastical authorities, for the Worcester annalist informs us that as there was no other equity than the king's will, the bishop's ransom was taxed at 500 marks and the prior's at 200. In 1297 perambulation was made of the forests of Feckenham and Kinver to put down the enclosures made since the time of Henry III.[8] The result of this was not satisfactory, so in 1299 a fresh perambulation was promised to separate

[1] *Giffard Reg.* (Worc. Hist. Soc.), pp. xvii, xviii.

[2] Giffard completed the fortifications of Hartlebury which had been begun by his predecessors. The licence to crenellate was issued in 1268 (*Giffard Reg.* p. xxviii.). In loyal hands it formed a valuable intermediate post between Worcester and Bridgnorth.

[3] *Ann. Mon.* (Rolls Ser.), iv. 476.

[4] Ibid. 484.

[5] Pat. 29 Edw. I. mm. 10, 14. There were serious complaints both in this and the next reign of the malpractices of recruiting agents who were often willing for valuable consideration to excuse the rich and able-bodied and enlist the poor, the halt, and the maimed. Some notion of the large sums obtained by one Malcolm Musard in Worcestershire will be found in Assize Roll 1038 (P.R.O.), 17 Edw. II. part ii.

[6] *Giffard Reg.* (Worc. Hist. Soc.), Introd. xxxv. and 361. The final agreement was in the year 1290.

[7] *Ann. Mon.* (Rolls Ser.), iv. 501.

[8] Ibid. 536.

the king's forests from the woods of his subjects, and a proclamation made to this effect in English at Worcester during July.[1] The next year Hugh le Despenser, a forest justice, held his court at the Hospital of St. Wulstan in Worcester. The delinquent foresters were tried, found guilty of offences against vert and venison, and fined. The king's order that the Charter of the Forest should be kept in all its details was publicly proclaimed in Worcester, and later in the year the king's justices with the knights and free tenants perambulated Feckenham Forest and fixed its boundaries. The Priors' Grove at Wolverley was also separated from the forest of Kinver.[2] Next year, 1301, the perambulation was confirmed by the king, and published at the castle.[3]

The strain of the Gascon war was felt in Worcestershire as in the rest of the kingdom. Both layman and clerk suffered from the excessive taxation. The protests of the Worcester clergy against the seizure of their wool and leather by the royal agents even reached the stage of a public excommunication, against which the king formally appealed,[4] and in the autumn of 1297 the county demanded seisin of their liberties before they paid the subsidy required.[5] The currency also became scant and depreciated, and a good deal of bad money was in circulation. For example, in August 1300, on the visit of the king's judges to Worcester, two Worcester citizens were brought before them charged with paying for wool and other goods with false coin known as pollards, and heavily fined.[6]

The county did not take much part in the struggles of the first quarter of the fourteenth century. Adam of Orleton,[7] one of the great leaders against the king, had his reward in being translated to the see of Worcester, but his work was mainly confined to the Gloucestershire portion of his diocese. There is little direct evidence, but it is possible, that most of Worcestershire was on the side of the Lords Ordainers in the struggle with Edward II., as one of their number, the 'Black Dog of Ardenne,'[8] the second earl of Warwick, Guy de Beauchamp, had considerable local influence. The insurrection in Wales in 1314 gave Worcester its usual importance as a military base, and that importance continued with the rise in power of the Despensers, who were the great marcher earls and the rivals to the earl of Lancaster. The death at Bannockburn of Gilbert de Clare and the marriage of one of his co-heiresses to the younger Despenser,[9] who thus became a considerable landowner in the shire, as shown by the Despenser arms still to be seen in the windows of some of the parish churches, must have increased the royalist influence in the county. There is, however, not much account of this beyond the occupation of the Severn valley by the royalist forces to prevent the marcher earls joining the earl of Lancaster at Doncaster. The story of the struggle which ended in the fall of the Despensers belongs more to Gloucestershire and Herefordshire than to Worcestershire.

From the death of Edward II. the importance of Worcestershire begins temporarily to decline, partly from the fact that invasion from Wales became less frequent, partly from the fact that the French war carried attention to

1 *Ann. Mon.* (Rolls Ser.), iv. 541.
2 Ibid. 544, 545.
3 Ibid. 548.
4 Ibid. 533. The actual publication, however, seems to have been contrary to the bishop's orders.
5 Ibid. 534.
6 Ibid. 546.
7 *Sede Vacante Reg.* (Worc. Hist. Soc.), pt. iii. p. x.
8 *Thom. of Walsingham* (Rolls Ser.), i. 115.
9 *Dict. Nat. Biog.* xiv. 415.

other matters. The war doubtless had its effect here as in other counties in keeping up a continual drain in men and money.[1] There can be no doubt that either from the war or from the pestilence the population of the county declined. This was not all, there was not merely a decline in population, but estates fell largely into the hands of men who were non-resident in the county. Sir John Beauchamp, of Holt, was with the king at the battle of Crecy, the victory which led Edward to quarter the arms of France, but there is not so much to tell of the county during Edward's reign. It was not until later, when the northern nobles united with the Welsh, that Worcester again became a centre of political interest.

With the accession of Henry IV. Worcester regained something of its old importance; and with one of its landowners, the young Mortimer, a possible claimant to the throne, the county might play an important part in any rebellion. Early in 1401 there were fears of a general Welsh rising; it was noticed that their students at the University had gone home, whilst the Welsh labourers outside the principality were everywhere throwing up their employment.[2] On 3 June, 1401, Henry IV. on his march to Wales came to Evesham and reached Worcester on 8 June; his expedition was not successful, as he could not bring Owen Glendower to a fight.[3] In October he again came to Worcester to muster his force for Wales, but returned to London, after leaving garrisons at various places, without striking any effective blow at the insurgents. In 1402 Glendower captured Sir Edmund Mortimer, the uncle of the young earl of March. When the king refused to permit his ransom, the prisoner made common cause with his captor, married Glendower's daughter,[4] and declared his intention of proclaiming Richard II. if living, and if not, the 'right heir,' the earl of March. A treaty of partition between the earl of Northumberland, Mortimer, and Glendower soon followed,[5] and the Percies rose in arms, but the climax of the struggle belongs to the history of Shropshire. In September, 1403, the king again came to Worcester, for life on the Welsh marches had become almost intolerable for the English settlers,[6] but he was unable to move for want of supplies, and applications to the clergy for help, in spite of the efforts of Archbishop Arundel, met with a miserable response.[7] After putting down the conspiracy of Scrope and Mowbray, and executing the archbishop and earl-marshal in 1405, Henry again devoted himself to Wales, and in September, on a return march to Worcester from a raid in the principality, lost most of his baggage.[8] At Worcester the clergy were assembled in council with a view to raising money, but a renewed proposal to plunder the bishops was, as two years before, indignantly resisted by the primate.[9]

The whole state of the county on the Welsh border during this reign was one of the great causes of grumbling, a continual expense involving repeated

[1] Details as to the constant requisitions of archers and men-at-arms, munitions of war, and money will be found collected from the Records in J. Noake, *Worcester Nuggets*, p. 27 sqq. An entry in Pat. R. 20 Edw. III. m. 26*d.*, informs us that a serious riot had occurred in Worcester not long before, the town bell had been rung to call the commonalty to arms, and the king's justices and their servants maltreated, and some of the latter killed. This would seem to establish the existence of a certain amount of discontent in the city.

[2] *Parl. R.* (Rec. Com.), iii. 457.

[3] Henry IV.'s own impressions as to this rising are contained in a letter from Worcester, printed in Nicolas, *Proc. and Ord. of Privy Council* (Rec. Com.), i. 133.

[4] Adam of Usk, *Chron.* (Royal Soc. of Lit.), p. 75.

[5] Ellis, *Orig. Letters*, 27.

[6] Nicolas, op. cit. ii. 77.

[7] *Ann. Hen. IV.* (Rolls Ser.), 373, 374.

[8] *Eulog. Hist.* (Rolls Ser.), iii. 408; *Ann. Hen. IV.* (Rolls Ser.), 414.

[9] Stubbs, *Const. Hist.* iii. 53.

calls on the freeholders. The history of the county from the death of Henry IV. almost to the end of the Wars of the Roses is not of striking character; the plotting of the Lollards with the Mortimers, if it existed, and the part played by John Oldcastle,[1] are points which are much disputed, and on which there is little real evidence.

The French war of the fifteenth century seems to have only affected Worcestershire in drawing from it men and money, and comparatively few persons of note were contributed by the county to the struggle. It was the last wish of Henry V. that the earl of Warwick, who had become the great county landowner, should be the tutor of his son Henry of Windsor.[2] The course of the intrigues between the royal dukes that ended in the loss of France and the general discontent had nothing to do with the county, and it was not until the duke of York, as the representative of the Mortimers, began to put himself forward as the popular leader, that the county was affected. In the struggle that followed not one of the great battles was fought within its borders, and it was only as a base and as a means of passage that Worcestershire has a part in the story of the Wars of the Roses. On the whole the county was probably Yorkist. Warwick, who had much influence, was one of the leaders of that party, the Mortimers were on the same side, whilst Bourchier, although he was now promoted to the primacy, had been, during his episcopate at Worcester, not unfavourable to the Yorkist cause. The absence of any Lancaster property or influence in the county must have told against the king. The earl of Shrewsbury was however a royalist and died for the king at Northampton. Whether the marches of Wales were included in what was made over to the duke of York in 1460[3] is not quite clear, but the effect of the compromise in that year must have largely consolidated the Yorkist influence in the county and its borders. Their position was still further strengthened by the victory of Mortimer's Cross in 1461.

For the better government of the Welsh marches a jurisdiction was established under Edward IV., which for two centuries had a most important effect on Worcestershire history. Ludlow was the great royal stronghold on the Welsh border and the chief residence, alternating at times with Bewdley, of an officer known later as 'President of the Welsh Marches,' whose duty it was with the members of the council, of which he was president, to keep order in Wales and its borders. Among the counties included under this jurisdiction was Worcestershire. The court enforced its own orders by its messengers, and seems to have proceeded on similar lines to the Privy Council, as if it were a local committee of that body. Started under Edward IV. it gradually became, under the Tudors and Stuarts, an arbitrary and dreaded power in the district.

The final battle in the Wars of the Roses was fought on 4 May, 1478, at Tewkesbury, just outside the county border, and many of the fugitives crossed the Severn into Worcestershire. Legend still points out spots at Bushley, where fugitives, including Queen Margaret herself, found hiding places.[4] Possibly Edward's vengeance on Warwick, whom he judged to be a traitor, was felt by the tenants at Hanley Castle and in the district.

1 His name is traditionally connected with the Nanfans of Birt's Morton Court, in Malvern Chase.

2 Stubbs, *Const. Hist.* iii. 94.

3 *Parl. R.* (Rec. Com.), v. 377, 378.

4 Probably at Payne's Place, Bonnett's End. See Dodeswell, *Hist. of Bushley* (Arch. Society Papers, xxiv. 219).

On 9 April, 1483, Edward IV. died. The most powerful man connected with the county at his death was Henry Stafford, duke of Buckingham, who represented the Plantagenets through Thomas Woodstock, and was married to Katherine Wydeville, sister of the queen. The young King Edward V., who had been for some time residing at Ludlow with Bishop Alcock as President of the Council, passed through Worcestershire to London. On his way he was met by the duke of Gloucester who, as Protector, now invested Buckingham with extraordinary powers in Wales and several English counties, and conferred upon him the offices of Chief Justice and Chamberlain in North and South Wales and of constable of the royal castles in Wales and the marches.[1]

On 26 June Gloucester declared himself king,[2] and was crowned on 6 July. The grants to Buckingham were now confirmed, and he was promised the royal moiety of the Bohun estates.[3] Yet by the autumn the duke, who had hitherto supported Richard, was in open revolt. This may be partially explained by an ambition that could no longer brook the limitations of a subject. He was probably aware that the attempt made by Henry IV. to bar from the throne the descendants of John of Gaunt and Katherine Swynford was legally invalid, but a chance meeting with Lady Stanley, between Worcester and Bridgnorth, reminded him that in his cousin Henry of Richmond was to be found the senior representative of the Beauforts,[4] whilst all the skill and craft of Bishop Morton were employed in the same cause. The evident unpopularity of Richard and the rumoured murder of the young princes may have finally decided him to support the marriage of Henry and Elizabeth, and thus aspire to the position of king-maker. Whilst the headquarters of Buckingham were at Brecon, Richard, who had made a progress through Worcester and thence to the north and through Lincoln, mustered his forces at Leicester. The line of the Severn once more became of supreme importance to both parties. Buckingham collected his men, intending to seize Bewdley and Worcester and march across England. He got as far as Woodbury Hill, overlooking the Severn valley, when he found that all the fords were held for the king by his own distant kinsman, Humphrey Stafford, of Grafton, while an extraordinary October flood, long remembered as the 'Duke of Buckingham's water,' rendered the crossings impassable, even if they had been unguarded. On 23 October a proclamation was issued offering pardon to all but the leader.[5] Buckingham's force gradually melted away and he was obliged to fly in disguise northwards towards Shrewsbury. Before the month was out he was a prisoner, and on the 2 November following, was executed at Salisbury.

The preparations for the invasion of England by the earl of Richmond had been mostly made in Wales, possibly with the connivance of the Council of the Marches. As in Buckingham's rebellion, so at Bosworth Field Sir Humphrey Stafford of Grafton stood loyally by King Richard, and at his master's death fled to sanctuary at Colchester. Concerned in the rising of Lord Lovell he again took sanctuary at Colnham in Berkshire, but his immunity was not allowed by the King's Bench, and, attainted in the first parliament of the new reign, he suffered at Tyburn. Of his extensive estates

[1] Pat. Edw. V. m. 3.
[2] T. More, *Life of Ric. III.* p. 79.
[3] Hall, *Chron.* (Ellis), 38*b*.
[4] *Parl. R.* (Rec. Com.), vi. 245; *Croy. Cont.* in Gale (1684), i. 567.
[5] Rymer, *Foed.* (Rec. Com.) xii. 204.

which thus came into the king's hand, Grafton was given to Sir Gilbert Talbot, with other property in Worcestershire. Land here and elsewhere was also given to John Darell, esquire, of the king's body, and John Pympe, esquire, in consideration of their service and losses.[1]

With the accession of Henry VII. a new era in the county history begins. With the increasing settlement and good order of Wales Worcestershire ceased to be of special importance politically, and the next 160 years furnish the story of her decline into an ordinary English county. Much of the land of the shire now passed into new hands. Not only at his accession, but all through Henry's reign there were constant attainders; one that largely affected the county was that of the earl of Warwick in 1498; a consequence of which was that a set of small men took the place of the large landowners. The new comers were never powerful enough to resist the royal will or the Court of the Marches, so that their existence tended to increase the power of the Crown. Simultaneously with the decrease of power in the lay landlords a decrease occurred in that of the ecclesiastical, the bishops ceased to be resident,[2] and the power that they had possessed as feudal lords departed. Their agents collected their rents but did no more, and what power they had they used for selfish motives. At the same time the small landowners tried to better their position by means of enclosures, and these formed one of the greatest grievances in Worcestershire as everywhere else. Trade increased, and the new owners found that it was profitable to develop the wool market for themselves, while from the trading class successful merchants invested their profits in land. Worcester still retained its position as a centre for the West Midlands, but it became a trading instead of a military centre, and from the accession of Henry VII. to the Civil War it developed into a depôt from which goods were distributed over the Welsh marches and South Wales.

The county of Worcester and the Welsh marches are especially associated with the memory of Prince Arthur, whose birth had been so ardently desired to strengthen the union of the Roses. His marriage by proxy[3] took place near Bewdley after early mass on Whit Sunday, 1499, though the actual marriage was solemnized in the autumn at St. Paul's Cathedral. For too short a time he maintained his court on the marches, and under the guidance of Sir Reginald Bray, a native of the county, and other wise counsellors ruled prudently and well, and is said to have settled an old and bitter feud between the towns of Bewdley and Kidderminster.[4] But in the early spring of 1502 the young prince in whose life so many hopes were centred lay dead at Ludlow. On St. Mark's Day his body was taken to Bewdley. Cold driving rain[5] and the deep mire of the road made it a toilsome and perilous journey. Thence, after a requiem mass on the morrow, the procession passed on to Worcester, where he was laid to rest in the cathedral. Over the tomb his father reared the stately chantry, which still, in spite of ignorant iconoclasm, is one of the chief glories of the church.[6]

[1] *Mat. for Reign of Hen. VII.* (Rolls Ser.), i. 506, and ii. 33.

[2] After 1497 the revenues of the see were devoted to the maintenance of an English political agent at Rome. And for forty years the titular bishops generally residing at Rome were Italians. *Worc. Dioc. Soc. Trans.* (1890), 94.

[3] Rymer, *Foed.* (Rec. Com.), xii. 756, sqq.

[4] Blakeway MS. cited by Burton, *Hist. of Bewdley*, 34.

[5] Leland, *Collectanea*, v. 373.

[6] In the Cathedral Library is a printed Sarum missal. On the binding is stamped the arms of England with a label impaling those of Aragon, possibly one of the few surviving relics of the funeral.

The dissolution of the monasteries did not affect the lay owners so much in this as in other counties. The bishop of Worcester retained most of his lands,[1] and the possessions of the abbot and convent of Westminster passed eventually to the dean and chapter. Bordesley went to the Windsors, Halesowen to the Lyttletons, and Dudley to the Dudleys. Evesham, Pershore, Great and Little Malvern also passed into lay hands, and their estates extended over a considerable area. The power of the Crown was greatly strengthened by the institution of lord-lieutenants in the middle of the sixteenth century. In the cases of counties in the area of the jurisdiction of the Court of the Welsh Marches it became the custom to appoint as lord-lieutenant not a different individual in each county, but the Lord President of the Council of Wales, and this remained the practice till the court was abolished at the end of the seventeenth century, thus greatly enhancing the power of the Crown. The legislation of Henry VIII. provided that Worcestershire was to be under the jurisdiction of the court and that Welshmen were not to purchase lands in Worcestershire.[2] Whatever force was at the disposal of the court for keeping order in Wales was also at its disposal for keeping order in Worcestershire. Thus was formed the nucleus of a royal force to maintain the law beyond what existed in an ordinary English county.

The central government, by its spies and informers, was often able to ascertain more accurately the state of the district than the local justices could do; for instance, in 1551 the Privy Council wrote to the magistrates ordering them to arrest certain coiners who had lately set up a coining house in Worcestershire and report on the matter to the Privy Council.[3] What took place as regards this case of coining went on with regard to other matters as well; the Privy Council continually received information on different matters, and commissioned agents to inquire and report. All through the latter half of the sixteenth century, under the Cecil rule, there was considerable local dissatisfaction which led more than once to consequences that might have been serious. For instance in 1570 the earl of Sussex, the President of the Council of the North, was ordered to send one Price, a lieutenant of Sir Thomas Manners' band, who was charged with exacting the sum of £51 from the poor men of Worcester, that he might return and make satisfaction. The same order was to be taken with Manners himself if he refused to disburse certain moneys and account for armour which he had appropriated.[4] The county also felt and complained of the heavy hand of the Court of the Marches. In 1574, Wylde, the member from the city, moved in the matter. On this the Privy Council wrote[5] to the attorney- and solicitor-general stating that a controversy had arisen to withdraw the city and county of Worcester out of the jurisdiction of the Lord President and Council of the Marches 'by the practyse of one Wylde, who hath ben therto animated by certein lawiers, having subscribed a boke to that effect.' The law officers were required to consider the matter with the Lord President and return to the Privy Council what they thought was the law.

The Privy Council did not stop here. Wylde was arrested by their order and committed to the custody of the knight marshal. He was subse-

[1] But see Stat. 1 Eliz. under which a good deal was taken away by what was called an exchange.
[2] 34 and 35 Henry VIII. c. 26.
[3] *Acts of Privy Council,* ii. 385.
[4] Ibid. vii. 358.
[5] Ibid. viii. 200.

quently bailed on condition that he would do nothing more in the matter of the jurisdiction of the Council of the Marches, but would submit to such orders as the Privy Council might make.[1] But even then Wylde was not out of his trouble, as the Court of the Marches proposed to have him arrested for the contempt shown of them by the action he had taken. The Privy Council however stepped in, sent for the Lord President of the Marches, and ordered him not to molest Robert Wylde by attachment or otherwise, but to suffer him to remain at Worcester without any trouble or molestation till their lordships had taken such order as they deemed advisable.[2] The matter ended in the jurisdiction of the court being fully maintained. The court was far too useful a body for the Privy Council to consent to any interference with it. How extensive was its jurisdiction will be seen from the action of the Privy Council on a petition in 1575[3] from Upton-on-Severn that the bridge over the Severn had lately decayed and the re-edifying of the same was very necessary. Accordingly the Privy Council wrote to the Council of the Marches directing them to order the justices of the peace in the shires under their jurisdiction to cause a collection to be made in each shire. The Privy Council later hit upon a method that they thought would meet the justice of the case. There was a payment of £40 a year 'which goeth out of the church of Worcester,' this together with fines imposed on careless parsons, they wrote to the Council of Wales, had better be used for 'the finishing that worke,' whereby 'they may repaire both the bridge and the faltes of the clergie.'[4]

Two years later, in 1577, the lawlessness of the marchmen was manifested in an assault on Anthony Powell, a messenger of the Privy Council, who was intercepted near Worcester by the friends and servants of Thomas Bury of Overwick and robbed of despatches which he was carrying to the President of the Marches. In the course of the affray one of the assailants received his death wound. Bury, by means of his friends, procured an inquest to be empanelled within the city of Worcester, and the jury brought in a verdict of wilful murder against the messenger and his companions. On hearing of this the Privy Council on the last day of the year gave orders that the assailants should be apprehended and required to furnish bonds or be committed with a view to further proceedings, and charged the sheriff and justices of the county to take measures for an open and impartial inquiry,[5] and to inform the Lords of the Council of the verdict.

John Russell, the sheriff of Worcestershire in 1578, was required by the Court of the Marches to appear before them, but this he declined to do, alleging that he had to attend the Privy Council. The Council of the Marches complained of his conduct to the Privy Council, who ordered him to attend the Court of the Marches, but wrote to the president directing that he should be discharged after some grave admonition without any further punishment,[6] 'albeit they liked not (in respect of the credit of the Court) his excuse made in that sort.'

It is difficult to say how far the Council of the Marches or the Privy Council possessed secret information as to the political action of the Catholics and their connexion with the conspiracies of the time, or how far their pro-

[1] *Acts of Privy Council,* viii. 204.
[2] Ibid. viii. 207.
[3] Ibid. ix. 17.
[4] Ibid. ix. 103.
[5] Ibid. x. 128.
[6] Ibid. x. 217.

ceedings, especially those during Whitgift's tenure of the see of Worcester, were the result of religious zeal. Whatever was the real reason, about 1580 the records of the Privy Council show increased activity against recusancy. In 1580 Thomas Throckmorton of Coughton, Ralph Sheldon of Beoley, and John Talbot of Grafton, were sent for to London; and from this date onwards the law was not allowed to remain a dead letter.[1] In 1581[2] the Privy Council sent to the Custos Rotulorum, Sir John Littleton, saying that as they had been informed that sundry persons excommunicated and refusing to go to church had been indicted, he was required to see that they should be proceeded against according to law, 'having also regard that other like offenders be likewise proceeded against in like manner without any favour or partiality.' In 1582 the Privy Council directed the bishops of all dioceses to return certificates of all persons who had been convicted and who did not conform;[3] and in June, 1582, directed the sheriffs and justices to take general action against recusants.[4] In 1586 the Privy Council ordered the sheriffs of the various counties to consider what sum could be raised by rates levied on the lands of recusants.[5]

In the crisis of 1588 urgent steps were taken, and in April of that year the President of the Council of the Marches was called on to make a new muster in the county. This seems to have brought out the fact that there was a shortness of weapons to arm the muster, and to supply this want the president was ordered to get arms and armour from the recusants. On 27 June orders were issued for the necessary mobilization should occasion arise,[6] which were followed on 28 July by a further order that the county should send up 400 men by 9 August.[7] A week before the date assigned, however, the order was countermanded and the 400 men were sent back,[8] and on 6 October warrants were directed by the Privy Council to the bishop of Worcester directing him to discharge the beacon watchers.[9]

The efforts of the Government to raise money to meet the expenditure to resist the invasion seem to have been well met by the city of Worcester, which had already shown its loyalty to the queen by a magnificent reception during her progress of 1575. Lord Pembroke, the President of the Welsh Marches, had directed them to raise a sum of £150. They not only raised the required amount but increased it to £200. In consequence of 'which dutyfull declaracion of their goodwill' the Privy Council informed Lord Pembroke that the city was to be spared from further assessment to be laid upon them by him.[10]

The zeal of the city was not universally copied in the county; William Dethicke of Obden declined to pay the loan to Her Majesty; he was accordingly brought before the Council and ordered not to depart without leave.[11] Edward Pitwaye of Shipton-on-Stour, who refused to answer for a sum of money required of him by privy seal, was also brought before the Council,[12] but upon persuading the Council that but for the inability of his estates he would have been willing to pay, he was discharged.

The city of Worcester had received a charter from the queen in 1558 confirming all previous charters and granting new privileges. It was probably

[1] *Acts of Privy Council,* xii. 166.
[2] Ibid. xiii. 146.
[3] Ibid. xiii. 376.
[4] Ibid. xiii. 451.
[5] Ibid. xiv. 15.
[6] Ibid. xvi. 138.
[7] Ibid. xvi. 195.
[8] Ibid. xvi. 215.
[9] Ibid. xvi. 303.
[10] Ibid. xvii. 136.
[11] Ibid. xvii. 144.
[12] Ibid. xviii. 210, 236.

on the strength of this grant that in 1590 the corporation put forward a claim to the Privy Council that they ought not to be mustered in the county outside the city limits. Whether the recent contributions of the town had softened the hearts of the Council is not clear, but on 7 February, 1590, they wrote to the earl of Pembroke, as President of the Marches, desiring him that whenever he should think fit to muster the forces of the city they should not be compelled to be mustered and trained out of their precincts and jurisdiction, but that his deputy-lieutenant or some of the justices of the peace of the county should be appointed to repair to the said city to take the view and muster of foot soldiers and horse according to the privilege.[1]

Although the danger of invasion had passed, demands were still made on the county for providing men and supplies for defence. On 26 September, 1589, the earl of Pembroke was ordered by the Council to have 400 men ready for service in Ireland, of which Worcestershire was to send a hundred.[2] In January, 1590, a further contingent of 200 men, to be got ready to march to Bristol to meet the Spanish invasion of Ireland.[3] Late in the same month another hundred were required,[4] and the mayor of Bristol was ordered on 15 February to have sufficient 'barkes and vessels' to convey them to Waterford, and the persons who had the conduct of the men were to be allowed 4*s.* for every coat and £18 8*s.* for conduct money, being at the rate of ½*d.* a mile for each mile they should cover to Bristol and eight days' pay for victual at 8*d.* a man per day.[5] Captain Tanner, who commanded the Worcester company, was empowered by the Privy Council to impress a surgeon and a drum.[6] On 1 March, 1590, the sheriff of Worcestershire was ordered to find eighty beasts as fresh meat for the navy.[7] On 15 March another hundred men were to be levied in the county and placed under the orders of Captain York and conducted by Lieutenant Mortimer,[8] for embarkation to Waterford[9] by the last day of March, 1589. This liability for Irish service, which the county shared with the others under the jurisdiction of the Welsh Marches, must have been a severe drain to the resources of the county. The more so as it was not merely that the county lost the labour of so many men, it was also rated for the support of the men it sent. In 1601 there was a complaint to the Sessions that five parishes which had sent fifty men to Ireland were rated at £3.[10]

So far as Worcestershire went the change of dynasty from Tudor to Stuart brought about very little change in the county administration. The attempt of certain Catholic conspirators to destroy James and his government had the sympathy and even the actual aid of some of the gentry of the shire. The ruinous fines for recusancy, even more than the occasional butchery of their priests, kept the Catholics in a constant state of unrest. There is a significant deposition preserved among the Sessions Papers that one John Hunt, the servant of Edward Harriotts, of Cookhill, had sworn by God that 'there would be knocking very shortly,' and that he would fight for his life before he went to church.[11] On the Herefordshire border, in the summer of 1605, armed recusants had resisted the sheriff and his officers.[12] The great Catholic families

1 *Acts of Privy Council,* xviii. 355.
2 Ibid. xviii. 142.
3 Ibid. xviii. 294.
4 Ibid. xviii. 329.
5 Ibid. xviii. 345.
6 Ibid. xviii. 350.
7 Ibid. xviii. 390.
8 Ibid. xviii. 420.
9 Ibid. xviii. 437.
10 *Sess. R.* (Worc. Hist. Soc.), p. 44.
11 Ibid. 67, 2 Aug. 1604.
12 *Cal. S.P. Dom.* Jas. I. p. 225.

of Worcestershire were the Winters of Huddington, the Sheldons of Beoley, the Talbots of Salwarpe, and the Habingtons of Hindlip. Of these the Winters and the Habingtons were certainly implicated. Winter paid with his life for his share in it. The Sheldons do not appear to have been involved, and the Talbots were only suspected from their family connexion with the Winters. As far back as 1580 John Talbot of Grafton had been sent up to the Privy Council charged with recusancy,[1] and had been made to reside with the dean of Westminster,[2] in order that the dean might confer with him and reduce him to conformity. The dean's labours do not appear to have been very successful, for Talbot did not conform. At the time of the Armada he was still in custody, but was ordered to provide for two demi-lances and three light horses.[3] In 1589 Talbot petitioned the Council that as he was suffering badly from the stone he might be allowed to enjoy the liberty of going six miles from his house in Clerkenwell, where he then by order resided, so that by exercising his corpulent body and receiving the wholesomeness of the air he might be better restored to his former health. This was allowed on condition that he avoided 'publicke places of assemblie of people as Paules Church and Westminster Hall,'[4] and later in the year he was permitted to make a journey to Worcestershire to despatch his business.[5] He was also allowed to sell all his armour remaining in Mr. Littleton's hands, and to dispose of what remained unsold.

After the discovery of the plot the conspirators reached Huddington, Winter's house, and thence crossed to Holbeach, in Staffordshire, a house of Stephen Littleton's, on their way seizing armour for their use at Hewell Grange, which belonged to Lord Windsor.[6] An attempt to get aid from Talbot of Grafton failed. He drove the messengers from his presence. Sir Richard Walsh, the sheriff of Worcester, had followed the rebels, and in the morning of 8 November his men began firing into the house at Holbeach. The two Wrights and Catesby were shot dead, Percy mortally wounded, Winter and Rokewood disabled and captured with Grant, Morgan, and a few others.[7] Both the Winters and their accomplices were executed for the plot, and the full sentence for treason was carried out. The house at Huddington still remains. On one of the walks in the garden by the moat local legend has it that Winter is still at times to be seen headless, bowelless, limbless, a visible witness to the methods of the English law in its sentences on traitors.

It was not until the January of the following year that a proclamation was issued for the arrest of the priests whose names had been connected with the plot. Gerard and Greenway escaped, Garnett had been at Coughton until the December previous, but had then moved to Hindlip, at the invitation of Oldcorne, Habington's chaplain. But the Council had information that Garnett was hid somewhere in the county, and in 1606 sent to Sir Thomas Bromley, the new sheriff, most peremptory orders to take him. The sheriff was to search Hindlip House most strictly, to pull down wainscots, bore the ground, drill the boards and chimney corners, examine the roofs, and search out concealed hiding-places. Bromley went to Hindlip, and under great difficulties carried out his mission. Mr. Habington and all his house-

[1] *Acts of Privy Council*, xii. 166. [2] Ibid. 169. [3] Ibid. xv. 394.
[4] Ibid. xvii. 198. [5] Ibid. xviii. 9.
[6] Ex. of W. Ellis, cited by Gardiner, *Hist.* i. 261.
[7] Add. MSS. 5459. T. Lawley to Salisbury, Nov. 14.

hold denied all knowledge of any priests. Bromley had given up all hopes of finding any, when two men crept from a secret place and surrendered through hunger and cold. They proved to be really Owen and Chambers, the servants of the priests. This was on 23 January, 1607. A week later, on the 30th, Bromley wrote that he had taken Garnett and Hall (Oldcorne) and conveyed them to his house (Holt Castle) to restore their strength for the journey to London, and he gives particulars of the other prisoners he made in what he calls 'this wearisome action.' In the May following Garnett was executed at Tyburn. Oldcorne, who had been sent back to Worcester, was there convicted and suffered death. Habington, though sentenced, was pardoned through the influence of powerful friends, confined to the county, and spent his time writing its history.

The old standing grievance of the jurisdiction of the Court of the Welsh Marches was again raised during the reign of James. It formed a subject of complaint that the Court of the Marches was in the habit of practically staying proceedings before the Court of Quarter Sessions and transferring the cases to themselves. It is said the Court of the Marches went even further, and heard cases that had already been decided by the ordinary courts of the land.[1] An attempt was again made in 1614 to get Worcestershire excluded from the Council's jurisdiction. Like the previous one it failed. The justices were, however, very grateful to Sir Herbert Croft, a Herefordshire man, who assisted in the attempt, and wrote thanking him for his endeavours to procure the exemption of Worcestershire from the Council of Wales, which the king had partially granted, and urging him to press for a total exemption.[2]

Another grievance that was much felt under the Stuarts was that of purveyance. The county had like all others to provide a certain quantity of food, nominally for the supply of the king's table. This was often compounded for by a money payment. In 1610 it was stated that Thomas Grove, who had contracted to satisfy the obligations of the county as regards purveyance, could not do it at the sum allowed. An ox cost from £10 to £10 10*s*., which was far above the sum the county granted.[3] The Worcestershire amount seems to have been 20 fat oxen, 20 fat muttons, 20 stirks, and 150 lambs.[4] The allusions to purveyance in the Sessions Rolls and elsewhere would suggest that it was found to be a very real burden on the county.

Military service in the county was not popular, and when they could people avoided attending the muster. Thomas Boys was ordered to attend; but upon his failure to appear he was bound over to perform such service as he should be commanded.[5] There was always a difficulty in getting the money to make the necessary payments for the muster. One John Hide, who owned a corn mill at Acton Beauchamp, refused to pay his rate for match and powder for training soldiers, and for the muster-master's pension. The other parishioners petitioned for an order to compel him to do so.[6]

Except these 'domestic details' there is little in the history of the reign of James I. to be told. The great point is that the policy of the government was piling up a number of petty grievances, each insignificant in itself, but each tending to make it unpopular, and the stress of the regu-

[1] *Sess. R.* (Worc. Hist. Soc.), p. ccxxix.
[2] *Cal. S.P. Dom.* 1614, p. 262.
[3] *Sess. R.* (Worc. Hist. Soc.), p. 154.
[4] Ibid. civ. 659.
[5] Ibid. p. 33.
[6] Ibid. p. 461.

lations fell not on the upper class, but on the lower middle classes and the yeomanry, in fact, on the very men who made up the parliament armies.

Charles continued his father's policy. In 1626 the idea of a forced loan was taken up, and commissioners were appointed, whose duty it was, first to lend themselves, and then to get other persons to do so. Athough there was a good deal of opposition, yet the loan met with some success. To get in arrears, and to quicken the commissioners, a letter was sent to those counties which had not paid in April, 1627. One of these was Worcestershire. The letter ordering the justices in sessions to get in the arrears is still among the sessions papers.[1] Early in the reign of Charles attention was again directed to the question of purveyance. The county was behindhand with its payments, and a letter was sent to the justices telling them they were in arrears for composition money due for His Majesty's household provisions.[2]

The financial necessities of Charles made him have recourse to various expedients to raise money. Among them was the sale of his forestal rights, two of the forests affected being Malvern Chase and Feckenham. The king's rights in Malvern Chase were purchased by Sir Cornelius Vermuyden for £5,000.[3] As early as October, 1627, Sir Miles Fleetwood had been engaged on the disafforestation of Feckenham, with a view to the improvement of the king's revenue.[4] The commoners in the forest seem to have suffered by the changes introduced, and there was a considerable amount of rioting and armed resistance to the enclosures made by the king's commissioners.[5]

There does not appear to have been any very special incident in the county history during the years of Charles's personal government. The county paid its ship-money, if not without a murmur, at least fairly well. The return for 1637 shows that out of the £3,500 assessed on the county and city £3,242 was collected and paid; the arrears for the county were only 35*s*., the rest was payable by the city.[6] One of the judges who in Hampden's case gave judgment for the Crown in favour of the legality of ship-money, Mr. Justice Berkeley, was a Worcestershire man, and possibly the knowledge that he held it to be legal may have had its weight in the county. Berkeley, however, fell upon evil times. His judgment in Hampden's case was greatly resented by the House of Commons. In 1641 he was in consequence of it impeached for high treason, arrested while he was sitting in court, and kept in prison until October. In September, 1642, the House of Lords convicted him, sentenced him to pay a fine of £20,000, and to be incapable of holding any office. But as parliament was pressed for money, he was let off on paying half. At the battle of Worcester in 1651 his house was burnt, and he had, until his death in 1656, to live in the stables.[7] Of all the Worcestershire royalists probably Berkeley received the harshest treatment.

With the Long Parliament complaints as to the government arose. The two members for the county were Sergeant Wylde and Humphrey Salway, and the first thing the county took up was the old subject of the Court of the Marches of Wales. All the old grievances are set out, and two are especially dwelt upon, that the court were judges both of fact and of law, and

[1] *Sess. R.* (Worc. Hist. Soc.), p. 432.
[2] Ibid. p. 397.
[3] *Cal. S. P. Dom.* 1630, p. 353.
[4] Ibid. 1627, p. 372.
[5] Ibid. 1632, pp. 289, 342, 424.
[6] Phillipps, MSS. cited in *Introd. to Sess. R.* (Worc. Hist. Soc.), p. clv.
[7] Foss, *Judges*, vi. 256.

so deprived the people of their birthright, trial by jury, and that proceedings before the Court of the Marches were no bar to proceedings in the ordinary courts of the land, and frequently persons were punished twice for the same offence.[1]

It 1642 it was clear that war would break out, and both sides took steps to raise men. The king issued the usual Commission of Array, and there being no resident lord-lieutenant, the commission was directed to certain gentry named in it. One of the most active was Sherrington Talbot of Salwarpe, who did his utmost to levy a force for the king. Sergeant Wylde, the member for the county, worked against him, and tried either to prevent any men being raised, or if they were, to get them officered by parliamentarians. To some extent Wylde was successful, his great achievement being that he got the magazine which contained the arms and accoutrements for the men when raised placed at Droitwich, a place which was under his direct influence. One point which raised a storm was the payment of the muster-master. The earl of Bridgwater, who was Lord President of the Marches, and so lieutenant of the county, tried to make the counties pay.[2] There is no record of what was done in Worcestershire, but in Shropshire the payment was resisted, and parliament declared the taking of it was extortion.

It is difficult to say what was the precise attitude of the county as a whole at this crisis. It is always said that it was conspicuously loyal, and there is some evidence to bear this out. Doubtless the majority of the magistrates were for the king, and as far as their local influence went probably the loyalty extended, but there was also a strong parliamentary minority, especially in the towns. The strongest evidence of the county loyalty is two presentments of the grand jury, one in 1642, and one in 1643, both, unfortunately, only fragments, which point to the fact that considerable supplies in money were raised for the king. The former speaks of 'payment of the money unto Colonel Sandys, all which we have in the . . . . of His Majesty's Commissioners appointed for the safety of the county of Worcester.'[3] Colonel Sandys of Ombersley was a strong royalist, and during part of the war acted as governor of Worcester. This payment to him therefore shows that the money in the hands of the commission, whatever might be its amount, was to be used for the king's purposes. The other document made in April 1643,[4] is also imperfect, but, fortunately, more of it has survived. From its contents it appears that in January, 1643, the sessions ordered £3,000 a month to be raised and paid monthly towards the payment of His Majesty's forces sent and raised for the defence of the county of Worcester. In the autumn of 1642, on the retreat of the earl of Essex from Worcester, the city was occupied by Sir William Russell for the king, and remained a royal garrison until it surrendered in July, 1646, at the end of the Civil War. The question early arose how the garrison was to be paid, and this document doubtless gives the answer, showing clearly enough that the grand jury of the county were resolved that Worcestershire should loyally and substantially support the king's cause. The order directs that the money was to be levied according to the assessment of the sum which had been raised to put down the Irish rebellion, and is also interesting for another reason, since it states that

[1] *Sess. R.* (Worc. Hist. Soc.), i. 684.
[2] Rushworth, *Hist. Coll.* iv. 281.
[3] *Sess. R.* (Worc. Hist. Soc.), 700.
[4] Ibid. 710.

the county ought to be free from other levies and from troops living at free quarters, showing that even at the outbreak of the war the licence which the German officers in the royalist ranks allowed, was felt as a grievance by the farmers and yeomen, a licence which ultimately led to the formation of the clubmen, and worked much disadvantage to the royalist cause.

It is difficult to give an exact idea of the pressure of the monthly contribution, but it may be put in this way: the county paid every month something less than what it had been asked to pay each year for ship-money, and every two months more than the whole contribution towards putting down the Irish rebellion.

On 22 August, 1642, Charles raised his standard at Nottingham.[1] He at once determined to march westward to join the troops that were being raised for him in South Wales. The exact point he was to make for was not settled—Chester, Shrewsbury, or Worcester. A consultation with one of the great Worcestershire royalists, Sir Thomas Lyttelton, led him to select Shrewsbury.[2] Marching parallel to the king was Rupert with the cavalry. Essex was at Northampton with orders to keep between the royal army and London, and to cut off the king from South Wales as far as possible. To carry this out Essex marched westward to Stratford-on-Avon and thence to Pershore. Such was the enthusiasm in the parliamentary ranks that one regiment ran shouting for two miles together and crying 'To Worcester, to Worcester,' and entreated their officers to march all night to get at the enemy.[3]

Before starting on his march Charles ordered a regiment of horse to Oxford to bring off some money that had been sent there for him, together with plate from the colleges and such recruits as could be enlisted. Byron, who was in command, carried out his instructions, and with a valuable convoy marched from Oxford to Worcester on his way to Shrewsbury. Hearing of Essex's advance, the king ordered Rupert to reinforce Byron and bring in the convoy, and Essex being informed of Byron's arrival at Worcester, allowed some of his cavalry under Col. Fiennes to march there in advance of his main body, and endeavour either to capture the convoy, or at least to get between Worcester and Shrewsbury so as to cut Byron off from his objective. Fiennes set off, reached Worcester early on 22 September and made a demonstration before it, then drawing off he crossed the Severn, placing himself in a position at Powick so that he could observe Essex's march and move into the Shrewsbury road to cut off Byron as soon as Essex marching from Pershore reached Worcester. Next day, the 23rd, Fiennes was told that Byron was starting for Shrewsbury; he at once marched to intercept him, and riding up a narrow lane that led into an open field at Wick, to his surprise found Rupert, who had marched from Bewdley to relieve Byron, with a considerable number of horse. As soon as Fiennes' men began to emerge from the lane Rupert charged them, they turned back into the lane, which soon became choked with men and horses. In an instant all was confusion and Rupert's troopers had an easy victory, driving back Fiennes down the lane, over the bridge, to the village of Powick. So great was the terror of the fugitives that they fled nine miles and more to Pershore, where meeting Essex's bodyguard of 100 picked men, they so discouraged them that they also turned and fled.[4] Rupert having routed

[1] Clarendon, *Hist.* ii. 290.
[2] Nash, *Coll. for Hist. of Worc.* i. 499.
[3] Wharton's letter, 26 Sept. 1642, *Arch.* xxxv. 324.
[4] Ludlow's *Memoirs*, 18.

Fiennes went back to Worcester, collected his men, and marched off that evening with Byron and the convoy to Tenbury. It arrived a day or two after at Shrewsbury in safety. This fight, known as the battle of Powick Bridge or Wick Field, was the first serious fight in the war, and established the superiority of the king's cavalry.[1] In spite of this skirmish, the parliamentary men were in stronger force, and on 23 September Rupert and Byron evacuated Worcester, which was at once occupied by Essex. There was some skirmishing round the north-western border of the county from Bewdley to Stourbridge during the next month. Charles was collecting men at Shrewsbury, and the royalist horse, who were often quartered at Bridgnorth, made frequent forays into Worcestershire, but no fighting of importance took place. On 15 October Charles started on his march for London, Essex left Worcester on 19 October to intercept him; on 23 October Edgehill was fought. No further contest of importance took place during the rest of the year in Worcestershire. The parliamentary troops abandoned Worcester, on which Sir William Russell took possession of it for the king, and it was held by the royalists until July, 1646.

In 1643 there was a good deal of fighting in the county. The king appointed Prince Maurice to the command of the forces within its limits. Early in April Maurice took over his command, and at once tried to check the movement of Sir William Waller, who was then at Gloucester. Crossing the Severn by Upton Bridge a series of manœuvres followed, of which on the whole Maurice had the best. Waller, however, determined if possible to keep Maurice to the west of the Severn, and for this purpose he occupied Tewkesbury in force, sending a detachment to hold the bridge at Upton, the only place where Maurice could recross the river. On Maurice's appearance the detachment retired; they were followed by the royalists, and a fight took place at Ripple between Upton and Tewkesbury. As at Powick, so here the parliamentary men could not stand up against the royalist cavalry, who rode them down, defeating and dispersing them. Having made good his passage over the Severn Maurice retired to Oxford.

About the same time Rupert was sent to recapture Lichfield, and ordered on his way to give the people of Birmingham a lesson for their disloyalty. On his march from Henley-in-Arden to Birmingham, Rupert with a considerable force found his passage barred at Camp Hill, in the extreme north-east of the county just outside Birmingham, by the townsmen and some few troops under the command of Captain Greaves of King's Norton. Any resistance to Rupert's attack was hopeless, his superiority in numbers being so overwhelming, but the Birmingham men determined to fight. They had thrown up some earthworks, behind which they stood and repulsed at least two direct attacks of the royalists. Rupert thereupon extended his troops on both flanks, who circling round took the Birmingham men in the rear while he himself attacked them in front. On this they turned and fled, Rupert following them into the town. The place was plundered and several houses fired, the damage being estimated at more than 20,000 pounds.[2]

Prince Maurice having drawn off his troops, Waller determined to try what a sudden attack on Worcester would do. He marched from Gloucester

[1] Cf. Letter of Falkland to Cumberland, 7 October, cited by Gardiner, *Civil War*, i. 31.

[2] Warburton, *Memoirs of Prince Rupert*, ii. 151.

on the night of 28 May, 1643, and attacked the town ; it was well defended, and although Waller took one or two positions near the walls on the outside which enabled him to place his guns advantageously, he could effect no lodgment, whilst the assailants lost heavily in a successful sally by the royalist horse. On the approach of a relieving force from Oxford, Waller relinquished the attack and retreated to Gloucester.[1]

The rest of the fighting during the year was mainly outside the county. In July Wilmot routed Waller at Roundaway Down ; this was followed by the surrender of Bristol to Rupert and the royalist siege of Gloucester. On Essex relieving the place in September, Charles and the royalist army retreated to Evesham, expecting that Essex would follow them.[2] He came, however, no further than Tewkesbury, setting off thence across the hills for London. Rupert and Charles marched to intercept him and instead of the battle taking place in Worcestershire it was fought in Berkshire, the first battle of Newbury.

In 1644 there was some fighting of a desultory nature on the south-west side of the county. Massey, the governor of Gloucester, was continually making raids from Gloucester along the line of what is now the Gloucester and Ledbury railway. Encounters were common, the most important being the battle of Redmarley. Massey had marched out to attack the royalists who were stationed near that place. Mynne, who commanded them, expected to be joined by some reinforcements from Worcester, but Massey attacked him in the early morning before the Worcester men arrived and drove him from his position. While he was trying to check Massey's advance he was killed, and his force utterly routed ; but when the Worcester reinforcements joined the fugitives Massey thought it prudent to retire.[3]

In May the parliamentary armies under Essex and Waller nearly surrounded Oxford, which had they done, Charles would in all probability have been captured. He, however, managed with a few troops to march between the two armies and to set off for Worcestershire. On the morning of 5 June he was at Burton-on-the-Water in Gloucestershire with some 6,000 men.[4] A great dispute arose between Essex and Waller as to which of them should follow him. Essex ordered Waller to do it, and Waller was obliged to obey, but he did it with a bad grace, and failed to pursue Charles with any rapidity. The king gained time, and for him time meant reinforcements. Charles reached Evesham and passed on to Pershore, breaking down the bridge over the Avon, a proceeding which, owing to hurry or mismanagement, cost him some eighty men, and thence reached Worcester,[5] where he remained a few days. While there he heard that Lord Denbigh was vigorously besieging Dudley castle, so he sent Wilmot to raise the siege. Wilmot made a furious attack on the besieging force and was nearly successful, but in the end retreated.[6] Charles had resolved to await Waller at Worcester, but on 9 June Sudeley castle surrendered to the parliamentary general and three days after the king advanced further up the Severn to Bewdley.[7] Waller followed him to Droitwich and Bromsgrove, but did not attack, on the ground that his

[1] Townsend MS. Nash, *Coll. for Hist. of Worc.* Supt. 87.

[2] *Engl. Hist. Rev.* xiii. 724.

[3] *Bibliotheca Gloucestrensis*, xciv.

[4] *Mem. of Col. John Birch*, p. 84 note.

[5] *Perfect Diurnal*, 10–17 June, 1644.

[6] Symond's *Diary* (Camden Soc.), 8.

[7] Warburton, *Memoirs of Prince Rupert*, ii. 417.

force was not strong enough. The king made a feint of advancing to Shrewsbury and Ludlow, then turning with his cavalry reached Worcester, sending his foot down the Severn,[1] and thence retired by Evesham[2] towards his headquarters. Waller, who had pressed beyond the royal army to prevent a junction with Prince Rupert was outmanœuvred, but turned and followed. After the battle of Cropredy Bridge and Waller's consequent retreat, Charles again marched to Evesham, where he stayed, and afterwards joined the force that was besieging Tewkesbury, but Massey threw in supplies and reinforcements, and ultimately the siege was raised.

Another incident[3] of 1644 should be mentioned. Sir Thomas Lyttelton as governor held Bewdley for the king. One of the local parliamentary leaders was a Colonel Fox, 'Tinker' Fox the royalists called him, from his alleged business, whose headquarters were at Edgbaston Hall just over the Warwickshire boundary. From this place he made raids into Worcestershire, planting two garrisons, one at Stourton castle and another at Hawkesley, the home of the Middlemores, a royalist Catholic family. While here he conceived the design of surprising the royalist garrison at Bewdley, and carrying the governor away prisoner. With a party of under 100 men he rode into the town, overpowered all resistance, took the governor from his bed and carried him off, finally sending him for safe custody to the Tower.

In the closing days of May 1645 Massey, the governor of Gloucester, as a last service in the district where he had done so much, marched up the Avon valley from Tewkesbury and stormed Evesham, thus cutting the line of communication between Oxford and Worcester. A little later Charles with his army marched into Worcestershire, staying at Inkberrow and Droitwich, while Prince Rupert reached Bromsgrove, marching thence to besiege Hawkesley House, held by Fox for the Parliament.[4] The royalist army then moved on into Staffordshire and continued the march which ended at Naseby. Charles' retreat from Naseby led him past Lichfield to Kidderminster, where the register records the burial of 'one of the wounded in the battle in Leicestershire,' and on to Bewdley, where the king remained two days,[5] thence to Hereford and South Wales to endeavour to raise a further army. Meanwhile the Scotch army advanced southwards to Alcester, it was said, on their way to Worcester, but turning aside they went to Droitwich, crossed the Severn at Bewdley, and marched on to besiege Hereford. Their sojourn in Worcestershire is of importance, as it seems probable that the shortness of supplies led them to plunder, and their plundering obtained for them great discredit, so much so that when a Scotch army came to the county six years later, the country people would have nothing to do with them; the remembrance of 1645 had utterly disgusted Worcestershire with the Scots.

Charles returned to Oxford, and having collected some troops marched again to Worcester on his way to raise the siege of Hereford. He stayed a day or two at Worcester, and then by way of Bromyard reached Hereford, the Scots on the retreat from Hereford crossed the Severn at Gloucester and marched through Evesham to Stratford-on-Avon. In 1646, even after the communications of the western army with Oxford had been severed,

[1] Symond's *Diary* (Camden Soc.), 14.

[2] Evesham, which had heartily welcomed Waller, was fined £200 and 1,000 pairs of shoes. Ibid.

[3] Vicar's *God's Ark* (1646), p. 217.

[4] Symond's *Diary* (Camden Soc.), 167.

[5] Burton, *Hist. of Bewdley*, 40.

Charles hoped to rally enough troops to unite with the French auxiliaries whose help he still expected,[1] and Sir Jacob Astley collected such remains of the royalist force as he could from various garrisons, and marched with them through Worcestershire towards Oxford. He was, however, met at Donnington, near Stow-on-the-Wold, by the parliamentary troops, where his men were defeated and dispersed, and he himself made prisoner.[2] Charles left Oxford at the end of April and gave himself up to the Scots. From their camp at Newark he wrote directions to the commanders of the different garrisons to surrender their forts to the Parliament. Acting on these instructions Colonel Leveson surrendered Dudley castle, Colonel Sandys Hartlebury castle. Worcester, however, refused to surrender and was besieged, from May until July, being one of the last towns that held out for the king. Scarcity both of ammunition and food, and the utter hopelessness of further resistance, appear to have been the reasons that led the royalists to surrender. The articles for the capitulation of Worcester included also the delivery to the Parliament of Strensham, Sir William Russell's seat, whilst Madresfield had already been precipitately, if not treacherously,[3] yielded during the investment of the city. With the surrender of these garrisons ended the first civil war in Worcestershire.

The county had suffered very severely. It was said, with what truth is uncertain, that the injury done to roads and bridges was at least £50,000, an enormous sum if the then value of money is considered. But the injury to the public was little to what private[4] persons suffered, mainly by the repeated plunderings of both sides. So much was this felt that armed bands of farmers and labourers in the last years of the war resisted attempts to carry off cattle or fodder. These men, calling themselves 'Club men,' were commanded by Edward Dineley, and on one occasion went so far as to attack Rupert and Maurice when on their march to Oxford.[5]

Although the county had suffered much from the war, a strong royalist feeling still prevailed among a certain class, and in the series of plots that took place from the time the Scots handed the king over to the Parliament to the time of his execution, there was hardly a day on which some royalist scheming was not going on. A plot formed by the officers of the Gloucester garrison and others against the Parliament had its headquarters at Broadway.[6] Another plot to raise men to march to the relief of Colchester was carried on by the celebrated Colonel Dudley. It ended in his imprisonment and condemnation to death, but he afterwards escaped.[7] Probably Worcestershire had had enough of war and was not anxious for further fighting, but when Charles II. started on his southward march after the skirmish at Warrington, it became necessary to decide the most suitable point to make for. As it was said that large supplies could be drawn from Wales the Scots turned aside to Worcester to wait for the Welsh reinforcements. This was contrary to the advice of Hamilton, who, it is said, urged an immediate advance on London.[8] Even on the Welsh border the king could hardly expect a warm welcome when

1 Gardiner, *Civil War*, iii. 79.

2 Clarendon, *Hist.* ii. 581.

3 Rushworth, op. cit. vi. 266.

4 Russell lost in stock timber and waste £20,000. Webb, *Civil War in Herefordshire*, note, p. 275. See also note p. 276 for details from a MS. estimate made in 1666 of the losses of the city of Worcester.

5 Webb, *Civil War in Herefordshire*, ii. 248.

6 Rushworth, op. cit. vii. 974.

7 *Dict. Nat. Biog.* xvi. 100.

8 Gardiner, *Commonwealth*, i. 433.

accompanied by the Scots, having regard to their conduct in 1645, which was still remembered. On 22 August Charles marched into Worcester, and was received by the corporation, a few troops of parliamentary horse under Lambert retiring sullenly across the Severn to Gloucester.[1] The proclamations[2] of the king ordering a levy *en masse* received a poor response. Fortifications[3] were thrown up in haste, especially on the south near the London road. The king also sent a brigade, under Massey, the former governor of Gloucester, to Upton, to hold the passage of the Severn and prevent his right being turned.

Cromwell, who had marched along the east coast, concentrated his men at Evesham, thus getting between Charles and London. In order to cut off the Scots from Wales and to shut them up in Worcester, Cromwell detached Lambert with a considerable force to take Upton, and to gain the west bank of the Severn. After a stiff fight the Scots were driven out and followed to Powick, a village three miles from Worcester. Cromwell then advanced from Evesham towards Worcester and drew up his men on the south side of the town in front of the Scotch forts, extending his left to the Severn, on the other side of which Lambert's outposts were stationed. Lambert had been directed to collect all the boats he could, and with these Cromwell constructed two bridges,[4] one over the Severn just above its junction with the Teme, the other over the Teme. On this being done, on 3 September Lambert and Fleetwood were ordered to drive the Scots from the line of the Teme and clear the west bank of the Severn by forcing them into Worcester. Fleetwood attacked the Scots at Powick Bridge, where at the beginning of the war Rupert had defeated Fiennes, but was repulsed and unable to carry the bridge. Lambert had crossed the Teme by the bridge of boats and attacked the Scots who were posted near its junction with the Severn, but had also been unsuccessful, having been repulsed more than once. Cromwell, seeing that the plan was likely to fail, marched a brigade over the Severn bridge of boats and ordered Lambert to renew the attack in front while he pressed on the rear and flank of the royalists. After some hard fighting this plan was successful, and the Scots were beaten back from hedge to hedge towards Worcester. The retreat of the Scots' left placed those at the bridge at Powick in danger of being cut off. To avoid this, they too retired; Lambert pressing on one flank with Fleetwood on the other soon converted the retreat into a rout. From his position on the cathedral tower Charles and his staff had seen the attempt of Cromwell to drive in the Scots' right wing. To relieve the pressure Charles ordered the Scots Cavalry under Leslie, who were drawn up on the Worcester side of the Severn, to cross the river and aid their comrades. This Leslie's men flatly refused to do. Charles, however, determined to make an effort. Collecting all the troops he could, he sallied from the south or Sidbury Gate, thinking that by forcing back Cromwell's right and centre, he would oblige him to recall his troops and so compel him to relax his attack on the Scots' right. Had the plan been carried out earlier in the day it might have been successful, but it was tried too late. The duke of Hamilton, who led the Scots' left, driving back the parliamentary

[1] Cary, *Mem. of Civil War*, ii. 335.

[2] *Engl. Hist. Rev.* v. 114.

[3] See proclamation (addressed to constables and tything men of Salwarpe) printed by J. Noake, *Worc. in Olden Times*, 157.

[4] Cromwell to Lenthall, 3 Sept. 1651.

troops from their position, stormed and carried their works; the Scots' centre led by Charles himself also gained ground and the whole parliamentary army began to retire. Had Charles been able to push his success home he would have won the day, but Hamilton's ammunition gave out and his men would not advance. Cromwell returned across the Severn and was able to stop the retreat. The parliamentarians had been so successful on the right that he could now afford to bring back some of his men from Wick, and with this reinforcement Cromwell charged the Scots. Hamilton fell mortally wounded, and his men gave way, retreating to their works. Fort Royal, at the south-eastern corner of the city walls, was stormed and its guns turned[1] on the fugitives crowded in the narrow streets. At the same time the parliamentary troops on the left of the Severn forced Worcester bridge and attacked the Scots' rear. This completed the rout. The town was soon a shambles, though Cromwell rode to the front through a hail of musketry to offer quarter.

Charles himself barely escaped along the Kidderminster road, and reached Stourbridge on his way to Boscobel. No victory was ever more complete, the Scots' army being practically destroyed. The feeling of many Englishmen was expressed in the memorable words of Hugh Peters to the militia men of the parliamentary army, 'When your wives and children shall ask you where you have been, and what news, say you have been at Worcester, where England's sorrows began, and where they are happily ended.'[2] The battle was indeed the last real fighting the county saw and its further history is a record of peace.

During the Commonwealth after Worcester fight there is nothing of any great importance in the political history of the county. The royalists were crushed by the fines they had to pay for their delinquency, and the Parliament men do not seem to have received any great reward ; Wylde who had done so much for the Parliament and had been made Chief Baron, was left out by Cromwell from all office. The Lygons seem to have got nothing, nor did the Lechmeres. Some smaller men may have profited a little, but although it is difficult and unsafe to rely too much on names, those, as far as can be ascertained, who acted as justices of the peace, grand jurors, coroners, high constables, and bailiffs are to a great extent the same under the Commonwealth as those who occupied similar positions before the war and also after the Restoration.

So far as evidence of documents exists the Restoration did not make so great a change in Worcestershire as in other counties. None of the Worcestershire royalists received any great reward, and but few of them got any return for what they had lost for royalty. It is difficult to say whether it was the result of the war or whether due to some other causes, but from the Restoration to the end of the seventeenth century it appears that the county was impoverished. This is borne out by the fact that there are few buildings that date from the last half of the seventeenth century, though there are many of the first half of that century and also of the next. The Sessions records in the reign of Charles II. are mainly occupied with two sets of documents. One consists of the measures for restoring order by attempts to

[1] Cromwell to Lenthall, 3 Sept. 1651. Cary, *Mem.* ii. 355.
[2] A *Perfect Diurnal*, cited by Gardiner, *Commonwealth*, i. 445.

deal with the wandering poor. Another very large class of documents is formed by the certificates under the Test Act. No one could hold any office unless he produced a certificate signed by the minister and churchwardens of some parish, and certified by two persons in the parish that they were well acquainted with the office holder, and that he had taken, at morning prayer after the sermon, the sacrament according to the rites of the Church of England. None of the great movements of Charles's reign seem to have had much effect in the county. The popish plot led to a number of searches in the houses of Catholics, and to the arrest of Father Wall (alias Johnson), who was hung as a priest at Red Hill, the last execution in the county of a priest as such. There were occasional riots as to enclosures, some as to Quakers, but on the whole there was nothing noteworthy. Under James II. things went on much the same. Persons who brought news of Monmouth's rebellion and alleged he had been successful and would soon be at Worcester were very properly indicted as spreaders of false news.[1] James himself paid a visit to Worcester, the first royal visit since the Restoration. The county was said to be a strong Jacobite stronghold, but the Revolution does not appear to have created any active opposition.

The same state of things continued under William III., but with this exception, that the thirty years since the Restoration had enabled the county to recover itself; both in trade and in other matters things appeared more prosperous. The age of town building commenced, and persons who had made fortunes by trade began to acquire considerable estates. In several instances the old landowners gave way to a new class of men who had made money by trade. In Anne's reign the great Worcestershire event was the feud between Bishop Lloyd and Sir John Packington,[2] the champion of high Tory views. The story has already been told under the ecclesiastical history, but its effect on the political history should also be noted; from about the same time dates the dividing line between the two great parties in their modern form.

Worcestershire had now ceased to be a place of any special importance, and sunk into an ordinary English county. Her Jacobitism was not strong enough to involve her in the troubles of 1715 or 1745, and she has not taken any special part in any of the great movements of the eighteenth or nineteenth centuries. Only two Worcestershire families have done much outside county work; the Lytteltons took a large share of public work in the eighteenth century, and Sir John Packington filled various cabinet offices in the nineteenth; but except these and Warren Hastings, the creator of modern India, Worcestershire men have done little, and the county has not been the scene of any important movements.

Still, at the present time, three Worcestershire men are in Mr. Balfour's government, Lord Windsor, Commissioner of Works, Mr. A. Chamberlain, Chancellor of the Exchequer, and the Hon. A. Lyttelton, Colonial Secretary. The political history of Worcestershire during the last two centuries and a half is mainly to be found in the history of its representation in the House of Commons.

As early as the year 1295[3] Worcestershire returned sixteen members of parliament, two knights for the shire, and two burgesses each for the city of

[1] Session decrees. [2] *Dict. Nat. Biog.* xliii. 92.

[3] W. R. Williams, *Parl. Hist. of the County of Worc.*, which furnishes an exhaustive account of the subject.

Worcester and the boroughs of Bromsgrove, Droitwich, Dudley, Evesham, Kidderminster, and Pershore. In the case of the boroughs, Droitwich excepted, we have no further record of representation till a much later period. The smaller communities were always glad to be quit of the payment of their members, the burden entailed by their parliamentary privilege. Droitwich seems to have been represented until 1311, but after the November Parliament of that year no returns are found till 1554, when the borough was again empowered to send members to Parliament by Philip and Mary. Evesham, by virtue of a clause in the charter of James I.[1] to the town, recovered its privilege of electing two members in 1604. Two years after[2] Bewdley was enfranchised, and received the right to return one member. On two occasions[3] during the Commonwealth, in 1654 and 1656, five members were elected by the shire. By the Reform Act of 1832[4] four members were allotted to the county, which was divided into two divisions. Droitwich[5] lost one of its representatives, but Dudley and Kidderminster were again enfranchised, receiving one member each. In 1867 Evesham lost[6] one of its members. The changes[7] made in 1885 were revolutionary. The county was divided into five single-member constituencies; the city of Worcester lost one member, whilst Bewdley, Droitwich, and Evesham were altogether deprived of their separate representation.

Amongst the knights of the shire will be found representatives of the chief county families. In 1301 and 1305 we find Robert Bracy[8] of Warndon, who had been undersheriff in 1298. An heiress of this family in the time of Henry V. married Thomas Lygon, himself a member for the county in 1467. In 1309 occur the names of Robert Sturmy and Robert de Somery, whose families were seated respectively at Sutton Sturmy and Dudley Castle.[9] Seven years later,[10] in 1316, we first meet as knight of the shire a member of the Lyttelton family, Thomas de Luttelton, who had married Juliana, heiress of Robert de Somery, his colleague in the county representation. Before the reign of Elizabeth the Attwoods, Beauchamps, Blounts, Staffords, Throckmortons, and many others of note did their duty to the shire by representing it in Parliament. Sir John Bourne[11] of Holt and Battenhall will be remembered as the bitter enemy of Bishop Edwin Sandys, the first Elizabethan bishop of Worcester. He first served as member for the county in 1554. John Lyttelton, member for the shire in 1584, was a Catholic, and concerned in the rebellion of the earl of Essex. He was saved from execution by the influence of Sir Walter Raleigh, but died in prison.[12] Lyttelton's brother-in-law, Sir Henry Bromley, knight of the shire in 1593, was also involved in Essex's rebellion. His estates forfeited to the Crown were restored by James I., and he proved his loyalty and also his attachment to the Anglican Establishment by his vigorous search for the priests implicated in the Gunpowder Plot.[13] Sir Thomas

[1] May, *Hist. of Evesham*, p. 472.

[2] Bewdley had risen to importance under the Tudors. According to Leland, in 1539 it was 'but a very new towne.' Cf. Burton, *Hist. of Bewdley*, p. 12.

[3] Williams, op. cit. pp. 46 sqq.

[4] 2 and 3 Will. IV. c. 64.

[5] 2 Will. IV. c. 45.

[6] 30 Vict. c. 102.

[7] 48 and 49 Vict. c. 23.

[8] Williams, op. cit. p. 2.

[9] Ibid. p. 4.

[10] Ibid. p. 6.

[11] An interesting letter from him to Francis Yaxley giving an account of his rural occupation will be found S. P. Dom. Eliz. vol. xi. 4 Feb. 1560.

[12] Williams, op. cit. p. 34.

[13] Ibid. p. 36.

Leighton of Feckenham, member in 1601, was a distinguished soldier,[1] and had married a relative of Queen Elizabeth. Among other offices he held that of Constable of the Tower.

In the reign of Charles I. we meet the familiar names of Sir Thomas Littleton of Frankley, Sir John Packington of Westwood, and William Russell of Strensham, all of whom fought bravely for the king. Littleton, who had offered in 1642 to raise a regiment of foot and a troop of horse for Charles I., has already been mentioned as the captive of 'Tinker' Fox. Russell of Strensham was with Prince Rupert at Powick, and 'the Roundheads pillaged his house to the bare walls.' Sir John Packington was one of the royal Commissioners of Array in 1642, and the Parliament took ruthless satisfaction from his property, especially in Buckinghamshire. Before Edgehill fight he had joined Charles I. with a troop of horse, but although captured and tried for his life, no witness could be got to give evidence against him on account of his great popularity, so he was acquitted and enlarged. In the Long Parliament[2] the shire was represented by John Wylde and Humphrey Salway, and the former served as chairman of several committees of the House. In the assembly known as Barebones Parliament Major Richard Salway and Colonel James were allotted to Worcestershire.[3] They were both active and zealous parliamentarians. The increased representation of 1654 and 1656 has already been mentioned. Among later local names of note we meet Bromley, Harley, Lechmere, Lygon, Pytts, Packington, Sandys, Ward, and Winnington. In 1715 Sir John Packington, Sandys and Thomas Vernon, though of different politics, stood jointly against Samuel Pytts, who professed himself a Tory, and were returned. One[4] of Vernon's election banners is still preserved at Hanbury Hall, with the inscription, 'For his most excellent majesty King George, For Peace and the Church of England as by law Established.' From this time till 1747, when two Tories were elected, the representation was divided between the two historic parties. In 1761[5] the members were again of different politics, the Tory being the Hon. John Ward, while William Dowdeswell was the Whig nominee, the leader of his party in the Commons from 1765–1775, and Chancellor of the Exchequer 1765–1766. Both members were Whigs from 1774–1784, but then or soon after this the opinions of Mr. Lygon underwent a change under the stress of the French Revolution. From 1806 till the eve of the Reform Act of 1832 both political parties had a representative amongst the county members, but in 1831 two Whigs were elected after a seven days' poll, the result being:—Hon. T. H. Foley, 2,034; Hon. F. Spencer, 1,765; and Hon. H. B. Lygon (Tory), 1,335.[6]

After the division of the county by the first Reform Bill East Worcestershire returned two Whigs by a considerable majority; in West Worcestershire, where parties were pretty equally divided, a Whig (Hon. T. H. Foley) and a Tory (Hon. H. B. Lygon) shared the representation. In the 1837 election for East Worcestershire there was a considerable Tory reaction, and the Whigs were beaten. From that date until the further division in 1885 the political colour of this constituency varied considerably from time to time. West Worcestershire, on the other hand, from 1841 until the present day has been

[1] *Cal. S. P. Dom. Eliz.* 1587, p. 443, and ibid. 1588, p. 474.
[2] Williams, op. cit. p. 42
[3] Ibid. 43.
[4] Ibid. 58.
[5] Ibid. 60 sqq.
[6] Ibid. 64.

invariably Tory or Conservative. The exigencies of space will not allow an analysis of the results since 1885 in the one-member constituencies, but it may be noted that the new western division, like the old West Worcestershire, has favoured the Conservative party ; at the election of 1900 all the members were Unionists.

The names of the burgesses who represented Worcester city are not so uniformly connected with the territorial aristocracy of the county as in the case of the knights of the shire, but many are worthy of note. In the 'John de Hornyngwold' elected in 1309 we may, perhaps, see an ancestor of an old Worcestershire family which represented the city at least as late as the middle of the last century.[1] In 1337, one of the members was named Thomas le Cartere, probably the man of the same name who with Henry le Carter was appointed[2] on 26 July of that year to buy for the king's use 400 sacks of wool at 9½ marks the sack. In the sixteenth and early seventeenth centuries at least, members were occasionally found amongst the wealthly clothiers of the city. Roland Berkeley, member in 1593, had been first master of the Clothiers' Company of Worcester under the charter of 1590, and from the considerable profits of his trade purchased an estate at Spetchley, which passed to his still more famous second son, Robert Berkeley, also member for the city in 1620 and 1624, afterwards impeached and now known as the upholder on the bench of the legality of the ship-money.[3] In the year of Charles I.'s accession the city had for one of its members Sir Henry Spelman, the eminent antiquary.[4] In 1689 occurs[5] the name of John Somers, afterwards the famous Whig Lord Chancellor. There was elected in the by-election in March, 1718, Samuel Sandys,[6] who sat for Worcester till his elevation to the Lords in 1743. Nicknamed the 'motion-maker' by Sir Charles Hanbury Williams, he will always be remembered as the untiring opponent of Walpole, and almost certainly the person whom Lord Chesterfield cruelly branded[7] as 'without any merit but the lowest species of prostitution, enjoying a considerable post got by betraying his own party, without having abilities to be of use to any other.' In 1747 Thomas Vernon, a Whig, was at the head of the poll, but the second in order, T. G. Winford, a Tory, was unseated on petition, and the seat adjudged to the second Whig candidate, Robert Tracy, the House resolving 'that the right of election is in the citizens not receiving alms, and admitted to their freedom by birth or by servitude or by redemption in order to trade within the city.'[8] Some notion of the expense of contesting Worcester may be derived from the experience of Colonel T. H. H. Davies, a popular Whig member who won a seat for Worcester in 1818 and, with the exception of the years 1835–7, held it till 1841. The 1818 election is said to have cost him £12,000, whilst even in 1826 his expenses amounted to £8,000.[9] Since 1885, when the city of Worcester was deprived of one of its members, the constituency has been consistently Conservative, and the seat is now held by the Hon. G. H. Allsopp.

One of the earliest members for Droitwich, after the resumption of its parliamentary representation, to hold high office in the state was Sir Thomas Coventry of Croome D'Abitot, who sat for the borough in 1620, afterwards

[1] Williams, op. cit. p. 78.
[2] Pat. 11 Edw. III. m. 15.
[3] Foss, *Judges*, v. 256.
[4] *Dict. Nat. Biog.* liii. 330.
[5] Ibid. liii. 222.
[6] Ibid. l. 293.
[7] *Old England or Constitutional Journ.* No. 1.
[8] Williams, op. cit. p. 103.
[9] Ibid. 109.

well known as Lord Keeper. The loyalty of Droitwich to Charles I. was of a signal character, and had been rewarded by a letter written with the king's own hand, in which the burgesses were assured that their faithful service should be laid up in his princely remembrance for their future advantage.[1] In 1646 Thomas Rainsborough and Edward Wilde displaced Porter and Sandys, disabled from sitting on account of their loyalty. After the Restoration, the Sandys, Winnington, and Foley families by turns exercised a predominant influence in the elections. In 1690, when two Whigs were returned, the earl of Bellamont and Philip Foley, Sir John Packington the defeated candidate, a Tory, petitioned against Foley's return. On this the House resolved,[2] 11 November, 1690, 'That the right of election is in the burgesses of the corporation of the Salt Springs of Droitwich, and that Mr. Foley is duly elected.' In 1726, on the decease of his uncle, Edward Jeffreys, Thomas Winnington[3] of Stanford Court was returned to the House of Commons, and proved a consistent supporter of Walpole. From 1743–1746 he held the office of Paymaster-general of the Land Forces. A curiously close election[4] occurred in 1747: Hon. S. Masham (Whig), 19; Thomas Foley, junr. (Tory), 19; Francis Winnington (Whig), 19; and Hon. Edwin Sandys (Tory), 18. On a petition being presented, Mr. Masham's name was erased, and Mr. Sandys' substituted for Thomas Foley's by the order of the House. In the following year,[5] to the great chagrin of the rival families, the burgesses of the Foley interest created several new burgesses of their party, and thenceforward the Foleys were supreme in the borough. In 1832 Droitwich was deprived of one of its members; from 1837 to 1874 it returned Sir John Packington, and in 1874 and 1880, the last election before the Reform Bill of 1885, John Corbett, a well-known local salt maker, was returned in the Liberal interest, the figures of the poll being: in 1874, Corbett, 787; Packington, 401: in 1880, John Corbett (L.), 857; G. H. Allsopp (C.), 368; and Ernest Jones (L.), 5.

In the case of the borough of Evesham, although no members seem to have been returned to the Commons between 1295 and 1604, we have a notice[6] of three persons summoned to a council at Westminster respecting trade in 1337. In all probability the original electors were the householders of the borough.[7] By the first enabling charter of James I. representatives to Parliament are ordered to be chosen of the 'bailiffs, aldermen, and burgesses of the borough.' The second charter of James I. substitutes 'mayor' for 'bailiffs,' but confirms the earlier directions.[8] It must be noted, however, that the first and several subsequent returns made under the second charter show that the franchise was in practice restricted to the incorporated burgesses. The return for 1620 is signed by the mayor, recorder, and thirteen capital burgesses under the common seal; and the members elected waived their right to their allowance, to the great relief of the town.[9] In consequence of a petition by Sir James Rushout, the unsuccessful candidate in 1669, it was decided by the House 'that the right of election was in the common burgesses of Evesham, and that the election was void, and

1 Nash, *Worc.* i. 305.
2 Williams, op. cit. p. 128.
3 *Dict. Nat. Biog.* lxii. 198.
4 Williams, op. cit. p. 133.
5 Nash, *Worc.* i. 304.
6 Willis, *Notitia*, pref. ix.
7 Cf. Glanville, *Reports*, xiv. (Committee for Elections, 1623).
8 May, *Hist. of Evesham*, p. 279.
9 Ibid. p. 281.

that Edward Field, the mayor, be taken into the custody of the sergeant-at-arms for his misdemeanour in making the return of the borough of Evesham, and denying the poll, and be reprimanded by the Speaker.'[1] As a result of this decision, Sir John Hanmer was finally elected in the last month of the same year. In the indenture executed under the common seal, forty-two persons, denominated 'burgesses,' beside 'many other burgesses,' are stated as parties together with the mayor. Even mere payers of scot and lot seem to have voted with the freeholders at this election.[2] The election of 1685 was made under the new close charter of 12 June, 1684,[3] and was confined to the mayor, aldermen, and capital burgesses only.

In the first return after the flight of James II. under the 'circular' of the prince of Orange the two old members, Henry Parker and Sir John Mathews, were again returned, but by a popular election. From 1715 until 1784 the Whigs[4] monopolized the representation of the borough except at the election of 1768 when a Tory named Durant was second on the poll. At the next election six years afterwards 400 electors voted, and the poll was kept open for three days.[5] The election of 1802 is noteworthy from the fact that for the first time since the Revolution, voters who claimed merely on their freehold qualification were rejected, although sixty-four suffrages of this character were tendered.[6] Five years later the question of the franchise was again raised. The poll was kept open six days and the result showed: William Manning (T.), 494; Sir Manasseh Lopes (T.), 334; and Humphrey Howarth (W.), 320. Lopes[7] probably owed his position to lavish bribery among the poorer freeholders whom, contrary to the procedure at the previous election, the returning officer admitted to the poll to the number of 122. Mr. Howarth declined to receive such votes himself, and on petition was declared duly elected in place of Sir Manasseh. But perhaps the most famous of all the Evesham elections took place in 1818. The poll was kept open for twelve days, and it is said that the expenses of the contest and the subsequent petition reached at least £20,000. Freeholders, in accordance with the decision of 1808, were not polled, the voters being either freemen, persons with an inchoate right to freedom, or payers of scot and lot. The Whig candidates were returned, the poll being: Humphrey Howarth, 410; W. E. Rouse-Boughton, 359; and Sir C. Cockerell, 341. On petition the Tory candidate was declared duly elected in place of Rouse-Boughton. The committee of the House further declared as the return for 1295 was not then forthcoming that Evesham was a new borough and the franchise vested in the corporation burgesses alone.[8] A comparison of the figures[9] of the election of 1826, when the suffrage was restricted to the burgesses of the corporation, is instructive: Sir C. Cockerell, 231; E. Protheroe, 137; and Patrick Grant, 87. The poll was kept open for four days, but the votes received were less than half those of 1818, and a considerable majority were those of non-residents. Bribery and corruption were rife

[1] Williams, op. cit. p. 147, quoting *Journ. of House of Commons*, ix. 110.

[2] May, op. cit. p. 286.

[3] Ibid. 453.

[4] The Rushout interest was predominant in the borough. In 1761 Sir John Rushout was returned, though not without a contest. May, op. cit. 290. In 1766 Horace Walpole alludes to Sir John Rushout as 'the oldest member in the House.' Walpole to H. S. Conway, 18 Oct. 1766.

[5] Williams, op. cit. p. 154.

[6] May, op. cit. p. 293.

[7] Lopes' later exploits in the way of bribery at Barnstaple and elsewhere in the west country are matters of common notoriety.

[8] May, op. cit. p. 296.

[9] Williams, op. cit. p. 157.

at the contest of 1830. Sir C. Cockerell was returned as a Whig and Lord Archibald Kennedy as a Tory, but both seats were voided on petition. A vivid picture has been left to us by an eyewitness of the spontaneous opening of inns, their lavish hospitality, and the liberal remuneration of the expenses and time of the independent voters.[1] By the first Reform Act the franchise was allowed only to freemen living within seven miles of the borough and ten-pound householders. On the first register thus revised there were 359 names, and both Whig candidates were returned at the election which followed. At the election to the first Parliament of Queen Victoria, the Hon. George Rushout and Peter Borthwick were returned in the Tory interest, but on the subsequent petition Lord Marcus Hill, afterwards Lord Sandys, the Whig nominee, was seated in place of Mr. Borthwick, who was found guilty of bribery.[2] By virtue of the Reform Act of 1867 Evesham lost one of its members. At the 1880 election Daniel Ratcliffe (L.) was returned by 382 to 372 given for Algernon Borthwick, afterwards Lord Glenesk ; on a petition the election was declared void for bribery. In July 1880 the last election before its final disfranchisement as a separate borough was held, when the poll stood thus: Frederick Lehmann (L.), 378, and F. D. Dixon-Hartland (C.), 376; but on petition and a scrutiny, the seat was awarded to Mr. Dixon-Hartland, who was declared to have received 375 votes, whilst his opponent was allowed only 372. Five years after the borough became merged in the county.[3]

Bewdley was first granted one member under the charter of James I., the bailiff acting as returning officer. Before 1832 local magnates, the Clares, Herberts, Foleys, Lytteltons or Winningtons usually exercised a preponderating influence on the elections, and the corporation often managed to secure large sums of money[4] as the price of the seat, which 'provided for many useful improvements being made in the town.'[5] Ralph Clare of Caldwell, near Kidderminster, was elected in 1642. In 1640 there was a struggle between the Clare and Herbert interest, but Sir Henry Herbert of Ribbesford was returned in the March election, and a petition against him was not proceeded with owing to the dissolution in the following May. In the autumn of the same year a double return was made, but Herbert was declared elected and Sir Ralph's election disallowed on petition. The struggle between the rival families was renewed after the Restoration in 1661, and when Sir Ralph Clare petitioned against Herbert's election, the House declared that Sir Henry Herbert was duly elected, and resolved further 'that the right of election is in the bailiff and 12 capital burgesses of Bewdley appointed by charter, 3 Jac. I., exclusive of all others.'[6] In 1673, the struggle was between the Herberts and Foleys. Philip Foley was returned, but on petition by Henry Herbert, son of the late deceased member, Foley's name was erased from the return. In 1679 Foley was again returned, and on an unsuccessful petition by Herbert, the House resolved that 'all the inhabitants of Bewdley have not a right to vote.'[7] In 1685 a Lyttelton, in 1689 a Herbert, and in 1694 a Winnington, represented the borough, and

[1] May, op. cit. p. 298. [2] May, *Hist. of Evesham*, p. 304. [3] Williams, op. cit. p. 162.

[4] According to the Corporation Accounts, Mr. Andrews, the sitting member, presented £1,000 in 1807 and £2,000 in 1808. Williams, op. cit. p. 174. The borough still, 1905, possess invested funds, the results of elections.

[5] Burton, *Hist. of Bewdley*, p. 47. [6] Williams, op. cit. p. 167. [7] Ibid. p. 168.

the early years of the eighteenth century witnessed a terrific struggle between the Herberts and Winningtons for the supremacy. Fresh charters granted by James II. in 1685 and Queen Anne in 1708 further complicated matters. For at least two years the town possessed rival corporations, who in the most solemn fashion annulled and declared void one another's proceedings. A double election was the result in 1708, but the House declared the Hon. Henry Herbert duly elected.[1] In 1768 there was a memorable contest between the Hon. Thomas (afterwards Lord) Lyttelton and Sir E. Winnington, which resulted in Lyttelton being unseated on petition.[2] Burgesses had been specially created in the Lyttelton interest, but were held to be of insufficient standing to vote at this election. For the thirty years following 1774 the Lyttelton influence was supreme in the borough. The patronage of the seat immediately before the first Reform Bill seems to have appertained to a wealthy local attorney, W. Aylesbury Robarts.[3] In 1832 the franchise was extended and from that year till 1847 Sir Thomas Winnington held the seat in the Whig interest. He was then beaten by a Tory, Mr. Ireland of Owsden Hall, who was unseated on petition. Two other Conservative returns were voided later, that of Sir R. Glass, of Atlantic Cable fame, in 1868 and Mr. Cunliffe in the year following. In the last case the seat was allowed on a scrutiny to the Liberal candidate, the Hon. A. Anson. In the last election at Bewdley as an independent borough, which was rendered necessary by the unseating on petition of the Liberal candidate, Charles Harrison, in April, 1880, who defeated the present Lord Chief Justice, Lord Alverstoke, another Liberal was returned with the following poll: Enock Baldwin, 611; W. N. Marcy, 491. Both candidates were men with a local connection.[4]

Of the boroughs re-enfranchised during the past century, it need only be remarked that at Dudley the influence of the Ward family was naturally very considerable, and that the borough was honoured in 1855 by having as its representative Sir Stafford Northcote, afterwards Lord Iddesleigh.[5] Kidderminster for several years afforded a seat to Robert Lowe,[6] later known as Lord Sherbrooke, whilst another member of some notoriety in his day was Baron Grant (né Gottheimer), unseated on petition in 1874. Since 1886 the borough has been represented by Sir Frederick Godson.

MILITARY HISTORY

The present Worcestershire Regiment includes four battalions of the line, the old 29th and 36th Foot, and two newly raised; of these the 36th Foot, with its once well-known grass-green facings, received the county title of the Herefordshire during the American War,[7] and its detailed history may be left to the volumes dealing with that county. Farrington's Regiment, as the 29th was called from its first colonel, claims to have been formed in the year 1694; but if full continuity[8] be essential to a regimental

1 Burton, op. cit. p. 45.
2 Ibid. 47.
3 Williams, op. cit. pp. 163, 175.
4 Ibid. 178.
5 *Dict. Nat. Biog.* xli. 195.
6 Ibid. xxxiv. 149.
7 Lawrence-Archer, *The British Army*, p. 271.
8 It was disbanded in 1697, and its re-formation was one of the last acts of the life of William III. Partial continuity at least may be claimed, as many of the old officers of the corps were appointed to the new establishment. Everard, *Twenty-Ninth Worc. Reg.* p. 10.

history, 12 February, 1702, is, perhaps, the more correct date. It would seem that the regiment had at first no special connection with the shire, though probably recruited in part within its limits, as on 30 May, 1702, one company at Worcester[1] was ordered to march to Knutsford and Altrincham, while other companies are mentioned as being at the same time at Bury St. Edmunds, Easingwold, York, and Knutsford.

It was not until the year 1782 that this distinguished corps, which had fought at Ramillies and defended Gibraltar, became officially attached to the county, and the commanding-officer was advised as follows: 'His Majesty having been pleased to order that the 29th Regiment, which you command, should take the county name of "The Worcestershire Regiment," and be looked upon as attached to that county, I am to acquaint you it is His Majesty's further pleasure that you should in all things conform to that idea, and endeavour by all means in your power to cultivate and improve that connection, so as to create a mutual attachment between the county and the regiment, which may at all times be useful towards recruiting the regiment.'[2] In conformity with this order a captain and ensign[3] are shown by the evidence of the muster-rolls to have been in Worcester during the latter half of 1782, doubtless on recruiting duty, and many good men were obtained for the corps.[4] The regiment was at this time in Canada, but in October, 1787, it returned to England, to find that a number of local recruits enlisted for their county regiment had been ordered to join the 43rd Foot, a blunder of the War Office which so disgusted the county that for many years local recruiting was ruined.[5] Before the Worcestershire Militia were called out at Worcester for their annual training in the following spring, the 29th were ordered to Pershore, and were then inspected and reviewed by Lieutenant-General Douglas. The regiment was in 1789 most ably and efficiently commanded, with Lord Harrington as colonel and Lord Cathcart as lieutenant-colonel.[6] In 1796, by Act of Parliament, 156 men were appointed to be levied for the army in the city and county of Worcester, and Colonel Enys endeavoured, with considerable success, to kindle local interest in the regiment, when the War Office repeated their previous blunder, and the 'quota men' raised in Worcester were ordered to be transferred to the 46th Foot.[7] During the war with revolutionary France, detachments of the regiment enjoyed a spell of service at sea, and in the famous action of the 1st of June, during the duel between the *Brunswick* and *Le Vengeur*, the men of the 29th on board the former vessel lost eleven killed and twenty-one wounded.[8] On 12 March, 1795, an order appeared in the *London Gazette* for the addition of a second battalion to the 29th Regiment, but before the end of the year this second battalion was directed to be incorporated with the first.

Probably the most glorious service rendered by the Worcestershire regiment was in the Peninsula. At Roliça[9] in 1808 they bore the brunt of the battle,

[1] Everard, op. cit. p. 12.

[2] H. S. Conway to Lieut.-Gen. Evelyn, or the Officer commanding the Twenty-Ninth Reg. cited by Everard, p. 97.

[3] Everard, op. cit. p. 213.

[4] Ibid. 98.

[5] Ibid. p. 104.

[6] Ibid. p. 105.

[7] Ibid. p. 213.

[8] Ibid. p. 155. The esteem and affection in which Lord Cathcart was held by the whole regiment is shown by the will of Capt. Saunders, killed on the *Brunswick*, who speaks of him as the father of the regiment, and recommends his orphan sons to his care.

[9] Owing to a clerk's blunder, 'Roleia' is the official name borne on the colours.

and it is recorded 'that the men of the regiment fought in queues and powdered hair, and carrying hairy packs of a pattern long forgotten, and the officers in cocked hats worn athwartships, in the fashion of the preceding decade.'[1] At the action with the 82nd they formed the 3rd brigade under Major-General Nightingale.[2] For the three following years the regiment saw continuous service against the French, and after Talavera its gallantry and discipline were mentioned in General Orders.[3] In the autumn of the same year Sir Arthur Wellesley wrote to Castlereagh, 'I wish very much that some measures could be adopted to get some recruits for the 29th Regiment. It is the best regiment in this Army, has an admirable internal system, and excellent non-commissioned officers.'[4] From the terrible carnage of Albuera only 96 men, 2 captains, and a few subalterns of the corps emerged unwounded. Many of the officers and men of the 29th, as in other famous Peninsular regiments, were of Irish birth, and Captain Humfrey was struck down by a round-shot while cheering on his men to the charge 'for the honour of Old Ireland.'[5] The monthly returns for 25 May of 1811 show that whilst the head-quarters were in Spain the depôt was at Droitwich and recruits were being sought at Manchester.[6] The story goes that when Lord Wellington inspected the hospitals at Elvas, after Albuera, he exclaimed, 'Oh, old 29th, I am sorry to see so many of you here.' To which the men replied, 'Oh, my Lord, if you had only been with us, there would not have been so many of us here.'[7] In October, 1811, the Worcestershire Regiment was ordered home to recruit, and Lord Wellington declared on their departure that 'the 29th landed with the army three years ago, and they have been distinguished in every action that has been fought in that period,'[8] whilst their divisional commander, Lieutenant-General Hill,[9] could not allow the regiment 'to quit the 2nd division of infantry without expressing to it his warmest approbation and thanks for its good conduct,' and his regret at being deprived of their services.'[10]

In 1814 the regiment was employed in the American War during the operations at Fort Castine,[11] whence it returned to Portsmouth. It was then ordered to Belgium, but was too late to form part of Wellington's Army at Waterloo, though the heavy firing was distinctly heard as the regiment pushed forward from Ghent towards the British head-quarters.[12] After forming part of the Army of Occupation in France, the regiment remained in the British Isles till 1826, when it embarked for Mauritius, where it continued until 1837,[13] when it went to India. During the Sutlej campaign the 29th suffered severely at Sobraon, and Captain Coker brought the regiment out of action when his senior officers were killed or wounded.[14] In the second Sikh War at Chilianwala one-third of the men who went under fire were killed or wounded. The regiment saw little active service from this time until the outbreak of the South African War, when the first battalion took part in the

[1] *Broad Arrow*, 2 October, 1886.
[2] Napier, *Peninsular War*, i. App.
[3] 29 July, 1809.
[4] Gurwood, *Wellington Dispatches*, iii. 496.
[5] Everard, op. cit. 321.
[6] Ibid. 326.
[7] Ibid. 327.
[8] Gen. Order, Freneda, 3 Oct. 1811.
[9] Gen. Order, Portalegre, 7 Oct. 1811.
[10] The Peninsular services of this distinguished corps formed the groundwork of the once popular novel *Caleb Balderston*, which was written by one of its officers. Lawrence-Archer, op. cit. p. 269.
[11] Lawrence-Archer, op. cit. p. 269.
[12] Everard, op. cit. 349.
[13] Ibid. 388.
[14] Ibid. 450. A monument to those who fell in the Sutlej campaign is placed in Worcester Cathedral.

operations in the Orange River Colony. And 'South Africa 1900–2' is now borne on the colours with the battles of India and the Peninsula, and the earliest honour of the regiment, 'Ramillies.'[1]

Amongst regimental nicknames of the 29th may be mentioned 'The Old and Bold,' 'The Guards of the Line,'[2] the 'Vein Openers,'[3] 'The Eversworded,' and 'Two and a Hook.' The lion is an old regimental device, and appeared on the crossbelt plate of the officers at least as early as 1796. The star is said to have originally been granted by George III.[4] Since the formation of the modern territorial regiment the white and red rose united has been allotted to it as its badge, whilst the castle on the helmet plate has been taken from the Worcestershire Militia. The modern regiment has retained the 'Royal Windsor March,' the quick-step of the old 29th, but its motto 'Firm' has been derived from the Herefordshire, the 36th of the line, which now forms its second battalion.

Another regiment may be mentioned in connection with the county history, the 89th, or 'Worcestershire Volunteers, which was raised in the county in 1779. Whilst on service in the West Indies it lost seven-eighths of its establishment within a year, and was disbanded at the peace in 1783. Three other regiments raised for service during the American War of Independence were largely recruited in Worcestershire, the old 87th, 88th, and 91st. They were also disbanded at the peace.[5]

The continuous history of the present militia battalions of the Worcestershire regiment dates from the year 1770, but it will perhaps be well to give a passing reference to some of the earlier levies. During the reign of Elizabeth continual musters were made for service in Ireland. Musters[6] taken in Worcestershire in 1574 and 1575 show that the numbers were 1,850 able men, 1,850 armed men, and 25 light horse. In the year of the Armada four bands of trained men, each 150 strong, were organized under Captains Geo. Winter, Robert Acton, Francis Ketley, and Thomas Bridges, besides 100 pioneers, 17 lances, 83 light horse, and 10 petronels,[7] with a proper provision of arms, ammunition, and transport. For several years[8] previous to 1588 considerable attention had been devoted to the organization of the musters as well in Worcestershire as in the rest of the country, and when the Spanish were expected to attempt a landing, the Worcestershire militia, with those of Warwick, Leicester, and Huntingdon, formed part of Sir Henry Goodyer's regiment attached to the force assigned for the defence of the Queen's Majesty. The general muster[9] of Worcestershire early in the reign of King James I. is

[1] Hart, *Army List*, 1905, p. 275 sqq.

[2] There may be some connection between this nickname and one of the regimental badges, a star. Cf. Letter from Horse Guards, 7 Aug. 1877. 'I am directed by H.R.H. the Field-Marshal Commanding-in-Chief to acquaint you that as the stars which were recently ordered to be removed from the pouches of the 29th Regiment were granted to that corps as a special distinction for service in the field, His Royal Highness, with a view to assimilation, as much as possible, of the pouches of the 29th Regiment to those of the Guards, has approved of white ammunition pouches being issued in lieu of black ones.' Cited by Everard, op. cit. p. 519. Another account is that the star is borne traditionally from their having once been brigaded with the Guards. Lawrence-Archer, op. cit. 273.

[3] This nickname was bestowed on the regiment by the citizens of Boston in America after a riot during which a party of the 29th Regiment fired on the people with fatal results, thus drawing the first blood in the War of the Revolution.

[4] Lawrence-Archer, op. cit. 272, but see previous note.

[5] Holden, *Hist. of Third and Fourth Batt. Worc. Reg.* p. 239, note.

[6] Add. MS. 33,276, f. 16.

[7] Harl. MS. 168, f. 171.

[8] *Cal. S. P. Dom. Eliz.* 1581–90.

[9] Stowe MS. 574, f. 26.

said to have numbered 5,600 able men with 2,500 armed men, 230 pioneers, 20 demi-lances, and 85 light horse. In this reign the array of the county was organized into trained bands, and on several occasions the local authorities were reminded by the central government that the state of the militia was becoming more important on account of the unsettled condition of Christendom, and that musters should be held yearly, with other directions.[1]

At the commencement of the Civil War, Sir John Packington, Samuel Sandys, Sir Thomas Lyttelton of Frankley, and Sherrington Talbot of Salways, were amongst the Commissioners of Array who raised forces for Charles I., and the city militia formed part of the garrison of Worcester. During the Commonwealth the standing army of the state left less room for the action of the militia, but on the fall of Richard Cromwell the old constitutional force was organized and prepared for any event, and when on 12 May Charles II. was proclaimed at Worcester, the militia were in attendance and fired volleys to celebrate the occasion. During the reign of Charles II. a troop of horse was kept up in the county under the command of Captain Wylde, whose duty it was to put down sectaries.

The county militia shared in the reorganization which followed the Restoration, and in 1667 were called out to disperse a rabble of some hundreds of apprentices who had attacked certain houses of ill-fame in the city of Worcester.[2] Thirty years after the county possessed[3] two troops of horse each sixty strong, and a regiment of foot of seven companies with 786 rank and file. The captains of horse were Lord Herbert of Cherbury, and William Bromley, probably of Holt. The lord-lieutenant, Charles, duke of Shrewsbury, was colonel of the foot regiment, and the lieutenant of his company was Chambers Slaughter of Brace's Leigh and Bransford; Sir James Rushout was lieutenant-colonel, and Edmund Lechmere of Hanley Castle was major, the captains being Richard Dowdeswell of Pull Court, William Walsh, Samuel Jewkes, and John Sheldon. A note is appended to the return stating that 'at the last muster they appeared full and in good order.'

The militia of the kingdom were apparently mustered every year for training until the reign of George I., but as the necessity for a standing army was gradually accepted by the nation, the militia suffered neglect. In 1715 they were called out for the annual training,[4] but they were only embodied twice between that period and their reorganization in the second half of the eighteenth century. Contemporary opinion is expressed by a writer in the *Craftsman*,[5] who 'would not be thought to mean that our militia are fit to defend our country or indeed for anything, besides furnishing the town with a ridiculous diversion, and cramming their guts at the expence of their industrious fellow-subjects. For this reason they are laid aside everywhere but in Middlesex. But it's absurd to suppose that the *militia* cannot be made useful.' The Seven Years' War almost denuded the country of regular troops, and as a French invasion was by no means impossible, the government determined to revise and organize afresh the old constitutional force. By Act of Parliament[6] a force

[1] *Cal. S. P. Dom. Jas. I.* 1619–1623, pp. 294 and 604.

[2] Ibid. *Chas. II.* p. 560.

[3] Eg. MS. 1626 (B.M).

[4] Holden, *Hist. of 3rd and 4th Batt. Worc. Reg.* p. 17. This is a work of exhaustive research, and must be the basis of any account of the Worcestershire Militia.

[5] 6 Jan. 1733, No. 340, quoted in *Gent. Mag.* iii. 10.

[6] 30 Geo. II. c. 25.

of 30,000 foot was to be raised in England and Wales selected by ballot[1] from men between the ages of sixteen and forty-five professing the Protestant religion.[2] Of these, Worcester city and county were expected to contribute 560. The annual training was to last twenty-eight days, and the period of service was fixed at three years. On embodiment the men received a guinea, known as a 'marching guinea,' and became subject to martial law, while their pay was the same as that of the line.[3] For the officers there was generally a property qualification.

On 27 July, 1758, a meeting[4] was held at the Talbot Inn, Sidbury, attended by the earl of Coventry, lord-lieutenant, and several deputy-lieutenants of the county, to discuss the raising of a local regiment, but owing to the reluctance of gentlemen to accept commissions, in some cases probably due to their objection to the ballot, which was highly unpopular in the country, the meeting was adjourned, and in spite of further attempts the regiment was not actually raised[5] till 1770. The first colonel was Nicholas Lechmere, Holland Cooksey was major, and the names of the captains were John Clements, Philip Moule, Samuel West, William Wrenford, Edward Baker, and Thomas Cornwall.[6] Of the silk colours the one was a 'Union, the other a green sheet with the arms of the earl of Coventry.'[7] The red coats of both officers and men were faced with green. The first training of the newly-raised regiment began 29 October, 1770, and was ended on the 24 November following. No untoward incident occurred beyond a duel between two of the officers, happily without a fatal result.[8]

The history of the regiment until 1778 was uneventful. In that year, in consequence of the alliance of France with the American colonists, the government embodied the militia,[9] and the Worcestershire regiment assembled on 20 April for permanent duty. On their march through London to Warley Common, in Essex, they were inspected by King George III. and the Prince of Wales at Turnham Green. According to the *London Chronicle* of 16 June, 1778, 'The Worcestershire militia seemed to be well-disciplined and as regular and decent a set of men as any internal corps.' Either in this year or shortly afterwards two brass six-pounders were attached to the regiment under the name of battalion guns. After the peace with America in 1783 the militia were disembodied, and at the same time the light company raised in 1779 and added to the Worcestershire regiment was entirely disbanded.[10] The year 1787 is of interest in the regimental history of the Worcestershire militia as then for the last time the officers carried spontoons, which were afterwards replaced by swords. On the outbreak of war with France the regiment was again embodied. Nicholas Lechmere, who had assumed the further name of Charlton, was still colonel, the lieutenant-colonel was J. W. Newport, while William Wrenford was major. It is a curious circumstance that on its first embodiment in 1778 the Worcestershire regiment was numbered twenty-nine, and on the second occasion thirty-six—the numbers of the old regiments of the line which now form the first and second battalions of the present

1 But substitutes were permitted.
2 This limitation existed until 1802.
3 Holden, op. cit. p. 19.
4 Ibid. p. 20.
5 This was decided upon at a meeting at Hooper's coffee-house, Worcester, on May 19.
6 Militia Letter Book, 1770.
7 A return of Arms, etc., cited by Holden, op. cit. 24.
8 Holden, op. cit. 26.
9 Warrant, 6 March, 1778.
10 Holden, op. cit. 47.

territorial regiment. The duties assigned to the Worcester militia during their second embodiment[1] were of a very arduous character, and on several occasions in Cornwall they were called upon to act vigorously in aid of the civil power. Lord Cathcart,[2] colonel of the 29th Regiment, met the Worcestershire militia at Salisbury in 1796 when they were *en route* for Kent, and wrote to his wife that 'they are a very fine regiment, and have been at pains to imitate the Worcestershire regiment of foot in dress and many other things.' On 6 May, 1795, Colonel Nicholas Lechmere-Charlton, the first colonel of the Worcestershire militia, who had brought his regiment to a rare state of efficiency, resigned his commission, and was succeeded by Lieut.-Col. J. W. Newport. In 1796 the dread of a French invasion had become so acute that supplementary militia were raised, the quota of Worcester county and city being fixed at 825.[3] Two years later these were called out and embodied under the Acts 23 Geo. III. c. 18 and 19, and whilst one half was drafted into the Worcestershire regular militia, raising it to ten companies, the other half of the supplementary recruits was formed into the 2nd Worcestershire[4] militia, or supplementary militia, under Ambrose St. John, Lieut.-Col. Commandant. This second battalion was paid off and disbanded in 1799.[5] The king's colour was a Union, and their regimental colour yellow.

The original Worcestershire militia did good service in Ireland,[6] whither they proceeded on service in the autumn following the battle of Vinegar Hill, and it was whilst there that the regiment was deprived[7] of its battalion guns. Between July and November 1799 nearly 500 men volunteered from the two battalions of the Worcestershire militia into the regular service, and in September of the same year the first battalion was ordered to return home, and received a warm and hearty welcome at the ever-faithful city.[8]

By the discharge of the supplementary men and the drafting of the volunteers into the line regiments the Worcestershire militia were reduced to the headquarters and light companies, and in the April following the Peace of Amiens they were disembodied by royal warrant, the Secretary of State who forwarded it bearing witness both to their 'uniformly good conduct' and their 'truly meritorious zeal and public spirit.'[9] In 1802 the restriction of service in the militia to Protestants was removed, and the establishment was fixed for the Worcester militia at eight companies, including a Grenadier and Light Infantry Company with 616 privates, besides officers, non-commissioned officers, and drummers.[10] Though temporary increases were made during the ensuing French war, this normal establishment existed in force till 1852. On the resumption of the French war the regiment was again embodied for garrison duty in England, and was now styled the 47th Regiment of the militia,[11] a number which it retained till 1833. In May, 1803, they were sent by forced marches to Gosport.

In 1808 a large number of local militia was raised,[12] the foundation for the new force being found in most cases in the existing volunteer corps, the

[1] It is probable that during this embodiment the facings of the regiment were changed to yellow. Holden, op. cit. p. 55.
[2] Everard, *Hist. of Twenty-ninth Reg.* p. 182.
[3] 37 Geo. III. c. 3 and 22. Even before June 1795 the county militia had been augmented by an additional company under Act 34 Geo. III. c. 16.
[4] Holden, op. cit. p. 74.
[5] Ibid. p. 100.
[6] For which it bears on its regimental colour the Harp of Ireland.
[7] Holden, op. cit. p. 91.
[8] Ibid. p. 95.
[9] W. O. Militia Letter Book, vol. ii. cited Holden, op. cit. p. 104.
[10] Stat. 42 Geo. III. c. 90.
[11] *London Gazette*, 1803, p. 710.
[12] Under Act 48 Geo. III. c. 3.

ballot being employed to supplement deficiencies ; those raised in Worcestershire will be referred to later. In 1809 and the following year the regular Worcestershire militia contributed as many as 6 officers and 311 men to the 7th Royal Fusiliers,[1] and during the whole of the French war the militia battalions were constantly depleted to fill the ranks of the line. Sir William Napier[2] even declares that at Talavera the greater part of the English troops engaged were 'raw men so lately drafted from the militia that many of them still bore the number of their former regiment on their accoutrements.' About this time the facings of the Worcestershire militia were probably changed from yellow to buff.[3] The regiment also received new colours, the regimental colour or county colour bearing the arms of the city of Worcester on a buff ground, while on the right-hand lower corner was the Irish harp already mentioned. The condition and character of the Worcestershire regular militia during these years of embodiment is borne witness to by Major-General John Hope in 1811 in his confidential report, in which he declares that he has seen few regiments equal to the Worcestershire in all points of drill and discipline.[4] In 1814, owing to the extensive volunteering into the line and the formation of provisional militia battalions for foreign service, the regiment in garrison at Portsmouth numbered little over 300 men. In 1814 these provisional battalions, the first of which contained a detachment of the Worcestershire militia, were sent to the south of France, but in June of the same year the first provisional battalion was recalled to England, and the Worcestershire detachment rejoined their regiment.[5] In August of this year the regiment was disembodied, but in June 1815 it was again ordered to be assembled for permanent duty,[6] and in October embarked for Ireland. In April 1816 they returned to England, and were finally disembodied at Worcester in the following month.

On account, probably, of the annual suspension of the ballot, there was no muster of the corps for training from this time until 1820, when the number assembled was 450, under the command of Colonel J. W. Newport, with Viscount Deerhurst as lieutenant-colonel, and T. H. Bund as major. In 1831 the permanent staff of the Worcestershire militia was of great assistance to the civil power during the disturbances which attended the struggle for the first Reform Bill.[7] From this time until the middle of the last century the history of the Worcestershire militia in common with that of other distinguished regiments of the old constitutional force is a history of dissolution and decay. By 1851, although the county regiment possessed an efficient adjutant, the serjeant-major was over seventy, the six serjeants nearly all as old, and the arms of the regiment, twelve flint muskets, were kept at Worcester gaol.[8]

The year 1852 saw the reorganization of the militia, and by order in Council the quota for Worcester county and city was fixed at 1,267, of which 789 men were to be raised in 1852 and 478 in 1853. Several officers who had done good service in their day retired through age and ill-health, amongst them Colonel T. H. Bund, who had joined as major in 1807 and succeeded Lord Deerhurst in 1843. He was seventy-eight years

[1] Holden, op. cit. p. 128. The distinguished service of the Royal Fusiliers at Albuera is a matter of common knowledge.
[2] *Hist. Pen. War*, ii. 145.
[3] Holden, op. cit. p. 129.
[4] Ibid. 135.
[5] Ibid. 149.
[6] Ibid. 154.
[7] Ibid. 176.
[8] Ibid. 185.

old at the time of his resignation, and was succeeded by Lieutenant-Colonel T. Clutton-Brook, whilst Major T. Clowes became lieutenant-colonel. By the end of 1852 nearly 800 volunteers had enlisted in the regiment,[1] the first training under the new system taking place in the following year. On 4 May, 1854, the colours carried by the regiment till 1886 were presented by Lady Lyttelton, wife of the lord-lieutenant of the county. During the embodiment consequent on the Crimean war, the regiment was for a time at Aldershot, where it earned an excellent reputation, and 450 men volunteered for foreign service.[2] At the review of 18 April, 1856, the Worcestershire militia furnished the Guard of Honour to Queen Victoria and the Prince Consort, and on 14 June following the corps, which since 1854 had ranked as the 67th Regiment of militia, was disembodied at Worcester, and the officers were entertained by the magistrates and gentry of the county 'to mark its appreciation of their services, and of the credit reflected on the county of Worcester by the behaviour of its militia.'[3] Colonel Thomas Clutton-Brook died in the last month of 1856, and Lieutenant-Colonel Clowes, who retained his rank, became commandant, resigning his commission to the regret of the whole regiment early in the following year, whereupon Major Thomas Webb became lieutenant-colonel and commandant. In 1857 the regiment was called out on permanent duty owing to the Sepoy mutiny,[4] and after a period of service in Ireland disembodied in May, 1858. The history of the next thirty years presents many features of regimental interest, but few that can be recorded in the space at our disposal. In 1870 Lieutenant-Colonel Webb resigned his commission as commandant, and was granted the honorary colonelcy of the regiment. He was succeeded as commandant by Major T. C. N. Norbury.

As a result of the army reorganization scheme of 1873, which brigaded the 29th, the 36th, and the Worcestershire and Herefordshire militia, a second battalion was formed in the following year, whose first commandant was Lieutenant-Colonel C. S. Hawkins.[5] The 200 men required to recruit the regiment to the number of 1,400 was raised in a fortnight. Their first colours were presented[6] by General the Hon. Sir Augustus Spencer, commanding the 5th Army Corps, in July, 1876, at Homington Down. The year 1881 was the date of the general order providing for the institution of territorial regiments, the line battalions of the Worcestershire Regiment being provided by the old 29th and 36th Foot, whilst under the new scheme the militia exchanged their buff facings for white. In 1886 the old Worcestershire militia, forming the third battalion of the territorial regiment, received new colours, at the newly-built barracks at Norton, at the hands of the Countess Beauchamp, the wife of the lord-lieutenant.[7] The later services of the county militia, now the fifth and sixth battalions of the Worcestershire Regiment, are fresh in the memory of all. The fifth battalion was embodied from 7 May to 15 October, 1900, and the sixth battalion from 8 May to 19 October of the same year, and also from 9 December, 1901, to 10 October, 1902, then gaining the honour, 'South Africa, 1902.'[8] On their return to Worcester in 1903 they were entertained at a dinner in the Shire hall.

[1] Holden, op. cit. p. 189. [2] Ibid. 202. [3] Ibid. 208. [4] Ibid. 211
[5] Ibid. 225. [6] Ibid. 228. [7] Ibid. 249. [8] *Army List*, July, 1905.

At the time of the French wars Worcestershire took its proper part in raising and maintaining volunteers for national defence. On the last day of November in the year 1803, George III., who had recently reviewed in Hyde Park, amid scenes of uncommon ardour and enthusiasm, the volunteers of London and Westminster, wrote to his confidant, the bishop of Worcester: 'We are here in daily expectation that Buonaparte will attempt his threatened invasion. . . . Should his troops effect a landing I shall certainly put myself at the head of mine and my other armed subjects to repel them; and as it is impossible to foresee the events of such a conflict, should the enemy approach too near to Windsor, I shall think it right the queen and my daughters should cross the Severn, and shall send them to your episcopal palace at Worcester. . . . Should such an event arise, I certainly would rather that what I value most in life should remain, during the conflict, in your diocese, and under your roof, than in any other place in the island.'[1] In the same year the effective rank and file of the Worcestershire volunteer cavalry and yeomanry numbered 501, whilst the volunteer infantry showed a muster roll of 3,803, of which the city of Worcester furnished 552.[2]

The Worcestershire Regiment of Fencible Cavalry, raised in 1796 and known in 1798 as the Regiment of Provisional Cavalry, and also in the following year as the Worcestershire Regiment of Light Dragoons, had comprised four troops—the Commandant's (Hon. John Somers Cocks), Major Henry Bromley's, Captain J. W. Long's, and Captain Thomas Webb's—each mustering between fifty and sixty officers and non-commissioned officers and rank and file inclusive.[3] On leaving Ireland on 17 January, 1800, where they had been stationed since 1799, they were thanked by Lord Cornwallis for their services,[4] and afterwards disbanded at Kidderminster on 12 April, 1800, with the honourable record of being the only regiment of provisional cavalry that volunteered to serve out of England.[5]

In 1803 the Worcestershire yeomanry was commanded by the Hon. J. S. Cocks, who applied to the War Office for 'the stipulated allowance for clothing of nine pounds per man for three years for three troops of Worcestershire Yeomanry Cavalry.' The third troop appears from his letter to have been an augmentation on a former establishment of two troops,[6] as the commandant had been notified by the lord-lieutenant on 19 August, 1803, of His Majesty's authorization to draw allowances for the equipment of this new third troop. The total complement of the corps was at this time 163. In 1804, while stationed at Gloucester from 29 October to 13 November, the three troops were commanded by Captains Geo. Deakin, Lavender, and Chambers, and kept up their numbers well.[7] The Stourbridge first troop of yeomanry cavalry was commanded in 1804 by Captain John Addenbrooke, and numbered 54 privates, 2 buglers, and 4 commissioned officers, but by 1815 the effectives, exclusive of officers, had sunk to 37.[8] The second troop of Stourbridge Volunteer Cavalry was commanded from 1813 to 1816 by

1 Geo. III. to Bp. of Worc., *Bentley's Miscellany*, xxvi. 519.
2 *Parl. Ret.* 1803.
3 W.O. Pay Lists Fencible Cavalry, 3,791 (P.R.O.).
4 Turberville, *Worc. in Nineteenth Century*, p. 218.
5 Holden, *Hist. of Third and Fourth Batt. Worc. Reg.* p. 65 note.
6 These two troops are said to have been raised about 1794. Holden, op. cit. p. 56 note.
7 It was still under the same commandant in 1815. W.O. Yeomanry Pay Lists, 4,050 (P.R.O.)
8 Ibid.

Captain Thomas Homfray, and averaged between 30 and 40 of all ranks.[1] From 1803 to 1815 Captain John Adams was in command of the Bromsgrove troop of light horse volunteers or yeomanry, and the total effectives besides officers usually numbered about 45.[2] The King's Norton Volunteer Cavalry under Captain H. Geast mustered during the same period rather fewer men, and this number in 1806 fell to 35 of the rank and file and 3 sergeants.[3] Captain Thomas Brettell was in command from 1804 to 1813, but during his term of office the total effectives of all ranks, which in May, 1805, amounted to 45, had by 1813 sunk to 17 privates, 1 trumpeter, and 1 quartermaster.[4]

The Wolverley troop of yeomanry cavalry usually mustered about 40 in the period 1804–1814, and was commanded by Captain James Knight.[5] The return of the Kidderminster troop of yeomanry in August, 1803, shows 1 captain (Sam. Steward), 2 lieutenants, 1 cornet, 2 sergeants, 1 trumpeter, and 40 rank and file, its full establishment, but in 1815, when Captain Homfray was commandant, the total effectives besides officers numbered 56.[6]

After the battle of Waterloo in 1815 the peaceful history of the yeomanry was only varied by occasional service in aid of the civil power during the period of social unrest which followed the peace. On 29 September, 1817, the mayor and magistrates of Worcester sent an urgent summons to Major the Hon. J. S. Cocks at Eastnor Castle requesting him to immediately muster the Worcestershire Regiment of Yeomanry Cavalry 'for the suppression of a riot now vigorously acting.'[7] The regiment was assembled, did its duty,[8] and was dismissed the same evening, but the next day there was a renewal of the disturbance, and again the mayor and magistrates applied to the commandant, 'We earnestly entreat that you will immediately muster them again for the ultimate suppression of the renewed grievances.' On the occasion of these troubles, known as the 'Freemen's Riots,' the yeomanry probably acted with considerable reluctance, and were in sympathy with the effort to prevent encroachment on Pitchcroft Ham.[9] In November of the same year there seems to have been trouble at Kidderminster, as Mr. John Roberts, J.P., wrote to Captain Boycot, in command of the Kidderminster Cavalry, 'I hereby require you will assemble your troops of Kidderminster Yeomanry Cavalry on actual service as soon as possible for the preservation of the peace of the borough.'[10] In 1831 the present regiment of yeomanry was formed by the earl of Plymouth. He was colonel, Lord Lyttelton lieutenant-colonel, and there were 10 troops and 40 officers.[11] During November and December, 1831, at the time of the Reform agitation, the Stourbridge and Upton troops and the Worcester Yeomanry were mobilized in aid of the civil power.[12] In 1850 the regiment mustered 11 troops, with 2 guns and 22 artillerymen.[13]

Lack of space will not permit us to further trace the history of the county yeomanry, which at present is known as one of the regiments of

[1] W. O. Yeomanry Pay Lists, 4,050 (P.R.O.). [2] Ibid. [3] Ibid. [4] Ibid.
[5] Ibid. [6] Ibid. Captain Homfray signed as commandant in 1807.
[7] The disquietude of the authorities seems to be here infused into their language. The writer had no doubt in mind the 'vigorous action' required of the gallant commandant. W.O. Yeomanry Pay Lists (P.R.O.).
[8] Turberville, *Worc. in Nineteenth Century*, p. 116. [9] Ibid.
[10] 25 Nov., W.O. Yeomanry Pay Lists, 4,050 (P.R.O.). [11] *London Gazette*, 25 May, 1831
[12] W. O. Yeomanry Pay List, 4,050 (P.R.O.). [13] Holden, op. cit. p. 57 note.

Imperial Yeomanry. The Queen's Own[1] Worcester Hussars showed by the good service of its contingent in South Africa the continuance of the loyal and gallant traditions of the corps. The uniform is blue with scarlet facings.

Of the infantry volunteers raised during the Napoleonic period the Loyal Worcester Regiment (the City Corps which had been formed in August, 1813, and for whose arms and equipment £2,500 had been raised)[2] was commanded from 1803 to 1808 by Lieut.-Colonel the Hon. G. W. Coventry, the first major being Samuel Wall, junior. The company officers in 1803 were Captains Elias Isaac, John Dowding (Grenadier Company), James Williams, H. Philpott, Thomas Carden, junior, M. James, John Duncan, and M. Barre.[3] The drills usually took place on Sundays so as not to interfere with the usual business of the men. In April, 1804, the Worcester Volunteers received from Lady Deerhurst their colours, which were afterwards consecrated in the cathedral.[4] After 1808 this regiment furnished recruits for the Worcester Local Militia under the command of Colonel Fernando Smith.

The commandant of the South Worcester Volunteer Regiment in 1803–4 was Thomas Bland, and in 1808 and 1809 the returns are signed by Colonel the Hon. W. B. Lygon. This corps was in 1803–4 the strongest in numbers of all the Worcester battalions and included the following companies: Ripple (Captain Ric. Clarke), Welland and Castle-Morton (Captain Wm. Boulter), Hanley Castle (Captain Thom. Hornyold), Mathon (Captain Robert Harrison), Great Malvern[5] (Captain John Benbow), Powick (Major W. A. Oliver, late Captain 64th Foot), Upton (Captain James Skey), Longdon (Captain John Stone), Madresfield (Captain R. Lygon); Captain Harrison acted as adjutant.[6] The South Worcester Volunteers received their colours on Hanley Common on 17 September, 1804, from Mrs. Lygon, who also gave the privates 100 guineas to drink the king's health.[7] Ultimately this regiment was merged in the South Worcestershire Local Militia under the Act 48 Geo. III. c. 3.

The North Worcestershire Volunteers included three companies raised in or near Bromsgrove with the King's Norton and Tardebigge companies. The Bromsgrove captains were John Lucas, Walter Brook, and Robert Andrews; Captain W. C. Russell was in charge of the King's Norton company and Captain J. Mence, junior, of the Tardebigge. The commandant was Lieut.-Colonel Wm. Villiers.[8] They were presented with their colours by Lady Beauchamp on 10 August, 1807,[9] and about a year later furnished the main body of recruits for the North Worcestershire Local Militia raised under the Act already cited.

The combined Loyal Evesham and Pershore Battalion of Volunteer Infantry were in 1804 under the command of Major-General Jeffrey Amherst as their lieutenant-colonel, and numbered, besides officers, 20 sergeants, 20 corporals, 8 drummers, and 391 privates. Henry Wigley was at this time major

1 The regiment was honoured with this title after forming an escort for H.R.H. the duchess of Kent and the Princess Victoria on their visit to Worcester in 1832.

2 Turberville, *Worc. in Nineteenth Century*, p. 225.

3 W.O. Volunteer Pay Lists, 4,589 (P.R.O.).

4 Turberville, op. cit. p. 226.

5 In the return of this company, which was under its proper strength, there is a note that no less than eleven privates had enlisted with the regulars. So the volunteers would seemed to have served as a very valuable nursery for the line.

6 W.O. Volunteer Pay Lists, 4,590 (P.R.O.).

7 Turberville, op. cit. p. 226.

8 W.O. Volunteer Pay Lists, 4,589 (P.R.O.).

9 Turberville, op. cit. p. 231.

and Jeremiah Martin, adjutant.[1] The ladies of Evesham worked colours for the battalion, which were presented on their behalf by Mrs. Perrott,[2] in April, 1804. In September, 1808, the battalion volunteered into the militia and was then known as the East Worcestershire Local Militia, and men were drawn by lot to complete their establishment.[3]

The West Worcestershire Volunteers included the Bewdley, Kidderminster, and Stourport contingents, and in 1806, and probably also in the previous two years, were under the command of Lieut.-Colonel John Jeffreys, who is returned in the printed Volunteer List of 1804 as commander of the Kidderminster companies. The complement of the Bewdley company in 1804 was 123 of all ranks. Captain Robert Pardoe was in command, James Pardoe, first lieutenant, and the second lieutenant was William Prattinton. In the same year the Kidderminster contingent mustered three companies from fifty to sixty strong, and the major in command was J. Turner.[4] Nearly all the men had done their twenty days' exercise. The Stourport Loyal Volunteers numbered between 120 and 130 of all ranks, and were under the command of Captain Richard Jukes, who notes on his pay-list and return: 'The whole of above-named men have been compleatly armed and accoutred at the expence of the inhabitants.'

The Droitwich Volunteers mustered, in the year 1804, 144 non-commissioned officers and rank and file, besides 2 captains, 2 lieutenants, and 2 ensigns under the command of Captain Edward Penrice.[5] The Elmley Lovett detachment at the same date could only show just over 40 of all ranks, under Captain G. F. Forester.[6] Dudley was well to the fore, as might have been expected, and raised four companies under Lieut.-Colonel the Hon. J. W. Ward, with Thomas Hawkes, Joseph Hately, William Boyle and Richard Moore as captains, Joseph Payton being adjutant and Major Wainwright second in command in 1804. Four years later Wainwright had apparently become commander, and in 1810 was succeeded by Lieut.-Colonel Hawkes. In 1808 the officials at the Horse Guards were worrying the Dudley corps for their current account for 1803, to which the adjutant replied, 'I have the honour to inform you that the Dudley Loyal Volunteer Infantry was not accepted till late in the year 1803, and that we omitted to draw any money upon account of services in that year. Of course we have no account current for 1803.'[7]

Other detached corps were the Feckenham (Captain R. B. Waldron), the Hanbury (Captain John Weir), the St. John's and St. Clement's (Captain John Hall), the Shipston (Captain J. B. Bellamy), Tenbury (Captain Edw. Wheeler), and the Witley Rifle Corps (Commandant Thomas Ld. Foley).[8] The Shipston company boasted a surgeon, John Horniblow, whilst the Tenbury contingent, a hundred strong, had all put in thirty days' attendance, and some more, during the year 1803.[9] Colours were presented to the Tenbury contingent by Mrs. Pytts, of Kyre House, in August, 1804.[10] The West Worcestershire Volunteers and some of the detached corps seem to have been

1 W.O. Volunteer Pay Lists, 4,589 (P.R.O.).
2 Turberville, op. cit. p. 226.
3 May, *Hist. of Evesham*, p. 408.
4 W.O. Volunteer Pay Lists, 4,590 (P.R.O.).
5 Ibid. 4,591 (P.R.O.).
6 Ibid.
7 Ibid.
8 Lord Foley's rifle corps had been raised in September, 1803. Turberville, op. cit. p. 225.
9 W.O. Volunteer Pay Lists, 4,591 (P.R.O.).
10 Turberville, op. cit. p. 256.

merged, after 1808, in the West Worcestershire Regiment of Local Militia, which was commanded by Lord Foley.

The volunteer enthusiasm again awoke in 1859 when the policy of Napoleon III. was regarded with grave suspicion in this country. Sir Thomas Phillipps, of Middle Hill, issued a Broadsheet entitled 'Reasons for a Rifle Corps,' which was sufficiently alarming: 'If any enemy should land and conquer the country, he will take away your cattle, your sheep, your horses, your pigs, your poultry, and your corn, at last, if not first, your wives and daughters!' In another sheet, as one of Her Majesty's deputy-lieutenants for the county of Worcester, he expressed his readiness to enroll the names of any gentlemen who were willing to form a company of the Worcestershire Rifle Corps. To this and other patriotic appeals the shire was not backward in its response, and possesses at the present time two battalions of volunteer infantry, with headquarters at the City of Worcester and Kidderminster respectively.[1] Contingents from these corps took part in the late South African War. A corps of heavy garrison artillery, the 1st Worcestershire, comprises four batteries, with headquarters at Worcester, Kidderminster, Redditch, and Malvern, and its affiliated cadet company at Malvern College.

[1] *Army List.* To the 2nd Volunteer Battalion of Infantry the Victoria Institute, Worcester, furnishes a cadet corps.

INDUSTRIES

INTRODUCTION

THE genesis of the industry of any county is usually determined by two factors, one its physical character and resources, the other the will, enterprise, and plastic power of man. Often a trade is rooted in the soil of a particular district, its very being depends on local and peculiar sources of supply. Occasionally, however, as in the case of the porcelain works of Worcester, foresight and initiative have created an industry which is wholly independent of its immediate surroundings.

The production of salt at Droitwich is coeval with authentic history, for in Domesday the Wich with its salt-making is a dominant feature and pervades the survey of the shire.[1] To the brine springs of the Keuper marls Worcestershire owes its oldest, perhaps its most characteristic, organized industry. And neither the salt works, the early iron-smelting, nor the Stourbridge glass, would have been practically possible but for the dense woodlands of the county such as the Forest of Feckenham. The importance at a later period of the northern coal-fields needs no insistence here, but we may mention the iron that lay close by, and the Silurian limestone, worked for centuries as a flux for that metal. The fire-clay mined in the district near Stourbridge, which was probably in origin an ancient exhausted soil, is world famous. It bears intense heat without melting, and is especially adapted for crucibles and fire bricks, being therefore essential for the prosecution of the local industries. The sandstones which occur with the coal-measures are worked for building use, while the lower Lias is not only burnt for lime, but, to a small extent, quarried for paving, and the alluvial clays furnish ample material for the brickmaker.

In regard to textiles it may be mentioned here that among the causes which led to the development of the old local industry of Kidderminster into fabrics where colouring formed a more leading feature, was the belief long accepted that the brilliancy and permanence of colour in the local stuffs was owing to the peculiar property of the River Stour in fixing their dyes.[2]

For the culture of fruit and its natural development, the production of cider and perry, Worcestershire has long been famous. The vale of Evesham and the valleys of the Severn and the Teme offer admirable sites for orchards and hopfields. Robert of Gloucester[3] under Henry III. celebrated the 'frut at Wircestre,' and Drayton[4] sang of Evesham Vale—

'Where full Pomona seems most plenteously to flow
'And with her fruitery swells by Pershore in her pride.'

The natural fertility of its river-valleys, improved by careful culture, still stands the county in good stead. During the distressing prevalence of bad trade in Worcestershire and Herefordshire in the year 1903, fruit-growing alone of the industries of the West Midlands showed any prosperity, and this was mainly due to the unusual crop in the Evesham district.[5]

Passing from the material and physical to the human factor in the origin and progress of our industries, we may briefly note the occasional stimulus derived from abroad. In England, generally, foreign immigration either introduced a trade entirely new, or consolidated and extended one previously existing which had hitherto been purely local. In Worcestershire we obtain our primary example in the glass manufacture of Stourbridge, where the skilled craftsmen of Lorraine, after previous settlement elsewhere in England, utilized the natural advantages of the neighbourhood and built up a substantial and extended business.

Again, as the cloth trade of Worcestershire decayed, partly perhaps through the competition of the water-power looms of Somerset and the adjacent counties, a new impetus was given to the manufacture of silken fabrics, and later of carpets, by the influence, direct or indirect, of foreign weavers, driven from France by the Revocation of the Edict of Nantes. Also on several occasions since, improvements in carpet-weaving, glove-making, and fruit-culture have been derived from an intelligent study of foreign methods.

[1] *V.C.H. Worc.* i. 268.

[2] Information kindly supplied by Mr. J. Brinton. See also Gibbons, *Kidderminster*, p. 52.

[3] *Met. Chron.* (Rolls Ser.), i. 10.

[4] Drayton, *Polyolbion* (Anderson, 1793, iii. 395).

[5] *Ann. Rep. Chief Inspector of Factories* for 1904 (1905), p. 52.

In the development of every trade which is not purely local, the provision of suitable means of communication with the surrounding country is of the first importance. As to land transit, probably from a very early period the salt of Droitwich was carried on pack-horses by the Salt Ways,[1] whilst in the eighteenth century traffic on the various roads had become so great that several Acts were passed for their repair. From one private Act[2] of Queen Anne for *Repairing the Highway or Road from the city of Worcester to the Borough of Droitwich*, we learn that the greatest part, being in length about six miles, by reason of the great and many loads and carriages of salt and other goods, which daily pass through the said road, had become impassable for the space of nine months in every year. And in the eighteenth century so great was the demand for the garden produce of Evesham that in one day from sixty to eighty horses were laden for dispatch to Birmingham market. By the first and second decade of the last century the roads had been so improved that wheeled vehicles were generally employed for transport and fewer horses were required.[3]

The further improvement of land transport by the construction of railways towards the middle of the nineteenth century gave an impulse to the industries of the county which can only be compared with the progress made eighty years before, when the chief canals were made. At Kidderminster, for instance, the advent of the railway coincided with the revolution in the manufacture of textiles brought about by the general introduction of the power-loom, and trade sensibly advanced.

Lack of space does not permit us to trace the various stages by which the iron-track compassed the county. It must suffice to say that the two leading systems now in possession are the Great Western and Midland. The Great Western railway enters the county at Church Honeybourne, passing through Evesham, Pershore, Worcester, and Droitwich to Kidderminster, Stourbridge, Dudley, and the north, a great artery of traffic linking the industrial centres of the county. To the west the Worcester and Hereford branch of the Great Western connects with Malvern and South Wales, a north-easterly branch from Stourbridge runs through Cradley and Rowley Regis to Birmingham, and a north-westerly up the Severn valley. A motor-car service is now being started to develop the resources of the fruit-growing districts. The other great arterial line, the Midland, passes from Birmingham through Bromsgrove, Droitwich, Worcester to Cheltenham and Bristol, while a branch from Ashchurch in Gloucestershire joins Evesham, Alcester, and Redditch. Finally, we may mention the line from Kidderminster to Tenbury, which unites with the Shrewsbury and Hereford. The last decade has witnessed[4] a signal advance in electric traction. We may instance the Kidderminster and Stourport electric tramway and the Dudley and District connecting with Stourbridge, Lye, and Wollescote, whilst others are open or in contemplation.

But the history of water communication in Worcestershire demands a more extended notice. A glance at the county map shows the Severn flowing from north to south by Wribbenhall, Bewdley, and Stourport, where it receives the Stour, and thence to Worcester. A little below Worcester it is joined by the tributary Teme and keeps onward in its course by Severn Stoke and Upton to Tewkesbury.

From an early period, in spite of serious difficulties in navigation, the 'king's high stream of Severn' had an increasing carrying trade. Barges and trows laden with wood, iron, madder, oil, wine, and other merchandise[5] passed up and down between Bristol and Bewdley, and often fierce disputes arose when the citizens of Worcester and Gloucester demanded tolls, or neighbouring landowners became too rapacious, while tow-paths or 'lyne-weyes' were apt to suffer overgrowth of brushwood and timber.[6] An Act of 1430 recites that the river Severn is common to all the king's liege people to carry and re-carry all manner of merchandise, as well in trowes and boats as in flotes, otherwise called drags. This comfortable doctrine, however, had not found favour with the neighbouring Welshmen and others who had assembled in great numbers arrayed in manner of war, seized and hewn in pieces the drags, and beaten their crews, to the intent that they should hire of the said Welshmen.

Edward IV., in the twelfth year of his reign, granted[7] the men of Bewdley various privileges, including freedom from dues and tolls, in return for their good service at Tewkesbury field.[8] But apparently only three years after the bailiffs of Worcester were again demanding from the men of Bewdley, as well as others, one penny from the owner of every boat that passed their bridge, and fourpence a ton on the laden merchandise.[9] Hence grievous complaints arose, and

[1] In 1326 the toll levied upon the salt carts in the manor of Feckenham produced 3*s*. 9*d*. and no more owing to the carters making use of other ways apparently free from toll. Mins. Accts. 1067, No. 26. See also *Sessions R.* Intro. clxx.

[2] 12 Anne Stat. ii. cap. 3.

[3] Pitt, *Gen. View of Agric. Co. Worc.* (1813), p. 147.

[4] *Directory of Elec. Lighting and Traction* (1905).

[5] See Depositions, Star Chamber Proc. Hen. VII. 4, and Bill, Star Chamber Proc. Hen. VIII. $\frac{4}{182}$.

[6] See *Parl. R.* v. 569*b*; Acts 9 Hen. VI. cap. 5; 19 Hen. VII. cap. 18; 23 Hen. VIII. cap. 12.

[7] *Cal. Pat.* 12 Edw. IV. m. 27.

[8] Depositions in Star Chamber Proc. Hen. VII. 4.

[9] Apparently the Council of the Marches at Ludlow 15 Hen. VII. regulated the toll to be levied on boats from Bewdley passing under Worcester Bridge. See Noake, *Worcestershire Relics* (1877), p. 65.

as a result an Act was passed in 1503[1] against certain officers of Worcester and Gloucester, who prevented vessels from passing unless they paid certain tolls, decreeing a heavy penalty if this extortionate practice was continued.

Thoroughly alarmed at this Act, Worcester as well as Gloucester petitioned[2] the Star Chamber that they should be allowed to continue the accustomed tolls. Otherwise, the bailiffs of Worcester expressed a fear that they might be unable to pay the fee farm of their city due to the king's highness. They drew a vivid picture of their bridge of stone, 'archyd and embowyd, by the whichich (sic) burge the kynges subjects have their passage between Englond and Walys,' as well as of their 'key or wharfe made of fre stone adioyning to the same river.' The tow-path the citizens apparently claimed as their freehold, for the use of which they were entitled to charge. As to the damage done, they declared that the boatmen with the 'seid cordys and with hokys and sparreys of yron drawith, hokyth, tyeith, and puttyth at the seyd burgge and greytly fretyth losyth, and often tymes brekyth and castyth down the stonys of the seyd burge,' and that the city of Worcester was put to grave expense for repairs.

As a consequence of these petitions a writ was issued 4 December, 1504, to the abbot of the Monastery of the Blessed Mary of Bordesley and divers laymen, to inquire as to the verity of the matter. The commission met on 17 January following at Worcester, and a number of masters, pursers, and others employed in the river craft, when examined, seemed, with some exceptions, to have borne out the general allegations of the Worcester authorities as to the levy of tolls, though certain communities were to be held more or less exempt. The fact seems to have been that Bewdley was becoming a considerable depôt for merchandise directed to Bristol and the south, and whilst the bargemen could scarcely have objected to a moderate toll when their goods were sold by their own free will and at their own price at Worcester, yet they did heartily resent a fine for merely passing beneath the bridge, or what was still worse, a compulsory sale at Worcester at a lower price than they could get nearer the coast.

It is clear that the authorities of Worcester were none too nice in their methods of compulsion. As certain petitioners of Bewdley averred[3] in the next reign, 'If your seid oratours refuse so to do contrary to their appetites, then they ryottuosly shete arrows and caste stones at them, and so for fere and drede of theyr lyves have compelled them to cum out of the kynge's hye streym with theyr merchandize, and to pay them the seyd summes of money, and also to make sale of ther merchaundize contrary to their myndes.'

In spite of petitions and inquiries the same practices seem to have continued. An Act of 1532 imposes a penalty of 40*s*. for hindering passengers on the banks of the Severn or demanding tolls. And as late as 1564 the bailiffs of Worcester were insisting on their customary dues from Tewkesbury men, who claimed exemption, and seizing their cattle in default.[4]

In spite of the notorious defects of the Severn navigation, very little was done until the nineteenth century to remedy them. Acts dealing with the towing-paths and their maintenance were passed from time to time, but only in the year 1842 were Commissioners appointed to raise money on the security of the Severn tolls and improve the navigation of the river. Locks and weirs were built between Stourport and Worcester, and thence to Gloucester, and gradually, in spite of considerable opposition, the canalization of the Severn was fully carried out. Now, at every season of the year, a depth of at least ten feet of water is maintained between Gloucester and Stourport.[5] As the Severn joins the Gloucester and Berkeley ship canal at Gloucester ships of 400 tons[6] can now go up as far as Worcester, but the bridge at Gloucester stops sea-going ships only thirty miles from Birmingham. Unfortunately, the Worcester and Birmingham canal can only admit barges of thirty tons or so, and its adequate improvement is most desirable, and would render speedy and effective the water communication between the Midlands and the sea.

In the seventeenth century some attention was given to the improvement of the various tributaries of the Severn. On 9 March, 1635–6, Mr. Secretary Windebank acquainted[7] his Majesty sitting in Council, that William Sandys, of Fladbury, in the county of Worcester, had undertaken at his own cost to make the river Avon passable for boats from Severn, where that river falls in near Tewkesbury, through the counties of Worcester, Gloucester, and Warwick into or near Coventry, and that he has been already at great charge therein, also that Mr. Sandys intends to make passable a good part of the river Teme lying towards Ludlow, whereby the said counties may be better supplied with wood, iron, and pitcoals, which they want. Commissions were issued to persons of quality to deal with claims for compensation, and it was ordered that every assistance should be given to the project.

1 19 Hen. VII. cap. 18.

2 Star Chamber Proc. Hen. VII. 4.

3 Ibid. Hen. VIII. $\frac{4}{182}$.

4 J. Noake, *Worc. Relics* (1877), p. 65, and compare deposition of John Southall, Star Chamber Proc. Hen. VII. 4.

5 Information supplied by J. W. Willis-Bund, LL.B.

6 Harcourt, *Rivers and Canals* (ed. 2, 1896), p. 478.

7 *Cal. S. P. Dom.* Chas. I. 1635–6, p. 280.

In May, 1661, as we learn from a letter[1] sent by A. Newport to Sir A. Leveson, there was a bill before the Lords for making a brook in Worcestershire navigable betwixt Severn and 'Shirbrige,'[2] that the coals there may be brought cheaper to Worcester, Gloucester, and these lower countrys, which will absolutely destroy all the water sale of coals out of Shropshire; yet it will certainly pass the Lords, whatever it does in the Commons.[3]

The parish registers[4] of Kidderminster furnish the information that coals were first brought to that town from Stourbridge by water on 6 March, 1665. This was probably in consequence of Yarranton's attempt to improve the navigation between Stourbridge and Kidderminster. His own account[5] of the matter is well worth quoting: 'The river *Stoure* and some other rivers were granted by an Act of Parliament to certain persons of honour, and some progress was made in the work, but within a small while after the Act passed it was let fall again. But it being a brat of my own, I was not willing it should be abortive; therefore I made offers to perfect it, having a third part of the inheritance to me and my heirs for ever, and we came to an agreement. Upon which I fell on, and made it completely navigable from *Stourbridge* to *Kederminster;* and carried down many hundred tuns of coales, and laid out near one thousand pounds, and there it was obstructed for want of money, which by contract was to be paid.'[6] Very little further of an effective character seems to have been done to improve the water-communications of the county until the great canal era of the eighteenth century.[7]

The two earliest canals then constructed were the Staffordshire and Worcestershire, or Trent and Severn, communicating with the Grand Trunk, and the Droitwich canal from that town to the Severn.[8] Acts were procured for these in 1766 and 1767, and the work was completed by the years 1770 and 1771. The impetus given to trade was very great. Prior to the construction of the Staffordshire and Worcestershire canal there were only a few cottages at Stourport constituting the hamlet of Lower Mitton; after this the town rapidly increased in importance as a depot for agricultural produce and manufactured goods and became a busy inland port. In a few years' time as much as £2,000 was occasionally paid on the Trent and Severn canal for the tonnage of one season's fruit alone northward bound, representing perhaps 7,000 tons.[9] Allusion has already been made to the important Worcester and Birmingham canal; the Act[10] for its construction was obtained in 1791. Another canal connects Birmingham, Dudley, and Stourbridge.

Having considered the natural resources of the county, foreign influence, and the means of communication, we must now give some account of the industries themselves. The more important from the historical point of view are treated in separate sections. We have only to notice briefly the remainder here. The first of these might legitimately claim separate treatment if the space available were not limited. From an early period Worcestershire has been famed for its orchards of apples, and especially pears. Drayton as he draws out the roll of English troops at Agincourt grants as its blazon to the county 'Worcester, a pear-tree laden with the fruit,' and an achievement on the arms of the city is 'Argent, a fess between three pears sable,' whilst in the *Polyolbion* the river nymphs of the shire 'full bowls of perry brought.'

Cider and perry were probably made in Worcestershire at an early time, though notices are curiously scanty in mediæval records.[11] During the Tudor period and the century following there seems to have been considerable development. The famous orchards in Worcestershire for the production of perry stood on the rising ground at Monkland Farm, Newland, between Malvern and Worcester, originally planted, if we may believe the country-side, by the Malvern monks. The variety is the Barland pear, so harsh and astringent in flavour that it is said that even the pigs have no love for it, but well adapted for the production of an excellent liquor. In a 'hit' or favourable season as many as 200 hogsheads have been obtained from the 70 or more trees at Newland, and at an average price of £3 a hogshead the perry obtained would be worth £600.[12]

Pears are not used for perry alone, but their juice is at times blended with that of the apple, or even the common wild crab, for the production of cider.[13] In the 'hit' of 1784 cisterns were formed in the ground when the casks gave out, but they did not answer and the liquor was

[1] J. Noake, *Worc. Nuggets*, p. 272.

[2] Apparently for 'Stourbridge.'

[3] This Bill must have been the origin of the Act 13 and 14 Chas. II. cap. 13, which applied both to the Stour and Salwarpe, and is no doubt the statute referred to in the quotation from Yarranton.

[4] Burton, *Hist. of Kidderminster*, p. 78.

[5] Yarranton, *England's Improvement* (1677), p. 66.

[6] Information as to some later proceedings in connexion with this project will be found in *Hist. MS. Com.* Rep. xiv. Ap. pt. vi. p. 386. House of Lords.

[7] Note, however, 24 Geo. II. cap. 39 for the better regulating of the navigation of the river Avon. Proprietors of the navigation were to keep the river cleansed.

[8] 6 Geo. III. cap. 97; 8 Geo. III. cap. 37, 38.

[9] W. Pitt, *Gen. View of Agric. of Worc.* (1813), p. 149.

[10] 31 Geo. III. cap. 59.

[11] *Herefordshire Pomona*, pp. 23 and 24.

[12] E. Lees, *Botany of the Malvern Hills* (1868), p. 62.

[13] Pomeroy on 'Gardens and Orchards,' in Pitt, *Gen. View of Agric.* p. 177.

spoilt. It is said that in Pershore the juice ran from the pear-hoards in currents into the common sewers.[1] At the present day a great deal of the coarse perry is undoubtedly consumed. It is often termed cider, which it closely resembles, and is mainly the drink of the farm labourers.

As to the general use of cider, even amongst the well-to-do in the seventeenth century, we have an interesting note[2] by Dr. Beale, that when 'the late king (of blessed memory) came to *Hereford* in his distress, and such of the gentry of *Worcestershire* as were brought thither as *prisoners*; both *king*, *nobility*, and *gentry* did prefer cider before the best *wines* these parts afforded.' About 1662 a hogshead of cider cost £1 14*s*., while one of strong beer was ten shillings cheaper, and in 1720 a bottle of cider was sold at 6*d*., equal to three shillings of our present money.[3] Under William and Anne the cider industry of the western counties received a considerable stimulus from the partial exclusion of French wines during the long Continental war. As Philips patriotically sang—

> 'What should we wish for more, or why in quest
> Of Foreign Vintage insincere and mixt
> Traverse the extremest world?'

But with the commencement of the nineteenth century the manufacture declined[4] both in quality and bulk. During the wars with Napoleon corn and meat rose in price, and farmers turning their minds to corn-growing and cattle, grubbed up many of their orchards, of which the most prolific were on plough land, and at the same time neglected to improve those that remained. Less care, too, was taken in the actual manufacture, whilst middlemen dealt with the deteriorated liquor at their will, and nauseous mixtures replaced the pure juice of apple and pear. Excellent cider and perry were, however, still to be had at the right places in the early nineteenth century. 'Tommy Hope' of the Three Tuns, a well-known Pershore character, had in his cellar a famous 'Balm-Perry,' as he called it, which was thirty years old. As dark as porter, possibly from a trace of iron in the juice, this perry was kept in vats holding about 500 gallons each. It was a memorable liquor.[5]

At the present time cider and perry are made in most districts of the county where orchards abound, and a fair number of merchants are engaged in the trade. In the case of two firms at least cider-making is combined with the production of beverages of the lighter kind. These are A. W. Smith & Co., of the Standard Works, Pershore, whose other speciality is in mineral waters, and G. Hopkins & Sons, of Sutton Brewery, Kidderminster, who manufacture lager beer.

The wild crab has already been mentioned as occasionally employed in cider-making. From its verjuice vinegar used at one time to be commonly made in the valley of the Teme and in other districts where the crab was plentiful.[6] Malt vinegar has now generally taken its place, and has a history of about a quarter of a century as an organized industry in the city of Worcester. The first factory seems to have been opened[7] near Silver Street, in 1781. The present works of Messrs. Hill, Evans & Co., Ltd., for making malt vinegar and British wines, cover nearly seven acres, and are of their kind probably the most important in the world. Certainly they possess a vat of 'record' size, 100 feet in circumference and 32 feet high, with a capacity of 114,821 gallons, three times that of the Great Tun of Heidelberg.[8] This industry is also carried on by other firms at Worcester, Evesham, and Stourport. And in this connexion we may mention the Worcester sauce manufacture of Messrs. Lea and Perrins.

A necessary mention of the hop-growing industry must precede any reference to brewing and malting. As early as the seventeenth century hops were grown in the county in considerable quantities, and in 1689 we find a presentment[9] of Mr. Goodie, the hop-weigher, for not weighing justly in the market of Worcester. Again, in 1731, an Act[10] of Parliament deals with the Worcester hop-market; and there seems to have been a considerable advance in the planting of gardens about the middle of the eighteenth century.[11] At Bewdley every Saturday there was a market for hops,[12] while the Teme valley was as noted[13] for its plantations as for its production of cider, and the great Worcester hop-market and fair are naturally magnified by all writers on the shire. It has been stated[14] that at the beginning of the nineteenth century there were 6,000 acres under hops in Worcestershire, but that the acreage had fallen to 1,625 by the fifth decade. If this estimate is correct there has been considerable recovery. The year 1855 is credited[15] with

[1] Pomeroy on 'Gardens and Orchards,' in Pitt, *Cen. View of Agric.* p. 179.

[2] Gen. Advts. concerning Cider in Evelyn's *Sylva and Pomona* (1679), p. 376.

[3] J. Noake, *Mon. and Cathedral of Worc.* p. 305.

[4] C. W. Radcliffe Cooke, *A Book about Cider*, p. 9. Mr. Cooke, whose efforts to revive interest in the cider industry are known of all men, quoted the opinion of Lord Ducie, p. 18, that in Gloucestershire, near Tortworth, 'occasional bands of Wenlock limestone seem to produce the best cider apples.'

[5] H. Stopes, *Cider* (1888), 25.

[6] *Herefordshire Pomona*, i. 107.

[7] Green, *Hist. of Worc.* ii. 23.

[8] *Worc. at Work* (1903), 5.

[9] *Hist. MSS. Com. Rep.* 35, i. (1901), 326.

[10] 4 Geo. II. cap. 25.

[11] *Universal Mag.* June, 1763.

[12] Postlethwayte's *Dict. of Trades and Commerce*, ii. 846.

[13] Camden, *Brit.* (ed. Gough, 1789), iii. 371.

[14] Turberville, *Worc. in the 19th Century*, p. 6.

[15] J. Noake, *Notes and Queries for Worc.* p. 228.

having produced a larger yield of hops than was ever before known in the shire, the Worcester district, which, however, includes Herefordshire, having paid a duty of £398,635 6*s.* 5¾*d.* The extent[1] now usually under hops is about 4,000 acres, and at Worcester from 30,000 to 60,000 pockets of local produce are sold in the season.[2]

In the days when ale formed the staple drink of Englishmen, there is hardly a record of a local court where we may not find some reference to brewing. It was, in fact, a necessary local and often domestic industry. The Corporation of Worcester were not behind their brethren in authority elsewhere in their regulations. Complaint had been made as early as the time of Henry VII. of the consumption of wood in the maltkilns, and it was ordered in the first year of Edward VI., 'That from the fest of All Saints to the fest of Purificacion neither bakers nor brewers shall buy noo woode by the cobbull lodde' under certain pains. The price of ale was fixed at regular periods, and 'sadde and discreete persons' were appointed to taste the brew. Their oath suggests a pleasing if somewhat formidable duty : 'You shall resort to every brewer's house within this city on their tunning day, and there to taste their ale, whether it be good and wholesome for man's body, and whether they make it from time to time according to the prices fixed. So help you God.' Occasionally the corporation seem to have assisted their officers personally in the task.[3]

The precise date when hopped beer, as distinguished from the old-fashioned ale, was first brewed in Worcester cannot be precisely stated. In 1554 there is said to have been no beer brewer in the city, but the lodgers of one Richard Moon were more desirous to drink beer than ale.[4] So the public taste was evidently changing here as in the rest of England. We shall be unable to trace the later history of the industry at any length, but an entry in the State Papers of the reign of Charles II.[5] throws an interesting side-light on the condition of the trade. This is a petition of Richard Colston to the king, showing that for ten months of his office of gauger of excise for the city of Worcester, by discovering many frauds of the brewers he has so enraged them that they conspire against his life, and indict him falsely for an assault on Anne Butler, a brewer. He prays for a reprieve in case he be found guilty by the partiality of the jury. Annexed to this petition is the examination of the said Richard Colston and one Sam. Young, taken before the mayor, Thos. Street, and other justices. They declare that having received several informations that Anne Butler often concealed her brewings, they searched her house on the 2nd inst. for concealed beer ; and before their departure drank two or three flagons, but they deny taking any liberties or using any violence. This entry is otherwise interesting as showing us a continuance of the mediaeval practice of brewing by women. At the present time Worcester and the chief towns of the county have several flourishing breweries of great local repute, which lack of space forbids us to enumerate particularly.[6]

Of the various textile manufactures cloth and carpets have received treatment elsewhere, and we have only to make a brief mention of linen, silk, and a few subsidiary and allied industries. In the Middle Ages flax was extensively grown near Kidderminster, and in 1335 the tithe was valued at 13*s.* 4*d.*[7] Later, Kidderminster was noted for mixed fabrics of linen and wool, and linen and silk. By the Statute 30 Chas. II. cap. 9 the watering of hemp or flax in the Severn was forbidden. Bromsgrove, which at one time, according to Leland's phrase, stood 'somethinge by clothinge,' afterwards developed an important local industry in the bleaching of cotton and dressing of flax. The factory known as the Buck House employed many hands, and the coarse linens[8] of Bromsgrove were well known in the markets. At the present time the manufacture of lint is carried on at the Charford Mills.

There are traces of silk manufacture in Worcestershire, even before the infusion of new life which followed the Revocation of the Edict of Nantes. On 3 October, 1692, we meet with the petition[9] of Edward Beardmore of Worcester, silk-weaver, showing that he was in arms for King Charles I., under the command of Colonel Sandys, in Captain Bathe's company, and that he has ever since been diligent in his calling. But by reason of 'the meaness of his trade' and other reasons, he is now reduced to poverty, and craves a beadsman's place in the cathedral church of Worcester. But it was not till after the influx of foreign refugees, and the stimulus they gave to English trade, that we find both Blockley and Kidderminster becoming the centres for a considerable manufacture of silken fabrics.

Blockley, which lies in the south of the county, astride an old main road between London and Worcester, and also on the Fosseway, returned only eighty-seven families in 1563. Owing to the opening of the silk mills in the first decade of the eighteenth century, this number had by 1757 more than trebled.[10] The builder of the first mill here, Henry Whatcot, died in 1718. Plenty of

1 *Encycl. Brit.* (new ed.), Suppl. Vol. 33, *Worc.*

2 Kelly, *Direct. Worc.* (1904).

3 J. Noake, *Worc. in Olden Times*, pp. 34–35.

4 J. Noake, *Worc. Relics*, p. 67.

5 *Cal. S.P. Dom.* Chas. II. 1668–9, p. 255.

6 See *Worc. at Work*, p. 22, and Kelly, *Direct. of Brewers and Maltsters.*

7 Burton, *Hist. of Kidderminster*, p. 172.

8 Camden, *Brit.* (ed. Gough, 1789), p. 359, and information kindly supplied by Mr. J. Brinton.

9 *Cal. S.P. Dom.* Wm. & Mary, 1691–2, p. 469.

10 Nash, *Hist. of Worc.* i. 101.

water-power[1] was available, and by 1825 eight mills were in full work. The silk-throwing thus established at Blockley was utilized for the Coventry ribbon industry, and in fact depended to a large extent on the employment of that town. Unfortunately the prospects which seemed to open out for silk goods in 1860, under the treaty then arranged between the French Empire and the British Government, were ruined by the reverses of 1870. The French Republic abandoned the Reciprocity Treaty, fashions also changed, and both Coventry and Blockley suffered greatly. At Blockley the trade is now extinct.

As the clothing trade of Kidderminster declined, mixed stuffs of worsted and silk were made under the name of Spanish poplins, as well as Irish poplins and crape. In 1755 was established the manufacture of figured and flowered silk, and in 1772 1,700 silk and worsted looms were at work.[2] In 1831 the silk and worsted looms had decreased to 340, and the carpet manufacture gradually displaced the other trades of the town. An additional reason for the loss of the silk trade at Kidderminster is that these stuffs, as well as bombazines, were sent to Norwich to be dressed and finished; as a result, in a few years Norwich annexed the whole process of manufacture to itself.[3] There seems also to have been a slight manufacture of silk goods at one time in other parts of the county, as in 1833 the Parliamentary Commissioners mention a declining ribbon factory at Evesham.[4] At the present time Benjamin Sanders and Sons have a factory at Bromsgrove for silk florentine buttons.[5]

The knitting of worsted hose flourished at one time in the south-east of the county. We have an early mention of the Le Hosiere in Brutestrete,[6] Evesham; and an entry[7] in the corporation book of the same town of 30 May, 1615, that on the admission of one Norton by purchase to the freedom of the borough it was ordained that no other foreigner should be permitted to exercise the same trade 'so long as Norton shall buy up stockings here.' Evesham and Pershore are both mentioned by Postlethwayte[8] in the middle of the eighteenth century as engaged in the hosiery trade, while Shipston-on-Stour[9] in 1751 had a considerable manufacture of the same kind. In the early part of the last century there were[10] at Bredon from sixty to eighty stocking frames, which employed about a hundred persons, dependent on that manufacture at Tewkesbury. As late as 1845 the historian[11] of Evesham speaks of this ancient industry as 'lingering on the outskirts—the dying embers of our ancient trade.'

At one time a considerable lace manufacture flourished at Worcester. Mr. Jackson's factory was first established there, in January, 1817, owing to the Luddite troubles in Nottingham, and was soon followed by others,[12] but it does not seem to have taken permanent root in the city.

The limited space at our disposal forbids us to give more than a cursory mention to the remaining industries of the county, interesting as many of them are, and worthy of more extended treatment, whilst a few will have to be left for notice in the topography. The parchment manufacture at Stourbridge and at Bengeworth still remains; that at Bengeworth[13] is of peculiar historic interest, as from the earliest times of the Abbey of Evesham parchment was, it is said, here made for the monks. As early as the reign of Elizabeth[14] paper seems to have been made in the county, and in Hurcote parish register[15] for 20 August, 1653, is a notice of Robert Gough, deceased, 'who dyed at Hurcote papar myll.' Books were printed[16] at Worcester as early as the sixteenth century by John Oswen, one of the early itinerant printers, and *Berrow's Worcester Journal* boasts of being the oldest newspaper in Great Britain, having been first published in 1690.[17]

Bewdley at the present time still possesses two local trades of old standing. The manufacture of horn goods was active here[18] in the eighteenth century, and seems of considerable antiquity. The firm of G. J. Humpherson and Son still produce drinking horns, powder flasks, and combs.[19] Brass-founding was introduced at Bewdley by the Bankes of Wigan in 1697, and the manufacture of Maslin (Mechlin), pans, kettles, and other articles, is now pursued at the Load Street Works of G. T. Smith and Sons.[20] There are also prosperous general brass-foundries at Oldbury, Halesowen, Dudley, and Kidderminster. At one time there was some manufacture of salt-petre in the county, and references may be found to it in the state-papers of the seventeenth century;[21] and finally, we may

1 We are indebted to Mr. J. Brinton for valuable notes on the silk trade of Blockley.

2 Burton, *Hist. of Kidderminster*, pp. 180–181.

3 Information kindly supplied by Mr. H. Brinton.

4 May, *Hist. of Evesham*, p. 495.

5 Kelly, *Direct. Worc.* (1904).

6 Evesham Chron. (Rolls Ser.), p. 211.

7 May, *Hist. of Evesham*, p. 313.

8 *Dict. of Trade and Commerce*, ii. 846.

9 Pocock, *Travels through Eng.* (Camden Soc.), ii. 280.

10 Pitt, *Gen. View of Agric.* p. 279.

11 May, p. 313.

12 Chambers, *Gen. Hist. of Worc.* (1820), p. 363.

13 Kelly, *Direct. Worc.* p. 467.

14 *Cal. S.P. Dom.* Eliz. 1601–3, p. 44.

15 Burton, *Hist. of Kidderminster* (1890), p. 187.

16 Burton, *Bibl. of Worc.* p. 3.

17 Kelly, *Direct. Worc.* (1904).

18 Camden, *Brit.* (ed. Gough, 1789), iii. Add. p. 358.

19 Kelly, *Direct. Worc.* (1904), p. 28.

20 Ibid.

21 *Cal. S.P. Dom.* 1625–6, Chas. I. p. 490, also 1629–31 pp. 95–103, and 1631–33 p. 183.

mention the brush-making of Worcester, which dates from the eighteenth century.[1]

The modern development of industry in Worcestershire is striking and extensive. The carriage and wagon and chemical works of Oldbury, the Midland Railway Works at Bromsgrove, Cadbury's chocolate works and colony at Bournville, Selly Oak, the King's Norton Motor Co., the cycle works at Redditch, the carriage works of Messrs. McNaught, Lord Dudley's Iron Works at Dudley, and the Vulcan Iron Works [2] of Worcester, the rope-spinning walks, boot and saddlery manufactories, with many others, would require a volume for their adequate description. It should be especially noticed that in the county manufactures, as elsewhere in England, electrical driving is on the increase, the power being usually obtained from a central station. Another recent and significant fact is that the cycle makers and repairers are giving increased attention to motors and motor-cycles, and as a necessary result saddlers and others dependent on trade connected with horses are suffering owing to the transition from horse to motor traction.[6]

A century's retrospect of Worcestershire industries shows us great changes. When that sturdy Englishman, William Cobbett, rode through the county, homework still prevailed, and he waxed eloquent [7] on the comparative comfort of the shire. 'There is no horrible misery here as at Manchester, Leeds, Glasgow, Paisley, and other hell-holes of 84 degrees of heat. There misery walks abroad in skin, bone, and nakedness. There are no *subscriptions* wanted for Worcester; no militia-clothing.' His remarks applied particularly to the glove-trade of Worcester, and the work done in the cottages amidst the fields and hop-gardens. Now for good or ill the factory system embraces a large portion [8] of the county industry, but ameliorated by a consideration for the workers which was unknown in Cobbett's time.

SALT

Salt being of such great value to man in all stages of civilization, and more especially in ancient times owing to the want of winter feeding for cattle, and the greater consumption of salt meat due to it, we shall expect to find the industry of salt-making one of very great antiquity. The examination of the salt industry of Worcestershire is rendered the more interesting from the fact that, with the exception of Cheshire, Worcestershire is the only county in England in which salt has been continuously worked to any great extent. That the springs of Droitwich might have been known to the Romans is possible from the discovery of Roman remains made in that place during the construction of the railway from Worcester to Birmingham, but the evidence afforded by these remains seems to indicate merely the existence of a villa and not any large settlement.[3]

With the exception of these remains the first evidence as to the existence of the saltworks is to be found almost at the beginning of the eighth century. From this time onward the industry can be traced as a growing one, and its importance realized. Ethelbald,[4] king of the Mercians, made a grant to the abbey of Evesham [5] about the year 717, of some land and buildings in a place described variously as Sele or Saltwich, 'where salt is wont to be made.' Grants appear to have been made in 836 [9] and 884,[10] by Mercian rulers, of lands and woods and everything connected with the manufacture of salt around Droitwich, at Hanbury and Himbleton. Again, in 964 [11] mention is made of the lease of two houses with four vessels, and everything rightly belonging thereto, for the cooking of salt in Upwic. King Edgar,[12] 972, endowed the church of Worcester with lands and five furnaces for the making of salt in 'Fepstone' or 'Phepson.' All these instances serve to show that the industry was steadily carried on, and that the privilege of saltmaking was one to be sought for, but, unfortunately, they do not throw much light on the process or extent of the work. It is, however, fairly certain that the water was pumped up and evaporated, the salt remaining in the pan.

Coming to the Domesday Survey of Worcestershire, very frequent mention is found of the springs at Droitwich, then called Wich. It appears that a great many outlying places, some as far distant as Oxfordshire and Gloucestershire,[13]

[1] *Worc. at Work*, p. 5.

[2] These works, which employ from 800 to 900 men, are specially noted for the manufacture of railway signals. Messrs. McKenzie and Holland are the proprietors.

[3] *V. C. H. Worc.* i. 210.

[4] Birch, *Cart. Sax.* i. 203.

[5] *Chron. Evesham* (Rolls Ser.), p. 73.

[6] *Ann. Rep. Chief Inspector of Factories*, 1904 (1905), p. 52. See also as to the increase of electrical driving generally, 1904 Report, p. 291.

[7] *Rural Rides* (1830), p. 510.

[8] In the county of Worcester in 1903 there were still 846 out-workers in the glove-industry, which, as Cobbett noted, is peculiarly adapted for this kind of labour, but apparently the numbers are diminishing, *Ann. Rep. of Chief Inspector of Factories*, 1903 (1904), pp. 196, 228.

[9] *Chron. Evesham* (Rolls Ser.), i. 583.

[10] Ibid. ii. 175.

[11] Ibid. iii. 317.

[12] Birch, *Cart. Sax.* ii. 583.

[13] *V. C. H. Worc.* i. 269.

possessed shares in these saltpits. The king and Earl Edwin seem in the time of King Edward to have been the principal holders. At the time of Domesday, 1086, the Sheriff Urse[1] had a large holding, which came to him by virtue of twelve separate estates, a good example of how scattered these rights had become.

As to the actual working of the salt not much is said by Domesday. Several technical terms appear, which do not explain much, but rather increase the difficulties. The pits or wells from which the brine was extracted appear as 'putei.' The most frequently used term is that of 'salinae'; these were apparently either the places in which the brine was boiled, or represented, according to Nash, merely shares of salt water measured out from the wells to those who had the right of making salt. Another term, 'hoccus,' it is now practically impossible to explain. Nash[2] suggests that it was a smaller measure of salt water; this is the only attempt at explanation which can be found. 'Plumbi' were apparently the leaden pans in which the brine was actually boiled. Three measurements were used, according to Domesday, for the salt when made. Of these a 'summa' was the equivalent of a horseload. A 'sestier' was another measurement not now capable of explanation. A third measure was a 'metta' or 'mit.' This word seems to have outlived the others, and to have been a purely local term. Habington,[3] to whom reference will again be made later, in his Survey of Worcester explains it as equal to about eight bushels. King Edward is stated to have had a share in five brine-pits. In Upwic, 54 saltpans and 2 'hocci,' paying 6*s.* 8*d.*; in another brine-pit, Helpenic, 17 saltpans; in a third brine-pit, Midelwic, 12 saltpans and ⅔ of a 'hoccus,' paying in all 6*s.* 8*d.* 'In five other brine-pits,' it is said, 'there are 15 saltpans.' From all King Edward had £52.

One of the most interesting sidelights, and one of the most important with regard to almost any industry at this time, is thrown by the mention of timber in Domesday. The consideration of fuel must have been a very important one at this time, especially since the destruction was not lightly tolerated. The woods of the bishop at Fladbury[4] are entered as supplying 'ligna ad salinas de Wich.' The Forest of Feckenham round Bromsgrove sent yearly 300 cartloads of timber, which produced 300 mits of salt. The monks of Westminster obtained 100 mits of salt and sent 100 cartloads of wood from Martin Hussingtree.[5] The usual proportion, in fact, seems to have been 100 mits of salt for 100 cartloads of wood.[6] The great destruction of timber necessary for the boiling seems to have, in fact, led to a restriction of the work at various periods.[7] Leland[8] states that this was the case in his time.

King John, in 1215, granted a charter to the town of Droitwich,[9] which may be taken as a proof of the growing importance of the industry, and had a great influence on the subsequent history of the town, as it became the foundation of a monopoly. The charter was of the usual kind, granting to the burgesses of Wich the vill with saltpits, etc., for the yearly rent of £100.

According to Habington[10] the town of Droitwich was in some way benefited by Richard, bishop of Chichester, 1245, a native of the town, who was canonized by Pope Urban in 1262.[11] He goes on to say that after his death the wells fell into disrepair. As evidence of this he quotes a writ directed by Henry III. to the sheriff that he should inquire into the deterioration of the salt wells. The sheriff replied that the cost of repairs would be not less than £40, because it would be necessary to pull down twelve houses standing round the wells before they could be got at to repair them. The date of these proceedings is given as 16 December, 1264.

During the reign of Henry III. there is another reference to the saltworks, which is interesting as showing that the burgesses of the town were endeavouring to monopolize the industry. This reference is contained in an inquisition held before Simon de Walter, when it was stated[12] 'that the prior of Worcester had his saltpit and was wont to boil his salt from time immemorial, and used a common bucket to pump his saltpit, for which he paid sometimes more and sometimes less, and the same prior was wont to have men to pump his pit, boil his salt, and repair his pans (plumbos). And the said prior always was in seisin of doing all the aforesaid things until the bailiffs of Wich (Droitwich) took the manor of the king and impeded him. And the said prior was wont to boil four pans, and the said bailiff forbad the men of the vill to do his work, which cannot be done by others than the men of that vill.' Reference to this dispute is again found in the reign of Edward III. On 14 July, 1342, there is an exemplification,[13] at the request of the prior of Worcester, of a writ close dated at Missenden, 22 August, 1252, 'charging the sheriff of Worcestershire to cause the prior to have such seisin in respect of his salt in the town of Wych and of the boiling of the same as he used to have from time immemorial, until prevented by the bailiffs of the said town, who had taken the manor from the king at ferm.'

That the burgesses of Droitwich were as

1 *V.C.H. Worc.* i. 163*b*.
2 *Hist. of Worc.* 1781–99.
3 *Surv. of Worc.* (Worc. Hist. Soc. 1899).
4 f. 172. 5 f. 174*b*. 6 f. 173*b*.

7 *Sede Vacante Reg.* (Worc. Hist. Soc.), 270.
8 *Itin.* (Hearne ed. 1769).
9 Habington, op. cit. ii. 298.
10 Ibid. ii. 300.
11 *Worc. Epis. Reg. Giffard* (Worc. Hist. Soc.), 23n.
12 *Worc. Inq.* (Worc. Hist. Soc.) pt. i. p. 13.
13 Pat. 16 Edw. III. pt. ii. m. 27.

careful of their privileges as the prior is shown by an inspeximus dated 19 December, 1330,[1] of their charter from John. One more mention made during this reign is interesting as showing that the name Wich was in some way coming to its modern form; a transition for which even Nash, though he makes one or two suggestions, can give no satisfactory reason. On 20 June, 1347, a licence,[2] in consideration of 12 marks to be paid to the king, was granted to William de Salewarp, clerk, and Thomas his brother, to alienate in mortmain a loft and also a salt-house of six pans of salt water (buleriam sex plumborum aquae salsae) in Dryghtwich to two chaplains to celebrate divine service daily in the church of St. Michael Salewarp for the souls of the faithful departed. From this time onwards occasional references are found in various proceedings of courts and in ancient documents to the works at Droitwich. These principally refer to shares acquired or alienated by different people at one time or another. In 1378 the burgesses of Droitwich obtained by the payment of a fine of 40*s.* an inspeximus of the charter dated 19 December, 1330, inspecting and confirming the one dated 1 August, 1215. Beyond these allusions, however, there is nothing to throw light upon the progress or fortunes of the town and its industry.

The first connected and critical account of the process of salt-making and the history of the town of Droitwich is to be found in Leland's *Itinerary*,[3] a work written about the year 1539. He begins[4] his account by stating that the great advancement of the town was by making salt, and that nevertheless the burgesses were for the most part poor because gentlemen had the gain and the burgesses the labour. According to this account there were then three springs or wells in the town. The first and best was situated on the right bank of the river: this one was double as profitable as the others. The two others were lower down the river on the left bank, 'almost at the very town's end.' Mentioning the principal well, Leland states that there was a tradition that in the time of Richard de la Wich, bishop of Chichester already referred to, the supply of water failed, and was restored by the intercession of the bishop. The memory of this man was, Leland states, kept up by an annual feast, on which day the principal well was adorned with tapestries, and drinking, games, and revels took place at it. There were a great number of furnaces for making salt around this well. Habington states that in the reign of Henry VII. there were five wells in three different places, in Upwich, Middlewich, and Netherwich. Comparing the different accounts, it appears that the great spring was at Upwich. There were at this time 360 furnaces at work, paying 6*s.* 8*d.* each to the revenue.

Just before Leland's account was written, Mr. Newport, who dwelt at Droitwich, had promoted a search for another brine pit. The remains of an old pit were found, which was identified by the timber placed round it to keep the earth from falling in. This part, however, was not occupied, either from a deficiency in the salt spring or to avoid interfering with the profits of the other three. In Leland's opinion, and, he says, in that of many others, it would have been quite possible to dig and find more springs. There were, however, two objections to this course. The first was the desire to restrict the supply of salt in order to keep up the price. The men of Droitwich had at this time such privileges that they alone could make salt, and they are said to have succeeded in preventing the opening of a salt spring discovered in another part of Worcestershire. The second and very serious objection to any extension of the works was the scarcity of fuel. The country around Droitwich is said to have been stripped of its timber. Wood was brought from places in the Forest of Feckenham, such as the neighbourhood of Bromsgrove, Alvechurch, and Alcester. Six thousand loads of wood were, as it was, used in a year at the furnaces. The wood is described as 'young pole wood, easy to be cloven.' Each furnace produced four loads of salt yearly, working only from Midsummer to Christmas. The people who worked about the furnaces are described as being 'very ill coloured.'

From this description the following conclusions may be drawn. The salt industry had by this time become one of considerable importance and of great value to those who were fortunate enough to have a share in it. The statement that the burgesses had all the labour and but little profit shows that the number of these shareholders was limited. Having fallen into the hands of a close corporation with the practical monopoly of the sale of salt, the output was restricted to keep up prices. Further development of the industry was prevented by lack of fuel. The salt supply, therefore, was not likely to increase until the monopoly could be broken down and a new kind of fuel took the place of wood.

Following on Leland's interesting account, the next most important entry regarding the Droitwich industry is found in the reign of James I., when Habington's *Survey of Worcestershire* appeared.[5] The interval which elapsed between Leland and Habington is made mention of only in lawsuits and wills, the shares in the saltworks apparently giving rise to fairly frequent litigation. Before dealing with Habington's description it may be mentioned here that in the last year of the reign of James I.[6] the bailiffs obtained a confirmation of their former liberties. The town

[1] Chart. R. Edw. III. m. 11, no. 22.

[2] Pat. 21 Edw. III. pt. ii. m. 26, p. 33*b*.

[3] Hearne (ed. 1769).

[4] Ibid. iv. p. 110.

[5] Habington, *Survey of Worc.* (Worc. Hist. Soc.).

[6] *Cal. S.P. Dom.* 1623–5, p. 346.

was incorporated. This charter, or renewal of charters, is of some importance, as it formed the principal plea in a suit which some time after had a great effect on the industry of salt-making in Droitwich.

In Henry VII.'s reign,[1] Habington states, there were five salt wells springing up in three separate places, named Upwich, Middlewich, and Netherwich. In his day only three of these remained, one in Upwich, two in Netherwich. The wells in Middlewich had perished, and there remained in their place nothing but waste ground. The stream running from Bromsgrove, the river Salwarp separated Upwich on the northern bank from Netherwich and Middlewich on the south bank. This brook ran close to the mouths of the pits, but the fresh water had no effect on the salt. Even, as sometimes happened in times of floods, if the fresh water overflowed into the pits no damage was done to the supply of brine, which remained unimpaired when the flood ran off. The supply seems to have been indestructible and inexhaustible. During the half of the year in which work was carried on, many hundred large vessels of salt water were drawn out daily except on Sundays and solemn feasts without diminishing the supply ; on the other hand, during the half of the year in which work stopped, the wells never overflowed nor suffered any detriment. The inhabitants have from time immemorial used 'rare justice' in the distribution of the salt water obtained from the wells. It was divided in various proportions or measurements known as saltphates walinge, plumbaryes, bullaries or boylaries of salt water. The best known name at this time was a phate. A phate[2] consisted of 216 large vessels of salt water. These vessels were of equal size, and were termed burdens of salt or brine ; both words appear in the account. The water on being pumped out of the well was first delivered to certain sworn officials, known as 'Magistri de la Beachin, masters of the Beachin or Tyes men.'[3] The water, owing to its varying quality, had to be divided in a certain proportion. The strongest water lay at the bottom of the well ; the water in the middle was not so strongly impregnated with salt, and the water at the top was weakest of all. Each phate, therefore, had a third part of each quality of water. To ensure this proportion, a phate was made up of twelve 'wickburdens,' each containing eighteen vessels of water. These eighteen vessels of water consisted of six vessels drawn from the bottom called 'first man,' six drawn from the middle called 'middle man,' six drawn from the top called 'last man.' In this way we have twelve times eighteen, that it to say, the 216 vessels of which a phate consisted. Although many great lords and even the king had been and were owners of phates, and though many had many phates and some only a share of a phate, yet each always had his proper share from 'first man,' 'middle man,' and 'last man.' The salt water having passed through the hands of the 'tyes men,' was then taken to 'seates,' formerly known as 'salinae' and 'domus salinae' (salt houses). This word 'salinae' certainly had a variety of meanings, representing either the saltpans, the houses in which the saltpans were kept, or sometimes a share of salt water, described in Habington's time as a 'phate.' In the salt houses the brine was boiled and converted into salt. The salt was then put into baskets made of twigs of sally, somewhat open to allow the moisture to run off. Four of these baskets, called barrows, containing about two bushels, made up a 'mit.' This is the term noticed above in the discussion of the Domesday[4] references to Droitwich. There were 400 of these phates in Upwich, besides some in Lowerwich. The owners of them before making salt had to give notice to the king's bailiffs of Wich, who committed the business to the 'master of the beachin,' whose office it was to see that the water was properly divided.

So important had the privilege of salt-making become that it is said that the possession of a phate, or no more than a quarter of a phate, in fee simple, carried with it the privileges of burgessship, which privilege descended in the same way as land by common law to the eldest son, but a burgess by birth might by grants of a portion of a phate make any of his relatives a burgess. A woman who was a burgess might also make her husband one in the same way. Nevertheless, though the purchase of a phate would not make a burgess, Habington says that of late years certain noblemen and others had been admitted to the borough. Of these he mentions John Talbot of Grafton, a connection of the earls of Shrewsbury, admitted in 1571 ; the Lord Keeper Coventry ; John, earl of Shrewsbury ; the bishop of Worcester ; Doctor Thornborough, and Thomas, Lord Windsor, all admitted a little later.

This account of the works is one of the fullest which can be found anywhere. It gives a very good impression of how jealously the separate rights were guarded, and, though it admits the entrance of certain new holders, says nothing of any extension of the industry. The work, it states, was still only carried on for half the year, no doubt owing to the same reasons as formerly; namely, the fear of oversupplying the market and the difficulty of providing sufficient fuel. It is rather curious that Habington, who lived within four miles of Droitwich and so thoroughly investigated this subject, should make no mention of the question of fuel, which must have continued to be one of great importance. Neither does he, unfortunately, give any idea as to

[1] Habington, *Survey*, ii. 296.
[2] Ibid. [3] Ibid. 297.

[4] See *V.C.H. Worc.* i. 269. Two barrows palewise in fess appear in the second and third quarters of the sinister half of the arms of the borough of Droitwich.

the total output, though, from his statement as to the large quantities of water pumped daily, it may be inferred that it was considerable. A time was, however, fast approaching when great changes were to take place. The monopoly was to be broken down and a new fuel was to take the place of wood.

For the history of Droitwich and its saltworks from the time of Habington down to the end of the eighteenth century we are principally indebted to Nash, who, in his *History and Antiquities of Worcestershire*, published in 1781, gathered up all the information given by previous writers, and brought the account up to his own time.

The renewal of the charter by James I. left the proprietors of the works firmly established in their monopoly. During the next two reigns and the interregnum nothing of very great importance is chronicled, though one or two interesting references to Droitwich and its saltworks are to be found. Droitwich appears to have suffered on at least one occasion during the Civil War. On 23 August, 1643, it is stated that 'Captain Croxton and Captain Venables, with their companies and others, went to Durtwich, and cut in pieces all the pans, pumps, saltpits, and works, carried some of their pans off; so their salt-making was spoiled, which served Shrewsbury and Wales and many other places of the kingdom. The provocation to this was that Lord Capel had issued a proclamation that none under his command should fetch any salt from Nantwich.' [1]

In 1655 [2] a more peaceable and useful scheme was projected at Droitwich. The land carriage of the salt to Worcester was attended with great expense.[3] Mention is now made of the first proposal to make the Salwarp navigable, and in this way to open a waterway between the works and the Severn. Two parliamentarians, Captains Yarranton and Wall, undertook for the sum of £750 to make the Salwarp navigable, and to procure letters patent for doing so from the Protector. The burgesses agreed to give them eight phates in Upwich, valued at £80 per annum, and three-fourths of a phate in Netherwich, for twenty-one years, as an equivalent for the £750. The scheme, however, fell through, owing to the poverty of the projectors and the unsettled state of the times.[4]

During the reign of Charles II. the thanks of the corporation were given to Winter Harris for extending the trade in salt. On 4 October, 1680, one Gardiner was encouraged to sell Droitwich salt at Berkley, in Gloucestershire, none having been previously sent to so great a distance. About this time the canal project was renewed by Lord Windsor.[5] He proposed to erect six locks for which he was to receive £199 in hand, or its equivalent, seven phates in Upwich; £80 more were to be given when the first lock was finished; £100 more for each of the remaining five locks. To raise these sums eight phates and a half in Upwich and one phate in Netherwich were to be set aside for twenty-one years. The work was begun, and as many as five locks were completed, and then the work was abandoned.

At this time there were in Upwich three hundred and eighty-seven phates, one quarter and two parts; in Netherwich best pit, twenty phates: and in the worst pit eleven phates and two quarters. The proprietors of phates in Upwich numbered one hundred and twenty-seven persons; in Netherwich best pit twelve persons, in the worst pit ten persons. The value of the phates varied at different times. At this time, 1680, a phate was valued at about £10, and salt was from 1*s*. 4*d*. to 2*s*. 8*d*. per bushel. The reign of William and Mary saw what was a regular revolution in the affairs of Droitwich and its salt industry. In 1688, and again in 1689, a bill was introduced which bore the title of *An Act for the Better Regulating the Salt Works in Droitwich*. From the arguments on behalf of and against the bill, it is clear that an attempt was being made to break down the monopoly of the owners of saltpits. The bill was passed with amendments in 1689,[6] and Nash seems to think that if anything it strengthened the monopoly. In the next year, however, Robert Steynor, described by Nash [7] as a person of considerable fortune, and an enterprising and undaunted spirit, broke through the monopoly by sinking two pits on his own freehold land in 1690. The corporation, in the person of Charles, duke of Shrewsbury, brought an action against Steynor, and litigation went on between the two parties until 1695.[8] The principal evidence put forward by the plaintiff was, first, that the digging of new pits was against the customs of the manor and borough. Every man had his share of brine and bullaries according to his estate; no one was allowed to have any more than was drawn and delivered by sworn officials. Secondly, a fee farm of £100 per annum was paid by the proprietors of the salt springs, and not charged on houses. Thirdly, that the springs which supplied the old wells ran through several persons' lands before emptying themselves into the pits. If these were interfered with the old pits would be ruined. Fourthly, that the salt was formerly only made for half the year to keep up the price and save fuel; that the defendant had sunk two wells, one about two hundred yards from the Netherwich springs, and another about two hundred yards from Upwich, near his house. That he was making three hundred and fifty bushels of salt a week, and as he was building a new salt

1 Burghall's *Diary* in Barlow, *Ches.* p. 168.

2 Nash, i. 306.

3 Ibid. 304.

4 Nash, i. 298, quoting records of corporation.

5 Ibid. i. 306.

6 *Hist. MSS. Com.* 12 Rep. App. pt. vi. p. 110.

7 Nash, op. cit. i. 298.

8 Exch. Depos. Worc. 8 Will. III. No. 15.

house might make two hundred more a week. That this brought down the price of salt and the value of the old pits. Fifthly, that the defendant's[1] action in sinking pits had caused a subsidence in the old pits at Upwich of about five inches. The proprietors of the salt rights really based their case on the charter of John, mentioned above, and especially on its renewal by James I., which had added some restraining clauses preventing anyone from digging new pits.

Mr. Steynor argued that the charter of John did not convey all the saltpits and works to the corporation, but merely such as were in possession of the crown at the time. He contended that a pit called Sheriffs Pit, and Lench's Lands where he had sunk a pit, were never in the crown. He produced Domesday Book in evidence, in which he showed that Earl Edwy had shares in the property, and also the bishop of Worcester. Finally, it was contended that the restraining clause of James I. was illegal, and that the bailiffs had no right to exclude all others from digging pits.[2]

After various trials, both in Chancery and in the King's Bench, it was finally decided on 24 January 1695, before the Lord Keeper, that Mr. Steynor might lawfully sink the two pits on his own freehold, draw brine thereout, make salt thereof, and dispose of the salt. These proceedings are said to have cost Mr. Steynor £6,000.

The effect of this decision of course was that people began to sink pits on their own lands, and found brine as good as in the old pit. The monopoly was destroyed, and the trade greatly increased. The price of salt fell from two shillings a bushel to fivepence.[3] This was a very serious blow to the proprietors of the old pits. They laboured now under several disadvantages from which the owners of new wells were free. They were, for instance, charged with the fee farm rent of £100 and other expenses, such as the payment of officials, from which the others escaped.

While these events were taking place and the breaking down of the monopoly gave so great an impetus to the production of salt, another matter of great importance also stimulated production. This was the introduction of the use of coal, which is stated to have taken place in 1691.[4] Coal was found to do quite as well as wood, and was not restricted in quantity in the same way as the latter. Another invention, attributed to Mr. John Pedmore and dating from this time, was the introduction of iron pans instead of leaden ones for boiling the salt.[5]

The proprietors of the old pits naturally made many efforts to evade the judgment given in the Steynor case and to recover their old influence. One such attempt was made in 1708 under cover of an act of parliament entitled *A Bill for the better preserving the ancient salt-springs in Droitwich,*[6] *and the rights of the proprietors thereof.* The plan proposed in this bill was to allow the old proprietors to bring the brine in pipes from Droitwich to Hawford, in the parish of Claines on the Severn; to empower the bishop of Worcester to convey to them in fee, in exchange for other lands, about twenty acres at or near Mythamhill and pit, whereon they might erect saltworks; and to subject the owners of the free pits to a portion of the fee farm and all expenses attending the project. The indefatigable Steynor appears to have led the opposition to this project, and through his efforts the bill was thrown out.

It is interesting to notice here the fate of this gentleman who played so important a part in the history of the industry. Nash tells us that he shared the fate of many other projectors and persons engaged in lawsuits; he spent an estate of above £1,000 a year, and for several years before his death received weekly pay from the parishes of St. Nicholas and St. Andrew; which allowed him 17*s.* a week in consideration of his former services. A sad fate for one who had done such good service to so many people. The monopoly having been broken down, the work was now carried on at the old pits, and by private owners at new ones in very much the same way as before. The decreased price in salt naturally increased the demand, and the substitution of coal fuel helped to increase the supply. So matters stood until in 1725 another revolution took place, making a most important epoch in the history of the industry.

Up to this time the wells had only been sunk down to a stratum of talc. In 1725 Sir Richard Lane, sometime mayor of Worcester, and member for that city, was informed by certain persons from Cheshire, that in that county the strongest brine lay lower than the pits in Droitwich were usually sunk. He therefore determined to bore through the talc at the bottom of a pit. Upon this being done, the strong brine rushed out with such violence that two men who were at work in the pit were thrown to the surface and killed.[7] This deep boring was of course promptly adopted by many other proprietors, with the result that there was now such a profusion of strong brine that large quantities of it were wasted, a curious change from the time when the brine was measured out with such nicety. This discovery had a very disastrous effect on the proprietors of the old pits, which now sank in value from £5,000 per annum to practically nothing. It had formerly been considered one of the safest

[1] Nash, op. cit. i. 298.
[2] Exch. Dep. 8 Will. III. No. 15.
[3] Nash, op. cit. i. 298.
[4] Camden, *Britannia* (ed. Gough, 1789), 362.
[5] Ibid. 362; Nash, op. cit. i. 300.
[6] Nash, op. cit. i. 298.
[7] Ibid. 299.

forms of investment, so that many charities were founded in it, jointures secured upon it, and every sort of trust money invested in it. Its fall in value created the greatest confusion and distress in the neighbourhood. Two hundred persons are said to have lost all their property, many schools, hospitals, and almshouses were also ruined.

On 16 September, 1773, Joseph Priddey, of Droitwich, informed Nash[1] that he had sunk several pits, and generally found it about 35 feet to the talc. Then came a stratum of talc about 150 feet in depth. Under the talc lay a river of brine 22 inches deep. Below the river was a hard rock of salt. When a hole was bored through the talc, the brine burst forth with most surprising force. In the next year the same man sunk a pit and found it 53 feet to the talc, 102 feet of talc, the river 22 inches deep, and then a rock of salt. He bored for 2½ feet into this rock but found no change in it. The cost of sinking a pit at this period was about £40.

Since the year 1725 the trade of the town had increased very much down to the time when Nash wrote. Several things would tend to this end. The greatly increased supply of brine brought the price of salt down to 5*d.* a bushel without the duty, from which it may be inferred that it was brought within the reach of more consumers. A canal was, and had been for a long time, a matter of great necessity to Droitwich. In 1755 Mr. Baker, a druggist from London, revived the scheme put forward in the bill of 1708 for conveying the brine in pipes to Hawford, on the banks of the Severn. In 1767 estimates were given by Mr. Brindley for constructing a canal[2] from Hawford to Droitwich. The proprietors began to dig their canal in 1768, and the first barge-load of coals passed along it in March, 1771.

Nash gives some interesting figures as to the production of salt, and also a description of the process in his day. During the period 11 November, 1769, exclusive, to 4 August, 1770, the amount produced was 480,340 bushels; the proprietors paid duty for 371,078 bushels; the remaining bushels were sold in bond.

In 1771 there were fifteen proprietors of the saltworks who occupied forty seats or pans for boiling the brine.

In 1772 there were eight pits, from which forty-five pans were supplied with brine. One pit, which was found to be too large, held 6,000 gallons, the others contained 800 gallons each.

The salt made in these pans and sold from 5 April, 1771, to 5 April, 1772, amounted to 604,579 bushels; of these 110,120 bushels were exported to foreign countries. £61,457 were paid to the salt office in London; this was nearly one-third of the whole salt revenue collected in England. The duty paid 1772–1773 rose to £72,169 2*s.* 11*d.* More salt was made in 1774 than had ever before been made. The year 1775 saw a decrease, owing to the American war. A duty of 3*s.* 4*d.* a bushel was at the time laid on white salt. If the duty was paid immediately on the first day there was a rebate of 3*d.* a bushel. If the salt was sent coastwise to any other part of England there was also an abatement of 3*d.* If the salt were exported to some foreign country the proprietor had only to give a bond as security for the duty, which bond was remitted on his proving that all the salt had been exported.

The process employed for making salt at this time was as follows: A little water was put into the pans to keep the brine from burning to the bottom, the pan was then filled with brine, and a piece of resin about the size of a pea thrown in to make it granulate fine. When the brine was boiling, the salt first incrusted at the top and then subsided to the bottom. When it had subsided, the 'wallers,' or persons employed in the seals, laded it out with an iron skimmer, and put it into wicker barrows, each containing about half a bushel, in the shape of a sugar loaf. It was then allowed to stand for some time to let the brine drain off. The salt was then dropped out of the barrow, and put into the oven to harden. The 'wallers' boiled a pan full of brine in about twenty-four hours. The drawing out the salt from the pan was called a 'lade.' Fourteen or fifteen hundredweight of best coal with great care boiled a ton of salt, or forty bushels, each bushel weighing fifty-six pounds. The salt is said to have been boiled very fast, which, with the resin, made it fine, but took away from its strength.

From contemporary analysis Droitwich brine is said to have been exceedingly pure, and heavily impregnated with salt.

A duty of 4*d.* a bushel was imposed on the foul salt used for manure. A good deal of fraud arose from this, and the salt was largely used, not for manure, but in the glass, soap, and many other trades. The extraordinarily high duties imposed for many years upon salt naturally led to a great deal of smuggling, and, it is said, much money was made by those employed in this way until the abolition of the duties brought smuggling to an end.[3] Some idea of the total output during the eighteenth century and of the extravagant duties may be derived from the following figures. The income[4] of the salt duty of 3*s.* 4*d.* per bushel was as follows:—1733, £115,708 5*s.* 6*d.*; 1734, £187,515 3*s.* 5*d.*; 1736, £195,291 19*s.* 9*d*; 1737, £206,184 19*s.* 6*d.* These exorbitant

[1] Nash, op. cit. i. 299.
[2] Ibid. 307.
[3] *Droitwich and its Neighbourhood*, 1875.
[4] Prattinton, *Gen. Hist.* 94.

duties were continued throughout the whole of the eighteenth century, and for practically the first quarter of the last century. The salt duty was altogether done away with in 1825, and the natural result was a great increase in the production, and a considerable fall in price to the consumer.[1]

The history of the industry has now been brought down to the beginning of the last century.

There remains to chronicle but one important event in connexion with the saltworks of the county. This took place in 1828. In that year were discovered the pits at Stoke Prior.[2] A Cheshire brine smelter, led on by the hope of discovering rock salt, made investigations in the district. These led to the discovery of brine springs and the erection of important saltworks. In 1875 there was even greater pumping power at Stoke than at Droitwich. Four brine-pits were in use. Fifty canal boats, four hundred railway vans, were in the possession of Mr. Corbett, the owner of the saltworks. Five thousand six hundred hands were employed in the industry after Mr. Corbett dispensed with women workers. The rate of production was about 3,000 tons a week, but the competition of Cheshire salt was severely felt.

The present production[3] of the combined works at Droitwich and Stoke Prior is 170,000 tons per annum. The works at Droitwich belong to the Salt Union, Ltd., with the exception of those formerly owned by Mr. John Bradley, not now worked, and those of Messrs. Boucher and Giles. This last firm obtains the brine from the Salt Union, who take over the whole of the salt manufactured.

The methods of salt production employed are as follows: Wells about 4 feet in diameter are sunk to a depth of 80 to 100 feet, the sides lined with sheets of iron well puddled with clay to prevent surface water, or fresh-water springs, from entering.[4] From the bottom of the well hollow copper rods are pushed down some 100 feet more until the brine is reached. After being pumped to the surface the brine is run into a large open brick reservoir, whence it is conveyed by pipes to the saltpans situated in various parts of the town. The average size of the saltpans is, for fine salt, 40 feet by 22 feet, and for coarse salt, locally known as broad salt, 80 feet by 22 feet, the depth in each case being about 18 inches. The pans are heated by huge fires beneath, and the brine boiled. The salt forms first a crust upon the surface and then sinks to the bottom of the pan. It is then raked to the side, and the mass, hot and wet, placed in wooden moulds, known locally as 'tubs.'[5] The salt sets almost immediately, and after draining for 20 minutes the solid mass, known as a 'bar' of salt, is withdrawn from the 'tub' and taken to the drying room. The 'bars' are piled in stacks ready, when thoroughly dry, for the market. It is interesting to note that the more quickly the brine is boiled the finer is the salt resulting, slow boiling producing the coarsest salt.

We may finally notice a curious circumstance which occurred in the year 1870. This was a remarkable falling off in the quality of the brine. Fortunately a few months afterwards the brine recovered all its old excellence as mysteriously as it had lost it.

Another source of prosperity for Droitwich was found in 1836,[6] when the Brine Baths, from which so many sufferers seek relief, were opened. In rheumatism especially, their efficacy has been proved again and again. No doubt the solvent action of the brine upon the hardened cuticle allows the dissolved salts to reach the nerve endings, and so by reflex action to stimulate the internal organs.[7] Besides common salt, chloride of magnesium, the sulphates of lime, alumina and soda, and even a trace of iodide of sodium, are found in the Droitwich brine. Nearer the railway station than the original Royal Baths, which had been greatly improved by Mr. Gabb and Dr. Bainbrigge, Mr. John Corbett, in 1887, built a new set of baths on higher ground, the St. Andrew's Brine Baths, opposite the Raven Hotel. With the view of increasing the attractions of Droitwich as a health resort, Mr. Corbett not only conservatively restored and enlarged the quaint and picturesque Raven Hotel, but built the Park Hotel in the Worcester Road. These improvements in bath and hotel accommodation have naturally led to a large increase of visitors, who take the cure by hot brine, douche, and vapour baths, while the swimming baths present the curious feature that owing to the specific gravity of the salt water the bather cannot sink. Though one of the youngest of our bathing resorts, in public estimation Droitwich promises to retain permanently its repute for its powerfully curative waters. And thus the oldest industry of the borough finds a new development and application quite unknown to the primitive saltworkers of the Domesday time.

[1] In addition to the duty a charge was made by the different corporate towns on the salt brought in. To avoid this the salt was taken round the town, and the road by which the salt was taken round Worcester was called Salt Lane. As the prison is in the street, the Worcester citizens in the last half of the nineteenth century changed the name to Castle Street.

[2] *Droitwich and its Neighbourhood*, p. 45.

[3] We are indebted to Mr. P. J. Pond for valuable notes on the salt industry of Droitwich.

[4] Brine weakened by fresh water is known locally as 'bastard' brine.

[5] The 'tub' is square in shape, but tapers slightly towards the top, and the size varies, the regulation sizes being for the contents to weigh 80, 100, 120 or 160 to the ton.

[6] Bainbrigge, *Droitwich Salt Baths*, 1871.

[7] P. A. Roden, M.B., *Droitwich and its Brine Baths*.

COAL MINING

To many, having in mind the notoriety of the town of Dudley as a mining centre, Worcestershire is synonymous with wealth in coal; but such can hardly be said to be the fact, for coal mining is not anything like the prominent and important industry in Worcestershire that it is, and has for long been, in the neighbouring county of Stafford. Colliery enterprise in the former county is in great measure restricted to the small portion of the South Staffordshire coalfield which extends into northern Worcestershire, and comprises an area of, perhaps, not more than 20 square miles.

The coalfields of Worcestershire are (1) the extension of the South Stafford field alluded to; (2) part of the Forest of Wyre field (about one-third of the field), in the north-east of the county; and (3) a small field with an area of less than one square mile, in the neighbourhood of the Lickey Hills, where a thin seam of coal, said to be about 2 feet in thickness, was once worked near the village of Rubery.

The coal measures of the great coalfield of Staffordshire and Worcestershire are divided, by Professor Lapworth and Mr. Sopwith in their report (Royal Coal Commission, 1905), into three divisions, viz.:

1.—*Upper Division* (or Halesowen Sandstone Group), grey and yellow sandstones and marls, with a few insignificant coals.

2.—*Middle Division* (Brick Clay or Espley Group), red, blue, and grey marls and clays, and green and yellow sandstones, etc.

3.—*The Lower Division* (or Productive Coal Measures Group), formed of grey sandstones and shales and fireclays, and containing the chief workable seams of coal and ironstones.

The upper division is only found in the southern portion, the middle division covering a large area of the field, the aggregate thickness of the two groups being from 600 to 1,000 feet. The lower or productive coal measures group covers a large surface area, but towards the southern extremity passes under and is worked below the Brick Clay and Halesowen Sandstone groups. And, though attaining a considerable thickness (somewhat less than 2,000 feet) in the northern part of the field, the seam gradually decreases to the south, so that in the Worcestershire section of the field its average thickness is from 500 to 600 feet only. It is in the productive group that the famous 'thick,' or 'ten-yard' coal is found, which is due to the coming together of some fourteen of the coal seams of the northern part of the South Staffordshire Coalfield, owing to the gradual thinning out of the intervening beds of shale and sandstone.

In the neighbourhood of Dudley the 'ten-yard' coal reaches its greatest thickness, and preserves in that district considerable uniformity. Mr. Jukes in his *Geology of the South Staffordshire Coalfield* gives the following section of the seam in the Horse Pasture, Corbyn's Hall.

	Ft.	In.	Ft.	In.
1. Roofs coal	—		3	2
White coal parting .	3	6	—	
2. White coal	—		3	9
3. Floors coal and batt .	—		1	6
4. Heath and tow coal .	—		3	6
5. Brassils coal. . . .	—		1	6
6. Fine coal	—		2	6
7. Veins coal	—		1	6
Stone coal parting .	0	8	—	
8. Stone coal	—		3	0
9. Patchell's coal . . .	—		1	0
10. Sawyer's coal . . .	—		2	0
11. Slipper coal. . . .	—		3	0
12. Benches or kid coal .	—		2	5
	4	2	28	10
			33	0

This is, of course, an unusual thickness for the seam to attain to, and 28 feet would be nearer the average in the Dudley district. As, however, we approach the boundary of the coalfield towards Lye Waste, near Stourbridge, a great change takes place in the character of this coal, it decreases in thickness, and the intervening bands of shale widen. A characteristic section taken at Tintam Abbey fireclay works showed:

	Ft.	In.	Ft.	In.
1. Top coal	—		7	0
Spoil (shale, etc.). .	5	0	—	
2. Middle coal. . . .	—		6	0
Spoil (shale, etc.) .	5	0	—	
3. Bottom coal . . .	—		6	0
	10	0	19	0
Total with partings			29	0

So considerable indeed is the deterioration in quality south of a line drawn from Birmingham to Stourbridge, due to the intermixture of non-carbonaceous matter with the coals, that, according to Dr. Lapworth and Mr. Sopwith 'a line joining the Manor Pits, near Halesowen, with the sinking near Wassel Grove, may be looked upon as marking the practical limit of the profitable Staffordshire coal seams in the southern direction.'

INDUSTRIES

That portion of the exposed part of the Forest of Wyre—or, as it is sometimes called, the Bewdley—coalfield which exists in Worcestershire will comprise, roughly speaking, not more than about 10,000 acres. Little was known about this field until of late years, and the question of its formation still excites much interest amongst geologists. The measures dip to the east at a gentle angle, and lie unconformably upon the Old Red Sandstone and Silurian rocks, 'along the western and southern edge of the coalfield and passing up with apparent conformity into the red so-called Permian strata along its eastern margin, except in the neighbourhood of Bridgnorth, where the coal measures are unconformably overlapped by the basement bed of the Trias.'[1] The coal seams which this field contains are both thin and of inferior quality. At Arley Colliery, near Bewdley, the strata have been penetrated to a depth of 454 yards, ultimately reaching a mass of basaltic rock, only one workable seam being found in the section, and that at a depth of 176 yards. The Shropshire portion of this coalfield would appear to contain coal of more value than that yet developed in the Worcestershire area, but in no part can the potentialities, with the knowledge so far to hand, be spoken of as great.

It may be interesting to trace the development of the coal-mining industry of Worcestershire from its commencement to the present day before forecasting the possible future of the industry. As to when coal came to be first worked in the county as an article of commerce there can be no degree of certainty. Coal was possibly first worked in Worcestershire in the thirteenth century, for we know that in the reign of Edward I. 'See Cole' as well as iron was being worked at 'Walsale,' in the neighbouring county of Stafford, and at Brierley Hill, and up to Dudley. And it is said that mines existed since 1300 along the outcrop of the measures by Netherton Hill.[2] We have, however, to come down to much later times before we find a record of a substantial trade in coal being carried on.

Dud Dudley's earliest experiments in substituting coal for charcoal in the smelting of iron in blast furnaces were made at Pensnett Chase, about the close of the year 1619; and though, owing to the persistent opposition of the charcoal ironmasters, his efforts were disastrous, yet coal did gradually come, some time after his day, to be used in smelting iron, and of course this led to a considerable development of the coal trade. The saltmakers of Nantwich also drew their fuel supplies from the Staffordshire coalfield[3] about this time, for they adopted coal in lieu of wood in the seething of the salt brine about the middle of this century, the use of coal in saltmaking being spoken of as a novelty at Nantwich in 1656.[4] At Droitwich coal brought from the Forest of Dean first began to be used about 1678.[5] Coal was, according to Dud Dudley,[6] also used in making glass near his dwelling in the neighbourhood of Stourbridge; and according to the same authority there were in the seventeenth century twelve to fourteen collieries at work, besides twice as many out of work, within a circuit of ten miles from Dudley Castle (partly in Staffordshire and partly in Worcestershire). The production, however, of any one of these collieries was small, the average output per mine being about 2,000 tons per annum, though the output of some reached as high a figure as from 3,000 to 5,000 tons. Their depth, also, was only from 24 to 60 feet, though in some instances nearly 120 feet was attained. How different from modern colliery practice in Britain, when the output *per diem* of some mines is equal to that for a whole year in the instances quoted above, and the depth from the surface is between 2,000 and 3,000 feet! But colliery enterprise, even at the present day, in the district under notice, cannot be said to have very greatly advanced, for the coal is very thick, exists at shallow depths, and a great portion of the better fuel has been extracted.

Probably this was the last district in which coal was quarried to any extent by surface or 'open cast' workings. A number of these existed in the middle of the seventeenth century and were known by the name of 'foot-rids.' Mr. R. L. Galloway, in his exhaustive *Annals of Coal Mining and the Coal Trade*, thus describes the mode adopted of working the thick coal (drawing his information in part from Dud Dudley's *Metallum Martis*): 'The colliers are described as beginning at the bottom (of the seam) and carrying working places (crutes or staules) about 2 yards in height as far forward and of such a breadth as was deemed expedient; then taking slice after slice of the coal upwards till they reached the top, making use of the small coals (which were left underground as of no value) as a platform for raising themselves to the upper parts of the seam. According to Mr. Bald, when this coal first began to be worked by means of pits, a distance of 20 yards all round was considered a sufficient area to be worked, after which a new pit was sunk' (*Edinburgh Encyclopædia*, art. 'Mine').

It is interesting to note that the word 'colliery,' which has long been in use to define a coal mine, was probably employed at this time, for as late as 1797 we find it spelled 'coalery,' in an article so entitled in the *Encyclopædia Britannica* of that date.

[1] *Report of Royal Coal Com.* (1905), Part iii. Report of Professor Lapworth and Mr. A. Sopwith.

[2] *Midland Mining Com.* First Report, p. 63.

[3] Houghton, *Collection*, vol. ii. p. 88. ed. 1727; *Phil. Trans.* 1669.

[4] *Chambers's Journal*, Jan. 1870.

[5] *Phil. Trans.* No. 142, p. 1059.

[6] *Metallum Martis.*

The spontaneous combustion of the coal, which to-day proves so troublesome in causing the dangerous underground fires in the coal mines of the Staffordshire and Warwickshire coalfields, was an anxiety as far back as 1686, for Dr. Plott, writing at that time, says:[1] 'All these things (I say) being put together, what can there else be concluded, but that some cole-pits may and doe fire of themselves, as 'tis unanimously agree'd they doe. Wednesbury (where the coal works now on fire take up eleven acres of ground), Cosbey, Ettingsall, and Pensnet in this County, as Mr. Camden will have it, whereas indeed the place He mentions then on fire, was Broadhurst on Pensnet in the Parish of Dudley and county of Worcester where he says a colepit was fired by a candle through the negligence of a groover, and so possibly it might; but as for the rest (which are in Staffordshire) 'tis agree'd they all fired natural of themselves, as they expect the shale and small-cole in the bottoms and deads of all the old works, will doe and have done, beyond all memory.'

Nash, in his *History of Worcestershire*, published in 1781 (ii. 212), refers to the collieries in the neighbourhood of Stourbridge and to the benefits derived from the construction of canals. He also makes mention of the clay as lying 150 ft. below the surface and about 45 ft. below the coal.

The use of coal in smelting iron led to the more extensive working of that fuel, but the depth at which it could be mined was very limited until the invention of the steam-engine by Newcomen enabled the mines to be better drained. The first steam-worked pumping-engine was erected at a Staffordshire pit in 1712; and Watt's engine of 1782, and his parallel motion patented in 1784, which allowed of the winding of coal being performed by steam in place of manual or horse labour, led to still further expansion in the trade.

But even as late as 1835[2] we find that the coal-pits in this district were very numerous and close together, and few of the pits were deeper than 450 or 600 ft. They were seldom more than 300 yards apart, or worked more than 10 acres.[3] According to the author of *Fossil Fuel*[4] (pp. 192–200), it was customary to sink a pair of pits, called a 'plant' or plantation, so near together that they could be worked by the same 'gin' or 'whimsey'; the ropes were either flat or round, made of hemp, and in some cases chains were used. The coal was conveyed to the towns by means of carts or by canal.

Coal-mining, in so far as individual collieries are concerned, has never been conducted on an extensive scale in the exposed portion of this coalfield either in South Staffordshire or in Worcestershire. Mr. Blackwell, in his report laid before Parliament (6 May, 1850), pointed out that whereas the colliery leases of the North (Newcastle district) averaged from 500 to 2,000 acres, and in Lancashire and Wales 25 to 250 acres, in the Staffordshire coalfield they were often not more than 10 or 20 acres, nor at the present time are the 'takings' of an extensive area. Of course, the large tonnage per acre (owing to the excessive thickness of the coal) accounts in great measure for this, and the shallowness of the mine necessitating but little capital to develop the concern allows of small areas being worked. Furthermore, many of the small concerns now at work are engaged in going over an area a second, or it may be even a third, time, extracting remains of ribs and pillars left to support the roof in a previous working.

The output of coal in the Worcestershire portion of the Dudley district was reckoned at about 700,000 tons for the year 1851, worth, perhaps, £200,000.[5] The output for 1904 was much about the same, viz., 737,208 tons, and the number of persons employed above and below ground at the mines was 2,559.

The profitable coals in the exposed coal-measure areas of Worcestershire are rapidly approaching complete exhaustion, so that any possible future developments in the coal-mining industry in the county are entirely dependent on the geological question; that is, on the existence of other or hidden fields, and the reader who may be peculiarly interested in the matter is advised to peruse the able sub-report to the Geological Committee on the concealed and unproved coalfields of district 'B' by Professor Lapworth,[6] where the prolongation of coal measures containing workable coal seams is exhaustively treated. Respecting the country lying between the Abberley and the Clent Hills, the learned professor arrives at the same conclusion as the late Professor Ramsay, given in the report of the previous Royal Coal Commission,[7] to the effect that it is 'unsafe to suppose that productive coal measures, like those of the more northern parts of South Staffordshire and Coalbrookdale, would be found in the synclinal area underneath the new red beds anywhere between the southern half of the Forest of Wyre and the northern end of the Clent and Lickey Hills.' Turning, however, to the country between Highley and Stourbridge, Professor Lapworth states: 'At the time when the previous Royal Coal Commission issued its report it was supposed that only the upper and

[1] *Nat. Hist. of Staffs.*

[2] 1835 *Report*, 3048.

[3] Ibid. 3027, 3023–24.

[4] Professor Jevons deemed that this work, the *Hist. of Fossil Fuel*, was written by John Holland. It was published in 1835, or in the same year that witnessed the publication of the valuable Parliamentary report.

[5] *Worc. in the Nineteenth Century*, by T. C. Turberville, 1852.

[6] *Final Report of the Royal Commission on Coal Supplies*, part ix. 1905.

[7] 1871.

less profitable coal measures existed throughout the whole of the Forest of Wyre coalfield; but within the last few years representatives of the more profitable or "sweet" coals of the Coalbrookdale area have been discovered and worked in its northern parts on the Highley Estates; and Mr. Cantrill has shown that the so-called Permian strata of the Enville country form the natural upward continuation of the Forest of Wyre coal measures. It is, therefore, not impossible that the lower or profitable coal measures may extend from the Highley district eastward far under the so-called Permians of that area, and lie at reasonable depths below the surface. As yet, however, this remains only a matter for more or less hopeful speculation.'

IRON

The north-eastern region of Worcestershire forms part of the mineral district commonly called the South Staffordshire coalfield. Hence, it is difficult to treat the iron or coal trade of Worcestershire as an independent industry separate from that of Staffordshire. The Worcesshire district includes Oldbury, Cradley, Stourbridge, Halesowen, and Old Swinford, and the detached part of the county round Dudley, embracing the parish of Netherton. At the most this district is never more than 4 miles in breadth and 5 in length.[1] The iron mines here seem to have been worked long before the utility and cheapness of coal for smelting purposes were discovered in the seventeenth century. Coal was, indeed, worked very early, and coal and iron mines are mentioned together.[2] But for long years wood, and not coal, was employed for smelting iron. And during that period the iron industry, at least in Worcestershire, seems to have assumed no great proportions. With the seventeenth century came the revolution in iron smelting and the real beginning of the iron industry in England.[3] This was due in the main to the discovery that coal was both a better and cheaper agent in the smelting of iron than wood. And this discovery was made just as a difficulty arose about the use of wood, and perhaps because that difficulty arose.

During the sixteenth century a great outcry was raised regarding the quantity of wood consumed in the iron furnaces, so much so that for a short time the trade in consequence seems to have declined.[4] In 1558 an Act was passed forbidding the use of timber for 'coals for the working of iron . . . growing within fourteen miles of the sea, or of any port of the rivers Thames, Severn, Wye.'[5] This, perhaps, was more directly brought into existence by the operations in the Weald of Sussex, but no doubt applied here also. Now came the most important event in the history of the iron trade in Worcestershire or elsewhere. This was the discovery and use of coal for iron furnaces by Dud Dudley[6] in the reign of James I. 'The leading place,' says Mr. Ashley, 'was secured to Great Britain by various circumstances, among which I should be disposed to place the enterprise of her sons in the first place . . . Dud Dudley was the greatest pioneer in this direction.'[7] In his book *Metallum Martis* (1665), he gives a most interesting account of how first he was taken from his studies at Balliol College, Oxford, in 1619, to manage his father's furnace and two forges at Pensnett, near Dudley; near which hamlet, and on the present rifle range, there now exist rough lumps of cinder, which probably mark the spot and are the refuse from this early working. There he found that 'within ten miles of Dudley Castle there be near 20,000 smiths of all sorts, and many iron works at that time within that circle decayed for want of wood (yet formerly a mighty woodland country).' Also his father's woods were disappearing, and the works were falling into ruin. Finding the coal very accessible, being so near to the surface that it was dug in open works, he began to use it for smelting iron. The result of this was a patent, obtained from the king by his father, on 22 February, 1621, for fourteen years.[8] But Dudley experienced the worst of ill fortune. First, in 1622, his forges and fineries at Pensnett and Cradley were

[1] There is also another smaller coalfield round Bewdley in the Forest of Wyre, and yet another in the Lickey Hills. See *V. C. H. Worc.* i. 11.

[2] Thus in 1292 Roger de Somery had a mine of 'seacoal' (that is, ordinary coal) and iron worth 40*s.* yearly in Dudley. *Worc. Inq.* i. 35.

[3] Blast furnaces had already been employed in the sixteenth century. Swank, *Iron in all Ages* (1892), 46 *seq.*

[4] *Hist. MSS. Com. Rep.* iii. (4), p. 72. Unwin.

[5] Stat. 1 Eliz. c. 15.

[6] Dud Dudley was a natural son of Edward, Lord Dudley, of Dudley Castle.

[7] Ashley, *Brit. Industries* (1903), p. 4.

[8] *Cal. S.P. Dom.* 1619–23, p. 349. *Specification of Pats. of Invention*, Lord Dudley. In this patent it is stated that the 'art and misterie' had not formerly been performed by any in England. It is true that in 1612 and 1613 respectively patents had been granted to Simon Sturtevant and John Rovenson to make iron with coal. But both, according to Dud Dudley, failed. Hence he obtained his patent. Both Sturtevant and Rovenson, like Dudley, wrote treatises, pointing out the benefits to be derived from their inventions: S. Sturtevant, *Metallica* (1612); John Rovenson, *A Treatise of Metallica* (pub. Thos. Thorp, 1613).

destroyed by floods; and later on he had to contend against the enmity of the other ironmasters who still used charcoal, whereas he could make iron both cheaper and better by using coal. However, he was ordered to send bar-iron to the Tower in 1623. This was examined and passed by the London ironmasters, with the result that when all monopolies were abolished in 1625 privilege was granted to Lord Dudley 'for melting of iron ewer.'[1] The ironmasters round Dudley naturally attacked his forges and destroyed them. In 1637 seventeen persons were indicted for assaulting and damaging the property of Alice and William Parkhouse, probably relations of the unfortunate Dud Dudley.[2] He then erected, first a new furnace at Himley, and then a forge at Sedgeley, making 7 tons of iron a week, 'the greatest quantity of pit-cole iron that ever yet was made in Great Britain.' These again were destroyed by the jealous ironmasters. Thus pressed, Dudley was forced to sue for a new patent, which he obtained in 1638.[3] Meanwhile patents for the same invention had been granted to others. They, however, were unsuccessful in their attempts,[4] and Dudley at length obtained the assistance of certain influential men.[5] Now everything seemed favourable to him, when, worst of all disasters, the Civil War broke out and shattered all his prospects. Dudley was an ardent royalist and lost all his estate and money in the war, being twice imprisoned and making two escapes.[6] During the Cromwellian period he suffered much at the hands of the ironmasters of Bristol and the Forest of Dean, who tried to force him to disclose to them the secret of his invention,[7] and compelled him to sell them his new works at Bristol. At the Restoration he applied in vain for a monopoly and renewal of his patent, and so finally gave up the practice of iron-making.

In his book, Dudley sets forth all the advantages of his new-found 'sea-cole iron' over 'charcoal iron'; namely, that it was raised more quickly, was cheaper by £3 per ton, much finer, especially the cast-iron, and used up all the small coal, which was otherwise wasted. Dudley himself had four forges near his house, Green's Lodge. They were: Green's-forge, Swin-forge, Heath-forge, and Cradley-forge. Of iron ore there were several kinds: Black-row-graines, a hard black iron; dun-row-graines, found in the clay; white-row-graines. And at a much lower stratum, Rider Stone, Cloud Stone, and Cannock or Cannot Stone, which only made red and cold-shere iron, both very brittle and not at all malleable.[8]

At the end of the book is an interesting account of the older methods of making iron. The earliest devices were 'foot-blasts or bloomeries, that was by men treading of the bellows, by which they could make but one little lump or bloom of iron in a day, not 100 weight.' 'The next invention was to set up the bloomeries that went by water for the ease of the men treading the bellows.' These made more iron and extracted a greater quantity of iron out of the slag: but they only made 2 hundredweight of iron in a day. The charcoal furnaces of his day made 2 or 3 tons of pig or cast iron in a day.[9] Dudley himself made only 1 ton a day with his pit (or sea) coal. But the quality of his coal was better and its cost less.

As a result of his efforts the town of Dudley became the centre of an important trade. Habington remarked that 'the inhabitantes, though certaynly descended from Seth, yet followe in professyon Tubalcain, the inventor of the Smythe's hammer: the rest are miners delving into the bowells of the earthe for our fuell, theyre profytt, and have all of them the reputation of bould spirited men.'[10] There seems to have been some little trade at Worcester also.[11] In 1620 the 'poor handicraftsmen that work at iron and steel' complained of the rise in price of articles of food owing to the 'engrossers.'[12] In 1677, according to Yarranton, there were still larger ironworks at Stourbridge and Wassal Grove, the manufacture having probably settled at the former town to avail itself of water power from the river Stour. At Dudley, and 10 miles round, were 'more people inhabiting and more money returned in a year than is in these four rich, fat counties I mention.'[13] Sow-iron, made of iron-stone and Roman cinders, found in the Forest of Dean, was sent to the forges of

[1] Stat. 21 Jas. I. c. 3.

[2] *Quarter Sess. R.* (Worc. Hist. Soc.), Introd. lxvi. and ii. 637. Dud Dudley had taken into partnership his nephew, Edw. Parkhouse, the son of his sister Jane, and Richard Parkhouse. *Metallum Martis*, p. 8, pedigree in the edition reprinted 1854.

[3] *Specification of Pats.* No. 117 (1638), Nos. 91, 113.

[4] *Cal. S.P. Dom.* 1637–8, pp. 16, 17, 482.

[5] David Ramsey, Sir Geo. Horsey, and Roger Foulke.

[6] Dudley gives an exciting account of his adventures—how first he was taken at Worcester; there he escaped and fled to London, where he was again captured and sentenced to be shot, but once more escaped. *Cal. S.P. Dom.* 1660–1, p. 202.

[7] Captain Buck and Captain John Copley. *Metallum Martis*, 21 seq.

[8] *Metallum Martis*, 40, 47.

[9] Ibid. 50.

[10] Habington, *Surv. of Worc.* (Worc. Hist. Soc.), i. 195.

[11] It has been stated that there were large smelting works here in Roman times. But probably the *scoriae* found there had been brought down the river to be smelted in the sixteenth century. *V. C. H. Worc.* i. 205.

[12] *Hist. MSS. Com. Rep.* iv. p. 121. The Worcester ironmongers were incorporated in 1598. Their minute book began in 1753 and ended in 1822. Town records quoted in J. Noake, *Worc. in Olden Times* (1849), p. 40.

[13] Viz. Warwick, Leicester, Northampton, and Oxfordshire. Yarranton, *England's Improvement by Sea and Land* (1677), 52 seq.

Dudley and Stourbridge, and there 'made into bar iron and small commodities and sent all over England.' Again, he remarks, there were 'in Worcestershire . . . mines of iron-stone that makes iron, not very good for use of all thyngs, but of excellent use for nails and many small commodities.' 'And in these countreys there are great quantities of pit-coals which are in all places near to the ironworks, and by the help of the coal the iron is manufactured with ease, cheapness, and advantage, whereby we have the trade of good part of Europe for these commodities.'[1] Yarranton himself had introduced the art of tinplate-working from Germany and Bohemia into Worcester, and actually improved it.[2]

About the same time we find another great family connected with the ironworks, the Foleys. Nash states that Richard Foley of Stourbridge, the founder of the family, was the owner of ironworks there.[3] His eldest son Richard lived at Longdon, and worked iron-stone and coal at his forges at Mear Heath.[4] His second son, Thomas Foley, 'from almost nothing, did get about five Thousand Pound per Annum, or more, by Iron-works, and that with so just and blameless dealing, that all Men that ever he had to do with, that ever I heard of, magnified his great Integrity and Honesty, which was questioned by none.'[5] He became very rich and purchased the manors of Old Swinford and Witley. His grandson Thomas bought the manor of Kidderminster, and in 1711 was created a peer as Baron Foley of Kidderminster.

The process of making iron was still much the same as when Dud Dudley first made it. Plot describes it in 1686. The best kind of iron at Dudley, he says, was a 'blew metal,' that made nails worth 10*s.* a hundred, and 'tough iron,' which was found for the most part at Rushall. The furnaces and forges were usually built near to one another. In them two tons of cast iron could be made in a day. In his time, too, slitting mills had just been erected. This was considered a great improvement for cutting iron. In addition there were new kinds of rollers and cutters.[6]

According to Plot, the latest effort to smelt iron with pit coal was made by a 'Mr. Blewstone, a High German, at Wednesbury,' which signally failed. In 1735 Abraham Darby began making iron with coal at Coalbrookdale in Staffs with more success than Dud Dudley or Mr. Blewstone.[7] In 1740 there were still two furnaces in Worcestershire making charcoal pig iron and producing 700 tons a year.[8] Charcoal then, in spite of all the inventions, was still much used.[9] From this date, however, coal or coke was more generally burnt in the furnaces, judging from the statistics for the year 1788. This coke was not the hard oven-made material which is now generally made as coke, but a soft fuel made from burning coal in open heaps or 'fires,' in which the coal was treated much the same as wood in the preparation of charcoal. There were now no furnaces in South Staffordshire and Worcestershire making charcoal pig-iron,[10] but this may have been in some measure due to the great demand for charcoal in the after processes of ironmaking, which would force the smelters to use coal, and to give up their prejudices. From 1760 onwards the great improvements made in the manufactures in England caused a marvellous increase in the iron trade everywhere.[11] In 1789, on the Stour alone, there were thirty works, slitting mills, forges, and wire mills.[12] In the same year at the newly arisen Stourport, too, one Thomas Banks established an iron foundry.[13] In 1796, in South Staffordshire and Worcestershire, there were fourteen furnaces, making 13,210½ tons.[14] Nash remarked that Stourbridge was famous for its ironworks; every kind was made, 'from pig to every minute article.'[15] At Wolverley

[1] Yarranton, *England's Improvement by Sea and Land* (1677), pt. 2 seq. p. 147. [2] Ibid. pt. 2, p. 151.

[3] Nash, *Hist. of Worc.* ii. 465 (1799). Another story associates the name of the founder of the Foley family, who was a fiddler living near Stourbridge, with the introduction of the first slitting mill into England, a knowledge of which he surreptitiously gained by visiting Swedish ironworks and fiddling for the workmen. Percy states that Richard Foley, the founder of the Foley family at Stourbridge, first a seller of nails and afterwards a forge master, died in 1657 at the age of 80 years. Swank, *Iron in all Ages* (1892), 48.

[4] Plot, *Nat. Hist. of Staffs* (1686), 158.

[5] R. Baxter, *Reliquiae Baxterianae* (1696), iii. 93. Baxter attributes this praise to him chiefly because he established a hospital at Old Swinford and endowed it with an estate worth £600 a year.

[6] Plot, *Nat. Hist. of Staffs*, 158 seq. (1686).

[7] R. Meade, *Coal and Iron Industries* (1882), 522; R. Hunt, *British Mining* (1887), 175.

[8] Meade, ibid. 522.

[9] Postlethwayt, *Considerations on the making of Bar-Iron* (1747).

[10] In Staffordshire (probably including parts of Worcestershire) that year there were six furnaces making 4,500 tons of coke pig-iron yearly, and three new ones expected to be in blast to make 2,400 tons. H. Scrivenor, *Hist. of Iron Trade* (1854), p. 87.

[11] The most important inventions were the cylindrical cast-iron bellows made by J. Smeaton in 1760, the steam engine by Watt in 1769, rolling iron into bars by Cort in 1783. Swank, *Iron in all Ages* (1892), 53 seq.

[12] Postlethwayt, *Dict. of Trade and Commerce* (1751); Camden, *Britannia* (Gough, ed. 1789), p. 357.

[13] Prattinton MS. iv. Bewdley (Soc. of Antiq. Lib.)

[14] The total number of furnaces in England was 124, making 125,079 tons. Meade, *Coal and Iron Industries* (1882), 523.

[15] Nash, *Hist. of Worc.* ii. 212 (1799). 'Within three miles of this town, but in the county of Stafford, the mines of coal are very extensive and the strata 40 yards thick, affording sufficient to last more than 1,000 years, supposing 120,000 tons to be raised each year from twenty pits, one half which belong to Lord Dudley.' Also 'About half a mile from Dudley is a

also there were three forges and plating and slitting mills, and 'almost every branch of the iron manufactory.' 'At the Upper Mill, cannon are bored: this is an ingenious invention and answers much better than casting them.'[1] The principal manufacturer there was one Mr. Knight, whose ancestors had 'acquired a very large fortune by the iron trade.' In 1800, round Dudley, six new furnaces were being built; and in 1806, when it was proposed to levy a tax on pig-iron, in the South Staffordshire district there were then forty-two furnaces making yearly 49,460 tons of iron.[2] The trade continued to increase in the same way[3] throughout the nineteenth century. In 1831, however, there was a great strike among the iron-workers. Eighteen furnaces were destroyed, and 3,000 workers thrown out of employment. This meant the decrease of 1,000 tons of iron a week. From the account of the strike the workpeople seem to have been justified, for they were very badly paid.[4]

Neilson's invention[5] in 1828 of hot blast marked the next era in the iron industry, and the larger outputs of iron which followed are mainly traceable to this discovery. Furnaces began to increase in size, more blast power was procurable from larger engines; but the use of the soft coke, before alluded to, retarded in Staffordshire the use of the higher blast furnaces which other iron districts began to adopt. By degrees, however, it was found necessary to procure hard coke from other districts—Durham, South Wales, and Yorkshire—to mix with the softer local fuel, and to take advantage of the economies which higher furnaces gave. Later on the waste gases, which then streamed in sheets of bright lurid flame from the furnace throats, casting a sort of aurora light on the sky at night as they flickered in the wind, and visible many miles away, were utilized for steam generation; and the adjoining neighbourhood, although deprived of the illumination, at all events gained freedom from much smoke and dust. This economy of fuel by utilization of the waste gas soon began to occupy the attention of the inventor, and the gas was further utilized for heating the air used in the furnaces. This was first heated in iron pipe-stoves, but the firebrick stove soon followed with its greater power of raising temperature; the first furnace in the Staffordshire district to adopt it being a Dudley one, Messrs. Cochrane & Co. of Woodside, Mr. Charles Cochrane of Stourbridge having done much to perfect the system.

After 1870 the extension of railways began to alter the conditions of the Staffordshire trade. A reduction of ten hours to eight hours per day, combined with the facilities for bringing in cheaper iron ores from other districts, began to affect the output of the ironstone in the mines of the South Staffordshire district. These stones were much as Dud Dudley described them, and were in many cases mined with the coal, but some of the seams were worked separately. They contain about 30 per cent. of iron on an average. The separately worked ores were the first to feel the altered conditions of the labour market, and only those parts of the district where they were in specially thick formation were able to mine them profitably. Hematite ores from Cumberland and from the Forest of Dean, oolites from Oxfordshire and Northamptonshire, began to be used as mixtures with the local stones (which latter had to be calcined before use), and also a large amount of the cinder known as 'tap and flue' which was made in the puddling and refining process. The growing size and height of furnaces also necessitated the increased use of hard coke, so that, with some few exceptions, where for special reasons and uses the old quality of iron is required, the present consumption of the South Staffordshire blast furnaces is largely supplied from elsewhere. Bar and sheet iron, which in the seventies attained its maximum production, soon began to feel the increasing competition of steel, which has become a formidable competitor.

Fortunately the Thomas Gilchrist process was applicable to the phosphoric pig-iron of the district; and though it was some time before advantage was taken of it, the beginning of the twentieth century has found three well-equipped steelworks. Two of these make their own basic pig-iron, and are following the most recent and advanced methods of steel practice. It is interesting, too, to note that one of these—the Round Oak Steel Works—is just on the border-land of the county of Worcester. The small Worcestershire portion of the district, too, figured largely in the old-established iron brands of bar iron, which made the South Staffordshire district famous in bygone years. 'S. C. Crown' and 'Lion' and 'Netherton' marked irons were and are made in Worcestershire, 'L.W.R.O.' close on the boundary; so that of the six 'marked' brands which have for many years ruled the prices of Staffordshire iron

spot of ground called by the country people the Fiery Holes: it consists of about 20 acres . . . . here were formerly many coal-pits, which as is supposed took fire by the carelessness of the workmen.' ii. Correc. and Add. 26.

[1] Nash, *Hist. of Worc.* ii. 212 (1799). Cor. and Add. p. 84. Wolverley lies in the Forest of Wyre coalfield.

[2] H. Scrivenor, *Hist. of Iron Trade* (1854), 98.

[3] In 1823 in South Staffs there were 81 furnaces, and in 1839 118, doubling the quantity of iron made. Meade, *Coal and Iron Industries* (1882), 525. In 1851 over a million tons was made yearly. Kendall, *Iron Ores of Great Brit.* (1893), 33.

[4] The iron-gatherers demanded an increase of 6*d.* per day: this was refused by the masters as impossible. The highest paid only received from 17*s.* to 25*s.* per week. *Worc. Herald*, 10 Dec., 1831, quoted in Prattinton MS. Gen. Hist. p. 100 (Soc. of Antiq. Lib.).

[5] The later history of this industry is kindly contributed by Mr. Francis Grazebrook.

markets, three at least are manufactured in the county of Worcester.

Dudley with its valuable deposits of coal and iron, its upheaved riches of silurian limestone, has latterly had to recognize the factor of exhaustion; but the past enormous mineral wealth has built round the town numerous industries, and has attracted capital into many trades which have formed valuable consumers of the product of its mineral. Like its ancient castle which formed a nucleus for its town, these parent industries have established a long series of industries and manufactures which, while developing in their own direction, sustain and absorb the local output of semi-finished product. Among these are chains and cables, pulley blocks, nuts and bolts, railway wagon and bridge building, fenders and fire-irons (the latter a special Dudley industry), pipes and bedsteads, safes and hollow-ware, besides the numerous smaller articles in which iron finds its use. Were it not for this vital local demand, this inland district, hampered with heavy railway rates to the ports for exported goods, would have felt more seriously than it has the competition of places more advantageously situated for seaborne traffic. While dealing with the associated industries, one must not forget the firebrick industry in which Stourbridge Clay is a name for the best class of refractory firebricks. The outcrop of the coal towards Stourbridge brings up the lower measures of the carboniferous deposit; these are principally fire-clays, some of which are of great value. The blending of these and their manufacture into various goods has built up a large and progressive industry in Worcestershire. The recent proving of the continuation of the coalfield to the north-west by the earl of Dudley at Baggridge will be an inestimable boon to the district, and will no doubt pave the way to further developments; but the district of South Staffordshire and its iron industry have already made a name in the history of civilization, to which the production of iron has so largely contributed.

TOOLS

It seems quite natural to find the trade of toolmaking in Worcestershire. In the northern part were all the materials necessary for making the implements. The trade centred round Dudley, Bromsgrove, and Belbroughton, especially the last place.[1] The chief articles made were scythes, shovels, pikes, and, in the Civil War, sword blades. The scythe-making industry was well established by the beginning of the seventeenth century. Probably it came into existence about the same time or soon after the smelting of iron ore had become a small industry in the county.[2] The earliest mention of scythe-smiths occurs in 1564.[3] Many of them, as is natural, bear the name of Smith, and others are Thomas Norton, Francis Heninges, Hugh Luke, William Perks, George Gilbert, John Cole, and John Waldron.[4]

The trade still continues to the present day in much the same places. Wolverley, Cradley, Belbroughton, and Hartlebury were centres of the manufacture in 1831, when 280 smiths were engaged in the trade.[5] Ten years later the number had increased to 398, by no means a large quantity.[6] Since then Pershore, Halesowen, and Stourbridge have taken up the trade.[7]

With this trade was connected another, due to the existence of the cloth industry in the county—that is, the manufacture of wool-cards. In 1572 the card-makers had a stall in Bewdley market.[8] In the sixteenth century the wire-drawers and card-makers suffered much from importation of foreign cards. Already, in 1548 and 1597, Acts had been passed forbidding their importation. They were so little obeyed, however, that in 1661 the card-makers of Worcester and other counties sent up a petition declaring they were nearly ruined by the foreign cards and by the hawking about of cards by 'vagabondious persons, void of habitation, who travelled from place to place, collecting old cards, from which they drew out the teeth, scored them, turned the leaves of the cards and reset the teeth in them, fixed them in new boards, and having counterfeited the marks of substantial card-makers, sold them to the country people.'[9] Next year a statute was passed forbidding all these abuses, especially the employment of old wire for new cards.[10] Little more is heard of the trade; probably it continued as long as the cloth trade was in existence in the county and died out with it.

NAILS AND CHAINS

Nail-making in some form or other was probably pursued in Dudley and the neighbourhood from the time when iron ore was first worked there.[11] But the earliest reference

[1] *Quart. Sess. R.* (Worc. Hist. Soc.), Introd. 36.

[2] See article on Iron.

[3] Chan. Proc. (P.R.O.), bdle. 188, No. 59.

[4] *Quart. Sess. R.* (Worc. Hist. Soc.), i. 263, 264; ii. 446, 471, 636.

[5] *Pop. Ret.* 1831.

[6] Ibid. 1841.

[7] Kelly, *Direct. for Worc.*

[8] Prattinton MSS. (Soc. of Antiq. Lib.), iv. Bewdley.

[9] Pet. in Corporation docquets quoted in Noake, *Worc. Nuggets* (1889), 272; *Jour. of House of Com.* viii. 28.

[10] Stat. 19 Chas. II. cap. 19.

[11] Cf. article on Iron. No mention of nailers is to be found in the Lay Subsidy Rolls, but Hutton makes it as old as the fourteenth century. Hutton, *Hist. of Birmingham*, 1835, p. 191.

does not occur until 1538, in the accounts for the building of Nonsuch Palace at Cuddington in Surrey. There it is recorded that English nails were bought from Reynolde Warde of Dudley, nailman, at 11*s.* 4*d.* the thousand.[1] In 1584 an Act was drafted to regulate the number of apprentices to be kept by a master, and 'nail-making is to be a trade of itself in those counties' (Staffs, Worc., and Salop).[2] Although the bill was not passed, yet its mere introduction implies some considerable trade in the district. From that time onwards through the sixteenth and seventeenth centuries this trade seems to have developed. No doubt the great progress and improvements in the production of iron bars gave the necessary impetus to an industry already existing. There are numerous entries in the Quarter Session Rolls of nailers during this period at Dudley, Cradley, Chaseley, Stourbridge, Hagley, Warley, Bromsgrove, and Pedmore.[3] It is said that a slitting mill for cutting iron into rods was established some time about 1686 by Richard Foley of Stourbridge. The great development in the smelting and manufacture of iron at the end of the seventeenth century must, too, have helped to improve and increase the nail trade. In 1727 there were said to be 2,000 nailers at Sedgeley alone.[4] The trade seems to have concentrated in the villages round Birmingham, alike in Worcestershire, Staffordshire, and Warwickshire. Hutton remarked 'that we cannot consider it a trade in so much as of Birmingham; for we have but few nail-makers left in the town; our nailers are chiefly masters, and rather opulent. The manufacturers are so scattered round the country that we cannot travel far in any direction out of the sound of the nail-hammer.' He also remarked on the number of women employed in the trade[5] at the time of his journey through the country in 1741.

The condition of the nailers throughout even to recent days appears to have been of the very worst and lowest. As early as 1713 an attempt was made to improve it by an increase in price of 6*d.* on every thousand nails, part of which was to go towards the education of the workpeople. They received only 3*s.* a week, working more than twelve hours a day.[6] Hutton gives them a very bad character, due to their fearful condition.[7] One of the causes of this may be that the organization of the industry differs from that of any other, in that little supervision is possible. 'There are no large manufactories in which numbers of nailers work under one roof. Nail-making by hand is essentially a home trade, practised in small sheds or shops attached to dwellings, in which not unfrequently the father, his sons, and daughters work together.' The 'forges are very rarely more than 15 feet by 12 feet (the ordinary size is 10 by 9 feet) and the only means of ventilation is by the door, and of lighting by two unglazed apertures, while the interior is filthily dirty.'[8]

Despite all this, at the end of the eighteenth century nail-making was very prosperous. At Bromsgrove 960 persons were employed in it in 1777.[9] Yet Nash said the number of nailers was greater still in Staffordshire, just on the borders of Worcestershire. Halesowen and the Lye near Stourbridge, were and still are great nail-making centres. Altogether from 35,000 to 40,000 were employed in the trade in his time, and about 200 tons of iron made weekly into nails. 'This comprises all ages and both sexes: both boys and girls begin to work by the time they are seven years old.'[10] Just then also the art of cutting nails, instead of forging them, had been discovered. As early as 1813 Bromsgrove was more especially noted for tacks and smaller nails of all kinds.[11] This branch of the trade still continues there. In 1831, 2,751 people were engaged in the industry in Worcestershire, by far the greater number occurring at Broms-

1 L. and P. Hen. VIII. xiii. (2) 132, 133. Flemish nails were only five shillings the thousand.

2 *Hist. MSS. Com. Rep.* iii. (2) 6. 'No one but those apprenticed and trained to it to practise it, and no apprentice to set up shop as a nailer unless he be 30 years old or married.' Every nailer employing two apprentices had to have also one journeyman.

3 *Quarter Sess. R.* (Worc. Hist. Soc.) i. 18, 86, 89, 90, 95, 99, 141, 232, 234, 269, 282; ii. 397, etc. These begin 1591 and end 1643.

4 Bradley, *Collec. for Improvement of Husbandry and Trade*, 1727, ii. 232.

5 Hutton, *Hist. of Birmingham* (1835), 192. After noticing the number of blacksmiths' shops, he said, 'In some of these shops I observed one or more females, stripped of their upper garments and not overcharged with their lower, wielding the hammer with all the grace of the sex. The beauties of their face were rather eclipsed by the smut of the anvil; or, in poetical phrase, the tincture of the forge had taken possession of those lips which might have been taken by the kiss. Struck with the novelty, I inquired whether the ladies in this country shod horses, but was answered with a smile, "They are nailers."'

6 From a pamphlet entitled *An Essay to Enable the Necessitous Poor to Pay Taxes*, quoted in *The Birmingham Trades* (Brit. Manufacturing Ser. ed. G. Ph. Bevan, 1876), 31.

7 'A fire without heat, a nailer of a fair complexion and one who despises the tankard, are equally rare among them. While the master reaps the harvest of plenty, the workman submits to the scanty gleanings of penury, a thin habit, an early old age, and a figure bending towards the earth. Plenty comes not near his dwelling, except of rags and of children.' Hutton, *Hist. of Birmingham* (1835), p. 192.

8 *The Birmingham Trades* (Brit. Manuf. Ser.) p. 31.

9 Prattinton MSS. (Soc. of Antiq. Lib.), vi. Bromsgrove.

10 Nash, *Hist. of Worc.* (1799), ii. Correc. and Add. p. 57.

11 Pitt, *General View of Agric.* (1813), 278.

grove.[1] But during the latter part of the last century the rapid strides made in the manufacturing of nails by machinery[2] completely displaced the hand-wrought nails in the markets, and the nail industry is now mainly centred in the large towns, Birmingham being the centre of the trade so far as the Midlands are concerned. But many of the manufacturing towns in the north of England supply a large quantity of machine-made nails, while there is a considerable importation from Germany. Here is one of the instances where the introduction of machinery has completely dislocated an old industry.[3] There are still, however, certain kinds of nails which are not produced by machinery; these and also the best horse-nails are still made by hand, but the demand for them is limited, and so, while there is a trade, the number of workmen exceeds the number of consumers.

The chain-making industry of Worcester, like the nailing, is a development of the iron and coal works in the district. Its area is very limited, being chiefly confined to Netherton, Cradley, and Lye, but it gives employment to a considerable number of persons, and has formed the theme for numerous and sensational articles and reports.[4]

The chain-making is of two kinds: the large heavy chains used mostly for ships and moorings, and the small chains. The first are made by a few firms only, as they require large capital and expensive machinery, together with the very best iron and work, and have to undergo a severe test. The great works are those of Noah Hingley and Sons, at Netherton, near Dudley, where large quantities of chains for the Admiralty and various shipping companies are manufactured. So important is the industry that a testing-house has been established by Lloyd's in the district, and all first-class chains are tested and marked there before being sent out.

The small chain manufacture is mainly done in shops or outhouses which adjoin or form part of the workers' homes. A fire like a blacksmith's, a large pair of bellows, a fixed hammer known as an oliver, are the chief requisites. The men get the iron from the masters and make so much chain. The quantity they have to produce in order to earn a living wage is considerable, so all hands, men, women, and children, are engaged in the business. It is naturally warm work, and those employed in it do not wear a superfluity of clothing, hence comes the fanciful description of the degraded state of the chain-makers. A good deal of distress often exists when work is slack, but the accounts of the horrors and degradations associated with chain-making are to a great extent created for sensation. It is probably one of the oldest industries in the county, and the one that has been least affected by modern innovations. The number of persons engaged in it is not large.

Another trade arising out of the iron industry is galvanizing. It is confined in Worcestershire to the watershed of the Stour, which divides in part of its course the counties of Worcester and Stafford. Large numbers of articles made of galvanized iron are turned out, and also the galvanized iron sheets. The chief point connected with the trade is the difficulty that arises in getting rid of the waste acid. If poured into the streams it is said to canker the boilers which take the water from this source; if poured into the sewers it is said to corrode them. The trade is not a very large one at present, and, with all the restrictions and difficulties which surround it in the way of disposing of its acid waste, does not seem likely to become so.

NEEDLES

Worcestershire can boast of the monopoly of at least one trade. Redditch and needles seem almost synonymous terms. It is not, however, a very ancient industry in the county.

Needle-making seems to have been an established trade in Buckinghamshire in the sixteenth century, when Redditch was but a small obscure village.[5] The tradition is that the industry was founded by Christopher Greening at Long Crendon about 1560.[6] There certainly was a family there of that name at that date, and Long Crendon a little later became celebrated for its needles.[7]

[1] *Pop. Returns* for 1831. Bromsgrove 1,169, Dudley 575, Old Swinford 539, Cradley 162, Northfield 122, King's Norton 97, Warley Wigorn 87.

[2] Tomlinson, *Cyclopædia of Useful Arts* (1866). In fact, it is only quite recently that nail-making by machinery has taken the place of the old hand industry. Many of the forging sheds still exist at the backs of the cottages round Bromsgrove, and some are still in use at the Lye and Halesowen.

[3] There has always been and still is great competition between the English and Belgian nailers. The latter are able to produce nails now at a cheaper rate. *The Birmingham Trades* (Brit. Manuf. Ser.), 31.

[4] See Baring Gould, *Nebo the Nailer*.

[5] Needles were first made in England by a Moor in Cheapside in Mary's reign, and again by Elias Crouse, a German, in 1566. Stow, *Annales* (1615), p. 948. The crest of the Needle-makers is now a Moor's head wreathed and couped at the shoulders. It was formerly an Apple Tree and Serpent.

[6] Some say 1650, but this seems a mistake. Tomlinson, *Cyclopædia of Art*.

[7] M. T. Morrall, *Hist. and Descrip. of Needle Making* (1866); A. E. Morrall, *Short Descrip. of Needle Making* (1886); Tomlinson, *Cyclopædia of Arts*; Shrimpton, *Notes on a Decayed Needle Land* (1897); *Birmingham Trades* (Brit. Manuf. Ser.), (1876), p. 101; Long Crendon Register, 1559, in *Home Counties Mag.* vi. 184.

From there some of the needle-makers probably migrated to the neighbourhood of Birmingham, and several small factories were set up on the river outside the town. About the end of the first quarter of the nineteenth century most of the Birmingham makers migrated to Redditch. The cause of the removal was doubtless the presence of emery stones in the river Arrow.[1] A horse-mill is said to have been established at Studley about 1700.[2]

From Redditch the industry spread to Bromsgrove, Feckenham, and the neighbouring villages. By 1790 the two places were well known for their needles and fish-hooks. Ten years later 400 people were employed in the industry at Redditch, and about 2,000 in the neighbourhood.[3] The oldest firms are those of Messrs. H. Milward and Sons,[4] and Messrs. Holyoakes and Gould, Messrs. Geo. Webb and Son, Feckenham Mills, Hemming, and Bartleet, while the Chillingworths had a large needle trade at the old forge mills near Redditch. Richard Hemming learnt the art of needle-making at a horse-mill at Sambourn, near Studley, close to Redditch, in the early part of the eighteenth century; John Mills had a water-mill, the first wholly occupied by needle-making, at Washford Mill in or before 1780.[5] But it was not till quite recently that Redditch became the most famous town for needles. At first the trade was practised chiefly by the workpeople in their homes, and both women and children as well as men were employed. Machinery was not used for their manufacture in Redditch till about 1828. It is stated by one of his descendants that in 1814 Peter Shrimpton came from Crendon to Redditch, and made netting, sail, mattress, and packing needles. Other members of the same family, Emmanuel, Jacob, and Titus, followed, and set up works there between 1830 and 1860. In 1830 there was a great strike at Redditch owing to the introduction of machinery for stamping the needles, and consequently much damage was done and eight men were imprisoned. Finally, the 'strikers' were persuaded to return and learn the new methods.[6]

In the late thirties drilled-eye needles were successfully brought out by William Green, of Astwood. Joseph Turner, of Redditch, in 1840 revived the practice of moistening needles with oil instead of water, which diminished the labour and did not corrode them so much. He encountered considerable opposition, and in consequence removed to Stratford-on-Avon, but finally returned to Redditch.[7] In 1843 Samuel Thomas introduced pointing-machines and the fan[8] for drawing away the dust from the grinder's wheel, in his works at the British Needle Mills in Redditch. After the needle-pointers' strike in 1846 the fan made its way and gradually won the approval of the men.[9]

As a result of these improvements the trade rapidly developed in the early part of the last century. Between 1841 and 1861 the population of Redditch doubled. In 1856 there were 100 manufacturers and 10,000 workmen in and near Redditch. In 1862 Messrs. Kirby Beard moved their works from Long Crendon to Redditch for greater convenience. Originally they were only needle merchants in London, but in 1850 they began making needles for themselves at Long Crendon.[10] In 1866 there were twelve firms engaged in the trade.

As closely connected with needle-making, and in some sense a natural development of that industry, we may mention here the manufacture of fish-hooks, which are probably produced in greater bulk in the Redditch district than anywhere else in England. William Bartleet and Sons, of the Abbey Needle Mills, will be familiar to most anglers as the makers of the Cholmondeley-Pennell eyed hooks in their improved forms. Harrison, Bartleet and Co., Richard Hemming and Son, and Henry Milward and Sons, may also be named amongst other firms equally well known, whom lack of space compels us to omit. Through the constant improvements effected in their manufacture the fish-hooks and fishing tackle of Redditch have become famous all over Great Britain, and are also in constant request by colonial sportsmen.

TILES

Tiles may roughly be classified as of two kinds, roofing and floor or wall tiles. In the history of their manufacture there is no interesting or vast development. Of neither was there any particular industry in any one place. Up to quite recent times both kinds of tiles were made as the need arose and at places near to the buildings for which they were required. In some towns perhaps there was some small

[1] The water-power furnished by the Arrow for turning mills was doubtless a consideration also.

[2] *Chambers' Edinburgh Journal*, 17 May, 1856, p. 317.

[3] Nash, *Hist. of Worc.* ii. 404. Mr. Sheward appears to have been one of the founders of the trade at Redditch, and occurs in documents of 1760–87 (W. T. Hemming, *Needle Region* (Redditch, 1877), p. 11). His windmill existed quite recently.

[4] This firm dates from 1730.

[5] Hemming, *Needle Region*, p. 14.

[6] M. T. Morrall, op. cit. p. 25.

[7] M. T. Morrall, op. cit. p. 23.

[8] Invented by Abraham, of Sheffield. Tomlinson, *Cycl. of Arts*. Shrimpton, *Notes on a Decayed Needle Land* (1897).

[9] M. T. Morrall, op. cit. p. 24.

[10] Shrimpton, *Notes on a Decayed Needle Land*.

local trade to supply the requirements of the neighbourhood; but on the whole it may be said to be as general and as necessary as the shoemakers' or bakers' trade. In the nineteenth century only have large centres of the industry arisen. This is due partly to the increase in population and partly to the greater facilities and cheaper means of communication and transport. Also the repeal of the taxes on bricks and tiles in 1839 and 1850 can have had no small effect on the development of the trade.[1]

A large number of workers appears to have been engaged in the tile trade at Worcester. The first information we have concerning them is in 1467 in the laws of the merchant guild.[2] There the tile-makers were forbidden to form any kind of organization as other trades. Everyone, even a stranger, was to 'be free to work with whom he likes,' and 'to come and go as he likes.' Nor were they to meet together in a union or 'parliament,' under pain of loss of franchise and a fine of 20*s.*; also every tiler was to mark his tile. These laws are curious. They show an entirely different spirit from that in which all other guilds were administered. For these latter, the rules were far more exclusive and rigid.[3] Among the tilers, however, free trade was made compulsory and the equality of all workers insisted on. It may be argued that this showed, not a more advanced condition of the trade, but rather a far inferior. The making of tiles at that period may have been such a rough and simple process that every man could superintend it for himself; and in that case the existence of masters and journeymen would only cause an enhancement of prices without any apparent compensating advantage. However that may be, the same rules were enforced again in 1497.[4]

The tile-houses in Worcester seem to have been situated in the north-eastern part of the city, at Lowesmoor, in the parish of St. Martin's. Habington relates that 'the Bishoppe had in hys Losemore clay-pittes apt to make tyle and brycke for which (as I take it) in the raygne of Henry the fourth hee receaved a rent, and I thincke from that tyme to thys the soyle theare or theare abouts hathe served makers of tyles and brycke, for without St. Martin's gate in Worcester was a house auncientlу called the Tylehouse which belounged to the Trinity.'[5]

[1] *Encyclo. Brit.* art. 'Tiles.'

[2] Toulmin Smith, *Eng. Gilds* (Early Eng. Text. Soc.), p. 351 seq. Nos. 57–78.

[3] Ibid. *passim.*

[4] Printed in Green's *Hist. of Worc.* (1796), app. lii.

[5] Habington, *Surv. of Worc.* (Worc. Hist. Soc.), ii. (1), 45. In 1221 there was a pottery at Sidbury, more to the south of the city in St. Peter's parish (*Pleas of Crown*, Selden Soc. No. 147), but it is not known that tiles were made there. A kiln thought to be Roman was found in Diglis near the river in 1860, and some tiles in St. Swithin's Street. *V. C. H. Worc.* i. 206, 207.

Again in 1650 a thousand tiles were ordered from Worcester for repairing the Bridge Chapel at Bewdley.[6] The trade there was still in existence in the seventeenth century. In 1700 there were some fields called 'clay pits' in Claines containing 18 acres, part of the estate of the late convent of White Ladies.[7]

In Yardley, however, at the end of the eighteenth century there was a flourishing trade in 'burnt tiles for covering houses.' At least 150,000 were made yearly. The clay there 'is of a peculiar good quality, and if well tempered and burnt would, notwithstanding the severest weather, last longer than the memory of man.'[8] At the present day Yardley has a reputation for excellent tiles and bricks. There are at least three firms there engaged in the trade.[9] At King's Norton also, quite close, there are four firms.

The history of the ornamental tile-making is more interesting, though just as obscure. In Worcester there appears to have been some trade in the fifteenth century, and even before, in connection with the cathedral and monasteries. In 1833 and recently two kilns were discovered at Malvern, and in 1837 in St. Mary Witton near Droitwich.[10] In these kilns were found tiles similar to those in the churches of Great and Little Malvern and in the cathedral of Worcester. The kiln at Malvern was situated about 200 yards from the priory church, and was probably erected by the monks when their church was built about 1450. Several of the tiles in Great Malvern Church bear the dates 1450, 1453, and 1456. Some are earlier still, of the fourteenth century, judging from the heraldic designs on them.[11] On these tiles were three kinds of ornamentation—armorial bearings, sacred symbols, and floral and other patterns. Sometimes they were laid singly and sometimes in sets of four and sixteen. They were usually made of red clay, with the pattern pressed out with a stamp. The spaces thus formed were then filled with a whitish liquid clay. Finally, the whole was faced with a yellow glaze, which imparted a rich colour to the red clay and improved the appearance of the tile.[12] Most of the tiles in Worcester Cathedral

[6] Prattinton MS. (Soc. Antiq. Lib.), Bewdley par.

[7] There are still large brickworks in Claines parish just outside the city of Worcester.

[8] Nash, *Hist. of Worc.* (1799), ii. 479.

[9] These are Messrs. Derrington and Sons, Henry Heming, and Arthur Lewis. Kelly, *Birm. Directory* (1904).

[10] *Gent's Mag.* 1844, May, 492; July, 25; 1833, Aug. 162; Oct. 301. In Card, *Dissertation on Antiq. of Priory of Gt. Malvern* (1834), app. there is a beautiful picture of the kiln found there.

[11] The arms are those of Hen. III. and Richard, king of the Romans.

[12] These tiles are fully described and depicted in Card, *Hist. of Malvern* (1834), p. 22; Nichols, *Encaustic Tiles* (1845); Shaw, *Specimens of Tile Pavement* (1858); Jewitt, in *Journ. of Brit. Arch. Assoc.* iv. 216; Wood-

are earlier, of the thirteenth and two following centuries; on the earlier ones the pattern of the trefoil is frequently inscribed, and on the later ones the oak and vine leaf. And at Malvern, in addition to the pavement tiles, there were some beautiful wall tiles.[1] From the number of tiles showing the Malvern and Droitwich patterns which are scattered all over and outside the county[2] it might be inferred that these two places were the centres of a fairly large industry from the thirteenth century onwards. Whether tiles were made there only, excavation alone can discover. At present there is no evidence to suggest there were other places. Tiles continued to be made at Malvern up to the sixteenth and seventeenth centuries. In the church there are some dated 1640.[3]

In the last century Mr. Chamberlain, who was engaged in the china works at Worcester, began making encaustic tiles there much about the same time as Minton began at Stoke. After he joined Messrs. Flight and Barr, the manufacture was still continued. When the latter removed to their new premises, the old premises were used solely for the making of tiles of all colours and designs under the management of Mr. Barr and Mr. Fleming St. John. In 1850 the works were sold to Messrs. Maw, who two years later removed to Broseley in Shropshire. Once more, in 1870, Mr. H. C. Webb revived the manufacture at Rainbow Hill, but this factory has ceased to exist.[4] Thus, from the thirteenth century onwards till recent times there has been an intermittent trade in tiles in the county of Worcester.

We may also mention here that in addition to ordinary brick-making there is a considerable amount of work done in the county in the production of what are known as blue bricks or Staffordshire bricks, and these derive their colour from the special clay of which they are made. They are much harder and more durable than the ordinary 'builder' bricks, and are invaluable for any work where strength is required, especially in a damp locality. For paving footpaths in populous districts they are now much in request. The chief centre of their manufacture is the region including Oldbury, Cakemore, and the Lye, and at each of these places there are large brickworks.

CHINA

The manufacture of china in Worcester is due entirely to exceptional circumstances. Worcester does not produce one single substance that is used in the manufacture of china, nor have Worcester people any special aptitude for the work. In the early part of the eighteenth century the clothing trade, which had been one of the great city industries, had almost died out owing to the migration of the clothiers to Gloucestershire and Somersetshire, and the loss of the trade caused the prosperity of Worcester to decline. Some of the citizens felt that a new industry might be introduced with advantage to take the place of the clothing trade, and to Dr. John Wall it occurred that china-making would be the most suitable. China was at that time fashionable, the taste for it had increased, and the demand exceeded the supply. Wall accordingly determined to set up a china manufactory in Worcester. He began about 1750 to carry on some experiments at a house now No. 33 Broad Street, and had got so far that in 1751 he and his associates took, on a lease for twenty-one years, a large house overlooking the river, where they began the Worcester china works. In the *Gentleman's Magazine*[5] for 1752 a view of the porcelain manufactory is given. At first the chief productions were imitations of oriental china, and to make the imitations perfect even the marks were copied. The ordinary forms were made on the wheel and

ward, *Hist. of Bordesley Abb.* (1866), 93, 107. The arms they bear are chiefly those of founders, such as the Despencers, Clares, earls of Gloucester, Beauchamps, de Bracis. On several, legends are inscribed: on one in the abbey church, Malvern, is the following:—

Thinke . mon . thi . liffe .
mai . not . eu . endure .
that . thow . dost . thi . self .
of that . thow . art surre
but . that . thow . gevest .
un . to the . sectur . cure .
and eu . hit . availe . the .
hit . is . but . aventure .

Card, *Hist. of Malvern*, p. 34. 'Sectur cure' in line 6 apparently means 'executor's care.' This occurs as far north as York, and as far west as the Wirral. On another, 'Miseremini mei, miseremini mei, saltem vos amici mei, quia manus Domini tetigit me.' And on a third, 'Mentem sanctam, spontaneum honorem Deo, et patrie liberacionem.' Nichols, *Encaustic Tiles*.

[1] Habington (Worc. Hist. Soc. 1899), ii. (2), 183.

[2] Similar tiles to those in the kiln at Malvern have been found at Gloucester and Hereford. *Gent. Mag.* July, 1844, p. 30. Others occur as far afield as Neath and St. David's to the west, and Heytesbury to the south (*Assoc. Archit. Soc. Reports*, xix. 156; *Brit. Arch. Assoc. Journ.* iv. 1848, 216).

[3] Cole, in his notes on Malvern Church, records under the window nearest the east end of the south aisle the following inscription in tiles: HERE LYETH THE BODY OF EDMUND REA LATE VICAR OF MUCH MALVERNE DECEASED THE 23 OF DEC. ANNO DO. 1640. *Gent's Mag.* July, 1844, p. 30, and Cole MS. (B.M.), x. 126.

[4] L. Jewitt, *Ceramic Art in Gt. Brit.* (1883), p. 154; R. W. Binns, *A Century of Potting in the City of Worc.* (1865).

[5] Aug. 1752, p. 348.

turned on the lathe;[1] the best were made from moulds. Being so successful with the imitation of oriental china, the makers tried their hands at imitating English patterns, and some very successful imitations of Chelsea were produced, and when these had been done with success imitations of Dresden and Sèvres followed.

On the discovery of china clay in Cornwall the Worcester Company entered into an agreement for twenty-one years for a supply of the clay for their works.[2]

One novelty was introduced at Worcester; printing on porcelain was first adopted there,[3] and it greatly facilitated the production of china. This process has usually been ascribed to Dr. Wall. Green, who subsequently wrote the history of Worcester, and is better known to us as an engraver, was employed in the factory from 1760 to 1764[4] as an apprentice to Hancock, who engraved the plates for the china. In his *History of Worcester*[5] he says that Worcester will be able to rival, and in fact supersede, the celebrated commodity of India.

Worcester china seems to have so far prospered that in 1768 a London agency was established 'up one pair of stairs at Giles's, in Cockspur Street,' for articles in the Dresden, Chelsea, and Chinese. It does not seem to have been very prosperous, for in 1776 the stock of Giles's chinaware and enamels was disposed of by auction. Young in his tour visited Worcester, and gives the wages then paid to the workmen employed in the factory, viz.—men 12*s.* to 75*s.*, labourers 6*s.* to 7*s.*, children 1*s.* to 3*s.* per week.[6]

On the expiration of the lease of the works in Warmstry House, the whole factory, with the secret of the process for making porcelain, was offered for sale by auction. The sale took place in 1772, when the price realized was £5,250. The Rev. Thomas Vernon, one of the original proprietors, was the purchaser, but he assigned the property a few weeks after to John Wall the younger,[7] and the company was reconstituted, the number of partners being six, of whom Dr. Wall was one. In 1776 Dr. Wall died, but the works continued to be carried on by the surviving partners until 1783, when they were sold to Mr. Thomas Flight, who had acted as the London agent of the company.

China-making had turned out a success. One of the workmen who had been employed there, Robert Chamberlain, in 1781 set up a factory on his own account in Diglis, on the site of the works now occupied by the Royal Porcelain Company.[8] In 1788 George III. paid a visit to the bishop of Worcester, who had been tutor to his son. He inspected Flight's china works, and from the visit the works first earned the right to call themselves the Royal Porcelain Manufactory. In a satirical account of the king's inspection, he is made to say,[9] 'I visited the china manufactory. The place has an infernal appearance. The man who described the works to me carried tobacco in his mouth. Charlotte says he smelt horribly. I find mixing with my people attended with many disagreeable circumstances.'

Chamberlain's firm throve; there was a keen rivalry between it and the Porcelain Company, and Chamberlain doubtless considered it good business, when Lord Nelson went to Worcester in 1802, that his firm were able to secure a visit to their works as well as his patronage, including an order for a breakfast service and two vases, one to have a miniature of himself supported by the figure of Fame, the other to have a likeness of Lady Hamilton.[10]

Chamberlain's china fetched high prices. A dessert service for the Princess Charlotte cost £201 19*s.*,[11] a dinner service for her £847 12*s.* a dinner service for the East India Company £2,170, a second somewhat plainer £2,019, a dessert, dinner, and breakfast service for the Prince Regent £4,047 19*s.* With such prices it is obvious that the business could not have been very extensive.

In 1820 a third firm, Grainger's, set up as china-makers, and carried on business until 1888. Some very beautiful specimens of work were produced by the manufacturers. About 1855 the firm began to manufacture a material called semi-porcelain for dinner services, which would stand a large amount of heat, and obtained some popularity.

In 1840 the two firms of the Porcelain Company, Flight and Barr, and Chamberlain's, united, a joint stock company was formed, and with various changes it has continued to the present time, the business now being carried on by a limited company as the Royal Porcelain Works. In 1888 the company bought up the china works which had been carried on by Grainger, and from that time until 1896 they were the only china-makers in Worcester; but in this year another firm, Messrs. Locke and Co., set up a manufactory for the production of a different grade of china. In 1900 a third firm, Hadley's, commenced business in Worcester, and turned out some very beautiful and artistic work, though not in any great quantity, but they have since been bought up by the Royal Porcelain Company.

At the present time there are only two distinct china works in Worcester, the Royal Porcelain Works, the descendants of the old manufactory established by Dr. Wall, and those of Locke and Co.

[1] Binns, *Century of Potting* (1877), p. 34.
[2] Ibid. p. 45. [3] Ibid. p. 49.
[4] Ibid. p. 7. [5] Vol. ii. p. 20.
[6] Six Months' Tour, ed. 1771, p. 306.
[7] Binns, op. cit. p. 119.
[8] Green, *Worcester*, ii. 22.

[9] *Royal Recollections*, p. 103.
[10] Binns, op. cit. p. 222. [11] Ibid. p. 233.

GLASS

The glass trade first became a substantial industry in England in the seventeenth century. There was no export trade until then. Glass had, of course, been manufactured in previous centuries. Window glass for churches was made in mediaeval times, and examples may still be seen in Malvern Church and other places in the county.

In Worcestershire the manufacture began at Stourbridge in the sixteenth century, and gradually developed with the general growth of the trade elsewhere until the county became one of the most important centres of the industry. One of the causes of this is a peculiarly fine clay found in the district round Lye, near Stourbridge. This layer of clay lies 'within a circle of not more than two miles,[1] taking the valley of the Stour and Lye as the centre, and at depths varying from three or four to a hundred and eighty yards from the surface. Its position in the strata is in all cases below the thick coal at distances varying from twelve to twenty-five yards; and it is generally overlaid by a shaly friable kind of coal called "batts," from twelve to twenty-four inches thick. The thickness of the seam varies from five or six up to forty inches. The quality is in some instances as hard as stone, having to be blasted with powder, and in others soft and easily workable. There is a great variation in its component parts, arising principally in the proportion of silica.'[2] This clay has a world-wide fame. Its fine quality makes it most suitable for moulding the pots in which the glass is melted. In fact, at the present day Stourbridge clay is held to be one of the most necessary ingredients for making glass-house pots. Plot, writing in 1686, remarked that 'the most preferable clay of any is that of Amblecot, of a dark blewish colour, whereof they make the best pots for the glass-houses of any in England; nay, so very good is it for this purpose, that it is sold on the place for sevenpence the bushell, whereof Mr. Gray has sixpence, and the workmen one penny, and so very necessary to be had that it is sent as far as London . . . . the goodness of which clay and cheapness of coal hereabout no doubt has drawn the glass-houses, both for vessels and broad glass, into these parts; their being divers set up in different forms at Amblecot, old-Swynford, Holloways-end and Cobourn brook.'[3] It is more than probable that the pots were made at Stourbridge some time before glass itself. A lease, it has been stated, was granted for digging glass-house pot clay there in 1566.[4]

Glass itself does not seem to have been made there before the seventeenth century. The manufacture began with the arrival of certain strangers from Lorraine. In September, 1567, licence was granted to John Quarre or Carré and Antony Becku (alias Dolin) for 21 years to make glass, provided that the works were opened before 24 June, 1568.[5] Accordingly, in 1568, Quarre or Carré and John Chevallier made a contract with 'Thomas and Balthazar de Hanezal, dwelling at Vosges in Lorraine,'[6] to come to England, bringing with them four gentlemen glaziers, and work for them for nine years.[7] The Hennezals apparently came soon after the agreement was concluded. With them seem to have come also members of the de Houx, de Thiéry, and du Thisac families, the two latter known in English as Tyttery and Tyzack. But as the du Thisac bear the same arms as the Hennezals, it is possible that they were all members of one family of Hennezal, distinguished by local appellations. They seem to have settled first in Surrey and Sussex, where Carré's works lay. After their nine years were over some of them perhaps left Carré, and about 1576 set up works at Buckholt, in Hants,[8] conveniently situated near extensive woodlands. They seem to have been very unpopular everywhere, on account of the quantity of wood they burnt in their furnaces, 'for as the woods about decay so the glassehouses remove and follow the

[1] Nash says the clay stands over a district 'not above half a mile square or about 200 acres.' Nash, *Hist. of Worc.* (1799), ii. 212.

[2] L. Jewitt, *Ceramic Art in Gt. Britain* (1883), 156.

[3] Plot, *Natural Hist. of Staffs* (1686), 121.

[4] L. Jewitt, *Ceramic Art in Gt. Brit.* (1883), 156. I cannot trace his authority.

[5] Pat. Eliz. pt. 11, m. 4. 33. *Cal. of S.P. Dom. Eliz.* 1547-80, pp. 297, 315, 477; Addenda (1566-79), p. 34.

[6] Glass-making was considered in no way derogatory to the rank of a French gentleman. In Lorraine there were four families belonging to the lesser nobility engaged in the trade, namely, de Hennezal, de Thiérry, du Thisac, and de Houx. Of these the Hennezals were the oldest. They were mentioned in the first charter of 1448 granted to the original glass-makers by Jean de Calabré. Their descendants still have glass-works in the province. Members of all four families seem to have come over to England, probably to avoid the religious troubles of France in the sixteenth century, but no less attracted by the expected profits. Beaupré, *Gentilshommes Verriers* (1847), pp. 41n., 11, and 39.

[7] Lansdowne MS. (B.M.), 59 fol. 194, 202. No. 76.

[8] Remains of a glass furnace have been found here and pieces of glass, one of which is ascribed to the fourteenth century and others to the sixteenth and seventeenth. See *Brit. Arch. Assoc. Journ.* xvii. 57; 70. *V.C.H. Hants*, i. 323n.

woods with small charge.'[1] From Buckholt they migrated, about 1599, to Newent, in the Forest of Dean, probably still in search of wood.[2] At this place they would hear of the excellent Stourbridge clay, and finding also that it was quite close to the great Forest of Feckenham, they migrated and finally settled down at a place called the Lye, or Lye in the Waste, on a hill still known as Hungary Hill, about two miles out of Stourbridge.[3] The later discovery of coal on the spot would induce them to stay there, since in 1615 the use of wood for furnaces was forbidden. It seems impossible to discover the exact date of their appearance in Worcestershire. Their names do not occur in the Subsidy Roll for 1603.[4] They seem to have arrived at Stourbridge about 1612.[5] In 1612, John, son of Paul and Bridget Tyzack, was baptized at King's Swinford, in Staffs, about three miles north of Stourbridge. And on the 9th and 16th December, 1615, Paul, son of Jacob Henzie, and Zacharias, son of Fowler Henzie, were respectively baptized at Old Swinford, in Worcestershire.[6] Joshua, son of Ananias Hensell, seems to have been the head of the family at Stourbridge.[7] In 1621 died Edward Henzey 'of Amblecoat in the parish of Old Swinford in the county of Staffs, glass-maker.' The name of Henzey appears[8] in the Old Swinford parish registers from 1615 to 1780, and in the King's Swinford from 1612 to 1729. The Tyzacks lived at Old Swinford from 1615 to 1729. The Tytteries first appear in 1622, and the de Houx in the following year. In addition to these, there are many other foreign names in the registers, such as Bigo, Durocker, Verelst, throughout the seventeenth and eighteenth centuries.[9] Their number cannot have been very large, for Habington, writing some time about 1636, and describing Stourbridge and Old Swinford, does not mention them at all.[10]

The glass-makers of Stourbridge must have worked under Sir Robert Mansell's patent; for he had the monopoly of all glass-making in England. In the Newcastle parish registers it is recorded that 'Edward Henzey, servant to Sir Robert Mansfield (sic), was buried.' If he was a servant of Sir Robert, then probably his relations in Worcestershire were also dependent on him. Sir Robert, however, seems to have experienced great difficulty in obtaining the full use of his monopoly.[11]

The foreign glass-makers at Old Swinford continued to work and increase and become wealthy. Already, in 1615, Paul Henzey had bought land in Bedecote near Stourbridge.[12] And by 1664 there were at least three glasshouses in King's Swinford and Old Swinford, called 'Coleman's Glasshouse, Hood Glasshouse, and Glasshouse in the Brottell,' all belonging to Joshua Henzey. But quarrels soon arose among these foreigners. Joshua Henzey wished to monopolize the whole trade, and so agreed to pay John Tyzack ten shillings a week to prevent him setting up another glasshouse. But one Paul Tyzack, seeing what profits Joshua Henzey was making, brought an action against him, complaining that his wages had not been paid, and declaring that he had earned twice or three times as much wage when working with Joshua Henzey.[13]

1 *Hist. MSS. Com. Rep.* xiii. pt. iv. pp. 65, 76.

2 Docquets quoted in A. Hartshorne, *Old Eng. Glasses* (1897). A. W. C. Hallen, *Les Gentilshommes Verriers* (Edin. 1893). *Encycl. Brit.* art. Glass.

3 Or it is possible they went to Newcastle-on-Tyne first, and then migrated to Stourbridge, some returning afterwards to Newcastle. H. S. Grazebrook, *Coll. for a Gen. of the Noble Families of Henry Tyttery and Tyzack* (1877), p. 13.

4 *Lay Subs. R.* 1603 (Worc. Hist. Soc.), 1901.

5 In a list of burials at Old Swinford, it is at least remarkable that, whereas in 1611 there were only 25, in 1612 there were 49. For the following years also the number remains about the same, except in 1636, when it was 90, the effect of the plague there. Prattinton MS. (Soc. of Antiq. Lib.), Old Swinford Par.

6 H. S. Grazebrook, *Coll. for a Gen. of the Noble Families of Henry Tyttery and Tyzack* (1877), et seq.

7 A descendant of the Henzies has in his possession a seventeenth-century painting on vellum of the arms, crest, and motto of the family (Arms gu. 3 acorns or; crest, 'a firebolt and fireball.' Motto 'Seigneur, je te prie garde ma vie'). Under this is written, 'This is the true coate of arms, with Mantle, Helmet, and Crest, pertayninge to the ffamily of Mr. Joshua Henzell of Hamblecot in the county of Stafford, gentleman, who was the sonne of Ananias Henzell de la Maison de Henzell, tout pré la village de Darnell en la Pie de l'Lorraine; which Arms of his anncestours were ther sett upp in the Duke of Lorraine's gallery windowe amongst many nobleman's coates of Armes there annealed in glasse.' Then follows a description of the arms. Hallen, *Les Gentilshommes Verriers, (French Gentlemen Glass-makers)*. (Edin. 1893.) For their pedigree see H. S. Grazebrook, *ut supra.*

8 H. S. Grazebrook, *ut supra.*

9 It is interesting to see the way in which these families continued to intermarry, though scattered all over the country, even as far north as Newcastle-on-Tyne, Glasgow, and Leith, and as far south as Sussex.

10 'Thys manor and paryshe of Swineford called Old Swineford, environed allmost with Staffordshire and Shropshire, as onely united unto as by neyghboringe Pedmore, and is nowe best knowne to us by a bridge over the ryver of Sture whereunto the Towne northward, a good dystance from the churche, extendethe itsealfe in a fayre and well inhabited streete, and not long synce inryched with a Frydaie Marcate, is commonly named Sturbridge.' Habington, *Survey of Worc.* (Worc. Hist. Soc.), i. 205.

11 Docquets printed in App. to *Old Eng. Glasses* by A. Hartshorne (1897), and H. S. Grazebrook, *ut supra.*

12 Prattinton MS. (Soc. of Antiq. Lib.), Private Rec. ii.

13 Spec. Depos. Exch. K.R. (P.R.O.), Mixed Cos. 19 Chas. II. East. No. 8.

From the documents of this incident it appears that there were works at Amblecote and Holloway End, as well as at Hungary Hill. It is sometimes stated that some of the first works were situated near Stourbridge railway station, for there are there some fields called Glasshouse Fields.[1] Joshua Henzey did not work alone. He took into partnership Robert Foley, probably to obtain coal for the furnaces. Foley was the great iron manufacturer, and it is possible that his family was already in possession of the coalfields of the district.[2]

The Henzeys were not the sole glass-makers. There were also English families engaged. One, Thomas Rogers, who had married Anne Tyttery,[3] died in possession of several glasshouses and warehouses, and was 'an eminent dealer in glass.'[4] His son, grandson, and great-grandson carried on the works. The great grandson, Thomas Rogers, built a large house at Holloway End, and was sheriff of Worcestershire in 1750.[5] Another clan of glass-makers were the Bradleys. They were an old family, and were closely connected with the Henzeys and Tytterys. One member, Thomas Bradley, who died in 1677, was described as a glass-maker in his letter of administration to his widow. Another Thomas Bradley, who died in 1691, was the owner of a glasshouse and lands in Dennis. Yet another Thomas Bradley had a 'glasswork' in Old Swinford in 1705, and John Bradley, glass-maker, was, with Edward Tyzack, broad-glass manufacturer of Amblecote, trustee to a marriage settlement in 1704. In 1699 one Mrs. Hunt had a glasshouse on the Heath[6] at Stourbridge.

The original families of Henry Tyttery and Tyzack seem to have died out at Stourbridge. The families became represented by the Bretells, Dixons, Pidcocks, and Bates, many of whom continued glass-makers.[7]

By the end of the seventeenth century the glass trade was flourishing at Stourbridge. In 1686 Plot had remarked that there were several glasshouses at Amblecote, Old Swinford, Holloway End, and Coalbourn Brook.[8] In 1696 there were said to be altogether eighty-eight glasshouses in England, and seventeen of these were at Stourbridge. Seven made window-glass; five, bottles; and five, flint, green, and ordinary glass.[9] Originally the Lorraine glass-makers came to England to make window-glass only, and teach the English their methods; although the latter had not altogether lost the art.[10] But they soon began making other kinds. Thomas Rogers made white glass and bottles, and one Edward Henzey broad glass.[11]

However, they seem to have excelled in making coloured window-glass. Dr. Pococke, travelling through England in 1751, 'came to Stourbridge, famous for glass manufactures, especially for its coloured glass, with which they make painted windows which is here coloured in the liquid, of all the capital colours in their several shades, and, if I mistake not is a secret which they have here.'[12]

In the eighteenth century stone glasshouse pots began to be a distinct industry. The clay for them had probably first attracted the Lorraine workmen. Nash has a very interesting article on it. In his time 'it is sent to the manufacturing towns all over England, Ireland, and Scotland, and a great deal exported.' The principal proprietors of it were Lord Foley, Edward Hickman, and Mr. Millward. So valuable was it that it was forbidden to be exported as fuller's earth, unless manufactured. 'For this reason it is often exported in the shape of bricks, which may sometimes be ground down and used as clay.' Concerning the kinds of glass, he noticed that 'broad glass has been manufactured here for several generations, ever since it was first brought into England from Lorraine . . . Crystal glass has long since been made here; but the art of cutting and engraving it was not long since brought from Germany to London, and from London hither.' Also he mentions plate-glass, crown-glass, bottles, and flint-glass.[13] The manufacture of cut-glass continued so to improve that by 1819 Stourbridge was already well known for it.[14]

Improvements now came fast. In 1780 George Ensall[15] erected a 'lear' for annealing, the first of its kind. It is stated that he went to Germany and Bohemia, disguised as a minstrel, and so obtained entrance into the

1 L. Jewitt, *Ceramic Art in Gt. Brit.* (1883), p. 156.

2 From a patent quoted in Nash, *Hist. of Worc.* (1799), ii. 365. See art. on Iron.

3 Probably the daughter of Daniel Tyttery, who was buried at Old Swinford, 30 Dec., 1641. H. S. Grazebrook, *ut supra.*

4 Their daughter married Henry Saunders, grandfather of Henry Saunders who wrote *Hist. and Antiq. of Shenstone. Bibl. Topog. Brit.* iv. pt. 4 (ed. 1794), Introd. p. 8. H. S. Grazebrook, *ut supra*, p. 16.

5 Ibid.

6 Prattinton MS. (Soc. of Antiq. Lib.), Old Swinford Par.

7 H. S. Grazebrook, *ut supra.*

8 All these places are in the ancient parish of Old Swinford, though the townships of Amblecote and Coalbourn Brook were in Staffordshire, while that of Lye was in Worcestershire.

9 Houghton, *Coll. for Improvement of Trade and Commerce* (1727), ii. 48.

10 A. Hartshorne, *Old Eng. Glasses* (1897), 159.

11 H. S. Grazebrook, *ut supra*, p. 16.

12 *Dr. Pococke's Travels through Eng.* (ed. Camden Soc. by J. J. Cartwright), i. 222. Some of this glass was in Hagley Church in his time, ii. 285.

13 Nash, *Hist. of Worc.* (1719), ii. 212.

14 Pinnock, *Hist. of Topog. of Counties of Eng.* (1819), Worc. p. 30.

15 Sometimes identified with the Hennezals. But the name Ensall occurs in a Worcestershire Muster Roll of 1539 before any Hennezal had come. L. and P. Hen. VIII. xiv. (1), 306.

glasshouse. The methods he learnt there he introduced into his own glasshouse at Stourbridge. In 1802 open and sheet moulds for pressing glass were first used by Charles Chasbie, and new designs for wine-glasses by Loxdale and Jackson, and James Chasbie, about 1804. Steam engines for cutting glass were introduced by Dudley and Dovey of Stourbridge. In 1824 and 1845 the processes for making crystalline, pressed glass, and enamelling, were much improved. As a result of these inventions the productions of the Stourbridge firms were among the finest at the exhibition of 1851.[1] In 1852 there were altogether twelve glass factories, employing 1,050 hands. There was also a great increase in the export of clay and in the making of bricks. In 1852, 46,000 tons of clay were being raised annually, and 14,000,000 bricks made, to the value of £50,000. The best clay for glasshouse pots was sold at 55*s.* per ton, and the 'seconds' or 'offal' clay at 10*s.* per ton. It is exported to North and South America, France, Holland, and Germany. There were, however, only four proprietors of the clay mines, and two firms renting them.[2] The largest works were 'Ruffords' clay works; 900 hands were employed in making bricks alone.

A new invention of this period was the making of clay retorts for gasworks, and clay baths veneered with porcelain instead of metal. This manufacture has steadily increased, and now for nearly all public baths these bricks are used.[3] Mr. Jewitt gives an interesting description of the treatment of clay for glasshouse purposes. 'After having been carefully selected, it is broken into small pieces by women accustomed to its appearance, who throw on one side all pieces of discoloured or irregular clay; it is finely ground by heavy edge-runners, and mixed with a certain proportion of ground potsherds (old broken burnt pots), the proportion of which varies according to the purpose for which it is used; it is then mixed with water and tempered with the foot, and allowed to lie not less than six or seven weeks so as to acquire great tenacity before being made into pots. These pots are built up by hand gradually, great care being taken that the last layer of clay is not allowed to become hard or dry, or it will not unite properly; neglect in this respect causing the pot to give way in the furnaces. The pots are dried very gradually, and are seldom fit for use under six to eight months. The ordinary clay is allowed to lie in large heaps, subject to the action of the atmosphere; and is then used in the manufacture of gas retorts, firebricks, etc. The quantity of bricks made annually in the district is about 50 millions.'[4] This was in 1883. The life of these pots is seldom longer than three weeks or a month; sometimes they last six weeks, sometimes one hour.

It is to be feared that of late years the making of glass, like many other trades of old standing, has suffered severely in the prevailing depression. The following may be mentioned as still engaged in the glass manufacture of Worcestershire. At Bromsgrove, Mr. Thomas Evans; at Stourbridge, Mr. Zachariah Haden. Also The Stourbridge Glass and Gripalite Tile Company, Ltd., and Messrs. Thomas Webb and Sons, Ltd., manufacturers of flint and coloured glass at the Stourbridge Glass Works. At Dudley, three firms: Messrs. Joshua Lane and Sons of Eve Hill; Mr. Richard Wilkes of Campbell Street; Mr. William Woodcock of Furnace Road, Dudley; and at Oldbury a firm of glass-shade makers, Messrs Wm. E. Chance and Co., of Church Bridge, who also manufacture 'antique' glass of the finest quality for church windows and the best domestic work. This product is the nearest approach now made to the beautiful old flashed and pot-coloured glass of an earlier time.[5] The great works of Chance Brothers at Spon Lane, where most of the glass for optical purposes and lighthouses is made, adjoin the county border.

CLOTH

The woollen industry from an early date formed the staple trade of England. At first the production of the raw material was alone attempted. English wool was found to be so far superior to any other, that it was eagerly sought for by all weavers and cloth makers of north-west Europe throughout the twelfth and thirteenth centuries. Soon the manufacture followed the trade in the raw material, and by the thirteenth century craft guilds of weavers and dyers were well established all over the country, and the State had begun to take measures for controlling and regulating the trade. Edward III. did his best to improve it by the introduction of Flemish weavers, and by the prohibition of the export of the raw material. With the fourteenth century arose the drapers, the retail merchants of cloth. The next century marked a great

[1] Messrs. Richardson of Wordesley, Davis Greathead of Stourbridge, Webb of Platts and Wood. *Birmingham Journ.*, 31 May, 1851.

[2] T. C. Turberville, *Worc. in the Nineteenth Cent.* (1852), p. 9. The following is an analysis of the best clay:—Silica, 72·516; Alumina, 20·264; Lime, 0·891; Peroxide of iron, 3·308; Protoxide of Manganese, 1·438; Phosphate of Lime, 1·533.

[3] T. C. Turberville, *Worc. in the Nineteenth Cent.* (1852), p. 9.

[4] L. Jewitt, *Ceramic Art in Gt. Brit.*, p. 157.

[5] From information kindly furnished by Mr. Wm. Pearce.

development. The clothier, the capitalist manufacturer, first made his appearance, superseding the older craft guilds. In the sixteenth century the trade was at its height. The discovery of new countries, and the development of the English navy, led to a tremendous increase of capital. Moreover, the religious and political troubles, which had ruined the trade abroad, only served to improve the English manufacture, by causing the migration of a large number of Flemish and other weavers to this country. But this supremacy did not last long. England's wool trade was soon to suffer in turn. It could not in any case have escaped the effects of the English financial and political troubles of the seventeenth century; but at the same time other European countries were beginning to recover. Spanish wool and Spanish cloth were imported into England, in spite of prohibitions. English weavers failed to improve the quality of their cloth and suit the material to the wants of their consumers. In the eighteenth century, partly owing to the great wool famine, and partly, perhaps, to economic difficulties, England was no longer the sole producer of wool or manufacturer of cloth. In the nineteenth century it partially recovered after the introduction of steam power. To-day its cloths are still held to be among the finest and best anywhere produced. But it is a manufacture based on imported material.

In all this Worcestershire played perhaps an unimportant part. But at one period the industry was certainly quite a substantial one in the county. In the sixteenth century it was most flourishing. Then it was said to have given employment to 8,000 people;[1] the county is mentioned by Thomas Fuller in a list of districts famous for cloth making, and the town of Worcester[2] gave its name to a fine broad-cloth, in the manufacture of which it excelled. Indeed, it was a county well adapted both for raising wool and for making cloth. The soil was fertile, and afforded good pasture for sheep. A number of streams served to turn the fulling and other mills. A navigable river provided easy communication to other parts of England or foreign ports. And the towns of Worcester, Kidderminster, and Evesham, formed centres for the manufacture and sale of cloth and wool. Thus it seems natural to find the woollen trade established in the county, though its history there can hardly be taken as a good illustration of the general development of the industry in England. The organization came later, and the decline earlier, than in many other counties. But still it played a part, however small, in the English trade as a whole.

Of the trade in the raw material there is little to learn. Worcester quite early helped to supply the foreign market. In 1280 and 1315 the Cistercian monastery of Bordesley, and the Benedictine abbeys of Evesham and Pershore, sold wool to Flemish and Florentine merchants. Even earlier, in 1273, an abbot, John of Bordesley, tried to pay off a debt to some Florentine merchants in wool.[3] Judging from the usual price in Worcestershire during the twelfth and thirteenth centuries, its wool was of an average quality.[4] But in respect of quantity it cannot have been a great wool-producing county. It only contributed 209 sacks and 16 lb. to the general levy granted to Edward III. in 1341, while Norfolk sent 2,206 sacks, Lincolnshire 1,265, and Gloucestershire 591.[5] In the fourteenth century, however, Worcester merchants travelled as far as Calais, taking, no doubt, the chief product, wool.[6] At the beginning of the next century these merchants felt themselves justified in demanding that a staple should be established in the borough of Worcester. This, however was refused on the petition of the merchants of the staple.[7]

The export, however, continued. In 1453 the decay of the cloth manufacturing trade was attributed to the export of wool at a very low price, in spite of the statutes made by Edward III.[8] Eleven years later it was enacted that no one was to buy wool except 'such as shall make cloth thereof,' under penalty of a fine equal to double the value of the wool purchased.[9] This statute can have been but little observed, for in 1484 a proclamation was issued to the inhabitants of the county, by which the exportation of yarn-cloth not dressed was strictly forbidden.[10]

However, the aim of these various statutes was not only to prevent exportation but also to crush out of existence the middleman, who first made his appearance with the development of the woollen trade in the fifteenth century. In 1488, 1530, and 1550 the old statute that

[1] *Infra.*

[2] Fuller, *Church Hist.* (Brewer, 1845), ii. 287.

[3] Cunningham, *Growth of Eng. Industry and Commerce* (3 ed. 1896), 624. Compare *Archaeologia*, xxviii. 221; *Trans. Royal Hist. Soc.* xviii. 148.

[4] *Cal. Pat.* 1334–8, 481; *Parl. R.* (Rec. Com.), ii. 138*b*.

[5] *Parl. R.* (Rec. Com.), ii. 131*b*. Heref. sent 140, Westmld. 156, Newcastle 73.

[6] Ibid. iii. 352*b*.

[7] Prattinton MS. (Soc. of Antiq. Lib.), Gen. Hist. 96; *Stat. Realm* (Rec. Com.), i. 332; *Parl. R.* (Rec. Com.), ii. 253.

[8] *Parl. R.* (Rec. Com.), v. 275*a*.

[9] *Stat. Realm* (Rec. Com.), ii. 410. Among other counties Worcester is mentioned. *Parl. R.* (Rec. Com.), v. 464.

[10] *Cal. Pat.* 1476–85, p. 519. If Worcester exported wool, she also supplied the foreign merchants in London: One Thomas White, of Broadway, husbandman, brought an action of debt against Thomas Wynnam, 'a man of power and might dwelling in a foreign shire in London,' for 12 sacks of Cotswold wool he had ordered and kept for six years. Early Chan. Proc. (P.R O.), bdle 66, No. 462.

only clothiers and merchants of the staple were permitted to buy wool in large quantities, was reinforced.[1] As a result of this, one Ralph Parsons, of Cropthorne, was twice brought up, in 1553 and 1555, for infringing the statute; the first time, however, the case was dismissed.[2] In 1567 one Spencer, of Broadway, was accused of the same offence.[3] During Elizabeth's reign there were several cases of 'engrossing'[4] and 'regrating' wool,[5] as it was called; and one case in 1566 of 'enhauncing' the price by keeping wool for a year after it had been shorn.[6] In 1577 the clothiers of Worcester declared the high price of wool was caused by the 'greedy covetousness of the merchant staplers.'[7]

The high lands east of Evesham seem to have afforded the best pasture for sheep. The husbandmen of Broadway, Bengeworth, and Cropthorne are more frequently mentioned than any others as dealers in wool. Much of the wool for the Worcester clothiers seems to have been supplied by the adjoining counties of Hereford, Shropshire, Staffordshire, and Warwickshire.[8] Yet in 1615 Worcestershire was mentioned as one of the five of the twelve cloth-making counties of England that had 'any store of woolle of their own breeding.' It even sent its wool to Gloucester, Devon, and Kent.[9] But it is absurd to say that this or any other county of England was self-sufficing at the period.

On the whole the trade can never have been very extensive. There is far more to learn about the manufactured article—cloth. That trade, one ambitious Worcester citizen states, originated in the seventh century, and continued to prosper without any break to his day.[10] For a more truthful account let us turn to the history of the craft guild. By its rise and development the growth of this or any other trade in the thirteenth and fourteenth centuries may be measured. In most towns of England craft guilds were in existence in the twelfth century. In Worcestershire at this period there are isolated notices of dyers at Worcester, and of weavers there and at Evesham and Feckenham.[11] In 1203 the men of Worcester paid a fine of 100 shillings that they might buy and sell dyed cloth, as they did in the time of King Henry.[12] This is a proof, perhaps, that there was but little cloth trade in Worcester then. For the restriction against the importation of woollen cloths, dyed or undyed (for the freedom from which the fine was paid), was in favour of the weavers, and not of the towns, which hitherto had dealt largely in foreign cloths, dyed by themselves. It was more profitable to import than to make cloth. By towns where weavers' guilds were established the fine was not paid, and hence the payment of a fine at Worcester indicates the absence of a guild at this date.[13] On the contrary it seems probable that in these early times whatever trade existed was in the hands of the monks.[14]

The Assize of Measures, again, was in force in Worcester, but our authorities are silent as to any guild. In 1218 Ralph de Wilitun, sheriff of Worcestershire, was bidden to look after the fair and assize of cloth, and to proclaim that no dyed, brown, or hauberk cloth was to be sold, unless it was of the measure required by the assize.[15] In 1221 complaints were made to the justices in eyre that the assize was not carried out.[16] In 1223 the bailiffs of Worcester were again commanded not to allow the fair and the cloth fair to extend beyond the fixed time of a week[17] for fear of injury to the other fairs. But in all this there is no evidence of any craft guild. Rather in Worcester the earlier organization, the merchant guild, seems long to have held its sway, and it kept in its own hands the management and monopoly of all industries. But it was not until 1227 that

[1] *Stat. Realm* (Rec. Com.), iv. 141. Stat. 22 Hen. VIII. cap. 1.

[2] Exch. K.R. Memo. R. (P.R.O.), 1 Mary Hil. 54; 2 and 3 Phil. and Mary Trin. 38.

[3] Ibid. 9. Eliz. Mich. 78.

[4] An 'engrosser' or 'brogger' or 'forestaller,' was one who bought up goods on their way to market, in order to make a corner and 'enhance' the price. A 'regrator' bought to resell in the same market.

[5] Wm. Wranford of Longdon in 1564 (Ibid. 6 Eliz. Mich. 379*d*.), William Brooke, alias Wover, of Broadway in 1565 (Ibid. 7 Eliz. Trin. 89), Joseph Phelps of Bengeworth in 1568 (Ibid. 10 Eliz. Trin. 94), Henry Inkbarrow at Evesham in 1599 (*Quart. Sess. R.* Worc. Hist. Soc. i. 18).

[6] Exch. K.R. Memo. R. (P.R.O.), 7 Eliz. Mich. 198.

[7] *Cal. S.P. Dom.* 1547–80, p. 550.

[8] A list of 'broggers' and 'engrossers' is given in Prattinton MS. v. Worc. City (Soc. of Antiq. Lib.), *Acts of P.C.* xix. 184, and Exch. Memo. R. (P.R.O.).

[9] S.P. Dom. 1615, vol. lxxx. No. 13, printed by Unwin, *Industrial Organisation* (1904), 188–9.

[10] *i.e.* sixteenth century, *vide infra*.

[11] Dyers of Worc. 1173, *Pipe R.* (Pipe R. Soc.), xix. 163; *Feet of F.* (Pipe R. Soc.), xv. 70; *Chron. de Evesham* (Rolls Series), 215 n.; *Bracton's Note Book* (ed. Maitland 1887), No. 1080.

[12] Madox, *Hist. of Exch.* (1769), i. 468.

[13] Pishey Thompson, paper on *Early Commerce of Boston* (Assoc. Archit. Soc. Rep. and Papers, ii. 363), and *infra* Dyers.

[14] In *Chron. de Evesham* (Rolls Ser.), p. 213, is the following note: 'et foragio unius equi et foragio certae quantitatis ad calefaciendum aquam ad pannos.'

[15] *Cal. Pat.* 1216–25, p. 153. This was the Assize of Measures of 1197 issued by the Justiciar, Hubert Walter, requiring, among other things, 'that woollen cloths, wherever they are made, shall be of the same width, to wit: of 2 ells within the lists and of the same goodness in the middle and sides'; the Act was to be administered by legal men appointed by each county, city, or borough.

[16] Worc. Eyre for 1221 printed in *Pleas of the Crown* (Selden Soc. 1887), No. 148.

[17] *Cal. Close* (Rec. Com.), i. 356; Ibid. i. 555, *vide infra*.

the citizens of Worcester obtained from Henry III. the right even of having a merchant guild with a hanse and other customs.[1] Free trade was not in any way permitted. 'None who are not of that guild shall do any merchandise in the said city or suburb, save at the will of the said citizens.' The grant was confirmed to the borough again by Henry IV., Edward III., and Richard II., when additional powers were given to the guild merchants of trying cases between merchants, and arresting for debt.

In Kidderminster the craft guild arose just as late. But there we meet with an early reference to the cloth trade. Before 1334 it was enacted 'that no manner of man within the Manner and Burrow off Ketherminster shall make any woollen cloth Broad nor Narrow without the Baylieft's Seall in payn of xxs for every defaulte, the one haulfe to the prince and the Lord and the Other to the Bayliefe.' The same rule applied to 'carsies' as well as to cloth.[2] And not only in these two towns was the trade in existence: there were weavers and dyers scattered all over the county, and fulling mills at Evesham and Kidderminster. However, by far the greater number of dyers, sheresmen, and weavers are found at Worcester,[3] which suggests that that town was the great centre of the trade, as it was the centre of local justice, in the county.

During the fourteenth century the industry was slowly developing, and Worcester cloths were becoming famous. In 1337 Evesham sent deputies to a 'Council in respect of trade,' to which only representatives of large trading centres were summoned.[4] In 1422 Benedictine monks were forbidden to wear Worcester cloth. Its fine quality made it more suitable for military men than for them.[5] Perhaps this progress was the work of the skilled Flemish weavers, some of whom seem to have penetrated as far as Worcestershire.[6] About 1453 there was a slight depression in the trade, attributed at the time to the export of wool at a low price.[7] Therefore in 1464 and 1467 the importation of foreign cloth,[8] and the exportation of English cloth not properly fulled was forbidden.[9] Finally, in 1484 a proclamation was issued to Worcester that no person was to 'carry beyond the sea any woollen yarn or cloth not fulled; but that the woollen yarn shall be woven and the cloth thereof made shall be fulled and shorn and fully wrought within the realm,' under very severe penalties.'[10] In spite of this there was 'used and accustumed grete cloth-makynge to be hadd wt yn the seid cite and sabbarbes of the same, and so occupied by grete part of the people ther dwellynge.'[11] The effect of this policy of protection was to give a great impetus to the cloth trade everywhere; 'the manufacture of cloth had increased with such extraordinary rapidity that it had grown to be a very important trade.'[12]

In 1467 we get the first definite piece of information concerning the craft guild in Worcester, although the merchant guild was still the ruling authority there. There are three sets of ordinances and rules for the crafts of weavers and walkers, all compiled within a short period.[13] The first two were made respectively in 1467[14] and 1497[15] by the merchant guild of Worcester among their own rules; the third was made by the craft of weavers, walkers, and clothiers themselves in 1522. It seems more convenient to treat these three sets of rules together than to take each one separately. In them we get a little insight into the organization of the industry.

In the ordinances of the guild merchants of 1467 the articles concerning the cloth trade relate chiefly to the assize of measures and the regulation of the pageants. In those of 1497 the greater number of rules for clothiers shows that the trade during those thirty years had become more important. There now appear more details of organization, and the craft of the drapers is first mentioned. By 1522 the

[1] Nash, *Hist. of Worc.* (1799), ii. App. 110; *Cal. Chart. R.* i. 23.

[2] Burton, *Hist. of Kidderminster* (1890), p. 171. The term kersey or carsey seems to have been applied to a kind of coarse cloth. There were, however, fine cloths of this make. It was chiefly exported to Holland. It was also commonly used for stockings before the introduction of knitted ones. Beck, *Drapers' Dict.* p. 179.

[3] *Lay Subs. R.* circa 1280 and 1332 (Worc. Hist. Soc.); *Chron. de Evesham* (Rolls Ser.), 215.

[4] May, *Hist. of Evesham* (1805), 312. v. *infra*, Dyers.

[5] Rock, *Textile Fabrics* (S. Kensington Mus., Art Handbooks, 1876), p. 65.

[6] The names of one or two 'Frenchmen' and 'Flemings' occur in subsidy rolls and municipal documents of Kidderminster. *Lay Subs. R.* (Worc. Hist. Soc.), 1 Edw. III. and *ex inf.* J. Brinton, Esq.

[7] v. *supra.*

[8] *Stat. of Realm* (Rec. Com.), ii. 410, Worc. is one of the counties mentioned.

[9] Ibid.

[10] *Cal. Pat.* 1476–85, p. 519. This proclamation, however, was soon repealed. *Cal. of Pat.* 1476–85, 494.

[11] Toulmin Smith, *Eng. Gilds* (Early Eng. Text Soc. 1870), 383.

[12] Cunningham, *Growth of Eng. Industry and Commerce* (1895), 434.

[13] Green, *Hist. of Worc.* (1796), app. Ordinances of Henry VII. In the ordinances of the Guild Merchants of Worc. in 1467 five crafts were mentioned, and as the regulations for the weavers and walkers occupy more space than those of any other, it might be inferred that the weavers and walkers formed one of them, if not the most important. Toulmin Smith, *Eng. Gilds* (Early Eng. Text Soc.) 371 seq.

[14] Printed in Toulmin Smith, *Eng. Gilds* (1870), 371 seq.

[15] Printed in Green, *Hist. of Worc.* (1796), App. pp. lviii. lxi. lxvii.

weavers, walkers, and clothiers, were making ordinances for themselves.[1] Either the merchant guild by that time was declining, or probably the weavers had separated from the merchants owing to the increased importance of their trade.

Throughout these ordinances the dominating note is the desire to ensure to the consumer the best possible material. For this purpose the greatest possible care was displayed, and every precaution taken, to compel the manufacturers to obey the assize, and to prevent them from injuring the trade by making cloths of a poor or bad quality. A wool weight was to be kept in the guildhall for the use of all spinners, who from the wording of the texts were for the most part women, working at home. The warp and woof together were to weigh 84 lb. according to the old assize, 90 lb. according to the new. The cloth was to be weighed both before and after it was woven, allowing 2 lb. for the waste and the thrums (knots). Finally it was to be examined by the searchers, and if approved of, sealed with the seal of the borough. Two searchers were appointed yearly, one to be a walker, the other a weaver, chosen by the whole craft of weavers and walkers; and the two chamberlains of the borough controlled all defaults. Moreover 'at every lombe within the citye or subarbs of the same oon journey-man at the leest' was necessary, under pain of a fine of 6*s.* 8*d.* from the master weaver, to ensure that the work was carefully done. In 1497 it was ordained that he who 'bryngeth to werpe any stuff to mak a hole cloth, that he bryng his hole warpe by hitself, and after that he shall bryng his hole wofe at oon or two severall tymes' to be weighed.

Some steps towards the modern system of industry may be observed. One of these was division of labour. One man did not perform all the processes necessary for making cloth. In 1467, there were 'spynners, websters, dyers, and shermen,' and people to 'dye carde or spynne, weve or cloth-walke'; and in 1497 cloth could only be sealed if it was 'warked manly walkyd, burlyd, and wrangle halfyd as a cloth ought to be'—these operations being performed by different workers.

Weavers and walkers were quite distinct. From which of these classes the retailer or draper was drawn it is difficult to ascertain.[2] It does not appear to have been the weaver or walker (for a little later the weavers with the walkers and clothiers formed a craft of their own), but rather perhaps the cloth finisher.[3] In 1497, it was enacted that 'an artificer might make a dagon of cloth of 8 yards to sell where he liked if he makes not divers of them . . . to the prejudice and hurt of the draper's crafte.' The drapers' craft, then, was in existence at this date, though it was not incorporated till 1551.

One of the most important points to the makers of the ordinances was the necessity for the craftsmen to attend the pageants and meetings. Perhaps it can be explained by the desire of the town to make the guilds recognize its authority by some outward sign. It is noticeable in the laws of 1467, and in those of 1497 it was remarked that the five pageants 'were to be better and more certenly kept than they have byn by for this tyme.' They must have formed a picturesque procession on Corpus Christi Day with their 'torchis and tapurs,' going to 'the lawde and worship of God,' the more important members in the livery, probably of scarlet cloth, which was to be renewed every three years. We have a survival of this in the flags of the Clothiers' Company with their arms. The company has still the remains of some of its old banners as well as its modern ones. It also possesses what is called a pall, said to have been used at the funeral of Catherine of Aragon, more likely at that of her first husband, Prince Arthur, which consists of fragments of old ecclesiastical vestments sewn together and is now in the Worcester Museum. On Corpus Christi day too, or the Sunday following, every craft performed its play. In 1522 every journeyman and master weaver was bidden to meet at the house of the Friars Preachers, and march with the walkers to the cathedral. There they met afterwards to settle up accounts and elect the new master and wardens. Four times a year they attended a dirge and mass of Requiem, and 'from them to a drynkyng if any be ordeyned.' Every one, even if only apprenticed, was to contribute to these processions either in wax or money—a larger amount if they had not served their time or if they were absent.

But already some of the later narrowness of these crafts was creeping in. 'No one was to be received into the clothing' unless he had been apprenticed seven years, was free of the borough, admitted by the advice of the master, wardens, and fellowship, after inquiry 'if he is of good name, sufficient goods and carring of wevyng and of his craft.' No one was to practise the trade unless he was made free of the company. Strangers were not permitted to have the same privileges as the

[1] Prattinton MS. (Soc. of Antiq. Lib.) Worc. City. These appear to be the first ordinances made by the craft.

[2] Ashley, *Early Hist. of Eng. Woollen Industry* (Amer. Econ. Assoc. 1887), 60. Here Mr. Ashley points out that the drapers might conceivably have arisen from either of the two groups, the cloth finishers and the wool dealers.

[3] There is also mention of two drapers between 1456 and 1467, namely, Richard Mychell, draper of Worc. (Early Chan. Proc. P.R.O. bdle. 26, No. 139), and Henry Lambe, draper of Worc. (Ibid. bdle. 29, No. 82). Noake relates that there was a fellowship of tailors and drapers in Henry VII's reign. Noake, *Worc. in Olden Times* (1844), p. 31.

inhabitants of the town. No wool was to be sold in the guildhall on market day till 'x of the belle,' and no stranger to buy till 'xi of the belle,' and a penny a todd (28 lb.) was charged as toll on all wool coming into the town. All wool was to be weighed by buyer or seller in the guildhall. Drapers and 'lynnynmen' were to sell only in the guildhall, and then pay twopence for their stalls, and fourpence in fair time. On the other hand any 'man or woman denysyn may sill linen cloth of their proper makyng without contradiction of eny person.' Even workpeople outside the town were not to be employed to the hurt of the poor commonalty of the town.

But this, as it seems, was an attempt to check the growth of the domestic system, which was evidently beginning to make itself felt in Worcester. It was this system which finally overthrew the guild system in the sixteenth century. And it was by this method that industry was organized throughout the seventeenth and eighteenth centuries, until it in turn was superseded by the factory system.[1] 'The central figure to be studied in the new organization of labour is the clothier. He buys the wool, causes it to be spun, woven, fulled, and dyed, pays the artisans for each stage in the manufactures, and sells the finished commodity to the drapers.' 'He was not an artisan but a capitalist manufacturer.'[2] He is evident in Worcester in 1467. The ordinances of this year show this in such rules as the following: 'to these seid artificers,[3] by maisters and makers of cloth, they should none other wyse be contented or payde but in mercery vitelle or by other meanes and not in sylver, that hath growen to grete hurte,' wherefore it was ordained that no workman should be compelled to 'ressyve nothinge in chaffare, but in gold or sylver of eny makers, chapmen, or syllers of cloth.' The 'maisters and makers of cloth' must have been the clothiers employing dyers, spinners, weavers, and other 'artificers' to make cloth for them, which they sold to the draper.[4] To pay these people, some capital was necessary, however small. It was this that gave them their importance in the sixteenth century and made all others engaged in the trade dependent on them. Again, every cloth was to be searched at Michaelmas as it went from the weaver to the walker, and from the walker to the owner, who is evidently the clothier. The clothiers formed a craft with the walkers and weavers in 1522, making their own ordinances. These clothiers were often graziers on a large scale. In fact, sheep-farming was the most lucrative, and therefore the most popular, pursuit in the sixteenth century.

One of the results of this was that business was more carried on in the country, and the towns in consequence declined. Naturally, the 'organized weavers of towns resisted, and public opinion held with them that the great wealth-producing industries of the country should be confined to the towns.'[5] So much was this felt in Worcestershire that in 1533–4 an Act was passed providing that after September, 1536, cloth should only be made in towns under a penalty of 40*s.* for every cloth. Worcester, Evesham, Droitwich, Kidderminster, and Bromsgrove, says the Act 'have byn in tymes past well and substancially inhabyted occupyed maynteyned and upholden by reason of makyng of wollen clothes called longe clothes short clothes and other clothes aswell whytes blewes and browne blewes, and the pore people of the same citie borowes and townes and of the Countre adjoyning to theym daily sett aworke as in spynnyng cardyng breakyng and sortyng of wolles, and the handy craftes there inhabytyng as weavers fullers sheremen and dyers have byn well sett a worke and had sufficient lyvyng by the same, untill nowe within fewe yeres passed that dyverse persones inhabityng and dwellyng in the hameletts thropes and villages adjoynyng to the seid Citie borowes and townes w^tin the seid Shire, for theire pryvate welthis singuler advauntages and commodities nothyng regardyng the mayntenance and upholdyng of the seid Citie Boroughes and townes ne the comen welthe of the seid handy craftys inhabytyng and dwellyng within the seid Citie Boroughes and Townes, ne the poore people which had lyvyng by the same have not only engrossed and takyn into theire handes dyverse and sondre fermes and become fermers grasiers and husbandmen, but also doo exercise use and occupie the mysteries of clothe makyng wevyng fullyng and sheryng within theire seid howses, and doo make all maner of clothes aswell brode clothes whytys and playne Clothes within theire seid howses in the Countres abrode, to the greate decay depopulacion and ruyne of the seid Citie townes and boroughes.'

This is an excellent illustration of the way in which the industry was carried on under the domestic system, and also of the useless attempts of the town clothier to recover control of the trade. And it 'shows clearly that the struggle between town and country was at this time due mainly to the rivalry, not of the craftsmen but of their employers.'[6] Landlords were forbidden to raise the rents of houses or cottages for the exercising of the craft, in the hope to induce clothiers to return to the towns. And all cloths were to be measured and sealed with the

[1] Ashley, *Early Hist. of Woollen Industry* (Amer. Econ. Assoc. 1887), 72 et seq.

[2] Ibid. p. 81.

[3] i.e. spynners, websters, dyers, shermen, and other laborers, or artificers.

[4] From this it would appear that at this date the makers were also the retailers of cloth. v. *supra.*

[5] G. Unwin, *Industrial Organisation in the sixteenth and seventeenth centuries* (Oxf. 1904), 85.

[6] *Stat. of Realm* (Rec. Com.), 25 Hen. VIII. c. 18.

seal of the town as they came wet from the mill: but this time the length and breadth of the piece of cloth was to be stamped on it, instead of being of a particular measure as heretofore.[1]

These measures resulted in a complicated condition of trade which is not altogether easy to describe. The circumstances of the time were indeed involved. We seem to detect various developments which are somewhat opposed in direction. One of these is a decline in the wool trade throughout the south and west of England, which lasted till far into the seventeenth century. Another is the migration of the trade from the towns to the country, and the consequent establishment of the domestic system of work done at home. To this migration the towns offer strenuous resistance, and at the same time it produces outside the towns a greater prosperity for the moment. The result is that we get conflicting statements as to progress or decay. The towns, in particular, exaggerated the evil, in the hope of procuring state restriction on the domestic system. A further complexity arises from the fact that the cloth now produced in the country was brought into the towns, to be sold there by the drapers. Therefore, while the cloth industry dwindled in the towns, its fall was in part compensated by a new form of business—that is, the selling of cloth by the drapers. On the other hand, the dislocation of trade threw town workmen out of employment and caused corresponding distress. This complexity in respect to the wool trade is further increased by the general troubles of the country due to the enclosures, the suppression of the monastic system, and other features of the age. In fact we are in a transitional period which is marked, like all such periods, by the co-existence of advance and decline in many complicated details.

First we may note how the craft guilds and city authorities made desperate attempts to bring back the trade to the towns and oust the country clothier. But the measures they took only tended more and more to drive the trade and the workpeople out of the town to places where they could work in greater freedom and ease. In a Chamber Order made in 1539–40, no foreign clothier was allowed to fetch yarn out of the city, and no foreign journeyman was to be employed before a citizen without the consent of the master and wardens. He was also obliged to bring a testimonial of his servitude, and pay 8*d.* to the poor. Disputes were forbidden, but when any did arise they were to be settled by the master and wardens. The company was allowed, when necessary, to levy an assessment on every loom in the city to pay off its debts or raise subscriptions. There were the same regulations for the pageants, processions, and meetings as in 1522, but the members were not to pay more than half a guinea each for their drums and ribbons. One of the great complaints against the guilds was that they exacted very heavy fees.

In 1540 we find a small advance. From this time forward the craft appears to have held its meetings in the Trinity Hall, originally part of the chantry or gild of the Trinity, in the parish of St. Nicholas,[2] with other 'occupacions' of the city, for the use of which they paid a geld yearly to the clerk of the Trinity Hall.[3] Definite possession of the hall was, however, not obtained till nearly a century later, in 1612.

Statements of contemporary writers about the condition of the trade at this time are naturally conflicting. In 1538 Latimer writing to Cromwell describes Worcester as 'behind (the times), an ancient and a poor city, and yet replenished with men of honesty though not most wealthy.' He explains its poverty and the idleness of the inhabitants 'by reason of their lady,'[4] that is, of their Roman Catholicism.

On the other hand Leland, writing in the latter part of Henry VIII.'s reign, noted that 'the wealthe of the Towne of Worcester standeth most by Drapering, and noe Towne of England at this present tyme maketh so many Cloathes yearly, as this Towne doth.' And Kidderminster, too, 'standeth most by cloathinge,' and Bromsgrove 'somethinge by cloathinge.'[5] The cloth trade was still carried on then in Kidderminster and Evesham, and also in other towns of Worcestershire, in Bromsgrove and Droitwich to some extent. Later Bromsgrove became noted for its coarse cloths and linen. An explanation of the prosperity of Worcester and these other towns would, perhaps, be that they became the centres for the sale of the cloth rather than the centre of the manufacture. This would seem the more true, when we find that in 1551 the craft of drapers and tailors, having become prosperous and important, were making their own byelaws and ordinances; and this points to a flourishing condition of the trade in general. The draper still seemed to be working himself, and was not solely a merchant, the rules relate chiefly to the tailors; no master was to finish a piece of work cut out by another, and no journeyman was to take work to be done out of his master's house. In fact, on the whole, the trade seems to have been at its height in the county generally about this time, and not so bad in Worcester itself, if we judge from the number of statutes passed to regulate the industry, and also from a statement made about fifty years

[1] This Act was confirmed in 1535–6, stat. 27 Hen. VIII. c. 12.

[2] See Topography.

[3] Noake, *Worc. in Olden Times* (1849), p. 18. See p. 293 below.

[4] *L. and P. Hen. VIII.* xiii. (2), 211. Also there were two Acts, one in 1536 and another in 1540, enforcing the building of houses in the city of Worcester. Stat. 27 Hen. VIII. cap. 22 and 32 Hen. VIII. cap. 18.

[5] *Leland's Itinerary* (Hearne, 3 ed. 1769), iv. 105. 109, 113.

later, showing that at this time there were about three hundred and eighty looms in the city, giving employment to eight thousand people.[1] Also it was enacted that 'hytt shall be lawful to the saide drapers and their apprentices to make women's hoses, as they heretofore have used without greeing with the saide taylors.'[2] The drapers in Worcester then were hosiers as well; later, they were united with the skinners and tanners. All actions were brought in the name of the city chamberlain who was secured from loss by the company.

No less plain is the effect of the domestic system in throwing out of work a large number of journeymen and smaller masters. The clothier found it cheaper to employ a number of apprentices. The Worcestershire clothiers wandered even as far as Kent in their search for work, to the great annoyance of the Kentish weavers. On the whole, the clothier seems to have treated his journeymen very badly, paying them with 'soup, candels, rotten cloth, stinking fish, and such like baggage.'[3] The craft guilds and town weavers received great support and assistance from the state in the enforcement of their regulations. There was a return to the old system of requiring all cloths to be made according to a prescribed length, breadth, and weight.[4] It seemed unfair, especially to workpeople, that any persons should have in their hands a great many men's livings.

The abuses in the making of cloth led to a very severe Act in 1552.[5] The statutes made for the Worcestershire cloth trade are typical of the whole policy of Edward VI.—a policy, that is, of extreme reform in every part of the state. The Acts, however, were so severe that in the next reign it was found necessary to moderate them to a great extent. The defects complained of were 'the mingling of Fell, Lamb's, and Fleese' wools, the making of thin cloth, the use of too little material, insufficient thicking, overstretching, stopping holes with flocks, and shrinking. It was enacted that all white cloths made in the city of Worcester, called Long Worcesters, were to be between 29 and 31 yards long, 7 quarters within the breadth, and to weigh 80 lb. All coloured cloths were to be 'well scoured, thicked mylled, and fullye dried.' All white cloths, called Short Worcesters, were to measure wet 23–25 yards long, and to every yard 1 inch, 7 quarters in breadth, and weigh 60 lb. at the least, with a penalty of 40*s.* for every cloth. Deficient cloths were not to be sealed, but were liable to the aulnager's fee. Drapers were to try cloths by weight and measure, and present the deficient ones, which were then to be forfeited. Clothiers were to repay the price of faulty clothes sold by them on penalty of a fine double the value of the cloth. Defective cloths that were exported were to be returned, and the name as well as the arms of the town was to appear on the seal, probably to assist the foreigner in identifying the place of manufacture and to make the country clothier bring his cloth into the town at least for sale. There was a very heavy penalty for counterfeiting the seal. In order, perhaps, to prevent any partiality on the part of the crafts, the mayor was made responsible for searching and sealing. Stretching was forbidden, and the use of tenters with wrenches. Cloths were not to be hard pressed to prevent shrinking. Wool to be made into broad-cloths and kerseys was not to be boiled with 'Gales rynde, barks of trees, or sawedust.'[6]

The makers of this statute were not only determined to prevent the decline of the cloth trade owing to these abuses, but also to increase the trade by other means. Thus, clothiers quitting their business after a certain rate without licence from three justices of the peace were not allowed to resume it.[7] Also in the same year the Act compelling seven years' apprenticeship was reinforced, an Act in the sole interest of the town craftsman and the town clothier.[8] This Act, however, was found too severe, and in consequence, on the petition of the town clothier, another was made in the first year of Queen Mary (1553), permitting the inhabitants of towns, where the trade had been carried on previous to the Act, to make cloth according to the first statute of 1552.[9] This must have been a blow to the craft guilds: for the one obligation it had been most necessary to have fulfilled before obtaining admittance to the guild was that of having served seven years' apprenticeship, which gave it control over all other members of the trade. This Act of 1553 abolished the necessity, opening the trade to a much larger number of people and making them in a small degree independent of the guild. But, at the same time, the country clothier was still liable to the 'apprentice' Act. It was only the town employer that was benefited by the repeal. 'That is, the determining feature in the legislation was the rivalry of town and country employers.'[10]

The reasons given for this Act were that many who had served five or six years' apprenticeship and were quite competent were prevented from working; also many had married clothiers' widows, who had made cloth for twenty years before. There is an interesting statement that

[1] Green, *Hist. of Worc.* App. Queen Elizabeth's visit to Worcester, p. xliv.

[2] Printed in Noake, *Worc. in Olden Times* (1849), p. 37.

[3] Printed in Pollard, *The Protector Somerset*, p. 214.

[4] *Stat. of Realm* (Rec. Com.), iv. (1), 136.

[5] Ibid.

[6] *Stat. of Realm* (Rec. Com.), iv. (1), 136.

[7] Ibid.

[8] Stat. 5 and 6 Edw. VI. cap. 8.

[9] *Stat. of Realm* (Rec. Com.), iv. (1), 232.

[10] G. Unwin, *Industrial Organisation* (1904), p. 85.

experience in the 'true sorting of wool,' the 'principal ground of clothmaking,' was only to be found in women as clothiers' wives and their women-servants, and not in apprentices. Women also performed most of the spinning of the yarn after it was sorted;[1] the clothier's wife must have been an important person, superintending all the processes for the preparation of the yarn for weaving or fulling, yet women were never able to become members of the guild, as they were on the continent. Here are also mentioned 'spullars of yarn' and 'forcers and cisters of wool,' besides sorters and spinners.[2]

These Acts were not only made but enforced. In 1555 Richard Yowle was brought up for selling fourteen long cloths, each of which lacked 4 lb., to Robert Luce of Old Jewry; both were to forfeit £28; that is, 40*s.* for each cloth.[3] In the following year, two Worcester clothiers, Roger Collynges and John Englysshe, were summoned to value a cloth which had been rolled and folded before it was sealed.[4]

In 1558 several clothiers from all parts, and probably from Worcester, after bringing their kerseys and coarse cloths to the great fair in London, at St. Bartholomew's, were so afraid of being fined that they confessed to the lords in council that they were not made according to the statute. Among others appointed to make the confession was Oliver Brigges of Bewdley.[5] This proves that the cloth trade was pursued in that town also, as well as in other places in Worcestershire. In the same year the other Act of 1555 was also moderated; the minimum weight was reduced from 84 lb. to 75 lb.; no one was to add a list after the cloth was made, except the Worcester clothiers, who were allowed the lists they had been accustomed to make previously.[6] It was only necessary for cloths to be sealed once; and those that were faulty were to be distinguished by the seal, and then they might be sold.

The town clothier still attempted to force the trade back into the town. It was enacted that no one might make cloth unless he lived in a market town and had been an apprentice for seven years. But existing clothiers in small towns and those not apprenticed for seven years might continue their trade.[7] This Act also shows that in spite of all hindrances the domestic system was growing apace to the impoverishment of the towns.

For information concerning the industry at the beginning of Elizabeth's reign, let us turn to the Exchequer Memoranda Rolls. There are to be found the names of the Worcestershire clothiers accused of different offences in the making of their cloth. In 1561 two cloths of the value of 60*s.* and £5 belonging to John Cowell of Worcester were forfeited for being sold unsealed, and moreover the same day snatched out of the hands of the aulnager by Richard Bolyngham.[8] In the same term a cloth belonging to John Englisshe of Worcester was seized for the same offence.[9] Francis Thorne of Hartlebury was accused of making forty clothes outside a market town, for which he was to pay a very heavy fine of £80.[10] The remainder of the entries for Worcester concern engrossing and regrating wool. Their interest for the cloth trade lies in the fact that from them it is possible to learn the names and importance of the clothiers who bought the wool. Most of the wool dealers came from Herefordshire and Shropshire, but all the clothiers came from the city of Worcester. The earliest is Richard Wheler,[11] the first, perhaps, of a family of clothiers who became important members of the trade later on in the seventeenth century. It is interesting to note, too, that he was a shoemaker as well as a clothier. Others are William Maddock, William James and John Hewes, both of whose names occur twice; George Warryngton,[12] Richard Claterbrooke, Edward Silvester,[13] John Halloway, Thomas Dowding, and George Cardemaker.[14] The descendants of the two last were clothiers in the next century.

In the summer of 1575 Queen Elizabeth paid a visit to Worcester. The city was decked out ready to receive her: its citizens were clad in their official robes. As the queen entered, she received the liberties of the city from the Deputy Recorder, a Mr. William Bellue, M.A., kneeling between the bailiffs. He afterwards, while all continued to kneel, delivered a speech to her for which he received £20. In it he described the rise and present condition of the cloth trade in the city. According to Mr. Bellue the trade began in the seventh century[15] and ever since was

1 *Supra.*

2 *Stat. of Realm* (Rec. Com.), iv. (1), 232.

3 Exch. K. R. Memo R. (P. R. O.), Mich. 2 and 3 Phil. and Mary, No. 42.

4 Ibid. East. 2 and 3 Phil. and Mary, No. 1.

5 *Acts of P. C.* 1556–58, 370–80.

6 A list was an edge or se vedge: it seems to have been the custom to add on a selvedge after the cloth was woven. All lists were now forbidden unless woven with the cloth, except at Worcester.

7 *Stat. of Realm* (Rec. Com.), iv. (1), 323.

8 Exch. K. R. Memo. R. (P. R. O.), Mich. 4 Eliz. 20, 21*d.*

9 Ibid. No. 21.

10 Ibid. No. 215. In 1551 John Thorne of Hartlebury, husbandman, was accused of making three long white cloths. Ibid. 5 Edw. VI. No. 7.

11 Ibid. 6 Edw. VI. Mich. 380*d.*

12 Exch. K. R. Memo. R. (P. R. O.), 6 Eliz. Mich. 379 and 379d, 378d, 376, 377, and 380*d.*

13 Ibid. 7 Eliz. Trin. 89, Mich. 198.

14 Ibid. 6 Eliz. Mich. 377, 376, 378.

15 The first part of the speech is lost, but that which remains seems to be the beginning of the history of the cloth trade . . . . I will for honor sake begyn with worthy Worfarnis, first Chrysten Kynge of Martia or Medle England, who of his kinglie affection

the 'onely relief and meyntenance of this citie;' it continued so to increase that 'in good and fresh memory of man, ther were . . . . three hundred and fowrscore great loomes, whereby eight thowsand persons wer well meyntained in wealth and abilitie besides masters and their children. Then florished this citie and became populus.'[1] But 'at this day . . . . . the wealth wasted and decayed, the bewty faded, the building ruined, the three hundred and fowerscore loomes' reduced to a hundred and sixty and about 5,000 people out of work, 'so that of all that was, ther is allmost nothying lefte but a ruynous citie, or decaied antiquities, such as we see.' This altered condition of affairs he ascribed to 'the changes of fortune and chance of tyme,' the breach of faith by merchants, and 'restraint of trafyqe' chiefly caused by pirates. But he concluded Her Majestie's visit prognosticated a more happy and prosperous estate.[2]

The case of the clothier seems to have been exaggerated by Mr. Bellue, whose love of rhetoric was doubtless greater than his love of truth.

The trade in the city of Worcester itself probably had declined owing to the migration of many of the clothiers into the country, where they bred their own sheep. There they had the raw material ready to hand, saving them the trouble and expense of depending on wool dealers. But even in Worcester there was still a fair number of clothiers. There are twenty-two mentioned in a list of those who bought their wool from 'embroggers' in 1589, and some of them, Thomas Walsgrove, Hugh Chandler, Humphrey Weaver, and William Pytt, must have driven a thriving trade, judging from the large quantities of wool they bought.[3] And one clothier in 1576, Richard Maie, was even able to lend a bishop's wife 200 marks to pay her debts.[4]

In any case, the citizens of Worcester were rewarded for their trouble and their kneeling by a charter of incorporation for their weavers, walkers, and clothiers[5] in 1590. The details of this charter introduce us to the industrial capitalist. The whole of this period is, indeed, marked by the rise of the industrial capitalist, with which was associated the re-assertion in a modified shape of the local industrial monopoly, partly in opposition to the attacks on the town trade by the country weaver and London merchant. One of the effects of this was the amalgamation, for greater strength, of kindred crafts and guilds. Thus united in a company, they formed a strong body, and were enabled to assert themselves in the revived municipal organization, and 'share in the benefits of the movement for the protection of town industries by legislation.' They were also better able to cope with the country weaver, and perhaps bring back the trade to the town once more, a point in which they could always count on the assistance of the State.[6]

The most important articles of the charter were those relating to the constitution of the guild. A master and four wardens were to be elected yearly, with thirty assistants, to continue in office so long as they behaved themselves. All of them were to take an oath of obedience; and 'convocations' were to be called occasionally by the master and wardens, where they could make their own ordinances. The master had the right of settling all disputes and levying fines: but those levied on weavers were to be employed for the relief of poor weavers only. The old rule of seven years' apprenticeship was once more laid down, and no one was to be admitted to the company without consent of the assistants, or the greater part of them. The weavers formed by far the larger part of the governing body of the guild, and throughout

towards this towne, abowte nyne hundred yeres past, by his charter granted and made Worcester a citie. Abowt which tyme the inhibitants here first began their marte of wooles and trade of clothynge. . . . . By thes most bountyfull benefytes by yor Majesties noble progenitors of worthiest memory, and by yor Hygness conferred unto us, wch for avoiding perplexitie we may not particularly remember, together with the painful labour, industrye and diligence of good citesyns, this citie of long tyme so increased in wealth, substance and beautifull buildings, and became so fortunate in the trade of clothyng as by the onely means thereof.'

[1] 'But why remember we the tyme past with such commendacion of the floryshing estate thereof? or why do we shewe yor Majestie of things that late wer' and now ar' not, with that greef of mynde? may we remember that Worcester, one of the most ancient cities of y^r kingdom, was some tyme wealthy, bewtifull, and well inhabited?'

[2] From Chamber Order Book of Worc. for year 1575, p. 122. 8. printed in Green, *Hist. of Worc.* (1796), App. p. xliii.

[3] Prattinton MS. (Soc. of Antiq. Lib.), v. Worc. City, p. 173.

[4] *Cal. S.P. Dom.* Eliz. 1547–80. p. 516. Being unable to obtain repayment he sent a petition to the queen as from one 'who gave unto your majestie the finest cloths in the worlde.'

[5] The bishop of Hereford pleaded for them with the queen on her return journey. 'Hit may please yor Majestie, so it is, their trade is not so good as it hath been, for the meytenance of their lyvyng, but their poor good willes and hartes your Majestie hath.' To which the queen answered, 'I perceive that very well, and I like as well of them as I ham liked of any people in all my progressive tyme in all my lyff.' Also it is related that in 1575 the clothiers petitioned for a charter. Prattinton MS. (Soc. of Antiq. Lib.), v. Worcester City, p. 144, *Cal. of S.P. Dom.* Eliz. 1581–90, p. 688. Nash says they received their charter in 1511. Nash, *Hist. of Worc.* (1799), ii. App. p. cxiv.

[6] Unwin, *Industrial Organization* (1904), pp. 40, 85, 95, seq.

seem to have been the more influential craft. The first master, Rowland Berkely, two of the wardens, Robert Rowland, *alias* Steynour,[1] and Thomas Fleete, *alias* Wallsgrove, and eighteen of the assistants, were weavers; the other two wardens, Hugh Chandler and Humphrey Jones, and eight of the assistants, were walkers, while only four assistants were clothiers; these were Francis Streete, William James,[2] John Edwards, and William Bagnall. Among the other assistants occur the names of Richard Nash,[3] Richard and William Hall, John Batchelor, Henry and Humphrey Hill, John Cowcher, John Maie, Humphrey and Thomas Weaver, Thomas Brooke, William Collombyne, William Collins, William King, John Ashely, and John Gorway.

Five years later the company began making their byelaws,[4] by right of their charter. In these laws there were the usual arrangements for electing officers and holding meetings, and a great number of regulations for apprentices and journeymen. All apprentices were to be enrolled before they could begin to work; only one apprentice could work at a loom with a journeyman, unless the apprentice was in his last year. Widows of weavers were allowed to continue their trade with a journeyman, but they could have no apprentices. An expelled member could not be received again without the consent of the whole company, nor could he have any dealings with any member of the company under penalty of a very heavy fine on both. A journeyman could not weave his own cloth, and if he was discharged he could not be again employed. On the other hand a master was not to take an apprentice to hinder or defraud a journeyman from his service, and journeymen of the city were preferred before foreign journeymen. These had to bring a testimonial and obtain the consent of the wardens before they entered the service of a master. If masters did not pay journeymen their wages the latter could complain to the company, and the case would be judged. Apprentices had the same right of complaining also, but they were not to be at liberty; they were to live at their master's house and be under him. Still, to be able to complain at all meant that they were not entirely at the mercy of their employers. Owing to the increase of population and the numbers employed in the trade in the fifteenth and sixteenth centuries, the class of journeyman had so increased, that all could not hope to become masters, and some regulations were necessary to protect them; and on the contrary some masters became so poor that they had to work as journeymen. A rule was made that if a poor master became a journeyman he could never again work as a master unless he was readmitted. It is impossible to know whether this was caused entirely by the selfishness of the masters and narrowness of the guilds or by the systems of monopolies. More probably it was due to the power of the capitalist manufacturer, who occupied 'many men's livings.'[5] A clause provided that the master and wardens have 'power to decide all controversies arising between clothiers and their masters and journeymen, concerning weaving of cloth or wages.' From this it might be inferred that disputes or strikes had already occurred, but there is no evidence in Worcester of any association of journeymen or smaller masters, as in Coventry and Bristol.

There was still a strong feeling against strangers coming into the city. No foreign weaver was to take yarn out of the city. If a foreigner did attempt to set up his trade or obtain work in the city, he would only be able legally to do so after much trouble and many fees. Even then it would be doubtful if he would be successful. There is one article which rather suggests that the so-called weavers were in reality clothiers, or at least performed some other processes in the making of cloth than merely that of weaving, or else paid for having them done. No master weaver was to weave anyone's cloth, 'warped before it comes to his house, unless it be the chayne or chaynes[6] of one of the same occupation': therefore the weaver must have made the warp as well as the woof.

The whole tenour of these laws seems to restore to the company the control of all persons connected with the trade. This had been the aim throughout the fifteenth and sixteenth centuries both of the State and the towns. No one was to work at all unless a member of the company. To give the guild their due, there may have been present also the desire to improve the trade. As will be shown later, however, the restrictions do not seem to have secured the desired effects.

Some details of the following years are known to us. In 1596 John Cowcher was made High Master, and William Fryser and William Collombyne wardens; and among the assistants were the old Worcester names of Thomas Chetle, Richard Nurse, Edward Mytton, and John Watts.[7] There were also weavers and tailors scattered all over the county in Bromsgrove, Chaddesley Corbett, Kidderminster, Benington, Hanley, and Lindridge.[8]

[1] Was bailiff in 1584 and 1586; died in 1622. *Visitations of Worc.* (Harl. Soc.)

[2] v. *ante.*

[3] John Nash, probably his son, a clothier, was mayor in 1633. He founded a hospital at Worcester; died in 1662. *Visitations of Worc.* (Harl Soc.).

[4] Quoted by Prattinton MS. (Soc. of Antiq. Lib.), v. Worc. City, p. 164.

[5] *Supra.*

[6] It seems probable that 'chayne' meant the frame on which the wool was warped.

[7] Prattinton MS. (Soc. of Antiq. Lib.), v. Worc. City, p. 171.

[8] *Lay Subs. R.* (Worc. Hist. Soc.), 1603.

In 1605 the trade was said to be flourishing in Worcester, and 125 were bound to the clothing trade alone.[1] This seems a very small number compared to the 3,000 in 1575[2] (then itself considered a very small number), and perhaps it meant only the clothiers.

In 1606 there was once more a return to the policy of enforcing certain prescribed weights and measures for Worcester and other cloth, and every precaution was taken to ensure the good quality of the cloth.[3]

In Evesham the clothworkers by 1608 were a company making their own laws, for on 1 December of that year it was enacted that the company should have 'their composition and booke of orders made according to a constitution in that behalf enacted, which accordingly was by publique consent of the Maior and Comon council made, confirmed, and sealed.'[4]

This year Richard Nurse had risen to be both bailiff and High Master of the Worcester weavers, and Richard Englishe a warden.[5] In the following year James Philips was High Master.[6] Before the year 1615 Rowland Berkeley, the first High Master, with Henry Hill and William Norris and John Sandbrooke left gifts to the company for the relief of the poor by right of their licence granted in 1609.[7] And again twelve years later Robert Yowle and Rowland Berkeley, with Nash and Thomas Chetle and others, bequeathed sums of money to the company for the benefit of young men exercising the trade.[8] Altogether the trade seemed very prosperous, and its members wealthy and well-to-do.

This prosperity, however, was but short-lived. With the end of the sixteenth century the decline of the trade began. It never again recovered its old prosperity. From this time onwards there were constant complaints in the county of Worcester, as everywhere in England, of the decline, so much so that it was necessary for the State to interfere to improve it. Sometimes it was attributed to the engrossing of wool. In 1615 the company of Worcester clothiers appointed a commissioner, John Gwynn, to prosecute all offenders against the statutes of Henry VI. and Edward VI. forbidding engrossing.[9] In 1616 there was an account sent up of the quantities of cloth in store in Worcester and other counties.[10] This was due to a petition of the Merchant Adventurers, who complained that their trade was thwarted owing to an edict in Holland prohibiting the use of dyed or dressed cloths, and also to the embrogging of wool. They advised that the export of wool should be forbidden. The Stuart policy of retaliation had a disastrous effect on trade, and especially on the cloth trade. In some places, where the industry had never become very large, it caused extreme depression, and often total ruin.[11] In 1622 a mandate was issued to the justices of the peace for Worcester and other counties to force the merchants to buy up the cloth, and persuade the clothiers to renew their work. Wooldealers were not to store up wool, but sell at a moderate price: 'those who have saived in profitable times must now be content to lose for the public good till the decay of the trade be remedied';[12] an excellent sentiment, but not exactly one to be felt by individuals practising the trade. There was said to be great distress, owing to so many spinners and weavers being out of work. The answer to this mandate by the justices of Worcestershire suggests that the trade was not so bad in that county as in others. 'There were fewer clothiers in the county, except those belonging to the city of Worcester, which, by its late charter, is exempt from county jurisdiction.' Also they said no disturbances had arisen in the county through lack of work.[13] But yet, in 1619 journeymen had been so badly paid that they 'struck,' and appealed to the bishop of Worcester and Sir John Packington, who seemed to have decided the case in their favour. At least they were to have 7*d.* a day. To obtain this the journeymen must have formed themselves into some sort of combination.[14] And again, the mayor, returning the contribution of Worcester levied in 1622, stated that 'the city living chiefly by clothing is much impoverished.[15] And in that year and 1624 there was a quantity of Worcester cloth still unsold at Blackwell Hall.[16]

[1] From docquets of county quoted in *Assoc. Archit. Rep. and Papers*, xv. 331.

[2] *Supra.*

[3] *Stat. of Realm*, iv. (2) 1137.

[4] Extracts from Evesham Corporation Records quoted in Prattinton MS. xii. Evesham (Soc. of Antiq. Lib.).

[5] Ibid.

[6] Mentioned in an indenture of a weaver apprentice in Ibid.

[7] Extracts from Corporation Records in Ibid. p. 175. *Cal. S.P. Dom.* 1603–10, p. 525. Licence to master and commonalty of weavers, fullers, and clothiers of Worcester to purchase lands in mortmain for the relief of the poor.

[8] From Corporation documents mentioned in *Assoc. Archit. Soc. Rep. and Papers*, xv. 331.

[9] Prattinton MS. v. Worc. City. (Soc. of Antiq. Lib.)

[10] *Cal. S.P. Dom.* 1611–18, 393–4.

[11] Perhaps this was the cause of a petition in 1628 sent from Max. Dancey, the king's water bailiff at Dover, and agent for Worcester and other clothiers, praying that he might exercise his office by deputy, and his agency for the advantage of at least 500 spinners and workfolks, or they would be undone. From docquets, quoted in Noake, *Worc. Nuggets* (1889), p. 270.

[12] *Cal. S.P. Dom.* 1619–23, p. 343.

[13] Ibid. p. 366.

[14] Four papers 'settling workmen's wages,' quoted in Prattinton MS. v. Worc. City, p. 174 (Soc. of Antiq. Lib.).

[15] *Cal. S.P. Dom.* 1619–23, p. 391.

[16] Ibid. p. 363, and 1623–5, p. 146.

Despite all this, Habington, writing in James I.'s reign, noticed that the magistrates of the city 'weare anciently honoured with the tytell of Merchantes, but nowe inryched with the name of Clothyers, a trade of surpassynge charity for clothinge not onely our own nation but foryne countries, and above all settinge so many poore folkes on wourcke in carding spynninge and suchelyke handmaydes of theyre trade as they surmount those who releyve beggars at theyre gates.' Also as to the quality of the cloth he remarked that 'theare was made in our age a Broadclothe in thys citty so exceedinge fyne as all that eaver weare before or synce could neaver yet showe the lyke.'[1]

About this time, too, in 1612, the clothiers obtained definite possession of Trinity Hall. This had become the property of Robert Yowle, Thomas Wylde, John Rowland, alias Steyner, Hugh Ashby, William Langley, and William Welbin. Robert Yowle, surviving some of the others, gave as far as in him lay, the Trinity Hall to the Weavers, Walkers, and Clothiers of the City of Worcester. John Rowland, alias Steyner, married the daughter and heir of Robert Yowle, and outlived his father-in-law and all the other feoffees. Robert Rowland, alias Steyner, his heir by Yowle's daughter, gave it to the Corporation of Weavers, Walkers, and Clothiers of Worcester, 'which his grandfather, Robert Yowle, before intended, and to his power performed.'[2]

In 1635 all the statutes of weights and measures were repealed, and the aulnager was given additional power. All clothiers and spinners were to register their names and seal their cloths. Worcester was put on the list of counties for which searchers and aulnagers were appointed. The State hoped by these means to relieve somewhat the distress in the trade, through the greater elasticity which the change brought about.[3]

Kidderminster still continued to be a centre of the cloth trade; in the charter granted to it in 1636 it was stated to be 'of great commerce for working and making of clothes,' and by reason thereof, and by the daily confluence of many thither, it is very populous.'[4] As the trade developed the clothier began to make various sorts of cloths, besides the fine white broad-cloth for which the county was celebrated. At Kidderminster a peculiar kind of cloth was made, usually termed, for want of other name, 'Kidderminster stuff'; it seems to have been a sort of linsey-woolsey, a mixed material of cotton and wool. The making of it was the staple industry of the town in Richard Baxter's time.[5] He makes some interesting remarks concerning the condition of the trade and those employed in it, which show that the cloth trade at this time was not a very profitable one in Kidderminster. 'My People,' he says, 'were not *Rich*: There were among them very few *Beggers*, because their common Trade of Stuff-weaving would find work for all, Men, Women and children, that were able: And there were none of the Trades-men very rich, seeing their Trade was poor, that would but find them Food and Raiment. The Magistrates of the Town were few of them worth 40*l.* *per An.* and most not half so much. Three or four of the *Richest* thriving Masters of the Trade, got about 500*l.* or 600*l.* in twenty years, and it may be lose 100*l.* of it at once by an ill Debtor. The generality of the Master Workmen, lived but little better than their Journey-men (from hand to mouth), but only that they laboured not altogether so hard.'[6]

In 1640 the Worcester clothiers petitioned against an order of the Council prohibiting the manufacture of 'say dyed cloths,' because they had been confused with Spanish cloths of the same make.[7] On bringing evidence, however, to show that it was a most useful sort of cloth, the order was withdrawn.[8]

But as we go on through the middle of the seventeenth century the cry still continues to be in Worcester, as all over southern England, the decay and decline of the cloth trade. The causes are more or less plain, though complex.

The plague in Worcester in 1638[9] cannot have improved matters. Moreover, the disturbed state of affairs throughout the country caused by the impending civil war might well be the cause of the complaints of the clothiers in 1641 that they could not sell their goods for ready money as heretofore, nor procure payments for their debts; the merchants saying 'that this is no time to pay money.' They attributed the deadness of trading to the 'tediousness' of putting justice in execution.[10] Another cause of the block in the trade was the quarrel between the clothiers and the merchants on the one side, and the middleman, usually styled factor or packer, on the other. The clothier would be his own middleman. The merchant would have the entire monopoly of the merchant trade, both wholesale and retail. But, for both, their time had gone by. It was as impossible at this period to monopolize a trade as to hope to dispense with the middleman.

In 1648 the clothiers of Worcester made a long petition against the patent of the merchant adventurers as sole merchants.[11] This perhaps

[1] Habington, *Sur. of Worc.* ii. 426 (Worc. Hist. Soc.).

[2] Ibid. See p. 297.

[3] *Cal. S.P. Dom.* 1625–49, p. 519.

[4] Quoted in Prattinton MS. Kidderminster (Soc. of Antiq. Lib.).

[5] About the time of the civil wars. *Baxterianæ Reliquiæ* (ed. 1696), pt. i. p. 89.

[6] Ibid. pt. i. p. 94.

[7] *Cal. S.P. Dom.* 1640, p. 188–9.

[8] Ibid. 210–11.

[9] Tract entitled *The Plague in Worcester.*

[10] *House of Lords MSS.* (Hist. MSS. Com.), Rep. iv. App. p. 62.

[11] Tract printed in 1645 entitled *A Discourse on Free Trade.*

resulted in the opposition to the repeal of the customs duty on cloth in 1650, for it was declared 'it would yet more bring our cloth out of request, as our Worcesters and generally all our fine cloth is already.'[1]

Another cause of decline is to be found in the narrowness of the administration of the trade. Thus, the governing body of the borough of Kidderminster was determined not to permit free trade. The crafts in that town must have been very small, for the municipal council made the bye-laws for all of them. The complaint was made by the council that the 'society of weavers of the stuffes called Kidderminster stuffes have received of late much dammage in reputacion of trading by the covetousnes and irregularity of some others of ye same profession and trade within ye said burrough, who for their own advantage have driven a privat trade of ye same stuffes deceitfully made both for measure and workmanship, by which means a scandall is fastened upon ye said trade, the traders therein much disparaged, the trade decayed, and the poore increased, who formerly by their labour therein were supported and mainteyned.'[2] It was more probable that this accumulation of evils was caused by the narrowness of the craft, which did not permit of free competition or improvement in the trade.

In addition to the usual rules for apprenticeship and the necessity of becoming a member of the company, there was a regulation that no master was to have more than three looms for linsey-woolseys unless he had special permission from the warden and company; and for the three years ensuing no one entering on the trade was to work more than one loom. With such regulations it was not to be expected that the trade would develop. The good quality of the cloth was still in the eyes of the makers of these rules far more important than the actual wants of the consumer, the profits of the producer, and the increase of capital. Worcester cloth was considered good enough for the uniforms of one of the oldest of the English regiments. Charles II., when at Worcester in 1651, ordered a quantity of red cloth amounting to the value of £453 3*s.* to be provided for the life guard on foot. Perhaps it was more the desire to please the inhabitants and company of drapers of Worcester (for it was they who sold the cloth) at such a critical moment than the excellency of the quality that evoked the order. The drapers, however, received no immediate payment, and had to wait until after the Restoration before they could even demand it.[3]

The Worcester clothiers experienced the effects of narrow regulations themselves when they endeavoured to sell their cloth at Blackwell Hall in London, and came into contact with the London Company of Clothiers. In 1663 they complained to the House of Commons that the regulations of the Company and the Common Council of London caused them great inconvenience in forcing them to stay longer in London, in the choice of agents, and in the increase in expense, in hallage fees and duties.[4] But there was one side of the industry which looked more hopeful. The manufacturers of Kidderminster stuffs obtained an Act for the regulation of their trade in 1671,[5] by which they could make themselves into a company with all the privileges of searching and sealing, etc. Particular stress was laid on the quality of the yarn. It was to be bought and sold in the public market-place, and in quantities (called a lea) of not less than 200 yards. Moreover, the warden of the company was to have control of all material made of wool only.[6] Six years later there were said to be 417 looms and 157 master weavers. Only one master weaver had seven looms, most had two or three.[7] Therefore the municipal authority had been able to enforce its rules, perhaps to the detriment of the trade a little later. It certainly refused welcome to the stranger. Foreign journeymen who came into the town were obliged to give their names and qualities, and the names of their last employers, with a security from their present masters to save the inhabitants harmless from their charge.[8] This, a general regulation to crush the Law of Settlement, shows how great a hindrance that was to trade, and how it must in many places have helped the decline of small local industries.[9]

In Worcester trade was so bad that the company had been forced in 1675 to levy an assessment of £20 on looms to defray the expenses of attending parliament and endeavouring to procure more frequent exportation. However, they only managed to raise £5 13*s.* 4*d.* from 39 weavers and 86 looms.[10] If this was the total number of looms in the city, the trade must have fearfully decreased during the seventeenth century.

King James II. visited Worcester in 1687, and

1 *Cal. S.P. Dom.* 1650, p. 22.

2 Bye-laws printed by Burton, *Hist. of Kidderminster* (1890), p. 175.

3 *Cal. S.P. Dom.* Chas. II. 1660–1, p. 300. Ibid. 1670, add. p. 661.

4 *Cal. S.P Dom.* 1663–4, p. 535. In 1678, by an Act of the Common Council for the regulation of Blackwell Hall for long Worcester cloths, 1½*d.* was to be paid to the porters for carrying it out of the hall.

5 *Cal. S.P. Dom.* 1670, p. 531 ; Stat. 22 and 23 Chas. II. cap. 8.

6 Printed in Burton, *Hist. of Kidderminster* (1890), 176.

7 Nash, *Hist. of Worc.* (1799), ii. 42.

8 *Cal. S.P. Dom.* 1670, p. 531 ; Stat. 22 and 23 Chas. II. cap. 8.

9 Bye-law quoted in Prattinton MS. xx. Kidderminster (Soc. of Antiq. Lib).

10 From old book of orders quoted in Prattinton MSS. v. Worc. city, p. 172.

although the way from the gate to the palace was covered with the famous white broad-cloth of Worcester,[1] yet no demand for further privileges for the trade is recorded. Perhaps it was in too bad a state to hope for recovery. Anyhow, his visit was not so fruitful as that of his predecessor Queen Elizabeth. Certainly in the accounts of subsidies on wool in 1686 and the two following years Worcester compares badly with other counties.[2] But at last the State recognized the condition of the cloth trade and made one attempt, however misguided or useless, to improve it. At the end of the seventeenth century a rather interesting law was made, forcing everybody to bury their dead in woollen shrouds under a penalty of £5.[3] Later, because this was not observed, parsons were ordered to keep registers of those buried, after an affidavit had been sworn before a justice of the peace, mayor, or other officer of the law.[4]

Andrew Yarranton, who began life as a linen-draper's apprentice,[5] and was later an expert on water communication, declared that the decline in the trade was due to the fact that the clothiers were entirely in the hands of the factors, who had turned merchants, and 'the trade is ruined by them.' If the clothiers attempted to 'relieve themselves and seek out any other way, the factors would joyn stock together' and buy their materials from other towns. This had been the case even in Kidderminster, where they had been obliged to borrow £5,000 or £6,000 to help to drive the trade.[6]

The day of the merchant adventurer was over. His place as the dealer in England was taken by the factors, drawers, and packers, whose business enabled them to become large wholesale agents. They employed others to ship the goods for them. Trade as a whole was greatly developing in the latter part of the seventeenth century, mainly owing to the improved state of shipping under Cromwell. There naturally followed greater division of labour, and greater competition, all tending to make trade more free.

It might have been thought that this tremendous development in shipping and export trade with the newly acquired colonies and elsewhere would have given an impetus to the woollen industry in general and helped to revive it. It is certain that Worcester clothiers did export their materials, for they joined in a petition with the other clothiers of the west of England against the bill to prohibit the importation of Bengaline, Indian, and Persian silks, because it would lessen the exportation of English manufactures to India, and of 'late years they hade provided for the East India trade very great quantities of woollen manufacture.'[7]

In spite of this, the trade did not improve. Perhaps all the profits fell into the hands of the company; perhaps the fine broad-cloth of Worcester did not suit the requirements of the consumers abroad; perhaps 'wool broggers' sold bad wool, and so the clothiers had no chance.[8] At any rate the trade never again tried to reassert itself. Its history in the eighteenth century is the tale of its final disappearance from the county. Like many other things in that century, it went to sleep. But for the cloth trade it was a sleep of death: it never again awoke. Just a few notes and entries here and there show that one or two clothiers struggled on, while the guild continued to exist chiefly for meetings, suppers, drinkings, and such like. By 1711 the trades were said to be far in debt; every master admitted was to pay double fees.[9] Nine years later the Clothiers' Company begged for more frequent shipping of their stock to Turkey. They complained that bullion was exported thither instead of their cloth.

Again in 1740 the clothiers of Worcester and the stuff weavers of Kidderminster petitioned against the exportation of wool, declaring it was the ruin of their trade.[10]

Some bye-laws were made and confirmed in 1723 and 1730, forbidding, even as late as this, the intrusion of 'foreigners' from other towns.[11] In 1725 masters were forbidden to spend more than 40*s.* on any entertainment except at the election of factors. Indeed, all the entries in the account book were for money spent on ribbons, and wine, and food, on 'stream days,' at the funerals of members and on the admission of new ones.[12] This was an illustration of what was occurring all over the country.

In all this gloom there were a few bright spots. In July 1743 one Joshua Wheeler, mercer of Worcester, obtained a patent for his 'new invented method of preparing woollen cloth and hats, so as to keep out the rain, without impairing

1 Green, *Hist. of Worc.* (1796), p. 295.

2 For Worcester only £150 is recorded; for Devon, £1,500; York and Lancaster, £1,600; Somerset, £800. *House of Lords Papers* (Hist. MS. Com.), Rep. i.

3 Stat. 18 and 19 Chas. II. c. iv.

4 Stat. 30 Chas. II. c. iii.

5 Burton, *Hist. of Kidderminster* (1890), p. 153.

6 A. Yarranton, *England's Improvement by Sea and Land* (1677), i. 98.

7 *House of Lords Papers* (Hist. MSS. Com.), Rep. ii. Ap. i. p. 244, and tract of 1698, entitled *Case of the Clothiers and Fullers of Counties of Gloucester, Devon, Oxford, Worcester, etc.*

8 *Journ. of House of Com.* xii. 150.

9 From Minute and Order Book printed in Noake, *Worc. in Olden Times* (1849).

10 *Journ. of House of Com.* xxiii. 657.

11 *Journ. of House of Com.* xix. 74, 84, 88, 91. Docquets quoted by Noake, *Worc. Relics* (1877), p. 156.

12 Extracts from Book No. 4, quoted in Prattinton MS. v. Worc. City, 175 (Soc. of Antiq. Lib.).

their strength or beauty.[1] Outside Worcester matters were much better. In Kidderminster the manufacture of linsey-woolseys had given place to the making of fancy materials. As early as 1717 one Mr. Greaves of London encouraged the manufacture of striped tameys and prunellas.[2] In 1748 yard-wide silk and worsted stuffs were made. In 1751 there were 2,000 inhabitants, and 'it drove a pretty good trade.'[3] In 1755 silk alone was made, 'figured and flowered for women's cloaks.' In 1756 'the inhabitants of this place are generally employed in the worsted silk manufacture and are supposed to amount to 4,000 and upwards. There are many of them lodged in small, nasty houses, for the most part crowded with looms and utensils,' not a very bright picture of the trade, but it shows how thriving the industry was.[4] In 1772 there were said to be 1,700 silk and worsted looms. Also at the same time a particular kind of quality for worsteds was invented by Pearsalls, like Marseilles quality, used for petticoats. Mixtures of silk and wool formed the prevailing industry until that in turn was superseded by the carpet trade.[5] So that Kidderminster by continually taking up new industries, or rather various parts of the textile trade, as the old ones became unpopular and unprofitable, became more and more prosperous and more and more important. Stourbridge, and also Kidderminster, were famous for a fine frieze cloth,[6] which was chiefly exported to the Dutch.[7] And Bromsgrove, in 1751, 'drove a considerable trade in clothing,'[8] though thirty years later it had entirely lost its industry in narrow cloth and friezes.[9] Spinning and weaving were carried on all over the county, at Winchcomb, and other places,[10] chiefly at this time, no doubt, to supply the yarn for the carpet looms. At Shipston-on-Stour there was once a shagg manufactory, the decay of which in 1789 had much reduced the town.[11]

By that time, however, the Worcester trade was non-existent. The Account Book was closed in 1787.[12] People were admitted to the company who were not members of the trade at all.[13] In 1789 the 'cloathing trade was entirely gone.'[14] In 1796 Trinity Hall, the symbol of the industry of the city, was sold by public auction.[15] The company itself still continues to the present day. It protects no longer clothiers, but orphans and widows of citizens, and gatherings of its members are usually for distribution of charity, and for dinners. It has been said that it held so much landed property that it could not expire.[16] In 1802 and 1822 laws and regulations were drawn up to inaugurate it more or less as a social society, since its work as a trading body was long ago completed, and as a social body it still exists.

Elsewhere the making of silk and woollen materials still prevailed. In 1807 there were 700 looms at Kidderminster. By 1831 the number was reduced to 340.[17] Stourbridge now seems to have excelled in making a peculiarly fine cloth from wool produced in the neighbourhood.[18] Bromsgrove was known in the first quarter of the nineteenth century for the manufacture of a coarse linen for sacks and also for wool carding and spinning yarn, chiefly for Leicestershire stocking weavers.[19] But by 1856 there was only one loom for wool in the town.[20] There was not long ago a small linen industry at the Brick House factory. Bombazines were till lately made at Bewdley as well as at Kidderminster, but the trade now no longer exists. As Stourport developed it became a small centre of worsted spinning. As far back as 1791 there is evidence of a cloth factory there. At the present time the trade consists of the making

[1] *Gentleman's Mag.* July, 1743. Similarly in 1732 a gentleman travelling through England remarked that Worcester 'subsists by woollen manufacture; is famous for making some of the best broad-cloth in England. It is almost incredible, the number of hands employed here and in the adjacent villages, in carding, spinning, and weaving.' Quoted in Prattinton MS. Worc. City, p. 1 (Soc. of Antiq. Lib.). This proves that the domestic system of industry was still in vogue. There was at any rate one clothier, Edward Cookesy by name, in Worcester. Ibid.

[2] Camden, *Britannia* (Gough, ed. 1789), p. 357; Nash, *Hist. of Worc.* (1799), ii. 43.

[3] Postlethwayt, *Dict. of Trade and Commerce* (1751), ii. 846.

[4] From a dissertation quoted in Prattinton—Kidderminster.

[5] Bombazines were sent to Norfolk to be finished and dressed, and thus Norwich gradually appropriated the whole trade. Burton, *Hist. of Kidderminster* (1890), 180; Nash, *Hist. of Worc.* ii. 45.

[6] Postlethwayt, *Dict. of Trade and Commerce* (1751), ii. 846.

[7] Nash, *Hist. of Worc.* (1799), ii. 45.

[8] Postlethwayt, *Dict. of Trade and Commerce* (1751), ii. 846.

[9] Prattinton MS. vi. Bromsgrove (Soc. of Antiq. Lib.).

[10] Add. MS. (B.M.) 23,001, pp. 159 and 64.

[11] Camden, *Britannia* (Gough, ed. 1789). Add. p. 369.

[12] Book No. 4, quoted in Prattinton MS. v. Worc. City, 175 (Soc. of Antiq. Lib.).

[13] Ibid. in Noake, *Worc. in Olden Times* (1849).

[14] Camden, *Britannia* (Gough, ed. 1789). Add. 365.

[15] From vol. iii. quoted in Prattinton MS. v. Worc. City (Soc. of Antiq. Lib.). The hall was reconstructed in 1805 to provide an upholstery warehouse, and pulled down in 1890. *Assoc. Arch. Soc. Reports*, 1891-2 (Worcester Report).

[16] Noake, *Worc. in Olden Times* (1849).

[17] Burton, *Hist. of Kidderminster* (1890), 181.

[18] Prattinton MS. xxxi. Stourbridge (Soc. of Antiq. Lib.); Pitt, *General View of Agric. of Worc.* (1813), p. 277.

[19] Ibid. 278.

[20] Noake, *Worc. N. and Q.* (1856). For its charter, etc. see p. 285.

of curtain and other stuffs.[1] With these exceptions, however, the cloth trade in Worcestershire died out with the decline of the domestic system.[2] In 1831 there were only twenty-one clothiers in the county; thirteen of these lived at Worcester.[3] In 1841 in the whole county there were 381 woollen spinners, and most of these doubtless sent their yarn to the carpet manufacturers of Kidderminster.[4] The factory system was never taken up by the Worcester clothiers,[5] perhaps because the trade was far too decayed to be revived by the introduction of steam power. And yet Worcester had all the natural advantages of other counties now famous for clothmaking; plenty of streams, on the borders of the Staffordshire coalfield, and a navigable river leading to the excellent port of Bristol. The Worcester clothiers must have been lacking in capital or initiative, or both. Nash attributed the decline to the avidity of the manufacturer in over-stretching the cloth, so that when dry it lacked full measure; and to his obstinacy in making a thick, heavy broad-cloth, when the Turks chose rather a thin spongy cloth which took a brighter dye.'[8] Another cause, he declared, and one that has had disastrous effects on trade in other towns besides Worcester, was the 'frequent and expensive oppositions for the elections of members of Parliament,' and the corruption that often follows. On the whole the manufacturers, whether owing to poverty or stupidity, neglected or despised new systems, new methods, and new inventions, and so were unable to compete with their more enterprising brothers in the north. Nash found it difficult to believe this and so made chance bear some of the blame. For, said he, 'trade is of that coy and fleeting nature that it easily makes itself wings and flies away. In Ancient days, I might mention, the cities of Tyre, Carthage, Alexandria, Venice, Florence, Genoa; in latter days, a familiar instance the clothing trade is gone from Worcestershire and Gloucestershire to the north of England; and it is sincerely to be wished that the great trade of this kingdom may not fly to the north or some distant kingdom.'[9]

CARPETS AND RUGS

The domestic use of carpets as floor coverings in England is comparatively modern, and equally so their manufacture. But even in the middle ages carpets had been imported for ceremonial occasions and placed before altars or chairs of State, or used as table covers. 'Divers tall ships of London' in the early years of the sixteenth century plied 'an ordinarie and usuall trade' to the Levant, carrying thither 'kersies of divers colours' and bringing back 'Turkie carpets,' besides spices, wine, and silks.[6] In the reign of Elizabeth, whose audience chamber possessed an eastern carpet, it was suggested 'that a singular good workman in the art of Turkish carpet-making' might advantageously be induced to settle here, while James I. gave liberal encouragement to works at Mortlake[7] in Surrey, directed by skilled weavers from Flanders, where both tapestry and carpets were produced.

The modern carpet manufacture of England, however, dates only from the Revocation of the Edict of Nantes and appears to have been first carried on at Wilton.

The linsey-woolseys of Kidderminster, to which Chief Justice Jeffreys referred in his scoffing description of Baxter's doctrine, were famous long before the origin of the carpet manufacture proper in the eighteenth century. These 'Kidderminsters,' as they were called, were especially in request for the hangings of rooms and beds. At Wenlock, in 1687, it was decided that a carpet of Kidderminster stuff should be obtained for the council chamber.[10]

In the reign of George II. (1735) a carpet factory was built on Mount Skipet, at Kidderminster, and probably Pearsall was the pioneer weaver of the flat two-ply reversible carpet, then and since known as 'Kidderminster,' though now more commonly made in Scotland. Meanwhile Henry Herbert, ninth earl of Pembroke, after long and careful inspection of the factories of France and the Low Countries, brought skilled artists and weavers to Wilton in 1745, and by their assistance placed its trade in a pre-eminent position. And only ten years later carpets resembling the imported product of Turkish looms were being made at Axminster in Devon. Thus the Kidderminster weavers found themselves faced with the most severe and skilled competition, and some new advance was

[1] Noake, *Worc. N. and Q.* (1856).

[2] Horsehair clothmaking was introduced into Worcester 60 or 70 years ago by Mr. Edw. Webb, and is still carried on by his son, Col. Albert Webb.

[3] *Pop. Ret.* 1831, p. 727.

[4] At the present there exist many wool-sorting sheds behind the houses at Pershore.

[5] In 1794 a machine was introduced in Kidderminster for wool-combing. It was very unpopular, and consequently a petition was sent up to Parliament begging for its abolition; for, worked by 1 man and 4 children, it could do as much as thirty men, therefore it meant certain ruin. Burton, *Hist. of Kidderminster*, p. 181.

[6] Hakluyt, *Voyages* (1810), ii. 206-7.

[7] *V. C. H. Surrey*, ii. 354.

[8] Nash. *Hist. of Worc.* (1799), ii. App. p. cxiv.

[9] Ibid. Correc. and Add. p. 93.

[10] Burton, *Hist. of Kidderminster* (1890), p. 180. We are indebted to this valuable history for many facts as to the Kidderminster trade.

necessary to enable them to hold there own. Again the impulse was sought abroad; John Broom, whose name should be remembered with that of Pearsall as a pioneer of the carpet trade, brought a Belgian weaver from Brussels, and about 1749 the first Brussels loom was set up at Kidderminster, and soon the looped-pile fabric was produced in large quantities. Only four years afterwards 200 houses were built, and new streets were laid out by Lord Foley to accommodate the increased population.

Gradually carpet-making became the staple trade of the town in spite of the bitter opposition of the master weavers of Wilton, and largely took the place of the decaying silk and worsted industry. In 1807 it was found that since 1772 the carpet looms had risen from 250 to 1,000, whilst the silk and worsted looms had fallen from 1,700 to 700. With the application of the Jacquard loom to carpet-weaving in 1825, the triumph of the growing industry was complete, and this in spite of the severe competition of the Scotch manufacturers, a resultant reduction of wages, and a disastrous strike. Of the 2,020 carpet looms at work in the town in 1838, over three-quarters were employed for the Brussels fabric, 210 for 'Kidderminster' carpet, and 45 for Venetians.

Before dealing with the later development of the industry at Kidderminster it may be advisable to mention other instances of carpet manufacture in the county. In 1796 forty looms were at work in Worcester; eleven at Mr. Watkin's factory in Silver Street, which after the visit of the king and royal family in 1788 was known as 'The Royal Carpet Manufactory,' and twenty-nine at the Lowsmoor factory of Mr. Parry.[1]

In Bewdley[2] a carpet factory was built about the year 1825 opposite the bridge, and worked by Messrs. Sturge and Lloyd. They were succeeded by Messrs. Pardoe, Hoomans and Co. of Kidderminster, who established a branch here, and on their retirement the hand looms were taken over by Messrs. Collins and Rose, but the business only lasted six or seven years, owing to the introduction of the power-loom elsewhere.

At Stourport a carpet and worsted mill was opened by the late Mr. George Harris, and in time the hand looms gave place to steam-power in the weaving sheds. The Severn Valley Mills are now worked by Messrs. T. B. Worth and Sons, and the Island Mills by the Textile Manufacturing Company (Anderson, Lawson, and Co.), whilst the output of carpets, rugs, and curtains is very considerable.

The history of the Kidderminster trade in the first half of the nineteenth century reveals a certain reluctance on the part of the masters to adopt new methods, and they hardly showed their accustomed enterprise in refusing to purchase the patent of the new tapestry, or printed Brussels, invented by Mr. Richard Whytock of Edinburgh in 1832, when first offered to them, while a similar coyness was exhibited later in respect to Bigelow's new power-loom. Possibly the apprehension of the expense of the transition period and the consequent unsettlement among the workers rendered them cautious; but in the second half of the nineteenth century the necessary advance was made, and a complete revolution effected in the carpet trade of Kidderminster. The old hand-looms with their tradition of family life were largely swept away, and the weavers and dyers gathered in vast factories and mills.

In the years 1844-5 Messrs. Pardoe, Hoomans, and Co. began the manufacture of the printed tapestry carpets already referred to, and in 1851 a still more important advance was made by their adoption of the power-loom for this purpose, whilst Messrs. James Humphries and Sons used steam-weaving for Brussels carpets in the year following, and the firm of Messrs. Brinton and Sons also laid down the necessary new machinery and broke up their obsolete looms. The impetus given to this great change by the late Lord Ward, afterwards earl of Dudley, must not be forgotten. He built large works with steam-power and plant in what is now known as Green Street, and looms were placed there by several manufacturers.

But the great transition was not effected without serious loss of property; hand-loom detached shops, as well as the old warehouses, became idle and untenanted. A large outlay was necessary for the new machinery, and distress was caused by lack of employment for the older hands. The year 1853, a time of disastrous strikes in Lancashire and Wales, was also marked by an unsuccessful struggle on the part of the carpet-weavers of Kidderminster.[3]

During the period of unsettlement between 1851 and 1861, the population of Kidderminster had decreased by nearly 4,000, but as the new conditions were understood and appreciated, prosperity again visited the town, and a fresh stimulus was offered by the opening of the railway in 1852. The development of worsted-spinning at this time and later was very significant. Several large mills specially intended for the supply of carpet yarns were built and furnished with machinery. Some of them absorbed the outlying mills within a short

[1] Green, *Hist. of Worc.* ii. 19.

[2] For much valuable information as to the carpet trade both in Bewdley and Kidderminster we are indebted to John Brinton, Esq. of Moor Hall, Stourport.

[3] Webb, *Hist. of Trade Unionism* (1902), 206; *Report of Conference of Carpet Manufacturers and Workmen, Kidderminster* (1853). For contemporary information on the later relations of masters and men, see *Rep. of Conf. of Manufacturers and Workmen before T. Hughes, Q.C., at Kidderminster* (1875) and *Moxon Loom Arbitration Proc.* (Kidderminster, 1879).

radius of Kidderminster, such as those at Chaddesley, Spennels, and Hoobrook, thus contributing to the enlargement of the town and the provision of employment for the scattered workers of the district.

Comparing 1850 with the present date it may be safely affirmed that the production of carpets in Kidderminster has increased three-fold, and that six times as much worsted yarn is spun annually. Nor must it be forgotten that the yarns are not only consumed in the local manufacture, but are also exported to other industrial centres at home and abroad.

About the year 1860 the manufacture of chenille carpets and rugs by hand-looms was introduced into Kidderminster from Glasgow. These looms were superseded by power-looms in 1880. This manufacture now forms an important branch of the carpet industry. In 1878 the patent rights of an American invention to weave Axminster pile carpets by power-loom completely altered the conditions of this branch of the trade, and brought Axminster carpets to a price in reach of the public. Mr. Michael Tomkinson, a Kidderminster manufacturer, secured the rights, the inventor erected a number of looms, and over 2,000 hands are now employed in this branch of the trade.

The Worcestershire Exhibition held at Worcester in 1882 gave the best possible illustration of the progress made at that date in the industries of the county. Not only were excellent examples of its textile products shown, but the operations of carding, preparing, and spinning were illustrated, and carpets woven on the looms by steam power. The machinery supplied by Messrs. Brinton and other well-known firms furnished a valuable object lesson in the vast advances made during the preceding half-century in the staple industry of Kidderminster.[5]

CAPS

The cap-making trade does not occupy a very prominent place in the history of British industries. It appears to have been most prosperous in Plantagenet times. Since then it has gradually declined,[1] and now it no longer exists. Hats of felt, straw, silk, and other materials have taken the place of round woollen caps, and it is only in the most recent times that the wearing of cloth caps has again become more common.

The centre of the trade in Worcestershire was Bewdley. From the small amount of information to be obtained, it appears to have come into existence there in the sixteenth century.[2] We know that it was transferred from Monmouth, but the date of transference is doubtful. Fuller, writing in 1662, said that 'on the occasion of a great plague hapning in this Town (Monmouth), the trade was some years since removed hence to Beaudley in Worcestershire, yet so that they are called Monmouth caps unto this day.'[3] But the trade was flourishing in 1570 at Bewdley, according to a statute forbidding the wearing of felt hats by persons who were neither knights nor in the possession of £200 a year.[4]

We have still earlier evidence in the complaints against the use of mills for scouring and thicking Bewdley caps. It was said to utterly ruin and spoil them, and was again and again prohibited by statute in 1483, 1512, 1530, 1552, 1566, and 1571.[6] Finally the attempts were found to be so unsuccessful that they were given up. Cappers too were frequently mentioned at this period in the Ribbesford parish registers.[7]

It is improbable that the industry was at all noteworthy before the latter half of the sixteenth century. For Leland, writing about 1549,

[1] Beck, *Drapers' Dict.* p. 52. Caps were exported to Gascony in 1377. *Parl. R.* (Rec. Com.), iii. 109.

[2] Prattinton thought it was established probably about the same time as at Gloucester, where one Thomas Bell first introduced it. He died 1566. Fuller, *Hist. of Worthies of Eng.*; Fosbrooke, *Hist. of City of Glouc.* (1879), 165. Coventry, quite close, was also celebrated for its caps. Prattinton MS. (Soc. of Antiq. Lib.), Bewdley.

[3] Fuller, *Hist. of Worthies of Eng.* (1811), ii. 116.

[4] Stat. 13 Eliz. cap. 19. Bewdley is mentioned among other places as supporting the trade. Also the importation of foreign caps was strictly forbidden by Stat. 3 Hen. VIII. cap. 15, and the prices were fixed: for caps or bonnets, 2*s.*; hats, 10*d.*; crown caps or single night caps, 6*d.* They also varied according to the wool—Leominster wool caps fetching 3*s.* 4*d.* and 2*s.* 6*d.*, while Cotswold wool ones sold for only 2*s.* and 1*s.* 6*d.* Stat. 21 Hen. VIII. cap. 19.

[5] In 1889 an attempt was made to form a syndicate controlling the important factories of Kidderminster. Although the scheme was dropped it led to considerable combination amongst existing firms, and the transformation of some into limited liability companies. Interesting details as to the history of the leading firms and their specialities of manufacture, which the exigencies of space debar us from citing, will be found in Burton, *Hist. of Kidderminster* (1890), pp. 185, sqq.

[6] *Parl. R.* (Rec. Com.), vi. 223*b*; Stat. 22 Edw. IV. cap. 5; 3 Hen. VIII. cap. 15; 21 Hen. VIII. cap. 9; 7 Edw. VI. cap. 8; 8 Eliz. cap. 11; 13 Eliz. cap. 19. There the various workmen are said to be carders, spiners, knitters, parters of wool, frisers, thickers, dressers, walkers, dyers, battelers, shearers, pressers, edgers, liners, and bandmakers. The money received as forfeitures for disobeying these statutes was 'employed to the maintenance of the mistery of capping in certain decayed towns of this Realm.' *Acts of P.C.* 1578–80, p. 26.

[7] They begin in 1574 and are printed in Burton, *Hist. of Bewdley* (1883), App.

does not mention it at all when describing the place. In fact he said that 'Beaudley is but a very new Towne and that of ould tyme there was but some poore Hamlett and that upon the Building of a Bridge there upon Severne and Resort of people unto it, and Commodity of the pleasant site, Men began to inhabit there and because that the plott of it seemed fayre to the Lookers it took a French name Beaudley quasi Bellus Locus. I aske a Merchant there of the Antientnesse of the Towne, and he answered mee that it was but a new Towne.'[1]

The capping trade seems to have been most prosperous in the first half of the seventeenth century.[2] Among other names of those engaged in the trade appear those of Thomas Farloe and Walter Palmer, who lived about 1666 and 1670. Their wealth and position enabled them to mint token coins of their own. Other names are Wowen,[3] Grove, Bowen,[4] and Griffin.[5]

In the regulations of 1665 made for the new Blackwell Hall, in London, Monmouth, Bewdley, and all other caps were forbidden for the present to be brought into the hall or pay hallage.[6] For what reason, it is unknown. The very fact that Bewdley caps were classed with Monmouth caps proves they were considered at least as good as the latter, if they had not altogether superseded them, as Fuller states.[7] The trade, however, was but short-lived. Only twelve years later Yarranton laments that 'the trade of making caps at Bewdley is grown so low that great part of the Ancient Capmakers in that town are wholly decayed, and the rest at this present are in a very low condition.' So bad was the trade that it was 'like in a few years to fall to the ground.' He attributed the depression to the monopolizing and control of the trade by two or three factors, who could practically pay as little as they liked for the caps. He urged the cappers to incorporate themselves by a charter, and to raise money by procuring part of a granary at Stratford-on-Avon, where corn was always cheap.[8] It is more probable that the decline of the trade was due to the introduction and popularity of felt hats in the seventeenth century. Owing, possibly, to the immigration of French refugees at this time, these hats became cheaper and more fashionable. They continued to be worn generally by all classes until the present century, when hats of straw and silk, and cloth caps, have again more or less taken their places.[9] Woollen caps were never again generally worn.

The clothiers and probably the cappers of Bewdley suffered so much from the lack of wool and its high price about the end of the seventeenth century that in 1701 and 1718 they sent petitions to the House of Commons demanding that means should be taken to prevent the transportation and smuggling of wool into France and elsewhere.[10] A little later in the eighteenth century the trade somewhat revived for a short period. Bewdley caps were worn by seamen, whose numbers rapidly increased at this period, owing to the naval wars. The caps were so much used by the Dutch seamen that their name was given to them.[11] In 1789 Dutch caps of Bewdley were 'valued for the excellence of the capping, and particularly the high-priced ones are much esteemed by the London dealers.'[12] This revival, however, was but short-lived. Fashion did not long favour Bewdley. Even sailors found other kinds of caps that suited them better. Already in 1825 the woollen cap trade was much decayed at Bewdley.[13] From that time it gradually declined and disappeared. In 1883 the trade was a thing of the past, and woollen caps were curiosities.[14] Rarely are they seen nowadays. The nearest approach to them are Tam o' Shanters, and they are made elsewhere than in Worcestershire and Bewdley.

[1] Leland, *Itinerary* (ed. T. Hearne, 1769, 3rd ed.), iv. 106.

[2] It was a very prosperous industry at the time of the civil war. In 1647 the Bewdley men were said to be implicated in what was known as the Broadway Plot, and among others the plotters calculated on 500 capmen from Bewdley.

[3] Prattinton MSS. (Soc. of Antiq. Lib.), Bewdley par. On Thomas Farloe's token was the shape of a heart with 'Tho. Farloe Capper in Bewdley'; reverse, Bewdley cap with a very high crown, on one side of which is 16, and on the other 70, and underneath, 'His halfe Peny.' Walter Palmer's was a high-crowned hat, with 'The Cap of Walter Palmer of' above, and 'Bewdley Capper 1666' below. Reverse, P over W E in a circle.

[4] Ribbesford Par. Reg., printed in Burton, *Hist. of Bewdley* (1883), App.

[5] Victuallers Recog., quoted in Prattinton MSS. Bewdley.

[6] Strype, *Stow's Surv. of Lond.* (1720), ii. bk. v. p. 277.

[7] *Supra.*

[8] Yarranton, *England's Improvement by Sea and Land* (1677), pp. 163, 194.

[9] In 1601 there were two 'feltmakers' at Stourbridge, and in 1679 one John Hill of Kidderminster was a feltmaker. *Quart. Sess. R.* (Worc. Hist. Soc.), i. 232. Burton, *Hist of Kidderminster* (1890), 221. Fuller quaintly remarked that 'nothing but Hats would fit the Heads (or humours rather) of the English, as fancied by them fitter to fence their fair faces, from the injury of wind and weather.' Fuller, *Worthies of Wales* (1602), 50.

[10] *House of Com. Journ.* xiii. 501, xix. 84.

[11] Postlethwayt, *Universal Dict. of Trade* (1751).

[12] Camden, *Brit.* (Gough ed. 1789), ii. 357. Ric. Willis, bp. of Gloucester, Salisbury, and Winchester, was son of a capper of Bewdley. He died in 1734. Nash, *Hist. of Worc.* (1799), ii. 279.

[13] Pinnock, *Hist. and Topog. of Eng.* (1825), vi. 27.

[14] Burton, *Hist. of Bewdley* (1883).

INDUSTRIES

FULLING AND DYEING

The existence of a cloth trade in any district necessarily implies the existence of another, an allied industry, of dyeing and fulling. In fact, the dyeing trade is even earlier than the cloth. For, when wool was exported to, and cloth imported from, Flanders and other places, it seems to have been usually dyed in England. In 1173 the dyers of Worcester paid Henry II. £12, 'which they owed to his enemies in Flanders.' From this it would seem that the king claimed the debt of the Worcester dyers to the Flemish weavers, because he was at war with Count Philip of Flanders, one of the allies of his rebelling sons.[1]

Again, the men of Worcester in 1203 purchased freedom to buy and sell dyed cloth as they had done in the time of King Henry I., since by this date the importation of woollen cloth had been forbidden.[2]

Many of the fulling mills in the early period of the industry seem to have belonged to the monks, who had in their hands much also of the cloth trade. On the estate of the monastery at Evesham were at least two fulling mills, one being situated at Burton,[3] and another at Bengeworth.[4] The trade seems to have been prosperous round Kidderminster. Near it, one William de Stour had a fulling mill at Mytton[5] in the reign of Henry III. About the same time also one Alfred the Fuller was said to hold land on which the hospital was formerly situated, near the great mill at Kidderminster.[6] The monks of Worcester had a fulling mill at Wolverley[7] in 1240. Later on, Robert Burnel, bishop of Bath, had a fulling mill at Kidderminster in 1292.[8] About the same date a mill is mentioned at Impney[9] and another at Overbury. In the Subsidy Rolls for the fourteenth century many fullers occur, and most of them seem to have lived round Kidderminster and Worcester, the centres of the trade.[10]

In the fifteenth century the trade must have been in close connexion with the cloth trade, which was well established in Worcester by that date. Cloth not properly fulled was strictly forbidden throughout the period ; as also the use of tenters for stretching, 'gig-mills' for thicking, 'gallisrynde, barks of trees, and sawedust' for kerseys. Fulling by foot was said to be far more efficacious than by the mills.[11] These rules continued to be enforced right down to the seventeenth century.[12]

Dyers and fullers are frequently mentioned together in the Quarter Sessions Rolls. One instance, the fulling mills of Robert Wilmot on the Stour at Hartlebury, occurs in the Civil War ; he had a protection that his mills and his cloth were not to be disturbed. At this period dyeing had become one branch of the cloth trade.[13] The fulling of Bewdley caps at this period must have helped to develop the industry.[14] An interesting entry occurs in 1594, when R. Lecavill and W. Harris obtained sole permission to plant 100 acres of woad in Worcestershire and in other places.[15] Worcester was more famous for its red cloth than its blue ; it was said to be of the 'purest scarlet,' and was ordered for the uniforms of part of King Charles II.'s army when he was at Worcester in 1651.[16] At Evesham in 1608 a monopoly of the trade of dyeing was granted to Richard Bradford of Tewkesbury on payment of £20, and later he was admitted to the freedom of the borough.[17] The trade, then, was still in existence at that place, as well as in Worcester. In the seventeenth century a particular kind of cloth called 'say' dyed cloth was made, which appears to have much resembled Spanish cloth. So much so that in 1640, in order to distinguish it, 'lists or yarn pricked into the lists' were forbidden to be sewn on it. Petitions, however, quickly arose complaining of the ruin that would ensue in the trade. After inquiries had been made, it was found that the manufacture was 'useful, the dye having endured the scouring and cleansing of the fulling mill continues the colour much better than dyed after it is fulled and thickened, and will be a means to advance the dressing and

1 Pipe R. Soc. xix. 165. Article by Pishey Thompson in *Assoc. Archit. Rep. and Papers*, ii. 363.

2 *Supra*, Cloth, 283.

3 *Chron. de Evesham* (Rolls Ser.), 211, 'Nicholai Fullonis, super aquam,' and 212. The date is 1206.

4 May, *Hist. of Evesham* (1845), 313. *Supra* (Topog.).

5 His name appears in the Maiden Bradley Chart. quoted in Burton, *Hist. of Kidderminster* (1890), p. 21, and in Excheq. Mins. Accts. $\frac{195}{21}$ *temp.* Hen. III. (P. R. O.)

6 From Wanley MS. printed in Burton, Ibid. p. 171. Madox mentions the lease of a messuage and land in Wick, by Alfred, son of Ketelburn, fuller of Kidderminster, dated about 1235. Perhaps this is the same man ; if so, he must have been fairly prosperous.

7 Burton, Ibid. p. 194.

8 *Worc. Inq. P.M.* (Worc. Hist. Soc.), pt. i. p. 43.

9 Ibid. p. 33 (3), *Worc. Epis. Reg. Sede Vac.* (Worc. Hist. Soc.), introd. p. 39.

10 *Lay Subs. R.* (Worc. Hist. Soc.), 1280, 1332, 1 Edw. I.

11 *Supra*, Cloth, pp. 283, 288, and Caps, p. 299.

12 *Supra*, Cloth.

13 *Quart. Sess. R.* (Worc. Hist. Soc.), introd. p. 36; *Hist. MSS. Com. Rep.* iv.

14 *Supra*, Caps.

15 Docquets quoted in Noake, *Worc. Nuggets*, p. 348.

16 *Supra*, Cloth.

17 May, *Hist. of Evesham* (1845), 313.

dyeing of cloth in England, by performing thereof as well, if not better, in some colours than they are done in Holland.'[1] Therefore a list of a particular width and kind was allowed. Whether Worcester profited by this concession or not is not related.

All kinds of fancy cloth and mixtures of wool and silk were made and worn at the end of the seventeenth and during the eighteenth centuries, and must have required more careful fulling and dyeing.[2] In spite of the decline in the cloth trade generally in Worcestershire in the eighteenth century, there were several fulling mills in existence about 1778. There was at Bromsgrove an 'overshot wheel and two stocks' for fulling and scouring of linsey-woolsey, the beating of hemp, the washing and 'backing' of coarse-linen yarn; and at Salwarpe was a stock of fulling mills having three overshot wheels and four stocks for fulling not only cloth and linsey-woolsey, but also Bewdley caps and leather.[6]

LEATHER

As a rule, some one or two towns are to be found in every county more especially devoted to the leather industry. In Worcestershire these appear to have been, first, Bewdley; second, and less important, Worcester. Bewdley owes the trade to its proximity to the Forest of Wyre, where oak bark was easily obtainable, then one of the most necessary ingredients in the process of tanning.

There seems to have been some kind of guild or company of corvesors in Bewdley in the fifteenth century.[3] In Worcester there was a barkers' craft in 1497, beside a curriers', corvesors',[4] and saddlers', which seem all to have been quite distinct from one another. The members of these crafts were forbidden by the merchant guild to buy or sell leather, either from the butchers or from foreign hide or leather merchants, except in open market, for 'grete custom of hids belongying to the baill's offis for the tyme beyng be loste and embesseld in tymes past of covert byeng of hids of persons strangers owte of open market.' All were forbidden to tan, dress, or use sheep skins, probably because the hide was not considered of a sufficiently good quality.[5]

Among the Exchequer Depositions during Elizabeth's reign several tanners are named at Worcester and one or two at Bewdley. Amongst those at Worcester were George Webb,[7] Richard Badelande or Bodeland,[8] and John Burford;[9] at Bewdley were Humphrey Hyll,[10] and William Mychell.[11] The tanners of Worcester, with the pewterers, plumbers, glovers, and whittawers, were incorporated in 1643.[12]

There is little to learn of the Bewdley tanners in the seventeenth century. That the trade continued to flourish is proved by the constant mention of tanners. One of them, William Mounoye, in 1591, made the first grant of money to the Grammar School. Other benefactors of their trade were John Crump and John Sheriffe.[13] Other tanners bear well-known Worcestershire names, such as John Burton, Richard Inett, Robert Pardoe, Richard Clare, John Hayles, John Bolton, and Fraunces Hill, perhaps a descendant of Humphrey Hill before mentioned.[14] A family more especially devoted to the industry was that of the Soleys or Sowleys of Sandbourne. One John Sowley was a tanner in 1592, and died in 1604. He had a son John, probably also a tanner, buried in 1652,[15] and the family appears to have lasted and thriven in Bewdley.[16]

At the end of the century the tanners of Worcestershire, as of all other counties, suffered very much from the duty which was laid on leather

[1] *Cal. S.P. Dom.* 1640, pp. 188–9; 210–11.

[2] *Supra*, Cloth.

[3] In one of the south windows of the chapel of Bewdley, built after the birth of Richard duke of York, son of Edw. IV. 1474, is a painting showing the guild or society of corvesors of Bewdley, instituted in honour of the Virgin Mary. There was also a chantry belonging to them. Prattinton MSS. (Soc. of Antiq. Lib.), iv. Bewdley Parish. 'Barkers' are mentioned at Evesham in 1346, 1461, and 1467. *Cal. of Pat.* 1346–8, 505; 1461–7, 415; 1467–77, 51.

[4] 'That no corvisor occupy no currier's crafte upon the said peyn of 6*s.* and 8*d.*' Green, *Hist. of Worc.* (1796), App. p. lxvi.

[5] Green, *Hist. of Worc.* (1796), App. lxv. The rules for buying in the market occur also in the laws of 1467. J. T. Smith, *Eng. Gilds* (Early Eng. Text Soc. 1870), p. 384. In both sets of laws there are some interesting rules for sanitation forbidding 'Sadelers Bochers Barkers ne Glovers' from dressing hides and skins below the Severn Bridge or making the river at the place into a sewer. Ibid. 396. Green, lxvi.

[6] Prattinton MSS. (Soc. of Antiq. Lib.), vi. Bromsgrove.

[7] Excheq. K. R. Memo. R. (P. R. O.), Mich. 6 Eliz. 91*d.*

[8] Ibid. 7 Eliz. East. 67.

[9] Ibid. 5 Eliz. Mich. 91.

[10] Ibid. 7 Eliz. Hil. 196*d.*

[11] Excheq. K.R. Memo R. (P. R. O.), Mich. 7 Eliz. Hil. 195*d.*

[12] Documents quoted in Noake, *Worc. in Olden Times* (1840), p. 30. The shoemakers, according to Noake, were incorporated in 1504. Ibid. p. 28.

[13] Prattinton MSS. (Soc. of Antiq. Lib.), iv. Bewdley parish.

[14] Ribbesford, par. reg. printed in Burton, *Hist. of Bewdley*, App.

[15] Ibid. from Halty MS.

[16] Ibid. App. p. 4, 9; Nash, ii. 38, 56, 272, 279.

coming from Ireland. In the many petitions sent up from Worcester, Bewdley, Droitwich, Bromsgrove, and Kidderminster, demanding its withdrawal, it is stated that many curriers and tanners had gone over to Ireland, and that the trade in consequence was dying out in England.[1] In 1718 the shoemakers of Worcester declared that the result of the duty was a great increase in the price of leather. Merchants bought up all the leather and exported it. Another grievance of this period was the exportation of English bark. Everywhere in Worcester this evil was felt, at Evesham and Shipston-on-Stour, as well as at Worcester and Kidderminster.[2] By this time sheep and lamb skins were no longer so unpopular as in the fifteenth century. But it was no less necessary to take measures to ensure that these skins were delivered to the tanners and glovers in as perfect a state as the ox-hides. In 1719 the glovers and skinners of Kidderminster, Bewdley, Stourbridge, and Worcester made a petition to this effect.[7] They do not, however, seem to have received any protection from Parliament. Whether the duty was the cause or not, certainly the leather trade at Bewdley declined during the eighteenth century. Hayley, writing about 1770, said that in his time there were only three tanyards at Bewdley; whereas he could remember or 'reckon by hearsay' at least twelve. These were Slade, Hayley, and the Nashes. Those that no longer existed were Soley, Paton, John Burton, Edward Crane, Humphry Back, Goodyer Wildsey, John Seayer, Robert Pardoe, Tyler Whatmore and Morris, and the Clares.[8]

The trade was still in existence at the end of the eighteenth century. During the nineteenth century, however, certainly at Bewdley, probably at Worcester, it seems to have fallen off considerably, but tanners still exist at both places.

GLOVES

The glove trade seems to have been established in England by the fourteenth century. Glovers' companies were incorporated at Chester, Coventry, Perth, and elsewhere by that time.[3] In 1378 English gloves were exported. In these early times the gloves seem to have been made of leather and not of wool or cotton. Only the stouter qualities were made in England, and for long years the finer ones were imported.

In the Lay Subsidy Rolls for Worcestershire the names of two individual glovers at Hampton and Benningworth appear in 1327 and 1358.[4] But there is no sign of any great industry there till much later. In the Laws of the Worcester Merchant Guild for 1467 and 1497 regulations were made for the glovers, concerning the preparation of the skins.[5] There they seem connected with the tanners and curriers. In 1561 the craft included 'glovers, poche-makers, and pursers,' and was said to be a company making its own bye-laws.[6] The glove trade seems to have developed in Worcester, as everywhere in the sixteenth century, owing to the protective laws of Edward IV., Henry VIII., and Elizabeth,[9] and the more common wear of gloves. In the Quarter Session Rolls from 1607 to 1617 glovers are constantly mentioned. Curiously enough, they occur more frequently at Evesham, Feckenham, and Pershore, than at Worcester.[10] One or two also came from Inkberrow, Ombersley, and Northfield. For Worcester, however, there is other information. A document dating from 1570 to 1662, in private possession, cited by Noake, contains the names of members admitted and apprentices enrolled during that period, but the details of the industry are obscure. Most probably the workpeople carried on the trade in their own homes in the neighbouring towns and villages, as they do now, while Worcester was the centre of the industry for the distribution and sale of the gloves.

In 1642 it was forbidden to make gloves of 'lynnen, cloth, or fustian' under penalty of a fine of 6*s*. 8*d*. for every offence.[11] Even as early as this therefore the manufacture of cotton or woollen gloves existed, and was ruining the leather trade. However, the leather glove industry at Worcester appears to have been in a

[1] *House of Com. Journ.* xviii. 71, 727, 740, 748.

[2] Ibid.

[3] Beck, *Gloves, their Annals and Associations* (1883), 135 seq.; Morris, *Chester in Plantagenet and Tudor Periods.*

[4] *Lays Subs. R.* (Worc. Hist. Soc.), 1 Edw. III. 1327, p. 72; Ibid. 1358, p. 37.

[5] Toulmin Smith, *Eng. Gilds* (1870), 371 seq.; Green, *Hist. of Worc.* (1796), App.

[6] Docquets of company printed in Noake, *Worc. in Olden Times* (1849), p. 30. By some authorities it is stated that the company was incorporated in 1497, and by many in 1661, but no evidence of this is to be found in the Pat. and Close Rolls or State Papers for those dates. Kelly, *Worc. Direct.*; Hull, *Hist. of Glove Trade* (1834), 57.

[7] *House of Com. Journ.* xix. 91.

[8] Prattinton MSS. (Soc. of Antiq. Lib.), Bewdley Parish; Camden's *Brit.* (Gough, ed. 1789), ii. 358.

[9] Stat. 3 Edw. IV. cap. 4; *Parl. R.* (Hist. MSS. Com.) v. 507; Stat. 5 Eliz. cap. 7; Beck, *ut supra.*

[10] *Quart. Sess. R.* (Worc. Hist. Soc.), i. pp. 35, 46, 63, 73, 89, 125, 161, 164, 216, 234, 245, 258, 259, 272, 279, 281, 336.

[11] Docquets printed in Noake, *Worc. in Olden Times* (1849), p. 31.

fairly flourishing condition in the sixteenth century. More laws were made, with the consent of the mayor and corporation, and in 1663 the glovers, including the whittawers, were united with the tanners, pouch-makers, pursers, saddlers, pewterers, brasiers, and plumbers.[1]

The glovers during the eighteenth century must have continued to increase. But there is nothing to be discovered concerning them until the end of the century. Then there were said to be 4,000 employed in the trade at Worcester and in the neighbourhood.[2] At that time it was the principal trade in the town. It had quite superseded the cloth industry, and outside the county Worcester was already famous for its gloves. In 1802 the number of hands had increased to 6,000, and there were 70 glove masters in that city alone.[3] The glove-making district also included Ledbury, Cradley, and Bosbury, and some other places in Herefordshire. In spite of a stoppage caused by the American War, the industry continued to prosper until 1826, when there were 120 glover masters.[4]

Then came terrible depression caused by the removal of the hitherto prohibition of the importation of foreign gloves in 1826.[5] Only a duty of 8*s.* on men's and 7*s.* on women's gloves was henceforth imposed. This was a great disaster for the Worcester trade, for French gloves were both better and cheaper. Loud were the complaints raised against this free trade policy. It was declared that it would ruin English trade altogether. Hundreds were quickly thrown out of work. In 1831 there were 1,000 men and a much greater number of women employed in the trade in Worcester and its suburbs.[6] In the following year, however, only 113 were in full and 465 in partial employ.[7]

The trade continued to decline for some time, and in 1840 the glovers of Worcester hoped to revive the trade by persuading the queen, through the bishop of Worcester, to wear their gloves and so make them fashionable.[8] But this attempt was all in vain. Yet it is difficult to believe that the trade was really in a bad state, and in danger of becoming obsolete. One account says that 30,000 men, women, and children were employed in it.[9] Another authority, perhaps more correct, declares that in 1849 the number of masters was reduced to 40, and only 8,000 hands were employed.[10]

Since then the trade has gradually recovered. The glove makers have awaked to the fact that they must help themselves and improve the quality of their gloves. All means have been taken to compete with the French glove makers both in quality and price, and many improvements have been introduced that save both time and labour, more especially one for sewing the gloves.[11] The chief firm now is Messrs. Fownes in Talbot Street. Their gloves are quite equal in make and cut to any French gloves, and are even more worn in England than French ones. But a great deal of the actual glovemaking is still carried on in the old domestic fashion in the houses of rural workers for many miles round Worcester.

1 Docquets printed in Noake, *Worc. in Olden Times* (1849), p. 31.

2 Nash, *Hist. of Worc.* (1799), ii. App. cxiv.; *Gent's Mag.* lx. 1160.

3 Noake, *Worc. Guide* (1868); W. R. *Concise Hist. of Worc.* (808), p. 42.

4 Turberville, *Worc. in Nineteenth Century* (1852), pp. 17, 230. In 1785 Pitt put a tax on gloves, Stat. 25 Geo. III. c. 55. It was repealed in 1794, Stat. 34 Geo. III. cap. 10, with the exception of the licence, and even this brought in so little and was found so unsuccessful that it was taken off in 1796, Stat. 36 Geo. III. cap. 80. This greatly helped to improve the trade everywhere. In 1812 the 'grouders, stoners, and white leather parers' demanded an advance of wages.

5 Col. Davies, the member for Worcester, petitioned as early as 1824 that gloves might be exempted from the general removal of prohibitions. But Huskisson replied that prohibitions must be done away with and a high protective duty of 30 per cent. substituted. *Worc. Journ.* 11 March, 1824. Mr. Dent, the great Worcester glover, went up to interview the Chancellor of the Exchequer and obtained that the import duties on dressed or undressed skins should be taken off on 5 July, 1825, and that the importation of foreign gloves was only to be permitted after 5 July, 1826, and on payment of a sum per dozen according to their quality. Ibid. 18 and 25 March. Complaints of the distress continued to appear all through January and February, 1826, and on 9 March a petition was presented demanding (1) the limitation of importation to a few ports, (2) the imposition of a licence on all selling foreign gloves, (3) the stamping of all gloves. (1) was granted, but the others refused. On 16 March there was said to be a slight improvement, and on 26 March the excise duty on skins was reduced, and London made temporarily the only port for the reception of foreign gloves. Ibid. See Hansard, xii. 1202 (25 March, 1825) and the statutes 6 Geo. IV. c. 105, 107 and 111, 7 Geo. IV. c. 48.

6 *Pop. Ret.* 1831, Enumeration Abstract, p. 726.

7 Col. Davies moved for a committee of inquiry into the glove trade, but lost the motion. A committee of operative glove makers drew up a petition demanding a duty on foreign gloves. *Worc. Journ.* 1 and 28 Feb. 1832. Hull, *Hist. of Glove Trade* (1834), p. 58. *Gent's Mag.* 1832, i. 165. It was argued that smuggling was as great as ever. Viscount Strangford was strongly against the repeal of the duty. Beck, *ut supra*, p. 176.

8 Beck, *Gloves, their Annals and Associations* (1883), 178.

9 Hull, *Hist. of Glove Trade* (1834), p. 59. The failure of the English glove trade was also attributed to the introduction of 'Berlin' and all kinds of cotton and silk gloves. Sir Robert Peel proposed to again reduce the duty on gloves. The Worcester glove makers, at a meeting, declared if this was carried, they would be obliged to cease to employ any men at all, and appealed for mercy. *Worc. Journ.* i. Ap. 1842.

10 Noake, *Worc. in Olden Times* (1848), 32.

11 Yet in 1867 even 11,000,000 pairs of foreign gloves, chiefly French, were imported. Geo. Dodd. *Dict. of Manufacturers* (1867), p. 151.

INDUSTRIES

FRUIT GROWING AND MARKET GARDENING

The origin of the fruit-growing industry in the Vale of Evesham, which at the present day forms such an important feature in the industrial history of the county, has never been properly traced. There is, however, little doubt that in the beginning it took its rise from the monks attached to the great Evesham abbey. In the seventeenth century it received an impetus from an Italian gentleman, one Francis Bernardi, who was agent from Genoa in this country. Objecting to some measure adopted by the Senate of Genoa, he resigned his post and retired to Evesham, where he amused himself with gardening. His son, a man of some note, says his father spent £30,000 in the indulgence of his horticultural tastes, partly at Windsor and ultimately at Evesham. In his famous 'tour' (about 1770) Arthur Young computes the area of garden-land at Evesham at between three and four hundred acres; he adds that the rent varies from 50*s.* to £3 per acre, and says the gardeners carried their products round the country to Birmingham, Worcester, Tewkesbury, Gloucester, Warwick, Coventry, Stow, etc., seeds to Stafford, Lichfield, Leicester, Nottingham, etc.; and asparagus to Bath and Bristol. The local historian, Tindal (writing towards the end of the eighteenth century), says that £10,000 were at the lowest valuation annually turned by the Evesham gardeners. May (a later local historian), writing about 1845, estimated the extent of ground within the borough then cultivated as garden-land at a little under 600 acres. By 1870 the area had increased to about a thousand acres. At the present time it is estimated that in the Evesham district alone the area under market-garden cultivation reaches a total of ten thousand acres, and that the whole of the gardening area (which is not solely in Worcestershire) is from twenty to twenty-five thousand acres.

The economic result of the establishment of this important industry in the southern part of the county is important and interesting. Formerly the district was purely agricultural; and in the surrounding districts still devoted solely to that industry the tendency is for the population to decline and the value of property to decrease. In the gardening area the population is increasing; that of Evesham has risen from 4,245 in 1841, to 7,101 at the last census (it is now estimated at 7,500); that of the adjoining villages of Badsey from 395 to 775; Hampton from 469 to 970; Offenham from 355 to 617; in fact, taking the Evesham Union area, one can almost pick out the market gardening from the agricultural parishes by the increase or decrease in the population.

Next to the fertility of the soil, and the climate, the most important factor in the development of the industry has been found in the facilities for distribution afforded by excellent railway services. From the figures given above it will be seen that till the advent of the railways the industry was a very small one; this was of course a necessity, from the perishable nature of the produce. Before the railways came some of the gardeners took their produce to Birmingham market by road, but it is obvious that market gardening thus fettered could never attain any very great dimensions. The opening of the Midland main line from Birmingham to Cheltenham, with stations at Eckington and Defford, helped matters to some slight extent; but in 1852 what is now the Great Western Railway was opened between Evesham and Worcester. Within a few years Evesham also had direct communication with Oxford and London on the east, while, a few years later, the Redditch, Evesham, and Ashchurch branch of the Midland Railway gave it access to Birmingham and the north on the one hand, and to Gloucester and Bristol on the other. The result was a great expansion of the area under cultivation. At the present time the system of distribution is nearly perfect. Through goods trains, filled with garden produce, run from Evesham every evening during the season (except Saturdays and Sundays) to all parts of the country, particularly Birmingham and the North, and to South Wales; and goods loaded at seven o'clock in the evening are delivered in the various markets early the following morning. For the Scotch traffic, special through expresses leave Evesham daily about noon, delivering the produce in Glasgow and Edinburgh early the next morning. From Evesham alone it is estimated that as much as two thousand tons of garden produce (chiefly fruit) is dispatched per week during the busy part of the season, without taking into account the large quantities loaded at other stations and sidings within the area, and excluding the large quantities now sent by passenger trains. For the goods traffic the railway companies have, in response to the wishes of the growers, constructed hundreds of specially-designed vans, ventilated in order to keep the produce cool; and their rates are on the whole reasonable. To some parts of the north of England, however, where a large population is centred, rates are excessive, and do not compare favourably with those to other districts.

A feature of the system of distribution that has sprung into favour within the last few years is the sending of small packages of produce by passenger train in response to prepaid orders. While the larger quantities of produce, sent by goods trains, are consigned chiefly to salesmen and dealers, by this new system the private consumer is brought into direct communication with the grower, and he can rely upon receiving freshly-gathered produce. Fruit picked late in the afternoon can be despatched at about seven o'clock in the evening, and will be delivered to the purchasers, even in Scotland, early next morning. Very many thousands of packages are thus sent off each season.

For many years the legal status of the industry was somewhat precarious. A man would plant out perhaps twenty acres of land with fruit—strawberries, asparagus, or other crops that are not of an annual nature; and there would be nothing except the landlord's sense of justice to prevent the tenant being turned out of his holding practically without compensation, or having his rent raised on his own improvements. In some few cases the landlord's sense of justice proved to be lamentably deficient; and hardships occurred, too, when land changed owners. What was known as the Evesham Custom recognized to a great extent the rights of the tenants; but at last came the Market Gardeners' Compensation Act, which, although it does not go so far as many people would like in the matter of retrospective action, places the industry in a safe position. Thanks largely to the security which this Act of Parliament gives, a great extension of the industry has taken place of late years.

With regard to the crops grown, sixty years ago they consisted chiefly of radishes, onions, peas, cucumbers, plums, and kidney beans. Cabbages were not grown, owing to the difficulty of getting them away. The plums were then chiefly the Old Orleans, greengages, a few Barleys, and the old Damsons (Dammas). The yellow cooking plum, known as the Pershore, was introduced about half a century ago, and owing to its hardiness and prolific yield was largely planted. In 1870 there was a great crop of plums (though the gardening area was then small, difficulties of transport rendered the marketing of the crop an impossibility), and as a consequence growers began to look round for varieties more choice than the Pershore. A well-known fruit grower of the name of Vardon, of Peopleton, grew better sorts, which were largely used, and nurserymen went into the matter on a large scale. The growers in the Evesham district were much indebted to the firm of Thomas Rivers and Sons, of Sawbridgeworth, who introduced many new varieties of plums, apples, and pears. Nowadays, although the Pershore plums and Damascenes are very largely grown, there is a strong movement in favour of choice kinds; new varieties which look nice and travel well are eagerly planted by the growers. Speaking of plums, it may be stated that thousands of tons are now sent direct to the jam factories.

An important event in the history of the industry was the coming to Offenham, in 1852, of the late Mr. James Myatt, who, after being in business as a market gardener at Camberwell, took seventy acres of agricultural land in this village, which he converted into market-garden ground. He was the pioneer in the growth of strawberries, cabbage, outdoor rhubarb, and the well-known Myatt Ashleaf potatoes. The Evesham gardeners, who at that time were not the enterprising set of men they are to-day, looked somewhat askance at his innovations, especially as strawberries were not grown in the Evesham gardens before 1870. In that year something like a quarter of an acre of land was planted with strawberries at Hampton; they did well, and another piece was planted out by another grower, which showed returns as high as £200 per acre. Within a few years strawberries were grown in all parts, and now a single train will have on board as many as twenty tons of this fruit, picked and on the rail by 7 a.m., and delivered in Birmingham by 8.30 a.m.; one early passenger train will convey as many as twenty or thirty tons, the dispatch continuing on all passenger trains throughout the day to Birmingham, the north of England, and other places.

Tomatoes, now so largely grown, were not introduced till as recently as 1884. They were in that year tried on a small scale, and the area under their cultivation gradually increased till 1887, which was a very hot summer, and suited them so well that one grower was induced to plant out an acre, no one having previously grown so many. This one acre gave a net return of £350. As was the case with strawberries, people then went in for tomato-growing with a rush.

It is unnecessary to deal in detail with other crops. Asparagus, for which Evesham is specially famous, has been grown for very many years. In all varieties of fruit and vegetables the growers are eager to get the most improved kinds, and to adopt the latest methods. Only this year a party of them visited the market gardens round Paris in search of information, and French methods of cultivation, especially as regards early vegetables for salads, are now being put in practice. Glass, too, is being erected on a somewhat large scale, and canning and cold storage works are also thought of. The brining of vegetables for pickles has been practised for some years. Flowers, particularly wallflowers and narcissi, are largely grown for market.

Where the balance of nature is upset to such a large extent the question of blight naturally forces itself upon the attention of growers. Some years ago blight of various kinds did an enormous amount of damage, and the growers formed the Evesham Fruit Pests Committee, a body which directed its attention to methods of prevention and cure. With the assistance of Miss Eleanor A. Ormerod as consulting entomologist, and of chemists and practical gardeners, the committee found means of dealing with almost all the kind, of blight that affected their crops ; and the results of their experiments, which were embodied in a widely-circulated ' Report,' were adopted, not only all over England, but in other parts of the world besides. Further knowledge has since been gained, and the combating of insect pests is now an important branch of a gardener's education.

Equally important is the use of artificial manures. The gardeners pay high rent for their ground, and raise numerous crops during the twelve months. In order to do this artificial manures have to be employed to a great extent, and the annual sum spent on these preparations reaches to a very large amount. In the matters of pruning and grafting the gardeners are well to the fore, thanks largely to the skilled instructors placed at their disposal by the Worcestershire County Council.

A tendency that has recently made itself manifest is the coming into the industry of young gentlemen with capital, who adopt gardening as a means of livelihood. They generally article themselves to one or other of the many well-known growers for a term, varying from one to three years, in order to learn the business, and then embark on their own account, with more or less success, dependent chiefly on their natural capacity and industry.

As to the future of the industry there is no reason whatever for believing that it is overdone. It has been overdone according to some people ever since it was established. With improved methods of distribution, such as prevail at the present day, there is a market for unlimited quantities of good and graded produce at remunerative prices. The tendency now seems to be in the direction of larger holdings, but the small man has as good a chance as ever he had ; and more fortunes will probably be made out of market gardening in Worcestershire than have been made in the past—and that is saying not a little !

AGRICULTURE

THE agriculture of Worcestershire varies a good deal in different parts of the county. Originally the land was farmed on the open field system. Round each village were small enclosures which the householders owned in severalty, then came large arable fields in which each householder had an allotment; often the allotments were redistributed either every year or every three years, but gradually the allotments became fixed and the same person held them year after year. In old deeds relating to land in the county these allotments are described as so many 'sellions of land in a certain common field known as, *e.g.*, Stanfield.' When the crops were got in all the pigs and poultry of the village were allowed to wander over the open arable fields. A similar system prevailed as to the pasture land. Large meadows known as 'hams' are still to be found in some parishes, in which each ancient houseowner has an allotment from which he takes his hay crop, and when that crop is gathered in the cattle and sheep of the houseowners are turned out on the meadow, the number that each houseowner can turn out being fixed and strictly adhered to. In addition to these commonable arable and meadow lands, in many parishes there were large tracts of waste on which all the lord's tenants were entitled to pasture. The forests occupied a great portion of the area of the county in early times, and there still remain considerable tracts of woodland over which common rights often exist. Thus the county consisted of a series of villages with small enclosures round each, a common arable field, a common pasture field, a waste, and a greater or less extent of woodland, in some cases subject to a right of lopping by the commoner for firewood and for repairs.

With such a state of things good agriculture was not to be expected, and no real improvement was made in cultivation until the middle of the eighteenth century, when a movement was begun to get rid of the commonable rights. This first began in the arable fields, the owners exchanging different scattered lots for others near together; a surrender or exchange of common rights being then made, the lots could be enclosed and held in severalty. In some cases this was done by deed, in others by Act of Parliament. This practice was subsequently extended to the meadows, so that the meadow allotments were all grouped together freed from the commonable rights. In this way each owner was able to enclose his land and cultivate it as he pleased, which led to a better system of manuring and farming being introduced. This process went on until about the middle of the nineteenth century; but although in a number of parishes the common fields have been got rid of, some of them still exist. The process had its drawbacks; it led to a great deal of the land falling into the hands of the large owners, for when once a man's cattle were confined to a small allotment instead of being able to wander over all the meadow land of the parish, he was prevented from keeping a sufficient amount of stock to enable him to make a living and so had to dispose of his lands. From a very early period complaints were made as to the enclosure of the waste lands in the county. There does not seem to have been a great objection to the enclosure of commonable fields, nor even of the waste if it was kept as a grass or arable field, but no building was allowed to be erected ; this was mainly to prevent an increase in the poor the parish would have to maintain. To be able to erect a house on the waste the consent of the lord of the manor and the sessions had to be obtained. By a statute of Elizabeth (31 Eliz. c. 7) no one could build a house unless he assigned four acres of land to it, and the sessions papers contain indictment after indictment against persons for neglecting to do this.

At the end of the eighteenth and the first half of the nineteenth centuries enclosures became very fashionable, and a very large area of land was enclosed.[1] Nash, writing at the end of the eighteenth century, says : 'Enclosures have been the fashion in Worcestershire as well as in other counties, though I much doubt whether they would have been so often applied for to parliament if the solicitors of the Acts, surveyors, commissioners, etc., etc., had not gained more money by this than the landholder and the tenants.'[2]

There can be little doubt that a great deal of the land enclosed was not fit for anything but pasture, and would have been better left unenclosed. In consequence of the fall in prices a good deal that was then broken up now hardly pays for cultivation. But on the whole the enclosures have been a great gain to the county in improving the agriculture.

The soil of the county is of several kinds ; the most usual is a stiff clay with a subsoil of marl, or a light loam overlying the gravel. The clay lands as a rule lie to the east of the Severn, the loamy lands in the vale of Evesham and the west of the Severn, but it is impossible to give any exact boundary of the different lands. The stiff clay lands are well adapted for corn growing, and were formerly, when corn was high, cultivated to a profit, but of late years the rents of these lands have fallen largely. The loamy land is mostly given over to special cultivations—fruit, hops, and vegetables. In the valleys, especially those of the Severn, Teme, and Avon, there are very rich meadow lands, but the upland pastures are not as a rule of very high quality. There are now[3] 261,238 acres of permanent pasture, 15,559 acres of clover and rotation grasses for hay, and 8,423 not for hay.

No particular breed of cattle is peculiar to the county ; Herefords are largely found west of the Severn, and there are many fine herds. These are also fairly numerous on the east; the Croom herd is celebrated both here and in America, but the prevailing cattle there are half-bred Shorthorns. Neither is there any county breed of sheep. In the west and north Shropshires are the prevailing kind, while in the east and south Ryelands and Cotswolds. The present amount of stock in the county is:[4]

Horses	22,019	Cows	73,516
Sheep	149,455	Pigs	41,174

About the beginning of the nineteenth century the county contained a large number of small enclosures and small farms, but from the abolition

[1] There are 129 inclosure awards in the office of the clerk of the peace at Worcester, ranging from 1735 to 1872, out of about 220 parishes in the county.

[2] Vol. i. p. 11.

[3] *Agricultural Returns*, 1905.

[4] Ibid.

of the common field system the small farmers were not able to live, and a movement began by which these small farms were thrown together. This was greatly extended towards the middle of the century, when large farms became the fashion, both from the view of cultivation and of sporting. Since the agricultural depression began at the end of the seventies a reaction has set in, and there seems now to be a desire to return to smaller farms. The figures as to the present size of farms in the county are :[1]

	1895	1904
Above 1 and not exceeding 5 acres . .	2,819	2,733
„ 5 „ „ 50 „ . .	3,427	3,558
„ 50 „ „ 300 „ . .	1,950	1,984
„ 300 acres	182	161
Total	8,378	8,436

Average size of farms in 1904 . . . . . 47·4 acres.

Under the Tudors and Stuarts the great staple grain was barley, as is shown by the measures taken by the Stuarts to keep down the quantity of malt made, both by decreasing the number of alehouses, and preventing the beer being made over-strong by the use of too much malt. In some of the Privy Council letters to the justices, when a scarcity was feared, this is plainly stated ; for instance, in 1625 the Lord Keeper Coventry wrote to the Worcestershire justices to see that the strength of the beer sold be so moderated that drunkenness be avoided and vain consumption of grain prevented.[2] In 1631 the Lord Keeper wrote again directing the justices during the present scarcity to prevent the maltsters making any greater quantity of malt than sufficient for necessary use, so that there might be more barley for the poor.[3]

Besides barley there was grown to some extent a mixture of barley and oats called 'munkorn' ; this is frequently mentioned in seventeenth-century papers, but does not occur afterwards. Oats never appear to have been grown to a very great extent, and it was not until the eighteenth century that any large area was planted with wheat ; then alternate crops of wheat and beans became a very favourite form of cultivation on the stiff soils. The four-course system does not appear to have been introduced until early in the nineteenth century (neither Marshall nor Nash mentions it), but from 1820 to 1880 it was the method of cultivation on most of the larger farms where the lease prescribed a course of farming and did not leave the tenant a free hand. Of late years, however, farmers have declined to take leases with specific covenants as to cultivation, and have been allowed the right to cultivate their farms almost as they please, subject to such restrictions as not to take two white straw crops two years in succession ; not to grow more than a fixed proportion of wheat in the last year of the tenancy; not to mow meadow land twice in the same year ; and not to break up permanent pasture. The customs prevailing on a tenant's leaving, in the absence of agreement, are, as regards Candlemas and Lady-day takings, that an outgoing tenant has the right to plant in the autumn or spring preceding the termination of

[1] Board of Agriculture Returns.
[2] Sess. Rec. p. 398.
[3] Ibid. 484.

his tenancy one-third of the arable land with wheat; he harvests this crop, takes away the corn, and leaves the straw and chaff for the use of the incoming tenant. He is entitled to the use and occupation of two rooms in the house, and a portion of the homestead and buildings, to spend and consume his hay, straw, and fodder until 1 May next after his tenancy ceases. He is to be paid for acts of husbandry necessary for the crops of his successors, and for the seed and sowing of clover, and grass seeds sown in the white straw crops in the spring before quitting. In practice the incoming tenant takes the offgoing wheat crop at a valuation made in the month of July. As regards Michaelmas takings the tenant, on quitting, is allowed a portion of the homestead and buildings, also to consume his hay, straw, and fodder, and to enjoy the portion of arable planted with roots until 1 May next after his tenancy expires; he also has till the same date a piece or pieces of grass land near the homestead locally called the 'bosey pasture.' He is entitled to be paid for acts of husbandry necessary for the crops of his successor, and for all clover and grass seeds sown in the white straw crops in the spring before quitting. In practice the incoming tenant at either of the three dates takes the unconsumed hay, straw, and roots at a fixed valuation.

Entries vary; the majority are at Michaelmas, but in some parts there are entries at Candlemas and Lady-day. Formerly the tenant was bound to consume on the farm all the hay, straw, roots, and green crops grown thereon; now he is permitted in most cases, having first obtained the landlord's permission, to sell a portion, bringing back an equivalent in manure or feeding stuffs; he is not allowed to break up old pasture. It was formerly common for the tenant to bind himself to a fixed rotation of crops, and particularly not to grow two white straw crops in succession. Now the general practice is that he only covenants to farm the lands in a good and husbandlike manner, keep them clear from weeds, and not impoverish them.

The landlord is practically responsible for outside repairs, the tenant doing the painting. The tenant has to keep the interior of the farmhouse and all gates, fences, and ditches in good order and condition, the landlord finding new gates and rough timber when required. The tenant is allowed a reasonable time for gathering and clearing away fruit [1] after the expiration of his tenancy.

Taken as a whole, although there are some brilliant exceptions, the Worcestershire farms are not highly cultivated; the statement of Nash,[2] 'Our farmers do not manage their hedges well, but put in too much dead wood, so that the live quick is killed,' is still correct. Many of the farms, especially the smaller ones, show a great want of care and neatness. In recent years there has been a great decrease in the amount of labour employed, and the cultivation of the average of the farms is not nearly so good as it was forty or fifty years ago. On some of the better farms the contrary is the case, and the land is as well farmed as any in England. In Worcestershire the question as to whether the land is clean or foul depends to a great extent on the season, as on the heavy land it is impossible to do any work in a wet season, and most of the small farmers have neither the men nor the desire to take advantage of every opportunity of cleaning the land. Hence there is a good deal of the stiff land that is very foul.

[1] Bund, *Law of Inexhausted Improvements*, 3rd ed. p. 147.

[2] I. ix.

AGRICULTURE

The great feature of the agriculture of the county is growing special crops—fruit, vegetables, flowers, hops. As far back as the thirteenth century[1] Worcester was noted for its fruit—which then meant apples and pears. In the time of the Civil War a Parliament soldier writing from Worcester to London speaks with wonder of the fruit. He says, 'Worcestershire is a pleasant, fruitful, and rich county abounding in corn, woods, pastures, hills, and valleys, every hedge and highway beset with fruit, but especially with pears, whereof they make that pleasant drink called perry which they sell for a penny a quart, though better than ever you tasted in London.'[2] Apples and pears are still grown to a very large extent. Formerly a particular class of pears, which were quite uneatable, was especially grown for making perry, but this custom has been dying out of late years, it being recognized that good perry can be made from sweet eating pears as well as from other sorts, and that the secret of success is far more in the selection of good quality than in the use of particular kinds of fruit. The old pear orchards that were allowed to grow up as they pleased are also dying out, whilst modern methods of cultivation by which far more care in pruning is bestowed on the orchards are coming into vogue, with excellent results both as regards yield and quality. No actual figures exist, but in the west and north-west of the county it is difficult to let a farm that has not some 'fruit' on it. As to the kinds of apples and pears grown they are usually divided into two sorts: 'pot fruit,' which is so called from the large baskets in which they are packed, locally termed pots—this means really fine fruit, fruit fit for the table, and possibly the kind of apple that is the most grown is the Blenheim orange; and 'cider fruit,' which includes all other kinds than that which can be sold for the table. From the cider fruit not only is the best cider made, but also a production called drink, which is made from all sorts and conditions of fruit, and is chiefly given to the agricultural labourers, who consume an incredible quantity of this vinegary fluid. In many cases it is still, in spite of Truck Acts, given as part of the wages of the labourers, who are paid so much a week in cash, and so much in cider. It is usually said that more pears are grown in the county than apples; whatever may have been the case at one time, apples are now the more favourite fruit of the two, possibly because apples come into bearing sooner, the old rhyme being still true that 'he who plants pears, plants for his heirs.'

Formerly it was the custom to plant the apples and pears in hedgerows. This, while it certainly added to the picturesqueness of the country, did not tend to produce good fruit, as the trees were never manured and seldom pruned. This habit is largely dying out; fruit trees are now usually planted in orchards, standards in pasture, bush fruit on arable land.

A considerable number of cherries are grown in some parts of the county, but this is not by any means universal; and if Nash's statement is correct that two or three tons were often sold in Worcester market before five o'clock on a Saturday morning, the sale in the Worcester market must have fallen off since his time.

From various statements in old writers, and also from the names of fields, it would seem that in the fourteenth and fifteenth centuries vines were

[1] Robert of Gloucester, *Met. Chron.* (Rolls Ser.), i. 10.

[2] *Archæologia*, xxxv. 328.

cultivated to a considerable extent in the county. The Vineyard is a field name of fairly common occurrence in Worcestershire.

The sessions records show that tobacco was never cultivated to any extent in the county. Under the Stuarts the parish constables in the presentments had to make a return of the quantity of tobacco grown in each parish; almost invariably the returns say 'No tobacco is grown.'

A special cultivation which has increased to some extent in certain parts of the county quite away from the market gardening districts is that of the potato. Round Hartlebury and the Kidderminster district large quantities of potatoes are annually grown. Neither flax nor hemp is grown in the county, in fact in many old leases their cultivation was expressly prohibited. The special cultivation most carried on is that of hops. It is not clear when they were first grown in Worcestershire. They are said to have been introduced into England in the reign of Henry VIII.; but beyond a passing mention at the time of the Civil War, there is but little evidence of this cultivation existing to any extent before the beginning of the eighteenth century. In 1710 a duty was placed on hops, and at that time the cultivation was well established. Up to 1886 the acreage of hop land did not increase very much, as any new hop land was subject to an extraordinary tithe, paid by the cultivator, which might reach a very high figure. Since the passing of the Act (49 and 50 Vict. c. 54) repealing the right to levy any extraordinary tithe on new hop grounds, the area under hops has increased. At the present time in Worcestershire the land so cultivated is about 3,000 acres. Some kinds of hops have had their origin in the county, notably one known by the name of a Worcestershire parish 'Mathon.' Hops are mainly grown in the Teme valley and between the Teme and Severn; very few are found in the south and east of the county.

A large district in the south of the county, of which Evesham is the chief market, is mainly concerned in the production of fruit and vegetables; of late years a large trade is springing up in flowers, especially in wallflowers, 'gillies' as they are locally termed, but this trade is yet in its infancy. The great cultivation of the district, which has almost entirely grown up in the last thirty years, is fruit and market gardening.[1]

In 1872 the total number of landowners in the county was 21,804, possessing 441,060 acres, with a gross estimated rental of £1,685,736. Since then the rent of agricultural land has fallen greatly, and having regard to the assessments under the Agricultural Rates Act it is now not above £1,250,000

[1] See the special section on this subject in the article on Industries, p. 305.

FORESTRY

In common with most of the counties in England, Worcester has an interesting history with regard to the woodlands with which it was probably once densely covered, and more especially as regards the portions of these, as well as of the open lands afterwards adjoining them, which were subsequently brought under the forest laws.

As full details have elsewhere been given regarding the geological features and the botanical characteristics of the county, it is unnecessary to recapitulate them here. So far as concerns the conditions which enable us to form some opinion as to whether or not the county was originally thickly wooded no better idea can be given than the following quotations from the Rev. Dr. Treadway Nash's *Collections for the History of Worcestershire*, i. (1781), vii., Intro., in which he gives a description of the county which can still be fairly applied : 'Rich in grain and fruit, having fine pastures, all the necessaries of life, with many articles tending to promote an extensive trade and various manufactures which the industrious inhabitants are enabled to carry on by means of different rivers, some proper for the working of mills, and others for the conveyance of goods ; the air is soft, warm, and healthy, there being but few lakes and little boggy land ; the soil south of Worcester is mostly a rich clay or marl ; north of the city it is chiefly gravel or sand.'

These equable climatic conditions favourable to the cultivation of fruit on the red marl and rich loamy soil, and the fact that it still has a rainfall of about 25 inches annually, seem to justify the conclusion that before the historic period the whole of the valleys and hills of Worcestershire must have been thickly covered with woodland trees. The fertility of the land readily explains the fact that now, out of a total area of land and water amounting to 480,064 acres (of which 3,419 are water), only 19,188 acres, or about 4 per cent., are classifiable as woods and plantations, while 2,901 acres are mountain and heath land used for rough grazing ; while its comparative remoteness from the royal capitals of Winchester and London previous to and during the middle ages explains the reason of Worcester not receiving more attention than was the case with regard to the continuance of afforestation and the chase, large enough though the afforestations undoubtedly were at one time.

It is unnecessary to say much here as to the condition of the county with regard to woodlands in the early historic times, as information on such matters will be found in other parts of the history. It was no doubt at one time entirely covered with woods. During the Roman occupation of Britain most of the district now contained in Worcestershire was densely wooded. There was a Roman outpost at Worcester, but the Malvern hills were left to the Britons who had their strongholds on the heights. It was long before even the Anglo-Saxon invaders acquired dominion over the Severn valley, but it was at length incorporated in the Mercian kingdom. We know next to nothing about the extent of the woodlands during the Saxon and Danish times.

With the gradual clearance of the primeval woodlands and their enclosure for purposes of cultivation, the deer and other game which abounded in the former were driven back into the depths of the woods. Used first of all as common hunting-grounds, and furnishing much of the food of the people, these tracts in course of time became something like sanctuaries for the herds of wild cattle and wild boars, deer, and other animals of the chase. The hunting rights regarding deer were subsequently usurped by those who had gradually acquired the status of large landowners ; and later on the Saxon kings, as overlords, reserved to themselves this right of the higher chase in many tracts, which thus became 'royal hunting grounds,' or 'king's woods' (*silva regis*). Without being able to trace accurately the process of the formation of these and of the 'king's land' (*terra regis*) from the original folc-land, we only know that when Egbert became the first king of all England he was the overlord of many such 'royal hunting grounds' scattered throughout the different counties.

By the end of the Norman or very early in the Plantagenet period, Worcestershire contained the four forests, Ambreslie or Ombersley, Horewell, Feckenham with Pyperode or Pepperwood, Malvern with Cors, and also part of a fifth, the Forest of Wyre, the principal portion of which lay in Shropshire.

By the charter of the Forest exacted from the child king, Henry III., in 1217, it was provided that all districts which Henry II. had afforested, after being viewed, were to be forthwith disafforested. Ombersley and Horewell came under this category, for they were not ancient demesne of the crown. There seems, however, to have been some hitch in the proceedings with regard to these two Worcestershire tracts, for a special charter was granted by the king approving of both of them being perpetually disafforested in October 1229.[1]

Ombersley forest began at the north gate of Worcester, and extended along the banks of the Severn; it had originally formed part of the great forest of Wyre. Horewell forest began at the south gate, and extended along the eastern road to Spetchley and across the Avon.[2]

Feckenham forest on the east of the county was of considerable extent; a small portion of it overlapped into Warwickshire. In the twelfth and thirteenth centuries it was sometimes termed the forest of Worcester. According to a perambulation, *temp.* Edward I., when it had been reduced to its old proportions, this forest began at the Foregate, Worcester, passed to Beverburn, by Stowe to Bordesley, round by Evesham to Spetchley, and so to Sidbury.[3] The records that tell the history of this forest in the thirteenth and fourteenth centuries are considerable and voluminous. All that can here be attempted is to give a few of the more salient points that have not yet been chronicled.

Pleas of the forest of Feckenham were held at Worcester in 1262. The list of essoins or excuses for non-attendance (chiefly for the substantial cause of death) of those summoned to the pleas numbered upwards of eighty. Eight charter claims of privilege were admitted; the first being a grant of Henry III., in 1230, to the abbey of Bordesley, of wardships over the woods of 'Holowege,' 'Tuneshale,' and 'Tardebigg.' There were about forty venison presentments for killing or hunting fallow deer, the earliest going back to 1246. The fines imposed by the justices, ere the delinquent was released, varied from 2*s.* to 5 marks. In several cases, such as the taking of four does by the earl of Gloucester in 1250, the order of the king was pleaded. There were forty-eight vert presentments (illegal cutting of wood), the fines for which were mainly 12*d.*, but rising occasionally as high as 40*d.* The two agisters presented their agistment rolls from 1249, their total receipts were £9 8*s.* 7*d.* The escapes of the forest produced £6 17*s.* 2*d.* But by far the largest assets for the crown at these pleas were from the encroachments and enclosures recorded by the regarders of Feckenham and Pepperwood (Popperod). The first on the list of new assarts (that is since the last pleas) was the prior of Kenilworth; he was fined 26*s.* 4*d.* for 7 acres; the highest was John Dabetot, 48*s.* 10*d.* for 13 acres. There were also many half-mark fines for wood waste. The court sat from day to day for three weeks.[4]

Of the pleas of the forest of Feckenham and Pepperwood held at Worcester in 1270 the rolls are exceptionally full and interesting.[5] The Feckenham vert offences since the last pleas numbered about 150; the usual fine was 12*d.*; in twenty-three of these presentments an alibi was established. There were twenty-eight additional vert convictions in the king's park of Feckenham. Eight membranes are occupied with eighty-seven separate presentments for venison offences against the fallow deer, the majority of which are concerned with several offenders. Among them a charge occurs for hunting in the forest with the dogs of the prior of Studley, the prior being privy thereto. The assarts and purprestures, as disclosed by the regard, occupy the two last membranes.

The next pleas of Feckenham were held ten years later, namely in 8 Edward I.; the rolls of this eyre are also full and detailed.[6] They open with a list of thirty-seven officials, who could not be present through death. The venison presentments were again very numerous. The heaviest fine (£30) was that imposed on Sir Walter Beauchamp. On the feast of the Purification, 1271, Sir Walter, with two grooms and many of his servants, hunted in the forest with three greyhounds and bows and arrows; and on Thursday before Christmas of the same year he again hunted, killed a doe, and took it, without warrant, to his house at Alcester. The justices obviously apportioned the fines according to the position of the defendants; other fines at this eyre, for almost exactly similar offences, varied from £20 to 40*s.* The venison offences in the bailiwick of Pepperwood are entered separately. The vert offences and the enclosures and encroachments, both old and new, are fully set forth.

For Feckenham, as in other royal forests, the verderers were elected by the freeholders in county court in the same way as coroners; but the crown claimed the right to remove unqualified and incapable holders of that office. Thus Edward I. removed a Feckenham verderer in 1274, directing the sheriff to proceed to a new election.[7] Again in 1287 two verderers were removed, one on the ground of old age, and the other because he had been appointed a gaol-delivery justice at Worcester and had often to be there, and hence could not properly discharge his duty as a verderer.[8]

[1] Close, 13 Hen. III. m. 2.
[2] Cox, *Royal Forests of Eng.* 227.
[3] Cox, op. cit. 228.
[4] Forest Proc. Exch. T. of Receipt, No. 227.
[5] Forest Proc. Exch. T. of Receipt, No. 229; they cover ten long membranes closely written on both sides.
[6] Ibid. No. 231.
[7] Close, 2 Edw. I. m. 2.
[8] Ibid. 15 Edw. I. m. 4, 3.

The following are a few of the numerous references to this forest on the Patent and Close Rolls during the reign of Edward I. In 1289 Walter Beauchamp had a royal gift from Feckenham of four bucks, and William Beauchamp, earl of Warwick, one of twenty bucks.[1] Pardon was granted in 1290 to the bishop of Worcester and three others on a fine of 500 marks for venison and vert trespasses in this forest.[2] A pardon was granted about the same time to the prioress of Westwood for like offences.[3] In this year grant was made to Eleanor the king's consort, who held the forest by Edward's grant, to hold pleas of trespass of both vert and venison through her stewards every six weeks, and to take vert fines due for the same to her own use as well as all attachments of indicted persons and venison trespassers, provided that the latter were imprisoned at Feckenham, and there bailed against the next eyre of the justices.[4] In the same year Walter de Aylesbury, forester, was pardoned all venison trespasses on condition of surrendering his bailiwick in Feckenham forest.[5] A special commission had been appointed to inquire into the trespasses charged against various forest ministers, and this was one of the results. In 1293 liberty of hunting with dogs the hare, fox, badger, and wild cat in all parts of this forest outside the great covert was granted to James Beauchamp whenever he desired save in the fence month, provided he took none of the king's deer and did not hunt in the warren.[6] The king made a considerable sojourn at Feckenham in April 1301; during that visit he pardoned William de Staplehurst for taking a buck and carrying it away.[7]

On 30 April 1290 Gilbert de Clare, the Red Earl, earl of Clare, Hertford and Gloucester, married Princess Joan D'Acres, daughter of Edward I., and received as part of the honour of Gloucester a gift of the forest of Malvern together with the smaller forest of Cors adjoining it, which therefore at once became disafforested, and thenceforth ranked only as chases.

With regard to Malvern Forest about this time, we are told that 'This was also a forest belonging to the king, formerly so much overrun with wood as to be called by the monk of Malmesbury[8] a wilderness. It extended in length from the River Teme in the north to Cors Forest in the south, and from the River Severn on the east to the top of Malvern Hill on the west, where there is still to be seen the remains of a trench drawn on the narrow ridge of this steep hill to divide the possessions of the bishop of Hereford from the chase and to limit the two counties: made upon a great controversy that happened between that bishop and the earl of Gloucester soon after this forest had been given to him.'[9] This 'great controversy' was compromised by the earl agreeing to deliver a brace of bucks and a brace of does each year to the bishop and his successors at the palace of Kemsey, an agreement which was formally confirmed by the king. Having thus ceased to be forests, no mention is made of Malvern or of Cors during the perambulations held in 1299. About 1540, Leland[10] said that 'the Chase of Malvern is bigger than either Wyre or Feckenham, and occupiethe a greate parte of Malverne-hills. Great Malverne and Litle also is set in the Chase of Malverne. Malverne Chase (as I here say) is in length in some place a XX mile, but Malverne Chase doth not occupi all Malverne hills.' In an old deed of 1650 it was 'said to contain in Worcestershire 7,115 acres, besides 241 acres called the Prior's Land; in Herefordshire 619 acres; in Gloucestershire 103 acres.'[11] The perambulation of Feckenham forest made in 1299 recorded the boundaries as they had existed in Henry II.'s time, 'when in the beginning of his reign he enlarged the same, and afforested all the following manors, villages, and hamlets, with their woods and commons, to the great detriment of the owners thereof; To wit, etc.' It also recorded 'the antient and right bounds of this forest,' and stated what ought to remain forest and what ought to have been disafforested in terms of Henry III.'s Forest Charter.

'Soon after this perambulation this forest was reduced to its antient limits, and all the manors and villages above mentioned were disafforested, Bromssgrove, with its members, Gaynardeshull Socker in Cadeshulley, le Shepeleye, Totenhulle, Cherleford, Kernford, Letesfield, Bercote, and Barndley, which though without the antient limits, yet were continued to be forest because they were the king's domain.'[12]

There is a bundle of Feckenham forest inquisitions of various years in the reign of Edward III.[13] of which the following abstract of one of 1363 must suffice as an example.

At an inquisition taken 36 Edward III. of the forest of Feckenham the jury said—that the fallen oaks at Workewode were the king's; that the abbot of Alcester took pasture within the

[1] Close, 17 Edw. I. m. 4. [2] Pat. 18 Edw. I. m. 3. [3] Ibid. m. 32.
[4] Close, 18 Edw. I. m. 13. [5] Pat. 18 Edw. I. m. 13.
[6] Pat. 23 Edw. I. m. 13. [7] Pat. 28 Edw. I. m. 18.
[8] William of Malmesbury said that before the Conquest it was a wilderness thick set with trees, in the midst of which some monks who aspired to greater perfection retired from the priory of Worcester and became hermits. The enthusiasm spreading, their number increased to three hundred, when they formed themselves into a society of the order of St. Benedict, elected Alwin to be their prior, and founded a monastery in 1083.
[9] Nash, op. cit. p. lxix. [10] *Itinerary*, vii. 13. [11] Nash, op. cit. ii. 125.
[12] Nash, op. cit. p. lxvi. [13] Forest Pleas, Wygorn, No. 319.

forest bounds; that the wood of the hospital of Brokton, called Merelay, lay waste; that Alexander Foliott had made encroachment at Bradley on the ground of the bishop of Worcester; that the bishop of Worcester had two deerleaps in the park of 'Aludchuch'; that the earl of Warwick had his park of Bewdley fenced so high that the king's deer could have neither ingress nor egress; that the abbot of Bordesley had a less high fence enclosing his field of Knottynghill; that John Bagley, lieutenant of Gilbert Chastelyn, the queen's steward at Feckenham, took does, etc.; that John Bagley, who was neither a forester nor sworn minister, had made attachment, contrary to assise, of a fallen oak at 'Workwode'; that the king's foresters in the bailiwick of 'Barwe' ought to have board (prandium et pastum) at Knottynghill one day a week, of the manor of the abbey of Bordesley, and on another day of the week at Burtley, of the manor of Grumbold Pauncefoot, and on another of the rectory of Hanbury, and of a fourth day at 'Sheltewode' of the abbot of Bordesley; that the foresters of 'Workewode' had board at 'Tonshall' of the abbot of Bordesley; that the forester of 'Lekehey' had board at 'Katteshulle' of the prior of 'Diddeford,' but it was withdrawn in favour of the payment for the lawing of dogs.

In the year 1600 a special commission was issued by Elizabeth as to Feckenham forest, to inquire what wood and timber trees had been cut down and carried away during the past seven years, and by what warrant and at what price.[1] But the report is not extant.

That portion of Wyre Forest extending into Worcestershire in Henry III.'s time appears to have been a tract about four miles broad in the north of the county, lying to the west and north-west of Bewdley. All that is now left of these woodlands are the Bewdley Woods.

Through his marriage with one of Gilbert de Clare's daughters, Hugh de Spencer acquired possession of the chases of Malvern and Cors, as well as other estates, whence they descended by marriage to the earl of Warwick, and later on partly to the wife of Richard, duke of Gloucester, and partly to the wife of his brother George, duke of Clarence. As Richard III. had no issue, these estates were inherited by Edward Plantagenet, son of the duke of Clarence, and on his attainder by Henry VII. they reverted to the Crown.

A special inquiry was made in 1592 as to 'the spoyle of hir Maties woodes in Wyer Forest in the countie of Wigor,' during the past five years. The evidence of fifteen witnesses shows that there had been a good deal of illicit selling of timber by officials.[2]

In 1600 another commission was appointed to inquire concerning the pales of Bewdley Park. The report of the second of these commissions is extant; it was to the effect that the three miles of the pales of this park, rails, posts, gates, stiles, deerleaps, etc. were in utter ruin and incapable of keeping in the deer or keeping out other men's cattle; that the mill and the house in the park were also in great decay, and that ten timber trees would be required to repair the mill and the house, and forty-two for the pales, with £25 for iron work and other necessaries.[3]

In 1608 another survey was taken which showed that Wyre and Feckenham forests and wastes contained 12,520 sound and 25,900 decaying timber trees, 603 acres of coppice in lease and 447 acres unleased, while Bewdley Park had 1,887 sound and 2,265 decaying timber trees.

Though Malvern Chase was not formally re-afforested on its coming into the possession of Henry VII., and though no Justice in Eyre (the chief officer essential to a forest) was appointed to it, yet it seems from an ancient parchment (at that time in the possession of Edmund Lechmere, esq., and transcribed by Nash[4]) to have been governed by rules which were, save in name, practically equivalent to the forest laws. Both the chase and the lordship of Hanley were in the honour of Gloucester, to which special privileges had been accorded. It had its own court-baron held every three weeks, and its lordship law-day held once a year. The lord of Hanley lordship held all the royalties of Malvern Chase, appointed the four foresters and a ranger there, and had all windfall wood. The chief forester held the chase by a rent of an axe and a horn, and was bound to maintain himself and another forester mounted, and two walking foresters, to keep the chase. His emoluments in money and wood, &c., were definitely laid down even to certain hens at Christmas and certain eggs at Easter, and his powers and duties were also prescribed. No sheriff's writ or warrant could be served within the lordship. The foresters had power to arrest any felon or murderer and bring him before the chief forester, who could 'sit upon the said felons or murderers in judgment, after the form of the common law, at a place there called the Sweetoaks, within the said chase.' If such accused were found guilty by the jury summoned from the four nearest townships, then 'according to the royalties and customs of the said chase he shall give judgment, that his head shall be stricken off at the said Sweetoaks with a certain axe, whereby, with other services, the said chief forester holdeth his lands of the lord. And then the dead body shall be carried up to Malvern Hill, to a certain place there called Baldyatt, and there to be hanged upon a gallows, and not to be taken down without license of the chief forester.' And as in the case of forests, there were verderers, viewers (regarders), and riders, 'which by their tenures and holdings of

[1] Special Commissions, Q.R. 2,509.
[2] Ibid. 2,499.
[3] Ibid. 2,511.
[4] Op. cit. pp. lxxiii–lxxv.

their lands have power to ride and to peramble the grounds.' If the hedges were allowed to grow up higher than the armpit of the verderer who measured it, the owner of the land was to be fined. Twice every seven years the regarders had to supervise the 'hombling' or 'lawing' of dogs. 'And such dogs as are found that may or will not be drawen through a strap of 18 inches and a barley-corn in length and breadth, shall be hombled, viz., the further joint of the two middle cleas to be cut clean away. And the master or owner of the dogs shall be amerced in 3*s.* 1*d.*'[1]

The forest of Feckenham was disafforested by a deed dated 23 June 1629. In the preamble to this it is recorded how, on 11 July 1627, a commission under the great seal had been issued stating that 'for the improving of His Highness's revenue, and diminishing his charge,' and also 'for the benefit and ease of his loving subjects, His Majesty was resolved to disafforest, improve, and convert to His Highness's best profit, amongst other forests, His Majesty's forest of Feckenham in the county of Worcester.' Sir Miles Fleetwood was appointed commissioner to survey the forest and its soil and woods, to ascertain how much thereof belonged to the king, and how much to his subjects, to treat with the owners of the soil, woods, common or other interest, also 'to bargain and conclude with them, and every of them, and to allow them either in common or in severalty such parcels of the said forest, answerable in value for their said several and respective interests, either in fee simple or in fee farm, by lease or otherwise, in money or other recompense, as their several interests should require,' and then to 'apportion and set out in certainty and in severalty' the lands allotted to His Majesty and to the various other owners concerned. Apparently the only other landowner beside the king was Edward Leighton, esq., who was 'lord of the manor of Feckenham, in the farm, and lord of the manor of Hanbury,' and the disafforestation deed of 23 June 1629 decreed that he should :—

> 'have, hold and enjoy, to him and his heirs for ever . . . . . fourscore acres of land lying in Monkwood, within the manor of Hanbury, and also all the coppices . . . . . . within the manor of Feckenham, called Queen's Coppice, Rainger's Coppice, Timber Coppice, Fearfull Coppice, and Red Slough Coppice, containing by estimation three hundred and threescore acres, freed and discharged from His Majesty's game of deer ; and also freed and discharged for ever hereafter of and from all common and claim of any right and title of common whatsoever.'

But it is not recorded what extent of land was allotted as common land or what acreage remained forming part of the Crown property.

Thus the ancient forests of Worcester had ceased to exist in 1629, so that this county was not affected by the *Act for the Limitation of Forests* in 1640, when the angry Commons, tired of the vexatious oppression of the forest laws revived under Charles I. and of new afforestations made by him, determined that the limits and boundaries of the royal forests should, once and for ever, be what they were in 1622.

Except in name, however, and as lacking a Justice in Eyre, Malvern Chase long continued to be governed very much like the forests. Part of it was now domain land of the Crown, while the rest was burdened with rights regarding the deer. Courts were held which adjudicated on matters concerning the vert and the venison. Thus, among the orders recorded at the lordship law-day of Hanley in 1540, it was ruled 'that none of the inhabitants of Colwell do staff-drive any of their cattle into the chase further than the shire-ditch, on pain of 20*s.*,' and again that none of the inhabitants of Colwell or Mathon 'do cross any of the chase-wood growing on this side of the shire-ditch, over the hill, upon payment of 20*s.*' But according to a decree in the Court of Exchequer, dated 18 November, 1632, Charles I. had shortly before then taken similar steps with regard to Malvern Chase as had previously been applied to the forest of Feckenham for the separation and allotment of the lands belonging to different owners, and 'one-third part of the waste or commonable lands lying or being within the said forest or chase,' was allotted to the king and granted by him to Sir Cornelius Vermuyden on 12 May, 1631, while two-thirds were divided among the commoners, 'discharged from His Majesty's game of deer there and of and from the forest laws and the liberties and franchises of forest and chase'—for Charles I. had revived the right of afforestation throughout the kingdom and the abuses of the forest laws in order to gain money, though no formal re-afforestation of Malvern appears to have been made. The bishop of Hereford, Sir Thomas Russell of Strensham, Sir William Russell, bart., of Witley, John Horniold, esq., and others had appealed against the royal action and against a previous decree made in the Court of Exchequer, where they now appeared as 'some of the defendants for and concerning the late forest and chase of Malvern in the counties of Worcester, Hereford, and Gloucester.' It was now held by the Court that by their previous decree 'the King's Majesty hath actually, and in a legal way, under the great seal of England, disafforested and discharged the said late forest or chase, and discharged all and every the lands, tenements, and hereditaments, within the limits and bounds

[1] The legal question of Malvern Chase is discussed by Mr. Turner in *Forest Pleas*, cix–cxiii.

thereof, of and from the game of deer, and the laws, franchises, and officers of forest and chase according to the purport and true meaning of the said decree.' Accusations were laid in the Star Chamber 'against the said Sir Thomas Russell, Sir William Russell, and divers others, for certain riots and other misdemeanours supposed to have been done in opposition and hindrance of the execution of the said decree, and of His Majesty's service concerning the said disafforestation'—which charges were denied by the defendants.

A serious dispute arose between Sir Cornelius Vermuyden, the grantee of the third part allotted to the Crown, and the two Russells, father and son, regarding the execution of the first decree of the Court of Exchequer, and to settle the matters at issue the case was remitted to the latter by an order of the Privy Council, dated 5 September, 1632, with instructions as to how the case was to be dealt with. Apparently Sir Cornelius Vermuyden wanted to have good land and well situated, and this was not what the Russells and others had agreed to in bargaining with Sir Robert Heath as His Majesty's Attorney-General. The result was a decree that Vermuyden's grant of the king's one-third share should be 'not of all of the best sort of land, but good and bad proportionately,' that the contracts made 'with several mean lords of manors' with regard to common should be satisfied out of this royal one-third, and that it should be divided and fenced from the other two-thirds. But apparently the newly-formed estate thus alienated in 1631 by grant at a yearly rental of ten pounds soon passed from the grantee, Sir Cornelius Vermuyden or his heirs, into the hands of Sir Nicholas Strode of the Inner Temple, because among the private Acts of 1664 was *An Act for Confirmation of the Enclosure and Improvement of Malvern Chase* (16 Car. II., cap. 5), in which he applied for and obtained an enactment that the 'decree so made for the division, enclosure, and disafforestation of the said forest and chase of Malvern, and all proceedings had thereupon, or in pursuance thereof, shall be ratified, confirmed, and allowed, and shall be good, effectual, and binding in law, against the King's Majesty, his heirs and successors, and all the respective lords, freeholders, copyholders, tenants, inhabitants, commoners, etc. . . any law, custom, or usage to the contrary in any wise notwithstanding.'[1]

The portion of Wyre Forest situated in the north of the county was apparently dealt with in much the same manner, for the lordship of Bewdley was the only part held under the Crown. It was granted to William Herbert, earl of Pembroke, and in 1674 the leasehold interest under the Crown of the manor of Bewdley was bought by Sir Francis Winnington, a successful lawyer, who purchased a reversionary grant for ninety-nine years after Herbert's tenure terminated.

The existing woodlands of the county of Worcester, aggregating 19,188 acres in 1895, contain no lands belonging to the Crown, but are entirely included in the estates of private landowners, the chief of whom are the earl of Dudley (Witley Court), the earl of Coventry (Croome Court), and Earl Beauchamp (Madresfield). Except this bald statement as to total acreage for the county no statistics have ever been published or are yet available as to the extent of the woodlands on the various estates, or regarding the acreage of the oak and the other highwoods, copses, and coppices throughout the county.

Most of the wooded tracts are to be found towards the northern part of the county. In the south and south-east there are but few large woods, though shady belts of woodland fringing the streams that come down from the uplands are sometimes connected with large wooded areas, as in the case of Ufmore Wood. Among the most extensive and interesting of the compact blocks are the Randans and Pepperwood, the ancient Pyperode which once formed part of Feckenham Forest, extending for about three miles from south-west to north-east near Bromsgrove, and the Bewdley Woods, which formed part of Wyre Forest. The former consist mostly of the typical English copse-woods; while the latter, though also consisting mostly of oak, contain few large trees owing to there being a good market for the wood as soon as it reaches pole-size. Many of the ridges along the valley of the Severn in the middle of the county are well covered with trees and underwood, and all over Worcestershire the small-leaved elm is one of the most characteristic features among the hedgerow timber, while the fences are often composed in part or in whole of holly, more especially on limy soil.

Among the objects of special arboricultural interest in Worcestershire are five celebrated oak trees. The 'Cowley Oak,' called 'Cowley's Oke' in an old manuscript survey of Malvern Chase in 1633, is the most conspicuous tree there for size and spread of bough. In 1893 it measured 27 feet in girth at 3 feet above the ground.[2] On rising ground a little way off the Tenbury and Bromyard Road in Kyre Park stands the 'Gibbet Oak.' This is supposed to have derived its name from having been used in the time of the Wars of the Roses for the hanging of spies and traitors, and two huge limbs extending at right angles to the stem, some 8 or 9 feet from the ground, seem well adapted for such a purpose. In 1893 it girthed 24 feet at 5 feet from the ground. The

[1] The best account of Malvern Chase is that which appeared in *Jour. of Forestry*, vol. v. by Mr. Edwin Lees.

[2] John Smith, in *Trans. of Royal Scottish Arboricultural Soc.* xiii. (1893), 45.

other three are all pollard oaks and extraordinary specimens of the ‘burring’ which results from lopping time after time. They are known as the ‘Great Burr Oak,’ the ‘Old Pollard Oak,’ and the ‘Devil's Oak.’ The first of these stands on the banks of the River Teme in the parish of Leigh, about one mile west of Bransford Bridge, and had in 1893 a circumference of 20 feet measured at 3 feet above the ground. But it has only a very short bole in consequence of the lopping. The ‘Old Pollard Oak’ stands in a field near the Severn, in the southern part of Malvern Chase, and has a girth of 17 feet at 3 feet over the ground. It has now horizontal limbs stretched out in a curious manner. The ‘Devil's Oak’ stands in a hedge by the side of the road leading to Sherrard's Green, below Great Malvern. Although it has a grotesque and fantastic appearance, yet its name does not arise from this circumstance, but from the fact of some sweeps being seen to emerge one misty autumn morning from its cavity, within which they had been taking shelter from the discomfort of a damp fog. It may perhaps be worth while remarking here that many of the celebrated oaks throughout England are considerably larger in girth than any of the most remarkable in Scotland. But the former are very often hollow, as the result of being pollarded long ago; while the latter are usually sound and solid, in consequence of their not having been topped and lopped in such manner.

SPORT ANCIENT AND MODERN

HUNTING

THE records of fox-hunting in Worcestershire at the beginning of the nineteenth century are very meagre. There does not appear to have been any recognized county pack until Mr. John Parker assumed the mastership about 1829. We believe that Lord Foley had hounds at Witley and hunted the country between the Severn and the Teme to the north of Worcester, because we find that a pack of good-looking hounds owned by a Mr. Adams of Ludlow about this time was purchased from Lord Foley, the then owner of Witley Court. This pack it was that formed the foundation of the Ludlow pack, always well known for its good appearance as well as for its prowess in the field. Mr. Parker, as we have said, was the first recognized master of the Worcestershire pack, and he was a leading character of his day. As a tenant farmer on the estate of Mr. Berkeley of Spetchley Park, he began with a pack of harriers, and although unaided by much in the way of subscription, he showed himself such an eminent sportsman that his hounds were ere long transformed into foxhounds, and the whole of Central Worcestershire was thrown open to him. 'Nimrod' describes Mr. Parker as a very fine horseman as well as huntsman, and a wonderful performer on moderate horses. He is noted as the man who fought the last duel that took place in the county, his opponent being Mr. Russell, afterwards Sir John Pakington, subsequently Lord Hampton and a Cabinet Minister. Mr. Parker also for a time, it is believed, hunted the Old Berkshire country. He spent all his means on hunting and neglected his farm, with the result that he died a pauper in the County Asylum at Powick. There exists an excellent picture of him and his hounds, the work of Woodward, a Worcestershire artist who was famous in his day, many of his works being still highly valued in the county. Woodward was especially happy in his portraits of horses.

When John Parker in 1836 resigned the mastership of the hunt he had practically created, hunting came almost to a standstill for want of subscriptions. Captain Chandler, however, was prevailed upon to take up the country, which he hunted until 1845, when further difficulty occurred; and for one season a committee under the chairmanship of the Hon. Dudley Ward (afterwards Lord Dudley) came to the rescue. Things took a turn for the better in 1847, when Mr. John Russell Cookes of Orleton undertook the mastership. He was a very popular landowner and a good sportsman, who bred and rode his own horses, which were usually thoroughbred. He had a coadjutor in Mr. John Watson of Waresley, who although not joint master was a thoroughgoing helpmate, and seldom was missing at a meet. In 1850 Mr. Cookes retired in favour of Major Clowes, another popular local sportsman. The latter carried on the mastership for four years until 1854, when Mr. Cookes again took the reins for two years, to be joined by Major Clowes in 1857. This happy partnership lasted for seven years, until 1864. In 1865 Mr. Harry Foley Vernon, now Sir Harry Foley Vernon, of Hanbury Hall near Droitwich, entered on the mastership. He was joined the following season by Mr. Henry Allsopp of Hindlip Hall (afterwards created Lord Hindlip). This partnership of influential landowners did much for the fortunes of the county pack, and lasted three years, when the late marquis of Queensberry came in as master for two seasons and hunted the hounds himself. On his retirement in 1872 a division of the county was decided upon. The earl of Coventry, who ever since he had come of age had been a leading spirit in the sport, proposed a friendly division of the county—he taking the western side, and calling it the Croome country after his seat, Croome Court near Upton-upon-Severn; and Mr. Henry Allsopp resuming the mastership of the eastern side, and retaining the title of the Worcestershire Hounds. The dividing line starting from Worcester city ran nearly north and south, the West Midland Railway and Spetchley being roughly the boundary towards the south, and the river Teme from Powick to Knightsford Bridge towards the north. The Worcestershire took all to the east of the line thus drawn, including the Droitwich country and both banks of the Severn to its junction with the Teme at Powick, and the Cotheridge and Martley country, including Witley to the east of the river Teme. The Croome country, including Spetchley and Grafton as far as Evesham and both sides of the Severn from Powick to Upton-upon-Severn, extended to the Malvern Hills and Suckley on the north, to the Bredon Hills on the south, and Strensham near Tewkesbury on the west. A fairer division could not have been mapped out, and thus the countries remain to the present day.

The old Worcestershire of John Parker's two days a week, now provided six days' sport a week and often eight.

Of the new Worcestershire Mr. Henry Allsopp held the mastership for only one season, being succeeded in 1874 by Mr. Frederick Ames, who, with the exception of the years 1877 to 1879, when Mr. Charles Morrell was master, carried on the country until 1896. To Mr. Frederick Ames the hunting men and women of Worcestershire owe a deep debt of gratitude, for during his mastership the pack and country reached the zenith of their career. Not only was Mr. Ames a most painstaking master in the kennel, but an indefatigable worker in the field and popular with farmers and landowners alike. His reign saw many seasons of fine sport, increased subscriptions, and large fields of horsemen, while in this period the Worcestershire pack claimed recognition at the Peterborough Hound Show. In 1897 the earl of Dudley succeeded Mr. Ames in the mastership, appointing Major J. O. Trotter as his field master. The latter, a fine horseman and good sportsman, unfortunately died in 1899; but the earl still carried on the mastership until the close of the season 1901–2, when, being appointed Viceroy of Ireland, he was succeeded by Mr. C. R. Mills. It is needless to say that the fortunes of the hunt did not suffer in any way during Lord Dudley's mastership. A first-rate stud of hunt horses filled the stables at Fernhill Heath, where it should have been mentioned that kennels had been built at the expense of the country about twenty years before, and with an excellent huntsman in Will Shepherd, who had been engaged in 1888 by Mr. Ames, hunting was carried on in first-rate style, attracting votaries from the neighbourhood of Birmingham and Staffordshire. It was in this era, about the time of the mastership of Major (afterwards Colonel) Clowes that the County Hunt Club was formed. The club has ever since held its annual ball early in January. The uniform of the hunt is a pink coat with blue collar.

The Croome country, which as already said was formed out of the division of the old Worcestershire country in 1872, was known as 'the earl of Coventry's until 1882, when the earl handed it over to Mr. Lort Phillips, a well-known Pembrokeshire sportsman, who however only held it for one season, being succeeded by an equally good sportsman in Mr. E. Walter Greene, a native of Suffolk, where his father was for many years a master of staghounds. Mr. Greene successfully hunted the country until 1889, when Mr. E. H. Lawrence Walker became master. In 1893 Mr. A. B. Wrangham succeeded Mr. Greene and held office until 1899, when the Coventry family, always the chief supporters of the pack, again took it, the Hon. Henry T. Coventry, second son of the earl, becoming master in 1899 and continuing until 1901, when he was joined by Mr. G. Dudley Smith. The Croome country is about 20 miles square, and embraces the Bredon Hill on the south, to Malvern and Suckley and Bransford on the north, taking in a great portion of the vale of Evesham as well as that of the Severn west of Worcester. It is a small flying country, but in the neighbourhood of Evesham and Pershore is rather cut up by the spread of market gardens. Owing, however, to the popularity of the earl of Coventry and his family, barbed wire has been well kept down, and foxes are plentiful.

As regards the Worcestershire country itself, it should be noted that it has undergone considerable change during the last fifty years. Much of the plough country on the eastern side, known as Hanbury Forest, and around Droitwich has, owing to the decline in the price of corn, been laid down in grass or remained uncultivated. This has improved its scenting and riding aspects, while on the other hand the increase of fruit-culture and hop-growing has curtailed much old hunting ground. The increase of building and population round Bromsgrove, Redditch, and Droitwich, too, has prejudicially affected the country. Railways have not materially injured it, and wire, although impossible to keep down altogether, is not of sufficiently frequent occurrence to interfere with hunting, except in suburban areas. The coverts which for the last sixty years have been the best preserved and good for sport are the Hindlip coverts—Goosehill and Broughton, the property of Colonel Beancroft—the Hanbury and Bentley woods, Mr. Haywood's gorse, Westwood, and Oakeley Wood—the Trenches, and Crowle Brick Kiln, Bishop's Wood, and the Elmley Lovett coverts, as well as Lord Windsor's coverts at Hewell and Barnt Green. On the western side of the Severn, the earl of Dudley's domain at Witley, Holt Spinneys, Shrawley, Monkswood, Cotheridge, and Ankerdine Hill have done well for the hunt.

It should be mentioned that three packs of foxhounds whose kennels are in adjoining counties hunt on the borders of Worcestershire. The Albrighton hunt in the neighbourhood of Stourbridge, over the Clent Hill and Church Hill; the Ludlow have dipped into the county at Tenbury, Eastham, and Shakenhurst, where the Wicksted family have always been great supporters of fox-hunting; the Ledbury hunt on the Herefordshire side, Eastnor Castle, Colwall, and West Malvern. It should also be mentioned that Mrs. Cheape, popularly known as 'The Squire,' since 1892 has kept a very brilliant pack of harriers at Bentley, between Redditch and Bromsgrove. In the year 1901, when Mr. Frank Phillips died, the Willenhall Harriers, with which, for eleven seasons, he had hunted at his own charge the country round Coventry, were given up. Mrs. Cheape then increased the number of her hunting days from 5 a fortnight to 4 a week, and till 1904, hunted the Willenhall territory in addition to her own.

Among the runs enjoyed by the Worcestershire Hounds, that which took place on Lord Hindlip's birthday, 19 February, 1886, deserves mention. It was the custom to meet on that occasion at Hindlip Hall, where a breakfast was given. At least 400 riders mustered in the field, but not a tithe saw the end of that great day's sport, and many were the winter bathers in Crowle Brook. The late Mr. John Watson of Waresley wrote the following account of the run at the time :—

'On 19 February, 1886, the Worcestershire Hounds met at Hindlip—a vast crowd assembled to meet Lord Hindlip. The small coverts in the park contained no fox, so a move was made to Oakeley Wood, which was also blank, and Hazelwood was equally unfortunate. Goosehill next claimed attention, and though the hounds had been twice through it on the 15th, two foxes were afoot as soon as the hounds entered this fine wood, of which Mr. Beancroft may be as proud as of his beautiful old hall of the seventeenth century. Both foxes broke on the Hanbury side. The hounds ran to the Church Laurels, then round the north side of the park, crossing at the end of the deer park, and disturbing another fox in the belt. Denton went on with the fox he had been running all the time, but several couples of hounds followed the lately-disturbed fox. The hunted fox ran over Hunting-trap Farm, leaving Goosehill close on his left, straight to the Trenches, through it, and ran the beautiful grass meadows on the other side of Crowle Brook to below Crowle Thrift, where he crossed, but did not go to the Thrift, preferring to go down wind. Thus leaving Churchill Wood close on the left, he went to Spetchley Station, then straight on down the flat for Botany Bay, when a fresh fox jumped up, some distance behind the pack, who were too intent upon the fox before them to notice all the shouting from the railway and elsewhere after the fresh fox. The hunted fox held on as if for the turnpike road to Stoulton, but left it on his right, and ran on by Wolverton's farm, crossing the railway near Hand's Brake and the Pershore turnpike road into Mr. Whittaker Wilson's park. He was run into there. When taken from the hounds he stood as if he had not a joint in his body. Time, one hour fifty minutes; distance from Hanbury Church to Caldwell, eleven and a half miles on the ordnance map, to which must be added the distance from Goosehill to Hanbury, and allowance for deviations would make some sixteen to seventeen miles. Unfortunately the brooks and the pace, though a very fine flat line and mostly grass, allowed but few to see this real good fox eaten at ten minutes to four.'

The hon. secretaries of the hunt, who have worthily served their county, have been Mr. Woodhouse, Mr. Price Hughes, and Mr. F. W. Morton, the last-named of whom resigned in 1904 to be succeeded by Mr. Stanley Webb.

RACING

The earliest obtainable record of racing in this county refers to August 1758, when a programme was provided for three days' racing at Worcester.[1] The meeting, however, can hardly be called a success, as there was in fact only one contest, in which a horse called 'Juniper' was victorious. For another event a bay horse belonging to a Mr. Giles started alone, and after that 'there was no horse present to run.' In 1762 there were three races at Worcester in as many days. In 1763 there was like sport. In 1767 there were two races for which only five horses competed. In 1769, the first year of the publication of the *Racing Calendar* as edited by Messrs. Weatherby, Worcester was the only recognized place for race meetings in the county. In this year Mr. Sidebotham's 'Cyrus' won the principal race. In 1771 the sport was of a very similar character. In 1784 occurs the first mention of races at Bromsgrove in addition to Worcester. At the former place there were three Plates of £50, two of which were won by Mr. Thornton's 'Copperbottom,' while at the Worcester Meeting there were only two events, no horses being entered for the third. In 1793 Tenbury was the scene of a meeting, but only one race was run, the victor being 'Eclipse.' At Worcester 'Little Flyer' was the best horse of that year.

We must now pass on to 1822, when the Worcestershire Stakes had grown in importance, there being now a sweepstakes of 10 sovs. each. Lord Stamford's 'Peter Lely' was the winner, beating 'Master Henry.' There was also a Gold Cup, which was won by the same horse. It may be noted that the celebrated horse 'Euphrates,' who started in ninety-five races and won thirty-eight of them, ran for the Gold Cup

[1] It is well to bear in mind that at this period races were run in heats.

at Worcester five times between 1823 and 1829, and gained it twice, being second on the other three occasions. In 1830 the races were further improved, and there was a Produce Race of 50 sovs. each, while the Worcestershire Stakes was now 20 sovs. each with 20 sovs. added. It was won by Mr. Beardwood's 'Independence.' The Gold Cup of 100 gs. was won by Mr. Ormsby Gore's 'Hesperus.' The Autumn Meeting of that year consisted of only two races. There is no doubt that at the end of the eighteenth century the intervals between the heats that made up the solitary race of the day were chiefly occupied in cock-fighting.

The racing records of Worcestershire since 1837 are somewhat voluminous. In that year there were five places of sport in the county, viz., Dudley and Tipton, Stourbridge, Tenbury, Upton-upon-Severn, and Worcester. The Dudley Meeting fell through about 1850 owing to the spread of the mines and the ironworks. Stourbridge continued to flourish, and was very popular up to 1858, but the increasing number of houses eventually swept away the course. Tenbury existed as a little country meeting till 1857, and sport has since been carried on by a small steeplechase meeting over a new course on the meadows near the Swan Hotel. The races at Upton-upon-Severn were held in September, and were on a small scale. In 1837 only three were run, one of which was for a stake of 2 sovs. each, with £10 added. In 1853 they seem to have fallen to a still lower level, as only two horses ran in the first race. The second was a 'walk over,' while the third was a Hack Stakes of 10*s.* each with a Silver Cup added, for which six horses competed. This meeting died a natural death, but was revived in 1870 with some success.

The Worcester Races, held on the Common Ground of Pitchcroft, close to the city, on the banks of the Severn, have always been popular and well supported. Ever since 1837 there have been two meetings a year, one in the summer for flat racing, and another in late autumn for steeplechasing. The jumping course at Worcester up to 1880 was one of the finest in England, and always attracted some of the best cross-country horses in training. Since that time, owing to the natural fences being done away with, the course has become more circumscribed and artificial, and consequently the Autumn Meeting has to some extent degenerated. A few years ago the Corporation obtained an Act of Parliament giving them complete control over the ground on which the races are run, and the land has now been fenced and leased for racing purposes to a committee of townspeople who own the grand stand. A charge for admission is now made, thus creating a gate-money meeting. The ground is perfectly flat, and in all races exceeding a mile the course is a figure of 8. Floods have been known to stop the sport.

Thanks to the patronage which has been extended to the Worcester Meetings by the earl of Coventry ever since he came of age in 1858, sport has been of a higher standard than was the case at an earlier period. In 1837 only seven horses competed for three races on the first day,[1] but on the second sixteen horses competed in four races, including the Gold Cup of 3 miles, which was won by a celebrated grey horse called 'Isaac,' whose portrait can still be found in many a parlour and study in the county. The growth and improvement in the Summer Meeting at Worcester can be judged by the returns of the sport for 1853 as compared with 1837. In 1853 there were eleven races, to which £350 added money was given, and no less than eighty-six horses competed. In the Worcestershire Stakes of that year, to which for the first time £100 was added, there were twenty-three starters. The improvement continued, and in 1870 there were fourteen races in the two days and £730 added money, competed for by seventy-eight horses. In that year Mr. E. Brayley won the Worcestershire Stakes with his four-year-old 'Chivalry,' by 'Rinaldo,' carrying 7 st. 10 lb. The Coventry Stakes, an important two-year-old race in those days, was instituted by the earl of Coventry. It was a sweepstakes of 10 gs. each with £100 added, and was won that year by Mr. George Payne's 'Farewell,' by 'Brother to Bird on the Wing,' which beat seven others. It was worth £260.

These were the halcyon days of the Worcester Meeting, for in the Autumn Meeting of that year no fewer than sixty-one horses ran for the flat races, not reckoning the steeplechases and hurdle races which were run at the same meeting and were very well supported.

In the early years of Queen Victoria's reign there were several influential residents who bred racehorses. The late Mr. Watkins at Ombersley had the stallion 'Distin,' and bred several good horses. Mr. Russell Cookes also was successful in a small way. Mr. John Watson for a great many years had a large breeding stud at Elmley Lovett, and afterwards at Waresley. Among his best sires were 'Blinkhoolie,' 'Cathedral,' 'Albert Victor,' and 'Chevron,' and probably the best horses he bred were 'Wisdom' in 1873, 'Geheimniss,' who won the Oaks in 1892, 'Christmas Carol,' and 'Martley,' which were placed in the Derby. Another good horse was 'Buckingham,' which was unfortunately disqualified for the Derby by the death of his nominator in 1893. Mr. Watson sold his yearlings annually at Doncaster, and always realized big prices. He was a first-rate judge and a thorough master of the science of breeding, but he never raced himself. Mr. W. E. Everitt, of Finstall Park near Bromsgrove, also kept for several years a stud of

[1] The system of running races in heats had before that date been abandoned.

thoroughbreds. His best sires were 'Paul Jones,' 'Cardinal York,' for whom he gave a long price, 'Martley,' and 'Knight of Malta.' This stud never turned out anything first-rate, but Mr. Everitt ran several that won races. 'Paul Jones' unluckily died prematurely, and 'Cardinal York' failed to beget any stock as good as himself. The earl of Coventry never went in largely for breeding at Croome, though he possessed two good stallions in 'Tim Whiffler' and 'Umpire,' and the celebrated brood mare 'Virago'; he was, however, fortunate in two mares of his own breeding, each of which in turn won the Grand National Steeplechase at Liverpool. These were 'Emblem' and 'Emblematic.' They were trained on the confines of the county by the late Edwin Weaver of Bourton-on-the-Hill.

The earl of Dudley once contemplated the formation of a breeding establishment for thoroughbreds on his Witley property near Woodhampton, but he relinquished the idea and gave up racing when he took to hunting and politics. Mr. James Best of Holt Castle has of recent years kept a few choice thoroughbred mares, from which he has succeeded in breeding some good racehorses, such as 'Golden Crown,' 'Gang Way,' 'Surety,' and 'Worcester.' Some of these he raced himself, and 'Worcester' won the City and Suburban Stakes at Epsom in 1896. Many yeomen farmers of this county have bred good horses. Mr. Edmund Herbert of Powick, a leading tenant of the earl of Coventry, was one of the earliest. Then there were the Myttons, whose 'Flash in the Pan' was the winner of the Chester Cup in 1864. The Walkers of Knightwick and the Notts of the Tenbury district always bred good steeplechasers. Mr. W. J. Halford bred the celebrated horses 'Fisherman' and 'Leamington' in the county. Mr. S. Darling, the father of the present trainer Sam Darling, was a Worcestershire man in this era, and both he and his son trained horses on Defford Common near Upton-upon-Severn. The well-known and very successful jockeys of their day, Tom Calder and F. Allsopp, were Worcestershire lads.

During the last twelve years some steeplechases have been established under the auspices of the Worcestershire Hunt at Crowle, over a course that formerly was used for the same purpose, and where point-to-point races are now held. All the farmers are entertained at luncheon, and a very jovial function is carried out in the interest of sport. Mention must be made of Mr. F. Webb, who acted for many years as clerk of the course at Worcester and was a well-known and much-respected sportsman, and of Mr. E. Bentley, a leading auctioneer of Worcester, who owned and ran some good horses, winning the Worcestershire Stakes in 1882 with 'Charaxus.' Mr. Bentley held an annual sale of thoroughbred stock at Worcester during the Summer Meeting. The Hon. Henry Coventry, the earl's second son, has during the last few years taken charge of his father's race and steeplechase horses, and trains them with much success in Croome Park as well as on Defford Common. On the borders of the county at Bromyard racing was carried on successfully for about a century until ten years ago, when owing to a dispute with the lord of the manor the downs became no longer available. Redditch, on the borders of the county adjoining Warwickshire, for many years enjoyed a race meeting which extended over two days, when the stakes, although small, were eagerly competed for. This was a favourite battle-ground with old Mr. Thomas Parr of Wantage. The Redditch fixture dropped out of the Calendar in 1870.

There is still in existence part of an old course on the common at Malvern Wells, but there is no record in the Calendar of races having been held there in modern times. They probably consisted of pony and galloway races, which were always popular at Malvern.

COURSING

In the earlier days of coursing in England of which we have any records, Worcestershire does not appear to have been celebrated for its breed of greyhounds or for its coursing meetings. The first meeting recorded in Thacker's *Annual* took place in 1841 at Ombersley in the park of Lord Sandys. A sixteen dog stake comprised the programme, and the meeting was judged by Mr. Wm. Butler Best, of Kidderminster, an amateur who, besides keeping a kennel of greyhounds, hunted a pack of harriers. This meeting was continued annually for some time, being judged on several occasions by Mr. John Hatton. In 1842 the first meeting at *Holt Castle*, about six miles from the 'Faithful City,' was held, when a thirteen dog stake and two matches were run off, Mr. William Webb, who some years previously had owned a strong kennel, being the field steward, and Mr. John Hatton the judge. The ground at Holt was principally arable land, the enclosures being large and intersected by low quickset fences which could not stop any greyhound or very moderate hunter. The land was at that time farmed by Mr. Pickernel, one of the leading agriculturists of the county as well as a good sportsman. Hares were always in abundance, and ran stoutly, affording excellent trials.

Mr. A. Bennet, who died a year or two ago, judged this, and subsequent meetings for some years from 1855, besides many others in the county. He was of course a professional judge. Charles Presdee, a Worcester professional slipper, was also engaged at most of the meetings in this and the adjoining counties. He was a good slipper, though scarcely to be compared with his contemporary, the celebrated Tom Raper, who at that time officiated at the Waterloo Cup and most of the big meetings in Lancashire and elsewhere. Presdee's great failing was a bad temper, and he was not always kind to his dogs. Although coursing has declined in the county, one of the most prominent performers with the slips is W. Souch, a Worcester man who resides at Sidbury near that city. Souch officiated in the Waterloo Cup of 1904.

A second meeting was held annually on the same estate at Holt Fleet; this was run principally on meadows adjoining the river Severn. The Holt Castle Meeting, held amid beautiful surroundings, was always the best patronized, and in the latter end of the fifties a handsome tea-service was given for the winner of the principal stake, which was secured by Mr. E. Watton's 'Woodman' (by 'Larriston'—'Fly'). Mr. Watton had some very good greyhounds, but some few years after the success referred to gave them up, as well as his business, to take charge of the kennel of Mr. C. W. Lea, who had expended a large sum of money in greyhounds, and for some years ran strong teams at most meetings of any note in England. He was the chief of the firm of Lea and Perrins, of Worcestershire sauce renown. Both Mr. Lea and his trainer 'Teddy' Watton are now dead. Mr. Warwick judged this meeting in 1862, and Heritage was slipper.

At the latter end of the fifties and beginning of the next decade, coursing meetings in the county were numerous, and the *Worcester Club* sprang into existence, the President being Sir E. A. H. Lechmere, Bart. Among the patrons who gave permission for coursing to take place over their estates were the earl of Dudley, earl of Beauchamp, earl of Coventry, The Right Hon. Lord Sandys, and Messrs. R. Berkeley, W. Berkeley, and W. Acton. Mr. W. Webb, who kept the Bell Hotel, Worcester, was the field-steward, and Mr. G. Finch, solicitor, hon. sec. Patrons of the sport who gave permission for other than club meetings were Lord Windsor, Sir H. F. Vernon, Bart., Colonel Rushout, and Messrs. C. Wicksted, E. V. Wheeler, and Lambert Nicholls. The following were the principal meetings held:—Holt Castle, Holt Fleet, Ombersley, Croome Park, Spetchley, Pull Court, Hundred House, Mamble, Newnham Bridge, Burford (Tenbury), Hanbury, Hagley, Droitwich, Grimley, Cotheridge, Evesham, Hewell, Bellbroughton, Chaddesley Corbett, Wolverton, Pensham, Somerville Aston, and Stone, near Kidderminster. At the latter place existed what was presumably the first club in the county—only a small affair, which came to an end after the formation of the Worcester Club. The late Mr. W. Butler Best had been one of the chief organizers of the Stone Meeting. The county cannot therefore boast of a very old club; though close by, in the bordering county of Salop, the Morfe Club was established in 1815, and counted one or two Worcestershire coursers among its members.

Unfortunately, after the passing of the Ground Game Act, nearly all the above meetings ceased to exist, and at the present time Hanbury, which lies between Droitwich and Bromsgrove, is the only arena where annual meetings are held. Thanks to the kindness of Sir H. F. Vernon good sport can always be assured, hares being plentiful and affording good trials. The ground is chiefly arable, but the going is good with large fields divided by quickset fences.

At most of the meetings in the county the ground coursed over was of a mixed character, fallows with other arable lands. Driving the hares, unless out of turnips or a spinney, had not come into vogue. The land, however, throughout most of the county is light, perhaps the heaviest going being on the Tenbury side; though at Newnham Bridge, on the estate of the late Mr. E. V. Wheeler (an all-round sportsman), some splendid meadows on the side of the river Teme afforded always excellent sport. At Croome Park, the seat of the earl of Coventry, the coursing was chiefly on turf. The small meeting held annually at Mamble, where a cup was run for, was on the estate of the late Sir Edward Blount, Bart.; the enclosures of both arable and turf were rather small with strong fences; the soil also is a strong clay. Later, however, the venue was on the adjoining estate of the late Mr. Charles Wicksted of Shakenhurst.

Two of the most successful coursers in the county in the old days were Mr. William Webb of Worcester and Mr. Charles Randell of Charlbury, and it will only be necessary to mention one or two of their principal performers. A good greyhound of Mr. Webb's was 'War Eagle,' a black dog whelped 15 April, 1847, height 25 inches, weight 62 lb., bred by his owner. When 'War Eagle' was at stud, he was put at the low fee of five guineas, but now such a one would be at fifteen or twenty guineas. During his four seasons, 1848 to 1851, he won twenty-five courses and lost four. His running career came to an end 25 February, 1851, while running his second course in the Waterloo Cup, when he dislocated his fetlock joint in jumping a ditch. His performances took place over all kinds of country. Another wonderful greyhound in this respect was Mr. Randell's 'Riot' by 'Bedlamite' out of 'Black Fly,' whose weight, according to Mr. T. Jones's *Courser's Guide*, was 49½ lb. The following is a summary of her performances:—In 1854, as a puppy, she won five stakes and lost three, her principal wins being at Newmarket (24 dogs), Altcar (16 dogs), and Burneston (16 dogs). In 1855 she ran in six stakes, winning three, namely, Newmarket (16 dogs), Ashdown (36 dogs), and Kenilworth (32 dogs). In 1854 she won four times and ran in four other stakes, the principal wins being Amesbury (24), Kenilworth (28), and Selby (32). In 1857 and 1858 she won four stakes, finishing up with the Caledonian Cup of 32 dogs. Almost as celebrated was her brother 'Ranter,' who, according to the same authority, won twenty-seven courses and lost six, amongst his wins being the Waterloo Purse. Mr. Jones, in his remarks about this dog, says, 'The success of Mr. Randell's kennel at this time was most extraordinary, and much of the credit is due to old John Weaver who trained.' At the Newmarket Meeting, March, 1855, Mr. Randell won with every dog he brought from Worcestershire. Mr. W. D. Deighton, who resided in the city of Worcester at a rather later date, had a strong kennel of greyhounds, and for a time ran in partnership with Mr. George Finch, the hon. sec. of the club. Mr. Deighton held a nomination in the Waterloo Cup for a number of years, and in 1871 ran in the semi-final of the Cup with 'Deodora's Daughter,' a red bitch by 'Patent'—'Deodora,' who afterwards won the Uffington Cup at Ashdown Park in 1873. Another good open-country greyhound owned by Mr. Deighton was 'Oakball' by 'Accident'—'Dewdrop,' who won several good stakes at Ashdown and other meetings, making a total of thirty-eight courses won and nineteen lost. 'Oakball' afterwards became the property of Mr. Richard Till. Mr. C. W. Lea, before mentioned, had several useful greyhounds, though he never achieved anything very extraordinary. One of his best was 'Let Go,' a black-and-white dog by 'Clyto'—'Stylish Lady.' In 1886 he won the Gosforth St. Leger for puppies, five courses, and the Waterloo Purse. Another prominent courser at the same period was Mr. W. H. Smith of Kidderminster, who is still alive, but has practically given up public coursing, although he still holds a nomination in the Waterloo Cup. Some of his best greyhounds were 'Countess of Sapey,' 'Jenny Jones,' 'Donald O'Kane,' and 'Nopal,' who won Colonel North's Cup in 1892 and the de Grey Cup in 1891, both at the Yorkshire Club meetings. 'Nopal' was by 'Greentick' out of 'Neilson,' the latter being the property of Mr. Lambert Nicholls of Grimley, near Worcester. In 1896 he nominated the Irish dog 'Wolf Hill' in the Waterloo Cup, who ran up to 'Fabulous Fortune,' and in 1899 his own bitch 'Countess Udston' divided the Purse with 'Quite Bright.' He also divided the stakes, though not the event, with Colonel North's 'Fullerton,' by withdrawing 'Dear Belle' after an undecided event. Mr. Nicholls began public coursing about 1880 with a dog called 'Daily Telegraph,' given to him by Mr. Deighton. 'Daily Telegraph' won him three small stakes, and Mr. Nicholls then purchased 'Morning Star' and 'Naomi' ('Misterton'—'Coomassie') and later 'Prenez Garde' ('Ptarmigan'—'Gallant Foe'), with all of which he was successful. The last-named bred him, amongst others, 'Neilson,' about the best greyhound he ever had, who won the City of London Stakes at Kempton Park, the Bracelet at Four Oaks, and many other stakes. She bred also 'Northern Star,' who won the City of London Stakes, and was sold for £150, 'Nilson' and 'Nell Gwynne,' and a later litter in which were 'Harlington' and 'Duke McPherson,' the latter, as the property of Colonel North, running up in his first season to 'Burnaby' for the Waterloo Cup. In 1883 Mr. Nicholls purchased 'Royal Stag,' and won the £1,000 stake at Kempton Park with him. Mr. Nicholls has owned numerous other winners. He has still a strong kennel, and is a nominator for the Waterloo Cup. In the latter part of the seventies Mr. Miller Corbett of Kidderminster was one of the leading spirits. He sold 'Plunger' to Mr. James Hinks of Edgbaston, for whom he ran up to 'Honeywood' for the Waterloo Cup in 1880. Other celebrities of that time were Mr. W. Braithwaite, owner of that good bitch 'Witchery,' Mr. Thomas Jones of Dudley, author of the *Courser's Guide*, and Mr. Wagstaffe, who now lives at Matlock. The veteran Mr. J. Hinks above mentioned is also still alive, but has retired from public coursing.

Dr. Walsh ('Stonehenge'), who became editor of the *Field* in 1857, was a Worcester man, and at one time practised his profession in that city. Dr. Walsh was born in 1810 and died 12 February, 1888. In 1853 as 'Stonehenge' he published *The Greyhound*, and in 1856 *British Rural Sports* and the *Coursing Calendar*. He was one of the committee who compiled the original coursing rules and founded the National Coursing Club.

ANGLING

The history of Angling in the county may be divided into three periods, forming an instructive lesson which our Fishery Boards would do well to take to heart. The periods are (*a*) before 1842, (*b*) from 1842 to 1878, (*c*) from 1878 to the present day. Before giving details of the fishing one or two general remarks on the rivers are necessary.

The largest in Worcestershire is the Severn, which, flowing from north to south, divides the county into two unequal parts. The western half, until the Teme is reached, is distant not more than ten miles from the watershed line, so that the few streams which fall in on this side are subject to very rapid rises, and in dry weather run very low ; angling in them is therefore very uncertain. The Severn before 1842 was tidal for some way into Worcestershire ; the exact point may be difficult to determine, but extraordinary tides were felt at Worcester, and ordinary spring tides at least as far as Upton. The result was that estuary fish were found for some distance up the river and its tributaries. At one time angling with a worm for flounders formed a favourite amusement.

The Teme is in character a wholly different river from the Severn ; it is a typical Welsh stream, and in its natural state must have been an angler's paradise, possessing deep pools, long fords, plenty of shelter for fish, and the purest water. For a long time it has been blocked by mill weirs, but they did not affect the trout : the decrease of the trout is due to other and modern causes. The tributaries of the Teme were also most beautiful brooks ; too much wooded perhaps for comfort in fishing, but full of trout, and affording to those who could fish under bushes capital sport. Only two of them still retain anything of their old state : the Leigh Brook which comes in at the Leigh Court Station, and the Rea which falls in at Tenbury. The line of the watershed is peculiar ; nearly all the brooks on the right bank are cut off from the Teme, and flow direct into the Severn until the Rea is reached.

On the right bank the Severn receives the Avon, in which there has been little change, and it still remains a fine river for coarse fish. Its present state dates from the middle of the seventeenth century, when it was made navigable ; but it is difficult to say what it was before that period. In the tributaries of the Avon there should be good fishing, but there is not, because the brooks flowing from the hills have been tapped in order to obtain water supplies at various points, with the result that they run almost dry in summer, and the fish either die a natural death or are taken out and destroyed. Only two streams are really perennial—the Stour which flows by Shipston, and the Arrow which flows past Redditch, the latter being greatly polluted in places.

Going up the Severn, on the right bank but two streams need notice : one is the Salwarpe, which comes in just above the weir at Bevere and used to hold good fish, but has to a great extent been ruined by the pollutions from Bromsgrove and Droitwich ; the other is the Stour, which comes in at Lincombe, but is terribly polluted by acid waste, carpet dyes, and all sorts of impurities.

Such is roughly the present state of the streams, it will be seen that Worcestershire is far from being an ideal angling county.

Before 1842 the streams were in a fairly natural state ; there was not much fishing, and what did exist was of a local character, mainly at the mills and villages on each stream. Records of fishing are few, but we are told here and there of the capture of large carp, trout, or a salmon. A huge eel of 10 lb. and a 4 lb. perch are mentioned as having been caught in the Avon. In some of the old guide books samlet-catching is mentioned as 'a genteel amusement,' at which a few dozen 'elegant fish' can be taken in a morning with a fly ; these are said to be excellent eating. The sessions papers show that from the seventeenth century onward there were prosecutions for using improper nets for salmon, but there is very little about rod-fishing.

The Severn would appear to have been far better adapted for angling in former days than it is now. From its entrance into the county at Bewdley to its exit at Tewkesbury it was a series of pools and fords, in the lower part between Worcester and Tewkesbury the tide rose and fell daily to some extent. Dace-fishing on the fords, a form of angling once largely practised, has quite disappeared, the fords having been dredged out, and the dace are decreasing. From the brooks and rivers large trout dropped down into pools where the tide was felt, and took up their abode there, tempted by the quantity of food obtainable in such places. They would take either a live bait or an occasional worm, but were chiefly to be caught spinning. These fish ran up to 10 lb., and afforded capital sport ; they were, in fact, to the Severn what the Thames trout are to that river ; but there are now no such pools and so no trout.

The other fish that gave most sport was the twait-shad, which running up about May in large numbers to spawn would take a bait greedily, and being strong and active fish afforded great sport. Large quantities were taken with rod and line, and a few are still thus caught.

Coarse fish during this time, so far as can be ascertained from existing records, were not very numerous. One hears of great quantities of bleak and sometimes of very large roach, but these were mostly pond fish or fish that had been carried by floods out of the main river into places from which they could not return. A roach of 4 lb. is said to have been taken in some disused clay pits near Upton, but as to these fish of past times, distance lends not only enchantment but size. Pike were comparatively rare, and confined to the large ponds on gentlemen's estates. Bream were only found in the Avon, and very large ones were said to have been caught there ; pieces of board 'the exact size' of monster bream are still shown in cottages. Curiously enough little is said about what is now the commonest fish of all, namely, the chub ; almost every mill on the Teme has a legend of a monster perch.

In 1842 two events of importance took place. An association was formed at Worcester for the protection of salmon in the Severn and its tributaries, which from that time onwards till the establishment of Fishery Boards in 1865 represented the angling interest; and an Act of Parliament was obtained in that year for improving the navigation of the Severn. The association was concerned with salmon and salmon only; but indirectly it helped the preservation of trout and grayling, and as the association did not concern itself with coarse fish these began to decrease in numbers. Indeed, it was a recognized thing that the fishermen might net out a large number of them in the spring months, when they were allowed to use a net with a smaller mesh. Four weirs were erected under the Navigation Act (Worcester, Bevere, Holt, and Lincombe), which had considerable effect on the river, as except for a short distance below each weir it was virtually turned into a canal, and the fords on which trout and grayling bred were done away with. Indirectly this improved the trout-fishing in the brooks where the trout found breeding grounds and food. Several causes, however, tended to injure the fishing: (1) The fish were now more easily 'poached,' as in hot summers there was nothing to prevent a small pool in one of these brooks being emptied and all the fish killed; this was done to a considerable extent. (2) The insufficiency of food made the fish in the brooks more hungry, and so they were more easily caught than in the river. (3) The enormous increase in the number of anglers who are sometimes unscrupulous in their methods; (4) and worst of all, the great increase in pollution. The galvanizing works on the Upper Stour have poured in acid waste, destroying not only fish but feeding-grounds as well; while the dye from the carpet works at Kidderminster has at times caused immense destruction. On the Salwarpe the sewage and other refuse from Bromsgrove and Droitwich have made the river in parts uninhabitable for fish.

While the tributaries were suffering the main river itself did not improve. About 1853 the Board of Health made the city of Worcester turn all its sewage, including therein its manufacturing refuse, into the river, and this, if it did not kill, at least deterred the fish from passing up and down. The river, too, was dredged for navigation purposes.

Although the salmon were to some slight extent protected, and with the salmon the trout, the coarse fish were kept down, and a state of affairs brought about which rendered the river and brooks much less fitted for producing fish than before. It should be said that the foregoing statements do not apply to the Teme, and it was on the Teme and its tributaries during this period that the Severn had to rely for maintenance of its stock of fish.

In 1856 another Navigation weir was put across the river at Tewkesbury. The effect of this was to cut off all tidal water from Worcester, extend the canalization of the Severn to that place, and prevent the ascent of the fish. In 1878 came the Freshwater Fisheries Act; but it has failed miserably, ruining the trout-fishing without benefiting the coarse-fishing. Practically the whole of the Severn from Stourport to Tewkesbury is now a canal in which trout will not live; for dredging has told on the supply of food, and pollution on the trout. At first coarse fish bred freely, but, finding the supply of food running short, they began to ascend the tributaries, and have now driven trout and grayling higher and higher up the stream. The whole of the Teme and most of the brooks are now given over to chub; not a trout is to be seen in the lower parts. Year after year they ascend higher, until the trout limit of Worcestershire is now about Ham Bridge, halfway down the river. If the present conditions continue there will soon be no trout below Tenbury. Another evil due to coarse fish resorting to the smaller streams has been that they are followed by pike, and many of the brooks in the lower Teme are now full of pike. They have so much food that they very seldom take a bait.

Such trout-fishing as remains in the streams of the county is strictly preserved. The angling for coarse fish is not so good as that on the Thames and Trent. In the Severn and many of the rivers only very small fish can now be caught. This is due to the fact that the large fish seldom stay in the river, but run up the tributaries in search of food, and the great increase in the number of anglers has made the fish so shy that it is almost impossible to get them to look at a bait. A form of angling very common in the summer is called a fishing contest. The members of some club take train to a certain spot on the river and fish for so many hours; each angler fishing from a measured length of the bank, say 5 yards. On some occasions there are really miles of anglers. Their places are settled by lot. The first prize is for weight of fish. All fish caught are weighed in, and a total catch of 4 oz. has a fair chance of a prize.

A word should be said on the methods of fishing. Most of it is bottom-fishing of the ordinary kind. Greaves, bullock's brains, and sometimes cheese are considered killing baits for chub, but the great bait for large chub is the smallest form of lamprey, locally called the *vamprey*. This is a most killing bait in the hands of a man who knows how to use it. The mass of anglers use worm, maggots, and wasp grub as the best all-round baits, and with these catch the largest number and largest variety of fish. For pike the favourite lure is a live bait or a dead gorge. Spinning is not so much in favour.

A certain number of anglers fish with fly, but these are the exception. The Birmingham and district anglers mostly use the ordinary baits in the ordinary way.

Worcestershire has, however, one unique bit of fishing, which, while it lasts, affords really good sport. It is confined to one spot (that part of the Teme below the lowest weir at Powick) and to one time of year. It only occurs at the present day if there is a wet May and some freshets towards the end of the month to bring up the fish. Then should the twait-shad come up the river to spawn, and while they remain in the fresh water at times, but only at times, they feed voraciously. The fish swim in small shoals of from six to a dozen, and run from ½ lb. to 3 lb. They seem to be never at rest, but always moving about. The tackle used is a stiffish rod, a fairly strong line, and a gut cast, attached to which is the bait made of green, red, or yellow worsted lapped round the hook exactly like a mackerel bait only smaller. A few turns of silver twist are an improvement. The line is leaded, and may carry one or more baits. The lure is thrown across the stream to the opposite side of the pool in a downward direction, and worked up stream by the method known as 'sinking and drawing.' The fish are strong and fight well, rushing about the pool and leaping out of the water, but, having a tender mouth, they require careful playing. Some persons use a large black fly with silver twist for a body, and this is at times very killing. The fish are most capricious; they will take splendidly for a time, then suddenly leave off and presently take greedily again. Large numbers are caught at times: one rod in 1904 got fifty in an evening, another rod on the opposite bank of the river, fishing in the same pool, caught none. The twait only remain in the river about three weeks; while they are up the sport is really good, but nothing like that enjoyed before the Tewkesbury weir was put in. There is a legend of a man who had a cart brought down to the river, which he filled with twait caught by himself in one day. Alas! those times, if they ever existed, are now no more.

SHOOTING

It might be expected from the nature of the country, and the variety of the game found, that Worcestershire was a fine shooting county; but if the test of good shooting is a big bag the term cannot well be applied. There is a fair head of game, moderate bags being often, it might be said constantly, made; yet for a big battue or record shoot it would be necessary to go elsewhere. In the south the ground is fairly level and is well adapted for game; in the west, however, it is very hilly, and although well adapted for wild shooting, harbours so much vermin as to make preserving difficult. The north of the county is now given over to manufactures and building, so that a large head of game cannot be hoped for; the east and centre have large woodlands which give good sport when they belong to single owners. There are certain drawbacks to shooting, especially partridge-shooting, in the west; the hop-yards of this district offer the birds shelter, from which it is not easy to dislodge them in the early part of the season. In the south to a large extent shooting is practised under difficulties owing to the damage caused to the market gardens. Many of the fields are small with high hedges, and it is difficult to mark birds if they are walked up, and still more to arrange for a drive; but there are some places where the fields are larger and these difficulties do not exist.

There is a large amount of woodland in the county, and added to this there is a good deal of rough land in places, which lends itself rather to the old than to the modern methods of shooting. In old times the forests which extended over most of the county doubtless held much game. Down to the time of the Civil War there were wild red deer in Malvern Chase and Feckenham Forest and in Wyre Forest to the end of the eighteenth century. In 1614 two men were indicted for killing a sore deer in the king's chase called Malvern Chase.[1] In the same year six men were indicted for entering the park at Rock and killing a doe.[2] In the previous century a petition to be appointed master of the game in the forest of Feckenham was presented to Cecil by Sir Thomas Leighton, who stated, as one of the inducements to grant it, that he intended to bring 500 deer from his own park in order to improve the breed in that forest.[3] The deer gradually became confined to parks, of which there were a fair number in the county. Many of them, such as Bordesley, Cookhill, and Grafton, have long since disappeared, but parks and deer still exist at Witley, Croome, Spetchley, Hanbury, Hagley, and Elmley Castle. Deer-stealing was a frequent offence down to recent years.

There were several franchises of free warren in the county; that is, the grantee of the right from the Crown had the entire right to the game irrespective of the ownership of the land. The beasts of warren, that is the game to which the grantee had the exclusive right, were hares, roes, conies, partridges, rails, quails, woodcocks, herons, and pheasants. Anyone, even the owner of the land, killing any of them within the

[1] *Sess. R.* (Worc. Hist. Soc.), p. 193.

[2] Ibid. p. 194.

[3] *Salisbury MSS.* (Hist. MSS. Com.), ix. 373.

limits of the free warren was guilty of an indictable offence. Thus in 1612 Richard Parks of Old Swinford was indicted for entering the free warren of Muriel Lyttleton, widow, at Hagley, armed with bow and arrows, and using setting nets called 'hayes' for taking hares.[1] At Bredon the Savages had a free warren, and in 1599 a man was indicted for shooting a hare in a common field there.[2] As the law then stood it was illegal to take game in places such as standing corn. In 1602 an Evesham man was indicted for hawking with hawks and spaniels in standing wheat[3] at Offenham. Two cases remind us that no person who had not the correct property qualification could take game nor keep dogs adapted for the purpose. In 1610 a labourer of Stoke Prior was indicted for having *Canis leporarius*—in English a greyhound;[4] and a man who lived at Crowle and had not lands of the yearly value of £10 was indicted for hunting a greyhound and did 'usually kill hares' with it.[5]

It was illegal to shoot game or pigeons with a gun loaded with 'hail shot,' as it was then called. One of the earliest cases recorded in the county is that of John Kennard of Powick, who in 1614 was indicted for discharging a gun charged with powder and hail shot at two partridges at Powick, and killing them. At that time a crossbow was the instrument used for killing game, but the usual and favourite way was hawking. There are no very early records of pheasants or grouse being killed; but as the grouse was not a bird of warren the owner of the land would be at liberty to kill it even in a free warren, provided he did so in a lawful way. The red grouse has disappeared from the list of county game, but not so very long ago. It still is found in Shropshire on the Brown Clee Hills, and occurred in Worcestershire until the end of the eighteenth century. Black game is still occasionally met with in Wyre Forest. In the old days the heron stood at the head of the game-list, but the reforms of William IV. deprived it of its position. Two heronries still remain in the county; one in Shrawley Wood and one at Croome, while another is found at Ragley just over the county border. Woodcocks were never plentiful; some, no doubt, have always bred in the great woods as they do now; but the large bags that are made in Wales and Ireland do not occur, the county lying outside the line of the migration of the woodcock.

Snipe used to be very plentiful when the lands adjoining the Severn and Avon were uncultivated marshes. The south and west of the county must have been a paradise for this bird, but the gradual changes in the land have led to the extinction of the snipe as a resident, and it now only occurs as a winter visitor. The draining of the Longdon Marshes in the middle of the nineteenth century put an end to Worcestershire wild-fowl and snipe-shooting. Ducks, teal, and sometimes geese, however, are winter visitors, working up from the Severn estuary; but comparatively few breed in the county, and no decoy now exists nearer than one on the Severn at Berkeley.

The shooting is now practically confined to partridges, pheasants, and rabbits. Before the Ground Game Act there were large numbers of hares; some were preserved for coursing and hunting, but many were killed in every big shoot. Now, owing to the fact that a good deal of the land is either let or owned in small holdings, hares have rapidly decreased. Another cause of decrease is the fact that in the market gardens they are killed without mercy. Landrails, which used to be common, and which usually figured in a September bag, are much less frequently killed now than formerly; it may be that they are scarcer, but it seems more likely that the custom of walking up the birds now in vogue leads to the flushing of fewer landrails than was the case when dogs were used.

One bird that has largely increased, thanks to the Wild Birds Preservation Act, is the wood-pigeon. In the west and centre of the county it is one of the commonest birds, but so wary that comparatively few are shot. There are no available records of very large bags of wood-pigeon.

Partridges are very numerous in some districts only on the clay lands of Worcestershire, and they form the largest part; partridges do not thrive as they do on lighter soil. The reason seems to be, that if the breeding season is wet, the young birds get draggled with the clay and many die; while if it is dry the old birds run far to water, and the young birds get lost or fall into the cracks in the soil which are caused by drought. In spite of these drawbacks there are a good head of birds, and fair bags can be obtained. There are several places where two guns walking up the birds average thirty brace all through September. Driving is not so common as in other parts of England, and when practised is not so successful. In the south of the county the red-legged partridge has become common, and is said to drive off the grey partridge; however this may be, there is no doubt that such heavy bags are not made as used to be recorded before the red legs became numerous; this is owing to their running powers, which the crops, sown in drills or rows, such as potatoes, permit them to exert to the greatest advantage.

Pheasants are fairly numerous; the wild ones breed well and turn out some strong birds. Considering the size of the county there is not much hand-rearing, although a considerable number of pheasants are bred annually at some places, such as Witley and Hewell. Probably the largest bag on a day's shoot would be found at Wood

[1] *Sess. R.* (Worc. Hist. Soc.), i. 171.
[2] Ibid. p. 18. [3] Ibid. p. 50.
[4] Ibid. p. 149. [5] Ibid. p. 150.

Norton; but here the Duc d'Orleans turns down birds for the day's shooting, as was the case in the great shoots of 1904 on the occasion of the king of Portugal's visit; but there are very few places in Worcestershire which, on their best day, produce a bag of 1,000 pheasants.

In some places rabbits are still found in large numbers, and probably the heaviest bags made are of them. The record bag is that made at Croome on 11 December, 1887, when eight guns, the Comte and Comtesse de Paris and the Duc d'Orleans, Lords Ribblesdale and Deerhurst, Mr. A. Payne, and the Hon. C. J. and H. J. Coventry killed 3,276.

Battue-shooting was probably mainly introduced into the county by the late earl of Stamford and Warrington at Enville just over the Staffordshire border, where, at times, very heavy bags were made. On several occasions the king when prince of Wales shot at Witley: on such occasions a large head of game was killed. In 1904 the duke of Connaught shot at Hewell, when in spite of bad weather a good bag was secured. These, however, are all exceptional cases. Yet in spite of all that has been said, if a person is contented with a moderate bag on each day of the season, there are few counties in which he will do better than in Worcestershire.

ATHLETICS

Worcestershire, although very badly off in the way of proper athletic grounds with cinder paths attached, is a strong centre of the Midland Counties Athletic Association; and during the summer months many most successful meetings are held. The county town generally supports two meetings during the year; the Worcester Foresters selecting Whit Monday for a capitally organized fixture with a varied programme of open and close events to attract the Bank Holiday crowd. The Worcestershire County Cricket Club take an 'off' Saturday usually in July for a more exclusive meeting which is supported by all the cricket enthusiasts of the district, and is an object lesson as regards management and arrangements. Kidderminster, perhaps, comes next after Worcester as an athletic centre. Here, on the August Bank Holiday, the Carpet Weavers Athletic Society hold a meeting which, if length of programme, value of prizes, and magnitude of attendance be considered, is the most important fixture in the county. Earlier in the year the Kidderminster Harriers utilize the Whit Monday holiday for a well-attended local gathering. The excellent ground of the Stourbridge Cricket Club in the centre of the town is particularly well adapted for an athletic fixture. The meeting of this club is the oldest in the county, and it has been held for many years on the first or second Monday in July. The names of some of the best of the Amateur Athletic Association championship competitors frequently appear on the programme. The Amateur Athletic Association Championships have been decided on the Stourbridge cricket ground, where a cinder track was laid down specially for the occasion. The Netherton Cricket Club also hold sports on a Monday in June with a large entry list and under very capable management. Two other clubs affiliated to the Midland Counties Athletic Association hold annual meetings, viz.:—The Malvern Friendly Society Athletic Club and the Stourport Boat Club, the latter body deciding their foot races in connexion with the regatta.

In other parts of the county, athletics are steadily developing. Evesham now has a fixture of some importance, and the Halesowen Football and Cricket Club also obtain an annual permit for a meeting from the Midland Counties Amateur Athletic Association. At Ombersley, Eckington, and Bredon the local Foresters and Friendly Societies have found athletic sports a sufficiently attractive feature to increase their funds. Pershore, formerly celebrated for its sports, in which horse-racing formed no inconsiderable part, has recently revived the fixture under the Foresters' supervision.

These are the chief athletic gatherings in Worcestershire, but innumerable village sports are held in connexion with local fêtes and flower shows at which small money prizes are given. A properly constituted athletic club, however, is sadly needed in the county. There is no dearth of running and athletic ability, but, without a central organization and a cinder track for practice, other games and pastimes hold out superior attractions during the summer and winter months to the young Worcestershire athlete.

It must be added that W. G. George, the holder of the world's one mile record, began his running career in Worcester and the neighbourhood.

GOLF

The history of golf in the county of Worcester commences with the establishment, in 1880, of the County Club at Malvern, which takes premier place, both by virtue of seniority and strength of membership. Not till it had been in existence for ten years did any rival club arise; but in 1890 courses were opened at Redditch (Ipsley G.C.) and at Kidderminster, and from that date clubs increased rapidly. Hagley, Blackwell, King's Norton, Pershore, Stourbridge, Dudley, and Robin Hood (Hall Green) followed each other in quick succession, and in the order named. Evesham, Broadway, Bromsgrove, and Droitwich came into being next; whilst Worcester City, the latest addition in 1899, has made such phenomenal progress that it already ranks third in the county as regards numbers. During the last nine years of the nineteenth century, therefore, fourteen clubs sprang into existence. Adding to this list the original County Club at Malvern, Lord Dudley's private course at Witley, the Malvern Working Men's Club, the Worcestershire Ladies' Club (Malvern), and the King's Norton Ladies' Club, there is a total of nineteen clubs formed during the twenty years 1880–1899. The important organization known as the Worcestershire Ladies' County Union dates only from 1903.

The list of professional golfers in the county includes the names of George and Harry Cawsey (Malvern), W. Lewis (King's Norton), E. Veness (Hagley), and A. Lewis (Moseley); the brothers Cawsey have both taken high places in the Open Championship meetings.

The most prominent amateur residing in the county is undoubtedly Mr. Edward Blackwell, whose splendid efforts to keep the Amateur Championship Cup on this side of the Atlantic furnish his latest claim to mention. Mr. Blackwell was for some time captain of the Kidderminster G.C., playing with their team in interclub matches. On two occasions his performances over the Malvern course have found place in the 'Record Book' of that club. Playing in a foursome on 16 February, 1891, he with his drive laid his partner, Mr. H. D. Acland, within putting distance on the first green (240 yds.), and the hole was done in 2; while on 17 November, 1900, playing against G. Cawsey, the club professional, his drive to the fifteenth green was hole high, 266 yards, and up a sharp rise, and at the sixteenth he was past the green (245 yds.). The wind was slightly in his favour, but the course was wet and heavy, and there was scarcely any run on the ball in either case. As mentioned elsewhere, Mr. Blackwell assisted Lord Dudley in laying out the course in Witley Park; and there he constantly plays.

Among many other first-class or almost first-class amateur golfers in the county, mention may be made of the following:—Messrs. E. F. Chance, W. M. and G. E. Grundy (both of them in the Oxford University team of 1904), W. R. Nash, C. Toppin, W. W. Low, H. Foster, Rev. Shirley Baldwin, for twelve years captain of the King's Norton G.C., and winner of the Finch Hatton Open Scratch Bowl (36 holes) at Harlech, in 1896, in a field of seventy competitors; S. C. Healing, who won the Midland Counties Championship in 1902, G. W. Blathwayt, R. E. Foster, Capt. W. L. Foster, and T. Hyde. All the above-named, being members of the County Club, and playing at Malvern frequently, may be reckoned as county golfers. To these must be added the names of Hon. A. Lyttelton (Hagley), Messrs. J. P. Humphries (Kidderminster), F. Woolley (King's Norton), C. A. Palmer (King's Norton), and T. W. Piggott (captain of King's Norton G.C.).

The *Blackwell* Club (to take the first in alphabetical order) was started in 1892, and has a membership of 100 men and 50 ladies. The links are close to Blackwell Station (M.R.) and three miles from Bromsgrove. It is a 9-hole course on pasture land, which is heavy during the summer months. The hazards consist of a pond, hedges, ditches, cart-tracks, etc. The Ladies' Club, though using the men's course, has its own captain and secretary; both of which offices are at present filled by Mrs. Holcroft, Coppy Hill, Bromsgrove, who holds the ladies' record for the double round.

The *Broadway* course was laid out in 1895 by H. Wilson (Rhosonlea), Viscount Lifford and Dr. Standring being the chief promoters. It has a membership of sixty. The links lie on the Cotswolds, just above the pretty village of Broadway, on pasture land with loam soil, the nearest station being Evesham (G.W.R.). In summer only 9 of the 18 holes are available. The hazards are all natural, and of a sporting character; whilst the bracing air and beautiful views are famous. The Bogey of the 18-hole course is 80. The Hon. Sec. is Dr. Standring, The Laurels.

The *Bromsgrove* Club was founded in 1895 by the late Mr. A. Dipple, aided by Messrs. F. J. Russon and John Stevenson. It has a membership of eighty men and twenty ladies. The course is at Slideslow Farm, half a mile from the town, and consists of 9 rather sporting holes, on pasture land, with sandy soil, and both natural and artificial hazards. Play is possible all the year round. The Bogey for the 9 holes is 41. The Hon. Sec. is John Stevenson, Esq., Rock Hill, Bromsgrove.

Droitwich dates from 1895, when the course was laid out by G. H. Cawsey, the Malvern professional; Mr. Thomas Townsend, Dr. Roden, and Dr. Jones being the chief promoters. It has but a small list of resident members—twenty-one men and seven ladies—but it is largely used by the visitors attracted to the place by the famous brine baths. The links are situated at Bay Meadow, near the town, and are on pasture land with a stiff loam soil. Summer play is difficult. The Bogey for the 9 holes is 35. There are both natural and artificial hazards. The Hon. Sec. is F. W. Sadler, Esq.

The *Dudley* links were laid out in 1893 by the famous 'Old Tom Morris,' who succeeded in making a most sporting little course of 9 holes in the Old Park, on ground which, having once been worked for coal, is now clothed with turf in good condition for play throughout the year. The inequalities of the surface lend themselves to the purposes of the game, providing plenty of natural hazards. The Rev. A. G. Maitland and Mr. Grazebrook were the founders. The club has ninety members. The links are under two miles from Dudley Station, while Netherton Station (G.W.R.) is nearer, and tram-cars run close to the course. The Bogey for the 9 holes is 40, and the professional record for the green (33) was made by James Braid in 1897; the amateur record (38) by Messrs. A. H. Bussage and J. W. Naylor. The Hon. Sec. is J. Nichols, Esq., Old Bank House, Dudley.

The *Evesham* Club, itself instituted in 1894, was amalgamated with the Pershore Club (1893) in the year 1904, and numbers seventy men and twenty ladies. The course is at Craycombe, eight minutes from Fladbury Station (G.W.R.), midway between Evesham and Pershore. It was laid out by Ross of Streetly, Messrs. G. Hogarth, O. J. New, and E. D. Lowe being the principal originators. The soil being sandy affords good play all the year round, although the links are on pasture land. They are somewhat hilly, but pretty and sporting, with good lies, excellent greens, and a sufficiency of natural and artificial hazards. The Bogey for the double round is 78, the Par score 70. The record for the 9 holes (34) is held by the late club professional, G. Stephenson. The amateur record—also 34—was made in 1901 by Mr. J. A. F. Moncrieff. The Hon. Sec. is J. G. Baker, Esq., Pershore.

The *Hagley* course is a short but beautifully situated one of 9 holes. It was originally planned in 1891 by Mr. E. F. Chance, but was subsequently lengthened. 'Monument Hill,' the site of the links, is two miles from Stourbridge. The course is somewhat hilly, but the turf gives good lies and excellent greens. The hazards are all natural, and though the soil is clay, play is feasible throughout the year. Viscount Cobham, Messrs. H. T. Williams, E. F. Chance, and W. H. Grazebrook were chiefly instrumental in founding the club, which at present reckons seventy members. The professional, E. Veness, was a pupil of Peter Paxton at Eastbourne, and came to Hagley in 1893. He holds the professional record of the green (67), the Bogey being 78. The amateur record (72) rests with Mr. W. H. Grazebrook, who is Hon. Sec. Many famous players have been associated with this club; amongst whom may be mentioned Messrs. E. F. and A. M. Chance, Hon. A. Lyttelton, W. R. Nash, G. Macpherson. Hagley won the Midland Counties Cup at Streetly, where the Messrs. Chance have also obtained the gold and silver medals.

The *Kidderminster* Club was founded in 1890 under the auspices of Dr. Waddell and Mr. A. H. Mague; its establishment marks the date at which the game began to make real progress in the county. The course of 15 holes—of which the first three are played twice to complete the normal round of 18—was planned by the brother of David Brown, for some time professional to the W.G.C. at Malvern. It has a membership of eighty men and twenty-five ladies; the latter having a short course provided for them on the men's links. The comfortable club-house stands within five minutes' walk of Kidderminster Station. The soil is sandy; and the natural hazards, consisting of an orchard (which must be carried), gorse, hedges, etc., are supplemented artificially. During the winter, when the low-lying parts are sometimes invaded with water, only 9 holes are available. The Bogey of the course is 81, and the green record (68) is held by Edward Blackwell, sometime captain of the club. Mr. Roger Brinton is the Hon. Sec.

After the County Club, *King's Norton* is undoubtedly the most important golf club in Worcestershire, numbering 182 members; with a ladies' club, using the same course with shorter tees, but with its own separate organization and a membership of fifty-five. The course was originally laid out in 1892 by David Brown, at that time the Malvern professional, for 9 holes only. But it was shortly afterwards extended to 18 holes under the energetic management of Mr. J. J. Tomson—the present Hon. Sec.—supported by W. Goodrick-Clark, Shirley Baldwin and A. H. Wolseley, Major Baldwin and others. Mr. Tomson first purchased the land on which the links are situated, leasing it to the club. But in 1900 he re-sold the property to the King's Norton Golf Club Estate Company, Ltd., which started with a capital of £6,700. The course is on pasture land, clay soil, with plenty of natural hazards, consisting of ponds, roads, pits, trees, hedges, etc., supplemented by some artificial bunkers. The charming club-house is within twelve minutes' walk of King's Norton Station (M.R.) and five miles from Birmingham. The Bogey of the present course is 77. The Par score (69) has been attained by the club professional, W. P. Lewis, while the amateur record (68) is held by Mr. F. A. Woolley.

The ladies' course was arranged by G. H. Cawsey, the club professional at Malvern, in 1895, the ladies who promoted it being Mrs. Symonds, Mrs. Elkington, Mrs. Holcroft, Miss Hart, and Miss Wolseley. The record of the ladies' green (79) is held by Miss E. Neville. The Hon. Sec. is Mrs. E. C. Bewlay, The Cottage, Moseley.

The *Moseley* Club, which has a 9-hole course, was laid out in 1892 under the superintendence of Messrs. H. Bewlay, F. H. Elderton, H. H. Greenway, T. Hadley, S. R. Lowcock, and H. V. Pryse. It is situated at Moseley, about four miles from Birmingham. The ground is undulating—the soil gravel and sand, while there are both natural and artificial hazards. Play is possible at all seasons. The Bogey score for the double round has now been reduced to 78. A. Lewis is at present the club professional. The Hon. Sec. is Mr. C. P. Newman, West Croft, Moseley.

The *Worcestershire* is the pioneer golf club in the county, if not in the Midlands. It has—including four life-members and six abroad—a list of 250 members, which is the nominal limit. The club took shape in 1880 under the initiative of Mr. T. H. Ashton, the Hon. and Rev. R. Moncreiff, Rev. H. Foster, Mr. T. Gilroy, Capt. Dowdeswell, and several other gentlemen. The course on Malvern Common was originally laid out for only 12 holes by William Allen of Westward Ho. Peter Paxton, who became the club professional in 1882, converted the 12 holes into 9, whilst Douglas Rolland, who followed Peter in 1888, in his turn extended the course to 18 holes. At the present time of writing (1904) a further important alteration is in progress, several acres of low-lying boggy land having during the last few months been drained at considerable expense with a view to lengthening the lower course and of avoiding some dangerous crossings. These links possess a great advantage in their well-defined division into a 'lower' and 'upper' course, with the club-house in the centre. The Midland Railway forms the dividing line, and is itself the first bunker on the upper course. The hazards are all natural—ponds, roads, and ditches on the lower course; the two railway lines, a high embanked road, whins, gravel-pit, etc., on the upper. The soil is gravel and clay, and as a rule the short common grass affords good lies for the greater part of the year. The greens are almost invariably in beautiful condition, but are often very difficult owing to their slopes and undulations. The comfortable club-house is within 300 yards of Malvern Wells Station (G.W.R.), and one mile from Great Malvern.

There has been an unbroken succession of first-class professionals in this club: Peter Paxton (1882), Douglas Rolland (1888), David Brown (1891), and George Cawsey (1898). D. Brown won the Open Championship in 1886, and stood ninth so lately as 1897. Malvern course has been the scene of many first-class encounters. Of these, one of the most notable was that between J. H. Taylor (at that time at Winchester) *v.* David Brown, in May 1896. On that occasion Taylor's phenomenal steadiness on unfamiliar and somewhat tricky greens is shown by the level scores in the 36-hole match, viz.:—A.M. 39 + 37 = 76, P.M. 38 + 38 = 76: Total 152, *i.e.* a difference of two strokes only between the best and the worst 9 holes. David Brown, though losing the match at 5 and 4 to play, put in the best 9 holes of the day, viz., 36 for the upper course in the afternoon; showing how pluckily he played a losing game to the very finish. Another fine contest took place at Malvern, 3 October, 1901, when Harry Vardon played George Cawsey on the latter's home green. The champion actually had the worst of it in the first 18 holes, but pulled up splendidly in the second round, eventually winning at 5 and 3, with three strokes to the good, Cawsey making a grand finish by winning the bye. The score read as follows:—

A.M.	Vardon 41 + 34 = 75.	
	Cawsey 37 + 36 = 73.	
P.M.	Vardon 36 + 35 = 71	Total 146.
	Cawsey 40 + 36 = 76	„ 149.

The professional record of the green has for some time been in the hands of George Cawsey. In 1901, playing for the Swann Medal in Malvern Working Men's Golf Club, he returned a score of 32 + 36 = 68, in which occurred no less than six threes; whilst on 15 July, 1903, playing with Capt. R. Taylor (Sherwood Foresters), he went round with 34 +31 = 65, in which were four threes, a brace of twos, one five, and the rest fours.

The amateur record has been also much lowered of late, and is now shared by Mr. W. M. Grundy and Mr. H. S. Pelham, members of the Oxford team (1904), who in 1903 both did the course in 70.

The full medal-course was, at the Easter meeting 1902, done by Mr. B. Middleditch in 36 + 35 = 71, a truly splendid performance; equalling the best round played by H. Vardon in the match against Cawsey already mentioned.

The following items are culled from the W.G.C. 'Record Book':—'On 23 May, 1892, David Brown, club professional, did the lower course in 49, using only one hand.' 'On 25 June, 1901, Mr. L. E. Radcliffe, in presence of two members of W.G.C., drove a golf ball from the summit of the Worcestershire Beacon (1,400 feet above sea level) on to the eighteenth green in eleven strokes, the ball being teed for each stroke.'

From the old records of the County Golf Club, which contain much interesting matter, may be extracted two personal items which illustrate the rapidity with which a born golfer develops without passing through the weary apprenticeship of most beginners.

In 1882, when this club was in its infancy, Mr. Edward F. Chance, who for a long time has been reckoned one of the finest players in Worcestershire, was started on his way with the surprisingly liberal handicap of 40! In less than a couple of years—before the close of 1883—he was holding his own with the best at a handicap of 2!

On the other hand the Rev. H. Foster, Malvern College, seems never to have been anywhere but at the top of the tree. For in the earliest days of his golfing career—the beginning of the eighties—he was persistently at the head of the club competitions, with a handicap varying from 2 to scratch. And now, after nearly a quarter of a century of play, he is at about the same mark. During the long period covered by the club's history, the course, both in its length and the condition of the green—the implements of the game—even its rules—have all been altered; but to every new condition the really good player easily accommodates himself.

These notes on the W.G.C. must not be closed without acknowledgment of the services rendered to the club by Mr. W. Paterson, who for more than twelve years (1890–1903) filled the post of Hon. Sec. and still continues a member of the Club Committee. The name of Mr. H. D. Acland should also be mentioned, he having acted as Hon. Sec. from 1888–1890, and as Hon. Treasurer from 1891–1902.

The *Worcestershire Ladies'* Club is the one ladies' club in the county which not only has a separate organization of its own, but plays on its own links. Founded in 1891 under the patronage of Rev. H. Foster, Messrs. E. F. Chance and Moore Binns, Mrs. E. Chance, Mrs. Lyon, Mrs. Jupp, and Mrs. Salisbury, it was laid out by David Brown (professional to the W.G.C.) on land opposite to the club-house. In 1894, however, the present 9-hole course was acquired above the men's upper course, and a charming little club-house was built close to the Malvern Wells Station (G.W.R.). The members number eighty-nine, with twenty-four men associates. The course is on sloping ground, with gravel and clay soil, which allows of play throughout the year. Such few hazards as it possesses are all natural. The Bogey score is 40, and the Par score 36. The record (72) for the double round is held by Miss E. C. Neville, who, with her sister, Miss Neville, was till recently a member of this club. The present Hon. Sec. is Mrs. Greenstock, 3, The Lees, Malvern. In the Midland Counties Team Competition this club has thrice been victorious, and in the Ladies' Open Championship has on two occasions won the silver medal and once the bronze medal. On the occasion of the inter-club matches permission is sometimes asked and granted by the W.G.C. to make use of the men's upper course in combination with the ladies' course; and mixed foursomes, in which the members of the W.G.C. are invited to take part, are an annual event.

The *Malvern Working Men's* G.C. may very properly be grouped with the other two clubs playing on Malvern Common. It is in fact an offshoot of the W.G.C., which does much to encourage it by throwing open the men's course for its use, and offering prizes for competition. Friendly contests between the two clubs also frequently take place; and it needs a strong team to get much the better of the M.W.M.G.C., as the professionals and leading caddies form in themselves a capable nucleus of golfing talent. The club was instituted in 1892, and numbers fifty members, all of whom naturally take an interest in the good condition and up-keep of the Malvern links, and its institution has been the means of removing possibilities of friction in connexion with common-land and commoners' rights.

Redditch (*Ipsley*) Club was founded in 1890 by the late Colonel Milward, M.P., and Mr. J. W. Whitehouse. It numbers only forty members. The links are situated on the Old Racecourse at Ipsley, distant from Redditch two miles. There are 9 holes, on pasture land, with a gravel and clay soil. The hazards are all natural, formed chiefly by the River Arrow and a small brook. Play is not possible between April and September. David Brown of Malvern laid out the course; the Bogey score for which is 38. The Hon. Sec. is Mr. J. H. Whitehouse, Ipsley Court, Redditch.

The *Robin Hood* course was laid out by A. Tunley in 1893, under the management of Messrs. W. E. Patterson, E. E. Fordred, H. Lowe, and A. B. Bowden, and is situated at Hall Green, four miles from Birmingham. It consists of 9 very sporting holes on park land with sandy soil and natural hazards—brooks, gorse, etc., are supplemented by artificial bunkers. Play goes on all through the year, Sundays included. The Par score of the green is 37, and the Bogey for 18 holes 78. The professional record of 70 is held by J. W. Whiting, and the amateur (78) by Mr. F. A. Byrne. It has its full complement of 100 members. The Hon. Sec. is Mr. A. B. Bowden, Burlington Chambers, New Street, Birmingham.

So long ago as 1890, the old racecourse at Pedmore, about a mile from Stourbridge Junction and Town Stations (G.W.R.), was used as a private golf course; but in 1903 Messrs. W. H. Hughes and E. T. Wright, of Old Swinford, established the *Stourbridge* Club, which now numbers seventy playing and fifteen non-playing men members and thirty ladies. It consists of 9 holes on common-land with a sandy soil. There are both natural and artificial hazards, and play is possible at all seasons. The Bogey score for the 9 holes is 42. This club, which for five years (1898–1903) was in abeyance, is once more prosperous. The course, though short, is reckoned one of the best and most sporting in the Midlands. There is a variety of natural hazards—gorse, whins, fog and bent, hedges and ditches, and a pool. The club sends a strong team to the Midland Competitions, which has generally done well. The Hon. Sec. is Mr. E. C. Lowndes, Beauty Bank House, Stourbridge.

The *Worcester City* is the youngest of the county golf clubs, and has made most remarkable progress during the five years of its existence (1899–1904). This is owing chiefly to the judicious and energetic conduct of its affairs by Messrs. H. W. and A. G. Spreckley, who, in conjunction with Messrs. Milne and Stephen and Rev. P. Norton, initiated it. It already numbers 108 men and 35 ladies. The links are on the Tolladine road, about a mile from Worcester Cross, and rather less from Shrub Hill Station. The course is on pasture land and marl soil, but play is possible at all seasons. It is rather hilly, but the glorious views and air make full amends for this. The hazards consist chiefly of hedges and wired fences, with a few artificial bunkers. The Bogey score is 39.

Witley (Lord Dudley's) is a sporting little 9-hole course. It was laid out in the deer-park at Witley Court in 1895 by the earl of Dudley and Mr. Edward Blackwell. Like all park-land, it is more suitable for winter than summer play. The hazards are all natural, a small lake, a spinney, and fences being most in evidence, and the greens are kept in excellent order. A fine exhibition was witnessed, 7 February, 1902, when the earl invited ten of the leading professional players to spend a few days at Witley Court for purposes of golf, inviting at the same time members of the principal golf clubs in the neighbourhood to witness the competition. Snow, which fell rather persistently in the morning, threatened to spoil the golf, but happily it ceased before noon, and the afternoon round was played under pleasant conditions. Some wonderful returns were made, and the indifference with which these fine players during the forenoon round treated the slippery tees and the jacketed balls on the putting greens was a revelation. The players engaged were J. H. Taylor (Richmond), J. Braid (Romford), H. Vardon (Ganton), A. Kirkaldy (St. Andrews), W. Auchterlonie (St. Andrews), G. Cawsey (Malvern), D. Herd (Littlestone), B. Sayers (North Berwick), J. White (Mitcham), and W. Fernie (Troon).

The first prize for the 36 holes was eventually won by H. Vardon with 153, the second by H. Kirkaldy with 154, and the third by D. Herd with 155.

Worcestershire Ladies' County Club was started in 1903 with the object of providing a team to represent the county in the annual Ladies' County Championship, promoted by the Ladies' Golf Union. It has for its President the countess of Dudley; and as Vice-Presidents, Lord Windsor, Messrs. E. F. Chance, Shirley Baldwin, and Edward Blackwell. Miss D. Spear, 3, The College, Malvern, is the Hon. Sec.

In 1903 Worcestershire was champion county[1] in the Northern Division, winning five matches out of six, the last being drawn. In the final struggle on the Sunningdale Links, Devonshire took the first place, Kent the second, Worcestershire the third. The Midland Division,[2] to which Worcestershire now belongs, was only formed during this present year (1904). Besides providing for the County Championship, the County Golf Club arranges for an annual individual Ladies' Championship for Worcestershire, the qualification being birth in the county, or one year's residence. In 1903 the championship meeting was held on the Worcester City links, and resulted in the victory of Mrs. Holcroft of the King's Norton Club.

Worcestershire has generally been well represented at the Midland County Competition, and during the last nine years the meeting has, on four occasions, been held on a Worcestershire course (King's Norton). In 1897 the Cup was won by a county team (Hagley), and again in 1898 (by King's Norton), whilst the Gold Medal was won by A. M. Chance (Hagley) in 1897, by E. F. Chance (Hagley) in 1898, and by S. C. Healing (Cheltenham) in 1902, all prominent members of the County Club at Malvern.

1 For the County Championship the counties are now (1904) grouped in four divisions (until 1904 there were only three divisions), viz. :—1. North. 2. Midland. 3. South East. 4. South West. Until this present year Worcestershire was reckoned as in the Northern Division, but has now taken its place more appropriately amongst the Midland counties. In each division each county plays home-and-home matches with the others, and the county winning most matches becomes champion of the division. The four divisional champions then meet on some metropolitan links, to play for the Championship of England and the Cup appertaining.

2 The Midland Golf Competition owes its inception to Mr. A. W. Still, Editor of the old *Birmingham Daily Gazette*, who, in 1895, offered, on behalf of the proprietors of his journal, a Challenge Cup for annual competition by clubs in the counties of Derby, Gloucester, Hereford, Leicester, Notts, Shropshire, Stafford, Warwick, and Worcester. The venue of the meeting is changed every year, and during the last nine years it has been held at King's Norton (4), Streetly (3), Handsworth (1), Sandwell Park (1), Hollinwell, Notts (1). In 1904, at King's Norton, no less than twenty-seven clubs, representing nearly all the above-mentioned counties, competed. The meeting takes place during the first week in May, and lasts for two days. The present chairman is Mr. J. J. Tomson, of King's Norton.

CRICKET

The history of Cricket in Worcestershire may be divided into three periods, very unequally distributed over fifty-six years. In the first period the team, usually known as Gentlemen of Worcestershire, was for the most part composed of amateurs, whilst after 1870 it blossomed into a minor county team of somewhat variable quality. The second period opens in 1892, when a capital eleven could be collected, which held the minor county championship in 1896 with only one defeat, and in 1897 and 1898 possessed an unbeaten record; finally, in 1899, reaching the third period by its inclusion among first-class counties.

1844–1892.—One of the earliest county records is that of the encounter on Hartlebury Common, 28 August, 1844, between Worcestershire and Shropshire. In a small scoring match Worcestershire was defeated by 9 wickets. In the return match, at Shrewsbury, 18 September of the same year, the side fared no better, as they lost by 61 runs, Ingle scoring 55 for the victors. In September, 1848, the county opposed I Zingari, and the match was rendered notable by a tremendous drive, Mr. Harvey Fellowes hitting a rising ball from Nixon 132 yards to pitch. Next year the Ombersley Club visited Leamington and were defeated by 5 wickets. Wisden, for the victors, scored 60 and took 8 wickets, whilst Armitage made 30 and dismissed 10 opponents. On 26 and 27 July, 1849, at Himley Hall in Staffordshire, the Gentlemen of Worcestershire, with four professionals, encountered I Zingari, who won by 9 wickets. In this match Lord Ward, afterwards Lord Dudley, always a great patron of the game, appeared for his county, and the professional, Sams, made 37. A fortnight later a capital struggle took place between Worcestershire and Herefordshire at Ombersley. Worcestershire won by 2 runs, the totals being 86 and 88, whilst the border county made 78 and 94. Although the games need not be individually enumerated, it may be broadly stated that down to 1889 Worcestershire and Herefordshire opposed each other in the majority of seasons.

Worcestershire cricket from the early fifties was mainly supported by the energetic enthusiasm of Lord Coventry. He was never a first-class cricketer, but could hit hard and bowl slow lobs. He was president of the Marylebone Cricket Club in 1859. One of his sons, Hon. Henry Coventry, who has played for the county, was in the Eton eleven of 1886, whilst another, Hon. C. J. Coventry, went out with the first cricket team to the Cape.

For some years the matches of the Gentlemen of Worcestershire were of a rather variable character. At Shrewsbury they were dismissed 13 August, 1862, for 69 and 33, Mr. J. A. Allen carrying his bat for 32 in the first innings. To him also is mainly due the victory in the return encounter with the Gentlemen of Shropshire, as he scored 28 and 33 not out, whilst Mr. J. C. Raybould claimed 7 of the Shropshire wickets in their meagre total of 29. The Gentlemen of Warwickshire for some time proved too strong for their western opponents, winning at Kiderminster by an innings and 35 runs in 1863, when Mr. David Buchanan took 11 wickets, and by an innings and 49 runs at Warwick in 1865, when the same bowler took 14 wickets. For Worcestershire in the latter match Hon. G. S. Lyttelton and Hon. C. G. Lyttelton each scored 45. It may be here mentioned that, 26 August, 1867, eleven Lytteltons beat Bromsgrove School by 10 wickets, the victorious side being composed of Lord Lyttelton, two brothers, and eight sons. The most famous of the family, Hon. Edward and Hon. Alfred Lyttelton, were then respectively only twelve and ten years of age.

Lord Coventry took the chair at a meeting at the Star Hotel, Worcester, 3 March, 1865, when a committee was formed to establish a county club and to find a suitable ground. That their efforts were rewarded is proved by the victory of the home side—cited both as Worcestershire and as Gentlemen of Worcestershire—on the county ground over Warwickshire by 5 wickets, 17 July, 1866. Hon. C. G. Lyttelton contributed 94 and Hon. G. S. Lyttelton 54 towards a total of 228. For the visitors Mr. B. T. Featherston scored a lively 65, and Mr. David Buchanan claimed 8 wickets. A trio of matches in August, 1868, demand attention. Warwickshire, without Mr. Buchanan, won by 16 runs, although Mr. W. Caldicott and Hon. G. S. Lyttelton had dismissed them for 45, and Hon. C. G. Lyttelton had scored 58. The United South of England Eleven were routed by Twenty-two of Worcestershire (including William McIntyre and Brewster) with 57 runs to spare. The only score over 20 in the game was made by James Lillywhite, jun., who went in last and knocked up 36. The veteran John Lillywhite and Dr. W. G. Grace both played for the visitors. Without the two crack Lytteltons, a severe defeat was suffered at the hands of Herefordshire, who won by 146 runs, that useful cricketer Mr. W. Caldicott alone being successful for the home side, with both bat and ball. The following year showed a worse disaster, the defeat being this time by an innings and 29 runs, Mr. J. Swire scoring 101 towards the Herefordshire total of 280. A close finish by 1 wicket gave a victory to the United South, playing Twenty-two Gentlemen of Worcester with Millward and Platts. In the score of amateurs were Lord Coventry, Mr. W. R. Gilbert, cousin of the Graces, and the parents of the Fosters and the Bromley Martins. Platts fairly earned his fee, for he contributed 12 and 35, and took 15 wickets. James Lillywhite by scoring 41 not out at the conclusion was responsible for the bare majority, while Southerton took 20 wickets.

The season of 1870 was hardly fortunate. Herefordshire could not bring the first encounter to a conclusion (although Mr. T. Bent made 94 not out), thanks to the stubborn batting of Mr. C. L. Kennaway and Mr. W. Caldicott, who each made over 70. But the return at Hereford was disastrous; for with the meagre total of 90 to face, Worcestershire was beaten by an innings and 2 runs, Captain Decie and Mr. G. Nice dividing the wickets. Shropshire also was victorious by 7 wickets, although Captain Decie now appeared for Worcestershire, scoring 49 and 28 and capturing six opponents. More successful were the Twenty-two of Worcestershire in the match with the United North, as this yielded a victory by 14 wickets. Dr. W. G. Grace and Mr. W. R. Gilbert going in first for Worcestershire made 74 and 11 respectively, the other 20 between them making 28. John Smith of Cambridge with 41 and 31 was the chief scorer for the eleven, who found Mr. R. F. Miles a formidable bowler. The champion made 38 in his second innings. In the return encounter *v.* Herefordshire, in 1871, four of the family of Lyttelton appeared for Worcestershire, but their efforts could not save a defeat by 1 wicket. This was mainly achieved by the batting of Mr. J. Swire, who carried out his bat for 78, being joined by the last man, Mr. W. H. Potter, when 17 runs were still required. Time alone had prevented Worcestershire from winning the first match in that year. Lord Coventry scored 94 and Dr. Hobbes took 7 wickets for 39 runs. On the other side Mr. E. Baker was both times undefeated, being credited with 43 and 101. The United South proved superior to Twenty-two Gentlemen of Worcestershire without professionals by the margin of 4 wickets. The feature of the match was that H. H. Stephenson replaced Pooley at the wicket and disposed of five opponents. Jupp made 33 and 39 not out, and Charlwood 41. Apart from 54 by Rev. J. C. Crowdy and 57 by Rev. H. Foster, the home batting offered a feeble resistance to Silcock and Southerton, five batsmen failing to score at either effort.

The feature of 1872 was the inauguration of the first Worcester cricket week, the M.C.C. being then met for the first time. The premier club won by 3 wickets, John West scoring 52 and Mr. H. W. Verelst 42. Herefordshire was defeated by 96 runs, Mr. W. E. Moore and Mr. E. Oakes being the chief run-getters, and Mr. A. Everill taking 4 wickets for 15. Mr. F. Bent for the losers made 35 and 38 not out. Next year for the M.C.C. Farrands took 10 wickets for 36 in Worcestershire's score of 67. In the second innings, however, Mr. A. H. Hudson made 66 and Mr. Caldicott 50, following up a good bowling performance—7 for 27. The game was drawn. A splendid victory by 9 wickets over Herefordshire in June, 1874, atoned for a heavy defeat at the hands of Warwickshire. The former game was rendered noticeable by the bowling of Mr. A. Bailey, whose 6 wickets for 13 runs was largely instrumental in dismissing Herefordshire for 28. This was followed up in 1875 by a total of 392 against the same county; Mr. H. T. Allsop scoring 119, Mr. F. E. Allsop 63, and Mr. E. P. Jobson 61 not out. The latter was often of service to the team, as was also Rev. H. C. Moncrieff—a useful bat. He alone proved efficient 27 July, 1876, when Herefordshire won by 10 wickets; his performance of 26 and 38 with 4 for 38 being better than the figures indicate. There was a lively conclusion—Herefordshire needed 50 to win. Of those Mr. C. E. Brown made 41 not out, with three sixes and two fives, having scored 63 at his first effort, whilst in the 42 of Mr. E. E. Stanhope were a seven and a six. A crushing defeat was inflicted on Staffordshire; the result showing an innings and 153 runs to the good. Rev. H. C. Moncrieff scored 75, and Mr. H. T. Allsop 96. The M.C.C. won the opening match of the Worcester week, but Hon. Edward Lyttelton showed his fine batting ability for the county by making 50 and 29. Mr. George H. Longman headed the Club total with 41, while the ground bowler Flanagan took 11 for 62, and Farrands captured 5 for 5 apiece. There is an extraordinary discrepancy about the report of the encounter between the Free Foresters and the Gentlemen of Worcestershire, which was the concluding fixture of the week. The match is either reported as drawn or else as a victory by 231 runs for the wandering club.

For years after this it is difficult to deal with the Worcestershire fixtures, because the county team often met regiments, towns, and schools, as well as other counties. A few matches, however, are worth collecting from the long list of agreeable but unimportant games. One curious fact is that when Somersetshire arranged to play Worcestershire in 1901 it was stated by the executives that the counties had never met before; whereas in 1877, at Boughton, Somersetshire scored 136 and 143 to Worcestershire's 59 and 30; in 1878 at Bath the latter was beaten by an innings and 47 runs, and in 1879 at Sherborne the game was drawn —Somersetshire with 5 wickets down in their second effort being still 82 runs behind Worcestershire's first score of 321.

In 1877 the draw with Warwickshire was notable for the bowling of Mr. R. P. S. Higgs, who dismissed seven Midlanders for 36, but at the second effort Mr. C. Smith made 81 for them. Next year for the M.C.C. John West took 7 for 12 and 5 for 47; Rev. F. W. Wright getting 68. In 1881 none of the four completed innings of Herefordshire against Worcestershire reached 100, but Shropshire totalled 435 against them; Mr. A. E. Payne heading the score with 105.

Three minor fixtures may here be mentioned. In 1878 the town of Malvern twice played the county of Herefordshire, winning by 8 runs (58 to 50) in the home encounter, and having much the best of the out match—a draw. For Pershore *v.* Rev. G. Swinden's eleven, 4 August, 1879, Mr. R. T. P. Tearne took the 10 wickets in 7 overs without a run being hit from them—seven of the wickets being clean bowled.

In 1884 Mr. J. F. Hastings made a century for the county against Shropshire, his 103 being a large proportion of the total of 261. The sole defeat was at the hands of the M.C.C., when Attewell took the 10 wickets for 48 runs. In 1885 Worcestershire went into Wales to find opponents, and Mr. O. F. Jacson scored 113 against Radnorshire. The burden of the bowling was borne by Tyler (the subsequent Somersetshire crack), whose slow deliveries were censured in December, 1900. In the county averages his 121 wickets cost 10 runs apiece. Mr. P. H. Foley had by this time begun his enthusiastic interest in the side, which eventually bore such good fruit. In 1886 Mr. Alexander Smith made 41 *v.* Shropshire, but the fixtures were of a modest character. The Oxonian, Mr. J. Foord Kelsey, was of use in every department. For the next few years the importance of the matches lies only in the fact that they paved the way for the subsequent invigoration of Worcestershire cricket; and though it was a probationary period for so many useful young cricketers, the game as played by the county did not rise above a fairly high club standard. Still, it may be mentioned that in all the fixtures in 1889 the Rev. M. B. Buckle averaged 42, whilst Millward was the best all-round man. In 1890, as a schoolboy, Mr. H. K. Foster was already displaying his aptitude for batting, averaging 53 with a total of 376—his biggest contribution being 179. Husband also exceeded the century, and Mr. E. P. Jobson averaged 31. Mr. E. E. Lea claimed 31 wickets for 9 runs each, whilst the Cambridge bowler, Mr. C. Toppin, took eleven for a similar average. For purposes of record it may be mentioned in concluding this section that Dr. W. G. Grace, Messrs. W. R. Gilbert, J. Cranston, Eustace Crawley, C. P. Foley, Hon. and Rev. Edward Lyttelton, Hon. Alfred Lyttelton, M.P., and Tyler have all played for Worcestershire, though their reputation as cricketers rests on their performances for other teams.

1892–1898.—The beginning of important county cricket in Worcestershire was mainly due to a remarkable batch of young cricketers at Malvern College, the majority of whom resided within the county. Rarely has a school of the same size turned out a greater number of notable bats. Mr. P. H. Foley, the enthusiastic secretary, gathered these promising lads and some fairly efficient professionals into a county team, which amply justified a more ambitious programme. At the outset Mr. P. H. Latham was on the side, but later passed into the ranks of Sussex. Worcestershire has since been named Fostershire, after the famous brothers, but at the period now dealt with Mr. Reginald Foster was only a lower boy.

Five victories against three defeats in 1892 afforded the new side encouragement. Although no one scored a century, Messrs. Latham, H. F. Foster, Carmichael, E. P. Jobson, and P. R. Farrant all exceeded 80, and ten of the side averaged over 20 for the season. Raynor, Rollings, Millward, and Willoughby divided 136 out of the 158 wickets captured. Against Worcestershire the highest total was 245 made by Shropshire (in a disastrous game at Swindon, when the visitors were dismissed for 26), but the third century was passed in the matches with Staffordshire, Wiltshire, and Herefordshire.

Next season was not quite so fair on paper, as four victories were set opposite five reverses, but some of the five drawn games were favourable. The Second Elevens of Surrey and Lancashire as well as two M.C.C. fixtures were in the programme. Messrs. Latham, Greenstock, and E. P. Jobson all exceeded the century, whilst both Wheldon and Straw made their earliest appearances. The highest aggregate was 357 against Herefordshire, but the best results were 287 *v.* the Lancastrian and 241 for 5 wickets *v.* the Surrey representatives. The side suffered from playing no less than 34 individuals. A. Smith headed the bowling with 45 wickets for 10 runs apiece. Out of twelve fixtures in 1894 four were won and as many lost. In batting, Mr. H. K. Foster with the meritorious average of 31, having an aggregate of 468, proved immeasurably superior to anyone else in that year's record in Worcestershire, while Millward bowled so effectively that his 52 wickets cost but 8 runs each. Raynor also gave considerable assistance. The remainder, however, failed deplorably.

Mr. P. H. Foley had been mainly instrumental in organizing the Minor County Championship which has stimulated the cricket of the competing shires, although thus far it failed to rouse general interest. Worcestershire came out head of the list in 1895, playing most matches and scoring most victories, but had to put up with two defeats (from Durham and Hertfordshire). Mr. G. E. Bromley Martin, the old Etonian and Oxonian, and Mr. E. P. Jobson, were of most use with the bat, whilst

Bowley showed the promise he never realized until 1900. Arnold bowled admirably, taking 48 wickets for less than 10 runs each. This year a number of extra matches were arranged, which were played in various parts of the county, and created interest in the doings of the Eleven.

Worcestershire easily headed the minor counties in 1896, experiencing only one defeat, inflicted by Northamptonshire at Stourbridge. The splendid form of Mr. H. K. Foster, who in 1895 had scored a memorable century in the University match, was the main feature. He averaged 45, his aggregate of 550 being almost double that of any other batsman on the side, while his rapid 176 against Hertfordshire was the chief contribution to the total of 382. Arnold was of great use with bat and ball and Mr. G. E. Bromley Martin fairly earned the second place in the averages. By this time Straw had become a capable stumper.

In the brilliant record of 1897 there was no defeat; and none of the extra fixtures with the Yorkshire or Surrey Seconds or the M.C.C. ended adversely. Arnold did noble work, averaging 36 for 367 runs and taking 88 wickets at a cost of 11 each. Bird also bowled well, and the Captain, Mr. H. K. Foster, averaged 33 with a wonderful 106 at Lord's *v.* the M.C.C. as his best piece of work. The side also seemed to play better together, and success naturally inspired a confidence well maintained in 1898, when the county was openly competing for elevation to first-class rank, an effort which was deservedly rewarded. Not only did Worcestershire win the Minor County Championship with an unbeaten record, but twice defeated the Surrey Second Eleven, which had not known a reverse for five seasons. The struggle, however, with the M.C.C. ended in defeat by a margin of 4 wickets, the county each time scoring 205, and the M.C.C. 202 and 209 for six. Yorkshire Second with several of the county playing had to make 270 in their second innings, which was accomplished by 3 wickets. All the victories over minor counties were with an innings to spare. The team showed very even form, Mr. R. E. Foster's 147 not out being the only innings over 80. The trio of Fosters headed the averages and did able work, next to them being Mr. G. E. Bromley Martin and Wheldon. Four bowlers took 231 out of 233 wickets, Wilson capturing 90 for 11 and Bird 81 for 13. The contrast between the express deliveries of the former and the good length slows of the latter proved very destructive.

1899–1904.—In their first season among the first-class counties Worcestershire showed creditable form. The performance in the home match *v.* Hampshire set a seal on the reputation of the side. Messrs. W. L. and R. E. Foster each made a century in each innings, 140 and 172 not out, and 134 and 101 not out. Together they added 161 in an hour and a half in the first innings, and more runs still in their undefeated second effort. This new record created a great sensation. Arnold and Wheldon proved a valuable pair of professionals, and the brothers Bromley Martin and Mr. W. W. Lowe, the ex-Cantab, whose bowling was penalized in 1900, were not far behind. The bowling, however, was quite ineffective. The two victories were over Leicestershire and Derbyshire, when Mr. H. K. Foster scored 160 in less than three hours, Mr. G. E. Bromley Martin 102 (their partnership yielding 207 in two hours), and Mr. W. W. Lowe 102 not out, the total being 507. Against this had to be set five defeats, one being at the sensational *début* in May, when Yorkshire only managed to win by 11 runs. Wilson took 8 wickets for 70, and though Wainwright scored a lucky 86, it was the bowling of Brown of Darfield which won the match, for he claimed the last 6 wickets for only 19 runs. Ten centuries were hit in county fixtures. Arnold in a two-day match with Notts scored 140 and *v.* London County 104, and was chosen for the Players at the Oval. Worcestershire were severely treated by the M.C.C. at Lord's, losing by 332 runs, Captain E. G. Wynyard scoring 89 and 81, Carpenter 40 and 60, Storer 64, and Mr. W. L. Murdoch 66, while Albert Trott captured 11 wickets for 103.

With a largely extended programme Worcestershire closed the century in dismal fashion, defeating only Hants, Gloucestershire, and Leicestershire (by 10 runs), and losing ten county fixtures as well as three of their four extra engagements. Mr. R. E. Foster headed the batting with an average of 32, but never equalled his masterly double century in the Gentlemen *v.* Players at Lord's, or his superb 171 for Oxford *v.* Cambridge—innings which will never be forgotten. The bulk of the batting was done by Mr. H. K. Foster, who scored 1,235 with an average of 30, and made centuries against Lancashire and Middlesex. Bowley improved notably, while Arnold and Mr. W. W. Lowe lent the most efficient aid. But the bowling fell below a good standard, Wilson's 107 wickets costing 23 runs each, though he took the last four against Leicestershire for 8 runs. It also needed an invaluable stand by Mr. W. P. Robertson and the veteran Mr. A. J. Webbe to save Middlesex from defeat, and in the home match against Yorkshire Worcestershire up to a certain point had the best of the game with the champions until Tunnicliffe scored a masterly 158, for which he batted five and a half hours. At Lord's *v.* the M.C.C., Bowley and Wheldon added 162 in two hours and a half.

With three more reverses than victories the season of 1901 looked less satisfactory than it really was, for after a disastrous start Worcestershire played the later fixtures with considerable success, the final victory by 342 runs over Gloucestershire being quite a notable achievement. Mr. R. E. Foster was not only the most prominent but the most consistent bat. The Malvern Captain, Mr. W. H. B. Evans, who obtained his colours as a freshman at Oxford next year and played the best innings in the University match, besides bowling so finely against Cambridge in 1903, unfortunately threw his services soon afterwards into the hands of Hampshire. Pearson made a favourable impression, and most of the other members of the side played up to their previous form. The feature of the more interesting season of 1902 was the considerable, if intermittent, success which attended the lobs of Mr. G. H. Simpson-Hayward, whose peculiar flick was acquired by practising with billiard balls. Unfortunately Mr. R. E. Foster could not come into the side until the middle of the season, nor was his brother so certain as of yore. Still, the eleven showed unmistakable promise of better things, and the new Irish wicket-keeper, Gaukrodger, proved not only excellent in his department, but a far better batsman than Straw. Wilson with his low delivery was often an effective fast bowler, and Arnold's invaluable work with bat and ball formed a notable feature. At their best a fine side, Worcestershire displayed considerable inequality in 1903, even though they obtained a higher place than ever before, being bracketed fifth with Notts. Wilson and Arnold sent Sussex back on a good wicket for 47, the latter bowler showing consistently fine form throughout the year, which caused him to be selected for both the metropolitan matches against the Gentlemen, and for the Rest against the Champion County. He was also chosen to go with the M.C.C. side to Australia, where he bowled with consistent steadiness. It should be added that thus far he is the only cricketer who has scored 1,000 runs and taken 100 wickets for the western county. In Australia, for the M.C.C., Mr. R. E. Foster made the highest individual score contributed by an Englishman in a Test Match at the Antipodes, a fine as well as notable innings. The great achievement of 1903 for Worcestershire was Mr. H. K. Foster's 120 against Yorkshire, a contribution comparable with any ever compiled in championship matches. Bowley came prominently forward as a free and forcing batsman, while the patience of Mr. W. S. Caldwell was of great assistance in a period in July when Worcestershire carried everything before them.

In 1904 and 1905 the county team, though displaying excellent form, appeared lacking in a capacity for finishing off matches which were in their favour. Bowley, Arnold, and the Fosters were again considerably superior to the rest in batting, while Burrows materially strengthened the attack, and Pearson at last seemed in a fair way towards justifying the high hopes which he had inspired.

Now that a higher standard of cricket has been reached by all the three first-class western counties, there is every probability that Worcestershire will eventually attain a more prominent position than has yet fallen to its lot.

MALVERN COLLEGE

The beginnings of cricket at Malvern were in many respects unique. The school stands well up on the side of the hill, with a slope running to the railway embankment which skirts the foot of the grounds. An excellent position from many points of view, but hardly suitable for the purposes of cricket, for at first no attempt was made to cut terraces or to level the ground. It is not easy to imagine what this hillside cricket can have been like, but there are two obvious possibilities about a wicket inclined at an angle of 45°. The break of the ball must have been measured by feet instead of by inches, and fielding on the lower slopes can have been no sinecure. Under such adverse conditions was cricket played at Malvern until the first terrace was cut. It was then that the original Senior Turf came into being, and even that level expanse of 100 yards square must have made a vast difference in the conditions of the game. As time went on, laborious excavations in the side of the hill yielded, at great cost, more and much-needed space. To-day the dimensions of the Senior Turf stand at 230 yards by 120 yards, and further extension is now hardly possible. Separated from the upper terrace by a high bank is the Junior Turf, and here more levelling is contemplated. Until a few years ago a public road ran between the Junior Turf and the Bath Field. Now the road has been diverted, the railings taken away, and the two grounds are one, in everything but their level. Besides the Senior and Junior, smaller grounds have been made; but it is not yet the privilege of all the boys to play on perfectly level wickets. Such a consummation is greatly to be desired, though unlikely to be realized for some years to come, as the difficulties of the work are only equalled by the expense.

There is something to be said in favour of a playground laid out in the form of terraces, and not least from a spectator's point of view. No better place than the bank of the Senior Turf could be found for watching a cricket match. Moreover, for the purposes of supervision, it is no small advantage to be able to command a view of several games in progress.

There are probably few cricket grounds in the country possessing truer or faster wickets than can be found almost anywhere on the

Senior Turf. A really slow wicket is almost unknown, and even after the wettest of weather the ground dries at an extraordinary pace. On the other hand, the wicket seldom, if ever, becomes fiery or bumpy; it wears well during the longest spell of dry weather. Heavy scoring is the natural result of this condition of the turf, and when the narrowness of the boundaries is taken into account, it may well be imagined that the Malvern batsmen, as a rule, fare better than the bowlers.

Among the improvements of late years, the pavilion deserves special notice. Facing the Senior Turf, it forms part of a block consisting of gymnasium, workshops, etc., and formerly was but a poor makeshift. In 1893 £1,000 was spent on a more pretentious building, which contains a spacious luncheon-room, and is all that a well-planned school pavilion should be.

As regards personal history, the assertion can be made with some confidence that, although the school was started in 1865, its reputation in the game is the outcome of the last fifteen years. It is evident that during the first twenty years of the school's existence there was a general lack of enthusiasm for cricket. There were no masters who devoted themselves to the task of instilling keenness, and as yet the appointment of men with athletic as well as other qualifications had not begun to find favour in the eyes of school authorities. Consequently we find that few cricketers of merit were produced during this period, and that there was hardly enough success to awaken enthusiasm or to establish a high standard of self-respect. It would be unfair, however, to pass over the names of the two Stratfords, A. Newnham, F. A. Curteis, and H. B. Watson. In 1886 the school was at a low ebb, and the number of boys had fallen to 180. Much interest was taken in lawn tennis, but cricket was generally looked upon as a game only to be played under compulsion. It was at this critical period in the athletic history of the school that for the first time a master was appointed to superintend the games. There can be no doubt that the marked success in the game which has raised the school's reputation to its present high level is due in no small measure to the new régime.

The organization of the cricket is as follows[1] :—On whole schooldays two hours at least are devoted to net practice, and it is needless to say that the style and improvement in play of the batters is carefully watched by those who are interested in coaching. There are three sets of nets on the Senior Turf, as well as those on the lower grounds. The Lower School is 'fagged' in turn for fielding at the senior nets. When practice is finished, the eleven and the aspirants to the eleven have a spell of fielding. On half-holidays, when there is no foreign match, cricket begins at half-past two and ends at six. The school is divided into thirteen or fourteen games, known under the name of clubs. The order of the clubs is nominally as follows :—Senior, Middle 1, Middle 2, Junior, Colts, Sixth, Seventh, and so on. Of these, the Senior, Middle 1, and Colts play on the Senior Turf, and it is the custom in these clubs for batsmen to retire after scoring thirty runs. In this way everyone can be sure of an innings during the afternoon, and no great tax is put upon the endurance of the players in the field, as it is unusual for a side to be at the wickets for more than an hour and a half. Besides the professionals, masters and others connected with the school play in the Senior. Middle 1 is practically a prefects' club, where those who cannot attain to the Senior may 'save their face.' The Colts' club contains the most promising young cricketers, who, in course of time, are drafted into the Senior. It is considered an honour to be included in this club, for the boys receive special attention, and have advantages in the way of good practice wickets at the Senior nets. The Colts' pitch is twenty-one yards long instead of the regulation twenty-two. That the organization of the club answers its purpose, is apparent from the number of 'colts' who ultimately make their way into the school eleven. The arrangement of games by houses does not find favour at Malvern, but there is an excellent system of house fielding. After tea on half-holidays the captain of each house brings out his first fifteen or so and gives practice in catching and fielding, while the house wicket-keeper stands at a stump ready to receive the ball as it is returned by the fielders. House matches are played on the 'knock-out' principle, and are fought out with intense keenness. Occasionally a half-holiday is devoted to a house match, but as a rule these matches are played at odd times on whole school days, while those not specially interested in the game are engaged in net practice. Calculations are frequently upset by altered conditions of the wicket, for a week may easily be spent in playing out the match.

In order to ensure regular supervision on the lower grounds, each one of the old colours has a certain number of clubs apportioned to him, and is held more or less responsible for the maintenance of good order and keenness in those clubs. Each club captain, too, is a person of some importance, for it is his duty to report cases of slackness or insubordination, and to attend weekly meetings at which the school captain and the cricket master are present. The club scoring-books are then inspected, and cases for promotion or the reverse are considered. Under this effective system it would be well-nigh impossible for talent to go undetected. No stone

[1] The success of modern cricket at Malvern is mainly due to the unceasing and enthusiastic efforts of Mr. Toppin.—Ed.

is left unturned in the effort to encourage keenness and to bring on likely cricketers. All the essentials of the game are insisted upon, but individuality is not repressed, and boys are left to form their own style by imitation, if they like, not by compulsion. No system could be effective without a spirit of keenness among the boys themselves, and no one is more eager to learn and more willing to listen to advice than the Malvern boy. Under these conditions it is not surprising that the school cricket has flourished of late years.

The best-known Malvern cricketers, besides those already mentioned, are P. H. Latham, the five Fosters, C. J. Burnup, H. H. Marriott, G. H. Simpson-Hayward, W. W. Lowe, R. B. Porch, E. H. Simpson, W. S. Bird, W. H. B. Evans, E. H. and A. P. Day. The school has not produced many bowlers of note ; the best are the Stratfords, Capt. Newnham, W. W. Lowe, G. H. Neville, and W. H. B. Evans. The face of the ground and the narrowness of the boundaries are all against slow bowling, and most of the successful bowlers have been fast or fast-medium.

The school plays matches every year with Repton and Uppingham. Shrewsbury, Rossall, and Sherborne have all been played at different times, but these matches have been discontinued for various reasons, mainly connected with distance. The fixtures with Repton show a curious record. Up to 1891 Malvern had not won a single match for thirteen years, but since that date can claim a large proportion of victories. With Uppingham only a few matches have been played, and nearly all of these have been drawn.

To face page 347.

TOPOGRAPHY

THE HUNDRED OF BLACKENHURST

CONTAINING THE PARISHES[1] OF

ABBOT'S MORTON
BADSEY (with Aldington hamlet)
BRETFORTON
CHURCH HONEYBOURNE
EVESHAM BOROUGH
All Saints St. Lawrence Bengeworth
GREAT HAMPTON
Little Hampton Township
NORTON
Lenchwick Tithing
NORTH AND MIDDLE LITTLETON
SOUTH LITTLETON
OFFENHAM
OLDBERROW
WICKHAMFORD

THE hundred of Blackenhurst consists of lands which in the eighth century are said to have formed part of the foundation grant of the monastery of Evesham. This grant is said to have comprised 67 'mansæ,' being on both sides of the River Avon, of which seven were in Willersey in Gloucestershire and nine in Bengeworth and Hampton,[2] the latter being afterwards claimed as part of the hundred of Oswaldslow. The great manor of Ombersley with its 12 'cassatæ,' 5 hides at Abbot's Morton, and land at Oldberrow, were the subjects of separate grants.[3] The town of Evesham forms the nucleus of the hundred which occupies the famous vale, but two parishes, Ombersley and Oldberrow, are quite detached.

By the time of the Domesday Survey the hundred of Fishborough (Fissesberge) had been formed, consisting of Evesham, Norton and Lenchwick, Oldberrow, Offenham, the Littletons, Bretforton, Badsey and Aldington, Wickhamford, Church Honeybourne, and Ombersley.[4] Hampton and Bengeworth, which had formed the subject of the famous quarrel between the churches of Evesham and Worcester, were included in the bishop's hundred of Oswaldslow,[5] but though many services there were claimed by the bishop the survey only assigned to him the geld.

The abbot's jurisdictionary hundred then contained only 65 hides, and to make it a perfect unit of the twelve hundreds at which the whole county was assessed, it was 'made up' by the 15 hides which lay in the city of Worcester, and 20 hides which lay in Doddingtree hundred.[6]

In less than 20 years after Domesday the hundred had been rearranged and its name changed to Blackenhurst (Blakehurst, Blacahurst),[7] but the reason for this change and the derivation of the new name have not been ascertained. The hundred of Blackenhurst is first mentioned in a charter of

1 According to the *Pop. Ret.* 1831.
2 Birch, *Cart. Sax.* i. 183.
3 Ibid. 171, 176, 181.
4 *V. C. H. Worc.* i. 306–7.
5 Ibid. 297, 307.
6 Ibid. 307a.
7 From confirmation in Chart. R. 25 Hen. III. m. 4. This confirmation was granted because the seal of the original charter was broken.

Henry I., the date of which has been fixed at 1100–1108,[1] by which the abbey received a grant and confirmation of the whole hundred to hold in frankalmoign.

It is not clear when Bengeworth and Hampton became detached from Oswaldslow and included altogether in Blackenhurst. About the middle of the thirteenth century, William Beauchamp of Elmley is said to have withdrawn his moiety of Bengeworth from the bishop's hundred to his own court of the barony of Elmley,[2] and this course was followed also by his son William Beauchamp, earl of Warwick.[3] Apparently during the quarrel the latter conveyed Bengeworth to the abbot of Evesham, and when the quarrel was finally settled there is no mention of Bengeworth.[4] In the Subsidy Roll of 1280[5] Hampton and Bengeworth are included in Blackenhurst, and from that date onwards have so remained. There is no evidence to show that the bishop of Worcester continued to exact service from these places, or that any arrangement was arrived at with the abbot concerning them. By 1280, Abbot's Morton, Sheriff's Lench, and Atch Lench, which at the time of Domesday had been included in the hundred of 'Esch,'[6] had been transferred to that of Blackenhurst,[7] in which they still remain.

The distance of Ombersley from the rest of the hundred led the inhabitants to compound with the abbot for their attendance at the hundred court. The amount paid by them for the privilege of not attending the court was known as 'Hundred Silver,' and in 1540 amounted to 108*s.* 5*d.* yearly.[8]

In 1760 Ombersley was by Act of Parliament included in Oswaldslow for fiscal purposes,[9] an arrangement maintained by subsequent Acts.[10] The population return of 1811 accordingly shows it in that hundred, in which it has since remained. This was apparently the first change in the extent of the hundred since the thirteenth century. In 1894 the parish of Oldberrow was transferred to the county of Warwick.

The abbot had complete jurisdiction within his hundred of Blackenhurst. He had soc and sac, and tol and theam and infangthef, his lands there were free and quit of shires and hundreds, and all secular service and scutage, except the service of four knights and a half.[11] One of the chartularies of the abbey states that in the hundred of 'Fisseberga' there were 65 hides,[12] 'in which the church of Evesham has such liberty that neither the sheriff nor any officer under the king[13] can there do any violence or seize or receive anything except by leave of the abbot, who has soc and sac and tol and theam.' The abbots who came immediately after the Conquest alienated much of the abbey's lands, and this document carefully limits the power of future abbots. 'No abbot is able to make "teinland" or to give any inheritance except for a term of life, or to give tithes or churchscot to any man, nor could any man retain it, because all those lands were given for the use of the church.'

1 *V. C. H. Worc.* i. 330*a*.
2 *Worc. Epis. Reg. Giffard* (Worc. Hist. Soc.), 75.
3 Ibid.
4 See under Bengeworth.
5 Printed by the Worc. Hist. Soc.
6 *V. C. H. Worc.* i. 307*b*, 308*a*.
7 *Lay Subs. R.* c. 1280 (Worc. Hist. Soc.), p. 81.
8 Mins. Accts. 31–2 Hen. VIII. L. R. 1330, m. 27*d*.
9 Stat. 1 Geo. III. cap. 2.
10 Ibid. 5 Geo. III. cap. 5; ibid. 6 Geo. III. cap. 9; ibid. 8 Geo. III. cap. 8; ibid. 38 Geo. III. cap. 5.
11 Chart. R. 25 Hen. III. m. 4.
12 Cott. MS. Vesp. B. xxiv. f. 41*d*.
13 'Potens persona post regem.'

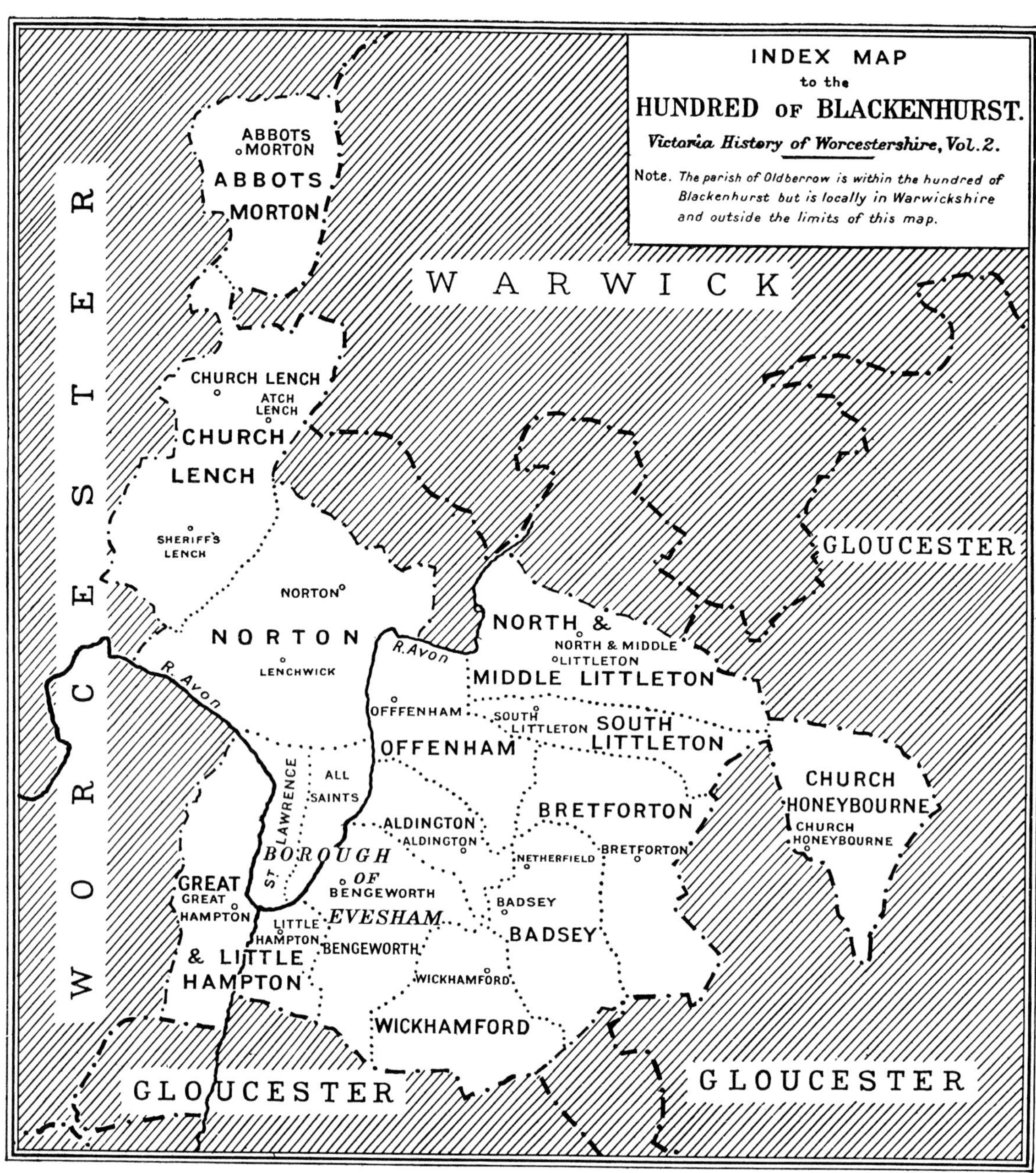

To face page 349

When the abbey was dissolved the hundred passed to the Crown, with whom it apparently still remains. The office of bailiff of the hundred and liberty was granted for life to Sir Philip Hoby, then to Sir Thomas, on whose death in 1567 a similar grant was made to his son Sir Edward Hoby[1] at a fee of 40*s.* yearly. In 1605, when the second charter was granted to Evesham, James I. granted the reversion of this office to the corporation of the borough to hold during the lives of John Kighley, son of Sir Philip Kighley, Philip Harris, son of Philip Harris, and Theophilus Baylie, son of the Rev. Lewis Baylie.[2]

[1] Pat. 9 Eliz. pt. 3, m. 27.

[2] May, *Hist. of Evesham* (ed. 1845), 454.

ABBOT'S MORTON

Mortun, Mortune (viii.–xi. cent.) ; Morton Abbas (xiii.–xvi. cent.) ; Abbot's Morton or Stony Morton (xvii.–xviii. cent.).

The parish of Abbot's Morton is situated on the eastern border of the county seven miles north of Evesham. A brook called Piddle Brook, which has given its name to the next parish of North Piddle, flows through the parish from south to north, then, turning westward, forms a portion of the northern boundary. From the valley of this stream, which is about 183 feet above the ordnance datum, the land rises towards the western boundary, where it reaches the height of 258 feet. The subsoil is keuper marl, and the surface is stiff red clay. The parish contains 1,474 acres ;[1] its population is entirely agricultural. The main road from Worcester to Alcester runs through the parish from west to east, sending a branch northward to the village. The nearest railway station is Alcester, some six miles distant, on the Barnt Green and Evesham branch of the Midland Railway, opened in 1876. Among other ancient place names we find Drayshott Hill Copse, Stoneway Copse, Mapleryding Copse, and Snell's Gutter.[2] An Enclosure Act for the parish was passed in 1802.[3]

MANOR In 708 Kenred, king of the Mercians, is said to have granted the land called Mortun to Egwin for the monastery at Evesham.[4]

The Piddle Brook formed one of the boundaries of Kenred's grant. In the time of Edward the Confessor Abbot's Morton contained five hides, but when the Domesday Survey was taken a large part had been leased out. The Survey states that it was held of the abbey of Evesham by Ranulf,[5] who was probably brother of Abbot Walter,[6] the first Norman abbot of Evesham, who succeeded Æthelwig in 1077. Abbot Walter is described in the chronicles as a young man, who, lacking in worldly wisdom,[7] declined to accept the homage of many tenants of the monastery, and bestowed their lands upon his own kinsmen.[8] Prominent among them was his brother Ranulf, to whom he probably gave land in Abbot's Morton and also Bretforton and Littleton (q.v.) in Worcestershire, and Kinwarton in Warwickshire. For about eighty years after the Domesday Survey, Ranulf's lands in Abbot's Morton followed the same descent as those in Bretforton(q.v.). About 1163–4, however, Randolph or Ranulf, son of William of Coughton, received a grant of the mill of Sambourne in Warwickshire from Abbot Adam and the convent of Evesham, and in return surrendered all claim to Abbot's Morton and lands in Norton and Hampton and a messuage in Evesham.[9] By another deed, probably executed at the same time, his brother Simon released to the convent his right in the same lands, and received in return a grant of Wrottesley and Loynton in Staffordshire.[10] By these conveyances this part of Abbot's Morton was restored to the possession of the monastery.

Of other less important tenants in Abbot's Morton during the twelfth century, mention may be made of Ralph the freeman, who is probably the Ralph of Morton elsewhere referred to,[11] Stephen and Robert de Wicke, each of whom held half a hide or two virgates.[12] There were besides nine 'virgatarii' and nine 'cotarii' who owed the ordinary service and customs to the abbot as their lord. Two virgates were appropriated to the chapel, and the village rendered yearly 60*s.* to the kitchener of the monastery and 40*s.* to the abbot.[13]

From the twelfth century until the dissolution of Evesham Abbey in 1539, the manor of Abbot's Morton was held by the monastery. During those centuries little is known of its history, and it is seldom mentioned in the abbey chronicles. In 1230–1 Abbot Thomas Marlborough bought a hundred acres of

[1] *Worc. Co. Coun. Handbk.* (1903), 149.

[2] Pat. 38 Hen. VIII. pt. 13, m. 7.

[3] Stat. 42 Geo. III. c. 36.

[4] Birch, *Cart. Sax.* i. 176.

[5] *V.C.H. Worc.* i. 307*b*. There seems to have been another manor of Morton which has been identified as Abbot's Morton, and which at the time of the Domesday Survey was the possession of Robert de Stafford, under whom it was held by Ernold. It had previously been held by Aethelwig, of whom it is said that he could betake himself where he would. (*V.C.H. Worc.* i. 311*b*.) The Survey states that there were '1 burgess who rendered 10*s.* and a saltpan that rendered 2*s.* and 8 mits of salt,' attached to the manor (*V.C.H. Worc.* i. 311*b*). This was probably the Morton which was held by Hervey de Stafford in 1212 (*Red Bk. of the Exch.* ii. 613). An abstract from Domesday Book given in Cott. MS. Vesp. B. xxiv. f. 6, also gives two Mortons in 'Leisse' or 'Esch' Hundred, but the burgage and saltpan are not mentioned as appurtenant to either. Robert de Stafford, who held the second Morton, became a monk of Evesham in 1088 (*Salt Soc. Publ.* ii. (1), 178, 182 ; Dugdale, *Mon.* ii. 18), and had previously granted Wrottesley to the monastery (Ibid.).

[6] Ibid. 261.

[7] *Chron. de Evesham* (Rolls Ser.), 96.

[8] Ibid.

[9] Cott. MS. Vesp. B. xxiv. f. 35.

[10] *Hist. of Family of Wrottesley*, by Major-Genl. Wrottesley, 8. The original deed was burned in the fire at Wrottesley in 1897.

[11] Cott. MS. Vesp. B. xxiv. f. 12.

[12] Ibid. f. 36 *d.*

[13] Ibid.

land at Morton and Lenchwick in Worcestershire and Sambourne in Warwickshire for the use of the abbots,[1] and immediately afterwards he built a house at Abbot's Morton 'in which the abbots might dwell when they went there.'[2]

From the Lay Subsidy Roll of about 1280 it would appear that Abbot's Morton was one of the least profitable manors in the Vale. It produced towards the subsidy only 39*s.* 6*d.*, of which the abbot paid 20*s.*[3]

In 1291[4] and during the fourteenth century Abbot's Morton was associated in some way with Atch Lench, at least for fiscal purposes.[5] In 1302–3 the manor seems to have been in the hands of Malcolm Musard, who is styled lord of Morton, and who then presented to the church;[6] probably he held only as lessee, as the convent afterwards resumed the right of presentation.[7] In 1401 an attack was made on the abbot's property there, and a commission was issued to inquire who were the culprits,[8] but the result is not known.

When the monastery of Evesham was dissolved in 1539, Abbot's Morton came into the hands of the Crown,[9] and so continued until 24 February, 1543–4, when Henry VIII. granted it to his last queen, Catherine Parr.[10]

In 1546 Queen Catherine leased it to Sir Philip Hoby,[11] son of William Hoby of Leominster and a distinguished diplomatist during three reigns.[12] It is said that his zeal for the reformation recommended him to Henry VIII., and on the dissolution of the religious houses a large share of the monastic spoils, including the greater part of the property of the abbey of Evesham in the Vale, passed to him by royal grant. The site of the priory of Bisham in Berkshire also came into his possession and became the chief seat of the Hoby family. On 28 August, 1546, he received from the Crown, for the sum of £201 11*s.* 5*d.* and in exchange for the reversion of the manor and advowson of Naunton Beauchamp, a grant of the reversion after the death of the queen of the manor and advowson of Abbot's Morton, to hold to himself, his heirs and assigns for ever by the service of a fortieth part of a knight's fee and the rent of £3 2*s.* 1½*d.*[13]

Sir Philip Hoby afterwards conveyed this manor with that of Offenham to John Hooper, bishop of Worcester, and Sir Richard Blount, in trust to the use of himself for life, and then to his issue male, and in default of such issue to his half-brother Sir Thomas Hoby and his heirs male, with contingent remainders to Richard and William Hoby, also half-brothers of Sir Philip.[14] This conveyance was confirmed on 8 April, 1552.[15]

Sir Philip Hoby died without issue on 29 May, 1558, seised of the manor of Abbot's Morton.[16] His wife Elizabeth survived him. His heir was his sister Mary, the wife of Brian Carter[17]; but in accordance with the settlement mentioned above Abbot's Morton passed to Thomas Hoby, and in 1559 Brian and Mary Carter levied a fine by which they surrendered to him all their right in this and other manors.[18] Thomas Hoby was knighted at Greenwich on 9 March, 1565-6, and about the end of that month was sent as ambassador to France.[19] He lived only a few months afterwards, dying at Paris on 13 July, 1566.[20] His son and heir Edward was then only six years of age, and during his minority his mother, who in 1574 married John Lord Russell, had the custody of his lands. Edward Hoby was knighted in 1582. Some time afterwards he became involved in great pecuniary embarrassment.[21] In June, 1588, 'the only moytie' of certain woods in Abbot's Morton was seized by the sheriff for debt; in the following year another distraint was made on them, and William Ownsted of London, who had purchased 'three parts' of the woods from Sir Edward Hoby, complained of the inconvenience he suffered by the property being still undischarged.[22] It was probably to extricate himself from his financial difficulties that Hoby disposed of a great part of the property which his family had acquired in Worcestershire. In 1595 he conveyed the manor of Abbot's Morton to his uncle Richard Hoby and Margaret his wife and the heirs and assigns of Richard.[23] The latter resided in the Seyne House at Badsey,[24] but very little is known of him.

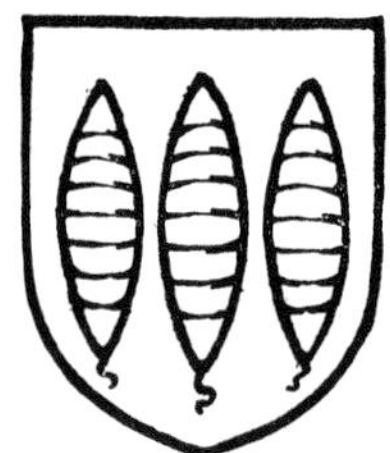

HOBY. *Silver, three weavers bottoms gules.*

Five years later Richard Hoby conveyed Abbot's Morton to Richard Mottershead and Ralph Hodges,[25] probably in trust for the purpose of getting rid of the entail. For some years afterwards there is no evidence to show who actually held the manor. In 1609, however, it was in the possession of Charles Ketilby and Elizabeth his wife.[26] Elizabeth was the daughter of Richard Hoby, and in 1587 had married Thomas Sheldon of Broadway, after whose death she married in 1596-7 Philip Kighley or Keightley of South Littleton, afterwards knighted, one of the tellers of the Exchequer.[27] Her second husband was deceased in April 1605,[28] and between this date and 1609 the manor of Abbot's Morton must have been conveyed to Charles and Elizabeth Ketilby, probably as part of Elizabeth's dower on her third marriage. In Trinity

1 *Chron. de Evesham* (Rolls Ser.), 275. This reference is probably to Norton, which was usually associated with Lenchwick.

2 Ibid. 276–7.

3 *Lay Subs. R. c.* 1280 (Worc. Hist. Soc.), 86.

4 *Pope Nich. Tax.* (Rec. Com.), 229b.

5 Ibid. and *Lay Subs. R.* 1332–3 (Worc. Hist. Soc.), 19.

6 *Sede Vac. Reg.* (Worc. Hist. Soc.), 68.

7 Ibid. 205.

8 *Cal. of Pat.* 1399–1401, p. 552.

9 Mins. Accts. 31–2 Hen. VIII. L.R. 1330, m. 22, 22*d.* Sundry rents in the city of Worcester were accounted for by the Crown bailiffs with this manor.

10 *L. and P. Hen. VIII.* xix. 645.

11 Close 38 Hen. VIII. pt. 3, No. 17.

12 For the Hoby family see *V.C.H. Berks.* under Bisham.

13 Pat. 38 Hen. VIII. pt. 13, m. 7. The rent of £3 2*s.* 1½*d.* was afterwards included in the fee farm rents conveyed to Lord Hawley and the other trustees for sale on 11 Nov. 1670. (Pat. 28 Chas. II. pt. ii.)

14 Chan. inq. p.m. 5 and 6 Phil. and Mary cxv. 74.

15 Ibid.

16 Ibid.

17 Ibid.

18 Feet of F. Div. Cos. East. 1 Eliz.

19 *Dict. of Nat. Biog.* xxvii. 55.

20 Chan. inq. p. m. 9 Eliz. cxlv. 3.

21 S. P. Dom. Eliz. clxxv. 7.

22 B. M. Add. MS. 15,903, f. 6.

23 Com. Pleas Recov. R. East. 37 Eliz. m. 3; Feet of F. Worc. Mich. 37-8 Eliz. For a further account of Sir Edward Hoby see the *V.C.H. Berks.* under Bisham, and also the *Dict. of Nat. Biog.*

24 Com. Pleas Recov. R. East. 37 Eliz. m. 3.

25 Feet of F. Worc. Hil. 42 Eliz.

26 Ibid. Trin. 7 Jas. I.

27 Information supplied by Mr. O. G. Knapp of Bengeworth, from the register of Badsey; Exch. Dep. Hil. 14 Jas. I. No. 20.

28 *Cal. of S. P. Dom.* 1603-10, p. 211.

term of 1609 they conveyed it to John Ketilby and John Hopkins.[1]

After this the manor became the property of Abel Gower of Boughton,[2] near Worcester, who on 1 December, 1622, granted it to Edward Lewis of Spernall, then incumbent of Abbot's Morton, and Richard Lewis and their heirs for ever.[3] Richard Lewis was a minor at his father's death, and the manor was in the custody of the Master of the Court of Wards until his majority.[4] By his will dated 30 October, 1652, Richard Lewis left Abbot's Morton to two of his sisters, Margaret the wife of William Folkingham and Elizabeth the wife of William Brooke,[5] although he seems to have had a daughter who married one Saunders and had a son Edward Saunders.[6] In 1664 William Folkingham and Margaret levied a fine of their moiety of the manor to the use of themselves and their children, and in default of issue to the use of Margaret absolutely.[7] William Brooke and Elizabeth settled their moiety on themselves for life, and in default of issue on the right heirs of Elizabeth.[8] A division of the property was made on 20 December, 1681, and both sisters and their husbands dealt with the manor by fine in the following year.[9]

Elizabeth Brooke died without issue, and by her will dated 17 July, 1687, left her moiety to her niece Elizabeth Gale, then Elizabeth Fisher, the daughter of her sister Sarah Lewis, who had married Robert Gale. In 1719 Elizabeth Fisher barred the remainder by suffering a recovery of her moiety, and by her will dated 11 November in the same year left it to her nephew William Gale, of North Piddle, the second son of her brother Lewis. In 1721 William Gale sold his moiety to John Ballard and John Ellins of Abbot's Morton for £175.[10]

In 1682 William Folkingham and Margaret had made a further settlement of their moiety, which Margaret afterwards bequeathed to her niece Joan Gale—sister of Elizabeth Gale or Fisher, to whom Elizabeth Brooke had left the other moiety—and in default of issue to her nephew Lewis Gale, brother of Joan, and Edward Saunders, grandson of Richard Lewis, Margaret's brother, for their lives, with the remainder to her right heirs.[11] Joan Gale is said to have died without issue, and Margaret Folkingham's moiety then passed to Lewis Gale, who presented to the church in 1699. Lewis had issue Edward, William, and three other sons. Edward is said to have become on his father's death the heir at law of Margaret Folkingham, but this seems to be an error, as Edward Saunders had not only a life interest under Margaret's will, but, as the grandson of Richard Lewis, had a prior claim.[12] On 1 May, 1711, Edward Saunders jointly with Rebecca his wife and William Saunders his son and heir conveyed the moiety of the manor to John Bulleine of Evesham, who seems to have held it until 1723. On 11 June of that year Edward Gale of Spernall, eldest son of Lewis Gale, jointly with Alice his wife, is said to have sold a moiety to John Ballard and John Ellins, who already held one moiety; it is not clear how he came to hold this share, however, and the conveyance may simply have been for the purpose of assuring the title of Ballard and Ellins in the moiety which they had purchased from his brother William Gale of North Piddle.[13] On 25 June, 1723, John Bulleine of Evesham and his wife Phoebe sold the moiety which they had acquired from Edward Saunders to John Ballard and John Ellins for £90,[14] and the moieties thus became again united. The conveyances to Ballard and Ellins seem to have been for the use of the latter, who presented to the church in 1727[15] and left the manor at his death to his son Edward Ellins, who was incumbent of the parish in 1736. Edward Ellins in turn bequeathed it to Robert, Christopher, and Ursula Hunt, the three children of Robert Hunt, the brother of his wife Anne.[16] It was afterwards sold by the Hunts to Thomas Cowley, in whose family it remained until about 1850, when it passed to the Perks family.[17] About 1890 Mr. Henry Perks of Inkberrow sold part of the manor to the Rev. Thomas Walker, rector of Abbot's Morton, on whose death, in 1904, it passed to his widow,[18] Mrs. Walker of Battenhall Manor, Worcester. Mrs. Walker died in 1905, and this share is now held by her representatives. The other part was sold to Mr. W. H. Bagnall of Charlton Kings, Cheltenham, who still owns it.[19]

Near the church is the Court Close, with traces of a moat, and there are in the village several old timber houses. A house described as the old Manor House was recently pulled down.[20] There is a tradition that the silver bells belonging to the abbot are buried near the moat.

In 1609, in a presentment as to highways, bridges, etc., from Abbot's Morton, it is stated that the whipping stocks and the other stocks had been repaired.[21]

CHURCH The church is dedicated in honour of St. Peter. It stands at the west end of the village street, being approached by a flight of steps, the ground rising rapidly from east to west.

The church consists of chancel with north vestry, nave with north transept and south porch, and west tower. Its history appears to have been that of many churches in the neighbourhood. At the end of the twelfth century there was a church with an aisleless nave and chancel, the chancel of which, at some time difficult to fix, but not later than the first quarter of the fourteenth century, was rebuilt of the full width of the nave. A north transept was added about 1340 and a west tower in the fifteenth century. The east gable of the chancel and all the south side of the church were faced with ashlar in the seventeenth century. A west gallery was put up in 1840, but certainly had a predecessor, as a dormer window on the south side of the nave, near the south-west angle,

1 Feet of F. Worc. Trin. 7 Jas. I.
2 Prattinton Coll. (Soc. Antiq.)
3 Ibid.
4 *Cal. of S. P. Dom.* 1635-6, p. 377.
5 Prattinton Coll. (Soc. Antiq.)
6 Ibid.
7 Ibid. and Feet of F. Worc. Mich. 16 Chas. II.
8 Prattinton Coll. (Soc. Antiq.)
9 Ibid. and Feet of F. Worc. Hil. 33-4 Chas. II. William Folkingham and Margaret, William Brooke and Elizabeth, Thomas Wormington senior, and Katherine, Thomas Wormington junior, Richard Pardoe, Wintour Harris and Katherine, conveyed it to Francis Ballard, William Grove, Samuel Saunders, John Ward, and Henry Hill.
10 Prattinton Coll. (Soc. Antiq.)
11 Ibid. 12 Ibid. 13 Ibid.
14 Ibid. As the other moiety was sold for £175, it is possible that this moiety was divided between Edward Saunders and Edward Gale and that the shares conveyed by the latter and John Bulleine respectively were fourth parts and not moieties as stated.
15 Nash, *Hist. of Worc.* ii. 178.
16 Prattinton Coll. (Soc. Antiq.)
17 Information supplied by Mr. Robert Hunt of Morton-under-Hill.
18 Information supplied by the late Mrs. Walker.
19 Ibid.
20 Information supplied by Mr. Hunt.
21 *Quart. Sess. R.*(Worc. Co.Coun.), 132.

inserted for the purpose of lighting such a gallery, is dated 1806. The latest addition is a small vestry to the north of the chancel. The walls of the church, where not ashlar faced, are of lias rubble with ashlar quoins; the roofs are of grey stone slates; the tower has, within the parapet, a gabled roof running east and west.

The east window of the chancel is of two trefoiled lights with a quatrefoil in the arched head, late fourteenth or early fifteenth century. It contains a little Flemish glass, one piece dated 1590, with scriptural subjects. In the north wall is the modern vestry doorway. In the south is a plain priests' doorway with square head, having on the west a single light square headed window and to the east a curious small three-light window, of the roughest workmanship, perhaps of seventeenth-century date. The head is

Abbot's Morton Church from Village Street.

square, with cinquefoiled lights and narrow cusped openings in the spandrels over them. The narrow openings are not glazed, but roughly blocked with small stones, and do not show inside the church. It looks like a copy of fifteenth-century work by a country mason ignorant of Gothic detail. The parallel in position between this little window and the miniature two-light thirteenth-century window at South Littleton is worth noting. The east and south walls of the chancel are ashlar faced, the work being dated by leaded letters and a date in the gable over the east window.

RL HE IH IT RE 1637.

There is no structural division between the chancel and nave beyond a flattened lath-and-plaster arch of the full span. The altar rails are of good detail, with turned balusters and a carved rail, probably late seventeenth century.

There is no arch from the church to the north transept, which has in its east wall a square-headed window of three trefoiled lights, and in the north wall a window of two trefoiled lights, with a quatrefoil in the head, both of the fourteenth century. The latter contains a few pieces of old glass, and in the quatrefoil some heraldry of comparatively modern date.

In the north wall of the nave is a blocked doorway with a low pointed segmental arch and square hollow chamfered abaci, c. 1200. There is a narrow chamfer on arch and jambs. In the south wall, which has three slight buttresses, and is ashlar-faced like the chancel, are two windows, and a doorway with a porch over it. The western of the two windows is a plain square headed single light; the other, east of the porch, has modern three-light wooden tracery under a square head. The doorway has somewhat coarse continuous mouldings, late fifteenth or sixteenth century. On either side of the porch are seats which are fifteenth-century pews of a simple and solid character.

Near the south-west corner of the nave is a small dormer window in the roof to light the gallery; in its plastered gable is the date 1806 pricked in the plaster.

The western tower of the fifteenth century has an embattled parapet with angle pinnacles in bad repair; of the gurgoyles only that at the south-west angle remains perfect. It is a very poor piece of work, the head of a bull—possibly the only survivor of a set of the evangelistic symbols. The belfry windows are of two lights with clumsy tracery in the heads, probably the work of local masons, and contrasting with the tracery of the two-light west window of the ground stage, which is well wrought and designed, and may be a ready-made piece of work bought and fitted to local jambs. A weathered string runs round the tower above the level of this window, and over it on the west face is a small square-headed slit. There are diagonal buttresses at the western angles of the tower. The font is modern, with a plain round bowl on an octagonal base. No old wood work is to be seen: there is a west gallery, as before noted, dated 1840, with a panelled front.

There are four bells,[1] the treble and third by Mears, 1842; second by Thomas Hancox junior, of Walsall, 1633; the tenor is a fifteenth-century bell from a Worcester foundry, inscribed—

'Virgenis (*sic*) egregie vocor campana Maria' (*sic*)

The church plate consists of a modern plated cup, paten, and flagon.[2]

Before 1812 there is one volume of parish registers beginning in 1728.

ADVOWSON From the earliest time of which we have record until the beginning of the nineteenth century the advowson of the church of Abbot's Morton followed the descent of the manor.[3] Between 1817 and 1822[4] it was conveyed by a member of the Ellins family—said by Dr. Prattinton to be the Rev. Edward

[1] Walters, *Trans. Worc. Arch. Soc.* xxv. 564, 581.

[2] Lea, *Ch. Plate, Worc. Archd.* 34.

[3] The churches in the Vale were chapels of the mother church at Evesham until the Dissolution, when they became parish churches. See Chant. Cert. Worc. xxv. no. 26.

[4] *Clerical Guide*, 1817 and 1822.

Ellins[1]—to T. Eades, Esq. The latter conveyed it about 1841 to G. J. A. Walker, Esq.,[2] from whom it passed to the Rev. Thomas Walker, rector of Abbot's Morton from 1861 to 1904 and joint lord of the manor. The representatives of his widow, Mrs. Walker, of Battenhall Manor, Worcester, are the present patrons.

The chapel is mentioned in 1206 as being held appropriated to the sacristy of the abbey, and in 1231-2 Abbot Thomas Marlborough again granted it for the same purpose.[3]

Early in the thirteenth century this church formed one of the causes of a dispute between the bishop of Worcester and the abbot of Evesham, as to the rights of the monks.[4] The dispute which had begun before 1206 [5] does not seem to have been settled until 1248-9, when the bishop's jurisdiction in the church and parish of Abbot's Morton was acknowledged by the abbot and convent. A vicarage seems to have been ordained to which the abbot and convent were to have the right of presentation; the vicar was to receive the obventions of the altar and mortuaries and the greater and lesser tithes, and was to bear all episcopal and archidiaconal charges, while it should be lawful for the abbot to have a private chapel in his manor at Abbot's Morton without prejudice to the mother church. This arrangement was confirmed in 1269.[6] A portion of the tithes was withheld, apparently as a pension, by the abbot,[7] and since the vicar received the great tithes he became practically rector, and a few years later is so described.[8] In 1291 the abbot's portion in the church of Abbot's Morton in tithes withheld was estimated at 13*s.* 4*d.*;[9] the total value of the church is not stated.

The procurations and synodals were released in 1877.

There is no nonconformist place of worship in the parish. There is a non-provided school, built in 1844, with provision for 56 children.

CHARITY Mrs. Elizabeth Walker by deed dated 26 July 1862 gave £174 towards the support of a Sunday School in Abbot's Morton. This sum is invested in Great Western Railway 4½ per cent debenture stock which is dealt with by the Official Trustees.[10]

BADSEY WITH ALDINGTON

Baddeseia (viii. cent.); Badesei (xi. cent.); Badseie (xvi. cent.).

The parish of Badsey, which formerly comprised the hamlet of Aldington, formed into a separate civil parish in 1883, lies in the south-east part of the county. It contains 1,882 acres, and in 1901 possessed 198 inhabited houses, of which 675 acres and 35 houses were in Aldington.[11] The subsoil is of lower lias and the surface is a fertile mould. The lands in the parish are chiefly laid out in market gardens. The Oxford, Worcester, and Wolverhampton branch of the Great Western Railway passes through Aldington; the nearest station to Badsey is that of Littleton and Badsey, in Offenham parish, opened in April, 1884. There is a siding for goods, chiefly vegetables, in Aldington, about a mile west of the station, opened in 1872. The village of Badsey is situated between the main road from Evesham to Broadway and the main road from Evesham to Chipping Campden, which latter runs through the parish nearly directly from west to east. From Badsey village a road passes southwards through Wickhamford and joins the main road from Evesham to Broadway.

Aldington forms the western part of the parish, stretching along the left bank of the Avon for about a mile. The hamlet is situated to the north of the Campden main road about a mile from Badsey, and from it a road runs to the north-west in the direction of Offenham. Two of the larger farms in the parish are Bower's Hill and Badsey Field, and Netherfield Close is an ancient place name still existing.[12]

Allies quotes from May's *History of Evesham* to the effect that about a mile distant from Badsey church, in a field called Foxhill, human bones and the bones of animals were found together with pieces of coarse dark gritty pottery, and rude slabs of stone occasionally laid kiln-wise and bearing marks of fire.[13] Roman coins and Edward I. pennies have also been discovered in the parish.[14]

An Enclosure Act for Aldington was passed in 1807 [15] and one for Badsey in 1812.[16]

Prattinton states in a 'note from a man on the road, July 1817,' that a wake used to be kept on Holy Thursday, but since the enclosure the farmers had endeavoured to put a stop to it. There used to be much cudgel playing at this wake[17] which is now abandoned. The chief scene of revelry was at the Royal Oak public-house near the spot where the road to Badsey turns off to the right from the main road, but the public-house was then shut up, and in 1807 the wake was kept in the angle of the road.[18] A few hundred yards to the east of the spot mentioned the main road turns at a right angle to the left, and shortly again as suddenly to the right.

MANOR Badsey is said to have formed part of the grant made by Offa, king of the East Angles, in 703, to Evesham Abbey,[19] while it is also stated that in 709 five and a half 'mansæ' there were included in the joint grant of Offa and Kenred, king of the Mercians, to that house.[20] Badsey was the property of the abbot and convent at the time of the Domesday Survey, which states that it had contained

1 Prattinton Coll. (Soc. Antiq.).

2 *Clergy List*, 1841 and 1842.

3 *Chron. de Evesham* (Rolls Ser.), 276. There was apparently an ordination between these grants, as it is stated in the latter that the sacrist had previously only received 3*s.* yearly.

4 See under Evesham Abbey, p. 119

5 *Cal. of Papal Letters*, I. 24, 25, 252.

6 *Worc. Epis. Reg. Giffard* (Worc. Hist. Soc.), 9 and 10; *Cal. of Papal Letters*, I. 252; *Chron. de Evesham* (Rolls Ser.), 191-4.

7 *Pope Nich. Tax.* (Rec. Com.), 217*b*.

8 *Worc. Epis. Reg. Giffard* (Worc. Hist. Soc.), 212; *Sede Vac. Reg.* (Ibid.) 210.

9 *Pope Nich. Tax.* (Rec. Com.), 217*b*.

10 *Digest of Endowed Charities, Worc.*, *Parl. Papers*, 1900, lxiii.

11 *Worc. Co. Coun. Handbk.* (1903), 148.

12 Chan. inq. p.m. 4 Jas. I. ccccix. 148.

13 Allies, *Antiq. of Worc.* 88.

14 *V.C.H. Worc.* i. 218 and information supplied by Mr. O. G. Knapp.

15 Stat. 47 Geo. III. c. 15.

16 Ibid. c. 45.

17 Prattinton Coll. (Soc. Antiq.).

18 Ibid.

19 *Chron. de Evesham* (Rolls Ser.), 71.

20 Birch *Cart. Sax.* I. 183. This charter, however, is marked as spurious in Kemble, *Cod. Dip.* I. 70.

six and a half hides in the time of Edward the Confessor.[1] Abbot Walter afterwards granted five virgates of this land to William, one of his Norman kinsmen,[2] to whom he also granted in inheritance the office of steward of the abbey lands, of which office he had deprived the prior.[3] William was succeeded by Philip the steward, probably his son, who is said to have held five virgates and a half, and who was contemporary with Richard Francis who held half a hide in Badsey by the service of going with a packhorse to carry the cloths of the monks throughout England at the expense of the abbot.[4]

In 1246–7 William of Evesham, steward of the abbey, brought a suit against Abbot Thomas of Gloucester because the latter would not permit him to hold the hallmote and hundred courts in the Vale of Evesham as his ancestors had held them from time immemorial, and had detained from him a daily corrody and other perquisites pertaining to his office. William appears to have won the case by default of the abbot,[5] and was probably restored to his stewardship.

Badsey : The Seyne House.

In the Lay Subsidy Roll of about 1280, William the Steward occurs under Aldington, which apparently included Badsey, and from the amount 20*s.* which he contributed it is evident that he was the wealthiest landowner there.[6] After this date, and some time before 1316, he conveyed his land in Badsey, which produced a rent of 60*s.* a year, to Abbot John Brokehampton.[7] Shortly afterwards, John Wellesley, knight, conveyed to the succeeding abbot, William of Cheriton, a messuage and two carucates of land 'which formerly belonged to William the steward of Evesham.'[8] Possibly Sir John Wellesley was William's heir, since he held and surrendered to the abbey the corrody which the steward and his heirs had held *ab antiquo* from the monastery.[9]

At an early date there appears to have been a house at Badsey for the use of the sick and blooded (*minuti*) monks of Evesham. In 1328 Abbot Chiriton assigned the lands above referred to as belonging to William the steward with all the tithes of sheaves there to the chamberlain, who, in return, was to render every year for the bettering of the clothes of the brothers £10 of silver. Buildings were to be erected in the garden to accommodate the sick monks, and as often as they or other monks of the monastery who had obtained permission from the prior wished to feed there they should receive from the cellar and kitchen the corrody belonging to them as fully as at the monastery.[10] On 8 March 1333–4 Thomas of Evesham, the king's clerk, had licence to alienate to the abbot and convent of Evesham a messuage with a garden and virgate of land in Badsey for the refreshment of the monks in sickness, and to find a chaplain to say one mass at the high altar in the convent church for his soul and the soul of Robert de Netherton his uncle, late a monk of the abbey.[11] Later on, Abbot Roger Zatton (1380–1418) appropriated the demesne lands of Badsey to the use of himself and his successors, abbots of the monastery, at the same time charging the lands with the payment of 10*s.* a year to the monks and three cartloads of straw for the beds of the monks and the blooded, to be taken from the manors of Aldington and Wickhamford.[12] This house for convalescents was granted in 1545, under the name of the 'Seyne house,' to Sir Philip Hoby;[13] it passed with the manor of Abbot's Morton to Sir Edward Hoby, and in 1595 Richard Hoby resided there.[14]

Badsey continued in the possession of the abbey of Evesham until its suppression in 1539. In 1535 it was annexed to Aldington, which seems to have been at that time the more important manor; the demesne lands were then on lease. In 1539 the manor came into the hands of the Crown, with whom it remained until 24 April, 1562, when Queen Elizabeth granted it, with that of Aldington, to Sir Robert Throckmorton of Coughton and his heirs, to hold in chief by the service of a twentieth part of a knight's fee.[15]

Sir Robert died seised of the manor on 12 February, 1580–1, leaving as heir his son Thomas, then forty-five years of age.[16] Thomas Throckmorton seems to have held it until 1589, when jointly with Margaret his wife, the daughter of William Whorwood, who had been Attorney-General of Henry VIII., he had licence from the Crown to alienate it to Rice or Richard Griffin,[17] in whose favour a fine was accordingly levied in Michaelmas term of the same year,[18] probably on Richard's marriage to their daughter, Margaret Throckmorton.

In 1598 the manor of Badsey passed from Richard and Margaret Griffin to Richard Hoby,[19] who two years later conveyed it by fine, with the manor of Abbot's Morton, to Richard Mottershed and Ralph Hodges.[20] For some years afterwards Badsey seems to have followed the same descent as Abbot's Morton. In 1609 Charles Kettilby and Elizabeth his wife conveyed it with the latter manor to John Kettilby and

[1] *V.C.H. Worc.* i. 306b. In an extent marked in the margin T.R.E. which occurs in Cott. Vesp. B. xxiv. f. 49d, five and a half hides are said to be in Badsey, and one and a half in Aldington.

[2] Cott. MS. Vesp. B. xxiv. ff. 12d.

[3] *Chron. de Evesham* (Rolls Ser.), 97.

[4] Cott. MS. Vesp. B. xxiv. f. 46.

[5] Assize R. Beds. 31 Hen. III. No. 4, m. 22d.

[6] *Lay Subs. R. c.* 1280 (Worc. Hist. Soc.), 83.

[7] *Chron de Evesham* (Rolls Ser.), 285.

[8] Ibid. 289.

[9] Ibid.

[10] Ibid. 291; Tindal, *Hist. of Evesham*, 108-9.

[11] Pat. 8 Edw. III. pt. i. m. 24.

[12] *Chron. de Evesham*, 309.

[13] Pat. 37 Hen. VIII. pt. 5.

[14] Com. Pleas Deeds Enr. 37 Eliz. m. 3.

[15] Pat. 4 Eliz. pt. 4, m. 46.

[16] Chan. inq. p.m. cxciii. 89.

[17] Pat. 31 Eliz. pt. 14, m. 27.

[18] Feet of F. Worc. Mich. 31 & 32 Eliz.

[19] Ibid. Trin. 40 Eliz.

[20] Ibid. Hil. 42 Eliz. See Abbot's Morton.

John Hopkins,[1] but the purpose of this conveyance does not appear. Richard Hoby is described as being 'of Badsey' in 1617,[2] and probably retained property in the parish until his death, which seems to have taken place there in February, 1616–7.[3]

The manor of Badsey was afterwards purchased by Sir Sebastian Harvey, alderman of London, who at his death left an only daughter and heir Mary, his widow, who afterwards married Sir Thomas Hinton, being administratrix of his property. Mary Harvey married John, the son of Sir Francis Popham, and about 1627 she and her husband presented a petition to the Council stating that Sir Thomas and Lady Hinton refused to surrender her share in her father's property, and asking redress. Litigation followed, and both parties, tired of the delay and expense, which was 'not so little as £20,000,' besought Lord Dorchester and Endymion Porter, a cousin of John Popham, respectively to use their influence with the Lord Keeper to terminate the matter, which was finally 'happily settled' in 1631.[4] Both parties then united in levying a fine by which the manor of Badsey was conveyed to trustees to the use of John and Mary Popham.[5] Mary survived her husband, who died without issue in 1638, seised of Badsey, leaving his brother Alexander as his heir.[6]

The subsequent history of Badsey is obscure. It is said to have been conveyed in the seventeenth century by one Christopher Popham to a member of the Wilson family on a thousand years' lease, but the conveyance has not been found. In 1866 Mr. Edward Wilson, a descendant of the lessee, sold the manorial rights and the churchyard to the Dean and Chapter of Christ Church, Oxford, who are the present lords of the manor.[7]

ALDINGTON (Aldintone, xi. cent.; Aunton or Aldington, xvi. and xvii. cent.) One 'mansa' here was included in the grant made to the abbey of Evesham by Kenred, king of the Mercians, and Offa, king of the East Angles, in 709.[8] Although it is not mentioned in Bishop Egwin's statement of the lands of the monastery in 714,[9] it occurs in Domesday Book as a berewick of the adjoining manor of Offenham.[10]

It is not clear when Aldington became separated from Offenham, but the change had evidently taken place during the twelfth century, when it had become connected with Bretforton, and the tenants of one of these manors are occasionally entered under the other. Thus Hugh son of Robert, a twelfth-century tenant, is stated to hold 2½ hides in Aldington,[11] while another entry assigns him to Bretforton (q. v.)[12]; and Robert Ewen, who was clearly a Bretforton tenant, appears in the Subsidy Roll of about 1280 under Aldington.[13] In 1291 Aldington had become joined to Badsey.[14]

Abbot Roger Zatton (1380–1418) is said to have built a great grange at Aldington,[15] which probably superseded an earlier one built by Abbot Randolph in the early part of the thirteenth century.[16]

In 1535 the clear annual value of 'the manor of Aldington with Badsey annexed' is given as £38 5*s.* 4*d.*[17] Together they rendered yearly to the abbey 18 quarters of wheat, 26 quarters of barley, and 10 quarters of peas and beans. The demesne lands of Aldington, like those of Badsey, were in lease.[18] On 12 December, 1538, the abbot and convent of Evesham granted a new lease of the demesne lands with the site of the manor of Aldington to Richard Pygyon for a term of 61 years.[19] In the following year the manor came into the hands of the Crown, to whose bailiffs Richard Pygyon and the other tenants paid their rents in 1540.[20] On 20 February, 1539–40, the grain rents already referred to, paid by the farmers of the manor of Aldington, probably including Badsey, were granted by Henry VIII. to Sir George Throckmorton.[21] In 1562 Queen Elizabeth granted the manor with that of Badsey to Sir Robert Throckmorton, son of Sir George, and his heirs.[22] It does not appear how or when Richard Pygyon's lease terminated; he probably[23] continued to hold from Sir Robert Throckmorton as he had formerly held from the monastery and afterwards from the Crown, or he may have been then deceased. The manor of Aldington then followed the descent of Badsey (*q. v.*) until 1598, when it was conveyed by Richard and Margaret Griffin to Philip Bigge,[24] second son of Thomas Bigge of Lenchwick, another conveyance to the same effect being executed in the following year.[25] Philip Bigge appears to have held the manor until 1614, when jointly with Hester his wife he levied a fine by which it was conveyed to William Courteen and John Mounsey,[26] apparently for the use of the former, who afterwards held it.

William Courteen, who was knighted in 1622, was one of the most prominent merchant traders of the period, and was connected with the Company of Merchant Strangers.[27] He incurred heavy losses by the failure of his attempt to colonize Barbadoes, which had been granted to him, his colonists being expelled by the earl of Carlisle in 1629. He was further embarrassed by the fact that large sums of money lent to James I. and Charles I. were never repaid.[28] In his time of prosperity he made extensive purchases of landed property, including several manors in Worcestershire. He seems to have settled the manor of Aldington on

COURTEEN. *Gold a talbot sable.*

[1] Feet of F. Worc. Trin. 7 Jas. I.

[2] Exch. Dep. Hil. 14 Jas. I. No. 20.

[3] A monument was erected to him in the church of Badsey by his step-daughter, Margaret Newman, wife of Richard Delabere (Nash, *Hist. of Worc.* i. 53). His mother, Katherine Hoby, was also buried at Badsey. (Ext. from Par. Reg. made by Mr. O. G. Knapp.)

[4] *Cal. of S.P. Dom.* 1627–8, 174, 497–8; ibid. 1629–31, 99, 281; ibid. 1631–33, 101; ibid. 1634–5, 151.

[5] Feet of F. Div. Cos. Hil. 6 Chas. I.

[6] Chan. inq. p. m. ccccxxxvi. 133.

[7] Information supplied by W. B. Skene, Esq., Treasurer of Christ Church.

[8] Birch. *Cart. Sax.* i. 183.

[9] Ibid. 190–1.

[10] *V.C.H. Worc.* i. 306*b*. The Survey assigns 1 hide to Aldington, but an extent which occurs in an abbey chartulary states that the abbey had at Aldington T.R.E. 1½ hides, 3 ploughs, 6 oxmen, and 2 bordars. (Cott. MS. Vesp. B. xxiv. f. 49d.)

[11] Ibid. f. 47.

[12] Ibid. f. 12.

[13] *Lay Subs. R. c.* 1280 (Worc. Hist. Soc.), 82–3.

[14] *Pope Nich. Tax.* (Rec. Com.), 229.

[15] *Chron. de Evesham* (Rolls Ser.), 304.

[16] Ibid. 261.

[17] *Valor Eccl.* (Rec. Com.), iii. 249.

[18] Ibid.

[19] Mins. Accts. 31-2 Hen. VIII. L.R. 1330, m. 14d.

[20] Ibid. m. 14–15.

[21] *L. and P. Hen. VIII.* xv. 563.

[22] Pat. 4 Eliz. pt. 4 m. 46.

[23] The lease of the 'site' of the manor and the demesne lands carried with it no manorial rights.

[24] Feet of F. Worc. Trin. 40 Eliz.

[25] Ibid. East. 41 Eliz.

[26] Notes of F. Worc. Mich. 12 Jas. I.

[27] *Cal. of S.P. Dom.* 1619–23, i. 45, 101, 170 et seq.

[28] *Dict. of Nat. Biog.*

Peter Courteen, his son by his first marriage, who was described as of Aldington when he was created a baronet in 1622,[1] and who died without issue in 1625.

Of Sir William Courteen and his son, Habington says that they 'leaft to Mr. William Corteyn, who now succeedethe them, yea, to us all, suche an example of bounty and pietie in beinge more like parentes than landlordes to theyre tenauntes, as all must needes prayse, and I wish all able gentellmen would imitate.'[2] Sir William Courteen died in 1636, seised of the manor of Aldington, leaving as his heir, William, his son by a second marriage, twenty-seven years of age.[3] His father's losses brought him into great difficulties, and all his efforts to secure repayment of sums lent to the Crown were unavailing. In 1614 his East India ships were seized by the Dutch, and two years later he became bankrupt.[4] Some time afterwards he withdrew to Italy and died at Florence in 1655, leaving a son William. In 1651 Aldington and other manors were claimed by the Committee for Sequestration,[5] who in Michaelmas term of that year conveyed it to John Pettyward.[6] Aldington was also claimed by many creditors,[7] and in 1665 it was sold to Thomas Foley, the celebrated iron-master, who was high sheriff of Worcestershire, and founder of Old Swinford Hospital, the parties to the sale being William Courteen the naturalist, grandson of Sir William, Samuel Baldwin, George Carew, William Willoughby, and William Cherry.[8] The manor remained in the Foley family for nearly a century and a half; in 1806, some time after the death of Thomas, fifth Baron Foley of Kidderminster, his property in Aldington, comprising about 250 acres, was sold to several persons. The manor was purchased by Mr. George Day, merchant of Evesham,[9] who in 1807 was lord of the manor, or reputed manor, of Aldington,[10] which was then apparently leased by him to William Preedy.[11] In Michaelmas term of 1808 the manor, described as Aldington Farm, was purchased from Mr. Day by Mr. James Ashwin for £12,000.[12] The latter left it to his second son Richard, on whose death in 1866 it passed by bequest to his nephew, Henry Ashwin, who was succeeded in 1892 by his son James Ashwin, Esq., of Bretforton, the present lord of the manor.[13]

SHRAWNELL PARK (Schrewenhulle, xiv. cent.; Srawnell, Shrawnehull, xvi. cent.) is said to have been first enclosed by William Cheriton, abbot of Evesham from 1317 to 1344, and to have been planted by him with oak, ash, and other trees.[14] He may possibly have intended it for the recreation of the sick monks in the infirmary which he founded there.[15] In 1535 'the pasture of Srawnell' was in lease at a yearly rent of 24*s*.[16] In 1542 the king granted to Sir Philip Hoby 'a park called Shrawnell,' described as being in the parish of Bengeworth.[17] This was probably, however, a wrong description, as two years later he received another grant in which the property is described as being 'in the parish of Badsey within the lordship of Aldington.'[18] In the latter grant a house called 'The Lodge' is mentioned. On his death in 1558 it was found that he died seised of this property and a number of tenements in Badsey,[19] which would seem to have then passed to his half brother Sir Thomas Hoby and afterwards to Sir Edward Hoby. On 31 January 1570–1 Lady Elizabeth Hoby, widow of Sir Thomas, who had the wardship of her son during his minority, applied to Sir William Cecil for timber out of Shrawnell Park for the repair of a bridge and certain mills in Evesham.[20]

Shrawnell afterwards passed to Francis Dineley of Charlton, who died seised of it in 1626, his heir being his grandson Edward Dineley, then aged twenty-four,[21] and continued in the Dineley family till the break up of their estates in the eighteenth century.[22]

The park seems to have lain along the banks of the Faulk Mill Brook,[23] and to be now represented by a farm called the Parks, standing near the Avon in the west of the parish.

A mill at Aldington is mentioned in the Domesday Survey,[24] and it is stated that Ralph, abbot of Evesham (1214–1229), bought a mill there and gave it to the almonry.[25] A mill at Badsey was held in the twelfth century by Philip the steward, who rendered for it 1 mark annually.[26] Mills were in existence at both places in 1535 and in 1540.[27] Aldington Mill seems to have been the more valuable; it was leased by the abbot and convent on 24 January 1538–9 to Thomas Bugden and Elizabeth his wife at an annual rent of 30*s*. 4*d*.[28] Badsey Mill produced an annual rent of 24*s*.[29] The mill at Aldington is still in existence.

CHURCH

Badsey church is dedicated in honour of St. James. There is a record[30] of its dedication by the bishop of St. Asaph on the feast of St. John, 1295. This may refer to a rebuilding of the chancel, as at Church Honeybourne and Bretforton.

It stands to the east of the main street of the village, in a churchyard[31] of some size, and consists of chancel with vestry and organ chamber on the north, a north transept, nave with south aisle and porch, and west tower.

The history of the building, to be deduced from existing evidence, is as follows: About 1120[32] was built an aisleless nave with north and south doorways,

[1] *Dict. of Nat. Biog.* He is there stated to be of Aldington, Northants, but there is no Aldington in that county.

[2] *Surv. of Worc.* (Worc. Hist. Soc.), ii. 257.

[3] Chan. inq. p. m. 12 Chas. I. ccclxxix. 96.

[4] *Dict. of Nat. Biog.*

[5] Abstracts of Claims to Delinquents' Lands.

[6] Com. Pleas Recov. R. Mich. 1651, m. 17.

[7] Abstracts of Claims to Delinquents' Lands.

[8] Feet of F. Worc. Mich. 17 Chas. II.

[9] Prattinton Coll. (Soc. Antiq.).

[10] Enclosure Act, Stat. 47 Geo. III. c. 15.

[11] Ibid.

[12] From a document in Mr. Ashwin's possession.

[13] Information kindly supplied by Mr. Ashwin.

[14] *Chron. de Evesham* (Rolls Ser.), 292.

[15] See p. 354.

[16] *Valor Eccl.* (Rec. Com.), iii. 249.

[17] Pat. 34 Hen. VIII. pt. 6, m. 33. The parishes adjoin, and part might have been in Bengeworth.

[18] Ibid. 35 Hen. VIII. pt. 9, m. 30; *L. and P. Hen. VIII.* xix. (1), 276.

[19] Chan. inq. p.m. 5 and 6 Phil. and Mary, cxv. 74.

[20] *Cal. of S.P. Dom.* 1547–80, p. 407.

[21] Chan. inq. p.m. 2 Chas. I. ccccxxiii. 74.

[22] See under Charlton.

[23] Mins. Accts. 31–2 Hen. VIII. L. R. 1330, m. 14, 14 *d*.

[24] *V.C.H. Worc.* i. 306*b*.

[25] *Chron. de Evesham* (Rolls Ser.), 262.

[26] Cott. MS. Vesp. B. xxiv. f. 50.

[27] *Valor Eccl.* (Rec. Com.), iii. 249, and Mins. Accts. 31–2 Hen. VIII. L. R. 1330, m. 14, 14 *d*.

[28] Ibid.

[29] Ibid.

[30] MS. Harl. 3763, f. 115.

[31] The churchyard was not enclosed towards the road till after the middle of last century.

[32] There is no evidence of earlier work above ground.

lighted by two windows, one in each side wall. There was probably a short chancel, narrower than the nave, of this date. At the end of the thirteenth century the chancel was rebuilt, of the full width of the nave, no doubt outside the lines of the older chancel, after the usual manner. There may have been structural alterations between these dates, but the evidence is not conclusive.

A north transept was added about 1330, and a west tower about 1450. The south doorway of the nave replaced an earlier doorway in the fourteenth century. In 1885 the south wall of the church was pulled down and a south aisle and porch built, opening to the nave with an arcade of four bays. The twelfth-century window from the south wall was built into the north wall of the nave to the west of the north doorway. A vestry was built on the north side of the chancel.

The main features of the church are as follows:—The east window of the chancel is of three lights trefoiled, late fourteenth century; the window arch within and without is made up of the moulded voussoirs of an early thirteenth-century arch set in a flattened curve; but whether originally belonging to this church or brought from elsewhere is not clear. There are no sedilia or piscina. The altar rails are good work of the late seventeenth or early eighteenth century. Against the north wall of the chancel is the monument of Richard Hoby, to the west of which is a modern arch opening to the organ chamber and vestry. In the south wall are two windows with a plain arched doorway between them. The eastern window in this wall is of two lights with a trefoil in the head, and may be of late-thirteenth-century date, part of the new work consecrated in 1295. The work is inferior to that in the chancels of Church Honeybourne and Bretforton, recorded to have been dedicated in the same year. The western window in this wall is of two trefoiled lights under a square head.

The chancel arch is modern:[1] before 1885 there was no arch between nave and chancel: no doubt the original east wall of the nave had been removed to make way for a screen and rood loft The north transept is of the fourteenth century, opening to the church by an arch of two chamfered orders, with small shafts and half-octagon capitals. The north window is modern, of two trefoiled lights, but retains its fourteenth-century rear arch; the east window is of two lights uncusped, of the fourteenth century; the west also of two lights, trefoiled, of the same date. In the north wall of the nave the original doorway, c. 1120, remains, though blocked. It is square headed, with a plain tympanum and semicircular arch and label over. The label is chamfered, with rosettes in relief on the inner face, and the arch has a line of incised zigzag. The lower edge of the tympanum is cable moulded, and the jambs are plain.

In this wall part of the internal dressings of the original window are to be seen: its east jamb and part of the head were destroyed at the building of the transept arch. To the west of the north doorway is a complete twelfth-century window, moved here from the destroyed south wall.[2] It is a plain, narrow, round-headed loop. All the outer face of this wall has been renewed in lias masonry. The door, built up in the north doorway, is ancient, though probably later than the doorway. The modern south arcade, of four bays, has pointed arches of two hollow chamfered orders on octagonal pillars with capitals and bases. In the south wall of the modern south aisle

Badsey Church from the west.

the doorway from the old south wall is inserted under a modern stone porch with a panelled gable. It has a plain chamfered arch and jambs, and retains its old wooden door with wrought-iron hinges. In its east jamb, outside, are remains of a holy-water stone.

The west tower is of the fifteenth century, of good design, with simple and effective details. It is of three stages with an embattled parapet with angle and central pinnacles and projecting gurgoyles, and has a stair turret at the south-east angle. The belfry windows are of two lights: the west window on the ground stage is a large tracery window of four cinque-

[1] A former description of the church speaks of the ancient chancel arch as 'supplanted by a trumpery curve not very dissimilar to a piece of bent timber.' May, *Hist. of Evesham* (1845), 243.

[2] See above.

foiled lights; a little old white and gold glass remains in the tracery. The tower arch is of two continuous orders. Two ancient gable crosses remain—one, of the fourteenth century, on the north transept, of good design, but with a curious effect, as it is set north and south instead of east and west.[1] The other, on the chancel gable, looks early, perhaps of the beginning of the thirteenth century or earlier, and is older than the gable on which it stands.

A stone, with the date 1653 in lead letters, in the same gable, is no doubt a record of repairs of the time. The roofs of the church are covered with grey stone slates, and in nave and chancel retain most of their old timbers, which may be of the fourteenth century. The work is simple; the chancel has arched braces, and in the nave the studs and collars give a half octagonal form. The transept roof timbers are modern.

The wooden pulpit[2] is octagonal on a modern stone base. It has some linen pattern panels probably of sixteenth-century date. There are no old pews. The communion table[3] is dated 1730, and forms part of the gift of William Seward, who gave the table, the ornaments over it, the other tables in the church, and the clock, reseating the church at the same time. A western gallery, now gone, was given by Thomas Byrd. The font has a plain modern octagonal bowl, standing on an early-fourteenth-century hexagonal stem with angle shafts and foliated capitals of excellent detail of the time. In the church are two oil-paintings attributed to Count Carlo Cignani (1628–1709) and Otto van Veen of Antwerp.

The monument against the north wall of the chancel is of early-seventeenth-century date, having the figures of Richard Hoby (ob. 11 February, 1616–17) and his wife Margaret, kneeling at a desk under an entablature carried by columns. Above are the Hoby arms, and on the panelled base of the tomb the figures of two sons and one daughter. The figure of Margaret Hoby is much damaged.

There are eight bells, the treble and second having been added in 1902. The rest are by Michael Bushell and William Clark of Evesham, 1706. These founders had a habit of dating their bells by chronograms, and on the tenor is the following inscription:—[4]

+ I H S

MVtaVIt VIgILans In seX nos CVra robertI

hILL IbI VIC: gVL CLark effICIt ano (*sic*) arte sVa.

The word ano is apparently a blunder.

The church plate[5] consists of an Elizabethan cup with paten cover, with dotted line ornamentation, and a pewter flagon and two plates.

The parish registers, complete from 1538, are contained, previous to 1812, in two volumes. A book of churchwardens' accounts of considerable interest, though not in perfect condition, exists. The earliest entries are of 1525.

ADVOWSON The advowson of the chapel of Badsey belonged to the abbey of Evesham until the suppression of that house in 1539. When in 1540 Henry VIII. erected the bishopric and established the Dean and Chapter of Westminster, he stipulated in the foundation charter for the maintenance of ten readers at the Universities of Oxford and Cambridge.[6] Two years later, on 15 August, 1542, he granted to the Dean and Chapter the rectory and church and the advowson of Badsey and Aldington and other property[7] apparently towards the support of these readers.[8] On 4 July, 1546, the Dean and Chapter surrendered the advowson to the king,[9] who on 11 December granted it with the rectory and church to the Dean and Chapter of Christ Church, Oxford,[10] who still remain the patrons.

The chapel of Badsey is mentioned in 1206.[11] One of the many charges brought against Abbot Roger Norreys in 1213 was that he had twice simoniacally sold this chapel and that of Bretforton.[12] From a very early date Badsey, Aldington, and Wickhamford seem to have been closely connected for spiritual purposes, and it is probable that for some time one chapel served for all three. In 1291 the value of the chapel of Badsey with Aldington and Wickhamford annexed was £15 6*s.* 8*d.*,[13] and in 1340 the 'chapel' of Badsey, Aldington, and Wickhamford is referred to.[14] In 1535 the clear yearly value of the chapel of Badsey was £5 6*s.* 8*d.* It was at that time in lease to Thomas James, chaplain and curate, for the term of his life.[15] Wickhamford had then a separate chapel, but the livings were still connected, since in 1542, when the Dean and Chapter of Westminster received the advowson, they were required to pay £3 11*s.* 4*d.* yearly to the vicar of Badsey, Aldington, and Wickhamford.[16]

It is stated in 1206 that the lesser tithes of Badsey and Aldington were applied to the repair of the spoons, cups, glass windows, etc., of Evesham monastery,[17] and the tithes of five yardlands in Badsey were appropriated to the sacristy.[18] The infirmary had two and a half marks yearly from the chapel of Badsey.[19]

In 1651 it appeared that the means and allowances which anciently belonged to the minister there were the tithes of about seven yardlands for Badsey and two in Aldington and all the privy and small tithes in the parish, being worth for the whole £20 yearly.[20]

In Badsey there is a meeting house for Quakers, and at Aldington a place of worship for Baptists.

The Council School at Badsey was built in 1895 as a Board School for Badsey, Aldington, and Wickhamford, and provides accommodation for 260 children.

[1] This is at any rate not a modern alteration.

[2] Its date is suggested by an entry in the churchwardens' accounts for 1529: 'resuyd for ye old pylpet iiijd.'

[3] Prattinton MSS. s. v. Badsey.

[4] From a MS. of 1660 it is known that the inscription on the old tenor—recast 1706—was: Det sonitum plenum Jesus et modulamen amoenum.

[5] Lea, *Ch. Plate Worc. Archd.* 31.

[6] Pat. 34 Hen. VIII. pt. 5, m. 5; Deeds of Purchase and Exchange, Box E, no. 76; *L. and P. Hen. VIII.* xvi. 154.

[7] *L. and P. Hen. VIII.* xvii. 395–6.

[8] Deeds of Purchase and Exchange, Box 2, no. 76.

[9] Ibid.

[10] Pat. 38 Hen. VIII. pt. 8, m. 19.

[11] *Chron. de Evesham* (Rolls Ser.), 213.

[12] Ibid. 241–2.

[13] *Pope Nich. Tax.* (Rec. Com.), 219.

[14] *Non. Inq.* 1340 (Worc. Hist. Soc.), 39.

[15] *Valor Eccl.* (Rec. Com.), iii. 235.

[16] *L. and P. Hen. VIII.* xvii. 396.

[17] *Chron. de Evesham* (Rolls Ser.), 209.

[18] Ibid. 211.

[19] Ibid. 213.

[20] Parl. Surveys of Church Livings, Lambeth, xvi. 430–1.

CHARITIES The following sums of money have been bequeathed for supplying bread to the poor of the parish:—Mr. Thomas Martin £5; Mrs. Jane Jarrett £5; Mr. Augustus Jarrett £20; Mrs. Elizabeth George £7; Mr. Jarrett Stevens £6. It is known traditionally that many years ago these gifts, amounting to £43, were laid out in the purchase of land lying in the common fields. By the Act of Enclosure, 1812, this land was exchanged for nine acres called the Old Lays, and the rent of £7 10*s.* derived from this land is distributed quarterly by the churchwardens in bread at the church, two-thirds being allotted to Badsey and one-third to Aldington.

Several dispersed pieces of land held by the parish from time immemorial were at the Enclosure exchanged for a piece of ground adjoining the Poor's Land. The rent from this land is expended in keeping the church in repair.

Under the will of Elizabeth Seward, dated 2 June, 1753, the parish of Badsey is entitled to 6*s.* monthly to be applied for teaching poor children to read. In 1830 there was a school-mistress in Badsey, appointed by the Baptist minister at Evesham, who had the teaching of nine poor children in consideration of this payment, and received day scholars from the parish at small weekly payments.[5]

BRETFORTON

Brethfortona (vii. cent.); Bratfortune (xi. cent.); Brackforton (xii. cent.); Bradforton (xvii. cent.).

The parish of Bretforton has an area of 1,706 acres, and in 1901 contained 139 inhabited houses.[1]

The parish slopes gently from south to north, and is traversed by three streams flowing westward from the Cotswold Hills to the Avon. The subsoil to the west is of lower lias, and to the north-east of oolite, and the surface is of gravel with pliable light mould. A large extent of the parish is devoted to fruit culture and market gardening, but formerly it was famed for the excellence and abundance of its corn. In 1782 and succeeding years the cultivation of hemp and flax was attempted by Joseph Cooper of Evesham, who is said to have obtained the bounty offered by the Acts of 21 and 26 George III. for their cultivation.[2] About the same time, Penny Hancock, a landholder in the parish, is said to have sunk for coal on the Manor Farm.[3]

The Oxford, Worcester, and Wolverhampton Branch of the Great Western Railway passes through the northern part of the parish, but the nearest station on this line, two miles distant from the village, is Littleton and Badsey, in the parish of Offenham. In 1904 a new station outside the parish was opened for Bretforton and Weston Subedge on the Great Western Railway line from Honeybourne to Winchcomb and Cheltenham then in process of construction.[4]

The village lies on the main road from Evesham to Chipping Campden, and near to it roads branch off north-east and north-west to South Littleton and Cow Honeybourne respectively. The old Worcester and London road which crossed the Avon at Twyford Bridge passed through the parish.

In the middle of the village is a small square known as the Cross, having the church on the west, while the present main road passes along its north side. The road has been diverted from the south side of the churchyard to the north, and formerly crossed the square diagonally from south-east to north-west. The parish stocks still remain to the south of the churchyard, though now in the garden of Mr. Ashwin, adjoining the church. On the south boundary of the churchyard is a stone wall in which are two narrow square-headed windows, belonging to a destroyed mediæval building, and elsewhere in the village are several old stone and timber houses.

Bretforton.

The Manor House, a little distance north-west of the village, is of considerable interest. The original

[1] *Worc. Co. Coun. Handbk.* (1903), 148.
[2] Shawcross, *Bretforton Memorials*, 148.
[3] Ibid. 150; *V.C.H. Worc.* i. 21.
[4] Information supplied by Mr. O. G. Knapp.
[5] *Char. Com. Rep.* xxiv. 501.

building was L shaped, the longer arm standing approximately east and west.[1] It is good work of the first half of the fourteenth century, rubble walling with ashlar dressings, having at the ground level a semi-circular barrel vault with chamfered stone ribs, lighted by small square-headed windows, and over it a hall now cut up into two stories, but probably at first open to the roof. Only one original window remains, a square-headed one of two trefoiled lights in the north wall. The east gable retains its finial, but with the exception mentioned all the windows are of the seventeenth century, with square heads and stone mullions, put in when the hall was divided into two stories. The roof-timbers, though of the original pitch, date from the same time, and are quite rough. At the north-west angle is a stone staircase turret lighted by several small windows, one of fourteenth-century date, but possibly not in its original position. The stairs are wooden, with good seventeenth-century balusters. About the end of the sixteenth century a wing was added to the original building, running north and south and joining it on the north-west. It contains nothing of special interest beyond the arrangements in simple patterns of the blue stone paving of the ground floor.[2] In 1635, as shown by a doorway which bears the date and W. C. on its label, another wing was added, running east and west, at the north-west of the sixteenth-century block. It has been a good deal altered, and has nothing of interest except this doorway, in the late Gothic work of the time. To the east of the house are the farm buildings, including a square pigeon-house which is partly mediæval, and a fine barn with porches, apparently of early fifteenth-century date, chiefly of timber construction on dwarf stone walls with buttresses. A small stream runs in front of the house, but there is no trace of a moat. To the north of the house is a large rectangular pond which may be in part ancient.

Bretforton Manor House.

Bretforton has been described as one of the pleasantest villages in the Vale of Evesham.[3] It has long been divided into the Upper and Lower Ends and The Cross.[4] At the latter a cross seems to have formerly stood, of which, however, there is now no trace.[5] Prattinton states that the base was in existence in his time, and that the cross had been removed from it within the memory of man.[6] Among modern field names are Porridge Yats, Cysters, Bull Butts, Berrythorn Close, Flax Ground, New Yats, Pumbleditch, Balham, and Dilham.[7] Larkborough is the name of one of the larger farms, and a field bears the suggestive name of Wickham Street Way.

The parish was enclosed in 1765,[8] and then contained 1,260 acres of commonable land.[9]

MANOR

Bretforton formed one of the largest of the gifts supposed to have been made by Kenred and Offa to the abbey of Evesham, their alleged grant here comprising twelve 'mansæ.'[10] At the time of the Domesday Survey it consisted of 12 hides, of which 6 seem to have been appurtenant to the manor of Offenham, and the remaining 6 to Wickhamford.[11] The former moiety continued indirectly appurtenant to Offenham, since it is stated to have been attached to Aldington,[12] which at the time of the Survey was a berewick of Offenham.[13] In Bretforton, as elsewhere, Abbot Walter alienated a considerable portion of the abbey's possessions. He is said to have given 3 hides and 1 virgate here to his brother Ranulf,[14] and 2½ hides to Hugh of

Bretforton Dovecote.

[1] The shorter arm, which stood at the south-east, has been destroyed.

[2] The stone comes from a quarry near by.

[3] Nash, *Hist. of Worc.* i. 18.

[4] Shawcross, *Bretforton Memorials*, 6; Stevens, *Mon.* App. II. 134; Mins. Accts. 31–2 Hen. VIII. L. R. 1330.

[5] Shawcross, *Bretforton Memorials*, 6.

[6] Prattinton Coll. (Soc. Antiq.).

[7] Shawcross, *Bretforton Memorials*, 174.

[8] Stat. 5 Geo. III. c. 27.

[9] Prattinton Coll. (Soc. Antiq.).

[10] Birch, *Cart. Sax.* i. 183, 191.

[11] *V.C.H. Worc.* i. 306b.

[12] Cott. MS. Vesp. B. xxiv. f. 6.

[13] *V.C.H. Worc.* i. 306b.

[14] Cott. MS. Vesp. B. xxiv. f. 11d.

Bretforton.[1] Although not mentioned in the Domesday Survey, Ranulf and Hugh were probably then in possession of their respective holdings. As Abbot Walter is said to have enfeoffed nearly all the military tenants of the abbey,[2] his brother Ranulf was probably one of the first of the abbey's knights 'who did the service of a knight in horses and arms,' the abbot finding their expenses while on the king's service.[3] As knights of the abbey, Ranulf and his successors made personal residence within its precincts until during the abbacy of Reginald (1130–49) the monastery apparently became cramped for room, and the abbot caused the removal of the knights' houses, which, it is said, had given the abbey the appearance of being besieged.[4] Ranulf subsequently assumed the name of Coughton, from Coughton in Warwickshire, which passed by some means into his possession. Major-General Wrottesley has shown him to be the founder of the existing family of Wrottesley,[5] and he was an ancestor also of the families of Kinwarton and Throckmorton.[6] It is probable that Aubrey, the abbot's sister referred to in an abbey chartulary as holding land in Hampton,[7] was the sister of Abbot Walter and of Ranulf, and that the lands quitclaimed by the latter's descendants in 1163–4 had descended to them by reason of this relationship. Similarly their title to lands in Norton surrendered at the same time must have been derived from Hugh, the nephew of Abbot Walter.[8]

Ranulf was still living in 1121, and as 'Ranulf de Cocton' witnessed the grant of Wixford by Abbot Robert and the convent of Evesham to Ralph Pincerna or Boteler in that year.[9] Towards the end of the twelfth century an extent in an Evesham chartulary shows his lands divided between the families of Kinwarton and Coughton,[10] and Major-General Wrottesley has suggested that upon his death he was succeeded by two sons, between whom his lands were divided according to the Norman custom known as *Paragium* under which the younger brother inherited equally with the elder.[11] Some time between 1151 and 1158 the names of Robert of Coughton and William his brother occur as witnesses to a grant made to Bordesley Abbey by Peter de Stodley,[12] and if not identical with the William and Robert mentioned in the Pipe Roll of 1130–31,[13] these two brothers must represent the next generation. Robert of Coughton must have died without issue, since he was succeeded by the two sons of his brother William.

These sons, Randolph, or Ranulf, and Simon, about 1163–4 restored Abbot's Morton (q.v.) to the abbey,[14] but Ranulf still retained the property which had descended to him in Bretforton.[15] He is probably the same Ranulf of Coughton whose name occurs in 1166 as one of the abbey's knights,[16] and who for his land in Bretforton is stated to have owed service to the king and to have paid geld for 1½ hides and owed suit at the courts of the hundred and of the county.[17] Ranulf was still living in 1174–5,[18] but he must have died shortly after that date, and was succeeded by his son Simon.[19] The latter was in all probability 'the knight of Coughton' referred to in the *Chronicle of Evesham* under the date 1206, when 3 hides of his land in Bretforton paid tithe to the sacrist.[20] Simon of Coughton was succeeded, according to Dugdale, by his son, another Simon, living in 1221,[21] who at his death left two daughters and co-heirs: Cecilia, who married John de la Mare, and Joan, the wife of William de Spineto.[22] There is no evidence to show whether either of these families held Bretforton, but some time during the thirteenth century the whole of the Coughton property there, 3 hides and a virgate, passed by some means which have not been ascertained to the Avenel family.[23] About 1280 five inhabitants of Bretforton held of the Avenel fee,[24] and nearly three centuries later part of Bretforton was still known as 'Bretforton Avenels fee.'[25]

Contemporary with Simon son of Ranulf of Coughton was Hugh son of Robert, who is stated to have held 2½ hides in Bretforton,[26] probably the same that Hugh of Bretforton had formerly held. Jointly with Payne son of Henry, who held land in Littleton, he owed the service of one knight's fee.[27] Hugh is also said to have held these 2½ hides in Aldington,[28] with which Bretforton was still closely connected.[29] He owed service to the king for half of his land, and did suit at the county and hundred courts and paid geld.[30] About 1206 a tenant of the abbey also named Hugh held at least 2 hides in Bretforton.[31]

[1] Cott. MS. Vesp. B. xxiv. f. 11 *d.*

[2] *Chron. de Evesham* (Rolls Ser.), 67–8.

[3] *Red Bk. of the Exch.* (Rolls Ser.), 301.

[4] *Chron. de Evesham* (Rolls Ser.), 98.

[5] Maj.-Gen. Wrottesley, *A Hist. of the Fam. of Wrottesley* (Salt Soc. New Ser. vi. (2), 10).

[6] Ibid. and Dugdale, *Warw.* ii. 748–9.

[7] Cott. MS. Vesp. B. xxiv. f. 49 *d.*

[8] Ibid. f. 31; Wrottesley, *op. cit.* 9.

[9] Harl. MS. 3763, f. 91; Wrottesley, *op. cit.* 12–13.

[10] Harl. MS. 3763, f. 59:—'Radulphus frater Abbatis Walteri habet in Withelega [Weethly] iii hidas de dominico. In Kinewarton iii hidas de dominico. In Stoke ii hidas de dominico. In Litelton ii hidas et dimidiam de dominico. In Bretferton iii hidas et i virgatam, dono Walteri Abbatis contradicente capitulo.' The date of this document is probably about 1130 (see Wrottesley, *op. cit.* p. 11). The same chartulary at f. 66 contains the following entry:—'Simon filius Ranulfi de Cocton tenet in Litelton ii hidas et dimidiam, et in Witheleia i hidam et dimidiam, et in Bretferton iii hidas et i virgatam et debet i militem. Ranulfus tenet in Kinewarton iii hidas, et in Witheleia i hidam et dimidiam et in Stoke ii hidas et dimidiam et debet i militem.' The amount held by Simon and Ranulf jointly corresponds exactly to that held by Ranulf the abbot's brother.

[11] Wrottesley, *op. cit.* 19.

[12] Madox, *Form. Angl.* 244; Wrottesley, *op. cit.* 19. The date must be between 1150 and 1158, as it is addressed to John, bishop of Worcester (1151–1158).

[13] See Wrottesley, *op. cit.* 19.

[14] Cott. MS. Vesp. B. xxiv. f. 35. The date has been fixed by Eyton at 1163–4, and the deed must have been executed between 1160, when Adam became abbot of Evesham, and 1168, when the Pipe Roll shows Simon to be lord of Wrottesley. See Wrottesley, *op cit.* 8–9. The witnesses to the two deeds are the same.

[15] Cott. MS. Vesp. B. xxiv. f. 50 *d.* 'Rand. de Koctun tenet xiii virgatas apud Bretferton,' etc.

[16] *Red Bk. of the Exch.* (Rolls Ser.), 301.

[17] Cott. MS. Vesp. B. xxiv. f. 50 *d.*

[18] A deed occurs in the Kenilworth chartulary by which Henry Clinton mortgages a mill to Ranulf Coughton for a sum of £10, to be repaid within a year from the first Feast of St. Michael after the surrender of the castle of Leicester, which took place in 1174. The deed mentions Ranulf's son Simon and his brother Simon. See Wrottesley, *op. cit.* 21.

[19] Cott. MS. Vesp. B. xxiv. f. 12:—'Simon filius Ranulfi de Coctun tenet in . . . Bretforton iii hidas et i virgatam.'

[20] *Chron. de Evesham* (Rolls Ser.), 211.

[21] *Warw.* ii. 748–9.

[22] Ibid.

[23] Harl. MS. 3763, f. 168:—'Feodum . . . tres hide et una virgata terre in Bretforton, quod vocatur feodum Avenel.'

[24] Stevens, *Mon.* ii. 134.

[25] Ct. R. Worc. bdle. 210, no. 24. Also called 'Bretforton Avenels' and 'Bretforton Awneles fee.' Ibid.

[26] Cott. MS. Vesp. B. xxiv. f. 12.

[27] Ibid.

[28] Ibid. f. 46 *d.*

[29] See above, p. 360.

[30] Cott. MS. Vesp. B. xxiv. f. 50 *d.*

[31] *Chron. de Evesham* (Rolls Ser.), 211.

The sacrist of the abbey of Evesham had a considerable interest in Bretforton, and in 1206 is said to have had there in demesne 55 acres in one field and 76 acres in another.[1] Five and a half virgates of land held in villenage also pertained to his office, besides the tithes from 4 hides of land there.[2] The sacrist's land apparently comprised altogether 2 hides, which were free from geld[3] and formed perhaps the 'Sexton's Farm' of later days.[4]

A curious scandal appears to have arisen in the time of Abbot Roger Norreys, who seems to have held an annual feast at Bretforton and to have squandered the rentals of the sacrist in luxury and drunkenness, spending, it is alleged, in one day what would have sufficed for many members of the church for a whole year.[5] His successor, Abbot Randolph, who succeeded in 1214, abolished the feast, considering it a great evil.[6]

In 1233 it is stated that Adam le Boteler held half a virgate of land in Littleton by the service of doing suit at the county court of Worcester for the abbey's property in Bretforton.[7]

The various alienations which had taken place in the thirteenth century considerably reduced the value of Bretforton to the abbey, but later on it recovered some part of its property here. Abbot Henry (1256–63), in the early days of his abbacy, purchased land from Ralph de Bretforton worth 50*s.* yearly,[8] which he assigned towards the maintenance of a chaplain to celebrate divine service daily in the monastery of Evesham, to redeem the negligence of the brethren in their celebrations, and for the souls of the abbots and brethren of the monastery and their parents, and for all the benefactors and founders of the house.[9] He also assigned to the convent towards his anniversary a rent of 20*s.* from Hugh Bartram, one of his tenants in Bretforton.[10]

Among the owners of land in Bretforton towards the end of the thirteenth century was John de Bampton, who in 1269 jointly with Amice his wife conveyed a messuage, land, and rent there to Adam, son of Ralph, and his wife Agnes.[11] Robert Ewen or Ywayn seems to have been at that time the richest and most important landholder in Bretforton;[12] he is entered under Aldington in the Subsidy Roll of about 1280,[13] probably because Bretforton and Aldington were closely connected, and the boundaries between them undefined. Besides his own tenement Robert Ewen also leased land from Adam Kauf, and had two tenants of his own fee,[14] and his holding was probably a mesne manor. He was still holding in Bretforton in 1327,[15] and was succeeded by his son John Ewen, whose son and heir John was living in 1348.[16] Thomas Ewen, son and heir of the latter John,[17] in 1365 conveyed a capital messuage and 2 carucates of land with rents, services, reversions, bondmen and their issue to Richard Patty of Bengeworth, chaplain, and others by whom the premises were conveyed to Abbot William Boys (1345–67).[18] The property was valued at the then considerable sum of £10 per annum. In 1366 Thomas Ewen completed the conveyance by granting a release of all actions to Abbot William and the convent.[19] A William Ewen in 1540 and in 1559 held considerable copyhold property in Bretforton, including 'a principal mansion' called 'Euanscourte.'[20] The Ewen family continued in Bretforton as late as 1694.[21]

Among other thirteenth-century tenants, Maud Smart and Alexander de Littleton held of the abbot's fee, and twenty-five men and three women 'of the abbot' apparently holding in villenage, and nine 'men of the sacrist' are also mentioned.[22]

It is probable that Bretforton is the 'Brecston' referred to in the taxation of 1291 as belonging to the abbey and valued at £2 14*s.* annually,[23] although the identification is not quite certain. If Bretforton is referred to, its value is below even the amount received from the lands above mentioned formerly belonging to Ralph de Bretforton and Hugh Bartram without taking into account any other tenements. Gradually, however, the convent recovered land there, and several times during the fourteenth century property of considerable value was transferred to the abbey.[24]

In 1535 the clear value of the abbey's property at Bretforton was £38 12*s.* 5*d.*, the demesne lands being then in lease.[25] On 4 January, 1538–9, the abbot and convent granted a new lease of the site of the manor and the demesne lands, together with the tithes, to John Harward and Agnes his wife, and Thomas Harward, younger brother of John, for the term of forty years,[26] and shortly afterwards the manor came into the hands of the Crown.[27] It was then a parish of itself, and comprised 'Bretforton Avenels' or 'Awnelesfe,' which contained the house known as Ewens Court, 'Bretforton Aldington Hernes or Herus,' and 'Wykewanheerus.'[28] Probably these last two distinctive names arose from the early division of Bretforton into two parts, one attached to Aldington, the other to Wickhamford, and the consequent uncertainty as to which place these lands really belonged.

Both John and Agnes Harward appear to have died before 5 March, 1560–1, when Thomas Harward

[1] *Chron. de Evesham* (Rolls Ser.), 211. Cott. MS. Vesp. B. xxiv. f. 13d.

[2] *Chron. de Evesham* (Rolls Ser.), 211.

[3] Cott. MS. Vesp. B. xxiv. f. 49d.

[4] Rev. W. H. Shawcross, in Bretforton *Par. Mag.* May 1904.

[5] *Chron. de Evesham* (Rolls Ser.), 260–1.

[6] Ibid.

[7] Ibid. 278.

[8] Ibid. 281.

[9] Ibid.

[10] Ibid. 282.

[11] Feet of F. Worc. 53 Hen. III. No. 25.

[12] Stevens, *Mon.* ii. 134, from Cott. MS. Nero D. iii. f. 243b.

[13] *Lay Subs. R. c.* 1280 (Worc. Hist. Soc.), 82–3.

[14] Stevens, *Mon.* ii. 134.

[15] *Lay Subs. R.* 1 Edw. III. (Worc. Hist. Soc.), 70–1. A Richard Ywain is mentioned in the *Chron. of Evesham* (p. 215), about 1206; he may have been holding land in Bretforton.

[16] De Banco R. 355, m. 5. John Ewen then sued several persons for messuages and lands in Bretforton which had belonged to his grandmother Joan, the daughter and heir of Adam son of Ralph de Bretforton, possibly the Adam son of Ralph mentioned above.

[17] *Anct. D.* (P.R.O.), D. 428.

[18] Ibid. B. 9439; Chan. inq. a. q. d. 39 Edw. III. (2nd nos.), 42; *Chron. de Evesham* (Rolls Ser.), 296.

[19] *Anct. D.* (P.R.O.), D. 428.

[20] Mins. Accts. 31–2 Hen. VIII. L.R. 1330, m. 19; Ct. R. bdle. 210, No. 24.

[21] Feet of F. Worc. Trin. 6 Wm. and Mary.

[22] Stevens, *Mon.* ii. 134, from Cott. MS. Nero D. iii.

[23] *Pope Nich. Tax.* (Rec. Com), 229.

[24] Pat. 8 Edw. III. pt. i. m. 18, where Henry of Ombersley, clerk, and William of Ombersley, chaplain, have licence to alienate to the monastery land and rent in Bretforton to the value of 100*s.* yearly; again, during the abbacy of William Boys (1345–67), Thomas Ewen's property, above mentioned, was acquired by the abbey: *Chron. de Evesham* (Rolls Ser.), 296, 307; Inq. a. q. d. 39 Edw. III. (2nd nos.), 42.

[25] *Valor Eccl.* (Rec. Com.), iii. 250.

[26] Mins. Accts. 31–2 Hen. VIII. L.R. 1330, m. 19*d.* and Lansd. MS. N. 578, f. 27 *d.* 28. This rent on the dissolution of the monastery of Evesham was paid to the Crown bailiffs. Ibid.

[27] Mins. Accts. 31–2 Hen. VIII. L.R. 1330, m. 19.

[28] Ibid.

surrendered to the Crown the lease granted to his brother,[1] and received another of the same premises to himself and his wife, with remainder to their son Thomas for life.[2] The lease of the site carried with it apparently no manorial rights, which remained in the Crown[3] until 29 June, 1566, when Queen Elizabeth granted the manor of Bretforton, including the site then under lease, and other lands to her favourite, Robert Dudley, earl of Leicester, and his heirs, in exchange for the manors of Watton and Beverley in Yorkshire and other lands in the counties of Kent and Rutland.[4]

In 1582 the earl of Leicester conveyed this manor and that of Hampton by fine to Sir John Huband, his high steward, and John Nuthall,[5] and in 1586 received a pardon on payment of a fine of £100 for having thus alienated the manor without licence of the Crown.[6] Sir John Huband and John Nuthall probably held Bretforton in trust to the use of Ambrose Dudley, earl of Warwick, brother of the earl of Leicester, to whom it passed on the death of the latter in 1588. In Hilary term of 1589, shortly before his death, Ambrose, earl of Warwick, conveyed the manor to Ralph Sheldon.[7] In 1595 Sheldon levied a fine by which Bretforton was conveyed to John Watson and his wife Ann, the former being apparently the son of John Watson of Bengeworth.[8] On 9 July, 1602, a fresh grant from the Crown was made to John Watson, George Langford, and John Gilbye and their heirs and assigns for ever.[9] The reason for this grant is not clear unless it was made for assurance of title. The manor seems to have continued in the possession of the Watsons, the court-baron of John Watson being referred to in an indenture of 1616.[10] In 1621 John Watson, senior, conveyed the manor to William Watson and Richard Purdewe,[11] probably in trust. There is evidence that John Watson held it in 1623,[12] and he probably continued in possession until his death in 1648.[13] In 1654 the manor of Bretforton was in the hands of William Watson, who was probably the son of John and Anne, and who jointly with John Watson,[14] possibly his brother, in Michaelmas term of that year conveyed it to Jane Pixley,[15] probably only for the purpose of barring a remainder.

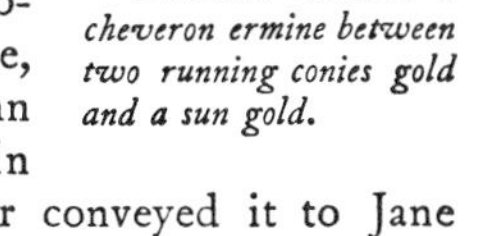

WATSON. *Azure a cheveron ermine between two running conies gold and a sun gold.*

In 1671 Thomas Watson,[16] who was possibly the nephew of William Watson, conveyed his manor or lordship of Bretforton, with all appurtenances, to William Bagnall.[17] This conveyance mentions the whole manor, but in 1679 William Bagnall acquired what is described as a fourth part of the manor from Capel Hanbury and Honora his wife and Anthony Crompe.[18] This fourth part of the manor possibly refers to the Grange estate, and has been identified as the Sexton's Farm or sacristan's land.[19] The Grange, with some 120 acres of land, is said to have been purchased by the Wylkes family from John Dudley and others, and to have been sold in 1612 to William Canning.[20] This William Canning two years before had married Anne Harward, daughter of Thomas Harward, holder of the advowson. He was a member of the famous family of Canning of Bristol, and had an estate at Foxcote in Warwickshire. Habingdon states, evidently in error, that he was lord of the manor of Bretforton, probably because he owned the Grange, which he is said to have rebuilt in 1635.[21] Seven years later, in 1642, he is said to have sold 'the Farm of the Manor of Bretforton' to Sir John Rous of Rouslench, from whose son, Sir Thomas Rous, it was purchased in 1649 by Sir William Sambach, who died in 1653.[22] In Michaelmas term of 1659, by a fine which possibly refers to the Grange, Anthony Sambach and his wife Elizabeth conveyed a messuage and about 200 acres of land with common of pasture to Anthony Crompe, John Crompe, and Thomas Ewens.[23] It is possible, therefore, that this property formed what is described as the fourth part of the manor which was conveyed in 1679 by Anthony Crompe and Capel and Honora Hanbury to William Bagnall,[24] who is stated to have acquired the Old Grange estate; [25] but it is not clear how Capel and Honora Hanbury had any interest in it.

On William Bagnall's death in 1688 the manor of Bretforton was held by his widow Elizabeth Bagnall, and passed about 1704 to their daughter Elizabeth and her husband, Thomas Lutwyche,[26] son of Sir Edward Lutwyche, of Lutwyche in Shropshire, Justice of the Common Pleas. Thomas Lutwyche was called to the bar of the Inner Temple in 1697 and became a Q.C. in Anne's reign. He has been described as an able lawyer and a high Tory.[27] At the time of his death, 13 November, 1734, he represented the borough of Amersham in Parliament. Thomas Lutwyche was succeeded by his son William, after-

BAGNALL. *Ermine two bars gold and a lion vert with a forked tail over all.*

[1] Pat. 3 Eliz. pt. 1, m. 5. [2] Ibid.

[3] As the perquisites of the manorial court are accounted for by the Crown bailiff during the Harwards' tenancy till the grant to Leicester, it is apparent that the Harwards did not hold the manorial rights. See Aug. Off. Mins. Accts. of lands of Evesham Abbey, 6–7 Eliz., No. 39, etc.

[4] Pat. 8 Eliz. pt. 7, m. 26.

[5] Feet of F. Div. Cos. Hil. 24 Eliz.

[6] Pat. 28 Eliz. pt. 11, m. 39.

[7] Feet of F. Div. Cos. Hil. 32 Eliz.

[8] Ibid. Worc. East. 37 Eliz.

[9] Pat. 44 Eliz. pt. 13, m. 29–31.

[10] Information supplied by Rev. W. H. Shawcross, vicar of Bretforton.

[11] Feet of F. Worc. Mich. 19 Jas. I.

[12] Information supplied by Mr. Shawcross from an indenture which refers to the court baron of John Watson, 1623.

[13] Bretforton par. reg. (ext. in Prattinton Coll.). His widow Ann survived him two years. Ibid.

[14] There were two brothers named John according to the *Visit. of Worc.* 1682–3, 101, and Com. Pleas. Recov. R. Mich. 1654, m. 23; but this is not borne out by the Bretforton parish register.

[15] Ibid.

[16] 'Thos., son of Mr. Thos. Watson and Cicelie his wife, baptized 1625.' Extract from Bretforton par. reg. in Prattinton Coll. (Soc. Antiq.).

[17] Feet of F. Worc. Trin. 23 Chas. II.

[18] Ibid. Hil. 30 & 31 Chas. II.

[19] Rev. W. H. Shawcross, *Bretforton Par. Mag.* May 1904.

[20] Ibid. and Habington's *Survey of Worc.* (Worc. Hist. Soc.)

[21] Rev. W. H. Shawcross in *Bretforton Par. Mag.* May 1904.

[22] Ibid. quoting documents in private possession.

[23] Feet of F. Worc. Mich. 1659.

[24] Ibid. Hil. 30 & 31 Chas. II.

[25] Rev. W. H. Shawcross in *Bretforton Par. Mag.* May 1904.

[26] From information kindly supplied by Rev. W. H. Shawcross, vicar of Bretforton.

[27] *Dict. of Nat. Biog.* On 6 November, 1723, he delivered a strong speech in parliament against the Bill for laying a tax on papists. Ibid.

wards high sheriff of Shropshire, whose possessions in Bretforton are said to have consisted in 1756 of Bretforton Farm, Bull House, a fourth part of the manor of Bretforton, with a yearly rent of 2 bushels and 1 peck of wheat, 9*d.* and a heriot issuing out of the lands of James West, and the advowson of the vicarage.[1] If the description in this document is correct, it does not appear how William Lutwyche came to hold only a fourth of the manor when apparently the whole of it passed from the Watsons through the Bagnalls to his family. Nash states that he was lord of the manor in his time,[2] but the Enclosure Act of 1765 does not give him this title. William Lutwyche died unmarried in 1773, leaving as his heirs his three sisters, Elizabeth, Anne, the wife of Nicholas Fazakerley, and Sarah, the wife of Thomas Geers Winford, of Astley. In 1773, the year of William Lutwyche's death, Penny Hancock, a member of an old Bretforton family, jointly with his wife Hannah, conveyed the manor by fine to William Tucker.[3] It does not appear how Hancock came to hold the manor, but he is said to have been in possession of the property in Bretforton known as the Manor Farm.[4] In 1785 the Lutwyche property in Bretforton is said to have been sold.[5] The manorial rights appear to have been extinguished at this time, and the manor to have become in abeyance. The old Grange estate is now held by the trustees of the late Mr. Wade Brown of Monkton Farleigh, Wiltshire. Mr. James Ashwin has an estate here. His family has long held property in Bretforton, and was allied by marriage with the families of Crompe and Timbril there. The Baldwin estate referred to by Nash passed to the Ashwins by the marriage in 1758 of Henry Ashwin to Mary, daughter of Richard Baldwin. Penny Hancock's estate is said to have been sold in 1829 and to be now held by the Rev. Seymour Ashwell.

LUTWYCHE. *Gold a tiger passant gules.*

Some extracts from the Court Rolls of the manor of Bretforton for the years 1550, 1551, 1559, and 1562 are preserved in the Public Record Office.[6] It is not quite clear whether the mill mentioned in the Domesday Survey[7] was at Bretforton or at Wickhamford. There seems, however, to have been one at Bretforton in 1291,[8] but by 1559 it had passed out of existence, the Mill Close 'on which was formerly a water mill' being then in the tenure of William Ewens.[9]

CHURCH The church is dedicated in honour of St. Leonard, and stands to the west of the village square known as the Cross, on a site raised considerably above the level of the street. A consecration is recorded[10] on the feast of St. Thomas the Martyr, 1295, by the bishop of St. Asaph. The church is mentioned as a chapel in 1206,[11] and in the Lay Subsidy Roll for 1358 as a church. It consists of chancel, nave with north and south aisles, transepts and porches, and west tower. The nave arcades are the earliest part of the church ; they belong to the end of the twelfth century, the south arcade probably a few years earlier than the north ; the north aisle walls, and possibly the south, contain masonry of this date. The chancel is of the full width of the nave, of good design and workmanship, much like the chancel at Church Honeybourne, but a little more advanced in detail. Its date is within a few years of 1300, and the record of a consecration in 1295, both here and at Church Honeybourne, points to a date in the last decade of the thirteenth century for its erection.

The transepts belong to 1340–1350, and the west tower to the fifteenth century. Both porches are modern.

The church is built of lias rubble walling with dressings of Broadway stone ashlar. The tower is ashlar-faced. The roofs are covered with stone slates, except those of the aisles, which are leaded.

The chancel has an east window of three trefoiled lancets within a pointed arch, the middle light being taller than the other two, and flanked by pierced spandrels. In the north wall are three windows, the first from the east being of two cinque-foiled lights under a pointed arch, with a small uncusped lozenge in the head ; the other two are trefoiled lancets. In the south wall the windows correspond to those on the north, but there is a plain priest's door between the second and third windows from the east. All these features are part of the original design—the windows are widely splayed on the inside, with chamfered rear arches, and a moulded string runs round the chancel both inside and outside, at the level of the sills. There are no sedilia, and the piscina is a drain in a plain square recess. There are three steps just west of the first pair of windows from the east. The roof has heavy moulded tiebeams and wall plates. All seats and fittings are modern. There is no chancel arch, but in its place a tiebeam with braces resting on fifteenth - century stone corbels. Here, as elsewhere, a former roodloft is no doubt responsible for the disappearance of the east wall of the nave. In the Prattinton manuscripts,[12] among other notes on this church, taken about 1825, is one that the chancel screen was removed about 1810. Part of the roodloft stair remains on the south side, entered from the south transept. The north arcade of the nave is of three bays, of late twelfth-century work. The pillars are round, with round capitals and bases. The arches are pointed, of two orders, the outer square and the inner chamfered ; the stone has been a good deal retooled. The capital of the eastern respond has a line of nailhead ornament ; that of the first pillar from the east is scalloped on the aisle side, with short spreading flutings, and towards the nave has a carving[13] of the legend of St. Margaret.

[1] From an indenture dated 3 May, 1756, in the possession of the owner of the advowson, quoted by Rev. W. H. Shawcross, *op. cit.*

[2] Nash, *Hist. of Worc.* i. 118. He states that 'William Lutwyche of Lutwyche, in Shropshire, is the present owner of the manor. And Mr. Richard Baldwyn has a considerable estate here, 1779.' But William Lutwyche is stated to have died in 1773. Possibly the fourth part of the manor refers to the area, not the manorial rights.

[3] Feet of F. Worc. Hil. 13 Geo. III.

[4] Shawcross, *Bretforton Memorials*, 150. It is possible that Penny Hancock was the descendant of William Hancock, who married Mary, the daughter of Anthony Crompe by his wife Joan, sister of Thos. Harward of Bretforton.

[5] Ibid. in *Bretforton Par. Mag.* May 1904.

[6] Ct. R. Worc. bdle. 210, nos. 23 and 26.

[7] *V.C.H. Worc.* i. 306*a*.

[8] *Pope Nich. Tax.* (Rec. Com.), 229.

[9] Ct. R. Worc. bdle. 210, no. 24.

[10] Harl. MS. 3763, f. 115.

[11] *Chron. de Evesham* (Rolls Ser.), 218.

[12] In the library of the Society of Antiquaries.

[13] Illustrated in the article on Early Christian Art for this county.

The capital of the next pillar has scallops interrupted by small human heads at the four cardinal points. The western respond has a plain moulded capital. In the west wall of the north aisle the line of the original roof is to be seen, the wall having been raised and the pitch of the roof altered in the fifteenth century.[1] The west window of the aisle is a trefoiled lancet of the fourteenth century, probably on the lines of a twelfth-century window. The eastern bay of this aisle is taken up by a small transept chapel of c. 1340. It has a fifteenth-century east window of three cinquefoiled lights, and a two - light north window of the fourteenth century with trefoiled lights and a quatrefoil in the head. In the west wall the opening to the north aisle is spanned by an arch of two square orders, with its southern springer resting on the abacus of the first pillar of the nave arcade. Prattinton mentions a 'panel roof with roses' as existing at the east end of the north aisle in his time. In the north aisle is a fifteenth-century window of local type with three cinquefoiled lights under a straight-sided four-centred head. To the west of the window is a fifteenth-century doorway with continuous mouldings, and a holy-water stone on the inner face of the west jamb. There is a modern stone porch, in the outer arch of which is hung a fifteenth-century door with a large wooden lock and wrought-iron scutcheons and hinges. The south arcade of the nave is of two bays, with pointed arches of two square orders, late twelfth-century work. The pillar and responds are round, with round capitals and bases; the capitals have tall fluted scallops. The western respond has in modern times been made into a pillar by being backed with a semi-circular ashlar shaft with half-capital and base, the piece of walling west of the respond being pulled down, and the space between the respond and the west wall spanned by a segment of an arch in imitation of the south arcade. The south transept is of the fourteenth century. It is wider than that on the north, the position of its west wall being fixed by the pillar of the south arcade, which is further to the west than the first pillar of the north arcade, as the three bays of the latter are necessarily of smaller span than the two-and-a-quarter of the former. It has a fifteenth-century east window of three lights, and a two-light fourteenth-century south window. In the west wall is a trefoiled fourteenth-century lancet, and in the south a trefoiled fourteenth-century piscina with a shelf. The south aisle has a three-light fifteenth-century window like that in the north aisle, and a plain four-centred doorway with a holy-water stone in the inner face of the west jamb. There is a modern stone porch, replacing a wooden porch, the marks of whose gable remain. As in the north porch, an old door is hung in the outer arch. The west window of the aisle is a large three-light tracery window of the fifteenth century. The west tower, of the fifteenth century, is faced with wrought stone. It is of three stages with embattled parapets and crocketed pinnacles, and has in the top stage two-light windows with a quatrefoil in the head on all four sides. There is a small modern square-headed west doorway with a single-light window over. The ground and second stages of the north and south sides are blank. From the nave a plain fifteenth-century doorway with a hollow chamfer on arch and jambs, now blocked, gave access to the tower. Over it was formerly a wooden west gallery. The pews in the church are all modern, but one in the south transept is made up with elaborately carved panels, one of which is dated 1615.

BRETFORTON CHURCH FROM THE CROSS.

The font is round, with a tapering bowl on a round stem, and a torus mould at base; it may be of the twelfth century.[2] Its wooden cover is dated 1721. A few small pieces of ancient glass remain.

On the gable of the north transept is an old gable-cross. There are six bells of 1823, by J. and N. Westcott of Bristol. They succeed a ring of five, of which the treble was by Henry Bayley of Chacomb, 1654, the second and third by Henry Farmer of Gloucester, 1622, the fourth by the same founder, 1612, and the tenor a mediæval bell from Nottingham, inscribed *Trinitate sacra fiat hæc campana beata.* The church plate consists of a plain cup with paten cover inscribed 1686 R.H. & S.B. No hall mark, but a maker's punch. The cup and cover were

[1] At the same date the north wall was refaced with ashlar.

[2] In the garden of Mr. Ashwin's house, west of the church, is an octagonal panelled font of the fifteenth century.

kept in a beehive straw case fitting to their shape.[1]

The registers begin in 1538, and are in good preservation.[2] The interior of this church has been completely stripped of its plaster, and the exposed rubble masonry pointed in black mortar, a proceeding which, while undoubtedly of assistance in dating the different parts of the church, is from all other points of view much to be condemned.

ADVOWSON The advowson of Bretforton belonged to the abbey of Evesham until the dissolution in 1539. It then came to the Crown, with whom it remained until 14 November, 1558, three days before the death of Mary, when it was granted, with the rectory and church, to Richard, bishop of Worcester.[3] It was restored to the Crown by one of the first Acts of Elizabeth's reign,[4] and on 4 October, 1586, it was granted to Sir Christopher Hatton and his heirs in fee in exchange for lands in Herefordshire.[5] The advowson afterwards passed from Sir Christopher Hatton to Edward Caryll of Harting in Sussex, who, jointly with his wife Elizabeth, in 1598 conveyed it with the rectory to Thomas Harward,[6] the lessee of the manor house, who presented the vicar in 1601. In 1613 Thomas Harward and his wife Alice conveyed the advowson to Nicholas Edmondes and William Canning,[7] probably in trust for the use of the latter, who in 1610 married their only daughter Anne,[8] and who resided at the Grange. Anne Canning died in 1618, and the advowson then passed to her husband, who presented in 1632. William Canning afterwards married Mary, the sister of Endymion Porter; their son Endymion Canning bequeathed a sum of money to the poor of Bretforton. The advowson afterwards passed to Anthony Crompe, who is said to have been a descendant of Joan, sister of John Harward, formerly lessee of the site of the manor.[9] Anthony Crompe presented to the living in 1664, 1668, and 1673.[10] In 1679, jointly with Capel Hanbury and Honora his wife he conveyed the advowson to William Bagnall,[11] then lord of the manor, who presented the vicar in 1681. The advowson afterwards passed to Elizabeth Bagnall, his widow, and then through their daughter Elizabeth to the Lutwyche family. William Lutwyche presented in 1760, and was succeeded as patron by his three sisters, Elizabeth Lutwyche, Ann Fazakerly, and Sarah Winford, who presented in 1775, 1780, and 1782. In 1785 they sold the advowson to Thomas Timbril, a resident of Bretforton,[12] who died in 1806. By a deed dated 16 April, 1791, Thomas Timbril granted the advowson to his son, the Rev. John Timbril, who was instituted vicar in November, 1816. He does not seem to have been popular with his parishioners, and declined to make residence in his parish, living as archdeacon of Gloucester at Beckford in that county.[13] In 1845 he conveyed the advowson by deed to Rear-Admiral George Morris of Thorney Abbey, Cambridgeshire, who in 1846 presented his son, the Rev. G. S. Morris, who probably became patron of the living on his father's death. The Rev. G. S. Morris died in 1889, and the advowson then passed to the Rev. Samuel Garrard, of Great Malvern, and from him to the Rev. Charles Eustace Boultbee, vicar of Chesham. Boultbee afterwards conveyed it to the Rev. John Peter Shawcross, whose brother, the Rev. W. H. Shawcross, is the present vicar.[14]

The chapel of Bretforton is said to have been twice simoniacally sold by Abbot Roger Norreys.[15] His successor, Abbot Randolph (1214–1229), gave 5 marks from the church to the frater or refectory to find cheese for the convent, and the next abbot, Thomas Marlborough, appropriated its whole income to the monastery.[16] In 1291 the chapel of Bretforton was worth £7 13*s.* 4*d.*[17]

In 1535 the tithes of lambs, wool, sheaves, and hay were let to farm for a yearly rent of £13 6*s.* 8*d.*[18] A few months before the dissolution of Evesham monastery these tithes were included in the lease for 40 years to John and Agnes Harward and their son Thomas before referred to.[19] They seem to have afterwards been the subject of several grants. On 17 May, 1575, they were given to John Dudley and others;[20] Sir Christopher Hatton on 4 October, 1586, received a grant of the tithes of corn in Bretforton, with the advowson of the church.[21] On 14 April, 1610, the tithes of lambs in or upon 25 yard lands were granted to Francis Kilborne and others 'to hold as long as it is in hand';[22] and on 24 March, 1611–12, Francis Philipps and others received a grant of all tithes of hay belonging to the office of hostilar of the late monastery, to hold as of the manor of East Greenwich in socage.[23] In 1670 the rent of £13 6*s.* 8*d.* paid by Anthony Crompe and Humphrey Loggine for the tithes of Bretforton was vested in the trustee for the sale of fee farm rents.[24] This rent was afterwards conveyed by Lawrence Ball and his wife Elizabeth to John Payne and Benjamin Rogers.[25]

The fine of 1773 by which Penny Hancock and Hannah Wilmot, his wife, conveyed the manor to William Tucker also conveyed to the latter 'all manner of tythe.'[26] There appear to be no rectorial tithes now payable in Bretforton.

[1] Lea, *Ch. Plate Worc. Archd.* 32.
[2] *Dioc. Conf.* 1899, *Digest of Par. Reg.* 16.
[3] Pat. 5 and 6 Phil. and Mary, pt. 2, m. 7.
[4] Stat. 1 Eliz. c. 4.
[5] Pat. 28 Eliz. pt. 2, m. 21–22.
[6] Feet of F. Worc. East. 40 Eliz.
[7] Ibid. East. 11 Jas. I.
[8] *Visit. of Worc.* 1619 (Harl. Soc.); Ext. from Bretforton Par. Reg. in Prattinton Coll. (Soc. Antiq.).
[9] Information supplied by Rev. W. H. Shawcross, vicar of Bretforton. See also *ante*, 363.
[10] Ibid.
[11] Feet of F. Worc. Hil. 30 and 31 Chas. II.
[12] Information supplied by Rev. W. H. Shawcross.
[13] Shawcross, *Bretforton Memorials*, 157. He is said to have incurred the displeasure of the inhabitants of Bretforton by cutting down a fine walnut tree which grew in the churchyard, and converting it into gunstocks.
[14] Information supplied by Mr. O. G. Knapp.
[15] *Chron. de Evesham* (Rolls Ser.), 241–2.
[16] Ibid. 275. The convent is here said to have had *three* marks for cheese from Bretforton church, and as this sum was not sufficient, Abbot Thomas gave the remainder to supplement this and other wants. Half a mark was to be given to the infirmary, a similar amount towards supplying sauce for cooking, half a mark on the day of St. Vincent, and again on the day of St. Odulph, for wine, and the remainder at the feast of Relics.
[17] *Pope Nich. Tax.* (Rec. Com.), 229.
[18] *Valor Eccl.* (Rec. Com.), 253.
[19] Mins. Accts. 31–2 Hen. VIII. L. R. 1330, m. 19 *d.*
[20] Pat. 17 Eliz. pt. 5.
[21] Ibid. 28 Eliz. pt. 2, no. 2.
[22] Ibid. 8 Jas. II. pt. 8.
[23] Ibid. 10 Jas. I. pt. 2.
[24] Ibid. 22 Chas. II. pt. 2.
[25] Feet of F. Worc. Hil. 34 and 35 Chas. II. In 1724, Thomas Little and Sarah his wife, Elizabeth Hale, widow, and Thomas Laight, conveyed the tithes of the fourth part of premises in Bretforton (Feet of F. Worc. Hil. 10 Geo. I.), and in 1727, Thomas and Elizabeth Timbril conveyed the tithes in one messuage there to John Timbril. (Ibid. East. 13 Geo. I.)
[26] Ibid. Hil. 13 Geo. III.

There is a Baptist chapel in the village.

The first notice of a schoolmaster in Bretforton is of John Kinman, who died in 1779. A Sunday school was opened about 1823. The village school was founded in 1847, two cottages being utilized for this purpose which themselves had once formed the vicarage. A School Board was formed in 1881,[1] and the school is now a Council School providing accommodation for 201 scholars.

CHARITIES Endymion Canning, of Brook, in the county of Rutland, by his will dated 4 May, 1681, gave £20 to the parish; William Bagnall by will dated 1688 bequeathed £10, and a similar sum was given by his widow, Lady Elizabeth, in 1712. These three charities have now been consolidated and the money invested in Consols, the interest of £1 5*s.* 8*d.* is distributed yearly to the poor.[2]

Mr. Henry Byrd by deed dated 29 July, 1858, gave 2 acres of land, the rent of which (£6) is distributed to the poor in clothing and coals on St. Thomas's Day.[3]

Richard Price in 1727 gave £20, the interest of which was to be devoted equally to the payment of a minister for preaching a sermon on Good Friday and towards bread for the poor.[4]

CHURCH HONEYBOURNE

Huniburne (viii. cent.); Church Honibourne (xvi. cent.).

The parish of Church Honeybourne is situated on the eastern boundary of the county, and with the exception of about 400 yards in the extreme north-west is entirely surrounded by Gloucestershire.

A stream flowing towards South Littleton forms the boundary between Church Honeybourne and Weston Subedge for about a mile, and just beyond the village of Church Honeybourne it is joined by another stream which flows through the parish past Poden in a north-westerly direction. The Roman road, Rycknield Street or Buckle Street, passes the village and runs northward, forming the western boundary of the parish for some distance. A road passes north-eastward to Pebworth, and Church Honeybourne is also connected by road with Cow Honeybourne, which is closely adjacent.

The Oxford, Worcester, and Wolverhampton branch of the Great Western Railway passes through the parish, and Honeybourne Station, opened in 1853, is about half a mile away from the village, and is partly in this and partly in Cow Honeybourne parish. A branch line connects this station with Stratford-on-Avon, and another is now (1904) on point of completion to Broadway and Winchcomb.

Church Honeybourne has an area of 1,339 acres, and there are twenty inhabited houses.[5] The population is almost wholly engaged in agriculture and market gardening. The subsoil is lower lias, and the surface is stiff clay. The chief crops raised are wheat, oats, beans, and barley.

The following place-names occur:—Sheppey, the Poult Close, Gosse Meadow,[6] Reins Close, Cowlease, the Old Gore.[7]

MANOR Church Honeybourne is said to have passed into the possession of the monastery of Evesham in 709, as the gift of Kenred and Offa, whose grant included 2½ 'mansæ' here.[8] It was the property of the abbey at the time of the Domesday Survey, and so continued until the suppression of the house in 1539. Its extent in the time of Edward the Confessor is variously stated as 2½ and 3 hides,[9] of which the monastery held 1 in demesne.[10] From the fact that it was for centuries the property of a religious house and afterwards of an ecclesiastical body, the manor of Church Honeybourne has little history.

The abbot rendered 4 marks towards the subsidy of about 1280 for his property here, and the chief tenants were then apparently Walter Balne, Roger de Poddeho, Stephen de Poddeho, and Thomas de Badesheye.[11] In 1291 the abbey's property in Church Honeybourne was valued at £4 13*s.* 4*d.*,[12] and about this date Abbot John Brokehampton (1282–1316) built a grange here.[13]

In 1535 the demesne lands were let to farm, and the revenue from the manor, including a rent of £20 from the pastures of Poden, was £30 4*s.* 2*d.*[14] On 28 December, 1538, the abbot and convent granted a lease of the site of the manor of Church Honeybourne with the demesne lands to John King and Agnes his wife, and John and Henry King their sons, for a term of sixty years at the yearly rent of 50*s.*[15] The manor came into the hands of the Crown in the following year; in 1540 its clear issues, including the rents from Poden, were £25 2*s.* 4½*d.*[16] On 5 August, 1542, Henry VIII. granted the manor to the then recently established Dean and Chapter of Westminster.[17] On Mary's accession, however, the monastery of St. Peter was refounded, and the manor of Church Honeybourne was granted to it on 10 November, 1556.[18] The dean and chapter being re-established by Queen Elizabeth, a fresh grant was made to them on 21 May, 1560.[19] Under the Act of 1649 for the sale of church lands, this manor, with others, was sold in 1651[20] to Sir Cheney Culpeper of Hollingbourne, Kent, the sale being confirmed in 1654.[21] At the Restoration Church Honeybourne returned to the possession of the Dean and Chapter of Westminster, who remained lords of the manor until 1869, when the manorial rights were vested in the Ecclesiastical Commissioners,[22] with whom they now remain.

[1] Shawcross, *Bretforton Memorials*, 123.
[2] *Char. Com. Rep.* xxiv. (1830); *Genl. Digest of Endowed Charities, Parl. Papers*, 1876, vol. 58.
[3] *Digest of End. Char. Worc. Parl. Papers*, 1900, vol. lxiii. This charity is there described as the charity of 'Austen, Pugh, and others (otherwise Byrd's Charity).'
[4] Shawcross, *Bretforton Memorials*, 118.
[5] *Worc. Co. Coun. Handbk.* (1903), 148.
[6] Close, 1651, pt. 56, no. 19.
[7] Pat. 36 Hen. VIII., pt. 22.
[8] Birch, *Cart. Sax.* i. 183.
[9] *V.C.H. Worc.* i. 307*a*; Cott. MS. Vesp. B. xxiv. f. 6.
[10] Ibid. f. 45 *d.*
[11] *Lay Subs. R. c.* 1280 (Worc. Hist. Soc.), 87.
[12] *Pope Nich. Tax.* (Rec. Com.), 229*a*.
[13] *Chron. de Evesham* (Rolls Ser.), 287.
[14] *Valor Eccl.* (Rec. Com.), iii. 250.
[15] Mins. Accts. 31–32 Hen. VIII. L. R. 1330, m. 16 *d.*
[16] Ibid. m. 17.
[17] *L. and P. Hen. VIII.* xvii. 392.
[18] Pat. 3 and 4 Phil. and Mary, pt. 5, m. 1–6.
[19] Ibid. 2 Eliz. pt. 11, m. 15–22.
[20] Close, 1651, pt. 56, no. 19.
[21] Ibid. 1654, pt. 11, no. 13.
[22] *London Gazette*, 13 August, 1869, 4524.

The name of *PODEN* [Poddenho, Poddenhomme (viii. cent.) ; Powden (xvi. cent.)] now survives as the name of a farmhouse and a few cottages lying a little to the south-east of the village of Church Honeybourne, and close to the Gloucestershire border. It is said to have been transferred with Church Honeybourne to the abbey of Evesham by Offa in 703,[1] while in another account it is included in the grants of Kenred and Offa to the abbey in 709.[2] From the eighth century until the Dissolution in 1539 Poden remained in the possession of the abbot and convent of Evesham. 'The pasture of Poden' seems to have been a valuable property, as in 1535 it was valued at £20, while the remainder of the abbey's lands in Church Honeybourne produced an annual rent of a little over £10.[3] About 1536 the pasture was coveted by one 'Master Wever,' one of the king's servants, who brought to Abbot Clement Lichfield the king's 'letters of instance' to grant him possession of it. Cromwell, however, was induced to accept a 'lytle fee' from the abbot, who represented to him that the pasture could in no wise be spared, 'for hyt is the chyff mayntenance of our Howsholde as well for the provision of our beffs as mutton and other necessaries.'[4] Cromwell then advised Abbot Lichfield to reply to the king that the pasture could not be spared, and 'the kyngs Hyghnes was ryght well contentyd.' But Wever in his disappointment bore the abbot a great grudge, and threatened that he had power to depose him and make whom he would abbot. Clement Lichfield in great distress wrote to Cromwell in 1538, begging his protection and deliverance from 'the malicyous suyts and vexacions which the said Gentylman doth dayly Imagyn against me.'[5] Wever, however, continued his suit for the pasture ; in 1539 he was said to have 'purchased' the king's letters for it, and Philip Hawford, who had succeeded Clement Lichfield as abbot, also wrote to Cromwell, requesting his intercession on behalf of the convent.[6] Wever's efforts to gain possession of Poden were unsuccessful, since it was granted to Sir Philip Hoby on 19 March, 1540, with the manor of Offenham.[7] On 14 May, 1544, he received a grant in fee of the reversion of these lands to himself and Dame Elizabeth his wife.[8] It appears from the latter grant that he paid the sum of £322 19*s.* 6*d.* for the manor of Offenham and his possessions in Poden,[9] the latter being held at an annual rent of £3 0*s.* 9*d.*[10]

On Sir Philip Hoby's death in 1558 Poden passed to his half-brother Thomas Hoby, and for some years followed the same descent as Abbot's Morton (q. v.). It was probably afterwards disposed of by Sir Edward Hoby, but its history for some years is somewhat obscure.

In 1640 Poden appears to have been held by Lord Edward Somerset, afterwards sixth earl of Worcester, the great supporter of the king during the Civil War, who in 1640 settled Poden on his daughter Lady Anne Somerset, in lieu of £4,000 left to her by Lady Dormer her grandmother.[11] Poden lay on the route from Worcester to Oxford, and was utilized for supplies to the continual reinforcements sent by the Somersets to the king.[12] It was sequestered with the rest of the earl of Worcester's property, and in 1652 had been granted by Parliament to Hugh Peters the Puritan extremist and his heirs. In 1651 Lady Anne Somerset, who had married Henry Howard, son of the earl of Arundel, claimed Poden from the Committee for Compounding, and on 17 January, 1655, the matter was settled by the payment to her husband and herself of £2,242 10*s.*, part of the arrears of rent due to the countess of Arundel, in lieu of their title to the lands settled on Hugh Peters.[13]

The latter at the Restoration was tried and condemned as an abettor of the death of Charles I., and was executed at Charing Cross on 16 October, 1660, with Harrison the Anabaptist and six others.[14] If Peters still held Poden at the time of his death it would revert to the Crown, and probably be restored to Lady Anne Howard, but it is not clear whether or not it did so. Towards the end of the eighteenth century Poden was held by Walwyn Graves of Mickleton, Gloucestershire,[15] whose family had possessed lands in Church Honeybourne at a much earlier date.[16] The property was held by the Graves family down to the time of the late Lady Graves-Steele, and was sold between 1860 and 1870 to the Sidebottom family, one of whom now holds it.[17]

GRAVES. *Gules an eagle gold with a silver crown in an orle of crosslets gold.*

Poden has been described by Nash and other writers as a manor,[18] but there is no evidence to bear out this statement.

CHURCH A priest is mentioned in the Domesday Survey,[19] and a church was probably in existence at Church Honeybourne from an early date.[20] In the beginning of the thirteenth century Abbot Randolph allotted 1 mark from its revenue towards the minutions or bloodlettings of the monastery.[21] Abbot Thomas Gloucester (1243–1256) also gave from it an annual pension of 6 marks to the bursar for the use of the convent,[22] and this arrangement was ratified and confirmed by one of his successors, William de Whitchurch.[23]

[1] *Chron. de Evesham* (Rolls Ser.), 71.
[2] Birch, *Cart. Sax.* i. 184.
[3] *Valor Eccl.* (Rec. Com.), iii. 250.
[4] *L. and P. Hen. VIII.* xi. 236–7.
[5] Ibid.
[6] Ibid. xiv. (i.), 520.
[7] Ibid. xv. 173.
[8] Pat. 36 Hen. VIII. pt. 22, m. 2 ; *L. and P. Hen. VIII.* xix. (i.), 380.
[9] Ibid.
[10] *Cal. of Com. for Compounding*, i. 566.
[11] Ibid. iii. 1705, 1706, i. 766.
[12] J. W. W.-B.
[13] *Cal. of Com. for Compounding*, iii. 1705–6, i. 766. In 1652 a fine had been levied by which Edward, earl of Worcester, Viscount Molyneux, and Henry Somerset (Feet of F. Worc. Mich. 1652), conveyed lands in Church Honeybourne to Richard Bowcher and George Chalncombe, and this fine may have reference to Poden.
[14] *Cal. of S. P. Dom.* 1660–1, 316 ; *Dict. of Nat. Biog.*
[15] Nash, *Hist. of Worc.* i. 198.
[16] In 1659 Richard Graves levied a fine in favour of Robert Jenkinson and William Child (Feet of F. Worc. Trin. 1659) ; in 1680 Samuel Graves made a conveyance to John Slater and William Blennerhassett (Ibid. Mich. 32 Chas. II.), and in 1714 Richard Graves and Elizabeth his wife conveyed to Caspard Frederick Heming, Graves Martyn, and John Brewster (Ibid. Trin. 13 Anne). All three conveyances were made in respect of lands in Church Honeybourne.
[17] Information supplied by Mr. O. G. Knapp.
[18] *Hist. of Worc.* i. 198.
[19] *V.C.H. Worc.* i. 307*a*.
[20] The vicar, in an appeal for funds for the repair of the church, states that there is a local couplet which runs :—
'When Evesham town was bush and thorn
'There was a church at Honeyborne'
and the dedication to St. Egwin may suggest an early origin for the church.
[21] *Chron. de Evesham* (Rolls Ser.), 213, note.
[22] Ibid. 280.
[23] Ibid. 282.

O. G. Knapp, photo.

Church Honeybourne: The Church from the South-East.

To face page 368.

A church is recorded to have been dedicated at Honeybourne by the bishop of St. Asaph on St. Egwin's Day, 1295.[1] It is dedicated in honour of St. Egwin. It stands on low ground on the west boundary of the parish, some distance from a main road, and consists of chancel, aisleless nave, south porch, and west tower with stone spire.

The chancel is of excellent design and detail, of the end of the thirteenth century. It is built of lias rubble with wrought stone dressings, the rubble having been thinly plastered externally. There are pairs of buttresses at the eastern angles, and a moulded string runs across the east wall below the window. The east window is of three trefoiled lights under a pointed arch. In the north wall are three trefoiled lancets, and in the south two, and a plain priest's door. A moulded string runs round at the level of the window sills. All windows have rear arches. The piscina has a trefoiled head under a moulded label with crockets of good naturalistic design. The general features of the chancel resemble those at Bretforton, but seem slightly earlier, and it is probable that it was this part of the church which was dedicated as recorded above. The chancel arch is modern. In the south wall of the nave east of the porch are two blocked and mutilated pointed arches. Their spacing suggests that they are part of an arcade of four bays opening to a south aisle of the length of the nave, but no traces of the two western bays remain, or of the aisle walls, and the aisle was probably of two bays only. In the walling which blocks the two arches are two two-light windows with modern tracery, but old jambs which seem to be of the fourteenth century. The south doorway of the nave is plain work of the fourteenth century, and does not appear to have been rebuilt.[2] To the west of the doorway is a large three-light fifteenth-century window with tracery in the head, retaining a few pieces of the original white and gold glass, one of which has ihs with the spear and sponge on a reed laid horizontally across the letters, and another MG in a monogram. High in the south wall are four fifteenth-century clearstory windows, each of two trefoiled lights under four centred arched heads. Over the south door is a porch entirely built of wrought stone. Its roof of stone slabs is carried on four arched stone ribs with chamfered responds. The outer archway has a four-centred arch with pierced quatrefoils in the spandrels under a square head, with a niche in the gable above. It has never had a door. In the north wall of the nave are three windows and a doorway. The first window from the east is of early fifteenth or late fourteenth century date, of two trefoiled lights with a quatrefoil in the head. The lines of the tracery are very good, and on the inner chamfer are remains of a painted decoration of red roses. The second window from the east is built up, only its rear arch showing. On the outer face of the wall no trace of the window is to be seen, and a fifteenth-century buttress occupies its place. The north doorway has a plain chamfered arch of the fourteenth century. It is blocked with masonry. To the west is a plain two-light window of early fourteenth century style. There is no clearstory on this side of the nave, but the wall has been raised to the height of the south wall when the existing fifteenth-century roof was put on. The lines of an earlier roof of steeper pitch are to be seen. The present roof has moulded ridge, rafters, and tiebeams, with carved braces and jacklegs resting on stone corbels in the form of angels bearing shields, now blank. The chancel roof is modern, as is all other woodwork in the church. The font is modern.[3]

The west tower is of the beginning of the fourteenth century, with an added belfry stage and spire of c. 1360–70. It opens to the church by a low segmental arch of two chamfered orders, now filled in with blocking, in which is a sixteenth-century doorway. Above the arch is a blocked doorway formerly leading to a gallery. All its stonework is modern, but it appears to be the successor of a late fifteenth-century doorway, and is evidence of the existence of a west gallery at that date. The stairs to the gallery remain in the tower; they have oak newels with carved heads of comparatively modern date.

The tower is only 9 feet square within the walls, and of very plain design, as regards the earlier part. There is a doorway of late fifteenth-century style in the south wall of the ground stage, and in the west wall a plain narrow square-headed light. There are two similar windows above it in the same wall, and one in the south wall. In the north wall are no openings. The belfry stage, which is an addition to the original work, is also severely plain, having square-headed single lights on the east and west, and nothing on the north and south. The plainness in this stage is clearly intentional, in view of the contemplated addition of a stone spire and the doubts of the builders as to the strength of the substructure. Their doubts were fully justified, as the tower has crushed badly beneath the added weight, and a large buttress at the north-west angle is a witness to the efforts of later generations to remedy the evil. At the south-west angle the original fourteenth-century buttresses still remain.

The spire is a fine octagonal stone broach with ribbed angles. There are square pinnacles at the four corners of the tower, and round the base of the spire two-light windows with gabled heads. The bells are hung at this level in two tiers. On the window mullions at half-height the mouldings are interrupted by square blocks with sunk quatrefoils on their faces, a late instance of a detail which occurs earlier in the century in the lantern of Pershore Abbey and elsewhere. In the upper part of the spire are four spire-lights, that on the south having a square opening below it.

There are five bells: the treble of 1731 by Abraham Rudhall; the second, 1797, by John Rudhall; the third and tenor, 1830, also by John Rudhall; and the fourth by Bagley, 1663. The old tenor had an interesting mediæval inscription, given by Prattinton: 'Orate pro bono statu omniū burgensiū de castro epī.' There is a corporate town in Shropshire of the name Bishop's Castle, but how this bell came to be at Church Honeybourne does not appear.

The church plate[4] consists of a communion cup of 1703 or 1705, inscribed with the initials 'H. P.' and 'E. O.,' a plated cup and paten, and a pewter flagon and alms dish. The registers are contained in three books, beginning in 1673.[5]

1 Harl. MS. 3763, f. 115.

2 See below for a further discussion of this point.

3 The octagonal bowl of an ancient font, found c. 1860 on an adjoining farm, stands in the tower.

4 Lea, *Ch. Plate Worc. Archd.* 32.

5 *Dioc. Conf.* 1899, *Digest of Par. Reg.* 16.

The architectural history of the church presents several difficult points. The chancel seems to be the oldest part of the existing building, and the nave and tower to have been built not long after, i.e. in the early part of the fourteenth century.

It will be noticed that in the churches of Bretforton and Badsey, which have a parallel history with Church Honeybourne as regards their chancels,[1] the chancels are of the full width of the naves, which are of the twelfth century. The same thing may have been the case here, but the rebuilding of the nave soon afterwards restored the former proportions. This being so, it follows that the blocked arches in the south wall of the nave are not earlier than the fourteenth century. The inference is that the windows in the blocking have been moved to their present position, and the S.S.E. buttress refaced to match the other when the aisle was pulled down. The fact that the arches and piers have been mutilated in the course of being blocked tells against the supposition that they were built and temporarily blocked, after a not uncommon fashion, in preparation for an aisle which was never finished. The south porch has a plinth on its west side and none on the east, which suggests that it was built against the west wall of the aisle, which could not, therefore, have been destroyed before the second half of the fifteenth century at earliest.

ADVOWSON The advowson of Church Honeybourne belonged to the abbey of Evesham from the earliest time until its suppression in 1539. It then remained in the Crown until 14 December, 1558, when the advowson, the rectory, and the church were granted by Philip and Mary to Richard, bishop of Worcester.[2] Probably on the accession of Queen Elizabeth the advowson returned to the Crown, as on 28 May, 1569, she granted the rectory and church to Sir Robert Throckmorton, to whose father, Sir George Throckmorton, the tithes had been granted many years before,[3] for a term of 21 years at a yearly rent of 15*s*.[4] On 29 May, 1577, the reversion of the expiration of Throckmorton's lease was granted to William Gourlay for 31 years;[5] and again, on 4 October, 1586, before even the first lease had expired, the rectory church and advowson were granted to Sir Christopher Hatton and his heirs in fee.[6]

The rectory was afterwards held in fee simple by Sir Edward Caryll, of Harting, in Sussex, who on 9 February, 1604–5, settled it upon himself for life; on his death it was to be held for five years by his eldest son, Sir Thomas Caryll, knt., who was to pay his father's just debts from its issues; it was then to pass into the hands of trustees by whom it was to be reconveyed and re-assured to Sir Thomas Caryll, if living, or if dead to the next heirs male of Sir Edward, and in default to his right heirs.[7] From Sir Thomas Caryll it passed to his two daughters and co-heirs—Mary who married Richard Viscount Molineux, and Philippa the wife of Henry Parker, Lord Morley.

On 15 May, 1645, it was sequestered for the delinquency and recusancy of Lord Molineux and Lord Morley.[8] In 1649 Sir Richard Molineux and others conveyed the rectory of Church Honeybourne to Sir John Dormer,[9] and by another fine of the same year he conveyed it to John Dormer and Richard Salway.[10] In 1699-1700 the rectory, advowson, and tithes were held by Pierce Mostyn and his wife Frances, Robert Dalton and his wife Elizabeth, Edward Burdett and Edward Gleast, who then jointly conveyed them to Edward and William Walker.[11] In 1733 they were conveyed by Francis Manby and his wife to Anne Walker, widow,[12] and in 1775 John Berkeley and his wife Jane conveyed the advowson of the vicarage to Rowland Berkeley.[13]

In the early part of the nineteenth century it was held by the Rev. Thomas Williams, who by his will dated 6 June, 1819, left it to his wife Jane, with remainder as to one moiety to his cousin Ann Halford, afterwards the wife of Thomas Johnson, Elizabeth Barker, and Ann Stapylton, the daughters of his cousin, Ann Hall, widow, and as to the other moiety to the brothers and sisters of William Allies of Alfrick. The Rev. Thos. Williams died 5 May, 1829, and his widow on 28 December, 1830. On 9 February, 1841, George, Jabez, and William Allies, Ann Johnson, Elizabeth Barker, and Ann Stapylton jointly conveyed the advowson to the Rev. Augustus Miles Carteret Stapylton, who raised mortgages on it in 1856 and 1859, and on 31 August, 1860, jointly with his mortgagees conveyed it to the Rev. Richard Poole, who presented himself to the living on the death of William Bonaker in 1869. On 16 December, 1872, it was conveyed by the Rev. Richard Poole to the Rev. Thomas Smyth, who succeeded him as vicar, and who on his resignation conveyed the advowson to Mrs. Coopland, whose son, the Rev. G. B. P. Coopland, now holds the living.[14]

The church was formerly a chapelry of Evesham, and from an early date the chapel of Cow Honeybourne, in Gloucestershire, was attached to it.[15] The latter belonged to the monastery of Winchcomb, and it appears that a controversy arose between that house and the abbey of Evesham respecting its possession.[16] By an undated agreement which appears in the Evesham chartularies the abbot of Winchcomb granted the chapel to the church of Honeybourne with all tithes and offerings, except the tithes of his demesne. The abbot of Evesham in return surrendered two acres of land which belonged to the demesne of Winchcomb; he also agreed to pay a silver mark annually to the abbot of Winchcomb, and to hold divine service in the chapel of Honeybourne on Sundays and on two weekdays and on feastdays. On all the greater feasts the men of Honeybourne were to attend the mother church at Evesham.[17]

1 See the accounts of these churches for the process involved.

2 Pat. 5 and 6 Phil. and Mary, pt. 2, m. 7.

3 *L. and P. Hen. VIII.* xv. 563.

4 Pat. 11 Eliz. pt. 1, m. 47.

5 Ibid. 19 Eliz. pt. 8, No. 18.

6 Ibid. 28 Eliz. pt. 2, No. 2.

7 B.M. Add. Ch. 18,899.

8 *Cal. of Com. for Compounding*, i. 739.

9 Feet of F. Worc. Trin. 1649.

10 Ibid. Trin. 1649. In 1670 the sum of £15 from the church of Church Honeybourne, paid by Edward Baldwin, was included in the sale of fee farm rents to Lord Hawley. (Pat. 22 Chas. II. pt. 2.)

11 Feet of F. Worc. Hil. 11 Wm. III.

12 Ibid. East. 6 Geo. II.

13 Ibid. Trin. 15 Geo. III.

14 From information supplied to Mr. O. G. Knapp by the Rev. G. B. P. Coopland from deeds in his possession.

15 *Nonarum Inq.* 1340 (Worc. Hist. Soc.), 40; *Valor Eccl.* (Rec. Com.), 253.

16 Cott. MS. Vesp. B. xxiv. f. 11; Harl. MS. 3763, f. 81.

17 Ibid. The only name which appears in the document and affords any clue as to the date is that of Simon, archdeacon of Worcester.

In later years the inhabitants of Honeybourne, probably Cow Honeybourne, while making their Pentecostal procession to Evesham, were attacked by the people of the Vale, and serious riotings and even murders occurred. They consequently appealed to Rome, and Pope Eugenius in 1442 absolved them from the necessity of joining the procession, but an offering of one farthing from each household was still to be made to Evesham monastery at Easter.[1]

CHARITIES Mrs. J. Williams left by her will a sum of £3,500 towards the augmentation of the living.

A sum of £6 yearly was left to the poor by the late Miss Coombs, and is distributed by the Vicar.

The children of Church Honeybourne attend a Council School in the adjoining parish of Cow Honeybourne, a School Board having been formed for the two parishes in 1894.

BOROUGH OF EVESHAM[2]

Homme, Ethomme, Hethomme (viii. cent.); Eovesholme, Evvesholme, Evsham, Eovesham (viii. to xv. cent.).

The borough of Evesham is situated in the broad and fertile vale of the same name which extends along the River Avon and southward and eastward to the Cotswold Hills. It is some fifteen miles south-east of the city of Worcester, with which it is connected by two roads — the London and Worcester road, which passes through Spetchley, Pinvin, and Fladbury, and the lower road which passes through Pershore, Cropthorne, Hampton, and Bengeworth. It has a station on the Oxford, Worcester, and Wolverhampton branch of the Great Western Railway, opened in 1852, and another on the Barnt Green, Evesham, and Ashchurch branch of the Midland Railway, opened in 1864. The high-road from Leicester to Bristol passes through the town, as does the road from Cheltenham to Leamington. The Avon, though navigable for small vessels, is little used for purposes of commerce, and the traffic that now passes through Evesham is mainly confined to the produce of the market gardens round it, although in mediæval times its position on one of the great highways leading into Wales made it an important centre. The abbot and convent of Evesham in 1538, pleading for the continuance of their house as an educational establishment, stated that it was 'the meetest house in all the country for such a purpose, being situate in wholesome air in the town of Evesham, through which there is a great thoroughfare into Wales.'[3] A few years later the Royal Commissioners for the Suppression of Chantries also described Evesham as a great thoroughfare from the marches of Wales to London.[4]

The plan of Evesham is like that of most English boroughs of mediæval origin, though somewhat modified by the proximity of the town to the river and the presence of the Bengeworth bridge as an important means of communication with the suburb and the country outside to the east. Thus we find the main thoroughfares radiating from the market-place of the town—the High Street running north, Bridge Street, leading to the bridge;[5] and Bewdley Street leading westward. Old names are retained in Cowl Street and Oat Street.[6] The market square is situated close to the site of the abbey, and the chief business of the town centres around this square and in Bridge Street.[7]

Evesham: Entrance to Churchyard from Market Square.

The town owed its origin[8] to the founding of a monastery on this site early in the eighth century,[9] and its development to the great abbey around which it grew up. In 1055 Evesham was granted the privileges of a port and given a market by Edward

[1] Printed in Nash, *Hist. of Worc.* i. 200–1. He states that the document was copied by Bishop Lyttelton from Petyt's MSS. in the Inner Temple Library.

[2] The best history of the borough is that of George May, *A Descriptive History of the Town of Evesham*, Evesham and London, 1845. The earlier history by Tindal (Evesham, 1794) is diffuse, and the account given by Nash in his *Collections for the History of Worcestershire* is brief and unsatisfactory.

[3] *L. and P. Hen. VIII.* xiii. (2), 360; ibid. xiv. (1), 532.

[4] Chant. Cert. Worc. 60, no. 35.

[5] Bridge Street (Brutstrete, Brutaynstrete, le Bruggestrete, etc., *Chron. de Evesham* (Rolls Ser.), 211, 217, 308) and High Street ('magno vico,' 'alto vico,' *Chron. de Evesham*, 211, 212, 269, 272, 307, *Anct. D.* (P. R. O.), D. 882) occur as early as 1206.

[6] Cowl Street (Colestrete) and Merstowe Green also occur in 1206 (*Chron. de Evesham*, 211, cf. ibid. 307), Le Longstrete in 1415 (*Anct. D.* (P. R. O.), D. 396), and Oat Street ('le Odestrete') in c. 1317–44 (*Chron. de Evesham*, 290).

[7] *Chron. de Evesham* (Rolls Ser.), 211–12, 217, 269, 272, 307; May, *Hist. of Evesham*, 159–60; Tindal, ibid. 210.

[8] The contention that the Roman station *Ad Antonam* was on the site of Evesham is shown to be untenable in May, *Hist. of Evesham*, 14–15, 365.

[9] *Chron. de Evesham* (Rolls Ser.), 17–20; Dugdale, *Mon.* ii. 1–3.

the Confessor, showing that the town had attained some importance.[1] It does not appear to have ranked as a borough, however, and in Domesday Book Evesham appears as a monastic town under the sole lordship of the abbot and convent. The abbot owned the mill with its revenue of 30*s*., and the general revenue of the town had almost doubled since the time of Edward the Confessor.[2]

There is no exact evidence in regard to the bounds of the borough of Evesham previous to its incorporation in 1604. The charter of that date gave the boundaries of the borough; but this charter was soon superseded by that of 1605; the boundaries given in which include in addition to the parishes of All Saints and St. Lawrence the suburb of Bengeworth on the other side of the river Avon; but in so far as they relate to Evesham proper they may perhaps be said to represent the ancient limits of the mediæval town.[3] In general the town comprised the two parishes of All Saints and St. Lawrence, and the boundaries extended from the south side of the bridge by the old Gild-hall along the Avon, including the Abbey Park and meadows towards the town, to the Abbey Park wall; thence along the River Avon to the ditch on the far side of Higden Close, by Chadbury Mill, and, following this ditch towards Lenchwick, to the highway and along it to Lenchwick Lane, otherwise Offenham Lane, and, following this lane, to Offenham or Twyford Bridge; then by the south side of this bridge back towards Evesham to the meadow known as the Paddock, which was included in the borough, as well as the Evesham mills with the land adjoining them, and from thence by the banks of the Avon 'unto certain houses called the Alms-houses, including the houses adjacent to the north side of Evesham Bridge, otherwise Bengeworth Bridge.'[4] These were doubtless the boundaries of the town in the later Middle Ages, as owing to its situation on a small peninsula changes in the bounds and area were not possible. The comparative isolation of the town, surrounded on three sides by the Avon, rendered any elaborate system of defences unnecessary, and we have no mention of such. In this respect Evesham is similar to many other monastic towns, though its abbey and the conventual buildings were shut off from the town and the country outside by strong walls.[5]

By the charter of 1605 the parish of Bengeworth on the other side of the Avon was incorporated with Evesham as part of the new borough, the boundaries of which have remained practically unaltered to the present day,[6] although of late years the town of Evesham has extended considerably to the north and west, and Bengeworth to the north and east.[7]

Although the Domesday Survey affords no evidence of the existence of a borough at Evesham, it is possible that the statement 'the men dwelling there pay 20*s*.' may point to the existence of an organized body of the townsmen, connected perhaps with the recently established market. It is noteworthy that in a survey of certain property in Evesham alienated by the abbots Robert (c. 1104–1122) and Maurice (c. 1122–1130)[8] it is stated that they granted away sixteen dwellings 'de burgo' besides other dwellings and lands there.[9] Again, in the same chartulary there is what appears to be a rental of Evesham, probably dating from the latter part of the twelfth century and containing the names of nearly two hundred inhabitants. This list divides the town into four parts, viz. Evesham ('in Evesham'), Greenhill ('de Ruinhulla'), the Barton ('de Bertona'), and the new borough ('de novo burgo').[10] The last division is suggestive, and there is distinct reference in the *Chronicle* to the 'old town' of Evesham.[11] It is possible, therefore, that during the twelfth century the town assumed the character of a borough. But in the absence of definite evidence, it can only be stated that during the Middle Ages Evesham belonged to the class of monastic towns, but had a semi-burghal character, for though lacking many of the privileges possessed by royal boroughs it had its own courts and officials, and its status was that of a mesne borough. It was summoned to send burgesses to Parliament in 1295 with many other boroughs under ecclesiastical lordship which enjoyed temporary representation, and it was also represented in the Parliament of 1337.[12]

Although it is known that burgages existed at Evesham in former times, there is little evidence respecting them. In a document[13] which corresponds very closely to and is probably an abbreviated form of the institutions of Abbot Randolph of about 1206,[14] it is stated that the sacrist received 20*s*. yearly from burgages in the town of Evesham, and in 1281 Joan de Tywe had licence to alienate in mortmain to the abbot and convent six burgages and 14*s*. rent there.[15]

1 *Chron. de Evesham* (Rolls Ser.), 57. 'Port' was a term used in Anglo-Saxon times for a mercantile town. It meant a place for the sale and purchase of goods (Kemble, *Saxons*, ii. 550).

2 *V.C.H. Worc.* i. 306; Merewether and Stephens, *Hist. of Boroughs*, i. 211; May, *Hist. of Evesham*, 154–56; Tindal, ibid. 49–50.

3 Owing to numerous discoveries of foundations outside the present urban portion of the borough, it has been conjectured that the mediæval town was more extensive than the modern borough, and that a decline in population and a decrease in the urban extent of the town took place after the dissolution of the abbey. Tindal, *Hist. of Evesham*, 202. It is said that in 1587 there were 200 houses and more in the parishes of All Saints and St. Lawrence. Exch. Dep. 29 Eliz. East. No. 12.

4 From the second charter granted by James I. dated 3 April, 1605, Pat. 3 Jas. I. pt. 15, and May, op. cit. App. xiv. 456–57; Tindal, *Evesham*, 342–363.

5 *Chron. de Evesham* (Rolls Ser.), 291–92, 351; Dugdale, *Mon.* ii. 20, 'Licentia pro abbatia firmanda et kernellanda'; cf. *Gent. Mag.* New Ser. (1856), i. 326–7; Tindal, *Hist. of Evesham*, 127; May, ibid. 40, 58, 64, 168.

6 Charter of 1605, Pat. 3 Jas. I. pt. 15; May, *Hist. of Evesham*, App. xiv. 457. For Bengeworth, see p. 397.

7 Information supplied by Mr. O. G. Knapp; cf. census return for 1901. The growth of Bengeworth is attributed chiefly to the extensive sale of building sites by Lady Northwick.

8 For these dates, which differ from those given by the *Chronicle*, see *Hist. of Family of Wrottesley* (Wm. Salt Arch. Soc.), 11, footnote 2.

9 Cott. MS. Vesp. B. xxiv. f. 11.

10 Ibid. f. 42–45*d*. The names of Randolph or Ranulf of Coughton (see Bretforton), and Bertram of Hidcote (Hidcote Bartram, Gloucestershire), who appear as military tenants of the abbey in 1166 (*Exch. Red Bk.* (Rolls Ser.) 301), occur in this list.

11 *Chron. de Evesham* (Rolls Ser.), 216.

12 *Ret. of Members of Parl.* i. 6, 115–6. William de Sodinton and Robert de Hales represented Evesham at the former Parliament, and Richard de Tapenhale, Nicolas de Neubury, and Robert de Bagdon at the latter.

13 Dugdale, *Mon.* ii. 24. It is very similar to the list of the sacrists' revenues given in the *Chron. de Evesham* (Rolls Ser.), 211, with this difference, that it gives the total amount: 'de burgagio in villa Evesham viginti solidos,' while the *Chronicle* specifies each tenement and its rent, and the addition of these rents gives the amount of 20*s*. 5*d*.

14 *Chron. de Evesham* (Rolls Ser.), 205 et seq. See also Cott. MS. Vesp. B. xxiv. f. 13.

15 *Cal. of Pat.* 1281–92, p. 8. She was possibly the descendant of William de Tywe, who is mentioned in 1256 as rendering certain rents to the sacristan of the abbey. (*Chron. de Evesham* (Rolls Ser.), 211.) The names of William, Richard, and Cecilia de Tywe occur in the twelfth century rental of Evesham already referred to (Cott. MS. Vesp. B. xxiv. f. 42).

But there is no evidence regarding the total number or extent of burgages in Evesham, nor can it be definitely stated when they ceased. No mention of a gild merchant has been found. There existed, however, an ancient building known as the Old Gild-hall, situated near the south-west corner of the bridge, and mentioned in the boundaries in the charter of 1605.[1] The townsmen of Evesham never, apparently, formed themselves into either a commune or a gild-merchant, but the trading companies or fraternities which are frequently referred to in the borough records for the seventeenth century may have been the survivals of earlier craft gilds.

The practical control of the town rested with the abbot and convent, whose steward presided over the court-leet, which at its Michaelmas sitting chose the two bailiffs for the ensuing year.[2] These bailiffs acted as governors of the town. It was their duty to conduct the proceedings in the borough court, held once in three weeks, to collect the taxes and tolls, to supervise the holding of fairs and markets, and in general to administer the internal affairs of the borough.[3] These bailiffs are first mentioned in 1303, when Simon de Eyleworth and Richard de Somburne in virtue of their office witnessed a grant of a messuage in High Street.[4]

In 1327 Edward III. granted letters patent to the bailiffs and the 'good men' of Evesham, giving them authority to levy special tolls on merchandize entering the town, for the purpose of paving the town.[5] Although a deed of 1392[6] shows that bailiffs were then in existence, they are not mentioned in a grant of pavage in 1401, the charter being directed to the 'good men of Evesham,' and the customs are to be levied under the direction of the abbot of Evesham.[7] This indicates that the abbatial influence was still paramount and that the bailiffs were hardly important enough to be mentioned.[8] But by the end of the fifteenth century the townsmen had gained greater independence. An agreement made with the abbot in 1482 shows that the bailiffs held the profits of court at a yearly fee farm of 20 marks paid to the kitchener of the monastery, but there is nothing to show how long this arrangement had been in force. The bailiffs who retired at Michaelmas had formerly been responsible although out of office for the rents then due, and had suffered great loss and inconvenience in consequence, and it was agreed that in future the rents due at Michaelmas should be collected by the incoming bailiffs. The fee farm, which had formerly been paid in equal portions at the Feasts of the Annunciation (25 March) and St. Michael Archangel (29 September), was henceforth to be paid at the Feasts of the Purification (2 February) and St. Peter ad Vincula (1 August), and the first term of the year was to begin at Michaelmas instead of at the Annunciation as formerly. The retiring bailiffs were to supply the cellarer, steward, and jury of the leet with the customary bread, cheese, and ale during the Michaelmas session of the court. This indenture was sealed with the seals of the abbot, prior, kitchener, and steward on behalf of the monastery, and with the seals of office of the retiring and the incoming bailiffs and of eighteen representatives of the townsmen on the part of the town.[9] As the power of the commonalty at Evesham increased the influence of the abbot grew less. According to contemporary testimony the last important abbot, Clement Lichfield (1514–1539), though a man of great ability, was able to exercise but a very indirect influence on the election of the bailiffs, and though his nominee was elected in some instances, the townsmen frequently disregarded his recommendation.[10] No doubt the disturbed state of ecclesiastical affairs in England from 1530 to 1539, and the extortion of the king and his ministers from the abbot, did much to weaken the authority of the ecclesiastical lord of the town.[11] Furthermore, the townsmen were becoming better organized, for we hear of a definite body of freemen, and of the bailiffs and ancients of the town disfranchising such as were not obedient to the constituted authorities, thereby depriving them of their privileges in the town and rendering them liable to such restrictions and tolls as were imposed on foreigners.[12]

1 Pat. 3 Jas. I. pt. 15, May, *Hist. of Evesham*, 199–200, 402, 456; Gross, *Gild Merchant*, i. 82. This building was possibly connected with the Guild of the Holy Trinity, seemingly a religious fraternity whose lands were in 1586 granted to Sir Christopher Hatton (Pat. 28 Eliz. pt. 2, no. 2). The old Gild-hall of Evesham was also known in the early part of the nineteenth century as 'The Key House at the bridge foot,' and was let as a workhouse by the churchwardens of All Saints' parish. It was sold and pulled down under the Evesham Bridge Act of 1853 (see under *Charities*, p. 395, also *Char. Commiss. Rep.* xxiv. 508 *et seq.* and *Genl. Digest of Endowed Charities*, 1876). Its site is said to be now occupied by Mr. Geo. Hunt's house. Close to it stood the 'King's fish board,' an oak board 'near eight inches thick' where fish was sold; the town crier used to proclaim what kinds of fish were to be sold there. The corporation books record an annual payment of 6*s.* and afterwards of 9*s.* 8*d.* to the holder of the fee farm rent for the king's board: Prattinton Coll. (Soc. Antiq.).

2 Cott. MS. Titus C. ix. fol. 10; May, *Hist. of Evesham*, 252 and note: 'Ad visum francisplegiæ tentæ apud Evesham die Sabbati in festo S. Michaelis Archangeli, anno regis ejusdem Henrici decimo, coram domino Humfrido Stafford, tunc ibidem senescallo.'

3 May, *Hist. of Evesham*, 115, 252–53, 258; Merewether and Stephens, *Hist. of Boroughs*, ii. 651, 1004–5; Dugdale, *Mon.* ii. 9; Tindal, *Evesham*, 212.

4 *Anct. D.* B. 8982.

5 *Cal. of Pat.* 1327–1330, 201; May, *Hist. of Evesham*, 370; Merewether and Stephens, *Hist. of Boroughs*, ii. 661–52. Another grant of the same nature was made in 1331. *Cal. of Pat.* 1330–4, 197.

6 *Anct. D.* B. 3547. Their names are given as witnesses to a deed,—(Ambr)esleye and Richard Lench.

7 *Cal. of Pat.* 1399–1401, 439. Merewether and Stephens, *Hist. of Boroughs*, ii. 791. See also grant of pontage in Pat. 14 Hen. III. m. 5.

8 As in other monastic towns the townsmen owed suit and service to the abbot. They had to grind their corn at his mill, and bake their bread in his ovens. In 1307 a private oven was destroyed, in 1388 all querns or hand mills in the town were destroyed, and in 1430 a horse mill was thrown down. May, op. cit. 83–84, 103, 162–63. *Chron. de Evesham* (Rolls Ser.), 214–15, 216.

9 *Anct. D.* (P. R. O.), B. 11, 136. Merewether and Stephens, *Hist. of Boroughs*, ii. 1004–5; May, *Hist. of Evesham*, 252. This indenture shows a considerable advance in independence on the part of the townsmen.

10 On one occasion he is said to have requested that John Matthews, his chief cook, might be chosen bailiff, but the inhabitants refused, saying, 'they would not seek their bailiff in the abbot's kitchen.' But upon the abbot providing himself with another cook for that year Matthews was chosen bailiff. On another occasion Abbot Lichfield's request was refused because the inhabitants 'did not like' his nominee. Exch. Dep. 29 Eliz. East. no. 12. May, op. cit. 253–54; Merewether and Stephens, *Hist. of Boroughs*, 1421, 1424.

11 Abbot Lichfield is said to have contributed large sums to the royal treasury from time to time, and paid at least £170 to Wolsey, besides numerous smaller sums to royal officers and servants. May, op. cit. 129–30; Dugdale, *Mon.* ii. 39.

12 Merewether and Stephens, *Hist. of Boroughs*, ii. 1425, 1428. As the freemen compounded with the bailiffs before being admitted, it is clear that the bailiffs had become the all-important officers in the town. They appear to have had maces borne before them in public by the sergeants-at-arms, whom they appointed. They also had the appointment of the 'bellman' or town crier. May, *Hist. of Evesham*, 252–53; Tindal, *Evesham*, 92 note.

The inhabitants of Evesham were doubtless not sorry to see the abbey dissolved, although to its presence the town had owed much of its growth and importance. But they still had to endure the hardship of having a mesne lord over them. The lordship of Evesham passed into the hands of the Crown with the remainder of the abbey property, and until 1546 it received the fee farm rent of 20 marks or £13 6*s.* 8*d.* paid by the bailiffs of the town.[1] On 2 October 1546 Sir Philip Hoby, the possessor of the greater portion of the abbey estate and buildings,[2] received letters patent which conveyed to him practically the whole town of Evesham[3] with great jurisdictionary privileges there. These included the right to hold view of frankpledge in Evesham, goods and chattels of felons and fugitives, three fairs every year with stallage, piccage, and customs of these fairs, a weekly market, all franchises, free warren and customs, and the power of holding courts.[4] The consideration for this grant was a payment by Sir Philip Hoby of £1,067 2*s.* 11*d.* He was to hold in free socage and not in chief, and it was stipulated that he and his successors should keep the bridge of Evesham in repair.[5] As lord of the town he continued to receive from the bailiffs the fee farm rent of £13 6*s.* 8*d.* He reserved to himself the power of appointing the steward of the court leet,[6] and to further increase his power in the town he persuaded the chief inhabitants to agree to a plan by which the jury nominated six candidates, three from each parish of the town, for the office of bailiff, and of these six the steward of the leet, acting under instructions, would 'prick' or indicate the two to be chosen.[7] This gave the new lord of the town much influence, though even his own bailiffs sometimes stood up for the rights possessed by the community, and the townsmen were not altogether submissive.[8] On the death of Sir Philip Hoby the overlordship of Evesham passed in the same way as the manor of Abbot's Morton (q.v.). It is significant that the Hoby family dealt with Evesham as a manor,[9] while the townspeople apparently looked upon it as a borough, and quoted their privileges. The different aspects taken by the lord and the inhabitants probably led to friction, as Sir Thomas Hoby is said to have threatened to 'sue the bailiffs and inhabitants respecting their privileges.'[10] In Sir Edward Hoby's time a famous suit occurred in the Court of Exchequer in 1583, when Queen Elizabeth questioned Sir Edward Hoby's right to control the courts of the town.[11] As a result of the royal claim a certain Bartholomew Kighley was made steward of the leet by letters patent, and attempted to hold the court-leet, informing the auditors that it belonged to the queen, and that Sir Edward Hoby had no right to hold courts. Disturbances over the courts became very numerous, and in 1585 almost resulted in a riot.[12] In April of that year courts-leet were held by the steward appointed by Sir Edward Hoby, and also by the steward appointed by the Crown. Sir Edward Hoby seems to have had the support of the majority of the inhabitants, and when the royal steward demanded entrance to the New Hall and charged the two sergeants in the queen's name to serve the court, they refused and kept the door 'with great staves and iron spikes in the end.' The queen's steward was then forced to hold the court in the market-place, under the New Hall, but the conduct of the boys of Evesham, apparently encouraged by their elders, deprived it of all dignity. They hauled a 'coken-stool' along 'through the face of the court' with a boy sitting on it, saying of the steward, 'He preacheth, he preacheth!' while they made a great noise, 'halloing' and crying 'A steward, a steward!' 'A court, a court!' 'A jury, a jury!' and 'The foreman of the jury should be set by the heels!' In the crowd which surrounded the court were many women who were prepared to pelt the steward and jury with stones if a quarrel arose.[13]

Sir Edward Hoby then took the whole matter before the Court of Exchequer and succeeded in establishing his right to nominate the steward of the court-leet. The decree of the court also recognized the right of the steward to name the two bailiffs from the six nominees of the jury. The bailiffs were to enjoy the same privileges as formerly, and in return for the profits from the fairs, markets, and courts were to pay to Sir Edward Hoby, his heirs or assigns, the ancient fee farm rent of 20 marks each year. Sir Edward and his successors were to retain 'the fines, reliefs, and other casual perquisites and commodities of courts.' The courts-leet were to be held in the new Town Hall twice yearly, and every three weeks a court was to be held in the old Booth Hall, and the general administration of the town was to continue as before.[14]

It was not until 1604 that the townsmen obtained their first charter from King James I., probably through the influence of the Rev. Lewis Bayly, the incumbent of All Saints' parish in Evesham, and chaplain to Henry, Prince of Wales, at whose request the

[1] Mins. Accts. 31–2 Hen. VIII. L. R. 1330.

[2] See p. 391.

[3] In St. Lawrence parish he received a messuage in 'Le Merstow' held by the vicar of St. Lawrence, 77 messuages, the building called 'Le old Sextrye,' a tenement called the Grange, and other property; in All Saints' parish 76 messuages, three watermills, all fisheries in 'Lez Fludgates' of these mills and in the River Avon from the mills to Offenham or Twyford Bridge, all the lane next the stream to the north of the town of Evesham, and other messuages and shops.

[4] Pat. 38 Hen. VIII. pt. ii. m. 11.

[5] Ibid.

[6] For Sir Philip Hoby see Abbot's Morton.

[7] It would seem, however, that a similar practice existed in the time of the monastery. Exch. Dep. 29 Eliz. East. 12.

[8] May, *Hist. of Evesham*, 254–55; Merewether and Stephens, *Hist. of Boroughs*, ii. 1423, 1425.

[9] After the agreement of 1482 at the latest there could not have been a manor of Evesham distinct from the borough; the latter seems to have evolved from the former, and probably with the grant of liberties to the townsmen the manor passed out of existence except in name, since it possessed no courts distinct from the courts of the town or borough. Thus in 1540 the crown bailiffs returned that there were no perquisites of court to account for from Evesham, all the amerciaments arising in the courts having been granted to the bailiffs of the town in fee farm. (Mins. Accts. 31–2 Hen. VIII. L.R. 1330.)

[10] May, *Hist. of Evesham*, 255. The condition of the town under the lay lords who followed the abbot in the lordship seems to have been one continued dispute between the town officers and the lord and disputes as to jurisdiction between various claimants. Merewether and Stephens, *Hist. of Boroughs*, ii. 1423–27.

[11] May, *Hist. of Evesham*, 256–57 and notes.

[12] Exch. Dep. 29 Eliz. East. no. 12.

[13] Ibid.

[14] Exch. Dec. and Ord. no. 12, ff. 275 and 337. Also enrolled on Memo. R. Mich. 29 and 30 Eliz. no. 392, f. 411. For an account of this Exchequer suit (Exch. Dep. East. 29 Eliz. no. 12), in which much interesting information as to the borough and its government, both before and after the dissolution of the abbey, was elicited, see Merewether and Stephens, *Hist. of Boroughs*, ii. 1420–28; May, *Hist. of Evesham*, 253–58. Tindal, in writing his *Hist. of Evesham* (1794), 92 *n.* knew of these depositions only in fragmentary form.

charter is said to have been granted.[1] By this charter the king incorporated the borough by the name of 'the bailiffs, aldermen, and burgesses of the borough of Evesham in the county of Worcester,' and granted them a common seal. Twelve aldermen and twelve capital burgesses were to form the common council of the borough, from the members of which two bailiffs—termed the high bailiff and the low bailiff—were to be chosen by the council.[2] The charter nominated the first bailiffs, aldermen, and capital burgesses by name, but made provision for future elections by the common council, which was also given the power to hold civil and criminal courts. Two burgesses to sit in Parliament were to be chosen by the bailiffs, aldermen, and burgesses, and two sergeants-at-mace were to be appointed for the borough. The charter further nominated a high steward of the borough and a town clerk, and placed the village of Bengeworth under the jurisdiction of the newly-incorporated borough.[3] This charter had not been long in operation before serious trouble arose in connexion with the government of the suburb of Bengeworth, and in 1605 King James granted the burgesses a second charter, again at the request of Henry, Prince of Wales, by which the burgesses of Evesham and the residents of Bengeworth were jointly incorporated by the name of 'the mayor, aldermen, and burgesses of the borough of Evesham, in the county of Worcester.'[4] This charter differed from the preceding one by creating the office of mayor, by reducing the number of aldermen to seven, and by making Bengeworth a part of the borough. It also sets forth that a recorder and chamberlain should be appointed, and that the mayor with these officers and with the aldermen and capital burgesses should constitute the common council. Furthermore, the officers of the borough were to be aided in the discharge of their duties by twenty-four assistants chosen from the burgess body.[5] To safeguard the rights of the burgesses in Bengeworth the charter expressly states that once in seven years at least an inhabitant of Bengeworth is to be chosen as mayor, and that that suburb is to be represented by two aldermen, four capital burgesses, and eight assistants.[6] In other respects this charter is similar to the previous one, and with very slight changes it has remained the governing charter of the borough down to the present time.[7]

The duties of the various borough officers were for the most part very clearly defined in the charter of 1605. The mayor took a solemn oath before his predecessor and the council that he would faithfully execute the office in all things. This oath was taken the first Thursday after Michaelmas, and having taken it the new mayor entered on the duties of the office for the ensuing year.[8] Prominent among these duties was that of acting as a justice of the peace within the borough and caring for the revenues arising from the courts. The mayor was also a judge of the king's court of record in the borough, over which he was to preside each week. He was also the king's escheator, and had to take account of all escheats and forfeitures within the borough, while as clerk of the market he was to hold the various assizes of bread, beer, weights and measures, and so forth with the aid of a jury of twelve lawful men. These special duties were apart from the mayor's general duty of upholding the charter and franchises of the borough, and of seeing that all ordinances enacted by the council were respected. He was always the chief presiding officer in council and court, and the office must have called for a considerable sacrifice of time and energy,[9] yet we hear of only one instance in which the fine for non-acceptance, allowed in the charter, was imposed.[10] One case occurs of a burgess begging to be excused from serving, having heard that the council were planning to elect him.[11]

The office of high steward, mentioned in the charter of 1605, was a merely complimentary post, the occupant having no real influence in borough affairs. He was chosen by the mayor and council to hold office during their pleasure, and the honour was generally bestowed for life on a person to whom the corporation were indebted or on some local magnate.[12] The recorder was also chosen by the mayor and council to serve at their pleasure, but he had important functions. The charter expressly stipulated that he was to be 'learned in the laws of

[1] Pat. 1 Jas. I. pt. 8. May, *Hist. of Evesham*, 258. The real mover in the matter was, without doubt, the Rev. Lewis Bayly, the Prince's chaplain. This divine was later given the see of Bangor, and in 1615 was chosen by the Evesham corporation as High Steward of the borough as a recognition of his services. Cf. E. A. B. Barnard, 'Old Times Recalled,' *Evesham Journal*, 25 Jan. 1902.

[2] Curiously enough this charter makes no provision for the creation of burgesses. Vacancies are to be filled 'out of the inhabitants of the borough,' May, op. cit. 279.

[3] An abstract of this first charter is given in May's *Hist. of Evesham*, App. xiii. 451–52; cf. also pp. 259–60. Although the preamble of this charter refers to 'divers charters and letters patent' to the burgesses granting franchises and liberties, it is doubtful if any such grants were made, as the borough seems to have existed by prescription alone.

[4] Pat. 3 Jas. I. pt. 15; May, *Hist. of Evesham*, 454–55; Tindal, ibid. 211.

[5] The first charter had not provided for assistants, May, op. cit. 452. They were possibly introduced into the charter of 1605 in order to give the burgess body more official representation. Lewis, *Topog. Dict. of Engl.* ii. 148, is mistaken in including the assistants in the common council, of which they formed no part.

[6] Pat. 3 Jas. I. pt. 15; May, op. cit. 461.

[7] This charter of 1605, 3 Jas. I. was dated 3 April. It is given in full in May, *Hist. of Evesham*, App. xiv. 454–484; Tindal, ibid. App. vi. 342, 363; and Nash, *Hist. of Worc.* i. 423–38. The original charter somehow fell into the hands of the late Mr. Halliwell Phillips, and was bought for the corporation at his sale. (Information supplied by Mr. O. G. Knapp.) For comments on this charter see May, op. cit. 260–61; Tindal, ibid. 202; Merewether and Stephens, *Hist. of Boroughs*, iii. 2143–45.

[8] May, op. cit. 460; E. A. B. Barnard, 'Old Times Recalled,' *Evesham Journal*, 16 May, 1903, where the oath is given in full.

[9] May in his *Hist. of Evesham*, 270–273, gives a list of the bailiffs and mayors of the borough to 1844.

[10] On 27 August, 1616, Mr. William Watson was disfranchised and fined £40 for not accepting the office of mayor: Ext. from Corpn. Bks. in Prattinton Coll. (Soc. Antiq.). A suit in the Court of the Marches respecting this fine followed in 1618 (ibid.), but the result does not appear. On 29 July, 1689, Hy. Halford was fined £20 for refusing the office of capital burgess, but by the next meeting he had accepted. In 1692 Joh. Frensham was fined £5 for refusing to act as assistant (Corpn. Waste Bk.). A case also occurs of an alderman and capital burgess being suspended in 1610 for 'discovering the Counsell of his brethren,' till he cleared himself. As the vacancy was afterwards filled up, he probably failed to exonerate himself: Ext. from Corpn. Bks. in Prattinton Coll. (Soc. Antiq.)

[11] Barnard, 'Old Times Recalled,' loc. cit. 1 Feb. 1902. This case occurred in 1685 in connexion with the proposed appointment of Thomas Bartlett, physician.

[12] May, *Hist. of Evesham*, 258, 462; Barnard, 'Old Times Recalled,' loc. cit. 25 July, 1903, see also ibid. 5 April, 1902; the office of high steward was held almost continuously by the Lords Coventry from 1630 onward.

England.'[1] He was present with the mayor and senior aldermen at the weekly court of record and also at the quarter sessions. It does not appear that he had any special salary or emoluments, and a deputy could be employed.[2] The appointment of the deputy rested with the council, however. In the case of the first recorder under the new charter the corporation ordered in 1608 that 'he must live in Evesham with his wife and children, and shall not depart from the same for the space of more than three weeks at any time without the consent of this Corporation.'[3] The chamberlain of Evesham was an important officer who was chosen from among the burgesses and held office at the pleasure of the council. He was to have charge of the revenues of the corporation and their muniments. He was also to keep the books and accounts of that body, and his duties soon became those of an ordinary town clerk.[4] Like the recorder he was without salary, but derived some income from the fees imposed by the court of record and at quarter sessions, as well as from fees paid at the admission of freemen.[5] The office appears to have been an honourable one, implying as it did active participation in the affairs of borough government. Each year at the feast of St. Matthew (21 September) the chamberlain had to render an account of his office to the mayor and council.[6] During the seventeenth century the office of chamberlain was held by but six different individuals in all.[7]

The mayor, recorder, and chamberlain were the higher officers of the borough. There were also several borough officers of less importance, notably the coroner, who was chosen from the capital burgesses or the assistants to serve during the pleasure of the council. He was to possess exclusive jurisdiction, as the charter granted that no royal officer should enter the borough on any official business. The coroner, therefore, acted as sheriff within the borough in addition to his ordinary duties.[8] He was without salary, but received a guinea for every inquest he held and half-a-crown for every burial certificate he issued, which provided some little income.[9] In spite of the lack of remuneration this office was a popular one as a stepping-stone to higher honours,[10] the office was held very frequently for only a few months, the holder resigning to accept a higher position.[11] The offices of steward of the leet and clerk of the market were vested in the mayor of the borough, who also had the appointment of two sergeants-at-mace to carry the maces before the mayor and to attend upon him. These sergeants also served in the borough courts, proclaiming the orders of the justices, executing processes, mandates, and other business of the courts.[12] In many respects these officers were like the modern constable, and they received a small sum each year from the mayor as well as certain fees from the service of processes and on the admission of freemen.[13]

Under the charter of 1605 the Common Council of the borough consisted of the mayor, six aldermen, twelve capital burgesses, the recorder, and the chamberlain—twenty-one persons in all. This council was self-perpetuating, aldermen and capital burgesses being elected for life by the council from among the body of burgesses.[14] Four of the aldermen, selected by the council, acted as justices of the peace, and in conjunction with the mayor and recorder as justices of gaol delivery.[15] The office of alderman brought with it however no special salary or privileges. The twelve capital burgesses had no special functions, but were eligible, together with the assistants, to the office of coroner.[16] The council was empowered to elect from among the burgesses twenty-four assistants to aid the mayor in the affairs of the borough. These assistants had little power, were without definite functions, and had no salary nor emoluments. Their only privilege was their eligibility to the office of coroner, but the position was honourable, and paved the way to membership in the council.[17]

The charters of 1604 and 1605 altogether ignored the claim of the Hoby family and their successors to the overlordship of the town, and gave to the borough powers already granted by letters patent to Sir Philip Hoby and never surrendered. The fee farm which the Hobys had received from the town the Crown reserved to itself, and this led to some difficulties during the seventeenth and eighteenth centuries. In 1596 Sir Edward Hoby, with Richard Shepham and John Gilbert, to whom he had sold the reversion, after Lady Russell's death, of the site of the abbey, conveyed all his rights in Evesham to Edward Grevill,[18] afterwards knighted, of Milcote, Warwickshire. In 1603–4 the latter sold his possessions and rights in Evesham. to John Woodward.[19] Immediately after Lady Russell's death in 1609 Sir Edward Hoby confirmed John Woodward in possession,[20] and in 1610 a fine was levied by Sir Edward Greville and Joan his wife, apparently for the same purpose.[21] The latter entirely disregarded the charter to the borough and claimed to convey not only the site of the monastery, but view of frankpledge, goods and chattels of felons and fugitives, fairs and markets and their customs, a court of piepowder, corrections of

[1] Of 1605, Pat. 3 Jas. I. pt. 15. May, op. cit. 462.

[2] Pat. 3 Jas. I. pt. 15. May, op. cit. 462–3, 465; Barnard, loc. cit. April, 1902.

[3] Barnard, loc. cit. 23 May, 1903.

[4] Charter of 1605, Pat. 3 Jas. I. pt. 15. May, *Hist. of Evesham*, App. xiv. 463–64. 'All manner of rents, fines, amerciaments, revenues, profits, commodition, and emoluments' were to pass through his hands.

[5] May, op. cit. 491; Barnard, loc. cit. 5 April, 1902.

[6] May, op. cit. 463–64. The first chamberlain was Russell Andrews, who had been town clerk under the previous charter.

[7] Barnard, loc. cit. 5 April, 1902, and 25 July, 1903, where lists of the chamberlains (1604–1758) are given.

[8] May, op. cit. 470–71. The duties of the coroner are given in the charter of 1605 (Pat. 3 Jas. I. pt. 15).

[9] Barnard, loc. cit. 5 April, 1902.

[10] Many of those whose names appear as coroners in the seventeenth and eighteenth centuries appear also in the list of mayors in later years. Several also fill lesser offices later. Barnard, loc. cit. 5 April, 1902, and 25 July, 1903; May, op. cit. 270–73.

[11] Barnard, loc. cit. 5 April, 1902, and 25 July, 1903. Lists are there given of all the coroners of Evesham from 1604 to 1758.

[12] May, *Hist. of Evesham*, 473; their maces were to be 'gilt or silver, engraved and ornamented with the arms of the Prince and heir-apparent of the kingdom of England.' Henry, Prince of Wales was the original patron of the borough. Barnard, loc. cit. 13 June, 1903.

[13] Barnard, loc. cit. 20 June, 1903; May, op. cit. 481.

[14] May, op. cit. 457–59, 460. Aldermen and capital burgesses had a special oath of office; see Barnard, loc. cit. 23 May, 1903.

[15] Pat. 3 Jas. I. pt. 15; May, op. cit. 468, 469–70. Their duties were 'from time to time to deliver the gaol of the borough aforesaid of the prisoners from henceforth to be committed to the same gaol on any account whatsoever.' Ibid.

[16] May, op. cit. 460, 471.

[17] Ibid. 260, 457, 459, 460, 471, for assistants and their position. In 1654 we have record of the swearing-in of a number of assistants. Barnard, loc. cit. 25 Jan. 1902.

[18] Feet of F. Worc. Hil. 38 Eliz.

[19] Ibid. Div. Cos. East. 1 Jas. I.

[20] Quoted in extracts taken by Dr. Prattinton from Mr. Rudge's MSS.

[21] Feet of F. Worc. East. 8 Jas. I.

weights and measures, and assize of bread and ale.[1] In 1615 John Woodward, knt., son of the above John Woodward, conveyed the site with all the rights above mentioned to Sir William Fleetwood and Sir David Fowles,[2] two of the magistrates appointed by the royal charter, who seem, however, to have acted in this case in a private capacity. In 1617 Sir John Woodward made a conveyance similar to that of 1615, in favour of Sir William Fleetwood,[3] and another in 1618 to Sir William and Sir Henry Kingsmill.[4] On 22 November, 1624, Sir John Woodward mortgaged his Evesham estate to Sir William Courteen,[5] who, in 1626, acquired all Woodward's interest in Evesham,[6] and on 1 March, 1633, settled it on his son William on the latter's marriage with Catherine, daughter of the earl of Bridgewater.[7] In 1649 a commission of bankruptcy was awarded against William Courteen, and in 1651 James Winstanley, Anthony Boys, and others conveyed Evesham to John Pettyward[8] for the purpose of sale. On 29 March, 1656, John Pettyward is said to have sold Evesham to Christopher Dodington and others,[9] and it shortly afterwards passed into the hands of William Courteen, the naturalist, son of William and grandson of Sir William Courteen. In 1664 he sold the manor of Evesham, the site of the monastery, frankpledge, markets, and fairs, and all other rights to Edward Rudge,[10] merchant, of London, in whose family the lordship of the borough of Evesham still remains, being now held by Edward Charles Rudge, Esq.

Since the Exchequer decree of 1587 the fee farm rent had been regularly paid by the bailiffs, and afterwards by the corporation of Evesham to Sir Edward Hoby and those who succeeded him as mesne lords. But according to the charter this rent was at the disposal of the Crown. Thus, in 1616 James I. granted it to John Allen for his life with the arrears unpaid for thirteen years,[11] and in 1624 to Giles Johnson for his life,[12] but the corporation denied that any payment had ever been made to either of these grantees.[13] In 1663 a thirty-one years' lease of the fee farm rent was granted as a concealment to Major Thomas Mucklow, who was to render £3 6*s.* 8*d.* annually to the Crown.[14] The corporation purchased Major Mucklow's grant, and for some years paid the rent reserved by the Crown, as well as the fee farm rent, to Mr. Rudge 'in their own wrong.'[15] When the charter of 1684 came into force they represented their case to the king, and were discharged from payment of the £3 6*s.* 8*d.* until 1691, when it was again demanded. A further appeal was then made, and the Court of Exchequer decided that the corporation was liable only for the rent of £13 6*s.* 8*d.* payable to Mr. Rudge as the successor of Sir Philip Hoby.[16]

After the charter of 1605 the lords of Evesham exercised no jurisdictionary influence within the borough, although from time to time they laid claim to certain rights there. Thus, during the eighteenth century the question as to the right of manor was several times raised, but never definitely settled. About 1726 some lead pipes, dug up in the churchyard of All Saints', were claimed by John Rudge as owner of the abbey site, and by the mayor on behalf of the corporation. Sir Thomas Pengelly, to whom Mr. Rudge submitted the question, was of opinion that all such property had become vested in Mr. Rudge. Again, in 1733, Mr. John Rudge, under letters patent granted to Sir Philip Hoby and never rescinded, laid claim to the tolls and other profits of markets and fairs in Evesham. He instituted a suit in chancery to recover them, but died before the case was brought to an issue. A bill of revivor was filed in 1740 by his son Edward Rudge, but the corporation of Evesham in replying insisted that Henry VIII. had no right to grant courts-leet to Sir Philip Hoby, and stated that immemorially they had held their franchise subject only to the ancient fee farm rent of £13 6*s.* 8*d.*[17]

In 1762-3 Edward Rudge instituted a suit in the Court of Common Pleas against Elias Andrews, the mayor of Evesham, for cutting down trees on the waste land of the manor, but he also died before the suit was brought to an issue.[18] From that time onward no question of the right or jurisdiction of the lord of the manor appears to have been raised.

The borough courts at Evesham consisted of a court of quarter sessions; the court of record, to be held, according to the charter of 1605, every Thursday, but seemingly held on a Tuesday in later times; a court-leet, and a view of frankpledge held twice a year by the mayor as steward of the leet, which was afterwards discontinued; and, finally, a court-merchant or court of piepowder incident to the holding of fairs and markets and in session during them.[19]

In addition to the charters in 1604 and 1605 Evesham received two later charters, the first in 1684,[20] and the second in 1688,[21] but as both were afterwards abrogated, and that of 1605 restored, they need but brief mention. The charter of 1684 imposed on the town by Charles II. on the surrender of the previous charter did not alter the limits of the borough or the title of the corporation.[22] The number of aldermen, however, was increased to nine,

[1] Feet of F. Worc. East. 8 Jas. I.

[2] Ibid. Mich. 13 Jas. I.

[3] Ibid. Mich. 14 Jas. I.

[4] Ibid. Hil. 15 Jas. I. These conveyances were probably mortgages.

[5] Prattinton Coll. (Soc. Antiq.).

[6] Feet of F. Worc. East. 2 Chas. I.

[7] Prattinton Coll. (Soc. Antiq.); *Dict. of Nat. Biog.*

[8] Com. Pleas. Recov. R. Mich. 1651, m. 17.

[9] Prattinton Coll. (Soc. Antiq.).

[10] Feet of F. Worc. Trin. 16 Chas. II.

[11] *Cal. of S. P. Dom.* 1611–18, 388; Pat. 14 Jas. I. pt. I.

[12] Ibid. 23 Jas. I. pt. 9. It is said to have been purchased after Johnson's death by Moore from the trustees of a workhouse (Prattinton Coll. (Soc. Antiq.)), but there is no evidence to bear out the statement.

[13] Prattinton Coll. (Soc. Antiq.).

[14] Pat. 15 Chas. II. pt. 4.

[15] Exts. from Corpn. Bks. in Prattinton Coll. (Soc. Antiq.).

[16] Prattinton Coll. (Soc. Antiq.).

[17] Exts. from Rudge MSS. in Prattinton Coll. (Soc. Antiq.).

[18] Prattinton Coll. (Soc. Antiq.).

[19] May, op. cit. 465–68, 472, 473–74, 479–80, for information in regard to these courts as given in the charter of 1605. Tindal, *Hist. of Evesham*, 212, says that about the year 1740 a woman was burned within the borough, being convicted of petty treason, this being the last instance of capital punishment at Evesham. See also May, op. cit. 318. Mr. Oswald Knapp has discovered a broad-sheet entitled 'The last dying Speech, Confession, Character, and Behaviour of Elizabeth Moreton, *alias* Owen, who was first strangled and afterwards burnt at Evesham, on Friday, the 10th of August, 1744, for poisoning her husband,' who was a maltster at Evesham. This probably refers to the case above mentioned, as petty treason would include the murder by a wife of her husband. (J. W. W.-B.) For the court of record and its duties see, in addition to the charter, Barnard, loc. cit. 30 May, 1903.

[20] Pat. 36 Chas. II. pt. 3, no. 2.

[21] Ibid. 4 Jas. II. pt. 12, no. 2.

[22] Barnard, loc. cit. 18 July, 1903, gives a quite detailed account of the surrender of the charter of 1605, including the order of surrender and the petition of the mayor, aldermen, and burgesses for a new charter. See also May, *Hist. of Evesham*, 261–265, and the abstract of the charter given in App. xiii. 352–53.

including the mayor; there were twelve capital burgesses as before, a recorder, a chamberlain, and a town clerk, a new official. These constituted the common council, from which all the higher officers were to be chosen. The number of assistants was reduced to twelve. Every member of the corporation had to take the oath of allegiance and supremacy and subscribe to all acts which had been passed, and no burgess was to exercise any suffrage until he had subscribed to the same oaths. Members of Parliament were to be elected by the mayor, aldermen, and capital burgesses alone, and, most important of all, the power was reserved to the Crown of removing at its pleasure any corporate officer, whomsoever, by Order in Council. To make the royal control more absolute the first mayor, aldermen, capital burgesses, and assistants of the borough under this new charter were named, as were also the high-steward, the recorder, the chamberlain, and town clerk, these last being life appointments. The mayor and corporation were given power to select the coroner and lesser officers. The Crown further appointed seven persons by name to be justices for life to act with the mayor, recorder, and four aldermen nominated by the council. Four of these justices were to be members of the common council as well. The whole object of the charter of 1684 was to bring the corporation under the royal control, especially in regard to elections to Parliament.[1] It was due to much the same cause that in 1688 the charter of 1684 was revoked, and a new one issued of exactly similar character, and containing the same provisions, save as regards the oaths to be taken, in the place of which it is declared that 'the king doth dispense all officers appointed in the said corporation, from taking the oaths of supremacy and allegiance, as likewise from that enjoined by the statute for regulating corporations, and from receiving the Lord's Supper according to the Church of England, and further from subscribing either declaration under the statutes of Charles II. as well as from all penalties or molestations in consequence thereof.' Finally, the Crown reserved the right of restraining from the exercise of office any future high-steward, recorder, or common councillor of the borough, who had not the approbation of the king under his sign manual.[2]

A few weeks after this grant of a new charter to Evesham, James II. issued a proclamation restoring to the corporations of English boroughs 'their ancient charters, liberties, franchises, and rights.'[3] This Act restored to Evesham its charter of 1605, which with slight modifications due to successive municipal reform acts in the nineteenth century has remained the charter of the borough to the present time.

In 1687 the common council drew up a set of by-laws, known as the 'Constitutions of the Borough of Evesham.'[4] The chief matters dealt with are the procedure in connexion with the election of the mayor, the duties of that officer as to voting in council, keeping accounts, holding courts and assizes, and so forth.[5] Other by-laws refer to matters of precedence among members of the council, to penalties for refusal of office, to the filling of vacancies in the council or among the assistants; to the care of the public records of the borough; to the regulation of apprentices, and their admission as freemen after their time of service has expired; to the fiscal system of the borough; to the duties of the freemen; to the duties of the chamberlain; to the regulation of the grammar school; and to the trading companies and fraternities within the borough.[6] These constitutions appear to have continued in use after the restoration of the charter of 1605.

Since the close of the seventeenth century little change has taken place in connexion with the constitutional history of the borough. In 1824 a local Act of Parliament was passed which provided for the sale of waste lands within the borough, and the expenditure of the money derived therefrom in 'paving, cleaning, lighting, watching, regulating, and improving the borough.' The common council were appointed as standing commissioners to carry out this act, but were to proceed in conjunction with other commissioners taken from among the principal inhabitants.[7] In 1833 Evesham was visited by parliamentary commissioners appointed to inquire into municipal corporations. Their report gives in brief the main features of the borough government, and is especially valuable in connexion with the borough officers and their duties and in regard to the courts. In the opinion of the commissioners the close character of the corporation was and had been productive of great evil in the town. Reference is made to the narrow spirit in which the governing body was perpetuated, and the care taken to exclude any of opposing politics. No dissenter had ever been elected, and very frequently obstacles had been placed in the way of admitting freemen, for political reasons, by the council.[8] Complaints were also made

[1] A short abstract of this charter containing the chief provisions and changes is given in App. xiii. of May's *Hist. of Evesham*, 452–53. The expense of obtaining this charter was very great, amounting to £102 16*s.* 6*d.*: Corpn. Waste Bk.; Barnard, loc. cit. 25 Jan. 1902. May gives the total as £104 16*s.* 6*d.* (op. cit. 264). £69 7*s.* 6*d.* was subscribed in the borough towards defraying the expenses of the charter.

[2] Pat. 4 Jas. II. pt. 12, no. 2; May, *Hist. of Evesham*, App. xiii. 453–54, where an abstract of James the Second's charter is given. The king's idea in doing away with the former oaths and tests was to secure the support of the corporation. In this, however, he signally failed. Macaulay, *Hist. of Engl.* (2 vols.), i. 492–93.

[3] May, op. cit. 268. This proclamation was issued on the advice of the bishops. It is dated 18 Oct. 1688.

[4] These 'Constitutions of the Borough of Evesham' are given in May's *Hist. of Evesham*, App. xv. 484–490. There are twenty-nine articles in all. Merewether and Stephens, *Hist. of Boroughs*, iii. 1829–31, give a résumé of the chief matters dealt with in these constitutions.

[5] This collection of by-laws is interesting as the first known attempt to supplement the charter by borough legislation. The attempt to regulate the companies and fraternities (May, op. cit. 485, and Merewether and Stephens, op. cit. iii. 1830) is of particular significance, as will be noticed later.

[6] The document is dated 21 July, 1687. Neither the name of Henry Parker, the recorder, nor that of Thomas Watson, the deputy recorder, appear in the list of witnesses, nor is the name of Richard Cave, the chamberlain, appended; but no minutes are signed by these officers during the year. The 'Constitutions' appear, therefore, to have been signed by the mayor, Edward Walker, and the aldermen and capital burgesses, to the number of thirteen, and by the two royal justices.

[7] *Report on the Corporation of Evesham*, in App. xvi. of May's *Hist. of Evesham*, 495. 'This is called the only local Act relating to the borough.' This Act is later referred to in the by-laws of 1839, May, App. xvii. sect. 7, where in order to enforce the Act policemen are to inform against every person 'committing any offence prohibited by the said Act.'

[8] *Report on the Corporation of Evesham*, sect. 15, May, *Hist. of Evesham*, App. xvi. 492, sect. 15, 'Every one who is known to entertain opinions at variance with those of the influential part of the corporation is carefully excluded from this body (*i.e.* the common council). No dissenter, however respectable, has ever been elected; and previously to 1818, when it was desirable to reduce the number of voters, obstacles, as we were informed, were thrown in the way of admitting persons intitled to their freedom by birth or servitude.'

of the administration of justice being biased by party leanings, but the commissioners were of the opinion that 'the municipal authority was vested in the best hands with reference both to intelligence and character to be found in so small a district.'[1] This report further sets forth the amount of the borough rate, levied instead of the county rate, for the seven years from 1826 to 1832, the highest return for any one year being £166 7*s.* 2*d.* in 1827, and the lowest £69 6*s.* 10*d.* in 1826; the return for 1832 was £141 16*s.* 7*d.* Furthermore, it appeared that the corporation was without property in the borough, save for one quit rent of 10*s.* and the tolls which brought in a revenue of something over £100 per annum, but this enabled them to more than meet necessary expenses.[2] The report showed that, while the government of the town needed to be made more representative, borough affairs were not badly managed, and the general prospects of Evesham were good.[3]

When the Act for the Regulation of Municipal Corporations came into effect in 1835, important changes took place in the government of the borough, tending to make it more representative. The mayor, aldermen, and councillors were henceforth to be elected by the burgesses at large. The criminal jurisdiction of the corporation was also taken away, and the court of record for civil suits discontinued.

In 1838, however, four special borough magistrates were provided, who, with the mayor and the magistrates of the county, were to hold petty sessions in the borough each week. Early in 1839 the reorganized corporation drew up a series of by-laws, ten in number.[4] In these it was enacted that any one elected to the office of mayor, alderman, councillor, auditor, or assessor who did not accept and qualify for such office within five days after notice of his election was to be fined, the fines varying with the importance of the office from £50 in the case of the mayoralty to £15 in the case of the auditor or assessor. Fines were likewise imposed for non-attendance at council meetings, save by reason of illness.[5]

During the seventeenth century there seem to have been eight trading companies in existence at Evesham, namely, the companies of the Mercers, Cordwainers, Clothworkers, Glovers, Ironmongers, Shoemakers, Drapers, and Innholders; the last three do not appear to have been as important as the first five, however, which are officially recognized as the trading companies of the borough by the constitutions of 1687.[6] The chief political importance of these companies was in connexion with the admission of freemen in the borough. It was the practice for all those admitted as freemen in the companies to become also freemen of the borough and pay the usual fees; and also, apparently, for apprentices who became freemen, by completing a seven years' apprenticeship to a resident freeman, to enter one of the Evesham companies, for in the minutes of council in 1608 it is recorded that Jonathan Smyth, an apprentice, residing in the borough, was enfranchised and made a freeman, 'the end and term of his apprenticeship being accomplished,' and, having paid a fee of 5*s.* for this freedom, became at the same time free of the company of Clothworkers.[7] Furthermore, in the constitutions of 1687 the twenty-first section is devoted to the companies and their abuse of the right of admitting freemen.[8] To remedy this abuse it was provided 'that the constitutions of the said respective five companies shall be revived . . . . subject always to the conditions following,' which were in the first place that no one belonging to the several companies should 'admit into their respective company any person until the master and wardens of such company . . . . and the mayor and common council of this borough shall have agreed thereunto under their respective hands in writing.' In the second place, no person admitted by the mayor and council was to exercise any trade falling under the jurisdiction of any of the existing companies until made free of that company.[9] In the third place, it was 'ordained that upon the admission of every or any person or persons into any or either of the said fraternities the person or persons so to be admitted as aforesaid shall first take the oath of a freeman and the other oaths mentioned in the late charter granted to this borough,' namely, the charter of 1684.[10] Fourthly, no person within the borough should fraudulently seek to have his apprentice created a freeman before the apprentice had done at least seven years' actual service. The proper procedure was for the master to cause the indentures of apprenticeship to be enrolled with the chamberlain of the borough within three months of their being taken out. If this were not done the master incurred the penalty of disfranchisement and the apprentice could obtain no benefit, as regarded the freedom of the borough, from the indentures.[11]

[1] Report on Evesham, sect. 18, May, op. cit. App. xvi. 493.

[2] Ibid. sect. 22, where a table of receipt and expenditure is given. For the year ending April, 1814, the borough paid government taxes to the amount of £5,188 7*s.* 11¾*d.* This large return was due, however, to the Pitt Property Tax, for after its repeal the tax for the year ending April, 1833, was but £1,378 8*s.* 10½*d.* May, op. cit. 318-19. For the local assessments of the borough in the early nineteenth century see ibid. 319.

[3] Report on Corporation of Evesham, sec. 25, May, op. cit. App. xvi. 495. The chief fault in connexion with the borough was its close corporation.

[4] May, op. cit. App. xvii. 495-497.

[5] Bye-laws of the Council, May, *Hist. of Evesham*, App. xvii. 495-97. Fining is sanctioned in the charter of 1605 (May, op. cit. 461-62) in the case of refusals of office. See also Barnard, loc. cit. 22 February, 8 March, 1902; 20 June, 27 June, 1903.

[6] Constitutions of the Borough of Evesham, art. xxi. May, op. cit. App. xv. 488-89; Barnard, loc. cit. 22 March, 1902. There is little in print regarding these companies, save what is contained in the above constitutions. There appears to have been also a Fellmongers' Company. In the Corpn. Waste Bk. of 1705 the following entry occurs:—'John Holloway, Glover, who is free of the Fellmongers' Co. is admitted to Freedom' [of the corporation]. Information supplied by Mr. O. G. Knapp.

[7] Barnard, loc. cit. 23 May, 1903. The company of Clothworkers was the third in rank of the companies. It was constituted in 1608 by the council, loc. cit. 30 May, 1903.

[8] May, *Hist. of Evesham*, App. xv. 488-89. Constitutions of the Borough of Evesham, 1687, sect. xxi. 'Item.—Whereas the inhabitants of this borough for the better regulations of their trades and occupations have formed themselves into divers companies and fraternities,' etc. There seems to have been considerable irregularity in regard to the admission of freemen and other such matters about this time, for, on 17 January, 1690, Richard Young, one of the aldermen, who had been mayor in 1670, resigned his office on account of 'the illegal proceedings of the Chamber in elections and making Freemen contrary to Law.' Barnard, loc. cit. 15 February, 1902.

[9] Thus it was that when freemen were admitted who wished to engage in trade in the borough they immediately joined one of the companies. Barnard, loc. cit. 23 May, 1903.

[10] These other oaths were the Oaths of Allegiance and Supremacy. May, *Hist. of Evesham*, App. xiii. 452.

[11] Constitutions of the Borough, 1687, May, op. cit. App. xv. 489. This was obtaining the freedom of the borough through servitude or apprenticeship. No one but a freeman could legally carry on trade in the borough by the charter of 1605.

Finally, it was to be lawful for the widow of a freeman to use the trade of her late husband during her widowhood, and the eldest son of a deceased freeman was to be made free by virtue of his father's copy, if required.[1]

The Evesham companies possessed special privileges and perquisites throughout the seventeenth and eighteenth centuries. They had a practical monopoly of the chief industries of the town, and they also seem to have been the recipients of small grants from the town treasury on special occasions.[2] The Parliamentary Commissioners in 1833 reported 'that an old privileged company, called the master ironmongers, complained that the corporation, although receiving a small fee on the admission of members, refused to assist them in the assertion of their exclusive privilege.'[3] As, however, these fees did not exceed 19*s.* a year, and were paid pursuant to the ancient constitution of the company, it was judged that as the corporation had ceased to exact fines from non-freemen for trading in the borough, 'it could scarcely be called to enforce exclusive privileges which would be mischievous were they not obsolete.'[4]

Previous to the incorporation of the borough in 1604 freemen had been admitted by the bailiffs, at the autumn meeting of the court-leet, on account of worth and standing in the community. They paid a small fee to the bailiffs and took an oath to be true franchised men and to obey the town officers. The bailiffs also seem to have had power to disfranchise any who were considered unworthy of being freemen.[5] The charters of 1604 and 1605 gave the mayor and common council authority to admit freemen, and non-residents could be chosen as freemen and enjoy all the rights which resident freemen enjoyed, including voting at borough elections.[6] The mayor and council availed themselves of their power to admit non-resident freemen, and in 1830 out of some 427 voters not more than 190 were resident burgesses. After the passage of the Reform Bill of 1832 the number of voters was reduced to 359, of whom about one half were resident burgesses.[7]

The borough of Evesham does not seem to have possessed a seal previous to its definite incorporation in 1605. The seal of the abbey and the individual seals of the bailiffs and of leading burgesses were appended to important municipal documents.[8] The charter of 1604, indeed, expressly states that the king grants a common seal to the borough. The seal there granted was procured the same year, and has since remained in use.[9] It is of silver, and bears on its obverse a shield of broad type having on it the arms of the borough. In honour of the heir-apparent these insignia are taken from the armorial bearings of the principality of Wales, the duchy of Cornwall, and the earldom of Chester, being 'Azure, a prince's crown over a garb of the earldom of Chester all Or, bound with the same, and Sable, between two ostrich feathers of Wales Argent, within a border of the third bezanty for the duchy of Cornwall.'[10] The edge and borders of the seal are ornamented in bead pattern and encircled with the words SIGILLUM . BURGI . EVESHAMENSIS. The reverse of the seal has in the central portion a picture of a strongly fortified and crenellated town, with houses, churches, and a round tower surmounted by a cross, and beneath, on a scroll, one end of which bears a palm, the other an olive branch, is the name EVESHAM, and underneath a rose. The legend around the edge is LIBER . AB . HENRICO . FACTVS . SVM . PRINCIPE . BVRGVS . 1604, a tribute to Henry, Prince of Wales, who had been instrumental in obtaining for the borough its first charter.[11]

There are two maces of silver gilt, 29 inches long, of date 1619–20 and London make. The mayor's chain and badge are modern. The corporation also possesses a loving-cup and a rose-water basin of silver given by George Carew of Aldington in 1660.[12]

Information as to the trade and commerce of Evesham during the earlier period of its history is scanty. There seems little doubt that in Anglo-Saxon times the town had considerable trade, for in 1055 it was created a port, or market town, by Edward the Confessor.[13] Nevertheless, no market is mentioned in the Domesday entry.[14] A weekly market was held in the borough during the later middle ages and likewise several fairs, by prescriptive right on the part of the abbot and convent.[15] A few years after the dissolution of the abbey, the royal commissioners appointed to inquire concerning the repair of the bridge stated that the 'towne of Evesham ys nowe at thys daye the best occupied market wekely and the greteste thorowfare of any towne in the said county of Worcester or in thenny part of this realme.'[16] The weekly market and three annual fairs, granted to Sir Philip Hoby in 1546, in all probability corresponded to those formerly held by the abbot.[17]

The control of the trade of the town must have rested largely in the hands of the abbot and the ecclesiastical officers, who enjoyed special privileges as

[1] May, op. cit. App. xv. 489. Such would be freemen by usage or inheritance; cf. ibid. App. xvi. 492.

[2] In certain articles of reform adopted by the council in 1736 clause no. v. reads 'That no more than twenty shillings shall hereafter be expended at any Rejoicing Night, exclusive of five shillings to the Ringers, and five shillings to each Company.' Barnard, loc. cit. 22 March, 1902.

[3] App. xvi. to May's *Hist. of Evesham*, 485.

[4] Report on the Corporation of Evesham, 1833, sect. 25, May, op. cit. App. xvi. 495. The last mention of restrictive measures occurs in the year 1700, though there may have been, and probably were, later instances.

[5] Exch. Dep. East. 29 Eliz. no. 12. Merewether and Stephens, *Hist. of Boroughs*, ii. 1424–25, testimony in Exchequer Court given by William Smith. Associated with the bailiffs in disfranchising were 'the ancients of the town.' Disfranchisement of a burgess or freeman made him liable to all tolls and taxes enforced on foreigners.

[6] Charter of 1605, May, *Hist. of Evesham*, App. xiv. 479–480. The oath taken by the freemen on admission is given in Tindal, ibid. 342, and in May, op. cit. 280.

[7] Report on the Corporation of Evesham, 1833, sect. 14, May, op. cit. 492; Barnard, loc. cit. The parliamentary history of the borough is dealt with quite exhaustively in May's *Hist. of Evesham*, cap. xiv.

[8] Merewether and Stephens, *Hist. of Boroughs*, ii. 1004–5.

[9] May, *Hist. of Evesham*, 259, so states, and there seems no reason to doubt his assertion, though it is possible that the corporation obtained a new seal after the grant of the charter of 1605. It appears to have had three seals in its possession in the seventeenth century. Barnard, loc. cit. 20 June, 1903.

[10] Nash, *Hist. of Worc.* i. 411; cf. May, *Hist. of Evesham*, 259–60.

[11] A representation of this side of the seal is given in May's *Hist. of Evesham*, 259, with the title 'The Borough Seal—actual size,' but this is clearly the reverse of the seal and not the obverse, as he calls it.

[12] *Corpn. Plate of Engl. and Wales*, Jewitt and Hope, ii. 441.

[13] *Chron. de Evesham*, (Rolls Ser.), 75.

[14] There is little doubt, however, that they existed, May, 253, 320.

[15] May, *Hist. of Evesham*, 320; *Chron. de Evesham* (Rolls Ser.), 216.

[16] Aug. Off. Misc. Bks. cxii. ff. 13 and 14.

[17] Pat. 38 Hen. VIII. pt. 2, m. 11.

to buying provisions.[1] Sales could be made only in the market-place of the town, and trading had to be carried on publicly. The market stalls or shops were in many instances owned by the abbey and were rented to traders and merchants.[2] Illegal trading, the use of false weights and measures, and the holding of unauthorized fairs or markets were offences severely dealt with by the lord of the town or by the king.[3] At Evesham, as elsewhere, the townsmen or tenants of the abbey shared in the privileges in respect to trade which the Crown granted to the ecclesiastics.[4] Thus in 1241 the men of Evesham were able to assert their freedom from all tolls, save twopence on the purchase of a horse in the market of the city of Worcester.[5]

Special tolls were frequently levied in the mediæval boroughs, and Edward III. several times empowered 'the good men and bailiffs of Evesham' to collect additional tolls on merchandise sold in the market-place in order to provide for the paving of the town.[6] Evesham at this time must have been a place of some commercial importance, for in 1337 it was summoned to send representatives to a council in regard to foreign trade, along with other of the chief trading towns of England. Evesham no doubt sent representatives on account of its woollen industry, for it occurs as one of the monastic houses supplying wool to the foreign market in a long Italian list of such places, bearing the date 1315, and doubtless it exported considerable quantities to Flanders and to Florence, the two great mediæval centres of the woollen industry.[7] The manufacture of woollen cloths went on also in the town, but was in a depressed condition in Henry the Eighth's reign through the competition of neighbouring hamlets, where cloth was being manufactured by free traders under no such restrictions as the journeymen and apprentices of the towns. Complaint was, therefore, made to Parliament in 1534 by the clothiers of Worcester, Evesham, Droitwich, Kidderminster, and Bromsgrove, and an act was passed[8] by which no one was to make cloths in Worcestershire but the residents of the towns mentioned, and in order to encourage craftsmen it was further ordered that rents of houses occupied by workers in cloth should not be raised above the rate current during the preceding years.[9] It is known that Evesham and Bengeworth were equipped with fulling and shearing mills previous to the dissolution, the fulling mill being situated in Bengeworth, across the river, and the shearing mill above the bridge in Evesham, and doubtless all cloth had to be fulled and sheared at the mills owned by the abbot.[10] After the dissolution greater freedom in respect of trade prevailed for a time, but at Evesham, as at other places, monopolies were granted during the late sixteenth and early seventeenth centuries.[11]

The charter of 1605 granted to the mayor, aldermen, and burgesses of the borough to have two markets every week, one on the Monday and the other on the Friday, and also three fairs in the year, the first to begin on the Monday of the second week after Easter, the second on the Monday after Pentecost, and the third on the feast of St. Silvina, 10 September, each fair to continue two days.[12] This charter also granted the corporation exclusive control over the trade of the town, prohibiting anyone not a burgess from exposing for sale any article save in gross and except at the time of fairs, the penalty being the forfeiture of the goods or their value to the mayor, aldermen, and burgesses.[13]

Although the charter of 1605 granted markets on Monday and Friday of each week, only the former day was used to any extent, Monday having probably been the accustomed day for the weekly market from mediæval times. There appeared to be some slight disposition to use Friday as well as a market day even in the last century, but the Monday market still remains the important one.[14] The three fairs granted by the charter proved insufficient for the needs of the borough and the country around it, and new ones were added until early in the nineteenth century six were held in each year, namely, one on 2 February, one on the second Monday after Easter, one on Whit Monday, one on the second Monday in August, one on 21 September, and one on the second Monday in December. At these fairs live stock and produce were sold, the September fair being famed for strong black horses from the country around.[15] In addition to the fairs it was the custom into the early part of the nineteenth century to hold each year two assemblies known as 'statutes,' or, more vulgarly, 'mops,' at

[1] *Chron. de Evesham* (Rolls Ser.), 216.

[2] Ibid. 210, 300.

[3] In 20 Hen. III. (1235–36) the liberties of Evesham were seized on account of false measures being used while the king was visiting the town. They were restored, however, upon the submission of the abbot and monks. May, *Hist. of Evesham*, 405; Nash, *Hist. of Worc.* i. 411; Dugdale, *Mon.* ii. 9 note *f*.

[4] Henry I. granted that the abbot and monks of Evesham and their servants should be exempt from toll throughout England for all goods which their men can attest to be their own property. Harl. MS. 3763, f. 82 *d*; Confirmation in Chart. R. 25 Hen. III. m. 4; May, *Hist. of Evesham*, App. viii; Tindal, ibid. 85.

[5] Dugdale, *Mon.* ii. 34, from Cott. MS. Vit. E xvii. f. 226; Tindal, *Hist. of Evesham*, 189.

[6] *Cal. of Pat.* 1327–30, p. 201; Merewether and Stephens, *Hist. of Boroughs*, ii. 651–52; May, 370.

[7] Cunningham, *Growth of English Industry and Commerce*, i. App. D, 550, 552; cf. Peruzzi, *Storia del Commercio e dei Banchieri di Firenze*, 71. The Italian designation for Evesham was 'Guesame in Chondisgualdo,' or 'Evesham in the Cotswolds.' There are suggestions in the Cott. MS. B. xxiv. that certain of the abbey tenants owed the service of carrying about the woollen cloth for sale. See under Badsey and Hampton.

[8] Stat. 25 Hen. VIII. c. 18; see also Cunningham, op. cit. i. 461–2; May, *Hist. of Evesham*, 312–13; Green, *Town Life*, ii. 97*n*.

[9] Ibid.

[10] May, *Hist. of Evesham*, 313; cf. 83, 162–163 in connexion with other mills.

[11] Thus on the 6 January, 1608, in consideration of £20 the council admitted Richard Bradford of Tewkesbury, dyer, as a freeman, and gave him the exclusive privilege of dyeing cloth in the borough, and on 30 May, 1615, Norton, who was admitted a freeman by purchase, was given the exclusive control of the trade in haberdashery. May, op. cit. 313; Barnard, loc. cit. 6 June, 1903. In regard to the alleged monopoly of brewing see May, op. cit. 406, and Barnard, loc. cit. 6 June, 1903.

[12] Charter of 1605, Pat. 3 Jas. I. pt. 15. May's *Hist. of Evesham*, App. xiv. 472. In regard to the market court it was enacted by the council in 1632 'that the mayor for the time being on every market day hereafter sit and be present in the Booth Hall at all times convenient during the market. And that with him likewise shall there sit the town clerk or his deputy, with the action book for the entry of actions. And that the sergeants of ye mace do likewise then attend there, that they may be the more ready for performing their duties in their several places,' etc. Fines are imposed for any defaults. Barnard, loc. cit. 20 June, 1903.

[13] Charter of 1605, Pat. 3 Jas. I. pt. 15; May's *Hist. of Evesham*, App. xiv. 473. In 1700 the council took action against those trading in the borough who were not free of the corporation. Barnard, loc. cit. 22 February, 1902.

[14] May, *Hist. of Evesham*, 321, says in 1844, 'There are still, however, some lingering vestiges of the Friday's market, such as the attendance of the county carriers on that day, together with certain signals of attempts at traffic displayed, in the immediate vicinity of the hall.'

[15] 'These faires of Evesham with that vale doe soe exceed for strong and able horses as they are often preferred from the Cart and plow to the Court and the tylt, and which is most laudable, to serve in the warres.' Habington, *Surv. of Worc.* (Worc. Hist. Soc.), ii. 74.

which servants out of employment, both agricultural and domestic, stood in rows to be inspected by possible masters or mistresses and, if satisfactory, hired.[1]

Various industries seem to have flourished at Evesham in the past, as is shown by the existence of the trading companies already mentioned.[2] The borough, however, developed no special industry, and its trade never extended much beyond its immediate neighbourhood. The manufacture of woollen goods, of silks and ribbons, of linseed oil, and of bone manure appear to have been of chief importance in the early part of the nineteenth century.[3] The parliamentary commissioners in 1833 reported that 'the trade of the town is small, but with the exception of a ribbon manufactory in a declining state, was stated to us to be in a prosperous condition.'[4]

EVESHAM: OLD HOUSES AT THE CORNER OF COWL STREET.

The remarkable fertility of the soil in the valley of Evesham has from an early period favoured the growth of the gardening industry. The abbey appears to have had large gardens and farms in and around the town, and after its dissolution these passed into secular hands and commanded large rents.[5] Gardening received a further impetus from the settlement at Evesham in the seventeenth century of the Genoese Francis Bernardi, father of the celebrated John Bernardi, who is said to have expended some £30,000 in laying out and cultivating his gardens.[6] During the seventeenth and eighteenth centuries this industry developed rapidly, and the market gardens of Evesham became famous, so that in the early part of the nineteenth century Evesham and its neighbourhood were supplying such places as Worcester, Birmingham, Dudley, Coventry, Warwick, and Cheltenham.[7] Practically all the available land within the borough had been turned into gardens by the middle of the last century, there being almost 600 acres under cultivation, and the greater number of the inhabitants were engaged in raising produce.[8] Market gardening has continued to be the main occupation, and the country all round the town is one vast garden. The area of land under fruit and garden crops, especially asparagus, is annually extending. A small amount of manufacturing of agricultural implements, of gloves, and of hosiery still goes on in the town.

Several times in its history Evesham was honoured with royal visits, although perhaps these were paid to the abbey rather than to the town. Henry II. appears to have been once there;[9] Henry III. paid several visits to it,[10] and stayed there before the battle of Evesham as Simon de Montfort's prisoner. Edward I. also came to it,[11] although once, according to the Worcester annalist, who had never a good word to say for the rival house, he avoided its monastery 'as if it were unclean,' and stayed at the abbot's grange at Offenham.[12] It appears that James I. of Scotland also spent some time at Evesham during his captivity in England. He was at Nottingham Castle until the middle of July, 1407, in the care of Richard, Lord Grey of Codnor, and was afterwards taken to Evesham, where he remained probably as an inmate of the abbey, in company with Griffin, son of Owen Glendower, until July, 1409.[13] In much later times Evesham was occupied as a royal garrison during the Civil Wars, but was stormed and taken from the Royalists by Colonel Massey on 26 May, 1645. Charles I. passed through the town several times, and after the battle of Cropredy Bridge stayed there several days, dating a letter from his 'Court at Evesham,'[14] said to be a house still standing in Bridge Street.

[1] May, *Hist. of Evesham*, 322. This was a common practice in the west of England at one time.

[2] May, op. cit. App. xv. 488–89. Constitutions of the Borough; very little is known of these companies. The tradesmen and merchants at Evesham in the seventeenth century issued a large number of interesting copper tokens for use in the internal trade of the borough. May, op. cit. 217–18; Barnard, loc. cit. 4 July, 1903.

[3] May, op. cit. 312-314.

[4] Report on the Corporation of Evesham, sect. 25, in App. xvi. to May's *Hist. of Evesham*, 495. The competition of larger manufacturing centres always militated against the development of home trade in Evesham.

[5] May, *Hist. of Evesham*, 315; Pope in his *Satires and Epistles*, bk. ii. epistle 2, speaks of the 'lords of fat E'sham' as 'large acr'd men.'

[6] May, op. cit. 316. Bernardi had gardens first at Windsor and then at Evesham. He had previously been the Genoese agent at London.

[7] May, op. cit. 316.

[8] May, *Hist. of Evesham*, 316. May notes that the garden land at his time commanded from four to ten pounds per acre a year in rent, sometimes even more in cases where it adjoined the town. Also that the average wage of a garden hand was then, 1843, ten shillings a week.

[9] *Cal. of Chart. R.* i. 11.

[10] *Cal. of Pat.* 1216–25, 376, 387; ibid. 1225–32, 524; *Cal. of Chart.* 97, 182.

[11] *Cal. of Pat.* 1272–81, 162; ibid. 1292–1301, 581.

[12] *Ann. Mon.* (Rolls Ser.), iv. 500. The grange at Offenham was on the road. Edward's reason for avoiding the abbey could scarcely have been because of the support and sympathy it had given to Simon de Montfort, because he had visited it in 1276 (*Cal. of Pat.* 1272–81, 162), eleven years after the battle of Evesham.

[13] *Dict. of Nat. Biog.*; *Cal. of Doc. Scot.* (Rec. Com.), iv. 777, where the following entry occurs:—1408, November 16. 'To Richard, Lord Grey of Codenore, chamberlain, at Evesham, for the expenses of the King of Scotland at vis. viii*d.* per diem, and of Griffin, son of Owain Glendourdi appe Gryffythe appe Richard at iii*s.* iv*d.* £40.' Issue Rolls (Pells) Mich. 9 Hen. IV.

[14] R. Symonds, *Diary of the Marches of the Royal Army during the Civil War* (Camden Soc.).

A. W. Ward, photo.

Evesham : South Chapel of Nave, St. Lawrence's Church.

A. W. Ward, photo.

Evesham Abbey : Doorway of Vestibule to the Chapter-house.

To face page 382.

CHURCHES AND OTHER BUILDINGS The principal buildings situated in the borough are the two parish churches of Evesham, St. Lawrence's and All Saints', the parish church of Bengeworth, St. Peter's, the Bell Tower of the Abbey, the Grammar School, the Town Hall, and Deacle's school, Bengeworth. The churches or, as they are originally called, chapels of St. Lawrence and All Saints were in all probability built to provide the inhabitants with suitable places of worship, so allowing the abbey church to be reserved for the inmates of the monastery.[1]

The church of St. Lawrence stands to the south-west of All Saints' church, and close to the south boundary of the churchyard. It consists of nave and chancel with north and south aisles, a west tower and spire, and a south chapel. A dedication of the church is recorded by the bishop of St. Asaph on 18 December, 1295, but the present building preserves no features of that date. It has suffered much from neglect and subsequent rebuilding, and its interest lies chiefly in the south chapel, which is a work of Abbot Lichfield's time, like that in All Saints' church. From Browne Willis's description [2] it appears that there was a corresponding chapel on the north side of the nave.[3] In 1730 the north arcade of the church, with the aisle and the north chapel, was destroyed, and a new wall was built on the line of the north aisle wall as high as the wall over the south arcade, and this wide space was roofed in a single span. The timbers used were too light, and the roof fell in. After this, the church stood neglected and in ruins for 106 years. In 1836 it was repaired,[4] the north arcade and clearstory rebuilt, with the north aisle, and much other work done which will be noted in detail.

The east end of the chancel is of much more elaborate design than the rest of the church. It is of late fifteenth or early sixteenth century date, and projects a few feet beyond the east gables of the aisles. It has tall and narrow two-light windows on the north and south, with transoms, very richly panelled angle buttresses, and a large six-light east window with tracery and transoms. The gable is set back from the line of the window, the extrados of whose arched head is exposed and forms a sort of coping. The wall surfaces are also panelled, a row of enriched quatrefoils running below the windows and above the moulded plinth.

The arcades of nave and chancel run continuously from east to west, and there is no chancel arch, but the site of the roodloft is shown by piers dividing the three bays of the chancel from the four bays of the nave. In both these piers are arched recesses with four-centred heads, that on the south being the roodloft doorway, while that on the north was put there to match the other at the rebuilding of 1836, and has no meaning. The south arcade has clustered shafts with four-centred arches; the wall surface above is panelled, and there are two two-light clearstory windows to each bay. The work is thin and poor, of late fifteenth or early sixteenth century date. The nave roof, in the form of a ribbed pointed wagon vault, dates from 1836. The aisle walls were at that time replastered and marked with false joints with the worst possible effect. The north arcade, which dates from 1836, with its clearstory, is a copy of the south arcade. The north wall of the north aisle is also entirely modern. It has three-light windows alter-

EVESHAM: VIEW OF THE TWO CHURCHES FROM THE WEST.

nating with pinnacled buttresses, and towards the east end a doorway into the north aisle of the chancel. The east wall of this aisle is old, and shows traces of an old window much larger than the present one, which dates from 1836. The east wall of the south aisle has the same history. The south windows and wall of this aisle are in the main ancient; the windows are tracery windows of three lights with poor detail. Under the east end [5] of this aisle was a vaulted charnel, the level of the floor over it being raised above that of the rest of the church as often happened in such cases. For this reason the vault was destroyed in 1836 to level the floor, and a flight of

[1] *Chron. de Evesham* (Rolls Ser.), 216. May, *Hist. of Evesham*, 168–69. A reference to the chapel of St. Lawrence occurs in the institutes or customs compiled at the abbey by Abbot Randolph about 1223, the chaplain being then one of the monks who was allowed a special corrody. Later, the chaplaincy was held by indenture from the abbot and convent. *Valor Eccl.* (Rec. Com.), iii. 255.

[2] *Mitred Abbies*, i. 90, 91.

[3] There is a drawing of this chapel in Thos. Dingley's *History from Marble* (Camden Soc. ii. 251).

[4] The repairs and alterations cost about £2,500, most of which was raised by voluntary contributions. May, *Hist. of Evesham*, 172–3.

[5] Ibid. 175.

steps leading down to the charnel from the aisle was also destroyed. There were two recesses in its east wall,[1] and a window next the churchyard. A brick arch was built instead of the vault, and the present access is by steps from the churchyard. The flat head of a blocked window east of the steps and another in the east wall are now the only external traces of the charnel.

The south chapel opens to the church with a panelled arch in which was formerly a low stone screen. It has a richly-carved and panelled stone fan vault, and contains a modern octagonal font, a fairly accurate copy of an ancient font taken away in 1836. In the east wall is a five-light window with a blank wall below, against which an altar stood ; on either side are tall canopied tabernacles for images coming down to the floor level. The south window is large, of five lights. The west wall is blank, but there are traces of the abutment of some building against the chapel at this point, the bonding of its plinth and parapet being still visible. The face of the masonry inside the chapel is so regular that it seems doubtful if any building was actually erected ; but on the other hand this seems the only position for the junction with the passage which formerly connected the great courtyard of the abbey with St. Lawrence's, and was still standing in Habington's time, who calls it 'a very great and curious walk to go at certain times to the little church to celebrate mass.' It had disappeared before Browne Willis wrote his account. The west tower opens to the nave by a lofty panelled arch, and has a stone vault with a bell-way in the crown. Across the arch is built a modern stone screen forming the front of a gallery, beneath which is the main entrance to the church through a west doorway in the tower. Over this doorway is a large four-light tracery window. The belfry windows are of two lights with a quatrefoil in the head ; their arch-mouldings have a fourteenth-century section, but otherwise nothing in the tower seems older than the fifteenth century, and probably the windows are not so old as they look. There is an embattled parapet with angle pinnacles and a short ribbed octagonal spire with remains of a foliated finial at the top. On the broaches of the spire are four short pinnacles. At the south-east angle is a projecting vice, entered from the churchyard, and finished at the level of the parapet with a conical stone cap. At the base of the parapet are a row of circular rain-water shoots, a curious feature which occurs in a slightly different form in the tower of South Littleton Church and elsewhere in the district. The number is so excessive that if it were not for their irregular spacing they might be intended as a merely ornamental feature. A few such shoots are to be seen on the tower of All Saints' Church. From a point a few feet below the parapet the angles of the tower are cut away, leaving diagonal faces which at a lower level are flanked by small buttresses. A pierced embattled parapet, with pinnacles over the buttresses, runs round the aisle walls, and is everywhere an addition of 1836 ; but the parapet on the south chapel, of much better design, is original. In the north wall of the tower outside, near the ground, is inserted a stone panel of good fifteenth-century style, representing the Crucifixion, with our Lady and St. John standing on either side.

The church contains no ancient fittings, but in the south aisle is a large fifteenth-century wooden coffer, and the communion table bears an inscription recording its gift in 1610 by Margaret Hay. There is one bell without inscription.

The church plate consists of two communion cups, dated 1838, and a standing paten of 1694, presented in 1838. There is also a flagon of 1847 and an alms dish of 1854, and a second alms dish of brass.

The register of baptisms and burials of St. Lawrence's begins 29 May, 1556, and is stated to have been 'newly written and trewly copied out of the other Bokes by John Wood, minister here, the first day of June, 1599.'[2] The register of marriages begins 1569.[3]

A chantry in honour of St. Katherine was founded in the parish church of St. Lawrence by the will of Robert Hynke, who gave certain lands and tenements to maintain a priest to say mass daily at the altar of St. Katherine. The date of the foundation does not appear. The priest was removable at the will of the parishioners.[4] There were besides three stipendiary priests 'of honest conversation and completely learned,' who were, perhaps, connected with the chantry in honour of the Holy Trinity, the Virgin Mary, and St. Clement, which is known to have existed here.[5] A Guild of the Holy Trinity is also mentioned.[6]

The church of All Saints occupies the north-east corner of the churchyard, which before the dissolution formed the layfolks' cemetery of the abbey. It is directly north of the site of the nave of the Abbey Church and north-east of the church of St. Lawrence. It consists of chancel with north vestries and organ chamber, north and south transepts, nave with north and south aisles and south chapel, and west tower with west porch. The building has undergone much 'restoration,' and the chancel and north aisle of the nave have been rebuilt. The west wall of the nave is the oldest part now standing ; it appears to belong to an aisleless twelfth-century church of which the west doorway, now the east doorway of the tower, and the south-west angle alone remain. The chancel before rebuilding seems to have been of the thirteenth century, and the north aisle of a somewhat later date in the same century. The north transept has some fourteenth-century details, and the south aisle, in which are fifteenth-century windows, is older than its windows. The north arcade and the south transept are of the fifteenth century, and the west tower, though it has several puzzling features, is probably not older than this time ; the south arcade, south chapel, and west porch are of the sixteenth century.

The main fabric of the church is built with lias rubble walling and Broadway stone dressings : the west porch and the Lichfield chapel and parts of the south transept are ashlar-faced. In the north wall of the chancel is a two-light fourteenth-century window, and the head of the door to the north vestry is of two orders with feathered cusping, fifteenth-century work. The east window is modern, and in the south of the chancel are modern copies

[1] Not further described in May's *Hist. of Evesham.*

[2] Prattinton Coll. (Soc. Antiq.).

[3] In 1653, 1654, and 1657 marriages took place before the mayor, and the banns were published three several market days in the market place of Evesham. (Ibid.)

[4] Chant. Cert. Worc. xxv. 26 and lx. 35. Robert Hynke's name does not appear in the *Calendar of Wills* published by the Worc. Hist. Soc.

[5] Pat. 28 Eliz. pt. 2, no. 2.

[6] Ibid.

of a fifteenth-century three-light window, and of a thirteenth-century lancet; there is also a small doorway. In the angle formed by this wall and the east wall of the south transept is a small blocked square-headed window; no signs of it are now to be seen from the inside. It is of the 'low-side' class, its sill being some three feet from the ground, and appears to be of the fifteenth century. The chancel arch is of two orders; it has been much repaired, but some of the stonework is ancient, and would seem to be of late thirteenth or early fourteenth-century date. Above it in the east gable of the nave are two two-light fifteenth-century windows, parts of which seem to be old. As there is no clearstory to the nave they light what would otherwise be a very dark part of the church, and may have been inserted to light the roodloft. In 1876 traces of wall paintings were found above the chancel arch, and the outline of the rood was visible.

In the north transept, or Derby chapel, the walls appear to belong to the early fourteenth century, and the rear arch of the north window is of that date, the tracery being modern. The transept opens to the nave by a wide arch of two plain chamfered orders without capitals or shafts, and to the north aisle by an arch like those in the north arcade, shortly to be described. The north and west walls of the north aisle have been rebuilt, and retain no old features except a niche in the west gable outside with a crocketed ogee head, poor work of the sixteenth century, under which is a seated figure of fifteenth-century style. At the south-east angle of the aisle, in the south wall, is a double recess with two trefoiled openings under a square head, and below them three trefoiled crocketed canopies over three niches, that in the middle being wider than the others. It has contained a figure or a group, and the side niches single figures, all of which have been cut away, leaving only the bases and rough wall behind as evidences. The whole looks as if it had been the reredos of an altar, and may not be in its original position. It is of the fifteenth century. The double niche above seems earlier, and possibly does not belong to the rest. The arch at the east end of the aisle had a wooden screen across it, of which some vestiges remained in the middle of the last century.[1]

The north arcade of the nave is of the fifteenth century, of three bays of very plain and shallow detail, the capitals being mere strings, and the archmoulds wide and shallow hollows between two plain chamfers. The capitals of the west respond and the first pier from the east are relieved by a narrow band of foliage carving. In the south-west face of the second pillar from the east is a crocketed trefoiled niche for an image; not an insertion, but part of the original work. A broken fifteenth-century figure now stands in it. The south arcade of the nave is of three wide bays; one bay, wider than the others, to the south transept, and two to the aisle. It is a coarse copy of the north arcade on a larger scale, and represents the latest step in the development of the building.

The south transept has a four-light east window with a straight-sided four-centred head of local type and fifteenth-century date and a form of reticulated tracery caused by the intersection of the mullions in lines following those of the straight-sided arch of the head. The south window of this transept and the windows of the south aisle, as well as the modern copy in the south wall of the chancel, are of the same type. In the west wall of the transept is part of a two-light window, blocked to the west by the Lichfield Chapel, and having its north jamb cut away at the time of the building of the south arcade, when the north end of this wall must have been destroyed. The south aisle has a west window and two south windows. Below the sill of the first window from the east on the south side are the lower parts of the jambs of a doorway whose head was destroyed by the building of the window. This may be only a barrow-hole, but the position is that of a south doorway to the nave, and the windows are probably insertions.

Against the west wall of the south transept is placed the fine tomb-chapel of Abbot Clement Lichfield, built by himself while prior of the abbey, and, therefore, before 1513. It opens to the church with a four-centred panelled arch, and has two windows on the south and one on the west of three lights with transoms and four-centred arched heads; below the windows runs a band of large quatrefoils, enclosing lozenge-shaped pateræ of carved foliage. The chapel is vaulted with two bays of richly-panelled and carved fan vaulting springing from shafts in the four angles of the chapel and the middle of the south wall. The middle of the north wall being taken up by the arch of entrance to the church, the vault springs at that point from a pendant on which are carved the letters C.L.P. for Clement Lichfield, prior. The east wall of the chapel is blank, and now has against it a modern altar and reredos: no traces of the original altar or its surroundings are to be seen. The abbot's monument was in the form of a brass inlaid in a marble slab.[2] The brass has long since disappeared. He died 18 October, 1546.

The west wall of the nave, as before noted, is the earliest part of the church. It is thick, and sets back on its east face at about 12 feet from the floor level. The west doorway, now leading to the space under the west tower, has a plain round outer arch with a square label chamfered on both edges and having broach stops at the springing. Its date is about 1180. Over the doorway is a low opening, with a trefoiled arch on the east face; all the masonry is modern, and its original date can only be guessed at. The tower, built against the west wall of the church, is only 8 feet square within. Its lowest stage forms, and has always formed, the west entrance to the church, and in the north jamb of its west doorway, on the inner face, is a holy-water stone. The arch of the west doorway is round and quite plain. It may be of any date, but the general character of the tower suggests that none of it is older than the fifteenth century. Over the doorway is a niche with a crocketed canopy. The tower is of three stages, with embattled parapet and angle pinnacles (the latter of very late style, sixteenth century), and a short octagonal stone spire with rolls at the angles and small spirelights, and a band of cresting round the spire near the top. The belfry windows are of two lights with trefoils in the heads. Against the west wall of the tower is built a west porch, with wide square-headed doorways on the north and south, only that on the north being used. The porch is faced with wrought stone, and has an

[1] May, *Hist. of Evesham*, p. 188.

[2] There is a drawing of the slab in Dingley's *History from Marble* (Camden Soc.), ii. 251.

embattled and pierced parapet with panelled angle buttresses and pinnacles. Below the cornice is a row of quatrefoils enclosing carvings; over the north doorway are five, having respectively a rose, a lis, three feathers, a pomegranate halved with a rose, and a crowned rose. If, as seems probable, this conjunction points to Prince Arthur, eldest son of Henry VII., the date of this porch is not likely to be later than 1502, the date of the prince's death. The porch has a plaster ceiling with moulded cross beams, having at their intersection a wooden boss carved with the Five Wounds encircled by the Crown of Thorns. The west wall of the tower up to the height of the ceiling of the porch was faced with wrought stone when the porch was built.

Externally the south aisle and south transepts have embattled parapets and pinnacles; the Lichfield chapel has a more elaborate parapet with pierced trefoiled openings. The south face of the south transept is of ashlar, as are the lower courses of its east wall; at the north end of this wall is a straight joint of wrought stone butting against rubble.

The font is of the fifteenth century, octagonal with panelled bowl and stem; it stands at the west end of the south aisle, and was formerly in the north aisle. The niche in the second pillar from the east in the north arcade may have some connexion with its original position.

The church plate consists of a communion cup with hall mark 1624 on the bowl (the stem may be older), inscribed 'Phillip Gardiner the elder gave 40*s.* towards this Copp: Edmund Young and William Bartlett, churchwardens'; a large paten with hall mark 1683; and a modern flagon, 1847. Also a large pewter dish dated 1688; two pewter flagons, 1722; and two pewter plates uninscribed.

In the eastern of the three windows in the north wall of the north aisle is a piece of fourteenth-century glass, formerly in the north window of the north transept, having a seated Majesty with right hand raised and the left resting on an orb.

The register of baptisms and marriages begins in 1539, and that of burials in 1538. There is one bell, without inscription.

There is mention of a chantry in honour of St. Mary the Virgin and St. George in All Saints' Church,[1] and it is probable that the two stipendiary priests 'indifferently learned and of honest conversation' who are mentioned in the chantry certificates were connected with this chantry.[2]

ADVOWSON In the early thirteenth century both churches were appropriated to the sacristan, who received from them 10 marks yearly.[3] At the dissolution they passed to the Crown, and the advowson is now held by the Lord Chancellor. The living of All Saints is a vicarage with the perpetual curacy of St. Lawrence annexed.

The Society of Friends have a meeting house in Cowl Street. This body was established in Evesham before 1655, and suffered much from the harsh and arbitrary action of the local magistrates. They met at the house of Edward Pitway in Bengeworth until in 1676 the present meeting house was erected.[4]

The Unitarian chapel in Oat Street was erected in 1737 as a meeting house for the Presbyterians, who first came into notice in Evesham about 1720.[5] There is a Baptist chapel in Cowl Street, a continuation of a congregation of Particular Baptists who first met about 1704 and erected a meeting house in Bengeworth in 1722. They removed to the present chapel in Cowl Street in 1788, when a part of the congregation seceded and founded the chapel in Mill Street where the Plymouth Brethren now worship.[6] There is also a Wesleyan Methodist chapel in Chapel Street, erected in 1808. The temporary Roman Catholic chapel, which was first opened for service in 1887, and formerly stood in Magpie Lane, was removed to High Street in 1903.

EVESHAM ABBEY The most important source of information on the history of the Benedictine Abbey of Evesham is the *Chronicle of Evesham*, the earlier part of which was compiled by Thomas Marlborough, abbot 1229–1236. It is continued by an anonymous writer to the death of Abbot Zatton in 1418. It is printed in the Rolls Series (1863), No. 29. The abbey was founded by Egwin, bishop of Worcester, 692–710, who became the first abbot. The foundation charter is dated 714.[7]

His church stood till the year 960, when it fell, the relics of St. Egwin being miraculously preserved from damage. A new church was begun at once, and seems to have been completed, but was possibly of inferior work by reason of the disturbed state of the abbey, in which the battle of monks against canons raged with unusual severity. At any rate, Abbot Manni (1044–1059) is said to have rebuilt the church on a larger scale than before, and its consecration is recorded in the *Anglo-Saxon Chronicle* under the year 1054.[8] From miracles told of St. Egwin it may be gathered that this church or its predecessor of 960 had a crypt with an altar in it.[9] There is also mention of an 'ecclesia Dei Genitricis,' but it is not clear whether this refers to a distinct building or to the church itself.[10] Abbot Manni also made a new and precious shrine for St. Egwin. His successor, Æthelwig (1059–1077), built a chapel of St. Nicholas, and contemplated a third rebuilding of the church, for which purpose he left to his successor five coffers full of silver.

Walter of Cerisy (1077–1104) carried on the work as his funds allowed, pulling down the old church little by little as the new work proceeded. The chronicler records this with evident regret for the destruction of the old building.[11] Abbot Walter, he says, liked the new style of building, and therefore destroyed the old work, which was at that time one of the most beautiful of its kind in England. The crypt was filled in with the fragments of the destroyed building. To raise money for the new work the abbot sent two of the brethren on a journey

[1] Pat. 28 Eliz. pt. 2, no. 2; ibid. 10 Eliz. pt. 3.

[2] Chant. Cert. Worc. lx. 34.

[3] Cott. MS. Vesp. xxiv. f. 13; *Chron. de Evesham* (Rolls Ser.), 210.

[4] May, *Hist. of Evesham*, 201; Joseph Besse, *Sufferings of the People called Quakers*, ii. 50 et seq.; Geo. Fox's *Journal* (8th ed.), i. 253. Pitway had been mayor in 1648; he was removed from the office of capital burgess in 1656 for signing a petition to Cromwell against the magistrates.

[5] May, *Hist. of Evesham*, 205.

[6] *Char. Commiss. Rep.* xxiv.; May, *Hist. of Evesham*, 208–10.

[7] *Chron. de Evesham* (Rolls Ser.), 17. Early dates for the foundation of monastic houses cannot be insisted upon.

[8] Ðæs ylcan ȝeares man halȝode þæt mynster on Eofeshamme on vi. Id. Octobris.

[9] *Chron. de Evesham*, 51.

[10] Ibid. 52.

[11] Ibid. 55.

through England with the shrine of St. Egwin. Before his death the crypt and eastern parts of the church as far as the crossing were built, with the four tower arches and one story of the tower, and presumably also the transepts.

No buildings are attributed to Robert (1104–1122), but Maurice (1122–1130) built the eastern range of claustral buildings, the chapter house, dorter, and parlour. Reginald of Gloucester (1130–1149) continued the building of the nave and completed the claustral buildings on the south and west, the frater, the outer parlour with chapel, the guesthouse with its camera, and the great kitchen. He also gave two large and two small bells, and built a wall round the whole monastery and its cemetery, intending to make a moat also, but abandoning the idea for fear the place would thereby be made so strong that the king would utilize it as a fortress.

William of Andeville (1149–1159) was too much occupied with repelling the attacks of William de Beauchamp and destroying his castle of Bengeworth to do much work to the abbey buildings, and his successor, Roger, *parvus sed factis magnanimus*, holding office for one year only, left no record of his rule but the mill by the bridge which connects Evesham and Bengeworth. Adam (1160–1191) finished the church and cloister, and put glass into many of the windows. He built the lavatory and laid on a supply of water, also the old infirmary, the reredorter and the bakehouse, brewhouse and granary, and made the two largest bells and the reading-desk in the chapterhouse.[1]

Roger Norreys (1191–1213) seems to have done evil consistently, and was finally deposed ; but in his time the central tower of the church was built to its full height, though apparently not roofed in for want of the money which the abbot wasted. So it happened that in 1207 the new tower fell on the presbytery and ruined it, destroying the shrine of St. Wistan and several others, and the high altar, though the shrines of St. Egwin, St. Odulf, and St. Credan were miraculously preserved.

Randulf (1213–1229) made 'speculam abbatis juxta aulam in curia de Evesham.' It is not clear what this was. He also pulled down the old guesthall and stable, presumably intending to rebuild them ; but this he did not do. In the church he made 'tres sedes abbatum,' perhaps the sedilia.

Thomas Marlborough (1229–1236), the compiler of the first part of the *Chronicle*, has put on record a long list of his own works as dean, sacrist, prior, and abbot. After the fall of the tower in 1207, here called the *first* fall,[2] he repaired the walls of the presbytery 'in modum pinnaculorum,'[3] to make a passage round the presbytery, which was not done before. This seems to mean that he built an eastern aisle to the presbytery. He also repaired the presbytery itself, with the roofs of the crypts adjoining the presbytery, and the greater part of the beams of the tower. Being made sacrist in 1217 he continued the repair of the presbytery, blocking up five arches of the presbytery and one before the entrance to the crypts. This was evidently for abutment to the central tower. Many minor works are also noted, as a lectern 'retro chorum,' and much repair of broken glass in the presbytery windows. When prior (1218–1229) he built two towers to the presbytery and made five stone roofs (*tabellata lapidea*) over five roofs of the crypt, and repaired that part of the church which is over the altar of St. John Baptist, after a second fall of the tower, and made it 'in modum pinnaculorum'[4] to make a passage round that part of the church with stone roof and towers.

The date of this second fall of the tower is nowhere given, but it was probably before 1217, and the blocking of the five arches of the presbytery in that year may have been undertaken in consequence. The presbytery was evidently remodelled after this second fall, being vaulted in five bays, ending at the east in a gable flanked by two turrets. Of the many other works recorded it must suffice to mention the great bell tower which Adam Sortes began[5]—this seems to be a separate building—the repair of the cemetery wall and the reredorter, and work done in the new infirmary. When abbot (1229–1236) he set up the rood and rood altar in the nave of the church, and made 'one of the vaults of the church behind the procession door from the cloister,' i.e. at the east end of the south aisle. He also added to the abbot's house. The church was completed in the time of Richard le Gras, and was dedicated in 1239.

The bell tower was set on fire by lightning in 1261,[6] and repaired in 1278,[7] only to be partly wrecked by a storm in 1291.[8]

John of Brokehampton (1286–1316) built the Lady Chapel,[9] with a vault with gilt bosses carved to represent the stories of various virgin saints. In his time the general rebuilding of the claustral buildings was undertaken on a scale of great magnificence. The chapterhouse was rebuilt,[10] with a fine vault and no central column,[11] and the east walk of the cloister with studies for the monks over it. Also the dorter, which was 'wide and excellent,' carried on vaults from one end to the other. A very valuable piece of information is here given as to the use of these vaults, which is generally a doubtful point. They were here divided into offices (*cameræ*), one for the *magister capellæ* and another for the sacrist, and also contained a misericord and other rooms. The reredorter had beneath it a long vaulted room for the use of the *minuti*,[12] the monks who had been let blood.[13] There were also built at this time the frater or refectory, the infirmary, the abbot's hall, with a splendid open timber roof and a two-story porch, the kitchen and pantry adjoining, the abbot's chamber ('camera'), 'painted with the story of Joseph,' with a small chapel, and a vaulted cellar under the chamber. The monastic kitchen was also rebuilt, and the bakehouse and brewhouse, with stables and chambers for guests, a guesthall, cellarer's chamber, etc.

1 This still exists, having been dug up on the site of the abbey in 1813, and is now doing duty as a lectern in Norton Church, see p. 419.

2 Op. cit. 265.

3 The east end of Abbey Dore Church might be so described. From the context it is clear that the meaning must be 'small gables,' and not 'pinnacles.'

4 See above.

5 Adam Sortes was expelled in 1207 by Abbot Roger Norreys.

6 *Ang. Sac.* i. 495.

7 Leland, *Collect.* i. 246.

8 Ibid. i. 248.

9 For the consecration of altars marking the completion of this work in 1295, see Harl. MS. 3763, f. 115, and also Cott. MS. Vit. E. xvii. f. 228.

10 Leland, *Collect.* i. 249, assigns this work to the year 1317.

11 'This house,' says the chronicle, 'by reason of its spaciousness and beauty is held to be one of the chief among the chapterhouses of this realm.'

12 This is probably the explanation of the room with a fireplace, in a similar position, at Netley Abbey.

13 *Chron. de Evesham* (Rolls Ser.), 287.

Under William of Chiriton (1316–1344) the work went on, the most important building being the great gateway,[1] with vaults, chapels, and rooms round it, embattled above, and adorned with stone statues of our Lady, St. Egwin, and the royal founders of the abbey. Another gateway was built 'in Bertona versus Merstowam,' and from it a stone wall to the river.

In the time of William Boys (1344–1367) part of the great grange in the barton was built, and the 'summer hall' with a chapel and chamber adjoining it standing between the frater and the great chamber of the abbot, also a chapel in the cemetery near the gate of the abbey.

John of Ombersley (1367–1379) built a chapel outside the abbey gate, close to the charnel chapel. He also rebuilt the north and west walks of the cloister.

Roger Zatton (1379–1418) built the bell tower of Evesham, and apparently rebuilt the presbytery of the church. He also built four cottages as bedehouses close to the cemetery gate.

At this point the *Chronicle* stops, and there is no record of the work of the remaining abbots until the time of Clement Lichfield (1514–1539).[2] He made alterations to the quire, and built the well-known bell tower which is now the chief feature of Evesham.

It seems clear that the Abbey Church and its surrounding buildings were destroyed within a few years of the dissolution. With certain reservations the site of the abbey and all buildings on it were granted to Philip Hoby, except all the bells and lead of the church and belfry.[3]

The buildings granted to Hoby were used as a quarry for building-stone. The great bell tower of Clement Lichfield was spared, perhaps because of its newness, and the great gateway of the abbey was left standing, but otherwise all the important buildings disappeared. Thomas Fuller[4] tells us that 'by a long lease it was in the possession of one Mr. Andrewes, father and son; whose grandchilde, living now at Berkhampsteed in Hertfordshire, hath better thriven by God's blessing on his own industry than his father and grandfather did with Evesham Abbey. The sale of the stones whereof he imputeth a cause of their ill successe.'

In Habington's time the site of the church was marked by a 'huge deal of rubbish overgrown with grasse.'[5] The abbey gateway, he says, 'though deformed with age, is as large and as stately as any at this time in England.'[6]

In 1726 a new impetus was given to the work of destruction by the finding of the heavy lead pipe already referred to on the north of the churchyard, which was traced in a line running south-east from the west porch of All Saints' Church across the churchyard to the site of the nave of the Abbey Church, on the eastern part of which a house called Hampson's House was then standing. This piece of plunder was the signal for more digging on any available part of the site, and we are told in a letter from Robert Crookes to John Rudge, of 13 July, 1726,[7] that 'Ashmore at the Crowne talkes of diggin the Cross churchyard, and doubts not (if noe other valuable goods) at least to finde a greate many valuable stones.'

This indiscriminate destruction seems to have been allowed to proceed unchecked, and it is not surprising to find that when the site came to be excavated by others than tradesmen in want of building materials, great part of the buildings had entirely disappeared, even to the foundations, and while the bases of the walls of the nave and transepts, with parts of the eastern range were still to some extent in place, the eastern part of the church was represented by foundations only and the remains of the crypt.

These excavations were begun in 1811 by Mr. Edward Rudge. They began near the arch, opening from the cloister to the chapterhouse vestibule, and resulted in the discovery of the north part of the east range, including the sacristy (?) and chapterhouse and part of the subvault of the dorter, together with the whole plan of the church, except the Lady Chapel and the south wall of the nave, of which not even the foundations remained. The plan of the buildings discovered, reproduced here from the *Vetusta Monumenta*, vol. v. pl. lxvii., can be approximately dated throughout with the help of the *Chronicle*. There seems to be no definite trace of the almost certainly apsidal eastern termination of the early church, which was probably destroyed by the alterations of 1207 and after; and of the Lady Chapel, built by John of Brokehampton, 1286–1316, only the foundations of the west end remain. The chapterhouse was ten-sided, with a diameter of 51 feet 6 inches, and was vaulted in one span without a central column. The materials of the building were rubble walling of lias faced with Broadway stone ashlar. To the east of the south transept is a rectangular room[8] or chapel with a crypt under it, in which were found several richly carved or painted architectural fragments. The length of the eastern range of buildings is unknown, as only the north end was excavated. This showed remains of a central row of columns, showing that it was vaulted in two spans. The space was divided by cross walls into several chambers, the use of which is mentioned in the *Chronicle* (see above). In one were the remains of a fireplace.

A number of burials were found in the church, some of which were identified, notably those of William of Chiriton,[9] 1344, and Henry of Worcester, 1263. But the most interesting was a disturbed burial in the north transept at a greater depth than the rest, with which was found a lead plate with this inscription:—

HIC REQUIESCIT DOMNUS ABBAS AELFRICUS HUIUS LOCI

ANIMA SUA REQUIESCAT IN PACE AMEN

proving the remains to be those of a Saxon abbot Aelfric, the exact date of whose death is not known, but who occurs as witness to a charter granted by King Ethelred[10] in 997.

With the exception of this burial nothing was discovered which belonged to pre-Conquest times. From the account of the re-building by Walter of Cerisy (1077–1104) it appears that the crypt of the

[1] *Chron. de Evesham* (Rolls Ser.), 291.

[2] Leland, *Collect.* iv. 70.

[3] For these reservations and their subsequent history see below, pp. 391, 392.

[4] *Church Hist.* 369.

[5] *Survey of Worc.* (Worc. Hist. Soc.), ii. 91.

[6] Op. cit. ii. 92.

[7] Quoted in *Vet. Mon.* v.

[8] At Shaftesbury Abbey a similar feature has been found by Mr. Doran Webb on the east of the north transept.

[9] Or perhaps John of Brokehampton, 1316. See *Liber Eveshamensis* (Henry Bradshaw Soc. 1893), p. 207, note on col. 139, line 31.

[10] Kemble, *Cod. Dipl.* iii. 303.

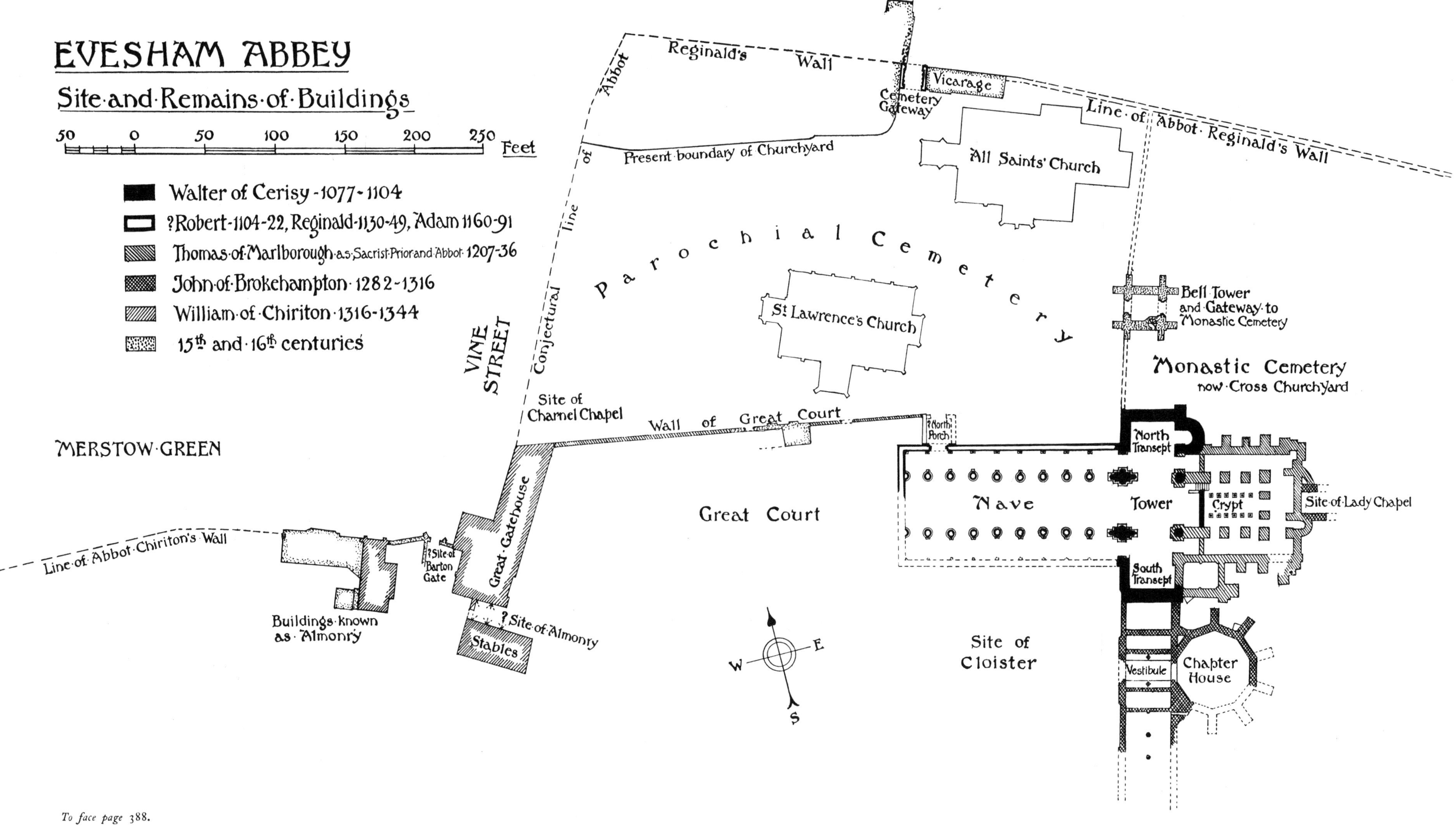

To face page 388.

on the south of the gatehouse and north of the building, now turned into cottages, which is called the Abbot's Stable on the plan in *Monumenta Vetusta*, v. pl. lxvii. If this is so, it follows that the buttresses of the gateway still remaining to the east of what is now called the almonry will belong to the barton gate, whose site has hitherto been placed at the west end of the building. A difficulty is, however, raised by the next words of the grant, describing the position of the storehouse, which is said to abut on the tower of the abbey gate north, and the garner south, and upon the 'Almery' west. No literal interpretation of the words will suit both the descriptions, and the question is difficult to settle without further exploration of the site. A positive identification of the 'Lord's Stable' of the grant with the building now known as the Abbot's Stable would go far to prove the point. Chiriton's boundary wall may still be traced running westward to the Avon from the 'Almonry.' The only parts [1] of the abbey church now to be seen in position are a piece of the west wall of the north transept and the bases of several piers adjacent to it, being part of Walter of Cerisy's work. The east wall of the market gardens which cover the site of the church and cloister, etc. runs southward from this point on the line and including parts of the west wall of the east range of claustral buildings. The only noticeable feature is the fine arch which formed the entrance to the chapter-house vestibule. Some way south of this arch the wall turns at a right angle eastward for a few feet, and then again southward, and finally westward. At this point part of the wall seems ancient and contains a plain late thirteenth-century doorway. It is not possible to be certain to what part of the monastic buildings it belonged.

The bell-tower built by Abbot Lichfield (1513–1539) is the only building which remains in anything like its original condition.[2] It is 110 feet high, faced with Broadway stone ashlar, of excellent detail and workmanship. It is in three stages, with double angle buttresses, the ground stage having wide four-centred archways under crocketed ogee hood-moulds in its east and west walls, leading from the parish churchyards to the open space now known as the Cross Churchyard, formerly the monks' cemetery. The abutment of the now destroyed wall which divided the monks' cemetery from that of the lay folk may be seen on the western buttresses of the tower. Both archways were designed for wooden doors. Over the west archway is a mutilated carving of three mitres, as in the Lichfield Chapel in All Saints' Church, while over the east archway is an inscription 'Qui gloriatur in Dno glorietur,' enclosing a defaced carving.[3] This stage of the tower was intended to have a stone vault, but there is no evidence that it was ever built. The east and west faces of the tower in all three stories are richly panelled, four tiers of panelling to each story, with arched heads to the panels, trefoiled or cinquefoiled. The north and south faces are quite plain on two stories, but in the top story are panelled like the rest. The tower is finished with an embattled and pierced parapet springing from a cornice below which is a band of quatrefoils, and at the angles are tall crocketed pinnacles ending in vanes, these last being added in 1717. There is a stair turret in the south-east angle, entered from the south side. In each face of the top story are two two-light windows with transoms—the part below the transoms being blank, with a quatrefoil piercing. On the second story there are four-light tracery windows on the east and west faces only. The windows of the top story on the west face were formerly blocked by a clock dial with two 'Jacks' above it.

The tower contains a clock and chimes, and a ring of eight bells, the first seven being by Abel Rudhall

Evesham Abbey: The Almonry.

[1] They owe their preservation chiefly to the fact that a house, called Hampson's House in 1726, was built over them.

[2] It is possible this bell-tower may have been preserved as others were elsewhere in monastic towns because the townsmen had certain rights in it for calling the inhabitants together in the case of 'fire or fray' and ringing the curfew.

[3] An anchor in an escutcheon, according to Dingley, *History from Marble* (Camden Soc.) ii. 250.

former church was not destroyed, but filled in with fragments of the Saxon building, so that it might be supposed to be still in existence buried beneath the later work. That the Saxon church occupied the same site as the present one may be assumed from the record of its gradual destruction as the new work went up, and it is possible that deep diggings on the site of the nave and crossing might bring to light some traces of it.

The line of the boundary wall of the abbey precinct and the position of the gates may be laid down with some accuracy. Reginald (1130–1149) is said to have built a wall round the whole monastery and its cemetery, and William of Chiriton (1316–1344) built the great gateway 'versus villam,' and another 'in Bertona versus Merstowam,' and from it a wall to the river. This wall was afterwards known as the Abbey-park wall.

Both the parish churches were included within the abbey precincts, with their churchyards, which were in fact the lay folks' cemetery of the abbey, the monastic cemetery lying to the east and separated from them by a wall running northwards from the north transept of the Abbey Church to the boundary wall. The great bell tower of Abbot Lichfield served as the gateway to the monastic cemetery, and probably took the place of an older gateway in the same position.[1]

The line of Reginald's wall from the bank of the Avon a little south of the bridge to the twelfth-century gateway which bears his name, close to All Saints' Church, is marked by a wall, mostly of modern date, which probably stands on the old foundations. The gateway, whose details seem rather earlier than Reginald's time, has lost its inner and outer arches, its upper part having been replaced by a timber structure in the fifteenth century.[2] Its remains consist of the wall arcades on either side of the entry, and the mutilated jambs of the inner and outer arches. It must always have been the entrance to the Abbey Church and cemetery from the town, and is mentioned as the cemetery gate in the form of installation of a newly-elected abbot.[3] Abbot Zatton (1379–1418) is said to have built four cottages as bedehouses [4] close to the cemetery gate. From this point there are no more traces of Reginald's wall, but existing boundaries suggest that its line was as shown on the plan. The wall [5] dividing the great courtyard of the abbey from the lay cemetery, which still exists in part, ran from what is probably the west wall of the north porch of the church to the boundary wall on the west, and near the point of junction stood the charnel chapel built by Abbot Boys (1344–1367) 'in the cemetery near the gate of the abbey.' Its substructures were found in 1832. To the south of this chapel stood the great gateway of the abbey, built by Abbot Chiriton (1316–1344).[6] It still remains, having been turned into a dwelling house in 1711, being gutted and refaced in the process. The removal of the plaster from its east face has revealed the lines of many of its blocked windows, and the inner arch of its great entry. In its north wall is a two-light fourteenth-century window.

From the south-west corner of the gatehouse the abbey boundary turns westward at a right angle. The lower part of a small gateway stands in the angle thus formed, and to the west is the picturesque building known as the almonry,[7] which, though much mutilated, retains some ancient detail, notably the stone lamp-niche here illustrated, and a fine carved sixteenth-century fireplace.

On its north front are two gables with good barge-boards and some seventeenth-century pargetting.[8] A reference to the description of the 'Almerye' in

Evesham Abbey : Stone Lamp-niche in Almonry.

the grant made at the suppression makes it doubtful whether the building whose position is carefully set down there can be that which now bears the name. From the plan here given it will be seen that the words of the grant, 'adjoining to the gate at the coming unto the said late monastery on the north, upon the Lord's stable on the south, upon the Basse court towards the east, and upon the Barton gate towards the west,' do not at all satisfactorily fit the position of the present 'Almerye,' but would very well describe the vaulted building whose remains still exist

[1] *Chron. de Evesham* (Rolls Ser.), 188.

[2] The interesting timber house east of the gateway, formerly used as the vicarage, was probably built at the same time. It contains a good stone fireplace in its west room on the ground floor, and part of a nearly contemporary wall decoration of painted canvas on a wooden partition.

[3] *Liber Eveshamensis* (Henry Bradshaw Soc. 1893), p. 154.

[4] It is possible that the mediæval timber buildings abutting on the north-west angle of the gate may be Zatton's bedehouses. In the apex of their north gable is the letter T, which throws no light on the question. The old vicarage would equally (perhaps better) suit the context.

[5] This wall contains a thirteenth-century doorway, and parts of a fifteenth-century building with two projecting chimneys.

[6] In the *Chronicle* its position is given as *versus villam*, which seems rather inaccurate, but as the cemeteries took up the whole of the north side of the abbey precinct, which was really the side *versus villam*, the great gateway opened as nearly 'towards the town' as the arrangement of the site allowed.

[7] A fourteenth-century building with later additions.

[8] A set of drawings of this building is published in *Trans. Brist. and Glos. Arch. Soc.* ix. 128.

of Gloucester, 1741, and the tenor by Thomas Mears of London, 1821.

The arms of the abbey, in allusion to the story of St. Egwin, were 'Azure a chain in chevron with a bolt at the dexter end and a horse-lock at the sinister between three mitres gold.'

When the monastery was dissolved a part of the abbey buildings was granted to Clement Lichfield for his life; the grant included the Chamberer's chamber, abutting upon ponds called 'Th' Abbottes Poles' on the east, 'le Basse Courte' on the west, 'le Abbottes Garden' on the south, and the building called 'Princes Chappell Chamber' on the north, a kitchen, a garden, a little curtilage, a house called 'le Taylours House' or 'le Aple House,' a little orchard called 'Calves Crofte,' and a pond within Evesham Park.[1] His successor in the abbacy, Philip Hawford, besides his pension of £240 yearly, received a grant for his life, or until he was preferred to an appointment of equal value, of 'le Almerye,' adjoining the gate of the monastery on the north, abutting on the Lord's Stable on the south, on a curtilage called the Base Court on the east, and on a gate called the Barton Gate on the west, the dove-cote above the Barton Gate, a garden called the Hynde Garden adjoining the Barton Gate, and the buildings called the Store House.[2] Certain buildings and gardens were also reserved for a Doctor Pryne or Prince and were known as Doctor Pryne's lodging.[3] Immediately after the surrender of the house a considerable portion of the fabric, including the abbey church, was destroyed, apparently by order of the commissioners. The stone from the demolished buildings was sold, but the people of Evesham claiming a share in the plunder are said to have made 'no little spoil'; and Philip Hoby, to guard his future interests in the place, was forced to pay men to watch nightly to prevent further waste.[4] He wrote to John Scudamore in October of 1539 or 1540, desiring to purchase the remainder of the stone 'for his necessity which shall shortly happen in building.'[5] Philip Hoby must have anticipated his grant, which was not made until 5 August, 1541.[6] He then received on a twenty-one years' lease the site of the monastery and the demesne lands of Evesham.[7] From this grant all the buildings given to Clement Lichfield and to Philip Hawford, or reserved for the officers of the Court of Augmentations, were excepted. On 30 July, 1542, Philip Hoby received a grant in fee of the premises already conveyed to him on lease, from which all buildings called 'Le Receipt' and 'those in which the records of the monastery remain' were also excepted.[8] Again, on 3 April, 1544, there were granted to him in fee the buildings excepted on the last grant, together with 'lez stewardes lodginges' and the dove-cote and garden attached to them, a sheep-cote containing fourteen 'lez beyes,' with a curtilage adjoining beside the town of Evesham, in St. Lawrence Parish, and a close called 'le Shepehouse Close,' alias 'le

Evesham: Bell Tower from the West.

[1] *L. and P. Hen. VIII.* xix. 276.

[2] Aug. Off. bk. ccxxxiv. f. 203; *L. and P. Hen. VIII.* xv. 542, 550.

[3] *L. and P. Hen. VIII.* xix. (1) 276. John Wodhouse, vicar of Bretforton, by his will dated 1530, left 'to Mr. Dr. Pryn viij mks. yf hyt shall pluyse hym to synge for me a whoole yere only hymselfe'; and also, 'ij Angell nobylls to pray for me as I wold for hym, and that should be whyle I lyvede.' Information supplied by Mr. O. G. Knapp.

[4] *L. and P. Hen. VIII.* xiv. (2), 148, where the letter is dated 31 October, 1539, and ibid. xvi. 93; where it bears the date 31 October, 1540.

[5] Ibid.

[6] Ibid. xvi. 721.

[7] Pat. 34 Hen. VIII. pt. vi. m. 33; *L. and P. Hen. VIII.* xvi. 721.

[8] Ibid. xvii. 322; Pat. 34 Hen. VIII. pt. vi. m. 33.

Lammes Close,' in St. Lawrence Parish; also the reversion of the buildings granted to Clement Lichfield, Philip Hawford, and Doctor Pryn, respectively, except the almonry and its gardens, and except also all bells and leaden roofs.[1] On 9 July, 1545, the almonry was also granted in fee to Philip Hoby,[2] so that Hawford had probably then been preferred to the deanery of Worcester.

When Sir Philip Hoby died the site of the manor or monastery passed to his brother Thomas, who in 1558 had licence to convey it to the use of his wife for life with remainder to his heirs male.[3] Immediately after the fine executed by Brian and Mary Carter in his favour,[4] Thomas Hoby accordingly made a settlement in favour of his wife of 'the site of the manor of Evesham' and certain pieces of land and pastures, the trustees being his two brothers-in-law, Sir Nicholas Bacon, Lord Keeper of the Great Seal, and Sir William Cecil, afterwards Lord Burghley; his father-in-law, Sir Anthony Cooke, and Richard Cooke.[5] When Sir Thomas Hoby died in 1567, Lady Hoby, who afterwards married John, Lord Russell, held these buildings and lands and had besides the custody of her son's possessions during his minority. On his coming of age in 1581, Edward Hoby confirmed her dower, and she continued to hold the abbey site till her death in 1609. During that time Sir Edward Hoby made several conveyances of property in Evesham,[6] and in 1595, jointly with his brother and heir apparent, he conveyed the reversion of the site of the monastery after his mother's death to Richard Shepham and John Gilbert.[7] In 1596 another fine was levied, by which Sir Edward Hoby, Richard Shepham, and John Gilbert, conveyed it, with all the rights and jurisdictions belonging to the former, to Edward Grevill.[8] From that time onward the site followed the descent of the overlordship.[9]

The remains of ancient masonry in the town, other than those already noted, are of little importance; but many houses retain parts of their ancient timber construction hidden by plaster or brick fronts. Fifteenth-century gables with carved bargeboards remain in several places, as at the south-east corner of the market-place, the north end of Cowl Street, the 'Almonry,' and elsewhere. In Bridge Street, No. 22, though much renewed, retains part of its fifteenth-century timber front, a doorway with carved spandrels, and a door with strap hinges. Of later buildings, Tower House, in the same street, and Dresden House, in the High Street, are worthy of notice, especially the latter, as fine examples of late seventeenth or early eighteenth century town houses. The date of Dresden House is approximately that on the head of a water pipe on the south side, 1692; and besides the fine wrought-iron railings and brackets carrying the door-head on the street front, it contains a good staircase, and panelled rooms and chimney-pieces of excellent design. In the garden

EVESHAM: OLD HOUSES IN BRIDGE STREET.

[1] *L. and P. Hen. VIII.* xix. (1), 276; Pat. 35 Hen. VIII. pt. ix. m. 30.

[2] Pat. 37 Hen. VIII. pt. v. The right of the Hoby family to the site of the monastery was several times questioned: Memo. R. Rec. East. 1 Mary, m. 13; Ibid. Mich. 3 Eliz. m. 127; Ibid. Trin. 9 Eliz. m. 73.

[3] Pat. 1 Eliz. pt. x.

[4] See p. 350.

[5] Feet of F. Worc. East. 1 Eliz.

[6] Ibid. Trin. 37 Eliz.; Pat. 28 Eliz. pt. 13; Ibid. 29 Eliz. pt. i.

[7] Ibid. Trin. 37 Eliz.

[8] Ibid. Hil. 38 Eliz.

[9] See p. 376.

A. W. Ward, Photo.

DRESDEN HOUSE, EVESHAM: CHIMNEY-PIECE IN GARDEN AND DOORWAY TO HIGH STREET.

To face page 392.

behind the house is a stone sun-dial dated 1720, a summer house contrived from an early seventeenth-century chimney-piece, which bears the arms of the town of Evesham and may have been formerly in the town hall, and a curious three-story garden house, c. 1750, known as the Temple, which has an elaborate plaster ceiling, and wooden panelling with the initials of Clement Lichfield, last abbot but one of the abbey. This is said to have come from the church, but the greater part at any rate is clearly of the date of the garden house.[1]

The Grammar School of the town, founded in the reign of Edward III.,[2] has been so often reconstructed that but a very small portion of it is older than the seventeenth century. Its much restored entrance porch retains the four-centred head of the doorway inscribed 'Orate pro anima Clementis abbat,' which therefore dates from after the death of Clement Lichfield, 18 October, 1546. The present town hall, a stone building standing on the west side of the market-place, was first built about 1580, the earliest known mention of it occurring in a deed dated 12 March, 1583.[3] It was of the customary type, of two stories with an open arcade below and a large room above. The arcade has been built up, and the whole so much repaired and enlarged at different times that very little of the original work is left. The arcade was put to various uses, sometimes serving as a threshing floor, sometimes as a provision market.[4] The central portion of the basement served until 1835 as the borough gaol and gaoler's residence, especially after the destruction of the ancient gaol in 1789. This part was later used as the municipal police station. On the upper floor is a large room formerly used for Quarter Sessions and Assizes, and still used for council meetings and public assemblies. A small room adjoining was erected for a council chamber in 1728. In 1834–35 the hall was renovated, and a new wing containing a modern iron staircase from the basement to the floor above was added at the expense of individual members of the corporation; [5] further repairs took place in 1897. On the north side of the market-place is a three-story fifteenth-century timber building, which is believed to be the Booth Hall, which stood at the top of Bridge Street near the present town hall, and continued to be used for public purposes after the town hall was built.[6] It is now cut up into shops and dwelling houses, and its ground story so much altered that it is not now clear whether it was originally open.[7] The market cross, which stood near the centre of the market square, was removed about 1760, and little record of it has been preserved.

Evesham and Bengeworth are connected by a stone bridge of three arches, erected during the mayoralty and mainly by the efforts of Henry Workman at a cost of £13,000, and opened on 13 March, 1856. The old stone bridge of eight arches, destroyed to give place to the present bridge, was one of the most interesting structures [8] in connexion with the borough. The original bridge, of which two arches on Bengeworth side showed the character, must have been a handsome one. It was erected in all probability during the first half of the twelfth century, and was certainly in existence in Abbot William Andeville's time (1149-59).[9] Since then it underwent so many repairs that it was practically rebuilt.[10] A grant of pontage was necessary as early as 1256.[11] In 1374 the bridge was broken by a flood,[12] and the central arch was rebuilt during the abbacy of Roger Zatton (1379–1418).[13] Abbot Thomas Newbold (1491–1513) rebuilt the arch at the Evesham end, and extensive repairs were also necessary in Clement Lichfield's time.[14] Shortly after the dissolution of Evesham monastery, the inhabitants of the town

EVESHAM : THE BOOTH HALL.

[1] Pococke, *Travels through England* (Camden Soc.), 277. The date must be 1750–1757. Information supplied by Mr. E. H. New.

[2] Chant. Cert. Worc. lx. 35. For its history see the article on 'Schools.' May, *Hist. of Evesham*, 130, 194–95, 196–97, also last part of charter of 1605, May, App. xiv. 480–483, establishing 'the free Grammar School of Prince Henry.' Barnard, loc. cit. 1 March, 1902, 'Repairs to School in 1706.'

[3] *Penes* O. G. Knapp, Esq. Bengeworth. Habington, writing sixty years later, attributes its erection 'to one of the Hobys.' It was probably built by either Sir Philip Hoby, who had intentions of building at Evesham when he first received a grant there, or his brother Sir Thomas; it was evidently in existence before Sir Edward Hoby attained his majority.

[4] May, op. cit. 198. In 1611 the Council desired that 'No person hereafter shall thresh or wynnow corn or set carts under the New Hall upon forfeit of 3*s*. 4*d*. for every offence.' Barnard, loc. cit. 6 June, 1903. See also Habington's account, *Survey of Worc.* (Worc. Hist. Soc.), ii. 75.

[5] May, *Hist. of Evesham*, 198–99.

[6] The Exch. Decree of 1587 ordered that the three weeks courts should be held in this hall. By 1687 it was disused as a hall and let by the Corporation as a dwelling house. In 1714 the Corporation paid £36 17*s*. 4*d*. for making a 'Gaole Roome' in the Old Hall.

[7] May, op. cit. 200.

[8] Ibid.

[9] *Chron. de Evesham* (Rolls Ser.), 100.

[10] May, *Hist. of Evesham*, 164, 360–62; Tindal, ibid. Barnard, loc. cit. 208-9, 27 June, 1903, 15 February and 8 March, 1902.

[11] Pat. 40 Hen. III. m. 5.

[12] Leland, *Coll.* i. 251.

[13] *Chron. de Evesham* (Rolls Ser.), 305.

[14] Aug. Off. Misc. Bks. cxxvii, f. 123–5.

petitioned Rich the chancellor that the king's receiver at Evesham might be instructed to have the bridge repaired, it being far in decay and ruin.[1] Commissioners were appointed by the Crown to inquire into the matter. The witnesses, the most interesting of whom was Clement Lichfield, the late abbot, stated that the monastery had always been responsible for the repairs of the bridge. The commissioners, whose report contains some interesting details,[2] stated that four of the eight arches were 'much ruyned and in farre decay' in the foundations; they found that the repairs could not be made 'one grote under £300,' and that the bridge could be kept in repair for £10 yearly. 'And truth it is, as we the said commissioners do well knowe, that alwaies are much habundance of rayne and wete and often grette frostes and ises . . . . with which said bridge therefore hathe byne and shall contynually be gretly charged and bourdeyned, and it no such time escapyd withoute grette hurte, and if the same bridge should fortune to fall, then should the said towne of Evesham and the most part of the country of the Vale there in short space be gretly impoveryshed,' because the inhabitants of the Vale would have no means of access 'with any caryage' to Evesham and its great market.[3] When the town was granted to Sir Philip Hoby in 1546 it was stipulated that he should keep the bridge in repair.[4] After the charter of 1604 this duty devolved on the corporation. In 1644 several of its arches were broken by the royal troops, and it was not thoroughly repaired until the time of Charles II.[5] If we are to judge from the records of the borough, constant repairs to the bridge were necessary from that time onwards, and at the time of its removal but little remained of the original structure.

CHARITIES

The following charities[6] for the purposes of general relief are in existence at Evesham:—

Thomas, Lord Coventry, by his will dated 31 August, 1657, gave £500, with which a yearly rent charge of £25 was purchased; this is distributed to the poor of the borough in sums of not more than 10*s.* each.

Philip Gardner gave tenements in Offenham, which about 1871 were sold and the proceeds invested in Consols to the amount of £239 1*s.* 6*d.* The income is distributed on 24 December among forty poor widows or poor persons of All Saints parish in money, clothing, coals, and bread.

From the charities of Mrs. Abigail Martin and the Rev. John Jephcott (will dated 3 March, 1712–3), chargeable on the same premises, £1 10*s.* is distributed annually to poor women of All Saints and St. Lawrence; £4 is also paid to the vicar of All Saints. A sum of 6*s.* 8*d.* formerly paid to the poor of St. Lawrence has been lost.

Elizabeth Gardner bequeathed £50 to aged persons unable to work; this was increased to £100 by her sister Ann and brother George Gardner; the latter also bequeathed £50 to the poor of Bengeworth and £100 towards teaching the children of Evesham to read. Certain premises in Evesham were accordingly charged with these bequests, and the sum of £10 issuing from them is allotted as follows:—£4 to St. Lawrence, £4 to All Saints, and £2 to Bengeworth.

Miss Harriet Smith by will dated 2 July, 1821, left £500 to the parishes of All Saints and St. Lawrence. The moiety belonging to All Saints has been invested in Consols to the amount of £238 8*s.* 6*d.*, the income from which is distributed in money at Christmas by the vicar and churchwardens to such poor persons as do not receive parochial assistance. The St. Lawrence moiety is invested, together with a sum left by Miss Horne, in Consols £334 11*s.* 6*d.*, the income from which is distributed in coals at Christmas to poor persons in All Saints parish.

James Mitchell gave 40*s.* to the poor of St. Lawrence out of premises formerly the George Inn. This sum is distributed at the church in bread on St. Thomas's Day and Good Friday.

Nicholas Field, by will dated 5 February, 1679, gave to the poor of St. Lawrence 20*s.* yearly, issuing from property in Evesham, to be distributed on twenty Sundays in the year, beginning on Epiphany Sunday; the distribution is made by the churchwardens.

Widow Lye, of Cropthorne, gave a tenement in Cowl Street, the rent to be divided between the poor of St. Lawrence and of Cropthorne. Formerly the churchwardens of St. Lawrence applied their share to general parish purposes; it is now given in bread weekly on Sundays between Christmas and Lady Day.

John New, by codicil dated 10 January, 1820, left £100, the interest to be distributed in bread among such industrious poor as have resided for twelve months in Oat Street, Cowl Street, Chapel Street, and Upper Mill Street, without distinction as to religious communion.

Leonard Fryer or Freer gave 52*s.* from property in Evesham to the poor of St. Lawrence, 1*s.* to be distributed in bread every Lord's Day. This charity, in abeyance in 1830, was afterwards recovered, and is in the hands of the churchwardens.

Lawrence Banks' Charity: According to the Benefaction Table in All Saints' Church, Lawrence Banks gave Amphlett's House, in St. Lawrence parish, that the poor there might have 12*d.* in bread every Sunday. The identity of the house has not been ascertained, but the churchwardens of both parishes receive 50*s.* yearly from a tenement in Bewdley Street, which is not referable to any other origin, and this sum, formerly included in the church fund, is now laid out in bread.[7]

George Drury, by will dated 1851, left £100 now in Consols to the amount of £96 17*s.* 11*d.*; the income is distributed in bread on Christmas Eve amongst the deserving poor of All Saints parish not receiving parochial relief.

Isaac Roberts, by will dated August, 1856, bequeathed £100, now invested in Consols £104 14*s.* 6*d.*; the

[1] Aug. Off. Misc. Bks. cxvii. f. 123–5.

[2] Ibid. cxii. ff. 13 and 14.

[3] Ibid. ff. 13 and 14. See ante, p. 371. This statement suggests that Twyford Bridge was not used for vehicular traffic, and Leland expressly states that it was 'for footmen.'

[4] Pat. 38 Hen. VIII. pt. ii. m. 11.

[5] Barnard, loc. cit. 27 June, 1903. This writer thinks that the historian May is mistaken in stating that after being broken in 1644 (May, *Hist. of Evesham*, 360), 'it stood for eighteen years a dreary monument of those doleful times,' and there seem good grounds for his view.

[6] The information respecting charities is taken from the *Charity Commrs. Rep.* xxiv. 502 et seq.; *Genl. Digest of Endowed Charities, Parl. Papers*, 1876, vol. lviii.; *Digest of the Endowed Charities for the County of Worcester, Parl. Papers*, 1900, vol. lxiii; and *List of Charities, Borough of Evesham*, printed for the Corporation, 1897. See also the account given in May's *Hist. of Evesham.*

[7] This charity does not appear in the corporation's printed *List of Charities*, 1897.

income is distributed by the vicar and churchwardens in bread among the poor of All Saints' parish at Christmas.

The following bequests have been made for educational purposes :—

John Gardner, by will dated 5 February, 1688, gave a quit-rent of £4 6*s*. 8*d*. payable by the Goldsmiths' Company of London, and another of 18*s*. payable by the churchwardens of St. Augustine's, London, for teaching twenty-five poor children of All Saints and St. Lawrence to read English. A dame school was supported by this charity until the foundation of the National Schools, to which the issues were then applied, until about 1894. In 1897 three years' receipts were in hand ; its subsequent application has not been ascertained.

Edward Rudge, by will proved 18 November, 1846, left personalty which was invested in Consols valued at £104 0*s*. 8*d*., the interest of which is applied to educational purposes.

The Workman Foundation : By deed dated 14 March, 1884, a mortgage, and Consols to the amount of £2,000, producing together an income of £61, were conveyed by Mr. Henry Workman to found exhibitions for deserving scholars in the Evesham Grammar School, tenable at any university in Great Britain. Mr. Workman, by will proved 22 January, 1889, bequeathed a further sum which has been invested in India three per cents., and its income of £8 18*s*. 8*d*. applied towards the augmentation of the salary of the headmaster of the Grammar School.

J. A. Roberts, by will dated 1857, bequeathed a mortgage of £400 and a sum of £92 16*s*. 2*d*. in a savings bank, producing a total income of £20 15*s*. 8*d*. to the Grammar School.

Thomas Mathews, by will dated 20 November, 1672, gave a rent charge of £5 towards apprenticing poor children born and bred in All Saints' parish. The bequest is dealt with by the churchwardens and overseers.

The following charities are applied towards medical relief and nursing :—

The Bonaker Trust Fund : According to the will of the Rev. W. B. Bonaker, proved in 1869, the interest and dividends of £8,762 14*s*. 3*d*. Consols are given to the Worcester General Infirmary, and in the admission of patients under this bequest preference is to be given to those nominated by the minister and churchwardens of St. Lawrence, Evesham.

The Bonaker Convalescent Charity was also established by Mr. Bonaker to promote by pecuniary assistance or otherwise the convalescence of poor invalids, and applies to the county generally, but poor persons dwelling in the parish of St. Lawrence have a preference.[1]

The following charities are devoted to ecclesiastical purposes :—

Edward Rudge, citizen and alderman of London, by will dated 17 November, 1640, left £400 to the churchwardens of Evesham to be laid out by them, by and with the advice of twelve of the 'ancientest and most substantial householders' for the maintenance of a lecturer to preach the Word of God in the parish church every Sabbath afternoon or upon some working day. He also bequeathed £200 to make a stock for the employment of the poor of Bengeworth. This charity in 1897 consisted of a rental of £50 from lands in Hampton, a sum of £831 2*s*., the produce of lands sold to the Railway Company, and a further sum of £172 2*s*. 8*d*. invested in new Consols in the name of the official Trustees of Charitable Funds. Two-thirds of the income is paid to the vicar of Evesham as an endowment, and the remaining third to the poor of Bengeworth (q. v.).

Church Fund, All Saints : The rents formerly issuing from the old Gild Hall, known at a later date as the Key or Quay House and let as a workhouse, with a yard adjoining, were applied to the repairs of the churches of All Saints and St. Lawrence. When the premises were sold under the Evesham Bridge Act of 1853 the proceeds were invested in Consols to the value of £1,106 10*s*., the income from which is applied as before.

Church Estate, St. Lawrence : This estate was the subject of an order of the Charity Commissioners dated 14 November, 1890. In 1897 it consisted of six messuages and cottages in Bewdley Street, two messuages in Vine Street, a cottage in Churchyard, the Fire Engine house in Vine Street, a cottage in Littleworth Street, a chief rent of 5*s*. 4*d*. payable out of land in Evesham, a stable in Swan Lane, and a garden near Mill Hill. In 1900 a sum of money invested in Consols to the amount of £67 11*s*. 6*d*. and termed Parish Property, also belonged to this estate. Its issues are applied with the rents from the above property to general church purposes.

Rev. W. B. Bonaker, by will dated 31 July, 1869, left a sum of money for the repair of the memorial windows in St. Lawrence's Church. This was invested in Consols amounting to £263 0*s*. 11*d*. in the hands of the Official Trustees, and according to the Charity Commissioners' printed report of 1900 was then accumulating.

Joint Church Estate of All Saints and St. Lawrence : This estate was also the subject of an order of the Charity Commissioners of 14 November, 1890. It consists of the Star Hotel, subject to the rent charge of £10 yearly in favour of the charities of Elizabeth, Ann, and George Gardner,[2] and of £93 7*s*. 8*d*. in Consols, the proceeds of the sale of a cottage in Oat Street. The income is divided between the churchwardens of All Saints and St. Lawrence, and devoted to church expenses.

Maltby's Charity : A Mr. Maltby of Brickland in Gloucestershire is stated on the Benefaction Table of All Saints to have given 13*s*. each from two houses in Evesham and a further 6*s*. from a house in High Street. The latter donation has been lost, but a rent of £3 received by the churchwardens of both parishes from a tenement in Oat Street was referred to Maltby's gift ; it was formerly absorbed in the church fund, but in 1830 was given in bread. Possibly this tenement is the cottage in Oat Street referred to above under the Joint Church Estate as having been sold.

Mary Bishop gave 40*s*. from two closes in Evesham to the ministers of All Saints and St. Lawrence, and

[1] The Rev. W. B. Bonaker originally left the money for these charities to Rev. Canon Bourne, of Weston Subedge, and Rev. Canon Ingram, of Harvington, both since deceased, to be used at their discretion. Some division of the money was effected, and Canon Ingram's son, the Rev. Arthur Winnington Ingram, applied his portion to secure nominations to the Convalescent Home at Weston-super-Mare. It is not known what happened to Canon Bourne's portion, as it has always been privately administered. (Information supplied by Mr. Oswald G. Knapp).

[2] See *ante*.

if there was no minister in either parish then to the poor of Evesham. The Benefaction Table of All Saints states that Robert Bishop in performance of the will of Mary Bishop, by deed dated 7 October, 1612, granted a rent charge of 20*s.* to the Corporation. In 1830 the property was in the hands of Edward Rudge, Esq., who paid £2 yearly to the vicar.

William Bond, by will dated 8 February, 1702, gave the moiety of the residue of his personal estate after his mother's death to the parishes of All Saints and St. Lawrence. He also gave £3 out of a close in Great Hampton to the minister of St. Lawrence, and this sum is still received by the vicar of Evesham.[1]

Baptist Chapel Charity: Elizabeth Seward, by will dated 2 June, 1753, left the interest and dividends of £350 invested in South Sea Stock towards the maintenance of the minister of the Baptist congregation in Bengeworth, the interest and dividends of £400 South Sea Annuities to teach poor children to read at the schools of Badsey, Evesham, and Bengeworth, and the interest and dividends of £400 South Sea Annuities to the Baptist minister for the support of monthly lectures in divinity. The congregation afterwards divided and removed to Evesham. In 1876 the precise amount of the stock could not be ascertained, but it formed part of a sum of £4,762 8*s.* 6*d.* Consols, and produced an income of £41 12*s.* 4*d.*, of which the minister received £12 6*s.* 4*d.*, a lecturer £14 13*s.*, and another £14 13*s.* was devoted to education, in which the parish of Badsey was entitled to share.

Ait Payment: One shilling to each of the parishes of All Saints and St. Lawrence issuing from an eyot in the Avon was recovered in 1830 by the Charity Commissioners and paid to poor widows in these parishes. Apparently, however, this charity has since been lost.

The charities of Dr. John Feckenham, Sergeant Cresheld, Sir Thomas Bigge, Thomas Watson, Savage, Palmer, Edmund Symonds, Robert Cookes, and others mentioned in the Corporation Books and on the Benefaction Tables of All Saints have also been lost.

John Pitts by will proved 1884 bequeathed £500 to each of the parishes of All Saints and St. Lawrence, to be invested and the income distributed to the poor in kind on 12 December yearly. The testator's personal estate proved insufficient, however, the bequest was reduced to £49 9*s.* 7*d.*, and the payment of this reduced sum was delayed pending the settlement of certain proceedings in Court.

BENGEWORTH

Bengwithe (viii. cent.); Bennicworte, Beningeorde (xi. cent.); Bengewrthe (xii. cent.); Beningwrthe, Bengeworthe (xiii. cent.).

The parish of St. Peter, Bengeworth, lies on the left bank of the River Avon, opposite to Evesham, with which it is connected by a bridge, rebuilt in 1856. It contains 1,360 acres, the greater part being laid out in market gardens and fruit grounds. The subsoil is lower lias, the surface gravel.

The houses of the main street, Port Street, have red brick fronts of the eighteenth century or later, but contain a considerable amount of timber framing, now for the most part hidden. The parish contains no domestic buildings of great interest, but the so-called manor house near the site of the old church has a little fourteenth-century work, and the Mansion House (O. G. Knapp, Esq.) is a sixteenth-century timber house re-cased and refitted in the early eighteenth century, with later additions. From the straggling hamlet which surrounded the prior's mansion in the early part of the thirteenth century,[2] Bengeworth gradually developed into the 'vill' of the Middle Ages,[3] and by the time of the dissolution seems to have become—probably from its proximity to the wealthy abbey of Evesham and its flourishing market, as well as its situation on one of the highways leading from Evesham—a fairly prosperous little country town. The monastery had there a fulling mill which they let to farm,[4] and which probably supplied the monks with cloth for their own use. The mill must have had a fair trade, since it produced a yearly rent of £6.[5] On 24 February 1538–9 it was let to Alice Gettesley or Gottesley for the term of her life.[6] This lease appears to have expired about 1566, and about this time two fulling mills came into existence in place of one. On 12 July, 1566, one of these was let to Anthony Rotsey for sixty years at a rent of 60*s.* annually,[7] and on 17 May, 1568, he was granted a lease of another mill for a similar term and rent,[8] so that the two mills produced exactly the same amount that one had formerly yielded. The fulling industry in Bengeworth has long since passed away. In the seventeenth and early eighteenth centuries there are traces of a glove manufacture at Bengeworth,[9] and up to the end of last century a number of women were employed in sewing gloves for the manufacturers in Worcester. Parchment making is said to have been an ancient industry here, and was common at the beginning of the eighteenth century, but by the middle of the nineteenth century it no longer existed.[10] Nail-making was also formerly carried on, but was nearly extinct in 1870. The nailers mostly lived in 'Nailers' Row,' in 'The Leys,' to the north of Port Street, where each house had its forge at which the family worked, the material being given out by local firms. There is also a ropewalk, now nearly disused, in the old 'Parsonage Close.'[11]

[1] The charities of Mary Bishop and William Bond are not mentioned in the Corporation's printed *List of Charities*, 1897.

[2] *Chron. de Evesham* (Rolls Ser.), 208.

[3] *Lay Subs. R.* 1358 (Worc. Hist. Soc.), 35.

[4] *Valor Eccl.* (Rec. Com.), iii. 23.

[5] Ibid.

[6] Mins. Accts. 31–2 Hen. VIII. L.R. 1330, m. 7–8. The name appears as 'Gotysley' in the parish registers.

[7] Mins. Accts. Worc. 16–17 Eliz. no. 35.

[8] Ibid.

[9] *Quart. Sess. R.* (Worc. Co. Coun.), 46. In 1705 John Holloway of Bengeworth, glover, was admitted to the freedom of the borough of Evesham. Information supplied by Mr. O. G. Knapp from the Corpn. Waste Bk.

[10] In 1712, John Rudge, of Bengeworth, parchment maker, eldest son of John Rudge, of Bengeworth, parchment maker, was admitted to the freedom of Evesham (Corpn. Waste Bk.), and Charles Acton, of Bengeworth, parchment maker, was party to a deed dated 1721, in the possession of Mr. O. G. Knapp, of Bengeworth. Only one firm, Paine & Co., appear in the directory of 1820, and in 1841 two names are found, Tipper and Goodall, who were the last to practise the art. (Information supplied by Mr. O. G. Knapp.)

[11] Ibid.

When the first charter was granted to Evesham in 1604, incorporating it as a royal borough, the suburb of Bengeworth was placed under its jurisdiction, but the residents there were granted no voice in the government of the borough. The inhabitants petitioned the king that their town might be incorporated with and form a part of the borough of Evesham, pointing out that many riots and disturbances had taken place and had passed unpunished, 'through the defect of good discipline and government in the said town.' Their request was accordingly granted, and their grounds of complaint removed by the charter of 1605,[1] and since that date Bengeworth has formed a part of the borough of Evesham.

About eighty years ago the foundations of a large apartment, with remains of two fireplaces, were discovered on levelling a bank in 'the moat orchard,' about 60 yards south-west of the old church. The dimensions of this room were given as 42 feet by 27 feet, and it was supposed to be the remains of the Beauchamps' castle. May, the local historian,[2] was, however, of the opinion that it was once the great hall of the prior's mansion, and not the castle, the position of which was clearly described as 'at the head of the bridge.'[3] An ancient building which may have formed part of the prior's mansion still stands to the west of the tower of the old church. It is partly of the fourteenth century, the roof timbers and a little lavatory with a trefoiled head on the first floor being of that date. It is sometimes called the 'manor house.'

The main road, which leaves the market-place of Evesham by Bridge Street and crosses the Avon by Bengeworth bridge, passes through Bengeworth by the principal street, 'Port Street,' and just beyond St. Peter's Church diverges, one branch passing westward to Chipping Campden, another south-westward to Stow-on-the-Wold. Port Street was probably the 'high street of Benigworth' referred to in a deed of apparently the thirteenth century.[4] Perhaps the earliest definite reference to it is in 1419, as 'le portstrete,' 'by the end of the bridge.'[5] The street now known as the Waterside, which runs south-eastward from Port Street parallel with and close to the Avon, was perhaps in existence in the fourteenth century. In 1343 William, son of John le Sclattare of Bengeworth, chaplain, conveyed to Richard Mareschal, chaplain, and others, a messuage in Bengeworth, 'over against the water of Avon';[6] and in 1391 another conveyance occurs of a messuage there 'opposite the water of Avon.'[7] The Waterside is continued as a main road, which passes through Little Hampton and Great Hampton and on to Pershore.

The Oxford, Worcester, and Wolverhampton branch of the Great-Western Railway passes through the northern extremity of Bengeworth parish before crossing the Avon into Evesham, which is the nearest station for Bengeworth. Bengeworth station, opened in 1864, on the Barnt Green, Evesham, and Ashchurch branch of the Midland Railway, is in Great Hampton parish about a mile and a half from Bengeworth.

The parish was enclosed in 1775.[8] Among place names 'le Bondende' occurs in 1540,[9] and others are Foxplace,[10] Bergmers, Haukspyrys,[11] Horsebridge Hill, Newborough, The Meer, The Shillboard, Shutmore, Broken Cross, Rudgeway, Monken Path, Friendacre furlong, Aunmore furlong, Bearcroft furlong, and the Dean furlong.[12]

Close to the bridge are the Workman Gardens, which also form a beautiful riverside promenade. They owe their formation to Mr. Henry Workman, to whose exertions the erection of the new bridge was mainly due, and who originated the idea of reclaiming from the Avon certain eyots which obstructed the stream, and of laying out the land thus gained as pleasure grounds. He raised the necessary funds by voluntary subscription, and the land was conveyed to the Corporation by deed dated 4 May, 1864.[13]

MANOR The history of Bengeworth during the centuries preceding the Domesday Survey depends almost entirely on the varying statements of two rival religious houses, who for many years were at issue for its possession. The monks of Evesham claimed that it was granted to their church by Kenred, king of the Mercians, in 708,[14] or jointly by Kenred and Offa, king of the East Angles, in 709,[15] while the Worcester monks stated that Bengeworth was included in the grant of Cropthorn made to them by Offa of Mercia in 780.[16] There is no contemporary evidence to bear out either of these statements, to which little credit is attached by authorities,[17] and the charters inserted by the annalist of the Worcester house in his chartulary, which partially cover the period between the original grant and the survey, are all open to suspicion. One of these charters states that Burhred, king of Mercia (852–874), and Aelhun, bishop of Worcester (848–72), gave land at Bengeworth, next the River Avon, under the extent of 10 'mansæ' to the church of Worcester.[18] This land Bishop Werefrith, the successor of Aelhun, granted to his kinsman and neighbour Cynelm, abbot of Evesham, who was to hold it for the term of his life, and was empowered to bequeath it at his death to any two heirs he might wish; it was then to revert to the see of Worcester.[19] The holder of the land was to give alms daily for the souls of King Burhred and Bishop Aelhun.[20] This grant is dated 907, but King Alfred, whose consent to the grant is mentioned, died in 901. In 980 Bishop Oswald is said to have granted land at Bengeworth to a knight named Aelfward for his life, with reversion to another knight named Edwin, if he survived Aelfward; Edwin might bequeath it to one or other of his brothers, on whose decease it was once more to return to the church of Worcester.[21] Again, some time between 1033 and 1038,[22] Bishop Brihteag is said to have given 5 hides of land there to his kinsman and chamberlain Atsere[23] or Azor, who at the

[1] See under Evesham, p. 375.
[2] May, *Hist of Evesham* (1834), 137.
[3] *Chron. de Evesham* (Rolls Ser.), 100.
[4] *Anct. D.* (P.R.O.), B. 3,540.
[5] Ibid. D. 884.
[6] Ibid. B. 4,062.
[7] Ibid. D. 546.
[8] Stat. 15 Geo. III. cap. 37, Priv.
[9] Mins. Accts. 31-32 Hen. VIII. L.R. 1330.
[10] Ibid.
[11] Pat. 36 Hen. VIII. pt. 24.
[12] In a deed of 1754 in Mr. Knapp's possession.
[13] *Digest of Endowed Char. Parl. Papers*, 1900, vol. lxiii.
[14] *Chron. de Evesham* (Rolls Ser.), 72.
[15] Birch, *Cart. Sax.* i. 183. See also ibid. 190.
[16] *Heming's Chartul.* (ed. Hearne), ii. 319; *Ann. Mon.* (Rolls Ser.), iv. 366.
[17] Kemble (*Cod. Dip.* I. 70, 167) marks both charters as spurious, and Mr. Round (*V. C. H. Worc.* i. 255) suggests that the monks of Worcester concocted Offa's charter nearly three centuries after its supposed date.
[18] *Heming's Chartul.* (ed. Hearne), i. 40.
[19] Ibid.
[20] Ibid.
[21] Ibid. i. 210.
[22] During Bishop Brihteag's episcopate.
[23] *Heming's Chartul.* (ed. Hearne), i. 269; *Chron. de Evesham* (Rolls Ser.), 97.

Conquest held it and did service for it at the bishop's pleasure.[1]

From the time of the original grants by the Saxon kings until the latter part of the tenth century, the Evesham house, unlike its rival, produced no charters in support of its claim to Bengeworth, and no statements are made in its chronicles in regard to the holders during that period. It is vaguely said to have been possessed by divers men from the time of King Edmund, probably Edmund the Elder (940–46) to the time of King Canute.[2] Five hides in Bengeworth then came into the hands of the latter king by forfeiture,[3] and had probably been held by one of the friends of Edric and Norman, who were put to death in the first year of his reign.[4] Canute granted the land which he had acquired to Brihtwin, one of his nobles, for his life with reversion to the monastery of Evesham.[5] These five hides appear to have afterwards passed to a holder named Aerngrim, during the period immediately preceding the Conquest. Bengeworth had therefore become divided into two portions of equal extent, held respectively by Aerngrim and Atsere or Azor,[6] both, according to Heming, the chronicler of Worcester, holding of the bishop.[7] By some means one of those moieties, with other lands claimed by the bishop, passed into the hands of Æthelwig, abbot of Evesham from 1059 to 1077, and hence arose the bitter quarrel between the church of Evesham and that of Worcester.[8] The chronicler of Evesham looked upon the acquisition of Bengeworth as one of the many good deeds of Abbot Æthelwig, and states that he was at much labour and expense in obtaining it from the bishop of Worcester, who had unjustly occupied it with other lands rightly belonging to the abbey.[9] A very different story is told by Heming, who states that Urse d'Abitot, the sheriff of Worcester, having possessed himself of Atsere's lands in Bengeworth, Aerngrim, the holder of the other moiety, fearing that he also might be dispossessed, sought the patronage of Æthelwig, and transferred his suit and service from the church of Worcester to the abbot. Very shortly afterwards, however, Aerngrim was ousted from his holding by the craft of Æthelwig, who by his eloquence and power, 'which made even the Normans fear him,' soon silenced the neighbours who cried injustice upon the act.[10] Both chronicles agree that Bengeworth—or part of it—was seized by the sheriff Urse, who, according to the Evesham version, only relinquished it when Æthelwig, in his devotion to his house, gave him in exchange lands which had formed part of his own inheritance.[11] Immediately after Æthelwig's death in 1077, Odo, bishop of Bayeux, 'that rapacious wolf,' is said to have obtained a writ from the king, his brother, authorizing him to take possession of certain lands which Æthelwig had held, among them Bengeworth,[12] and he further forced a gemot of five shires to assign these lands to himself,[13] while Urse the sheriff again entered into actual possession, apparently as Odo's under-tenant, of that moiety of Bengeworth which had been held by Atsere,[14] retaining besides Acton Beauchamp and Bransford which Abbot Æthelwig had given him in exchange.[15] Odo is stated to have afterwards issued a writ by which he surrendered Bengeworth to the abbey as its right, his surrender being confirmed by the king,[16] and Abbot Walter the successor of Æthelwig apparently recovered Aerngrim's estate there.

The quarrel with the church of Worcester, of which Bengeworth was one of the subjects, was continued by Abbot Walter, and was finally settled by the court of four shires at Gildenberga.[17] Before that court the abbot appeared bringing as his only testimony the relics of his monastery, including the bones of its sainted founder,[18] who had won for it from the Saxon kings such a rich endowment, while the bishop produced in support of his claim a charter the authenticity of which is doubted.[19] The quarrel so far as it concerned Bengeworth seems to have been both territorial and jurisdictionary; in the first—although Geoffrey, bishop of Coutances, is said to have testified that Bishop Wulstan had proved four hides there to be of his fee[20]—Worcester gained nothing. Abbot Walter proved his right to only five of its ten hides, and one of these five afterwards passed into the possession of Urse d'Abitot, who also managed to retain Atsere's moiety.[21] With regard to jurisdiction, Abbot Walter acknowledged that Bengeworth was within, and owed suit, 'fyrd and geld' to the bishop's hundred of Oswaldslow,[22] in which it is accordingly returned in the Domesday Survey.

The two divisions of Bengeworth probably became two manors; that held by Urse d'Abitot descended to the Beauchamp family by the marriage of Walter de Beauchamp to Emmeline the daughter and heir of Urse. In the early part of the twelfth century the whole of Bengeworth is stated to belong to the hundred of Oswaldslow, the abbot of Evesham still holding four hides and Walter de Beauchamp six.[23] In a survey of the abbot's manor, taken probably about the middle of the twelfth century, the names of twenty-eight bordars, including three smiths, are mentioned.[24] The Beauchamps had by this time fortified their position by erecting a castle at the head of the bridge which connected Evesham and Bengeworth, and during the abbacy of William de Andeville (1149–59) considerable friction seems to have existed between his house and that of Walter de Beauchamp, son and successor of William. The latter, taking advantage of the wars in Stephen's reign, crossed the Avon into the abbot's territory, destroyed the walls of the abbey cemetery, and laid waste other property of the church;[25] for these sacrilegious acts he was at once excommunicated with his accomplices by Abbot William, of whose courage the chronicler is very proud.[26] An encounter followed between the abbot's men and those of William de Beauchamp, in which many of the latter were killed, among them a knight named Abetot, who was buried, unreconciled

1 *V. C. H. Worc.* i. 297.
2 *Chron. de Evesham* (Rolls Ser.), 84.
3 Cott. MS. Vesp. B. xxiv. f. 34.
4 *Chron de Evesham* (Rolls Ser.), 84. Norman himself is said to have held Hampton closely adjoining. (Ibid.)
5 Cott. MS. Vesp. B. xxiv. f. 34.
6 *Chron. de Evesham* (Rolls Ser.), 97; *Heming's Chartul.* (ed. Hearne), i. 269.
7 Ibid.
8 See *V. C. H. Worc.* i. 253–6.
9 *Chron. de Evesham* (Rolls Ser.), 94–5.
10 *Heming's Chartul.* (ed. Hearne), i. 270.
11 *Chron. de Evesham* (Rolls Ser.), 95.
12 *Heming's Chartul.* (ed. Hearne), i. 273.
13 *Chron. de Evesham* (Rolls. Ser.), 97.
14 Cott. MS. Vesp. B. xxiv. f. 10 *d.*
15 *Chron. de Evesham* (Rolls Ser.), 95.
16 Cott. MS. Vesp. B. xxiv. f. 28. Printed in *Chron. de Evesham* (Rolls Ser.), xlviii. See footnote (2) *V.C.H. Worc.* i. 254.
17 See *V. C. H. Worc.* i. 253–6.
18 *Heming's Chartul.* (ed. Hearne), 81.
19 *V. C. H. Worc.* i. 255.
20 *Heming's Chartul.* (ed. Hearne), i. 77.
21 *V. C. H. Worc.* i. 297*a*, 307*a*.
22 *Heming's Chartul.* (ed. Hearne), 75, 296.
23 *V. C. H. Worc.* i. 325*b*.
24 Cott. MS. Vesp. B. xxiv. f. 34.
25 *Chron. de Evesham* (Rolls Ser.), 100.
26 Ibid.

to the Church, outside the cemetery at Elmley.[1] The abbot carried his victory still further, took possession of William de Beauchamp's castle, and destroyed it to the foundations; and, having done so, he made and consecrated a cemetery there.[2] A plot of ground adjacent to the north-east angle of the bridge was still known in the early part of the nineteenth century as 'the castle,' and probably pointed out the site of the Beauchamps' stronghold. Considerable traces of the moat were also to be seen, though said to be arched over.[3] The cemetery which the abbot made there must therefore have disappeared, since it could not have occupied the same situation as the cemetery, now closed, which surrounded the old church.

By 1206 the abbey's manor at Bengeworth seems to have become an important one. The manor house or court was at that time assigned to the prior, with the fields pertaining to it, and the garden, fish-pond, and meadow within the court, and all messuages in the fields around it, 'from the house of Thomas Algar to that of Walter Ballard.' Prior Thomas Marlborough afterwards abbot, had exchanged for this property certain land in Littleton which he had bought from Ralph Despencer. It is stated that since the value of Bengeworth was at that time less than the Littleton land, the prior was to feed twenty-five poor persons on the anniversary of Prior Thomas from its issues. The meaning of this statement is not quite clear. The prior had also to find a candle on the day of St. Wistan and another on the day of St. Credan to burn before the shrines of these saints.[4] To his office pertained also the greater and lesser tithes of Bengeworth from the lands and men of the monastery there.[5]

About the middle of the thirteenth century Bengeworth once more formed a bone of contention, the opposing parties on this occasion being Walter Cantilupe, bishop of Worcester, and William de Beauchamp of Elmley Castle. Among other complaints made by the bishop, William de Beauchamp was stated to have withdrawn his manor of Bengeworth from the hundred of Oswaldslow to his court of the barony of Elmley without the consent of the bishop and to the prejudice of the liberty of Oswaldslow.[6] For this and other reasons William de Beauchamp suffered excommunication from the bishop, a sentence confirmed by Pope Innocent IV.[7] Peace was made between the parties in 1251,[8] and a settlement of the disputed points made in 1257.[9] The quarrel, however, was resumed by Walter Giffard, Cantilupe's successor, with William, earl of Warwick, son of William de Beauchamp above mentioned.[10] The bishop proposed that the earl should surrender to him, by gift or sale, the manor of Bengeworth.[11] This the earl refused to do,[12] and in 1268 bestowed it instead on the monastery of Evesham in free and perpetual alms.[13] Bengeworth then probably dropped out of the quarrel, which was finally settled in 1280, the abbot of Evesham being appointed by the earl of Warwick as one of his arbitrators.[14] On 15 November, 1280, the year after the Statute of Mortmain was passed, Edward I. confirmed the manor to the convent. The fact that the bishop of Worcester was one of the witnesses to this confirmation points to an amicable settlement between all parties.[15] A part of Bengeworth seems, however, to have remained in the Beauchamp family at least for a time. In the Lay Subsidy Roll of about 1280, Lady Ankaret de Beauchamp held property there which must have been considerable, judging from the amount she paid—20*s*.[16] She was probably a kinswoman of the earl, and may have had a life interest in the manor; but no condition touching her tenure is mentioned in the earl's charter, and it is quite possible that she was simply the abbot's tenant.[17] The two parts of Bengeworth having thus become united, it is probable that they were erected by the convent into one great manor.

Beauchamp, Earl of Warwick. *Gules a fesse between six crosslets gold.*

The taxation of 1291 proves that Bengeworth was one of the abbey's most valuable properties, being worth £27 18*s*. 1¼*d*. annually;[18] and it shows also the division of its revenues between the various officials of the abbey. The convent had there six carucates of land, each carucate worth 30*s*.; from fixed rents and commutation for services they had £4 4*s*. 9¼*d*.; the kitchener had rents worth £4, and from two mills £1 10*s*.; the pittancer had rents valued at four marks; the custodian of the altar of the Blessed Mary had rents worth £2; the almoner had £2; the sacrist £2, and the sub-sacrist £1.[19] From that time until the dissolution little is known of the history of Bengeworth. When the strife which had agitated the monastery in earlier years concerning it had ceased, its history must have become the ordinary history of a monastic manor. The convent continued to increase its property there from time to time, and Bengeworth is mentioned in the annals of the monastery only when some new acquisition was made or its issues turned to some fresh purpose.[20]

1 *Chron. de Evesham* (Rolls Ser.), 100.
2 Ibid.
3 May, *Hist. of Evesham* (1845), 164.
4 *Chron. de Evesham* (Rolls Ser.), 208.
5 Ibid.
6 *Worc. Epis. Reg. Giffard* (Worc. Hist. Soc.), 75.
7 *Ann. Mon.* (Rolls Ser.), i. 140, 142; iv. 440.
8 Ibid. iv. 102, 440.
9 Ibid. 445.
10 *Worc. Epis. Reg. Giffard* (Worc. Hist. Soc.), 75.
11 Ibid. 77.
12 Ibid.
13 Harl. MS. 3763, f. 121 *d*. and Cott. MS. Nero D. iii. f. 245. The latter manuscript gives the date, being the year in which William de Beauchamp succeeded to the earldom.
14 Thomas, *Worc. Cath.* App. 31–2.
15 Harl. MS. 3763, f. 118 *d*.; Chart. R. 8 Edw. I. m. 1, no. 8.
16 *Lay Subs. R.* c. 1280 (Worc. Hist. Soc.), 87.
17 Her name appears in this Subsidy Roll, also under Hob Lench, Great Comberton, and Naunton Beauchamp.
18 *Pope Nich. Tax.* (Rec. Com.), 229.
19 Ibid.
20 In 1220–1, Abbot Ranulf had acquired from Ralph Untoge and his wife Alice a messuage in Bengeworth (Feet of F. 5 Hen. III. no. 30). William of Whitchurch, during whose abbacy William de Beauchamp surrendered his manor (*Chron. de Evesham* (Rolls. Ser.), 283), is stated to have further acquired certain rents in Bengeworth, Evesham, and elsewhere, from which he assigned 20*s*. towards the refreshment of the monks on his anniversary (ibid.). On 10 July, 1291, John of Whitchurch had licence to alienate to the abbot and convent a messuage, two virgates of land, and 30*s*. in rent in Atch Lench and Bengeworth (*Cal. of Pat.* 1281–92, p. 440). Abbot John of Brokehampton (1282–1316) acquired from William Marshall there a rent of 28*s*. (*Chron. de Evesham* (Rolls Ser.), 284); William of Cheriton (1317–44) a tenement which had belonged to Avice of Bampton, valued at 12*s*. annually (ibid. 290). William Boys (1345–67) acquired from the lord of Aston Somerville two virgates of land worth 30*s*. per annum, which he afterwards assigned to the infirmarer (ibid. 294), from Nicholas Porter two tenements with five cottages worth 20*s*. yearly, and from John Grenehulle, chaplain, a tenement with two cottages worth 10*s*., and a

In 1535 the demesne lands of Bengeworth were let for a term of years, and the clear value of the abbey's possessions there was estimated at £59 13*s.* 8*d.*[1] In 1538 this lease seems to have terminated, since on 16 January the site of the manor and the demesne lands were let to William Phillipps and his wife Agnes, and their sons Thomas and Richard, for 72 years, or as long as any of them should live.[2] When in 1539 the monastery of Evesham was dissolved, the manor came into the hands of the Crown; its total issues during that year amounted to £91 5*s.* 2*d.*[3] For some years it continued in the Crown, the courts being held by the Crown bailiffs, and gradually, as various tenements were granted out, its issues decreased. With the site of the manor and the demesne lands there was also leased a parcel of land lying in the fields of Bengeworth and known in 1540 and for some years afterwards as 'The Brodeland'[4]; but subsequently this name was altered into 'The Lord's Lands.'[5] In 1553 the site of the manor was still under lease to the Phillipps family, but some time during the latter part of this year or the early part of 1554 the lease terminated, either by death or surrender, and on 1 September, 1554–5, the site and demesne lands passed into the possession of William Swift on a twenty-one years' lease at the yearly rent of 106*s.* 8*d.*[6] Swift does not appear to have held the site for this period, since in 1565–6 it was granted, with the demesne lands, to Philip Tolley the Crown bailiff there for twenty-one years.[7] The latter died about 1571, when a fresh lease for twenty-one years was granted to his executors, Fulk Bellows and John Whetely.[8] In 1574 the reversion in fee of this lease was granted to Robert Dudley, earl of Leicester, and his heirs, in exchange for other lands, to hold of the manor of East Greenwich in free socage and not in chief.[9] Some time afterwards the site passed to the Bigge family, but it is not clear at what date the conveyance took place. Thomas Bigge, the brother-in-law of Sir Philip Hoby, already held the rectory, and in 1574 he is returned as the 'farmer' of the lordship or manor and accountable, with Bartholomew Kightley, the bailiff, for its issues.[10] In 1576 Thomas Bigge acquired from Bartholomew Kightley certain lands in Bengeworth called 'Atlams Lands,'[11] which had been granted by letters patent on 3 April of that year to Christopher Hatton,[12] from whom Kightley had shortly afterwards purchased them.[13] On 2 August, 1577, Christopher Hatton was further granted a grange in Bengeworth, being part of the manor and certain lands there, in lieu of lands which he surrendered to the queen,[14] and on the following day he sold this property to Thomas Bigge.[15] The latter must, therefore, have held property of considerable value in Bengeworth, and it is probable that between 1574, when the grant was made to Lord Leicester, and in 1581, when Thomas Bigge died, some conveyance was effected by which Bigge acquired the reversion of the site. The latter's son may however have purchased it, as he did the rectory of Bengeworth, in which he had formerly only a life interest. He certainly held the site of the manor in 1601, when he conveyed it with other premises to his brother, Philip Bigge, and Henry Neale, in trust to the use of himself for life with remainder to his son Thomas in tail male, and in default to his sons Clement and Samuel.[16] It is probable that during the early part of the seventeenth century, when all or nearly all the property which had come to the Crown from the monastery of Evesham had been granted out at a reserved rent, the manor of Bengeworth fell into abeyance, and courts for it were no longer held. On 26 June, 1610, a grant of the lordship or manor of Bengeworth was made by King James I. to George Salter and John Williams,[18] but this grant was surrendered on 19 June of the following year,[19] and Thomas Bigge, who had been knighted in 1603, continued in possession until his death on 4 May, 1613.[20]

BIGGE. *Silver a fesse engrailed*[17] *between three martlets sable with three golden rings on the fesse.*

At the time of his death he was seised of the site of the manor of Bengeworth held in free socage of the manor of East Greenwich.[20] His son Thomas then succeeded him, and had livery of the site of the manor of Bengeworth on 20 November, 1617.[21] In the following year he jointly with his brother Samuel, who had by the lack of issue to Thomas and the death of his elder brother Clement, become his heir apparent, conveyed the manor by fine to George Hemsworth, Francis Heaton, and Thomas Bolles,[22] in trust to the use of Thomas himself for life with remainder to Samuel.[23] Thomas Bigge, knight and baronet, died on 11 June, 1621,[24] and was succeeded by Samuel Bigge, his brother. His widow Anne before 1626 married Sir John Walter, a chief baron of the Exchequer.[25] Samuel Bigge did not have livery of his possessions in Bengeworth until 5 December, 1626.[26] He appears to have afterwards conveyed Bengeworth to William Courteen, who in 1636 conveyed the manor to Sir Edward Littleton, his brother-in-law, and Thomas Coppyn.[27] The history of Bengeworth for some years afterwards is obscure. William Courteen[28] through many heavy losses became bankrupt in 1643, and if he actually held Bengeworth

tenement formerly belonging to Thomas Eddeby worth 5*s.* (ibid. 294). The same abbot assigned to the office of almoner £8 6*s.* 8*d.*, issuing from lands in Bengeworth, Evesham, and Saintbury, in Gloucestershire (ibid. 299). Abbot John Ombersley (1367–79) acquired all the tenements in Bengeworth which formerly belonged to John Dykun (ibid. 300). Roger Zatton (1379–1418) is stated to have repaired tenements at Bengeworth which had perished by fire, and he erected a new cattle-shed at the 'court of Benge' (ibid. 304). In 1392 Thomas Patty granted to Abbot Roger five messuages, a toft, and two acres, in Bengeworth and Offenham (*Anct. D.* B. 3547). Possibly this was the property referred to in the Chronicle as acquired by Abbot Roger at great expense (*Chron. de Evesham* (Rolls Ser.), 306).

1 *Valor Eccl.* (Rec. Com.), iii. 248.
2 Mins. Accts. 31–2 Hen. VIII. L.R. 1330.
3 Ibid.
4 Ibid.
5 Ibid. 4–5 Eliz. no. 36.
6 Pat. 1 and 2 Phil. and Mary, pt. 10.
7 Ibid. 8 Eliz. pt. 2.
8 Ibid. 13 Eliz. pt. 6, m. 4.
9 Ibid. 16 Eliz. pt. 1, m. 5.
10 Mins. Accts. 16–17 Eliz. no. 35.
11 Close, 18 Eliz. pt. 10.
12 Pat. 18 Eliz. pt. 13, m. 1.
13 Close, 18 Eliz. pt. 10.
14 Pat. 19 Eliz. pt. 8, m. 39.
15 Close, 19 Eliz. pt. 14.
16 Chan. inq. p.m. 2 Chas. I. ccccxxiii. 75.
17 As on monument of Sir Thos. Bigge; see p. 420.
18 Pat. 8 Jas. I. pt. 37, m. 14.
19 Close, 9 Jas. I. pt. 20, m. 12–15.
20 Chan. inq. p.m. 12 Jas. I. cccxli. 45.
21 Fine R. 15 Jas. I. pt. 2, no. 36.
22 Feet of F. Worc. Trin. 16 Jas. I.
23 Chan. inq. p.m. 2 Chas. I. ccccxxiii 75.
24 Ibid.
25 Ibid.
26 Fine R. 2 Chas. I. pt. 2, no. 30.
27 Feet of F. Div. Cos. East. 12 Chas. I
28 See under Aldington, Badsey.

it was probably involved with his other estates in the maze of litigation which followed.[1] But in 1656 it was dealt with by Thomas Freame and Charles Fox,[2] and again in 1659 when they conveyed it to William Windowe probably for the purpose of a settlement and division.[3] Charles Fox was the son of Michael Fox of Chacombe, Northamptonshire, who had married Catherine, the sister of Samuel Bigge,[4] while Thomas Freame was probably the son of Elizabeth Bigge, another sister, who had married Thomas Freame of Lypiatt, Gloucestershire.[5] It is possible, therefore, that William Courteen may have held Bengeworth from Samuel Bigge on lease or in mortgage, since on the latter's death without issue his sisters or their descendants became his co-heirs. The manor seems to have been divided into three parts, of which one-third went to Thomas Freame and another third to Charles Fox; the remaining third probably passed to Anne, another sister of Samuel Bigge, who had married John Wright of East Meon, Hampshire,[6] and in 1660 was conveyed by William Wright, possibly her son, to Thomas Knyvett.[7] Thomas Freame of Lypiatt left three daughters and co-heirs:[8] Elizabeth, who married Thomas Clutterbuck; Anne, who married Thomas Chamberlain; and Sarah, who married Henry Windowe,[9] who each held a ninth part of the manor of Bengeworth. In 1666 Anne Freame, junior, conveyed her share to Thomas Chamberlain, senior, Thomas Higgs, William Windowe, and Thomas Bridges,[10] probably for the purpose of a marriage settlement. In 1673 Sarah Freame levied a fine conveying her ninth part to William Selwyn, Silvanus Wood, Philip Sheppard, and John Griffin,[11] probably for a similar purpose, and in 1683 the three sisters and their husbands sold their portions, a third in all, to Sir Thomas Haselwood.[12] In 1679 and again in 1680 Gilbert Batty and his wife Elizabeth claimed to convey another third by fine to John Lloyd,[13] though in 1683 in a conveyance to Sir Thomas Haselwood, to which John Lloyd and his wife Dorothy were also parties, they dealt with only 'two parts of the third part,' i.e. two-ninths of the whole.[14] It was probably the remainder of this share, 'a third part of a third part,' which Sir Thomas Haselwood acquired from Francis Ancell in 1684,[15] and in the same year Sir Thomas also purchased the remaining third from Richard White, clerk, and his wife Mary.[16]

Although it would thus appear that the whole manor passed to Sir Thomas Haselwood, it is probable that one or more of these conveyances simply confirmed a previous sale, and that a part of the manor still outstanding in other hands passed subsequently to the Rushout family. Thus the 'moiety of the third part of the third part,'[17] i.e. one-eighteenth of the manor and of the rectory conveyed in 1661 by Henry Waller and Hester his wife to Richard Howe, has not been accounted for, and possibly other shares remained outstanding. From this time onwards for about a century 'the manor,' a term that had lost its strict legal use, is dealt with by the Haselwood and Rushout families respectively, and has, therefore, a double descent.

By his will dated 7 May, 1716,[18] Sir Thomas Haselwood left the manor in trust for his eldest son Thomas, with remainder to his other sons and his daughters respectively. On 2 February, 1721–2, Thomas Haselwood executed a deed of bargain and sale, and suffered a recovery by which he barred the entail, and immediately afterwards the trustees appointed by his father's will conveyed Bengeworth to other trustees to the use of Thomas for his life, with remainder to his only son, James Haselwood, subject to an annuity of £170 charged on it for the use of Ann, the wife of Thomas, for her life.[19] James Haselwood accordingly succeeded his father, and dealt with Bengeworth in 1737.[20] He seems to have become involved in pecuniary difficulties, and in March of 1739 he mortgaged the manor or site of the manor of Bengeworth to the Rev. Bernard Wilson, D.D., of West Keal, Lincolnshire, and Francis Say, the latter's trustee, who had advanced £10,000. In September, 1743, Haselwood borrowed from Wilson a further amount, and on 18 and 19 March, 1744, the principal and interest, as well as his mother's annuity, being still unpaid, he conveyed to Wilson in satisfaction of his debts the manor or lordship of Bengeworth, and by a further conveyance in August, 1745, confirmed the latter in possession.[21] In July, 1747, Wilson mortgaged Bengeworth to Thomas Musgrave, but it was not until 24 June, 1749, that he acquired from the two sisters of James Haselwood, Dorothy and Lucy, and Francis Turner Blythe, the husband of the latter, all their interest in the property; in January, 1753, a conveyance for the same purpose was made by Ann, the widow of Thomas and mother of James Haselwood.[22] By his will dated 27 June, 1767, Dr. Wilson bequeathed his real estate to his great nephew, Robert Wilson Cracroft, son of Robert Cracroft of Hackthorn, Lincolnshire, who in 1774 acquired from William Linthwaite of Newark, and Mary his wife, all their interest in the property, the latter being the cousin and heir-at-law of Dr. Wilson. In 1776 Joseph Musgrave, the nephew and heir of Thomas Musgrave, to whom the manor had been mortgaged in 1747, released and confirmed it to Robert Wilson Cracroft, who had paid off the mortgage.[23] In 1777 Cracroft again mortgaged the manor to William Wynne, LL.D., and in 1781 he conveyed it to Sir Jacob Wolff of Chumleigh and Thomas Cracroft of West Keal as trustees, who were to sell it, paying off the mortgage and investing the residue on behalf of his brother John Cracroft, in view of the latter's

1 *Dict. of Nat. Biog.*; Kippis, *Biog.*

2 Feet of F. Worc. East. 1656.

3 Com. Pleas Recov. R. East. 1659, m. 151.

4 Baker, *Northants*, i. 590. Clement Bigge, of Lenchwick, by his will (*Abst. of Wills P. C. C. Soame*, pp. 85-6) bequeathed to 'my godson Samuel Foxe, a brace of jacobins to be used as his godmother and aunt think fit,' and speaks of his sister Catherine Fox of Chacombe.

5 Monument in Norton Church, and will of Clement Bigge, above cited.

6 Monument in Norton Church. He had two other sisters, Mary and Ursula, of whom nothing is known, and who probably died young.

7 Com. Pleas Recov. R. Mich. 1660, m. 93.

8 Rudder, *Glouc.* 293.

9 *Visitation of Glouc.* 1682-3, pp. 203-4.

10 Feet of F. Worc. Hil. 17-18 Chas. II.

11 Ibid. East. 25 Chas. II.

12 Ibid. Trin. 35 Chas. II.

13 Ibid. Hil. 30 and 31 Chas. II. and Trin. 32 Chas. II.

14 Ibid. Trin. 35 Chas. II.

15 Ibid. East. 36 Chas. II.

16 Ibid.

17 Ibid. Trin. 13 Chas. II.; Com. Pleas Recov. R. East. 13 Chas. II. m. 55.

18 Proved P.C.C. 7 January, 1720.

19 Information supplied by Mr. O. G. Knapp from documents in his possession.

20 Com. Pleas Recov. R. Mich. 11 Geo. II. m. 150.

21 Information supplied by Mr. O. G. Knapp from documents in his possession.

22 Ibid.

23 Ibid.

marriage. Apparently, however, this sale did not take place, and in 1789 John Cracroft had succeeded to his brother's property in Bengeworth. By deeds of lease and release in October of that year he directed that his estates in Bengeworth, 'except the manor or lordship or reputed manor or lordship of Bengeworth,' should be sold.[1] It is not clear why this exception should be made unless Cracroft had discovered that he had no legal title to the manor; the Enclosure Act of 1775 had stated that Robert Wilson Cracroft was simply rector impropriate of the parish, and had recognized Sir John Rushout as lord of the manor, which was said to be co-extensive with the parish.[2] It has not yet been ascertained when Bengeworth first passed to the Rushout family; but as early as 1674 Sir James Rushout is said to have leased a messuage there to one Nathaniel Watson.[3] His son, Sir John Rushout, dealt with the manor in 1718,[4] in 1729, and in 1761.[5]

CRACROFT. *Vert a dance silver bendwise with three martlets sable thereon.*

The Cracroft estate in Bengeworth was put up for auction on 26 May, 1789, but withdrawn and subsequently sold by private treaty for £16,000 to Charles Welsh on behalf of Sir John Rushout, son of the before-mentioned Sir John, who was to retain £8,000 of the purchase-money to pay off Wynne's mortgage.[6] On 15 October, 1789, the premises, excepting the manor, were confirmed to Sir John Rushout, afterwards created Baron Northwick, who by a codicil to his will dated 11 January, 1793, bequeathed his real estate lately bought to his wife, Rebecca Lady Northwick, and two trustees.[7] In June, 1802, Lady Northwick, jointly with her trustees and Sir William Wynne, the mortgagee, sold this property for £31,000 to Richard Whitehouse Jennings for the use of John Robins, acting on behalf of Charles Thellusson of Finsbury Square, London.[8] In the following month Thellusson borrowed £21,000 from one Woodford, and in 1804, as security, mortgaged the premises to him, again excepting the manor. Soon afterwards the property was sold in lots.[9] These conveyances, however, affected only the property which had descended from the Haselwoods to the Cracrofts. The manor as held by the Rushouts remained distinct, and is still held by this family, being now in the possession of Lady Northwick.[10]

RUSHOUT. *Sable two leopards and a border engrailed gold.*

CHURCH The church is dedicated in honour of St. Peter,[11] and is a modern building (1870–1), consisting of chancel, north and south transepts, nave of four bays with aisles, and a south-west tower with spire. The site is at the east end of the street of Bengeworth at the junction of the main roads to Bretforton and Broadway, on ground rising from west to east, and about as high above the river level as the Evesham churches on the other bank. The only relic of the old church preserved is a black and white marble monument to John Deacle (ob. 1709), founder of a charity school in the parish. His effigy in white marble reclines, resting on one elbow, and above is a pediment carried on black marble columns, with a shield of arms.

There is a very good view from the south-east of the old church of Bengeworth in May's *History of Evesham* (1845 ed. p. 219). It had a chancel with north and south aisles, an aisleless nave, and a west tower with a spire very like that of St. Lawrence, Evesham. The tower was also the west porch, and had a vaulted lower stage. The old church stood to the south of the main street, approached from it by a short road. It was pulled down, except the base of the tower, when the new church was built. The churchyard is of irregular shape, enclosed by a brick wall, and surrounded by houses. The base of the tower appears to be of the early fifteenth century, and has a west doorway of two chamfered orders, and small blocked windows in its north and south walls. Of the vault above mentioned only the wall ribs remain; it appears to be of the date of the tower. The east arch of the tower is low pitched, following the line of the vault, and over it is a blocked doorway to a former west gallery. The broken remains of a plain fifteenth-century font, and a few mural tablets, one to Thomas Watson, 1561, are placed in the tower.

The church plate consists of a large communion cup of 'Puritan' type, with paten cover, dated 1627, and inscribed 'The gift of Edward Rudge, 1628,' and a small cup and cover of the same type, dated 1636. There are six bells, recast, after the rebuilding of the church, by William Blews and Sons, of Birmingham, 1873. The registers begin in 1539, the early paper-book not being extant; prior to 1812 there are four volumes: i. 1539–1722; ii. and iii. 1734–1810, interrupted by iv., which contains baptisms from 1808 to 1812. There is a fifteenth-century window in the north wall of the nave of Norton Church, which was formerly in the old church here, and the stone sedilia at Norton are made of material brought from the same place.

ADVOWSON Bengeworth was a chapelry of the church at Evesham until the dissolution.[12] On 5 August, 1541, the rectorial tithes there were granted to Philip Hoby,[13] who on 2 October, 1544, received a further grant to himself, his heirs and assigns for twenty-one years, of the Parsonage House, a court, a small '*stagium*,' a close called the Parsonage Close, and other appurtenances.[14] Sir Philip Hoby by his will left his interest in the rectory to his brother-in-law Thomas Bigge and his wife Maud, and after their

[1] Information supplied by Mr. O. G. Knapp from documents in his possession.
[2] Stat. 15 Geo. III. cap. 37, Priv.
[3] Prattinton Coll. (Soc. Antiq.).
[4] Com. Pleas Recov. R. Trin. 4 Geo. I. m. 116.
[5] Ibid. Hil. 1 Geo. III. m. 75.
[6] Information supplied by Mr. O. G. Knapp from documents in his possession.
[7] Ibid.
[8] Ibid.
[9] Ibid.
[10] Information from Lady Northwick's agent.
[11] There is a tradition that the church was formerly dedicated to the Holy Trinity, but there is no evidence on the point except that this dedication occurs in Bacon's *Liber Regis*. The reference in the *Chron. de Evesham* (Rolls Ser.), 84, so often associated with Bengeworth, is clearly to the famous church of the Holy Trinity founded by Leofric and Godiva at Coventry.
[12] *Pope Nich. Tax.* (Rec. Com.), 219*b*. *Valor Eccl.* (Rec. Com.), 255.
[13] *L. and P. Hen. VIII.* xvi. 721.
[14] Quoted in Pat. 4 Eliz. pt. v. m. 3.

Bengeworth: The Old Church, pulled down 1871.

A. W. Ward, photo.

Hampton Church from the North-West.

To face page 402.

decease to their eldest son.[1] The grant to Sir Philip Hoby does not appear to have carried the advowson, which on 14 November, 1558, a few months after his death, was granted to Richard, bishop of Worcester,[2] and probably afterwards returned to the Crown by the Act of the first year of Elizabeth's reign.[3]

In 1562 Thomas Bigge appears to have petitioned the Crown for a fresh lease of the premises left to him by Sir Philip Hoby and on 5 December of that year he was granted the Parsonage House with appurtenances as above,[4] to hold for term of his life, with remainder to his son Thomas and then to his son Philip for their lives.[5] In 1587–8 the rectory, church, and advowson, with the reversion of the tithes and property conveyed to Thomas Bigge, were granted by letters patent to Edward Downing and Miles Dodding and their heirs to hold of the manor of East Greenwich in free socage;[6] the grantees to pay a yearly rent to the Crown, and certain sums towards the stipends of the master and assistant master of the Grammar School at King's Norton. On 13 February, 1592–3, Thomas Bigge, the second of that name, purchased the advowson from these grantees,[7] and for some years afterwards it followed the descent of the manor. On 21 March, 1606, for some reason not ascertained, a fresh grant of the Parsonage House was made to Thomas Hyde, Sir William Kelligrew, Anthony Thorolde, Richard Fancotte, and Sir Thomas Bigge, their heirs, administrators and assigns,[8] but the Bigge family continued to hold the advowson.[9] Samuel Bigge held it in Habington's time,[10] and although Thomas Watson is said to have had it in his possession in 1670,[11] still it seems to have passed to the co-heirs of Samuel Bigge, and is dealt with in all the fines concerning the manor from 1656 until 1684,[12] when all interest in it came by purchase to Sir Thomas Haselwood. It then followed the descent of the manor and was sold to the Rev. Bernard Wilson in 1745. The latter seems to have conveyed it to the Rev. John Tregenna, whose daughters and co-heirs afterwards held it. In Trinity term of 1767, Thomas Biddulph and Martha, Thomas Rogers and Margery, John Barnard and Anne, and Catherine, Jane, and Sarah Tregenna, jointly levied a fine by which the advowson was conveyed to the Rev. William Talbot,[13] of Reading, who presented in 1771. Charles Henry Talbot, probably his son, was patron of the church in 1775, and Robert Wilson Cracroft, of Hackthorne, in the county of Lincoln, was rector impropriate.[14]

About 1836 the advowson passed from Mr. Talbot to the Rev. W. Allies,[15] and from the latter to the Rev. William Harker, who became patron about 1846.[16] Harker is said to have conveyed it to the Rev. William Pitt MacFarquhar, and the next patron was Mrs. Marsden, who in 1861 presented her son, the Rev. Samuel E. Marsden, afterwards bishop of Bathurst.[17] Mrs. Marsden some years later conveyed the advowson to the Rev. William Bentley, afterwards called the Rev. William Corry de Bentley Corry, vicar of Bengeworth, on whose death his trustees conveyed it in 1897 to Samuel Buchanan Smith, Esq., of Salisbury, who now holds it.[18]

CHARITIES John Deacle, the founder of the Free School, by will dated 24 July, 1706, bequeathed a sum of £2 10*s*., which is distributed on Sundays in bread at the church to aged and indigent persons.[19]

Edward Rudge: From this charity [20] one-third is distributed by the churchwardens to the necessitous poor of Bengeworth in small sums on Christmas Eve.

Andrew Ordway, who died 13 July, 1712, gave 20*s*. yearly to the poor. This sum, which issues from a rent-charge, was formerly distributed by the churchwardens in bread on Sundays after divine service; in 1876 it was given in money, but is now given in bread.[21]

John Martin, of Little Hampton, yeoman, by his will dated 28 February, 1713, gave property in Little Hampton, from which the vicar of Bengeworth receives £10 annually as an endowment. This charity is now called the Church Charity.[22]

Frances Watson, by will dated 7 September, 1727, gave £100 to be distributed weekly in bread by the minister and churchwardens of Bengeworth. This sum was decreased to between £80 and £90 by the failure of the persons to whom it was entrusted, but by other contributions again raised to £100, which was laid out in the purchase of a turnpike road bond on the tolls of Evesham and Cheltenham. It was afterwards invested in a mortgage from which the income of £5 is distributed in bread.[23]

Thomazine Watson, by her will dated 2 September, 1737, bequeathed £150, with which a house and land in Ashton-under-Hill were purchased, and this property has since been exchanged for a cottage, garden, and orchard in Bengeworth; two-thirds of the rent is given to the vicar of Bengeworth, and the remaining third is distributed to the poor in bread by churchwardens.[24]

Mrs. Shaw, by deed dated 1862, conveyed a sum of money, which has been invested in Consols to the amount of £324 15*s*. 3*d*., to be devoted to educational purposes. £150 has been applied to new buildings at Bengeworth National Schools, and no interest will be available until this is repaid, except £2 annually paid to the Provident Society.[25]

Miss Phoebe Porter, of Birmingham, by will proved 1861, bequeathed a sum of £666 13*s*. 4*d*. in Consols the income from which is distributed by the vicar and, churchwardens in coals, blankets, and warm clothing.[26]

Gardner Charity: A sum of £2 from the charities of Elizabeth and George Gardner (see Evesham) is

1 Pat. 4 Eliz. pt. v. m. 3.

2 Ibid. 5 and 6 Phil. and Mary, pt. ii. m. 30.

3 *Stat. Revised*, i. 487.

4 Pat. 4 Eliz. pt. v. m. 3.

5 Ibid.

6 Ibid. 30 Eliz. pt. xv. m. 4.

7 Close, 35 Eliz. pt. vi.

8 Pat. 3 Jas. I. pt. xiv.

9 Chan. Inq. p.m. 12 Jas. I. cccxli. 45; Fine R. 15 Jas. I. pt. ii. no. 36; Feet of F. Worc. Trin. 16 Jas. I.; Chan. inq. p.m. 2 Chas. I. ccccxxiii. 75; Fine R. 2 Chas. I. pt. ii. no. 30.

10 *Surv. of Worc.* (Worc. Hist. Soc.), ii. 179.

11 Pat. 22 Chas. II. pt. ii.

12 See descent of manor.

13 Feet of F. Worc. Trin. 7 Geo. III.

14 Stat. 15 Geo. III. cap. xxxvii. Priv.

15 *Clerical Guide*, 1817 to 1836.

16 *Clergy List*, 1841 to 1846.

17 Information supplied by Mr. O. G. Knapp of Bengeworth.

18 Ibid.

19 *Char. Commrs. Rep.* xxiv.; *List of Charities, Evesham Borough.*

20 See under Evesham.

21 *Char. Commrs. Rep.* xxiv.; *Digest of Endowed Char. Parl. Papers*, 1876, vol. lviii.; *List of Charities, Evesham Borough.*

22 Ibid.

23 Ibid.

24 Ibid.

25 Ibid. and information supplied by Mr. O. G. Knapp.

26 *Digest of Endowed Char. Parl. Papers*, 1876, vol. lviii.; *List of Charities, Evesham Borough.*

distributed in bread on Sundays by the churchwardens.[1]

The Church Charity consists of £183 1*s.* 7*d.*, invested in Consols, the income from which is applied to church repairs. Its origin has not been ascertained.[2]

John Pitts by will proved 1884 bequeathed £500 to be invested and its income distributed among the poor. The testator's pure personal estate proved insufficient, the bequest was very much reduced and its payment is still delayed.[3]

GREAT AND LITTLE HAMPTON

Hantune (xi. cent.).

The parish of Great and Little Hampton is situated on the southern border of the county, immediately south of Evesham, from which it is separated by the River Avon. The Merry Brook forms the western boundary for some distance, and the River Isbourne,[4] flowing northward through the parish, divides the village of Great Hampton on the west from that of Little Hampton on the east; near its junction with the Avon it is crossed by a mediæval bridge with stone ribs, apparently of the fourteenth century. This bridge has now fallen into decay, and a new one is being built close to the site of the old. The land slopes generally to the banks of the Avon, which in the north are somewhat liable to floods. The greatest height is attained at Clarke's Hill, a little to the north of the village of Great Hampton, from the summit of which there are beautiful views of the town of Evesham rising from the opposite bank of the Avon and of the famous vale stretching away to the Cotswold Hills. On the slope of this hill tradition says the vineyard belonging to the monks of Evesham was situated. Probably it lay on the western side of the ridge sloping to the west and south, which would seem much better adapted to the cultivation of the vine than the steep bank facing the river and the east winds,[5] on which some writers have believed they could trace the remains of terrace cultivation.[6]

At the time of the Domesday Survey the vineyard was newly planted, and in it certain of the abbot's tenants in Hampton were required to do service.[7] At the Dissolution it had been turned into pasture land,[8] which in 1544 was granted to Richard Andrews.[9]

The road from Evesham to Pershore and thence to Worcester passes westward through the villages, and at Little Hampton the road to Winchcomb, Cheltenham, and Tewkesbury branches off to the south. In 1727 the inhabitants of Hampton petitioned the Commons against a Bill for repairing the road from Broadway to Evesham, setting forth that it was not the real highway from London to Worcester, the real and nearest way passing through Hinton and Pershore; this road may still be traced through Child's Wickham and Hinton, after which it is lost.[10]

The Evesham and Ashchurch branch of the Midland Railway passes through the parish; Bengeworth Station at Great Hampton on this line was opened on 1 October, 1864, when the mayor and corporation of Evesham made the journey in the first train which ran to Ashchurch.[11]

The parish contains 1,693 acres and 191 inhabited houses.[12] The subsoil is lower lias, and for the most part the surface is strong clay. Much of the parish is meadow land, but market gardening is carried on to a considerable extent.

Among former place names the following occur:—Greneweye,[13] Daves Croft, Farcenett, Whitsonfarthings—the latter being held at an annual rent of 13 pence payable at Pentecost[14]—Mylnefurlong, Singmeade or Snigmeade,[15] and Dirton Acres.[16] In 1634 it was asserted that Giles Washbourne and Thomas Ordway of Bengeworth had ploughed up a highway called 'The Procession Way' in Little Hampton, and John Clemens of Evesham had by hedging, ditching, and fencing, turned an ancient footway leading between Gloucester and Evesham from its ordinary course and forced travellers to go over 'the Corn Lane.'[17]

An Enclosure Act for Great and Little Hampton was passed in 1776.[18] The Enclosure Award is now in the custody of the clerk to the parish council.[19]

MANOR It appears that the abbey of Evesham was endowed at its foundation early in the eighth century with certain lands in Hampton; according to one authority these lands were the gift of Kenred of Mercia in 708,[20] while another states that they were bestowed on the abbey by Kenred and Offa jointly in the following year.[21] The evidence of a copy of the later grant shows that the lands conveyed comprised 9 'mansæ' in Hampton and Bengeworth, and from subsequent grants it would appear that 5 of these were in the former place.[22] Hampton is also said to have been included in the grant of Cropthorn, made by Offa of Mercia to the church of Worcester on 23 September, 780, and to have then consisted of 15 'mansæ.'[23] The convent of Evesham, however, seems to have remained in possession of the property originally granted to it until 988, when Ethelred the Unready seized its 5 'mansæ' and bestowed them on his servant Norman, to hold for the term of his life and to dispose of at his death to any

[1] *Digest of Endowed Char. Parl. Papers*, 1876, vol. lviii.; *List of Charities, Evesham Borough.*

[2] So described in *Digest of Endowed Char. Parl. Papers*, 1876, vol. lviii.; it does not appear in the printed *List of Charities, Borough of Evesham.*

[3] *Digest of Endowed Char. Parl. Papers*, 1900, vol. lxiii. See under Evesham.

[4] Called the Vincell in Nash, *Hist. of Worc.* Introd. I. lxxxvii.

[5] *V.C.H. Worc.* i. 307a.

[6] It is said to have been formerly known as Vineyard Hill. In a field book of a parish survey made probably by Nathan Izod in the early part of the nineteenth century a field on the western side is called 'The Vineyard.' Information supplied by Mr. O. G. Knapp.

[7] Cott. MS. Vesp. B. xxiv. f. 28.

[8] *Valor Eccl.* (Rec. Com.), iii. 249.

[9] Pat. 36 Hen. VIII. pt. 3, m. 6.

[10] *Journals of the Commons*, 19 March, 1727.

[11] Information supplied by Mr. O. G. Knapp from the *Evesham Journal.*

[12] Worc. Co. Coun. Handbk. 1903, p. 148.

[13] Anct. D. (P.R.O.), B. 4170.

[14] Pat. 15 Eliz. pt. 2.

[15] Ibid. 31 Eliz. pt. 14.

[16] Ibid. 10 Jas. I. pt. 5.

[17] *Quart. Sess. R.* (Worc. Hist. Soc.), 560, 575.

[18] Stat. 16 Geo. III. c. 49, Priv.

[19] Information supplied by Mr. Knapp.

[20] *Chron. de Evesham* (Rolls Ser.), 72.

[21] Birch, *Cart. Sax.* I. 183 from Cott. MS. Vesp. B. xxiv. f. 68.

[22] See later.

[23] Birch, *Cart. Sax.* I. 328. *Ann. Mon.* (Rolls Ser.), iv. 366. Mr. Round thinks this charter was forged by the Worcester monks to support their claim (*V.C.H. Worc.* i. 255).

heir he might appoint.[1] In this grant the Avon, the Isburne (Esburne) and the Merry Brook (Mœr brook) are mentioned as boundaries.[2] In 1017 Norman was put to death by King Cnut, and his possessions in Hampton were shortly afterwards granted to his brother and heir, Leofric, Earl of Coventry.[3] Early in the Confessor's reign the latter, jointly with Godiva his wife, restored the 5 'mansæ' which had thus come into his hands to the monks of Evesham[4]; the grant was confirmed by the king,[5] and probably took place between the years 1043 and 1044.[6] It seems that Hampton was again lost by the monks, but was recovered by Abbot Æthelwig between 1070 and 1077.[7] On the latter's death it is said to have been seized by Odo, bishop of Bayeux, whose claim was successfully opposed by Abbot Walter.[8] Hampton then became one of the subjects of the great dispute between the church of Evesham and that of Worcester,[9] and the actual result of the proceedings which followed seems to have been to confirm the former in possession while the bishop gained nothing, since the Domesday Survey states that he had no service from Hampton except the geld due to his hundred of Oswaldslow.[10] The abbey's property at Hampton at the time of the Survey comprised 5 hides, which were said to form part of Cropthorn,[11] one of the possessions of the bishop. A survey of the hundred of Oswaldslow taken during the early part of the twelfth century states that the abbot of Evesham held 15 hides at Hampton of the manor of Cropthorn, 5 hides paid geld, and 10 were free by the king's writ.[12]

Here, as in other manors of the monastery, Abbot Walter displaced some of the Saxon tenants by one of his own Norman relatives, giving to his sister Aubreye 3 hides and 1 virgate.[13] Contemporary with her was Ailward, who held 1½ virgates free.[14] It is quite possible that Aubreye's lands in Hampton were those surrendered to the abbey during the twelfth century by Ranulf and Simon of Coughton, the descendants of her brother Ranulf, in consideration of property in Staffordshire.[15]

In 1130 William de Melling and his brother Simon restored to Abbot Reginald and the convent certain lands belonging to the church of Evesham, which they held in Hampton and Norton, and placing their surrender upon the altar abjured all claim to them.[16] The abbot in return, 'from pure good will' (*pro caritate*), gave them 20 marks.[17] In the latter years of the twelfth or the beginning of the thirteenth century,[18] William Pintelthein held ½ a hide of land in Hampton by the service of going with his horse throughout England to carry the cloths which the monks made;[19] a further ½ virgate had also been granted to him at his wish by Abbot Adam, which had been held for many years by Arnold 'de Celario.'[20] William Pintelthein was quite possibly the 'William le Thein of Hampton' who in 1220–1 surrendered his land in Hampton by fine to Abbot Randolph.[21] Contemporary with him were Henry the clerk, who held ½ a hide, Ralph a virgate, Richard a virgate, Hugh Sorel a virgate, Geoffrey Marshall 2 acres, Perruc at Lorteburne, and Ralph Arnald who held a croft called Lillinghom.[22]

In 1206 the precentor of the abbey received from certain land in Hampton[23] 5*s.* yearly, which was applied towards the finding of ink for the writers and colours for illuminating, and necessaries for binding and for the organs;[24] the sacristan also received a similar sum from land there.[25]

Towards the subsidy of about 1280 Hampton rendered £10 4*s.* 10*d.*, of which the abbot paid £2 13*s.* 4*d.*[26] For some reason which does not appear, Hampton is omitted from the temporalities of the abbey of Evesham in the taxation of 1291, and little is known of it during the middle ages except that Abbot John Ombersley towards the end of the fourteenth century decided to let it out to farm.[27] In 1535 the demesne lands were under lease, and in 1539 the manor came into the hands of the Crown.[28] On 5 August, 1541, certain lands in Hampton were granted to Sir Philip Hoby with the site of the monastery of Evesham,[29] but the manor itself remained in the Crown until 1566, when Queen Elizabeth granted it with Bretforton (q.v.) to Robert Dudley, earl of Leicester.[30] On 8 July, 1575, Leicester received a confirmatory grant to himself and his heirs with the condition that he should pay £4 annually from the issues of the manor towards the salary of the curate there.[31] In 1580 he levied a fine by which he conveyed Great and Little Hampton to Sir John Huband, his high steward, John Dudley and John Nuthall,[32] probably in trust. On 9 January, 1580–1, another grant was made to him of the manor of Great and Little Hampton to hold in chief

DUDLEY. *Gold a lion vert with a forked tail.*

[1] Cott. MS. Vesp. B. xxiv. f. 30; *Chron. de Evesham* (Rolls Ser.), 84. The latter states that these lands were taken away from the monastery in the time of Edmund Ironside (1016).

[2] Cott. MS. Vesp. B. xxiv. f. 30.

[3] Ibid. and *Chron. de Evesham* (Rolls Ser.), 84.

[4] Ibid.

[5] Cott. MS. Vesp. B. xxiv. f. 30d.

[6] Living, bishop of Worcester, is mentioned as a witness, and as he died on 23 March, 1045–6 (Stubbs' *Episcopal Succession*), and another witness, Stigand, bishop of Elmham, was consecrated in 1043 (ibid.), the grant must have taken place between those dates. Eadsive, archbishop of Canterbury, and Aelfric, archbishop of York, also witnessed the grant.

[7] *Chron. de Evesham* (Rolls Ser.), 94.

[8] Ibid. 97.

[9] See *V.C.H. Worc.* i. 253 et seq.

[10] Ibid. 297a.

[11] Ibid. 297a, and 307a.

[12] *V.C.H. Worc.* i. 325b. Another survey, however (Cott. MS. Vesp. B. xxiv. f. 6), taken probably about the middle of the twelfth century, states that it only contained five hides, and that these were in Oswaldslow.

[13] Cott. MS. Vesp. B. xxiv. f. 49d.

[14] Ibid.

[15] See under Abbot's Morton and Bretforton.

[16] Cott. MS. Vesp. B. xxiv. f. 27.

[17] Ibid.

[18] It was after the time of Abbot Adam (1160–1191), 'Abbas Adam ei accommodavit, ad tempus pro Judea, quam predictus Willielmus duxit in uxorem.' Cott. MS. Vesp. B. xxiv. f. 31d.

[19] Ibid. He 'gelded with the others and made service to the king, "et debet ire cum runcio suo per totam Angliam ad portandum pannos cujuslibet monachi in expensa abbatis."'

[20] Ibid.

[21] Feet of F. Worc. 5 Hen. III. no. 29.

[22] Cott. MS. Vesp. B. xxiv. f. 31d.

[23] Ibid.

[24] *Chron. de Evesham* (Rolls Ser.), 210.

[25] Ibid. 211.

[26] *Lay Subs. R.* c. 1280 (Worc. Hist. Soc.), 81.

[27] *Chron. de Evesham* (Rolls Ser.), 303.

[28] Mins. Accts. 31–2 Hen. VIII. L.R. 1330, m. 10d.

[29] *L. and P. Hen. VIII.* xvi. 721.

[30] Pat. 8 Eliz. pt. 7, m. 26.

[31] Ibid. 15 Eliz. pt. 2, m. 20.

[32] Feet of F. Div. Cos. Hil. 22 Eliz.

by the service of a fifteenth part of a knight's fee and the annual rent of £38 16*s.* 6¾*d.*,[1] but it does not appear why this grant was necessary. In the following year the earl of Leicester conveyed this manor with that of Bretforton (q.v.) to Sir John Huband and John Nuthall, and Hampton afterwards passed with the latter manor to Ambrose, earl of Warwick.[2] In 1589 the latter, with Anne his wife, had licence from the Crown to convey it to Ralph Hockenhull,[3] who seems to have been a maker of saltpetre of the city of London,[4] and accordingly a fine was levied in Easter term of that year by which Ralph and George Hockenhull acquired it.[5] About the same time the earl of Warwick and others had licence to alienate to Edmund Langston a part of the demesne lands.[6]

Some years afterwards, on 11 October, 1616, John Martin is said to have died seised of the manor or manors of Great and Little Hampton, which he held of the Crown,[7] but there is no evidence to show when this property had passed into his possession. He was succeeded by his son William, then aged thirty-six,[8] who had livery of the manor on 25 November, 1616.[9] It would appear from subsequent evidence that the manor shortly afterwards became subdivided, and the fee farm rent issuing from it was paid by the various tenants.[10] The Martin family in 1652–3 held only a portion of the demesne lands, and their property is said to have consisted of a part of the 'great farm of Little Hampton.'[11] In 1652–3 John Hill, to whom the fee farm rent had passed, sued John Barnard, William Stiles, Thomas Thorne, Giles Harewell, clerk, Thomas Martin, William Martin, and Robert Martin for its payment,[12] and again in 1661 he brought an action against Robert Martin and others for the same purpose.[13] One of the witnesses in the former suit stated that there were then two or three freeholders and some leaseholders in Great and Little Hampton, that the leases were held for 2,000 years, and had been granted in the time of Queen Elizabeth, and confirmed in the time of King James.

Although it would thus appear that the manor had fallen into abeyance, it was dealt with during the eighteenth century by the Dineleys of Charlton. In the reign of Elizabeth they had acquired the right of free fishing in the Avon and the Isbourne in Great and Little Hampton,[14] and in 1658 Edward Dineley, afterwards knighted, had dealt with land and rent there.[15] In 1666 John Martin and his wife Mary conveyed to him a small quantity of land in Little Hampton,[16] and probably he purchased other parts of the manor. Apparently the first member of the Dineley family who dealt with the whole manor of Great and Little Hampton was Sir John Dineley Goodere, grandson of Sir Edward Dineley, who immediately after succeeding to the estates in 1739 jointly with his only son Edward, who died shortly afterwards, suffered a recovery to bar the entail.[17] For some years afterwards the manor of Hampton followed the same descent as that of Charlton.[18] When unhappy family quarrels had ended in the murder of Sir John Dineley Goodere on board the *Ruby* man-of-war at Bristol on 17 January, 1740–1, and the execution of his brother, Captain Samuel Dineley Goodere,[19] R.N., for his instigation of the crime, Hampton passed with the other Dineley estates to John Dineley or Foote, nephew of Sir John and brother of Samuel Foote, the celebrated comedian.[20] John Dineley Foote dealt with it in 1741,[21] and some time afterwards it passed to his cousin Edward Dineley Goodere, the elder son of Captain Goodere, who in 1751 suffered a recovery by which Hampton passed to one John Pitt,[22] but it is not clear whether this was an actual conveyance or simply for the purposes of a trust. Goodere, who died a lunatic in 1761, was the last of his family to hold Hampton. In the Enclosure Act of 1776 one Thomas Ramell is styled lord of the manor.[23] In 1765 he had conveyed land and rents there to Charles Beaufoy,[24] and he was probably succeeded in Hampton by the Beaufoy family.

Dineley. *Silver a fesse sable with a molet between two roundels sable in the chief.*

In the early part of the nineteenth century the manor was held by John Hanbury Beaufoy of Upton Gray, Hampshire, who died on 28 November, 1836. His Hampton property appears to have been vested in Louisa, the wife of Robert Toovey Hawley of Bridgefield, Hampshire, for his life, with remainder to her son Henry John Toovey Hawley in tail male.[25] The latter died on 20 May, 1874, leaving a son and heir William Henry Toovey Hawley, and Mrs. Hawley died on 20 December, 1875. By this time the estate was heavily encumbered, and having been disentailed, was conveyed on 3 April, 1876, to George Thomas Woodroffe of New Square, Lincoln's Inn, who sold it on 17 October, 1876, to James Goddington Ledsam of Weoley Park, Selly Oak. The latter sold the estate by auction on 3 June, 1889, when the house and reputed manor were bought by Thomas

[1] Pat. 23 Eliz. pt. 3, m. 13. The yearly rent of £38 16*s.* 6*d.* arising from the manor of Great and Little Hampton was granted by Queen Elizabeth to Thomas Greene, 1602-3 (Pat. 45 Eliz. pt. 1). On 16 February, 1613-4, it was granted to Queen Anne for her life (ibid. 11 Jas. I. pt. 13), and on 19 January, 1619-20, it was granted to Lawrence Whitaker and others (ibid. 17 Jas. I. pt. 3). Richard Hill and Grace his wife, John Hill, of Hollowe, and Susan his wife conveyed it by fine to John Hill, of Gray's Inn, in 1647. (Feet of F. Worc. Mich. 23 Chas. I.).

[2] Pat. 28 Eliz. pt. 11, m. 39. Camden states that Robert Dudley, earl of Leicester, having erected a hospital in the town of Warwick, willed and directed that his brother the earl of Warwick should make good any deficit in its revenues from the manor of Great Hampton in Worcestershire (*Magna Brit.* vi. 222).

[3] Pat. 31 Eliz. pt. 14, m. 14.

[4] *Cal. of S. P. Dom.* 1581-90, p. 612-3.

[5] Feet of F. Worc. East. 31 Eliz.

[6] Pat. 31 Eliz. pt. 14, m.

[7] Chan. inq. p.m. 14 Jas. I. ccclv. 77.

[8] Ibid.

[9] Fine R. 14 Jas. I. pt. 1, no. 18.

[10] Exch. Dep. Hil. 1652-3, no. 9.

[11] Ibid.

[12] Ibid.

[13] Ibid. Mich. 13 Chas. II. no. 3.

[14] Feet of F. East. Worc. 39 Eliz.; see also ibid. East. 12 Chas. I.

[15] Ibid. 1658.

[16] Ibid. Hil. 17 and 18 Chas. II.

[17] Com. Pleas Recov. R. Hil. 12 Geo. II. m. 8.

[18] For the full descent of the Dineley family see Charlton, Cropthorn.

[19] See *Dict. Nat. Biog.*

[20] Ibid.

[21] Com. Pleas Recov. R. Hil. 15 Geo. II. m. 193.

[22] Ibid. Mich. 25 Geo. II. m. 45.

[23] Stat. 16 Geo. III. cap. 49.

[24] Com. Pleas Recov. R. Trin. 5 Geo. III. m. 195. In 1713 one Mark Romell had dealt with land in Hampton. Ibid. Trin. 12 Anne, m. 59.

[25] Information supplied by Mr. O. G. Knapp, of Bengeworth, from documents in his possession. Mr. Beaufoy's will was dated 4 December, 1823, and proved P.C.C. 9 February, 1837.

William Butler, M.R.C.V.S., of Bengeworth, the present owner.[1] The manorial rights have apparently long fallen into disuse.

A grange is said to have been built at Hampton by Abbot John of Brokehampton (1282–1317),[2] but no trace of it now exists.

The Domesday Survey states that there were then two mills at Hampton,[3] but in the thirteenth century and subsequently only one is mentioned.[4] In 1538 a watermill with a fishery was leased by the abbot and convent to Thomas Dingley or Dineley and Agnes his wife and their heirs for sixty-two years at a yearly rent of 46*s.* 8*d.*[5] The lord was to keep the mill in repair, and if the mill at Evesham could not be worked by reason of floods, then the abbot might grind at the mill of Hampton without paying toll.[6] This mill was included in the grant of the manor to the earl of Leicester on 8 July, 1573.[7] It is still in existence and stands on the River Isbourne about a quarter of a mile from the village of Little Hampton. The fishery which the Dingleys held with the mill seems to have been in the River Isbourne, and extended from the croft called Dames or Danes Croft, formerly belonging to the sacrist of the abbey, to the fields of the lord of Hinton (Hinton on the Green) [8] in Gloucestershire. In 1597 William Savage conveyed the right of free fishing in the Isbourne and the Avon to Francis Dineley and his son Francis,[9] and this right was afterward dealt with by the descendants of the latter.[10]

A fishery in the River Avon within the manor of Hampton was also granted to Sir Philip Hoby and his heirs to hold in socage on 2 July, 1547.[11]

CHURCH The church is dedicated in honour of St. Andrew, and stands on rising ground on the left bank of the Avon, and close to the main road from Pershore to Evesham. The building is all of one date, and the record of the building of a chancel [12] here by Abbot John of Brokehampton (1282-1316) refers to an older church, of which nothing is left standing, though pieces of twelfth-century stonework are to be seen built into the walls. The church consists of chancel with modern north vestry, nave with south porch, and tower between nave and chancel. With the exception of the vestry, the rebuilt east wall of the chancel, and the south porch, the whole is of one date, c. 1400, good, solid work, with large and simple details, and walling of rubble masonry with ashlar dressings. The roofs are covered with stone slates. The east window of the chancel [13] is of three trefoiled lights with tracery in the head; the north wall is blocked by the vestry, and in the south wall are two windows, one of two trefoiled lights, and the other, at the west end, of a simple cinquefoiled light under a square head. Between these windows is a plain doorway. There is a plain piscina and no sedilia.

The tower is narrower than the nave, whose north and south walls enclose it, forming bays on each side covered internally with pointed barrel vaults, and externally with flat-pitched roofs of stone slabs. Each bay is lighted by a window of two trefoiled lights under a straight-sided four-centred head. This form of arch is common in the district in the fifteenth century, and occurs in all the nave windows of the church, an early instance of its use. The tower is of three stages, with unusually large angle dressings. It has an embattled parapet with pinnacles and gargoyles at the angles. The four belfry windows are of two trefoiled lights with no tracery in the head. The lowest stage of the tower has a ribbed vault with a bell-way in the crown of the vault, and opens to nave and chancel with massive pointed arches of two orders with large hollow chamfers; the mouldings are continuous, finishing on large stops three feet from the floor level. On either side of the east arch, on both east and west faces, are stone corbels about 10 feet from the floor, to carry the front and back beams of the roodloft. At the north-east angle of the tower is a projecting vice, which also served as the rood stair; the doorway which opened to the roodloft remains, having a modern door made up of old material. The vice is entered by a doorway in the north-west angle of the chancel, which retains its ancient door.

The nave has on each side two two-light windows of the same type as those north and south of the tower, with north and south doorways between the windows. The north doorway is blocked, and has a plain double chamfered arch of two orders. The south doorway has a four-centred arch under a square head with carving in the spandrils. Over it is built a stone porch, of the fifteenth century, but an addition to the original design. It has a roof of stone slabs carried on arches, and an outer archway with a square head over a four-centred arch with pierced spandrels. Over the arch is a plain niche. In the east jamb of the south doorway, outside, is a recess once containing a holy-water stone.

The west window of the nave is of three trefoiled lights with tracery of two sixfoiled openings in the head. There are diagonal buttresses at the western angles of the nave, which is much overgrown with ivy. A plinth of good detail runs round the nave walls. Where not hidden by the ivy it may be seen that the lower parts of the nave wall above the plinths are mostly faced with wrought stone, while the upper parts are in rubble work, suggesting a re-use of the materials of the previously existing church, as far as they served.

The plan of the church, unusual at the time of its building, gives a very effective proportion to the interior, which is elaborately decorated with modern painting.

The font is ancient, with a plain tapering round bowl on a square base; it is probably of the twelfth or thirteenth century, but has no detail which might help to fix its date. The chancel roof retains its old trusses; pieces of carved Jacobean woodwork have been used to make a reredos and panelling on the east wall of the chancel. The pulpit is modern, carved in Jacobean style. There were five bells by W. Bagley, 1702; there are now six, by Carr of Smethwick. The church plate [14] consists of a modern chalice and paten, purchased in 1860, and an Elizabethan cup with paten cover of 1571. The cup is

1 Information supplied by Mr. O. G. Knapp.
2 *Chron. de Evesham* (Rolls Ser.), 287.
3 *V. C. H. Worc.* i. 307a.
4 *Chron. de Evesham* (Rolls Ser.), 211. *Valor Eccl.* (Rec. Com.), 250.
5 Mins. Accts. 31-2 Hen. VIII. L.R. 1330, m. 10d.
6 Ibid.
7 Pat. 15 Eliz. pt. 2, m. 20.
8 Mins. Accts. 31-2 Hen. VIII. L.R. 1330, m. 10d.
9 Feet of F. Worc. East. 39 Eliz.
10 Ibid. East. 12 Chas. I.
11 Pat. 1 Edw. VI. pt. 9; Chan. inq. p.m. 5 and 6 Phil. and Mary, cxv. 74.
12 *Chron. de Evesham* (Rolls Ser.), 287.
13 Reset in a rebuilt wall.
14 Lea, *Ch. Plate Worc. Archd.* 32.

cracked and not in use. The registers begin in 1539.[1]

In the churchyard near the south porch are the base and steps of a cross; the base is panelled with quatrefoils.

In 1904, after the writing of this account, a north chapel and vestry were added to the chancel, overlapping the tower. The north window of the tower was taken out and reset as the east window of the new chapel. All the modern paintings were removed, and the woodwork at the east end.

ADVOWSON The church of Hampton, like most of the churches in the vale, was a chapelry of the mother church of Evesham until the dissolution.[2] From that time the advowson followed the same descent as Badsey (q. v.), and is now held by the dean and chapter of Christ Church, Oxford. The living is a rectory impropriate.[3] A grant of £500 towards building a parsonage was made by the Ecclesiastical Commissioners out of the Common Fund in 1881.[4]

CHARITIES John Martin by will dated 28 February, 1713, left £10 yearly to the minister of Hampton, 25*s.* for teaching poor children to read and to learn the Church Catechism, 10*s.* for bread to the poor on Christmas Day, and 5*s.* to the parish clerk. The residue of his rents was to be applied towards apprenticing boys and girls whose parents lived in the parish of Hampton; and he further directed that lands should be purchased for the use and benefit of the minister of Hampton for ever.[5] This charity now produces a gross income of £207, of which £169 10*s.* is spent on education, £15 on apprenticing, the minister receives £10, any addition to this sum having been declined, £2 10*s.* is expended on coals and bread for the poor, while the remaining £10 is given to the parish of Bengeworth.[6] A dame school was started under this bequest, but replaced by the public elementary school, now a council school, built partly by money from this charity in 1873, under a scheme of the Charity Commissioners.[7]

Henry Workman by will proved 22 January, 1889, bequeathed a sum which has been invested in Consols to the amount of £205 13*s.* 1*d.*; from the interest and dividends, amounting to £5 13*s.*, clothing is distributed to poor people, whether receiving parochial relief or not, on Christmas Eve.[8]

John Pitts by will proved 1884 bequeathed a sum of £500 to be invested and its income distributed in kind to the poor of Hampton on 12 December yearly. As in the case of Evesham (q. v.) and other places mentioned in the bequest, this sum was much reduced by the insufficiency of the testator's pure personal estate, and the payment of the reduced sum is still delayed pending the settlement of certain proceedings in court.[9]

NORTH AND MIDDLE LITTLETON

Lutleton (viii. cent.); Luthlet, North Luttelton (xiii. cent.).

The parish of North and Middle Littleton lies on the eastern border of the county. It extends from the Avon to the Roman Road known as Icknield Street, which in the Saxon boundaries of the Evesham lands is described as 'the old way which the natives call No Man's Land, otherwise Buckle Street' ('Buggildestret').[10]

The parish contains 1,706 acres and 78 inhabited houses.[11] The land rises gradually from east to west, where Cleeve Hill, partly in this parish and partly in that of Cleeve Prior, is 200 feet above the Ordnance datum; at the extreme west of the parish also the land rises to the same height. The subsoil is almost wholly of lower lias, but at Cleeve Hill from the level of the Avon upwards the marl of the Keuper and the black shales of the Rhœtic formation are exposed. On the top of the terrace the surface soil is dark and of good quality, and to the east of the parish is a stiff but not poor clay. The parish is almost wholly agricultural, but market gardening is gradually extending over a great portion of it. The road from Cleeve Prior to South Littleton passes from north to south through the parish, sending out branches westward to Offenham and eastward to the villages of North and Middle Littleton respectively. A road running eastward connects the villages with Pebworth in Gloucestershire.

The villages of North and Middle Littleton are adjacent, and are situated in the centre of the parish, about half a mile from the Cleeve Prior and South Littleton road. The nearest railway station is Littleton and Badsey, on the Oxford, Worcester, and Wolverhampton branch of the Great Western Railway; it is two miles away, and was opened in April, 1884.

Papermaking was carried on here early in the nineteenth century, and became a somewhat important industry in the neighbourhood, employing many hands; but the business becoming unprofitable, the extensive buildings fell into ruin and were finally taken down. There was before the introduction of railways an active business carried on in the stone and lime trade. The quarrymen lived in both North and South Littleton, but most of the quarries were in North and Middle Littleton. Flagstones of good quality were raised, and among the workers were some skilled handicraftsmen,[12] as is shown by the elaborately worked headstones in the churchyards. This trade has now vanished.

Among the place-names in the parish are Hossage, Harrow Hill, Pickersham Meadow, and Short Dole. At the south end of Cleeve Hill is a mound having the appearance of an ancient tumulus, which can hardly be the result of quarrying; and to the north of this there is a low embankment along the ridge of the hill which may indicate Roman work. In the field between the village and Cleeve Hill fragments of

[1] *Dioc. Conf.* 1899, *Digest of Par. Reg.* 17.

[2] *Pope Nich. Tax.* (Rec. Com.), 219*b*; *Valor Eccl.* (Rec. Com.), 111, 256. In 1535 it was on lease for the term of his life to John Higgins, chaplain and curate, who, in his will dated 4 October, 1588, describes himself as vicar of Cropthorne, and desires to be buried there.

[3] Parl. Surv. of Ch. Liv. Lambeth.

[4] *Lond. Gaz.* 10 June, 1881, 2963.

[5] *Char. Commrs. Rep.* xxiv. 522.

[6] *Digest of Endowed Charities, Parl. Papers*, 1876, vol. 58.

[7] Ibid.

[8] Ibid. 1900, vol. lxiii.

[9] Ibid.

[10] Birch, *Cart. Sax.* i. 184.

[11] *Worc. Co. Coun. Handbk.* (1903), 148.

[12] R. F. Tomes, *Littleton Notes* in the *Evesham Standard.*

imperfectly-burned glazed pottery are thickly scattered over the surface of the land, and with them are sometimes associated much-corroded small coins of Roman appearance.

Camden states that there was formerly a medicinal spring upon the top of a hill called Harrow Hill in North and Middle Littleton, and that it was 'of a sovereign virtue for the cleansing of sore and ulcerated eyes, and though the water of it is of a soft taste, yet by its distillations from the rock it naturally petrifies things thrown into it.'[1]

It appears that until 1540 the three Littletons formed one parish, which was known as Middle Littleton.[2] The Act for the enclosure of North and Middle Littleton and for making compensation for tithes was passed in 1811.[3] A survey of the manor taken in 1557 states that there were then upon the lordship 'many fair elmes.'[4]

MANOR Thirteen 'mansæ' in Littleton formed part of the endowment of the monastery of Evesham at its foundation early in the eighth century; this grant is said to have included 'the three Littletons,' and is claimed by one of the chartularies[5] of the abbey to have been made by Ethelred of Mercia in 703, while another[6] states that it was made by Kenred and Offa five years later. From that time until the suppression of the house in the sixteenth century the Littletons were held uninterruptedly by the abbot and convent of Evesham. Abbot Walter alienated a portion of the abbey's lands here, as in other places. To his brother Ranulf he granted 2½ hides,[7] and to Hugh Travers 5 virgates, without the consent of his chapter.[8] Neither of these holders are mentioned in the Domesday Survey, though they were probably then in possession. The Littletons were at that time divided into two parts, one containing 7 hides and forming a distinct manor,[9] the other 6 hides, forming part of the manor of Offenham.[10] The former may correspond to North and Middle Littleton, and the latter, as it adjoins Offenham and Bretforton, which was also attached to Offenham, might be South Littleton.

Ranulf's lands in Littleton probably descended to the Coughton family with his property in Abbot's Morton and Bretforton (q.v.) During the thirteenth century the Coughton family appear to have parted with their property in the Littletons, and about the reign of Edward I. their 2½ hides were held by Hugh de Norfolk and Adam de la Lee.[11] Major-General Wrottesley states that the former was tenant by courtesy, being the second husband of Joan, daughter and co-heir of Simon Coughton.[12] The subsequent history of the Coughton lands in Littleton has not been ascertained.

Towards the end of the twelfth century Payne Travers had succeeded to Hugh Travers's 5 virgates,[13] for which he owed knight service;[14] and among other tenants, Payne son of Henry, held 9 virgates, Richard son of Augustine 1 hide, Ralph Despenser 3 virgates, and Geoffrey Withelard 1 virgate; the last three named paid geld.[15] The alienations which had taken place must have considerably reduced the value of the Littletons to the monastery. The abbot paid only 2 marks towards the subsidy of about 1280, while the whole amount paid was £4 6*s.* 8*d.*, more than the total value of the abbey's property in 1291, which was only £4 4*s.* 7*d.*[16] Considering the extent of the Littletons this was a very small amount, but gradually a portion at least of the alienated land seems to have been re-acquired by the convent. In 1206 Ralph Despenser's land had been bought and given to the prior;[17] and Abbot John of Brokehampton, about the end of the thirteenth or the beginning of the fourteenth century, acquired for the convent a messuage and 3 virgates of land in South Littleton which had belonged to Peter Grynel.[18] On 15 October, 1313, John of Whitchurch, perhaps a relative of Abbot William of Whitchurch, had licence to alienate in mortmain to the abbot and convent a virgate and 5 acres of land and 20*s.* of rent in Littleton to find a chaplain to celebrate divine service daily in the church of St. Egwin, Evesham, 'for his soul and the souls of his ancestors, and for all Christian souls.'[19] He had previously in the reign of Edward I. given the monks a certain rent there without the king's licence, for which he was afterwards pardoned.[20] The property which he thus bestowed on the convent was worth altogether 65*s.* 10*d.* yearly.[21] On 27 May, 1315, John de Littleton had a similar licence to convey to the abbot and convent a messuage, 3 virgates, and 8 acres of meadow in Littleton—apparently then let to Avice de Bampton—which were of their fee and worth £2 18*s.* 4*d.* yearly.[22] This property is elsewhere stated, however, to have consisted of only 12 acres and to have been in North Littleton.[23] Besides these, Abbot William of Chiriton also acquired a messuage and a carucate of land in South Littleton which had belonged to Adam le Boteler, and a messuage and a virgate which had been held by Henry Payne.[24] Two tenements and 2 virgates in North Littleton were afterwards obtained by Abbot William Boys,[25] and in 1392 Richard Plomer and others granted tenements in mortmain in South Littleton and elsewhere to the monastery.[26] In 1535 the value of the abbey's property in the three Littletons had increased to £37 16*s.* 4*d.* Middle Littleton was evidently then regarded as the chief manor, to which North and South Littleton were attached.[27] On 16 December, 1538, the abbot and convent granted a lease to John Aldington of Middle Littleton, yeoman, Margaret his wife, and Thomas and John his sons, of 'all that their scite or mansion place and mansion' of their manor of Middle Littleton, with the demesne lands, and tithes of wool, lambs, and hay for seventy years at the yearly rent of 24 quarters of barley and 12 quarters of wheat, good and clear winnowed, to be delivered on the 25th March; £6 rent at Michaelmas, four

[1] *Mag. Brit.* vi. 224.
[2] Mins. Accts. 31–2 Hen. VIII. L.R. 1330, m. 17.
[3] Stat. 51 Geo. III. cap. 35.
[4] Harl. MS. 606, f. 18.
[5] *Chron. de Evesham* (Rolls Ser.), 71.
[6] Birch, *Cart. Sax.* i. 183, from Cott. MS. Vesp. B. xxiv. f. 68. This charter is supposed by Kemble to be spurious.
[7] Cott. MS. Vesp. B. xxiv. ff. 6, 11 *d.*
[8] Ibid.
[9] *V.C.H. Worc.* i. 307 *a.*
[10] Ibid. 306 *b.*
[11] Harl. MS. 3763, f. 168.
[12] *Hist. of Family of Wrottesley*, 17.
[13] Cott. MS. Vesp. B. xxiv. f. 11 *d.* 12.
[14] Ibid. and *Exch. Red Bk.* (Rolls Ser.), 301.
[15] Cott. MS. Vesp. B. xxiv. f. 12.
[16] *Pope Nich. Tax.* (Rec. Com.), 229.
[17] *Chron. de Evesham* (Rolls Ser.), 208.
[18] Ibid. 285.
[19] *Cal. of Pat.* 1313–17, p. 28–9.
[20] Ibid. p. 397.
[21] *Chron. de Evesham* (Rolls Ser.), 285.
[22] *Cal. of Pat.* 1313–17, p. 291.
[23] *Chron. de Evesham* (Rolls Ser.), 290.
[24] Ibid.
[25] Ibid. 295.
[26] Ibid. 306, and Inq. a. q.d. 16 Rich. II. pt. 1, no. 155.
[27] *Valor Eccl.* (Rec. Com.), iii. 250.

great loaves, each loaf containing 'the tere of a strike of wheat,' and two capons on the feast of St. Stephen as before time it hath been used and accustomed.[1]

In 1557 the manor of Middle Littleton, with North and South Littleton, was granted to John Elliott and Alexander Chesnoll, apparently for the use of the former,[2] who is described as citizen and 'merchant venturer' of Bow Churchyard, London.[3] He sold the manors shortly afterwards to James Longworth, who held a court for them in 1558, and a little later conveyed them to Sir Rowland Hill, knight, of London.[4] The latter seems to have settled the Littletons on his niece Alice, daughter of John Barker or Coverall of Wolverton, and on her marriage with Sir Thomas Leigh[5] they passed to the Leigh family. Sir Thomas Leigh was Lord Mayor of London in 1558; he died in 1571 seised of 'the manors of North, Middle, and South Littleton,' which he held in chief by knight service.[6] His son Roland Leigh, thirty-one years of age, was the next heir, but the Littletons continued in the possession of his mother Alice. In 1575 she conveyed them to John Croftes, Nowell Lloyd, and John Freer, probably in trust.[7] They seem to have next passed to Sir William Leigh of Newnham Regis, Warwickshire, third surviving son of Sir Thomas Leigh, who in 1593 conveyed them by fine to his elder brother Thomas Leigh of Stoneleigh, afterwards knighted.[8]

HILL. *Azure two bars silver with a quarter of the arms of* WILBRAHAM of Woodhey, which are *sable a cheveron silver between three broad arrow heads silver with a wolf's head razed sable and two molets gules on the cheveron.*

In 1598, Sir Thomas Leigh, by a fine to which Sir William Leigh, and his son Francis Leigh, and John Leigh, were parties, conveyed the manors to William Bond, the son of his sister Winifred, who had married Sir George Bond, Lord Mayor of London.[9] John Colles and Winifred his wife, possibly the daughter of Sir George Bond, made another conveyance to the same effect,[10] and in the following year, jointly with William Bond and his wife Katherine, conveyed the manor to William Quarles, Leonard Barr, and Richard Wright, probably for the purposes of a settlement.[11] In 1605, William Leigh, son and heir of Roland Leigh and grandson of Sir Thomas Leigh, who had not been a party to any of the above conveyances, levied a fine[12] by which he conveyed all his interest in the manor to his cousin William Bond, who had then been knighted.

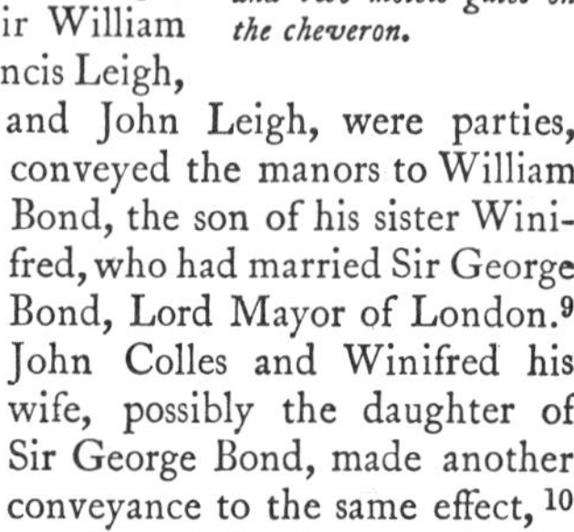

LEIGH. *Gules a cross engrailed silver with a silver lozenge in the quarter.*

In 1609 Sir William Bond and his wife Katherine levied a fine by which the Manor of Middle Littleton, apparently including North Littleton, was sold to Sir Matthew Carew, Master in Chancery, 'a knight practised in wars abroad and well beloved at home,'[13] and Alice his wife,[14] and from this date South Littleton had a separate descent.

BOND. *Silver a cheveron sable with three bezants.*

North and Middle Littleton afterwards passed to Edward, son of Sir Matthew Carew, who jointly with his wife Eleanor dealt with them as 'manors' in 1655, when they were conveyed to Francis Kenward,[15] and again in 1659 when they were conveyed to Robert Raworth and Thomas Prichard.[16]

In 1690 the manor of North and Middle Littleton had passed into the possession of Sir James Rushout, baronet, who then dealt with it by fine,[17] and from that time it has remained in the Rushout family; Lord Northwick, who died in 1887, devised it to his wife for life, and she is lady of the manor at the present time.

In Elizabeth's reign free fishing in the Avon pertained to the manor.[18]

May, in his *History of Evesham*, states that Mr. Fisher Tomes, of Welford, near Stratford-on-Avon, in 1845 had in his possession an original court roll of the manors of Littleton from 1525 to 1539.[19]

CHURCH

Middle Littleton[20] church stands to the east of the manor house on a level site. It consists of chancel with north vestry and organ chamber, north and south transepts, nave with south porch, and west tower. It was much 'restored' in 1871, and in the Prattinton MSS. there is a statement that it was 'ceiled, beautified, and repaired, in the year of our Lord 1793, by Smith, of Pebworth, architect.' Before 1871 the chancel appears to have been of the end of the thirteenth century; it is now modern, retaining an original east window of three trefoiled lights under an arched head, pierced in the spandrels between the heads of the lights, and in the north wall a single thirteenth-century lancet. In the same wall an arch opens to a modern vestry and organ chamber, in which is a sixteenth-century wooden chest with a linen-pattern panel at one end. In the south wall of the chancel are two lancets and one three-light window, all modern; the chancel arch is also modern. The north transept is of the fourteenth century, having in its

[1] Prattinton Coll. (Soc. Antiq.) from a lease in the possession of Edward Rudge in July, 1817. The 12 quarters of wheat and 24 quarters of barley were leased on 23 February, 1539–40, to Sir George Throckmorton for an annual rent of £7 4*s.*; the lease was renewed in 1552 (Pat. 31 Hen. VIII. and ibid. 6 Edw. VI. m. 6.).

[2] Pat. 3 and 4 Phil. and Mary, pt. ix. An extent of the manor at this time appears in Harl. MS. 606, f. 17–18.

[3] Chan. Proc. Ser. ii. bdle. 94, No. 1.

[4] Ibid.

[5] Burke's *Peerage*.

[6] Chan. inq. p.m. 14 Eliz. clxi. 91.

[7] Feet of F. Div. Cos. Mich. 17–18, Eliz.

[8] Ibid. Worc. East. 35 Eliz.

[9] Feet of F. Worc. Hil. 40 Eliz.

[10] Ibid.

[11] Ibid. Mich. 41-2, Eliz.

[12] Ibid. Mich. 3 Jas. I.

[13] Habington, *Surv. of Worc.* (Worc. Hist. Soc.), says that 'Inquiring of an inhabitant here, who though very plain in appearance yet was witty and not unlearned, how many in succession were lords of Middle Littleton since the abbey's reign, he answered the owners changed so often as they confounded his memory.'

[14] Feet of F. Worc. Hil. 7 Jas. I.

[15] Ibid. Trin. 1655.

[16] Ibid. East. 1659.

[17] Ibid. Hil. 2 Wm. and Mary.

[18] Ibid. Div. Cos. Mich. 17-18 Eliz.; Ibid. Worc. East. 35 Eliz.; Ibid. Hil. 40 Eliz.

[19] *Hist. of Evesham*, 238-9.

[20] There is no church at North Littleton.

east wall a trefoiled single light of that date, and a trefoiled piscina with a shelf. The north window is also of the fourteenth century, of two trefoiled lights with a quatrefoil in the head. There is a modern arch between transept and nave. The south transept is a chapel built by Thomas Smith, who by his will dated 14 October, 1532, bequeathed to his chapel a sum of money and a cow, and a chalice and vestments, desiring that he should be buried in it. His brass has long disappeared. Prattinton,[1] who visited the church in July, 1817, says that the stone robbed of its brass still remained, and a small figure of a man with a cap or bonnet and a gown, and at his feet an oblong space for the inscription, could still be traced. Habington[2] gives the inscription in full: 'Praye for the soule of Thomas Smithe who under the License of my Lord Abbot of Ewsham, made this chapele of his proper cost, on whose soule Jhesu haue mercy. Amen.' The chapel is lighted by an east and two south windows, all of three cinquefoiled lights under a square head. The parapet is embattled.

The nave is of the thirteenth century. Of the north wall nearly the whole has been rebuilt and two modern windows inserted; the blocked north doorway remains, just to the west of the north transept. It is of plain fourteenth-century work, with a continuous chamfer on its outer arch and jambs. The south doorway is modern. It opens to a large fourteenth-century porch, which has had an upper room, now destroyed, lighted through a slit in the south gable. Smith's chapel is built against its east wall. The windows in the south wall of the nave are (1) a three light fifteenth-century window with a segmental-arched head, and (2) a thirteenth-century lancet. On the western buttress of this wall is a mediæval sundial. In the west wall of the nave is a fifteenth-century doorway into the tower, of the same character and workmanship as that at Offenham, with large roughly carved spandrels and a battlemented cornice with pateræ over the arch. On either side of it are the jambs and rear arches of thirteenth-century lancets, blocked by the building of the west tower. The heads of these windows are higher than those in the nave. They cannot have long remained open, as the tower, though obviously not contemplated when they were built, appears itself to be of the thirteenth century as regards its lower stages, having lancets in its west and south walls on the ground stage, perhaps the west windows of the nave reset. In its north wall is a small modern doorway. The tower is built with a straight joint against the nave wall, and the nave gable remains and is clearly to be seen on the first floor of the tower—the east wall of the tower being built on it. The thirteenth-century masonry stops at the level of the belfry floor, and the walls are much thinner from this point and belong to the fifteenth century, at which time the upper story was added and diagonal buttresses built at the west angles of the tower. A weathered string was also inserted at half height. The belfry stage has an embattled parapet with angle pinnacles and gurgoyles at the angles and centres, those at the centres of each face being larger than the others. The belfry windows are the same on all four faces, of two trefoiled lights with cusped openings over them under a square head.

All roofs in the church are modern, but the pews in the nave are mostly ancient; they have heavy moulded top rails and tracery-panelled ends, and fronts or backs where adjoining a passage; on one pew linen-pattern panels occur. The pulpit is a half octagon, of fifteenth-century woodwork, most probably re-used to serve its present purpose. The font, which is of the twelfth century, though some of the ornament seems to be a later addition, has a round tapering

Middle Littleton Church.

bowl on a round stem. On the bowl is a band of incised lozenges enclosing devices of leaves, crosses, chevrons and the like, and below is a cable mould.

Parts of the chancel screen were remaining in 1845,[3] and a great deal of the ancient pavement of glazed tiles, as well as a sanctus bell turret on the east gable of the nave. On the north transept an old gable cross still remains. There are a few fragments of ancient glass in the east window of the chancel.

There are five bells, by Matthew and Henry Bagley, 1685. Prattinton gives their inscriptions, and says that there is also a small bell dated 1071. This bell at the present time stands on the floor of the nave of South Littleton Church, near the south door. The date is a blunder for 1701. The communion cup[4] has the date letter for 1571; it has a band of floral ornament and traces of gilding. The parish

[1] Prattinton Coll. (Soc. Antiq.).

[2] *Surv. of Worc.* (Worc. Hist. Soc.), i. 324.

[3] May, *Hist. of Evesham*, 1845, s.v.

[4] Lea, *Ch. Plate Worc. Archd.* 33.

registers[1] begin in 1661, and are contained in four books. In the Lansdowne MS. 1233 in the British Museum are some extracts from an earlier register from 18 July, 1595, to 1652.

In the churchyard is a cross standing on three steps and a base. The shaft is ancient, and a modern head has been fitted to it. There was formerly a sundial on the top of the shaft.

On the development of the plan of the church little need be added to the above account. The chancel, which before its rebuilding was probably c. 1290, is as wide as the nave, c. 1220, and as the church has never been cruciform this points to the usual widening at a rebuilding. The east window clearly belongs to the class found at Church Honeybourne and Bretforton, and may be due to that energetic builder Abbot John of Brokehampton.

The manor house stands to the west of the church, adjoining the churchyard. It is a picturesque building with mullioned windows of late sixteenth or early seventeenth-century date. Behind it is a farmyard, and on the other side of the yard the great stone barn built by Abbot John Ombersley in 1376,[2] 130 feet by 42 feet, standing east and west, with two gabled porches on each of the long sides. Of these porches the eastern pair have been pulled down, but otherwise the barn is in excellent condition. It is built of rubble masonry without wrought stone angles and buttresses, and square-headed slits for windows. On each long side are eight buttresses, and at each end three. The gable copings remain, and on the east gable and the south-west porch gable the original stone finials are still in place, in the form of trefoils with pointed leaves on long slender stems bending outwards at the top—a very graceful and effective design. Two ranges of wooden posts divide the internal area and support the wide span of the roof.

A tithe barn was mentioned in the lease of the manor of Middle Littleton to John Aldington in 1538.[3] One half of it was to be held by the lessee, and the other half, 'the western end containing five bays and a half,' and the garner-house belonging to it were to be reserved to the abbot and convent of Evesham, who were to keep their own half in repair.[4]

At the east end of the churchyard is an ancient stone building, now divided into cottages, having in its west wall, which has been reduced in height, the lower part of a two-light fourteenth-century window with a transom.

ADVOWSON From the monastery of Evesham the advowson of North and Middle Littleton passed to the Crown and followed the same descent as Badsey (q.v.), being now in the hands of the dean and chapter of Christ Church, Oxford.

In 1206 the lesser tithes of the three Littletons were given up to the use of the guest chamber, with the exception of Payne's nine virgates, the tithes of which as well great as small were appropriated to the sacristan.[5]

The Society of Friends has a meeting house in North Littleton which is used also by other denominations.

There is a non-provided school at North Littleton at which children of South Littleton are accommodated, affording places for 145 children.

CHARITIES From time immemorial the churchwardens have held four acres of land in North Littleton.[6] They possess also a yearly rent charge of £1 issuing out of a farm now the property of Lady Northwick and a sum of £53 18*s.* invested in Consols, the proceeds of a sale of two cottages in 1874. The income is applied towards church expenses.

John Millard, by will dated 16 August, 1811, left a sum of £5 towards providing surgical and medical aid for the poor of the parishes of North Littleton and Offenham. This has been invested in Government stock to the amount of £59 7*s.* 2*d.* for North Littleton, and the income of £1 12*s.* 8*d.* is used to pay part of the subscriptions of the Littleton Club.

He also bequeathed a sum of £5 yearly to the Sunday school at North Littleton.[8]

SOUTH LITTLETON

South Luttultone (xiii. cent.).

South Littleton has an area of 813 acres and contains seventy-seven inhabited houses.[7] The land is higher at both the eastern and western ends of the parish than in the centre, in each case rising to over 200 feet above the ordnance datum. A stream passes through the parish from north to south, and after passing the village is joined by Shinnell Brook, flowing westward from the direction of Church Honeybourne. The village is situated on the road which leads from Cleeve Prior southwards and joins the main road from Evesham to Chipping Campden in Badsey Parish. Roads also pass westward from the village into Offenham Parish and thence to Evesham, and eastward, joining the Roman Icknield Street or Buckle Street near Honeybourne Station. The Oxford, Worcester, and Wolverhampton branch of the Great Western Railway runs for a short distance through the southern part of the parish, and Littleton and Badsey Station, opened on 25 April, 1884, is about a mile from the village. The subsoil is of lower lias, and the surface is a dark coloured soil of good quality, while in the extreme east is a little hazel loam. The occupation of the people is agricultural, and market gardening is spreading considerably in the parish. Hops have been cultivated to a small extent from an early period.

[1] Dioc. Conf. 1899, *Digest of Par. Reg.* 17.

[2] *Chron. de Evesham* (Rolls Ser.), 301.

[3] Prattinton Coll. (Soc. Antiq.), from lease in the possession of Edward Rudge, Esq. in 1817.

[4] On 21 March, 1721-2, leave was granted by the dean and chapter of Christ Church, Oxford, for the removal of three bays of a barn which stood near the vicarage house to the ground near Sheen Hill, 'being in the occupation of Edward Smith, of North Littleton, that he may have a convenience of improving the glebe land' (Prattinton Coll. (Soc. Antiq.)), but this cannot refer to the stone barn, which is complete at both ends; nor is the advantage of removing three bays of a *masonry* building to a distance evident. The barn referred to must have been wooden.

[5] *Chron. de Evesham* (Rolls Ser.), 211, 216.

[6] In 1602 Philip Kighley was the tenant of half an acre of land known as Church Meadow for which he rendered to the churchwardens a yearly rent of 10*s.* (Prattinton Coll. (Soc. Antiq.), quoting from Chwdns. Acct. Bk.)

[7] *Worc. Co. Coun. Handb.* (1903), p. 148.

[8] *Char. Com. Rep.* xxiv. 524.

A. W. Ward, photo.

MANOR HOUSE, MIDDLE LITTLETON.

A. W. Ward, photo.

HOUSE AT SOUTH LITTLETON.

To face page 412.

Among the place names are Sheenhill, abbreviated to Shinill in 1770, Hoborne and Cort Harton. A field called Cow Leasow shows traces of considerable arable cultivation before it became the meadow indicated by its name. The name Vineyard Orchard also exists. Narval is the name of a farm in the parish.

MANOR South Littleton passed with North and Middle Littleton into the possession of the monastery of Evesham early in the eighth century. It was probably the Littleton which was attached to the manor of Offenham at the time of the Domesday Survey and which contained six hides.[1] It afterwards became separated from Offenham, at what date it does not appear, and being then grouped with the other two Littletons, followed their descent until 1609, when Middle Littleton (apparently North and Middle Littleton) was conveyed by Sir William Bond and Katherine his wife to Sir Matthew Carew.[2] South Littleton seems to have then become a separate manor.

About 1636 it would appear that the manor was purchased by Thomas, first Baron Coventry, Lord Keeper of the Great Seal; in 1628 a conveyance of a free fishery in South Littleton in the water of the Avon had been made to Lord Coventry, Hugh Dashfield, and Arthur Bickerton by Humphrey Aylesworth, clerk, and Elizabeth his wife.[3] The manor house was in the possession of John Lord Coventry in March, 1681, when he granted a lease of it, with his lands in the parish and the fishery in the Avon, to Francis Tayler for three lives, for a fine of £1,872, £5 a year rent with freedom from heriot.[4] The manor remained in the Coventry family till comparatively recent times, when it passed by will to two brothers named Williams, and by the son of one of them was sold in 1875 to the then tenant of the manor house, Edward Callow Crump. In 1882 it became the possession of Colonel Robert Bourne, of Cowarne Court, near Ledbury, who now holds it.

Abbot John of Brokehampton (1282–1316) is said to have built a grange at Littleton,[5] perhaps South Littleton; he also built a windmill there,[6] but no mill is mentioned in the survey of 1535.[7]

The Lytteltons of Frankley at one time held property in these parishes, from which they are said by Nash to have taken their name.[8] They seem to have originally held land in both North and South Littleton; John Lyttelton probably surrendered to the convent all his holding in the former by the conveyance of 1315;[9] but the family in 1535[10] still retained a messuage and appurtenances in South Littleton, which are said to have been usually allotted to the widows.[11] This property is stated to have been disposed of during the reign of Queen Elizabeth.[12]

LYTTELTON. *Silver, a cheveron between three scallops sable.*

The parish was probably enclosed at an early date. A terrier dated 1635 states that in the first or second year of King James's reign there had been 'an exchange division and inclosure agreed betweene the lord and tennentes of the whole fieldes.'[13] The Enclosure Act relating to North, Middle, and South Littleton, passed in 1811, however, affected a small extent of land in the parish.[14]

CHURCH South Littleton Church is dedicated in honour of St. Michael,[15] and stands to the west of the village street on a level site. It consists of chancel, north transept, aisleless nave, south porch, and west tower. The evidence to be obtained from the building as it now stands shows that there was a church here in the twelfth century, of which the nave was rebuilt at the end of the century and the chancel late in the thirteenth century, leaving only the chancel arch of the early building standing. The north transept was added about 1330, and the west tower built against and over the west gable of the nave in the fifteenth century, the gable being left unaltered except for the removal of its coping and the making of a small doorway through it to the tower. Doorways from nave to tower are more common than tower arches in this district, and the process of development described is no doubt the reason for this in many cases. In the sixteenth century the south side of the church received three new windows and a priest's door, but no further changes in the plan of the building took place. The old chancel arch stood till 1883. The base and steps of a cross are to be seen in the churchyard.

The earliest work to be seen is in the north, south, and west walls of the nave, c. 1200; this agrees very well with the recorded dedication in 1205. The whole building has been modernized, and the chancel, transept, and north wall of nave for the most part rebuilt. The chancel has diagonal buttresses at the eastern angles. The east window is of three trefoiled lights with quatrefoils in the head—late fourteenth century. In the north wall are two windows—one modern, the other, to the west, a small square-headed light of the fourteenth or fifteenth century, now filled with pieces of old glass, mostly fifteenth century. In the south wall are three openings. To the east is a miniature two-light window, c. 1280, cut out of one stone. It has trefoiled main lights and a quatrefoil in the head—the label is also worked on the stone. To the west of it is a plain sixteenth-century doorway with a low four-centred head, and adjoining it a sixteenth-century window of two uncusped ogee lights with plain uncusped tracery under a square head. Inside the church the sill of this window has been cut down, and the lower part of the west jamb of the doorway cut back to make a seat—possibly the sedilia. In Prattinton Coll. is a drawing (c. 1820) showing the lower part of this window blocked up. The upper part of the west jamb of the doorway is carried by a grotesque head corbel. Over door and window are labels with dripstones carved to represent the heads of (i) possibly a layman, (ii) an abbot or bishop, (iii) a beast with long ears, perhaps a horse; the second dripstone being common to both labels. Near

1 *V.C.H. Worc.* 306*b*.

2 Feet of F. Div. Cos. Hil. 7 Jas. I.

3 Ibid. Worc. East. 4 Chas. I.

4 R. F. Tomes, 'Littleton Notes' in the *Evesham Standard.*

5 *Chron. de Evesham* (Rolls Ser.), 287.

6 Ibid. 284.

7 *Valor Eccl.* (Rec. Com.), iii. 250. A dove-house worth 7*s.* 6*d.* a year was then in existence.

8 Nash, *Hist. of Worc.* ii. 104.

9 Pat. 8 Edw. II. pt. 2. See North and Middle Littleton.

10 Ibid. 27 Hen. VIII. pt. i. m. 46.

11 Prattinton (Soc. Antiq.) quoting a note by Bishop Lyttelton in the Habington MS.

12 Nash, op. cit. ii. 104.

13 R. F. Tomes, 'Littleton Notes' in the *Evesham Standard.*

14 Stat. 51 Geo. III. c. 35.

15 A dedication is recorded 1 September, 1205, Prattinton Coll. (Soc. Antiq.), from a note by Mr. Gough in his copy of Nash given to the Bodl. Lib.

the south-east angle of the chancel is an interesting pillar piscina, thirteenth century, with a stopped and chamfered shaft and modern base. Above the bowl is a recess with a shelf and a triangular head. In the north wall is a square locker, into the back of which some fifteenth-century glazed tiles have been built. They bear, among other devices, the five wounds of Christ, a shield with sword and cross keys, and the arms of De Clare.

The chancel arch is modern, 1883, replacing a small twelfth-century arch flanked by squints. The north transept is of the fourteenth century, in great part rebuilt, and opens to the nave by a modern arch. It has small trefoiled single lights in its east and west walls, and a two-light fifteenth-century window with segmental rear arch in the north wall. To the south of the east window is a recess for a piscina, with a shelf and straight-sided head. To the north of the same window a half-octagonal bowl with ears at the lower angles is built into the wall, piscina-fashion, below a modern recess with a triangular head. It appears to be a holy-water stone.

The north wall of the nave has been rebuilt, and contains a plain blocked roundheaded doorway with square abaci chamfered, and a small chamfer worked on the jambs. Towards the west end of the wall is a small thirteenth-century lancet, and there are two modern windows. The south wall of the nave has three windows, the first two from the east being of three lights, of the same detail and date as the west window in the south wall of the chancel; the third window is a single trefoiled light of the fourteenth century. The south doorway is placed about midway in the wall and is like that on the north, but with a chamfer worked on the arch and a little more detail on the abacus; the date of both is c. 1200. On its eastern jamb is a small consecration cross. Over it is a wooden porch, parts of which, especially the entrance arch, are of the fourteenth or early fifteenth century, on a modern masonry base.

All roof timbers in the church are modern, but a fair number of fifteenth-century pews remain in the nave, with tracery panels on their fronts and ends, and heavy moulded cappings. In 1843 a good deal of the ancient pavement of glazed tiles remained in position. The pulpit is octagonal, made up of pieces of fifteenth-century woodwork. The west tower[1] is of the fifteenth century, of two stages, with an embattled parapet. The angle pinnacles no longer exist. The string at the base of the parapet has a number of square shoots for rain-water, a curious arrangement which occurs in a slightly different form in the tower of St. Lawrence's church, Evesham. The belfry windows are of two lights; that on the west is more elaborate than the rest, having cinquefoiled lights with a quatrefoil in the head, and an embattled transom. On north and south the windows have two simple trefoiled lights, and on the east trefoiled lights with a plain cross in the head—a curious but clumsy piece of detail. The tower is built against the west end of the nave with a straight joint, and the line of the nave gable is clearly to be seen inside the tower, surmounted by the later masonry. The lower windows of the tower are plain square-headed loops in the south and west walls. Those lighting the ringing floor have rear arches made up of pieces of fourteenth-century window-heads. The tower is entered from the church by a low doorway, the head of which is made of two fourteenth-century window-heads, with the tracery roughly cut down and set parallel to each other on the east and west faces of the wall. The jambs of the doorway are modern.

The font has a round tapering bowl, with a double cable-mould at the top edge and a single mould at the base. On the bowl are four incised circles enclosing three floral devices and a cross. This bowl is of the twelfth century, and is fitted with a modern shaft with zigzag ornament. There are three bells,[2] the treble and tenor being the work of a Worcester founder of the fifteenth century. They are inscribed respectively:

Treble: SOLVE JUBENTE DEO TERRARUM PETRE CATENAS.

Tenor: AD LAUDEM CLARE MICHAELIS DO RESONARE.

The second bell, formerly by T. Hancox, senior, of Walsall, 1628, was recast by Taylor of Loughborough, 1901.

The church plate[3] consists of a cup, flagon, and pewter alms dish. The cup is Elizabethan, of the fringed stem pattern, with a double line of dotted ornament, 5¾ inches high, and 3 inches across the top. The parish registers[4] begin in 1538 and are contained in four books, the earliest being the original paper book. An entry in this register states that on 18 October, 38 Henry VIII. (1546), Master Clement Wyck [Lichfield], Bachelor of Divinity and some time abbot of the monastery of Evesham, died and was buried in the parish church of All Hallows in Evesham, 'the wyche gave to our church before he died 3 kyne to have masse and dirge with sertan refreshyng to the Parysheners at every yeres mynde for ever.'[5] An entry in the Chantry Certificates of the reign of Edward VI. states that in the parish of South Littleton 'there was gyven by dyvers parsons for the mayntenance and fynding of ij. lampes and certen tapers within the said parishe iiii. kyne presed at xii*d.* the kow.'[6]

ADVOWSON The advowson is now held by the Dean and Chapter of Christ Church, Oxford, having descended in the same manner as that of North and Middle Littleton (q. v.).

The children of the village attend the school at North Littleton.

CHARITIES John Dafforne, who died in 1728, bequeathed to the poor the sum of £20, with which a cottage known as 'Lampit's Cottage' was purchased; its rent of £1 is distributed in bread.[7]

Miss Ann Tomes, who died in 1826, left a similar sum, which has been invested in Consols to the amount of £21 7*s.* 1*d.*; the income of 12*s.* 9*d.* is given in bread.[8]

Church property: Six cottages and 6 acres of land formerly held by the churchwardens have been sold, and the proceeds invested in Consols £176 18*s.* 8*d.*, the income from which is devoted to church repairs.[9]

[1] This tower, like many other church towers, was used as a pigeon-house in the sixteenth century, and probably earlier.

[2] H. B. Walters, *Proc. Worc. Arch. Soc.* xxv. 564, 580.

[3] Lea, *Ch. Plate Worc. Archd.* 33.

[4] Dioc. Conf. 1899, *Digest of Par. Reg.* 18.

[5] Lansd. MS. 1233, f. 31.

[6] Chant. Cert. Worc. lx. No. 73.

[7] *Char. Commrs. Rep.* xxiv.; *Digest of Endowed Charities, Parl. P.* 1876, vol. lviii.

[8] Ibid.

[9] Ibid.

South Littleton Church : South Side of Chancel.

A. W. Ward, photo.

Middle Littleton : Barn built by Abbot John Ombersley, 1376.

To face page 414.

G. Shute, by will dated 1838, bequeathed a sum of money which has been invested in Consols, £97 13*s.* 10*d.*; the income of £2 18*s.* 7*d.* is distributed in money.[1]

John Pitts, by will proved 1884, bequeathed £300 to be invested and its income distributed to the poor of South Littleton on 12 December every year. This bequest, as in the case of Evesham (q. v.), has been much reduced, and its payment is apparently still delayed.[2]

Anne Harris, widow, who died in 1638, bequeathed £5 to be distributed yearly to the poor; but this charity has long since disappeared.[3]

NORTON

Nortune, Nordtona (viii. cent.); Nordtune, Nortune (xi. cent.).

The parish of Norton, with the hamlet of Lenchwick,[4] lies immediately north of Evesham. The River Avon separates it from Offenham in the south-east and from Cropthorne in the south-west, and a tributary stream forms the boundary line between this parish and that of Harvington. Another stream flows southwards past Lenchwick and joins the Avon at Chadbury Mill.

NORTON VILLAGE STREET.

The land has a general slope from the north-west, where Hipton Hill is 336 feet above the Ordnance datum, to the banks of the River Avon, which in some places are low and liable to flood.

The Barnt Green, Evesham, and Ashchurch branch of the Midland Railway passes along the eastern side of the parish; there is a station at Harvington about a mile north-east of the village of Norton, opened in 1866.

The main road from Evesham to Worcester runs just within and almost parallel with the southern boundary of the parish for some distance. The road from Evesham to Alcester passes through it in a northward direction, and on this road, about 3 miles north of Evesham, the village of Norton is situated. A branch of it running north-west reaches Lenchwick, a mile south-west of Norton, and continues to Church Lench. From Norton a road to the east reaches Harvington, and from Lenchwick are roads to the east and south joining the main roads.

The parish of Norton and Lenchwick has an area of 2,656 acres and contains 97 inhabited houses.[5]

1 *Digest of Endowed Charities, Parl. Papers*, 1876, lviii.

2 Ibid. 1900, lxiii.

3 *Char. Commrs. Rep.* xxiv.

4 Described as a tithing in the Population Returns of 1811 and 1831. In the Cott. MS. Vesp. B. xxiv. f. 53, Lenchwick is said to contain 10 hides.

5 *Worc. Co. Coun. Handb.* (1903), 148.

The population is mainly engaged in general agriculture and market gardening. The parish is situated on a tongue of the lower lias which stretches northward between two arms of the red marl, while to the south is a small outcrop of the Rhaetic formation. The surface soil is in some places sandy, but it is chiefly loam and clay.

A bridge known as Twyford[1] or Offenham Bridge[2] formerly spanned the Avon between the parishes of Norton and Offenham, and it is said that some traces of it can still be seen when the river is low. It was described by Leland as a narrow stone bridge for footmen. In 1615 the bridge was in a state of decay, and it was not known by whom it ought to be repaired; it was said to be in the parish of Offenham,[3] although the actual boundary between Norton and Offenham is in mid-stream. On the Norton bank, and close to the ferry, a strip of land known as Dead Men's Ait or Eyot projects into the Avon, and here tradition says Montfort's troops suffered great slaughter in attempting to cross the river in their flight after the battle of Evesham.

The following place names occur:—Coulde Knaveshill,[4] Could Kenan Lane,[5] Colekeran, Longesnalle,[6] Asken Corner, Upper Sytch, Long Dragon Piece, and Swatman's Ground.[7] The small islands in the River Avon close to Chadbury Mill were formerly known as 'Lez Byttes,' 'Lez Golleys,' and 'Heynam Pyte.'[8] The common fields of Norton and Lenchwick were enclosed in 1735.[9]

MANOR Seven 'mansæ' in Norton and one in Lenchwick are said to have been given by Kenred and Offa in 708 to Bishop Egwin for his newly founded monastery of Evesham.[10] Towards the end of the tenth century the abbey of Evesham and its lands were seized by Alfhere,[11] ealdorman of Mercia, and bestowed by him on Freodegar, a monk, who became abbot. The latter shortly afterwards exchanged the abbey with 'a certain powerful man named Godwin' for Towcester. Godwin, however, does not seem to have been able to obtain possession of all the abbey lands, but among those he held was Lenchwick, which perhaps included Norton.[12] After Godwin had retained some of the abbey lands for several years, Abbot Brihtmar redeemed them from him about 1010, but in 1013 Godwin again seized them, and Lenchwick seems to have once more passed into his hands. On his final expulsion by Abbot Aelfward in the following year, Lenchwick was once more restored to the monks.[13] Shortly afterwards, probably between the years 1017 and 1023, Abbot Aelfward 'and his household of Evesham,' leased 6 hides at Norton to Aethelmar.[14] Again, in 1058, Bishop Aldred, with the consent of the convent, granted 2 'mansæ' or hides of bocland and a meadow there to his servant Dodda for the term of his life.[15]

Norton and Lenchwick were held by the monastery of Evesham at the time of the Domesday Survey.[16] The lands seem to have been then divided among various tenants, whose names however do not appear. Abbot Walter is said to have given 6 hides and 1 virgate of the 10 hides which the monastery held in Lenchwick to 'his men.' Probably this included the 3½ hides which he gave to his nephew Hugh, who seems to have been still in possession towards the middle of the twelfth century,[17] and to have been succeeded by his kinsmen, the Coghtons, who surrendered his lands to the abbey about 1164.[18] According to a survey of the abbey lands apparently made about that date, Turstan and Thurkil were then each holding 1 hide of the demesne land. Huttebrand had ½ a hide and 12 acres, and Godwin of Hooknorton had ½ a hide[19] also of the demesne, whether of the enfeoffment of Abbot Walter or not it is not quite clear. Half a hide of land was also held by William Guthmund of the abbey,[20] and passed from him to his descendants, since Hugh Guthmund died seised of it in 1266.[21] In the twelfth-century survey mentioned above, Randolph is stated to have held ½ a hide and ½ a virgate and 12 acres, and various other small holdings are mentioned.[22] In Norton, as in Hampton, William de Melling and Simon his brother seemed to have despoiled the convent of a part of its property, but in 1130 they made a full restitution of all they had seized.[23]

Abbot Randolph (1214–29) is stated to have cleared and brought into cultivation a considerable extent of land at Lenchwick, and a grange was built and a vivary or stew pond made by him there.[24] Consequently, in 1291, Norton and Lenchwick seem to have been among the abbey's most valuable possessions, being worth £13 10*s.* 3*d.* yearly.[25]

In 1535 Lenchwick was probably the chief manor, and its clear annual value was £25 7*s.* 8*d.*, the demesne lands being retained in the abbot's hands.[26] Norton was valued at £15 18*s.* 2*d.* yearly.[27]

During 1538 the abbot and convent seem to have granted new leases of most of their property in Norton and Lenchwick,[28] including the demesne lands, which were let to farm to John Wheler and others.[29] In the following year the abbey of Evesham was dissolved, and the manor of Norton and Lenchwick came into the hands of the Crown, with whom it

[1] Mins. Accts. 31-2 Hen. VIII. L.R. 1330, m. 13-4; Chan. inq. p.m. 5 and 6 Phil. and Mary, cxv. 81.

[2] Ibid. cxv. 74.

[3] *Quart. Sess. R.* (Worc. Co. Coun.), 210.

[4] Ibid. 563.

[5] Ibid. 573.

[6] Ibid. 688.

[7] Allies, *Antiquities*, 339.

[8] Mins. Accts. 34-5 Hen. VIII. No. 179, m. 6d.

[9] Stat. 5 Geo. III. c. 39.

[10] Birch. *Cart. Sax.* i. 183; *Chron. de Evesham* (Rolls Ser.), 72, mentions only Norton, which is there said to have been given by Kenred alone.

[11] *Chron. de Evesham* (Rolls Ser.), 79.

[12] Ibid. 79, 80.

[13] Ibid. 80-84.

[14] B.M. Add. Ch. 19,796.

[15] Ibid. 19,801.

[16] *V. C. H. Worc.* i. 306*a*.

[17] Cott. M.S. Vesp. B. xxiv. f. 53, and Harl. MS. 3763, f. 59.

[18] See under Bretforton.

[19] Cott. MS. Vesp. B. xxiv. f. 53.

[20] Ibid. For one virgate of it he went to the county court and the hundred court, and for the other made service to the king and gelded and paid tithe in grass and wool and lambs to his lord.

[21] Inq. p.m. (Worc. Hist. Soc.), pt. i. 9. Hugh did suit at the abbot's court from three weeks to three weeks, and two suits at the two great hundred courts of the abbot yearly, and one suit at the county court of Worcester from month to month.

[22] Cott. MS. Vesp. B. xxiv. f. 53. For his half hide Randolph owed suit at the county and hundred courts. It is said that Alvric the prior of Evesham unjustly freed him from these services.

[23] Ibid. f. 30.

[24] *Chron. de Evesham* (Rolls Ser.), 261–2.

[25] *Pope Nich. Tax.* (Rec. Com.), 229. The abbey's property was afterwards increased by Abbot William Boys (1345–67), who is stated to have acquired from Henry Chester two virgates of land and a close at Norton valued at 13*s.* 4*d.* annually. *Chron. de Evesham* (Rolls Ser.), 294.

[26] *Valor Eccl.* (Rec. Com.), 249.

[27] Ibid.

[28] Mins. Accts. 31–2 Hen. VIII. L.R. 1330, m. 11 and 12.

[29] Ibid.

remained for some years. In 1542 some pasture and meadow lands in Lenchwick were granted to Sir Philip Hoby,[1] and in the following year Richard Andrews and Nicholas Temple received a close and pasture at Twyford Bridge, in the tenure of Thomas Dineley, to whom they afterwards had licence to alienate this property.[2] On 15 January, 1550–1, the manor of Norton with Lenchwick, with the mills of Chadbury and a fishery from the island there, was granted to Sir Philip Hoby[3] and his heirs to hold in chief by the fortieth part of a knight's fee.[4] Sir Philip died on 29 May, 1558, seised of the manor, which the inquisition states was settled for life, in failure of issue male to himself, on his sister Magdalen or Maud and her husband Thomas Bigge, with remainder to his brothers, Thomas, Richard, and William.[5] Sir Philip Hoby leaving no male issue, Norton and Lenchwick should have passed in accordance with this settlement to Thomas and Magdalen Bigge. It would appear, however, that the manor was held instead by Thomas Hoby, half brother of Sir Philip, and for some years it followed the same descent as Abbot's Morton (q.v.).[6] When Edward Hoby, son of Sir Thomas, attained his majority in 1581, he conveyed Norton-cum-Lenchwick to his cousinThomas Bigge,[7] afterwards knighted, son of the before-mentioned Thomas Bigge, who had died on 25 June, 1581, and for some years this manor followed the same descent as that of Bengeworth (q.v.).

In 1618 Thomas Bigge, jointly with Samuel his brother and next heir, conveyed the manor to Thomas Bolles, Francis Heaton, and George Hemsworth,[8] probably for the purposes of a settlement. Sir Thomas Bigge died 11 June, 1621, but the inquisition was not taken until 1626, five years afterwards,[9] and livery of his lands was granted to his brother Samuel on 5 December of that year.[10] His widow Anne, on whom he had settled the manor for life, had in the meantime married Sir John Walter, chief baron of the Exchequer, who in 1630 was forbidden to act as judge.[11] In Trinity term of 1625 Sir John and Lady Walter had, jointly with Samuel Bigge and his sisters and their husbands, levied a fine by which the manor of Norton and Lenchwick was conveyed to Sir Charles Montagu and Sir Edmund Sawyer,[12] probably trustees for Sir William, afterwards Baron, Craven of Hampstead Marshall,[13] a distinguished soldier of the time, who took an active part in the Thirty Years' War.

Lord Craven was in possession of the manor in 1633. In 1645, on the marriage of his cousin, Sir William Craven of Combe Abbey, with Elizabeth, third daughter of Ferdinand, Lord Fairfax, the Parliamentarian general, he settled the manor on Sir William and Elizabeth for their lives, with remainder to the heirs male of Sir William, and reversion in default to John, Lord Craven, Baron Ryton, brother of William, Lord Craven, for his life, and then to Thomas Craven, Sir William's brother, and his heirs male, and afterwards to Anthony, another brother, and his heirs male.[14] Sir William Craven died in 1655, and his only son William died a minor ten years later. A new settlement seems to have then become necessary, and accordingly in 1667 the manor was conveyed by William, Lord Craven, Thomas, Lord Fairfax, Henry Arthington, Thomas Craven, Sir Anthony Craven, and Sir William Craven, to Sir John Baber and Ralph Marshall.[15] Lady Craven, however, retained the manor[16] in dower in accordance with the terms of the marriage settlement until her death. Norton and Lenchwick seem to have then passed to Sir Anthony Craven, knight and baronet, of Sparsholt in Berkshire, cousin once removed to Sir William Craven of Lenchwick and also to William first Lord Craven. In Trinity term of 1697 Sir Anthony Craven suffered a recovery by which the manor was conveyed to Sir Edmund Wiseman of London,[17] probably only for the purpose of a marriage settlement.[18]

CRAVEN. *Silver a fesse between six crosslets fitchy gules.*

The manor afterwards passed to Charles Craven, cousin twice removed to Sir Anthony, governor of Carolina during the reign of Anne. He dealt with Norton and Lenchwick in 1719,[19] and in 1736 suffered a recovery probably to bar the entail.[20] One of the bells of the church of Norton bears his name and the date 1723.[21] He is stated to have sold the manor to Sir Edward Seymour of Maiden Bradley,[22] and as the latter died in 1741, the conveyance by which he acquired Norton and Lenchwick probably took place between 1736 and 1740.

SEYMOUR. *Gules a pair of wings gold.*

By his will, dated 3 October, 1740,[23] Sir Edward Seymour directed that the manor should be sold, and the money arising from the sale divided between his three sons, Edward, Francis, and William. The sale did not take place, however, and the manor was held jointly by these heirs. Edward Seymour in 1750 became 8th Duke of Somerset, and is said to have settled his share on his daughter, Lady Mary Seymour,[24] who in 1759 married Vincent John Biscoe, of Austin Friars, and on her death in 1762 her third of the manor passed to her husband, who held it in 1765.[25] William Seymour, of Knoyle in Wiltshire, died in 1746 without issue, and left his share to his brother Francis, of Sherborne, who thus held two-thirds. On the death of the latter in 1761 this share passed to his son Henry, who held it in 1765.[26] The subsequent descent of Norton and Lenchwick is somewhat obscure. It is said to have passed to the Cocks family, and to have been sold by them to the Hollands.[27]

1 Pat. 34 Hen. VIII. pt. 6. m. 33.
2 *L. and P. Hen. VIII.* xviii. 536, 541.
3 See Abbot's Morton.
4 Pat. 4 Edw. VI. pt. 9, m. 31.
5 Chan. inq. p.m. 5 and 6 Phil. and Mary, cxv. 74.
6 Feet of F. Div. Cos. East. 1 Eliz.; Chan. inq. p.m. 9 Eliz. cxlv. 3.
7 Feet of F. Worc. Mich. 23 and 24 Eliz.
8 Ibid. Trin. 16 Jas. I.
9 Chan. inq. p.m. 2 Chas. I. ccccxxiii. 75.
10 Fine R. 2 Chas. I. pt. 2, No. 30.
11 *Dict. of Nat. Biog.*
12 Feet. of F. Worc. Trin. 1 Chas. I.
13 *Quart. Sess. R.* (Worc. Co. Coun.), 513.
14 B.M. Add. Ch. 1799.
15 Feet of F. Worc. Hil. 18 and 19 Chas. II.
16 Pat. 22 Chas. II. pt. 2, m. 1.
17 Com. Pleas Recov. R. Trin. 9 Wm. III. m. 8.
18 According to Burke's *Peerage* he married Theodosia Wiseman, who was possibly the daughter of Sir Edmund.
19 Com. Pleas Recov. R. Mich. 6 Geo. I. m. 135.
20 Com. Pleas Recov. R. Trin. 10 Geo. II. m. 209.
21 Prattinton Coll. (Soc. Antiq.).
22 Nash. *Hist. of Worc.* ii. 195.
23 Proved 16 April, 1741
24 Nash, *Hist. of Worc.* ii. 195.
25 Stat. 5 Geo. III. cap. 39.
26 Ibid.
27 Information supplied by J. W. W.-B.

About the year 1846 the estate of Lenchwick and Chadbury was sold privately by Edward Holland, of Dumbleton, M.P. for East Worcestershire and afterwards for the borough of Evesham, to H.R.H. the Duc d'Aumale, at whose death in 1897 it passed to his great-nephew, Henry, Duc d'Orleans, who is now lord of the Manor of Norton and Lenchwick. His residence is at Wood Norton, west of Chadbury, and overlooking the Avon. The present fine mansion, built in 1897, stands on the site of a previous keeper's cottage, which was added to from time to time, until the present house was erected. The Duc d'Aumale largely added to the estate by buying further land from adjoining owners.

The Duke of Orleans bears the whole arms of France.

CHADBURY (Chaldelburi, viii. cent.; Chadbery, xiv. cent.). The hamlet of Chadbury is situated on the main road from Evesham to Worcester, about 2½ miles from the former, and close to the River Avon. Between 701 and 703 Ethelred of Mercia granted it, under the name of the castle of Chadbury,[1] to Bishop Egwin for the monastery of Evesham. It afterwards became a part of the manor of Norton and Lenchwick, and is only mentioned in connection with its mill. Chadbury mill stands on the Avon about a quarter of a mile from the village on the Evesham side. It was probably one of the two mills mentioned in the Domesday Survey as being in Norton.[2] The rent arising from it in 1206 was appropriated to the kitchen of the abbey of Evesham.[3] By a conveyance of the reign of Henry III. the lessee of the mill and the lands belonging to it was to render yearly to the cook of Evesham 25*s.* and forty sticks of eels, or, if so many were not taken, 1½*d.* for each stick.[4] In 1535 a rent of 40*s.* was received from this mill.[5] On 10 June, 1538, two water-mills, called Chadbury mills, were let by the abbey and convent of Evesham to Thomas Dinely and his wife Agnes, and their heirs,[6] but the term for which the lease was granted does not appear.

Chadbury mills were included in the grant of the manor to Sir Philip Hoby on 15 January, 1550–1.[7]

TWYFORD (Thuiford, viii. cent.; Tuiford, xiii. cent.). Although the name of Twyford now survives only in Twyford House and Twyford Farm, the place seems to have been of considerable importance in former times. In 703 Kings Ethelred and Offa gave to Bishop Egwin divers lands for the endowment of Evesham Abbey, which lands, together with twenty 'mansæ' in Twyford, were afterwards seized by Osward, brother of Ailward, subregulus of the Hwiccas, but on Stratford-on-Avon being given to him by Bishop Egwin, he returned Twyford to the bishop.[8] Twyford is stated to have been afterwards held by the bishops of Worcester,[9] but was later restored to the abbey, and probably formed a part of the manor of Norton and Lenchwick. The mill of Twyford was probably one of the two mills in Norton and Lenchwick mentioned in Domesday.[10] In 1206 it yielded a yearly rent of 28*s.* and forty sticks of eels, which was appropriated, like that of Chadbury, to the kitchener of the abbey.[11] In 1225 two mills were stated to be in existence at Twyford, and formed the subject of a plea between Akina, formerly the wife of Henry of Twyford, and William of Brumarton.[12] No mill exists here at the present day. It is known that the gallows of the abbot of Evesham stood at Twyford.[13]

CHURCH Norton Church is dedicated in honour of St. Egwin.[14] It is mentioned in 1206 as belonging to the sacristy of the abbey, and a consecration of it is recorded in 1295, but no part of the existing building is as old as the thirteenth century. It stands to the west of the main road from Evesham to Alcester, and south of the village of Norton. Its site is level, but there is a general fall to the north, the village being on comparatively high ground. The churchyard was not enclosed till 1844.

The church consists of chancel, north transept, aisleless nave with south porch and west tower. It has suffered much from the restorers. The walling throughout is of lias rubble, with ashlar dressings, and all roofs are of grey stone slates. The chancel is of the fifteenth-century; its details are unusually coarse and heavy, though the work is not inaccurate. The east window is of three lights trefoiled, with normal fifteenth-century tracery in the head. In the north wall is a two-light window with a coarsely worked label and large square dripstones. The east window in the south wall is of the same pattern, and to the west of it is a priest's door, with a flattened segmental head and no moulding beyond a broad chamfer. The west window in this wall is a wide cinquefoiled single light under a square head with a heavy label like the rest. There are short diagonal buttresses at the east angles, and the face of the east wall sets back above a coarse square-edged string about eight feet from the ground—showing either a correction of a mistake in the original setting-out or a rebuilding of the upper part of the wall. The set-back is about one inch at the south-east angle and five inches at the north-east. The chancel arch is modern and quite plain; there was no arch before 1844. The north transept opens to the church with an arch of two chamfered orders. The transept appears to be of the fourteenth century; all details are very simple. There are two square-headed two-light windows in the east wall, one blocked by the tomb of Sir Thomas Bigge, to be described later. The north window is of four lights, with tracery formed by the intersection of the mullions—the main lights are trefoiled with acutely pointed heads. The west window is like those on the east. There are short diagonal buttresses at the north angles, and a short buttress in the middle of the north wall below the window. It is to be noted that the east wall of this transept is considerably east of the line of the chancel arch.

Of the nave, the north wall only is ancient; the two buttresses at its west angle are of the fourteenth century, and the line of a former gable shows at this angle. There are two windows in the wall—one of

1 *Chron. de Evesham* (Rolls Ser.), 18, 71. 'Castellum de Chadelburi.' The mound that would seem to be an earthwork is an outcrop of the Rhætic beds and is not artificial.

2 *V.C.H. Worc.* i. 306*b*.

3 *Chron. de Evesham* (Rolls Ser.), 217.

4 *Anct. D.* (P.R.O.), B. 1923. See also Cott. MS. Vesp. B. xxiv. f. 53.

5 *Valor Eccl.* (Rec. Com.), iii. 249.

6 Mins. Accts. 31–2 Hen. VIII. L. R. 1330, m. 12.

7 Pat. 4 Edw. VI. pt. 9, m. 31.

8 *Chron. de Evesham* (Rolls Ser.), 18, 72–3.

9 Ibid. 73.

10 *V.C.H. Worc.* 306*b*.

11 *Chron. de Evesham* (Rolls Ser.), 217.

12 *Bracton's Note Book*, iii. 22.

13 *Hund. R.* (Rec. Com.), ii. 282.

14 *Chron. de Evesham* (Rolls Ser.), 210.

four lights, with fifteenth-century tracery, brought here from the destroyed old church of Bengeworth, and the other a modern square-headed window of two trefoiled lights. There are two added fifteenth-century buttresses in the length of the wall, and the fourteenth-century north doorway has been taken out and now does duty at the east entrance of the churchyard. It is of curious construction, the head being in three stones forming three sides of an octagon, with a wide chamfer. From the soffit of each of the three sides two cusps project, the effect being decidedly clumsy. A fifteenth-century label has been placed above it. The south wall of the nave is entirely modern, with the south porch; but the old south doorway, similar to that formerly on the north, has been reset, with some pieces of fifteenth-century stonework built into the wall over it. Before the 'restoration' of 1844 the west end of the nave was roofless, and the east half was closed in by a lath-and-plaster partition. A contemporary account of the work says that the nave walls were rebuilt 'avoiding the obstruction of arches and pillars by omitting the ancient side-aisles.'[1] This implies that arcades existed before the restoration; but if so they have left no traces. A drawing of the church dated 1843[2] shows that the line of the present south wall of the nave is the same as that of the former south wall, which would allow only two or three feet for a south aisle if a south arcade existed, and there has never been a north arcade.

The western tower, of the fifteenth century, opens to the church with a low pointed arch with semi-octagonal responds and capitals of poor detail. The tower is of two stages with diagonal buttresses at the west angles. It has a plain west doorway, now of modern masonry, and above it a window with two cinquefoiled ogee-headed lights under a square head. There is a weathered string at half height; in each face of the upper stage is a two-light square-headed window, the main lights having trefoiled ogee heads. There is a good embattled parapet with angle pinnacles, and gurgoyles at the angles and centre of each face, and the tower is finished with a gabled roof within the parapet, running east and west. There is an old gable cross on the north transept. The roofs are in the main modern, but the chancel retains one fifteenth-century truss with moulded cambered tie-beam, and jacklegs resting on corbels carrying brackets with pierced spandrels. The principals have a collar and moulded arched braces. All pews, etc., are modern, but the pulpit contains some late sixteenth and seventeenth-century carved detail, and at the east end of the chancel some old linen-pattern panelling[3] is to be seen. The seventeenth-century communion table and church chest are in the north transept. There are modern stone sedilia (1887), made from the tracery of a window formerly in the old church of Bengeworth. The lectern is of very great interest; it is in the form of a sloping desk with carved sides, resting on a short round shaft with foliated cap and moulded base with spurs. The cap, shaft, and base, are modern, but the desk, of white marble, is admirable work of the twelfth century. It is about 2 feet 4 inches square over all, sloping from about eighteen inches high in front to six at back, the vertical sides being carved with scrolls of foliage in high relief. The lectern is set to face west. A beast's head with long ears projects from the foliage on the north and south sides, and two human heads with close curled hair and short rounded ears are on the east side. The middle of the west face is taken up by a seated figure of an abbot or bishop in mass vestments. His head is bare[4]; he wears amice, chasuble, dalmatic, stole and alb; the feet are broken away; the right hand is raised in blessing; the left holds a crosier, with a plain curled head, turned to the left. At the upper angles of the west face of the lectern are pinholes of half an inch diameter, probably for the attachment of branches for lights. The upper face is sunk, leaving a projecting rim to keep a book in place. The lectern was dug up in 1813 on the site of Evesham Abbey, and a description, with illustrations as accurate as might be expected at the time, is published in *Arch.* xvii. 278. Mr. Rudge, the writer of the description, is inclined to identify it with the 'lectricium retro chorum' made by Thomas de Marleberge in 1217–8, when he was sacrist. But the style of work will not admit of this identification. It is certainly of an earlier date, about 1150–70, and is perhaps the 'lectricium capituli' made by Abbot Adam 1160–1191.[5] The font stands at the west end of the nave. It is of the fifteenth century, octagonal, with quatrefoiled panels on bowl and shaft. There are two quarries of old glass with fleurs-de-lis in the head of the north window of the north transept.

There are six bells—the fifth by Barwell, 1901, the rest by Richard Sanders of Bromsgrove, 1723.[6]

The church plate[7] consists of an Elizabethan cup with paten cover with a floral-band ornamentation, hall mark 1571, and a plain plate, from its appearance part of a service, with hall-mark 1686, inscribed 'The gift of A. Craven.' The flagon and alms dish are of pewter, date 1679. The parish registers[8] are contained in four books, beginning from 1538.

In the north transept are three fine tombs of the Bigge family. That against the east wall is of Sir Thomas Bigge, 1613, and Ursula, his wife, daughter of Clement Throckmorton, of Hasely, Warwick, 1601. The figures of Sir Thomas and his wife kneel at a double desk with books, under a panelled arch flanked by columns, with a cornice setting out over the columns, and carrying three shields of arms: (i.) Bigge, impaling Throckmorton; (ii.) Bigge, with mantling and crest; (iii.) as (i.) In the spandrels of the arch over Sir Thomas, Bigge; over his wife, Throckmorton. On the base, below the kneeling figures, are the small figures of four sons and five daughters, with shields of arms showing their marriages. Over the eldest son: Bigge, impaling Wytham of Ledston, Yorks. Over the eldest daughter: Fox of Chacombe impaling Bigge; over the second daughter, Wright of Eastmayn (Eastmeon, Hants), impaling Bigge; over the third, Freame, of Lypiatt, Gloucs., impaling as before.

Against the north wall is an altar tomb with enriched cornice and projecting pilasters with shields of arms. It probably had a canopy, now gone. On it are the recumbent effigies of Thomas Bigge, 1581, and his wife 'Maudlen,' sister of Sir Philip Hoby, 1574. On the west side of the tomb are the arms of

[1] May, *Hist. of Evesham*, 1845. [2] Ibid.

[3] Found by a former vicar, Rev. H. G. Bath, in an attic of Lenchwick manor house or a cottage adjoining.

[4] The top of the head is damaged.

[5] Illustrated in the article on Early Christian Art in this volume.

[6] Walters, *Proc. Worc. Arch. Soc.* xxv. 587.

[7] Lea, *Ch. Plate Worc. Archd.* 33.

[8] Dioc. Conf. 1899, *Digest of Par. Reg.* 18.

Bigge; on the south face (i.) Dineley impaling Bigge; (ii.) Bigge impaling ? Morton; (iii.) Bigge impaling Throckmorton. In panels between the pilasters are small figures of four daughters and two sons. The inscription belonging to this tomb is fixed to the wall above it, below an acutely pointed shield with Bigge impaling Hoby.

To the west of this tomb, against the north wall, is an alabaster altar tomb with black marble panels, carrying four black marble columns which support an alabaster tester with panelled soffit. On the tester stand: (i.) a helm; (ii.) the arms of Bigge in an oval with a strapwork frame; (iii.) the Bigge crest. All these are in alabaster. The tomb is that of Sir Thomas Bigge, baronet, 1621, and the arms are differenced by having the fesse engrailed [1] with the Ulster scutcheon on the middle of the fesse. The effigy is of alabaster, recumbent. On all three tombs the male effigies are in armour.[2] In this transept are hung several banners, and two tabards with helms, crests, gauntlets, and swords. One tabard, over the tomb of Sir Thomas Bigge, bears the arms of Craven. On the second tabard is the same coat quartering a second coat for Craven of Appletreewick.

A chapel dedicated in honour of St. Michael [3] appears to have been formerly in existence at Lenchwick, but was in ruins at the end of the eighteenth century.[4] The two chapels of Norton and Lenchwick are mentioned in 1206 as appropriated to the sacristy of the abbey of Evesham.[5]

ADVOWSON On 24 January, 1541–2, Henry VIII. granted the rectory and church, advowson of the vicarage and tithes, to the dean and chapter of Worcester,[6] who still remain the patrons. The grant was confirmed on 22 May, 1547,[7] and again on 8 March, 1608–9.[8]

There is no Nonconformist place of worship in the parish, but attached to the Mansion of the Duc d'Orleans at Wood Norton is a Roman Catholic Chapel. There is a non-provided school at Norton affording accommodation for 103 children.

CHARITIES Lady Ann Walters during her lifetime gave £50, and by her will bequeathed a similar amount, towards educating the poor children of Norton and Lenchwick. £50 of this gift was deposited in a house in Blackfriars, which was burned in the Great Fire of 1666, and a quantity of molten silver saved from the ruins was ordered by the Commissioners of Charitable Uses to be sold. The sale produced £22, and a total sum of £45, the residue having apparently been lost, was invested in a rent charge of 32*s*., which was formerly in abeyance, but is now regularly paid towards the support of a Sunday school.[9]

OFFENHAM

Huffam (viii. cent.); Afanhamme (xi. cent.); Uffenham [10] (xiii. cent.).

The parish of Offenham lies along the left bank of the River Avon, and on the south-west is bounded by the Badsey brook flowing into the Avon from Badsey. The land slopes from the east of the parish, where at Bennett's Hill, near South Littleton, it is 142 feet above the Ordnance datum, towards the banks of the Avon and of Badsey brook; about the centre it is above 100 feet. The Avon banks in the north-western corner of the parish are low and liable to floods. The old Oxford, Worcester, and Wolverhampton Railway, now the west midland branch of the Great Western Railway, passes through the southern portion of Offenham, where is situated the station of Littleton and Badsey, opened in April, 1884, and the Aldington siding for goods, chiefly vegetables, opened in 1872.

The parish is intersected by several roads; but the only main road, that from Evesham, terminates at the centre of the parish, where it sends out three branches. Perhaps the most important road in former times was that part of the old road from Worcester to London, which, branching off from the Roman road, the Buckle Street, and from the main road leading from Evesham to Chipping Campden, passes through Bretforton, crosses the railway at the Littleton station, and runs along the southern part of Offenham to what is now known as the Offenham boat or ferry across the Avon near the south-western corner of the parish, where a stone bridge known as Offenham or Twyford bridge formerly spanned the river.[11] A branch of this road, known as Three Cocks Lane, passes north-eastwards through the parish to the Fish and Anchor ford on the Avon.

Offenham village lies a little to the north of this latter road and close to the river. No road passes through it. The village consists of a short street containing the church, school, and vicarage, and here stands also the Court Farm, a farmhouse built on the site of the old grange or abbot's house, of which only some foundations remain.

The parish of Offenham has an area of 1,235 acres and 133 inhabited houses. The subsoil is of lower lias and the surface in some parts is gravelly. The population is almost entirely engaged in agriculture and in market gardening; the latter has greatly increased of late years, especially as to fruit. Large quantities of strawberries are grown, and it is here that the variety Myatt's British Queen was originated. There are several quarries in the parish, but now little used, as the stone is of inferior quality; they were possibly those worked at the time of the Domesday Survey, which states that a team of oxen were employed in drawing stone to 'the church.' [12] There are also lime kilns near the Fish and Anchor ford.

The following ancient place-names occur:—Dickstreate, Hawkefeild,[13] Sheepditch, Blakemister.[14] The last name survives in Blackminster Lane, and Hobs Hole is another existing place-name. Roman coins have been discovered in the parish.[15] In 1887 twenty

[1] This Habington considers to be 'contrary to reason.' *Survey of Worc.* (Worc. Hist. Soc.), ii. 217.

[2] For an account of these monuments, c. 1640, see Habington, loc. cit.

[3] Nash, *Hist. of Worc.* ii. 196.

[4] Ibid.

[5] *Chron. de Evesham* (Rolls Ser.), 210.

[6] Pat. 33 Hen. VIII. pt. 5.

[7] Ibid. 1 Edw. VI. pt. 9.

[8] Ibid. 6 Jas. I. pt. 12.

[9] *Char. Commrs. Rep.* xxiv; *Digest of Endowed Charities, Parl. Papers*, 1876, vol. lviii.

[10] It is so pronounced locally at the present day.

[11] See Norton and Lenchwick.

[12] *V. C. H. Worc.* i. 306*b*.

[13] Pat. 29 Eliz. pt. 11.

[14] Chan. inq. p.m. Jas. I. ccccvi. 65.

[15] *V. C. H. Worc.* i. 219.

skeletons were found near Faulk Mill. They were discovered in the black earth overlying a bed of gravel that was being worked for road material, and in the same earth were found some copper or bronze Roman coins. In the manor house is a fine carved oak mantelpiece bearing the arms of Haselwood. Near the house extensive foundations have at various times been discovered, probably belonging to the grange, built about 1300, by Abbot John of Brokehampton. The remains of a moat are evident. On the Avon, where it forms the northern boundary of the parish, were formerly a weir and locks, but since the railway company have acquired the Avon navigation, they have fallen into disuse. A scheme has been lately put forward to restore them.[1]

convent.[5] In 1058 three acres of meadow land 'in Afanhamme, which St. Oswald gave Bercstane in the land,' were included in the grant which Bishop Aldred, with the consent of the monastery, made to his servant Dodda, for life.[6]

Offenham seems to have been an important manor at the time of the Survey, Littleton—probably South Littleton—Bretforton, and Aldington, being appurtenant to it.[7] It is there stated to have contained one hide, free from geld.[8]

Until the Dissolution, Offenham continued to be held by the abbot and convent, and during that period little is known of its history except that it was a favourite place of residence of the abbots. On 17 March, 1289, Edward I., avoiding Evesham as if it

Offenham Village, showing the Maypole.

MANOR Offenham was from very early times connected with the monastery of Evesham; it is said to have formed part of King Offa's gift to the abbey in 703;[2] it is also claimed to have been given by Kenred and Offa in 709, the extent of their gift being one 'mansa.'[3] In 976 it was seized with the abbey by Alfhere, ealdorman of Mercia, and for some years afterwards its history was similar to that of Norton (q.v.).[4] When Godwin was finally expelled by Abbot Aelfward, Offenham seems to have been held in undisputed possession by the

were unclean, visited Offenham, and stayed there three days.[9] In 1237–8, and again in 1392, small grants of property and land there were made to the monastery.[10] In the early part of the thirteenth century, during Randolph's abbacy, the houses of Offenham are said to have been burnt down, and the grange was re-erected by the abbot.[11] John of Brokehampton (1282–1316) is also said to have built a grange at Offenham,[12] and John Ombersley erected an outer gate with a chamber above it and a stable adjoining it.[13] At the existing manor-house or grange, abbot

[1] Information supplied by J. W. W.-B.

[2] *Chron. de Evesham* (Rolls Ser.), 71. This is probably only from the name. It is, however, very doubtful if the modern way of writing the name Offenham is the true one, and whether the real name was not Avon Ham corrupted into Uffenham. and so into Offenham. The Evesham forgeries are so extensive and numerous that all early charters connected with it are doubtful. J. W. W.-B.

[3] Birch, *Cart. Sax.* i. 183. This charter is probably spurious.

[4] *Chron. de Evesham* (Rolls Ser.), 79; ibid. 80-1.

[5] Ibid.

[6] B. M. Add. Ch. 19801. See also Norton.

[7] *V. C. H. Worc.* i. 306b.

[8] Ibid. In a statement of the hidation of the lands of Evesham monastery it appears to have contained two hides, one of which was geld free. (Cott. MS.Vesp. B. xxiv. f. 3.)

[9] *Ann. Mon.* (Rolls Ser.), iv. 500.

[10] Feet of F. Worc. 22 Hen. III. No. 11; Inq. a. q. d. 16 Rich. II. pt. 1, No. 155.

[11] *Chron. de Evesham* (Rolls Ser.), 261.

[12] Ibid. 287.

[13] Ibid. 301.

Roger Zatton (1379–1418) rebuilt the hall,[1] with a sideboard ('le copbord') [2] on one side, and a parlour ('le perler') on the other, and a dovecot within the court. Offenham was one of the few manors the demesne lands of which were then retained in the abbot's own hands [3] instead of being let out at farm, possibly on account of the abbot's frequent residence there.

On 24 April, 1539, however, a few months previous to the dissolution of the monastery of Evesham, a lease of the demesne lands was granted, under the seal of the convent, to Arthur Collarde, Edmund Charlett and others, the abbot retaining 116 acres in his own hands for the use of his house.[4] Shortly afterwards, by the suppression of Evesham Abbey in 1539, the manor came into the hands of the Crown, and on 19 March, 1539–40, Henry VIII. granted it, with all other possessions of the abbey in Offenham, and certain property at Poden in the parish of Church Honeybourne, to Philip Hoby and Elizabeth his wife, to hold in tail by the service of a tenth part of a knight's fee and the yearly rent of £7 3*s*.[5] On 25 May, 1544, this grant was confirmed, and as it probably seemed unlikely he would have an heir, according to the above limitation, a further grant in fee of the reversion of the manor of Offenham, with the lands at Poden, was obtained by Philip Hoby, his heirs and assigns, by the same service and rent as before and on payment of the sum of £322 19*s*. 6*d*.[6] On 22 June he had licence from the Crown to convey the manor to Anthony Denny and Maurice Berkeley, gentlemen of the privy chamber, William Butt, senior, and Thomas Starnold of the household, in trust to the use of himself and the lady Elizabeth his wife, and his heirs male, with contingent remainder to his brother John and his heirs male, and then to the right heirs of Philip.[7] Some years later a further settlement was made in which John Hooper, bishop of Worcester, and Sir Richard Blount, acted as trustees.[8] John Hoby, mentioned in the previous settlement, was probably then deceased.

For some years afterwards Offenham followed the same descent as Abbot's Morton (q.v.). In 1583 Sir Edward Hoby, jointly with Margaret his wife, the daughter of Henry Cary, Lord Hunsdon, conveyed 'the site' of the manor of Offenham to his cousin, Sir Thomas Cecil, afterwards Earl of Exeter, and Dorothy his wife.[9] Sir Thomas Cecil acquired by this conveyance the manor house, with the park, and a portion of the tithes,[10] but the manorial rights probably remained with Sir Edward Hoby, who continued to hold property there. During the latter part of Elizabeth's reign Sir Edward Hoby had licences to alienate various lands and tenements in Offenham,[11] and at the time of his death, in 1616, he was seised of only a tenement and a small quantity of land there.[12] These were said to be held in chief by the service of a fourth part of a knight's fee.[13] The manorial rights probably fell into disuse when the manor-house and demesne lands were conveyed to various people. No mention is made of them in the inquisition on Sir Edward Hoby, with whom they should have remained.[14] Sir Edward left as his heir his brother, Sir Thomas Posthumous Hoby,[15] who does not seem, however, to have held the manor of Offenham.

The site of the manor, which had come into the hands of Sir Thomas Cecil in 1583, afterwards passed from him to the Haselwood family, but it is not clear at what date the conveyance took place. In 1600 Philip Parsons and his wife Anne conveyed the tithes in three messuages in Offenham to Thomas Haselwood,[16] and the family seem to have been living there early in the seventeenth century.[17] In 1650 Francis, the son and heir of Thomas Haselwood, levied a fine by which he conveyed the site of the manor of Offenham to Samuel Dingley and Edwin Baldwyn,[18] possibly for the purposes of a trust. In 1682 Sir Thomas Haselwood dealt with 'the capital messuage or mansion house in Offenham in possession of Humphrey Mayo, gentleman,' and with other property there.[19] The manor house afterwards passed with part of the demesne lands into the hands of the Freemans of Batsford, from whom it went to Philip Parsons of Overbury. William Parsons, son of the latter, died in 1714, leaving an only daughter, Mary, who in 1735 married William Bund of Wick. It continued in the possession of the Bunds until 1840, when they sold it to the Digbys of Coleshill, who now hold it.[20]

HASELWOOD. *Silver a cheveron gules between three owls sable with three lozenges ermine on the cheveron, and a chief azure with three hazel branches gold.*

The Haselwoods still retained property at Offenham until the middle of the eighteenth century. About that time James Haselwood mortgaged it with his manors of Wick Burnell, Wick Warren and others, to Bernard Wilson, clerk, into whose hands it ultimately passed by fine in 1746.[21] The property then became sub-divided, and passed into various hands, and is now mostly held by small owners.

PARK A deer park was in existence at Offenham towards the end of the fifteenth century. Abbot John Norton is said to have provided that the brothers of the monastery of Evesham should have a deer from it on his anniversary, and to have stocked it for that purpose.[22] It was apparently granted, with the manor, to Sir Philip Hoby, for it was included in the conveyance from Sir Edward Hoby to Sir Thomas Cecil in 1583.[23] In 1626 Francis Dineley died seised of a park called the New

1 *Chron. de Evesham* (Rolls Ser.), 304.

2 'In mediæval halls there is frequently a recess in the wall at the end behind the screen, which appears to have been used for the sideboard or cupboard.' Parker's *Gloss. of Arch.*

3 *Valor Eccl.* (Rec. Com.), 248.

4 Mins. Accts. 31-2 Hen. VIII. L. R. 1330, m. 13-14.

5 *L. and P. Hen. VIII.* xv. 173.

6 Ibid. xix. 380. In 1695 John Jones, clerk, conveyed to Sir William Powlett the rents arising out of the manor of Offenham. (Feet of F. Worc. Trin. 7 Wm. III.)

7 *L. and P. Hen. VIII.* xix. 507.

8 See Abbot's Morton.

9 Feet of F. Worc. East. 25 Eliz.

10 Ibid.

11 Pat. 28 Eliz. pt. 4, m. 23; 30 Eliz. pt. 11, m. 24; 31 Eliz. pt. 6, m. 27.

12 Chan. inq. p.m. 16 Jas. I. ccclxx. 59.

13 Ibid.

14 Possibly as the demesnes became separated from the services the manorial rights were lost.

15 Chan. inq. p.m. 16 Jas. I. ccclxx. 59.

16 Feet of F. Worc. Hil. 42 Eliz.

17 *Genealogist*, i. 43.

18 Feet of F. Worc. Mich. 1650.

19 Information supplied by Mr. O. G. Knapp from documents in his possession.

20 Prattinton Coll. (Soc. Antiq.) and information supplied by J. W. W.-B.

21 Feet of F. Worc. Hil. 19 Geo. II.

22 *Chron. de Evesham* (Rolls Ser.), 339.

23 Feet of F. Worc. East. 25 Eliz.

A. W. Ward, photo.

OFFENHAM CHURCH : EAST DOORWAY OF TOWER.

To face page 422.

Park in Offenham, his heir being his grandson Edward, son of his elder son Francis, aged twenty-four years.[1] This park was still clearly defined some years ago by a fosse and a bank, which were known as the 'deer's leap,'[2] but all traces of it have now passed away.

In 1650 there pertained to the manor a free fishery in the water of the Avon.[3]

There was a mill at Offenham at the time of the Domesday Survey[4]; in the early part of the thirteenth century there were more than one, a yearly rent of 10*s.* arising from them being appropriated to the kitchen of the abbey, while 6*s.* 8*d.* from Faulk Mill (Fokemulne) was similarly applied.[5] In 1237-8 a conveyance was made to Abbot Richard of mills and land in Offenham.[6] Only one mill was mentioned in 1291, however, and that from its value being the same was probably Faulk Mill.[7] In 1540 Faulk Mill with a fishery in 'Stokebroke' was worth 43*s.* 4*d.* yearly.[8] It is still in existence and still called Faulk Mill; it stands about half-a-mile from the village of Offenham on Badsey Brook, a small tributary of the Avon.

CHURCH Offenham church, dedicated in honour of St. Milburg, stands to the south of the village and west of the main street. It consists of chancel, with north vestry; nave, with north aisle, and arcade of four bays, south porch, and west tower. The whole church, except the tower, was rebuilt in 1861, retaining nothing of the old work. The tower is of the fifteenth century, of three stages, with embattled parapet and angle pinnacles, having projecting gurgoyles at the angles and centre of each face. The belfry windows are of two trefoiled lights with tracery under a square head with a label. The west window in the ground stage is a single ogee trefoiled light with a crocketed label and flanking pinnacles. Below it is a seam in the masonry as if a west door had once existed. The tower is entered from the church by a lofty fifteenth-century doorway with double doors hung to open into the tower. Its east face is of elaborate though coarse work, with an arched head 10 feet high to the crown, under a heavy square label with pateræ. The large spandrils are carved with a flower and coarsely-cut leafwork radiating from it. A similar doorway on a smaller scale occurs at Middle Littleton. The font is octagonal with enriched quatrefoil panels on the bowl and panelled stem of the fifteenth century. There are six bells—the treble and second by Taylor of Loughborough, 1897; third, 1732; fourth and fifth by W. Clark of Evesham, 1701; and the tenor by J. Rudhall, 1830.

The church plate[9] is modern, and consists of a cup, paten, flagon, and salver.

The registers[10] begin in 1538, the original paper book being preserved. There are three other books in fair condition.

ADVOWSON The advowson of Offenham belonged to the abbey of Evesham until the suppression of that house, when it passed in the same way as the advowson of Badsey (q. v.); it is now held by the dean and chapter of Christ Church, Oxford. In 1871 the Ecclesiastical Commissioners endowed the living with £43 6*s.* 8*d.* a year out of the Common Fund.[11]

The chapel of Offenham was appropriated to the sacristan of the abbey as early as 1206.[12] In 1291 it was worth £5 6*s.* 8*d.* yearly.[13] In 1535 it was on lease to John Warren, chaplain and curate for the term of his life, and its clear value was £6 11*s.* 2*d.*[14] A considerable portion of the tithes appears to have been commuted by Sir Thomas Cecil in 1584.[15] In 1813 an attempt was made by petitioning Parliament to deal with the tithe. It was alleged in the petition that the inclosed land was subject to great and small tithes, the estates were intermixed and much dispersed and incapable of further improvement. The petitioners sought to bring in a Bill to enable them to make exchange and exonerate the parish from tithe. Nothing seems to have come of this after the Tithe Commutation Act. An extraordinary tithe was imposed on the market gardening, and this continued until 1886, when it was abolished.[16]

CHARITIES By will dated 16 August, 1811, John Millard directed that a sum should be raised out of his personal estate sufficient to produce £5 yearly when laid out in Government funded property; this sum was to be applied towards the establishment of a Sunday School where poor children should receive an elementary education. With the consent of the Charity Commissioners the principal sum, about £500, was about 1853 applied towards the cost of erecting the National School. Millard bequeathed a further sum, now invested in Consols to the amount of £59 7*s.* 2*d.* in the hands of the official trustees, towards providing surgical and medical aid for the poor.

Brent's Charity. Mrs. Brent bequeathed £100 towards the support of a school; this sum was first laid out in the purchase of an India Bond, and afterwards with its interest, and a further £13 10*s.* given by John Millard, was invested in Consols. From 1812 to 1815 no school was carried on as it was desired to accumulate the principal, but from 1815 to 1820 nine children from Offenham were sent to the National School at Evesham. On the establishment of a school at Littleton the children were sent there, and finally, when a National School was established at Offenham itself, £7 of the interest of this charity, which in 1876 consisted of £266 13*s.* 4*d.* in Consols, was devoted to its support, the remaining £1 being given to the Sunday School.

W. Kerry, by will dated 1835, gave a sum invested in Consols to the amount of £162 14*s.* 10*d.*, the interest of which is also devoted to the support of the elementary school.

The Poor Land consists of an acre and a half of grass land, the rent of £7 from which is distributed in bread.[17]

The non-provided school at Offenham affords accommodation for 130 children; a new infant school is now being built by the Worcestershire County Council. There is a Baptist chapel, built in 1871.

1 Chan. inq. p.m. 2 Chas. I. ccccxxiii. 74.
2 Noake, *Guide to Worc.* 289.
3 Feet of F. Worc. Mich. 1650.
4 *V. C. H. Worc.* 306b.
5 *Chron. de Evesham* (Rolls Ser.), 217, and Cott. MS. Vesp. B. xxiv. f. 48.
6 Feet of F. Worc. 22 Hen. III. No. 11.
7 *Pope Nich. Tax.* (Rec. Com.), 229.
8 Mins. Accts. 31–2 Hen. VIII. L. R. 1330, m. 13–14.
9 Lea, *Ch. Plate Worc. Archd.* 33.
10 Dioc. Conf. 1899, *Digest of Par. Reg.* 18.
11 *London Gazette*, 16 June, 1871, 2804.
12 *Chron. de Evesham* (Rolls Ser.), 210.
13 *Pope Nich. Tax.* (Rec. Com.), 219*b*.
14 *Valor Eccl.* (Rec. Com.), iii. 255.
15 Feet of F. Worc. Hil. 26 Eliz.
16 Information supplied by J. W. W.-B.
17 *Char. Com. Rep.* xxiv. 526–7.

OLDBERROW

Hulebarwe (viii. cent.); Oleberge (xi. cent.); Huleberge, Ulleberwe (xiii. cent.); Wolbarowe (xvi. cent.); Ouldborough (xvii. cent.).

The parish of Oldberrow, now in Warwickshire for all administrative purposes, is quite detached from the rest of Blackenhurst Hundred, and is about 15 miles north and a little to the east of Evesham. It stretches into Warwickshire a long, narrow strip, in no place a mile wide, Beoley, the only Worcestershire parish which touches it, forming its north-western boundary, which is half a mile in length. The land is undulating, and slopes from the north-west, where Oldberrow Hill is 513 feet above the Ordnance datum to the south-east, where the height is under 300 feet above the same level. A small stream flowing eastward into the river Alne forms the north-east boundary for three-quarters of the distance. No main road passes through the parish, but just beyond the north-west boundary a road from Henley in Arden passing through it meets the main road from Birmingham to Alcester. The village lying towards the south-east of the parish is connected by road with Morton Bagot, Ullenhall, and Henley in Arden, and a road to Wootton Wawen connects them with the main road from Birmingham to Stratford-on-Avon. The nearest railway station is at Henley in Arden, opened in 1894 as the terminus of a branch line from the Oxford and Birmingham section of the Great Western Railway two miles to the west of the village. Oldberrow contains an area of 1,236 acres. The subsoil is keuper marl, the surface soil loam and clay. Wheat and beans are grown, but much of the land is under pasture. The population is very small, and almost entirely engaged in agriculture. Among the names of fields are Wharnap Hill, Great Cadboro', Banner's Hill, Puck Meadow, and Gospel Bit.[1] Among former place-names the following occur:—Quagg, Cowlehill,[2] Hill Forge Croft, Thistlecroft, Leatrench, Park Meadow,[3] Farbarrows, Hollow Croft, and Coppice Close.[4]

MANOR

In 709 Kenred of Mercia gave 12 acres in Oldberrow to Bishop Egwin towards the endowment of the newly-founded monastery of Evesham.[5] The grant was afterwards apparently confirmed by Beortulf of Mercia about the middle of the ninth century.[6]

After the Conquest Oldberrow apparently passed out of the hands of the monks and became one of the subjects of the dispute settled by the court of seven shires at 'Gildeneberga.'[7] Abbot Walter conclusively proved his right to it, however, and it was included in the writ which Odo, bishop of Bayeux, addressed to Wulstan, bishop of Worcester, and the sheriffs of Worcester, Gloucester, and Warwick, directing that the church of Evesham should hold in peace certain lands, of which it had been unjustly impleaded.[8] At the time of the Survey, Oldberrow was again in the possession of the monastery. Although the extent of cultivated land then remained the same as in Beortulf's grant, outside the 12 acres there seems to have lain a considerable stretch of woodland, part of the forest of Henley in Arden, which probably furnished food for swine and employment for the two swineherds mentioned in the Survey.[9] Shortly afterwards Robert, a monk of Jumièges, who became abbot of Evesham in 1104, and who is stated to have distributed many of the lands of the abbey among his friends[10] without the consent of the chapter, gave Oldberrow to Simon Despenser, who rendered for it an annual rent of 25*s*.[11] The monks appear to have made efforts to regain it, and even excommunicated Simon, but the latter continued to hold it,[12] and from him it passed to his descendants,[13] in whose hands it remained until the beginning of the fourteenth century.

In the twelfth century Oldberrow was held by Ralph Despenser, probably the same who about 1150 held land in Littleton.[14] On his death, which occurred before 1190, a dispute seems to have arisen respecting the succession to Oldberrow. Simon his son then had assize of mort d'ancestor against Thurstan, son of Simon,[15] but the identity of the latter and the grounds on which he based his claim do not appear, though he was probably successful, as the manor seems to have descended in the direct line of a Thurstan Despenser who lived in the latter part of the twelfth century, and who had two sons, Walter and Aumary.[16] His son Walter, to whom Henry II. had granted the manors of Worthy in Hampshire and Stanley Regis in Gloucestershire,[17] died before 1204 without issue, and was succeeded by his brother Aumary.[18] Oldberrow was certainly held by the latter's grandson, Adam Despenser, in 1252[19] and about 1280.[20] Adam, who died in 1294, leaving as his heir his son Aumary,[21] is said during his lifetime to have given this manor to the latter. On 1 May, 1311, Aumary had licence to alienate the manor of Oldberrow in mortmain to the abbot and convent of Evesham[22] during the abbacy of John of Brokehampton.[23] Many years afterwards, in 1346–7, the two

[1] Allies, *Antiquities*, 338.

[2] Mins. Accts. 31–2 Hen. VIII. L.R. 1330, m. 20*d*.

[3] Com. Pleas Recov. R. Worc. Trin. 16 Geo. III. m. 59.

[4] Prattinton Coll. (Soc. Antiq.), quoting from terrier of 1714.

[5] Birch, *Cart. Sax*. i. 181–2; *Chron. de Evesham* (Rolls Ser.), 72.

[6] Cott. MS. Vesp. B. xxiv. f. 34*d*. and 35. See Birch, *Cart. Sax*. i. 181–3. Beortulf reigned from 838 to 851 (*Flor. of Worc*.).

[7] Cott. MS. Vesp. B. xxiv. f. 24. *Chron. de Evesham* (Rolls Ser.), app. to preface xlviii.

[8] Ibid.

[9] *V. C. H. Worc*. i. 306*b*.

[10] *Chron. de Evesham* (Rolls Ser.), 98.

[11] Cott. MS. Vesp. B. xxiv. f. 8d.

[12] Ibid. 'Simon Dispensator tenet Uleberga pro 25 solidis dono Rodberti Abbatis sine capitulo et super excommunicationem Sancte Marie et Sancti Egwini patronis nostris.'

[13] From subsequent evidence (*Cal. of Chart. R*. i. 414) these appear to have been the Despensers who held Great Rollright in Oxfordshire by the serjeanty of being a steward of the king, and who probably derived their name from that office: *Testa de Nevill* (Rec. Com.), 308*b*.

[14] Cott. MS. Vesp. B. xxiv. f. 9.

[15] Pipe R. 2 Rich. I. m. 4. 'Simon filius Radulphi debet cs. pro habenda recognitionem de morte patris sui de villa de Ulleberga versus Turstinum filium Simonis. Summonendum est in Oxinfordscira.'

[16] *Rot. Chart*. (Rec. Com.), i. 126.

[17] Ibid. and Cartæ Antiquæ D.D. 9, 10, 11.

[18] *Rot. Chart*. (Rec. Com.), i. 126.

[19] *Cal. of Chart. R*. i. 414, where it is wrongly identified as Holborough (in Inkberrow).

[20] *Lay Subs. R. c*. 1280 (Worc. Hist. Soc.), 88.

[21] Inq. p.m. 23 Edw. I. No. 31.

[22] *Cal. of Pat*. 1307-13, p. 337.

[23] *Chron. de Evesham* (Rolls Ser), 284.

daughters and coheirs of Aumary, Agnes the widow of Thomas of Birmingham and Agatha the wife of John Coningsby, sued the abbot of Evesham for this manor. They stated that their grandfather Adam had given it to their father Aumary and his wife Lucy in fee tail, that Aumary had consequently no right to alienate it, and that on his death it should have descended to them 'per formam donationis.' The abbot in reply stated that Aumary held the manor in fee simple and not in fee tail, and this defence was held to be sufficient; and judgment was given for the abbot.[1] Two messuages in Oldberrow, with fields adjacent, worth 2 marks annually,[2] were also acquired by Abbot William Chiriton from John Nutelyn, who probably held under the Despensers in Oldberrow as in Stanley Regis.[3]

In 1535[4] the manor was let to farm with the demesne lands for the sum of £4 1*s*., and the sale of wood produced the sum of 13*s*. 4*d*. yearly.[5] Three years later, on 8 December, 1538, the abbot and convent granted a lease of the 'site' of the manor and the demesne lands to Richard Smith, alias Court, Agnes his wife, and Edward, John, and Thomas their sons, for a term of sixty years at the same rent as before.[6] On the surrender of the monastery of Evesham in 1539 the manor of Oldberrow came into the hands of the Crown.[7]

On 24 April, 1542, Henry VIII. granted Oldberrow with various manors in other counties to Sir Edmund Knightley of Fawsley, Northamptonshire, a chief commissioner for the suppression of the religious houses, and Lady Ursula his wife, in consideration of the sum of £98 15*s*. 10*d*., and in exchange for certain manors and lands in the counties of Northampton and Buckingham.[8] Sir Edmund was to hold Oldberrow in tail male with remainder to his brother Sir Valentine Knightley, and then to the right heirs of his mother, Lady Joan Knightley, then deceased.[9] On 3 June, 1542, Sir Edmund Knightley wrote to John Scudamore, Receiver of the Court of Augmentations for the county of Worcester, desiring to be put in possession of the manor and to receive the moiety of his yearly rents there.[10] He died in September of the same year, and none of his children surviving him, the manor of Oldberrow passed to his brother Sir Valentine Knightley in accordance with the terms of the grant. The latter in 1557–8 had licence from the Crown to convey it to Sir John Spencer and others, possibly for the purposes of a trust.[11] Sir Valentine died in 1566 seised of Oldberrow.[12] From his will, dated 26 December, 1564, it appears that this manor, with that of Burgh Hall in Staffordshire and other lands, was settled on his third son Thomas in tail male, with reversion in default to the heirs male of Sir Valentine, and then to his right heirs. In the meantime it was vested in trustees, of whom his eldest son, Richard Knightley, was one, who were to apply its issues to the maintenance of his younger sons, except his second son, Edmund, and to the provision of a marriage portion for his daughter Anne.[13] In 1593 Thomas Knightley, jointly with Elizabeth his wife and his elder brother Sir Richard Knightley of Fawsley, conveyed Oldberrow to Thomas Crue and Nicholas Stanton,[14] probably in trust. On 10 October, 1605, on the marriage of his son Richard with Jane, daughter of Sir Edward Littleton of Pillaton Hall, Staffordshire, a settlement was made by which the manor was conveyed in trust to the use of Thomas for his life, and then to his son Richard and his heirs by Jane his wife.[15] Thomas died on 28 November, 1621, and was succeeded by his son Richard, then over forty years of age.[16] In 1647 Richard Knightley and Jane his wife and their son Richard conveyed the manor to Humphrey Salway and Samuel Knightley,[17] in trust on the marriage of the younger Richard with Anne, daughter of Sir William Courteen and widow of Essex Devereux. Richard had previously married Elizabeth, daughter of the famous John Hampden, and on his death in 1661 Oldberrow seems to have passed to Richard his son by this marriage. The latter died unmarried in Paris on 5 October, 1665, and this manor and his other possessions came to his half-brother and heir, Essex Knightley of Fawsley, on whose death, on 20 April, 1670, his estates descended to his only child Anne, who in 1688 became the wife of Thomas Foley of Dudley and of Stoke Edith, Hereford, created Baron Foley of Kidderminster in 1711. In 1694 Thomas Foley and Anne conveyed Oldberrow by fine to Robert Harley and Humphrey Hetherington,[18] and for some years afterwards its descent is obscure.

KNIGHTLEY. *Quarterly ermine and paly gold and gules with a border azure.*

FOLEY. *Silver a fesse engrailed between three cinqfoils with a border sable.*

In 1716 the manor was in the hands of Richard Hilton and Mary his wife, who in Michaelmas term of that year levied a fine by which they conveyed it to Robert Fulwood.[19] The latter seems to have held it until 1741, when it was acquired by Thomas Bree and George Butter for their joint use, with reversion to the heirs of the former.[20]

In 1742 the manor house, Oldberrow Court, with 257 acres of arable meadow and pasture and coppice woods, was advertised for sale, and is stated by Prattinton to have been bought by a Mr. Parrot of Coventry.[21]

Oldberrow was held in 1776 by Mary Packwood of the borough of Warwick, widow of Gery Packwood, and Charles Porter Packwood, their son and heir, who in June of that year jointly suffered a recovery by which the manor was settled in fee simple

[1] De Banco R. 347 m. 168*d*.
[2] *Chron. de Evesham* (Rolls Ser.), 290.
[3] *Orig. R.* (Rec. Com.), i. 148.
[4] *Valor Eccl.* (Rec. Com.), 248*b*.
[5] Ibid.
[6] Mins. Accts. 31-2 Hen. VIII. L.R. 1330, m. 20*d*.
[7] Ibid. Wrottesley in the county of Stafford was said to be then annexed to Oldberrow.
[8] *L. and P. Hen. VIII.* xvii. 165; Pat. 34 Hen. VIII. pt. 1, m. 17.
[9] *L. and P. Hen. VIII.* xvii. 165.
[10] Ibid. 221.
[11] Pat. 4 and 5 Phil. and Mary, pt. 15, and Habington, *Surv. of Worc.* (Worc. Hist. Soc.), ii. 236.
[12] Chan. inq. p. m. 8 Eliz. cxliii. 54.
[13] Ibid. where the will is quoted.
[14] Feet of F. Worc. East. 35 Eliz.
[15] Chan. inq. p. m. 20 Jas. I. ccccxxxvii. 75.
[16] Ibid.
[17] Feet of F. Div. Cos. East. 23 Chas. I.
[18] Ibid. Hil. 6 Wm. and Mary.
[19] Ibid. Worc. Mich. 3 Geo. I.
[20] Ibid. Mich. 15 Geo. II.
[21] Prattinton Coll. (Soc. Antiq.), quoting *Worc. Journ.* 1742.

on the latter.[1] Nash states that it was afterwards sold by 'one Packwood'—possibly Charles Porter Packwood—to the trustees of Robert Knight, earl of Catherlough,[2] whose seat was at Barrells, Henley-in-Arden, Warwickshire, adjoining Oldberrow, and who died in 1772 without legitimate male issue.[3] His trustees were Sir Henry Burrard, William Snell, and William Jacomb,[4] who, acting apparently on instructions contained in Lord Catherlough's will, seems to have purchased Oldberrow Manor, and to have conveyed it to his natural son Robert Knight. The latter held it in 1826.[5] On his death it was sold by his trustees on 20 June, 1856, to Mr. William Newton of Whateley Hall, Castle Bromwich, who died in 1862, and was succeeded by his son Mr. Thomas Henry Goodwin Newton, the present lord of the manor.

KNIGHT, EARL OF CATHERLOUGH. *Silver three bends gules and a quarter azure with a spur and its leathers gold.*

Many of the houses in the parish are said to have been pulled down by Mr. Robert Knight,[6] and Oldberrow now consists of the church, the rectory, three farmhouses, and two cottages.

On 3 January, 1252–3, Henry III. granted to Adam Despenser a weekly market on Wednesday at his manor of Oldberrow and a yearly fair there on the vigil, the feast, and the morrow of St. John the Evangelist[7] (26–28 December).

In 1291 the church of Oldberrow was valued at £4 6*s.* 8*d.*[8] In 1535 it was stated to be a rectory worth £4 annually.[9]

CHURCH Oldberrow Church is dedicated in honour of the Blessed Virgin Mary, and is of the simplest possible form, a plain rectangle with no division between nave and chancel. It was entirely rebuilt in 1875, the old features being reset. The east window is of the fourteenth century, with three trefoiled lights, the mullions intersecting in the head. In the north wall, at the east end, is a narrow pointed lancet with an outer reveal for the glazing, early thirteenth century. West of it is a modern recess to the east of the modern chancel screen; beyond this is a wide single light with a trefoiled head, made of a piece of tracery from a larger window. The north doorway has a fourcentred head in one stone, on which is a cross in a sunk circle flanked by two trefoiled sinkings, rough work of the fifteenth century. Towards the west end of this wall is a modern single light. In the south wall, beginning from the east, are: (i.) a single trefoiled fourteenth-century light; (ii.) a small twelfth-century round-headed light with an outer reveal; (iii.) west of the screen, a modern window of two cinquefoiled lights; (iv.) the south doorway, opposite the north doorway, having a sharply-pointed fourteenth-century arched head with a plain chamfer over it is a modern wooden porch. The west window is modern, of two lights with tracery under a square head. From the west end of the nave roof rises a modern wooden bell-turret with a pyramidal roof. Its detail, as is that of all the modern woodwork, porch, screen, and seats, is very good. A turret of similar design, but ancient, and showing traces of having been used as a pigeon-house, is to be seen at the neighbouring church of Morton Bagot.

In the chancel in the south wall is a square locker and a twelfth-century pillar piscina, of which the bowl only is ancient.

The font has a shallow, round bowl, with a necking at the base; its stem is in the shape of four engaged shafts on a square base. It may be of the twelfth century. On the bowl an incised design of foliage is repeated four times. The whole has been tooled over but seems to be ancient, and is shown in a drawing in the Prattinton Collection dated 1826.[10]

There are three bells,[11] the treble being uninscribed, but of the ancient long-waisted shape. It may be as old as the thirteenth century. The second and tenor are by John Martin of Worcester, 1674.[11]

The church plate consists of a cup (1787) and a large paten of 1830.[12]

The parish registers are complete in six books from 1649.[13]

Dr. Prattinton states that he examined the registers of Oldberrow on 26 August, 1826. He found that the earliest register had been exposed to damp, and was in such a state as scarcely to admit of examination without injuring it. What remained of it was carefully preserved in a paper marked 1546 to 1646, but there seemed to be entries as early as 1539.[14] The second register was marked on the outside 1646 to 1671, and the third 1674 to 1729.[15]

Habington notes in his *Survey of Worcestershire*[16] that in the east window were the arms of the abbey of Evesham: 'Asure, a cheyne with a horslocke in cheueron betweene three bishops' miters,' and those of Owlborough, 'Gules, a fesse betweene 3 owles Argent,' with figures of three persons of the Owlborough family and a mutilated inscription, 'Orate pro animabus Johannis Owleborough . . . ejus . . . Johannis filii.'[17]

OWLBOROUGH. *Gules a fesse between three owls silver.*

The abbey arms are still in this window.

ADVOWSON The advowson of Oldberrow seems to have been held by the Despensers and to have passed from them with the manor in 1311 to the abbot and convent of Evesham,[18] with whom it remained until the suppression.[19] It was then granted to Sir Edmund Knightley with the manor, and followed its descent until it came into the hands of Thomas and Anne Foley, though it

[1] Com. Pleas Recov. R. Worc. Trin. 16 Geo. III. m. 59.

[2] Nash, *Hist. of Worc.* ii. 204.

[3] *Complete Peerage*, ii. 197.

[4] Studley Deeds in the library at Stratford-on-Avon, and information supplied by Mr. A. C. Coldicott, of Henley-in-Arden.

[5] Prattinton Coll. (Soc. Antiq.).

[6] Ibid.

[7] *Cal. of Chart. R.* i. 414.

[8] *Pope Nich. Tax.* (Rec. Com.), 219*b*, 239*b*. [9] *Valor Eccl.* (Rec. Com.), iii. 258.

[10] In the library of the Society of Antiquaries.

[11] Walters, *Trans. Worc. Arch. Soc.* xxv. 552.

[12] Lea, *Ch. Plate Worc. Archd.* 24.

[13] Dioc. Conf. 1899, *Digest of Par. Reg.* 4.

[14] Prattinton Coll. (Soc. Antiq.).

[15] Ibid.

[16] Op. cit. (Worc. Hist. Soc.), ii. 236.

[17] The Roger de Ulbarwe who seems to have been connected with the adjoining Warwickshire parishes of Lapworth and Tanworth may possibly have been a member of this family, of whom, however, no trace has been found in Oldberrow. *Cat. of Anct. D.* (P.R.O.), iii. 58-9; ibid. iv. 96.

[18] *Chron. de Evesham* (Rolls Ser.), 284.

[19] *Sede Vac. Reg.* (Worc. Hist. Soc.), 203, 232.

is not mentioned until the inquisition taken upon the death of Thomas Knightley in 1622.[1] It is said to have been sold by the Foleys to William Holyoake in 1705 for £110.[2] In 1754 Thomas Chambers and Mary and John Holyoake conveyed it to William Tibbatts;[3] on 5 August, 1758, Holyoake mortgaged it to one Underhill for £150, and on 25 November, 1761, sold it to the Rev. John Peshall of Guildford for £500.[4] It still remains in the Peshall family, the present patrons being Mrs. Peshall and the incumbent, the Rev. Samuel Peshall.[5] The living has recently been annexed to Morton Bagot, and is now known as Oldberrow cum Morton.

There is no Nonconformist place of worship in the parish.

The children of Oldberrow attend the National School at Ullenhall.

CHARITIES Edmund Court some time before 1780 conveyed to trustees certain property in Henley-in-Arden, Warwickshire, to the use of the poor of Oldberrow. The houses, becoming ruinous, were pulled down before 1830,[6] and the material was sold for £12 10*s*., which was distributed in kind amongst the most deserving poor. The land is let for £5, which is given away on St. Thomas's Day and Whitsunday to sixteen or eighteen persons, chiefly widows, who when once placed on the list continue to receive the charity for their lives.[7]

Francis Court settled certain property for the payment of 5*s*. yearly to the poor, and a similar sum was left by Richard Freeman. These two charities were distributed on St. Thomas's Day with that of Edmund Court.[8]

WICKHAMFORD

Wikewane (viii. cent.); Wiguene (xi. cent.); Wykwanford (xvi. cent.); Wykewantford (xvii. cent.).

The parish of Wickhamford is situated in the south-east of the county, to the east of Bengeworth. It has an area of 1,266 acres, and contains thirty-three inhabited houses.[9] The land slopes gently upward from the valley of a branch of the Badsey Brook, which flows through the parish from south to north. The subsoil is lower lias, and the surface is a rich mould. Nearly the whole of the parish is devoted to market gardening and fruit culture, and asparagus is largely grown. The main road from Evesham to Broadway and Stow-on-the-Wold passes through the parish about half a mile south of the village, with which it is connected by a branch road running northward to Badsey.

The village consists of a single street of small houses, running north and south, bounded towards the north by the buildings of the manor house.

The railway stations of Evesham on the Great Western and the Midland Railways, opened in 1852 and 1864, and of Littleton and Badsey on the Great Western Railway, opened in April, 1884, are about equally distant from the village to the north-west and north respectively. Among the place-names in the parish are Green Street, Pitcher's Hill, Came's Acre, and Coomb Nap.[10]

MANOR Three 'mansæ' in Wickhamford passed into the possession of the monastery of Evesham early in the eighth century as part of the foundation gift of Offa of Essex in 703,[11] or of the joint gift of Offa and Kenred in 709.[12] At the time of the Domesday Survey Wickhamford was held by the abbey and contained 3 hides.[13] Among the free tenants of the abbey there during the twelfth century were Walter Trusselun or Frusselun, who held 1 hide, and John de Wickwana, who held 1 virgate.[14]

In 1291 the abbey's possessions at Wickhamford were valued at £9 6*s*. 9½*d*.;[15] and from the improvements afterwards made by Abbot Roger Zatton (1379–1418)[16] the manor seems to have increased in importance. On 10 March, 1528–9, the abbot and convent granted a lease of the demesne lands with the site of the manor to William Spon or Sponer and his assigns for a term of fifty-one years,[17] and this lease remained in force when the manor came into the hands of the Crown.[18]

The manorial rights were held by the Crown until 1561–2, when the manor of Wickhamford was granted to Thomas Throckmorton and Margaret his wife and their heirs to hold in chief by the service of the twentieth part of a knight's fee.[19] They remained in possession of it until 1594, when they levied a fine, to which their son John Throckmorton was a party, by which the manor was conveyed to Samuel Sandys and Mercy Culpeper his wife.[20] It is then described as consisting of fourteen messuages, 1,100 acres of land, and a mill.[21] Samuel Sandys was the son of Edwin Sandys, bishop of Worcester, afterwards translated to York. He purchased the manor of Ombersley and considerable property round Evesham, and died seised of Wickhamford on 18 August, 1626, leaving as his heir his son Edwin. The manor was, however, held by his widow Mercy until her death in 1629; Edwin had predeceased her on 6 September, 1626, leaving a son Samuel,[22] to whom the manor then passed.

THROCKMORTON. *Gules a cheveron silver with three gimels sable thereon.*

Wickhamford after this date followed the descent of the Sandys family,[23] being dealt with at various

1 Chan. inq. p.m. 20 Jas. I. ccccxxxvii. 75.
2 Nash, *Hist. of Worcs.* ii. 204.
3 Feet of F. Worc. Mich. 28 Geo. II.
4 Nash, op. cit. ii. 204.
5 Clergy List, 1904.
6 A statement of charities was made in that year by Thomas Hayes, churchwarden, and is quoted in the Prattinton Coll. (Soc. Antiq.).
7 Ibid.; *Char. Commrs. Rep.* xxvi. 554–5; *Gen. Digest of Endowed Char.* Parl. Papers, 1876, vol. lviii.
8 Ibid.
9 *Worc. Co. Coun. Handbk.* (1903), 148.
10 Allies, *Antiquities*, 336.
11 *Chron. de Evesham* (Rolls Ser.), 72.
12 Birch, *Cart. Sax.* i. 183. This charter is marked spurious by Kemble, *Cod. Dip.* i. 70.
13 *V. C. H. Worc.* i. 306*b*.
14 Cott. MS. Vesp. B. xxiv. ff. 9 and 45.
15 *Pope Nich. Tax.* (Rec. Com.), 229*a*.
16 *Chron. de Evesham* (Rolls Ser.), 304.
17 Mins. Accts. 31–2 Hen. VIII. L.R. 1330, m. 15*d*.
18 Ibid.
19 Pat. 4 Eliz. pt. ii. m. 1.
20 Feet of F. Worc. Trin. 36 Eliz.
21 W. and L. inq. p.m. 22 Jas. I. xl. 49.
22 Ibid.
23 See Ombersley. Wickhamford is said to have been leased by Samuel Sandys and his wife Mercy, and Dame Penelope his mother, to Field Whorwood of Nethercote, Oxfordshire, for forty years from 15 February, 1637. *Visit. of Oxon.* (ed. Sir Thos. Phillipps), 32.

times for the purpose of marriage settlements. Thus, in 1657 it was conveyed by Samuel and Mary Sandys to Sir John Pettus, of Cheston Hall, Suffolk, royalist, deputy-governor of the royal mines and author of various books on metals, on the marriage of their son Samuel with Elizabeth Pettus, only daughter of Sir John. In 1694 Samuel Sandys and his wife Elizabeth, and Edwin Sandys their son, conveyed the manor to Sir James Rushout and William Bromley,[1] Edwin Sandys having married Sir James's daughter Alice. In 1743 Samuel Sandys of Ombersley and Wickhamford was created Baron Sandys of Ombersley, and was succeeded by his son Edwin Sandys, who died without issue in 1797. Five years later his niece Mary, dowager marchioness of Downshire, was created Baroness Sandys of Ombersley with remainder to her second son, Arthur Moyes William Hill, and his younger brothers and their heirs male successively, failing which to his eldest son Arthur, marquess of Downshire, and his heirs male.

SANDYS. *Gold a dance between three crosslets fitchy gules.*

HILL, MARQUESS OF DOWNSHIRE. *Sable a fesse silver between three spotted pards passant gardant with three scallops gules on the fesse.*

The manor remained with the family until about 1860, when it was purchased by the late J. P. Lord, who resided near Worcester, whose trustees still hold it.[2]

Abbot Randolph (1214–1229) is said to have built a grange at Wickhamford;[3] and one of his successors, Roger Zatton (1379–1418), also erected a tithe grange there, next the fishpond, and afterwards a great grange in the same court.[4] He also rebuilt a tenement called Hodysplace, 'on which he spent at least 20 marks.'[5]

The manor house stands near the church, and has a picturesque half-timbered east front, with gables facing east at either end. No features appear to be older than the sixteenth century, though parts of the walls may be earlier. In the room now used as a dining-room, on the south side of the house, is a wide fireplace with a flat four-centred stone arch and a seventeenth-century panelled wood chimney-piece with inlaid patterns in the panels. The large fishpond of the monastic grange remains, and a round stone pigeon-house. Between the house and the church stood the great stone barn, now destroyed.

The Domesday Survey mentions a mill at Wickhamford.[6] In 1206 it was leased for a rent of 8*s*., which was appropriated to the kitchener of the monastery;[7] some time afterwards, its holder having died while the king had the custody of the abbey, the next abbot, Thomas of Marlborough, retained it for the use of the convent.[8] In 1291 it was said to be worth 6*s*. 8*d*. yearly,[9] and in 1535 it had again been leased at an annual rent of 8*s*.[10] In 1540 it produced, with a parcel of land anciently belonging to it, the rent of 26*s*. 8*d*.[11] The mill is still in existence, and stands on the Badsey Brook about a quarter of a mile from the village of Wickhamford.

CHURCH

Wickhamford Church, dedicated in honour of St. John the Baptist, stands on low ground near a small brook to the north of the village, and separated from it by the manor house and its grounds. It consists of chancel, nave with south porch, and west tower.

The chancel is of the thirteenth century, rough-cast externally, having a fourteenth-century two-light east window, of which only the jambs and mullion below the springing remain, as the rebuilding of the gable in brick has destroyed the head, which is replaced by a wood lintel. In the north wall are two plain thirteenth-century lancet windows, that to the east blocked by the Sandys monument to be described below; the other, also blocked, is, like the corresponding window in the south wall of the chancel, at a lower level than the rest. In the south wall are two windows, and a door with a square chamfered head. The western window is a thirteenth-century lancet, that towards the east being of the fourteenth century with two trefoiled ogee lights and a trefoil in the head. There is a small arched recess for a piscina, and on the east wall, south of the east window, a defaced wall-painting of our Lady and Child, on a red ground, of late thirteenth-century date. The altar rails are good turned-work of the eighteenth century. The greater part of the north side of the chancel is taken up with the Sandys monument. The chancel arch is of the fourteenth century, of two chamfered orders dying out at the springing.

The nave is of the fourteenth century, refaced externally with ashlar in the sixteenth, and retaining of its original features, beside the chancel arch, only the first window from the east in its north wall, of two trefoiled lights with a quatrefoil in the head, and the quoins of the external south-east angle. The south doorway with a low four-centred head, and the windows east of it, of two trefoiled lights with a square head, are of the sixteenth century, and the south porch may be the same. At the west end of the south wall is a round-headed window of seventeenth or eighteenth century date, to light a now destroyed west gallery. In the north wall, beside the window already described, is a sixteenth-century window of two uncusped lights under a square head. The nave roof retains its ancient framing, with tie-beams, queenposts, collars, and purlins; in the east bay windbraces also occur. Above the chancel arch at the level of the plate of the nave roof runs a beam with fifteenth-century cresting, which is returned some six feet along the north and south walls of the nave. The roof over this length is boarded in to the underside of the collars with oak boarding divided into panels by moulded oak ribs, and over the beam the wall is boarded in to the same height. On this boarding are painted the royal arms of Charles II., dated 1661, doubtless the successors of a painting of the doom (which may still exist beneath the later paint) surrounding the rood. Whether the rood was also painted or carved in relief there is nothing to

[1] Feet of F. Worc. and Oxf. Mich. 6 Wm. and Mary.
[2] Information supplied by J. W. W.-B.
[3] *Chron. de Evesham* (Rolls Ser.), 261.
[4] Ibid. 304.
[5] Ibid. 305.
[6] *V.C.H. Worc.* i. 306*b*.
[7] *Chron. de Evesham* (Rolls Ser.), 217.
[8] Ibid. 276.
[9] *Pope Nich. Tax.* (Rec. Com.), 229.
[10] *Valor Eccl.* (Rec. Com.), iii. 250*a*.
[11] Mins. Accts. 31–2 Hen. VIII. L.R. 1330, m. 15*d*.

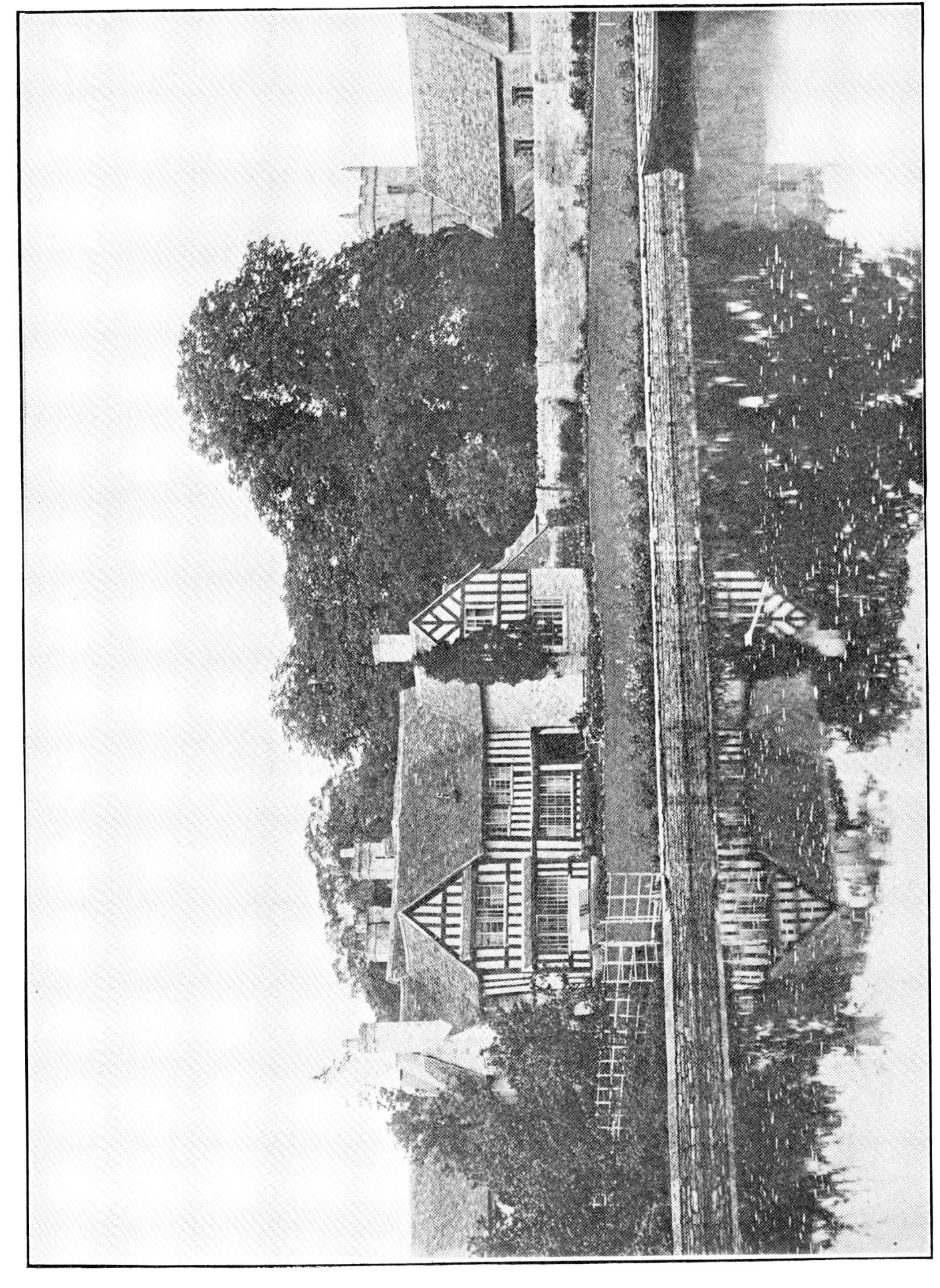

WICKHAMFORD: EAST FRONT OF THE MANOR HOUSE.

To face page 428.

Wickhamford Church : The Sandys Monument.

To face page 429.

show, but in the middle of the panelled ceiling where it joins the upright boarding is a series of wavy lines alternately white and blue, with a black border, which looks as if it may have formed part of a nimbus over the head of Christ.

The west tower is of three stages, ashlar faced, of the sixteenth century or later. On the ground stage it has a square-headed west window of three trefoiled lights, on the first story a single round-headed light on north, south, and west, and in the belfry a two-light window with pointed uncusped lights and a vesica in the head on the same three faces, with a square-headed two-light window on the east. It has an embattled parapet with small angle pinnacles. It opens to the church with a plain pointed arch, with a string of renaissance detail at the springing, seventeenth or eighteenth century.

The seating of the nave consists of high eighteenth-century pews, into the ends and doors of which are framed an interesting series of carved panels, mostly of the linen pattern, of which there are several types, the more elaborate having vine leaves and grapes at top and bottom. The pew next to the pulpit has six richly-carved panels, apparently French work of the late fifteenth or early sixteenth century. The pulpit has the reading desk and clerk's desk below all fitted with carved panels like the pews. The pulpit is octagonal, and appears to retain, within a later casing, a fifteenth or sixteenth century pulpit of which the inside only can now be seen, of very solid construction, with panels framed into angle posts. The outer casing has carving in high relief in panels of cherubs' heads and standing figures of saints, seventeenth-century work, and perhaps Flemish. The clerk's desk has six panels of sixteenth-century English work of the type most widely known by its occurrence at Layer Marney Hall in Essex. At the west end of the nave over the tower arch is a row of panels which formed the front of the west gallery, now destroyed. Three of these are seventeenth-century work in high relief, the rest linen panels. In an account of the church in May's *History of Evesham* (1845) it is mentioned that 'several pieces of carving have been added to the panels of a later and too elaborate character.'

The Sandys monuments in the chancel were very elaborately repaired and repainted some time since, and are fine specimens of this kind. They consist of two panelled alabaster altar tombs against the north wall, under one long tester carried by round arches springing from five black marble columns with Corinthian capitals. The arches are ornamented with charges from the Sandys coat, and the soffit of the tester is panelled. Against the wall at the back of the tomb are similar arches, carried alternately on pilasters, and corbels in the form of angels holding shields. The tomb to the east is at a somewhat higher level than the other, but the tester is of the same height throughout. On the eastern tomb lie the alabaster effigies of Sir Samuel Sandys (1626), 'eldest son to that famous prelate Edwyn, archbishop of Yorke,' and his wife Mercy (Culpeper), 1629. On the second tomb are the effigies of Sir Edwin Sandys (1626), son of Sir Samuel, and his wife Penelope (Buckley), who died in 1680. The date of the monument is about that of the death of Sir Edwin Sandys, and the effigy of his wife is that of a young woman. The inscriptions, which are very short,[1] are on the cornice of the tester, on the top of which stand two alabaster shields, gilded and coloured, with crest, helm, and mantling, flanked by twin obelisks. Alternately with these are small alabaster figures, partly gilded, of Faith, Hope, Charity, and Time. On the fronts of the altar tombs are kneeling figures of children, with in some cases shields above them denoting their marriages. On Sir Samuel's tomb are four sons and seven daughters.

On Sir Edwin's tomb are five sons and three daughters, but no shields; their father dying young, none of them were married at his death, and this helps to fix the limit of date for the tomb. At the back of the tomb, under the arcade, above the figures of Sir Samuel and his wife, are an oval with the Sandys coat, and a lozenge with the Culpeper arms and various alliances. On the spandrel of the arch between these shields are the arms of Sandys impaling Culpeper, and below, on the shield held by an angel, an impaled shield showing the full bearings of Sandys and Culpeper. The same arrangement is followed over Sir Edwin's tomb, with the Sandys and Buckley arms.

The font is modern, with a round tapering bowl and octagonal shaft and base; it stands under the tower.

There is one bell, by Matthew Bagley, 1686.

There is a communion cup with paten cover of 1571, and a pewter flagon and alms dish, dated 1692.[2] The registers begin in 1538.[3]

ADVOWSON Wickhamford was a chapelry of the mother church at Evesham until the dissolution. It seems to have been connected with the chapel of Badsey and Aldington, as in 1291 their value was given jointly as £15 6*s.* 8*d.*,[4] and in 1535, though each chapel appears to have had its own curate,[5] Wickhamford is stated to have been annexed to Badsey.[6] It was then in lease to Nicholas Wyke, chaplain and curate, for the term of his life.[7] It is referred to in 1540 as the parish church.[8] After the dissolution it followed the same descent as Badsey, and is now held by the dean and chapter of Christ Church, Oxford.

In the early part of the thirteenth century the lesser tithes of Wickhamford were appropriated, with those of Badsey and Aldington, to the repair of the spoons, cups, and glass windows of Evesham monastery.[9]

In 1574 the churchwardens of Wickhamford held ½ virgate of land and the pasture for certain animals,[10] but no church land or charities are mentioned in the Charity Commissioners' Reports.

The children of Wickhamford attend Badsey Council School. There is no place of worship for Nonconformists in the parish.

[1] But see Habington, *Surv. of Worc.* (Worc. Hist. Soc.), ii. 314, for the original inscriptions.
[2] Lea, *Ch. Plate Worc. Arch.* 33.
[3] Dioc.Conf.1899, *Digest of Par.Reg.* 19.
[4] *Pope Nich. Tax.* (Rec. Com.), 219*b*.
[5] *Valor Eccl.* (Rec. Com.), iii. 255, 256.
[6] Ibid. 253*a*.
[7] Ibid. 256*b*.
[8] Mins. Accts. 31–2 Hen. VIII. L. R. 1330, m. 15*d*.
[9] *Chron. de Evesham* (Rolls Ser.), 209.
[10] Pat. 16 Eliz. pt. 12.

BIRMINGHAM REFERENCE LIBRARY

TOPOGRAPHICAL MAP. – SECTION IV.

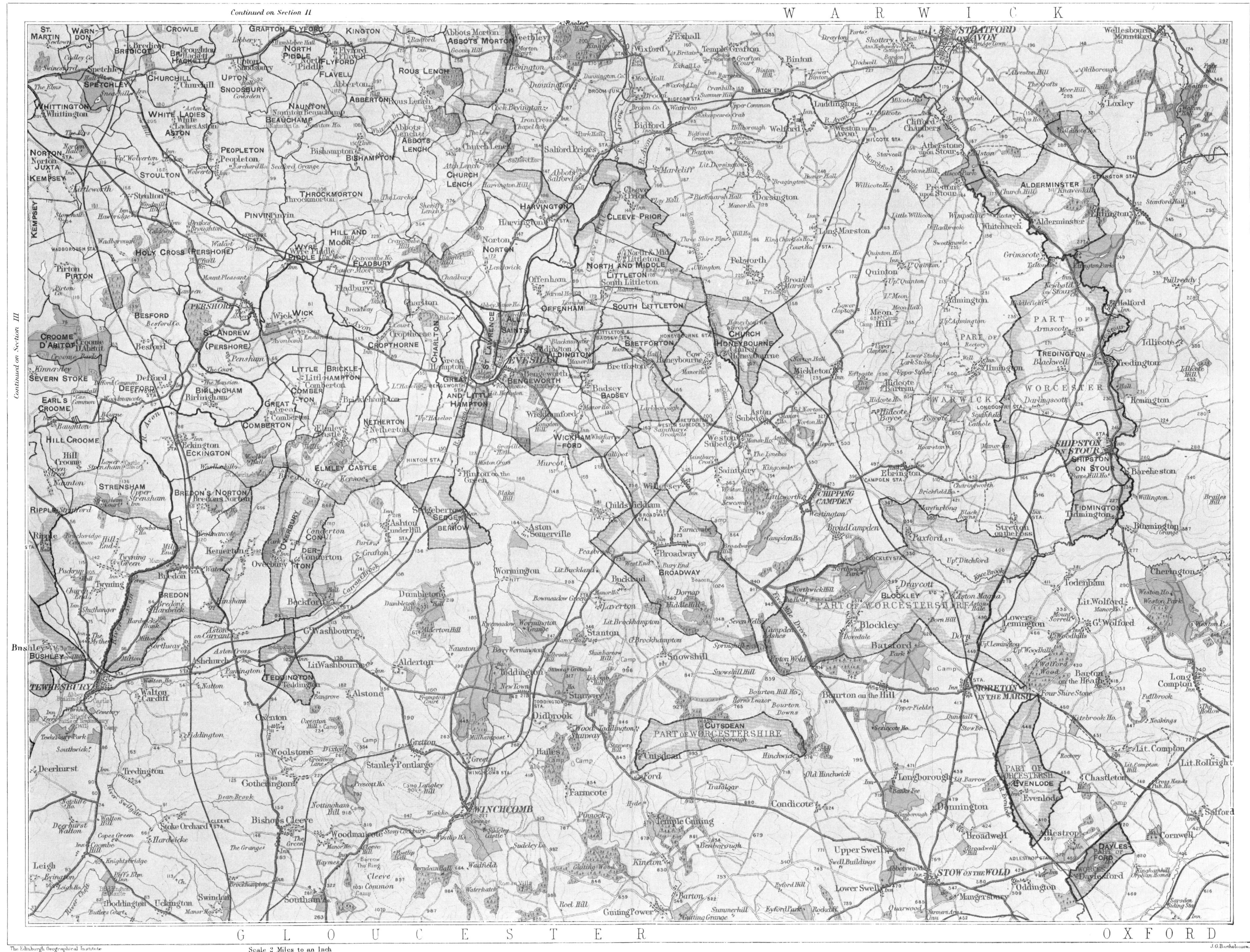

TOPOGRAPHICAL MAP. – SECTION III.

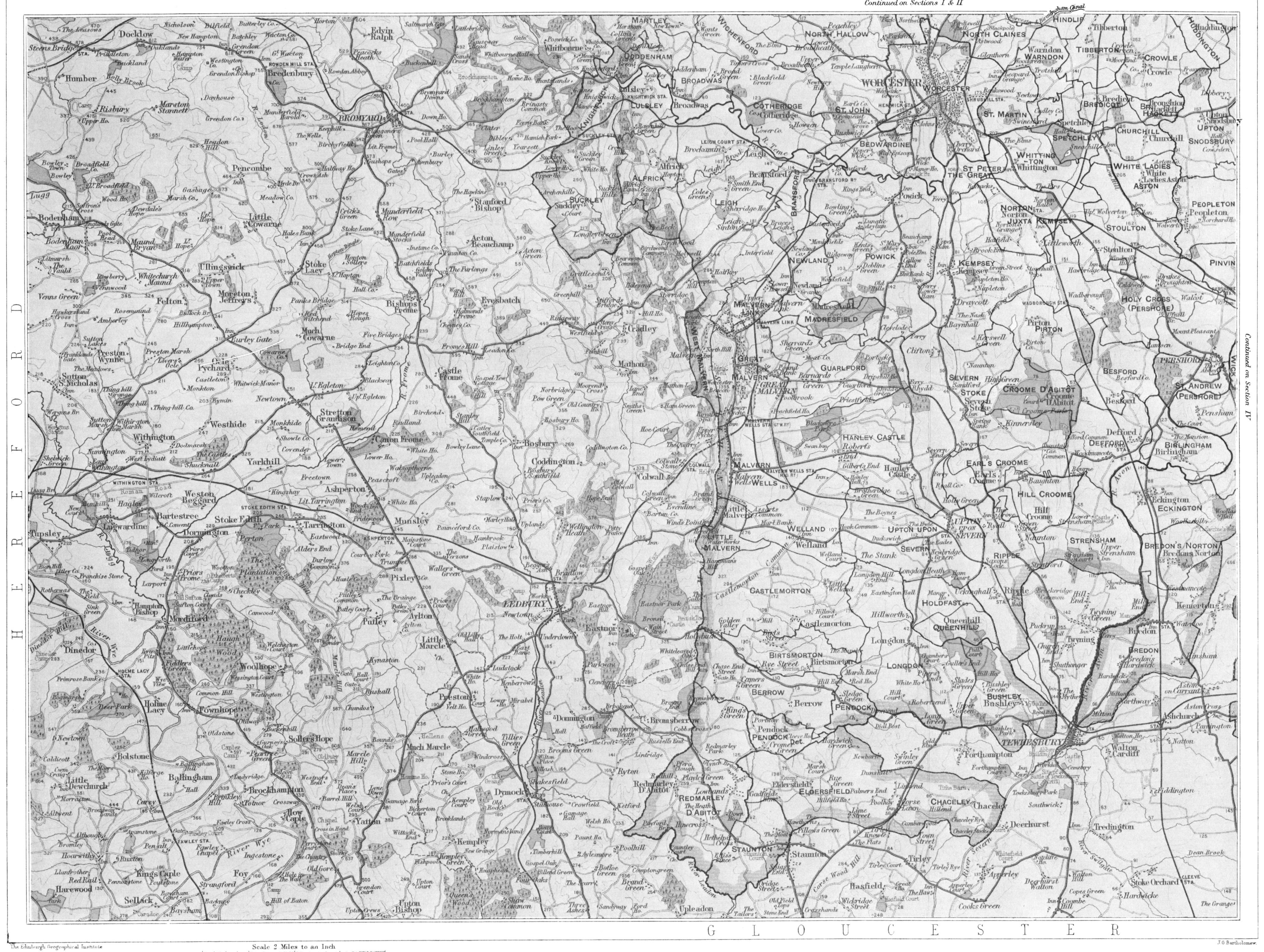

TOPOGRAPHICAL MAP. – SECTION II.

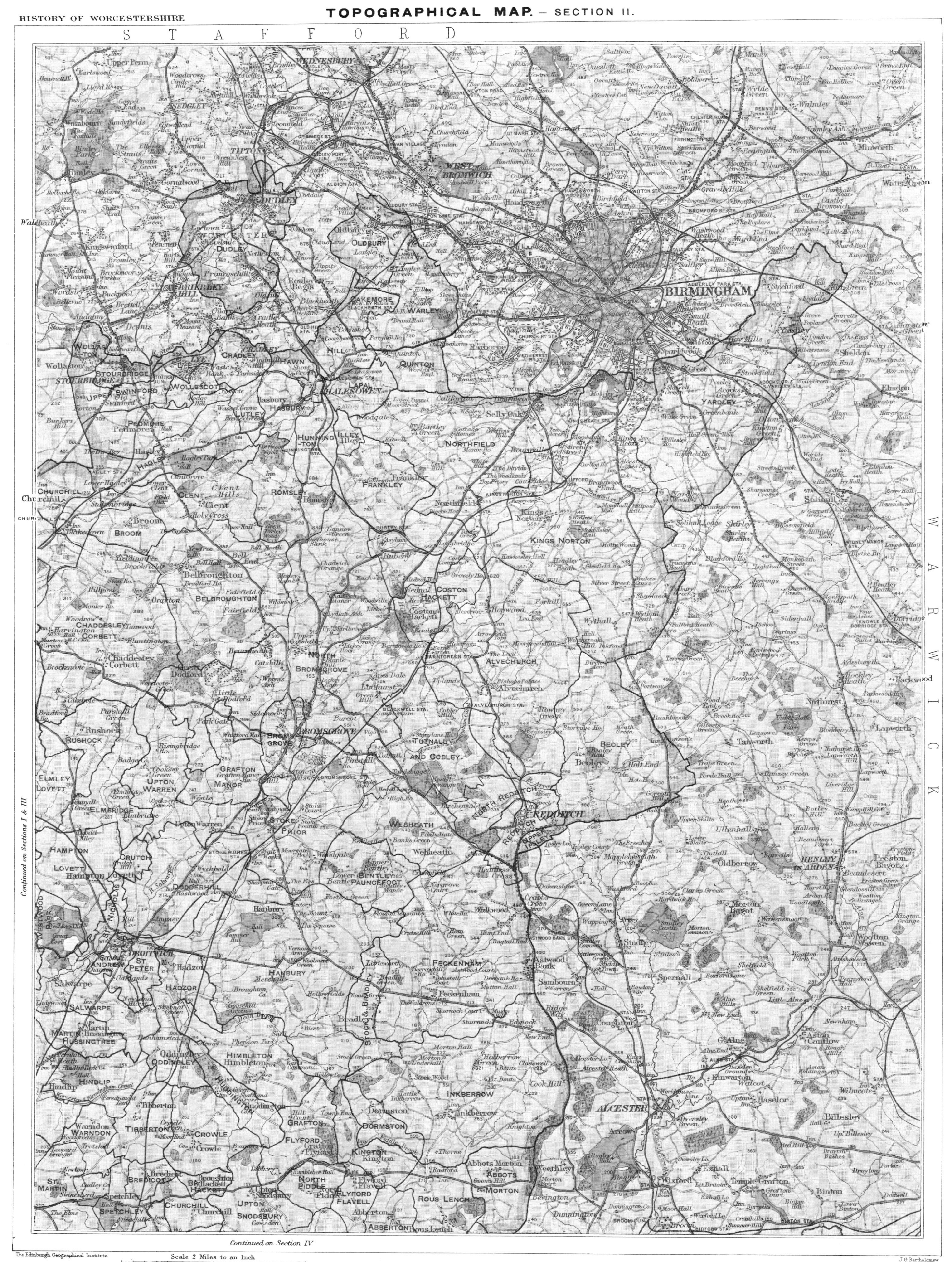

TOPOGRAPHICAL MAP. – SECTION I.

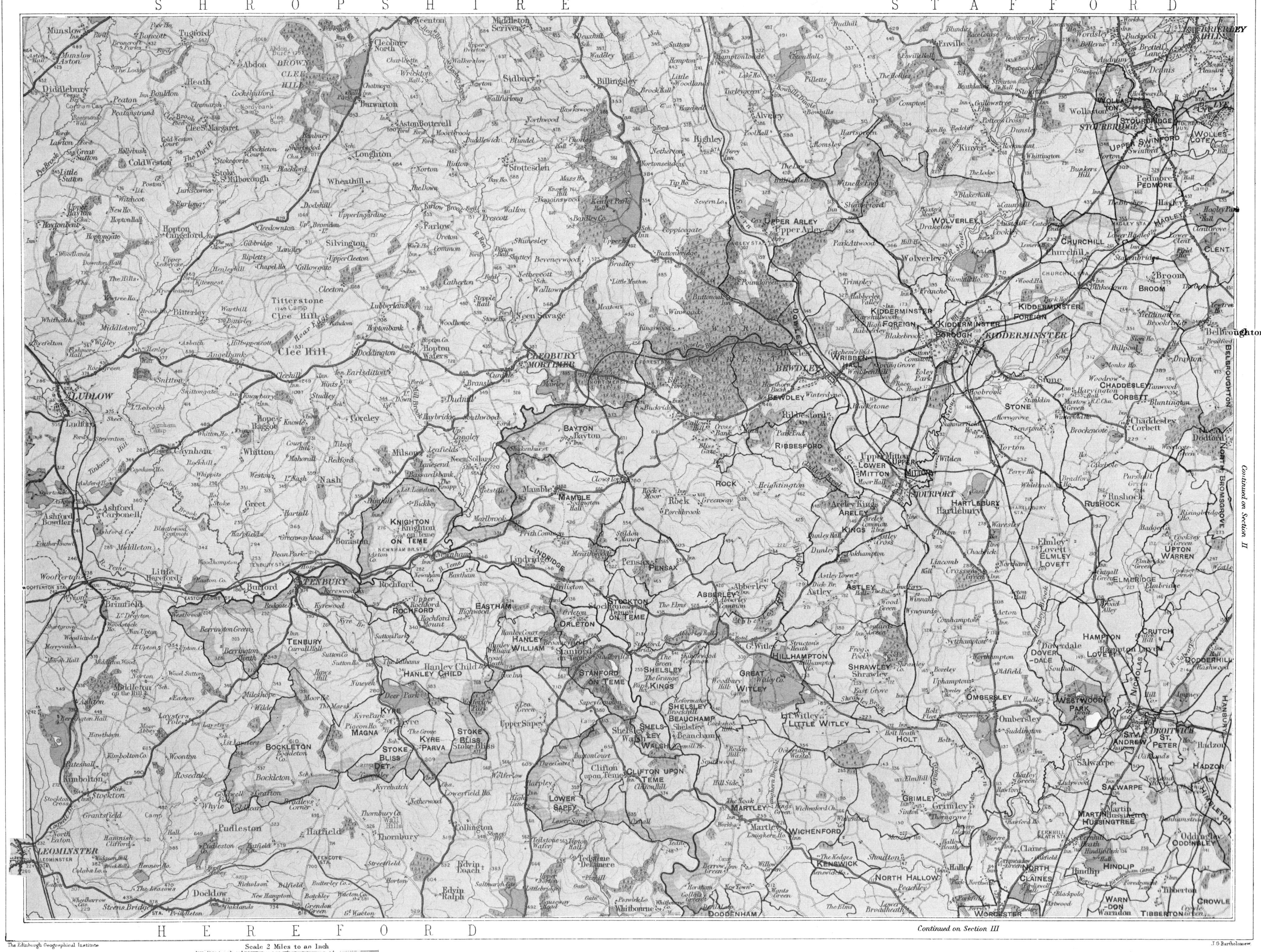